# WORLDMARK ENCYCLOPEDIA OF THE NATIONS

Volume 6

ISSN 1531-1635

# WORLDMARK
## ENCYCLOPEDIA OF THE NATIONS

# WORLD LEADERS

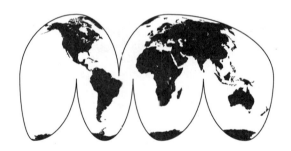

Formerly published by Worldmark Press, Ltd.

*GALE GROUP*

*Detroit*
*New York*
*San Francisco*
*London*
*Boston*
*Woodbridge, CT*

## Gale Group Staff

**Shelly Dickey,** Project Editor
**William H. Harmer,** Contributing Editor
**David Riddle, Jennifer M. York,** Assistant Editors
**Rita Runchock,** Managing Editor

**Mary Beth Trimper,** Composition and Electronic Prepress Manager
**Evi Seoud,** Assistant Composition and Electronic Prepress Manager
**NeKita McKee,** Buyer

**Kenn Zorn,** Production Design Manager
**Michael Logusz,** Graphic Artist

ISBN 0-7876-0511-5 (set)
ISBN 0-7876-0512-3 (volume 1)
ISBN 0-7876-0513-1 (volume 2)
ISBN 0-7876-0514-X (volume 3)
ISBN 0-7876-0515-8 (volume 4)
ISBN 0-7876-0516-6 (volume 5)
ISBN 0-7876-4809-4 (volume 6)
ISSN 1531-1635

Printed in the United States of America

10 9 8 7 6 5 4 3 2 1

# CONTENTS

For Conversion Tables, Abbreviations and Acronyms, Glossaries, World Tables, Notes to the Tenth Edition, and other supplementary materials, see Volume 1.

# EDITORIAL STAFF

*Editor in Chief:* Timothy L. Gall

*Senior Editors:* Jill Coppola and Mary Sugar

*Associate Editors:* Alana Andrews, Chandra P. Balasubramani, Glennon K. Brady, Lynne Brakeman, Nelia Dunbar, Rebecca N. Ferguson, Susan Bevan Gall, David M.Goodrich, Nese B. Guendelsberger, Robert Halasz, James Henry, Jeneen M. Hobby, Kim Humiston, Roman Jakubowycz, Daniel M. Lucas, Elizabeth Park, Caroline Sahley, Ann P. Standley, Susan Stern, George Sutcliffe, James Scott Volpe, Craig B. Waff, Jennifer Wallace, Rosalie Wieder, Douglas Wu, Michael Zannoni

*Cartographers:* Maryland Cartographics, Inc.; Scott B. Edmonds, President: Stephanie K. Clark, Deborah G. Freer, Tracy R. Morrill, Justin E. Morrill, Judith G. Nielsen, John P. Radziszewski

*Copy Editors:* Deborah Baron, Janet Fern, Mary Ann Klasen

*Typesetting:* Bridgette Nadzam, Brian Rajewski, Deborah Rutti

*Data Input:* Judith Raday Arth, Dawn Babos, Lee Ann DeWolf, Janis K. Long, Maggie Lyall, Cheryl Montagna, Deborah Ridgway, Tajana G. Roehl, Karen Seyboldt, Kira Silverbird, Karen J. Sippola

*Proofreaders:* Deborah Baron, Jan Davis, Janet Fenn, Ruta Marino, Jennifer Wallace

*Editorial Assistants:* Katie Baron, Jennifer A. Spencer, Daniel K. Updegraft

# NOTES

## TO WORLD LEADERS

"World Leaders" becomes Volume 6 of *Worldmark Encyclopedia of the Nations* (WEN) with this, the Tenth Edition. The 191 entries in "World Leaders" provide biographical profiles of the person who is the head of the nation's government and who bears primary responsibility for the country's policy. Thus, the focus of "World Leaders" is on the head of the government (e.g., the prime minister) rather than on the head of state (the monarch) when these two roles are not played by the same individual. In some cases, the person who appears to be running the country may not be in the position traditionally designated as that of the nation's leader. In those cases, the person generally acknowledged to be in charge has been profiled, even though there may be questions as to the legitimacy of his or her claim to authority. "World Leaders" focuses on the nations of the world: leaders of protectorates, governments in exile, and heads of territories seeking independence are not included.

Profiles are arranged alphabetically by country, and begin with the leader's name and title, accompanied by a recent photo except where none was available. The introductory sections provide a brief summary of the nation's status, including location, geography, and characteristics of society. A map of the country, in context with neighboring nations and/or bodies of water, accompanies each entry. (Researchers seeking more detailed information on any aspect of the country and its people may refer to the full country entry in the appropriate volume of WEN.) Sections profiling the leader's personal background may include date and place of birth, education, influences, and occupations and pursuits prior to entering political life. The leader's rise to power, leadership, and his or her domestic and foreign policy positions are discussed in subsequent sections. Finally, the leader's official mailing address is provided, along with a list of sources used in preparing the profile. The profiles were researched and written by knowledgeable experts, whose names and institutional affiliations appear at the end of each entry.

## ABBREVIATIONS

The following abbreviations are used in the entries:

| | |
|---|---|
| CAF | Communauté Financière Africaine |
| CARICOM | Caribbean Community |
| EC | European Communities |
| EU | European Union |
| GNP | Gross National Product |
| GDP | Gross Domestic Product |
| IMF | International Monetary Fund |
| UK | United Kingdom of Great Britain and Northern Ireland |
| UN | United Nations |
| US | United States of America |
| USSR | Union of Soviet Socialist Republics |

**AP/Wide World Photos:** de la Rua Bruno, Fernando (Argentina: photo by Gerardo Horovitz); Wajed, Hasina (Bangladesh); Izetbegovic, Alija (Bosnia and Herzegovina); Jelavic, Ante (Bosnia and Herzegovina); Radisic, Zivko (Bosnia and Herzegovina); Buyoya, Pierre (Burundi: photo by Molly Bingham); Hun Sen (Cambodia); Azzali, Assoumani (Comoros: photo by Jean-Marc Bouju); Kabila, Laurent (Democratic Republic of the Congo: photo by Ricardo Mazalan); Sassou-Nguesso, Denis (Republic of the Congo: photo by David Guttenfelder); Guei, Robert (Cote d'Ivoire); Douglas, Rosie (Dominica); Noboa Bejarano, Gustavo (Ecuador: photo by John Moore); Mbasogo, Teodoro Obiang Nguema (Equatorial Guinea: photo by John Riley); Afwerki, Isaias (Eritrea: photo by Michel Euler); Mitchell, Keith (Grenada: photo by Lynne Sladky); Jagdeo, Bharrat (Guyana: photo by Shirley Bahadur); Wahid, Abdurrahman (Indonesia: photo by Itsuo Inouye); Abdullah bin Hussein al-Hasem (Jordan: photo by Yousef Allan); Tito, Teburoro (Kiribati: photo by Katsumi Kasahara); Vike-Freiberga, Vaira (Latvia); Lahoud, Émile (Lebanon); Mosisili, Pakalitha (Lesotho: photo by Themba Hadebe); Konare, Alpha Oumar (Mali: photo by Ruth Fremson); Koirala, Girija Prasad (Nepal: photo by Binod Joshi); Clark, Helen (New Zealand: photo by David Hallett); Aleman, Arnoldo (Nicaraugua: photo by Anita Baca); Makamura, Kuniwo (Palau: photo by Marty Ledhandler); Kagame, Paul (Rwanda: photo by Jean-Marc Bouju); Mitchell, James (Saint Vincent and the Grenadines: photo by Ricardo Figueroa); Rakhmonov, Imomali (Tajikistan: photo by Sergei Karpukhin). **EPD Photos:** Meta, Ilir (Albania: Republic of Albania Department of Information); Bouteflika, Abdelaziz (Algeria); Molné Marc Forné (Andorra: Government of Andorra); Dos Santos, Jose Eduardo (Angola: Embassy of The Republic of Angola); Bird, Lester (Antigua and Barbuda: Antigua and Barbuda High Commission); Kocharyan, Robert (Armenia: President of the Republic of Armenia); Howard, John Prime Minister (Australia: Australian Consulate General); Schüssel, Wolfgang (Austria: Hopi Media, Vienna/Austrian Press and Information Service); Aliyev, Heydar (Azerbaijan: Embassy of the Republic of Azerbaijan); Ingraham, Hubert (Bahamas); Hamad, Sheikh (Bahrain: Bahrain Government); Arthur, Owen (Barbados: Government of Barbados); Lukashenka, Alyaksandr Hrihoryevich (Belarus: Government of Belarus); Verhofstadt, Guy (Belgium: Office of the Prime Minister); Musa, Said (Belize: Government of Belize); Kerekou, Mathieu (Benin: Embassy of the Republic of Benin); Wangchuck, Jigme Singye (Bhutan: SAARC); Banzer, Hugo (Bolivia: Embassy of Bolivia); Mogae, Festus (Botswana: Government of Botswana); Cardoso, Fernando Henrique (Brazil: Presidencia da Republica Brazil); Kostov, Ivan (Bulgaria: Government of the Republic of Bulgaria); Compaore, Blaise (Burkina Faso: Government of Burkina Faso); Bolkiah, Hassanal (Brunei Darussalam: Embassy of Brunei Darussalam); Biya, Paul (Cameroon: Presidence de la Republique du Cameroun); Chretien, Jean (Canada: Office of the Prime Minister); Monteiro, Antonio Mascarenhas (Cape Verde: Embassy of Cape Verde); Patasse, Ange Felix (Central African Republic: Republique Centrafricaine); Deby, Idriss (Chad: Presidence de la Republique du Tchad); Lagos, Ricardo (Chile: Lagos Presidential Campaign); Zemin, Jiang (China: photo by Yao Dawei, Embassy of The People's Republic of China); Pastrana, Andrés (Colombia: Embassy of Colombia); Rodriguez, Miguel Angel (Costa Rica: Embassy of Costa Rica); Mesic, Stjepan (Croatia: Office of the President); Castro, Fidel (Cuba: CSU Archives); Clerides, Glafcos (Cyprus: Embassy of Cyprus); Zeman, Milos (Czech Republic: Ministry of Foreign Affairs of the Czech Republic); Rasmussen, Nyrup (Denmark: Royal Danish Embassy); Guelleh, Ismael Omar (Djibouti: Ambassade de Djibouti en France); Fernandez, Leonel (Dominican Republic: Presidencia Republica Dominicana); Mubarak, Hosni (Egypt: Egyptian Presidency); Flores, Francisco (El Salvador: Presidencia de la Republica); Meri, Lennart (Estonia: Office of the President); Zenawi, Meles (Ethiopia: Embassy of Ethiopia); Chaudhry, Mahendra (Fiji: Government of Fiji); Lipponen, Paavo (Finland: Embassy of Finland); Chirac, Jacques (France: Embassy of France); Jammeh, Yahya A.J.J. (The Gambia); Shevardnadze, Eduard (Georgia: Government of Georgia); Schröder, Gerhard (Germany: German Embassy); Rawlings, Jerry (Ghana: Permanent Mission of Ghana to the United Nations); Bongo, Omar (Gabon: Office of the President); Simitis, Costas (Greece: Permanent Mission of Greece to the United Nations); Cabrera, Alfonso Portillo (Guatemala: Embassy of Guatemala); Conte, Lansana (Guinea: WebGuinee); Préval, René Garcia (Haiti: Embassy of the Republic of Haiti); Flores, Carlos Roberto (Honduras: Permanent Mission of Honduras to the United Nations); Orbán, Viktor (Hungary: Embassy of the Republic of Hungary); Oddsson, David (Iceland: Althingi, the Icelandic Parliament); Vajpayee, Atal Behari (India: Indian Parliament); Khatami, Mohammed (Iran: Presidency of the Islamic Republic of Iran); Hussein, Saddam (Iraq: Permanent Mission of Iraq to the United Nations); Ahern, Bertie (Ireland: Embassy of Ireland); Barak, Ehud (Israel: Government of Israel); Patterson, Percival James (Jamaica: Consulate of Jamaica); Mori, Yoshiro (Japan: Government of Japan); Nazarbayev, Nursultan (Kazakhstan: Government of Kazakhstan); Moi, Daniel T. Arap (Kenya: Government of Kenya); Kim Jong II (Democratic People's Republic of Korea—North Korea); Kim Dae-Jung (Republic of Korea—South Korea: Embassy of the Republic of Korea); Jabir III (Kuwait: Government of Kuwait); Akayev, Askar Akayevich (Kyrgyzstan: Government of Kyrgyzstan); Siphandone, Khamtay (Laos: Government of Laos); Taylor, Charles (Liberia: Government of Liberia); al-Qadhafi, Muammar (Libya: CSU Archives); Hans Adam II (Liechtenstein: Government of Liechtenstein); Adamkus, Valdas (Lithuania: Office of the President); Juncker, Jean-Claude (Luxembourg: photographic Library of the Luxembourg Press and Information Service); Trajkovski, Boris (Macedonia: Republic of Macedonia); Ratsiraka, Didier (Madagascar: Embassy of the Republic of Madagascar); Muluzi, Bakili (Malawi: Government of Malawi); Mohamad, Mahathir (Malaysia: Embassy of Malaysia); Gayoom, Maumoon Abdul (Maldives: Republic of Maldives); Fenech-Adami, Eddie (Malta: Malta Ministries Office); Taya, Maaouya Ould Sid Ahmed (Mauritania: Presidence de la republique); Ramgoolam, Navin (Mauritius: Government of Mauritius); Note, Kessai (Marshall Islands: Embassy of RMI); Zedillo Ponce de Leon, Ernesto (Mexico: Office of the President); Falcam, Leo A. (Federated States of Micronesia: FSM Government); Lucinschi, Petru (Moldova: Office of the President); Ranier III (Monaco: Principality of Monaco); Amarjargal, Rinchinnyam (Mongolia: Embassy of Mongolia); Chissano, Mohammed VI (Morocco: Moroccan Government); Joaquim, Alberto (Mozambique: FRELIMO); Than Shwe (Myanmar: Embassy of the Union of Myanmar); Nujoma, Sam (Namibia: Office of the President); Kok, Wim (Netherlands: Royal Netherlands Embassy); Obasanjo, Olusegun (Nigeria: Embassy of the Federal Republic of Nigeria); Stoltenberg, Jens (Norway: Office of the Prime Minister); al Said, Qaboos Bin (Oman: Government of Oman); Musharraff, General Pervez (Pakistan: Islamic Republic of Pakistan); Moscoso Rodríguez, Mireya Elisa (Panama: Office of the President); Morauta, Mekere (Papua New Guinea: Office of the Prime Minister); Gonzalez Macchi, Luis (Paraguay: Office of the President); Fujimori, Alberto Kenyo (Peru: Embassy of Peru); Estrada, Joseph (Philippines: Office of the President); Kwasniewski, Aleksander (Poland: Office of the President); Guterres, António Manuel de Oliveira (Portugal: Embassy of Portugal); Khalifa al-Thani, Hamad bin (Qatar: Government of Qatar); Constantinescu, Emil (Romania: Office of the President); Putin, Vladimir (Russia: Office of the President); Douglas, Denzil (Saint Kitts and Nevis: Office of the Prime Minister); Anthony, Kenny Davis (Saint Lucia: Embassy of Saint Lucia); Fahd Bin Abdul Aziz al-Saud (Saudi Arabia: Government of Saudi Arabia); Wade, Abdoulaye (Senegal: Government of Senegal); Kabbah, Ahmed Tejan (Sierra Leone: Office of the President); Goh Chok Tong (Singapore: Government of Singapore); Dzurinda, Mikulas (Slovakia: Government of the Slovak Republic); Kucan, Milan (Slovenia: Government of Slovenia); Ulufaalu, Bart (Solomon Islands: Office of Tourism); Mbeki, Thabo Mvuyelwa (South Africa: Embassy of South Africa); Aznar, José Maria (Spain: Embassy of Spain); Kumaratunga, Chandrika (Sri Lanka: Embassy of the Republic of Sri Lanka in Austria); al-Bashir, Omar Hassan Ahmed (Sudan: Office of the Prime Minister); Wijdenbosch, Jules Albert (Suriname: Republic of Suriname); Mswati III (Swaziland: Government of Swaziland); Persson, Göran (Sweden: Embassy of Sweden); Ogi, Adolph (Switzerland: Government of Switzerland); Al-Asad, Hafez (Syria: Embassy of the Syrian Arab Republic); Chen Shui-bian (Taiwan: ROC Government Informations Office); Mkapa, Benjamin William (Tanzania: Embassy of the United Republic of Tanzania); Leekpai, Chuan (Thailand: Office of the Prime Minister); Eyadema, Gnassingbe (Togo: Office of the President); Taufaahau Tupou IV (Tonga: Tonga High Commission); Panday, Basdeo (Trinidad and Tobago: Ministry of Public Administration and Information, Republic of Trinidad and Tobago); Ben Ali, Zine El Abidine (Tunisia: Embassy of Tunisia); Ecevit, Bulent (Turkey: photo by Burhan Ozbilici); Niyazov, Saparmu-rad Atayevich (Turkmenistan: Office of the President); Ionatana, Ionatana (Tuvalu: Tuvalu Government); Museveni, Yoweri Kaguta (Uganda: Office of the President); Kuchma, Leonid Danylovich (Ukraine: Office of the President); al-Nuhayyan, Sheikh Zayid bin Sultan (United Arab Emirates: Government of UAE); Blair, Tony (United Kingdom: Brit-ish Information Services); Clinton, Bill (United States of America: The White House); Batlle, Jorge (Uruguay: Office of the President); Karimov, Islam Abduganievich (Uzbekistan: Embassy of the Republic of Uzbekistan); John Paul II (Vat-ican: Apostolic Nunciature in the United States); Chavez, Hugo (Venezuela: Office of the President); Le Kha Phieu (Vietnam: Government of Vietnam); Saleh, Ali Abdullah (Yemen: Office of the President); Milosevic, Slobodan (Yugo-slavia: Government of the Federal Republic of Yugoslavia); Chiluba, Frederick Jacob Titus (Zambia: Embassy of the Republic of Zambia); Mugabe, Robert (Zimbabwe: Office of the President).

# AFGHANISTAN

## Interim Profile

The Soviet withdrawal from Afghanistan did not create peace and stability. After fighting the Soviets, the *mujahidin* (Muslim rebel tribesmen) captured Kabul in April 1992, then battled among themselves for control of the country. In November 1994, a new group formed, composed of former Islamic theology students. Known as Taliban (Student of Religion), it captured Kabul 27 September 1996 and now controls 90% of Afghanistan.

The Soviet Union sent troops into Afghanistan on 27 December 1979, in part to keep Afghanistan pro-Soviet. After the Soviets withdrew on 14 February 1989, superpower relations warmed, and the outside parties to the Afghan conflict sought political settlement. Since late 1989 the US proposed to the Soviet Union a mutual cutoff of military aid to the combatants. Moscow finally agreed on 13 September 1991 after the failed August coup attempt reduced Moscow's abilities to support Communist regimes in the Third World. Russia, the Soviet Union's successor in international affairs, then dropped its insistence that Afghan president Najibullah participate in a transition regime, and on 18 March 1992, a UN special envoy persuaded Najibullah to step down once the interim government was formed. Najibullah's announcement set off a wave of defections, primarily by Uzbek and Tajik ethnic militias, and his regime collapsed. Joining with the defectors, prominent mujahidin commander, Ahmad Shah Masud (of the Islamic Society, a largely Tajik party headed by President Burhanuddin Rabbani) sent his mujahidin into Kabul, paving the way for a new regime to be installed in April 1992.

## THE MUJAHIDIN AND THEIR INFIGHTING

Seven Sunni Muslim resistance parties formed a broad coalition against the Soviets in 1985. Their victory over Najibullah in April 1992 brought these parties to power in Afghanistan, whereupon they warred among themselves for ultimate control. Alliances continually shifted after President Rabbani took office in June 1992. Rabbani was supposed to leave office in December 1994 but refused on the grounds that political authority would disintegrate totally.

Another major force is the Uzbek militia of General Abdul Rashid Dostum, whose break with Najibullah in early 1992 helped overthrow the Communist regime. In January 1994, Dostum led an unsuccessful rebellion against Rabbani, then fought Rabbani until the Taliban takeover created an alliance in October 1996 with Rabbani against Dostum.

Shia parties, generally less active against the Soviet occupation than were the Sunni parties, have joined the infighting. In early June 1992 Iranian-backed Hizb-e-Wahdat (Unity Party, an alliance of eight Shia Muslim groups) agreed to join the mujahidin regime but broke with Rabbani in January 1994. The Shiite party fractured in 1995 when its patron, Iran, backed Rabbani against Taliban. When Taliban captured the western Herat area in September 1995, the action destabilized Iran's border with Afghanistan. One Hizb-e-Wahdat faction (Khalili) stayed loyal to Dostum while another (Akbari) joined Rabbani. Both factions of Hizb-e-Wahdat are opposed to Taliban.

Gulbuddin Hekmatyar, head of a faction of the Party of Islam, opposed the new government from its beginning in April 1992 and especially Rabbani's presidency. Hekmatyar met with Rabbani in March 1993 and agreed that Rabbani would remain president and Hekmatyar would become prime minister, but the agreement was not implemented. On 1 January 1994, Hekmatyar, Dostum, Hizb-e-Wahdat, and other mujahidin factions unsuccessfully attempted to seize power from Rabbani. On 26 June 1996, Hekmatyar switched sides again and joined Rabbani's government in Kabul. As of early December 1996 Hekmatyar and Rabbani are planning to oust Taliban from Kabul, but Hekmatyar's forces are greatly reduced so that he will not add significantly to the anti-Taliban coalition.

## THE RISE OF TALIBAN

Consisting of Islamic clerics and students from seminaries that sprung up in Pakistan among the communities of Afghan refugees, the Taliban movement came into being after the war against the Soviets and Najibullah. Taliban seized control of the southeastern city of Qandahar in November 1994 and continued to gather strength.

In February 1995 Taliban routed Hekmatyar out of his positions outside Kabul and demanded that Rabbani surrender. Rabbani refused, Taliban rejected UN efforts to include it in a peaceful transition, and an 18-month stalemate around Kabul ensued. In its drive to Kabul, Taliban amassed about 25,000 troops, a few hundred tanks, and about 10 combat aircraft. In September 1996 Taliban victories east of Kabul led Rabbani/Masud's outer defenses to crumble, and the government withdrew to the Panjshir Valley north of Kabul. With the Taliban capture of Kabul, Masud joined forces with the other factions fighting the Taliban. This

group, known as the Northern Alliance, continues to fight in the north.

In the Spring of 2000, the Taliban, claiming a series of defections from the Rabbani/Masud camp, began preparations for a renewed offensive to gain the remaining part of Afghanistan not under their control.

The Taliban is led by mujahidin fighter-turned-religious scholar, Muhammad Omar. He is thought to have been born in Kandahar in 1962. Described as a determined man with one eye, Omar fought against the Russian forces as a deputy Chief Commander in the Harakat-i-Inqilab-i Islami party of Mohammad Nabi Mohammadi during the Soviet occupation of Afghanistan in the 1980s. During the fighting, he was wounded and lost one eye. He is married and has four wives. Virtually unknown until the Taliban's capture of Kandahar, Omar remains a mysterious figure who refuses to speak to journalists directly. It has been reported that he rarely travels and has yet to visit the capital. He reportedly has strong ties with Bin Laden and other radical Islamists and has been harsh in his imposition of Islamic law on the Afghan people. His detractors claim that Omar is a nominal figure controlled by Pakistan's intelligence agency. On 3 April 1996, about 1,000 Muslim clergymen aligned with the Taliban cause chose Omar as "Amirul-Mumineen" (Supreme Leader of the Muslims).

Since taking control, the Taliban movement has lost international support as it has tried to impose strict adherence to Islamic customs and has harshly punished and even executed transgressors (Anderson). It forbade women from working outside the home (except health workers), closed girls' schools, and imposed a strict Islamic dress code. As a result,

the UN and other aid organizations, including UNHCR, UNICEF, Save the Children, and Oxfam, have cut back or ceased operations in protest or for lack of available (female) staff. Yet some observe that Taliban has brought order by disarming independent militiamen. It has opened roads, leading to a greater availability of food in areas under its control. There are even reports that complaints among the citizens have caused the Taliban to ease some restrictions. In January 2000, the coordinator of United Nations relief programs, Erick de Mul, reported that the realities of daily life were softening some of the Taliban's extremist positions. Some girls are going back to school, and a limited number of women in critical occupations like health care are re-entering the workforce.

In June 2000, the UN undertook a major effort to inoculate Afghani children against polio. Donkeys and bicycles were employed to transport thousands of volunteers in urban and rural areas. Both sides in the fighting agreed to a cease-fire to allow the immunization to take place.

## OUTSIDE INVOLVEMENT IN THE CONFLICT

Instability in Afghanistan opened the way for Pakistan, Iran, Saudi Arabia, and Russia to promote their own interests. Like the US, Pakistan prefers a stabilized Afghanistan, in part to avoid the ethnic Pashtuns in Afghanistan and Pakistan from uniting, but also to assist in trade with the Muslim states of the former Soviet Union. Pakistan hopes that Afghanistan will host the gas and oil pipelines to be built from the Central Asian states to Pakistan. Furthermore, Pakistan wants to repatriate the 860,000 Afghan refugees in its borders. Pakistan's relations with the Rabbani government had always suffered from its past favoritism of Gulbuddin Hekmatyar. Lacking influence over Rabbani, Pakistan cultivated the Taliban, providing political and "some material assistance," according to US officials. The stalemate improved somewhat when Rabbani offered to rebuild the Pakistan Embassy in Kabul, which Afghans burned in September 1995 to protest Pakistan's support for Taliban. Since Taliban took control of Kabul, however, Pakistan has been the only country to formally recognize its new government. Now that Taliban's chief Pakistani patron, Interior Minister Nasrullah Babar, has been removed from power along with Prime Minister Benazir Bhutto, some believe Pakistan might back a negotiated solution to the Afghan conflict.

Iran has moved closer to the Rabbani regime since late 1995, regarding western Afghanistan as within its natural sphere of influence and a route to the Central Asian states. Rabbani's party and Herat province are dominated by Tajiks, who are descended from Persian-speaking inhabitants of what is now Afghanistan. Since September 1995, when Taliban captured Herat, Iran has provided fuel, funds, and ammunition to the Rabbani government. Iran also hosts the former governor of Herat and his few thousand fighters who might, with Iranian help, try to retake Herat. Iran has become an active mediator. On 29–30 October 1996, it hosted an international conference on Afghanistan. Pakistan and Saudi Arabia did not attend, and the US, which has no diplomatic relations with Iran, boycotted the meeting as well. In an editorial in the Washington Post (4 November 1996), Iran's ambassador to the UN pointed out that the US and Iran have common interests in resolving the Afghan conflict.

About 1.3 million Afghan refugees still live in Iran, with some 500,000 integrated into Iranian society. In mid-1994 Iran reportedly began forcing Afghan refugees to leave Iran and return home, although Iran denies any forcible repatriation.

Russia invaded Afghanistan to weaken the Islamic movements in the Muslim states of the former Soviet Union. Russia had supported Rabbani by supplying military equipment and technical assistance to prevent Taliban from gaining power. Russia also wanted to prevent an influx of narcotics into Russia from Afghanistan and the Muslim states of the former Soviet Union. Russian fears of Islamic fundamentalism and instability have been heightened by conflict in Tajikistan. Russia is helping defend the Tajik government against 5,000 Tajik Islamic rebels who conduct raids into Tajikistan from Afghan territory, reportedly accompanied by Afghan mujahidin. (The Afghan government denies that it is aiding Islamic fundamentalist opponents of the Tajik government although it acknowledges that Afghan leaders outside government control may be doing so.) Some suggest that Russia is using Afghan instability to justify its continued presence in the Muslim republics, such as Tajikistan.

Former Communist elites still in power in Uzbekistan, Tajikistan, and Turkmenistan wish to prevent their own Islamic oppositionists from using Afghanistan as a base. Uzbekistan has been helping Tajikistan suppress Islamic rebels who receive aid and shelter in northern Afghanistan. Uzbekistan reportedly has close ties to Dostum, the Uzbek commander in Afghanistan. But Turkmenistan and other states stand to benefit from Taliban power since construction of a proposed natural gas pipeline from Turkmenistan through Afghanistan might then be built. Meanwhile, Afghanistan's Uzbeks, Tajiks, and Turkmen show no desire to unite with ethnic brethren in those Muslim states, nor have those former Soviet republics expressed territorial designs on Afghanistan.

During the Soviet occupation, Saudi Arabia channeled hundreds of millions of dollars to the Afghan resistance, particularly to Sunni Muslim leader Abd-I-Rab Rasul Sayyaf and his Ittihad Islami (Islamic Union) and, to a lesser extent, Hekmatyar. Sayyaf thus stemmed his adherence to the Wahhabi sect of Sunni Islam, also dominant in Saudi Arabia. Sayyaf, a Rabbani ally, also opposed the Iran-backed Shia militia Hizb-e-Wahdat, consistent with Saudi objectives to limit Iran's influence in Afghanistan. The Saudis (and the US) temporarily stopped aiding Hekmatyar and Sayyaf in March 1991 when they supported Iraq against the US-led coalition in the Gulf War.

Saudi Arabia, which practices a strict brand of Islam, seems to be backing Taliban since it counters Iran. The Saudis expect that a stable Afghanistan might make building the gas pipeline a reality. A Saudi company, Delta Oil, is a partner of Los Angeles-based Unocal in that proposed project.

## THE HUMANITARIAN CRISIS

Afghanistan faces major humanitarian problems. Over two million Afghan refugees, three-quarters of whom are women and children, are living in Pakistan and Iran. Another 500,000 Afghans are displaced internally. Afghanistan has suffered about two million dead, leaving 700,000 widows and orphans and about one million Afghan children who were born and raised in refugee camps outside Afghanistan. About 200,000 have been killed by mines, and the UN estimates that 10 million mines remain buried in Afghanistan, rendering much farming and grazing land useless. The UN High Commission for Refugees (UNHCR) estimated in December 1992 that, in addition to the 200,000 killed, 400,000 have been injured since the Soviet invasion. The US State Department estimates that mines cause 100 additional injuries every month.

## UNITED NATIONS PEACE EFFORTS

The UN has been viewed as a credible mediator by all sides. UN mediators Mahmoud Mestiri and Norbert Holl failed to arrange a peaceful transition prior to the Taliban takeover in Kabul. Their plan was similar to those advanced by UN officials and former King Zahir Shah: a permanent government to be chosen through a traditional Afghan selection process, such as a *loya jirga*, a grand assembly of notable Afghans. The plan underwent several modifications to make it more palatable to Taliban, which opposed dealing with any mujahidin groups.

Norbert Holl has mediated since Taliban's victory. His plan includes a cease-fire; demilitarization of Kabul (which would be policed by a neutral security force); and dialogue toward a broad-based transition government. To advance the plan, Holl organized a one-day UN-sponsored international meeting of the outside parties to the Afghan conflict. No Afghan factions were invited, and no concrete results have materialized. On the eve of the UN meeting, Taliban asked the UN to recognize its rule and to give it Afghanistan's seat at the UN.

The UN denies that it backs the return of King Zahir Shah to Afghanistan as a transitional leader. Some factions, such as the National Islamic Front of Afghanistan, support the return of the king, because his rule is remembered by many Afghans as an era of peace, stability, and human rights. Others believe the king is out of touch with modern Afghan politics and that in any event his rule failed to exterminate the Communist Party in Afghanistan.

## REFERENCES

"Back to War in Afghanistan." *The Economist,* 31 July 1999, p. 33.

"Living with the Taliban." *The Economist,* 24 July 1999, p. 39.

*New York Times,* 27 March 1996.

US Department of State. *Country Fact Sheet: Afghanistan,* 6 June 1994.

*Washington Post,* 2 March 1995.

**Profile researched and written by Kenneth Katzman, Ph.D. (12/96; updated 6/2000).**

# ALBANIA

Ilir Meta
Prime Minister
*(pronounced "ell-EAR MET-a")*

*"We shall make clear that those who do not respect laws might end up in jail."*

The Republic of Albania is situated in southeastern Europe and is bordered to the south by Greece, to the east by the former Yugoslav Republic of Macedonia, to the north by Serbia-Montenegro, and to the west by the Adriatic Sea. The total area is 28,748 sq km (11,100 sq mi), of which over two-thirds is mountainous and the rest river valleys and coastal lowlands.

The country's total population is about 3.4 million. Over 90% are ethnic Albanian, with Greeks comprising most of the rest. Outside of the country's borders live about an equal number of ethnic Albanians, mainly in the Kosovo region within Serbia, and also in Macedonia, Greece, and Italy. Most Albanians are of the Muslim religion; however, atheism is also widespread as a result of an official ban on religious worship from the 1960s to 1990. The Albanian language has two main dialects, the Geg and the Tosk.

The country's gross domestic product has been estimated at US$5 billion, and per capita income at US$1,490. The national currency is the *lek*. Albania's natural resources include oil, gas, coal, and metals. Agriculture and mining constitute the largest industries.

## POLITICAL BACKGROUND

Albania experienced a brief period of independence in the 15th century but was otherwise subjected to foreign rule. Independence was finally gained in 1912 after four-and-a-half centuries of Turkish Ottoman rule. The Paris peace conference after World War I reestablished the national state, and Albania became a member of the League of Nations. Italy occupied the country in 1939, followed by Germany in 1943. The Communist-led National Liberation Front (NLF) resistance movement, assisted by the Yugoslav partisans, took power in November 1944. Its leader, Enver Hoxha, headed the party and the country for four decades, until his death in 1985.

The Hoxha era was known for its extreme internal repression and isolationist tendencies. Albanian industries and agriculture were collectivized. The population was rigidly controlled by the ruling Albanian Party of Labor (the Communist Party) and its secret police apparatus. In foreign policy, Hoxha's regime pursued increasingly isolationist tendencies. Albania broke away from Yugoslav tutelage after the 1948 split between Yugoslav leader, Tito, and Soviet leader, Stalin. Ties with the USSR were broken in 1961, and Albania withdrew from the Warsaw Pact in 1968. China became its main ally in the 1960s, but that relationship cooled in the 1970s, leaving Albania almost completely isolated.

Albania was the last East Central European country to embark on democratization and market economic reforms in the 1980s. Hoxha's successor, Ramiz Alia, was considered somewhat less repressive and began to increase Albanian exposure to the outside world, while maintaining the Communist Party's exclusive hold on power. Large student demonstrations in December 1990 pushed the Alia government to accept multi-party elections. Albania held its first free elections in 45 years in March 1991. Although its fairness was questioned by outside observers, the Albanian Party of Labor (renamed the Albanian Socialist Party) won two-thirds of the vote and formed a government under Fatos Nano. Following large-scale strikes and demonstrations, the Nano government ceded power in June 1991 to a coalition government including the Socialists and the opposition Democratic Party. Members of the Democratic Party were given most of the key economic positions and were primarily responsible for initiating new economic policies. However, in December 1991, the Democratic Party withdrew from the national stability government, forcing new elections.

General elections held in March 1992 resulted in a resounding victory for the Democratic Party, which gained 62% of the vote. The Socialist Party won only 25% of the vote (down from more than 67% the previous year). In April 1992, the new People's Assembly convened, Alia resigned as the last communist leader in Albania, and Parliament elected Democratic Party chairman, Sali Berisha, to the presidency. The Democratic Party dominated a cabinet under Prime Minister Aleksander Meksi. In the following years, the Berisha-led government became increasingly autocratic, and the Democratic Party undertook measures to stifle political opposition. Former Socialist leaders like Fatos Nano were arrested.

Albania's next parliamentary elections were held on 26 May and 2 June 1996. Amidst charges of voting fraud, virtually all opposition parties pulled out before polling ended and boycotted the second round. The Organization for Security and Cooperation in Europe (OSCE), as well as other international observers, noted serious irregularities during the vote, including fraud, ballot stuffing, intimidation, and coercion tactics. The Democratic Party won almost all of the parliamentary seats. The new parliament was inaugurated on 1 July, but the Socialist Party boycotted the session. Berisha nominated a new government under Prime Minister Meksi on 11 July 1996.

Beginning in late 1996, numerous popular yet high-risk investment schemes collapsed, prompting violent riots in many Albanian cities. Over the previous two years, the so-called "pyramid schemes" promised exorbitant returns on investment, attracting over $1 billion. The collapse of these schemes led to widespread demonstrations, as many Albanians blamed the government for corruption and mismanagement in regulating the investment enterprises. In early March 1997, the demonstrations turned into armed rebellion in numerous cities in the south as anti-Berisha rebels stormed arms depots. Up to 2,000 Albanians were killed in the ensuing conflict. Thousands more fled to Italy and other countries. After international mediation, Berisha dismissed the Meksi government, appointed a new broad-based government headed by a Socialist, and agreed to hold parliamentary elections by June 1997. About 7,000 multinational troops were deployed to Albania in order to provide a stabilizing presence and assist in the delivery of humanitarian aid.

New elections were held under close international scrutiny on 29 June and 6 July 1997. The opposition Socialist Party won a landslide victory at the expense of Berisha's Democratic Party. In parliament, the Socialist Party won an absolute majority of 101 out of 155 seats. Berisha resigned on 23 July. The parliament elected Socialist Rexhen Mejdani to the presidency. Mejdani named Fatos Nano to be prime minister of the Socialist Party-led government, which was sworn in on 25 July 1997. Relations between the ruling Socialist Party and Berisha's Democratic Party remained extremely contentious after the 1997 vote. The Democratic Party called for a boycott of some sessions of parliament and favored early elections. Albania appeared on the verge of chaos again in mid-September 1998 when the murder of a prominent Democratic Party member led to violent demonstrations. Government authorities quickly regained control of sites that had been stormed by Democratic Party supporters. Nano accused Berisha of attempting to stage a coup. The US, the European Union, and other international organizations condemned the violence and appealed to all parties to work toward a peaceful solution. Nano resigned after failing to secure a cabinet reshuffle at the end of the month. The Socialist Party nominated Pandeli Majko to succeed him. Majko was sworn in on 2 October 1998. A little over one year later, in the wake of bloody conflict between ethnic Albanians living in neighboring Kosovo and Serb forces who wanted to reclaim the land, President Mejdani appointed Ilir Meta to the post of prime minister. On 27 October 1999, Meta took over the post.

## PERSONAL BACKGROUND

Ilir Meta was born in Skrapar, Albania, on 24 March 1969. In 1999 when he took office, he was the youngest prime minister in Europe. He is married with one child. His wife, Monika Kryemadhi, is the Vice President of International Socialist Youth. Meta graduated from the Economic Faculty of the Tirana University. In his youth he had a brief career as an amateur weight lifter. He joined the Socialist Party in 1990. Even though this party had split from the Communist Party, Meta has always insisted that he was never a member of the Communist Party. He had been a longtime friend of

outgoing Prime Minister Pandeli Majko, and most politicians thought that Meta and Majko would eventually link up to be a powerful political team. However, on 27 October 1999, Meta replaced Majko as prime minister of Albania. Meta has been described as an administrator who likes compromise and has friends in both the Democratic and Socialist Parties. He is known to be ill at ease at formal events.

## RISE TO POWER

Meta first became formally involved in politics in 1991 when he joined the newly formed Socialist Party (PSS). Prior to joining PSS, he had been a leader in the Young Albanians Euro-Socialist Forum, and as such was granted membership in the International Socialist Youth. In 1992 he was elected Deputy Chairman of the Socialist Party, which dealt mainly with international relations. He has been the representative to Parliament from the place of his birth Skrapar (Skrpar) in 1992, 1996, and 1997. In 1996 Meta was elected Secretary of Foreign Relations of the Socialist Party, and in 1997 he served as the Socialist Party's Secretary of State for Euro-Atlantic integration. Meta had always been a friend of Majko, whom he replaced. He served in Majko's government as deputy prime minister and shared many of Majko's views. During the period of interethnic conflict in Kosovo (1999), a region in Yugoslavia that both ethnic Albanians and ethnic Serbs claim, Meta served as governmental manager. Meta was elected leader of the Socialist Party by a vote of 68–45 over Mekbule Cecosi (who would have become Albania's first woman prime minister had the outcome been reversed). Meta was recommended for the position by Fatos Nano, Majko's predecessor. The crisis in Majko's government, related to the economy and the ethnic conflict in Kosovo, triggered President Rexhep

Meidani's decision to make a change in the government leadership and to appoint Meta as the new prime minister.

## LEADERSHIP

At the time of Meta's election as prime minister, Albania was suffering from widespread governmental corruption. One of Meta's first political actions upon taking office was to fire the minister of public economy and the minister of state. These two cabinet members stood accused of fraudulently issuing licenses to gas and oil companies that gave these ministers money in exchange for control. Meta promised that his government would weed out corrupt officials and those who did little government work. He accused many members of Parliament of doing little or no work, passing the time by reading newspapers or doing crossword puzzles. Meta stated that his goals as prime minister would be to streamline the government and improve roads. He announced that his government had negotiated a loan of $45 million from the European Bank to finance the rebuilding of a hydroelectric plant at Bistrica and to repair the road from Durres to Qafa Thana and the road from Elbasan to Librazhd. Meta stressed that to repay the loan taxes would have to be increased, and pledged to increase wage taxes by 8% for public administration employees.

## DOMESTIC POLICY

The main objectives of Meta's new government were to restore civilian order and reform the police department. He stated that the police needed to reestablish a sense of trust with the citizens of Albania and that the government would do its best to control corruption within the police department. In the past, Albanian citizens have been victims of various pyramid schemes run by government officials. Meta said that the police force would have to increase its level of professionalism. Also included in these reforms will be a restructuring of the judiciary system in order to restore a sense of law and order. Lawyers would be required to work within the system (instead of taking bribes). Meta announced a plan to revise history textbooks to remove negative descriptions of Turkey and Greece. He promised fair treatment for all Greeks residing in Albania and an end to all hostilities. He pledged improvement of roads and services in these minority communities that had previously been neglected. He also promised to improve electrical supply to the Greeks living in the area of Sarande. In his address to Parliament, Meta told the citizens of Albania that they have to work with the government and be prepared to make sacrifices in order to achieve a higher standard of living. He has stated that his policies would be a continuation of governmental policies and that there would be no radical changes.

## FOREIGN POLICY

When Meta took office, the Foreign Minister, Paskal Milo, remained in that post. Albania has assured many foreign governments, including those of Turkey and Greece, that the new government plans to bring peace and stability to the region. Meta has already made a trip to Greece and has assured the Greek government that the minority Greek population in Albania would be respected. He also promised that educational rights for Greeks in southern Albania would be protected. Albania has been encouraging Greece to invest in Albanian projects. The Greek Prime Minister, Costas Simitis, promised Meta's government that Greece would issue work permits to more than one-half million Albanians now living in Greece. Meta is thought to have sympathies toward Western (capitalist) governments. He has always said he was never a member of the Communist Party, but he does have an allegiance to his supporter, Fatos Nano, who has Communist alliances. The main foreign policy problem for the new government is dealing with the Albanian refugees in the former Yugoslavian territory of Kosovo. In an effort to help these refugees, Albania has withdrawn the oil embargo against Montenegro, another neighboring country involved in the Kosovo conflict. Albania still favors complete independence for Kosovo, but the government does not wish to cause problems in the area at this time. Albania wants to improve its economy in order to gain admittance to the European Union. Meta has stated that the implementation of the Stability Pact (cooperation with Albania's neighbors) for southeastern Europe is one of the prime objectives for Albania's foreign policy for the year 2000. Also, in order for Albania to gain standing in the rest of Europe, it must improve its relations with western European countries. According to foreign minister Milo, the European Union Council of Ministers is expected to approve a feasibility study on Albania in 2000.

## ADDRESS

Office of the Prime Minister
Tirana, Albania

## REFERENCES

Albanian.com. [Online] Available http://www.albanian.com (Accessed 2000).

Economist Intelligence Unit. *Country Profile, Albania, 1998-1999.*

*Europa World Yearbook 1998.* Europa Publications Ltd., 1998.

Foreign Broadcast Information Service, October-November 1998.

Frosina Information Network. [Online] Available http://www.frosina.org (Accessed 2000).

US Department of State. *Country Reports on Human Rights Practices for 1997, Albania.* March 1998.

Zickel, Raymond and Walter Iwaskiw. *Albania, a Country Study.* Washington, DC: US Library of Congress Federal Research Division, 1992.

**Profile researched and written by Gail Rosewater (2/2000).**

# ALGERIA

## Abdelaziz Bouteflika
### President

*(pronounced "ab-DEL a-ZEEZ BOOT-ah-FLĪCK-ah")*

*"Today, the time has come for a new impulse in the awakening of the national consciousness which will help eliminate violence in the acts and the minds, fully reinstate social peace and get over a crisis for which the state's deliquescence holds a considerable responsibility."*

The second-largest country in Africa, Algeria is located in North Africa, between the Mediterranean Sea in the north and the Saharan desert in the south. It borders Morocco on the northwest, the Western Sahara and Mauritania on the southwest, Mali and Niger on the south, and Tunisia and Libya on the east. Algeria has an area of 2,381,741 sq km (919,487 sq mi), of which more than 80% is desert.

The Algerian population of more than 31.1 million grows at an annual rate of 2.1%. Arabic is the official language, yet French is widely spoken and used as the language of commerce. Ethnically, Algerians are of an Arab-Berber stock. Islam is the religion of 97% of the people. The local currency is the *dinar.* Algeria's primary exports are natural gas, crude oil, phosphate rock, iron ore, citrus fruits, and dates.

## POLITICAL BACKGROUND

Algeria gained its independence from France in 1962, following a long and bitter struggle. The FLN (National Liberation Front) led that struggle and would dominate Algerian politics for the next three decades. Since 1979, the nation's problems have had two main features: a deep economic crisis and a violent societal challenge led by Islamist militants. Several factors brought this situation about, including the failure of the development strategy, the authoritarian nature of the government, and the rise of a very powerful Islamist movement. From 1965 to 1978, under President Boumedienne, Algeria engaged in a socialist development strategy that focused on heavy industries. The state controlled all natural resources, nationalized foreign assets, used centralized economic planning, and created a large public sector. This strategy achieved some positive results in economic growth, employment, education, health, and other services. However, by 1979 its negative effects started appearing, including a bloated bureaucracy, distribution bottlenecks, a rampant inflation, major structural dislocations, a growing income inequality, and a very poor agricultural performance, which in turn, stimulated urban migration and food scarcity. Moreover, society grew dependent on the state for almost every need without necessarily being required to be productive or efficient.

After Boumedienne's death, his successor, Chadli Benjedid, responded to the economic crisis with mostly ad hoc and ill-coordinated reform measures that were driven more by political imperatives than economic rationality. The power of the only legal party in Algeria, the FLN, was increased while the sphere of political expression was curtailed further. The reforms failed to halt economic deterioration not only because of their inadequate nature, but also because of resistance among workers, conservative elements of the ruling elite, and managers of the public sector. The sharp drop in oil prices in 1986, which translated into a 42% drop in Algeria's oil revenue, made economic revival almost impossible. This, in turn, aggravated the social contradictions and increased people's resentment against the state and its leaders. In the first week of October 1988, major youth riots shook the country and led to the fiercest repression ever, with the resulting deaths of some 500 people.

Following the tragic events of October 1988, the constitution was amended to permit a multi-party system. Within months, several political parties and independent associations were born. The most important ones were those affiliated with the Islamist movement, headed by the Islamic Salvation Front (FIS), which based its appeal on a plan to establish an Islamic republic governed by the *shariah* (Islamic law). The FIS became the main opposition party and won the most seats in the nation's first multi-party municipal elections of June 1990. In the first round of parliamentary elections of December 1991, it captured 188 out of 430 seats while the ethnically-based FFS (Front of Socialist Forces) obtained 25 seats. The FLN captured a mere 15 seats. Between the two elections, the Islamist challenge grew even bigger and led to a violent showdown with the army. Thousands of people were arrested, including the two FIS leaders, and a state of emergency was instituted in the summer of 1991. In January 1992, the army canceled the parliamentary elections, pushed President Benjedid to resign, banned the FIS, and put the formal reigns of the country in the hands of a High State Council. The Islamists responded to these developments by staging an armed rebellion that would last for many years and cause the death of more than 100,000 people.

In the midst of an intricate and violent political stalemate, economic redress became even more difficult and pushed Algeria to agree to an International Monetary Fund (IMF) structural adjustment program as a condition to the debt rescheduling the country needed. By the end of May 1994, Algeria was also engaged in a new series of political reforms. After attempts at dialogue with the jailed FIS leaders had failed, the state turned to a firmer repression of radical Islamists and an overture toward moderate opposition parties—both Islamist and secular. In January 1995, most opposition parties (including the banned FIS) met in Rome and agreed on a national platform for resolving the crisis, but

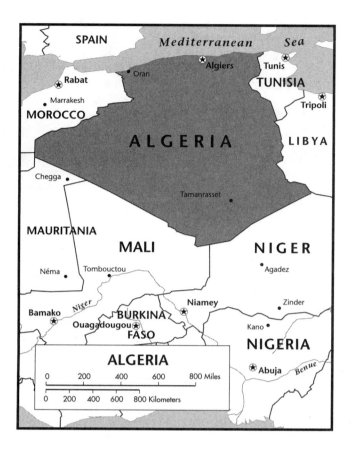

the government rejected it. A multi-party presidential election was held later that year, and incumbent general Liamine Zeroual won by 61% of the vote. A new political party, the RND (National and Democratic Rally), was created to support his candidacy. In 1996, a constitutional amendment was introduced. It reconfirmed Islam as the state's religion, prohibited parties based on "religious, linguistic, racial, gender, corporatist or regional" grounds, and reinforced the powers of the president. A second parliamentary chamber, the Council of the Nation, was created. New parliamentary elections held in June 1997 resulted in Algeria's first multi-party parliament. The main winners were RND, FLN, and the moderate Islamist parties, MSP (Movement of Society for Peace) and *al-Nahda* (Renaissance). The RND and the FLN constituted a pro-government coalition that controlled an absolute majority and seven ministerial posts each. The Islamists were also awarded seven posts.

Economic and security conditions continued to worsen, and thousands of people were killed. The Islamist violence widened and new organizations, mainly the Armed Islamic Group (GIA) and the Army of Islamic Salvation (AIS), engaged in a series of killings. Their victims were not only military and police personnel, but also civilians and foreigners. The state countered with measures that left scores dead and thousands jailed. It was in this context that Zeroual decided in the fall of 1998 to resign from the presidency, well before the end of his term, and call for a new vote in April 1999. Abdelaziz Bouteflika quickly became the candidate favored by the military and many elements in society.

## PERSONAL BACKGROUND

Abdelaziz Bouteflika was born on 2 March 1937 in the Moroccan town of Oujda, near the Algerian border. In 1956, he joined the Algerian nationalist movement, which was fighting for independence from France. When Algeria gained its independence in 1962, President Ahmed Ben Bella appointed Bouteflika to be minister of youth, sports, and tourism. The following year he became the foreign minister. Despite the overthrow of the Ben Bella government by Colonel Houari Boumedienne in 1965, Bouteflika was able to retain his post until 1979. As foreign minister, he distinguished himself by successfully articulating Algeria's economic and political nationalism in the 1970s. He led negotiations with France that preceded the 1971 nationalization of the hydrocarbon industry. Bouteflika chaired the 1974 United Nations' special session on the new international economic order. He also made Algeria's influence bear on the nonaligned movement.

After the death of Boumedienne in December 1978, Bouteflika was considered a possible successor. However, he lost the ensuing power struggle, and the military imposed Colonel Chadli Benjedid as Algeria's new president. Bouteflika remained in the government as minister without portfolio and advisor until 1980 when Benjedid dismissed him. The following year, Bouteflika was accused of having embezzled close to $12 million while he was foreign minister. Bouteflika abandoned Algerian politics and spent 16 of the next 19 years in exile in Switzerland. There he worked as a consultant to several Persian Gulf nations.

## RISE TO POWER

In February 1999, Bouteflika returned to Algeria after a group of top military, political, and business leaders persuaded him to run in the upcoming presidential elections. Six other candidates were on the ballot, but two days before the elections they decided to withdraw from the vote after the state refused to act on their complaints on electoral irregularities. By default, Bouteflika became the only candidate. This situation hurt the credibility of both the poll and its winner. Bouteflika had secured the support of the military and that of the FLN, the RND and MSP parties. Being from the era of the authoritarian but well-liked President Boumedienne, he was thought to be the ideal person to lead his country out of its deep and multidimensional crisis. According to official results, he won the election on 15 April 1999 by 73.79% of the vote cast, becoming the first civilian president since 1965.

## LEADERSHIP

During his electoral campaign and in his first presidential speech on 29 May 1999, Bouteflika promised to work hard to restore the trust of Algerians in their institutions, something which he regards as essential for ending political violence in the country. This may prove difficult, however, because of the alleged election rigging that hangs over his victory. Moreover, he will have to prove that his mandate comes from the people and not from the army, which still holds real power in the country. Backed openly by the RND, FLN, MSP, and *al-Nahda* movement, Bouteflika, has been called the "consensus candidate." To find a solution to the violent crisis, he pledged to negotiate with political parties, "except those whose hands are stained with blood."

Bouteflika seems committed to solving the crisis, but he needs to convince elements in the government and the army who may resist his plan. He is likely to nominate a prime minister who would not only support his policies but would also gather support for them in parliament. In order to brush aside the accusation concerning his electoral victory, it is probable that Bouteflika may either co-opt some leaders of that opposition by offering them positions in his government, or may call for new parliamentary elections in order to enhance the legitimacy of his rule.

## DOMESTIC POLICY

In his first speech, Bouteflika acknowledged that the state's institutions are ailing from abuses of authority, inefficiency, waste, and corruption. He indicated that social cohesion and peace depended on a regeneration of the state, which must be based on the rule of the law and on the promotion of the interests of the entire nation. The new president seems aware of the multitude of complex problems that the country must address in order to pull itself out of its current crisis. Among the tasks at hand are a much needed reform of the educational system, a better orchestrated economic reform, a firm and tangible encouragement of private investment, the modernization of agriculture, and special attention to the country's youth and its difficulties. He reaffirmed Algeria's Islamic and Arab-Berber identity and called for the renewal of regional integration efforts.

Just like his predecessors, Bouteflika seems committed to reviving the economy and to addressing the most urgent social grievances while maintaining law and order. His task is huge, complex, and not without risks. He must secure support from the army and the government, and also among the most important elements of civil society. Radical Islamists will remain a major challenge and are likely to continue their violent pressure on the state, which will in turn respond with firm repression against their most radical elements, and an invitation to dialogue to those seeking a political solution to the crisis. Bouteflika has little time to alleviate his people's problems, to eliminate the conditions that led to the rise of the societal rebellion, and to quell political violence. If he does not succeed quickly, the challenge might grow bigger and lead to an uncontrollable situation that would further aggravate the current vicious cycle of civil violence and military repression.

Despite good intentions, Bouteflika does not seem to be responding in a coherent, concerted fashion to his country's many problems. In May 2000, 30 members of the national assembly signed a petition to be presented to the president expressing dissatisfaction over the limited amount of legislative work completed over the last 12 months. The president, due to his interests and experience in foreign policy, seems more interested in mediating international crises in the region than attending to the country's domestic problems.

## FOREIGN POLICY

The United States and some Western European countries have criticized the way the last presidential election was conducted, but they have refrained from criticizing Algeria's human rights practices. This tolerance has always been predicated on there being at least a semblance of a democratic process in place. The last election failed to offer such semblance.

At the time when Bouteflika was foreign minister, Algeria played a central role in anti-colonialism, the nonaligned movement, the call for a restructuring of the international system, and the establishment of a new international economic order to help poor countries develop and gain economic independence. It has also fulfilled an important role within the Organization of Petroleum Exporting Countries (OPEC). Algeria has been a staunch supporter of the Palestinian struggle for statehood and has, since 1975, given moral and material support to the Western Sahara liberation movement (POLISARIO) in its struggle against Morocco's annexation of former Spanish Sahara. However, since the 1980s, Algeria has taken a low-key position in international relations, and has worked on developing its relations with the West and on diversifying its economic partners. It has succeeded in changing its image from a radical to a mature, moderate, and respected semi-industrialized country. Under Bouteflika's leadership, Algeria is expected to remain committed to the issues and principles mentioned above and to a pragmatic orientation. Bouteflika has begun to try to reestablish Algeria's influential role in world affairs in general, and among the Third World in particular, by attending mediation efforts in various trouble spots. However, in doing so he is jeopardizing the ability of his government to address the needs of his own people, which are at a crisis point due to years of civil conflict and deprivation.

## ADDRESS

Presidence de la Republique
El Mouradia
Algiers, Algeria

## REFERENCES

*Economic Crisis and Political Change in North Africa.* Westport, CT: Praeger, 1998.

*Foreign Affairs,* July/August 1998, vol. 77, no. 4.

*Le Monde,* various issues.

*Le Monde Diplomatique,* various issues.

*The Middle East and North Africa 2000.* London: Europa Publications, 1999.

*Middle East Journal,* 1996, vol. 50, no. 1.

*The New Global Economy: North African Responses.* Boulder, CO: St. Martin Press, 1996.

*New York Times,* 17 September 1998, 15–18 April 1999.

*North Africa Journal,* 23 May 2000.

Spencer, William. *The Middle East.* 8th ed. Guilford, CT: Dushkin/McGraw-Hill, 2000.

Stone, Martin. *The Agony of Algeria.* New York: Columbia University Press, 1997.

Zartman, L.W. *Collapsed States: The Disintegration and Restoration of Legitimate Authority.* Boulder, CO: Lynne-Rinner, 1995.

**Profile researched and written by Azzedine Layachi, St. John's University (9/99; updated by Kathryn L. Green, Ph.D., California State University, San Bernardino 6/2000).**

# ANDORRA

## Marc Forné Molné
### Executive Council President
*(pronounced "MARK for-NAY mol-NAY")*

*"We must insist on the values that can allow mankind to survive: respect for human rights, the fundamental importance of the individual, the conservation of our natural and historical heritages."*

The Principality of Andorra, despite its name, has been a constitutional republic since 1993. It is a landlocked state between Spain and France, and its culture, economy, and political life reflect the influence of those two neighboring countries. One of the smallest countries in the world, Andorra has only 450 sq km (174 sq mi) of territory, making it slightly more than twice the size of Washington, D.C. The capital city is Andorra-la-Vella. Andorra's population has been estimated to be approximately 66,000—only 18,000 of whom are Andorran citizens. More than 60% of its inhabitants are Spaniards, and most of the rest are French nationals. Its large foreign population is comprised of migrant labor seeking employment in its tourist industry and light manufacturing companies, and of wealthy individuals residing in Andorra because of its status as a tax haven. Andorra uses both the Spanish *peseta* and the French *franc* as official currencies. Catalan, spoken primarily in northeastern Spain, is the official language, but most residents speak French and Spanish as well. Ethnically, Andorran citizens are indistinguishable from their French and Spanish neighbors. The population is overwhelmingly Roman Catholic. There is no state religion in Andorra, and the Constitution explicitly permits all faiths. Andorra produces raw tobacco, cigarettes, and cigars, but its economy is built around tourism and a growing banking industry.

## POLITICAL BACKGROUND

Andorra has been considered a state since the 13th century, but only recently has its population attained a large measure of control over the country's affairs. Archaeological evidence indicates that Andorra's mountain valleys were inhabited as early as 4000 BC. During the early Christian era, the Romans encouraged resident tribes to surrender their nomadic life and form settlements there.

In 1278 the French Count of Foix and the Spanish Bishop of Urgel became the "co-princes" of the country, granting Andorra nominal independence but retaining authority over its foreign contacts and trade. For centuries, Andorra was an anomaly among states. Councils of Andorrans exercised an element of self-expression; at the same time, ultimate authority rested in the hands of the co-princes. The state was therefore neither a principality nor a republic.

France and Spain ultimately spurred the Andorrans to assume greater responsibility over their own affairs and to move towards more democratic practices. For most of Andorra's history, there was no functioning executive office within the government. Local councils and a national legislative body provided day-to-day governing authority. Until 1970, the vote was given only to males who were from families that had lived in Andorra for at least three generations. In that year, women obtained the vote. Few foreigners were allowed to gain citizenship. The Andorrans permitted no political parties and no labor unions. In 1975, the Spanish dictator Francisco Franco died, and Spain embraced democracy. From that moment, Spain, together with France, encouraged reform in Andorra. In 1981, an institution with vague executive powers was created, but efforts to codify a coherent body of law and a constitution failed. In 1993 Andorrans declared their independence. A Constitution gave Andorra sovereignty over most of its domestic affairs, trade, and general foreign policy.

France and Spain, however, continue to guide important aspects of life in Andorra. French and Spanish officials oversee Andorra's judicial system. Appeals to an ultimate court of jurisdiction are heard in courts in either France or Spain. Andorra has a small army comprised of males who own firearms. They have not been engaged in a conflict for over 700 years, and today their duties are largely ceremonial. France and Spain maintain responsibility for Andorran defense policy.

The growing foreign population has provided much of the capital for Andorra's economy. By the 1970s, foreign nationals began to seek a greater definition of their rights, including eligibility for citizenship and the right to organize. Andorrans, in a minority in their own country, had traditionally sought to limit foreigners' rights. The Constitution is a compromise in that it recognizes foreigners' aspirations by opening the door to citizenship but preserves political power in the hands of the indigenous population. Political parties and unions are now legal. Andorran families of long standing dominate political life. Foreigners may gain citizenship after 30 years of residency or if they have lived in the country since before 1975. Conservative Roman Catholic traditions are strong in Andorra. Although women may vote, few have succeeded in politics or business.

The Executive Council President is chosen by the General Council, which has 28 members and is elected every four years by a direct vote of all citizens over 18. The Executive Council President appoints the cabinet, but the General Council may bring down the government at any time by a majority vote. These practices resemble a parliamentary system, with the Executive Council President and the cabinet functioning as the executive branch, and the General Council as the legislature. The most important cabinet offices are foreign affairs, finance, the economy, and justice.

Power is fragmented among several parties. In the legislative elections of 16 February 1997, more than 80% of eligible voters cast ballots. The Liberal Union/Liberal Party of Andorra (Unio Liberal/Partit Liberal Andorra—UL), a center-right party, won more than 50% of the vote and 16 seats on the General Council; the center-left National Democratic Group (Agrupament Nacional Democratic—AND) won about 20% of the vote and gained six seats. Three smaller parties—conservative New Democracy (Nova Democracia—ND), the National Democratic Initiative (Initiativa Democratic Nacional—IDN), and the Union of Ordinc People (Unio del Poble d'Ordino—UPO)—each won two seats. The UL formed a government for the second time (first was in 1994), again under Marc Forné Molné.

## PERSONAL BACKGROUND

Marc Forné Molné became Executive Council President in 1994 when the General Council removed Oscar Ribas Reig on a vote of confidence motion. Forné (the custom in Andorra is to use the second name as the last name) was born in 1947, educated as an attorney, and is a practicing Roman Catholic. He has been active in Andorran political life since the 1970s, but restrictions on political organization meant that he and other political figures in Andorra kept a low profile until the passage of the Constitution in 1993. In that year he founded the Liberal Union party.

## RISE TO POWER

The government of Oscar Ribas fell because he was exploring the possibility of instituting a broader system of taxation in order to combat a growing budget deficit. By a vote of 20 to 8, the General Council removed his government on 25 November 1994; only the members of his own party voted for him. Forné was chosen to replace him because he was viewed as a well-educated moderate who would continue reform, but at a slower pace. Forné assumed power on 21 December 1994. Forné remained Executive Council President following the 1997 elections when his party won the majority of seats in the General Council.

## LEADERSHIP

Forné believes that for Andorra's prosperity to continue, the country must gradually become more engaged in the outside world. Forné opposed Ribas's efforts to institute broader taxation, and instead has concentrated on strengthening Andorra's links to the outside world in order to attract trade and investment. His leadership is evident in several steps taken shortly after he rose to power. In 1995, he attended meetings of the United Nations in New York and used the occasion to hold discussions with a number of current and future potential trading partners. In 1996, Forné's government took a firm stand on a key international issue by signing the Non-Proliferation Treaty. Signatories of this treaty do not possess chemical, nuclear, or biological weapons pledge not to obtain them in the future. The treaty could prove to be an important step in the effort to stem the sale and development of weapons of mass destruction in the aftermath of the Cold War. The Forné government is expected

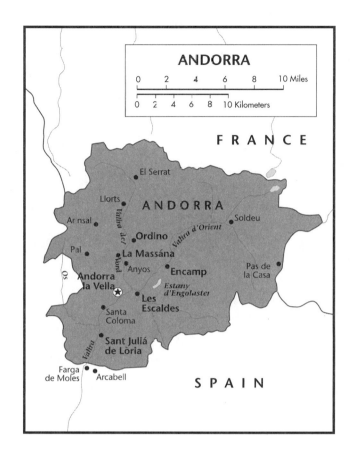

to continue to support positions in the security field that promote peaceful relations among nations.

## DOMESTIC POLICY

Andorrans had traditionally pursued agriculture to make their living. While sheep are still raised and the traditional crops of tobacco and potatoes are still sown, Andorra's livelihood now depends upon tourism and an emerging service industry of financial institutions. Domestic policy therefore centers upon efforts to assure that outside guests and capital continue to flow into the country. There is no income tax in Andorra, a tradition that has attracted wealthy residents, who live in the country and, in some cases, establish financial institutions such as banks and insurance companies. Andorra has tight banking secrecy laws to encourage the continued presence of such institutions. The US government and several European governments have expressed concern that such laws encourage money laundering and the investment of illegally gained capital in Andorra.

Raising revenue has become an important problem for Andorra's government. Because large numbers of foreign laborers have been necessary to build Andorra's many hotels and restaurants, there has been a need to construct housing, hospitals, and schools for these laborers and their families. In addition, it has been necessary to improve roads, lay sewer lines, and undertake a range of other tasks endemic in countries experiencing rapid growth—and to accomplish such efforts without an income tax. Some steps have been taken to keep the Andorran treasury at least partly filled. Foreigners must pay an annual levy in order to maintain the right to stay in the country. This annual levy provides funds for a substantial part of the country's budget. A small import tax on the large amount of consumer goods brought into the country for sale to visitors also supplies revenue for the country's treasury. The only tax on the individual Andorran citizen is a modest fee collected for telephone and electricity use. The Andorran government has run a deficit since the early 1990s, and methods short of an income tax are being considered to raise further revenues.

## FOREIGN POLICY

Andorra has no armed forces trained for combat, and its defense policy is handled by France and Spain. In part because it is landlocked between two large, powerful neighbors with which it is on good terms, Andorra has no apparent need for armed forces and defense arrangements beyond protection or assistance that France and Spain provide.

From the mid-1980s, France and Spain attempted to nudge Andorra not only towards independence and democracy, but into firmer contacts with the outside world. To some extent, this effort by Andorra's neighbors was economically based: citizens from France and Spain sought greater certainty from their Andorran hosts when applying for work or residence permits. Politically, Paris and Madrid wished to see these workers gain rights of representation, something that was not allowed until a constitution guaranteeing such rights could be adopted. Independence in March 1993 was quickly followed by openings to the outside world and the establishment of civil and political norms common in European democracies. In July 1993 Andorra joined the United Nations. It has established diplomatic and trade relations with a number of countries, such as China, Cuba, South Korea, and Indonesia, from which it imports raw materials or finished goods for re-sale to foreign visitors. Although it has diplomatic relations with these countries, it has no diplomatic representation except in Paris, Madrid, and New York, at the United Nations. Andorra's ambassador to the UN is also its ambassador to the United States. As a further step towards marking its place as an independent, democratic state, in October 1994 it joined the Council of Europe, an international institution that sets standards for human and civil rights.

The Spanish and French governments have encouraged Andorra to take advantage of the European Union's free trade regulations by developing export industries. Through an agreement with the European Union, Andorra obtained the right to export to EU countries with minimal tariffs on its goods. Tension between the countries of the EU and Andorra developed during the 1990s because of growing evidence of widespread cigarette smuggling through Andorra. European nations estimated that they were losing about 400 million euros (US$428 million) in tax revenue from illegal sales of cigarettes through Andorra. In 1998, the government took action to enforce customs laws and enacted regulations to make smuggling specifically illegal. As of 2000, no strong legitimate export industries had been established.

Andorra's future may well depend upon its continued efforts to mesh into broader European life. Because it depends heavily upon its neighbors and foreign guests to survive, Andorra is likely to continue to be accommodating to France and Spain when those countries insist upon changes of policy. In the 21st centruy, Paris and Madrid are most likely to urge reform of citizenship laws in order to provide a guarantee of rights for long-time foreign residents who wish to become Andorrans, as well as a softening of the banking secrecy laws in order to limit the flow of illegal capital into the country.

## ADDRESS

Office of the Cap de Govern
Andorra-la-Vella
Andorra

## REFERENCES

Bureau of Democracy, Human Rights, and Labor. US Department of State. 1999 Country Reports on Human Rights Practices. [Online] Available http://www.state.gov/www/global/human_rights/1999_hrp_report/andorra.html (Accessed March 10, 2000).

Duursma, Jorri. *Self-Determination, Statehood, and International Relations of Micro-states: The Cases of Liechtenstein, San Marino, Monaco, Andorra, and the Vatican City.* New York: Cambridge University Press, 1996.

Forné Molné, Marc. Speech delivered before the United Nations, 24 October 1995.

Ganz, Michael T. "Oh, Andorra." *Swiss Review of World Affairs*, January 1994.

**Profile researched and written by Paul E. Gallis (8/96; updated 3/2000).**

# ANGOLA

### Jose Eduardo Dos Santos
### President

*(pronounced "HOE-zay ed-WAHR-doh dose SAN-tose")*

*"I vow to struggle for strengthened national unity for the fulfillment of the worker-peasant alliance, and for the building of people's power."*

The Republic of Angola is situated on the Atlantic (west) coast of Africa, just south of the Congo River. It is bordered to the north and east by Zaire, to the southeast by Zambia and to the south by Namibia. The national territory covers 1,246,700 sq km (481,354 sq mi) and includes the enclave of Cabinda in the northwest. The capital is Luanda. Angola's 11.2 million people are primarily Bantus, who come from four distinct groups: the Bakongo in the northwest, the Kimbundu in the north-central region, the Ovimbundu in the south-central region, and the Chokwe in the east. Portuguese is the official language; of the several African languages, none is sufficiently universal to be adopted officially.

The unit of currency is the Kwanga; inflation has rendered it virtually worthless both at home and abroad, which has allowed a black market to flourish. The Angolan economy, once prosperous and still with massive potential, has been devastated by civil war. The per capita GDP has been estimated at $1,000. Exports, notably coffee and diamonds cannot be transported out of the country because the primary railway has been crippled for years. Potentially the bread-basket for all of southern Africa, Angola relies on massive food imports to avert widespread famine. Guerrilla activity has driven the peasants off the land, either to cities or neigh-boring countries. Cabinda's offshore oil reserves generate more than 85% of government revenue and attract private foreign investment despite the political instability of the country.

## POLITICAL BACKGROUND

Angola is the largest of Portugal's former African colonies, first settled in the late 15th century by Portuguese navigators who were seeking trade routes to India. In 1951, the colony was designated an Overseas Province of Portugal, making it an integral part of the Portuguese state. Guerrilla opposition to colonial rule began in 1961 and continued for 13 years, even in the face of substantial Portuguese military presence. By 1974, there were three major independence movements, each operating in a different area of Angola. The National Front for the Liberation of Angola (FNLA) controlled a great deal of the north and had established a government-in-exile in the Congo as early as 1963. The central region, plus Cabinda, was controlled by the Soviet-backed Popular Movement for the Liberation of Angola (MPLA). Eastern and southern Angola were in the hands of the National Union for the Total Independence of Angola (UNITA).

Independence for Angola became a real possibility in 1974 when a coup d'etat overthrew the Portuguese government. On 15 January 1975, the leaders of the three independence movements, Holder Roberto (FNLA), Jonas Savimbi (UNITA), and Agustinho Neto (MPLA), met with Portuguese representatives. The parties agreed that Angola would obtain its independence effective 11 November 1975, the 400th anniversary of the founding of Luanda. In the interim, Angola was to be ruled by a Portuguese high commissioner and a three-person Presidential Collegiate composed of representatives of each of the independence movements.

At midnight on 11 November, after the departure of the high commissioner, Neto announced the establishment of the People's Republic of Angola, under MPLA auspices. Concurrently, FNLA and UNITA, which had formed an alliance in the preceding months, announced the establishment of the rival Democratic People's Republic of Angola. A long and arduous civil war ensued. For years, the Angolan war was considered a classic example of East-West conflict, with MPLA receiving support of the Soviet bloc, and UNITA and FNLA receiving aid from the West. By 1979, the FNLA's forces were virtually eliminated, and in 1984 the remaining FNLA guerrillas surrendered.

Under the terms of the 1975 constitution, the head of government was the president. The cabinet was composed of the president, three ministers of state, and 21 ministers; the president could hold ministerial positions. In 1991 a series of amendments provided for the establishment of a multi-party democracy. Legislative power was vested in the National Assembly, with 220 members elected for four years on the basis of proportional representation.

In 1992, relatively free and fair elections were held for the presidency and the legislature. Of the 11 presidential candidates, Jose Eduardo dos Santos won 49.6% of the vote to Jonas Savimbi's 40.1%. Savimbi repudiated the results as fraudulent and refused to participate in a run-off. In the legislative elections, the MPLA scored 53.7% of the vote to UNITA's 34.1%, giving the ruling party a 129 to 70 seat advantage over UNITA. Holden Roberto's FNLA received only 2.1% (5 seats), and the others took the remaining 16 seats.

In 1994, dos Santos and Savimbi signed the Lusaka Protocol, which gave new hope for a peace settlement. In 1995, international sanctions were imposed on UNITA though sanctions have been violated repeatedly. In 1997, a government of national unity provided for power-sharing

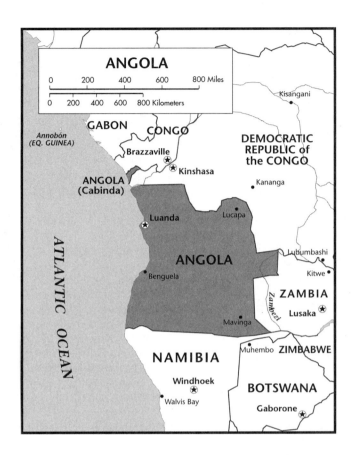

between the MPLA and UNITA, but resumption of the war in violation of the Lusaka Agreement rendered this arrangement ineffective. While the National Assembly functioned nominally, the war severed major sections of the country from Luanda, especially cutting off rural areas from MPLA government services. An estimated 2.6 million persons were thought to be internally displaced in 1999. Dos Santos announced elections for late 2001.

## PERSONAL BACKGROUND

Jose Eduardo dos Santos was born in Luanda on 28 August 1942. His father was a bricklayer. Dos Santos was educated at the Liceu Salvador Carreia during the Portuguese colonial administration.

In 1961, dos Santos joined the MPLA in its fight for Angolan independence. He fled Angola later that year for exile in the Congo where he was a founding member and vice president of MPLA Youth, based in Kinshasa. He served as MPLA representative in Yugoslavia and headed the MPLA office in Brazzaville. In 1963, dos Santos was one of a group of students sent on MPLA scholarships to study in the USSR. He graduated as a petroleum engineer in 1969 from the Institute of Oil and Gas in Baku. He completed a course in military communication shortly before returning to Angola in 1970, where he participated in the war against the Portuguese as a member of the Cabinda guerrilla front.

## RISE TO POWER

Dos Santos began his rise through the MPLA ranks in 1974, when he was named second in command of Telecommuni-

calions Services for the MPLA Second Politico-Military Region in Cabinda. He was also chosen as a member of the Provisional Readjustment Committee for the Northern Front. In September of the same year he was appointed to the MPLA Central Committee and was ranked fifth on the Political Bureau.

At the formation of the first MPLA government in November 1975, dos Santos was named chairman of the MPLA and Minister of Foreign Affairs. He moved on to the position of coordinator of the MPLA Foreign Relations Department. He was Central Committee Secretary for several departments, including Education, Culture and Sport, National Reconstruction, and Economic Development and Planning. In 1978 he was named Minister of National Planning, first Deputy Prime Minister and head of the MPLA's National Planning Committee. President Neto went to the USSR for medical treatment in September 1979, and before leaving he designated dos Santos to take charge of the government during his absence. Neto died in Moscow on 10 September 1979. Thereupon, the central committee "unanimously and by strong acclamation," elected dos Santos to succeed Neto as president of the MPLA. He took office as president of the People's Republic of Angola on 21 September 1979.

## LEADERSHIP

When dos Santos assumed the presidency, the country was still in the midst of post-colonial reconstruction. Although the potential for sustained economic expansion was enormous, productivity was low. Political institutions were weak or non-existent. Dos Santos committed himself to improve both areas. He also insisted on military security and resisted international efforts to undermine the regime. Dos Santos and his government have been hampered by a paucity of trained personnel and the skilled manpower necessary to implement development plans. Economic progress throughout his tenure has been devastated by the civil war.

In spite of his lofty ambitions to devolve power to the people, dos Santos has been a pragmatist. He has invited assistance from the East and West as befits the needs of the government. In the early 1980s, Cuban troops were defending American oil installations against attacks from UNITA guerrillas funded by the American taxpayer. With the end of the cold war, dos Santos no longer could play the superpowers against each other. Economic and institutional interests have taken a back seat to the civil war, and dos Santos has given priority to the survival of his regime.

## DOMESTIC POLICY

President dos Santos is faced with an economy devastated by war and neglect, the reconstruction of which will be a long and arduous process. Agricultural production has not yet returned to pre-independence levels, and massive food imports are required to feed the nation. Diamond and coffee production has fallen or is in UNITA's hands, which has resulted in a decline in foreign exchange earnings. Transportation is seriously hampered by war-related damage.

The appointment of a new economic team in January 1999 provided some hope that public finance would improve. However, a widening of the exchange rate between the official and parallel rates, and a World Bank announcement in May to discontinue lending because of war, rampant corruption, and lack of transparency, dimmed those hopes. Inflation in 2000 was expected to fall from 1999 levels as the government brought monetary growth under control.

The government attempted to reorganize mining by appointing a new minister, but key mining areas remained under rebel control or subject to rebel attacks. Nevertheless, De Beers planned to build a $30 million diamond processing facility in Luanda. Government has prioritized rebuilding transportation infrastructure both road and rail into the interior. Civil service reform is needed to reduce bloated ranks and better compensate those who merit it. On the bright side, real GDP growth rose in 2000 to 6.5% on the basis of rising oil production.

Huge crop shortfalls and seed corn shortages were expected into 2000 because of unharvested crops, and consumption of seed corn for survival. People fleeing their villages virtually left crops to be stolen, burned, or rot. Relief agencies expected to feed thousands of returnees after the October–November planting season. In health, the government emphasized vaccinations, maternal and child care, malaria prevention, AIDS prevention, and provision of essential medicines, but many areas in the country have no health facilities or access to medical care.

The government's offensives in 1998 and 1999 resulted in thousands of government troop casualties. In April 1999, the government began drafting 21-year-olds, something it had not done since 1991. In May 2000, the war was entering a guerrilla stage to which the Angolan army was less suited.

## FOREIGN POLICY

Dos Santos has supported Angola's neighbor to the north, Laurent Kabila, since his campaign to overthrow Mobutu in 1997. After the Rwandese and Ugandan invasion of Congo in 1998, Angola came into the war on the side of the SADC states along with Zimbabwe and Namibia to Kabila's

defense. Angola has agreements with Congo Brazzaville, Congo Kinshasa, and Namibia to allow its troops to operate on their soil. The spread of the war into Namibia and the pressure on Zambia to honor the sanctions, have strained relations with these neighbors. Key members of the international community presently seek to apply UN sanctions against UNITA to prevent it from obtaining weapons, and at the same time, protect their oil, diamond, and other commercial interests in Angola. The UN's current mandate in Angola is heavily restricted following Kofi Annan's declaration of the failure of the Lusaka Protocol.

## ADDRESS

Gabinete do Presidente

Luanda, Angola

## REFERENCES

Africa News Online. [Online] Available http://www.africanews.org/west/stories/1999_feat1.html (Accessed June 2000).

Africaonline. [Online] Available http://www.africa-online.com (Accessed June 2000).

*Africa Report,* various issues.

*Current History,* various issues.

Economist Intelligence Unit, *EIU Country Reports,* 28 February 2000.

Integrated Regional Information Network (IRIN). [Online] Available http://www.reliefweb.int/IRIN (Accessed June 2000).

Martin, Phyllis. *Historical Dictionary of Angola.* 1980.

*New York Times,* various issues.

USAID Country Strategic Plan, Angola 2001–05.

Wolfers, Michael and Jan Bergerol. *Angola In the Front Line.* 1983.

**Profile researched and written by Alison Doherty Munro (7/90); updated by Robert J. Groelsema (6/2000)**

# ANTIGUA AND BARBUDA

**Lester Bird**
**Prime Minister**
*(pronounced "LES-ter BURD")*

*"Comrades, the Antigua Labour Party, which has successfully guided this nation to the economic and social heights it has attained, is ready to lead it into the new century. On these strong foundations we have already laid, we will build a nation strong and healthy, a country robust and prosperous, a society that is just, fair and based on merit."*

Antigua and Barbuda (pronounced "ann-TEE-guh" and "bar-BYOO-duh") is made up of two islands along the outer edge of the Leeward chain of the Eastern Caribbean. Its 64,000 inhabitants live on 322 sq km (170 sq mi).

Ethnically, 95% of the population are descendants of West Africans who were imported as slaves. The remaining 5% are of European, Asian, Middle Eastern, or mixed descent. The official language of the country is English although an English dialect is widely spoken. Christianity is, by far, the dominant religion, with Protestants accounting for more than 85% of adherents.

Major exports include refined petroleum and petroleum products, crawfish, cucumbers, tomatoes, coconuts, sisal, salt, straw products, and lumber. However, tourism is the major foreign exchange earner. The national currency is the Eastern Caribbean (EC) dollar.

## POLITICAL BACKGROUND

Before the arrival of Columbus in 1493, the Amerindians settled Antigua and Barbuda. The name "Antigua" was given to the area in honor of Santa Maria la Antigua of Seville. English planters from the island of St. Kitts first colonized the country in 1623. After a brief period of French occupation, in 1667, it became a British possession through the Treaty of Breda. The country remained a British subject until 1981 when it became independent.

Although these two islands are 48 km (30 mi) apart, they have one government and form one independent state. Antigua and Barbuda is a constitutional monarchy in which the Queen of England is the titular head of state and is represented through a governor general. The legislature is comprised of a bicameral parliament with the council of ministers as the executive, headed by the prime minister. The bicameral legislature is made up of two chambers: an elected House of Representatives and an appointed Senate. The Senate (the upper house) has 17 members named by the governor general, 11 of whom are appointed on the advice of the prime minister. Of the remainder, four are named after consultation with the opposition; one is recommended by the Barbuda Council, which is also vested with the authority to raise local revenue; and one is named at the governor general's discretion.

The House of Representatives (lower house) has 19 members: 17 members who are elected every five years or at the dissolution of parliament, one ex-officio member, and one

Speaker. The opposition leader is normally chosen from the leading minority in parliament.

There are five political parties in the country. The ruling party, the Antigua Labour Party (ALP), led by Lester Bird, has dominated Antiguan politics since the 1960s. Other parties include the United Progressive Party (UPP), led by Baldwin Spencer, and a coalition of three opposition political parties—the United National Democratic Party (UNDP), the Antigua Caribbean Liberation Movement (ACLM), and the Progressive Labor Movement (PLM).

## PERSONAL BACKGROUND

Lester Bryant Bird is the son of the former prime minister, Vere Bird Sr. Before his retirement in 1994, Vere Bird had been the longest-serving prime minister in the English-speaking Caribbean. His son Lester was born on 21 February 1938 and attended the Antigua Grammar School. Bird is unique in that he is one of the few Caribbean leaders who excelled in competitive sports, academics, and politics. Between 1956 and 1957 he represented Antigua and the Leeward Islands in cricket. He also won a bronze medal for the long jump at the Pan American Games. In 1962, he entered the University of Michigan to study law and represented that institution in track and field. He gained the distinction of admission to the Honorary Fraternity Sphinx at the University for all-round performance as an academic athlete. In 1969, Bird was admitted to the bar at Gray's Inn. He remained in private law practice until 1976.

## RISE TO POWER

On his return to Antigua, Bird became involved in politics, following in the footsteps of his father—a prominent trade union leader and political figure. In 1971, Bird became chairman of the ALP. This political party was aligned with the Antigua Trades and Labour Union (ATLU) and was led by his father, then chief minister and minister of planning. Between 1971 and 1976, he was nominated senator of the Upper House and served as leader of the opposition until 1976 when he was elected to parliament. Between 1976 and 1981, he was named deputy premier and minister of economic development, tourism, and energy. In 1980, he was re-elected to parliament with an increased majority and appointed to the post of deputy prime minister and minister of foreign affairs, economic development, tourism, and energy. He was re-elected to parliament in 1989 and served as minister of external affairs, planning, and trade. During his tenure as minister in his father's administration, Bird served as acting prime minister on several occasions.

In 1994, Vere Bird stepped down as leader of the ALP and was replaced by his son. In that same year Lester Bird led his party to an electoral victory. He served as prime minister and minister of external affairs, planning, and services. In March 1999, Antigua and Barbuda held its fourth general election since the country gained independence. Lester Bird again led his party to electoral victory, and the ALP won 12 of the 17 seats in the House of Representatives. Bird continues to serve as prime minister. In addition, he holds the following government posts: minister of CARICOM and OECS affairs; minister of defense; minister of external affairs; minister of legislature, privatization, printing, and electoral affairs; minister of telecommunications and gambling; minister of public works, sewage, and energy; and minister of urban development and renewal.

## LEADERSHIP

Bird's initial term as prime minister was marred by controversy within the party regarding allegations of corruption against the previous administration. Lester's brother, Vere Jr., was accused of fraudulent behavior when he served as minister of public works in his father's administration. Despite this, Lester was able to restore the confidence of the nation in his administration. The ALP's overwhelming victory at the polls in 1999 is a reflection of that confidence.

Another major task that confronted Lester Bird when he began his first term, was to ensure that there was continued growth in the Antiguan economy. Again, his success in this arena is noteworthy. Despite a 4.5% decline in the GDP in 1995 due to two destructive hurricanes, Bird was able to turn this situation around the following year. Increases in construction activity and tourism brought a 4% rise in the GDP.

Bird's first five years as prime minister did not conclude without criticism. He has been accused of selling out Antigua to foreign investors. However, Bird has countered this argument by stating that "investors bring jobs and development that have made Antigua one of the most prosperous Caribbean nations." The nation of Antigua and Barbuda boasts an unemployment rate of only 5% even though more than 3,000 citizens from the island of Montserrat have immigrated there. Bird attributes this low rate of unemployment to the economic initiatives of the ALP, which seeks to create more jobs. Bird now has to fulfill his promise of providing full employment for the people of Antigua and Barbuda.

His second term in office will be no less challenging than the first as Bird has to ensure continued economic growth and reduce the size of the external debt.

## DOMESTIC POLICY

One of the most significant economic changes which has taken place for public servants is an increase in minimum wage. The ALP increased the minimum wage to EC$1,000 per month on 1 August 1997. National savings also increased from EC$770.4 million in 1997 to EC$834.4 in the first nine months of 1998. Bird attributes this increase to the fact that people now have greater disposal income; hence, they are able to save more. The tourism sector has also seen a slight

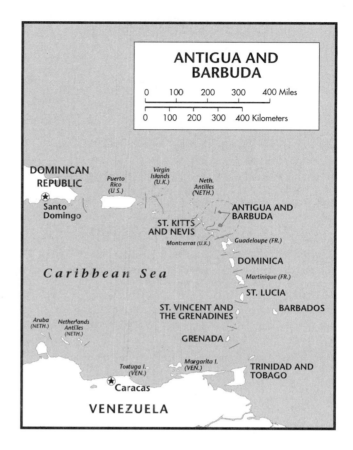

increase despite the damage done by the 1995 hurricanes. This increase has been seen mainly in cruise ship arrivals, which rose by 4.4% in the first nine months of 1998. The number of stopover visitors, however, declined by 7.8% during the same period due to hurricane damage to tourist facilities. The rate of inflation is one of the lowest in the region.

The ALP ensured efficient tax collection during their term in office. A Tax Compliance Unit was established with the objective of improving the tax collection systems of the Ministry of Finance. Central government revenue rose by 6.3% in the first half of 1996 when compared with the same period in 1995. Trade tax collections rose by 15.3%. In the tourism sector, collections from the cruise sub-sector rose by 13.3%. Overall, tax collections increased by 7.7% during the first six months of 1996.

The economy of Antigua and Barbuda has continued to be one of the strongest in the region. Bird has promised no new taxes during his second term in office. He strongly states that "our present tax base is sufficient to pay our way. Our goal is not to take money from the people's pockets, but to put more money in them." Although no new taxes will be introduced, Bird intends to make the tax system more efficient by providing an incentive scheme for tax and customs duty and by improving the tax administration and collection machinery. During his second term in office Bird intends to increase government revenue through economic expansion in tourism and the offshore financial sector.

Bird also intends to practice the politics of inclusion during his second term in office. People in the private sector who are trained and qualified will be invited to discuss government plans and make suggestions. This, Bird argues, will empower the people to make decisions about the future of their country.

## FOREIGN POLICY

Antigua and Barbuda continue to have strong extra-regional ties with the United States, Britain, and Canada. The nation participates in several international organizations, such as the African, Caribbean, and Pacific Countries (ACP), Caribbean Community and Common Market (CARICOM), International Monetary Fund (IMF), Organization of Eastern Caribbean States (OECS), United Nations Educational, Scientific and Cultural Organization (UNESCO), and the World Health Organization (WHO), among others.

The ALP has pledged to give continued assistance to countries within the region. Bird has already demonstrated his willingness to assist others by absorbing natives of Montserrat who had to flee their homeland due to volcanic eruptions. Other nationals from the region have also been given employment in Antigua and Barbuda, especially in the fields of nursing, teaching, and law enforcement. Bird sees this as a positive step towards Caribbean integration. By providing others with employment, he has stated, "we [Antiguans] benefit as much as they. It is not a one-way street." However, during the last general elections, Bird promised that priority would be given to Antiguans in employment.

Bird has managed to give Antigua and Barbuda a more outward-looking development policy, especially in the OECS and CARICOM. As minister of external affairs, Bird participated in several international forums and has sought to address global issues that not only affect Antigua and Barbuda but the entire Caribbean region.

## ADDRESS

Office of the Prime Minister
Factory Road
Antigua

## REFERENCES

Alexander, R. *Biographical Dictionary of Latin America and the Caribbean*. Greenwood Press, 1988.
*The ALP Manifesto Document*, 1999.
*Caribbean Contact*, February 1993.
*Caribbean Week*. St. Michael, Barbados: 1998.
*The Jamaica Daily Gleaner*, various issues.

**Profile researched and written by Rachael Boxill and Ian Boxill, University of the West Indies, Jamaica (9/99; updated 2/2000).**

# ARGENTINA

### Fernando de la Rúa Bruno
### President
*(pronounced "fair-NAHN-doh de lah ROO-ah")*

*"My government has a clear and simple strategy: growth, growth and growth."*

The Argentine Republic is located on the southern half of the South American continent and extends to the southernmost tip of the continent. It is bordered to the east by the Atlantic Ocean and Uruguay, to the northeast by Brazil and Paraguay, to the northwest by Bolivia, and to the west by Chile. It is the second-largest country in South America, with a total area of 2,766,890 sq km (1,073,400 sq mi) and a population of approximately 36 million. Argentina also claims the Falkland Islands (which are known locally as the *Islas Malvinas*), the South Sandwich Islands, South Georgia, and part of Antarctica. The capital is Buenos Aires, and 13.9 million people live in that metropolitan district.

Argentina has long been a country of immigrants; 97% of Argentines are of European descent, primarily Spanish and Italian. The official language is Spanish; other important languages spoken in Argentina are reflective of the European immigrant populations: Spanish, French, German, Italian, and English. There is also a significant Arabic population in the northwestern part of the country. The official religion is Roman Catholicism, and 92% of Argentines are Catholic.

Argentina's major exports are agricultural products, primarily grain and beef grown on the pampas. The Argentine unit of currency is the *new peso* which replaced the *austral* in January 1992; it is fixed at parity with the US dollar. Inflation is less than 4%; however, unemployment is 14% (December 2000). GDP has been estimated at US$8,600.

## POLITICAL BACKGROUND

Argentina's Western political history dates to the 16th century when Spanish explorers first visited the region. Spain established a permanent colony in what is now Buenos Aires in 1580. In 1776, Spain created the Vice-Royalty of *Río de la Plata*, and Argentina became a flourishing port and an integral part of the Empire. On 9 July 1816, Argentina formally declared its independence from Spain under the leadership of José de San Martín, who was a dominant force for national independence throughout the continent. The defeat of the Spanish brought with it a protracted period of conflict between federalist and centralist forces in Argentina to determine the future structure of the nation. The constitution of the Argentine Republic was promulgated in 1853. Conservative forces dominated until 1916, when Hipolito Yrigoyen, the candidate of the *Unión Cívica Radical*, was elected president in Argentina's first free popular election. Yrigoyen was overthrown in 1930 by a military coup. This event established a pattern in Argentine political history of alternating between civilian and military governments, which persisted until December 1983 when the Radical candidate Raúl Alfonsín assumed the presidency. In July 1989, Alfonsín ceded power to his constitutionally elected successor, the first time that had occurred since 1928.

One of the legacies of Argentina's history is the phenomenon of Péronism, a mass movement created in the 1940s by Juan Domingo Péron, who came to power in a 1943 military coup. Péron was elected president in 1946, and in 1948 he created the Péronista Party, a movement focused on social programs and nationalist ideology. Labor unions and the working poor were the overwhelming basis of support for Péronism and in 1951 contributed to Péron's re-election as president. Overthrown in 1955, Péron returned from exile in 1973 and was re-elected president of Argentina. He died in office, and it was the chaos of his wife's administration that precipitated the 1976 coup. The fact that many of the nation's political woes stem from the Péronist period notwithstanding, the ideology remains a potent force in Argentine politics, and it emerged essentially unchanged after the military dictatorships of the 1970s and 1980s. The country returned to democracy in 1983 after seven years of brutal military rule. At least 10,000 and perhaps as many as 30,000 Argentineans "disappeared" during military rule. The prosecution of former military leaders charged with human rights abuses remains a major issue in the country.

Argentina is a republic, the national leadership of which is vested in the president, who since 1995 is elected every four years and may succeed himself in office. Congress is composed of a 72-seat Senate, members of which are directly elected to six-year terms, and a 252-seat Chamber of Deputies, whose members are directly elected to four-year terms. The voting age is 18, and voting is compulsory for all Argentines between 18 and 70.

## PERSONAL BACKGROUND

Fernando de la Rúa Bruno was born on 15 September 1937 in the province of Córdoba. He is married to Inés Pertiné. They have three children. De La Rúa graduated with honors from a military secondary school, and received a law degree from the University of Córdoba. At the same university, he later earned a Doctor of Laws degree for his thesis: "Extraordinary Appeal to the Court of Cassation in the Argentine Legislation." De la Rúa is a devout Roman Catholic with strong anti-abortion views. In his efforts to fight government corruption and maintain transparency, he revealed personal

ARGENTINA

0      250      500      750 Miles

0    250    500    750 Kilometers

assets of about $1 million during the presidential campaign. He has close family ties to the military.

## RISE TO POWER

De la Rúa began his political career in his youth. By age 26, as a member of the Radical Civic Union, he was named an advisor to the Ministry of the Interior during the presidency of Arturo Illia (1963–66). By April 1973, he had been elected senator to represent the federal district. Later that year, he was a member of the failed presidential campaign for Ricardo Balbín. Shortly after, he served as legislator in the Upper Chamber until the military coup of 1976. In 1983, de la Rúa couldn't manage to win enough support for his presidential aspirations. But with the backing of his party, he was elected senator with more than 60% of the vote. In May 1989, he was again elected senator, but he lost the post to political maneuverings and was removed by agreement between minority parties. Yet, he remained a powerful political force within his party, becoming president of the important capital committee and a national deputy for the party. By 1992, he was president of the party's block of national deputies and had again been elected senator (1992–2001 term). One of his

most important political victories came in 1996 when he became the first freely elected mayor of Buenos Aires. Before 1996, the president selected the mayor. As mayor, de la Rúa turned a $600 million deficit into a surplus and helped improve many of the city's services. Based on his success with the city and his calls for honest government, de la Rúa became his party's presidential candidate and was elected with 48.5% of the vote in October 1999. He took office the following December, promising to focus on the economy.

## LEADERSHIP

Of sober personality, even boring by some measures, de la Rúa is a dramatic contrast to Argentina's last president, the Péronist *bon vivant* Carlos Saul Menem. Menem was charismatic and flashy, and his private and public life often intermingled, much to the chagrin of Argentineans. De la Rúa deliberately played off Menem's highly personalized politics during the presidential campaign, even though Menem was not a candidate. In his publicity spots, before moving on to campaign themes de la Rúa declared, "I am boring." Even though he delivers presidential speeches and interviews in a sleep-inducing monotone, de la Rúa is a respected centrist, a politician who has been capable of building consensus among disparate political parties. He may have to rely on those skills if he is to survive the presidency. By some measures, he is the weakest president in Argentinean history. To win office, his Radical party aligned itself with Frente del País Solidario (Front for a country in Solidarity or Frepaso), a left-center coalition of parties that gained respect and votes for its fight against government corruption. Frepaso and the Radicals came together under the umbrella of the Alianza (alliance) to back de la Rúa for president. His election was seen as a rebuke to Menem's Justicialist (Péronist) Party, which had been in power for 10 years. Menem was widely popular at first, but during his second term his administration was criticized for widespread corruption and cronyism.

De la Rúa's Alianza fell four deputies short of gaining control of the lower house of Congress. The Senate remained in control of the Justicialists, as did 14 of the country's 24 provinces. The Alianza lost the governorship of Buenos Aires Province, the nation's richest and most populated. That means de la Rúa will have to rely heavily on his powers of persuasion to gain approval for his economic and social reforms. Working in his favor is his image as an honest politician. During his four-decade political career, de la Rúa has carefully cultivated a scrupulous image. When sons Antonio and Fernando allegedly used their father's political clout to get better grades at the University of Buenos Aires in 1998, de la Rúa publicly rebuked them and called for a formal investigation. In his campaign for the presidency, he promised a government free of corruption and cronyism, themes that appeared throughout his political campaigns. He revealed his own earnings and promised to wage a war against corruption.

## DOMESTIC POLICY

In March 2000, the World Bank reported that 10 million Argentineans, or 29%, lived in poverty. Another 7% lived in extreme poverty. More dramatically, 43% of Argentinean children lived in poverty. Argentina's economy is no longer growing at the frantic double-digit pace of the early 1990s, when Menem's policies included massive privatization of government enterprises. After seven years of steady growth, the economy slowed in 1998 and entered a recession in 1999. By the time de la Rúa took office, unemployment was at 14%, and the federal government faced an $11.5 billion fiscal deficit. Immediately after taking office, de la Rúa declared a national economic emergency and said improving the economy would be the main priority of his government. It was not just the federal government that was in trouble. At least five provinces had not paid their workers and teachers for months. The province of Corrientes was so badly in debt that de la Rúa suspended its government and put the province directly under federal control. Argentina's economic problems were tied to the Asian and Russian economic crisis. The economic recession in Brazil, one of Argentina's most important trading partners, had a major impact on the Argentinean economy.

In his first month in office, de la Rúa convinced Congress to approve a new budget that sliced the deficit in half. He reiterated his commitment to continued parity between the peso and the dollar, and borrowed $7.5 billion from the International Monetary Fund. The loan allowed Argentina to swap bonds for new debt at lower interest rates. In his commitment for austerity, he slashed his own staff. To increase the competitiveness of Argentinean goods, he lowered fuel, highway tolls, and freight prices. To reverse high unemployment, he proposed a plan to stimulate small- and medium-size companies and break up monopolies. He promised higher taxes for the wealthy and long prison sentences for tax evaders. Like Menem before him, de la Rúa has promised to improve social conditions in his country, but even his Minister of Social Development and Environment acknowledges little can be done in the short term. "Poverty is with us, and will be with us for a while," Graciela Fernández Meijide said.

## FOREIGN POLICY

Despite economic problems with its largest economic partner, Brazil, de la Rúa remains committed to MERCOSUR, the Southern Common Market. Paraguay and Uruguay are members of the free trade bloc, and de la Rúa wants MERCOSUR to consider other members. A key strategic partner could be Chile, which has established strong economic ties to Argentina. Relations between the two nations have continued to improve steadily as former border disputes were settled amicably. As presidential candidate, de la Rúa severely criticized the former Chilean dictator Augusto Pinochet, who was arrested in London in October 1998 for human rights violations. But as president, de la Rúa said the fate of Pinochet, who was released on humanitarian grounds in March 2000, was strictly a Chilean issue. After his election, de la Rúa paid tribute to the soldiers who lost their lives fighting against the British for the Falkland Islands. He reiterated Argentinean sovereignty over the islands but said he would seek a peaceful resolution to settle the issue.

The United States and Argentina have maintained diplomatic relations since 1823, including those periods where relations between the two countries were strained, most notably during the military dictatorship of the 1970s and 1980s. Since the reintroduction of democracy, relations have steadily improved.

## ADDRESS

Casa Rosada
Buenos Aires, Argentina

## REFERENCES

"After These Elections, Don't Cry for Argentina." *The Christian Science Monitor,* 28 October 1999, p. 21.
"Argentina's Mr. Boring Plods to Victory by Default." *The Economist,* 4 September 1999, p. 39.
"Forget the Honeymoon in Argentina." *Business Week,* 15 November 1999, p. 280.
"New President Introduces Big Economic and Labor Changes for Argentina." *The New York Times,* 1 March 2000.
President of Argentina. [Online] Available http://www.presidencia.gov.ar (Accessed March 30, 2000).

**Profile researched and written by Ignacio Lobos (4/2000).**

# ARMENIA

## Robert Kocharyan
## President

*(pronounced "kochar-YAWN")*

*"There can be no real freedom and democracy if employment and minimum standards of living are not ensured."*

The Republic of Armenia is bordered by Georgia to the north, Iran to the south, Turkey to the east, and Azerbaijan to the east and south. It has a total land area of 29,800 sq km (11,620 sq mi).

The population of Armenia has been estimated at 3.4 million, with over 40% residing in the capital city of Yerevan. The country is essentially ethnically homogeneous. The official language is Armenian, a distinct Indo-European language, though Russian is widely spoken. A majority of the population (90%) belong to the Armenian Apostolic (Orthodox) Church, one of the oldest churches in Christendom.

Armenia's currency, the *dram,* was introduced in November 1993. The economy suffers from the lingering effects of a 1988 earthquake that killed 25,000 and left 500,000 homeless. Nearly 400,000 refugees fled to Armenia when conflict erupted in neighboring Azerbaijan. That country's refusal to allow trade or transhipment of goods through its territory to Armenia has further damaged the Armenian economy. GDP has been estimated at US$9.2 billion, and per capita GDP at about US$2,700.

## POLITICAL BACKGROUND
Persia and Ottoman Turkey divided Armenia into eastern and western portions from the 16th to18th centuries. Russia took over Persia's holdings in 1828. During World War I, Ottoman Turkey carried out forced resettlement and other harsh policies against Armenians that resulted in up to 1.5 million deaths. This national genocide remains a contentious issue in Armenian-Turkish relations.

Armenia declared its independence in 1918, following the Russian revolution. The Bolshevik army regained control of Armenia two years later, and it was named part of a Transcaucasian Soviet Federated Socialist Republic in 1922. Armenia became a separate union republic within the Soviet system from 1936 until its collapse in 1991. A referendum on independence was held on 21 September 1991. It was approved by 99% of the voters, and independence was declared two days later.

Beginning in 1988, conflict engulfed Nagorno Karabakh (NK), an enclave within neighboring Azerbaijan populated largely by ethnic Armenians. The legislature of NK has called for unification with Armenia, while Azerbaijan has resisted the secession of its enclave. Emigration of 350,000 Armenians residing in Azerbaijan and over one million Azerbaijanis residing in Armenia followed conflict in both states. In 1993, Armenian forces gained control over NK, occupying 20% of Azerbaijani territory. A cease-fire has held fitfully since May 1994, but talks on a political settlement remain inconclusive.

## PERSONAL BACKGROUND
Robert Setrakovich Kocharyan was born on 31 August 1954 in Nagorno Karabakh. He graduated with honors from the Yerevan Polytechnical Institute in 1982, majoring in electrical engineering. Kocharyan was politically active as a youth and eventually joined the Communist Party. In 1987–89, he was secretary of the Silk Mills Committee. Kocharyan resigned from the Communist Party in 1989 and now claims to be nonpartisan. He is married to Bella Aloyan. They have two boys and one girl. For recreation Kocharyan enjoys soccer, basketball, and swimming.

## RISE TO POWER
Since early 1988, Kocharyan has been one of the top leaders of the Karabakh Committee, dedicated to freeing NK from Azerbaijan domination. He helped organize paramilitary forces that fought against the Azerbaijani armed forces. Kocharyan was elected a deputy to the Supreme Council (legislature) of Armenia, serving from 1989 until 1994, and was named to its presidium. In 1991, he was elected to the Supreme Council of NK. When the Azerbaijani armed forces mounted an offensive in August 1992, Kocharyan was named the chair of the NK Defense Committee and prime minister of NK. He organized a successful counteroffensive that led to NK control over its territory and surrounding areas. In December 1994, Kocharyan was elected by the NK Supreme Council to the newly created post of president of NK. He was re-elected in November 1996.

Armenian president Levon Ter-Petrosyan appointed Kocharyan to the post of prime minister in 1997. Many observers believe that the appointment of this highly popular war hero was an attempt to garner greater public support for Ter-Petrosyan's regime. As prime minister, Kocharyan worked on rebuilding areas still suffering from the 1988 earthquake, on reducing tax evasion, and stamping out corruption in the police and military forces. He revamped the cabinet and established ties with myriad political parties, which benefitted him when he ran for the presidency of Armenia.

Ter-Petrosyan announced in September 1997 that he had accepted a peace plan proposed by the Organization for Security and Cooperation in Europe (OSCE) as a basis for resolving the NK conflict that would require "compromises" from Armenia. The two-stage plan called for NK Armenians to withdraw from most territories outside of NK and for international peacekeepers to be deployed, followed by discussion of NK's status. The announcement caused open criticism by Kocharyan. *"Yerkrapah,"* a legislative faction and militia group composed of veterans of the NK conflict, called for the resignation of Ter-Petrosyan. Many members of Ter-Petrosyan's legislative faction defected. Heated debate in the legislature culminated in his resignation on 3 February 1998. The duties of acting president devolved to Kocharyan.

An extraordinary presidential election was declared for 16 March 1998. The main contenders were Kocharyan, Vazgen Manukyan (who had run against Ter-Petrosyan in 1996 and was head of the National Democratic Union), and Karen Demirchyan (head of the Armenian Communist Party from 1974 until 1988). The top two vote-getters in the first round were Kocharyan and Demirchyan. No candidate achieved the required majority vote (over 50%), so a runoff election was scheduled for 30 March 1998. Many voters were attracted to Demirchyan because of nostalgia for the relative economic security of his Soviet-era rule over Armenia, and because Kocharyan at times appeared too low key and soft-spoken as a campaigner. Improving his appeal to the voters and benefitting from added endorsements from political groups such as the Armenian Revolutionary Federation (ARF), Kocharyan won the runoff election. He was inaugurated on 9 April 1998 as Armenia's second president since independence.

## LEADERSHIP

Kocharyan's presidential campaign stressed national traditions and values. In his inaugural speech, Kocharyan pledged that his administration "will act as a partner and advisor to its citizens." He promised that his government would guarantee freedom of speech and religion, allow the "unhampered functioning" of political parties, and ensure minority ethnic rights.

Kocharyan's campaign platform and inaugural address stressed the need for government intervention to rehabilitate industrial production and to create jobs. He called for government investments in Armenian industry, small and medium-sized businesses, and the creation of jobs. Kocharyan pledged to make the tax system fairer and clearer and to fight against illegal business activity, while offering protection to legal businesses. He favored low-interest loans for small businesses and the elimination of government impediments to the creation of new businesses. Kocharyan also pledged to carry out social programs. His platform called for increased wages and pensions, free medical care for the indigent, and improved integration of refugees into Armenian society by clarifying their status and providing housing.

At his inauguration, Kocharyan called for constitutional amendments to clarify relations between the presidency, the ministerial government, and the legislature. He also proposed a clarification of the powers of the Constitutional Court. These constitutional changes would enhance democracy by preventing power from being concentrated in the hands of one person. He proposed changes to 70 articles of the constitution to strengthen the legislature, increase the independence of the judiciary, bolster economic reforms, and permit dual citizenship. A package of amendments would be prepared by

a proposed constitutional commission, and the amendments would be submitted to a popular referendum.

Kocharyan urged greater ties with the Armenian diaspora, including a possible constitutional change to allow dual citizenship. He intended to continue the policy he followed as president of NK—to promote the integration of the economies, financial and educational systems, and culture of NK and Armenia. Kocharyan observed that NK and Armenia each had legislatures and presidents, but this constituted "one body and two heads....No force will dare or even stand a chance to divide that body." At the same time, Kocharyan stressed that NK's ultimate status depended on the wishes of its people.

## DOMESTIC POLICY

Kocharyan has called for a strong security system with an efficient and disciplined army as the best way to maintain peace in the region. His cabinet was initially composed of many professional economists as well as holdovers such as defense minister Vazgen Sarkisyan and national security minister Serzh Sarkisyan (later named head of the presidential staff). However, his government has been roiled by several changes in the prime ministership. Kocharyan's appeals to the diaspora were reflected in his appointment of Varden Oskanyan, a former US citizen, as foreign minister. He rewarded the Armenian Revolutionary Federation for its support by naming an ARF leader (who pledged nonpartisanship) as minister of education and culture. Kocharyan also called for the development of civil service standards to prevent nepotism in acquiring government posts. He pledged that the activities of government officials would be public and open to oversight and that they would declare the sources and amount of their incomes to foster both democratic and noncorrupt governance. After legislative elections in May 1999, the strong showing of the Unity bloc of parties led Kocharyan to accept the bloc's co-head, former defense minister Sarkisyan, as the new prime minister. Sarkisyan's assassination in October 1999 (see below) led to the appointment of Aram Sarkisyan, who was in turn ousted by Kocharyan in May 2000.

Kocharyan has expressed his determination to turn Armenia into the leading economic power in the region. Kocharyan placed partial blame for Armenia's current economic slump on the previous government's lassitude regarding economic reforms. He has called for the development of small and medium-sized enterprises in such sectors as mining, chemicals, machine tools, and electronics. The Armenian Statistics Department reported in February 2000 that economic growth in 1999 exceeded 3%, with the best performance in industry. Inflation was about 2%. Minister of Privatization Pavel Kaltakhchan stated that the government budget had received more than expected amounts from privatization during 1999. He reported that Armenia had privatized 1,500 large-scale enterprises and about 7,000 small enterprises over the past six years, that it planned to transfer another 500 enterprises to private ownership in 2000, including large plants and factories, and that 75% of Armenia's gross domestic product is being produced in the private sector. Negative economic trends in 2000 flowed from policy paralysis and a lack of investor confidence following the October 1999 government assassinations, however. The government in early 2000 was forced to reduce its planned budget spending by $32 million, and further cuts were anticipated. Kocharyan increasingly criticized Prime Minister Aram Sarkisyan as unable to exercise the budgetary and tax discipline necessary to pay government wages and pensions.

Illustrating the ongoing challenges to rule faced by Kocharyan, on 27 October 1999, gunmen entered the legislature and opened fire on deputies and officials, killing Sarkisyan and Demirchyan, two deputy speakers, the minister and former president of Nagorno Karabakh Leonard Petrosyan, and three others. The purported leader of the gunmen claimed they were targeting Sarkisyan and were launching a coup to "restore democracy" and end poverty, and took dozens hostage. President Kocharyan rushed to the legislature and helped negotiate the release of the hostages, promising the gunmen a fair trial. The killings appeared the product of personal and clan grievances. Abiding by the constitution, the legislature met on 2 November and appointed Armen Khachatryan as speaker (a member of the majority Unity bloc), and Kocharyan named Sarkisyan's brother Aram the new prime minister the next day, seeking to preserve political balances. Political infighting has intensified. Appearing to implicate Kocharyan in the assassinations and

hence force him from office, the military prosecutor investigating the assassinations (and linked to the Unity bloc) detained a presidential aide, who was released by court order in April. The Unity and Stability factions in the legislature also threatened to impeach Kocharyan in April 2000. Seeking to combat these challenges to his power, Kocharyan in May 2000 fired his prime minister and defense minister. In a national address on 3 May 2000, Kocharyan explained the firing by stating that the "constitution demands close work between the government and the president....Political games have become a way of life within the executive while at the same time the economic problems are snowballing."

## FOREIGN POLICY

Kocharyan has proposed enhanced cooperation with the Commonwealth of Independent States (CIS), including further development of traditional relations with Russia. One of his top priorities is to establish better relations with the neighboring states of Iran and Georgia. He has called for greater involvement in regional economic cooperation and for strengthening relations with countries such as the United States and EU states, and organizations such as the UN.

Kocharyan has been critical of the OSCE-sponsored peace process, stating that it was unlikely to succeed in mediating an end to the NK conflict. Both Armenia and NK reject the OSCE's proposal of broad autonomy for NK as part of Azerbaijan. Instead of talking through mediators, he has stressed direct talks with Azerbaijani president, Heydar Aliyev. He has encouraged all Armenians to support negotiations that would ensure self-determination for NK, its safe existence within secure borders, and its "permanent geographical ties" with Armenia.

The Kocharyan government has called on Turkey to accept responsibility for the "genocide" of 1.5 million Armenians during World War I as a precondition for improved relations. This stance has prevented an improvement of relations because Turkey refuses to admit that it carried out a genocide.

In line with a campaign proposal, Kocharyan has set up a government board to establish closer relations with ethnic Armenians living outside its borders—to help with cultural issues and facilitate trade and investment. By establishing closer ties, it is hoped that the diaspora will play a greater role in Armenian foreign policy.

## ADDRESS

Office of the President
19 Marshala Bagramyana St.
Yerevan, Armenia 375016

## REFERENCES

"Armenia: Prime Minister Missed Chance to Revive Economy," Foreign Broadcast Information Service (FBIS), 5 May 2000.

"Armenian Paper Says President Centralizing Power," FBIS, 3 May 2000.

"Armenian President Urges Karabakh Deal Based on Equality," FBIS, 4 May 2000.

"Armenian TV Interviews President," FBIS, 13 March 2000.

Bremmer, Ian and Ray Taras. *Nations and Politics in the Soviet Successor States.* Cambridge: Cambridge University Press, 1993.

*Country Studies: Armenia, Azerbaijan, and Georgia.* Washington, DC: Government Printing Office, 1995.

*International Spectator,* April–June 1997.

*Journal of Democracy,* July 1997.

*Journal of South Asian and Middle Eastern Studies,* Summer 1997.

"Kocharyan Ousts PM, Hits 'Political Games' in Executive," FBIS, *Central Eurasia: Daily Report,* May 3, 2000.

*Los Angeles Times,* 5 February–2 April 1998.

*The Nationalities Question in the Post-Soviet States.* London: Longman, 1996.

*New York Times,* 9 February 1998, 30 March 1998.

*PlanEcon Review and Outlook for the Former Soviet Union.* Washington, DC: PlanEcon, 1998.

"Political Crisis in Armenia 'Gaining Momentum,'" FBIS, 4 May 2000.

Smith, Graham. *The Transcaucasus in Transition.* Washington, DC: The Center for Strategic and International Studies, 1994.

Suny, Ronald G. *Looking Towards Ararat: Armenia in Modern History.* Bloomington, IN: Indiana University Press, 1993.

*Temple International and Comparative Law Journal,* Fall 1995.

*Wall Street Journal,* 4 February 1998.

*Washington Post,* 4 March 1998.

**Profile researched and written by Jim Nichol, Library of Congress (5/2000).**

# AUSTRALIA

**John Howard**
**Prime Minister**
*(pronounced "JON HOW-ard")*

*"We have an obligation as a decent society to look after those people who, through no fault of their own, can't get a job. But we have the right to ask of those people who are so protected and supported that they should give something back to the community in return. Now, I think that's a fair Australian principle."*

The Commonwealth of Australia is situated in the South Pacific and Indian Oceans, southeast of Asia. To the north are Indonesia and Papua New Guinea, and to the east is New Zealand. Including the island of Tasmania, which lies to the southeast, the country has a total area of 7,682,300 sq km (2,966,151 sq mi), a land mass about equal to the continental United States. Australia also claims vast territories in Antarctica. It is the sixth-largest country in the world and the smallest continent. Australia is, for the most part, a vast plateau, in which 75% of the continent has an elevation between 152 and 457 meters (500 and 1,500 feet). It includes many deserts, and most of its lakes and streams contain water for only part of the year. Only 6% of the land is suitable for farming. Unlike all other continents, it has no mountains of truly alpine structure and elevation. Many of the plants and animals found in Australia are unique to the country, including the kangaroo, koala bear, wombat, barking lizard, and platypus.

English is the principal language, reflecting the country's colonial heritage. A variety of aboriginal languages are also spoken. Australia has an estimated 18.7 million people, almost wholly Caucasian. Only 1–2% of the people are aborigine and Asian. The majority of Australians live in the principal cities of Sydney, Melbourne, Brisbane, Adelaide, Perth, and Canberra. The largest city is Sydney, home to 3.7 million people. Major religious affiliations are Anglican (26%), Roman Catholic (26%), and other Protestant denominations (24%). Many non-Christian faiths are practiced as well, including Judaism, Islam, and Buddhism.

With a per capita GDP of nearly US$21,200, Australia is one of the world's most advanced industrial countries. Only 6% of the labor force is engaged in agriculture, while 70% is employed in manufacturing or service industries. The main products are wool (of which Australia is the world's largest exporter), beef, steel, copper, coal, uranium, machinery, and transport equipment. Australia imports petroleum, computers, manufactured goods, and industrial raw materials. Its major trading partners are Japan, the US, the UK, and New Zealand. Trade with a variety of Asian countries has increased in recent years. The unit of currency is the Australian dollar.

## POLITICAL BACKGROUND

The original inhabitants of Australia form only a small minority of the current population. The country's name is derived from the Latin *Terra Australis Incognita*, a term used to describe an undiscovered "great south land" that Spanish and Portuguese explorers set out to find in the 16th and 17th centuries. The island was first sighted by Europeans, as they charted new trade routes to the East Indies. The most famous was Captain James Cook, who found the island in 1786, and claimed the eastern part for Great Britain as New South Wales. Originally established as a British penal colony, the first shipment of convicts arrived on 26 January 1788. The discovery of economic potential and the immigration of free settlers eventually ended the island's status as a penal colony in the 1840s. In 1901, Australia became an independent Commonwealth.

On 6 November 1999, 55% of Australian voters rejected a referendum to replace the British monarch, Queen Elizabeth II as their head of state. Thus, Australia remains a democratic state within the British Commonwealth of Nations, although 45% of those who voted would like to see the country become an independent republic. As of 2000, the formal head of state is Queen Elizabeth II, who is represented by an appointed governor-general. Real political power rests in the Parliament, which is bicameral. The lower house, the House of Representatives, has 148 members who are elected for three-year terms, each representing a single electoral district. The upper house, the Senate, has 76 members who serve six-year terms. Each senator is one of 12 who represents a single state. Most legislation is initiated in the House and sent to the Senate for ratification. Like many parliamentary systems, the House of Representatives is the more powerful of the two. The party or coalition of parties that controls the House also forms the government. Though the prime minister is traditionally a member of the House, cabinet ministers are often members of the Senate. The government need not hold a majority in the Senate and usually does not. Voting in national elections has been compulsory since 1924, and voter turnout in national elections generally exceeds 95%. The franchise extends to every citizen over the age of 18. There are five major political parties in Australia. Those currently in power are the Liberal Party and the National Party, conservative parties which have always governed in coalition anytime they held a majority in Parliament. In 1996, they replaced the left-leaning Labor Party, whose leader, Paul Keating, resigned from the post after losing the election to John Howard. The Liberal-National coalition was returned to power in a 1998 election when Howard defeated Kim Beazley, the new Labor Party leader. The two smaller parties, the Democratic Labor Party and the Australian Democratic Party, have been influential, primarily in the Senate.

## PERSONAL BACKGROUND

John Winston Howard was born in the working class Sydney suburb of Earlwood on 26 July 1939. His father was an automobile mechanic who ran his own small business. Howard attended Canterbury Boys High School and went on to the University of Sydney, where he earned a law degree. He worked for a private law firm in Sydney for many years before entering politics. Howard is married and has three children.

## RISE TO POWER

Howard's career in electoral politics began in 1974 when he won a seat in Parliament representing the Sydney district of Bennelong, a seat he has held ever since. Under the last Liberal government, led by Prime Minister Malcolm Fraser, Howard served as the minister for business and consumer affairs. He achieved recognition by rewriting the Australian Trade Practices Act, which prohibited boycotts on businesses and trade unions. Howard served as finance minister from 1977 until 1983 when the Labor Party came to power. In 1982, he was elected deputy leader of the Liberal Party and went on to become its leader in 1985. He led the party into the 1987 elections but lost. Two years later he was ousted from the party leadership, a position he did not regain until 1995.

Upon his reelection as party leader, Howard campaigned vigorously to oust the Labor Party. He benefited from the fact that the Labor Party had been in power for 13 years by capitalizing on the impression that Paul Keating was out of touch with ordinary citizens. However, the primary issues that were stressed in his election campaign were economic. At the time, Australia had run up a record foreign debt of $180 billion and was suffering from high unemployment. While Howard had advanced a conservative agenda during his previous tenure as party leader, in this campaign his message was altered. Learning that unabashed free-market capitalism would not win votes, Howard moved to a middle ground in the 1996 campaign, by appealing to voters whom he had earlier derided or ignored, such as blue-collar workers who had grown disaffected with Labor. Making campaign promises that required more than $6 billion in government spending, he was prepared to forsake a balanced budget rather than break any of those promises. His success in the election amounted to the biggest victory for the Liberals since the formation of their party in 1944. The Liberal-National coalition won 95 seats in the House, the largest majority of any party in 21 years. In 1998, voters returned the ruling Liberal-National government for a second term, although results were far less dramatic. The coalition saw its majority cut to only 10 seats.

## LEADERSHIP

Howard once boasted that he was the most conservative leader the Liberals ever had. In keeping with that image, one of his first priorities has been to embark upon reforming labor laws, with an eye toward weakening the position of labor unions and increasing the power, flexibility, and efficiency of businesses. The Liberals would outlaw compulsory union membership, abolish unfair-dismissal laws,

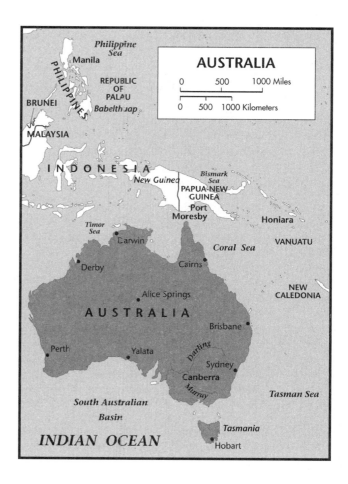

replace union-negotiated pay awards with contracts negotiated at individual workplaces, and end the monopoly of the powerful Maritime Union on shipping. Accused of declaring war on organized labor, Howard responded by stating that while he has no intention of destroying the trade union movement, he is determined to carry out the Liberal platform, which was "clearly laid out" before the voters.

Claiming that his election represented an "emphatic mandate" to change after 13 years of Labor rule, Howard also indicated that his conservative government would take a tougher approach to people collecting unemployment benefits, ensuring that only those genuinely entitled to a benefit would receive payments.

## DOMESTIC POLICY

Upon assuming office, Howard announced a series of economic measures. Accusing the outgoing government of leaving the country's finances in tatters, he proposed spending cuts of $8 billion, the sale of the government's 50.4% stake in the Commonwealth Bank of Australia, and the sale of Telstra, the publicly-owned communications company. He also promised action to increase job opportunities and reduce the unemployment rate, which stood at 8%. At the same time, he promised tax rebates for people who use private health insurance, rather than the government health plan, and a new $1 billion fund to attack environmental problems.

By 1998, Howard's main policy objective was to overhaul Australia's inefficient tax system by cutting income tax rates and imposing a 10% tax on all goods and services, including food. The Labor Party responded with a counter proposal to lower income tax rates for the poor, while taxing luxuries and capital gains. Howard also proposed to sell off the publicly-owned telecommunications company, Telstra—a move feared by rural Australians, who worry that private companies might not continue to provide services to the more remote parts of the nation's vast hinterland.

A major factor in the 1998 elections was the rise of the populist One Nation Party. Led by Pauline Hanson, this party has its main power base in the northern state of Queensland. Hanson's party, which advocates stopping all non-white immigration to Australia and ending welfare spending on aboriginal Australians, had won almost a quarter of the vote in Queensland. With this impressive showing, it was thought that One Nation might play a significant role in the 1998 national elections. Hanson predicted that she would end up with enough seats at the national level to hold the balance of power. As it turned out, One Nation took only 8% of the vote, and Hanson lost her own seat in the House of Representatives.

Howard called a constitutional convention in 1998 to reconsider Australia's status as a monarchy (Queen Elizabeth II of Britain is still the nominal head of state). Although Howard is personally opposed to this change, he agreed to allow a national referendum on the subject on 6 November 1999. Although the opinion polls indicated that just under 10% of voters favored retaining the monarch as Australia's head of state, 55% of voters on the referendum rejected a change. At issue is what form the government will become if Australia becomes an independent republic. Voters also rejected a new preamble to the constitution, written by Howard himself, that would have recognized rights of aborigines (indigenous Australians) for the first time. Howard would like to see constitutional change fade into the background, but the debate over Australia's status as a Commonwealth nation was still heated in 2000. The 2001 general election will include a vote on the simple question of whether to keep the monarchy or to become a republic. If the voters approve change, the specifics of the consitutitonal change will be considered later.

## FOREIGN POLICY

As a member of the British Commonwealth, Australia's foreign policy, for most of its history, centered around relations with Britain, the Commonwealth nations, the US and Western Europe. Keating had changed that focus in recent years. He believed that Australia was a part of Asia and that relations with the Asia-Pacific region should be given greater attention.

Howard came to office promising to reverse that focus. During the 1996 campaign, he accused the Keating government of turning its back on Australia's old friends in Europe and North America. He pledged to rebuild the strong ties that had existed previously. Within hours of his victory, Howard dismissed that vision. He has since sought to reassure both his countrymen and governments in the region by pointing out that the desire to have close relations with Europe or the US is not inconsistent with the continuation of deepening integration of Australia into Asia. Two-thirds of Australia's foreign trade is conducted with Asian countries, and Howard has pledged to boost political and economic links with its Asian neighbors. At the same time, however, he has stated that Australia would not sacrifice its "values and principles" simply for better trade relations with its neighbors.

Relations between Australia and the nations of Southeast Asia have become increasingly important to Howard. His tax cut plans are based on assumptions about continued robust economic growth in Australia and the Southeast Asian region. Those assumptions are threatened by the regional economic crisis that began in 1997. So far Australia has remained immune from most of the fallout of this crisis, but its dependence on regional trade could eventually make it vulnerable. Many Southeast Asian leaders see Australian economic intervention as one solution to their crisis. In light of this situation, the rise of One Nation (with its overtly anti-Asian message), coupled with calls for higher tariffs, has severely strained relations with Asia. Howard has made an effort to improve relations by distancing himself from remarks critical of human rights abuses in Malaysia and other Southeast Asian nations.

## ADDRESS

Office of the Prime Minister
Parliament House
Canberra, ACT 2600
Australia

## REFERENCES

*ABC-Clio, Kaleidoscope,* 1998.
*Business Week,* 18 March 1996.
*Chicago Tribune,* 3 March 1996.
*The Economist,* 20 June–10 October 1998; 13 November 1999.
*Financial Times,* 29 September–5 October 1998.
*The Guardian,* 5 March 1996.
*New York Times,* 4 October 1998.
*Reuters Asia-Pacific Report,* 15 March 1996.
*Straits Times,* 10 October–14 November 1998.
*Time Magazine,* 21 September–26 October 1998.
*Times of London,* 3 March 1996, 2 October 1998.

**Profile researched and written by Erik Gilbert, Arkansas State University, (3/99; updated 5/2000).**

# AUSTRIA

Wolfgang Schüessel
Chancellor
*(pronounced "SHOE-sel")*

*"We have a declaration where everything is enshrined, 'a yes' to human rights, 'a yes' to Europe, 'a yes' to guarantees for our minorities."*

The Republic of Austria is a landlocked nation that is located in the center of Europe. Germany and the Czech and Slovak Republics are to the north; Switzerland and the tiny principality of Liechtenstein are to the west; Italy and Slovenia are to the south; and Hungary is to the east. Austria's total area is 83,858 sq km (37,378 sq mi). The population has been estimated at 8.1 million. The unit of currency is the *schilling*. German is the official language; small minorities of Austrians have nevertheless preserved different mother tongues, for example Slovenian in Carinthia and Croatian and Hungarian in Burgenland. Austria's religious affiliation is 81% Roman Catholic, 5% Protestant, and 14% nonreligious, atheist or other. Austria's major exports are machinery and transport equipment, iron and steel, paper and paper products, and chemicals. Tourism plays an important economic role as well. The per capita GDP has been estimated at US$22,700.

## POLITICAL BACKGROUND

Austria became a small republic with its present borders established by the Treaty of St. Germain in June 1919. It was annexed by Nazi Germany in March 1938 but reestablished under Allied occupation in May 1945. Following its liberation, Austria was occupied by the four Allied Powers: the US, UK, France, and the USSR. In 1955, with occupation ending, Austria officially adopted neutrality as its foreign policy. Soon thereafter, Austria was admitted to the UN.

Austria is a federal republic in which the executive power is divided between the federal president (Dr. Thomas Klestil) and the federal cabinet. The president is elected for six years by popular suffrage. The president acts as a head of state, appoints the cabinet, and calls parliament into session. He can dissolve the Nationalrat (National Council) during its four-year legislative period but must obtain consent of the cabinet, which is the real power center and is led by the chancellor. The parliament is a bicameral legislature and consists of the Nationalrat with 183 members and the Bundesrat (Federal Council). The president appoints the chancellor (Wolfgang Schüessel), who must maintain a majority in the Nationalrat. This feature makes the Austrian government a parliamentary system. In reality, the president is more or less a ceremonial state figure while the chancellor acts as the head of government.

Austria is a multi-party democracy with an electoral system based on proportional representation. The voting age is 18, and every citizen over the age of 19 is eligible to run for Parliament. The two preeminent parties since the end of World War II have been the People' Party (OVP) and the Social Democratic Party (SPO). There have been three minority parties: the Freedom Party (FPO), the Green Party (GPO), and the small Liberal Party. The OVP is similar to the British Conservative Party, representing the moderate right; the SPO can be compared with the British Labour Party, representing the moderate Left. The FPO is a mixture of different rightist attitudes, ranging from conservatism to fascism, built upon pan-Germanic traditions. The Green Party is an environmental party with certain leftist, pacifist, and feminist goals.

## PERSONAL BACKGROUND

Wolfgang Schüessel was born on 7 June 1945 in Vienna. After primary school, he attended secondary school at the Schottengymnasium, where he obtained his higher school certificate in 1963. He then studied law at the University of Vienna where he graduated as a Doctor of Law in 1968.

## RISE TO POWER

Schüessel was Secretary of the parliamentary People's Party (OVP) from 1968 to 1975. He served as General Secretary of the Osterreichische Wirtschaftsbund (Austrian Economic Federation), which is a constituent organization of the OVP, from 1975 until April 1991. On 24 April 1989, Schüessel became Federal Minister for Economic Affairs in the coalition government formed by the Social Democratic Party of Austria (SPO) and the OVP under the Federal Chancellor Dr. Franz Vranitzky. At the 30th Annual Congress of the OVP on 22 April 1995, Schüessel was elected leader of the OVP. On 4 May of the same year he was sworn in as Vice Chancellor and Federal Minister for Foreign Affairs in the Vranitzky IV cabinet. He continued to hold these positions in the Vranitzky V cabinet after the general elections in December 1995. Beginning 28 January 1997, Schüessel functioned as Vice Chancellor and Federal Minister for Foreign Affairs to the Federal Chancellor Viktor Klima. By 1 July of 1998, Schüessel was serving as president-in-office of the Council of the European Union.

Upon assuming the rotating presidency of the European Union, Schüessel called for a transition period of up to 10 years before a new member's citizens would be allowed to live and work anywhere in the EU community. He claimed it was Austria's goal to maintain gradual access to the labor markets, reflecting general Austrian sentiment opposing EU enlargement.

In Austria's October 1999 elections, the far-right Freedom Party tied Schüessel's People's Party for second place, with the Social Democrats taking the lead. The prospect of a coalition government between the three parties created a national and international frenzy as the Freedom Party's leader, Joerg Haider, had in the past expressed support for Nazi ideology. Schüessel, awaiting his appointment to the chancellery, vowed to take his party into opposition. President Thomas Klestil made it clear he was unhappy at the prospect of a government that included the Freedom Party, but the results of the October 1999 elections left him with no choice but to swear it in. Consequently, Schüessel was sworn in as Federal Chancellor on 4 February 2000 alongside his controversial coalition partner, Joerg Haider.

## LEADERSHIP

Upon accepting the position of chancellor, Schüessel, along with Haider, was forced by Klestil to sign a statement renouncing the nation's Nazi past and promising to adhere to European priorities and values. Despite some 2,000 protestors against Haider thronging the streets of Vienna, Schüessel expressed the importance of working with Haider, not excluding him but making him part of the mainstream

work. Critics doubted Schüessel's ability to control Haider. The Green Party even called for a vote of no confidence in parliament as early as 9 February 2000; however, Schüessel survived. Then, in outlining his government program to parliament, Schüessel rejected international concern over the inclusion of the extreme-right group in his government. He stated his administration believed in tolerance and democratic values. He also emphasized commitment to the European Union. Other policies included handling the problem of illegal immigration, a priority of the Freedom Party.

## DOMESTIC POLICY

Schüessel's administration developed a safeguard against the Freedom Party in the form of a negotiated treaty. He stated, "We have a declaration where everything is enshrined, 'a yes' to human rights, 'a yes' to Europe, 'a yes' to guarantees for our minorities."

## FOREIGN POLICY

The swearing-in of the Freedom Party to Austria's coalition government prompted unprecedented sanctions on Austria by the European Union. The European Union acted to isolate Austria, one of its own members, claiming the government was working against its own democratic principles. Schüessel responded with surprise, emphasizing that such an alarmist response was unfounded and unnecessary as Austria had every intention of adhering to European values. He was adamant that his government intended to maintain the same quota of immigrants and refugees as in previous years, which he noted was a proportionally higher number than other European countries. Although EU sanctions were carried through, Switzerland did receive Schüessel in March 2000. While Switzerland is not a member of the EU, its welcome of Schüessel in effect undermined Austria's diplomatic isolation in Western Europe. Despite Haider's resignation as leader of the Freedom Party on 1 May 2000, EU sanctions still stood as of 1 June. On 5 June 2000, Schüessel called for his 14 EU counterparts to propose a way of ending Austria's political isolation at the summit meeting in Portugal later in the month.

## ADDRESS

Federal Chancellery
Ballhausplatz
A-1010 Vienna
Austria

## REFERENCES

BBC News. [Online] Available http://news.bbc.co.uk/ (Accessed June 2000).
"Heil Hader?" *The Economist,* 13 March 1999, p. 61.
"Far-right Turn." *The Economist,* 9 October 1999, p. 4.
"Fascism Resurgent?" *The Economist,* 9 October 1999, p. 57.
**Profile researched and written by Jill Coppola, 6/2000.**

# AZERBAIJAN

## Heydar Aliyev
## President
*(pronounced "HEY-dar AL-I-yev")*

*"We will never allow anyone to disturb the social and political stability
and the healthy climate that have been established."*

The Azerbaijan Republic is bordered by the Caspian Sea to the east, Iran to the south, Russia and Georgia to the north, and Armenia to the west. Azerbaijan has a total land area of 86,600 sq km (33,436 sq mi). Major administrative subdivisions include the Nagorno Karabakh Autonomous Region (NK, now formally abolished as a political entity) and the Nakhichevan Autonomous Republic (NAR). The capital is Baku, a major port on the Caspian Sea.

The total population has been estimated at 7.9 million. Extended economic hardship and conflict have contributed to the emigration of over one million Azerbaijanis and the concentration of a majority of the citizenry in Baku and other urban centers. About 13 million ethnic Azerbaijanis reside in neighboring Iran. While Azerbaijan's language and ethnic background are heavily Turkish, Iran influences its religion and culture. Ethnically rather homogeneous, nearly 90% of the population is Azerbaijani, less than 5% Russian, and the remainder Lezgin and other groups. The official language is Azeri, a Turkic language, but Russian is also spoken.

Azerbaijan introduced its own currency, the *manat,* in August 1992. Since the late 19th century, Azerbaijan exported oil and natural gas to the former Soviet republics and elsewhere. In the late 1990s, Azerbaijan began to export its sizeable oil resources through refurbished pipelines through Georgia and Russia to the Black Sea. Chemical and textile industries are other major employers. Cotton, grain, tea, citrus fruit crops, livestock, dairy products, and fish are important sources of revenue. Azerbaijan is also a major wine and spirits producer.

## POLITICAL BACKGROUND

In 1828, Russia took full control of most of the area of present-day Azerbaijan. Following the 1917 Bolshevik revolution, Azerbaijan declared its independence. The first independent Azeri state, also the world's first secular Muslim state, lasted only three years, from 1918 until 1921. Russia's Red Army invaded the country and suppressed its independence effort. Azerbaijan was declared a part of Soviet Transcaucasia in 1922 and became a separate Union Republic in 1936. During the Stalin era, Azerbaijan suffered from the travails of collectivization and the purges.

With the disintegration of the USSR, Azerbaijan was able to regain its independence in 1991. Ayaz Mutalibov was popularly elected to the post of president in an unopposed contest denounced as undemocratic by opposition parties. In 1992, Mutalibov was ousted by the Azerbaijani Popular Front (APF) and other opposition forces following Azerbaijani military losses in combating separatism in Nagorno Karabalj (NK, a region comprised of 180,000 ethnic Armenians).

The chairman of the Supreme Soviet, Yakub Mamedov, was named acting president and retained this position until he, too, was forced from power as a result of continuing military defeats in NK. Mutalibov tried to regain power but was forced to flee the country after APF-led crowds stormed the Supreme Soviet building and presidential palace. The APF assumed power, and APF leader Abulfaz Elchibey was elected president in June 1992. His government was soon discredited by further military losses in NK, and an internal uprising brought Heydar Aliyev to power In June 1993.

## PERSONAL BACKGROUND

Heydar Aliyev was born in the Nakhichevan Autonomous Republic (NAR) in 1923. His parents were both blue-collar workers. Aliyev graduated in 1957 with a degree in history from Azerbaijan State University. A widower, he has a grown son and daughter and five grandchildren. Aliyev is a practicing Muslim.

## RISE TO POWER

Aliyev's involvement in politics began in 1941 when he worked for the All-Union People's Commissariat of Internal Affairs (NKVD or secret police). He officially joined the Communist Party in 1945 and held a series of responsible posts in government and state security in NAR until 1949. From 1950 to 1964, he worked in the Azerbaijani Ministry of State Security (later renamed the KGB). In 1964, he became the deputy chairman, then in 1967–69 chairman of the Azerbaijani KGB. In 1969, he was named first secretary of the Azerbaijani Communist Party (ACP) Central Committee, purging Azerbaijani nationalists and overseeing state-directed economic development.

Aliyev assumed leading Soviet party posts in the 1970s. In 1971, he became a full member of the Soviet Communist Party Central Committee and in 1976 became a candidate member of the Politburo. He supported the Soviet intervention in Afghanistan in 1979. Because of these efforts, Soviet general secretary Leonid Brezhnev awarded him several Orders of Lenin and other medals. In 1982, he became a full member of the Politburo, the ruling body of Soviet politics. From 1982 until 1987, he also served as

## AZERBAIJAN

0　　50　　100 Miles

0　　50　　100 Kilometers

T'Bilisi ✪

RUSSIA

CAUCASUS MTS.

GEORGIA　Balakän

Zakataly

Akstafa　　Shäki　Quba　Khachmaz

Yerevan　Toviz　Kura

ARMENIA　Gyanja (Kirovabad)　Mingachevir

Sevana Lich　Yevlakh　Göychay

SER CAUCASUS MTS.　Bärdä　AZERBAIJAN

Nagorno-Karabakh　Aghjabädi

Agdam　Stepanakert　Ali Bayramly

Shakhbus　Aras

Nakhichevän

Ahar

Khvoy　TALISH MTS.

IRAN

Caspian Sea

Sumqayyt

Baku ✪

Apsheron Peninsula

Alyat

Salyan

Pushkin

Länkäran

Astara

deputy chairman of the Soviet Council of Ministers (equivalent to the vice prime minister).

Despite his support for the election of Mikhail Gorbachev as general secretary of the Communist Party in 1985, Aliyev was ousted from the Politburo two years later and relieved as party leader in Azerbaijan, accused of corruption. Aliyev lived in Moscow as a private citizen under pension for the next three years.

Upon returning to Azerbaijan in July 1990, Aliyev received a rapturous welcome from kneeling crowds of up to 30,000 individuals. He was elected to the Azerbaijani and NAR Supreme Soviets two months later on a nationalist platform, receiving over 95% of the popular vote. In July 1991, Aliyev resigned his Communist Party membership and, after the abortive coup against Gorbachev, called for total independence for Azerbaijan. Noting that Mutalibov had supported the coup plotters, he denounced Mutalibov's bid for the Azerbaijani presidency and orchestrated a ban on presidential voting in NAR. In September 1991, he was named chairman of the Supreme Soviet of NAR (renamed the Supreme *Majlis*).

An abortive attempt by the Elchibey government to disarm Suret Huseynov's paramilitary forces in the town of Ganja precipitated the fall of his government and provided the opportunity for Aliyev to assume power. Huseynov, a corps commander in NK, had been fired by Elchibey and blamed for defeats in NK. Returning to his hometown of Ganja in 1993, Huseynov amassed forces and weaponry (obtained from the departing Russian military) that posed an increasing threat to the Elchibey government. In early June 1993, the government launched an attack aimed at defeating Huseynov's forces. This attack was easily repulsed, and

Huseynov began to march on the Azerbaijani capital of Baku, precipitating a government crisis. Elchibey endorsed Aliyev's election as the new legislative speaker, in effect conceding some power to his political nemesis in a futile bid to retain power. Threatened by Huseynov's approaching forces outside the capital, Elchibey fled Baku, returning to his home village in NAR.

Although Elchibey still claimed to be president of Azerbaijan, Aliyev announced that he was assuming responsibility and power as acting head of state, fulfilling his drive to regain political power. On 24 June, a bare quorum of legislators met and formally stripped Elchibey of his presidential powers, transferring them to Aliyev. A 29 August referendum overwhelmingly expressed lack of confidence in Elchibey's rule, opening the way for a new presidential election. This took place on 3 October 1993, with Aliyev winning almost 99% of the vote against two minor party candidates.

## LEADERSHIP

During the years when he was out of power, Aliyev retained popularity among many Azerbaijanis, including ex-Communist Party members and supporters in NAR. He was particularly respected among most in NAR since he had given preference to Nakhichevans in filling government posts when he was the party leader. He has several popular nicknames, including "Heydar Baba" (Grandfather Heydar). He also championed autonomy rights for NAR. As war losses in NK increased and the economy declined during 1992–93, calls for the return of Aliyev grew stronger.

In late September 1994, police and others launched a purported coup attempt. Aliyev hinted at Russian involvement. After defeating the attempted coup, Aliyev accused Huseynov of major involvement, forcing the paramilitary commander to flee his country. This and several other alleged coup attempts triggered mass arrests of Aliyev's opponents.

An Aliyev-drafted constitution was approved by 91.9% of voters in a referendum in November 1995. It strengthens presidential power, establishes a new legislative system, declares Azerbaijani to be the state language, proclaims freedom of religion and a secular state, stipulates ownership over part of the Caspian Sea, and gives NAR quasi-federal rights. The president appoints and removes cabinet ministers (the *"Milli Mejlis"* consents to his choice of prime minister), submits budgetary legislation, and appoints local officials. Aliyev made several concessions to encourage the participation of prominent opposition parties in the October 1998 presidential election, including formal abolition of censorship and the adoption of some changes to electoral laws. However, most opposition parties chose to boycott the election, claiming that pro-Aliyev forces were in control of the electoral commissions. Of the six registered candidates, the major "constructive opposition" candidate was Etibar Mammadov of the NIP. Aliyev was elected to a second five-year term, receiving over 76% of 4.3 million votes cast, with runner-up Mammadov receiving 11.6% of the vote. Most international observers judged the vote to be not "free and fair," though also noting that the election demonstrated some improvement in political pluralism.

Aliyev has moved cautiously and adroitly to consolidate his power, displaying skills as a professional ex-Communist

Party politician and security chief similar to those of president Eduard Shevardnadze in neighboring Georgia. He faces possible contenders for power in Mutalibov (who continues to have a following within Azerbaijan), the opposition party coalition (among which the Musavat Party, headed by Isa Gumbar, appears prominent), and NIP head Mammadov. As of early 2000, Elchibey, still the head of the APF, was interested in regaining the presidency, but polls indicated that his popularity had waned though he was still respected as an elder statesman on nationalist issues.

## DOMESTIC POLICY

During his 1998 presidential campaign, Aliyev stressed that he planned no major changes in domestic and foreign policy if re-elected. At his inauguration, he stated that the increasing political stability since his election in 1993, the 1995 legislative election and constitutional referendum, and his October 1998 re-election had "proved to the world that a democratic, legal, and civilized state is under construction in Azerbaijan." He pledged to pursue continued dialogue with political opposition forces, stating that "democracy is impossible without opposition." He praised the economic assistance Azerbaijan had received from the International Monetary Fund and World Bank and declared that "we will move forward along the path to a market economy." He pledged to combat corruption among governmental officials. In late 1998, Aliyev responded to the Asian and Russian economic crises by calling for increased tax collection and privatization efforts and an end to unnecessary inspections and other interference in the work of private industry. His goals include finding ways to attract foreign investment, combating corruption in law enforcement and elsewhere in government, and aiding the poor and refugees. Despite this impressive economic agenda, Aliyev appears to be launching a new crackdown on political dissent and making efforts to restrict freedom of the press.

## FOREIGN POLICY

Aliyev has stated that Azerbaijan seeks to maintain good relations with all countries, especially its neighbors. In practice, Azerbaijan's relations with foreign states have been guided by their position regarding continued Azerbaijani sovereignty over NK. Aliyev has reiterated that he would not agree to any settlement of the NK conflict that violates the "sacred" principle of the sanctity of Azerbaijan's existing borders and its territorial integrity. Aliyev has continued Elchibey's policy of pursuing close ties with Turkey. Ties with Iran have been rocky, influenced by Iran's growing trade relations with Armenia and sensitivity between Azerbaijan and Iran over the status of Iran's ethnic Azerbaijani population. In early 2000, Aliyev visited Iran and called for improved economic, cultural, and political ties.

Aliyev has endeavored to involve foreign firms in the development of oil and natural gas resources in order to give these countries an interest in Azerbaijan's continued independence. In his inaugural address, Aliyev hailed the recent successes of Azerbaijan's foreign policy. He noted the many foreign delegations that have visited his country and the many agreements signed. He is particularly proud of having hosted the European Union-sponsored Silk Road Conference in 1998, at which transport development in the region was discussed.

At a news conference in February 2000 following his visit to the United States, Aliyev stated that the US and Azerbaijan have good relations. However, he has criticized a US law that limits aid to Azerbaijan as an "unfair decision." Sources of friction with Russia include the rejection of a predominantly Russian peacekeeping force in NK, allegations of a Russian "tilt" toward Armenia in NK peace talks, and the refusal to permit Russian troops to patrol its borders. In early 1997 Russian president Boris Yeltsin admitted that some Russian weaponry had been transferred to Armenia without authorization, fueling Azerbaijan's view that Russia tacitly supports Armenia in the NK conflict. In meeting with Russian's then-acting president Vladimir Putin in late January 2000, Aliyev reported that Putin praised Azerbaijan's treatment of ethnic Russians in Azerbaijan and recognized that Azerbaijan was not aiding separatism in Russia's breakaway Chechnya region, an earlier point of contention.

In 1999 and early 2000 Azerbaijan and Armenia continued trying to resolve their long-standing dispute in the NK conflict. NK is located within Azerbaijan's borders but has a population consisting primarily of ethnic Armenians. During a September 1999 summit of Baltic and Black Sea political leaders in Yalta, Aliyev met with Armenia's president, Robert Kocharyan, and the two leaders attempted to arrive at an official status for the disputed region that would be agreeable to both countries. Armenians wanted the region to be granted de facto independence while the Azeris proposed making it an autonomous republic, basically the same designation accorded it when it was part of the former Soviet Union. International hopes that a statement of intentions could be signed by the two sides at the November 1999 OSCE Summit were not met. The Summit Declaration endorsed "a lasting and comprehensive solution" to the NK conflict (and did not reaffirm Azerbaijan's territorial integrity). Bothe Kocharyan and Aliyev called for the OSCE to foster the creation of a Caucasian regional security system (though they disagreed on details). Such a system was also discussed when the two presidents met with then-acting president Vladimir Putin in Moscow in late January 2000.

## ADDRESS

Ulitsa Lermontova 63
Baku, Azerbaijan

## REFERENCES

Agence France Presse, 13–15 September 1998.
Azerbaijan News Distribution List, HABARLAR-L, 11–20 October 1998.
*Bakinsky rabochii*, 18 July 1998, 8 August 1998.
*FBIS Daily Report: Central Eurasia*, June–October 1998.
Reuters News Agency, 11–21 October 1998.
*RFE/RL Daily Report*, June–October 1998.
*Washington Post*, 12–13 October 1998.

**Profile researched and written by Jim Nichol, Library of Congress (3/99; updated 5/00).**

# THE BAHAMAS

### Hubert Ingraham
### Prime Minister
*(pronounced "HYOO-bert ING-rum")*

*"It is time for change in this country."*

The Bahamas is a nation of islands, an archipelago that stretches southeasterly for more than 805 km (500 mi) south of Florida to the edge of the Caribbean Sea. The chain comprises more than 700 islands, but less than 30 of them are actually inhabited. The total land area amounts to 13,939 sq km (5,382 sq mi). According to estimates, these islands have a total population of 284,000. The smallest of these islands, New Providence, boasts 65% of the nation's population, most of whom live in the capital city of Nassau. The other significant island, in terms of population concentration, is Grand Bahama, which has approximately 15% of the population.

Like many of the other English-speaking Caribbean countries the Bahamas was colonized by the British during the 17th century, although the Spanish were the first Europeans to "discover" the islands. African slaves were brought by the British to work on plantations. The current racial composition is 85% of African descent and 10% of European descent, with the remainder being of mixed races. The official language is English, although a local dialect is widely spoken. The overwhelming majority of the population is Christian, with approximately 23% Catholics. The official currency is the Bahamian dollar. Tourism is the most important industry. The major exports include refined petroleum and petroleum products, poultry and fish products. The per capita GDP is $20,100.

## POLITICAL BACKGROUND

The 1973 Bahamian constitution established a parliamentary system, very similar to the British model. The head of state is the British sovereign who is represented by the Governor General. The duties of the governor general include appointing the prime minister, cabinet, and leader of the opposition. Political power and responsibility for running the government reside with the prime minister, who is the leader of the majority party in the house. The opposition leader is usually the head of the majority opposition party in parliament.

The bicameral parliament consists of the Senate and House of Assembly. The Senate is comprised of 16 members appointed by the governor general, nine of whom are appointed after consultation with the prime minister, four on the advice of the opposition and three after consultation with others at his discretion. The House of Assembly consists of 49 elected members. Suffrage is universal over the age of 18.

All of the islands, except for New Providence, are administered by district commissioners whose legal authority is limited to local concerns. District commissioners are responsible for law and order administered through local courts.

There are four political parties in the Bahamas. The two major ones are the Progressive Liberal Party (PLP) and the ruling Free National Movement (FNM), which is the product of a merger between the United Bahamian Party (UBP) and the Free Progressive Liberal Party (FPLP). Although there are no fundamental ideological differences between the FNM and the PLP, the FNM appears to have more grassroots support while the PLP seems to draw much of its support from big business and the elite.

## PERSONAL BACKGROUND

Hubert Alexander Ingraham was born on 4 August 1947 in the small and remote village of Cooper's Town on the island of Abaco. He was educated at Cooper's Town Public School, Southern Senior School, and Government High School and Evening Institute. Trained as a lawyer, Ingraham clerked in the chambers of McKinney, Brancroft, and Hughes and was called to the Bahamas Bar in 1972. He is a senior partner in the firm Christie, Ingraham, and Company. In July 1993, Ingraham became a member of the British Privy Council. He is married and has two children.

## RISE TO POWER

Although Ingraham is the leader of the FNM, he started his career as a member of the PLP. In 1976 he was elected chairman of the PLP. As chairman he was instrumental in reforming and strengthening party branches throughout the Bahamas in preparation for the PLP's landslide victory in 1977. In that year Ingraham was elected as a member of parliament for Cooper's Town, Abaco. In 1982 Ingraham again ran as a member of the PLP and again won his seat. Following this electoral victory he was appointed minister of housing and national insurance. Ingraham served as a cabinet member until 1984 when he resigned following policy conflicts with the PLP's leadership. He subsequently joined the FNM. Following the death of the FNM's leader Sir Cecil Whitfield in 1990, Ingraham was elected leader of the party. In August 1992 he defeated his long-time colleague and rival, Sir Lynden Pindling, to become the Bahamas' second prime minister. Ingraham was returned to power in 1997 following general elections with an even larger margin of victory (34 out of 49 seats). The next election is scheduled to be held in March 2002.

## LEADERSHIP

Ingraham is perceived to be a grassroots leader. Following his electoral victory he came out on the street and shook hands with the people, laughing and joking with them. It was this easy-going, populist style which allowed Ingraham's party to win 32 of the 49 seats in the 1992 election. Having served the first term, he was able to increase his margin of victory by two seats in the 1997 election. Considered something of a maverick, especially since he resigned from the PLP in 1984, Ingraham has begun to fulfill several 1992 campaign pledges. Trading in illicit drugs, mainly for the US market, is a major problem in the Bahamas, since many of the small islands and cays are used by drug traffickers in their smuggling activities. Ingraham promised to take measures to eliminate the illegal drug trade. In 1995 relatives and members of the country's business and political elite were arrested for trafficking in cocaine. Ingraham was also successful in getting legislation passed which reduced the salaries of government ministers and legislators. He has taken steps to repeal the controversial Immovable Property Act (which limits ownership of property) and implemented programs to make the Bahamas the leading environmentally sensitive tourist destination in the Caribbean.

## DOMESTIC POLICY

The Bahamas is considered to be one of 37 high-income countries in the world. The principal source of that income is tourism, which employs 50% of the Bahamian workforce and accounts for approximately 72% of its GDP. Today the Bahamas is the most popular tourist destination in the Caribbean. In 1995–96 growth was modest, due mainly to the influence of increased government spending. This policy helped to reduce unemployment, which now stands at approximately 15%.

Earnings from tourism, offshore banking, shipping, and oil sectors have been used to pay off a trade deficit that amounted to $724.2 million in 1995. Almost 80 cents of every tourist dollar goes towards importing foodstuff for the tourist sector.

On assuming office in 1992, Ingraham moved quickly to deal with the devastation caused by a hurricane which affected large sections of the Bahamian society and economy. Cleanup costs were estimated to be $250 million. In 1993 he reshuffled parliament and transferred a number of matters in his portfolio to other cabinet ministers. In 1999, Category-4 Hurricane Floyd struck the northern and central islands, costing a loss of $70 million in tourism; however, the year's total revenues were expected to be $1.4 billion. Ingraham's government launched an aid package for elderly and indigent victims.

As promised during the general elections, Ingraham appointed a commission of inquiry in 1992 to look into the management of state-run enterprises. A report published in 1995 gave details of widespread mismanagement within the national airline, Bahamasair, and the national telephone company, Batelco. The report also alleged that two former cabinet ministers had received bribes relating to the purchase

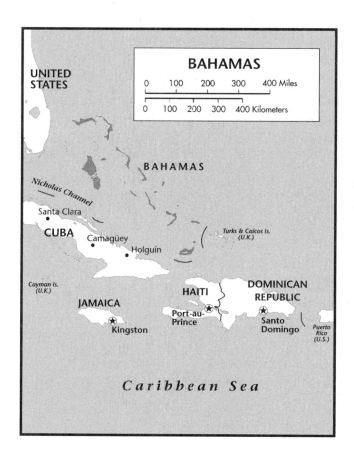

of aircraft for the airline. It recommended the removal of senior officials from the telephone company as well.

Ingraham has announced a program of privatization for commercial banks and state enterprises. For instance, he has already sold state-owned hotels on the island of Grand Bahama.

Despite promises to develop manufacturing, this sector remains relatively insignificant under the Ingraham administration. Although exports of pharmaceutical products and salt increased in 1995, the Bahamas is still not a member of the Caribbean Common Market (CARICOM)—a treaty of 15 Caribbean countries to cooperate in the areas of foreign policy and trade. While the Bahamas is a signatory to the Treaty of Chaguaramas which established CARICOM in 1973, it only participates in the areas of functional cooperation and the coordination of foreign policy.

## FOREIGN POLICY

Historically, the Bahamas has limited its foreign policy initiatives to the Commonwealth states, the Organization of American States, the Caribbean Community (CARICOM), the African Caribbean and Pacific (ACP) nations, and the United Nations. As a member of the ACP it is a signatory to the Lome Convention. The Bahamas is also a member of the IMF, the World Bank (IBRD), and the Inter-American Development Bank. The country is party to 31 treaties and agreements with the US, which cover such issues as defense, extradition, consuls, trademarks, and property. Diplomatic relations were established with El Salvador and Honduras in 1992 and with Kuwait In 1994.

The Ingraham administration, like its predecessor, has continued the "pro-Western" approach to international diplomacy, with an emphasis on Bahamas-US relations. One major reason for this is that 80% of the Bahamian tourists come from the US. However, these relations have been strained due to the aggressive attitude which the US has displayed with regard to bank secrecy laws and the illegal drug trade. Ingraham has taken steps to repair strained relations with Cuba and Haiti resulting from an influx of refugees from these two countries. However, little change is expected as Haitians are now routinely deported by the Ingraham government. Thousands of Haitian refugees have been deported since Ingraham came to power in 1992.

Although Ingraham had promised that the Bahamas would play a much greater role in CARICOM, this has not yet materialized. In 1992 Ingraham stated that he would be reporting the outcome of all CARICOM meetings to the Bahamian people. This, he argued, was necessary in order for his country to become an integral part of the Association of Caribbean States and the CARICOM community at large. However, at the July 1997 meeting of heads of government, the Bahamas opted not to become a member of the CARICOM Single Market and Economy (CSME). This group was formed to deepen the regional integration movement, by allowing for the free movement of some categories of people, free trade, investment, and travel within the region. Since Haiti has joined CARICOM, it is doubtful whether the Bahamas will become a member of CSME in the near future.

## ADDRESS
Office of the Prime Minister
Rawson Square
Nassau, Bahamas

## REFERENCES
*Caribbean Contact*, July–August 1992.

*Caribbean Countries: Economic Situation, Regional Issues and Capital Flows*. Washington, DC: The World Bank, 1988.

*Caribbean Development Bank Annual Report 1995*. Bridgetown, Barbados: Caribbean Development Bank, 1996.

*CARICOM Perspective*, April–June 1987.

*Daily Gleaner*, 4 September 1992.

*Economic and Social Progress in Latin America 1994 Report*. Inter-American Development Bank, 1994.

*Encyclopedia of the Third World*. New York: Facts on File, 1987.

*Personalities Caribbean*. Jamaica: Personalities Ltd., 1983.

*Trinidad Guardian*, 21–22 August 1992.

*World Outlook 1989*. London: Economist Intelligence Unit Ltd., 1989.

Profile researched and written by Ian Boxill, University of the West Indies, Jamaica (7/97; updated 3/2000).

# BAHRAIN

## Hamad Bin Isa al-Khalifa
## Emir

*(pronounced "HA-mad bin EE-sah all-kah-LEEF-ah")*

*"I am assuming the rule of Bahrain, relying on God, exerting all the effort possible to serve our country and our people by following the policy charted by the great departed."*

The State of Bahrain is located 24 km (15 mi) off the coast of Saudi Arabia and 28 km (17 mi) off the coast of Qatar in the Persian Gulf. The country consists of 35 islands covering a total area of 691 sq km (267 sq mi). Bahrain Island, which is 80 km (50 mi) long and has a width of 13 to 24 km (8 to 15 mi), is the largest island in the archipelago.

The total population has been estimated at 629,000, 80% of whom are believed to be ethnic Arabs. The other 20% are of Iranian origin. Like other countries of the Gulf, Bahrain's population includes a large number of migrant workers who reside in Bahrain but are not considered citizens. Approximately 25% of the total population are non-citizens. More than 90% of Bahrainis are Muslims, 75% of whom belong to the Shi'a branch of Islam while the other 25% are Sunnis. Bahrain's Christian population numbers about 43,000 while some 49,000 residents practice other religions. The ruling al-Khalifa family belongs to the Sunni branch of Islam. The official language is Arabic. Bahrain's currency is the *dinar*. The major industries are petroleum processing and refining, aluminum smelting and fabrication. The per capita GDP has been estimated at $13,100.

## POLITICAL BACKGROUND

For much of the 17th and 18th centuries Bahrain was ruled by Iran. In 1783, the Arab Utub tribe ended Iranian rule, and members of its main branch, the al-Khalifa, established themselves as rulers. In 1861, faced with threats from Iran and Ottoman Turkey, Bahrain sought assistance from the United Kingdom and agreed to become a protectorate. In return for British protection, the government of Bahrain agreed to abstain from piracy and the slave trade. Furthermore, Bahrain agreed not to establish relations with any foreign country without British approval. Although Britain and the Ottoman Turks acknowledged Bahrain's independence in 1913, the country remained under British control. The al-Khalifa family, however, maintained its position of prominence under British rule.

In 1970, a United Nations commission recommended total independence. The state of Bahrain became fully independent on 15 August 1971 under the rule of the al-Khalifa family. At first, a form of parliamentary government was established, and elections for a Constituent Assembly were held in December 1972. A year later, the National Assembly was elected. In August 1975 the prime minister resigned, charging that the Assembly had made it impossible for the government

to function. The emir dissolved the Assembly and asked the prime minister to form a new government.

At present, Bahrain is administered by a 16-member cabinet, headed by Prime Minister Sheikh Khalifa bin Sulman al-Khalifa and dominated by the members of the al-Khalifa family. In September 1998, in addition to the position of prime minister, eight other positions in the cabinet were filled by members of the al-Khalifa family. They also play an important role in lower administrative positions.

Although Sheikh Khalifa is the head of government, effective power was in the hands of his elder brother, Sheikh Isa Bin Sulman al-Khalifa. Under the constitution of 1973, the emir is the head of state and commander in chief of the armed forces. He has the power to conclude treaties and international agreements and to establish diplomatic relations with other countries. Sheikh Isa died of a sudden heart attack on 7 March 1999 after a 38-year reign. His eldest son, Crown Prince Hamad, assumed the throne within hours of his father's death.

## PERSONAL BACKGROUND

Hamad Bin Isa al-Khalifa, which translates to "Hamad son of Isa al-Khalifa," was born 20 January 1950. He is an experienced military officer. Hamad received his education in Britain at the Moons Officer Candidate School and Sandhurst Military Academy. He has subsequently studied at the US Army Command and General Staff College at Fort Leavenworth, Kansas. He has been the crown prince and designated heir since 1964. Hamad became a qualified helicopter pilot in 1978 and was a permanent member of the Helicopter Club of Great Britain. He speaks English, rides well, and enjoys water-skiing. Hamad used to play basketball and football with his soldiers and is fond of tennis and falconry. He has three sons and two daughters.

## RISE TO POWER

The al-Khalifa family dominated Bahrain before independence and has continued to do so. The political career of Sheikh Isa (Hamad's father) began in June 1953 when he represented his father at the coronation of King Faisal of Iraq. In 1956, after a series of disturbances in Bahrain's capital city of Manama, Isa was named to head the municipal council by his father, the ruling emir. He subsequently held a variety of administrative posts, including a position on Bahrain's administrative council and president of the education committee.

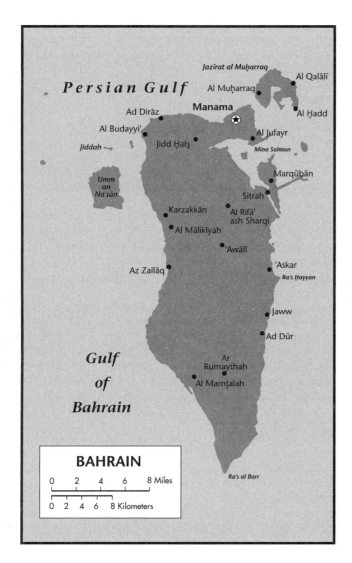

Isa's leadership status was formally recognized on 31 January 1958 when he became the designated heir apparent to his father. Over the next two years, because of his father's failing health, Crown Prince Isa came to play an increasingly important role in governing Bahrain. He also became the acting head of the al-Khalifa family council. This council, which is still in existence today, consists of the senior members of the al-Khalifa family and is primarily responsible for family matters, including disbursement of oil profits and other favors among members of the clan and their associates. The al-Khalifa council confirmed Isa as the new ruler of Bahrain on 16 December 1961. He subsequently guided Bahrain through the Organization of Petroleum Exporting Countries (OPEC) oil crisis and the Gulf War, steering a largely pro-Western course. In recent years Sheikh Isa had delegated authority to his brother, the prime minister, and to his son Hamad. As commander-in-chief of the Bahraini Defense Force and National Guard, Hamad played a prominent role in suppressing internal dissent in recent years.

## LEADERSHIP

Sheikh Isa presided over the transformation of Bahrain into a modern society, but he continued some of the traditional practices common in the Bahraini society for centuries. One of these is a public assembly known as the *Majlis*. At these assemblies anyone, regardless of their social or citizenship status, can directly petition the emir concerning any issue and ask him to personally adjudicate the matter. This traditional tribal practice, which is common in many Gulf states, provides citizens with direct access to the ruler. It is thought that Sheikh Hamad will continue this practice. He has not had much opportunity to demonstrate any particular style of leadership, but in his first months as emir, he took several liberalizing steps that made observers hope he might eventually move the country toward true democracy. He made several overtures to the beleaguered Shiite majority, including allowing Shiites into the army for the first time and releasing hundreds of Shiite political prisoners, most notably Sheik Abdul Amir al-Jamri, the country's best-known Shiite dissident. Observers believe that his approach to dissent and to disputes with Bahrain's neighbors, however, especially Qatar, will be heavier handed than his father's.

## DOMESTIC POLICY

Bahrain's economy is heavily dependent on oil. Its oil reserves, however, are much smaller than that of its neighbors, and it is estimated that they will soon be exhausted. Recognizing this fact, Bahrain's leaders have tried to diversify the country's economy. Their efforts, however, have produced mixed results. Outside of the oil sector, the most successful industrial enterprise has been aluminum production. In cooperation with British, French, Swedish, and US companies, the government built Bahrain's first aluminum smelter in 1969, with an annual capacity of 120,000 metric tons (132,240 tons). The company, known as Aluminum Bahrain (ALBA), has been the most successful non-oil industrial venture. In 1996, ALBA increased is production to 418,441 metric tons (461,245 tons) of aluminum, making it one of the largest aluminum smelters in the world. There are several industries that further process ALBA's output, including a joint venture between the government of Bahrain and a German firm that produces atomized aluminum for export.

Another successful industrial venture has been the Arab Shipbuilding and Repair Yard Company (ASRY). Jointly owned by the members of the Organization of the Arab Petroleum Exporting Countries (OAPEC), ASRY began operation in 1977. In the early 1980s, ASRY experienced financial problems caused by the oil glut and the decline in shipping in the Gulf. The "tanker war" between Iran and Iraq, enabled the company to recover. By 1987 it began to show a profit.

Bahrain has also achieved success in the service sector. The oil boom of the mid-1970s transformed Bahrain into the financial capital of the Gulf. By 1988, not counting domestic banks, 65 international commercial and investment banks had established branches in Bahrain. Some of these have since closed as oil prices dropped in the 1990s, but recently Bahrain has become the Gulf's Islamic banking center. Islamic banks either charge no interest or only minimal interest in an attempt to reconcile modern banking practices with Islam's prohibition on interest.

The oil income has enabled the government to rapidly expand social services. Bahrain's constitution provides for free education and health service for all citizens. The student population rose from 50,000 in 1971 to 86,000 in 1986. By 1983, Bahrain had 397 physicians, 6 hospitals, 27 health centers, and 16 child-care centers. The drop in oil prices, however, has adversely affected these social programs. The opening of a proposed Arab Gulf University has been postponed due to lack of funding.

The main domestic challenge facing the new emir comes from Bahrain's Shi'a community. Although the Shi'as constitute a majority of the population, they are underrepresented among the political and business elite. In recent years "fundamentalist" elements in the Shi'a community, possibly supported by Iran, have challenged the regime. The situation is further complicated by a rising unemployment rate (estimated to be as high as 18% for Bahraini citizens), demands from across the religious and economic spectrum for greater citizen participation in the functioning of the government, and resentment of the large number of foreign workers in Bahrain. In 1994, a charity-sponsored running race, whose participants were mostly foreign workers, was violently disrupted by villagers who were upset by the participation of women. Some of the villagers were arrested. A month later, rioting erupted all over the main island when cassette tapes of sermons by a Shiite imam from Manama began to circulate. These tapes condemned the presence of women in a foot race, the large number of foreign workers in Bahrain, and the decline of moral standards. They called for a revival of the 1973 constitution, which had allowed for a representative assembly. At least 40 people have died in civil unrest in the last decade. The US Navy, which maintains a strong presence in Bahrain, has placed a curfew on its sailors for fear that they might be attacked. Sheikh Hamad must find a way to restrain dissent in order to protect Bahrain's reputation for stability, which has been an essential ingredient in attracting foreign investment.

## FOREIGN POLICY

In general, Bahrain maintains friendly relations with its neighbors. In recent years, however, relations with Iran have been problematic. For much of the 20th century Iran has claimed sovereignty over Bahrain. This claim is based on Iran's former control over the islands in the 17th and 18th centuries. In 1970, the government of Iran announced that it has no objection to Bahrain's gaining independence from the UK, but it did not renounce its earlier claims. After the Iranian revolution of 1979, prominent elements within Iran again called for Iranian control of Bahrain. However, in April 1980 Teheran officially renounced all claims to Bahrain. Although for the time being this issue is moot, it has nevertheless complicated relations between the two governments.

Of more immediate concern are allegations that Iran is providing support for fundamentalist Islamic groups in Bahrain. After the Islamic Revolution, some Iranians called on Bahrain's Shi'a community to rise up against the al-Khalifas. Radical elements within Bahrain's underprivileged Shi'a community seem to have been receptive to these suggestions. In December 1981, 60 Bahraini Shi'as were charged with plotting to assassinate key officials and members of the royal family. The government of Bahrain alleged that the group was supported by Iran. Another plot to overthrow the government was discovered in 1985. In December 1988, Iran

was implicated in an alleged plot to sabotage Bahrain's oil refinery. Relations with Iran have improved, and since 1990 a Bahraini ambassador has been in Teheran. In 1992, a protocol for industrial and commercial cooperation was signed. In August 1999, Sheik Hamad responded positively to an invitation to visit Iran by that country's president, Mohammad Khatami.

In recent years, Bahrain has also had problems with its Arab neighbor and fellow Gulf Cooperation Council (GCC) member, Qatar. Both countries claim sovereignty over three regions: the island of Hawar, the Fasht al-Dibl coral reef, and the Zubara region. In 1986, troops from Qatar arrested Bahraini workers on Fasht al-Dibl. In 1996, Sheikh Hamad publicly rejected an offer by Qatar to build a causeway connecting Qatar to Bahrain. He is viewed as being unfriendly to Qatar, and Qatari officials are concerned about the possibility of increased tension between the two nations.

In its relations with other countries Bahrain generally follows the lead of Saudi Arabia. Like Saudi Arabia, Bahrain's foreign policy is pro-Western and generally favorable to the United States. Bahrain supported the allies in the 1990–1991 Gulf War. Currently, Bahrain is home to the largest US naval base in the region. Sheikh Isa offered a site to the US Navy, discreetly at first because of the probability of popular resentment against a foreign military presence, then openly during and after the 1990–1991 Gulf crisis. He later signed a security pact with the US.

Sheik Hamad is expected to continue Bahrain's close ties with the US; however, problems complicate the relationship. Early in 1999 Sheik Isa's government protested US and British air strikes against Iraq provoked by Saddam Hussein's refusal to cooperate with UN weapons monitors and UNSCOM (UN Special Commission) demilitarization measures. Another major problem in Bahrain's relations with the US is American policy pertaining to the Arab-Israeli conflict. Like many other Arab countries, Bahrain does not recognize Israel and has often been critical of US support for Israel. Signs indicated that relations with Israel appeared to be thawing. Ministerial level talks took place, and in 1995 Israeli television reported that Bahrain was considering opening a consulate in Jerusalem. However, unhappiness about the 1997 decision to construct new Jewish settlements in disputed territory seems to have temporarily chilled relations between the two countries.

## ADDRESS
Amiri Court
FOB 555
Riffa Palace
Manama, Bahrain

## REFERENCES
Childs, Nicholas. *The Middle East Review,* 1989.
*The Economist,* various issues.
*Financial Times,* 8 March 1999.
*The Middle East and North Africa,* 1999.
*New York Times,* 7 March 1999.

**Profile researched and written by Erik Gilbert, Arkansas State University (9/99; updated 2/2000).**

# BANGLADESH

### Hasina Wajed
### Prime Minister
*(pronounced "Ha-SEEN-a Wah-HEED")*

*"We want to run the country on the basis of national consensus to give our people freedom from poverty, hunger, exploitation, terrorism and injustice."*

Among the world's poorest nations, the People's Republic of Bangladesh (formerly East Pakistan) is located in Southern Asia. Nearly surrounded by India, except for a short south-eastern frontier with Myanmar and a southern coastline of 575 km (357 mi) on the Bay of Bengal, Bangladesh has a total area of 143,998 sq km (55,598 sq mi), roughly the size of Wisconsin. Most of this area is a flat alluvial plain, consisting of the delta of three major river systems: the Ganges (or Parma), the Brahmaputra (or Jamuna) and the Meghna. Alluvial deposits from these rivers make the region extremely fertile for growing rice, the country's most important food crop, and jute, the most important cash crop.

The population of Bangladesh has been estimated at around 120 million. With 825 persons per sq km (2,137 per sq mi), Bangladesh is one of the most densely populated countries in the world. More than 95% of the people are ethnic Bengalis who speak *Bangla*, the country's official language. Minorities include Urdu-speaking Biharis and tribal groups living in the Chattagram Hills. English is widely spoken among the country's educated elite. Bangladesh is a predominantly Muslim nation, and Islam is the state religion. Hindus, who number about 12 million, make up the country's largest religious minority.

Bangladesh has a developing economy which is primarily agrarian; nearly 80% of the people earn their livelihood farming rice, jute, sugarcane, wheat, and tea. Economic progress and diversification have been hobbled by a burgeoning population, few natural resources, lack of skilled labor, and a limited industrial base. Moreover, recurring floods and other natural disasters that adversely affect agricultural production also take a toll on the nation's economic performance. All these factors combine to make Bangladesh heavily dependent on foreign aid and assistance. The country's main exports are garments, fish products, jute, and leather goods. Its principal trading partners are the European Union, the United States, and Japan. The unit of currency is the *taka*.

## POLITICAL BACKGROUND
When British rule in India ended in August 1947, the country was partitioned to create a new independent nation, Pakistan. Comprised of the Muslim-majority areas in the northwest and northeast of British India, Pakistan came into existence as a country divided in two parts, West and East Pakistan, whose people, though sharing a common religion, were separated by nearly 1,600 km (1,000 mi) of Indian territory

and differences in language, culture, and traditions. Over the years, West Pakistan's economic and political domination of the more populous East Pakistan sharpened awareness of these differences among many East Pakistanis, fueling Bengali nationalism and demands for greater autonomy. Spear-heading this call was the Awami League, a leading political party in East Pakistan. In late 1971, India and Pakistan fought a war which ended with the surrender of Pakistani troops in East Pakistan and the independence of Bangladesh on 16 December 1971.

Attempts to establish a parliamentary system failed when the government proved unable to cope with the challenge of reconstructing and rebuilding an economy and civil society devastated by war. Amidst growing political and economic anarchy, a state of emergency was declared and most consti-tutional rights were suspended. Opposition parties were suppressed, and Bangladesh became a one-party state, plagued by coups and counter-coups. A popular uprising on 6 December 1990 paved the way for parliamentary elections and ended 16 years of political instability.

Under the present system, Bangladesh has a unicameral legislature, the *Jatiya Sangshad* or People's Assembly, comprised of 330 members. Three hundred members are directly elected from single-member constituencies for five-year terms on the basis of universal adult franchise. Thirty seats are reserved for women members who are indirectly elected to five-year terms by the directly elected members. The leader of the party with a majority in the *Jatiya Sangshad* serves as Prime Minister and is vested with full executive powers as head of government. The Prime Minister appoints a Council of Ministers, or Cabinet, whose members admin-ister the departments that carry out the government's functions. The President plays a largely ceremonial role as Head of State and is indirectly elected by the *Jatiya Sangshad* to serve a five-year term.

The country's main political organizations are the Awami League (AL), the Bangladesh National Party (BNP), the *Janata* Party and the *Jamaat-e-Islami* Party. Parliamentary elections held in June 1996 brought the Awami League to power after a hiatus of more than 20 years. The AL won 146 of the 300 directly elected seats in the *Jatiya Sangshad* and formed a government with the parliamentary support of the *Jatiya* Party's 31 members. As of February 2000, the AL has an absolute majority with 177 seats in the 330-member Parliament.

## PERSONAL BACKGROUND

Hasina Wajed was born on 28 September 1947 in Tungipara, a village in the Faridpur district of Bangladesh. She attended Eden Intermediate Girls' College where she was actively involved in student politics. In 1968 she married Dr. M.A. Wajed Miah. During the War of Liberation in 1971, Hasina Wajed, her husband, and her parents and siblings were all taken into custody by Pakistani authorities. After Bangladesh won its independence, her father became the new nation's first prime minister. Hasina Wajed resumed her formal education, completing a graduate degree in Bengali from Dhaka University in 1973. On 15 August 1975, Hasina Wajed lost her parents and her three brothers to assassins' bullets. For the next six years, Hasina Wajed remained abroad in self-imposed exile. In 1981 she returned to Bangladesh to take up the leadership of her slain father's political party, the Awami League.

Since her return, Hasina Wajed has devoted her time and energy to reviving the Awami League's political fortunes and restoring her father's legacy. Friends and associates describe her as a warm and kindly person. She is enormously popular with the Awami League's rank-and-file workers, who call her *Apa* or sister.

## RISE TO POWER

Hasina Wajed received her baptism in politics as a youth when she served as a contact between her father and the Awami League's student activists. But it was not until 1981, after the Awami League elected her to head the party, that her political career began in earnest. To many in the AL, Hasina Wajed's relationship to Sheikh Mujib and association with his formidable legacy made her the one person capable of healing divisions within the party's hierarchy and commanding the allegiance of the party's faithful supporters. While familial ties thrust Hasina Wajed into a role denied most women in male-dominated Bangladeshi society, her subsequent ascendance to the nation's highest office must be credited to her tireless and resolute leadership of the Awami League's long march back to power. In 1986 Hasina Wajed became a Member of Parliament and the country's youngest leader of the parliamentary opposition.

On 19 March 1996, the newly elected *Jatiya Sangshad* convened briefly to pass the Thirteenth Constitutional Amendment which provided for the appointment of a non-partisan, interim government solely to supervise fresh elections. Amidst a great deal of rancor, polling took place on schedule. Even though security was tight, outbreaks of violence were reported, but they did not deter a heavy voter turnout which set a new record for parliamentary elections in the country. Foreign observers who monitored the polls found that the elections were largely free and fairly conducted. The results, an Awami League victory, vindicated Hasina Wajed's personal and political odyssey. She was sworn in as Prime Minister on 23 June 1996.

## LEADERSHIP

The election of an Awami League government holds the prospect of a fresh start towards the long-term political and economic stability the country desperately needs. Providing this stability is the principal challenge facing Hasina Wajed, who now has to translate her skills as an opposition leader into the more demanding task of responsibly administering a

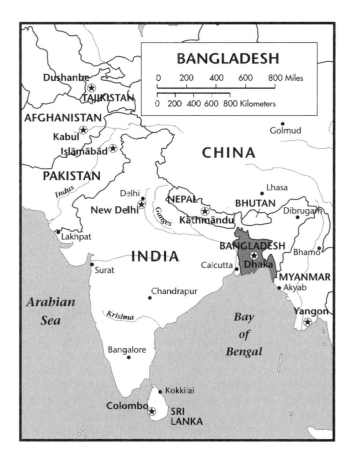

nation that too often seems ungovernable. She has to take the lead in convincing her allies and her foes to place the nation's interest above their own parochial ambitions, and not succumb to the temptations of political opportunism and vindictiveness. In speeches and public appearances following the elections, Hasina Wajed has repeatedly stressed her responsiveness to the people's will and their trust. She has disclaimed personal ambition and said that she values the people's affection more than the privileges of power. She considers the government the servant and not the master of people and has promised an accountable, transparent, and incorruptible administration. She has called for unity and cooperation among all political parties.

Hasina Wajed has also made overtures to the BNP, inviting it to join in a government of national "consensus." The offer, however, was refused, a spokesman for the BNP harshly calling it an ill-disguised attempt to reinstate one-party rule. There is, in fact, little liking between Hasina Wajed and the BNP leader, Begum Khaleda Zia. Each believes the other was involved in some way in the killing of her own father. The cycle of accusations, recriminations, strikes, and political violence has continued to plague Bangladeshi politics. With a four-party alliance of opposition parties committed to forming an electoral coalition to fight the general elections planned for 2001, the leadership of Hasina Wajed will be tested to the utmost.

## DOMESTIC POLICY

Bangladesh's endemic problems of poverty, overpopulation, and illiteracy have made economic development, or what Hasina Wajed calls "economic salvation," a top priority for the country's policy makers. Following the battering taken from a spate of strikes, work-stoppages, and other disruptions of commerce prior to the June 1996 elections, the first years under the Awami League government saw the GDP grow at over 5% with inflation held well in check. In its election manifesto, the AL jettisoned its earlier commitment to socialist economics and nationalization of key industries, and embraced the free-market philosophy of its BNP rival as the route to economic progress. The government has repeatedly stated its intention of opening the economy further and improving the climate for foreign investment. Its success in introducing pro-private sector policies, however, has been mixed. Trade has been liberalized, and new sectors of the economy opened to private sector development. But reforms, such as privatization of industries, have faced stiff opposition from interest groups, such as labor unions, government bureaucrats, and opposition politicians.

By the summer of 1997, popular discontent with Prime Minister Hasina Wajed's pro-Indian policies, her efforts to privatize public sector industries, and her apparent inability to deal with economic problems such as power and water shortages saw a return of the politics of "hartal" (strikes). Opposition parties began organizing a series of anti-government protests, strikes, and demonstrations that interrupted the daily life and normal business activities of the people. The disruptive impact of such actions on Bangladesh's economy was magnified by the devastating floods that hit the country during the summer of 1998. The total cost of flood damage was estimated at over US$2 billion, with agriculture being particularly hard hit. Losses were such that the government had to appeal to the international community for aid, both in food supplies and in emergency financial loans. Estimates suggest that if it had not been for the floods, Bangladesh might have achieved a growth rate approaching 7% in 1998.

By January 1999, the economy showed signs of recovery, but it has yet to achieve the growth rates necessary to help relieve Bangladesh's widespread poverty. The specter of political instability remains, with the government facing the disruptive tactics of the opposition parties—a situation that will likely continue up to the next elections. Other serious domestic problems that have still to be effectively dealt with include the law and order situation, corruption, an entrenched bureaucracy, and human rights issues. The AL government, however, has had successes in the area of domestic policy. A peace agreement signed in December 1997 ended the tribal insurgency in the Chittagong Hill Tracts. The discovery and development of natural gas deposits under the Bay of Bengal has helped ease Bangladesh's power crisis while completion of a major bridge across the Jumna River has improved links between the northwest and others areas of the country. Creation of a new system of local government promises to encourage participation of the people, especially traditionally disadvantaged groups, such as women, in the political process. Hasina Wajed has also introduced specific legislation aimed at reducing gender violence. Other government initiatives include creation of permanent Commissions to oversee elections and law reform, as well as plans for a Human Rights Commission and an Ombudsman.

## FOREIGN POLICY

Bangladesh enjoys cordial relations with the main global powers influential in the region: the US, China, and Japan. Ties with these countries center primarily on trade and economic assistance, but recently the US and Bangladesh have begun closer military cooperation. Bangladesh has provided troops for UN peacekeeping missions in Bosnia, Haiti, and the Iraq-Kuwait frontier—regions where the US has staked its strategic interests.

The main focus of the government's foreign policy agenda has been to resolve outstanding issues with its neighbors. India and Bangladesh have been at odds over sharing and managing common water resources since the mid-1970s when India built the Farakka Barrage, 18 km (11 mi) upstream from its border with northwestern Bangladesh, to divert water from the Ganges River to Calcutta. In December 1996, however, the two countries signed a 30-year water-sharing agreement, with India also receiving road transit rights across Bangladesh territory to its remote northeastern states. January 1997 was marked by an official state visit to Bangladesh by India's Prime Minister H. D. Dev Gowde, the first such visit in 20 years. The peace accord in the Chittagong Hill Tracts helped improve relations with India further by permitting the repatriation of Chakma refugees who had fled to India. Bangladesh has had less success in dealing with the repatriation of stranded Pakistanis (Bihari refugees) left over from the civil war. The government also continues to face the problem of *Rohingya* refugees from Myanmar, but tensions along the border have eased to the point where they no longer constitute a major foreign policy challenge for the AL government.

## ADDRESS

Office of the Prime Minister
Tejgaon
PABX-88160-79

## REFERENCES

*Bangladesh: Economc Trends and Outlook.* US Department of Commerce, National Trade Data Bank, Sept. 3, 1999.

*Country Profile: Bangladesh 1995–96.* The Economist Intelligence Unit Ltd., 1996.

*Europa World Yearbook.* "Bangladesh: Introductory Survey." London: Publications, 1999.

Hasina, Sheikh. "Bangladesh's Foreign Policy." *Presidents & Prime Ministers*, September 1999, p. 21.

Hossain, Golam. "Bangladesh in 1995: The Politics of Intransigence." *Asian Survey*, February 1996, vol. 36, pp. 196–203.

Shebabuddin, Elora. "Bangladesh in 1998: Democracy on the Ground." *Asian Survey*, January–February 1999, vol. 39, no. 1, pp. 148–155.

Zubrzycki, John. " A Poor Country Finds Hope In a New Woman Leader." *The Christian Science Monitor*, 24 June 1996, p. 7.

**Profile researched and written by Taufiq Rashid, Indiana University (9/96); updated by Deryck Lodrick, University of California (5/2000).**

# BARBADOS

Owen Arthur
Prime Minister
*(pronounced "O-wen AR-thur")*

*"No country can ever truly develop unless it finds the means of engrossing everyone
in the task of nation building, whatever their class, creed, color or political persuasion."*

With a total area of 430 sq km (166 sq mi), Barbados is the easternmost island in the Windward chain of the Caribbean countries. The population has been estimated at 259,000. Its racial composition reflects a population that is 80% African, 16% mixed, 3% European, and 1% East Indian. The official language of the country is English although a Barbadian or Bajan dialect (a mixture of English and Africanisms) is widely spoken. The overwhelming majority of the population is Christian, 70% of whom are Anglicans.

The local currency is the Barbados dollar. Major economic activities include tourism, sugar production, and manufactured goods (mainly electrical equipment and chemicals). The per capita GDP has been estimated at $11,200.

## POLITICAL BACKGROUND

Originally settled by the Arawak Indians, Western civilization credits a Portuguese explorer for the discovery of the island in 1536. It was the Portuguese who named the island "Los Barbados" after the ficus tree that grew there in great abundance. The British later settled Barbados in 1627. The current population is descended from African slaves who were brought to the country by the British to work on the sugar plantations.

Barbados is a democratic, self-governing country, functioning through a governor general appointed by Queen Elizabeth II of Britain and a prime minister who is usually the leader of the majority party in the House of Assembly. The prime minister presides over a cabinet selected from party members in the legislature. The bicameral legislature consists of the House of Assembly with 28 elected members and the Senate with 21 members, 12 of whom are drawn from the majority party, 2 from the opposition, and 7 are appointed to represent social, religious, and economic interests.

Barbados boasts of having the third-oldest parliament in the world. However, universal adult suffrage was not introduced until 1951, 15 years before Barbados achieved its independence in 1966. Barbados has three political parties. The Barbados Labor Party (BLP) and the Democratic Labor Party (DLP) have traditionally monopolized the political life of the country. The third party is the recently formed National Democratic Party (NDP), a faction which broke away from the DLP.

## PERSONAL BACKGROUND

Owen Seymour Arthur was born in Barbados on 17 October 1949. He gained his primary and secondary education at All Saints Boys School, Coleridge and Parry School, and Harrison College. He attended the University of the West Indies (UWI) in Barbados and Jamaica, the latter on a post-graduate scholarship. Arthur holds a Bachelor of Arts degree in economics. He began his working career in Jamaica as a research assistant on the Faculty of Social Sciences at the UWI. However, Arthur's career has largely been one of a technocrat. In 1974, he became assistant economic planner at the Planning Agency in Jamaica and within five years was appointed chief economic planner. Between 1979 and 1981, Arthur served as director of economics at the Jamaica Bauxite Institute. He represented Jamaica at the United Nations Conference on Trade and Development (UNCTAD) Intergovernmental Group of Experts on the transfer of technology in 1975 and 1976 and was a member of the Caribbean Technology Policy Studies Project between 1977 and 1978. Arthur has also served as a member of the board of directors of the Jamaica Scientific Research Council.

In 1981, Arthur returned to Barbados and took up the post of chief analyst in the ministry of finance and planning. Two years later, he joined the Institute of Social and Economic Research, UWI, Cave Hill Campus, Barbados. In 1985, he returned to the ministry of finance and planning as a parliamentary secretary for one year, before assuming the post of part-time lecturer in the Department of Management Studies at the UWI.

## RISE TO POWER

Arthur's entry into the political arena was in many ways difficult. He faced two by-elections in the same year. In 1984, Arthur's party, the BLP, went to court to contest the outcome of a by-election that was officially won by his opponent in the DLP, Sybil Leacock. The High Court later ruled that there should be a new poll, which was subsequently won by Arthur. Since then, he has never lost an election in his constituency.

Prior to 1983, Arthur was the consummate technocrat who worked as an economist under Prime Minister Michael Manley's democratic socialist government in Jamaica. When Arthur became a member of the BLP, the leader of the party and prime minister of Barbados, Tom Adams, projected him as a bright young economist with future leadership potential. In 1983, Arthur was made a member of the Barbados Senate and chairman of his party. Following his 1984 victory at the polls, Arthur became a member of Parliament. In 1985 and 1986 he served as parliamentary secretary in the ministry of finance. After his party's defeat in two successive elections

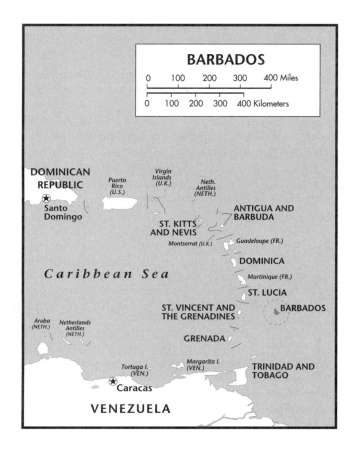

between 1986 and 1994 by the DLP, Arthur was made opposition leader and leader of the BLP.

Arthur became Barbados' fifth prime minister on 6 September 1994 when he successfully led the BLP to an electoral victory, capturing 19 of the 28 seats in the House of Assembly. In the election of January 1999, Arthur was again successful. This time his party won by an even greater margin. The BLP took 26 seats while the opposition Democratic Labour Party won only two seats in the House of Assembly.

## LEADERSHIP

Arthur has always been described as a grassroots leader because of the close relationship that he has with people of all levels of society. He has a strong number of socialist ideals, having been influenced by the Michael Manley administration during the 1970s. He is the first and only professional economist to become prime minister in the English-speaking Caribbean, and he continues to approach economic matters with much caution.

Arthur promotes "the politics of inclusion" that encourage nation-building by the entire population. This has been a major factor in Arthur's success as a political leader. He has argued that no one in society should be excluded from the development process.

Arthur has proved to be a skillful politician and an able leader. His administration brought growth to the Barbados economy and during the run up to the general elections of 1999, Arthur successfully attracted politicians from the opposition DLP to his party. He also received the endorsement of Richie Haynes, leader of the NDP.

With an emphasis on cultural emancipation and economic development, it is expected that Arthur will take Barbados into a Republic status. He has also promised to transform Barbados into the smallest developed country in the next century.

## DOMESTIC POLICY

The United Nations Development Program (UNDP) ranks Barbados as the developing country with the highest Human Development Index (HDI). Notwithstanding, economic growth has been inconsistent. The country experienced a recession during the latter part of the 1980s to the early 1990s. The BLP, under the leadership of Arthur, sought to end this recession and stimulate economic growth when they began their term in office in 1994. Since then, the GDP has increased significantly. In 1996, GDP grew by 4.5%, which was twice the recorded rate for 1995. Several factors influenced this rise in GDP: increases in stopover and cruise ship visitor arrivals, greater agricultural production, more construction activity, and increases in service activity.

Agricultural output increased significantly. In 1996, sugar production expanded by 53.5%. As a result, Barbados was able to satisfy its export quota to Europe. In 1997, the amount of sugar produced was 4.9% higher than in the previous year. Non-sugar output increased by 7.7% in 1996 but decreased marginally the following year.

Tourism also grew during 1996 and 1997, with an increase of 4.4% and 6.1% respectively. This led to an increase in the amount of construction activity, including three new hotels, the expansion and renovation of a number of existing properties, and the construction of a marina and associated facilities.

The rate of unemployment decreased from a rate of 23.1% in 1992 to 16.2% in 1996 and 15.9% in 1997. This is in keeping with Arthur's aim to develop human resources within the country, a policy that has been welcomed by both the private and the public sectors. The BLP also seeks to create an information system that is aimed at facilitating universal and public access to manpower, labor market, and working conditions in Barbados. In addition, the recently elected government seeks to implement a national minimum wage that will ensure a satisfactory standard of living for all working Barbadians.

Arthur's belief in free universal education will be further demonstrated as he continues to provide free access to post-secondary and tertiary level institutions in Barbados and the University of the West Indies. He promises to spend $100 million on education through a new strategy named "Edutech 2000" over the next seven years. This new strategy seeks to modernize existing schools, increase the use of information and multimedia technologies, and enhance teacher training. It hopes to strengthen the educational institutions through curriculum reform, as well as administrative reform in the Ministry. This is in keeping with the BLP view that full employment in Barbados can be achieved, but only if individuals are trained with relevant skills.

The BLP seeks to promote the construction of houses for all income groups through the National Housing Corporation (NHC) while implementing measures to reduce building costs for all sectors of the community.

## FOREIGN POLICY

Barbados seeks to strengthen its relations with the US, Canada, the UK, Ireland, and the Commonwealth by negotiating for new trade and economic relationships. As a member of the Caribbean Community and Common Market (CARICOM), Arthur continues to negotiate for entry into a Free Trade Area of the Americas and promotes Barbados as a gateway for extra-regional investment in the region. Barbados will continue to play an active role in shaping the new order through its involvement in several international organizations, such as the United Nations and the World Trade Organization.

Arthur has recognized that a single market and economy within CARICOM will provide Barbadian entrepreneurs and workers with greater economic opportunities. Therefore, he continues to promote the implementation of this policy. Arthur said that his aim is to make Barbados the most competitive Caribbean country by the year 2005. Looking ahead to 2005, Arthur announced that he has already begun negotiations with the European Union and the North American Free Trade Area. In his annual televised speech to the House of Assembly (1999), Arthur said that for Barbados to compete on the world market, it must curtail excessive consumer demand driven by easy access to credit, and Barbados must seek to reverse the trend of falling exports and declining tourism.

As part of the ongoing effort to stimulate trade and tourism, Barbados signed a new Air Services Agreement with the UK on 23 June 1999, replacing an agreement signed in 1971. The new agreement will expand coverage and improve the transport of people, cargo, and mail.

In a step toward a single Caribbean market, Arthur announced in July 1999 that Barbados would lift the ban against importing soft drinks. Later, in August, he pressured Trinidad and Tobago to lower oil prices. Because of treaties, Barbados is locked into buying oil from within the region, and Arthur complained that Trinidad and Tobago were charging above world market prices for gasoline and diesel fuel.

Although Barbados still has no representation in any of the African capitals, Arthur intends to systematically develop cultural and economic links with Africa by promoting, through trade missions, tourist and cultural exchanges. He has already appointed an African ambassador. The Commission for African Affairs will be used to promote people-to-people contacts.

Arthur intends to play a leading role in the Association of Caribbean States, especially in having the Caribbean Sea recognized by the international community as a special area for environmental protection. So far, Arthur has proved to be an able leader within CARICOM and the wider world. Barbados was the host country for CARICOM during the 1997 visit of US president, Bill Clinton. He has either led or participated in a number of high-level international trade missions, including a Commonwealth mission to the World Trade Organization.

## ADDRESS

Office of the Prime Minister
Bay Street
St. Michael, Barbados

## REFERENCES

*Barbados Advocate*, various issues.
*Barbados Labour Party Manifesto 1999*. Bridgetown, Barbados: Barbados Labour Party, 1999.
*Caribbean's Top 100 Public Companies 97–98*. St. Michael, Barbados: Lefferts Place, 1999.
*Weekend Nation*, various issues.

**Profile researched and written by Ian and Rachael Boxill, University of the West Indies (6/99; updated 2/2000).**

# BELARUS

### Alyaksandr Lukashenka
### President

*(pronounced "al-ak-SAHN-der loo-kah-SHEN-kah")*

*"There is no exit from [our] situation without help from Russia."*

Bounded by Russia on the east, Latvia and Lithuania on the north, Poland on the west, and Ukraine on the south, Belarus occupies some 207,700 sq km (80,200 sq mi) and has been a major east–west passage in both war and peace for more than 1,000 years.

Its current population is estimated to be 10.4 million, 80% of whom are ethnic Belarussians, 12% ethnic Russians, with the remainder including Poles, Ukrainians, Tatars, and a scattering of other smaller nationalities. Its capital, Minsk, is also the capital of the Commonwealth of Independent States. Belarussian is the official language, but Russian, which is closely related to Belarussian and spoken by most Belarussians (including President Lukashenka), also enjoys a privileged status. A distinct cultural community since at least the 10th century, Belarus has been subjected to outside influences because of its location. Intense russification took place under both the tsars and the Soviets. The Belarussian nation includes followers of the Belarussian Autocephalous Church, the Russian Orthodox Church, the Unitate Catholic Church, and the Roman Catholic Church.

Following the collapse of the Soviet Union, the Belarussian government introduced the *rubel* as a parallel currency to the Russian *ruble*. Because of hyperinflationary policies, the Belarussian *rubel* rapidly lost ground to the Russian *ruble*. At the center of Belarussian politics in 1993 and 1994 have been efforts by Minsk to conclude an economic union with Moscow. To date, these efforts have been unsuccessful, with the Yeltsin government apparently having concluded that the costs of such a union would be too high for Russia.

Historically, Belarus has been a major industrial region even though it lacks significant raw material resources. By the 1980s, industry accounted for over 60% of the economy. While that percentage has declined somewhat given the economic difficulties following independence, Belarus still sees itself as an industrial society. Among the most important products are agricultural machinery, computers, machine tools, and petrochemicals. Belarus's agricultural sector is a net exporter to the Commonwealth of Independent States.

## POLITICAL BACKGROUND

Because of its geographical location and the absence of any naturally secure borders, Belarus often has been a battleground among more powerful countries and an important east–west trade route between Europe and Russia. After the fall of Kievan Rus' in 1240, most of the territory of what is now Belarus fell under Polish and then Lithuanian influence.

Russia absorbed the area during the partitions of Poland in the 18th century and formalized it as the so-called "pale of settlement" for Jews in the Russian empire.

Because the region's economy could not support the burgeoning population and because of the tsarist government's restrictions on Jews, more than 1.5 million Jews and Belarussians fled to America and to the Russian Far East in the 50 years preceding the 1917 Russian revolution.

Like so much of the Russian borderlands, Belarus was the site of major fighting during World War I and the Russian Civil War, with Red, White, Polish, and some indigenous Belarussian forces all playing a role. In 1922, Belarus became one of the founders of the USSR and began to assume its current borders. Those were enlarged in 1924, at the expense of Ukraine and Russia, and further increased after the Molotov-Ribbentrop Treaty in 1939, at the expense of Poland.

Under the Soviets, Belarus was subjected to intense russification, and seldom represented a challenge to Moscow's policies. But in the 1980s, that situation began to change: a Belarussian People's Front was organized, albeit with its initial headquarters in Vilnius, Lithuania, after the Chernobyl nuclear accident contaminated much of Belarussian territory. Adding to a nationalist upsurge was the discovery of mass graves from the Stalinist terror of the 1930s at Kuropaty and other locations.

Along with other republics of the former Soviet Union, Belarus held competitive elections to a new parliament in March 1990, but significantly, the conservative Communists dominated that body. Nonetheless, in response to the nationalist Popular Front, the parliament declared Belarus a sovereign state within the USSR in July 1990. At the time of the August 1991 coup in Moscow, the leader of the Belarussian parliament backed the coup leaders: he was subsequently deposed and Belarus declared its independence. His replacement, Stanislav Shushkevich, a nuclear scientist who had helped expose the consequences of Chernobyl, led Belarus toward independence via the Commonwealth of Independent States.

But if Shushkevich was a reformer, Belarus's prime minister Vyacheslav Kebich was not. A longtime Communist party functionary, he resisted change, rejected efforts to have a referendum on early elections, and ultimately led the parliament in deposing Shushkevich. In March 1994, the parliament adopted a new constitution to replace the Soviet-era one, and this document created the position of president as chief of state and called for elections, which were held on 10 July 1994. In these elections, Alyaksandr Lukashenka unexpectedly triumphed, winning 80% of the vote on an anti-corruption and pro-Russian platform. Two years later, Lukashenka proposed constitutional reforms that disbanded the sitting parliament, creating a bicameral body chosen in controversial elections in November 1996. In addition, Lukashenka extended his own presidential term, which was to have ended in 1999, until 2001. Throughout the latter half of the decade, Belarus pursued political and economic union with Russia. Various agreements were signed by the two countries, but as of 1999 the proposed integration had not yet been implemented.

## PERSONAL BACKGROUND

Born on 30 August 1954 in Vitebsk oblast, Lukashenka graduated from the Mohylev Pedagogical Institute and the Belarussian Agricultural Academy. Following a brief teaching career as a historian and two years as a Soviet border guard, he worked in the collective farm system, rising to become the manager of the Gorodets State Farm in the Mohylev region in 1987. In 1990, he became a deputy in the Belarussian Supreme Soviet. Married with two children, Lukashenka speaks Russian and a Belarussian patois rather than formal Belarussian. His wife, also a teacher, is not interested in politics. Lukashenka himself has been handicapped by a serious back problem that has required frequent hospitalization.

## RISE TO POWER

Lukashenka first attracted public notice when he formed a parliamentary faction called "Communists for Democracy" and when he was the only Belarussian deputy to vote against the establishment of the Commonwealth of Independent States. He wanted to retain or restore the USSR, a position he maintained more or less consistently into early 1994.

But Lukashenka's breakthrough to political prominence came when he was named chairman of the Interim Parliamentary Anti-Corruption Committee. Although that body was created by conservative Communists who wanted to drive reformist parliamentary chairman Shushkevich from office and, thus, open the way for Prime Minister Kebich to take power, Lukashenka exploited his mandate to move against corruption in all parts of the Minsk administration. For that reason and because of his often flamboyant personal style, Lukashenka earned his nickname as the "Belarussian Zhirinovsky." (In this context, it is perhaps instructive to point out that his two "idols" are US President Theodore Roosevelt and Soviet secret police chief Feliks Derzhinsky. Drawing on popular unhappiness with the deteriorating economy, Lukashenka swamped his opponents in Belarus's first presidential elections.

In the first round on 23 June 1994, Lukashenka led a six-man field with 45.1% of the vote. Because he did not receive a majority, however, he faced a run-off with the number two candidate, Prime Minister Kebich. In that second round, Lukashenka received 80.1% of the vote, trouncing his opponent and driving him from office.

## LEADERSHIP

Lukashenka's populist style, his willingness to exploit the mass media, and his ability to reach out to the population

were reflected in his campaign for the presidency. Often saying contradictory things to different audiences, he played to the anti-incumbent mood of a population that had suffered greatly since independence, promising to prosecute the mafia and imprison or deport corrupt officials. He frequently said that Belarus could not survive without a closer union with Russia, one involving not only monetary links but political and military ones as well. But at the same time, he often worked closely behind the scenes with the old and corrupt party elite—the very people he was publicly attacking.

Lukashenka's cabinet has included enthusiastic economic reformers and partisans of independence. But others—particularly in the "power ministries" of defense and internal affairs—have been deeply conservative and pro-Russian, a mix suggesting that Lukashenka wanted to play one faction off against the other.

A major feature of Lukashenka's tenure as president has been the quest to increase his own power and his suppression of political dissent. In 1996 he pushed through a series of constitutional reforms that enhanced the power of the presidency and extended his presidential term from five years to seven years, or until 2001. After disbanding the elected legislature, he handpicked a Soviet-style "rubber-stamp" parliament. The referendum that approved the reforms was declared invalid by the country's Constitutional Court, and Lukashenka's political opponents attempted to elect their own legislators and president but faced a wave of arrests, interrogations, beatings, and disappearances. Lukashenka has retained his grip on power and in 1999 instituted a renewed crackdown on his remaining opponents. In September, a prominent opposition figure, Victor Gonchar, was reported missing.

## DOMESTIC POLICY

Lukashenka has been very reluctant to engage in massive reforms lest they result in social upheaval. As of 1999, Belarus still had a tightly centralized Communist-style economy that was yielding hyperinflation and shortages of consumer goods, and the World Bank was withholding further loans unless market reforms were implemented. Many entrepreneurs have left for Russia, and observers estimate that the private sector has shrunk from 30% to 10% of Belarus' economy as entrepreneurs have decamped to Russia.

## FOREIGN POLICY

Lukashenka's foremost foreign policy objective has been the campaign for union with Russia. Although a bilateral treaty with Russia calling for military and political cooperation was signed in 1996, implementation has moved slowly. At the end of 1998, new agreements provided for a single currency, tax and customs unions, and other measures. A further agreement authorizing an economic alliance between the two countries was approved by both of their parliaments and signed by Lukashenko and Russian president Boris Yeltsin at the end of 1999.

## ADDRESS

Office of the President
220010 Minsk, Belarus

## REFERENCES

*Belarusian Review,* 1992–94.

"In Big Daddy's Shadow: Belarus Dictator Alexander Lukashenko Maintains a Soviet-Style Grip on His Long-Suffering People." *Time International,* 17 May 1999, vol. 153, no. 19, p. 42.

*PlanEcon Review and Outlook,* February 1994.

*Political Handbook of the World.* NY: CSA Publications, 1999.

*Radio Free Europe/Radio Liberty Research Report,* 7 January 1994.

"St Sasha of Minsk." *The Economist (US),* 9 October 1999, vol. 353, no. 8140, p. 61.

Vakar, Nicholas. *Belorussia,* 1956.

Zaprudnik, Jan. *Belarus,* 1992.

**Profile researched and written by Paul A. Goble, Carnegie Endowment for International Peace (11/94; updated 6/2000).**

# BELGIUM

**Guy Verhofstadt**
**Prime Minister**
*(pronounced "Fer-HOFE-stott")*

*"This country must function better and rebuild its image in the world."*

The Kingdom of Belgium lies in the northwest corner of Europe and shares borders with France, Luxembourg, Germany, and the Netherlands. Even by European standards, Belgium is a small country with a total area of 30,153 km (11,781 sq mi), making it smaller than Switzerland or the Netherlands.

The population of Belgium has been estimated at 10,182,000. The country enjoys religious homogeneity, with approximately 90% of its citizens being Roman Catholic. However, the Belgian people are divided linguistically, with attendant social and cultural differences that are expressed in a contentious political climate. The northern part of the country, known as Flanders, is largely Flemish-speaking (57% of the population, one-fifth of whom also speak French). The southern part of the country, known as Wallonia (and its people as Walloons), is French-speaking (43% of the population). An eastern sliver of the country, near the German border, is German-speaking (1% of the population).

Belgium is a highly industrialized country, but the more prosperous industries are in the Flemish-speaking region, a development that has caused political divisions between north and south. In the 1990s, economic growth in Flanders was four times that of Wallonia. The per capita GDP has been estimated at $23,400. Principal exports include iron, steel, petroleum products, and chemicals. Banking and other service industries, concentrated in the capital city of Brussels, are also important. The unit of currency is the Belgian *franc*.

## POLITICAL BACKGROUND

Centuries of rule by the Spanish, Austrian, French, and Dutch ended in 1830 when Belgium won its independence. The country became a constitutional monarchy in which sovereign power theoretically lay with the monarch. Since 1993, the head of state has been King Albert II, son of the popular and long reigning (1951–93) Baudouin I. Like all Western European monarchies, the focus of Belgian politics is its parliament. In the 1990s, the Belgian parliament was reorganized and reduced in size. The parliament is bicameral, with a Chamber of Representatives having 150 seats and a Senate having 72 seats. The Chamber is directly elected, with proportional representation. Forty members of the Senate are elected in the same fashion, while 31 are elected indirectly, with the heir to the throne filling the final Senate seat. Elections for parliament must be held at least every four years. Voting is compulsory. In 1981, the minimum voting age was lowered from 21 to 18.

Belgium has a multi-party system as a result of its linguistic diversity and its system of proportional representation. In the June 1999 elections, nine parties received sufficient votes to be considered important in the political process. For nearly three decades, three principal "families" of parties have received the vast majority of electoral support: the Christian Democrats, the Socialists, and the Liberals. Since the 1970s, each of these parties has divided formally into French- and Flemish-speaking branches. In the 1990s, two new parties emerged: the "Ecolos," or Greens, and *Vlaams Blok,* a racist party with growing strength in Flanders.

The June 1999 elections saw an upheaval in Belgian politics. Political scandals and the perception of poorly managed government led to the ousting of the coalition of Christian Democrat Jean-Luc Dehaene. The temporary escape from prison of a notorious pedophile revealed deep discord among community and national police forces and caused a public outcry. A series of bribery and corruption charges against high-ranking officials, yielding a number of convictions in December 1998, brought the long-powerful Christian Democratic Party (CVP) of Dehaene into disrepute. The final blow against the government came in early June 1999 when health inspectors discovered that dioxin, a cancer-causing agent, was present in chicken feed. The European Union charged the Belgian government with covering up information about the presence of dioxin in the food chain and banned the sale of Belgian chicken in EU-member states. The long-ruling Christian Democrats were thrown out of office. The Liberals, traditionally ranking third behind the CVP and the Socialists, prevailed with the largest number of votes. Not since 1937 had the Liberals been able to name a member of their party as the head of government. Guy Verhofstadt replaced Dehaene as prime minister on 12 July 1999.

## PERSONAL BACKGROUND

Verhofstadt was born in Dendermonde, Belgium, on 11 April 1953. He lived much of his early life in Ghent, where he studied in a high school emphasizing Greek and Latin studies. Verhofstadt received a law degree from the Rijksuniversiteit in Ghent in 1975. He is married to a professional opera singer, with whom he has a son and a daughter. His passions are opera, bicycling, and the study of Italian culture.

## RISE TO POWER

Politics has been in Verhofstadt's blood since his university days. From 1972 through 1974, he headed the Flemish Liberal Student Party, which served as a training ground in the party's ideas and taught its members how to shape an agenda and put together leadership teams. In 1977, Verhofstadt became the political secretary to a senior Liberal Party politician, Willy De Clercq. De Clercq was masterful at forging compromises behind the scenes and in bringing disparate elements in the party together. As political secretary, Verhofstadt learned from direct involvement how the party was structured and how power was utilized.

Verhofstadt was a strong advocate of free markets from the 1970s through the mid-1990s. The Liberal Party is a pro-business party, with strong support from a variety of white-collar businesses, including private financial institutions. For some in Belgium, Verhofstadt's devotion to the free market was once considered too rigid. Socialists, Christian Democrats, and some of the country's newspapers derided him as "Baby Thatcher" due to his admiration for former British Prime Minister Margaret Thatcher. Nonetheless, he was widely viewed as having a brilliant legal mind. In 1982, at the age of 29, he became president of the Flemish Liberal Party. From 1985 until 1988, while the Liberals were a junior partner in a coalition government, Verhofstadt served as a vice prime minister and as minister of state for the budget. Out of power, in 1988, the Liberals named him to their "shadow cabinet" in a position-in-waiting should the party rejoin or lead a government. It was rare for someone so young to rise so quickly. The Belgian French press referred to Verhofstadt as "the big blue bad boy" due to his considerable height, the color associated with his party, and his sometimes rough, ardently ambitious ways.

## LEADERSHIP

Verhofstadt had twice attempted to form governments when the Liberals had not won a plurality of the votes. In 1991 and again in 1995, after initial failures by both Christian Democrats and Socialists to form governments, he had stepped in but was unable to forge a coalition. Bitter rivalries within his own party had impeded his efforts as much as opposition from other parties. His failure to form a coalition in 1995 weighed particularly heavily upon him. He resigned his leadership of the Liberal Party and decided to take time away from politics.

He moved temporarily with his family to Italy, where he spent over a year reading and reflecting. From all accounts, this year was an intellectually formative one. When he returned to Belgium in 1997 to take a seat in the Senate and once again lead his party, his political views were substantially broader and less ideological. While in Italy, he had developed an interest in the environment. He also saw that, while Italy had a contentious political culture, its governing institutions functioned quite well. He began to take a greater interest in the efficiency of governmental institutions and in policies that might curtail corruption. No longer was his focus strictly on the business community and the free market.

Upon returning to his home, he declared that Belgium "is still a country afflicted by politicization, scheming, wheeling and dealing—the country of missed opportunities." This would be a central theme in his rise to government leadership.

The 1999 parliamentary election campaign gave Verhofstadt ample opportunity to exhibit his broadened interests and ideas, as well as his ample leadership skills. During the campaign, his party hammered at the corruption of elements of the Belgian political elite, some of whom had recently been convicted of bribery. While Verhofstadt accepted political horse trading as necessary to the functioning of a multi-linguistic nation, he repeatedly told voters that the line must be drawn at under-the-table payments from the business world to political parties and at cronyism. He referred scathingly to the "kleptocracy" that was running the country. The campaign took place in a contentious atmosphere. A racist party was demanding that immigrants be sent out of the country. Flemish nationalists verbally attacked the Walloons, their poorer neighbors to the south, as draining away public resources. For the first time in many years, the idea that the country might split into separate states, a Dutch-speaking north and a French-speaking south, was raised as a serious option by political commentators and a growing band of local politicians.

The parliamentary election results of 13 June 1999 left the Liberals with 41 seats in the Chamber, the most of any party. The Socialists won 33 seats, and the "Ecolos" (Greens) won 20—the last a striking development for a party little more than a decade old. The Christian Democrats fared poorly. Normally, forming a coalition in Belgium requires several months of negotiation among the leading parties. The daunting task of coalition building again seemed at hand because the three strongest parties had many divergent views. The Liberals remained at heart a free-market party of business, with considerable support from the intellectual community as well. The Socialists remained the party of the workers and the lower middle class and in opposition to free-market policies that might throw its supporters out of work in hard economic times. The Greens often villified the business community as bent on making money at the expense of the environment and of the interests of the every-day citizen.

Verhofstadt's concerns over the environment, his desire to end corruption, and his intention to make the institutions of government function persuaded the Socialists and the "Ecolos" to join the Liberals in a government after only a month of bargaining. Verhofstadt is serving as prime minister with a cabinet that holds nine Liberal ministers, eight Socialist ministers, and four "Ecolo" ministers. The new government took power on 12 July 1999 and controls 94 of the Chamber's 150 seats.

## DOMESTIC POLICY

It is in domestic policy and style of governing that Verhofstadt may represent a break with the Belgian past. He has pledged to fight corruption and restore a functioning democracy. Verhofstadt has promised to stop the rivalries between local and national police and to end political appointments to judicial posts. For the latter, he would abjure political pressure and allow a Supreme Council of Justice to appoint judges based on their merits, not on their political affiliation. True to his Liberal Party tradition, Verhofstadt has promised to reduce costs to businesses by lowering the amount of money that they must contribute to employee pension systems. Although his Socialist coalition partners did not welcome this position, he promised them that he would take measures to revive Belgian industry. This would be accomplished by selling state assets to profitable private enterprises that might endure and create jobs and by continuing the previous government's policy of allowing mergers with Belgian companies by more profitable foreign companies. To the "Ecolos" he pledged that Belgium would end reliance on nuclear power between 2015 and 2021.

## FOREIGN POLICY

Verhofstadt sees little need for change in the country's foreign policy. Belgium's small size and catastrophic losses in the two World Wars have led it to pursue membership in a range of international organizations aimed at preserving peace and building prosperity. Belgium has proved a strong ally in NATO and an enthusiastic supporter of a long-term European Union effort to build not only an integrated economy but ultimately a joint foreign and defense policy with other member states. The headquarters of both NATO and the European Union Commission are in Brussels, a symbol of the country's dedication to international institutions.

Verhofstadt supported the Dehaene government's effort to join the European Monetary Union (EMU), which occurred on 1 January 1999. The 11 EMU members of the European Union have converged the values of their currencies in order to reduce cross-border financial costs and to create a fully common economic market. Verhofstadt has sharply criticized nationalism as a force leading to conflict. In doing so, he has clearly signaled that he opposes moves by any of his Flemish-speaking or French-speaking countrymen to divide Belgium into two states. As a way to build stability across the continent, Verhofstadt supports a continued but cautious expansion of both European Union and NATO membership to include newly democratic states in central Europe.

## ADDRESS

Office of the Prime Minister
16 rue de la Loi
1000 Brussels, Belgium

## REFERENCES

*Financial Times*, 2 September–11 June 1999.
*International Herald Tribune*, 13 July 1999.
*OECD Economic Outlook*, December 1998.
*Washington Post*, 4 February 1999.

**Profile researched and written by Paul E. Gallis, Congressional Research Service (12/99; updated 2/2000).**

# BELIZE

### Said Musa
### Prime Minister
*(pronounced "sa-EED MOO-sa")*

*"Our new economic initiatives are designed to inject substantial long-term capital into export industries and tourism while ensuring that the environment is protected and that the people participate in and benefit from development."*

Belize is situated on the Caribbean coast of Central America, south of Mexico and east of Guatemala. It has an area of 22,965 sq km (8,867 sq mi) and a 280 km (174 mi) coastline. The north of the country consists of limestone lowlands, the south is dominated by the Maya Mountains, and off the coast lies the world's second-largest barrier reef, with dozens of small islands. The largest town is Belize City, with some 55,000 people. Belize City (the former capital) was twice ravaged by hurricanes, in 1931 and 1961, so a new capital, Belmopan, was built inland in 1970.

The estimated population stands at 236,000, composed of 44% Mestizo (Spanish and Indian); 30% Creole (primarily African descent); 11% Ketchi, Mopan, and other Maya Indian; 7% Garifuna (African and Carib Indian); and 8% white, East Indian, and other. Migration is changing the ethnic composition of the population as most of the thousands of Belizeans who move to the United States are Creole while thousands of Spanish-speaking Central Americans have migrated into Belize. Although the official language is English, the majority of the population now speaks Spanish. Most ethnic groups also speak Creole, a language derived from a mixture of English and various African languages.

Most schools are government-supported denominational schools, chiefly Roman Catholic. Approximately 58% of the population is Roman Catholic; the rest mainly Protestant, including Anglican, Methodist, Baptist, Mennonite, Nazarene, Jehovah's Witness, and Pentecostal. There are also small groups of Mormons and Bahai.

The economy is chiefly agricultural (citrus, sugar, and bananas are the major exports), supplemented by fishing, small-scale industry (fertilizer, beverages, cigarettes and food processing), and most recently tourism and offshore banking, two of the most dynamic sectors. The United States is Belize's biggest trading partner. The unit of currency is the Belize dollar.

## POLITICAL BACKGROUND
Belize, a member of the British Commonwealth, has a Westminster-style parliamentary system. A British colony until 1981, known until 1973 as British Honduras, Belize became independent in 1981. Queen Elizabeth is the formal head of state, represented in Belize by an appointed governor general, who plays a ceremonial role. The legislature consists of a National Assembly comprised of an eight-member appointed Senate and a House of Representatives, members of which are elected in 29 constituencies at least every five years. The head of government is the prime minister, who in the parliamentary system commands a majority in the legislature. The prime minister and his cabinet are usually the leader and members of the majority party in the House of Representatives.

Party politics began in Belize in 1950 when the People's United Party (PUP) was formed, and it won the first election with universal adult suffrage in 1954. Belize achieved internal self-government in 1964, and complete independence on 21 September 1981. The PUP, led by George Price, dominated politics for 30 years, until the United Democratic Party (UDP), which was formed by a coalition of small opposition parties in 1973, won the 1984 election under the leadership of Manuel Esquivel. Although frequently riven by tensions among its constituent parties, the UDP has remained viable in opposition as well as in government, returning to power again in the elections of 1993.

In August 1998, the PUP was returned to power with 60% of the popular vote, winning 26 of the 29 seats in the House of Representatives. Voter turnout was estimated at over 90%, the highest in the country's history. Said Musa, the party leader, became the nation's third prime minister. The next National Assembly elections are scheduled to be held in August 2003.

## PERSONAL BACKGROUND
Said Wilbert Musa was born in San Ignacio on 19 March 1944, the son of Belizean Aurora Gibbs and Palestinian immigrant Hamid Musa. After attending primary and secondary school in Belize, he went to Manchester, England, where he received a law degree from Manchester University in 1967. He married the former Joan Pearson in 1967.

Musa returned to Belize in the late 1960s, serving as Circuit Magistrate (1967–68) and Crown Counsel (1968–70), then going into private practice, setting up the law firm of Musa and Baldermos in 1970. He also became involved with the United Black Association for Development (UBAD) and was co-founder of the People's Action Committee (PAC) and the Society for the Promotion of Education and Research (SPEAR), which with UBAD eschewed party politics in favor of popular organization. But after the PAC/UBAD alliance broke up, Musa joined the Peoples United Party, making an unsuccessful bid for parliament in 1974. By joining the PUP, he believed he could be more effective in what he considered the country's major challenge, increasing popular participation in government and political life.

## RISE TO POWER

Appointed senator in 1974, Musa joined Senators Harry Courteney and Assad Shoman in persuading the party to adopt a revised constitution, one designed to increase party democracy and rank and file participation. In 1979, Musa was elected from the Fort George Division and became a member of cabinet, serving as Minister of Education, Attorney General, and later Minister for Economic Development. With Shoman, then Minister of Health, he sought to expand the principles of party democratization to government itself and in 1982 challenged the party leadership, issuing a public declaration that the economic crisis then engulfing the region could only be solved by increasing democracy and opening participation "to strengthen and deepen democracy in Belize." The two Ministers also worked successfully to gather support for Belizean independence within Latin America and the international community.

Defeated in 1984, when the PUP won only 7 of the 28 seats, Musa was elected party chairman in 1986 and worked to expand party membership and attract new leaders. He was victorious in the next general election in 1989, serving in the PUP government as Foreign Minister, Minister of Economic Development, and Minister of Education. Musa held onto his seat in 1993 when the PUP narrowly won the popular vote but captured only 13 of 29 seats, the number having been increased to avoid the possibility of a tied House. In 1996, George Price, PUP founder and Belize's prime minister in all but two governments, stepped down as party leader. The previous year Musa had solidified his position in the party with the support of John Briceño, a young Mestizo politician with a solid following in the northern districts, the base of Musa's primary rival, Florencio Marin. Musa defeated Marin in the election for party leader, becoming only the second person to fill that post.

## LEADERSHIP

Musa's leadership has been consistently characterized by efforts to open the political process to the broad masses of Belizean people, believing that fundamental to their participation is the freedom from economic deprivation and want. Thus he has focused within the party to increase party democracy and attract new, especially younger, leaders and while in government has concentrated on the liberalization of education and media and the implementation of a sustainable economic development strategy based on a partnership between government and the private sector. During his first term, as Minister of Education, Musa initiated a series of social studies texts that made the colony's history accessible to school children for the first time, also discussing issues of nationalism, imperialism, and racism. During his second term, Musa implemented an open media policy in Belize, transferring the government-owned television and radio stations to a public/private corporation and granting licenses to competing broadcasters. He also moved decisively to resolve one of the most controversial policies of the previous government, severing the dependent link between Belize's

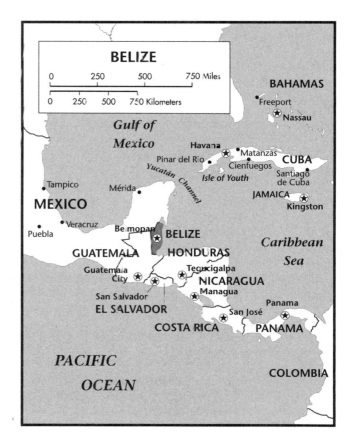

only post-secondary institution, the University College of Belize (UCB), with the US Ferris State University in Michigan, while nevertheless continuing to support UCB. In 1992, he authored the government's economic development plan, stating: "The urgent task at hand is to raise income and productivity for sustainable growth while also securing human development and social equality for all."

Upon taking office as Prime Minister in October 1998, Musa announced that the controversial timber licenses granted on Mayan lands in Toledo, a largely rural district in the south, would be subject to review. He also appointed the first Mayan cabinet member, naming Toledo Representative Marcial Mes as Minister of Rural Development, thus signaling the importance of integrating the nation's indigenous peoples more closely into its economic development. In perhaps another effort to expand the nation's political class by diversifying its leadership, he named one of two newly elected women representatives, Dolores Balderamos Garcia, to the cabinet as Minister of Human Development, Women, and Youth. He named Sylvia Sarita Flores, a Garifuna, to be speaker of the House, and Betty Zabaneh as president of the Senate.

Musa's commitment to party democracy placed him on the party's left-wing, and his early years in politics were ones of successive internal struggles with those content with the party's tight control of education and media as well as the political process. His commitment to third-world liberation struggles, including those in Cuba and Central America, as well as his participation in the People's Action Committee, with its avowedly anti-government stance, brought anti-communist attacks from inside his party as well as from the opposition, charges which were renewed again in the most recent election. Amiable and well-liked, however, Musa has an easy style which effectively denies the image of a left-wing ideologue. For four years, the UDP leadership repeatedly accused him of wrongdoing while in government, hiring special investigators and seeking to remove him from parliament. Ultimately, the accusations went nowhere and in fact were widely regarded as a form of political victimization. In 1999, Musa made an historic visit to Cuba, reinforcing the friendly relationship of the two countries by awarding Comondante En Jefe Fidel Castro with Belize's highest award for a non-Belizean: the Order of Belize.

## DOMESTIC POLICY

Perhaps the most innovative aspect of current domestic policy is the commitment to political reform, long a Musa priority. Beginning in 1994, SPEAR, revitalized in the mid 1980s as an independent NGO, carried out nationwide public hearings on constitutional reform, arguing that under the existing Constitution, there is "tremendous concentration of state power in the hands of the executive." SPEAR proposed a number of reforms, which were adopted by a coalition of 100 NGO organizations and presented to both parties in February 1998. The major proposals were adopted by the PUP and incorporated into its electoral manifesto, including the creation of a presidential office, distinct from the National Assembly, a measure designed to more clearly separate executive and legislative power, a more independent judiciary, and a strengthening of local government. A coalition evaluation of the government's first 100 days called political reform the area of "greatest achievements," especially commending the formation of a political reform commission headed by an NGO umbrella development group.

There is no doubt that Belize's small, insecure, and dependent economy remains the party's major challenge, however. The PUP campaigned against a stagnant economy, caused by excessive taxes, promising to abolish the widely unpopular 15% value-added tax (VAT) at the beginning of the next fiscal year (April 1999) and to revise the 1.5% tax on gross business receipts. Asked about lost revenues, Musa talked about growth-led development, targeting a 60% increase in GDP and increasing per capita GDP from the current $2,750 to $4,000. The new government also promises to create 15,000 new jobs and build 10,000 new homes—primarily through economic stimulation and private sector investment—and increase spending on education and social services.

Tourism, which became the most important sector of the economy in 1997, fell off slightly in 1998. The new government is expected to continue to promote its growth, including the development of "eco-tourism," encouraging small-scale, environmentally sensitive development. Offshore financial services is a fast-growing newcomer; by 1997 there were some 6,000 international business companies (IBCs) registered in Belize. Facilitated by a 1996 offshore banking act allowing nonresidents to conduct banking and related business in foreign currencies, securities, and assets, the first offshore bank was established in November 1998.

## FOREIGN POLICY

While Belize considers itself an ally of democracy and depends upon good relations with the United States, it has also consistently supported third world nationalist movements—including the Palestine Liberation Organization and the Polisario Front (fighting for the independence of Western Sahara), along with Cuba. Belize has good economic and political ties with both Mexico and the Caribbean Community (CARICOM), to which it belongs, and has joined both in the 25-member Association of Caribbean States (ACS), created in 1995. However, export competition from Mexico and Guatemala, along with concern about Mexico's continued appeal to Belizean consumers, may cause new strains. Belize has joined other CARICOM nations in opposing the US campaign against European Union import preferences for Caribbean products, especially bananas. In December 1998, the new government launched a vigorous "Buy Belizean" campaign, aimed at the growing number of consumers who travel north to Mexico to shop.

While the economy remains the major challenge, the government can also be expected to renew efforts to achieve a permanent settlement of the country's most volatile political issue, its relationship with neighboring Guatemala, which has long claimed Belize. The issue, and the political divisions surrounding its resolution, effectively delayed Belizean independence for at least a decade. Even after independence, a British garrison remained in Belize to support the tiny Defense Force against any Guatemalan threat. In the late 1980s, however, Guatemala, concerned about its growing international isolation, indicated its willingness to resume negotiations on settling the dispute. In 1991, Guatemalan president Jorge Serrano recognized Belize's right to self-determination, and the two countries agreed to establish diplomatic relations. The PUP pledged to enact legislation stating that Belize would not claim its territorial sea rights beyond three miles in the south and would undertake mutual development projects, including tourism and agro-industry, in a Joint Development Zone.

Initially endorsed by the UDP leadership, the terms of the agreement, embodied in the legislation, encountered widespread opposition, especially in the south, long neglected economically, and provoked a split in the opposition coalition. The UDP leadership then reversed itself, proposing legislation not take effect until a referendum was held. The government passed the Maritime Areas Act (MAA) in January 1992, amended to state that it would be subject to a national referendum. Then, in May 1993, Britain announced that its troops would be reduced and eventually withdrawn from Belize, and three weeks later, Serrano was overthrown and replaced. In the midst of this uncertainty, the PUP leadership, confident that its mandate would be renewed, called a general election for 30 June even though their term did not expire until September 1994. But the PUP underestimated the depth of Belizean concerns on this issue, which intensified with the fear that 5–10% of the GDP—and some 3,000 Belizean jobs—would be lost with the British withdrawal.

After the UDP victory in June, the MAA, while not repealed, was never put to a referendum, and the issue was again put on hold. In Guatemala, the new government acknowledged the interim agreement but declared that until a final treaty was concluded, its claim remained valid. In late 1993, however, Belize and Guatemala pledged to refrain from using force against each other and on 1 January 1994, Britain handed over security responsibilities to Belize and began its troop withdrawal. This was completed in 1996, and September talks resumed between Belize and Guatemala on normalizing relations. These continued in November 1998.

Long-standing fears about Guatemala, stemming from its more developed economy and large and growing population, as much as its more powerful military, keep the issue volatile in Belize and make broad-based economic development a central policy issue. Perhaps recognizing this, the PUP made economic empowerment of the south part of its election manifesto. More equitable and participatory development in both urban and rural areas will be essential in gaining the support of all Belizeans on any negotiated agreement.

**ADDRESS**
Office of the Prime Minister
Belmopan, Belize

**REFERENCES**
Barry, Tom. *Inside Belize* Albuquerque, NM: Inter-Hemispheric Resource Center. 1992.
*Central America Report.* Guatemala City: Inforpress Centroamericana, 11 June 1998; 4 September 1998.
*Europa World Yearbook.* London: Europa Publications Ltd., 1999.
*Journal of Commerce,* 14 January 1998.
*Miami Herald,* 20 November 1994; 20 June 1997; 21 December 1998.
Shoman, Assad. *Thirteen Chapters of A History of Belize.* Belize City: Angelus Press, 1994.

**Profile researched and written by Karen Judd, Ph.D., New York City (6/99; updated 3/2000).**

# BENIN

## Mathieu Kérékou
## President

*(pronounced "mah-tee-OO kay-ray-KOO")*

*"I formulate the wish that the entire country will live in peace, concord and tolerance, and the democratic gains will be consolidated in order to create the proper conditions for a stable, durable, peaceful and harmonious development."*

Known as the Republic of Dahomey before December 1975, Benin was a former French colony until independence was granted on 1 August 1960. This West African nation borders on Nigeria to the east, Burkina Faso and Niger to the north, and Togo to the west. With an estimated population of 6.3 million inhabitants and a land mass of 112,622 sq km (43,483 sq mi), Benin is a small country compared with its neighbors.

Despite its size, Benin is composed of more than 40 ethnic groups. The largest indigenous groups are the Adja, Bariba, Fon, and Yoruba. While the official language is French, the principal spoken languages are Fon and Yoruba in the south and Bariba and Fulani in the north. The dominant group is the Fon-Adja, accounting for approximately 60%, while the Bariba and Yoruba account for 10% and 9% of the population respectively. The Beninois are primarily animist (70%), with the remainder being equally divided into Christians in the south and Muslims in the north. The life expectancy at birth is 51 years for males and 56 years for females. The literacy rate is 37%.

The economy of Benin is mostly based on agriculture, which employs more than 50% of the population. The main agricultural products are cassava, yams, cotton, and maize. Benin has traditionally run massive trade deficits, but principal exports are cotton and energy products. The leading trading partners are France, United States, and the People's Republic of China. The per capita GDP has been estimated at US$1,300. Cotonou, the economic capital, and Porto Novo, the political capital, are its largest cities. The national currency is the CFA *franc*.

## POLITICAL BACKGROUND

Benin has withstood six coups, autocratic rule, and a Marxist-Leninist experiment, but in the 1990s Benin became a model for democratization in Africa. Major Mathieu Kérékou seized power on 26 October 1972 and dictated one-party rule, nationalization of private enterprises, and a Marxist ideology. His regime suffered from corruption on many levels. Amid mounting political pressure, Kérékou convened a National Conference in 1990 that ushered in multi-party democracy. For the first time in African history, an incumbent leader was defeated at the ballot box as Nicephore D. Soglo, an economist and technocrat, replaced Kérékou, on 24 March 1991. His regime was criticized for adhering to impossible demands by the International Monetary Fund (IMF) that resulted in a major electoral

defeat for Soglo's Benin Renaissance Party (PRB) in the 28 March 1995 national assembly elections. In 1996, the voters turned Soglo out and gave Mathieu Kérékou a second chance.

The present political structure is a product of the February 1990 National Conference. The new constitution, approved by referendum on 2 December 1990, instituted a multi-party presidential system. The president is elected by universal suffrage for a five-year term, renewable once. In presidential elections, a single candidate must win a majority of the votes. If there is no majority winner, then the two candidates with the most votes participate in a two-way runoff election. The National Assembly consists of 83 deputies serving four-year terms. To check executive authority, the Constitution guaranteed an independent judiciary and a Constitutional Court, an Economic and Social Council, and a media regulating authority.

Local government consists of six provinces subdivided into 86 districts and 510 communes while local administration, appointed by the national government, is assigned to elected provincial, district, town, and village councils.

## PERSONAL BACKGROUND

Known as "Django" to close family and friends, Mathieu Kérékou was born on 2 September 1933 at Koufra, Natitingou in the Atakora province of northern Benin. His father was a soldier from the Bariba ethnic group. He was prepared for a military career, in a country where military service was seen as a way to increase opportunities for a better life. He attended primary and secondary schooling for children of soldiers at Kati in Mali and St. Louis in Senegal and then went to Officers School at Frejus, France. Kérékou served with the French army until 1961 after which he joined the national army upon Dahomey's independence.

Kérékou began his political career as a military aid to President Hubert Maga (1961–63). Initially, he did not take an active role in the political administration of the government, preferring to manage military affairs. In 1980, he converted to Islam and took the name Ahmed. Unofficial sources allege that he subsequently converted to Christianity and became a born-again Christian. Kérékou maintains residences in Cotonou and northern Benin.

## RISE TO POWER

Mathieu Kérékou first attracted public attention as the commander of a paratroop unit at Ouidah that played an important role in the 1967 coup that overthrew General

Soglo. Although a key player and later chairman of the Revolutionary Military Council 1967–68, which was responsible for organizing the coup, Kérékou did not assume a cabinet position in the subsequent government of President Alley. However, he continued to play an important behind-the-scene role as the most powerful military figure. In 1968, during the civilian administration of Dr. Emile Zinson, he furthered his education in France and subsequently returned to take a more active role in government.

By 1970, the government floundered as three men bickered and jostled for power in a rotating presidency. To stop this ineptitude, Kérékou staged a coup on 27 October 1972 and threw Ahomadegbe out of power. His paratroopers from Ouidah took over the capital by symbolically toppling the gates of the presidential palace. Kérékou assumed the position of President, Prime Minster, and Minister of Defense, detained all previous government officials, and set up a commission to investigate their corruption. He formed a government composed entirely of army officers under the age of 40.

The first part of his presidency was characterized by adherence to Marxist-Leninist ideology. Banks, schools, oil distribution centers, and the insurance sector were nationalized. On 30 November 1975, Kérékou renamed the country "People's Republic of Benin," adding a socialist twist to the great 17th century Kingdom of Benin.

Beginning in the mid-1980s, Kérékou adopted a more pragmatic approach by encouraging the development of private enterprise. Yet the economy continually suffered from mounting debts, budgetary imbalances, and border disputes with neighbors. The IMF austerity program in 1986 provoked widespread strikes by students, teachers, and civil servants over the nonpayment of salaries. The army also increased its pressure for political change.

In February 1990, Kérékou convened a national conference, which ultimately led to multiparty elections, and his defeat on 25 March 1991 by Soglo. Having received only 32.4% of the vote, Kérékou asked "forgiveness from the victims of the deplorable and regrettable incidents" that took place during his 17-year reign. He stated his "deep, sincere and irreversible desire to change." Granted full amnesty by the Soglo government, he went into retirement conducting his social and business life late into the night at his Cotonou home.

Kérékou became politically active again after Soglo's Benin Renaissance Party (PRB) suffered a humiliating legislative defeat in the National Assembly elections on 28 March 1995. The subsequent presidential elections on 3 March 1996 pitted four major veteran politicians: Mathieu Kérékou, Nicéphore Soglo, Adrien Houngbedji, and Bruno Amoussou, who received 34.08%, 37.07%, 18.72% and 7.39% of the votes respectively. In the runoff elections on 18 March, Kérékou won the support of candidates Houngbedji and Amoussou, in addition to former 1991 presidential candidate Albert Tevoedjre. In a stunning turnaround, Kérékou defeated incumbent president Soglo 52.49% to 47.51%. Despite initial protests about foreign intervention and electoral irregularities, Soglo left the presidential palace and Kérékou made a triumphant return in an inaugural ceremony on 4 April 1996. In the ceremony, he evoked the name of God repeatedly and promised a government of national unity. One of Kérékou's

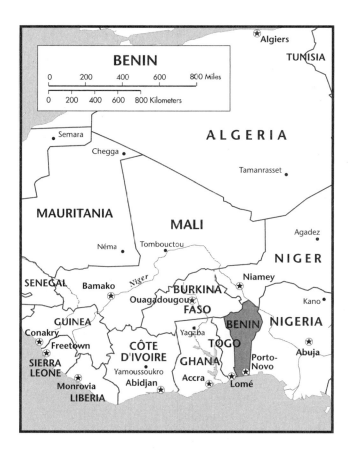

first acts was the creation of the Prime Minister's Office and appointment of Adrien Houngbedji, who supported Kérékou's runoff bid. Kérékou announced that the Prime Minster's responsibility would be the "coordination of government action and relations with institutions."

## LEADERSHIP

Kérékou is considered a charismatic and pragmatic leader. Most Beninois regard him as "The Chameleon" who repeatedly changed policies in order to ensure political survival. The nickname originated from his motto: "the branch will not break in the arms of the chameleon." Kérékou's leadership abilities were developed during his tenure as a military officer where he rose from the rank of Lieutenant to Brigadier General. In 1972, before staging his coup, Kérékou distinguished himself by successfully ending an army mutiny and winning strong support within the upper echelons of the army. He was then credited for rehabilitating a fragmented and demoralized military and became its undisputed leader.

During his first 17 years as president, Kérékou survived many attempted coups including one in January 1977 led by "colonel" Bob Denard and a group of armed Europeans and Africans. His administration was ruthless and dictatorial. One coup plotter, Michel Ailpe was allegedly shot trying to escape after Kérékou caught him having an affair with his wife.

Having renounced his Leninist tendency before the 1991 multiparty elections, Kérékou now defines "revolutionary" according to psychological and theological frameworks. While Kérékou's major support base is northern Benin, he must also maintain the consensus of many politicians representing different ethnic and regional interests. Until elections in 2001, he will be obliged to work with an opposition-dominated parliament and will have to balance IMF austerity with labor's demands for raises and benefits.

## DOMESTIC POLICY

Economic growth that benefits the entire population has been the major focus of the Kérékou administration. During the presidential campaign, he repeatedly spoke about the need to alleviate the hardships of the average citizen brought forth by IMF controls over the national economy. While the campaign rhetoric won widespread support from a public that saw little or no benefit from IMF-imposed fiscal and monetary austerity, Kérékou has created a dilemma. International agencies and donors expect him to continue austere economic policies that toppled his predecessor. Increased privatization and severe limits on government spending led to debilitating strikes and huge losses of customs revenue.

Kérékou may also be losing popularity for having tightened libel laws. In November last year, the Higher Audiovisual and Communication Authority (HAAC) authorized eight commercial and seven non-commercial radio stations along with one TV station and three satellite-TV stations. The decision reflected the will of the 1991 National Conference to break the state monopoly on airwaves. However, stations must subscribe to the state-owned Benin News Agency (ABP), which distributes national and international news at exorbitant rates. Furthermore, under a new defamation law, journalists face up to five years in prison or a fine up to US$17,000 for libel.

Finally, the government is beset by trafficking of children, and by drug traffickers who operate with impunity despite a tough anti-trafficking law enacted in 1997. Confusion over which government agency should enforce the law and how it should be enforced give traffickers and money launderers free reign in the country. Heroin, cocaine, and marijuana are moved in moderate amounts through Cotonou, which serves as a transshipment point between Nigeria and the United States via Europe.

## FOREIGN POLICY

The two foreign policy areas that the Kérékou administration must concern itself with are good relations with neighboring countries and the maintenance of foreign aid. Relations with Benin's neighbors deteriorated during the Soglo administration because their military leaders feared Beninois democracy. However, tensions with Niger and Nigeria have lessened since Kérékou's election and since Obasanjo's election in Nigeria. A border issue over refugees seeking political asylum from the military regime of Sani Abacha was resolved in April 1996. In June 1999, Benin began withdrawing its 140 troops from Guinea-Bissau. In December

1999, Benin strained relations with Togo over its bid to host the African, Caribbean, and Pacific trading partners accords, which Togo has hosted since 1975. Benin will be a beneficiary of the future West African gas pipeline.

Foreign and multilateral aid is vital for the economic survival of Benin. Kérékou has had to convince donors and international relief agencies that he is committed to market reforms. While IMF-initiated structural adjustment policies under Soglo have been credited with restoring budgetary health, they have led to increased unemployment and hardships for the vast majority of Beninois. Faced with tremendous domestic pressure for an expanded government role, Kérékou has had to balance austerity with growth. In December 1999, US$30.4 million became available for private sector development through the International Development association (IDA).

## ADDRESS

Office of the President, BP 1288
Cotonou, Republic of Benin

## REFERENCES

Africa News Online. [Online] Available http://www.africanews.org/west/stories/1999_feat1.html (Accessed May 2000).

*Africa Research Bulletin*, February–April 1996.

*Africa South of the Sahara, 1999*. London: Europa Publications Ltd., 1999.

Africaonline. [Online] Available http://www.africa-online.com (Accessed May 2000).

Banks, Arthur, Alan Day, and Thomas Müller, eds. *Political Handbook of the World, 1995–96*. Binghamton, NY: CSA Publications, 1995.

"Benin: General Chameleon." *Africa Confidential*, 26 April 1996.

Brockman, Norbert C. *An African Biographical Dictionary*. Santa Barbara, CA: ABC-CLIO, 1994.

Decalo, Samuel. *Historical Dictionary of Benin*. Third Edition. Lanham, MD, and London: Scarecrow Press, Inc., 1995.

Economist Intelligence Unit, Ltd. *EIU Country Reports*, 26 January 2000.

Integrated Regional Information Network (IRIN). [Online] Available http://www.reliefweb.int/IRIN (Accessed May 2000).

*Keesing's Record of World Events*. February–April 1996.

Rake, Alan. *Who's Who in Africa*. Metuchen, NJ: Scarecrow Press, Inc., 1992.

*USAID/Benin: Results Review and Resource Request* (R4), 31 March 2000.

*West Africa*, 1–7 April 1996, pp. 497–500.

**Profile researched and written by Robert W. Compton, Jr., Department of Political Science at Binghamton University (SUNY) (7/96; updated by Robert J. Groelsema 5/2000).**

# BHUTAN

## Jigme Singye Wangchuk
### King

*(pronounced "JIG-mee SEEN-gay wang-CHOOK")*

*"We will slowly and gradually develop into a constitutional monarchy."*

The Kingdom of Bhutan is a small landlocked nation encompassing 46,620 sq km (18,000 sq mi). The country is bordered to the east, south, and west by India and to the north and northwest by China. Located in the Himalaya Mountains, Bhutan is a rugged mountainous country with great extremes in climate. The southern slopes of the mountains receive heavy rainfall and are covered with thick forests. The low foothills in the south are extremely hot, and the Great Himalayas in the north are extremely cold.

The population has been estimated at 1.95 million, with an annual growth rate of about 2%. The two major cities—the capital, Thimphu, and Phuntsholing on the border with India—have estimated populations of 27,000 and 10,000 respectively. About 60% of the population is comprised of native Bhutanese, who live in the eastern portion of the country. About 15% of the population descends from Tibetan immigrants and can be found in the western part of Bhutan. Most of the remainder of the population, about 25%, are Nepalese and live mainly in the south. There is a small percentage of Lepchas, originally from Sikkim in India, and Paharias, who live in the southern foothills. There is also a small percentage of Santals, descendants of migrants from India's Bihar state. About 70% of the Bhutanese are Buddhists, and about 25% are Hindus. The remaining 5% are mostly Muslims.

The Bhutanese unit of currency is the *ngultrum*, but the currency of India, the *rupee*, also circulates freely in Bhutan. The per capita GDP in Bhutan has been estimated at US$1,000. In 1999, the country introduced its first income tax for residents earning more than US$100 per month, with rates ranging from 5% to 30% and the first deadline for filing tax returns set at February 2000. The major Bhutanese exports are cement, talc powder, fruit products, alcoholic beverages, dolomite, rosin, cardamom, coal, timber, yak hair, yak tails (for fly whisks), handicrafts, oranges, vegetables, and potatoes. On 2 June 1999, the twenty-fifth anniversary of King Jigme Singye Wangchuk's coronation, Bhutan's first television station began broadcasting.

## POLITICAL BACKGROUND

Bhutan's political history is intertwined with its religious history. A dual theocratic system evolved in which religious institutions were administered by the *je khempo,* or Head Abbot, while civil power was retained by a high officer known as the tiruk desi. During the 18th and 19th centuries the country encountered constant political strife that undermined the authority of the high officer and increased the power of regional governors. In 1885, the high officer sought aid from China to crush the power of the governors, but one of the regional governors, Ugyen Wangchuk, turned to the British for support. By 1907 Ugyen Wangchuk had consolidated his power enough to be named Bhutan's first hereditary king. In 1910 Bhutan and the UK signed a treaty allowing the UK to "guide" Bhutan's foreign affairs providing British India would not interfere in the internal affairs of Bhutan. Bhutan made the same arrangement with independent India in a treaty signed in 1949.

Since 1969 Bhutan has functioned as a limited monarchy although the country has no constitution. The king is appointed from the royal hereditary line by the legislature and may be removed by a two-thirds vote. The late King Jigme Dorji Wangchuk (1952–72), father of the current king, undertook reforms to help modernize the country's political institutions (serfdom was not officially abolished until his rule). A *Tshongdu* (National Assembly) was created in 1953 in which a majority of the members were elected by the people while others were either appointed by the king or by the regional monastic bodies. In 1965 the King established a Royal Advisory Council and three years later a Council of Ministers to bring more Bhutanese into the political system. The *je khempo* also maintains considerable authority in the country, and most levels of government contain members from Buddhist monasteries. The current monarch, Jigme Singye Wangchuk, has continued his father's political reforms. In 1998, he relinquished his position as Head of Government and transferred many of his executive powers to a cabinet elected by the National Assembly. He also introduced into law a provision under which the king would abdicate in favor of his hereditary successor if the Assembly supported a vote of no-confidence by a two-thirds majority.

Political parties are illegal. An opposition party, the Bhutan State Congress, which primarily represents the Nepalese minority, has its headquarters in India. The country is divided into 16 districts, each governed by a district officer appointed by the king. Popular elections, in which each family is granted one vote, are held at the village level every three years.

In 1968 an eight-member High Court was established to hear appeals from decisions made by local headmen and magistrates. The final appeal is made to the king.

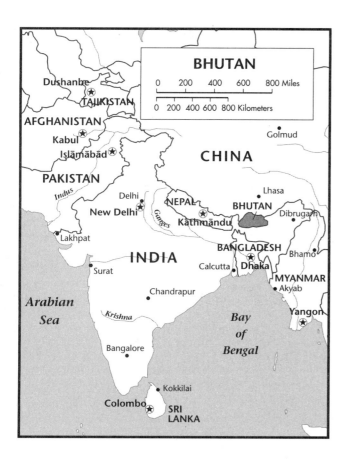

## PERSONAL BACKGROUND

Jigme Singye Wangchuk was born on 11 November 1955. He received his early education in Bhutan and then spent one year studying at North Point in India. In 1965 he went to England to continue his studies, but he returned in 1970 to Bhutan to attend the Ugyen Wangchuk Academy. As the son of the reigning King, Jigme Singye was granted many privileges and never personally experienced the poverty of many of his citizens. He rarely travels abroad. Like other Bhutanese he is an avid sportsman; it is reported that he plays basketball every day.

In 1988 Wangchuk officially married the four sisters to whom he had been privately married for the previous nine years. At the time of the official marriage, Wangchuk already had eight children, four boys and four girls. The King's reason for making his marriage public was to confirm the succession to the throne of his eight-year-old son, His Royal Highness Prince Jigme Gesar Namgyal Wangchuk.

## RISE TO POWER

Crown Prince Jigme Singye Wangchuk was installed as king on 24 July 1972 following the death of his father three days earlier. The *Tshongdu*, along with the Royal Advisory Council, had already agreed that the new king should be vested with full powers. This decision had been facilitated by the fact that Wangchuk had been made Crown Prince in March of that year. Additionally, in May he had been made *Tongsa Penlop*, a privileged position similar to that of the Prince of Wales.

The quick response by the political and religious elites of the country to Wangchuk's accession indicated the widespread consensus that had already been formed around the new king. At the time of taking the throne, the new king was the world's youngest ruling monarch.

## LEADERSHIP

Immediately upon taking the throne, the new king announced that he was determined to follow in his father's footsteps. He indicated that he planned to slowly and gradually develop the country into a constitutional monarchy. And he made it clear that there was a division of power between the head of the monastery and the king. In all religious matters, he contended, the *je khempo* is the deciding authority, and for the state administration, the king will have his final say.

However, the powerful Buddhist clergy retains great influence. The *New York Times* in 1988 reported that the clergy was able to prevent large-scale tourism because it feared that outside influences would hurt national character and the morality of the young. The word "revered" has often been used to describe the people's attitude toward the king. But Wangchuk still retains a lingering mistrust in delegating authority. The legislature does little more than rubber stamp bills initiated by the monarch. However, it has also been suggested that there has not been much demand for greater political participation by the populace. Bhutanese society has had a reputation for nonviolence and tolerance. In 1988 Wangchuk turned his attention to reforming the country's civil service. He reduced the number of bureaucrats, which also weakened somewhat the influence of the religious sects that had played a substantial role in government, and rationalized the salary system.

## DOMESTIC POLICY

Bhutan is one of the poorest countries in the world. But until recently the country had been totally self-sufficient in food. Most people live by subsistence farming or herding; together they account for about 95% of the country's economy. The natural resources of the country, including timber and swift-running waters for hydroelectric plants, remain little utilized.

Historically, economic development has not been allowed to undermine cultural traditions. However, the 1959 Chinese invasion of Tibet and the massing of Chinese troops on the Sino-Bhutan border led Wangchuk to undertake a modernization program out of fear that Bhutan would suffer the same fate as Tibet. In 1962 the government embarked on a series of five-year plans, relying heavily on Indian assistance, to build the country's infrastructure and develop its resources. Considerable improvements have been made in agriculture, irrigation, and road transportation. The country has come to rely on financial assistance from not only India, but also the UN and other international organizations. With widespread illiteracy (over 90%) and an unskilled labor force, dramatic improvements in living standards are unlikely to occur quickly, although the government has been attempting to improve this situation. During the 1990s, economic growth was slow, largely because of Bhutan's internal problems. Since 1997, however, the economy has been expanding at over 6% per year, and this has been reflected in increased government domestic spending. Fully 30% of the 1998–99 budget was allocated to social services, with a particular emphasis on schools and medical facilities.

The most pressing domestic issue, besides economic development, has been the status of the Nepalese minority and Tibetan refugees. Members of the Nepalese community have felt discriminated against in both political affairs and economic matters. They have formed a party-in-exile to pressure the Wangchuk regime for reforms, although their emphasis has been more on the liberalization of immigration and increased electoral representation in the government rather than a demand for a complete restructuring of Bhutanese political institutions.

Tibetan refugees resettled in Bhutan in the aftermath of the 1959 Tibet revolt against Chinese rule. However, many of the refugees refused Bhutanese citizenship in hopes of returning to their country. In 1979, in light of their uncertain status, the Bhutan government issued expulsion orders to those who refused to become citizens of Bhutan. Most of the refugees at that point agreed to accept citizenship, while those who refused went to India. Nonetheless, at the dawn of the 21st century their integration into Bhutanese life remains incomplete, and they suffer from the same lack of representation as the Nepalese.

## FOREIGN POLICY

As expected, given the 1949 treaty signed between India and Bhutan, India plays a major role in Bhutan's relations with the rest of the world. However, beginning in the late 1970s, Bhutan began moving away from its reliance on India for guidance in foreign affairs. The country has played a more independent role in the nonaligned movement and has joined a number of international organizations including the World Bank, the International Monetary Fund, and the Asian Development Bank. A major break with previous practices occurred in 1980 when the country established direct diplomatic relations with Bangladesh and allowed that country to open an embassy in the capital city, Thimphu. It has also entered into direct negotiations with China to resolve a border dispute between the two countries. India, however, continues to play a dominant role in foreign affairs, and most countries have their representative to Bhutan in New Delhi rather than Thimphu. In 1985, Bhutan was a founding member of the South Asian Association for Regional Cooperation (SAARC).

Contact with other countries remains limited. The country retains quotas on the number of tourists allowed to visit although in 1988 the government did buy its first passenger jet in order to promote tourism. Tourist arrivals in 1999 numbered about 7,000. The Tourist Authority of Bhutan is being renamed the Department of Tourism and plans significant increases in tourist fees for 2001 as the government tries to control the growth of the tourist industry. No formal diplomatic relations exist between the US and Bhutan although the US State Department has indicated that informal and friendly contact is maintained between the two countries.

Two recent events, more than anything, reflect Bhutan's changing outlook to the world beyond its borders. In late 1998, for the first time ever, foreign (non-Indian) financial institutions were allowed to purchase shares in the Bhutan National Bank. And in 1999, after two years of debate, officials allowed the nation to be connected to the global Internet. It remains to be seen how such changes will impact Bhutan and its people.

## ADDRESS
Royal Palace
Thimphu, Bhutan

## REFERENCES
*Asian Recorder*, 25 June –1 July 1914.
*Bhutan: A Kingdom in the Himalayas*, 1972.
*Current Biography*, 1956.
*Europa World Yearbook*, 1999.
*Far East and Australasia*, 1999.
*History Today*, December 1986.
"India Refuses to Intervene to Resolve Nepal's Bhutanese Refugee Problem." *The Associated Press*, 11 September 1999.
*Keesing's Contemporary Archives*, 11–23 June 1974.
*Keesing's Record of World Events*, various issues.
*New York Times*, various issues.
"Television's Final Frontier." *The New York Times Magazine*, August 22, 1999, p. 42.

**Profile researched and written by Lawrence Marcus (7/90; updated by Deryck Lodrick, University of California 5/2000).**

# BOLIVIA

## Hugo Banzer
## President
*(pronounced "OOH-gow BUH-n-sir")*

*"I have fought and will fight again for Bolivia. I have decided to lead a political movement with clear and well defined goals. I will lead a political force that will consolidate the democratization process initiated in my previous government."*

The Republic of Bolivia is a landlocked country in the center of South America. Bordering Brazil to the north and northeast, Paraguay to the southeast, Chile and Peru to the west, and Argentina to the south, Bolivia is the least developed country in South America. Bolivia's 1,098,580 sq km (424,264 sq mi) occupy a large segment of the Andes highlands and a part of the Amazon jungle. Its 7.4 million inhabitants are mostly of Quechua (30%) and Aymara (25%) descent. Creoles, or *mestizos* (30%), and people of European descent (15%) account for the rest. Although there are three official languages, Spanish is used primarily in large cities in the business world while Aymara and Qechua are spoken mostly in rural towns and among indigenous communities. More than 40% of the population speak Spanish as their second language. The literacy rate, at 80.1%, is one of the lowest in South America. The population is predominantly Roman Catholic. In recent years, however, evangelical Protestant movements have made some gains and now comprise 8% of the population. Infant mortality stands at 67.5 per 1,000 births, the highest in South America. Life expectancy, only 60 years, is the lowest in South America. With *Sucre* as its legal capital, Bolivia's economic and political center is La Paz, located at 3,658 m (12,000 ft) above sea level in the Andes highlands. La Paz with its 1,200,000 inhabitants, Santa Cruz (690,000), and Cocachamba (400,000) are the largest cities.

The unit of currency is the boliviano. The per capita GDP has been estimated at US$3,000. A set of privatization policies were introduced to foster economic growth in this poorest South American nation. Bolivia's main legal exports are natural gas, zinc, tin, gold, soya, silver, wood, and sugar. The country is also a major supplier of coca paste, which is refined into cocaine for the international drug trade. Imports include raw and capital goods for industry, transport equipment, and consumer products.

## POLITICAL BACKGROUND
Bolivia gained its independence from Spain in 1825. Domestic instability and conflicts with neighboring states have marred its history since that date. In regional conflicts, Bolivia has lost territory to Brazil, Chile, Paraguay, and Peru. No country in Latin America has experienced as many military coups: on average about one every other year since independence. A 1971 coup overthrew the government of General Juan Torres and brought Colonel Hugo Banzer to power.

According to the 1967 constitution (revised in 1994), Bolivia is a unitary republic. A bicameral congress composed of a 27-member Senate and a 130-member Chamber of Deputies holds legislative power. Voters elect members of both houses for four-year terms. Executive power is vested in the president who appoints the ministers of state. The president is elected directly for a four-year term; if no candidate wins a majority of votes, the Congress chooses the president. Although voting is mandatory for all adults 21 years or older (18 or older if they are married), compliance is low—particularly in rural areas.

Bolivia has an electoral system based on proportional representation, that fosters the existence of several mid-size political parties. The four largest parties are the National Revolutionary Movement (MNR), the Leftist Revolutionary Movement (MIR), the National Democratic Alliance (AND), and the Citizen's Solidarity Union (UCS).

## PERSONAL BACKGROUND
Hugo Banzer Suarez was born on 10 May 1926 in the town of Concepción, in Bolivia's sparsely-populated Eastern province of Santa Cruz. He came from a family of pure Spanish blood in this ranching region noted for its fierce independence. He was educated at La Paz and entered the Bolivian Army Military College, graduating as a cavalry lieutenant. After routine postings he was selected to receive training at the US Army School of the Americas in Panama, beginning a lengthy association with the US. In 1960 he received training at the Fort Hood, Texas, Armored Cavalry School. He is married to Yolanda Prada and has five children.

## RISE TO POWER
After several years commanding the key Fourth Cavalry Regiment, he was sent to Washington as military attache, a post of great prestige. There, he expanded his already wide circle of American friends (chiefly military) and perfected his English. In this period he also served under President Rene Barrientos Ortuno as minister of education. In 1969 Banzer returned home to the prized position of director of the military academy. He developed close ties with leaders of the two largest political parties in Bolivia at the time, the National Revolutionary Movement (MNR) and the Bolivian Socialist Front (FSB).

A series of short-lived democratic and military governments followed the Barrientos regime, until General Juan Jose Torres seized power in 1970. His ten months in office have been described as the ten months of emergency. Torres nationalized some tin and zinc mines in order to gain support from the middle class and the left. At the same time he launched a campaign to exile some of his political opponents. Among those exiled was the former military academy commander, General Banzer. Torres's chaotic leadership encouraged internal military disobedience. His shifting economic and social policies further alienated whatever popular support he enjoyed. Given this political climate, it was not difficult for General Banzer to lead a successful military coup that overthrew the Torres government on 22 August 1971.

## LEADERSHIP

Banzer ruled the country with an iron fist, exiling opponents and repeatedly violating human rights. During his tenure more than 15,000 people were arrested, 19,000 had to seek asylum in foreign countries, and 200 were killed for political reasons. A 1974 massacre of more than 100 peasants marked the most notable case of human rights violations during the Banzer regime. His supporters correctly claimed, however, that Banzer's human rights record was much better than that of the military governments of Brazil, Argentina, Uruguay, and Chile.

A populist leader, Banzer focused on controlling inflation, fostering economic growth, and bringing order to a country that had experienced decades of unstable military dictatorships and short-lived civilian governments. Though Banzer encouraged foreign investment, his restrictive policies regarding union activity and constitutional liberties led to opposition from labor leaders, clergymen, peasants, and students. In a well publicized summit with Chilean leader Augusto Pinochet, Banzer was unable to secure an agreement which would have given Bolivia access to the Pacific Ocean. The failure of this diplomatic effort also took its toll on his popularity.

An economic crisis, the failed accord with Chile, external pressure from the United States, and internal pressure from opposition groups forced Banzer to schedule presidential elections for July 1978. His hand-picked successor, General Juan Pereda, was the winner. However, the election results were nullified by an electoral commission because of widespread allegations of fraud. Pereda himself led a successful coup against the Banzer government, only to be overthrown a few months later in yet another military coup.

In 1980 Banzer founded the National Democratic Alliance (AND) party, one of the largest opposition groups. He has since run as a presidential candidate in every election. In 1985 he obtained the first plurality of votes, but Congress chose Víctor Paz Estenssoro. In 1989, after placing a close third, Banzer's party threw its support to Jaime Paz Zamora, the leftist candidate. Paz Zamora's MIR party members had been persecuted during the Banzer dictatorship of the 1970s. The surprising alliance between the MIR and the AND prevented Sanchez de Lozada, the front runner, from being elected in 1989. It all but guaranteed that Banzer would have MIR support in future elections.

The 1997 elections once again failed to produce a clear winner, and negotiations between the five largest parties were needed to select the next president. Banzer secured support from the MIR and UCS. After having tried five times, he

finally succeeded in becoming the democratically elected president of Bolivia at the age of 71.

Today Banzer is the charismatic and undisputed leader of the National Democratic Alliance. His military past and experience as a former president give him a political stature far beyond that of any of his political rivals. His populist rhetoric and criticism of the harsh economic policies of his predecessor, make Banzer popular among the working class and rural population. It is clear, however, that he will have difficulty keeping his unlikely electoral coalition together during his five-year term. Having been elected with the support of the left-leaning MIR and the entrepreneur-led UCS, Banzer will find it difficult to push his legislative agenda through Congress. It is unclear, as well, whether the AND will survive as a political party and what sort of relationship will develop between the elected AND legislators and the former dictator.

## DOMESTIC POLICY

Banzer has promised to implement effective social welfare policies. He has pledged to aid the elderly and government workers displaced by the privatization efforts of the previous government. He has repeatedly stated that the economic modernization plan of the Sanchez de Lozada government must not be undertaken at the expense of working Bolivians. However he has failed to clearly state his own economic policies. Analysts believe that Banzer will continue the Sanchez economic policies despite his campaign rhetoric.

Based upon his previous tenure as president, we should expect a combination of populist policies and tight economic controls. Banzer knows that, in order to foster growth, he must move forward with Sanchez de Lozada's privatization plan for state enterprises. His campaign statements have many investors worried. In order to calm them it is likely that Banzer will send strong signals to the international financial community that he intends to move ahead with the privatization process. Banzer needs to deliver high growth rates. For that to happen he must attract foreign investors—particularly from the US, Bolivia's largest trading partner. Therefore, no significant change in economic policy is anticipated in the near future.

Banzer is expected to adopt some social programs aimed at helping the dispossessed and rural poor. His campaign pledged to introduce reform without hurting those in need. This will most likely result in food subsidies and greater investment in education, health, and the elderly. However, Banzer must maintain a balanced budget. In order to fund meaningful social programs, his government needs to find ways to improve the tax collection system. Social unrest is expected to be reduced because Banzer enjoys strong support among both the military and labor unions.

## FOREIGN POLICY

Regional economic integration and securing access to the Pacific Ocean are top foreign policy priorities for the Banzer government. He will most likely seek to further develop trade with the Mercosur countries (Brazil, Argentina, Uruguay, and Paraguay) and its neighbors, Peru and Chile. In order to achieve such a goal, investment in road construction and transportation will be needed. The question of access to the Pacific Ocean will likely resurface as Bolivia opens its market to Chilean investors.

Banzer's election received a decidedly lukewarm response from Washington. In an effort to improve that relationship he has promised to take a hard stance on drug trafficking. However, an increased American military presence in Bolivia is unlikely to occur. Many rural poor depend on coca leaf production to survive, and alternative crops have not been successfully introduced. Moreover, the economic impact of drug money is so significant that curtailing drug production could trigger a recession. His success in distancing himself from drug lords and fighting corruption will most likely determine the level of economic support that Banzer will receive from the US.

## ADDRESS

Office of the President
Palacio de Gobierno
Plaza Murillo
La Paz, Bolivia

## REFERENCES

"Bolivia—To the Barricades." *The Economist,* 15 April 2000, p. 32.

*CIA World Fact Book.* [Online] Available http://www.odci.gov/cia/publications/nsolo/factbook/b1.htm (Accessed June 2000).

CNN. [Online] Available http://cnn.com (Accessed 30 May–5 June 1997).

*The Economist,* 9 August 1997.

*El País.* [Online] Available http:www.elpais.es (Accessed 7–9 June 1996.

Klein, H.S. *Bolivia: The Evolution of a Multi-Ethnic Society.* Oxford: Oxford University Press, 1992.

*La Jornada.* [Online] Available http://www.serpiente.dgsca.mx/jornada/ (Accessed 2 June 1997).

"The Net Spreads Wider Still." *The Economist,* 27 February 1999, p. 34.

Olsen and Associates Currency Exchange. [Online] Available http://www.olsen.ch/ (Accessed 20 July 1997).

**Profile researched and written by Patricio Navia, New York University (8/97; revised 4/2000).**

# BOSNIA-HERZEGOVINA

### Ante Jelovic (Croatian); Zivko Radisic (Serbian);
### Alija Izetbegovic (Bosniak, Muslim)
### (Three-member presidency with rotating chairmanship)

*"The time and tasks ahead of us demand new initiatives, new ideas and approaches which will not primarily depend on the national positions of every single Bosnia-Herzegovina presidency member and his affiliation to the Serb, Bosniak, and the Croat people in Bosnia-Herzegovina."*

Bosnia-Herzegovina, one of five successor states to the Socialist Federal Republic of Yugoslavia (SFRY), is located in southeastern Europe, between Croatia to the north and west and Serbia-Montenegro (also known as the Federal Republic of Yugoslavia) to the east. Its land area is 51,128 sc km (19,741 sq mi). Bosnia refers to the entire republic, except for the mountainous southwestern region of Herzegovina.

The population of Bosnia has been estimated at 3.5 million, of whom 44% are Muslims (also called Bosniaks), 31% ethnic Serbs, 17% ethnic Croats, and 7% others, including those of mixed background. The breakdown of Muslim, Serbian Orthodox, and Roman Catholic religious communities closely corresponds to the ethnic breakdown. Before the 1992–95 war, many parts of Bosnia-Herzegovina resembled an ethnic patchwork. Ethnic cleansing and displacement of hundreds of thousands of people during the war have brought about a much greater separation of the three communities. The official languages are Bosnian, Serbian, and Croatian.

The official currency of Bosnia is the convertible *marka* (KM), pegged to the German *deutschemark* (DM). The Yugoslav *dinar* circulates widely in the Republika Srpska, while the Croatian *kuna* circulates in Croat-dominated areas.

## POLITICAL BACKGROUND
In 1908, the Austro-Hungarian empire formally annexed Bosnia. The move provoked neighboring Serbia, which coveted Bosnia because of its large Serbian population. When a young Bosnian Serb assassinated Austrian Crown Prince Ferdinand in Sarajevo in the name of Serbian national unity, World War I began. In 1918, Bosnia was incorporated into the newly formed Kingdom of Serbs, Croats, and Slovenes (later renamed Yugoslavia). During World War II, the Nazi puppet state in Croatia annexed all of Bosnia. This period saw mass murder of Serbs by the ruling Croatian fascists, as well as massacres of Muslims and Croats by Serb nationalists. The communist Partisans, led by Josip Broz, popularly known as "Tito," led the resistance. After the war, Bosnia-Herzegovina became one of six republics in the reconstituted Yugoslavia. Tito ruled from 1945 until his death in 1980.

In the 1980s, Bosnia, like the other republics, experienced rising anticommunist and nationalist sentiment. In 1990, a number of independent political parties were formed, including nationalist Muslim, Serb, and Croat parties. Multiparty elections were held in November 1990, based on a system of proportional representation by nationality. The nationalist parties ran on a platform of defense of their cultures, but none of them called for dismembering Bosnia. The election resulted in a parliament divided along ethnic lines. The presidency of the republic included two members from each of the three ethnic groups, plus one ethnically mixed member. Alija Izetbegovic, head of the Muslim Party of Democratic Action (SDA), was chosen to lead the presidency.

The three nationalist parties formed a coalition government. The Bosnian government at first did not seek independence but rather promoted remaining in a new Yugoslav federation. In March 1991, however, the presidents of Serbia and Croatia secretly agreed to partition Bosnia between them. By fall 1991, working closely with Belgrade, the Bosnian Serb Party (SDS) had established numerous "Serbian autonomous regions" throughout Bosnia and began forming its own militias. The SDS declared a "Serbian Republic of Bosnia and Herzegovina," uniting these regions. In January 1992, an independent Serb republic in Bosnia was created, claiming over 60% of the Republic's territory. Meanwhile, the European Union backed the idea of holding a referendum on independence as a preliminary move to international recognition. The Bosnian Muslim and Croat communities voted overwhelmingly in favor of independence, but the Bosnian Serb leadership called for a boycott of the vote.

In April 1992, Bosnia-Herzegovina gained recognition from the European Union and the US as an independent state. About the same time, Serbian irregular forces, backed by the Yugoslav Army, launched attacks throughout the republic. They quickly seized more than two-thirds of the Bosnian territory, carrying out policies of "ethnic cleansing" to drive non-Serb populations out of their territory. More than two million people were driven from their homes, creating the greatest flow of refugees in Europe since World War II. An estimated 200,000 persons were killed. Fighting between ethnic Croats and Muslims in 1993–94 also resulted in "ethnic cleansing" by both sides. In response to US and European pressure, Bosnian Croat and Muslim leaders agreed to a cease-fire between their communities and to the formation of a Muslim-Croat federation in Bosnia-Herzegovina. In this way, the Croat and Muslim communities were officially allied against their common Serb enemy.

Numerous international attempts to negotiate a peace settlement failed. UN peacekeepers on the ground, with a mandate to provide humanitarian aid to the victims of the war, were unable to keep the peace. In August 1995, a NATO bombing campaign, coupled with a series of successful

Muslim-Croat counteroffensives against the Bosnian Serb forces, brought the parties to the negotiating table. Serbian president Slobodan Milosevic accepted responsibility for the Bosnian Serb leadership. After three weeks of negotiations at Wright-Patterson Air Force Base in Dayton, Ohio, the presidents of Bosnia, Croatia, and Serbia agreed to a wide-reaching peace accord in November 1995.

Under the terms of the Dayton peace agreement, Bosnia-Herzegovina maintains its current external borders. Internally, it comprises two equal entities, the Muslim-Croat Federation and the Republika Srpska. Each entity has its own parliament and government with wide-ranging powers, as well as its own armed forces. Each entity may establish "special parallel relationships with neighboring states," meaning Croatia and Serbia. At the all-republic level, there is a joint presidency, council of ministers, and a bicameral legislature.

Under the accords, the Bosnian Federation received roughly 51% of the territory of Bosnia-Herzegovina while the Republika Srpska received 49%. The parties to the accords could not agree on who would control the Brcko region, a strategic northeastern corridor between the Serb-held regions. The status of Brcko was submitted to binding arbitration. In March 1999, a tribunal determined that Brcko would have its own multi-ethnic autonomous government. The military part of the Dayton accords committed the two sides to maintain the cease-fire and separate their forces. A NATO-led force was deployed to ensure implementation of the military section of the agreement. The accords required the parties to cooperate fully with the international war crimes tribunal for

the former Yugoslavia. The agreement included guarantees on the right of refugees to return to their homes and on the protection of human rights. A civilian Office of the High Representative was created to oversee implementation of the civil aspects of the agreement.

Implementation of the military aspects of the agreement proceeded smoothly, although NATO had to extend its initial one-year deployment numerous times. In June 1998, NATO pledged to keep its peacekeeping force in Bosnia until a self-sustaining peace is achieved. Civilian implementation has been mixed. General elections were held in September 1996 and September 1998. Municipal elections were held in September 1997. The three nationalist parties have continued to dominate the political scene although the moderates have increased their share of the vote with each election. In the 1998 elections, Izetbegovic was reelected to the Muslim seat of the joint presidency, hard-liner Ante Jelavic won the Croat seat, and Zivko Radisic was elected to the Serb seat.

Central Bosnian government institutions have remained largely deadlocked by interethnic disputes. In December 1997, the High Representative acquired greater powers to impose decisions and has since imposed numerous measures and forced the dismissal of obstructionist officials. Many indicted war criminals, mainly Bosnian Serbs, remain at large. NATO forces have seized a few, and others have turned themselves in voluntarily. Aid from international donors has facilitated the reconstruction effort in Bosnia and spurred economic growth. The effort has not, however, led to a self-sustaining recovery. A key shortfall in peace implementation has been the inability of the vast majority of refugees to return to their former homes, especially in areas controlled by a different ethnic group.

## PERSONAL BACKGROUND AND RISE TO POWER

### Ante Jelavic

Born on 21 August 1963 in Croatia, Ante Jelavic studied engineering at the Technical Military Academy in Zagreb, specializing in missile systems and rocket fuels. He joined the Croatian Democratic Union (HDZ) party in 1990 while serving in the Yugoslav People's Army (JNA). From August 1991 to April 1992, he volunteered with the Croatian army, which was engaged in fighting against the JNA. Later, he became active in Bosnian Croat affairs, first with the Bosnian Croat militia and then with the Bosnian Federation defense ministry.

At the Bosnian HDZ's fifth party convention in May 1998, Jelavic was elected party chairman by an overwhelming majority of party delegates. His ascendancy to the head of the powerful HDZ party was unexpected, given President Tudjman's endorsement of another candidate. (The Bosnian branch of the HDZ is affiliated with the HDZ ruling party in neighboring Croatia.) In the September 1998 national elections, Jelavic soundly beat two challengers to become the Bosnian Croat representative to the tripartite Bosnian presidency.

Widely regarded as a Croat nationalist, Jelavic has not been considered to be a strong proponent for the integration of Bosnia's communities although he has professed support for the Dayton peace agreement. Jelavic claims Bosnian citizenship through his parents, who were both born in Bosnia. Jelavic and his wife, Iva, have three children.

## Alija Izetbegovic

Izetbegovic was born on 8 August 1925 in Bosanski Samac in northern Bosnia. He received a law degree from the University of Sarajevo. He was actively involved in politics by 1946 when he was arrested for "pan-Islamic activity" by the former Yugoslavia's Communist government and imprisoned for three years. After his release, he worked in the legal profession. He was arrested again in 1983 for his activities on behalf of Bosnia's Muslim population, receiving a prison sentence of 14 years, of which he served five before being released.

With the collapse of Communism in Eastern Europe, Izetbegovic founded the Party of Democratic Action (SDA), a secular, nationalist Bosnian Muslim organization, in 1990 and led the party to victory in multi-party elections in May of that year, becoming the head of a seven-member collective presidency representing all three of Bosnia's major ethnic groups and presiding over the country's declaration of independence in 1992. He remained the leader of Bosnia's Muslims during the civil war that immediately followed independence and was a co-signer of the 1995 Dayton Peace Accords. In 1996, Izetbegovic was elected to the Muslim seat on Bosnia's new tripartite presidency and was reelected to this post for a four-year term in 1998.

## Zivko Radisic

Zivko Radisic, the Serb member of Bosnia's joint presidency, was born on 15 August 1937 and received his education in political science. In 1977, he was elected to a five-year term as mayor of Banja Luka. Radisic entered national politics in 1982 when he became defense minister in the Communist regime of the former Yugoslavia. Between 1986 and 1990, he left this post to become director of the Cajavec electronic equipment company but reentered politics in 1991, becoming secretary of the Yugoslav Chamber of Commerce. Radisic took part in the Bosnian civil war, serving in the Serbian military. He has also been president of Serbia's Socialist Party.

In September 1998, he was elected to his first term as the Serb member of the tripartite federal presidency. Radisic is married and has two children.

## LEADERSHIP

The joint presidency of Bosnia and Herzegovina consists of three members, one representing each of the country's three main ethnic constituencies (Bosniak, Serb, and Croat). Members are directly elected by voters in one of the country's two political entities (the Republika Srpska for the Serb member; the Bosnian Federation for the Muslim and Croat members). Chairmanship of the joint presidency rotates among the three members, with each occupying the post for eight months, during which time he is the country's official head of state. The Serb member, Zivko Radisic, acceded to the chairmanship on 13 October 1998, followed by Croat Ante Jelavic on 15 June 1999 and Bosniak/Muslim Alija Izetbegovic in February 2000.

The major presidential responsibilities are in the area of foreign policy and include relations with foreign countries and international organizations, appointment of ambassadors and other international representatives, negotiating treaties, and cooperation with nongovernmental organizations. The members of the presidency are also responsible for presenting an annual budget to parliament and executing parliamentary decisions.

In its first years, the tripartite presidency has been viewed as a marginal institution and the least effective of all of the joint Bosnian institutions. Further progress is seen as contingent on the ability of the three members to work together productively.

## DOMESTIC POLICY

Progress on refugee returns remains a key priority. Of the more than two million Bosnian refugees and displaced persons at the end of the war, less than 600,000 had returned to their homes by mid-1999. Most of those who returned have settled in areas where they represent the ethnic majority. Minority returns have been minimal, especially to the Republika Srpska. During the course of the NATO air operation against Yugoslavia in March–June 1999, Bosnia accepted 70,000 Kosovar refugees. Most have since returned, but many thousands may remain in Bosnia. Another issue of concern has been the status of the strategically located town of Brcko, claimed by the Serbs since 1992 but declared an autonomous neutral district by UN High Representative Carlos Westendorp in March 1999, a decision protested by Serbian officials including then-joint-presidency chairman Zivko Radisic, who briefly resigned his position but later retracted his resignation.

Continuing economic reforms, countering organized crime, and promoting economic growth represent other domestic priorities. Bosnia's economy experienced significant growth in the first postwar years, largely fueled by the inflow of massive international reconstruction aid. Another ongoing issue facing the Bosnian leadership is the status of indicted war criminals at large in Bosnia. Former Bosnian leaders Radovan Karadzic and Ratko Mladic, both under indictment for war crimes, remain under international arrest warrant.

## FOREIGN POLICY

The international community has remained intensely involved in Bosnia's affairs. NATO's mandate continues, and the UN High Representative continues to exercise expanded executive powers. An international donors' conference for Bosnia was held in May 1999. Two months later, Bosnia hosted a summit meeting of leaders from more than 30 countries and international organizations. The meeting launched the Balkan Stability Pact, an initiative to strengthen peace and stability, deepen democracy and civil society, and promote economic reforms throughout southeastern Europe, including Bosnia.

In November 1999, to mark the fourth anniversary of the Dayton peace accords, the three members of Bosnia's joint presidency addressed the UN Security Council, pledging to strengthen national institutions bridging the divided country's two political entities. They also made several specific joint proposals, including the institution of a common national passport for all Bosnians, a 15-member secretariat for the presidency, and the formation of a multi-ethnic border patrol and a peacekeeping unit to aid UN troops already in place.

## ADDRESS
Presidency
Marsala Tita
71000 Sarajevo
Bosnia-Herzegovina

## REFERENCES
Banks, Arthur and Thomas Muller, eds. *Political Handbook of the World*. Binghamton, NY: CSA Publications, 1999.

The Economist Intelligence Unit. *Country Profile, Bosnia-Herzegovina, 1998–99.*
*Europa World Yearbook 1998*. London: Europa Publications Ltd., 1998.
Foreign Broadcast Information Service, various issues.
US Department of State. *Country Reports on Human Rights Practices for 1998, Bosnia-Herzegovina*. February 1999.

Profile researched and written by Julie Kim, Congressional Research Service (12/99; updated 6/2000).

# BOTSWANA

### Festus Mogae
### President
*(pronounced "FES-tus Mo-HIGH")*

*"There is national consensus that most of the policies are in place. Most of the criticism from both the opposition and our backbenchers is that they are not being vigorously implemented."*

The Republic of Botswana is a landlocked country in southern Africa, bordered by Namibia to the west and north, Zimbabwe to the northeast, and South Africa to the south and southeast. The national territory encompasses 581,730 sq km (224,607 sq mi) and the southern and western regions are geographically defined by the Kalahari Desert. The capital is Gaborone, which is located in the southeast near the border with South Africa. Approximately 80% of the 1.5 million inhabitants live in the eastern strip, which is the most developed region of Botswana.

The Tswana ethnic group makes up 55–60% of the population; Kalanga account for 25–30%; Kgalagadi, Herero, Basarwa ("Bushmen"), Khoi ("Hottentots"), and whites make up the remaining 5–10%. The official language is English, with Setswana and Ikalanga also widely spoken. Christianity is practiced by some 60% of the people while 40% profess indigenous beliefs.

Botswana's economy is among the best performers in Africa, with annual growth rates averaging more than 10% during the period 1976–1991. While growth has not been as rapid recently, Botswana has weathered the African economic decline better than most countries, and the government has maintained budget surpluses and significant foreign reserves as recently as 1996. Per capita income is approximately $3,600. That figure masks the fact that subsistence farming and cattle raising predominate in the country, with 80% of the population engaged in agriculture. The currency is the *pula*. Unemployment is high, running near 20%; inflation is less than 8%. Significant natural resources include diamonds, copper, nickel, salt, soda ash, coal, iron ore, and silver.

## POLITICAL BACKGROUND

The Batswana, a term which refers both to all citizens of Botswana as well as to the country's major ethnic group, arrived from neighboring South Africa during the Zulu wars in the early 1800s. Hostilities between the Batswana and Boer settlers from the Transvaal in the late 19th century led the Batswana to appeal to the British for help. In 1885, the British government put Bechuanaland, (as Botswana was formerly known), under its protection. The northern territory remained under direct British administration and became what is now Botswana.

In 1920, two advisory councils were established, representing Europeans and Africans. 1934 brought proclamations regularizing tribal rule and powers. A European-African advisory council was formed in 1951. Ten years later the constitution established a consultative legislative council. In 1964, the British accepted proposals for democratic self-rule. The seat of government was moved to the new city of Gaborone in 1965. These developments, along with the formation of political parties in 1960, were the precursors to general elections held in March 1965 and independence in September 1966.

Botswana boasts one of the few flourishing constitutional multi-party democracies in Africa. Since independence, elections have been freely contested and held on schedule. The constitution provides for a president elected every five years in a national election who, as of the 1999 election, is limited to two terms. The cabinet is drawn from the National Assembly and includes a vice president and a flexible number of ministers. The National Assembly is elected to a five-year term and consists of 40 elected and 4 appointed members; it is expanded every 10 years after the national census. Suffrage is universal, and the voting age was set at 21 upon independence but was lowered to 18 by constitutional reforms enacted in 1995. The House of Chiefs is an advisory body representing the eight major subgroups of the Batswana; any legislation with ethnic implications must be referred to the House of Chiefs.

The first president of the Republic of Botswana was Seretse Khama, the former heir to the chieftainship of the Bamangwato ethnic group and a founder, in 1962, of the Bechuanaland (later Botswana) Democratic Party (BDP). The BDP won 28 of 31 seats in the legislative assembly during the 1965 election, and Khama became prime minister and later president. He was reelected to the presidency three times, although the BDP faced challenges from several opposition parties which gained support during that period. Nonetheless, the BDP retained the greatest majority in all succeeding governments.

Khama died in 1980 and was succeeded by his vice president, Quett Ketumile Masire, another BDP founder. He was elected in his own right in 1984 and was reelected twice. During his 18-year tenure, Masire was able to maintain power for the BDP despite significant internal tension and rising support for opposition groups. The 1990s were marked by concern regarding a successor to Masire within his party, by corruption scandals that forced the resignations of the vice president and three ministers, by increasing demands for electoral reform, and by sporadic rioting which reflected rising social discontent. In January 1998, Masire announced that he would resign the presidency in favor of Festus Mogae,

his vice president. This resignation was intended to allow Mogae to build support prior to the 1999 election.

## PERSONAL BACKGROUND

Festus Gontebanye Mogae was born 21 August 1939 in Serowe, a town of about 35,000 in the eastern part of Botswana. He earned a Bachelor of Arts degree in economics from Oxford University in 1968 and a Master of Arts degree in development economics from Sussex University two years later. Mogae is married with three children. He has received numerous honors and awards, having been given the presidential Order of Honour of Botswana in 1989 and made an *Officier de l'Order Nationale* in both Cote d'Ivoire and Mali.

## RISE TO POWER

Upon completing his education, Mogae returned to Botswana and embarked on a career in the government bureaucracy, serving in the Ministry of Finance and Development as a planning officer, as director of economic affairs, and as permanent secretary. He has also held a variety of posts in international organizations, including the International Monetary Fund, the African Development Bank, the International Bank for Reconstruction and Development, and the Commonwealth Fund for Technical Cooperation. In addition, he has served on the board of directors of several major corporations.

In January 1982, Mogae was named permanent secretary to the president and secretary to the cabinet in Masire's government. Ten years later, he was named minister of finance and development planning and in September 1992, (amid a corruption scandal that forced the resignation of the

vice president), Mogae was named vice president. He remained in that post, his reputation intact and untarnished by the scandals that periodically erupted within the administration, until 1998. On 31 March 1998, Masire stepped aside, and Mogae became the third president of the Republic of Botswana.

## LEADERSHIP

Mogae was seen by many to be a compromise successor to Masire, whose tenure was, in later years, marked by dissension within the BDP ranks. Masire's decision to step down and allow Mogae to take over the presidency can be viewed as an indication of his confidence that Mogae would be able to mend the rift in the party prior to 1999 elections. This was a significant challenge facing Mogae in the period prior to those elections, since the party had split in two, with a division between the moderate and conservative factions of the leadership. Shortly after his inauguration, Mogae reshuffled his cabinet and reassigned leaders of the factions to portfolios designed to keep them more involved in government issues, with less time to pursue activities that erode party unity. Many observers expected Mogae to select one of the two faction leaders as his vice president, but instead, in a move that many viewed as politically shrewd, he named Lt. General Ian Khama to that post. Khama is popular in his own right and is the son of Botswana's first president. He is respected by both party factions and brings with him the grassroots support that Mogae himself lacks.

Eighteen months later, Mogae's Botswana Democratic Party (BDP) won 33 of the 40 parliamentary seats in the general elections held on 16 October 1999. The remaining seats went to the Botswana National Party (six seats) and the Botswana Congress Party (one seat). Festus Mogae was inaugurated as president based on the landslide win of his party in these elections.

Mogae comes to the presidency with ample government experience, having the distinction of serving under both of the country's post-independence presidents. Even prior to assuming presidential powers, Mogae indicated that he would concentrate on implementing policies of his predecessor, especially those targeting job creation and poverty, with just a few refinements. Thus it is unlikely that Mogae's administration will herald a significant departure from that of Masire.

Precisely because Botswana's democracy is stable, the likelihood of political crisis is remote. Political issues that have the potential to paralyze or destroy other African governments are readily handled by the democratic institutions that have developed in Botswana. Thus Mogae should be able to devote a significant amount of attention to retaining the BDP leadership.

## DOMESTIC POLICY

At the time of independence, Botswana was ranked as one of the 20 poorest nations in the world. Since then the economy has become among the strongest in Africa, averaging an annual growth rate of more than 10% during the 1976–1991 period. This was due primarily to the discovery and exploitation of huge mineral resources, most notably diamonds. Botswana is now Africa's third-largest mineral producer. Mining has transformed the economy. The nation's infrastructure and manufacturing sector have been improved, while social services have been expanded. Job creation has been impressive as well, with formal sector employment growing at nearly 10% in the 30 years since independence.

Growth at these high levels, especially when it is predicated on a expansion in one particular sector, is hard to sustain. Thus it is not surprising that Botswana's economy cooled down during the 1990s, but nevertheless maintained a respectable 4–5% annual expansion. The government had anticipated this slowdown in its development planning and adjusted budget items accordingly. In February 1997, the government unveiled its seventh National Development Plan, which was the blueprint for the economy through 2003. It emphasizes sustained and sustainable economic diversification, encouraging private sector growth.

Unemployment is perhaps the single most troublesome factor on the economic horizon. Because of a decrease in the number of Batswana working abroad and a reorganization of parastatal enterprises, some 21% of Batswana are unemployed. Job creation has slowed to a crawl, with some estimates putting it at only 1% in recent years. The government was also forced to scale back a planned expansion of the mining sector due to a lack of skilled labor in the country. There has been a rapid population influx to the cities from rural areas, but these are largely unskilled workers whose contribution to the growth of the economy is negligible and whose presence has strained social and government services. In April 1998, in response to these factors, the administration embarked on an ambitious public sector spending program; 3.5 billion *pula* (US$1 billion) was earmarked to build schools, clinics, and offices.

The Mogae government continues to encourage foreign investment in the national economy and has developed partnerships with some international corporations. Diversification will depend, in part, on increasing economic investment from abroad. Economic ties to other southern African countries have proven beneficial in the past, and there is no reason to expect these ties to erode in the future.

## FOREIGN POLICY

Botswana's foreign policy has historically put a premium on economic and political integration in southern Africa. This has led to the development of the 12-nation Southern African Development Community (SADC), to which Gaborone is host. The SADC has been the primary vehicle for diplomacy in the region, as well as an instrument of regional development. Post-apartheid South Africa has been welcomed as a partner in these regional initiatives.

The Southern African Customs Union (SACU), which includes Botswana, Namibia, Lesotho, Swaziland, and South Africa, dates to 1910. The SACU has provided duty-free access for Botswana's exports to the larger market in South Africa. However, South Africa's dominant role in the union became increasingly troublesome to other members. Barriers to the import of non-South African capital and consumer goods have caused a good deal of controversy. In 1995, an effort was made to renegotiate the terms of the SACU agreement.

Botswana maintains friendly diplomatic relations with most African nations, as well as with many European and Arab nations. The country is a member of the UN, where it established a reputation for consensual, constructive participation during its term on the Security Council. Botswana tends to exhibit solidarity with the African consensus on most international matters and was a member of the so-called "front-line states," which gave crucial support to the independence movements in Zimbabwe and Namibia, as well as in the opposition to apartheid in South Africa.

US-Botswana relations have been warm since independence, with the US viewing Botswana as a force for stability in Africa. The US has had a significant presence in the country, providing development aid for the past 30 years. In December 1997, after 30 years, the Peace Corps ended its mission in Botswana, leaving behind a legacy of assistance in education, business, health, agriculture, and the environment. The United States Agency for International Development (USAID) also closed out its programs in 1996, although as of 2000 Botswana continues to benefit from USAID's initiative for southern Africa as a whole.

## ADDRESS

Office of the President
Private Mailbag 001
Gaborone, Botswana

## REFERENCES

*Africa South of the Sahara 2000*. London: Europa Publications Ltd., 2000.

*Background Notes: Botswana*. US Department of State, October 1997.

"Biography of H.E. The President Festus Gontebanye Mogae." Republic of Botswana.

"Botswana ruling party wins landslide victory, 33 seats in parliament." *BBC Worldwide Monitoring*, 19 October 1999.

*Business Day Online*. [Online] Available http://www.bday.com (Accessed 11 November 1997, 7 April 1998).

*Namibian*. [Online] Available http://www.namibian.com (Accessed March 2000).

*New African*. [Online] Available http://www.africalynx.com (Accessed March 2000).

**Profile researched and written by Alison Doherty Munro (9/98; updated by Ezekiel Kalipeni, University of Illinois 3/2000).**

# BRAZIL

## Fernando Henrique Cardoso
## President

*(pronounced "fair-NAHN-do en-REE-kee car-DO-so")*

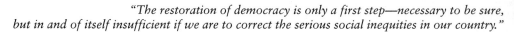

*"The restoration of democracy is only a first step—necessary to be sure,*
*but in and of itself insufficient if we are to correct the serious social inequities in our country."*

The Federative Republic of Brazil dominates the South American continent, encompassing 8.5 million sq km (3.29 million sq mi), which represents 40% of the continental land mass. Brazil is bounded to the east and northeast by the Atlantic Ocean; to the north by French Guiana, Suriname, Guyana, and Venezuela; to the west by Colombia and Peru; to the southwest by Bolivia and Paraguay; and to the south by Argentina and Uruguay.

Home to more than 171 million people, Brazil is the sixth most populous country in the world. The population comprises four major groups: those of Portuguese descent, whose ancestors colonized Brazil beginning in the 16th century; descendants of Africans who were brought as slaves to Brazil; Europeans and Asians who began emigrating in the mid-19th century; and indigenous peoples, primarily of Tupi and Guarani language groups. The national language is Portuguese. More than 80% of Brazilians profess the Roman Catholic faith; others belong to Protestant sects or practice spiritualism.

The unit of currency is the *real*. The Brazilian economy is diverse and export-oriented. Economic expansion occurred at an annual rate of 0.5% in 1999, up from 0% in 1998. Inflation was 8% in 1999, and unemployment stood at 7.7%.

## POLITICAL BACKGROUND

Claimed in 1500 by the Portuguese navigator Pedro Alvares Cabral, Brazil was ruled from Lisbon as a colony until 1808. In that year, fleeing Napoleon's army, the Portuguese royal family established the empire's seat of government in Rio de Janeiro. In 1821, the royal family returned to Portugal, leaving Prince Dom Pedro as regent of the newly established Brazilian kingdom. On 7 September 1822, Dom Pedro proclaimed Brazil's independence from Portugal and declared himself Emperor Dom Pedro I. His son, Dom Pedro II, ruled from 1831 to 1889 when a bloodless and unchallenged coup, led by Army Marshall Deodoro da Fonseca, established the United States of Brazil as a federal republic.

During the first 40 years of its republican history, Brazil was a constitutional democracy. In 1930, a military coup established the civilian, Getulio Vargas, as president. He remained dictator until 1945 when the nation returned to democratic practice. Alarmed by a spiraling economic downturn and growing social instability, the military intervened once again in 1964. Army Chief of Staff, General Humberto Castelo Branco, led a bloodless coup against the left-leaning administration of President Joao Goulart. Castelo

Branco became president and eventually assumed dictatorial powers. All political parties were banned. Successive military governments ruled Brazil until 1985 when a majority faction in the electoral college chose Senator Tancredo Neves as the next president, the first civilian to occupy that office since 1961. Although Neves died unexpectedly prior to his inauguration, his vice president, Jose Sarney, was sworn in as president in April 1985. In 1989, direct presidential elections were held for the first time in 29 years, and Brazilians elected Fernando Collor de Mello. Amid allegations of corruption and mismanagement, Collor resigned from office in 1992, and Vice President Itamar Franco completed his term. This smooth transition was hailed as a rebirth for the nation—the crisis and succession having been managed entirely within the dictates of constitutional procedure.

Upon the return to civilian government in 1985, Brazil moved quickly to re-establish fundamental democratic processes. In May 1985, a constitutional amendment re-established direct elections by universal suffrage. The right to vote was extended to illiterates (20% of the population). In 1987, a Constituent Assembly was seated and began debate on the new Brazilian constitution. The final draft was approved by the National Congress and promulgated on 5 October 1988.

The Constitution contains 245 highly specific articles, some of which remain controversial. The fundamental points establish Brazil as a federal republic of 26 states and the Federal District. A bicameral National Congress exercises legislative authority. The Federal Senate is composed of 81 members, who serve eight-year terms. The Chamber of Deputies is elected every four years by a system of proportional representation. The 1988 Constitution stipulated that executive power be held by a president elected to a five-year term. In 1994, the term was changed to four years. Two years later, the Constitution was altered to allow a president to serve more than one term in office. Presidential elections are structured in a two-round system. The first round is open to all comers. The second round is a contest between the two top contenders from the first round, unless a candidate receives an outright majority of votes cast.

## PERSONAL BACKGROUND

Fernando Henrique Cardoso was born into a wealthy military family in Rio de Janeiro on 18 June 1931. His academic training as a sociologist was perhaps in part responsible for his left-of-center political sympathies in his youth.

These brought him into direct conflict with the governing military regime.

An internationally recognized scholar, whose works have included seminal theories of development and dependency, Cardoso fled his academic position at the University of Sao Paulo in 1964 for exile in Chile. He returned in 1968, anticipating reappointment, but was instead arrested by military authorities. Barred from teaching in Brazilian universities, Cardoso founded the Brazilian Analysis and Planning Center (Cebrap), a research center where he provided a haven for other blacklisted academics. Viewed by the authorities as a hotbed of radicalism, Cebrap was bombed by right-wing terrorists in the 1970s. Shortly after that, Cardoso fled into exile again, this time as a visiting lecturer at prominent universities such as Oxford, Princeton, Yale, Berkeley, and Stanford.

Cardoso is married to Ruth Correa Leite, an anthropologist at Cebrap. The couple has three adult children and several grandchildren. In addition to his native Portuguese, Cardoso is fluent in several languages, including English, French, and Spanish. He has been awarded the Grand Cross of the Order of Rio Branco, the Grand Cross of the Order of Merit of Portugal, and has been named a chevalier in the French Legion of Honor.

## RISE TO POWER

Cardoso was drawn back to Brazil in response to the government's gradual re-opening of the political system, which would culminate by 1986 in the return to civilian national government. In 1978, he made his first foray into electoral politics, running for the Brazilian Senate. He was elected as an alternate. In 1979, he gained the vice-presidency of the Brazilian Democratic Movement Party (PMDB). He became a regular senator in 1983 after a vacancy was created by state gubernatorial elections. Cardoso ran unsuccessfully for mayor of Sao Paulo in 1985. The following year, he was elected senator for the state of Sao Paulo. In 1988, Cardoso helped to create the Brazilian Social Democratic Party (PSDB), a political movement with a left-of-center orientation. In late 1992, he joined the cabinet of the newly installed president, Itamar Franco, as foreign minister.

The following year, Franco prevailed upon Cardoso to become Brazil's finance minister, the fourth in eight months. Although not an economist by training, during his tenure Cardoso crafted the *Plano Real,* an anti-inflationary economic stabilization plan that was critical to the nation's plans to restructure its international debt. The plan was shepherded through Congress by a determined Cardoso and was put into effect in July 1994. The approval of the plan allowed Brazil to renegotiate the payment of its foreign debt on favorable terms. The plan's implementation reduced inflation from 50% to less than 2% in less than 3 months. The skill with which Cardoso negotiated the adoption of *Plano Real* and the budget that went along with it gave rise to speculation about Cardoso's political aspirations. In May 1994, Cardoso formally declared his intention to run for the presidency, as the candidate of the PSDB.

Both the 1994 and the 1998 elections were nominally contested by a number of candidates from across the political spectrum. The real race in both elections, however, was with Luis Ignacio "Lula" da Silva, a candidate from the Workers'

Party (PT). In 1994, Cardoso immediately took second place in the polls behind da Silva. As the effects of *Plano Real* took hold, Cardoso was able to close the gap and win the election on 3 October 1994.

On 4 October 1998 Cardoso again defeated da Silva in first-round balloting. The most hotly debated topics during the campaign were the anticipated reform of the pension system and the need to come to terms with the IMF over a new $27 billion line of credit. Despite a deepening economic crisis and the prospect of austerity measures in the immediate future, Cardoso won almost 52% of the vote to da Silva's 34%. Although voting is compulsory in Brazil, nearly 36% of eligible voters failed to cast ballots in the 1998 elections. This fact indicates a growing disaffection for the political process among some sectors of Brazilian society.

## LEADERSHIP

Inaugurated on 1 January 1995, Cardoso took the reins of a nation seen by most analysts to be poised for an increasingly significant role in the international community. Since 1995, Brazil has grown into that role, and all indications are that the country's importance will continue to increase. Much of the credit for Brazil's international presence must go to Cardoso himself. He is widely regarded as one of the hemisphere's most impressive presidents. He is articulate and well-read, has a firm grasp of the mechanics of politics, is a skilled negotiator and consensus builder, and is popular among Brazil's poor, despite economic hardships wrought by some of the austerity measures imposed during his first term in office.

Throughout the campaign in 1998, Cardoso made it clear that the next four years would be difficult ones for the nation. He did not make empty campaign promises but forthrightly stated his intentions, knowing that they were potentially unpopular. He raised the specter of increased taxes, announced his intention to come to terms with the IMF, and vowed to continue his drive to reform social security and the civil service. His honesty was welcomed by a society well aware of the serious problems facing their nation.

Cardoso began his second term with a majority in Congress slightly smaller than that which he enjoyed in his first term. His five-party coalition won 381 of the 513 seats in the lower house, 15 seats fewer than previously. In the Senate, his coalition won 67 of the 81 seats, a loss of two. Although the president's support in Congress has declined slightly, it seems that the new coalition is slightly less contentious than its predecessor. Thus it appears that Cardoso has the votes he needs to address the worsening economy.

## DOMESTIC POLICY

It should come as no surprise that economic issues are the predominant factor of Cardoso's domestic policy. The economy was hit hard by the Asian currency crisis, and decreased international confidence in the Brazilian economy weakened the *real*. In a period of six weeks in the summer of 1998, the government was forced to spend more than $30 billion in foreign reserves to avoid currency devaluation. Devaluation, it is feared, would re-ignite the hyperinflation of the early 1990s, as well as dampen international confidence and investment in the economy. Foreign capital left the country at an average rate of $1 billion a day during the first part of September 1998. This indicated that international confidence was already shaken. Economic growth has slowed, making it difficult to pursue the reforms that are required for the continued success of the *Plano Real*. These include tough measures against tax evasion—a phenomenon so widespread it has been referred to as a national pastime and costs the government between $25 and $30 billion annually—as well as government spending cuts to control the deficit. Cardoso has vowed to continue his efforts to privatize state-owned monopolies, a course he pursued with great success during his first term. He also intends to cut the government payroll and reform the social security system. All of these measures, however necessary they may seem, will likely face an uphill battle in Congress.

Cardoso acknowledges the very real toll exacted by Brazil's wildly skewed income distribution and has vowed to continue to make issues of social justice a priority of his administration through aggressive creation of jobs and economic opportunity. During the first two years of his second term, the economy has recovered slightly, but unemployment and inflation have remained high at 7.7% and 8% respectively, and real wages have also declined by more than 3% in 1999.

## FOREIGN POLICY

Brazil was a founding member of the Common Market of the South (MERCOSUR), a free trade pact among Brazil, Argentina, Uruguay, and Paraguay created in 1995. It was established in response to the North American Free Trade Agreement (NAFTA) and the European Union, and unites 200 million consumers with a combined gross domestic product of $1 trillion. Cardoso has stated his intention of pursuing other regional alliances. The president's fluency in languages other than Portuguese has made him a popular figure abroad. Presidential elections in Argentina, Chile, and Uruguay in 1999 have made Cardoso the senior president in South America, and he is expected to strengthen relations with Argentina's Fernando de la Rua and Chile's Ricardo Lagos, two presidents who also ascribe to social democratic ideas.

Brazil's relationship with the US has always been good and will likely remain so throughout Cardoso's term. Problematic issues of intellectual property rights have been resolved, and progress continues in the areas of the environment and trade. Cardoso's intention to remove restrictions on foreign investment in key Brazilian industries and to eliminate trade barriers will only strengthen relations. Joint ventures in medical, space, and environmental research between the two countries signal the cooperative nature of that relationship. The US offered crucial support to Brazil during its round of negotiations with the IMF, which produced a $21 million relief package. Cardoso visited the US in 1995 and again in 1999, hoping to win back the confidence of investors. US president Bill Clinton traveled to Brazil in 1997. Each government recognizes the importance of the other to their respective economies and works closely to preserve that relationship.

## ADDRESS

Gabinete do Presidente
Palacio do Planalto
Praca dos Tres Poderes
70150 Brasilia, D.F.
Brazil

## REFERENCES

*Boston Globe*, 4 October 1998, 20 October 1998.
"Brazil Local Loot." *The Economist*, 15 May 1999, p. 38.
"Cardoso, Fernando Henrique." *Current Biography*, October 1996, p. 9+.
*Chicago Tribune*, 5 October 1998.
*Financial Times* (London), 19 August–13 October 1998.
*Hemisphere: A Magazine of Latin American and Caribbean Affairs*, vol. 6, no. 1, winter/spring 1994.
*Journal of Democracy*, 1996.
*Los Angeles Times*, 15 September 1998, 4 October 1998.
*New York Times*, 17 May–21 October 1998.

**Profile researched and written by Alison Doherty Munro (3/99; updated by Patricio Navio, New York University 4/2000).**

# BRUNEI

## Hassanal Bolkiah
## Sultan

*(pronounced "HAH-soh-nol boal-KYE-ah")*

*"We have tried it. We had elections before 1962 and we had a few political parties, but people competed against each other and chaos resulted."*

Officially known as the Sultanate of Brunei (*Negara Brunei Darussalam*), Brunei is situated on the northwest coast of the island of Kalimantan (Borneo), most of which is Indonesian territory, and faces the South China Sea. Both of its two parts are surrounded by Sarawak, which is part of Malaysia. Brunei has a coastline of about 161 km (100 mi). Its total area is 5,765 sq km (2,226 sq mi), and its capital is Bandar Seri Begawan. The population has been estimated at 323,000. The unit of currency is the *Brunei* dollar.

The official language is Malay, and ethnically Brunei is comprised of Malay, 64%; Chinese, 20%; with indigenous races and others, 16%. Its religions include Islam, Buddhism, Christianity and animism. The terrain is heavily forested, and the crops include rice, sugarcane, and fruit. Its natural resources consist almost exclusively of petroleum and natural gas, which together account for 99% of Brunei's exports. Brunei's per capita GDP has been estimated at $17,000.

## POLITICAL BACKGROUND

Brunei has been a center of human settlement since at least the 8th century AD, and by the 13th century it was an Islamic state. The Sultan of Brunei ceded Sarawak to James Brooke, an English adventurer in 1841, and Brunei was then placed under British protection in 1888. The country was occupied by Japanese forces from 1941 to 1945. After the war, Brunei was a protected state, with the UK taking responsibility for its defense and foreign relations until 1 January 1984 when it became a fully independent nation.

Brunei is a monarchy. Under the provisions of the Constitution promulgated on 29 September 1959, sovereign authority is vested in the sultan. As the head of state, the sultan presides over a Council of Ministers and is assisted and advised by a Legislative Council, a Religious Council, a Privy Council (to deal with constitutional issues), and the Council of Succession. Hassanal Bolkiah is the twenty-ninth Sultan in a royal line that stretches back in time further than any other existing monarchy. He came to the throne by virtue of having been first born. Since 1962, when a state of emergency was declared, the Sultan has had virtually absolute political power, and at this time there are no political parties operating in Brunei.

## PERSONAL BACKGROUND

Born on 15 July 1946, Hassanal Bolkiah Mu'issaddin Waddautah is the first son of the late Sultan Muda Omar Ali Si Fidem. In childhood he was educated by tutors at Istana

and also went to school in Brunei and Kuala Lumpur, Malaysia. At the age of 15, in 1961, Hassanal Bolkiah was installed as the crown prince and invested with family order of Darjah Kerabat First Class. While attending Britain's Royal Military Academy at Sandhurst, he was suddenly recalled to succeed his abdicating father. Although he did not finish his education, the academy later awarded him an honorary commission. Installed as the new ruler of Brunei on 5 October 1967, Hassanal Bolkiah's official coronation took place on 1 August 1968 in a lavish ceremony.

Hassanal Bolkiah is one of the most accessible leaders in the world. He has no bodyguard, and he moves among his people with ease, frequently making helicopter tours of outlying villages. His hobbies include fancy cars and polo, and he loves sports. He is also considered to be one of the top three wealthiest men in the world with a fortune of $30 billion. He is married to Her Majesty Raja Isteri Penigran Anak Hajjah Saleha and Her Royal Highness Penigran Isteri Hajjah Mariam. He has ten children, four princes and six princesses.

## RISE TO POWER

Initially accepting his father as the power behind the throne, Hassanal Bolkiah gradually sought to take over the reins of government and by the early 1980s he was able to assert his authority. With the passing away of his father in 1982, Hassanal Bolkiah became the undisputed supreme authority in Brunei, and he enjoys almost absolute respect and loyalty from his people today. The Sultan shares his power with only a handful of close relatives. When he established a cabinet upon the attainment of independence in 1984, he named himself as the prime minister and minister of finance and home affairs, and he appointed members of his immediate family to hold other key government positions.

## LEADERSHIP

Political activity is muted in Brunei, as there is no real basis for it in the "Shellfare state" with its wide range of welfare benefits. There are no elections. The Brunei People's Independence Front formed in 1966 was deregistered in early 1988 because of inactivity; the Brunei People's National United Party founded in 1968 also appears to be defunct. In May 1985, the Sultan agreed to the formation of the Brunei National Democratic Party (BNDP), but at the same time prohibited all government employees (about 40% of the country's work force) from joining, thus depriving the party

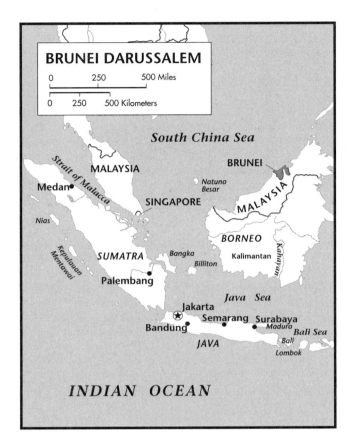

**BRUNEI DARUSSALEM**

0   250   500 Miles

0   250   500 Kilometers

South China Sea

MALAYSIA

BRUNEI

Strait of Malacca

Medan

Natuna Besar

SINGAPORE

MALAYSIA

Nias

BORNEO

Kepulauan Mentawai

SUMATRA

Bangka

Kalimantan

Billiton

Kahayan

Palembang

Java Sea

Jakarta

Semarang   Surabaya

Bandung

Madura

Bali Sea

JAVA

Bali

Lombok

INDIAN OCEAN

shares. Brunei's per capita income is one of the highest in the world, and the citizens of Brunei receive free health care and generous state pensions. There is no income tax, and government loans are freely available at an annual interest rate of 1%. Brunei's balance of trade is consistently favorable, and government revenues consistently exceed expenditures.

However, the petroleum sector was adversely affected by depressed prices on the world oil market in the 1980s. Also, in 1987, the country's reserves of petroleum were estimated to be sufficient for production at current levels for only 27 years more. Thus, Brunei faces the problem of how to diversify its economy and move away from total dependence on a dwindling resource. In 1985, the Sultan's government proposed a 20-year master plan to broaden the economy, suggesting development of a microchip and optics industry. In 1986 the government introduced a fifth National Development Plan, which was designed to reduce reliance on petroleum and natural gas income and to achieve self-sufficiency in food production. The government provides technical training in order to generate more attractive jobs. The Sultan's long-term objective is to turn Brunei into a center for banking, trade, and financial services.

One of the Sultan's major achievements was the establishment of the Sultan Haji Hassanal Bolkiah Foundation in 1992. The foundation is a gift from the Sultan to his people and focuses on, among other things, financing research-related works, particularly in the fields of knowledge.

## FOREIGN POLICY

As the ruler of a small country, Hassanal Bolkiah tries to protect his nation's independence by maintaining a defense relationship with the UK and by strengthening ties to neighboring Asian states. In the past, both Indonesia and Malaysia had territorial disputes with Brunei and supported the Sultan's political opponents. In addition, Malaysia regularly called upon the UK to "decolonize" Brunei and advocated UN supervision of elections in the sultanate. However, recently relations between Brunei and its neighbors have improved. In July 1980, the Sultan paid the first official visit to Malaysia in 17 years. In September 1987, Brunei and Malaysia announced a joint plan to produce defense equipment. In October 1984, Hassanal Bolkiah met with Indonesia President Soeharto at Jakarta, and Indonesia subsequently denied any territorial ambitions in regard to the sultanate. In September 1987, Hassanal Bolkiah offered an interest-free loan of $100 million to Indonesia for industrial and transport projects. In 1986, at the request of the US, Hassanal Bolkiah sent $10 million to the Nicaraguan contras.

Following independence, Brunei became a member of the Association of Southeast Asian Nations (ASEAN), the Commonwealth, the Organization of the Islamic Conference, and the UN. In 1999, the Sultan began discussing the creation of a Philippines-Brunei Joint Commission for Bilateral Cooperation with the Philippines' president Joseph Estrada.

## ADDRESS

Office of the Prime Minister
Istana Nurul Iman
Bandar Seri Begawan, Brunei

## REFERENCES

*The Far East and Australasia*, 1989.

of a potential source of support. The members of BNDP were mainly Brunei Malay businessmen and young professionals, and their political agenda was to gain government support for Brunei Malay commercial interests. The new party quickly split into two factions in October 1985, with one of the resulting parties proposing radical changes; not surprisingly, it was squelched by the government. The BNDP was finally dissolved by the authorities early in 1988 after it had openly demanded the resignation of the Sultan as the head of government, the lifting of the 26-year-old state of emergency, and democratic elections.

Hassanal Bolkiah favors maintaining the status quo and opposes any rapid development which might bring about social and economic change. To this end, Hassanal Bolkiah places great emphasis on Islamic values and strongly promotes Islam to keep his Brunei Malay power base stable. Malays enjoy preferential treatment and numerous benefits, while 90% of the ethnic Chinese inhabitants have been classified as "non-citizens," thus ceasing to qualify for many state benefits.

## DOMESTIC POLICY

Brunei is the third-largest oil producer in Southeast Asia after Indonesia and Malaysia, and the Sultan's government has been heavily involved in developing its rich natural gas and petroleum resources. Enormous wealth has been generated from royalties on both oil and liquified natural gas. Oil is produced by Brunei Shell Petroleum and Brunei Shell Marketing, in both of which the government now holds a 50% interest; gas is produced by Brunei LNG, in which the government, Shell, and Mitsubishi of Japan hold equal

*Far Eastern Economic Review,* 10 March 1988.

Hinton, Horold C. *East Asia and the Western Pacific 1988,* 1989.

Leake Jr., David. *Brunei: The Modern Southeast Asian Islamic Sultanate,* 1989.

Schelander, Bjorn. *Brunei: Abode of Peace.* Honolulu: Center for Southeast Asian Studies, School of Hawaiian, Asian and Pacific Studies, University of Hawaii, 1998.

**Profile researched and written by Junling Ma (7/90; updated 3/ 2000).**

# BULGARIA

### Ivan Kostov
### Prime Minister
*(pronounced "E-vaughn KOS-tofv")*

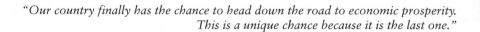

*"Our country finally has the chance to head down the road to economic prosperity.
This is a unique chance because it is the last one."*

Bulgaria is situated in the Balkan peninsula in southeastern Europe. Its territory covers 110,910 sq km (42,822 sq mi). It shares borders with Turkey, Greece, Macedonia, Yugoslavia, and Romania. To the east lies the Black Sea. About three-quarters of the countryside is mountainous. The country's total population has been estimated at 8.2 million. Of this number, ethnic Bulgarians comprise 85%; ethnic Turks 8.5%; Roma (Gypsies) 2.6%; and Pomaks (Bulgarian Muslims) 2–3%. Most Bulgarians belong to the Bulgarian Orthodox Church. Other religions practiced in Bulgaria are Islam, Catholicism, Protestant Christianity, and Judaism. Most people speak Bulgarian, a Slavic language written in the Cyrillic alphabet. The other significant language in Bulgaria is Turkish, spoken by the ethnic Turkish minority.

The national currency is the *lev*. Bulgaria was traditionally an agricultural country, but industrialization accelerated during the communist period. Major industries include machinery, metallurgy, and fuel and chemical production. Major agricultural products include tobacco, grain, wine, and produce.

## POLITICAL BACKGROUND

Bulgaria remained under the control of the Ottoman Empire until the end of the 19th century, gaining autonomy in 1878 and complete independence in 1908. Badly defeated in the second Balkan war of 1913, Bulgaria twice chose to ally itself with the losing side in World Wars I and II. The Soviet Red Army drove out Axis forces from Bulgaria in September 1944. The Bulgarian Communist Party deposed King Simeon in September 1946 and declared Bulgaria to be a People's Republic.

Communist leader Todor Zhivkov came to power in Bulgaria in 1954 and remained in power until 1989, the year of democratic revolutions throughout Eastern Europe. Under communism, Bulgaria was known as the most faithful ally of the Soviet Union among the communist Eastern bloc. Bulgaria did not have a well-organized dissidents' movement, and the regime did not embark on limited market economic experimentation, as other East European countries had. In 1989, opposition to Zhivkov grew, and a coalition of more than 20 opposition groups formed the Union of Democratic Forces (UDF). Meanwhile on 10 November 1989, the Bulgarian Communist Party politburo forced the resignation of Zhivkov in a "palace coup." Beginning in January 1990, round table negotiations between the Communist Party and the democratic opposition opened the way for new

democratic elections in June 1990. With about 90% of eligible voters participating, the Bulgarian Socialist Party (BSP), the former Communist party, nearly won a majority of the vote. The UDF came in second with 36%, winning all of the urban centers by a large margin but losing the vote in the countryside.

The parliament passed a new constitution on 13 July 1991. Elections to the new parliament, now called the National Assembly, were held on 13 October 1991. This time, the UDF won a slight plurality, with 34% of the vote. The Bulgarian Socialist Party (BSP) came in close second with 33%. The UDF allied with the Movement for Rights and Freedoms (MRF) and formed Bulgaria's first entirely non-communist government on 8 November 1991, headed by Filip Dimitrov of the UDF. The first direct presidential elections, held on 19 January 1992, brought incumbent President Zhelyu Zhelev, a founder of the UDF, to the presidency for a five-year term.

The Dimitrov government significantly improved Bulgaria's international reputation as a country swiftly transforming into a democratic state with a market economy. Politically, however, signs of trouble began to emerge by mid-1992. Tensions increased between the coalition partners of the UDF and MRF, and divisions within the UDF also became apparent. On 28 October 1992, the MRF, allied with the Socialist Party, voted in favor of a motion of no-confidence in the Dimitrov government, an action which led to its resignation. The political crisis lasted two months, as the parties could not agree on a new cabinet. Finally on 22 December 1992, the MRF nominated economics professor Lyuben Berov (unaffiliated) to be prime minister.

Beginning in 1993 and continuing in 1994, the Berov "government of experts" withstood numerous challenges. The most substantial differences arose between the UDF (especially former Premier Filip Dimitrov), on the one hand, and the Berov government and President Zhelev (one of the founders of the UDF) on the other. The UDF repeatedly sought to force the resignation of the Berov government. A currency crisis and the serious illness of Prime Minister Berov in March 1994 prompted President Zhelev to withdraw his support for the Berov government in April of that year. In May 1994, Prime Minister Berov himself introduced a vote of confidence in his government for a three-month period. On 2 September 1994, the Berov government submitted its resignation to the parliament, ending a tenure which lasted far beyond most expectations. President Zhelev dissolved parliament and set 18 December 1994 as the date for early elections—nearly one year before scheduled.

Early elections for the 240-seat National Assembly were held on 18 December 1994. The Socialist Party won 43.5% of the vote and 125 seats in parliament, an absolute majority. The UDF came in second with 24.2% of the vote and 69 seats. Socialist Party head Zhan Videnov became Bulgaria's prime minister on 25 January 1995.

Economic reforms under the Videnov government stalled. The Bulgarian economy suffered a shrinking gross domestic product, high inflation, and a collapsing currency. In the political arena, the Videnov government and President Zhelev remained at odds over numerous issues, especially economic policy and foreign policy priorities. Within the BSP, a reformist faction began to demand Videnov's resignation by mid-1996.

Bulgaria held presidential elections in October and November 1996. In a move to unite the non-Socialist opposition parties, the UDF, Agrarian Union, and the Movement for Rights and Freedoms agreed to put forth a joint candidate determined by a primary election. On 1 June, incumbent President Zhelev ran opposite UDF candidate Petar Stoyanov, and Stoyanov defeated Zhelev by a wide margin. In the first round on 27 October, opposition candidate Stoyanov led with about 44% of the vote. Socialist candidate and former culture minister Ivan Marazov trailed with 27%, and Bulgarian Business Bloc candidate George Ganchev pulled in 22%. In the second round on 3 November, Stoyanov won nearly 60% to Marazov's 40%. Stoyanov's victory marked a turning point in Bulgarian politics. The opposition, buoyed by Stoyanov's victory, set sights on forcing early parliamentary elections in 1997. Stoyanov was sworn in as president on 19 January 1997.

Facing growing internal and external opposition, Prime Minister Videnov resigned from office and party leadership at the BSP party congress in December 1996, reversing earlier vows not to relinquish power. New Socialist Party leader Georgi Parvanov pledged to form a new Socialist-led government. Tens of thousands of Bulgarian citizens, however, launched demonstrations on 3 January 1997 against the Socialist government and in support of opposition demands for early elections. On 10 January, riot police violently broke up a blockade of the parliament building by demonstrators. Outgoing President Zhelev refused to offer the Socialist Party a mandate to form a new government under the BSP's prime minister-designate, Nikolay Dobrev. Western economic and financial institutions warned that economic stabilization efforts and outside financial assistance could not begin until a new government was put in place.

President Stoyanov upheld a constitutional requirement to offer a governing mandate to the Socialist Party in late January but urged the BSP not to accept it. He rather urged them to work out a consensus arrangement on emergency economic policies and early elections. With its approval of a new cabinet line-up on 3 February, the deeply divided Socialist Party appeared set for a stand-off. The next day, however, President Stoyanov, the BSP, and the opposition announced an agreement, reached "in the name of civic peace," on holding early elections in mid-April 1997.

On 19 April, Bulgaria held new parliamentary elections. The United Democratic Forces coalition (comprised of the Union of Democratic Forces, the Popular Union, and the Bulgarian Social Democratic Party) came in first with an absolute majority of the vote (52.3%) and seats in parliament (137 out of 240). The Socialists were defeated but came in second with 22.1%. A new government led by UDF leader Ivan Kostov was approved by parliament on 21 May 1997.

## PERSONAL BACKGROUND

Ivan Kostov was born in Sofia, the capital, on 23 December 1949. He graduated from the Karl Marx Higher Institute of Economics in 1974. Kostov also studied mathematics and earned a degree in mathematical modeling at the Saint Kliment Okhridski University in Sofia. In 1984 he earned a PhD in economics at the Technical University of Sofia. Kostov became an associate professor of economics at the Technical University in 1991. Kostov is married to Elena Grigorova, and has two daughters, Yana and Mina.

## RISE TO POWER

Ivan Kostov became a member of parliament after the first democratic elections in 1990, in which the Socialist Party won a slight majority. He served on the economics and budgetary committee in parliament. During the coalition UDF-Socialist government in 1990–91, Kostov served as finance minister. He became the leading force behind Bulgaria's first efforts at radical economic change, and became known as a *Akamikaze* reformer. Kostov continued as finance minister in the UDF-led government (1991–92).

After the UDF government fell in late 1992, Kostov returned to parliament as a member of the opposition.

After the UDF lost to the Bulgarian Socialist Party in the December 1994 elections, the UDF leadership elected Ivan Kostov to take over the party chairmanship from former prime minister, Filip Dimitrov. Kostov's main objective was to broaden the support of the party among the electorate before the next elections. He strove to restructure the party to increase party cohesiveness and unity. By February 1997, Kostov transformed the UDF into a single party.

## LEADERSHIP
Under Kostov's leadership, the UDF transformed from an umbrella organization of 15 disparate and often quarrelsome parties into a single political unit. The UDF moved away from its hardline and intolerant anti-communist stance and began to present itself as a viable political alternative to the Socialists. The UDF rallied non-Socialists to support Petar Stoyanov's bid for the presidency in late 1996 and led daily demonstrations throughout Bulgaria in early 1997, demanding early elections.

During the early 1997 election campaign, Kostov pledged to institute fundamental changes in Bulgaria's policies. He emphasized accelerating economic reforms, combatting organized crime and corruption and seeking membership in NATO and the European Union. Though not personally as popular as President Stoyanov, approval ratings for Kostov have remained high. Kostov's biggest challenge may be in upholding cohesiveness and unity within the ruling UDF, especially if planned economic reforms do not soon bring positive results.

## DOMESTIC POLICY
The Kostov government's foremost priority is to lead the country out of its economic crisis. He hopes to achieve financial stabilization, accelerated privatization, tax and banking reform, crime reduction, and the elimination of corruption. One of the government's first tasks was to adopt a new budget and introduce a currency board. Foreign governments and international financial institutions have begun to provide aid and other assistance to Bulgaria.

In contrast to the situation in neighboring Yugoslavia, ethnic relations in Bulgaria have largely improved in recent years. Notably, relations between Bulgaria's ethnic Bulgarian and Turkish populations have vastly improved since the time of communism.

## FOREIGN POLICY
Bulgaria's foreign policy environment has been completely transformed since the end of the Cold War. Bulgaria was once the closest ally of the Soviet Union and a member of the Warsaw Treaty Organization (WTO) and the Council for Mutual Economic Assistance (CMEA), all of which dissolved in 1991. Since then, the government has sought to foster improved relations and eventual integration with the West, especially Western Europe, as well as act as a stabilizing force in the Balkans. Bulgaria has enhanced political, economic, and security links to Western institutions, such as the Council of Europe, the European Union, and NATO. Bulgaria signed onto NATO's Partnership for Peace program in February 1994 and has been an active participant in the initiative. An association treaty with the European Union came into force in February 1995.

The dissolution of both the Soviet Union and Yugoslavia presented Bulgaria with some difficulties. The ongoing conflict in Yugoslavia severed trading links with the West. Bulgaria's observance of UN economic sanctions against Serbia-Montenegro cost substantial economic losses. Bulgaria remained concerned about continued instability in the Balkans. After the Dayton peace agreement for former Yugoslavia was reached in November 1995, the government swiftly suspended trade sanctions against Serbia and sought to normalize bilateral economic relations. Bulgaria has supported other regional institutions such as the OSCE and the Black Sea Economic Conference.

Prime Minister Kostov has unequivocally favored Bulgaria's relations with and accession to the EU and NATO. In February 1997, the interim government issued a declaration that Bulgaria would seek full NATO membership. Though not among the three countries invited by NATO in July 1997 to begin accession negotiations, the Kostov government will continue to press for Bulgaria's eventual membership. In mid-July 1997, the European Commission could not recommend Bulgaria for membership in the EU because of the state of its economy, although it did note that Bulgaria was on its way to meet the political criteria for membership.

In 1999, Kostov pursued full-speed-ahead reform with the support of President and fellow reformer Petar Stoyanov. By year's end, these policies had contributed greatly to Bulgaria's standing as a stable country in the region.

The unabashedly pro-Western stance of the government was in evidence as soon as the NATO airstrikes against Yugoslavia began in late March. Although the overwhelming majority of Bulgarians opposed the conflict (as was the case in neighboring Greece and Macedonia), the Bulgarian government supported NATO's action wholeheartedly and even went to the length of permitting Turkish warplanes to fly over Bulgaria on their way to targets in Yugoslavia. As one headline summed up this policy, the pro-NATO policy was indeed a "brave gamble" for Bulgaria. Not only did nearly all Bulgarians oppose the war, Bulgaria itself suffered from the continuation of hostilities. Errant NATO missiles struck suburban Sofia; the bombing of Yugoslavia cut off Bulgaria from the Danube River, its primary trading route; and expected economic growth declined by over half, from 5% to 2%.

In the final analysis, however, Bulgaria's gamble paid off. NATO's recognition of Bulgarian support for the war effort bodes well for Bulgaria's desire to be included in a subsequent expansion of the Atlantic Alliance. The United States also extended much needed economic assistance.

Following the end of hostilities, Stoyanov and Kostov continued their pro-Western reform-minded diplomacy. In the spring, Bulgaria reached agreement with Macedonia on its language. Prior to this settlement, Bulgaria considered Macedonian to be a western Bulgarian dialect, thereby negating a claim to a distinct Macedonian national identity. Stoyanov and Kostov also reached agreement with Albania on an oil pipeline to run from the Bulgarian Black Sea port of Bourgas to Albania's Adriatic port of Vlore.

## ADDRESS

Prime Minister
Veliko Narodno Subraine
Sofia 1000
Bulgaria

## REFERENCES

*The Economist,* 26 April 1997, 27 February 1999.

*Financial Times* (London), 19–25 April 1997.
*New York Times,* 20 January–8 May 1997; 28 February 2000.
*Time,* 27 January 1997, 6 September 1999.
*The World Factbook.* Washington, DC: Central Intelligence Agency, 2000.

**Profile researched and written by Julie Kim, Library of Congress (7/97; updated 3/2000).**

# BURKINA FASO

### Blaise Compaoré
### President
*(pronounced "BLEHZ comp-pah-OAR-eh")*

*"If there is famine in any African country, then there is famine in Burkina Faso,
if there is illness in any African country then Burkina Faso is ill."*

The Republic of Burkina Faso is a landlocked nation in West Africa. It borders Mali on the northwest and Niger on the northeast; to the south and southeast are Benin and Togo; to the south and southwest Ghana and Cote d'Ivoire. Burkina Faso's total area equals 274,200 sq km (or 105,870 sq mi).

The population has been estimated at 11.6 million, with an average density of 28 people per sq km. Although French is the national language of administration, more than 60 African languages are spoken throughout the country; principal among these are More, Jula, and Fulfulde. Burkina Faso encompasses a large variety of ethnic groups, including the Mossi (50%), the Peul (10.4%), the Lobi-Dagari (7%), and others. In terms of religious practice, statistics vary widely. Some studies suggest that more than 50% of Burkinabè citizens practice traditional African religions while 25–30% are Muslims, and 10–15% are Christians.

The unit of currency is the *Communauté Financière Africaine (CFA) franc*. Burkina's principal food crops are millet and sorghum. Its primary exports include cotton, unworked gold, karite nuts, peanuts, sesame seeds, livestock, hides, and skins. Burkina's major trading partners are France and Cote d'Ivoire. The per capita GDP has been estimated at $1,000.

## POLITICAL BACKGROUND

Burkina Faso is a former French colony, known until 1984 as Upper Volta. The country gained its independence from France in 1960 and has been under military rule since 1980. At that time, Colonel Saye Zerbo overthrew the government of Sangoule Lamizana and abolished the 1977 constitution. Important political actors in Burkina have traditionally included the powerful trade unions, the traditional chiefs, and military officers.

In 1983, however, the established pattern of Burkinabè politics was overturned by the formation of the National Council for the Revolution (CNR), headed by Captain Thomas Sankara. Under Sankara, political activity was extended into the countryside, where peasant farmers were mobilized by grassroots organizations known as Committees for the Defense of the Revolution (CDRs). But Sankara aroused opposition among established groups who feared that their privileged positions would be threatened by his revolutionary principles. In 1987, Captain Blaise Compaoré led a successful coup in which Sankara was killed.

## PERSONAL BACKGROUND

Blaise Compaoré was born in 1950 in Ziniaré, a village near the capital city of Ouagadougou. He is the eldest of seven children from a prominent military family. Following his family tradition, Compaoré joined the army in 1971 and underwent infantry training in Montpelier, France. He received further military training at the officers school in Yaoundé, Cameroon, returning to Burkina Faso as a second lieutenant. He was later sent to Morocco for para-commando training. Compaoré is married to Chantal, daughter of the late president of Cote d'Ivoire, Houphouet Boigny.

## RISE TO POWER

After his return to Burkina, Compaoré was stationed at the Po garrison, headquarters of an elite commando unit of Burkinabè paratroopers. He developed friendships with several young officers at Po, including Captain Thomas Sankara. When Sankara was appointed commandant of the para-commando school at Po in 1974, he brought in Compaoré as his deputy. Seven years later, when Sankara obtained a ministerial position in the Zerbo government, Compaoré became commander of the Po garrison.

Compaoré led a paracommando revolt in 1983, which resulted in the formation of a radical government headed by Sankara. Compaoré was generally regarded as second in command to Sankara in the new government. Officially, he held the post of minister of state of the presidency, and later became minister of justice as well. Compaoré also maintained his command of the Po paratroopers. He participated in the arrest of political dissidents, including former presidents Yaméogo and Zerbo.

During 1987, personal disagreements between Sankara and Compaoré became increasingly evident. Sankara began to lose his grip on the direction of the regime. On 15 October 1987, fearing that he was going to be removed from power, Compaoré seized power in a bloody coup that resulted in the assassination of Sankara. At least 80 other people lost their lives, including 13 of Sankara's advisors and guards. At the time, Compaoré denied having ordered the deaths, but he justified the coup by claiming that Sankara had planned to have him murdered. Reaction, both internationally and internally, was highly negative. Compaoré declared himself president on 18 October 1987, becoming Burkina Faso's sixth head of state since its 1960 independence.

## LEADERSHIP

Compaoré denounced Sankara as a traitor to the revolution and declared his intention to initiate a "rectification" of the revolution. He ruled through the Popular Front, made up of many of the groups that had originally backed Sankara. In early 1988, Compaoré began dismantling some of the governmental structures that Sankara had put in place, starting with the replacement of the CDRs by revolutionary committees that were, at this point, disarmed. Committees were to be elected by each village, each office or factory, and each military unit. Local committee members then were to select representatives of regional and national committees. He also began appeals for more private investment, dropped some unpopular taxes, raised the salaries of public officials to generate support among civil servants, and repressed most political opposition through arrest and torture. In 1988, the Popular Front initiated negotiations with the IMF and the World Bank, a move rejected by the previous government. Opposition to Compaoré has come periodically from within the military. The president responded to military unrest in late 1988 by ordering the death of several soldiers accused of plotting against the government.

Compaoré has attempted to stabilize a political system historically divided by factionalism among the powerful left-wing organizations and trade unions. However, he has been unable to mobilize widespread popular support for his regime. In April 1989, the government sponsored the creation of the Organization for Popular Democracy Labor Movement (ODP-MT) in an attempt to unify the many small leftist organizations in the Popular Front. Some progressive leaders strongly against this move were ousted from the Popular Front.

Compaoré's own party formally abandoned Marxism-Leninism in 1991 and endorsed the new constitution that was accepted by referendum. It provided for a president elected for a 7-year term by universal suffrage and a bicameral national legislature, composed of a 107-member Assembly of Deputies and a 178-member Chamber of Representatives. The president appoints the prime minister, who appoints the Council of Ministers. Local government consists of 30 provinces divided into 250 departments, further divided into communes administered by mayors and municipal councils.

Compaoré was successful in his first bid for the presidency in December 1991. He ran uncontested, with opposition parties boycotting the polls. With a low 25% voter turnout, Compaoré was frequently called the "badly elected" president. After opening the political process to other parties, legislative elections were held in 1992. Twenty-seven parties participated, with Compaoré's ODP-MT winning 78 of the 107 seats. The next strongest party, the National Convention of Progressive Patriots allied with the Social Democratic Party, won 12 seats.

In February 1996, the CDP (Congress for Democracy and Progress), a new pro-Compaoré political party, was formed. The following year, the Compaoré-controlled Assembly approved constitutional amendments that removed restrictions on the renewal of the presidential mandate, allowing Compaoré to run again and increasing the number of parliamentary seats to 111. In 1997 parliamentary elections, 13 political parties and 569 candidates contested the 111 seats.

Compaoré's CDP won 101 seats, further increasing his tight control on the government.

On 15 November 1998, voters were asked to choose between Compaoré and two other contenders. Many observers claimed that the contenders were convinced to run by the president's people in order to legitimize the political process and prevent another unopposed election. A coalition of opposition parties had, as in 1991, called for a boycott. Fifty-eight percent of the electorate turned out, and Compaoré polled 87.53% of the ballots cast, becoming the only Burkinabè president to complete his term of office and be re-elected.

In December 1998, the body of Norbert Zongo, editor-in-chief of an independent weekly newspaper and an outspoken critic of the government, was found along with three others in his car. The bodies were burned, and bullet holes were found in the car. Zongo had been investigating the mysterious death of Compaoré's brother's driver, and speculation is that he was getting to close to the truth. Zongo's funeral brought an estimated 50,000 mourners into the streets, with rioting and looting in several cities. The public outcry, at home and abroad, forced Compaoré to establish an independent commission to investigate. Signs of a political assassination then forced him to compose a committee of elders to investigate unpunished political crimes. As of August 1999, the independent commission arrested three presidential guards in connection with the driver's death, but no arrests had been made in the Zongo case.

The elder's council recommended a government of national unity as a way out of the crisis. Some members of the

CDP, fearing for their own safety, have taken to arming militias; others have called for immediate parliamentary elections. "The Collectif," as the coalition of opposition parties, unions, and human rights groups is called, has demanded that Compaore's brother and six guards suspected in the killing be arrested and stand trial. They have also demanded the immediate and complete reform of the justice system. The matter has superseded the ruling party's ability to contain it, and even if resolved transparently, it will likely change the face of Compaore's government.

## DOMESTIC POLICY

Unlike the majority of African nations today, and despite the large number of ethnic groups represented, Burkina Faso does not have any significant ethnic conflict. French colonial policy basically destroyed pre-colonial points of ethnic power. However, labor and student protests continue to be a major source of social unrest. The Compaoré government endures frequent criticism for repression of its opposition, including charges of torture. The country is blessed with a well-functioning civil service and relatively infrequent charges of corruption. Great labor migration has produced a population on the move, with young Burkinabè men often working outside of the country. This movement makes it difficult to form cohesive organizations, but it is also difficult for the state to wipe out opposition.

Burkina Faso is one of the world's poorest countries. Subsistence agriculture accounts for over 40% of the nation's GDP and employs around 85% of the labor force. Since most crops rely on natural rainfall for irrigation, GDP fluctuates with annual levels of rainfall. Burkina has sustained a chronic trade deficit although remittances from Burkinabè migrant laborers in neighboring countries and receipts of official development assistance from donors help to offset imbalances in the current payments account. In fact, the export of labor is Burkina's greatest revenue producer. The level of national debt increased dramatically during the late 1980s, with debt servicing now absorbing up to 25% of export earnings. In comparison with other developing nations, Burkina Faso's debt servicing burden is actually modest. However, the fragility of the economy and its dependence on subsistence agriculture greatly limits its ability to recover from any sudden economic downturn or bad harvest. Industry is limited to assembly and agro-processing plants.

## FOREIGN POLICY

When Compaoré took power in 1987, many West African states condemned the assassination of Sankara and the formation of the Popular Front. The following year, Compaoré conducted a series of diplomatic visits to neighboring countries in an attempt to normalize relations. Since then, Burkina Faso has established close ties with Cote d'Ivoire and Togo—two countries which had been hostile to the Sankara government. Compaoré has assumed active mediation and regional peacekeeping roles in Africa, helping to resolve internal conflict in Togo and assisting in negotiations between Tuareg rebels and the governments of Niger and Mali. He has sent troop contingents to Rwanda and to the military observer mission in the Central African Republic.

In June 1989, Burkina received the chairmanship of the Economic Community of West African States (ECOWAS), a regional group which includes all West African nations. Compaoré has also improved relations with France that had grown cool under Sankara's leadership. His rebuilding efforts were so successful that Burkina Faso was chosen to host the Franco-African summit in December 1996. Compaoré has managed to maintain links with Libya that had been forged under Sankara. In February 1998, he met with the presidents of Mali, Niger, Chad, Sudan, and Libya for the creation of a sub-regional cooperation group: the Sahara-Sahelian Community States Rally (RCES in French). The group is headquartered in Tripoli, and the first chairman is Muammar Qadhafi of Libya. In June 1998, after a good deal of politicking, Compaoré was elected chairman of the Organization of African Unity, giving him an international platform.

Relations with the US have been strained by Burkina's ties with Libya. In January 1989, the US recalled its ambassador after Compaoré denounced the American downing of two Libyan planes. Relations between the two countries were further strained when Burkina's assistance to Liberian rebel leader, Charles Taylor, became known. In 1997 and 1998, Compaoré moved to join the regional peacekeeping force of ECOMOG. This action helped to improve relations with the US.

Compaoré has traveled extensively to seek bilateral trade agreements and private investment with other nations in the developing world. Trade agreements have been signed with Malaysia. India has agreed to complete a rail line to the manganese ore deposits in the northeast section of the country.

In December 1998, Compaoré's human rights record came into question with the unsolved death of Norbert Zongo, editor-in-chief of an independent weekly newspaper and an outspoken critic of the government. Amnesty International and numerous international human rights organizations called on the government for an independent investigation and report. As of August 1999, no arrests had been made in the Zongo case.

## ADDRESS

Office of the President
03 B.P. 7030
Ouagadougou 03
Burkina Faso

## REFERENCES

AfricaNews. [Online] Available http://www.africanews.org/west/burkinafaso/ (Accessed June 2000).
*Africa Report*, September–October 1991.
*Africa South of the Sahara*. 27th edition. London: Europa Publications, Ltd., 1997.
*Agence France-Presse*, 13–18 November 1998.
*Encyclopedia of Africa South of the Sahara*. New York: Charles Scribner's Sons, 1997.
Englebert, Pierre. *Burkina Faso: Unsteady Statehood in West Africa*. Boulder, CO: Westview Press, 1996.
*The Hindu*, 12 November 1997.
*New Straits Times* (Malaysia), 24–27 April 1998.
PanAfrican News Agency. [Online] Available http://www.africanews.org/PANA/ (Accessed June 2000).

Rake, Alan. *Who's Who in Africa: Leaders for the 1990s.* Metuchen, NJ: Scarecrow Press, 1992.

*Star-Tribune Newspaper of the Twin Cities Minneapolis-St. Paul,* 12 November 1989.

UNICEF-EPP Statistics. [Online] Available http://www.unicef.org/statis/ (Accessed June 2000).

United Nations Humanitarian Information Unit, UN-IRIN-West Africa. [Online] Available http://www.reliefweb.int/emergenc (Accessed June 2000).

*Washington Post,* 17 March 1997.

**Profile researched and written by Kathryn Green, California State University, San Bernardino (3/99; updated 2/2000).**

# BURUNDI

## Pierre Buyoya
## President

*(pronounced "pee-AIR boo-YOH-yah")*

*"We have to bring back democracy, but how long it will take, we don't know; it could be 12 months, 18 months or more."*

The small, landlocked Republic of Burundi lies in the center of Africa, bordered by Rwanda to the north, Tanzania to the south and east, and Zaire to the northwest. Lake Tanganyika forms the southwestern border of the country. Bujumbura is the capital. With a population estimated at 5.7 million living on an area of only 27,834 sq km (10,747 sq mi), Burundi ranks among the most densely populated countries in Africa. The unit of currency is the Burundian *franc*. Burundi has three ethnic groups: the Hutu (85% of the population), the Tutsi (14%) and the Twa (1%). Burundi is heavily Christianized: 65% of the population belong to the Roman Catholic Church, and 14% are members of Protestant churches. Much of the population, including many Christians, continue to practice indigenous religions.

Burundi's per capita income has been estimated at $740. Agricultural production dominates the economy, with coffee and tea being the primary exports. There is little industry other than the processing of coffee, cotton, and tea; the extraction of vegetable oil; and small-scale wood mills.

## POLITICAL BACKGROUND

In contrast to most African countries, Burundi existed as a political unit prior to European colonial rule. Nevertheless, German and (after 1916) Belgian rule profoundly affected Burundi's political future by exacerbating ethnic divisions and concentrating power in the hands of the Tutsi minority. Burundi gained independence in 1962 as a constitutional monarchy under a Tutsi king. After political gains by the Hutu majority in 1965, Tutsi leaders moved to reassert their own power, leading to a bloodless coup in November 1966 that installed Tutsi army captain Michel Micombero as president.

Conditions for the Hutu deteriorated under President Micombero, as they were gradually excluded from the army and administration. In 1972 fears of a potential Hutu rebellion led to massacres in which approximately 150,000 mostly professional and intellectual Hutu perished. Ethnic relations continued to degenerate during the 11-year rule of Colonel Jean Baptiste Bagaza, who deposed Micombero in 1976.

Major Pierre Buyoya first came to power in a 1987 coup. Beginning in 1988 he initiated a program to ease ethnic tensions by bringing Hutu into the government. His reforms culminated in a multiparty presidential election in June 1993 in which Buyoya ran as the candidate for the Union for National Progress (UPRONA) and received 32% of the vote

compared to 64% for Melchior Ndadye, a Hutu from the Front for Democracy in Burundi (FRODEBU). Contrary to expectations, Buyoya agreed to step down and urged his supporters to accept the results of the vote.

After taking office in July 1993, Ndadye, the first Hutu leader of Burundi, attempted to appease opponents by appointing Tutsi from UPRONA to a number of important posts, including prime minister. Nevertheless, many Tutsi refused to accept his authority as president, and in October 1993 Ndadye was killed in a coup attempt. Although the coup ultimately failed to bring down the government, it initiated a period of ethnic conflict, violence, and instability that continues today. In the months that followed Ndadye's assassination, thousands of people were killed in ethnic clashes throughout the country. Ndadye's successor as president, Cyprien Ntaryamira, was himself killed several months later in a plane crash in Kigali, Rwanda, that also killed Rwandan president Junvenal Habyarimana. Ntaryamira's successor, Sylvestre Ntibantunganya, served from April 1994 until he was deposed by Buyoya in a July 1996 coup.

## PERSONAL BACKGROUND

Pierre Buyoya was born in Burundi in 1949. His background is nearly identical to two of his immediate predecessors in office. Like both Micombero and Bagaza, Buyoya came from Rutovu in Bururi province and was part of the historically low-status Hima subgroup of the Tutsi. He graduated from the Royal Military Academy in Brussels and received additional training in Germany before returning to Burundi to assume an army post. Although a high-ranking officer, Buyoya was little known outside of the military before his 1987 coup.

## RISE TO POWER

During the decade that President Bagaza held power, he earned a reputation as a hard-liner. He excluded Hutu from nearly all government and military posts and outlawed public discussion of ethnicity. His ethnic extremism, intolerance of dissent, and attacks on perceived threats to his rule (particularly the Catholic Church) made him increasingly unpopular. On 3 September 1987, while Bagaza was attending a summit of francophone states in Quebec, a group of military officers took power in a bloodless coup. The officers created a 31-member Military Committee of National Salvation to lead the country and named Major Buyoya as president of the Third Republic.

During his seven years as president, Buyoya oversaw a transition to democratic government and gained a reputation as a moderate. After losing the June 1993 elections, he voluntarily left office and insisted that his supporters back the new president. Buyoya subsequently withdrew from the national spotlight but remained influential in the military. The October 1993 coup attempt was apparently carried out by soldiers associated with Bagaza, and Buyoya's refusal to support them helped to ensure their failure.

Following Ndadye's assassination, ethnic clashes left more than 50,000 dead, but violence diminished after several weeks. The country remained relatively calm following Ntaryamira's death in April 1994, but under his successor, President Ntibantunganya, security conditions gradually deteriorated. By late 1994, both ethnic groups had formed civilian militias and had begun to terrorize Burundi's population. Militia attacks drove most Hutu out of the cities and most Tutsi out of the countryside, creating for the first time a geographic division between the two groups. The military, who remained overwhelmingly Tutsi, frequently supported the Tutsi militia, leading Ntibantunganya to declare in March 1995 that a genocide had begun against Burundi's Hutu.

Meanwhile, Ntibantunganya began to face increasing opposition from Hutu who felt he was too moderate. In mid-1994 former Interior Minister Leonard Nyangoma fled Burundi and from exile in Switzerland organized a faction called the National Coalition for the Defense of Democracy (CNDD). A military wing of the CNDD operating out of Zaire began to launch guerilla attacks on Tutsi communities in northern Burundi. In 1996 CNDD attacks on Tutsi gradually spread throughout the country, and the military responded with increasing repression against the Hutu population. With violence spreading and becoming more intense, rumors surfaced in mid-1996 of a potential military coup, possibly to be led by former President Bagaza. Buyoya, who was in the US preparing to teach at Yale, evidently planned his coup to preempt action by Bagaza's supporters. While in the US, he apparently gained promises of international support, based on his reputation as a moderate. He cut short his American sojourn, returned to Burundi, and announced that he had relieved Ntibantunganya of his duties and was taking power.

## LEADERSHIP

During his first term as president, Buyoya gained a reputation as a supporter of democracy and a moderate on ethnic issues. After taking power Buyoya initially seemed little different from his predecessors, showing no inclination to relinquish Tutsi political dominance. However, after clashes in northern Burundi in mid-1988 left several thousand dead, including many Tutsi, Buyoya launched an aggressive program to ease ethnic tensions, naming a Hutu prime minister and placing Hutu in other important government posts. In 1992 Buyoya supported the adoption of a bill of rights and a new constitution that legalized political party competition. He organized multiparty elections and gained international acclaim for peacefully handing over power after his June 1993 electoral loss.

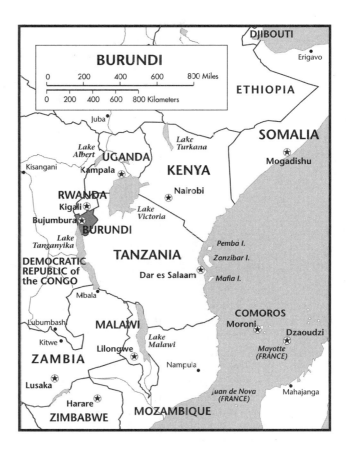

Buyoya's second coup, in July 1996, received a much less enthusiastic response. While some people were relieved that a relative moderate had taken power, Buyoya's support was limited among both Hutu and Tutsi. After taking power Buyoya defended his coup as due to declining security conditions, and promised to again ease ethnic tensions and bring peace to Burundi. He named a Hutu prime minister and Hutu to other cabinet posts and promised that no punitive action would be taken against ousted president Ntibantunganya and his supporters.

Nevertheless, few Hutu have supported Buyoya's return to power. They blame him for the failed democratic transition because as president, he brought no Hutu into the military—the real center of power in Burundi. The Tutsi-dominated military, in which Buyoya remained influential, figured in much of the violence that began in 1995 and showed little regard for President Ntibantunganya's authority. While Buyoya has blamed Hutu rebels for the instability in Burundi that necessitated his coup, most Hutu blame the military itself for creating instability. Some Hutu leaders have claimed that Buyoya intentionally set up Burundi's democracy for failure, so that he could play the role of peacemaker and return to office with international support.

Many Tutsi are also mistrustful of Buyoya. Tutsi leaders accuse Buyoya of betraying the national interest by transferring power to the Hutu in 1993. Tutsi leaders such as Charles Mukasi, head of UPRONA, have urged Buyoya to take a hard line against Hutu guerillas. Buyoya suggested in a letter to former President Julius Nyerere of Tanzania that he might be willing to meet with CNDD rebels, which prompted a group known as Youth Solidarity for the Defence of

Minority Rights (SOJEDEM) to accuse him of "high treason." Because SOJEDEM, UPRONA, and other groups pushed Tutsi civilians to take a more extreme position, Buyoya had to rely heavily on the military. But even within the military his support was limited since factions associated with Bagaza also supported a hard-line position. With the population of Burundi increasingly polarized, Buyoya's position was tenuous.

## DOMESTIC POLICY

Buyoya's primary domestic policy concern since regaining power has been establishing law and order in Burundi. He has attempted to accomplish this by appeasing the Hutu and by using force extensively. Immediately after the coup Buyoya suspended the constitution and dismissed the national assembly, then he appointed Hutu to his government. In September he lifted a ban on political parties and restored the national assembly. Members of FRODEBU refused to participate, however, as long as the constitution was suspended. Buyoya also announced a three-year transition back to democracy, designed to allow time to establish order and adopt a new constitution.

In the weeks following Buyoya's return to power, Bujumbura remained relatively calm, but in the countryside the military launched an operation to root out guerillas. Since the CNDD guerillas are based in Zaire, this operation was targeted primarily against Hutu civilians considered sympathetic to the rebels. According to Amnesty International and the UN, more than 10,000 civilians were killed in the first three months after the coup. Thousands of other Hutu civilians fled into Tanzania, Rwanda, and Zaire. Given this extensive use of military force, few Hutu were wooed by Buyoya's political overtures.

In 1998 Buyoya's regime reached a political agreement with the opposition-dominated National Assembly, which adopted a Transitional Constitutional Act and a transitional political platform. This agreement brought the predominantly ethnic Hutu opposition party FRODEBU into the Cabinet. Buyoya holds power in conjunction with a political power structure dominated by members of the Tutsi ethnic group, and political parties operate under significant restraints. The judiciary is controlled by the ethnic Tutsi and is not impartial.

In 1999, the government struggled to impose curfews and other regulations aimed at curbing attacks by rebels and warring ethnic factions. The efforts were largely unsuccessful, however, as the country continued to be ravaged by violent civil unrest. Thousands of refugees are homeless or living in makeshift camps while malnutrition and disease overwhelm them.

## FOREIGN POLICY

Buyoya's July 1996 coup received mixed international response. Although publicly condemning the coup, many Western governments have privately supported Buyoya's return to power, believing that as a moderate he can bring peace to Burundi. Burundi's neighbors, however, have taken a surprisingly strong position against the coup. Immediately following the seizure of power, an emergency meeting of leaders of east African states implemented an economic blockade against Burundi, which was widely enforced. According to the new prime minister, more than US$162 million were lost in the first three months of the blockade.

Buyoya's main foreign policy concern has been gaining support for his regime. While officially calling for a return to democracy, Western governments have become increasingly open about their support for Buyoya. In an October trip to Africa, the US secretary of state attempted to persuade the east African states to end the blockade, but their leaders subsequently reiterated their intention to isolate Burundi. Buyoya attempted to appeal to the leaders of the neighboring states by expressing a willingness to negotiate with the CNDD rebels, but the continuation of government-sponsored violence undercut his message of moderation. However, with conditions swiftly deteriorating in eastern Zaire and the possibility of international intervention, Buyoya's promise to restore order gained greater international support.

Finally in 1999, after three years of economic sanctions against Burundi, East African nations met and voted to lift the sanctions. As one of the world's most heavily indebted nations, Burundi also qualified for debt relief from the United States. The economy of Burundi continued to flounder, however, with income from coffee exports declining due to lower world demand and global oversupply, and ongoing civil unrest and violent conflict between Hutu and Tutsi factions undermining the development of enterprise and commerce.

Instability in neighboring Democratic Republic of the Congo has caused governments of nations in the region, including Burundi, Rwanda, and Uganda, to send troops to support Congolese Tutsi in their attempts to restore security to border regions.

## ADDRESS

Office of the President
Bujumbura
Burundi

## REFERENCES

Bigumandondera, Ferdinand. "Ninety Days After Buyoya's Putsch." *Panafrican News Agency*, 25 October 1996.
"Burundi Begins Sending Home Hutu Villagers as Talks Near." *New York Times*, 10 February 2000, pA19.
"Burundi: Murder and Manhunts." *The Economist (US)*, 23 October 1999, p. 50.
DesForges, Alison. "Failed Coup or Creeping Coup." *Current History*, May 1994.
Guichaoua, Andre. *Les crises politiques au Burundi et au Rwanda, 1993–1994*. Universite des Sciences et Technologies de Lille, 1995.
Lemarchand, Rene. *Burundi: Ethnocide as Discourse and Practice*. New York: Cambridge University Press, 1994.
Reyntjens, Filip. *L'Afrique des Grands Lacs en Crise: Rwanda, Burundi, 1988–94*. Editions Karthala, 1994.
*United Nations Chronicle*, various issues.

**Profile researched and written by Timothy Longman, Vassar College, Poughkeepsie, NY (12/96; updated 3/2000).**

# CAMBODIA

### Hun Sen
### Prime Minister
*(pronounced "HUN she-YEN")*

*"I must respond to the expectations of... the people,
who want to see a new government function better and be stronger
and more effective than before."*

Cambodia is one of the smallest nations in mainland Southeast Asia, occupying 181,035 sq km (69,898 sq mi). Its neighbors include Thailand on the west and north, Laos on the northeast, and Vietnam on the east. The Gulf of Thailand, to its southwest, provides Cambodia's only access to open waters. Its varied topography consists of a level central plain formed by the Mekong River basin and mountains in the country's southwest and southeast regions. The tropical climate brings 50 to 80 inches of rain annually in the lowlands and about twice as much in the mountain regions. About 75% of Cambodia's land is forested, and 16% is considered arable. The Mekong River flows southward from Laos through eastern Cambodia, and the Tonle Sap Lake serves as its natural flood reservoir.

Cambodians are a relatively homogeneous people, with the Khmer comprising 90% of its 11.6 million inhabitants. The remaining population consists of Vietnamese (5%) and Chinese (1%). The official language is Khmer, but French and local dialects are also spoken. The literacy rate is 74%, and life expectancy for males and females is 48.8 and 51.8 years, respectively. Theravada Buddhism, which has a long history in the region, is the major religion.

The Cambodian economy is based primarily on agriculture and forestry, which employs more than 80% of the population. Rice farming and milling, forestry, fishing, and rubber production represent major economic activities, with timber, rubber, fish, and precious stones serving as important sources of foreign exchange. With a per capita GDP of $700, Cambodia is one of the poorest countries in Southeast Asia and depends heavily on international aid. The national currency is the *riel*.

## POLITICAL BACKGROUND

Cambodia's long history dates to 200 BC with the formation of kingdoms known collectively as *Funan*. Khmer kingdoms first appeared in the 5th century AD, the most famous of which is Angkor (9th to 15th centuries). A Hindu-Buddhist kingdom, located in northwestern Cambodia, it is the site of the famous temple complex known as Angkor Wat. At its peak in the 12th century, the Khmer empire dominated much of present-day mainland Southeast Asia. Pressure from Thailand and Vietnam threatened the sovereignty of Cambodia in the 19th century, and King Ang Duong requested French protectorate status.

After 90 years of French colonial rule, Cambodia gained independence in 1953 under the leadership of Norodom Sihanouk. Since independence, Cambodia's history has been marked by civil war, foreign invasions, bloody revolution, and four types of political systems: a constitutional monarchy headed by Sihanouk (1953–70); a military-dominated republic led by General Lon Nol (1970–75); a communist regime led by Pol Pot (1975–79); and a socialist republic led by Hun Sen (1979–92).

The 1970–79 period was particularly brutal. Sihanouk was overthrown as head of state in a coup led by Lon Nol, paving the way for civil war. Simultaneously, Cambodia was dragged into the Vietnam War upon the invasion of American and South Vietnamese troops. It is estimated that American planes dropped 500,000 tons of bombs and destroyed countless villages and farms. When the Khmer Rouge emerged victorious in April 1975, the leadership of Pol Pot imposed a radical and murderous social revolution involving the systematic relocation, torture, and execution of educated Cambodians and urban residents. The capital of Phnom Penh became a ghost town as an estimated 2 million people (almost 25% of the total population) perished. Meanwhile, repeated border conflicts reached a climax in 1978 when Vietnam invaded Cambodia. In January 1979 Cambodia fell to the Vietnamese and Pol Pot's followers fled to the countryside to carry on their revolution.

From 1979 to 1992 the country was in a state of civil war with factions loyal to Pol Pot, the monarchy, and the Vietnam-installed regime. The Hun Sen period, however, is generally viewed as a significant improvement over the Lon Nol and Pol Pot regimes.

## PERSONAL BACKGROUND

Relatively little is known about Hun Sen. He was born on 4 April 1951 in the Stung Trang district of the Kompong Cham province. He was educated in Phnom Penh at Wat Tuk La'ak school prior to joining the Khmer Rouge in 1970. Hun Sen left Phnom Penh when a communist partner was arrested. He fled to eastern Cambodia, where he initially became a courier for a local communist leader. Hun Sen rose to the rank of commandant in Pol Pot's Khmer Rouge army by 1976 and received further military and ideological training. He is married and has six children.

## RISE TO POWER

Hun Sen broke with Pol Pot in 1977 and allied himself with Vietnamese forces. His political fortunes were greatly enhanced by the Vietnamese invasion of Cambodia. When

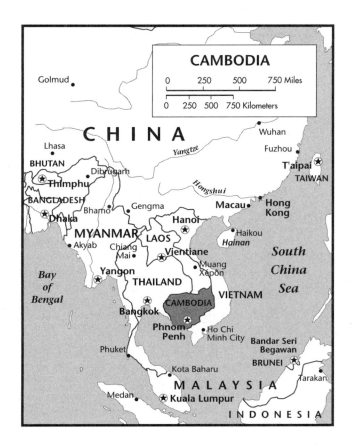

CAMBODIA

0    250    500    750 Miles

0  250  500  750 Kilometers

Vietnamese armies captured Phnom Penh in 1979, Hun Sen became part of a new government supported by Vietnam. Having developed cordial relations with the Vietnamese, he became one of the preferred choices for political leadership. In the new government established by the People's Revolutionary Council, he became minister of foreign affairs and vice premier in 1979. Hun Sen moved rapidly to the center of power in the following years by becoming a member of the Politburo of the Peoples Revolutionary Party (PRP) in 1981 and then chairman of the Council of Ministers of the PRP and premier in 1985.

In 1989, Vietnamese troops withdrew from Cambodia, setting the stage for national reconciliation. A peace agreement, drafted by five permanent members of the UN Security Council, was signed in October 1991, opening the way toward a comprehensive settlement involving the largest peacekeeping mission in UN history. The United Nations Transitional Authority in Cambodia (UNTAC) had a budget of $2.8 billion and a staff of 22,000 soldiers and civilians from more than 50 countries. UNTAC was responsible for preparing the country for democratic elections by supervising the government's departments of foreign affairs, information, finance, defense and public security, and for laying the legal and administrative framework for a democratic society.

Despite widespread violence orchestrated by the Khmer Rouge and Hun Sen's forces in the 1993 national elections, 90% of the Cambodian electorate voted. However, Pol Pot's Khmer Rouge boycotted the elections and maintained its guerilla campaign. The royalist FUNCINPEC Party, led by Sihanouk's eldest son, Ranariddh, received 45% of the vote and 58 of 120 National Assembly seats. The incumbent

Cambodian Peoples' Party (CPP), led by Hun Sen, received 38% and 51 seats. Questions about electoral irregularities threatened the peace agreement until Sihanouk persuaded both Ranariddh and Hun Sen to become co-prime ministers. On 21 September 1993, the National Assembly ratified a new constitution that resurrected the monarchy under King Norodom Sihanouk. With his new powers, Sihanouk appointed Prince Ranariddh as first co-prime minister and Hun Sen as second co-prime minister. An uneasy relationship between Hun Sen and Ranariddh followed.

## LEADERSHIP

As a communist nation, party and governmental positions are equally important in Cambodian politics. The 1993 constitution defined the political system as a multi-party democracy with separate legislative, executive, and judicial powers. In spite of this, Cambodia remained largely authoritarian, with power centered in personalities rather than institutions. While Ranariddh was able to wrap himself in the symbolism of royalty and tradition, Hun Sen had to appeal to populism. Considered to be a fiery orator, he conveyed an aura of competence. Most analysts considered him to be enthusiastic, intelligent, and sincere. He was also viewed as being a shrewd politician who understood the importance of political alliances and the practicalities of governing.

On 7 July 1997, Hun Sen staged a bloody coup, and Ranariddh was ousted from power. International criticism, including an Association of South East Asian Nations (ASEAN) decision to defer Cambodia's admission, led to strained foreign relations and a poor international image after the coup. Western nations suspended foreign aid and refused to recognize the Hun Sen government. International pressure forced Hun Sen to hold national elections on 27 July 1998 in order to legitimize his government.

Hun Sen's Cambodian People's Party won over half of the votes cast, securing 64 of 122 National Assembly seats. However, it lacked the two-thirds majority of parliamentary seats necessary to form a government. Hun Sen was forced to enter into negotiations with Ranariddh's royalist FUNCINPEC party, which had won the second-largest percentage of the vote. An agreement to form a coalition government was reached and approved by the National Assembly on 1 December 1998 after months of political uncertainty and civil strife. According to the terms of the agreement, Ranariddh is the Assembly president while Hun Sen is the sole premier and recognized ruler of Cambodia. The new coalition government gives Hun Sen an opportunity to restore foreign trust and redevelop a working relationship with Ranariddh.

## DOMESTIC POLICY

Hun Sen's coup had a chilling effect on the domestic scene and threatened the entire framework of the 1993 peace agreement. As a result of the July 1998 elections and the power-sharing agreement worked out in November, Hun Sen is now in a stronger position. However, his legitimacy remains significantly lower than it had been during his previous coalition government. Cambodian society is polarized as never before. Citizens have expressed their disapproval of Hun Sen by rioting and protesting after the 1998 elections. On the positive side, the last remaining leaders of the Khmer Rouge surrendered to the government in December 1998, ending 30 years of civil war.

The Cambodian economy has been severely damaged as foreign investment and aid ceased due to political uncertainty following the coup. For Hun Sen to succeed, he needs to stabilize the political situation and regain the trust of his coalition partners and the people. Once this is accomplished, foreign aid and investment will likely resume. An aggravating factor is the Asian economic crisis, which lowered demand for Cambodian primary products in neighboring countries. As a result, tax revenues decreased, and Cambodia experienced a severe budget deficit. A further aggravating factor is opposition leader Sam Rainsy, who, citing corruption, asked international lenders in March 1999 to refuse aid to the Cambodian government.

Also in 1999, the need to hold the surviving Khmer Rouge leaders accountable for the 1975–79 genocide, in which an estimated two million Cambodians died, dominated the news. As the whole Khmer Rouge top echelon, minus Pol Pot who died in 1998, was taken into custody in 1999, international pressure increased for their trial and punishment. The United Nations called for an international genocide tribunal, with the support of four members of the Security Council. The fifth, China, supported Hun Sen's wishes for a Cambodian trial. Hun Sen was willing to compromise to the extent of allowing foreign judges and prosecutors to participate and to give assurances that the trial would not be delayed. This did not allay suspicions that local courts would hold mere show trials shadowed by the threat of renewed warfare with remaining Khmer Rouge troops. At peace for the first time since the early 1970s, Cambodia's government pledged reductions in the size of its military and police, cutting military spending and corruption. Thousands of "phantom soldiers" who existed only on paper were to be cut from army payrolls.

## FOREIGN POLICY

Historically, Cambodia has aligned itself with the Soviet bloc, maintaining close ties with its neighbor, Vietnam. After the 1993 elections, closer ties with the US and ASEAN countries were gradually established. In 1995 and 1996, both the US and Japan promised increased foreign aid and investment. Hun Sen's 1997 coup deferred Cambodia's admission into ASEAN and led to the termination of Western aid and investment.

Following the formation of the coalition government in 1998, Hun Sen sought to repair the damage. Japan and the European Union (EU) announced the resumption of economic links with Cambodia. He continued to appeal to other countries for the reinstatement of foreign economic investment and aid. As evidence of cooperation was vital for Cambodia's chances of gaining membership in ASEAN and

achieving its long-term economic and security goals, Hun Sen reassured member states that he planned on working with FUNCINPEC and Ranariddh to promote domestic stability at an ASEAN meeting in December 1998. In May 1999 Cambodia was finally accepted as the tenth member of ASEAN, earning the country new respectability and the opportunity to participate in regional policy conferences.

Relations with Taiwan and Vietnam have demanded much of Hun Sen's attention. When the Cambodian government agreed to import hazardous waste and garbage from Taiwan, the decision led to a series of riots in Sihanoukville. Hun Sen's environmental minister requested that Taiwan take back the 3,000 tons of toxic waste deposited in the port city. Controversy over the clean-up continued into 1999. Finally, in March 1999, the responsible party (Formosa Plastics) pledged to remove the toxic wastes. Human rights activists who had been arrested for protesting the toxic dumping were released, and the government banned future import of toxic waste.

Finally, during a June 1999 visit by Vietnamese Communist Party officials, Vietnam and Cambodia agreed to end border disputes.

## ADDRESS

Office of the Prime Minister

Phnom Penh, Cambodia

## REFERENCES

*The Age (Australia)*, various issues, 1998.

Albin, David and Marlowe Hood. *The Cambodian Agony.* M.E. Sharpe, Inc., 1987.

*Cambodia in Review.* Royal Embassy of Cambodia to the US, November 1998.

Cambodian Online. [Online] Available http:// www.cambodian-online.com (Accessed November 1999).

*Far Eastern Economic Review*, 30 July 1998, 13 August 1998.

"Helping the Other Guys (International Donors Try to Change Cambodia's Politics)." *The Economist (US)*, 27 February, 1999, vol. 350, no., 8108, p.39.

Martin, Marie Alexandrine. *Cambodia: The Shattered Society.* University of California Press, 1994.

Mydans, Seth. "Cambodia: UN Rejected." *New York Times,* 11 February 2000, pA6.

*South China Morning Post*, 23 October 1998, 13 November 1998.

*Sydney Morning Herald*, 14 November 1998.

Wain, Barry. "Cambodian Leader Holds Grip on Power After Years of War and Bloody Coup." *Wall Street Journal*, 9 July 1999, p. A12.

*Washington Post*, 5 December 1998.

**Profile researched and written by Robert W. Compton, Jr., Western Kentucky University (3/99; updated 2/2000).**

# CAMEROON

## Paul Biya
## President
*(pronounced "BEE-yah")*

*"We are determined to stick with democracy. We know that our democracy is not perfect, but we are doing everything to improve it."*

The Republic of Cameroon, located in Central Africa, has an area of 475,442 sq km (183,569 sq mi). It lies on the gulf of Guinea and is bordered by Equatorial Guinea, Gabon, the Congo, the Central African Republic, Chad, and Nigeria. The physical geography of Cameroon is quite diverse, ranging from dense rainforest in the south to thorn steppe in the north.

Cameroon has a population of 15.5 million inhabitants. The country is experiencing rapid growth, averaging 3% a year. Approximately two-thirds of the people live in rural areas. The main ethnic groups are semi-Bantu Highlanders, Northwestern Bantu, and Sudanic Northerners. The largest cities are Yaounde, the capital, and Douala, the economic and industrial center. Official languages are French and English.

The national currency is the CFA *franc*. The per capita GDP is US$2,000. Major exports include coffee, cocoa, and cotton. Principal trading partners are France, the US, Germany, Belgium, and Guinea.

## POLITICAL BACKGROUND
The former German protectorate of Kamerun came under the administration of France and Britain in 1916. The French-controlled area (about 80% of today's Cameroon) gained its independence in 1960, with Ahmadou Ahidjo as its president. After a 1961 referendum, the British section was divided between Nigeria and the former French Cameroon. Federalism was replaced by a unitary state in 1972.

Since independence, Cameroon has had a highly centralized, autocratic political system with a strong Executive, a judiciary under the control of the Executive, and a National Assembly dominated by the ruling party. Until 1990, Cameroon had a single-party, the Cameroon National Union (CNU), later renamed the Cameroon People's Democratic Movement (CPDM/RDPC).

As democratization swept over Africa in the 1990s, President Paul Biya's authoritarianism began to buckle. In 1990, multiple parties were allowed, but Biya was widely accused of stealing the 1992 elections from SDF candidate, John Fru Ndi. Biya agreed in May 1993 to hold the Great National Constitutional Debate. In 1994, 16 opposition parties formed a loose alliance, dominated by John Fru Ndi's Social Democrats to work for constitutional and electoral reform. In December 1995, the National Assembly adopted a number of amendments, which were promulgated in 1996. They included a reformed judiciary, a 100-member Senate (one-third of its members appointed), regional councils, and

extending the presidential term to seven years, renewable once. Municipal elections were also held in 1996 in which the opposition emerged victorious in nearly every city. In May 1997, legislative elections were condemned by the opposition and international observers as fraudulent, leading to the opposition's boycott of the presidential elections later that October. As of March 1998, the government had not established the Senate, regional councils, nor had it met the opposition's demands for an independent electoral commission.

## PERSONAL BACKGROUND
Paul Biya was born on 13 February 1933 in Mvomeko, Sangmelima District, Southern Cameroon. His family belonged to the Boulou minority ethnic group. Biya received his early education at a Catholic mission school. He gained admission to Edea and Akono Junion Seminaries at the age of 14 to be trained for the priesthood. After seven years of study, he went to the *Lycee General Leclerc* to obtain a secondary school certificate in philosophy. This allowed him to pursue university studies in France, where he specialized in law and political science. Biya has been married twice. His first wife died in 1992. He remarried in 1994 and has three children.

## RISE TO POWER
Biya's political career was directly linked with that of former President Ahmadou Ahidjo. In 1962 he served the Ahidjo government as delegate in charge of foreign missions. Five years later he was named director of the president's civil cabinet and secretary general. Promotions continued until 1975 when Biya was named prime minister, making him Ahidjo's legal successor.

Ahidjo's resignation as head of state in 1982, for reasons of ill health, stunned the entire country. It was initially thought that Ahidjo intended to remain firmly in control as party chief with Biya acting as his puppet. However, in 1983 Biya reshuffled the cabinet and removed several longtime Ahidjo associates. The same year he announced the discovery of a coup plot and formally implicated Ahidjo, who resigned his post as party chief and retired to France. The following month, Biya was elected president of the CNU and in 1984 was elected president of the Republic.

The new government was soon challenged by another coup attempt. Ahidjo, who lived in exile in France, was again accused of being behind the plot. Biya tightened security, purges followed, and 46 of the plotters were executed. A

1985 party congress gave Biya firm control over the party and government.

## LEADERSHIP

After 18 years in power, Biya's record of accomplishments is thin. According to local press reports, he averages more than 100 days off per year, mostly outside the country at his luxurious estates in Europe. He is reported not to have convened his government even once in 1995 and rarely met with ministers. In 1997, analysts noted that he avoided the office, leading to speculation that his government was adrift and in disarray.

For most of his rule, he has presided over economic decline and unprecedented corruption. Critics talk about a 30% rule, meaning that nothing goes through the Finance Ministry without a 30% fee. However, after topping Transparency International's list of most corrupt countries for the past two years, Biya is eager to clean up his government's act, has dismissed government ministers accused of corrupt practices, and announced an anti-corrution campaign in his New Year 2000 address.

Biya risks leaving a legacy of subverting political reforms. Although he caved in to demands for multi-party democracy in 1990, he manipulated voter registration, vote counting, and other phases of the electoral process in national-level elections. In spite of a law authorizing private media, he has not promulgated it and has kept a tight grip on the broadcast media. His government has cracked down harshly on dissidents, particularly those from the Anglophone provinces. Amnesty International has reported that human rights abuses were common during the 1990s. In April 2000, about 100 alleged secessionists in Kumba, a major town in English-speaking southeastern Cameroon, were detained by police for sabotage.

Biya has an opportunity to demonstrate leadership on the issue of national unity. The Anglophone secession movement continues unabated, with some members calling for greater autonomy through a federal structure. The Southern Cameroon National Council has submitted application to the UN for membership as the Republic of Southern Cameroon and has attempted to invalidate the 1961 plebiscite.

## DOMESTIC POLICY

Biya faces severe domestic constraints, exacerbated by the political chaos following the 1997 elections. There are continuing reports of human rights violations. The government, however, has managed a coalition bridging the north–south divide, and with divisions rife in the opposition, the government had ample opportunity to assert a domestic policy in April 2000.

Despite having presided over nearly a decade of economic disarray, Biya's policies may have turned a corner in 1999. Prospects for economic growth in 1999 were good based on a recovery in oil prices and other export commodities, and further progress in economic reforms. An increase in real GDP was expected from 4.4% in 1998–99 to 4.9% in 1999–2000. The CFA *franc* was expected to remain weak, further benefiting exports. In addition, the three-year enhanced structural adjustment facility (ESAF) approved by the IMF in August 1997 was considered successful and would likely pave the way for the next three-year ESAF to 2003. The Paris Club

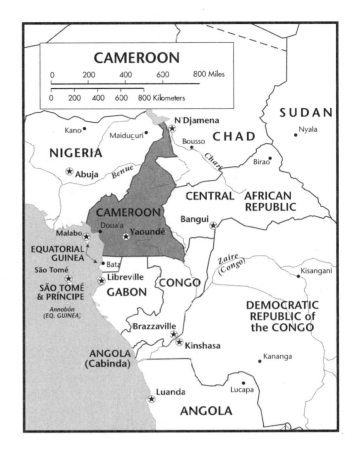

and non-Paris Club donors therefore were likely to reschedule debt, and Cameroon might become eligible for Bretton Woods assistance to the heavily indebted poor countries (HIPC).

While there were other bright spots in 2000 having to do with privatization and investment, the proposed construction of a 1,050-km (652-mi) buried pipeline to the port of Kribi on the Atlantic coast was cast into doubt as Royal Dutch Shell and Elf Aquitaine considered pulling out of the project. Exxon and the World Bank remained committed to it. If the deal goes through, the access fees alone from the pipeline would bring millions of dollars each year to the Cameroon treasury.

## FOREIGN POLICY

In 1995 Cameroon became a member of the British Commonwealth. Its application was widely seen as an attempt by the government to lessen the Anglophone criticism of Francophone domination. It remains to be seen if there will be any practical impact for the Republic from this membership.

In 1996–97 Biya served as chairman of the Organization of African Unity, stepping down in June 1997. Though this position gave him an international stage, negative reports of his domestic policies lessened the impact that the office could have provided.

A dispute with Nigeria over the Bakassi peninsula has lasted several years. Cameroon has detained more than 120 Nigerian prisoners of war and civilians since the cessation of hostilities in early 1996. The Biya government has been unable to obtain information on its missing soldiers. The dispute was submitted to the International Court of Justice in 1994. In 1999, the International Court of Justice (ICJ) in the Hague declared inadmissible Nigeria's request for an interpretation of the 11 June 1998 judgement concerning the Land and Maritime Boundary between Cameron and Nigeria. Both countries have pledged to resolve their differences peacefully, and Equatorial Guinea has offered to moderate the dispute.

A further irritant is provided by armed insurrection groups within neighboring Chad. Fighting has spilled over into the north of the Republic. At the end of November 1997, a Chadian opposition party called on Biya to refuse extradition of three Chadian rebels. With its own poor record on human rights and internal dissent, the extradition request places the government in an uncomfortable position. The granting of temporary asylum to Congolese refugees has also caused some problems within the country near the border with CAR.

Amnesty International is an outspoken critic of the Biya regime. It has issued several critical reports alleging a blatant disregard for human rights—citing arrests, beatings, torture, and continuing detention of opposition supporters to justify their claim.

## ADDRESS

Palais de l'Unite

1000 Yaounde

Republic of Cameroon

## REFERENCES

*Africa Confidential*, various issues.

Africa News Online. [Online] Available http://www.africanews.org/central/cameroon/stories (Accessed May 2000).

*Africa South of the Sahara*. London: Europa Publications Ltd., 1999.

*Africa Update*, Fall 1996.

Africaonline. [Online] Available http://www.africa-online.com (Accessed May 2000).

*Cameroon Acualite*, various issues.

*Cameroon Tribune*, various issues.

Economist Intelligence Unit, Ltd. *EIU Country Reports*. 5 February 2000.

Integrated Regional Information Network (IRIN). [Online] Available http://www.reliefweb.int/IRIN (Accessed May 2000).

IPS News Service. 6 November 1997.

*La Nouvelle Expression*, various issues.

Le Messager Journal d'Information et de Debat. [Online] Available http://www.cybernum.com/messager/ (Accessed Fall 1997).

*New York Times*, 14 October 1997.

Presidence de la Republique du Cameroon homepage. [Online] Available http://www.camnet.cm/celcom/homepr.htm (Accessed May 2000).

United Nations Department of Humanitarian Affairs Integrated Regional Information Network for West Africa. [Online] Available http://www.reliefweb.int/emergenc (Accessed May 2000).

U.S. Department of State. *Background Notes: Cameroon*.

*Washington Post*, 25 October 1997.

**Profile researched and written by Kathryn L. Green, California State University, San Bernardino (3/98; updated by Robert J. Groelsema 5/2000).**

# CANADA

### Jean Chrétien
### Prime Minister
*(pronounced "ZHAN KRIH-tyehn")*

*"I will try to bring us together by appealing not to what divides us, but what unites us."*

Canada, which occupies the northern part of North America, is a vast but sparsely populated country. Canada's land area is 9,203,210 sq km (3,553,363 sq mi), and its population is 31,000,000. Most Canadians live in the country's southern region, within 161 km (100 mi) of the US border. Reflecting its colonial heritage, the official languages are English and French. The largest religious denominations are Roman Catholicism (46%) and Protestantism, the latter represented mostly by the United Church of Canada (16%) and the Anglican Church of Canada (10%). The unit of currency is the Canadian dollar. The country's major trading partners are the US, Japan, the European Community, South Korea, Taiwan, and Mexico. Its major exports are machinery, wood products, automobiles, chemicals, oil, and agricultural products.

## POLITICAL BACKGROUND

Canada was a former colony of Great Britain. Unlike other nations, it did not achieve independence by means of revolution. Instead the process was a gradual one, culminating in the British North America Act in which the British parliament awarded self-rule in 1867. Its last formal legislative link with the UK was not severed until 1982, and Canada remains a member of the Commonwealth of Nations. As such, the head of state is Queen Elizabeth II of England. She is represented by the governor-general, a post currently held by Romeo A. LeBlanc. However, the roles of the Queen and governor-general are largely ceremonial.

Real political power lies with the prime minister and the parliament. The parliament consists of a Senate of 104 members appointed for life and a House of Commons of 301 members elected from single-member constituencies for maximum terms of five years. The House of Commons is the stronger of the two bodies and carries out the day-to-day governance of the country. The majority party in the House of Commons forms a government, and its leader becomes the prime minister. Currently the Liberal Party, led by Jean Chretien, holds a small majority in parliament with 155 seats. The official opposition is the Reform Party, led by Preston Manning. Other major parties include the Bloc Quebecois (BQ), the Progressive Conservatives, and the New Democratic Party (NDP).

Canada has a well-developed federal system in which power is shared between the national and provincial governments. Each of the country's 10 provinces has a lieutenant governor and a legislature, from which a premier is chosen.

The provinces enjoy a large measure of autonomy and are responsible for matters including education, municipal affairs, direct taxation, and civil law. This autonomy is especially important to Canada's largest province, Quebec, which was originally settled by the French, and is the only province with a French-speaking majority. National unity has always been a particular challenge in Canada because of the desire for separatism on the part of many in Quebec.

## PERSONAL BACKGROUND

Jean Chrétien was born in rural Shawinigan, Quebec, on 11 January 1934, the 18th of 19 children. His father was a machinist, who was deeply committed to the Liberal Party and acted as an organizer in local politics. Young Jean inherited his father's love of politics and by the age of 12 was working for the Liberal Party. After attending schools in Shawinigan, Jollette, and Trois-Rivieres, Chrétien entered Laval University to study law. Admitted to the bar in 1958, Chrétien joined a law firm in Shawinigan and served as director of the bar of Trois-Rivieres in 1962-63. He was first elected to the House of Commons in 1963, representing the constituency of St. Maurice-Lafleche. Jean Chrétien married Aline Chaine in 1957. They have three grown children.

## RISE TO POWER

Chrétien's rise to the top of Canadian politics was long in coming. Throughout his career he has held most of the top cabinet positions in Canada's government. In July 1965, after being reelected to the House of Commons, Chrétien was appointed parliamentary secretary of Prime Minister Lester B. Pearson. Over the next decade-and-a-half, he served in a variety of ministerial posts, including national revenue, Indian affairs and northern development, treasury, industry, trade and commerce, finance, justice, constitutional negotiations, and energy and resources. Thus, before becoming prime minister, he had gained experience in virtually every facet of Canadian government.

On 16 June 1984, Chrétien unsuccessfully ran for the leadership of the Liberal Party against John Turner. After the election, Turner appointed him to serve as deputy prime minister and secretary of state for external affairs. Unfortunately, Turner's government was short lived. In September 1984 the Liberals were swept from power by the Conservative Party, led by Brian Mulroney. The Conservatives won 211 seats in the House of Commons, the largest majority ever in Canadian politics. There were angry recriminations after

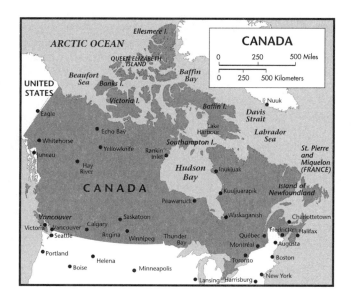

to do so for another 18 months, but he determined that it was best to go to the polls while the Liberals remained popular. However, instead of bolstering his parliamentary strength, Chrétien barely managed to hang on to a majority, as his 58-seat majority was reduced to 4. Chrétien was blamed for running a lackluster campaign and letting the agenda and tone be set by Reform leader, Preston Manning. Moreover, the regional fragmentation that was evidenced in 1993 became even greater in 1997. Not only did Reform and BQ draw from a regional base, so too did the Conservatives, who won all their seats in the East, and the Liberals, who won 101 of their 155 seats from Ontario alone.

It is now up to Chrétien to enforce discipline in his party in order to ensure passage of the Liberal agenda. In early 2000, he faced an attempt to challenge his leadership by finance minister, Paul Martin, author of the deficit reduction plan and quite popular in the party. However, as one supporter of the prime minister said, Chrétien is at his best when others underestimate him. Chrétien stood firm, announcing his plan to run for a third term.

## DOMESTIC POLICY
When Chrétien came into office he inherited an array of economic difficulties which had cost the Conservatives the 1993 election. Facing slow growth, high unemployment, and an out-of-control budget deficit, Chrétien sought to revive the economy by bringing social spending under control. Under a program of strict austerity measures, his government managed to bring the budget deficit close to zero, keep inflation in check, and spur economic growth. However, the unemployment rate barely fell, remaining at 9.5% by the time Chrétien called the 1997 election. Because of his poor showing in so many provinces, Chrétien promised to change his focus. Responding to Conservative voters along the East Coast, who have felt the effects of cuts in social programs but have not benefited from economic growth, he promised to spend more money for job creation and social programs.

By far the biggest problem that Chrétien has had to face during his tenure has been the increasing regional fragmentation that threatens to split the country in two. At issue is the province of Quebec, whose secessionist Bloc Quebecois was the official opposition party until mid-1997. Outnumbered more than two to one by English speakers, Francophone Quebeckers have long sought constitutional recognition as a "distinct society" within the Canadian federation. Amidst complaints of being treated as second-class citizens, Quebec has twice since 1980 held a referendum to decide on the question of leaving Canada and becoming an independent country. In 1995 the province came within a small margin of voting for secession, as the federalists (those who support unity) won with only 50.6% of the vote. Chrétien, from Quebec but adamantly opposed to a split, only began to vigorously campaign against secession when it appeared that the federalists might lose. In the end, it was the Anglophone vote which tipped the balance. Lucien Bouchard, who led the secessionist movement and is currently premier of Quebec, has vowed to continue the fight for an independent Quebec, promising another referendum in the years to come. However, Chrétien has moved to thwart a renewed fight by working to provide the constitutional recognition that Quebec has sought.

this crushing defeat, with Turner accusing Chrétien of not fully supporting him in the election. Exasperated, Chrétien resigned from the Conservative-dominated House of Commons in February 1986 and returned to the practice of law. However, Chrétien was still powerfully attracted to politics, and polls indicated that he remained one of the most popular politicians in Canada. Thus, when John Turner announced his resignation as Liberal Party leader in May 1989, Chrétien declared his candidacy. On 23 June 1990, Chrétien was elected leader of the Liberal Party. In December 1990, he was elected to Parliament and sworn in as leader of the opposition on 21 December.

Brian Mulroney resigned as prime minister in June 1993, his popularity at an all-time low. His position had become untenable because of the deteriorating economy, which was suffering under the burdens of low growth, high unemployment, and massive deficits. Mulroney was replaced by Kim Campbell, whose survival depended upon her ability to convince Canadians that her party had a viable strategy for economic renewal. As elections had to be held by November, according to the constitution, Campbell was left with little time to develop and implement her own policies. In the October elections, the Conservatives were rejected outright. Campbell lost her own seat, and the party retained only two of the 153 seats it held. Chrétien's Liberal Party won 178 seats, guaranteeing it a comfortable majority. On 4 November 1993, Jean Chrétien was sworn in as prime minister, 30 years after he first entered parliament.

## LEADERSHIP
The result of the 1993 election left Chrétien as the leader of the only party with a national following, as all other major parties were either regionally based or held too few seats to remain influential. This situation gave him a great deal of latitude to cut social spending and attack fiscal problems, such as cutting the budget deficit and reforming social security. Chrétien's success in these efforts, and the economic expansion which accompanied them, prompted him to call early elections in the hopes of solidifying his majority to enact further reforms. Chrétien took a large gamble when he called for a vote in June 1997. Constitutionally, he was not required

The consequence of this longstanding conflict has been a backlash, especially in the Western provinces, resulting in the success of the Reform Party. Drawing the bulk of its support from British Columbia and Alberta, Reform politicians have expressed resentment toward Quebec, questioning its demands for special treatment. Led by Preston Manning, the Reform Party has said it would be willing to let Quebec go rather than give it special recognition and preferences. With Reform now the official opposition in parliament, there is concern that Manning will galvanize nationalist sentiment in Quebec, further exacerbating what has been called the "balkanization" of Canada.

In addition to the difficulties of regional fragmentation, Chrétien has also had to address the grievances of Canada's Native American population. In the face of increasing economic expansion, many tribes have protested that they are being disregarded, and several have turned to militant tactics to make their grievances known. Adopting a more traditional conception of land ownership and usage, many groups are questioning the idea that "Canadian" is their only identity. In 1999, the governmnet established a new territory, known as Nunavut, whose population of 25,000 is 85% Inuit.

## FOREIGN POLICY

Canada is a member of the UN, NATO, and the OECD. Chrétien has played an increasingly active role in global politics. His government has supported the expansion of the NATO alliance, favoring the admission for former Cold War enemies Poland, Hungary, and the Czech Republic. He has also given Canada a high profile role in UN peacekeeping efforts, sending troops to more countries than any of its allies.

Chrétien describes Canada's relationship with the United States as his country's most important foreign tie, and has appointed his nephew as ambassador to the US. Chrétien claims to have much in common with US President Bill Clinton, and the two maintain a strong and friendly association. Still, Chrétien has kept a safe distance form his southern neighbor. He is careful to avoid the appearance of being too pro-American and not sufficiently protective of Canadians' national interests.

Generally, there is a friendly atmosphere of cooperation across the border. This is most evident with respect to NAFTA, the North American Free Trade Agreement. This agreement is designed to eliminate all trade barriers between Canada, the US, and Mexico. It was approved by all three countries in 1993 and is being slowly implemented over the next several years. In addition to removing trade barriers, it also allows for disputes to be addressed by resolution panels. This process keeps most conflicts contained and prevents them from becoming openly political. Still, critics of NAFTA contend that Canada is being dwarfed economically by the US and that the political fragmentation of the country is a result of its deeper economic ties to the US.

While Canada and the US generally enjoy friendly relations, there remain points of friction between them. Chrétien has clashed with the US over fishing rights in Pacific waters off the Canadian coast. He has also been an outspoken critic of American policy toward Cuba. The US has, since 1996, sought to punish companies from around the world that do business in Cuba. Several Canadian business-people have had their visas to enter the US revoked. Several firms may eventually be the target of lawsuits in US courts, their assets in the US threatened with seizure. Though President Clinton has put an indefinite ban on any lawsuits, Chrétien has threatened retaliation against American firms operating in Canada if Canadian firms are ever sued.

## ADDRESS

Office of the Prime Minister
Langevin Block
Parliament Buildings
Ottawa, Ontario K1A 0A2
CANADA

## REFERENCES

*Agence France Presse,* 3–10 June 1997.
Brooke, James. "Chretien Dismisses Fears of Rightward Trend." *New York Times,* 20 March 2000, p. A6.
———. "Canada: Chretien Defiant." *New York Times,* 15 March 2000 p. A6

**Profile researched and written by Mary Sugar (4/2000).**

# CAPE VERDE

### Antonio Mascarenhas Monteiro
### President

*(pronounced "mas-ca-RAIN-yas mon-TAIR-oh")*

*"The people elected me because I was the candidate that represented democracy and this is the important factor that made the difference."*

Cape Verde is a nation made up of 10 islands and five islets. The archipelago nation is situated in the Atlantic Ocean approximately 500 km (311 mi) west of Dakar, Senegal. Sao Tiago (Santiago) is the largest island at 922 sq km (356 sq mi); it is also the location of the capital, Cidade de Praia. Mindelo on the island of Sao Vicente, is the other main population center and the major port of the country. The total population is approximately 406,000, with a density of 84.7 people per sq km. Cape Verde has a high birth rate with an average of 6.12 children per family. Government efforts to curb population growth through family planning programs and legalization of abortion have not met with much success. Significant migration off the islands eases what would otherwise be an even greater burden. It is estimated that well over twice as many Cape Verdeans live outside the country (primarily in the US, the Netherlands, Italy, and Portugal) as in the islands. The remittances sent home by these overseas Cape Verdeans are a significant source of income for the island population. Except for Sao Tiago, where the majority of the population is of African descent, most of the Cape Verdean people are of mixed African and European descent. The official language is Portuguese, but the vernacular is Crioulo, a mix of Portuguese with African vocabulary and syntax. Despite a concerted educational effort, illiteracy for those over 15 years of age averages 28.4%. Life expectancy is 63.5 years for males and 71.2 years for females. Approximately 96% of the population is Roman Catholic.

The islands are of volcanic formation and many are rugged, rocky, and deeply eroded. They are also very dry and experience periodic droughts of some severity. Sao Vicente has almost no potable water and relies on a desalination plant for the city of Mindelo. Due to poor soil, erosion, and frequent drought conditions, Cape Verde relies on international relief for most of its food supply and receives the second-highest level of aid per capita in the world. Eighty percent of this aid comes in the form of straight grants. Cape Verde continues to receive such substantial international support because the government has shown itself to be concerned with keeping its debt-servicing costs as low as possible. This international confidence has allowed the government to keep a high degree of control over the distribution of aid and thus has been able to direct its resources to projects in keeping with its national development plans. Cape Verde's chief exports are bananas, tuna, and lobsters. Its principal trading partners are Portugal, the Netherlands, Spain, Brazil, and the US. The unit of currency is the *escudo*.

## POLITICAL BACKGROUND
The Cape Verde islands experienced the longest period of European colonization of any African nation. The Portuguese remained in direct control of this island archipelago from 1460 to 1975. In their struggle for independence from Portugal, beginning in the 1950s, the people of Cape Verde linked their fortunes to that of Guinea Bissau on the West African mainland under a unified movement, the PAIGC (African Party for the Independence of Guinea-Bissau and Cape Verde), formed in 1956. This movement was headed by Amilcar Cabral, whose father was Cape Verdean and whose mother was Guinean. Due to Cabral's influence on other independence movements in the region, Cape Verde and Guinea-Bissau hold an important position in African nationalist history. The armed struggle against the Portuguese lasted from 1963 until 1974 when a negotiated peace settlement was arranged. While achieving independence for themselves, the Portuguese African resistance movements, including those of Angola and Mozambique, had succeeded in bringing down the fascist Portuguese government in Lisbon. Elections were held in June 1975, and the Republic of Cape Verde was declared formally independent from Portugal on 5 July.

Amilcar Cabral was assassinated in 1973 in a Portuguese-backed coup attempt. The secretary general of the PAIGC, Aristides Pereira, became president following the 1975 elections. For the first few years of independence, Guinea-Bissau and Cape Verde attempted to pursue a formal union. In 1980 Cape Verde was officially declared a single-party state under the PAIGC, with all other political parties banned. However, that same year the president of Guinea-Bissau, Luiz Cabral (brother of Amilcar Cabral and considered a Cape Verdean through his father) was removed from office in a coup. The Cape Verdeans responded by separating from the PAIGC and forming in 1981 a separate party, the PAICV (African Party for the Independence of Cape Verde).

For the next 10 years Aristides Pereira ruled over Cape Verde but also oversaw the transition to a true multi-party democracy. In the mid-1980s non-PAICV members became increasingly and openly involved in public life, including election to the national assembly. The Pereira regime also began the process of privatization that has been increased in recent years.

The government consists of a president elected for five-year terms under direct universal suffrage. The National Assembly, a unicameral legislature, contains 72 members elected for five-year terms by proportional representation.

The prime minister is elected by the National Assembly and officially appointed by the president. The prime minister appoints the council of ministers from members of the Assembly.

## PERSONAL BACKGROUND

Antonio Mascarenhas Monteiro was born 16 February 1944 on the island of Sao Tiago to Manuel Gomes Monteiro and Ernestina Varela dos Reis Mascarenhas Monteiro. After completing primary and secondary school education in Cape Verde he proceeded with legal studies in Portugal at the Universities of Lisbon and Coimbra. From 1974 to 1977 he was an assistant at the Catholic University of Louvain in Belgium in legal studies and held a research position at the Inter-University Center for Public Law in Louvain.

President Mascarenhas is married to Maria Antonina Bettencourt Pinto with whom he has two daughters and one son.

## RISE TO POWER

Mascarenhas joined the PAIGC in 1969 but broke away from it in 1971 and continued to pursue an interest in law, African constitutional development, and human rights. Returning from his legal studies in Belgium in 1977, he was appointed secretary general of the National Assembly (ANP—Assembleia Nacional Popular), which position he held until 1980 when he became president of the ANP by appointment of the Supreme Court. He served in this capacity for 10 years. In this judicial position he obtained significant international experience and exposure, participating in international judicial meetings on human rights and the Organization of African Unity. Mascarenhas moved fully into the political arena in 1990 when he declared his candidacy for president, unaffiliated with any political party. Under the Cape Verdean constitution, a presidential candidate cannot be a member of a political party.

In the same year, the Movimento para Democracia (MPD) issued a manifesto calling for a multi-party system, and President Pereira followed with the announcement that the next presidential elections would be held on the basis of universal adult suffrage. The MPD called for political plurality under its coordinator, Carlos Veiga. In September 1990 Cape Verde officially became a multi-party state, with the stipulation that political parties should not be formed on the basis of religious affiliation or geographical region. The MPD was registered as a new party with its first congress being held in November 1990 in Praia. Veiga was elected chairman and the party declared its support for Antonio Manuel Mascarenhas Gomes Monteiro in his presidential bid. President Pereira confirmed that he would seek reelection. In the January 1991 legislative elections—the first multi-party elections in lusophone Africa—the MPD captured 56 of 79 seats, with the PAICV gathering the remaining 23. Veiga was sworn in as prime minister of a provisional government. In the February 1991 presidential elections 73.5% of the voters favored Mascarenhas, and he took office in March. President Mascarenhas stood unopposed for reelection in 1996 and won 80% of the votes, but with a low turnout of only 45% of the electorate. The next election was scheduled for February 2001.

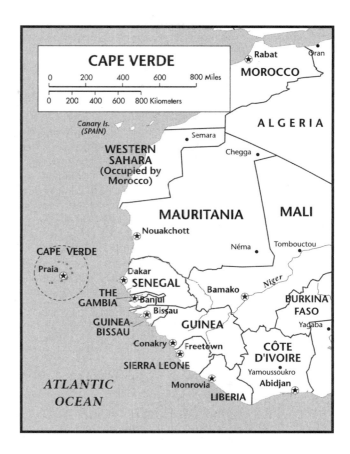

## LEADERSHIP

A new constitution was instituted in September 1992, formally declaring the Second Republic and emphasizing human rights, equality of all citizens, a commitment to democratic principles, and full participation of all citizens. Much of this constitutional document is fully in line with the principles and ideals for which President Mascarenhas has been working since beginning his legal studies in Belgium. He has continued, during his presidential tenure, to participate in international conferences on human rights and in inter-African commissions on civil disturbances and constitutional transition in Africa. For this work he has been awarded the Grand Collar of the Order of Freedom by the Portuguese government.

President Mascarenhas continues to preside over a lively, multi-party democracy. In the December 1995 legislative elections the MPD obtained 50 seats in the legislatively reduced 72-seat Assembly; the PAICV took 21 seats. Two other parties, the UCID and the PSD, contested the elections but received little public support.

## DOMESTIC POLICY

The domestic policy of any Cape Verdean government is closely connected to the continual economic struggle for survival on these islands. In 1995 it was estimated that fully 25% of the work force was unemployed, and a further 26% was under-employed. Only 10% of the land is arable, which is made even worse by the series of droughts that have been experienced in the 1980s and 1990s. Less than 10% of the arable land is under irrigation. A holdover from the colonial period is a tenure system of absentee landlords, which discourages those actually farming the land from making any improvements. Despite these deficiencies, fully 40% of the working population is engaged in agriculture (including forestry and fishing). Yet agriculture contributes only around 20% of the GDP and provides only about 10% of the domestic food requirements. The Pereira regime instituted extensive dike construction and tree planting to attack the dual problems of erosion and water retention, and Mascarenhas's government has continued these programs. Soil conservation and improved irrigation techniques are expected to more than double the land area under cultivation by the year 2000. The main cash crop exports are bananas, arabica coffee, groundnuts, castor beans, and pineapples. The principle food crops are maize, beans, cassava and sweet potatoes. Beans and maize are intercropped staples. Half of Cape Verde's irrigated land is in sugar cane, which is used to produce a local alcoholic beverage. The government is attempting to reallocate this land to staple and cash crops.

Fishing is a source of possible increased revenue. Currently tuna and lobster are major export products. The government hopes to increase training and credit facilities for the largely artisanal fishing industry in order to improve the status of this sector in the national economy. In addition, fish canning installations for anchovies, tuna, and mackerel have been opened by a Spanish/Italian consortium.

In a continued effort to encourage foreign investment, the government enacted a free-zone enterprise law in 1993, giving tax and custom duties exemptions to firms engaged in export-only production. Other economic initiatives currently underway are ship-building and repair facilities, promotion of the islands as an air traffic refueling station and tourist destination with the construction of a new international airport planned on Praia, and a ship registration agency in Mindelo.

## FOREIGN POLICY
Cape Verde pursues a neutral, nonaligned foreign policy and expends quite a bit of effort in seeking out sources of development aid. They have made substantial gains in this direction through grants from both Israel and Arab states and have also opened new diplomatic embassies and offices in the People's Republic of China, South Africa, Sweden, Hong Kong, Spain, Singapore, the United Kingdom and the United States. Cape Verde remains in close contact with lusophone Africa through PALOP (African Peoples of Portuguese Official Language), with Portugal and Brazil. These seven countries (Cape Verde, Guinea-Bissau, Angola, Mozambique, Sao Tome and Principe, Brazil, and Portugal) formed a lusophone organization to promote cooperation on development and cultural issues in July 1996. Cape Verde also has had observer status since 1977 with the francophone ACCT (Agency of Cultural and Technical Cooperation) and is currently debating full membership. Guinea-Bissau has switched its currency to the French West African franc. It remains to be seen if Cape Verde will take this step as well. The Central Intelligence Agency reports that Cape Verde has become an increasingly used transshipment point for illicit drugs from Latin America and Africa bound for Europe.

## ADDRESS
Presidencia da Republica
Cidade de Praia
Santiago, Cape Verde

## REFERENCES
*Africa South of the Sahara.* 25th ed. London: Europa Publications Ltd., 1996.
Cape Verde Home Page. [Online] Available http://www.umassd.edu/SpecialPrograms/caboverde (Accessed June 2000).
Davidson, Basil. *The Fortunate Isles, A Study in African Transformation.* London: Hutchinson; Trenton, NJ: World Press, 1989.
———. *No Fist is Big Enough to Hide the Sky.* 2nd ed. London: Zed Press, 1984.
Lobban, Richard A. *Cape Verde: Crioulo Colony to Independent Nation.* Boulder, CO: Westview Press, 1995.
———. *Historical Dictionary of Cape Verde.* 3rd ed. Metuchen, NJ: Scarecrow Press, 1995.
"Where History Stopped By." *New York Times,* 7 March 1999.

**Profile researched and written by Kathryn L. Green, California State University, San Bernardino (6/97; updated 3/2000).**

# CENTRAL AFRICAN REPUBLIC

**Ange-Félix Patassé**
**President**
*(pronounced "AN-je pa-TASS-a")*

*"Today I am president of all Central African men and women without exception...
Let us...reconstruct the Central African Republic, our dear and beautiful country
which is in an unprecedented state of ruin."*

The Central African Republic (CAR), which was known as the Central African Empire between 1976 and 1979, is a landlocked nation located in the geographic center of the African continent. It shares a northern border with Chad a southern border with both the Republic of Congo and the Democratic Republic of Congo, and its western and eastern frontiers are shared with Cameroon and Sudan respectively. The total area of the CAR is 622,984 sq km (240,535 sq mi). The south-central and western portions of the country contain the bulk of the population while the east-central and northeast portions of the country remain sparsely inhabited. The largest cities are the capital of Bangui, Bouar, and Berberati.

In 1992, the population of the CAR was estimated at 3,445,000. There are more than 60 different ethnic groups including the Aka or Babinga peoples sometimes referred to as pygmies, though the Baya, the Banda, the Manja, and a group known as the Oubanguian or Riverine, comprise almost 90% of the population. The national language is Sango, which is widely spoken throughout the country, though the official language is predominantly French, which is used in government. The people of the CAR are approximately 25% Roman Catholic, 25% Protestant, 15% Muslim, while the remainder practice a variety of indigenous religions, including animism.

The per capita GDP has been estimated at $1,640. The unit of currency is the *Communauté Financière Africaine (CFA) franc*, a currency that the CAR shares with Chad, Cameroon, Republic of Congo and Gabon. The five nations which hold the CFA *franc* have an arrangement with the French Treasury to manage their balance of payments and guarantee the exchange of the CFA *franc* for the French *franc*. The Central Africans grow cotton, coffee, and tobacco for export and cultivate manioc, corn, millet, sorghum, and peanuts for food crops. Diamonds and timber are harvested for export, and the country also contains reserves of uranium and gold.

## POLITICAL BACKGROUND

The CAR is a former French colony known as Oubangi-Chari that was part of a larger federation of French colonies grouped under the name *Afrique Equatorial Francaise*. It gained independence from France in 1960, as did most of the French colonies in Africa. However, the CAR maintains close cultural, economic, and political ties to France, based on both the continued importance of the French language and the

reliance on French foreign assistance. The country's first modern political leader was Barthélémy Boganda. Boganda is seen as the "father" of the CAR, though he died in a plane crash prior to formal independence. His successor and the nation's first president was David Dacko, who served until 1965 when he was overthrown by Jean-Bedel Bokassa in a military-led coup d'etat. Bokassa was president until 1976, then a self-proclaimed emperor until 1979 when he in turn was removed by a French-supported coup that briefly returned Dacko to the presidency. Bokassa's regime was internationally known for its personal excesses and a brutal record of human rights violations. Dacko's return to power was followed by a hastily drafted new constitution and a presidential election he managed to win by the narrowest of margins, 50.2% of the total vote. One of Dacko's opponents in the 1980 presidential election was Ange-Félix Patassé, who won the second largest portion of the vote, 38.1%. Dacko's narrow victory and his own inability to broaden his support base ultimately led to his decision to step down from the presidency in September 1981 in favor of André Kolingba, the army's top general. Kolingba ruled the CAR until the summer of 1993 as both a military authority and a civilian head of a one-party government, *Rassemblement Démocratique Centrafricain*. In September 1993, Kolingba lost the presidency to Patassé in the first real multi-party election in 12 years in the face of economic collapse and growing international pressure for reform.

## PERSONAL BACKGROUND

Ange-Félix Patassé comes from the northwest border region and is a member of a small ethnic group called the Sara. People of Saga origin, along with the larger ethnic groups of the Baya and the Banda, had long been excluded from political power by the minority, but politically influential, Riverine people. Given these historical conditions it is remarkable that Patassé was able to enter the civil service in his twenties and rapidly advance into higher levels of authority. During the Bokassa years he held numerous ministerial posts, including Transport and Communications, Public Health, Tourism, and Telecommunications. Patassé was dismissed from the government in 1978 and left the country in January 1979 to form an opposition in France to the Bokassa regime. He returned shortly after the coup that removed Bokassa but was arrested trying to leave the country in November 1979. Along with several members of his family, he was jailed for a time in the infamous Ngaragba

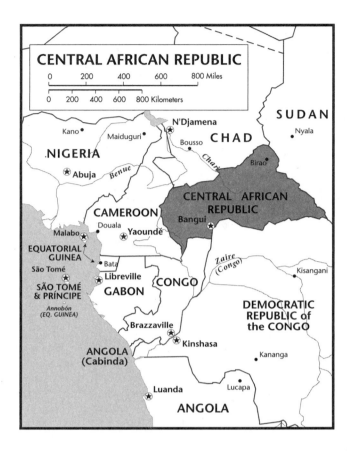

**CENTRAL AFRICAN REPUBLIC**

prison in Bangui, well-known for torture and mistreatment of prisoners.

## RISE TO POWER

Since 1980, Patassé and the *Mouvement pour la Libération du Peuple Centafricaine* (MPLC) have comprised the most consistent and, in some measure, the most effective opposition to both the Dacko and Kolingba governments of the 1980s and early 1990s. This was accomplished despite the fact that Patassé spent a large portion of the 1980s in hiding in his own country or in exile in France, Chad, or Libya. Although he was able to maintain an active core of support, his absence from the country and his former association with the Bokassa regime hindered the development of a large and consistent base of support within the country. His most consistent base of support had been among the peoples of the northwest and north-central portions of the country and among the young and unemployed of the major urban areas, particularly the capital of Bangui.

In the election held September 1999, 10 candidates were on the ballot for the office of president, including Ange-Félix Patasse and former presidents André Kolingba and David Dacko. Official results declared President Ange-Felix Patassé the winner although the other nine candidates charged that Patassé intimidated voters into supporting his candidacy. Patassé reportedly won 51.6% of the vote of the one million votes cast (out of 1.7 million registered voters), with Kolingbe winning 19.3% and Dacko 11%.

## LEADERSHIP

Patassé's task of rebuilding the economy and infrastructure in the CAR is a large one. In his own words, the country is in a state of ruin. The challenges he faces would be significant for any president, given the current economic and political conditions. The nation's schools have been essentially shut down for three years; the civil service has been on strike for months and unpaid for over a year; and France, the CAR'S chief financial donor, has reduced the overall amount of its financial support for the government. Moreover, Patassé will have to work hard to increase the base of his support in the nation's legislature, the National Assembly, if he hopes to enact the necessary programs and reforms. His slim chances of finding a political solution improved somewhat when his party, MPLC, strengthened its position in the National Assemby in the 1998 parliamentary elections, increasing their number of seats from 34 to 47 of the 109 seats; however, the opposition parties are still the majority by one seat.

Patassé's main leadership challenge will be to reorganize and regain the support of the country's civil service, which remains the most politically active and economically important group in the country. In the 1980s, as much as 95% of the CAR's annual receipts went toward the payment of salaries for public employees. The UN estimates suggest that up to 50% of the capital's population is supported directly by salaries paid to the 70% of all civil servants who are posted in the capital. Attempts at reform have had some success, but shortage of financial resources and long term structural problems in the domestic economy will make the reform of the civil service particularly difficult. Citing progress in the area of reform, in mid-1999 the International Monetary Fund extended an $11 million loan to CAR to help the government catch up on nine months of back payment owed to about 20,000 government workers.

In addition to the need to reform the civil service, Patassé faces a major hurdle in the need to develop a trust and respect for the democratic process among both politicians and the general population. In a country long accustomed to arbitrary and authoritarian rule, engendering a spirit of compromise and national unity will be a major task.

The success of his reforms will be tied to his ability to form alliances within the National Assembly, gain the support of the people who supported his opponents in the elections, and convince the international community, particularly France, to support the rebuilding of the country.

## DOMESTIC POLICY

In addition to the leadership issues mentioned above, the challenge to the Patassé-led government will center on health care, revitalization of the agricultural sector and the continuation of the market-based approach to the pricing of its two key exports, coffee and cotton. The manufacturing sector remains very small (8–11% of GDP), and efforts to encourage its expansion will require additional foreign support and the further development of its potentially large hydro-electric generating capacity.

## FOREIGN POLICY

Since independence in 1960, maintaining an atmosphere of cooperation between France and the government of the CAR has been the key foreign policy objective. It is without doubt the single most important political and economic relationship for the CAR. The new government will require continued French assistance and financial support for reform to succeed. However, it is also true that due to its landlocked position on the continent and the economic and political practicalities which follow, the CAR has actively attempted to foster close relations with its neighbors. Former president Kolingba summed up this two-pronged focus of foreign policy in a 1986 speech: "Our foreign policy is based on good relations with our neighbors and particularly favored by a linkage to France as the understanding between our two countries is total."

The French view the CAR's location as central to maintaining a presence in sub-Saharan Africa, reflected in the continued presence of French troops, and as a venue for maintaining French culture and language in the developing world. The 3,000 French expatriates who live in the CAR are more often than not technical advisors or aid workers who draw salaries from various French aid programs. Moreover, the French view their continued presence in the CAR as both a buffer against Libyan expansion in Chad (another former French colony) and an area of its former empire it wants to protect against encroachment by another power. Patassé has benefitted politically from this relationship both in terms of his ability to remain in opposition to the government while living in France during the 1960s and by the application of French pressure to the former regime to hold multi-party elections and accept the results.

Despite the historic relationship, France has been increasingly reluctant to continue direct support of the CAR government without some hope of improvement in its financial condition in the foreseeable future. This has led to growing pressure from the international community, particularly the IMF, the World Bank, and the UNDP, in attempts to reform the public structure of the Central African economy, with an emphasis on privatization and market prices for its commodities.

## ADDRESS

Presidence de la Republique
Bangui, Central African Republic

## REFERENCES

*Africa Report*, November/December 1993.

Africaonline. [Online] Available http://www.africa-online.com (Accessed March 2000).

"Central African Republic: Worsening conditions amid deepening poverty," UN Integrated Regional Information Network (IRIN). [Online] Available http://www.africanews.org/west/stories/1999_feat1.html (Accessed October 1999 ).

*The Economist*, 6 March 1994.

Kalck, Pierre. *Historical Dictionary of the Central African Republic*. Metuchen, NJ: Scarecrow Press, 1992.

*Le Monde Diplomatique*, March 1994.

*The Universal Almanac*, 1994.

**Profile researched and written by Raymond P. Webb, Milton Academy (3/94; updated 3/2000).**

# CHAD

## Idriss Déby
## President
*(pronounced "IH-driss DEH-bee")*

*"I am the president of all Chadians,...any development effort is only possible in national unity."*

The Republic of Chad became independent from the French Equatorial African Federation in 1960. It has a land area of 1,284,000 sq km (495,800 sq mi) and is bordered by Libya, Niger, Nigeria, Cameroon, Central African Republic, and Sudan. The country's official languages are Arabic and French, but more than 100 languages are spoken within the country. The largest ethno-linguistic group is the Sara peoples, accounting for about a quarter of the population. They are concentrated in the central parts of the southern river basins. Speakers of Niger-Congo languages live to the west of the Sara peoples. Saharan language speakers are concentrated in the Lake Chad region and Arabic speakers, divided among themselves by tribal rather than ethnic affiliations, predominate in the north and east. Tubu nomads reside in the Tibesti massif and Ennedi and Borkou plateaus. The country is as diverse religiously as it is linguistically with approximately 50% of the population practicing Islam, 30% Christianity, and 20% practicing traditional African religions. The population has been estimated at 7.6 million. Approximately one-fifth of the population is urban, with about one-half of these urban dwellers living in the capital of N'Djamena. Life expectancy is 49 years and the literacy rate is 48%. The currency of Chad is the CFA *franc*. The per capita GDP has been estimated at $1,000. Chad's primary exports are raw cotton, with live cattle and meat placing a distant second and third place. Its major trading partner is France.

## POLITICAL BACKGROUND

Since gaining its independence from France in 1960, Chad has been wrought with war and political turmoil. Numerous coups and takeovers have disrupted the political process and destroyed political institutions. By June 1982, Hissène Habré had used his troops to take the capital by force, quickly achieving recognition for his government by the international community.

Idriss Déby, former commander-in-chief of the Chadian army, formed a military unit in Sudan and began an invasion of eastern Chad. By December of 1990, he had taken the capital at the head of his troops and dissolved the assembly. A period of democratic transition began with Déby authorizing political parties in 1991 and a national conference to work out the transition process in 1992. Numerous postponements of a new constitution and elections followed. Finally, in July 1996 Déby won the long-awaited presidential election.

## PERSONAL BACKGROUND

Idriss Déby was born in Fada, a village in the Ennedi province of eastern Chad in 1952. His father was a shepherd of the Zughawa ethnic group. He achieved his baccalaureate and then joined the military officers school in N'Djamena. In 1976 he traveled to northern France where he obtained a professional pilot's license at l'Institut Aeronautique Amaury de la Grange at Hazebrouck. After returning to Chad, he became a second-lieutenant in the Forces Armées du Nord (FAN) that successfully brought Habré to power in 1982. He became commander-in-chief of the Chadian armed forces, Forces Armées Nationales Tchadiennes (FANT), where he achieved great success against Libyan troops in 1983. The French were so impressed with his desert fighting tactics that they began to call him the "cowboy of the desert." His military success began to make Habré fear him as a possible rival. Déby therefore quietly arranged for additional military training in France. He was replaced as chief of the armed forces by his cousin, Hassan Djamous. Upon completion of his training course, he returned to Chad and was appointed advisor for security and defense, with his cousin Djamous remaining as chief of the armed forces. Déby is married with four wives, one of whom was the wife of his deceased father—an obligatory custom of the Zughawa. He is the father of 10 children.

## RISE TO POWER

In the late 1980s, Hissène Habré became worried about possible rivals and began an increasingly repressive period of arbitrary arrests and executions. He created a security force consisting solely of members of his own ethnic group and equipping them better than the forces of which Déby and his cousin were in charge. The favoritism towards this force provoked a rebellion of the regular forces. Déby and his cousin were warned that their lives were in danger and fled the capital.

Déby made his way to the Sudan, where he formed the Patriotic Movement of Salvation (MPS) and began a reconquest of Chad. Déby's mission was completed by December 1990, having obtained military equipment from Libya, his former enemy. The French acquiesced to his designs by withholding support and information on Déby's troop movements and location from Habré. Habré fled the capital, allegedly with car loads of stolen funds, and Déby took charge of the country.

Though Déby declared his intention of moving toward a democratic government, the process moved slowly. Political parties were recognized in 1991, and a national conference to work out the transition began in January 1993. It concluded its work with a transitional charter and prime minister elected by the delegates. Déby was to remain as president and chief of the armed forces during the transition period. This period was expected to last one year, with the possibility of a one-year extension. In 1995 Déby finally set up a national independent commission. A draft constitution was ready for referendum vote in March 1996. The new constitution, which was approved by the voters in a 71% turnout, set up a president elected by universal suffrage for a five-year term with eligibility for re-election to one more five-year term.

During the election campaign, Déby was careful to travel to all regions of the country and even to apologize to the electorate in some areas that had experienced harsh treatment from his troops. He was the designated candidate of the MPS, which had been reformed into a political party. But he campaigned as the Republic Front candidate, a coalition made up of 12 political parties. Fifteen candidates were eventually accepted for the official list, including many of the major political and military figures and representing a wide range of viewpoints. The turnout in the first round of voting was 69%. The second round achieved a 77% turnout, with Déby garnering 69% of the votes. The legislative elections that followed in January and February 1997 brought Déby's MPS an absolute majority of 63 of the 125 assembly seats, with nine other parties sharing the remaining 62 seats. New elections are scheduled for 2001.

## LEADERSHIP

Considering the votes received by other candidates and abstentions, Déby only received one-third of the possible votes in the 1996 elections. Voting patterns reflected a north–south polarization—one of the greatest problems that continues to confront the president. In addition, 40 political parties presented candidates in the election, revealing potential sources of opposition, and the number has grown still further since those elections.

In the reform effort that faced Déby after his election, an armed force of over 40,000 needed to be reduced to 25,000. The army had been his source of support, and its reorganization and reduction was to be a test of Déby's commitment to a civilian government. However, though the trappings of the 1996-approved constitution have been put in place, Déby continues to exercise an authoritarian style of government.

A vocal opposition objects to the established unitary political system and would prefer a federal state system. They believe that there is a severe imbalance of power between the executive and legislative branches under the 1996 constitution and that the lack of an independent judiciary is hampering the emergence of a democratic state. The political opposition continues to be harassed, detained, tried, and imprisoned. Freedom of the press is also under attack. The president continues to face a seeming majority of the citizens from the southwest provinces in opposition to his rule. The success of the oil consortium plans to mine and export significant petroleum reserves in the region, so needed by the impoverished Chadian economy, is dependent on the government forming a working alliance with political leaders

of this region in order to bring about the peaceful conditions needed for such mining.

## DOMESTIC POLICY

In the period since his election, President Déby has engaged in a series of agreements with various political opposition groups and cease-fires with several rebel groups. However, off and on again armed rebellion continues in the northern and southern regions of the country, severely testing the military's ability to maintain order. In addition, serious charges of human rights abuses by the government have not seemed to lessen.

Soon after his election Déby moved to prevent the formation of a vocal Islamic opposition that had begun to cause unrest in the south. Church groups voiced concern over links between new converts in the south of Chad and the Sudan. The new minister of the interior published a decision in August 1996, dissolving all Islamic religious associations and designating the High Council of Islamic Affairs as the sole organization responsible for Islamic affairs in Chad.

The economy of Chad is of a very narrow range with agriculture providing employment for over 70% of the work force. Infrastructure is poorly developed, making transport of people and goods very difficult and expensive. Due to drought in the 1980s, Chad was forced to import about 75% of its food, placing further strain on its ability to import needed equipment for infrastructure development. Manufacturing consists mainly in the processing of agricultural products, particularly cotton. Chad's cotton and sugar production and refining industries have been badly hurt by illicit imports from Nigeria. In fact, illicit trade makes it difficult to even provide solid statistics for trade figures for the Chadian economy.

Power to run manufacturing is scarce, and electricity charges are among the highest in Africa. Successful development of the projected oil refineries could substantially encourage the development of the manufacturing sector by reducing Chad's reliance on expensive oil imports to run its generators. Déby has shown his understanding of the importance of this resource development and the June 2000 World Bank decision to assist in financing the oil pipeline between Chad and the Cameroonian port at Kribi will provide a much-needed boost to the prospects for economic development of this impoverished country.

Chad experiences severe budget deficits each year with expenditures about three times the level of revenue collected. There is thus an extreme reliance on foreign aid. Chad's trade picture is no better, experiencing large deficits due to low production levels and high transport costs. Chad has been able to achieve high concessionary loan terms, which has enabled it to keep its debt servicing low. In addition, when the CFA *franc* was devalued in 1994, France responded by canceling Chad's official debt. However, over 70% of Chad's debt is to multilateral institutions and thus not eligible for debt relief. Since the CFA currency devaluation in 1994, Déby has cooperated well with the IMF and World Bank and has been rewarded with favorable subsidies and loans. Public finances have been reorganized; public sector employment has been held down; and spending on infrastructure development has proceeded well. The economy has responded favorably with much-improved growth figures for 1997 and 1998.

## FOREIGN POLICY

Since the 1996 election Déby has moved to repair and solidify relations with neighboring countries. In August 1996 a tripartite Chad-Sudan-Central African Republic summit was announced to set up a regional integration program. In November 1996, Chad and Libya met for their third joint commission and reaffirmed their desire for cooperation. Déby has also sought and received economic and political linkages with various Arab states.

International human rights groups have documented abuses under Déby's regime carried out by his soldiers. In October 1996, Amnesty International strongly criticized the French government, charging them with "silence or complicity" in the face of arrests and executions being carried out by Déby's government. Amnesty's attacks were directed against France because approximately 800 French troops were then stationed in Chad. France responded by claiming no knowledge of abuses and no authority to intervene. They have considered a reduction in the number of French forces based in Chad. Though the French are only tepid in their support of Déby, they recognize the strategic importance of Chad in relation to contemporary trouble spots on the African continent and do not want to lose their military position there.

In January 1995, the Esso-led oil consortium, Chad, and Cameroon signed a pipeline management agreement, which was to have oil moving from southern Chad to the Cameroonian port of Kribi by 1999, thus further solidifying relations between Chad and Cameroon. However, turmoil in the region, weakening of resolve of some consortium partners, and international environmental and human rights concerns have delayed the project. Overruling these concerns, on 6 June 2000, the World Bank agreed to lend US$39.5 million to Chad and US$53.4 million to Cameroon to help build the 1,070-km (665-mi) pipeline. Exxon Mobil is the lead company in the pipeline project and had required, before it would proceed further with the project, that the World Bank participate in the project in order to protect private company investment from possible future nationalization of the company by Chad or Cameroon. Most of the funding for the project comes from private sources. The Chadian opposition has not responded favorably to the World Bank's decision, strongly condemning its funding due to their claims of government corruption, embezzlement, and drug trafficking.

## ADDRESS
Presidence de la Republique
N'Djamena
Republic of Chad

## REFERENCES
*Africa Confidential,* 17 March 1995, vol. 36, no. 6, pp. 4–5; 10 May 1996, vol. 37, no. 10, pp. 4–5.

*Africa Research Bulletin,* January–November 1996, vol. 33, nos. 1–11.

*Africa South of the Sahara.* 29th ed. London: Europa Publications Ltd., 2000.

*Africa Who's Who.* 2nd ed. London: Africa Books Ltd., 1991.

Chadian Embassy home page. [Online] Available http://www.chadembassy.org/ (Accessed June 2000).

Integrated Regional Information Network for West Africa. [Online] Available http://www.reliefweb.int/IRIN (Accessed May–June 2000).

International Boundaries Research Unit, University of Durham. [Online] Available http://www-ibru.dur.ac.uk/ (Accessed June 2000).

*Jeune Afrique,* 10–16 July 1996, no. 1853, p. 15; 7–10 August 1996, no. 1857, pp. 33–35.

*Keesing's Record of World Events,* March 1996, p. 40983; April 1996, p. 41033; July 1996, p. 41178; September 1996, p. R8.

*National Post,* 7 June 2000, p. C02.

*New York Times,* 6 June 2000, p. A3

*West Africa,* 22–28 July 1996, p. 1133; 2–18 August 1996, p. 1261; 19–25 August 1996, p. 1301; 9–15 September 1996, p. 1421.

**Profile researched and written by Kathryn L. Green, Ph.D., California State University, San Bernardino (6/2000).**

# CHILE

**Ricardo Lagos**
**President**
*(pronounced "Ree-CAR-doe LA-gos")*

*"We must end the two Chiles. No longer can we accept an unjust nation where the rich live comfortably while too many people live in poverty."*

The Republic of Chile lies upon a long, narrow strip of land, covering 4,275 km (2,650 mi) along the Pacific coast of Latin America, bordered by Peru and Bolivia to the north, Argentina to the east, and Cape Horn to the south. Easter Island (Isla de Pascua), the Juan Fernandez Islands, and many other small islands to the west and south also form part of Chile. The Andes Mountains separate Chile from Argentina, leaving Chile relatively isolated within Latin America. The total Chilean land area covers 736,905 sq km (284,520 sq mi), excluding the claimed Antarctic territory. Chile claims ownership to 1.2 million sq km (463,320 sq mi) of the Antarctic.

Chile has an estimated 14,974,000 inhabitants. Approximately 90% of the population is mestizo, which is mixed Spanish and Amerindian. About 8% is Amerindian, and about 2% is European. Of Amerindians, the Araucanians (also known as Mapuches) are the largest in number and most well-known. Most Chileans are Catholic, but an increasing number, some 18–20%, have become Protestant. The capital of Chile is Santiago.

Chile's wealth has traditionally been found in its natural resources; however, it is now becoming a modern industrial nation. Exports include minerals, nitrates, fish meal, wood products, and fruit and vegetables. Chile has long remained the world's leading producer and exporter of copper. Chile has had success with its economy in the last decade, during which growth averaged 6% a year and was accompanied by a substantial increase in real wages. Chile obtains more than 25% of its gross domestic product from its exports, which increasingly include not just products but capital and know-how. Chile invests about 28% of its GDP, a relatively high percentage, which should promote continued wealth. The per capita GDP has been estimated at US$12,500. Despite a slump in the economy in 1999, when unemployment reached about 11%, optimism for future growth remains high. The Chilean unit of currency is the *peso*.

## POLITICAL BACKGROUND

The Republic of Chile gained its independence from Spain in 1818, and by the mid-20th century had become one of Latin America's most advanced and stable nations. In 1970, Chileans elected to the presidency Salvador Allende Gossens, an enthusiastic Marxist who represented a coalition of five left-wing political parties, and for the next three years, Chile had a socialist government. Repeated violent clashes between pro- and anti-government forces, as well as covert US inter-

vention against the Allende government, led to chaos and a deteriorating economy. Allende's government was overthrown on 11 September 1973 by the Chilean military, with help from the US government and significant support from Chile's middle and upper classes. The military formed a four-man junta government composed of the commanders-in-chief.

General Augusto Pinochet Ugarte, commander-in-chief of the Army, soon came to dominate the other three. All political activity was banned, Congress was dissolved, and censorship and repression followed. Pinochet proclaimed himself president in 1974 but ruled Chile as a ruthless dictator for the next 15 years. Pinochet's goals were the eradication of socialism and the construction of a modern capitalist nation-state. Those unfortunate Chileans who opposed the dictatorship faced the possibility of imprisonment, torture, and death. Several thousand were murdered, while thousands of others were exiled. Opposition to Pinochet, however, continued throughout his rule. Pinochet gave signs of retaining power indefinitely, but national and international pressure to return the country to democracy continued to increase through the 1980s. In Chile, key political alliances between former foes led to a more unified voice against the dictatorship.

By 1988, Pinochet was forced to hold a national plebiscite, a yes or no vote on whether he should remain in office. Pinochet was confident that he would stay in power, but Chileans overwhelmingly voted to return Chile to democracy. The plebiscite led to presidential elections in 1989, with the right-wing candidate closely allied to Pinochet. The respected Christian Democrat Patricio Aylwin Azocar was backed by a center-left coalition of parties that supported a return to democracy. The coalition, known as the Concertación por la Democracia, or Concert of Parties for Democracy, brought together an unlikely alliance of former political foes like the Christian Democratic Party and the Socialist Party. The politically important Party for Democracy, an amalgamation of reformed leftists and centrists, was part of the Concertación.

Aylwin, the country's first freely elected President since Allende, was inaugurated in March 1990. His election was hailed as a victory for democracy, but Pinochet's power had not diminished at all. During his regime, Pinochet helped write a new constitution that favored the military with unprecedented independence. The constitution, promulgated in 1981, came into full effect in 1989.

Under the constitution, Chile has three official branches of government: the executive in the form of a president, the legislative, and the judicial. The president is elected by direct popular vote to a six-year term and is not eligible for re-election. The bicameral legislature consists of a 47-seat Senate and a 120-seat Chamber of Deputies. The judicial branch consists of the Supreme Court, which has 17 judges appointed for life by the president. When the court has a vacancy, the judges submit five names to the president from which the president must make his appointments. A two-thirds vote in the legislature is needed to change the constitution.

Pinochet also had named key allies to just about every important position of power in Chile, from university presidents to Supreme Court judges. His political maneuvers allowed him to remain head of the armed forces until 1998 when, as dictated by the constitution, he became a senator for life. The constitution also had allowed Pinochet and his allies to name eight senators for life who were sympathetic to the military. These senators have prevented Congress from reaching the two-thirds majority needed to make constitutional reforms.

Because of these serious obstacles, Aylwin and the Concertación were unable to return Chile to complete democracy. Nor could Eduardo Frei Ruiz-Tagle, another Concertación candidate elected to the presidency in 1994, bring the military under civilian control. The military, with occasional threats from Pinochet, continued to assert its independence.

Economically, the country continued to improve under the Concertación presidents. Aylwin had promised not to alter the basic market-oriented economic structure developed under Pinochet, and that promise was kept. Also, nations that were not willing to do business with Pinochet now flocked to invest in Chile. The wine, agriculture, and tourism industries flourished during the 1990s, and the economy continued to expand at a high rate until late 1998–99 when the Asian economic crisis, lower prices for its exports, and a decrease in tax collections led to a fiscal crisis. Aylwin retired on 11 March 1994 with an approval rating of more than 50%. Frei, also a member of the Christian Democratic Party and son of former president Eduardo Frei Montalva, took office with promises to spend more to help the poor.

In October 1998, the arrest of Pinochet in London on charges of human rights violations shocked Chileans and spun the Frei administration into a serious crisis. The military demanded his return and pressured Frei's government to break relations with England and Spain, which were seeking the extradition of Pinochet. The British government cited health and humanitarian reasons when it released Pinochet after 16 months of detention. Pinochet returned to Chile in March 2000 to a different political climate. Aged and disgraced by the detention, Pinochet had become a political liability even for the right.

The Socialist Ricardo Lagos was inaugurated president just a few days after Pinochet's return. Lagos immediately called for a new constitution and major political reforms. In the meantime, Pinochet was facing nearly 80 separate charges of human rights violations in Chilean courts.

## PERSONAL BACKGROUND

Ricardo Lagos was born into a middle-class family on 2 March 1938 in Santiago, the only son of Don Froilán Lagos, a small landowner, and Emma Escobar, a teacher. Lagos was only eight when his father died, leaving his mother to raise him. He received a law degree from the University of Chile in 1960 and a PhD in Economics from Duke University in 1966. Lagos has worked as professor, attorney, and secretary general of the University of Chile. He has spent the bulk of his adult life in politics.

## RISE TO POWER

Lagos' interest in politics began while he was a university student. At 18, he was elected president of a student group. In 1961, he left the Radical Party after it backed the conservative Jorge Alessandri for president, and he moved ideologically closer to the Socialists. During the Allende administration, he was named secretary general of the University of Chile and was the president's choice to be ambassador to Moscow. But he was never to take that post. The military coup on 11 September 1973 and the repression that followed forced Lagos to leave for Argentina, and later the United States, where he taught at the University of North

Carolina until 1975. From 1976 to 1984, Lagos worked as an economist for United Nations agencies. He began to take a more active role in the opposition to Pinochet when he returned to Chile in 1978. In the early 1980s, Lagos and many other Chileans founded the Alianza Democratica (Alliance for Democracy) to oppose military rule. He was president of the alliance in 1983–84, becoming a prominent voice for the left. In 1986, leftist rebels attempted to assassinate Pinochet. In the crackdown that followed, Lagos and many other opposition leaders who were not involved in the plot against the dictator were detained. Lagos spent 20 days in prison. In 1987, Lagos founded the Party for Democracy (PPD), which pressed for an end to the dictatorship.

During the yes/no plebiscite campaign for continued Pinochet rule, Lagos traveled throughout the country encouraging Chileans to let go of their fears and register to vote. In a now famous televised political roundtable, Lagos pointed a finger to the camera and said "you, Mr. Pinochet are responsible" for violations against human rights. Lagos' defiance boosted his political career, and his direct attack on Pinochet was credited for loosening the fear that gripped Chileans. He played a pivotal role during the plebiscite, but it was not enough to bring him to office. His ties to the left hurt him during the 1989 campaign for a Senate seat, gaining only 30% of the vote. But President Patricio Aylwin named him minister of education. In one of his most notable actions, he prohibited schools from preventing pregnant girls from attending classes.

In 1993, with the backing of the PPD, Lagos sought to become the Concertación's second presidential candidate, but he was defeated in the primaries by Eduardo Frei Ruiz-Tagle, who went on to become president. Frei named Lagos minister of works. He used the post to build a solid reputation as a capable technocrat. By 1996 and 1997, polls consistently named Lagos as one of the most important political figures in Chile and the most likely person to become Chile's third freely elected president since Pinochet. At least within the Concertacion no one measured up to Lagos' stature. During a primary to decide the Concertación's presidential candidate in May 1999, Lagos received 71.34% of the vote to defeat Andrés Zaldívar, a Christian Democrat and Senate President who received 28.7% of the vote. At first, Lagos was an overwhelming favorite to win the presidency over the conservative candidate Joaquín Lavín, a former member of the Pinochet government. But Lavín's appeal to working classes, growing dissatisfaction with the Concertación, and a troubled economy after many years of growth hurt Lagos. In the December 1999 election, Lagos and Lavín, who distanced himself from Pinochet after his arrest, finished in a virtual tie, with a little more than 49% for each candidate. While Lagos finished slightly ahead of Lavín, he did not gain the necessary 51% of the vote to avoid a runoff election. With the key backing of influential DC member Soledad Alvear, and votes from Communist Party members, Lagos narrowly defeated Lavín, 51.3% to 48.7%, for the presidency in the January 2000 election. On 11 March, Lagos was inaugurated President.

## LEADERSHIP

Lagos' inauguration speech symbolized his decade-long efforts to straddle a center position in Chile's highly polarized politics. He acknowledged his leftist roots by paying tribute to Allende's widow, calling her a "representative of Chile's dignity." As Chile's first president of the 21st century, Lagos carefully pointed to the unresolved and painful issues of the Pinochet era. But he quickly moved to a theme of unity, mentioning prominent conservatives who have played a major role in shaping the history of the country. Lagos' careful approach has been one of the most telling characteristics of his political career, despite the defiant shaking of a finger at Pinochet in 1988.

He has courted the working classes, often delivering hard-hitting speeches about Chile's unjust social system. Yet, he has never displayed the fiery rhetoric of his leftist predecessors, who called on Chileans to take over factories and land. Lagos has been careful to avoid polarizing the country's upper classes and the Concertación's conservative partners, the Christian Democrats. He has courted prominent US businessmen and has promised to leave virtually untouched the country's free market economic policies. His moderation has angered the Communists and Socialists, many of whom don't consider Lagos to be one of their own. Much like Britain's Tony Blair, Lagos believes nations do not have to embrace the United States' model of capitalism. Yet, he does not hold that Socialism is the answer. Instead, they tout a "Third Way" in which the government has a greater regulatory role in a free market economy. This is a key point for Lagos, who has described himself as a social democrat. He wants to increase workers' rights decimated by the Pinochet regime without angering industrialists who worry Lagos' proposed changes could simply lead to strikes.

Lavín's surprising results at the polls means Lagos faces the difficult challenge of maintaining the delicate balance that so far has kept the center-left Concertación in power for more than a decade. Many Chileans have become increasingly more disillusioned with the center-left coalition. Once the undisputed voice of democracy, the Concertación has been criticized for reverting into a political machine that hands out coveted government jobs to a small elite.

Lagos has been described as having a sober personality, and distaste for impulsiveness. He is considered an efficient technocrat and admired for a no-nonsense approach to government. He chose cabinet ministers carefully, stressing their expertise rather than party affiliations. Among his 16 cabinet members, there are five women, a reflection of his personal views on equal rights for women. The make up of the cabinet also is a reflection of the power structure of the Concertación: 7 Christian Democrats, 4 Socialists, 3 from Lagos' own Party for Democracy, and 2 Radical Social Democrats.

Aylwin and Frei were unable to make reforms to the constitution engineered by Pinochet. A conservative Supreme Court and Senate that remain sympathetic to the former dictator also will hinder Lagos. Congress, by a 113–27 vote, approved a constitutional reform titled "Dignity of the ex-President" shortly after Lagos' inauguration. The law allows Pinochet to keep his Senate salary and immunity if he is forced to resign his post. Lagos has promised he will guarantee the independence of the judiciary if Pinochet is brought to trial.

An able minister during the Aylwin and Frei administrations, Lagos is perceived as a leader who can get things done.

For thousands of poor Chileans, Lagos represents the best opportunity to improve their lives.

## DOMESTIC POLICY

Chileans look to Lagos to finally end Chile's long transition to democracy. Yet, how to bring it about remains a matter of contention and a difficult political battle for the president, who believes only a new constitution will signal an end to the transition. Unlike Aylwin and Frei, Lagos has taken a stronger and more public stance towards reform. Engineered by Pinochet, the constitution severely limits civilian control of the armed forces. It prevents the president from appointing and removing military leaders and prevents civilian oversight of the military budget. Lagos also wants to get rid of appointed senators, mostly Pinochet supporters who have prevented constitutional reforms. Lagos has called for military budget cuts and the creation of a professional and better army staffed by volunteers. Military service is compulsory in Chile.

Yet, Chile's conservative leaders are unlikely to back constitutional reforms without assurances that Pinochet and other military and police leaders will be allowed to retain immunity for human rights violations. Some Christian Democrats have even rejected giving the president the right to appoint and fire military leaders.

Dealing with delicate military issues is only one of Lagos' many domestic challenges. He has promised a great deal to the working classes, and it is unclear how much of it he will deliver in his six years as president. He has promised to create 300,000 new jobs and build thousands of new homes for the poor. Unemployment insurance, better education, and health care are also part of his domestic plans. Aylwin and Frei managed to dramatically reduce extreme poverty during their administrations. But Chile experienced a major fiscal crisis in 1998–99 caused by the Asian economic crisis, lower prices for Chile's exports, and a large decrease in tax collections. In 1999, unemployment reached 11%, forcing Frei to spend $90 million to create 64,000 jobs. With rising oil prices in 2000, and depressed copper prices, Lagos may be forced to follow an austere fiscal policy during his first year in office.

While Lagos favors privatization of some state-owned properties, his government is likely to hold on to its most important industries and most profitable industries. They include Codelco, a copper corporation, Enami, a mining company, and Enap, an oil company.

## FOREIGN POLICY

Lagos has promised he will not tinker with his country's free trade policies. He will seek tighter relations with the Mercosur trade bloc of South America. Joining Mercosur has increasingly gained more importance as trade with Argentina continues to grow. Chile has been so far unsuccessful in establishing a free-trade agreement with the United States, but Lagos is not expected to give up as the country continues to seek other economic alliances elsewhere.

In an interview with *El Mercurio,* Chile's largest daily newspaper, Lagos said the country needs to establish key alliances with other South American nations to counterbalance the great trading blocs of North America, Europe, and Asia. Without an alliance, Latin America does not stand a chance to compete, he said. He also wants greater economic and political coordination in Latin America similar to the European Union.

Lagos said he is willing to renew relations with Bolivia if that country is willing to enter diplomatic talks without preconditions. Bolivia, which lost access to the Pacific Ocean in the War of the Pacific of 1879–83, has been pressing Chile for access to the sea.

## ADDRESS

Officio de Presidente
Santiago, Chile

## REFERENCES

"The Irony of Chile's Full Circle." *The Christian Science Monitor,* 21 January 2000.

"A Light of Democracy: Chile's New Leader Spreads Gospel of Hope." *The Washington Post,* 18 January 2000.

"Socialist Takes Office in Chile with Nod to the Poor, and the Market." *The New York Times,* 12 March 2000.

"Socialist Is Charting Middle Way for Chile." *The New York Times,* 11 February 2000.

"Women Key to Victory in Chile's Vote." *The Christian Science Monitor,* 14 January 2000.

**Profile researched and written by Ignacio Lobos, journalist, (3/2000).**

# CHINA

## Jiang Zemin
## President

*(pronounced "jee-AHNG dzuh-MEEN")*

*"We should firmly persist in taking economic development as our central task and unify, in a dialectical way, the Four Cardinal Principles, to ensure that our modernization drive progresses successfully on a correct path."*

The People's Republic of China is located in central and eastern Asia. Its total area is 9,561,758 sq km (3,691,795 sq mi), making China the third-largest country in the world. With a population of 1.247 billion, it is also the world's most populous nation. China is a climatically and geographically diverse nation with primarily temperate climate in most of the nation, but dense tropics in the south, warm and humid coastal regions, and frigid northern and Tibetan regions. Of the total land mass, only 10% is cultivated regularly. Some of the world's longest rivers, including the Yangtze and Yellow rivers, and the world's highest mountains are located in China.

China is a relatively homogeneous nation, linguistically and ethnically, with the Han Chinese comprising 93% of the population. The remaining 7% consists of minorities such as the Manchus, Mongols, Tibetans, and Uigurs. Mandarin Chinese is the official language, and the literacy rate is 82%. The largest cities are Shanghai, Beijing (the capital), and Tianjin.

Sixty percent of the labor force is engaged in agriculture and forestry, while another 25% is involved in industry and services. The *renminbi yuan* is the national currency. China's major trading partners include Japan, Taiwan, Hong Kong, the United States, and the Newly Industrialized Nations (NICs) of Asia. Its primary exports are textiles, consumer electronics, armaments, toys, and raw materials. Over the past 10 years, the booming Chinese economy has grown more than 10% annually. The per capita GDP has been estimated at $3,600.

## POLITICAL BACKGROUND

The People's Republic of China was proclaimed in 1949 following a lengthy civil war when Communist leader Mao Zedong consolidated power and forced the Nationalist forces under Chiang Kai-shek to flee to the island of Taiwan, located off China's southern coast. The Chinese Communist Party (CCP) transformed the political, economic, and social system of the country by emphasizing socialist egalitarianism combined with a nationalistic drive toward modernization. The 1982 constitution specifies that supreme political power resides in the National People's Congress (NPC), but real power lies in the Politburo of the CCP Central Committee, with crucial decisions made by a small circle of the CCP select Standing Committee of the Politburo. The NPC's 3,000 members meet annually and elect most of the leading

government officials, including the president, vice president, premier, and vice premier.

The State Council, similar to the cabinet in other countries, is the top executive organ of the national government, and it reports to the CCP Secretariat, which encompasses the Central Committee and the Politburo. All senior members of the State Council also hold concurrently significant influence within the party. The State Council is headed by Li Peng, who was acting premier from 1987 to 1989 and premier since 1989. At the local level, China is divided into 22 provinces with representation consisting of provincial and municipal People's Congresses further decentralized by prefectural, city, county, and town assemblies.

## PERSONAL BACKGROUND

Jiang Zemin was born on 17 August 1926 in Yangzhou City, Jiangsu Province, to Jiang Shangqing, a Communist who was probably killed by Nationalist forces during the civil war. Allegedly, his family consisted of intellectuals: his grandfather was a doctor of Chinese medicine and famous painter; his father and uncle were men of letters. During his youth, Jiang attended an American missionary school and then enrolled at Jiaotong University in Shanghai. He participated in anti-Japanese activities and narrowly escaped capture by Japanese troops. He joined the Communist Party in 1946 and graduated in 1947 with a degree in electrical engineering.

After graduation Jiang worked as manager of a variety of state-run factories. In the early 1950s, he served as the first deputy director of the Yimin No. 1 Foodstuffs Factory in Shanghai, then as chief of the electrical machinery section of the Shanghai No. 2 Designing Division of the First Ministry of Machine Building Industry. He later became commercial counselor at the Chinese embassy in Moscow and worked as a trainee at the Stalin Automobile Factory in 1955. Upon returning to China in 1960 and until approximately 1970, he worked as a mechanical engineer and director of the power subplant in an automobile factory in Changchun. Then he became deputy director of the Shanghai Electrical Equipment Science Research Institute and subsequently director of the Wuhan Heat Power Machinery Research Institute. During that time, he went to Romania as a representative of the First Ministry of Machine Building Industry.

While little is known with certainty about the specifics of Jiang's life during the Cultural Revolution (1965–69) and the years up to 1976, he emerged in 1978 as advisor to the First Ministry of Machine Building. From 1980 until 1982 he was

vice minister of the State Administrative Commission for Import and Export Affairs. Concurrently, he held positions of vice minister of the State Foreign Investment Commission (until March 1982) and vice minister of the Electronic Industry, a position he held until June 1983. Subsequently, he was appointed minister of the Electronics Industry (until June 1985) and elected to the CCP Central Committee.

Jiang's political future improved dramatically when he was appointed mayor of Shanghai in 1985. As mayor, he worked tirelessly to modernize the city by attracting foreign investment, including major hotels, and by establishing a modern golf course. While many citizens considered him ineffective, Jiang's capitalistic endeavors gained him favorable attention in Beijing and the West. He became secretary of the Shanghai CP and was elected member of the powerful Politburo of the CCPs Central Committee in November 1987. Jiang remained secretary of the Shanghai CP until June 1989 when he was elected a member of the Standing Committee of the CCP Politburo and secretary general of its Central Committee. Leading up to and during the Tiananmen Square massacre, when the military attacked student protestors killing and injuring upwards of 15,000 people, Jiang continued to press for economic reform while calling for tight control over civil liberties and political reform. In June 1989, he was appointed General Secretary of the CCP.

He is married to Wang Yeping, his high school sweetheart, who formerly headed a Shanghai engineering research institute, and the couple has two children. Jiang speaks Russian, English, and Romanian; he reads French and Japanese. His hobbies include reading poetry in English and singing American songs from the 1940s.

## RISE TO POWER

Observers suggest that Jiang's appointment as General Secretary of the CCP after the Tiananmen Square massacre reflected a policy among the Chinese political elite to contain

the damage resulting from unfavorable international reaction. Jiang is telegenic and eloquent; he appeared on television to justify the government's action and subsequently warned about the dangers of Western values. In November 1989, Jiang replaced Deng Xiaoping as chairman of the Central Military Commission. In an interview with *US News and World Report* (12 March 1990), he said, "We do not regret, or criticize ourselves for the way we handled, the Tiananmen event, because if we had not sent in troops I would not be able to sit here today."

As General Secretary, Jiang continued to call for economic reforms, stating that "poverty is not socialism," but simultaneously restating the need for political order and stability in China by calling for a socialist democracy. As the ruling gerontocracy left the political scene, he consolidated power gradually by appointing allies. On 27 March 1993, Jiang became president by succeeding the aged Yang Shangkun. Since becoming president, Jiang has cultivated close ties with the military and the party bureaucracy to solidify his position and has become more visible on the international stage by traveling abroad, even meeting President Clinton at the Pacific Rim summit. In 1995, he launched an anti-corruption drive of local officials with the support of the National People's Congress.

Upon the death of Deng Xiaoping on 19 February 1997, a new generation of leadership moved to consolidate power. The ruling troika consists of Jiang as CCP secretary general and president; Li Peng as premier; and Zhu Ronji as vice premier. Jiang considers himself, at the present, equal among the three.

## LEADERSHIP

Over the next few years, Jiang seeks to consolidate his power over the party and the bureaucracy, but he needs to carefully position himself among rivals who prefer a collective form of leadership. Sino specialists expect a period of instability with the military and bureaucrats seeking to increase their power. He needs to perform well if he is to retain power. Maintaining economic growth, successfully integrating Hong Kong back into China, and dealing with rising ethnic tensions in the northwest provinces will test his ability.

Jiang maintains a pragmatic approach—preferring gradual political liberalization within the structure of the CCP and continued economic growth as the centerpiece of his vision for a new China. In many ways his technocratic background, coupled with his experience in international affairs, are seen as assets. The reform of the bureaucracy and the problem of low productivity of state enterprises are issues that, if satisfactorily resolved, would increase Jiang's support among party members and the bureaucracy. Given Li Peng's (his major rival) continuing unpopularity, Jiang stands to gain from any successes. On the other hand, failures during this transitional period could weaken his power base and lead to an all out power struggle.

## DOMESTIC POLICY

The cornerstone of Jiang's domestic policy is the maintenance of growth. To accomplish this, he needs to encourage continued direct investment in technology, promote the reform of an unprofitable state sector, and continue to draw foreign investment into China. Another major goal is the alleviation of poverty, which is caused by inequitable distribution of benefits derived from economic growth and by poor performance of the agricultural sector in many provinces.

After years of rapid growth, the Chinese economy suffers from some significant structural flaws. In particular, glaring differences between the coastal regions and the hinterlands threaten the unity of the nation. These regional differences not only contribute to massive migrations into Shanghai and Guangdong, but also cause resentment by poorer provinces that view the richer regions as benefiting from excessive governmental attention at their cost. Also, richer provinces resent public spending in poorer regions. Jiang needs to alleviate the severe economic differences among the regions without weakening the growth of the coastal areas.

Another serious domestic issue is the restructuring of state enterprise operations, which have become a severe budgetary burden. Jiang claims that these enterprises must change their methods of operation in order to succeed in a socialist market economy. Over the past two years, the Chinese government began a major privatization campaign. The government has become concerned about a potential backlash against the government resulting from increased social problems related to economic changes. Recently, the government cracked down on a religious sect, the Falun Gong, resulting in increased international condemnation of the country's human rights practices.

In 1995, foreign investment amounted to US$38 billion, of which US$11 billion was concentrated in the Shanghai region. Not only is it important for Jiang to maintain the flow of money into China, but the government needs to promote investment in the interior of the country. In particular, agricultural productivity must be improved in many regions where gripping poverty and hunger are a way of life. The rush to industrialize has left interior regions largely neglected. Even though labor costs are low in these regions, the infrastructure is not conducive to large-scale foreign investment. In 1999, the Chinese economy slowed, making it necessary for Jiang and the Chinese leadership to "look abroad" for economic growth.

## FOREIGN POLICY

Jiang has major obstacles to overcome in the international arena. Over the years, China's reputation has suffered internationally over its treatment of political prisoners and dissidents and continues to remain tarnished in the aftermath of the Tiananmen Square massacre. Issues of fair trial and prison conditions have enraged Western human rights activists. Contributing to this problem is the lack of democracy in China, as measured by Western standards. Jiang is a leader well versed in Western ways, and he is likely to seek to improve China's image abroad. However, recent allegations of campaign donations to American political parties have also drawn the attention of many China critics.

Jiang is likely to criticize the West for its intervention into Chinese domestic affairs while simultaneously moving to placate its critics by pointing to the unique problems of modernization that the country faces.

As the Chinese economy grows and its export-led-growth strategy produces significant trade surpluses, critics in the US are likely to question China's dedication to free trade principles. Significant pressure will continue to emanate from the White House with calls for the reform of Chinese copyright protection laws and labor laws. However, in order to maintain its high growth, Jiang realizes that exporting increasingly higher value-added products is necessary. In order to do this, Jiang needs to convince the foreign business community that China's domestic political and economic situation is stable and that reforms of the legal and investment codes are forthcoming.

The Chinese military began a process of modernizing its forces recently, and that process is likely to continue into the 21st century. Meanwhile, the perennial Taiwan problem, the return of Hong Kong and Macau, and constant attacks from Western critics of Chinese democracy and human rights have combined to increase nationalism within China. From a security standpoint, Asian neighbors have expressed concern over China's growing economic and military power and how that may fuel rising Chinese nationalism and consequent military action. However, Jiang showed his moderate approach recently by reassuring investors and the West that he would not interfere with Hong Kong's internal affairs. His overall success in foreign policy will be measured by his ability to assuage neighboring nations that China is a peaceful nation and gain entry into the World Trade Organization (WTO).

## ADDRESS

Office of the President
Beijing, People's Republic of China

## REFERENCES

Banks, Arthur, et al. *Political Handbook of the World, 1995–96.*

*China Daily,* 4–6 March 1997.

*Current Biography Yearbook, 1995.* New York: H.W. Wilson, 1996.

*The Economist,* 22 February–1 March 1997; 1 May–25 September 1999.

*Far Eastern Economic Review,* 6 March 1997.

*New York Times,* 23 February 1997; 12 September 1999; 28 September 1999; 1 October 1999.

*Nikkei Weekly* (Tokyo), 24 February–3 March 1997.

*Who's Who in the People's Republic of China.* New York: K.G. Saur, 1991.

**Profile researched and written by Robert W. Compton, Jr., Western Kentucky University (5/97; updated 5/2000).**

# COLOMBIA

### Andrés Pastrana
### President
*(pronounced "AN-dress Pass-TRA-na")*

*"We must all unite around the supreme objectives of reaching peace, reactivating the economy, and achieving social justice."*

The Republic of Colombia is located in the northwest corner of South America. Bordering Ecuador and Peru to the south, Brazil to the southwest, and Venezuela to the east, Colombia is the only South American country with a coastline on both the Pacific and Atlantic Oceans. Colombia connects the South American continent with the Central American isthmus through a narrow and densely forested border with Panama. In total, the country occupies 1.2 million sq km (440,000 sq mi).

Colombia is the third most populated country in Latin America, with more than 39 million inhabitants. Its population is 58% mestizo (mix of Spanish and indigenous), 20% white, 14% mulatto (black and indigenous), 4% black, and 4% Amerindian. A majority of Colombians are nominally Roman Catholic (95%), but in recent years Protestants have made important gains in urban areas. Population growth stands at an annual rate of 1.61%. Improvements in health conditions have helped infant mortality decline to a rate of 24.7 deaths per 1,000 live births. Life expectancy is now 70.28 years for males and 76.09 years for females. The literacy rate has also increased in recent years, and now stands at 91.3%.

The economy has grown at an average of 2.5% over the past decade. Total GDP is expected to reach over US$254 billion in 1998. Exports amounted to US$11.3 billion in 1998 while imports totaled US$14.4 billion the same year. Colombia's leading trading partners include the US (39%), European Union (26%), and Venezuela (8.5%). The nation's main exports are petroleum, coffee, coal, bananas, and fresh cut flowers. Colombia imports industrial equipment, consumer goods, chemicals, and paper products. With a labor force of more than 12 million, the major source of employment is services (46%), followed by agriculture (30%), and industry (24%). The Colombian currency is the *peso*.

The illegal production and sale of cocaine has served as an important source of financial resources for the informal economy. Colombia is the world's largest processor of coca derivatives and the main supplier of cocaine to the US and other international markets. More than 50,000 hectares (123,550 acres) of coca leaves are cultivated illegally, and the estimated profits from illegal drug production and export is more than $4 billion annually.

## POLITICAL BACKGROUND
Originally inhabited by tribal groups dominated by the Chibchas, Colombia was first visited by Spanish sailors as early as 1500. Yet, the first permanent European settlement was not established until 1525. Declared a Spanish colony in 1549, Colombia was organized into the vice-royalty of New Granada in 1717, along with what are now Venezuela, Ecuador, and Panama. Under the tutelage of South America's liberator, Simón Bolívar, the country began its quest for independence. With the defeat of the Spanish army in 1819, the Republic of Gran Colombia was formed as an independent state comprising the territory of the former vice-royalty. Two further wars created the autonomous states of Venezuela and Ecuador (1830) and Panama (1903).

The political history of Colombia has been dominated since independence by two opposing groups, eventually organized as the *Partido Liberal* (PL) and the *Partido Conservador* (PC), which is historically linked to the followers of Simón Bolívar, Colombia's liberator and first president. The PC helped to create a strong centralized government. The PL contributed a separation of church and state and universal suffrage to the political landscape.

Colombian politics is marked by extraordinary violence. Citizens resort to arms to resolve political differences to a degree unmatched on the continent. Three presidential candidates were assassinated during the 1990 campaign, and others had attempts made on their lives. The election of Cesar Gaviria in 1990 brought an opportunity for political peace. A new constitution was written in 1991, and several guerrilla groups entered the political arena after being demobilized. By that time, drug lords had come to replace guerilla leaders as the main threat to political and social stability. The leader of the powerful Medellin drug cartel, Pablo Escobar, was imprisoned but eventually managed to escape. At that point, Gaviria declared war on drug cartels and was killed in a 1993 confrontation.

Demand for drugs in the US remained high, and despite government efforts to eradicate coca leaf plantations, the influence of drug lords contaminated the country. The 1994 presidential elections showed the extent to which drugs had invaded every aspect of the nation's life. Liberal candidate, Ernesto Samper won the election, but accusations of drug-related campaign financing almost toppled his government months after his inauguration. Lack of credibility and a continuous need to disassociate his government from drug lords made Samper's four-year term a difficult one. Though the economy remained strong, impeachment procedures against Samper created a climate of political instability. The US pressured his government to make significant progress in the war against drugs, but distanced itself from Samper and his Liberal Party.

## PERSONAL BACKGROUND

Born in the capital city of Bogotá on 17 August 1954, Andrés Pastrana is the son of former president, Misael Pastrana (1970–74) and María Cristina Arango. As a member of the political and social elite, Pastrana traveled extensively throughout the country during his father's electoral campaigns and presidential term. Pastrana attended private school at the Colegio San Carlos de Bogotá and graduated from Colegio Mayor Nuestra Senora del Rosario Law School in Bogotá. Pastrana also received a graduate degree from Harvard University's Center for International Affairs. He is married to Nohra Puyana and has three children.

Upon his return from Harvard. Pastrana co-founded the *Guión* magazine and, in 1979, established the *Noticiero TV Hoy* television news program. As director of *TV Hoy,* he was awarded the prestigious King of Spain International Journalism Award and the Colombian National Simón Bolívar Journalism Award. During his years as a television journalist, Pastrana gained a reputation for serious news reporting and economic conservatism. He took a strong stand against drug trafficking and government corruption.

## RISE TO POWER

As a media personality and son of a former president, Pastrana had little difficulty getting elected to the Bogotá City Council as an alderman. In 1988, he was kidnapped by the Medellín drug cartel but escaped unharmed. At that point Pastrana became one of the most outspoken opponents of the government's policies against drug trafficking and internal violence. He ran a successful campaign for mayor of Bogotá and was elected to the Congress in 1991. Pastrana quickly became a leader of the Conservative Party and secured its nomination for the 1994 presidential elections. He narrowly lost to Ernesto Samper of the Liberal Party. Shortly after the election, Pastrana made public a series of tapes that linked Samper with the Cali drug cartel. He then led a civic movement demanding the president's resignation and later his impeachment by parliament. The Liberal Party's control of Congress allowed Samper to retain his position, but Pastrana used the drug scandal as a launching pad for his next presidential campaign.

During the 1998 campaign Pastrana accused Liberal Party candidate Horacio Serpa of corruption and ties to the drug cartels. Serpa had defended the president when he served as his minister of the interior but tried to distance himself from Samper during the electoral campaign. A second challenge came from the independent candidacy of Noemi Sanín. As a former member of Pastrana's Conservative Party, Sanín served as a cabinet member under several Liberal Party administrations. She became a strong spokesperson against corruption in the Samper government after the drug-related campaign finance scandal was made public. Sanín attacked both the Samper government and the alternation of power between the Liberal and Conservative parties. In the first round of voting, Serpa received 34.5% of the vote, Pastrana

came in second with an extremely close 34.4%, and Sanín took a surprisingly high 25.7%. A run-off election between Serpa and Pastrana was held on 19 June 1998. Turnout was high, with more than 12 million Colombians going to the polls out of an eligible 20 million voters. Pastrana's main ally was the high turnout rate in urban areas, where the Conservative Party is strongest. He received more than 6 million votes (50.45%) to Serpa's 5.6 million (46.5%).

## LEADERSHIP

Pastrana's election represents the first Conservative Party victory in a decade. He is faced with a Congress controlled by the opposition party and a country with growing unemployment. The economy is not growing fast enough to eradicate poverty. Pastrana must deal with widespread corruption, a growing problem of civil violence, crime, and ransom kidnappings. The leftist guerillas launched an offensive against the Samper government but have indicated a willingness to negotiate with Pastrana.

However, the biggest challenge to the Pastrana government is the growing influence of drug cartels. The 1991 Constitution made it almost impossible for drug lords to be extradited and judged outside Colombia. Pastrana has indicated that he would oppose extradition as well and would, instead, strive to improve the legal system in Colombia. The high demand for drugs in the US poses a most difficult challenge to any leader in Colombia. Peasants are faced with deteriorating coffee prices. The development of alternative crop production is slow and coca leaf production represents a sound alternative. The crop grows almost naturally in the highlands and is paid at rates several times higher than coffee or other crops.

The multi-million dollar drug business has also corrupted many among the military, government officials, and businessmen. Pastrana has made an issue of eradicating drug production from the country. His government will most likely attempt to form a broad civic coalition to put an end to drug-related violence and to reconvert the nation's economy to reduce dependence on coca leaf production.

## DOMESTIC POLICY

Pastrana must focus on three important domestic issues. First and foremost, he will address the issue of violence. Pastrana campaigned on a pledge to end Colombia's long-running internal conflict. The country's second-largest rebel group, the National Liberation Army (ELN), has said it will seek to negotiate peace. The larger Revolutionary Armed Forces of Colombia (FARC) has signaled it is likely to do the same if Pastrana grants its demand for the demilitarization of a large area. He will attempt to disarm paramilitary forces and better equip the police to reduce the growing violence in cities and rural areas. During his first two years in office, he has pushed to established talks with the guerrillas and advance in the pacification process in rural areas, but little progress has been achieved.

Secondly, Pastrana has pledged to deal with the production of illegal drugs. Crop conversion programs and economic development in rural areas and in the highlands will constitute his leading remedies to reduce illegal agricultural production of coca leaf. Tackling the drug problem will be a difficult challenge, for which he will need support from the international community. Although the US has fully backed Pastrana, illegal narcotic production has not decreased substantially.

Finally, Pastrana is expected to focus on ways to foster economic growth. He has already pledged to reduce the value-added tax from 16% to 12%. He will likely launch an aggressive program to develop infrastructure and housing. His government has pledged to privatize some services and reinvest these resources on education and health care, particularly for rural children. However, it is unlikely that he can take on a more aggressive social program if tax reduction is adopted. Moreover, he needs to have his program approved by parliament, where the opposition Liberal Party holds a commanding majority. The negative effect of the Asian economic crisis hurt Colombia's economy. The Economy shrank by 5.2% in 1999.

## FOREIGN POLICY

Over the past several decades Colombia has emerged as the world's leading cocaine exporter. Its drug cartels are the most successful organizations for the production and export of this illicit drug. Many argue that the drug problem should be solved primarily at the consumption end, by targeting demand rather than production. If other countries reduce consumption of cocaine, Colombian peasants would stop producing it. Pastrana endorses that view as well, but also points to the violence and corruption that drug production has caused in his country. He will probably attempt to get financial support from industrial and drug-consuming countries to develop programs for agricultural conversion and the development of alternative crops. In order for this effort to be successful, the US government will have to play a key role.

## ADDRESS
Palacio de Gobierno
Casa de Narino
Carrera 8A, No. 1–26
Santa Fe de Bogotá, Colombia

## REFERENCES
*CIA World Factbook.* [Online] Available http://www.odci.gov/cia/publications/factbook/co.html (Accessed September 1998 and April 2000).

CNN. [Online] Available http://CNN.com (Accessed September 1998 and April 2000).

CNN En Espanol. [Online] Available http://CNNenEspanol.com (Accessed May and June 1998).

"Colombia's New Antidrug Plan: President Andres Pastrana Arango." *Time International,* 4 October 1999, p. 31.

*El País.* [Online] Availabe http://www.elpais.es (Accessed June 1998).

"Reform of Congress Sought in Colombia." *The New York Times,* 31 March 2000, p. A12.

*El Tiempo de Bogotá.* [Online] Available http://www.eltiempo.com/ (Accessed May-June 1998).

*Encyclopaedia Britannica.* [Online] Available http://www.eb.com/ (Accessed April 2000).

US Department of State. *Background Notes: Colombia.* [Online] Available http://www.state.gov/www/background_notes/colombia_197_bgn.html/ (Accessed January 1997).

Weymouth, Lally. "Battling 'the Bad Guys': Colombia's President vs. Drug Lords, Leftist Rebels and Right-wing Paramilitaries." *Newsweek,* 14 February 2000, p. 50.

**Profile researched and written by Patricio Navia, New York University (9/98; revised 4/2000).**

# COMOROS

**Assoumani Azali**
**President**

*"I have seized power to save the Comoros from falling into chaos and anarchy."*

Located in the Indian Ocean, between Mozambique and the northwest coast of Madagascar, the Federal Islamic Republic of the Comoros is a chain of three small volcanic islands covering a total area of 1,862 sq km (719 sq mi). The population of the Comoros has been estimated at 563,000, with over half the people living on the main island, Grand Comore, where the capital city of Moroni is located. In addition to Grand Comore, the Comoros are comprised of Anjouan and Mohéli. In 1977, they assumed the Swahili names Njazidja, Nzwani, and Mwali.

Arabs who settled on the islands brought Islam to the Comoran culture. More than 99% of Comorans are Sunni Muslim. The linguistic heritage of the Arabs can also be felt in the Comoros where Arabic, along with French and Comoran (a mixture of Arabic and Swahili) are the national languages.

The Comoran economy is based on the local currency called the Comoros *franc*. Known as the "perfume islands," the Comoros grew famous for their exports of perfume essences, as well as vanilla and cloves. Comoran farmers also produce cassava, sweet potatoes, rice, maize, coconuts, coffee, cacao, and bananas. Major imports include meat, rice, and petroleum products. Despite their strategic location in the Mozambique Channel, none of the islands have been able to develop a viable economy, leaving the Comoran people among the poorest in the world. Per capita GDP has been estimated at $700.

## POLITICAL BACKGROUND
Like other islands of the Indian Ocean, the Comoros were settled by successive waves of explorers, traders, and colonists. During the 15th and 16th centuries, Malayan and Arab traders and immigrants settled on the archipelago. Later slaves were brought to the islands and more immigrants arrived from neighboring Madagascar and the African continent. During the 16th and 17th centuries, French, Dutch, Indian, and Chinese traders also made their way to the islands. Native Comorans were often enslaved and exported to other French-occupied territories in the Indian Ocean (e.g. Mauritius, Reunion, and the Seychelles) to work on sugar plantations.

An Islamic political structure was established during the 15th century by Shirazi Arab traders, who settled on the islands of Grand Comore and Anjouan. These settlers divided the 2 islands into sultanates and eventually expanded their rule over the islands of Mayotte and Mohéli. The Shirazi introduced a dynamic economic system and built a booming center of commerce where rice, spices, and slaves were traded in abundance. Indeed, as trade on the islands grew, so too did competition among sultanates for the rich European merchants' business. This competition led to strife and warfare between various sultanates. In the late 1700s, Sakalava slave raiders from the coast of Madagascar attacked the Comoros with such furor that they virtually depopulated the island of Mayotte. Following the defeat of the Sakalava kingdoms at the hands of the Merina, many liberated slaves returned to Mayotte and Mohéli. In the mid-1800s Comoran traders began importing captives from East Africa and disseminating the human cargo to the plantation economies of other Indian Ocean islands. This trade proved lucrative for Shirazi businessmen and contributed to the formation of a three-tiered social system with Shirazi elites, middle-class traders, and slaves.

France officially acquired Mayotte (the fourth island in the archipelago) in 1843 and by 1886 had taken control of the remaining three islands. The French governor-general of Madagascar administered the entire island territory. In 1947, the Comoros became an overseas territory of France and did not gain internal independence until 1961. Full independence was not achieved until 1975 when 96% of Comorans approved a national referendum to split from France. However, the population of Mayotte rejected the referendum, opting instead to remain a dependency of France.

Since independence, there have been numerous shifts of power in the Comoros, almost always precipitated by a military coup d'etat. President Ahmed Abdallah was designated president of the government council and head of state in July 1975. By August of that same year he was deposed by Ali Soilih, who seized power with the help of the now infamous French mercenary, Bob Denard. This political instability would continue for the next 25 years.

After four unsuccessful coup attempts during the mid-1970s, Soilih was overthrown in 1978 by Denard and 50 of his mercenaries. The coup plotters replaced Soilih with Ahmed Abdallah and Soilih's former deputy, Muhammed Ahmed—effectively creating a co-presidency. Nevertheless, Denard would continue to effectively rule the Comoros for the next 11 years.

Following the 1978 coup, France resumed aid to the Comoros that had been suspended during the Soilih administration. In October 1978, a new constitution for the Comoros was approved by 99% of the electorate, officially changing

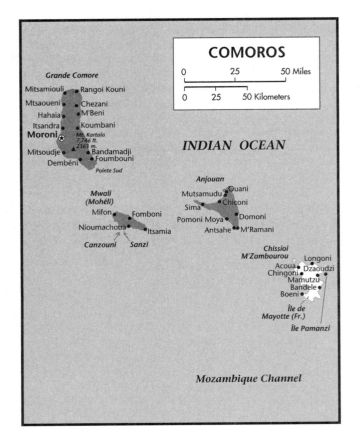

by instability: the periodic dissolution of federal assemblies, charges of corruption, strikes, and several attempted coups. On 25 September 1995, Denard returned to the Comoros and took control of the government, forcing Djohar into exile. Captain Ayaiba Combo headed the "transitional military committee" and claimed responsibility for the coup. In October of that same year, Combo handed power over to two civilian opposition party leaders: Said Ali Kemal and Mohamed Taki Abdulkarim. Thus, interim officials again ruled the Comoros until another set of elections could be organized, and a political transition could be achieved.

The elections of March 1996 involved 15 candidates and were well contested. Mohamed Taki Abdulkarim won the race and, for the first time in the nation's history, presided over a peaceful political transition. Peace in the Comoros, however, was short lived. By 1997, the country was gripped by economic and social crises and fell prey to secessionist fervor. Recognizing that the state was once again in disarray and disgusted by the greed of politicians in the capital, the people of Anjouan decided in August 1997 to break from the union and declare independence. Indeed, the Anjouanais sought to rejoin their former colonizer, France, in a territorial arrangement similar to the French-Mayotte accord. The secession movement also took root on Mohéli, which also asserted its independence from Moroni, further destabilizing the nation. Complicating the matter further is the fact that more than 70,000 Anjouanais live on Grand Comore and make up about half of the "national" army's approximately 800 men. This dynamic has created an ethnic division that runs deep in the military.

Taki's tenure as president was short lived. He died from an apparent heart attack in November 1998. The president of the Comoran Supreme Court, Tadjiddine Ben Said Massonde, took office as interim president on 6 November 1998. But the Massonde administration had little success in returning the Comoros to stability. Anjouan and Mohéli reasserted their demands for secession, which heightened political and ethnic tensions on Grand Comore. Indeed, tensions surrounding the secessionist debate spiraled out of control in April 1999, leading to three days of rioting in the capital, during which businesses were looted and destroyed, and hundreds of Anjouanais were forced to flee Moroni.

The chaos ended on 30 April when Colonel Assoumani Azali, the army chief-of-staff, staged a bloodless coup, overthrowing Massonde and restoring order to the streets of Moroni. While this event marked the eighteenth coup attempt in the Comoros 24-year history, and the fourth to succeed in ousting a sitting government, Comorans greeted it as a "necessary evil" to reestablish security and calm in the nation.

## PERSONAL BACKGROUND

Born around 1959, a native of Grande-Comore, Azali received his military training in Morocco and France. He was the army chief-of-staff under presidents Djohar and Taki. While little has been written about Azali, he has the reputation for being authoritarian and a blunt administrator.

## LEADERSHIP

When Azali seized power, the Paris-trained officer declared that he had intervened "to save the Comoros from chaos and

the name of the nation to the Federal Islamic Republic of the Comoros. Under this new constitution, individual autonomy for each island was guaranteed. Individual governors were elected and a 38-member federal assembly, comprised of representatives from each of the islands, was put into place. Although the assembly was meant to represent all of the political parties in the Comoros, it voted in 1982 to create an official state party, the *Union Comorienne pour le Progres* (UDZIMA).

In 1984, Abdallah was elected to another six-year term. Buoyed by his new mandate, he set out to extend and consolidate his power. One year later, Abdalllah succeeded in abolishing the office of prime minister, and, in 1989, pushed through a constitutional amendment which would allow him to run for a third term for the presidency. On 26 November 1989, members of the presidential guard, under the direction of Denard, assassinated Abdallah.

The Comoran constitution proscribed that Said Mohammed Djohar, the president of the Supreme Court, assume the role of interim head of state. Denard and his supporters, however, continued to maintain *de facto* control of national political and military power. Indeed, Denard and his band of mercenaries remained ensconced in Moroni until France intervened, and they fled to South Africa.

Djohar held elections in February 1990 that were widely viewed as fraudulent and later annulled. Opposition parties were allowed two months to organize but were still narrowly defeated by the sitting interim president: Djohar received 55% of the vote while the leader of the *Union Nationale pour la Democratie aux Comoros* (UNDC), Mohamed Taki Abdulkarim, received 45%. Djohar's presidency was marked destruction." Moreover, as head of a heterogeneous army that is being torn by ethnic loyalties, it is also thought that Azali seized power, at least in part, to avoid further internal strife among his forces.

Following the ousting of Massonde and his reformist prime minister, Abbas Djoussouf, Azali was sworn in as president on 5 May 1999, taking the positions of premier and defense minister as well. He dissolved all elected institutions in the country, suspended the constitution, and announced that he would form a 12-person executive body called the "Committee of State," consisting primarily of civilians and young technocrats, that will remain in place until elections can be organized. Yet it is clear that Azali intends to keep his hands firmly on state controls. At the president's inauguration ceremony, a new charter was officially endorsed endowing Azali with sweeping legislative and administrative powers.

## DOMESTIC POLICY

The bid for secession by Anjouan and Mohéli and the resulting constitutional crisis will remain the priority of the archipelago's military-led government. Azali has vowed to remain in power until an agreement to keep the Comoros Republic intact is signed and implemented. He said that elections could not take place until Anjouan signs on to an Organization of African Unity (OAU) brokered agreement. Signed in the Madagascar capital of Antananarivo, the so-called "Antananarivo Agreement" gives each of the three islands its own parliament, local government, and the presidency of the Comoran federation, to rotate between them every three years. However, it is unlikely that the forces pushing for secession will soon acquiesce to the government's entreaties to accept increased autonomy and political representation while remaining in a national union. The Azali regime is reportedly considering sending an OAU peacekeeping force to Anjouan to disarm the secessionists, but this is unlikely unless the Comoran government's relations with the OAU improve. Meanwhile, Azali's government has outlawed demonstrations and is actively seeking to restore security and discourage anti-Anjouannais and Mohélian hysteria on Grand Comore.

In addition to ensuring law and order and defusing nationalist sentiments in the Comoros, the immediate goal of the Azali administration will be to win the support of civil servants by providing them with regular and timely paychecks. At the same time it seems clear that the military government will also try to marginalize the political opposition. The fact remains, however, that Comorans today are faced with falling living standards and a deteriorating economic situation that impoverishes the vast majority of the archipelago's citizens.

## FOREIGN POLICY

Building up the Comoran economy will not be an easy task and will largely depend on the support of the international community, namely international financial institutions and donors. Although Azali's coup appeared to be popular among Comorans, it was vociferously denounced by the OAU, France, and South Africa—sponsor of the OAU's mediation efforts. Indeed, the military government has not been recognized by any foreign nation. This fact presents the Azali administration with the daunting challenge of winning international recognition and legitimacy and securing vitally needed International Monetary Fund (IMF) and World Bank assistance.

## ADDRESS

Beit Salaam Presidential Palace
Boite Postale 421
Moroni, Comoros

## REFERENCES

*Africa Research Bulletin*, 1–30 April 1999.
CNN Interactive. [Online] Available http://cnn.com/WORLD/africa/99005/02/comoros.reaction.ap/ (Accessed 5 May 1999).
CNN Interactive. [Online] Available http://cnn.com/World/africa/9905/06/BC-COMOROS.reut/indel.html (Accessed 7 May 1999).
*EIU Country Report: Tanzania and the Comoros*, London: Economist Intelligence Unit, 2nd Quarter, 1999.
*Human Development Report*. New York: United Nations Development Program, 1998.
*Jeune Afrique*, 11–24 May 1999.
*La Lettre de l'Ocean Indien*, 8 May 1999.
*National Geographic Atlas of the World*, 6th edition. Washington, DC: National Geographic Society, 1992.

**Profile researched and written by Timothy W. Docking, Boston University (9/99; updated 2/2000).**

# CONGO
## DEMOCRATIC REPUBLIC OF THE

### Laurent Kabila
### President
*(pronounced "ka-BEE-la")*

*"My long years of struggle were like spreading fertilizer on a field. But now it is time to harvest."*

The Democratic Republic of Congo, formerly known as the Republic of Zaire, is the third-largest country in Africa. The country covers 2,345,406 sq km (905,562 sq mi), most of it contained within the Congo River basin. The population of 50.5 million is comprised of more than 200 ethnic groups. Peoples of Bantu ethnicity make up the largest sector, with minorities of Sudanese, Nilotes, Pygmies, and Hamites. The official language is French, but over 400 Sudanese and Bantu dialects are also spoken. Congo's economy is based primarily on mineral extraction. Cobalt and copper are the principal exports; other minerals commercially exploited include diamonds, gold, silver, zinc, manganese, and tin. Agricultural products include coffee, rubber, cocoa, and tea. Congo also has offshore oil reserves. Despite these assets, it is the fourth-poorest nation in the world, due largely to mismanagement and corruption. Per capita GDP has been estimated at US$710. Hyperinflation has been eroding what little value the currency had. The unit of currency is the *nouveau zaire*.

## POLITICAL BACKGROUND

The territory once known as the Belgian Congo gained independence from colonial rule on 30 June 1960, with Patrice Lumumba as prime minister and Joseph Kasavubu as head of state. In less than a week, the armed forces had mutinied, and Katanga province threatened to secede. United Nations troops were brought in to maintain order. Kasavubu dismissed Lumumba in September 1960. Later in the same month, the government was overthrown by then-Colonel Joseph-Desiré Mobutu. He returned power to Kasavubu in February 1961.

UN troops left the country on 30 June 1964, but political chaos once again erupted. Another struggle for the presidency took place between Kasavubu and the newly designated premier, Moise Tshombe, head of Katanga province. On 24 November 1965, Mobutu led a second bloodless coup. This time he declared that he personally would assume the presidency for a period of five years and proclaimed the "Second Republic."

Mobutu declared that his would be a government by decree. These decrees would have the power of law unless parliament voted to reverse them. In March 1966, faced with intransigent parliamentary opposition to most of his reforms, Mobutu stripped the legislature of the bulk of its power and rescinded its right to debate his decrees. A new constitution was adopted in June 1967. Presidential elections, in which Mobutu ran unopposed, were held in late 1970, and he was

elected to a seven-year term. Elections were again held in 1977 and 1984, with Mobutu as sole candidate. Though elections were also held regularly for the national legislature, the sole legal political party was Mobutu's *Mouvement Populaire de la Revolution* (MPR). In 1971, the Government of Zaire and the executive council of the MPR were merged into the National Executive Council, further solidifying Mobutu's political domination. He personally appointed provincial governors and their cabinets, leaving them with little real authority.

In the early 1970s Mobutu undertook a campaign of Africanization of the former Belgian Congo. The name of the country was changed to Zaire, place names were changed from French colonial to African, and many individuals took African names. Following closely on the campaign for authentication came "*Mobutisme*," whereby Mobutu was elevated to the stature of "Father and God of the nation."

In King Leopold's shadow, Mobutu considered Zaire his personal fief. He diverted foreign aid, siphoned profits from the country's highly profitable mines, and thus amassed a personal fortune estimated at US$7 billion. Following his example, a public culture of corruption ensued, which observers labeled kleptocracy, or government by theft. Indeed, its pervasiveness once led Mobutu to admonish his bretheren: "When you steal, steal cleverly," meaning, I understand you are stealing from the state, but at least invest your ill-gotten gains in the country. This piece of advice was freely given though not practiced.

The threat to Zaire's strategic importance to the West subsided following the collapse of the Soviet Union. To placate Western donors, Mobutu opened a national dialogue with the Zairian people and convened a series of hearings around the country. More than 5,000 individuals and organizations submitted written critiques, revealing to Mobutu the deep and pervasive dissatisfaction with his rule. Devastated by the criticism, he announced far-reaching reforms. He declared that a new prime minister would be named to form a transitional government. A new constitution was drafted that limited the executive power of the president, at least theoretically. Political parties were legalized, and a popular presidential election was proposed but never took place. Dissidents were allowed to resume political activity, and exiles were permitted to return to Zaire. Mobutu reneged on his promises, and unable to postpone real reform further, he was driven from power in May 1997 by Kabila's allied forces. He died soon after in exile from prostate cancer.

## PERSONAL BACKGROUND

Laurent-Desiré Kabila was born in Ankoro, a small town on the banks of the Congo River in North Katanga. He studied philosophy in France and later became a member of the Assembly of North Katanga, in which he supported Patrice Lumumba. Officially, he is married with six children; his son Joseph is a commander in the rebel army, which Kabila leads.

Much speculation surrounds Kabila's personal life, particularly because he has kept his personal affairs from the public eye. Kabila's public image is that of a revolutionary; however, Che Guevarra once dismissed him as a trader and diamond black marketer. Kabila has apparently changed his religion from Muslim to Christian. Many Congolese suspect that one of his sons was mothered by a Tutsi. Rumors link Kabila romantically to the famous Congolese singer-dancer Tshala Mwana. He is believed to be 57 years old.

Most of Kabila's political career was conducted in opposition to Mobutu. He went into exile after the murder of the nation's first prime minister, Patrice Lumumba, and began plotting rebellion. He spearheaded several unsuccessful insurrections over the course of the next three decades, some from within Zaire and others from neighboring Tanzania. Kabila traveled extensively in East Africa and formed close ties with Yoweri Museveni in Uganda, and Paul Kagame, formerly a Rwandan rebel of the Front Patriotic Rwandais (FPR). Kagame became president of Rwanda in April 2000.

## RISE TO POWER

Kabila's fortune changed in the 1990s as Mobutu's unpopularity, the withdrawal of superpower support for him, and internal pressures for democratization mounted. Kabila's Alliance of Democratic Forces for the Liberation (AFDL) of Congo-Zaire was able to secure the backing of neighbors Rwanda and Uganda, both of whom provided critical financial, logistical, and troop support to him. Besides Kabila, the AFDL founders included Bugera, a Rwandan Tutsi; Masasu, the son of a Tutsi mother and Shi father; and Ngoma, a Congolese and the first leader of AFDL.

With the support of his allies, Kabila's Alliance swept from the east to Kinshasa in a matter of months, meeting little resistance from Mobutu's ill-trained and poorly paid troops. Mobutu's army made a bloody last stand in Kenge, some 200 km (124 mi) from Kinshasa, but was decisively defeated. Kabila rejected US- and South African-led negotiations for a ceasefire, and he refused to allow Mobutu to preside over a transition to elected government. Mobutu fled on 16 May 1997; Kabila arrived in Kinshasa on the evening of 20 May 1997.

## LEADERSHIP

For most of his first three years of rule, Kabila has had to direct the reconstruction of an impoverished country at war Upon assuming power, Kabila announced that the country's natural resources belonged to the AFDL. He also made symbolic changes renaming the country, "The Democratic Republic of Congo," and reverting to the 1960 independence flag and national anthem. Kabila named 13 ministers on 22 May 1997. He abolished the position of prime minister to consolidate the power of the presidency. Many people considered this a snub of the former prime minister, Etienne Tshisekedi. Kabila promised a new constitution within 60 days of his takeover.

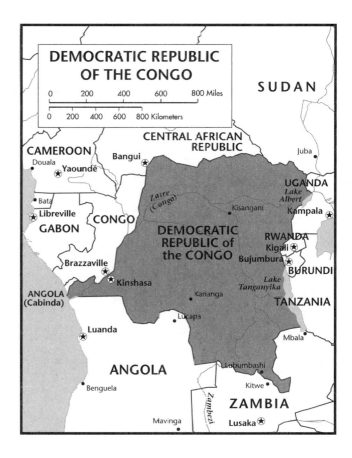

Prior to his inauguration on 28 May 1997, Kabila banned political parties, except the AFDL, and excluded most members of opposition parties from his cabinet. Until a new constitution could be established, Kabila ruled without a legislature and appointed judges. He protected his Rwandan allies from international condemnation by refusing to allow human rights groups access to areas where Hutu refugees had been massacred. When evidence of the massacres could not be refuted, he agreed to allow humanitarian agencies to investigate.

Kabila faced his first test of authority within days of proclaiming himself president. After being excluded from the new government, Tshisekedi announced that he viewed Kabila as another dictator and organized a protest in direct violation of Kabila's ban on political activity. In response, government soldiers were brought in to halt the demonstration. They fired shots in the air to disperse the crowd of 1,000 and detained 50 young protesters who demanded Kabila's resignation.

His second test occurred in August 1998 when Rwandan troops tried to abduct him at his Kinshasa residence. By 1998, only two of the founding members of the AFDL remained. Ngoma had been killed, and Masasu imprisoned by Kabila, leaving Bugera (a Tutsi) to succeed Kabila in the event of his departure. This situation made Kabila extremely vulnerable, particularly in view of Rwanda's territorial aims and his mostly unpaid debt to his former allies.

The third and major test was the invasion and subsequent war. Though fighting between Rwandan and Ugandan troops in May 1999 unveiled their opportunism, Rwanda accused Kabila of harboring the Interhamwe while Uganda came to the support of its ally. Rebellious factions within Congo, ostensibly protesting the lack of political reform but hoping to capitalize on the war, received backing from these neighbors. Without the military intervention of Zimbabwe and other SADC states, Kabila most certainly would have been defeated.

In the near term, Kabila's future depends on the success of the Lusaka Accords and the UN peacekeeping effort underway. In the longer run, it will depend on the resolution of unsettling issues among the Great Lakes countries, particularly the Tutsi, Hutu, and other ethnic cleavages in these countries. In the meanwhile, a democratic transition has been postponed indefinitely.

## DOMESTIC POLICY

The Democratic Republic of Congo must attempt to erase the legacy of 32 years of pervasive corruption and economic mismanagement of one of the world's most richly endowed countries. Instead of being among the richest African nations, Congo is very nearly the poorest with low levels of formal economic activity, poor public sanitation, transportation, and communications systems. Cellular phones have replaced the dysfunctional telephone system. Health and education have been the hardest hit. Civil servants are rarely paid, and what they earn is not enough to support themselves.

Kabila has vowed to promote peace and prosperity in Congo and has crafted what is being touted as a free-market economy with a human face. Kabila's spokesmen promised to create an economy of balance, where every participant gets his share and where government intervention insures that the economy is not a disaster at the social level. About a month after taking power, Kabila suspended the heads of 50 state enterprises created during Mobutu's reign. These were primarily cronies of the deposed leader, who used the companies to enrich themselves. He also announced plans to nationalize the nation's largest private television station, which was owned by a Mobutu supporter.

In 1997, the new government reviewed all economic agreements and concessions. Kabila ended the monopoly that the DeBeers company held on exporting diamonds and nationalized an important rail company run by a Belgian-South African conglomerate. Otherwise he was actively encouraging foreign investment in the economy, with the proviso that it had to contribute to the general interest of the country.

Since the August 1998 invasion, the government depreciated the *franc* four times to keep up with inflation. Its macroeconomic policies have not worked and have consisted mainly in cracking down on exchange bureaus. In November 1999, the government struggled to find the foreign exchange it needed to pay for food and fuel imports. The severe shortage of foreign exchange caused recurrent fuel shortages, a steady depreciation of the *franc,* and fed inflation because most goods are imported. The government also faced a possible uprising from civil servants angry over low salaries.

## FOREIGN POLICY

Congo has been the focal point of Africa's first continental war, and Kabila has had to cut a number of deals with his neighbors to stay in power. The year 1998 saw a dramatic reversal in relations between DROC and its former AFDL allies. The DROC had broken off diplomatic relations with Uganda and Rwanda, and hostilities had broken out between these former bedfellows. Zambian President Frederick Chiluba arranged talks between Laurent Kabila and the rebels. In April 1999, Kabila and President Yoweri Museveni of Uganda signed a ceasefire brokered by Colonel Muammar Gaddafi. The presidents of Chad and Eritrea attended this mini-summit.

Former Botswana president, Masire, has also mediated the Lusaka Accord and its implementation. Relations with the US and with France have improved after 1998. Cohen and Woods International, a well-known public relations firm, has represented the Kabila government in the US. Plans were underway in May 2000 to send some 5,000 UN peacekeepers to monitor the Accords.

## ADDRESS

Presidence de la Republique
Kinshasa
Democratic Republic of Congo

## REFERENCES

Africa News Online. [Online] Available http://www.africanews.org/west/stories/1999_feat1.html (Accessed May 2000).

Africaonline. [Online] Available http://www.africa-online.com (Accessed May 2000).

*Boston Globe,* 27 March–1 June 1997.

Congo 2000. [Online] Available http://www.congo2000.com (Accessed May 2000).

*The Economist,* 17 December 1994–24 May 1997.

Economist Intelligence Unit, Ltd. *EIU Country Reports.* 1999.

Integrated Regional Information Network (IRIN). [Online] Available http://www.reliefweb.int/IRIN (Accessed May 2000).

*L'Express,* 7 November 1996.

*MacLeans,* 7 April 1997.

*Mail and Guardian* (Johannesburg), 2 May 1997.

*New Republic,* 14–28 April 1997.

*New York Times,* 18 May 1997.

*Newslink Africa,* 7 October 1996.

*Newsweek,* 24 February–31 March 1997.

*Raleigh News and Observer,* 17–20 May 1997.

*Time,* 24 March–26 May 1997.

*US News & World Report,* 29 May 1995–26 May 1997.

Young, Crawford, and Thomas Turner. *The Rise and Fall of the Zairian State.* Madison: The University of Wisconsin Press, 1995.

**Profile researched and written by Alison Doherty Munro (6/97; updated by Robert J. Groelsema 5/2000).**

# CONGO
## REPUBLIC OF THE

### Denis Sassou-Nguesso
### President
*(pronounced "DEN-ee SAH-soo en-GESS-oo")*

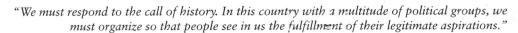

*"We must respond to the call of history. In this country with a multitude of political groups, we must organize so that people see in us the fulfillment of their legitimate aspirations."*

The Republic of Congo lies in Western Africa, bordering the South Atlantic Ocean and Gabon to the west, Cameroon and Central African Republic to the north; the Democratic Republic of Congo (formerly Zaire) lies across the Congo River to the country's east and south. The capital is Brazzaville. The national territory encompasses 342,000 sq km (132,047 sq mi), which spans the Equator.

The country's total population is approximately 2.7 million people, of whom are 48% Kongo in the south, 20% Sangha, 12% M'Bochi in the north, and 17% Teke in the central area of the country. There were fewer than 10,000 Europeans (primarily French) in the country prior to political unrest in 1997, and many of these were evacuated. French is the official language, but African languages—especially Lingala and Kikongo—are spoken by many Congolese. About half of the people in the Congo Republic are Christians and almost as many (48%) practice animist religion. There is also a small (2%) Muslim population.

The Congolese economy, or what remains of it after the political turmoil in 1994 and 1997, consists primarily of two distinct sectors: village agriculture and handicrafts. Forestry, once the mainstay of the Congo Republic's economy, has been supplanted by oil, which provides about 90% of government revenues and exports. Other exports include lumber, plywood, sugar, cocoa, coffee, and diamonds. The Congo Republic imports intermediate goods, capital equipment, petroleum products, and construction materials. The currency is the *Communauté Financière franc* (CFA Fr), also called the Central African *franc*.

## POLITICAL BACKGROUND
Part of the French colonial system dating back to the 19th century, the territory known as the Republic of the Congo became autonomous within the French Community in 1958. Full independence followed on 15 August 1960, and the country held its first presidential elections in 1961. Longstanding ethnic tensions led to the eventual resignation of President Abbé Fulbert Youlou. The *Mouvement National de la Revolution* (MNR), a Marxist-Leninist party, was established in 1964 as the sole political party in the country. Conflict between the MNR and the army led to a military coup in 1968, headed by Captain Marien Ngouabi, who had emerged as the principal player in Congolese politics. December 1969 saw the replacement of the MNR with a new Marxist-Leninist party, the *Parti Congolais du Travail* (Congolese Worker's Party or PCT). Ngouabi remained in

power, despite increasing ethnic and political tensions, until his assassination in 1977. The new government was unable to control the military governing committee and the left wing of the powerful PCT and was forced to relinquish power to a provisional committee. In March 1979 the president of that committee, Colonel Sassou-Nguesso, was appointed President of the Republic.

## PERSONAL BACKGROUND
Denis Sassou-Nguesso was born in 1943 in the town of Edou, in the Congo Republic's northern district of Owando. After graduating from the local primary schools, he attended secondary school in the city of Loubomo. Sassou-Nguesso obtained a degree from a teacher's college and taught school briefly, during which time he became involved with a radical youth movement that played a critical part in the nation's independence and subsequent politics. He left teaching to join the army and trained as an officer in Algeria and France. Sassou-Nguesso was commissioned a second lieutenant in 1962 and was appointed commander of the autonomous military zone of Brazzaville. In the army, the young officer excelled and, over time, received increasingly important assignments and promotions. By the early 1970s, he had attained the rank of colonel. Sassou-Nguesso is married to Marie-Antoinette. The couple has a number of children.

## RISE TO POWER
In addition to his military duties, Sassou-Nguesso became increasingly active in politics. He came to be considered a protégé of President Marien Ngouabi, who ruled from 1968 until 1977. President Ngouabi appointed Sassou-Nguesso to the position of minister of defense in 1975. Soon afterwards Sassou-Nguesso was named to a special revolutionary general staff. In 1977, he became vice president of the PCT military committee. In that same year, President Ngouabi was assassinated and succeeded by Sassou-Nguesso's rival, Joachim Yhombi-Opango, a former chief of staff. Yhombi-Opango was more sympathetic toward the West than the former Marxist regime. Economic problems, and Yhombi-Opango's attempts to resolve them, brought him into conflict with the left wing of the PCT. In February 1979, he was forced to relinquish power to a provisional committee appointed by the PCT. As president of that committee, Sassou-Nguesso was appointed President of the Republic the following month.

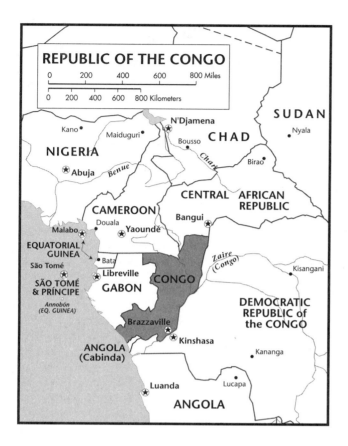

## REPUBLIC OF THE CONGO

LEADERSHIP

Sassou-Nguesso immediately undertook to temper the course charted by previous governments. Elections for a national people's assembly were held in July 1979 and a new socialist constitution was approved. Sassou-Nguesso promised that exiles opposed to the regime could return to the country without fear of repression. He adopted an increasingly pro-Western foreign policy and a liberal economic policy. In 1984, Sassou-Nguesso was reelected, both to the chairmanship of the party's central committee and to the presidency for another five-year term. Despite continued ethnic tensions and a floundering economy, Sassou-Nguesso was once again reelected in 1989.

The legislative elections held in September 1989 were historic. The list of candidates that was presented to the voters included, for the first time, candidates that were not members of the PCT. This was the first of many changes to come, no doubt precipitated by the dramatic changes occurring in Eastern Europe and the Soviet Union. Two months later Sassou-Nguesso announced a series of reforms intended to liberalize the economy, to reduce the role of the state, and to foster private enterprise.

Increased political pressure forced the Sassou-Nguesso government to gradually abandon its Marxist-Leninist orientation. Trade union activity served to hasten the movement toward a multi-party system, and the PCT announced that political parties would be immediately permitted to register, that a transitional government would take power in early 1991, and that a national conference would take place to decide the nation's future. In 1992 general elections, the *Union Panafricaine pour la Démocratie Social* (Panafrican

Union for Social Democracy or UPADS) won a majority in both houses of the parliament. Pascal Lissouba, a former prime minister and head of UPADS, succeeded in winning the presidency with 36% and 61% of the votes in successive rounds of a two-round election.

Conflict within the government quickly ensued. UPADS and the PCT attempted to form a coalition government, but the PCT left the alliance after being denied ministerial posts it had been promised. The PCT immediately allied itself with the *Union Pour le Renouveau Démocratique* (Union for Democratic Renewal or URD). The PCT-URD pact created a new majority in parliament and demanded the right to form a new government. When they were unable to win an outright majority in the National Assembly, the PCT-URD leadership formed a rival cabinet and encouraged a campaign of civil disobedience, which turned violent as militias loyal to Sassou-Nguesso clashed with government security forces. Despite repeated attempts to disarm the militias, violence continued to escalate from 1993 through 1997. Combatants were divided primarily along ethnic and political lines, both among the militias and within the nation's armed forces. Brazzaville itself was partitioned into three zones, each one controlled by supporters of one of the three principal political factions: districts in the north were held by Sassou-Nguesso's supporters; those in the south were controlled by Lissouba's; and the Bacongo suburb was held by Bernard Kolelas, chairman of the PCT-URD coalition. For four months in 1997 Brazzaville became a war zone as these factions fought for control of the city. Most of the residents fled, and the fighting reduced the capital to a ghost town. Finally, on 15 October, President Lissouba was forced to leave the country and Sassou-Nguesso declared himself to be the victor and new leader.

After being inaugurated on 25 October, Sassou-Nguesso lost no time in naming a new government, relying heavily on old allies from his previous administrations. He declared a willingness to work with anyone who severed ties to the former president. While this position lends credence to his stated goal of forming a government of national unity, it also represents a pragmatic attempt to win support from the south and central regions of the country—something he will require if he is to remain in power.

Sassou-Nguesso has promised to hold elections at some unspecified future time. Since the democratic transition from a one-party state, his party has never won a majority in parliament. Sassou-Nguesso grew accustomed to running unopposed for the presidency, and as of 2000, he has not set a date for elections.

DOMESTIC POLICY

Sassou-Nguesso's highest priority must be to rebuild the shattered Congolese economy. Already crippled from the violence of 1993–94, the nation was brought to an economic standstill by the fighting in 1997. More than 80% of the population was urban-based prior to the war, and the two principal cities withstood the heaviest damage. As former residents trickle back from neighboring Bagon, Cameroon, and Angola (where they fled during the fighting), they have been faced with rebuilding homes destroyed in the war and to living without the most basic of services. Fighting between the military and rebel followers of former perime minister

Bernard Kolelas continued to displace citizens well into 1999. The economic infrastructure, from roads to sanitation and beyond, was devastated. As of 2000, Congo Republic is one of the few countries not to have direct access to the Internet.

The President has accepted humanitarian assistance from the West, but will need to arrange for IMF and World Bank assistance in rebuilding the nation. Oil production, the country's economic mainstay, will be instrumental in financing these programs, but oil revenues are subject to the vagaries of the world commodities market and can fluctuate widely with demand. Further complicating the situation is the fact that oil-production is centered in the south, Lissouba's stronghold. The instability in the region due to the lingering civil war could lead to the government losing control of its most significant source of revenue. Thus, Sassou-Nguesso's economic agenda will be driven at least in part by his need to maintain political peace with opposition parties.

## FOREIGN POLICY

Despite his ideological background, Sassou-Nguesso's foreign policy during his previous tenure was remarkable for its pragmatism. With the fall of communism and the collapse of the Soviet Union, Sassou-Nguesso turned to the West to capitalize on the oil boom of the late 1980s. It was this change in focus that, in some ways, forced Sassou-Nguesso to adopt a more moderate political position than his Marxist-Leninist affiliation might otherwise have warranted.

Recent hostilities in the Congo Republic highlighted the role that international actors have come to play in sub-Saharan Africa. Sassou-Nguesso's military campaign was largely financed by France. Lissouba had broken the French monopoly on oil extraction, awarding some concessions to US companies. The French, in supporting Sassou-Nguesso, clearly hope that he will reinstate that monopoly.

Relations with the US are likely to remain unchanged. The country is not, in itself, of great importance to US strategic interests other than those of oil companies. The US government tends rather to view the Congo Republic as part of a regional sphere, in which Angola takes priority. This, in part, explains the almost total lack of response to the involvement of Angolan troops in the war. Any support the US gives will likely bring with it subtle pressure to open up the political system and move toward free elections.

Relations with its African neighbors are, for the most part, cordial. The Congo Republic played an important role in brokering the Cuban withdrawal from Angola and the move towards Namibian independence from South Africa. Angolan troops also played a significant role in Sassou-Nguesso's victory, largely as punishment to Lissouba for supporting UNITA, a rebel movement which fought the Angolan government for two decades. A longstanding border dispute with the Democratic Republic of Congo (formerly Zaire) remains unresolved as of 2000.

## ADDRESS

Office of the President
Brazzaville
Republic of Congo

## REFERENCES

AfricaNet. [Online] Available http://www.africanet.com (Accessed March 2000).

"Background Brief on Congo-Brazzaville." Nairobi: United Nations Department of Humanitarian Affairs: Integrated Regional Information Network.

*Boston Globe,* 16 October 1997.

*The Economist,* 11 October 1997, 10 April 1999.

*Republic of Congo: An Old General of Leaders in New Carnage.* New York: Amnesty International, 1999.

*US News & World Report,* 27 October 1997.

**Profile researched and written by Alison Doherty Munro (3/98; updated 3/2000).**

# COSTA RICA

## Miguel Angel Rodríguez
## President
*(pronounced "mee-GEL an-HEL rod-REE-gez")*

*"Only by helping each other will we be able to move forward."*

The Republic of Costa Rica is bounded on the north by Nicaragua and on the southeast by Panama, with coastlines on the Pacific Ocean and the Caribbean Sea. The total area is 51,060 sq km (19,730 sq mi). One-fifth of the land lies less than 122 m (400 ft) above sea level. The rest is highlands and volcanic chains.

The population is estimated at 3.7 million, growing at a rate of 2.06% annually. Ninety-six percent of the people are white and *mestizo,* with the remaining 4% being black, Indian, and Chinese. While Spanish is the official language, English is also spoken in some areas. About 95% of the population is Catholic, the remainder being predominantly Protestant. There are small but active Jewish and Buddhist communities as well. The infant mortality rate is 13.5 deaths per 1,000 live births and life expectancy is 75.7 years. A high literacy rate (94.8%) and good access to basic health care and education make Costa Rica the most developed country in Central America.

The per capita GDP has been estimated at $6,700. Average annual growth was 5% in 1999, up from 3% in 1998. During the 90s, the economy expanded at an average of 1.2% annually. Unemployment stood at 5.6% in 1998, but much underemployment has also been reported. While the country exported about $3.9 billion in 1998, it imported more than $4.5 billion that same year. The unit of currency is the *olón,* named after Christopher Columbus.

The years 1994–98 were difficult for the Costa Rican economy. The international price of coffee and bananas, the country's main exports, remained low. The exploitation of rainforests was slowed to protect the environment, causing unemployment in the export sector and a trade balance deficit. Tourism, however, has continued to expand, with eco-tourism becoming one of the fastest growing industries. Costa Rica has not escaped the phenomenon of globalization. Recent years have seen the rapid growth of *maquilas* or finishing plants, attracted to the region by low labor costs. Some view these unregulated "sweat shops" as a disturbing trend. Costa Rica, however, has more environmental protection laws and labor regulations than other Central American and Caribbean countries. In addition, high literacy levels and a productive workforce has attracted more highly skilled industries than its neighbors. The economy recovered strongly in 1999 in part due to the austerity measures implemented in Rodriguez's first year in office.

## POLITICAL BACKGROUND
In the pre-Colombian period the region was inhabited by several small and independent indigenous tribes. Christopher Columbus reached Costa Rica in 1502, at Puerto Limón, on the Caribbean coast. Permanent European settlement was not consolidated until 60 years later when the indigenous tribes were suppressed. For the next 300 years Costa Rica remained a Spanish colony, but never played a significant role in the regional economy. Coffee and bananas were the principal cash crops. Most of the native population did not survive, and the colony was too poor to import many African slaves. Spaniards were not attracted to the region because it lacked mineral deposits. In fact, when other areas of Central America were reorganized as *intendencias* of the Spanish Crown in the 18th century, Costa Rica remained under the control of Nicaragua.

The entire Central American region declared independence from Spain in 1821. However, the failure of this unified effort led Costa Rica to become an independent nation in 1838. A coffee-based economy helped development in the late 19th century. The construction of a railroad between Cartago and Puerto Limón encouraged the development of a banana-based economy in lands that were previously inaccessible.

In 1890, Costa Rica celebrated the first truly democratic elections in Central America. There has been a tradition of strong democratic institutions ever since. Religious toleration was guaranteed and public education made mandatory. The growth of a national business sector and labor unions in the Caribbean region led to the development of progressive, socialist, and communist parties.

Economic ties with Germany and Italy affected Costa Rica negatively during World War II, paving the road to power for a progressive alliance of liberals, communists, and Catholics. Following the international trend of strategic alliances to defeat Germany, Costa Rica's president, Rafael Angel Calderón, forged an anti-fascist alliance that governed until 1949. However, the landed coffee-producing elite opposed Calderón and a brief civil war followed. The anti-government forces, led by José Figueres Ferrer, were successful and a revolutionary junta took power. A 1949 constitution, set up by the victorious junta, abolished the army and established the present governmental system.

The president is elected to a four-year term and cannot be reelected for consecutive terms. The president, two vice presidents, the 57 members of the unicameral Legislative Assembly, and 87 municipal authorities, are all elected on the same day every four years, by universal adult suffrage. Costa Ricans are proud of their democratic traditions. The president becomes somewhat of a "lame duck" on the day of his election, and weak party discipline often means that majorities in the Legislative Assembly are hard to create and precarious. Because the president cannot run for a second term, he depends on his cabinet to initiate legislation. All budgetary matters must be passed by the legislature, which also appoints judges to the Supreme Court for eight-year terms. There are many autonomous governmental institutions which can ignore presidential authority. The result is that the Costa Rican presidency is a weak office compared to many in Latin America.

The major political party is the *Partido de Liberación Nacional* (PLN), which is descended from the groups which won the 1948 civil war. José "Pepe" Figueres founded the party, won the presidency three times, and is still revered. The party has traditionally promoted a strong welfare state, a leading economic role for the central government, and a managed economy. The size of the government has always increased under PLN administrations. However, international pressure from the IMF has forced the PLN to adopt more free market features and to reduce the size of government.

The second major party, the *Partido Unidad Social Cristiano* (PUSC), is descended from the defeated government coalitions of 1948, and from the followers of Rafael Calderón Guardia. The various anti-PLN groups formed a unity coalition, and created the PUSC in 1984. The party favors a free-enterprise, market approach to economics, and a much reduced bureaucracy and national budget. In the past, the PUSC has benefited from anti-PLN sentiment. In recent years political commentators have noted large areas of informal political agreement in national policies and priorities between these two leading parties.

## PERSONAL BACKGROUND

Born in 1940 in San José, Manuel Angel Rodríguez is one of five siblings. He attended the University of Costa Rica, earning degrees in law and economics. Upon graduation, he married Lorena Clare and moved to the US to pursue a graduate degree. He relinquished his fellowship in protest against the US invasion of the Dominican Republic, but proceeded to earn a doctorate in economics from the University of California at Berkeley in 1966. Upon his return to Costa Rica, Rodríguez began teaching at the University of Costa Rica. In 1976 he joined the faculty of the Universidad Autónoma de Centroamérica.

As a professor of economics, politics, and law, Rodríguez has written several books, articles, and newspaper columns. Among his better known works are (published in Spanish): *The Myth of Socialist Rationality, The Judicial Order of Freedom,* and *Freedom and Solidarity.* A practicing Catholic, Rodríguez is said to read the Bible regularly and enjoys literature. The Rodríguezes had three children, one of whom died as an adolescent.

## RISE TO POWER

Shortly after his return from Berkeley, Rodríguez was appointed director of the National Planning Office, a cabinet post in the José Joaquín Trejos administration. He also chaired Costa Rica's Central Bank. Later, in the same admin-

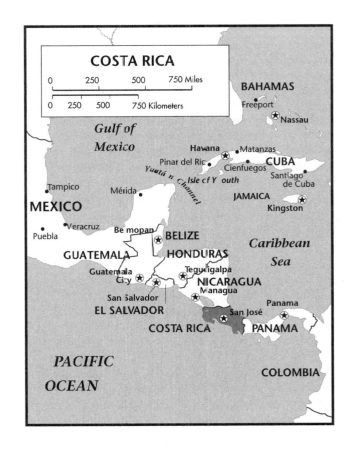

istration, he was named chief of staff. When the PUSC lost the 1970 election, Rodríguez returned to his academic post and took charge of some family businesses—building a small fortune in cattle, meat, and milk. He also served on the board of directors for banks and other financial institutions.

In 1987, Rodríguez made an unsuccessful bid for his party's leadership. He was defeated by Rafael Calderón Sol, who was elected president in 1990. That year, Rodríguez headed the parliamentary ticket of the PUSC and was elected to the 57-member Legislative Assembly. He was elected president of the Assembly in 1991 and began building a more successful bid for the leadership of his party and eventually for the presidency. Rodríguez worked diligently to pass legislation that encompassed a broad range of issues. Some of his better-known initiatives were a new electoral reform, the constitutional reforms to provide guarantees for the private sector, the creation of an agency to regulate public services, and a new energy law. He also sought international support by active participation in the International Christian Democratic Organization. In 1993, Rodríguez was nominated as the presidential candidate of the PUSC. However, his electoral campaign proved unsuccessful, losing by 2% to José María Figueres.

Rodríguez secured his party's nomination for the 1998 presidential elections. He campaigned diligently and enjoyed a comfortable lead in the polls throughout the campaign. Despite low voter turnout, he was able to win 46.8% of the vote. The president and his two vice-presidents will govern with a PUSC majority in the Assembly (30 of the 57 seats).

## LEADERSHIP

During the Figueres administration, Rodríguez opposed the government's effort to foster growth through fiscal expansion. Figueres had difficulty controlling inflation, maintaining a favorable trade balance, and increasing exports. These issues became favorite campaign themes for Rodríguez. The slow economic growth and growing income inequality helped him gain popularity. Rodríguez succeeded in convincing the electorate that Figueres and the PLN candidate were unable to stimulate the economy.

During the campaign Rodríguez was criticized for allegedly using public funds to help run his meat and milk businesses. He was also accused of having ties to the Mexican political godfather, Carlos Hank, whom Rodríguez visited during his electoral campaign. Rodríguez promptly admitted his mistake and severed all ties with Hank and other Mexican officials. He is generally regarded as honest and hard working, although the accusations made during the electoral campaign cast a shadow of doubt on his otherwise clean record.

## DOMESTIC POLICY

Rodríguez plans to concentrate his efforts on reducing the huge budget deficit, which stood at $3.6 billion in 1997. Some of his priorities will be to privatize inefficient state enterprises, generate cash for key social programs, and attract foreign investors to foster economic growth. He is expected to invest heavily in infrastructure and continue to develop the tourist industry. Unemployment is expected to increase because of the privatization of state enterprises and the planned reduction in the government bureaucracy. Labor unions, historically opposed to privatization efforts, may pose a significant threat to Costa Rica's political and social stability if popular support is not sought. In order to avoid a recession, Rodríguez will most likely propose a long-term plan to achieve these goals. The good economic results of 1999, with a reduction in inflation, unemployment and a strong economy growth have helped Rodríguez improve his popularity among the public. When he completes his first half of his four-year term in May 2000, he will enjoy more popular support than when he was originally elected.

## FOREIGN POLICY

Rodríguez is expected to seek trade agreements with other Latin American nations, particularly Mexico and Chile. He has many friends among Mexico's political elite, and his connections with Christian Democrats in other countries, such as Chile, will be beneficial as well. Costa Rica will most likely continue to act independently of the US but will remain an ally on major international issues. As an active member of the Organization of American States, the Rodríguez government could play a major role in helping soften political and economic relations between Cuba and the US.

Costa Rica played an important role in peace negotiations that ended the Central American wars of the 1980s. With peace at hand, Rodríguez could now lead the process of regional economic integration. His first international trips were to the US, neighboring Central American states, and the Summit of the Americas held in Santiago, Chile.

## ADDRESS

President
Casa Presidencial
San José 1000
Costa Rica

## REFERENCES

Bethel, Leslie. *Central America Since Independence.* Cambridge: Cambridge University Press, 1991.
CIA World Fact Book. [Online] Available http://www.odci.gov/cia/publications/nsolo/factbook/co.htm (Accessed April 14, 2000).
CNN. [Online] Available http://cnn.com (Accessed 31 January–1 February 1998).
"Costa Rica Decries High Prices." *The Oil Daily,* August 16, 1999.
La Nación. [Online] Available http://www.nacion.co.cr/ (Accessed 31 January–3 February 1998).
La Prensa Libre, (Costa Rica). [Online] Available http://www.prensalibre.co.cr/ (Accessed 31 January–2 February 1998).
World Bank Group. Country Profiles: Costa Rica. [Online] Available http://www.worldbank.org/html/extdr/offrep/lac/costaric.htm (Accessed 14 April 2000).

**Profile researched and written by Patricio Navia, New York University. (6/98; revised 4/2000).**

# COTE D'IVOIRE

## Robert Guei
### General, President (de facto)

*"Acts of defiance and insubordination are unacceptable because a refusal to abide by the wishes of the public is refusal to accept the primary principles of democracy."*

The Republique de Cote d'Ivoire (Republic of Ivory Coast) is located in West Africa with a 507 km (315 mi) Gulf of Guinea coastline as its southern border and Liberia and Guinea to the west and northwest, Mali and Burkina Faso to the north and northeast and Ghana to the west. Its area is 322,463 sq km (124,503 sq mi). There are three vegetation zones in Cote d'Ivoire: a narrow coastal/lagoon region, a central forest belt covering approximately one third of the country, and a grassy woodland northern region. There are four major rivers draining north-south into the Gulf of Guinea: the Comoe, the Bandama, the Sassandra, and the Cavally (moving from east to west). They are only navigable a short distance from the coast due to rapids created by the primarily southward-sloping plateau nature of the Ivoirian topography.

The population of Cote d'Ivoire is approximately 15.8 million. The literacy rate is 48.5%. Average life expectancy at birth is 46 years. The population is not evenly distributed: the northeast and southwest have very low population densities. The population growth rate for the country, once one of the highest in the world at 3.8%, had decreased by 1999 to 2.35%. There are over 60 recognized ethnic groups, each with its own language, and many of the languages have several distinct dialects. The major ethnic/language groupings are the Akan, Mande, Kru, and Senufo. Approximately one third of the population is foreign, with a 6% annual rate of immigration. The official language of the country is French. Cote d'Ivoire has one of the largest French communities in Africa, numbering approximately 30,000 in 1999. There is also a substantial Lebanese population (estimated variously between 100,00 to 300,000) living mostly in the urban areas of the country. Traditional African religions, frequently termed animism, are practiced by 18% of the population, Islam by 60%, and Christianity by 22%. Islam and evangelical Christian sects are gaining in converts. The official political capital of the country is Yamoussoukro, but the economic capital and most of the government offices remain in the former capital of Abidjan, which has a population estimated at 2.5 million. The Abidjan unemployment rate is estimated at 22.4%. There is a distinct urbanization process for the Ivoirian population and immigrant community, with an estimated annual urban population growth rate of 6.21%.

The Ivoirian unit of currency is the CFA *franc*. The per capita GNP is US$1,680. The primary Ivoirian exports are cocoa, coffee, cotton, bananas, palm oil and kernels, pineapple, and rubber. In 1998 approximately 38% of the export revenues came from coffee and cocoa. Timber exports, which used to be of primary importance for the country, have fallen greatly due to over-harvesting. Cotton production has increased and the country is now third in cotton production for African countries. Expanding rubber production is another healthy sign in the diversification of the Ivoirian economy. In food crops, Cote d'Ivoire is self-sufficient in cassava, yams, plantains, and maize. It produces 40% of the meat that its population uses.

## POLITICAL BACKGROUND

Colonized by the French and part of the French West African Federation, Cote d'Ivoire received its independence in 1960 under Felix Houphouet-Boigny. Houphouet-Boigny was a member of the French National Assembly and minister in the French government before his country's independence, and he continued to maintain very close ties with France throughout his 33-year presidency. When Houphouet-Boigny died on 7 December 1993, he was succeeded by Henri Konan Bedie, the president of the National Assembly, in accordance with the succession rules outlined in Article 11 of the nation's constitution. He remained in power until 24 December 1999, when a military coup took place. The mutinying army placed General Robert Guei in power, thus making him the de facto president. While the United States, Canada and other nations were quick to condemn the coup, many citizens of Cote d'Ivoire reportedly welcomed it as an improvement to the authoritarianism and corruption of the Bedie regime.

Until the December 1994 coup, Cote d'Ivoire had a constitutional democracy, with a constitution that had been amended several times. Upon claiming power, Guei set his own institutions in place, forming the Conseil National de Salut Public (CNSP), or "National Committee of Public Salvation," with nine senior military officers as members and himself as head. CNSP's stated goals were to create the conditions necessary for democracy and to organize free elections. Guei also created a transition government from members of the major opposition parties, and assigned it the task of rewriting the constitution. A referendum on the new draft constitution was scheduled for 23 July 2000.

## PERSONAL BACKGROUND

At the time of the 1999 coup, General Guei was 58 years old, a military man with a history of conflict with then-President Felix Bedie. In 1990, he was made military chief of Cote

**COTE D'IVOIRE**

d'Ivoire, only to be fired from the post five years later after criticizing Bedie for using the military to suppress student riots. Later appointed minister of sports, he was dismissed from that position for unknown reasons shortly after the 1996 Olympics. In 1997, President Bedie ordered him removed from the military altogether for allegedly having plotted a coup attempt two years earlier. In contrast to his adversarial relationship with Bedie, General Guei was, at the time of the coup, a strong ally to opposition leader Alassane Ouattara, of the Republican Rally (RDR) party.

## RISE TO POWER

General Guei came to power during the army's takeover of the Cote d'Ivoire government on 24 December 1999. The spark igniting the coup appears to have been the government's withholding of all wages earned by the nation's soldiers when they served as UN peacekeepers in the Central African Republic. Guei has stated that he wanted to restore the country to democratic rule and hold general elections within the year. He also stated his desire to restore the dignity of the military, eroded by poor salaries and inadequate equipment, and to free the political prisoners, members of the opposition RDR party who were jailed for damages caused during their political rallies.

## DOMESTIC POLICY

Guei faces major challenges, both economic and political. To bring stability back to Cote d'Ivoire, it is necessary that he continue some of the programs begun by his predecessors to manage the nation's debt load and diversify its economy. Cote d'Ivoire has a very high level of external debt per capita: it totals nearly US$20 million with a population of only 15.8

million. Forty percent of its export earnings go toward debt servicing. Because agriculture is responsible for 33% of the country's GDP, its economy is vulnerable to shifting world market prices for its agricultural commodities and particularly that of its two major exports: coffee and cocoa. In January 1994, the CFA *franc* was devalued against the French *franc*, from 50 CFA to 100 CFA to one French *franc*. Since that time, the country's economy has shown steady growth; however, in 1999 this trend slowed due to reduced export earnings and disruptions in the political environment. In the first half of 1999 export earnings dropped 30% for cocoa and coffee; earnings from palm and rubber exports suffered as well. A slow economy will make it difficult for Guei to appease the army. It is important that Guei continue the programs of economic diversification that his predecessors Houphouet-Boigny and Bedie attempted in the past. This diversification will include more emphasis on crops besides cocoa and coffee as well as the establishment of new processing and light industrial firms.

Guei's second major challenge is political. He must maintain control of the military, and banish the rumors of "unease" that began spreading within two weeks his taking power. Actions of rebellion have taken place at isolated barracks, apparently in response to continued low wages and perceived favoritism in the promotion of some in the army to governmental position. Guei's lack of total control over the military was demonstrated in March 2000, when troops ignored his command to dismantle the barricades around the television and radio stations.

Guei appears to be attempting to maintain neutrality in the debate over electoral qualifications, the results of which would determine whether popular candidate Ouattara would be able to run. At the time of the coup, there was suspicion that the military takeover was designed to place Ouattara in power, a view supported somewhat by Guei's assigning several of Ouattara's party members to high government posts. However, within a few months, all but one of the RDR cabinet members were removed from service, and it seemed less likely that Guei had Ouattara's candidacy in mind. As of July 2000, it was not clear whether Guei himself intended to stand for election.

## FOREIGN POLICY

The French armed forces have a 600-man contingent at a base near the international airport at Port Bouet. Immediately following the coup, Guei banned France from sending more troops to its permanent garrison. France had already sent in troops, but withdrew them, saying that the situation seemed stable. France urged other European nations to maintain a dialogue with the Cote d'Ivoire during the transitional period and beyond. This support is critical, since so much of the nation's economy is based on the export of agricultural products to other nations and the receipt of European aid and loans from international banking institutions, some of which was suspended as a result of the coup.

Since taking power in December 1999, Guei has met with some international leaders, including Liberian President Charles Taylor and UN Assistant Secretary-General for Political Affairs Ibrahima Fall. Both encouraged a speedy return to democratic rule for the nation, a goal Guei also claims as a priority. But for the most part, Guei seems to be keeping his own council. When invited to attend the June OAU Summit, he declined, saying that his government and country need to evolve at their own pace, not at the behest of outsiders who are not fully aware of the circumstances.

Cote d'Ivoire's borders are secure, though in the past it has faced a large refugee problem from the civil conflict in Liberia.

## ADDRESS

Presidence de la Republique de Cote d'Ivoire
Yamoussoukro, Cote d'Ivoire

## REFERENCES

Africa News. [Online] Available http://www.africanews.org/ west/ivorycoast/stories/ (various articles; accessed 1 July 2000).

United National Office for the Coordination of Humanitarian Affairs. Integrated Regional Information Network. [Online] Available http://www.reliefweb.int/IRIN/wa/ countrystories/cotedivoire/ (accessed 11 June 2000).

BBC News. [Online] Available http://news2.thls.bbc.co.uk/hi/ english/world/africa/ (various articles; accessed 11 June 2000).

CIA. *The World Factbook 1999.* [Online] Available http:// www.odci.gov/cia/publications/factbook/iv.html (accessed 15 June 2000).

Columbia University Area Studies, African Studies. [Online] Available http://www.columbia.edu/cu/libraries/indiv/area/ Africa/Cote.html (accessed 15 June 2000).

IRIN. [Online] Available http://www.reliefweb.int/IRIN/wa/ countrystories/cotedivoire/ (various articles; accessed 18 June 2000).

US Department of State FY2000 Country Commercial Guide: Cote d'Ivoire. [Online] Available http://www.state.gov/ www/about_state/business/com_guides/2000/africa/ cote_divoire_ccg2000.pdf (accessed 15 June 2000).

**Profile researched and written by Patricia Hale (6/2000).**

# CROATIA

## Stjepan Mesic
## President
*(pronounced "stee-YEH-puhn MEH-sitch")*

*"We all want Croatia to become a truly democratic society. We are committed to strengthening all of the institutions of the rule of law: to ensuring full respect of human and minority rights, freedom of the media, and to establishing a stable and lasting framework for the market economy and socially just society."*

The Republic of Croatia, one of the successor states to the Socialist Federal Republic of Yugoslavia, is bordered by Slovenia on the north, Hungary on the northeast, and Yugoslavia and Bosnia-Hercegovina to the east. Croatia has a 5,790 km (3,590 mi) coastline along the Adriatic Sea.

The entire country covers an area of 56,488 sq km (21,810 sq mi), and has a population of about 4.7 million, of whom 78% are Croats, 12% are Serbs, and the remaining 10% include Muslims, Hungarians, and Italians. The official language is Croatian, written in the Latin alphabet. The country is mostly Roman Catholic, 76.5%; with the Serb minority being Eastern Orthodox, 11.1%.

The official currency is the Croatian *kuna*. Croatia has a per capita GDP of US$5,100. Forty-four percent of the Croatian economy is concentrated in the industry and mining sector (especially textiles, food, and chemicals); 16% in trade; 10% in transport and communication; 9% agriculture; and 5% in tourism.

## POLITICAL BACKGROUND
With the collapse of the Habsburg Empire after World War I, political representatives of Croats and Serbs in Croatia voted to join with the kingdom of Serbia in a new Kingdom of Serbs, Croats, and Slovenes (Yugoslavia). But the authoritarian rule of the Belgrade-based governments and of the Serbian king caused resentment in Croatia. In a compromise meant to stabilize the country in the face of imminent war in the rest of Europe, Belgrade in 1939 granted Croatia limited autonomy. But the events of World War II soon overwhelmed Yugoslavia, and the advancing German army in April 1941 declared an independent Croatian state, ruled by a small fascist group called the *Ustaša*. This group ruled through terror, targeting Serbs for extermination or forced conversion to Roman Catholicism.

After the war, Croatia was included as one of the six republics of Marshal Tito's communist-ruled Yugoslavia. Although manifestations of national sentiment were suppressed, the 1960s saw an upsurge of Croatian national feelings, triggered by economic reforms which sought to decentralize the country and thus cede more power to local officials. By 1971, a full-scale Croatian Spring was underway, in which support for Croatian nationalism was a means of expressing dissatisfaction with the existing system. The ruling League of Communists of Croatia (LCC) co-opted the nationalist issue in an attempt to gain legitimacy and to keep the nationalist wave from getting out of control. In 1971 and 1972, however, Tito cracked down on these Croat reformists, purging them and replacing them with more conservative officials, but also giving Croatia and other Yugoslav republics a greater degree of autonomy.

After Tito's death in 1980, conservatives in the Serbian leadership sought to quash reemerging reformist trends and to reimpose a greater degree of centralization of the ruling party and state, in particular by trying to subvert the leadership of the other Yugoslav republics. The result was that by 1989 the previously conservative Croatian party, reacting to Serbia's pressures, came under the control of more liberal forces who in December of that year scheduled the republic's first multiparty elections for April 1990. The elections, held after the final breakup of the January 1990 Congress of the federal League of Communists of Yugoslavia, were won by the Croatian Democratic Community (HDZ). The HDZ was comprised of Croat nationalists ranging from far right émigrés with connections to the wartime *Ustaša* regime, to moderate, democratically-oriented officials who had been thrown out of the Communist Party in the purges of the early 1970s. Running on a platform calling for an independent Croatia within a Yugoslav federation, the HDZ won 205 of the 356 seats in parliament, with about 44% of the vote. In the presidential election, HDZ candidate Franjo Tudjman won with 55% of the vote. He remained in office until his death in 1999.

## PERSONAL BACKGROUND
Stjepan Mesic was born in the eastern Croatian town of Orahovica on 24 December 1934. His family espoused communism, fighting against Nazi Germany and the Ustaša during World War II. He studied law at Zagreb University, the oldest established learning institution in Croatia, where he became a prominent student leader. Mesic is married and has two daughters and two grandchildren.

## RISE TO POWER
During the Croatian Spring of the 1960s and 1970s, Mesic promoted the Croatian Nationalist movement against Tito and was jailed in 1971 for one year in the Stare Gradiška prison. After his sentence was over, Mesic joined Franjo Tudjman's National Democratic Union (HDZ) as secretary, later becoming Croatia's first Prime Minister (in the Yugoslavian Federation) in 1990. He is credited with helping to create the first independent Croatian government since the middle ages. The next year, he was appointed to the rotating

Presidency of the Socialist Federal Republic of Yugoslavia (SFRY), but quickly withdrew from the post under criticism from Serbians, when Croatia declared independence on 5 December 1991. He was made speaker of the Croatian Parliament (Sabor) in 1992, but became increasingly disenchanted with Tudjman's authoritarian style of government. By 1994, Mesic had withdrawn from the HDZ with other top officials, creating the Croatian Independent Democrats (HND) which split in 1997, part of which helped to build the HNS party. Mesic presided over the Zagreb branch of the HNS and was vice president of the entire HNS until his presidency on 18 February 2000.

## LEADERSHIP

Mesic's personality reflects an openness and hope for change and ethnic reconciliation for the Balkans that is reflected in his policies and demeanor. After his election to the presidency, he appointed Ivica Racan to the office of Prime Minister.

## DOMESTIC POLICY

Croatia has an executive and judiciary that are difficult to separate, which makes the transition to democracy harder in the somewhat authoritarian government. To correct this situation, Mesic has discussed his intention to limit the power of the presidency, with the exception of supreme command of the armed forces and the ability to disband parliament and call early elections. Early in 2000, Mesic called meetings with top advisors to help create the transition from the semi-presidential system to a parliamentary system, with a balance of power between the executive, legislative, and judiciary systems.

## FOREIGN POLICY

Croatia has been pressured into cooperating with the International Tribunal for War Crimes in the Hague, turning over several officers accused of atrocities in the war in Bosnia. Croatia was admitted to the Organization on Security and Cooperation in Europe and the UN in 1992, and to the Council of Europe in 1996. Croatia is a member of the NATO-linked Partnership for Peace, but NATO or EU membership will not happen for some time yet. Croatia was granted observer status in NATO parliament in April 2000, and the EU began negotiations on an Agreement for Stabilization and Association with Croatia in the same month. Mesic's foreign policy is strongly Pro-European and Western, looking for entrance to the European Union as soon as possible by making the economic adjustments necessary for such an event.

Despite intense international coordination in the restructuring mission of the Balkans, Croatia and its neighbors have retained their territorial animosities. Croatia and Italy are still arguing over property rights on the Dalmatian coast from World War II and earlier. Slovenia wants a part of Croatia that will give direct access to the sea in the Adriatic. Serbia and Montenegro dispute Croatia's claim to the Prevlaka Peninsula in southern Croatia because it is the entrance to Boka Kotorska in Montenegro. There is also a growing

number of ethnic Serbians re-entering Croatia, who will demand adequate representation in the Croatian government or look to Serbia for freedom.

## ADDRESS

President of the Republic
Villa Zagorje
Pantovcak 241
10000 Zagreb, Croatia

## REFERENCES

Croatia. [Online] Available http://www.croatia.hr/president.html (Accessed April 2000).

*Danas* (Zagreb), 1990–92.

*Globus* (Zagreb), 1992–94.

OMRI Daily Report. [Online] Available http://www.omri.cz/Publications/DD/Index.html (Accessed April 2000).

President of Croatia homepage. [Online] Available http://www.predsjednik.hr/ (Accessed April 2000).

Radio Free Europe/Radio Liberty analysis and reports. [Online] Available http://www.rferl.org/ (Accessed April 2000).

Republic of Croatia homepage. [Online] Available http://www.tel.fer.hr/ (Accessed April 2000).

Short review of the Economy of Croatia. [Online] Available http://www.svne.fer.hr/HR/hr-intro.html (Accessed April 2000).

**Profile researched and written by Mary Sugar (4/2000).**

# CUBA

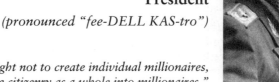

## Fidel Castro
## President

*(pronounced "fee-DELL KAS-tro")*

*"As Marxist-Leninists we fight not to create individual millionaires,
but to make the citizenry as a whole into millionaires."*

The Republic of Cuba is situated in the Caribbean Sea, 145 km (90 mi) south of Florida. This archipelago is composed of two main islands, Cuba and the Isle of Youth (formerly Isle of Pines), and about 1,600 keys and islets. Its total area is about 110,860 sq km (42,803 sq mi). In addition to the US, Cuba lies in close proximity to Jamaica, Haiti, the Dominican Republic, and Mexico.

Cuba's population has been estimated at 11.1 million inhabitants, of which about 66% were considered white, 22% mulatto, and 12% black. The official language is Spanish. About 49% of the population declare themselves non-religious, 40% Catholic, 3% Protestant, 2% African-American Spiritualist, and 6% other.

The unit of currency is the *peso*. Cuba's main exports are sugar (73% of export earnings), petroleum products, nickel ore, citrus fruits, and fish products. Its main imports are mineral fuels and lubricants, machinery, transport equipment, and cereals.

## POLITICAL BACKGROUND
According to the Constitution of 1976, Cuba is a unitary socialist republic, in which the Communist Party of Cuba is the leading force of society and the state. The state is responsible for the organization and direction of the economic life of the country, in accordance with a central social and economic development plan. Legislative authority resides in the National Assembly of People's Power, which is composed of 589 deputies. Deputies are elected for five-year terms by direct vote of all Cuban citizens over the age of 16.

The National Assembly of People's Power elects a Council of State (31 members) which represents the Assembly between sessions. The president of the Council of State is the official head of state and the head of government. Moreover, the president presides over the Council of Ministers, which is the highest ranking executive and administrative organ. The Executive Committee is led by the president and includes the first vice president and the vice presidents of the Council of Ministers.

## PERSONAL BACKGROUND
Fidel Castro Ruz was born on 13 August 1926 (some sources state 1927) on his family's sugar plantation near Biran. His father had come to Cuba from Galicia, Spain, as an immigrant laborer, but eventually became a landowner. Castro attended Jesuit schools in Santiago de Cuba and later entered the Jesuit *Colegio Belen*, a preparatory school in

Havana. In 1945 Castro began his studies in the Faculty of Law of the University of Havana, where he soon became president of the University Students' Federation. In 1947 Castro joined a force that was training to overthrow the dictatorship of Rafael Trujillo in the Dominican Republic, but which was disbanded by the Cuban government after only a few months in training. Later, in 1948, Castro participated in a violent uprising in Colombia, known as the *Bogotazo*, while he was attending a student congress there.

After becoming a lawyer in 1950, Castro spent much of his time defending the poor. As a member of the liberal *Partido del Pueblo Cubano* (also known as the *Partido Ortodoxo*), Castro became a candidate for parliament in the national elections scheduled for June 1952. In March 1952, however, General Fulgencio Batista overthrew the elected government of President Carlos Prio Socarrás and established a military dictatorship.

Castro reacted to the coup by submitting a petition to the Court of Constitutional Guarantees, in which he accused the dictator of having violated the Constitution of 1940. When his petition was rejected, Castro organized a small rebel force of 165, which on 26 July 1953 attacked the Moncada Barracks in Santiago de Cuba, with the hope of provoking a popular uprising in the Oriente province. The attack was a failure; about half of the rebels were killed and most of the rest were captured, including Fidel Castro and his brother Raúl. During his trial, Castro defended himself by giving a speech which later would become known by the phrase, "History will absolve me." Castro was found guilty and sentenced to 15 years in jail.

In 1955 Castro was released under a general amnesty. For a period of time, he tried to present a non-violent opposition to the regime, but was denied access to the mass media. Unhappy with the situation in his country, Castro left for Mexico where he organized the "26th of July" movement with Cuban exiles who were anxious to return to Cuba and overthrow the Batista dictatorship.

## RISE TO POWER
On 2 December 1956, Fidel Castro, his brother Raúl, Ernesto "Ché" Guevara (an Argentinean doctor whom they met in Mexico), and a force of about 82 men landed on the north coast of the Oriente province. The trip from Mexico was made on an old yacht, *Granma*, that had been acquired with money donated by deposed president Prío-Socarrás. Shortly after their landing, the rebel group was met by the Batista

forces, and most of the rebels were killed. A few of the survivors, including the brothers Fidel and Raúl Castro and Ché Guevara, escaped to the Sierra Maestro Mountains, where they regrouped and began recruiting new members. Beginning in early 1958, the rebel movement gained a series of victories against the Batista forces, which encouraged massive civic resistance in the cities.

The growing success of the rebel forces led to increasingly brutal repression by the Batista forces. In early 1958, the administration of US president Dwight Eisenhower suspended arms shipments to Cuba, accusing Batista of having violated agreements with the US by using the weapons not for national defense, but to fight internal enemies. This decision increased public disenchantment with Batista. Finally on New Years Day 1959, Batista accepted his defeat and went into exile in the Dominican Republic. The next day Fidel Castro and his "26th of July" movement marched into Havana and assumed control of Cuba.

## LEADERSHIP

In the four decades that Castro has ruled Cuba, he has proven to be a skillful politician and a survivor. Castro has not only consolidated his power domestically, but has also survived many international challenges, especially from the US. Initially Castro's revolution had widespread support not only from the Cuban population, but also from many Americans, who had been shocked by the abuses of the Batista dictatorship. (The US government recognized the new Cuban government within days of its victory.)

Moreover, the first provisional government was composed of a broad coalition of forces that had opposed Batista, ranging from former Batista officials who had broken with the dictatorship to liberal and Marxist groups. From the beginning, however, Castro's "26th of July" movement was the leading group within the coalition.

In the early days of the revolutionary regime, there were numerous arrests and executions of former members of the Batista dictatorship. The new government ruled by decree and promised that elections would be held within 18 months. The government began an agrarian reform and started nationalizing industrial enterprises, most of them owned by US companies. These policies were not popular with many Cubans, some of whom went into exile. The US companies that had been expropriated with little compensation were, of course, also unhappy with the new regime. Additionally, Castro's nationalistic rhetoric and critical view of the previous involvement of the US in Cuban politics further weakened relations with the Eisenhower administration. Moreover, in early 1960 Cuba signed an agreement with the Soviet Union to purchase Soviet oil in exchange for Cuban sugar. Soon afterwards the US cut the quota for sugar imports from Cuba, and the Eisenhower administration broke relations with Cuba.

In January 1961, John F. Kennedy was inaugurated as US president. On 11 April 1961, a US-sponsored force of about 1,300 Cuban exiles landed on Cuba's southern coast (the Bay of Pigs) with the purpose of overthrowing Castro. The invading forces were soundly defeated in what proved to be a major embarrassment for the Kennedy administration. After the invasion, Castro consolidated his power, and in December

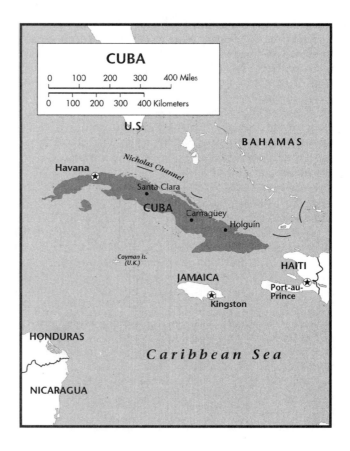

1961, proclaimed Cuba to be a communist state with a Marxist-Leninist program.

In October 1962 the tension between Cuba and the US reached its highest level after Soviet missiles with nuclear warheads that had the capability of reaching the US were discovered in Cuba. After a US-imposed naval blockade and several days of tension between the superpowers, the Soviet Union withdrew its missiles and the US agreed not to invade Cuba. After surviving this ordeal, which was considered to be the worst international crisis since World War II, Castro moved closer to the Soviet Union and other Socialist countries. In 1964 his government was ostracized by Latin American countries when the Organization of American States (OAS) imposed diplomatic and commercial sanctions against Cuba.

In 1965, with the consolidation of the revolution, groups that had supported the revolution were united into the Communist Party of Cuba. In 1972, Cuba became a full member of the Council for Mutual Economic Assistance, and thus received preferential trade from the Soviet Union and Eastern European countries. Throughout this period, Castro continued to be the undisputed leader of the Cuban Communist Party and of Cuba.

In 1976, after being approved by a popular referendum, Cuba's first constitution since the revolution came into force. The same year, the National Assembly of People's Power elected the members of the Council of State with Castro as president. Since then Castro has been re-elected several times and as of 2000 continued to lead the Communist Party of Cuba.

## DOMESTIC POLICY

Under Castro, Cuba's economy was transformed from a capitalist economy, which was extremely dependent on US investment, to a socialist economy. The Cuban state not only owns most enterprises but also sets economic plans for all sectors of the economy. In terms of economic development, the Castro government has been successful in addressing many of the problems that affect developing countries. For example, advances have been made in terms of life expectancy, health services, housing, living conditions, and education.

In the early 1990s, however, Cuba suffered a severe decline prompted by the collapse of the Soviet Union and consequent termination of favorable aid and trade arrangements that had supported its economy. This resulted in shortages of petroleum and basic raw materials, which seriously affected production. To deal with this crisis, Castro was forced to soften many of his fundamental socialist principles and move toward a more market-oriented economy. A graduated income tax, price increases on goods and services, and limited individual private enterprise were introduced. Government subsidies to inefficient state enterprises were reduced. Business laws were revised and the banking system was restructured to facilitate foreign investment. The government reported that GDP declined by 35% from 1989–93 (the years following the loss of Soviet aid) but since then GDP has been increasing, reportedly by 1.2% in 1998.

At the 1997 party congress, Castro endorsed policies intended to maintain the status quo for as long as possible. Sheer necessity has forced him to seek foreign investment in state companies, allow some limited self-employment. In 1999, the government announced that it would use the euro as the official currency for trade with European nations, although the US dollar would not be eliminated completely.

## FOREIGN POLICY

The survival of the Castro regime has, from the very beginning, been threatened by active US opposition, which reached its height in 1961 during the US-sponsored Bay of Pigs invasion. The Castro government has also had to deal with a continuous US embargo. The Helms-Burton Act, introduced in March 1996, imposed sanctions on those countries trading with, or investing in, Cuba. Its controversial Title III provision allowed US citizens to prosecute any foreign corporation or investor with business dealings involving property that had been expropriated during the Castro regime. Faced with strong opposition from the European Union, Mexico, and Canada, the Clinton administration imposed a temporary moratorium on Title III.

While the US continues to enforce many provisions of its trade embargo, in 1999, new regulations were proposed to allow the sale of food, medical equipment, and agricultural supplies to nongovernmental entities in Cuba. Investment by other nations in joint ventures has been steadily increasing since the mid-1990s. Economic relations with Russia improved significantly with the signing of a trade protocol, under which Cuba will provide Russia with sugar in exchange for petroleum.

The Castro government has tried to break its relative isolation by improving relations with other countries, a policy which has met with some success. In 1988 diplomatic relations were established with the European Community. Cuba signed a number of accords in 1992 establishing diplomatic relations with republics of the former Soviet Union. Full diplomatic ties were resumed with Colombia in 1993 and Chile in 1995. In 1998, Castro welcomed a visit by Pope John Paul II, the country's first-ever papl visit; he also lifted his 1969 ban on the celebration of Christmas. In 1999, for the first time since assuming power, Casto allowed a Protestant open-air religious service to take place. He also welcomed visits by leaders from African nations and Cambodia to explore the improvement of relations and international cooperation.

## ADDRESS

Office of the President
Palacio de Gobierno
Havana, Cuba

## REFERENCES

*The Economist,* 3 February 1990; 8 May 1999; 24 July 1999.
*Europa World Yearbook 1998.* London: Europa Publications Ltd., 1998.
*Granma,* 8 April 1990.
*Latin American Research Review,* Vol. 1, 1990.
*New York Times,* 13 April 1990, 12 October 1997.
*Washington Post,* 12 April 1990.
*World Factbook 1999.* Washington, D.C.: Central Intelligence Agency, 2000.

**Profile researched and written by Claudio Hidalgo-Nunez. (7/90; updated 9/97; updated 3/2000).**

# CYPRUS

### Glafcos Clerides
### President
*(pronounced "GLAHV-kos kleh-REE-dees")*

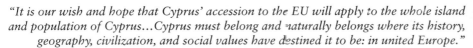

*"It is our wish and hope that Cyprus' accession to the EU will apply to the whole island and population of Cyprus…Cyprus must belong and naturally belongs where its history, geography, civilization, and social values have destined it to be: in united Europe."*

The Republic of Cyprus, the third largest island in the Mediterranean Sea, is located south of Turkey and west of the coast of Syria and Lebanon. It has a total area of 9,251 sq km (3,572 sq mi).

The population has been estimated at 754,000 inhabitants, of which 81.6% are Greek Cypriot (including Maronites, Armenians, and Latins) and 18.4% Turkish Cypriot. The religious composition reflects the ethnic division of the Republic. The Greek Cypriots are predominantly Eastern Orthodox, while the Turkish Cypriots are Sunni Muslim. In addition to Greek and Turkish, English is widely spoken.

The unit of currency is the Cypriot pound. The per capita GDP has been estimated at $13,000. Most Cypriot exports are directed toward the European Union and the Middle East. They consist of fruits, beverages, cement, clothing, footwear, and minerals. Major imports come from the European Union, Japan, and the Middle East. They include petroleum and petroleum products, consumer goods, and other agricultural and industrial products.

## POLITICAL BACKGROUND

Cyprus has played a major role in the history of the Eastern Mediterranean. Its pre-historic settlements date to the 6th millennium BC. Early in the 2nd millennium BC, the Greeks established their first city kingdoms on the island and introduced their language and culture. The Turkish Cypriot community established itself following the Ottoman conquest of 1571. The island was ceded by the Ottomans to the British Empire in 1878 and remained a crown colony until 16 August 1960, when it became an independent state. The constitution of Cyprus was drafted on the basis of a political compromise reached in 1959 by the governments of Britain, Turkey, and Greece.

The 1959 constitution required the election of a Greek Cypriot to the presidency and a Turkish Cypriot to the vice presidency, by separate communal electoral rolls. The Turkish community was granted disproportionate representation in all branches of the government along with extensive veto powers and separate voting majorities. Constitutional lawyers have described the Cypriot constitution as "unique and unprecedented." Difficulties in the implementation of this constitution and the unwillingness of the Turkish Cypriots to accept amendments led to intercommunal clashes late in 1963. At that point the Turkish Cypriots withdrew from the government of Cyprus.

The interference of Greece and Turkey in the affairs of Cyprus hampered the UN-sponsored intercommunal talks from 1968 through 1974, which sought revisions to the constitution. Following a coup against the elected president of Cyprus by the junta ruling Greece at the time, Turkey invaded Cyprus on 20 July 1974. Turkey claimed a right to intervene militarily under the Treaty of Guarantee, which was one of the independence treaties. Since then, nearly 39% of Cyprus remains under Turkish army occupation. The two communities had co-existed throughout the island, but were forced to relocate by the Turkish army. Nearly 50% of the population of Cyprus became refugees. Turkey introduced some 85,000 Turkish settlers in the occupied areas. Turkish troops, estimated at 35,000, control a dividing line that runs roughly on an east-west direction from Famagusta to the east, through the capital city of Nicosia, to the town of Morphou on the northwest of the island.

The government of Cyprus, under the control of the Greek Cypriots, retains international recognition and membership in all international organizations. The Turkish Cypriots have established separate political and administrative institutions in the area occupied by the Turkish army. In 1983, following a unilateral declaration of independence, the Turkish Cypriots established the Turkish Republic of Northern Cyprus, which has been proclaimed illegal by UN Security Council Resolution 541 (1983) and by all other major international organizations. This "state" is not recognized by any nation except Turkey. Since the Turkish invasion of 1974, the government of Cyprus and the leader of the Turkish Cypriots, Raouf Denktash, have undertaken talks to amend the constitution of Cyprus and to reunify the island. These talks have been held under the "good offices' of the UN secretary general. As of 2000, they have not succeeded. The Turkish Cypriots seek the establishment of a loose bi-zonal confederation, with minimal contact between the two communities. The government of Cyprus hopes to establish a functional and viable federation in which all Cypriots enjoy rights guaranteed by European conventions.

## PERSONAL BACKGROUND

Glafcos Clerides was born in the capital city of Nicosia on 24 April 1919. He is the son of the eminent Cypriot barrister, John Clerides. Educated in Cyprus at the prestigious Pancyprian Gymnasium of Nicosia and in Great Britain, Clerides received his LLB in 1948 from King's College, University of London. He was called to the Bar at Gray's Inn

in 1951, and practiced law in Cyprus from 1951 to 1960. During World War II he joined the Royal Air Force and was shot down in 1942. While a prisoner of war Clerides attempted several escapes, succeeding in his fourth try. Clerides met his wife Lilla, a Bombay Indian, in London. They were married in 1946. They have one daughter, Katerina, an attorney and member of the Cypriot House of Representatives. He is the author of a four-volume work entitled *Cyprus: My Deposition*. This book reviews the Cyprus problem and gives a personal account of Clerides' 40 years as presidential advisor, constitutional negotiator, and politician.

## RISE TO POWER

Clerides was active in the Greek Cypriot struggle for self-determination and union with Greece *(enosis)* in the 1950s. He took part in the constitutional negotiations prior to independence. In 1960, Clerides was elected to the Cypriot House of Representatives, serving as its speaker/president until 1976. With his legal background and experience, Clerides led the Cypriot government's negotiating team at the London Conference (1964), which was convened to avert the breakdown of the constitution. He was also the Cypriot negotiator in the UN-sponsored intercommunal talks from 1968 to 1976. Following the collapse of the junta that briefly took control in 1974, Clerides became acting president of Cyprus until the return of President Makarios.

In 1969, Clerides formed the Unified Party. Seven years later he founded the Democratic Rally, with leading members of his former party and other center and center-right political figures. Both of his parties were conservative. Since the 1985

parliamentary election, the Democratic Rally has emerged as the largest Greek Cypriot party in the House of Representatives. Clerides ran unsuccessfully for the presidency in 1983, losing to the incumbent president, Spyros Kyprianou. He also ran and lost in the 1988 presidential elections against George Vassiliou, a newcomer to Cypriot politics. Clerides was elected as the fourth president of the republic on 14 February 1993, unseating Vassiliou. He was reelected in a run-off election by 50.8% of the popular vote and began his second five-year term on 28 February 1998.

## LEADERSHIP

Clerides has received support from the Democratic Rally, the largest Greek-Cypriot party in the House of Representatives. The Socialist party, EDEK, withdrew its support when Clerides announced in late 1998 his decision to cancel plans to deploy a Russian surface-to-air missile system. Other small liberal parties and defectors from Kyprianou's Democratic Party have joined in support of the Clerides government. The Community Party of Cyprus (AKEL) is the main source of parliamentary opposition.

## DOMESTIC POLICY

Cyprus is an upper middle-income country with a free market economy. Government five-year economic plans provide an appropriate climate for the flourishing private sector. Agriculture accounts for less than 6% of GDP, industry some 17%, while tourism and services amount to 48%. Since the mid-1970s, Cyprus has become a regional center for foreign offshore companies and banking and is the third-largest registry for commercial vessels in the world. The economy suffered severe dislocations in the aftermath of the Turkish invasion of 1974, because most substantial economic resources and productive capacity were located in the occupied north of the island. Since that time, sustained foreign assistance, hard work, and a sound economic recovery program have transformed Cyprus into the showpiece of the Eastern Mediterranean—with low inflation and unemployment.

Because of its small and open economy and its heavy reliance on tourism, the Cypriot economy is affected by external developments. Cyprus has had an association agreement with the EU since 1973, which was upgraded in 1987. Three years later, Cyprus applied for full membership. In December 1997, the European Council agreed to include Cyprus in the next phase of EU expansion. Accession negotiations with Cyprus commenced on 30 March 1998. All Cypriot presidents coming from the ideological center/center-right have supported dynamic growth policies, the concept of Cyprus acting as an economic and political bridge between Europe and the Middle East, and the full membership of Cyprus in the EU.

The political problems confronting Cyprus since independence have dominated the domestic and foreign policy agenda of all presidents. Thus, the quest for membership in the EU and active participation in organizations such as the UN, the Nonaligned Movement, and the Commonwealth have been important objectives of all administrations as they seek to reunify the island, to protect the rights of all Cypriots, and assure the sovereignty and territorial integrity of their country.

In his second inaugural address, Clerides committed himself to work for a peaceful and prosperous Cyprus—one in which all citizens will live in conditions of complete security and will enjoy equal opportunities for economic and social progress as members of the EU. He has also proclaimed his readiness to continue talks with the Turkish Cypriot leadership under the "good offices" of the UN secretary-general. His basic negotiating priorities include a solution based on a bi-communal and bi-zonal federation, the demilitarization of Cyprus, the implementation of the "three freedoms" (movement, settlement, property ownership) for all Cypriots, and the integration of Cyprus in the EU at the earliest possible time.

Clerides also called for improving public administration, emphasizing merit, and improving the productivity of the public sector. In view of the economic and social challenges facing Cyprus, he called for a renewed partnership between the public and private sectors to achieve the needed economic and social growth. Because of the contribution of tourism to the GDP, Clerides has called for cooperation with the private sector to develop a balanced tourist policy and tourism infrastructure, without hampering the development of other productive economic sectors. Finally, Clerides has outlined measures for combating drugs, while improving education, health, women's rights, and the environment. In each of these areas, he hopes to keep his country's policies at par with those of other EU states.

## FOREIGN POLICY

Clerides has stressed that a solution to the Cyprus problem will reflect the principles of the UN Charter and of the European Convention on Human Rights. He declared that the integration of Cyprus in the EU will be a priority of his administration because it would be an effective guarantee for the security and rights of all Cypriots and a means of achieving constructive cooperation between the two communities.

During his second term, Clerides will be striving to unite Cyprus under a viable UN-brokered solution (the framework of which was rejected in June 1999 by Turkish Cypriot leader Rauf Denktash) and to integrate a united Cyprus in the EU, which is expected to have a positive effect on the overall economy and improve the standard of living for both communities.

## ADDRESS

Office of the President
Presidential Palace/Proedriko Megaro
Nicosia, Republic of Cyprus

## REFERENCES

*Cyprus Almanac 1997.* Nicosia: Public Information Office, Republic of Cyprus.
"Cyprus: Talks about Talks." *The Economist,* 4 December 1999, pp. 49–50.
*Cyprus: Background Notes.* US Department of State, 1988.
*Cyprus Bulletin,* 1 January–3 March 1998.
Joseph, Joseph S. *Cyprus: Ethnic Conflict and International Politics: From Independence to the Threshold of the European Union.* Basingstoke: Macmillan, 1999.

**Profile researched and written by Van Coufoudakis, Indiana University-Purdue University, Fort Wayne (6/98; revised 3/2000).**

# CZECH REPUBLIC

**Milos Zeman**
**Prime Minister**
*(pronounced "MEE-los TSAY-mun")*

*"This government will not be a government against citizens or an arrogant government above citizens, but it will be there to serve the people."*

The Czech Republic is a small, landlocked country in central Europe consisting of two lands, Bohemia and Moravia. To the country's west lies Germany; to the north, Poland; to the south, Austria; and to the east, Slovakia. Its total area is 78,900 sq km (31,560 sq mi).

The population is about 10.3 million. Czechs comprise 94% of the total, and Slovaks around 3%. Smaller percentages of Poles, Germans, Hungarians, and Roma (Gypsies) also live in the Czech Republic. About 40% of the population are Roman Catholic; 40% have no religious affiliation; 5% are Protestant; 3% are Orthodox; and 13% have other religious affiliations.

The government began a process of overhauling the formerly centrally-planned economy in 1991. The Czech economy now has all the characteristics of a free market, with approximately 75% of GDP produced in the private sector. Primary exports include machinery and transport equipment, industrial goods, agricultural products, minerals, and chemical goods. Nearly two-thirds of its trade is with European Union countries. The GDP at per capita purchasing power parity has been estimated at $11,300. The unit of currency is the *koruna* (Kc).

## POLITICAL BACKGROUND

The Czech Republic and Slovakia gained independence as a unified state in 1918 at the end of World War I, with the fall of the Austro-Hungarian Hapsburg monarchy. The idea of Czecho-Slovak nationalism emerged during the late 19th century and received strong backing from the victorious Allied powers, especially the US under President Woodrow Wilson. During the inter-war period (1918–39), Czechoslovakia became the only economically prosperous and stable democracy in central and eastern Europe. Nevertheless, in 1938 the Western powers allowed for Czechoslovakia's dismemberment at the hands of the Nazis. The Czech lands were incorporated into the Third Reich while Slovakia became an independent puppet state. In 1948, Communists seized power in a reunified Czechoslovakia. The country was ruled as a single-party dictatorship and satellite of the Soviet Union. The first attempts at resistance came during the 1968 "Prague Spring" when Alexander Dubcek introduced some democratic reforms within the Communist Party. Dubcek's effort to create "socialism with a human face" was crushed later that year by Warsaw Pact troops. The "Prague Spring" inspired the formation of several dissident groups, of which

the Charter 77 Movement, led by playwright and dissident Vaclav Havel, was the most prominent.

In late 1989, the Czech and Slovak protest movement, led by the Czech Civic Forum and the Slovak Public Against Violence, swelled to many thousands. It would eventually lead to the peaceful end of communist rule in a "Velvet Revolution." Havel was named president in December 1989. Czechoslovakia's first free elections were held on 8 June 1990. The Civic Forum and Public Against Violence won impressive victories. The new government began a radical overhaul of the country. New elections, held in 1992, reinstated a center-right government. Continuing progress, however, became stalled by discord between the Czech and Slovak lands. Despite continuous popular support for the federal state, increasing differences emerged between the two most prominent politicians of the two republics, Vaclav Klaus of the Czech Republic and Vladimir Meciar of Slovakia. These differences led to the eventual split of the Czech and Slovak Federal Republic, taking effect on 1 January 1993.

Under Klaus' leadership, the newly independent Czech Republic experienced numerous economic achievements: impressive growth, low inflation, and low unemployment. In the June 1996 elections, however, the center-left Social Democratic Party (CSSD), led by Milos Zeman, narrowed the gap with Klaus' Civic Democratic Party (ODS). The ODS won a plurality but lost their parliamentary majority and were forced to form a minority government. In return for support in parliament, the opposition Social Democrats gained leadership positions in parliament. Relations between the government and opposition remained acrimonious. In addition, the Czech economy became mired in numerous scandals that were attributed mainly to the lack of adequate regulatory controls over entrepreneurial activities. In 1997, the Klaus government introduced numerous stabilization measures. In the fall, however, after his party became linked with charges of corruption, Klaus' government resigned. President Havel appointed a caretaker government for a six-month term under central bank governor, Josef Tosovsky.

In June 1998 elections, the CSSD won a plurality of the vote with 32.3%. The ODS came in second, performing better than was expected, with 27.7% of the vote. Other parties that passed the 5% threshold for parliamentary representation included the Communist Party (KSCM) with 11%, the Christian Democratic Party (KDU-CSL) with 9%, and the Freedom Union (US) with 8.6%. The CSSD was allocated 74 seats in the 200-seat lower house of parliament. The ODS got

63 seats; the KSCM, 24 seats; the KDU-CSL, 20 seats; and the US, 19 seats. After failing to achieve a coalition agreement with other parties, the CSSD leadership worked out an agreement with the opposition ODS to form a single-party, minority CSSD government. Havel, who was re-elected to a five-year term in January 1998, appointed Zeman of the CSSD to serve as prime minister on 17 July 1998, despite reservations about CSSD-ODS accord.

## PERSONAL BACKGROUND

Milos Zeman was born on 28 September 1944 in the town of Kolin. He left Kolin to attend the Advanced School of Economics in Prague and graduated with a degree in economics in 1969. During the "Prague Spring" of 1968, Zeman joined the reform-minded Communist Party led by Alexander Dubcek. After the fall of the reform movement and Czechoslovakia''s occupation by Warsaw Pact troops, he was expelled from the Party. Zeman's employment opportunities were limited during the "normalization" period. For fourteen years he worked as a researcher in physical education, founding the prognosis center that was dissolved in 1984 due to critical political studies. In 1985, he found employment at an economics research institute where he studied the prognostic modeling of social systems. He then worked in agricultural organization until he was fired in 1989. During the 1989 "Velvet Revolution," Zeman was involved with the non-communist Obcanske Civic Forum. Zeman is married to Ivana, his second wife. They have a daughter, Katerina. Zeman also has a son, David, from his first marriage.

## RISE TO POWER

Zeman entered the Federal Assembly of the Czech and Slovak Federal Republic as head of the budget committee in 1990 and again following the 1992 federal elections. He joined the Social Democratic Party (CSSD) in 1992 as leader of the Prague branch, becoming party chairman in 1993. In the 1996 elections, the CSSD came in second place behind the ruling Civic Democratic Party (ODS), substantially increasing its strength in parliament. As a result of negotiations with the ODS, the CSSD won leadership posts in parliament, with Zeman becoming chairman of parliament. Relations between Prime Minister Klaus and Zeman's opposition CSSD remained contentious. As Klaus' political and economic difficulties increased in 1997, Zeman's CSSD grew in popularity. The CSSD was expected to perform well in early elections scheduled for June 1998. It received the largest share of the vote, but less than a majority. Zeman was unsuccessful in his attempts to build a majority coalition with smaller parties, such as the Christian Democratic Party and the Freedom Union. Instead, he concluded an agreement with Klaus' ODS on forming a single-party minority government. President Havel named Zeman to be prime minister on 17 July 1998, and his cabinet was sworn in the following month. In accordance with the CSSD-ODS agreement, ODS legislators did not participate in the vote of confidence, thus enabling the CSSD to prevail over the remaining opposition.

## LEADERSHIP

Under Zeman's leadership, the CSSD steadily increased its popularity. In 1992, the CSSD won 6.5% of the vote. In 1996, its share increased to 26% and came to 32% in the 1998 vote. During the 1998 campaign, Zeman emphasized a

"clean hands" program that would tackle corruption and give greater emphasis to social welfare issues. However, Klaus led an effective campaign and his ODS party surged to second place. After the vote, Zeman was unsuccessful in his attempts to build a majority coalition, even though he offered to give up the premiership and other key posts in exchange for a coalition agreement. Some observers speculated that Zeman might even lose his mandate to lead the government if Klaus and the ODS managed to reconstruct their former ruling coalition. Instead, Zeman worked out an unorthodox agreement with Klaus that allowed the CSSD to take power with minority support in parliament (74 out of 200 seats).

These circumstances have led observers to doubt the ability of the CSSD government to carry out its program or even complete its four-year term. While supportive of the CSSD, Czech public opinion has generally registered less enthusiasm for Zeman himself. Notwithstanding his recent political successes, Zeman has indicated that he may not continue in politics for very long. Early in his tenure as prime minister, Zeman announced that he would seek retirement by the year 2002 at the latest. His stated intention is to encourage the development of successors within his party.

## DOMESTIC POLICY

The CSSD took over a government with many domestic policy items on its agenda. The Zeman government aims to fight organized crime, increase economic transparency, and accelerate economic growth. He hopes to make the economy grow and still run a budget deficit. Zeman has promised to slow down the privatization of state banks, put tariffs on imports, raise the minimum wage, and increase welfare, while continuing to subsidize housing and energy costs. Welfare reform legislation and new laws on political party financing, part of the CSSD's "clean hands" campaign, are also priority issues for the Zeman government. In 1999, Zeman renationalized some of the country's ailing firms and implemented a series of interest rate cuts in the aftermath of Russia's August 1998 financial collapse that severely affected the Czech economy. The CSSD and opposition ODS agreed to propose constitutional changes, most likely regarding the electoral system. The Zeman government also aims to speed up the harmonization of Czech laws to European Union law, required before entry into the EU. It is unclear how much power the Zeman government really holds to fulfill its policy objectives, with only minority support in parliament and with the ODS in control of the parliamentary leadership. The ODS may exercise considerable influence on the government in its "silent coalition" with the CSSD even though it is not directly responsible for governmental action.

## FOREIGN POLICY

Since the "Velvet Revolution," the primary foreign policy goal of successive Czech governments has been to integrate into Western security and economic structures, especially NATO and the European Union (EU). The new foreign minister, Jan Kavan, has stated that he expects no radical changes in the basic tenets of that policy.

In 1997, the Czech Republic was invited, along with Poland and Hungary, to join NATO. Accession protocols with the Atlantic alliance were signed in late 1997, and the parliament ratified accession in April 1998. Czech troops had already served with NATO in peace-keeping operations in Bosnia since the end of 1995. While in opposition, the CSSD had long insisted that entry into NATO be subject to a popular referendum; but Zeman dropped this condition once in power. The Czech Republic became a full NATO member on 13 March 1999.

The process of accession into the European Union began in March 1998, along with four other central European countries and Cyprus. The Zeman government has identified Czech entry into the EU by 2003 to be a key foreign policy priority.

## ADDRESS

Office of the Prime Minister
Lazarska 7
11348 Prague 1, Czech Republic

## REFERENCES

Central European Online. [Online] Available http://www.centraleurope.com (Accessed 24 April 2000).

*Czech Republic Country Report 1998–99.* Economist Intelligence Unit.

*Financial Times,* 14 May 1998, 23 June 1998.

*Foreign Broadcast Information Service,* various issues.

"Little to Cheer About." *Time International,* 29 November 1999, p. 26+.

"Odd Couple: Czech Republic." *The Economist,* 11 July 1998, p. 54.

*Washington Post,* 7 December 1997.

"The Zeman Puzzle." *The Economist,* 27 June 1998, p. 53.

**Profile researched and written by Julie Kim, Library of Congress (12/98; revised by Mary Sugar 4/2000).**

# DENMARK

## Poul Nyrup Rasmussen
## Prime Minister

*(pronounced "NU-rop RAS-mussen")*

*"The [1998] election results show a clear choice of what road toward positive change the public wants to follow into the 21st century. Denmark is off to a good start."*

The Kingdom of Denmark is situated in the north of Europe, between the Baltic and North seas. Its southern border with Germany is the only land connection to the continent. Denmark consists of the Jutland peninsula along with 100 inhabited islands, including the large Arctic island of Greenland and the Faroe Islands in the North Atlantic, which are self-governing territories. Denmark proper has an area of only 43,092 sq km (16,638 sq mi), with a population of 5.4 million. The capital city is Copenhagen.

The population is 95% Scandinavian in origin, but a significant immigration during the past 30 years has eroded the previous homogeneity. Likewise, 95% of the Danish people are Lutheran in religious affiliation, and Danish is their first language.

Danes enjoy one of the world's highest standards of living, with a per capita GDP equivalent to $23,300. Denmark exports machinery, meat, dairy products, and chemicals. Its principal imports are machinery, heavy industrial products, and raw materials. The monetary unit is the Danish *krone* or crown.

## POLITICAL BACKGROUND

Denmark has been a constitutional monarchy since 1849. The present constitution dates from 1953 and establishes a unicameral parliament, the *Folketing*. Executive power is vested in the monarch, currently Queen Margrethe II, who appoints the prime minister and his cabinet. In practice, the queen's role is purely ceremonial, as she must consult the parties in the *Folketing* in making her choice, and the parliament can dismiss any minister or government by a majority vote of no confidence. Likewise, the prime minister can dissolve parliament and call new elections at any point during the four-year electoral term.

The *Folketing* is composed of 179 seats, most of which are elected by a system of proportional representation (parties gaining at least 2% of the vote receive seats in proportion to their share of the popular vote.) This has produced a multi-party system, with 10 parties currently represented in the diet. Since the establishment of parliamentary democracy in 1901, no single party has held a majority; thus, governments have been based on coalitions of parties. Denmark has mainly been governed by a series of minority governments that had to bargain continuously in order to get a majority of the *Folketing* to support individual legislative matters. The Radical Liberals are just left of center, but have often supported non-socialist coalitions on domestic issues; the Left

party is ideologically to the right of the Conservatives; and the Progress Party has been outflanked by the Danish People's party on the far-right of the political spectrum.

## PERSONAL BACKGROUND

Poul Nyrup Rasmussen was born in 1943 and grew up in the city of Esbjerg. His parents were both from the working class, but Nyrup Rasmussen benefited from the expansion of Danish higher education. He passed the university entrance examinations in 1962 and commenced his study in economics at Copenhagen University. He completed his masters degree in 1971. By this time, Nyrup Rasmussen had already become politically active in Social Democratic youth and student organizations. He has been married twice previously and is currently married to another leading Danish politician, Lone Dybkjaer, a former Social Liberal minister and current member of the European Parliament.

## RISE TO POWER

After completing his education, Nyrup Rasmussen became a staff economist with the National Labor Confederation (*Landsorganisationen* or LO). From 1980 until 1986 he served as chief economist for the LO. In 1986, he became director of the Wage Earners' Inflation Fund (*Loenmodtagernes Dyrtidsfond*). Nyrup Rasmussen was elected to parliament in 1988, after the chair of the Social Democratic Party and former prime minister, Anker Joergensen, had stepped down. As part of the new generation of Social Democratic leaders, Nyrup Rasmussen was elected vice-chair while his friend and former labor minister, Svend Auken, became chair. Although the Social Democrats gained seats in the 1988 and 1990 parliamentary elections, Auken's leadership style alienated some members of the party leadership. Nyrup Rasmussen's less confrontational style brought him considerable popularity among the public and among his colleagues in the *Folketing*.

Public opinion polls showed a strong base of support for Nyrup Rasmussen, who managed to stay close to all of the Social Democratic Party's many factions. His ability to relate to parties both to the left and right of his own suggested a possible advantage over the more controversial Auken. The strife led to an extraordinary party congress in April 1992 to consider the leadership issue. The congress elected Nyrup Rasmussen by a two-thirds vote. In 1993, after the conservative government of Prime Minister Poul Schlüter was forced to resign because of a scandal, Nyrup Rasmussen, as

skilled tactician, he waged an effective campaign, and his Social Democrats gained seats in the 11 March elections. Nyrup Rasmussen continued with his minority government, relying upon a divided opposition not to gain the single additional vote necessary to defeat his government. In March 2000, seeing the support for his government drop dramatically, Rasmussen reshuffled the cabinet and brought in Ritt Bjerregaard, a former European Union commissioner and popular with the voters. The main challenge came from the growing popularity of the far-right Danish People's Party, which accused the government of being soft on immigration.

## DOMESTIC POLICY

Economics and especially public finance dominate Danish politics. The economic upswing that started under his predecessors accelerated during Nyrup Rasmussen's first five years in office. Danish economic growth has been steady at about 3%, government budgets moved into surplus in 1995, and international balance of payments stayed positive. The result was a significant fall in public and international debt and a notable fall in unemployment, from nearly 12% when Rasmussen became prime minister in 1993 to about 7.1% in 1998. Inflation remained modest at just over 2% a year. While global and domestic factors played a role in these gains, policy changes were also significant. Nyrup Rasmussen's government tightened eligibility requirements for unemployment and other social welfare benefits. In particular, unemployed youth were required to go into training, education, or publicly-supported jobs. These "activist" measures were a sharp change from a previously permissive system of benefits. Nyrup Rasmussen was able to convince labor leaders that these changes were needed in order to maintain overall economic and social health. Difficult industry-union collective bargaining in the spring of 1998 underscores the delicate economic balance.

Containing public budgets in a generous welfare state is a difficult process because many expenditure decisions are made at the local level. Expanding post-secondary education and training opportunities, expensive transportation infrastructure projects, and encouraging enterprise have become staples of Danish politics. Dissatisfaction with growing waiting lists for health care has proven another challenge to the government. Denmark provides universal tax-financed health care for all residents. Private care is available for those willing to pay, but hospital procedures are done overwhelmingly in public hospitals. Compared to other affluent European countries, Danish health care costs are modest, but they are always under pressure from medical inflation and popular desires to reduce waiting lists. Efforts to increase hospital efficiency and patient choice have been introduced in the 1990s, but financial and personnel limitations have kept gains small.

Another contentious domestic issue has been the treatment of non-European immigrants and refugees, who have become increasingly visible during the past decade. They number less than 5% of the population, but in a previously homogeneous society, the change in many urban neighborhoods has been striking. All of the main political parties preach tolerance and support for this group, but public opinion has become skeptical of liberal admission and integration policies. While anti-foreigner violence has been minimal, the public debate

leader of the largest opposition party, was given the next chance to form a government.

## LEADERSHIP

Nyrup Rasmussen skillfully assembled a majority coalition. Joining his Social Democratic Party were three small centrist parties: the Social Liberals, Christian Democrats, and Center Democrats. His first priority was to work out a compromise on Danish relations with the European Union, since the Maastricht Treaty on European union had been defeated in a 1992 national referendum. Other priorities were to accelerate economic recovery and reduce continuing high unemployment.

The fragile coalition survived its first 18 months but lost some ground in the September 1994 parliamentary elections when the Christian Democrats lost all of their parliamentary seats. Nyrup Rasmussen carried on with a minority government, including the remaining two center parties. In 1996, the weakened Center Democrats withdrew from the coalition, fearing for their parliamentary existence. Nyrup Rasmussen continued with the Social Liberals, a traditional ally. Minority government required complex parliamentary bargaining, and Nyrup Rasmussen succeeded in patching together support on successive issues from a wide range of parties, including the Conservative Party. Only the Liberals, the second largest party in Denmark, stood as the main opposition under the effective leadership of Uffe Ellemann-Jensen.

Despite disappointing local elections in November 1997, Nyrup Rasmussen called a sudden parliamentary election in February 1998, six months before they were due. Ever the has grown increasingly harsh, especially on the political right. The Progress Party has long been opposed to liberal refugee policies, and even the Conservative Party has had its hard-liners. In 1996, hard-liners in the Progress Party formed a new Danish People's Party with curtailing immigration and "repatriation" of many refugees as a prime goal. These concerns are felt even by the progressive Social Democrats. Many municipal governments, typically Social Democratic, face severe social, educational, and economic challenges in accommodating immigrants. Nyrup Rasmussen's appointment in 1997 of Thorkild Simonsen as interior minister was an effort to find a moderate compromise on the issue. Not surprisingly, immigration and related issues were prominent in the March 1998 parliamentary elections, which saw the Danish People's Party gain 7.4% of the vote.

In spite of explicit assertion to the contrary ahead of the 1998 election, the government introduced fresh fiscal cutbacks and early retirement reforms in June 1998. Many traditional leftwing voters were obviously upset by this sudden policy reversal. The budget cutting by this and previous coalition government has brought vigorous economic growth to Denmark. Average growth rates between 1994 and 1999 were nearly 3% per year. Unemployment dropped from 12% in 1994 to 6% in 2000.

## FOREIGN POLICY

Nyrup Rasmussen has focused on four foreign policy goals since 1993. First has been a desire to clarify Denmark's ambiguous relationship to the European Union. Second has been the continuation of an active Danish presence in NATO, Baltic regional issues, and overall European security. Third has been a desire to keep the US fully engaged in European affairs. Fourth has been a commitment to pragmatic Nordic cooperation, especially to global order and development through the UN.

In June 1993, Nyrup Rasmussen delivered a convincing majority to a revised Maastricht European Union Treaty that had been narrowly defeated in the May 1992 referendum. Denmark has resisted "union" measures that would limit its independence in monetary, environmental, and social matters. It was not surprising that nearly half of his opening speech upon winning reelection in March 1998 discussed the EU and the national referendum ratifying the Amsterdam Treaty of 1997 (which elaborates several elements of EU governance as

well as expansion into east central Europe). That referendum was held on 28 May 1998, and the treaty was supported by 55.1% of the voters. This outcome was credited to Nyrup Rasmussen's energetic campaign in favor of the treaty and is seen as a personal victory for him. His next hurdle is to convince the Danish electorate to endorse Economic and Monetary Union. The referendum will take place in late September 2000, and all the main political parties are in favor of accession by 2002.

Doubts about NATO and the US that characterized the Social Democrats in the 1970s and 1980s have disappeared. Denmark quickly approved the inclusion of Poland, Hungary, and the Czech Republic into NATO, and Danish military units have served in the Balkans under UN, European, and NATO auspices. In July 1997, Nyrup Rasmussen welcomed Bill Clinton for the first visit ever by a US president while still in office. This visit signaled a desire on the part of the Nyrup Rasmussen government for Denmark to play a more prominent role in world affairs.

## ADDRESS

Prime Minister's Office (*Statsministeriet*)
Christiansborg
DK-1218 Copenhagen K, Denmark

## REFERENCES

*The Economist*, March 1998.
*The Financial Times*, 24 February 2000.
*Finansredgoerelse 97* (Public Finance Report 1997). Copenhagen: Ministry of Finance, 1997.
*Janet Matthews Information Services, Hilfe Country Report*, 20 October 1999.
*Morgenavisen Jyllands-Posten*. Arhus and Copenhagen, 1998.
*OECD Economic Outlook*, No. 62. Paris: Organisation for Economic Cooperation and Development, 1997.
*OECD Economic Surveys: Denmark*. Paris: Organisation for Economic Cooperation and Development, 1996.
*Politiken*. Copenhagen, 1998.
Tiersky, Ronald. *Europe Today; National Politics, Integration and European Security.* Boulder, CO: Rowman and Littlefield, 1998.
*Times* (London), March 1998.

**Profile researched and written by Eric Einhorn, University of Massachusetts at Amherst (9/98; updated 3/2000).**

# DJIBOUTI

### Ismail Omar Guelleh
### President
*(pronounced "EESH-mail O-mar gu-ELL-a")*

*"The port of Djibouti is the country's major source of government revenue. We are ready to lay down the foundation for cooperation among port authorities in the surrounding region."*

The Republic of Djibouti, formerly known as French Somaliland and subsequently renamed the French Territory of Afars and the Issas, became an independent republic in May 1977. Located in the Horn of Africa, just south of the Bab el Mandeb Strait, Djibouti occupies the strategic entrance into the Red Sea. Its neighbors include Ethiopia to its north and west, Somalia to the southeast, and Eritrea to its northwest. With a total land area of 23,310 sq km (9,000 sq mi), Djibouti consists of a coastal plain and plateau, separated by central mountains. Most of the land is volcanic desert, and the climate is hot and arid. Due to a shortage of precipitation, drought and water shortages are common. Djibouti has no arable land and is 9% permanent pastures.

An estimated 447,000 people live in Djibouti, with approximately 383,000 residing in the capital, Djibouti. The country's main ethnic groups include the Issa—of Somali descent—accounting for 60% of the population; the Afars for 35%; and French, Arabs, Ethiopians and Italians for 5%. French and Arabic are the official languages; however, Saho-Afar and Somali are widely spoken. Ninety-four percent of the population is Muslim, and 6% is Christian. With a literacy rate of 46.2% and life expectancy of only 49.1 and 53.2 years for men and women respectively, Djibouti is a poor country with a per capita GDP of $1,200.

Most economic activity is centered around the capital and port city of Djibouti, but the majority of Djiboutians are pastoral nomads. The country's main trading partners include Great Britain, France, and Somalia. Djibouti imports 97% of its food and is heavily dependent on foreign aid to survive. The national currency is the Djibouti *franc*.

## POLITICAL BACKGROUND

Formerly a French colony and overseas territory, Djibouti became independent in 1977 following a referendum in which an overwhelming majority (98.9%) voted to sever ties with France. During the colonial period, French administrators favored the Afar minority over the Issa majority, laying the foundation for post-independence ethnic distrust and conflict.

Following independence, the Issa supported the *Lingue Populaire Africaine pour l'independence* (LPAI), which was later renamed *Rassemblement Populaire pour le Progress* (Popular Rally for Progress, RPP). Its leader was Hassan Gouled Aptidon. The RPP and Aptidon dominated post-independence Djiboutian politics. Initially Aptidon sought to create a balanced government consisting of both Afars and

Issas by naming Afars to the cabinet, but his efforts failed to halt rising ethnic tensions. In December 1977, Prime Minister Dini and four other Afar cabinet members resigned. By 1981, Djibouti became a one-party state with only RPP-approved candidates standing for legislative elections in 1982 and 1987. By the mid-1980s, ethnic tensions between the Afars and the Issas increased, resulting in violence by 1989. In 1991, the *Front Pour la Restauration de l'Unite et de la Democratie* (Front for the Restoration of Unity and Democracy, FRUD) began a full scale guerrilla war against the government. Many Afar leaders were arrested, detained, and tortured during the first part of the 1990s. With mounting international criticism and the loss of French support due to severe human rights violations, Aptidon agreed to political change. Multiparty elections followed a constitutional referendum in December 1992, despite widespread electoral fraud and opposition boycott. The FRUD boycott ensured total victory for Aptidon's party. Meanwhile, by the mid-1990s, factional rivalry split FRUD, and some members entered into negotiations with the government and subsequently agreed to a power sharing arrangement. In December 1997, legislative elections resulted in RPP-FRUD capturing all 65 seats. Aptidon decided to retire due to old age and mounting health problems, paving the way for presidential elections in 1999.

The current constitution, approved in a September 1992 referendum, states that executive power is vested in the president, elected by universal adult suffrage for six-year terms. The prime minister, appointed by the president, presides over the cabinet, known as the Council of Ministers. The national legislature, the Chamber of Deputies, consists of 65 members elected to five-year terms by universal suffrage and through a party-list proportional representation system. Djibouti is a unitary state divided into five administrative districts called *cercles*.

## PERSONAL BACKGROUND

Ismail Omar Guelleh, the nephew of former president Aptidon, was born in 1947 in Dire-Dawa (Ethiopia) to Omar Guellah and Moumina Rirache of the Issa ethnic group and Mamassans sub-clan. During his youth, Guelleh attended a primary school based on Koranic principles, first in Dire-Dawa and then in Djibouti. In 1968, he began his employment with the French colonial administration, rising to police inspector by 1970.

In 1975, Guelleh, left his employment with the French colonial administration and became an independence activist with the LPAI, working as part of an editorial committee for *Popular,* a pro-independence newsletter. Later, he launched his own newspaper, *Djibouti Today,* pressing for Djibouti's independence.

From 1975 to 1977, Guelleh participated in several delegations abroad to negotiate for the country's independence. He visited Libya and Somalia to obtain foreign support. After independence was achieved, Guelleh became an important leader and Aptidon's chief-of-staff. He occupied that position for the next 22 years.

Guelleh is married and has four children.

## RISE TO POWER

Guelleh's rise to power commenced when he became an integral part of Aptidon's administration in 1977. As chief of staff, he was responsible for maintaining domestic security. He actively cultivated the support of the armed forces and the RRP. Since its formation in 1979, Guelleh steadily advanced in the party hierarchy. In 1983, he became a member of the party's central committee. In the following years, he served on a variety of party committees and became its vice president in 1996.

As former president Aptidon's health deteriorated, Guelleh assumed increased responsibility for daily governmental affairs. Using his political base within the military and police in addition to the RPP, he developed a solid reputation within the government and party. In particular, he enjoyed strong support from Aptidon and the Issa community—who referred to him by his initials, IOG.

When Aptidon decided not to seek another term because of his deteriorating health, Guelleh became his hand-picked successor. During the campaign, Guelleh stressed the importance of economic development, nation-building, and peaceful relations with Djibouti's neighbors. He spoke about the need to maintain an orderly transition in government based on his experience and ties to Aptidon. In the 9 April 1999 election, Guelleh garnered 73.89% of the vote while his opponent, Moussa Ahmed Iddris, obtained only 26.11%. Guelleh dominated in rural districts but still managed to poll 62% in the capital. Despite charges of fraud by the opposition, the Chamber of Deputies certified the elections, and power was transferred from Aptidon to Guelleh on 7 May 1999.

## LEADERSHIP

While Guelleh enjoys significant support from the Issa community and the military, Djibouti remains an ethnically divided society. Most Issas remain suspicious of him, and he needs to demonstrate his leadership skill independent of Aptidon.

The recent alliance between RPP and moderate members of FRUD creates a unique opportunity to reduce ethnic conflict in Djibouti. Despite allegations of electoral irregularities, Guelleh has broad support in the country. He needs to maintain a working relationship with Aptidon but at the same time must develop his own leadership appeal.

Guelleh's administration will seek to create a more ethnically balanced government by reaching out to the Afar minority. He will emphasize economic development and

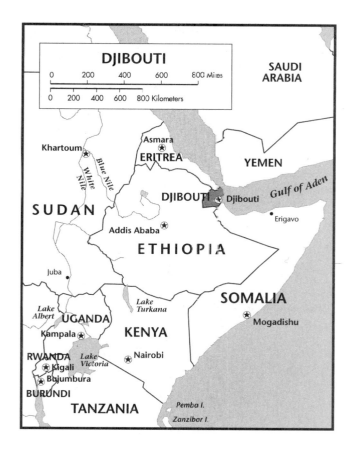

growth as the primary foundation for a prosperous Djibouti. Indeed, with the economy having declined over 10% in the mid to late 1990s, Guelleh represents a hope for the future.

## DOMESTIC POLICY

Guelleh's primary areas of domestic concern include economic development and ethnic harmony. Current statistics reveal that over 40% of the labor force remains unemployed, but the overall economy has stabilized after several years of negative growth. The economy remains heavily dependent on foreign aid, and repeated cuts in international aid during the 1990s worsened the overall economic picture. Coupled with these difficulties, increased military expenditures from 1991–94, to quell an insurgency, resulted in the government's inability to meet its international loan obligations that exceeded $250 million. International Monetary Fund (IMF) loans worth $6.8 million could not be disbursed because Djibouti failed to complete economic reforms after riots and strikes ensued. The government failed to meet interest payments in 1996. However, the problem was partially alleviated by a 1998 IMF line-of-credit for $2.8 million.

Two major developments offer hope for Djibouti's long-term economic growth. First, the discovery of natural gas reserves could potentially end the country's reliance on foreign aid. Second, capital expenditures on port facilities and the persistent war between Ethiopia and Eritrea have created a shipping boom in Djibouti. As a consequence of the Ethiopia-Eritrea conflict, Ethiopia became increasingly dependent on Djibouti for cargo transport. Based on Guelleh's ties to Ethiopia (his birthplace), a favorable environment for port commerce is likely to continue for the foreseeable future. There are plans to revamp the port's facilities and create an industrial zone and free port to complement the existing free trade zone.

Ethnic tensions between the Afars and the Issas remain a constant threat to domestic stability. In the 1980s and 1990s, conflict increased to the point that some Afars began to participate in armed conflict against the incumbent government. In 1995, negotiations between FRUD and the government yielded positive results, with one faction demobilizing and participating in the electoral process. However, continued Issa dominance of government and the military remain a major problem. Guelleh needs to expend significant resources and effort to diffuse potential conflict.

## FOREIGN POLICY

Since independence, Djibouti has maintained close relations with France and the Arab world, receiving significant foreign aid and development assistance from both sources. In addition, much of the country's trade is with France. Relations with Somalia remain troubled with the influx of Somali refugees into Djibouti. Adding to this, Somalia has extended territorial claims over Djibouti in the past and harbored FRUD insurgency rebels. To balance the Somali threat, Aptidon maintained close security relations with France.

Relations began to deteriorate when French troops left Djibouti, creating security and economic problems. The international community criticized Aptidon's worsening human rights record during the period of FRUD insurgency. France suspended economic aid and refused to bail out Djibouti during its budgetary meltdown during 1995 and 1996. The election of Guelleh opens the door for better relations with France and the West. While France did not certify the elections as free and fair, the French have endorsed Guelleh's election as a positive initial step toward multiparty democracy. Given Djibouti's need for foreign investment and its security concerns, Guelleh will seek to improve ties with France, which will, in turn, help diffuse an increasingly serious deficit-of-payment problem.

Having been born in Ethiopia, Guelleh enjoys the support of that country and promises greater economic integration. He campaigned on a program of increased ties with Ethiopia for economic and territorial security. Since the fighting between Ethiopia and Eritrea increased in 1997–99, relations between Ethiopia and Djibouti have been strengthened. The two countries remain desperately dependent on each other for survival, and Guelleh has announced his intention to seek an economic and political federation with Ethiopia. However, close ties with Ethiopia resulted in conflict with Eritrea. In November 1998, Djibouti severed diplomatic relations with Eritrea on grounds that the latter provoked conflict with Ethiopia. Guelleh will continue to favor Ethiopia over Eritrea in this conflict.

## ADDRESS

Office of the President
La Presidence BP 6
Djibouti, Republic of Djibouti

## REFERENCES

*Addis Tribune* (Ethiopia), April-May 1999.
*Africa Confidential,* June 1997.
Africa News Online. [Online] Available http://www.africannews.org (Accessed February 2000).
*BBC World News,* various issues.
*Europa Yearbook,* 1999.
*Global Studies: Africa,* 8th edition. 1999.
Ismail Omar Guelleh, campaign. [Online] Available http://www.ismail-omar.com/ (Accessed February 2000).

**Profile researched and written by Robert W. Compton, Jr., Western Kentucky University (9/99; updated 2/2000).**

# DOMINICA

## Roosevelt (Rosie) Douglas
## Prime Minister

*(pronounced "ROW-zee DUG-lass")*

*"I think the world has mellowed. Who would have thought 20 years ago that Nelson Mandela would have been freed, that racism would be the issue it is today? I don't think I have mellowed. I think the world has come around to my way of thinking."*

The Commonwealth Dominica is a Caribbean island about one-half of the way from Puerto Rico to Trinidad and Tobago. Its total area of 750 sq km (290 sq mi) consists of one island a bit larger than four times the size of Washington, DC. Roseau is the capital city. The population, estimated at 65,000, is of African and Carib Amerindian descent and is primarily Roman Catholic (73%). English is the official language, though many use a French patois. The per capita GDP is $3,300. The unit of currency is the East Caribbean dollar (EC$). The country's traditional agricultural exports include bananas (50%), soap, vegetables, grapefruit, and oranges. In recent years the country has worked to develop an eco-tourism trade to replace its historic reliance upon agriculture as the chief source of income.

## POLITICAL BACKGROUND

Carib Amerindians supplanted the island's indigenous Arawak people in the 14th century. Columbus landed in November 1493. In 1635, France claimed Dominica, and shortly thereafter French missionaries became the first European residents of the island. Dominica remained officially neutral for the next century, but the attraction of its resources remained; British and French lumbermen harvested timber in the 18th century. France eventually became predominant and established an active settlement. However, as part of the 1763 Treaty of Paris, the island became a British possession. In 1831, reflecting a more liberal official British racial policy, the brown privilege bill accorded political and social rights to free nonwhites. Three blacks became members of the legislative assembly the following year. Following the abolition of slavery in 1838, Dominica became the only British Caribbean colony to have a black-controlled legislature in the 19th century. In 1865, the colonial office replaced the elective assembly with one that consisted of one-half elected members and one-half appointed. Finally a Crown Colony government reestablished itself in 1896. Following World War I, an increase of political consciousness and unrest throughout the Caribbean led to the formation of the representative government association, which won one-third of the popularly elected seats of the legislative assembly in 1924 and one-half in 1936. Shortly thereafter Dominica became part of the Leeward Island Administration and was governed as part of the Windwards until 1958 when it joined the West Indies Federation. In 1967 Dominica, among other islands, became a self-governing state within the West Indies Associated States. On 3 November 1978, the Commonwealth of Dominica gained its independence from the United Kingdom. The Dominica Freedom Party, under Prime Minister Eugenia Charles, the Caribbean's first female prime minister, ruled from 1980 through 1995. The United Workers Party, led by Mr. Edison James governed until the February 2000 election.

## PERSONAL BACKGROUND

Roosevelt Douglas was born in Portsmouth, Commonwealth of Dominica, on 15 October 1941. He is the scion of a plantation-owning elite family. He did his pre-university studies at Dominica Grammar School and St. Mary's Academy. When he was 12, Douglas went to Canada to study agriculture. He took a Diploma in Agriculture from Ontario Agricultural College in 1963, but he eventually switched to political science and became leader of the Sir George Williams Progressive Conservative student organization in 1964. He received a Bachelors Degree in Political Science and Economy from Sir George Williams University and did his Post-graduate Studies at McGill University. In 1969, Douglas—by then a 16-year resident of Canada, a landed immigrant, and a student at McGill University—participated in a months-long dispute over charges of racism leveled against a professor. The dispute led to the occupation of several floors of the Henry F. Hall Building (then part of the Sir George, now Concordia College) and erupted into violence on 11 February 1969. The police arrested 97 students and charged Douglas with obstructing the use of private property. He was found guilty in a jury trial. In 1973–74, he served 18 months of a two-year prison sentence and was then deported. Douglas received the 1974 Black National Award in Toronto, Canada. Forced out of Canada, he returned to Dominica.

## RISE TO POWER

Upon return to Dominica from Canada, Douglas founded the Popular Independence Committee that struggled to end British rule. Dominica gained independence in 1978, and Douglas served briefly as an appointed senator. However, Hurricane David devastated the island in 1979. He invited Cuban troops to help the clean up effort, leading to his firing, apparently as a condition for US relief. Douglas has maintained close contacts with the Cuban government, and today the Dominica Labor Party has more than 400 Dominicans educated in Cuba. His friendships with Cuba, Libya, and Iraq led to the United States banning Douglas from entry for 15 years in the 1970s, 1980s, and 1990s. During that same time, he headed Mataba, a Libyan-based organization that financed and trained guerrilla movements in Africa, until

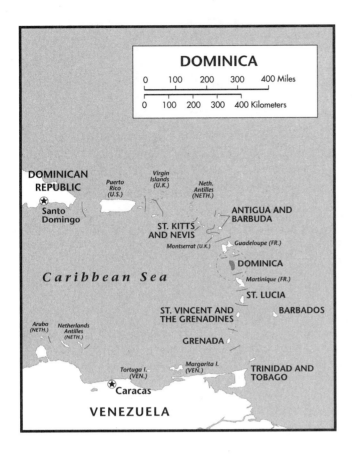

**DOMINICA**

0 100 200 300 400 Miles

0 100 200 300 400 Kilometers

DOMINICAN REPUBLIC

Santo Domingo

Puerto Rico (U.S.)

Virgin Islands (U.K.)

Neth. Antilles (NETH.)

ANTIGUA AND BARBUDA

ST. KITTS AND NEVIS

Montserrat (U.K.)

Guadeloupe (FR.)

DOMINICA

Martinique (FR.)

ST. LUCIA

BARBADOS

ST. VINCENT AND THE GRENADINES

Caribbean Sea

Aruba (NETH.)

Netherlands Antilles (NETH.)

GRENADA

Tortuga I. (VEN.)

Margarita I. (VEN.)

TRINIDAD AND TOBAGO

Caracas

VENEZUELA

it disbanded in 1995. In 1994, Douglas assumed leadership of the Dominica Labour Party (DLP), and after the 1995 election he assumed the shared position (with Brian Alleyne) of Leader of the Opposition. He served as an elected member of Parliament from 1985–95. The results of a by-election in 1996 left Douglas as the sole Leader of the Opposition, a position which he held until assuming the prime minister's position in February 2000. Throughout the 1990s, Douglas nurtured lasting relationships with Labor Party leaders in Europe, including Tony Blair, prime minister of the UK. In May 2000, the Canadian government officially pardoned Mr. Douglas.

## LEADERSHIP

An ongoing challenge for Mr. Douglas is that his government is in coalition with the conservative Dominica Freedom Party, led by the new Tourism Minister, Charles Savarin. Douglas must balance the needs of two, often opposing, political views. Also, to satisfy a campaign promise, the government has initiated a corruption probe of the Edison James' Administration.

## DOMESTIC POLICY

The new government faces numerous problems with which Douglas must deal: education and youth training, persistently high unemployment, lack of health care, an inadequate infrastructure, and a continued dependence upon the agricultural sector. Douglas faces an external debt of close to US$200 million and a gross national product of approximately US$248.3 million. The unemployment rate has remained at least at 20% for most of the past 10 years, and Douglas will

need to address the need for economic development early in his administration. Thus in June 2000, Prime Minister Rosie Douglas participated in the inauguration of EC express airline in Dominica, a step taken to enhance the country's tourism market. Dominica has promoted tourism heavily since 1990 as a way to end the country's economic dependence on bananas. After a sluggish start in the early 1990s, tourist arrivals jumped by 7.3% in 1993, 11.3% in 1994 and 5.4% in 1995, to reach a total of 68,838 visitors in that year. Since then total visitor arrivals have remained steady at over 68,000.

## FOREIGN POLICY

One of the critical elements of the LDP's successful campaign to replace United Workers Party focused on Douglas' criticism of the country's Economic Citizenship Program. For much of the 1990s Dominica provided foreigners with passports in exchange for investments totaling millions of dollars. At the end of 1999, there were an estimated 1,000 such citizens, largely from Russia, China, Europe, and the United States, with most residing outside Dominica. Douglas promised to end the practice, and shortly after taking office, his government did suspend the practice. In April, 2000, Dominica resumed selling passports to foreigners, after reviewing and "fundamentally changing" the program to eliminate abuses. Douglas has sought new investments from Libya and other old allies, but said he has also worked for closer economic relations with Europe, Canada, and the United States. He insisted that his government would not be anti-West, noting that the United States provides most of Dominica's 200,000 annual tourist visitors.

In May 2000, Prime Minister Douglas held successful talks with officials of the International Monetary Fund (IMF) on a request by Dominica for aid to repair damage done by Hurricane Lenny in November 1999. His government has also been able to obtain pledges of assistance from a number of governments. One of these is the French Government, which has given a commitment to improve the Melville Hall and Canefield airports to increase air traffic.

## ADDRESS

Office of the Prime Minister
Government Headquarters
Box 121
Roseau, Dominica

## REFERENCES

The Associated Press. 7 February 2000.
BBC News. [Online] Available http://news.bbc.co.uk/ (Accessed 1 February 2000).
CaKaFete. [Online] Available http://www.cakafete.com (Accessed May 2000).
*The Chronicle.* [Online] Available http://www.delphis.dm/ thechronicle/index.html (Accessed September 1999–May 2000).
Encyclopedia Britannica. [Online] Available http:// www.search.eb.com/ (Accessed May 2000).
Latin American Newsletters, Ltd. 22 February 2000.
*The Los Angeles Times,* 27 February 2000.

**Profile researched and written by John Ranahan, Oberlin, Ohio (5/2000).**

# DOMINICAN REPUBLIC

### Leonel Fernández
### President
*(pronounced "LAY-oh-nell fair-NAHN-dezz")*

*"There is no democracy where there are empty stomachs."*

Known by its inhabitants as *la Republica Dominicana*, the Dominican Republic is located in the West Indies. It occupies the eastern two-thirds of the island of Hispañola, which it shares with Haiti on the west. To the north lies the Atlantic Ocean, with the Mora Passage on the east separating the island from Puerto Rico. To the south lies the Caribbean Sea. Covering an area of 48,442 sq km (18,704 sq mi), the terrain is dominated by a central mountain chain and several lesser ranges. Despite the country's subtropical location, it enjoys a moderate climate, well suited for agriculture.

Spanish is the Dominican Republic's official language, reflecting its colonial heritage. The predominant religion is Roman Catholicism, which receives state support. Nearly two-thirds of the country's 8.1 million people live in the northern and eastern regions, where farmland is excellent, and water is plentiful. However, more than one million people live on the southern coast, in the capital city of Santo Domingo. The largest city in the Dominican Republic, it is also the nation's economic and cultural hub. Ethnically, about 75% of Dominicans are of mixed European and African descent while the remaining 25% of the population is made up of non-mixed blood whites and blacks. Haitians make up the largest minority group.

Life expectancy is 70 years of age, but infant mortality rates remains high at 42.5 deaths per 1,000 live births. Per capita GDP has been estimated at US$5,000.

The Dominican economy is based largely on agriculture, with its chief products being sugar, coffee, cocoa, and tobacco. However, there is also a strong mining sector which produces gold, silver, and nickel. In recent years, tourism has become a significant source of income. Primary imports, half of which come from the United States, include foodstuffs, petroleum, manufactured goods, chemicals, and pharmaceuticals. Major trading partners are the United States, the European Community, Mexico, and Venezuela. The unit of currency is the *peso*.

## POLITICAL BACKGROUND

The Dominican Republic is a representative democracy in which all citizens may vote once they reach 18 years of age, or even earlier if they are married. The country's 1966 constitution divides power among three branches: legislative, judicial, and executive. This similarity to the US constitution is no accident. After years of dictatorship under Rafael Trujillo, the country was in the midst of civil war when the US invaded in 1965. The invasion was ostensibly to protect American citizens, but was also meant to curb the growing influence of leftist rebels and prevent their success. After establishing an inter-American peacekeeping force, the US assisted the Dominicans in the formation of a new government. Following the US model, legislative action is conducted by a bicameral National Congress, which consists of the Senate and the Chamber of Deputies, whose members face election every four years. The Senate's 30 members each represent a province while the chamber's 120 deputies are apportioned by population. Executive power is vested in the president who is elected to a four-year term. The president has the authority to appoint provincial governors and to remove them as well. He is also commander-in-chief of the armed forces although military commanders have also wielded great power as well.

There are four major political parties in the Dominican Republic: the Dominican Liberation Party (PLD), led by Leonel Fernández, the Social Christian Reformist Party (PRSC) of former president Joaquin Balaguer, the Dominican Revolutionary Party (PRD), led by José Peña Gomez, and a smaller party called the Democratic Union (UD). As in the United States, the party of the president does not necessarily enjoy a majority in the Congress. Currently the president's PLD has only one seat in the Senate and 12 in the Chamber of Deputies.

## PERSONAL BACKGROUND

Leonel Antonio Fernández Reyna was born in Santo Domingo on 26 December 1953. When he was seven years old, he moved to New York City with his mother, attending elementary and high school in Manhattan. He learned to speak English so well that his accent is that of a native New Yorker. He acquired a taste for such artifacts of American culture as rock music and basketball—a sport he still plays with considerable skill to this day. After completing high school he moved back to the Dominican Republic to attend the Autonomous University of Santo Domingo, where he studied law. After graduation, he practiced law and continued his studies, earning a doctorate in law and politics. He joined the PLD when it was founded in 1973 by former President Juan Bosch, whom Fernández has referred to as his teacher and guide.

## RISE TO POWER

Fernández worked his way steadily and silently up the party hierarchy, holding a variety of positions. He remained

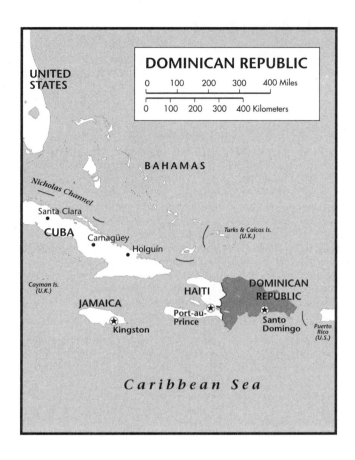

## DOMINICAN REPUBLIC

presidency from "falling into hands that are not really Dominican." On election day the president made sure his followers knew which way to vote; he turned up to cast his own ballot just as ostensibly as he had refrained from doing in the first round.

For his part, Fernández generally refrained from the racial accusations, concentrating his energy on the issues of economic growth and an end to corruption in government. Yet passions ran high. Fernández claimed that there was an international campaign based in Madrid, Washington and Caracas which was supporting Peña Gomez. Violent clashes between the parties resulted in at least ten deaths during the campaign, with one instance of shots being fired at Mr. Fernández. The decisive factor in the end proved to be the unity of the two parties behind Fernández, whose combined strength was just enough to give him a majority. On 30 June 1996, in elections described as free and fair by international observers, he was elected president with 51 percent of the vote. He was the first candidate to be elected from the Dominican Liberation Party.

On 16 May 2000, Hipolito Mejía of the Dominican Revolutionary Party was elected president; Fernández had been constitutionally prevented from seeking reelection. Although Mejía garnered less than half of the vote, the other two leading candidates dropped out of the race to avoid a runoff and Mejía was thus declared the winner. Mejía has promised to increase social spending when he takes office on 16 August 2000.

## LEADERSHIP

At 42 years of age, Fernández was the youngest elected president of his country, and a marked contrast to his octogenarian predecessor. He has been called the Benjamin Netanyahu of his country, in reference to the young new Israeli prime minister who also lived for several years in the United States. Yet while Fernández has great familiarity with the United States, its customs and culture, he is roundly acclaimed as being "Dominican to the core."

Fernández faces several obstacles to his leadership. He has very few allies in the Congress. His party captured only a handful of seats, and the alliance with Balaguer's PRSC broke down shortly after the election. The PRSC joined forces with Gomez's party, whose combined power will allow them to block any legislation and judicial appointments they oppose.

A bigger challenge for Fernández is to overcome the shadow of former president Balaguer, whose influence continues to resonate throughout the country. He continues to hold the levers of power in Congress; the courts are filled with Balaguer appointees, and so is the military. Furthermore, Fernández's alliance with Balaguer during the election strengthened the perception that the new president is indebted to his predecessor and cannot truly be an independent president. "He didn't sell his soul to the devil," said one observer, "but he leased it." Fernández counts those charges, stating that "I assume the presidency without having my hands tied. Calling me Balaguer's prisoner was campaign rhetoric by my opponents to discredit me." Staking out his independence might thus be aided by the break with Balaguer. It will make the passage of legislation more difficult, but Fernández can now be less concerned about souring relations with the man whose legacy he intends to challenge.

relatively unknown until he was selected as Juan Bosch's vice-presidential running mate in 1994. When Bosch stepped down after his defeat, Fernández assumed the party leadership.

Fernández's primary competitors in the 1996 election were José Francisco Peña Gomez of the PRD and Jacinto Peynado of the PRSC. While Peña Gomez had unsuccessfully run for President, Fernández and Peynado had never run before. Both men had been overshadowed for years by former presidents, Joaquin Balaguer and Juan Bosch. This time, however, neither of these veteran politicians chose to run. Bosch decided to back his party's younger nominee, and Balaguer was prevented from running for a seventh term by a 1994 constitutional reform. He agreed to step down at the end of a two-year term after pressure mounted in the wake of the 1994 elections, which were widely believed to have been rigged to ensure Balaguer's victory. With both of the old party leaders out of the picture, and Balaguer refusing to vote as a signal of his disdain for the entire proceeding, the race became competitive. No candidate won a clear majority in the first-round, so a runoff election was scheduled between the two candidates with the most votes, Fernández and Peña Gomez.

At this point, Bosch and Balaguer, who had been political enemies for decades, joined forces to oppose Gomez. Their alliance was widely seen as racially motivated with a nationalistic twist: Gomez, who is black, was accused of being a Haitian. The implication was that he was a Haitian agent who had a secret plan to unite the two countries under black rule. Some of the accusations went so far as to suggest that Gomez would use voodoo to accomplish this task. President Balaguer himself claimed that it was necessary to prevent the

After four years in government, he will retire with high levels of popularity. He fought corruption; the economy expanded at a healthy rate; and he successfully attracted new investment to foster economic and human capital development.

## DOMESTIC POLICY

Fernández comes to office not only as a new president, but as the first leader of a new political era in the Dominican Republic, determined to reform the entire political arena. Balaguer, who served as president for six terms and has run in every election since the early 1960s, was also a loyal aide to Rafael Trujillo, the dictator who ruled from 1930 until his assassination in 1961. Thus the ascent of Fernández represents to many a major departure form the "*caudillismo*" of the past and an opportunity to build a lasting democracy which is not marked by one-man rule and fraudulent elections.

One of the president's first targets is the widespread corruption in government. Focusing on the subject as a major theme of his campaign, Fernández assailed the great poverty of the many and the "outlandish amassing of wealth by the few." To that effect he plans to go after many of the country's state-owned companies, not only to root out their corrupt practices, but also to embark on a program of privatization. Denouncing the statist policies of his predecessor as inefficient, Fernández plans to sell off some businesses and enter into joint ventures on others—something which he says will help his country to compete in the global marketplace. Among those industries targeted are the utilities, mining, the national airline, and even sugar, which was once the backbone of the economy but now requires government subsidies to stay afloat.

Fernández intends to reduce the emphasis on large public works projects in favor of social spending on education, welfare, and social security. This will be difficult to accomplish since the government is burdened by a $4.5 billion foreign debt and is committed to spending millions of dollars on projects begun by Balaguer. Still, Fernández has pledged to relieve the poverty faced by most Dominicans. To raise money, he has proposed a gas tax and the sale or reorganization of inefficient businesses. He is also making efforts to attract foreign investment and to promote the already strong tourist industry. It is the country's strengthened democracy that represents the greatest long term asset to its economic outlook. As one businessman said, "the fact that we've been able to hold democratic and clean elections will help attract foreign investment."

## FOREIGN POLICY

A small country with little strategic significance to the world's great powers, the Dominican Republic has been able to stay out of most major international conflicts. Since the country lies within the US sphere of influence and receives most of its foreign aid from the US, good relations with its powerful neighbor have been a cornerstone of its foreign policy. To that end, Fernández plans to foster a close relationship in the areas of immigration control and anti-drug programs, though he has been critical of Washington's policy toward Cuba.

Relations with neighboring Haiti have long been strained. Even before he was inaugurated, Fernández was beset by problems with Haiti, whose president refused to attend the inauguration due to the tenor of the electoral campaign. In addition to the harsh words before the election, about half a million Dominicans of Haitian descent were prevented from voting in the first round, and thousands of black "illegal immigrants" were deported before the polling took place. In protest, President Preval stayed home and sent the foreign minister in his place. In an effort to repair relations, Fernández will make an official state visit to Haiti—only the second time in 50 years that a Dominican president has made such a trip.

In an effort to increase foreign aid and investment, Fernández met with the Spanish prime minister, Jose Maria Aznar, at a summit in Santo Domingo. The two agreed to begin cooperation on a range of issues but left one major issue unresolved. Spain has repeatedly asked the Dominican government to extradite five men who have been living in Santo Domingo since 1989. Sought by the Spanish as suspected terrorists, they were granted asylum by President Balaguer on the condition that they do not leave the country. While Fernández suggested that they might eventually be sent back to Spain, no agreement was reached. Instead, the two governments agreed to cooperate in combating terrorism.

## ADDRESS
Oficina del Presidente
Santo Domingo, D.N.
Dominican Republic

## REFERENCES
"Calling the Blind Man's Bluff." *The Economist*, 25 September 1999, p. 40.
*Caribbean Update*, 1 July 1996.
*The Economist*, 6 July 1996.
*Financial Times*, 5 September 1996.
*Latin American Weekly Report*, July–September 1996.
*The New York Times*, July–September 1996.

**Profile researched and written by David Bernell (9/96; revised by Patricio Navio 4/2000).**

# ECUADOR

## Gustavo Noboa Bejarano
### President

*(pronounced "goo-STAV-oh no-BO-ah bee-jah-RAH-no")*

*"Ecuador is in the worst crisis of its history."*

The Republic of Ecuador is located on the western coast of South America, north and west of Peru and south and west of Colombia. Ecuador has an area of 272,045 sq km (105,037 sq mi). The Galapagos Islands, a famous wildlife sanctuary, are also a part of Ecuador. With a tropical climate in the coastal area, the country also encompasses land in the drier and colder Andean region. Ecuador's highest mountain, the Chimborazo, reaches 6,267 m (19,000 ft) and forms part of the Andes mountain chain that extends from Colombia in the north to Argentina and Chile in the south.

Ecuador is a densely populated country of 12.6 million-people. With about one-third of the land area of Chile, Ecuador's population is almost equal to that of Chile. The capital city, Quito, is located in the Andean region. The Pacific port of Guayaquil, in the coastal region, is equally important for the country's economy. About 55% of all Ecuadorans are mestizo (mixed Spanish and Amerindian), 25% Amerindian, 10% black, and 10% Spanish. Ecuador's population grows moderately at a 1.93% increase per year, with more than 37% under the age of 15. The infant mortality rate of 33.4 deaths per 1,000 live births is somewhat higher than most South American nations, but lower than Bolivia and Peru. Life expectancy is 71.4 years. Approximately 95% of the population considers itself to be nominally Roman Catholic, but practicing Catholics are much fewer in number. Protestant churches have made important gains in recent years, particularly in urban areas.

Ecuador's main natural resources are petroleum, fish, rubber, and timber. The country's major exports are primary products, most notably oil, bananas, rubber, and shrimp. A positive trade balance, mostly a result of high oil prices in recent years, has kept the foreign debt at a relatively low level of $12.5 billion. Ecuador's main trading partners are the US (32%), other Latin American nations (30%), and the European Union (20%). Japan and other Asian countries have also entered the Ecuadoran market in recent years, but this trade has not grown as rapidly as in other Latin American nations. Per capita GDP has been estimated at US$4,800. Inflation has remained somewhat high in recent years; in 1998, it reached 43%. Unemployment stood at 12% in 1998, and underemployment is common in rural and coastal areas.

## POLITICAL BACKGROUND

At the end of the 15th century, the Incas from Peru conquered much of what is now Ecuador, uniting the various indigenous groups then living in the area. In 1534, the short-lived Incan rule was brought to an end by the arrival of the Spanish, who set up their colonial system, which lasted nearly 300 years. In 1822, Ecuador won its independence from Spain when General Antonio Jose de Sucre was victorious in the Battle of Pichineha. After an eight-year confederation with Colombia and Venezuela, Ecuador became an independent republic in 1830.

For most of the time since independence, Ecuador has been ruled by a small elite of European ancestry, who engaged in fierce struggles for power amongst themselves. During much of the 19th century the conservatives ruled, drawing their support largely from the wealthy landowners and the Roman Catholic Church. In 1896, however, the Liberal Party took over, ending the strong influence of the church and shifting power toward the military and business leaders. By 1925, widespread dissatisfaction with the failure of government to address Ecuador's economic and social problems resulted in the disintegration of the political system.

Between 1925 and 1948 Ecuador saw a succession of 25 presidents or heads of state, none of whom served a full term in office. Between 1948 and 1960, however, the country enjoyed a brief period of political stability. Each of the three presidents who served during that 12-year period, though affiliated with different political parties, pursued similar programs of increasing political participation, economic development, and moderate social reform.

During the 1960s and 1970s, political instability returned, along with a period of military rule and frequent coups. In 1978, the country moved toward the restoration of democratically-elected civilian government, adopting a new constitution and holding elections in 1979. The first civilian elected under the new constitution was Jaime Roldos Aguilera, a charismatic young lawyer from Guayaquil. Two years later Roldos was killed in a suspicious plane crash, and the next year the Ecuadoran Roldosista Party (PRE) was formed to continue the policies and programs which Roldos had advocated. However, since the return to civilian rule, no political party has become dominant in Ecuadoran political life.

In 1996 the *Roldosistas* elected their first president. Abdala Bucaram, the former mayor of Guayaquil and a businessman of Lebanese extraction, scored a surprising upset victory over his opponent. Bucaram's ability to govern depended largely on his relationship with the Congress and the country's financial and business community. His fortunes with the deeply divided and contentious Congress, however, were not promising. Bucaram also faced formidable economic challenges. Perhaps the greatest of these was to make good on his campaign promise to redress the widening gap between rich and poor while keeping the financial and business sectors from panicking. Shortly after taking office, Bucaram abandoned his populist platform in favor of the policies of his predecessor. This ignited the disappointment and disaffection of the poor, who had supported his election. Widespread charges of corruption, nepotism, and incompetence also began to surface. When he introduced harsh austerity measures, curbing government subsidies to balance the budget, and sending utility rates soaring, violent street protests began to occur with increasing frequency.

On 6 February 1997, six months after taking office, Congress ousted Bucaram following two days of massive popular protests against his economic measures. Congress chose Fabian Alarcon to serve as interim president. In the May 1998 elections, candidate Jamil Mahuad was elected to the presidency. Mahuad had promised economic reforms, but by late 1999, the country's indigenous peoples had grown disenchanted with his policies, which had done nothing to improve their social and economic situation. Massive banking scandals also had tainted his administration. In January 2000, Mahuad announced plans to replace the *sucre,* the national currency, with the US dollar, to stabilize the economy and end chronic inflation. Indigenous peoples said the plan would destroy their savings, driving them further into poverty. On 21 January 2000, thousands of indigenous peoples led by the Ecuadoran Confederation of Indigenous Nationalities (CONAIE) marched to Quito to protest "dollarization" of the economy. With aid from the military, they ousted Mahuad from office. A three-member junta, which included a prominent leader of CONAIE, held power for a few hours. The junta was dissolved after the United States and other nations threatened to isolate Ecuador if it did not return to democracy. Congress named Vice President Gustavo Noboa Bejarano as president of the country despite protests by Mahuad and indigenous leaders.

## PERSONAL BACKGROUND

Born in the coastal city of Guayaquil, Noboa was 62-years-old when Congress approved his ascension to the presidency. He is the second of nine siblings, has six children and five grandchildren. Never a politician at heart, Noboa spent most of his career in academia, 10 of those years as rector and law-school dean at the Catholic University. Described by friends as a Christian Democrat in ideology, Noboa never joined any of Ecuador's political parties. Yet, he was often invited by presidents to join their cabinets, offers he declined to remain head of the university.

## RISE TO POWER

Despite his self-imposed distance from politics, Noboa's name always came up at times of crises. When a vice-president was accused of corruption, he was invited to take his post. Several times, he was asked to become a minister, rejecting all offers. And when President Abdalá Bucaram was being pressured to resign, some Ecudorans wanted Noboa to take the post. Noboa did not completely lack political experience. He had served as governor of the province of Guayas, and had served

on a sensitive security and trust commission during the peace process between Perú and Ecuador. In 1998, Noboa became Vice President to President Jamil Mahuad. Noboa maintained a low profile during Mahuad's brief presidency, gaining respect for leading reconstruction work in Pacific Coast communities devastated by El Niño storms in 1997 and 1998.

As Mahuad's presidency fell deeply into crisis, Noboa maintained silence. He was in Guayaquil during the Indian and military takeover of government buildings on 21 January 2000. Mahuad fled the government palace, and within hours a three-man junta claimed to govern the country. The coup was immediately condemned by several nations, including the United States and the Organization of American States. They demanded an immediate return to democracy. General Carlos Mendoza dissolved the junta and allowed Congress to select Noboa as president on 22 January despite Mahuad's protests that he had been illegally removed from his post. Noboa said little about the coup or Mahuad and immediately restored democracy during his swearing-in ceremony on 24 January.

## LEADERSHIP

Integrity and honesty are often mentioned as Noboa's most important assets. Yet, Noboa will need to rely on strength and determination to keep Ecuador and his presidency on course. Noboa became the country's sixth president in just four years in a country where hugely popular presidents have quickly fallen out of favor. Ecuadorans have lost faith in their political institutions. Polls in early 2000 suggested that most people in Ecuador do not trust the government and favor a referendum on dissolving Congress and the Supreme Court. Two days after his inauguration, Noboa pleaded with his countrymen to build a better society. "My government will be one of order and peace, one that believes in justice and equality for all, a government that will surmount all obstacles to reach mutual benefits for all."

Noboa has managed to earn the trust of the army, a key to staying in power. Former President Mahuad had angered many top military leaders for reaching a peace agreement with Perú that ended a border dispute that dated to 1941. In many Ecuadoran sectors, the peace agreement was seen as a capitulation to Peruvian demands. Military involvement during the 21 January insurrection was seen as a direct rebuke against Mahuad. Noboa's government promised to punish officers who were directly involved in the coup, creating a potentially dangerous situation. While Noboa's integrity remained unchallenged, he is still a member of Ecuador's elite and distrusted by many indigenous peoples. Establishing a strong relationship based on mutual trust with indigenous leaders will be one of his most difficult challenges. In early 2000, several indigenous leaders criticized his government for doing little for their communities. Disagreements with indigenous leaders led to the resignation of one of Noboa's top cabinet members.

## DOMESTIC POLICY
Noboa faced major tasks early in his presidency: maintaining order after Mahuad's ouster, establishing the US dollar as the currency of the nation, stabilizing an economy in crisis, and improving relations with the powerful Ecuadoran Confederation of Indigenous Nationalities (CONAIE), which along with the military had helped depose President Jamil Mahuad. CONAIE grew in power in the late 1990s, and its members became more militant as they made more demands from government. Among the poorest in the country, indigenous peoples had established themselves as a powerful force by the turn of the 21st century. With the ouster of Mahuad, they showed they had the political will to force changes. Noboa understood that forging an amicable relationship with CONAIE was necessary to ensure success during his presidency and met often with its leaders early in his presidency. Yet, Noboa suffered his first setback with the resignation of his minister of government, Francisco Huerta, who had been appointed in January 2000 to negotiate and improve relations with CONAIE. Huerta resigned in April 2000, saying he had been unable to reach any common ground with the confederation. Noboa had asked Huerta to help formulate a plan for social and economic improvements for indigenous peoples. His resignation underscored the power of CONAIE, whose leaders threatened to continue protests against the Noboa government. CONAIE leaders accused Noboa's government of moving rapidly to "dollarize" the economy, but of moving slowly to improve the lives of indigenous peoples. Indigenous leaders warned Noboa he had three to six months to avert a social explosion. Early in 2000, Indigenous leaders pressed Noboa's government to hold a referendum on the dissolution of Congress and the Supreme Court. Some polls suggested that nearly 75% of the population supported having a referendum. CONAIE began to collect the needed 600,000 signatures for a referendum.

Noboa said little could be done until the "dollarization" of the economy was in place. His government inherited a fiscal crisis. The country's GDP had contracted by 8% in 1999, and unemployment had become a severe problem. The *sucre*, the national currency, lost two-thirds of its value in 1999. Former President Mahuad had suggested adopting the US dollar as the country's currency to stabilize the economy. It derailed his presidency. Yet, Noboa said Ecuador had no choice but to adopt the dollar and privatize state enterprises to stimulate the economy. Noboa said both measures were the best tools to stabilize the economy, control rampant inflation and attract foreign investment. Congress approved his economic measures in March 2000, and the government began an official campaign titled "Get to Know the Dollar" to educate Ecudorans about their new currency. The currency switch was to be completed by September 2000 when all but the smallest of transactions were to be done in dollars. Yet, the economic situation was expected to remain precarious, with no assurances that the switch to the dollar would cure the country's economic problems and prevent social unrest. The International Monetary Fund said Ecuador would have to make difficult decisions to ensure the success of "dollarization," including major increases in fuel and drastic cuts in government expenses. In exchange for loans, Ecuador agreed to keep its budget deficit to 4% of GDP and aim for economic growth of 0.9%.

## FOREIGN POLICY
Noboa's first task as president was to regain respect—and chiefly economic aid—from the international community. While Mahuad said he would not challenge Noboa's presidency, the Organization of American States said Mahuad's ouster represented a danger to democracies in the Americas. Noboa took steps to calm international concerns, stressing democratic measures and a willingness to institute transparency in government. The OAS later supported the new government.

The International Monetary Fund, the World Bank, and other international lenders agreed to loan Ecuador $2 billion to ensure a smooth transfer from the *sucre* to the dollar. The money was to be disbursed during a three-year period starting in 2000.

## ADDRESS
Excelentisimo Presidente de la Republica
Palacio Nacional
Garcia Moreno 1043
Quito, Ecuador

## REFERENCES
*Christian Science Monitor*, various issues.
CNN Online (English and Spanish). [Online] Available http:// www.cnn.com/ (Accessed April 2000).
*Los Angeles Times*, various issues.
*New York Times*, various issues.
*Washington Post*, various issues.

**Profile researched and written by Ignacio Lobos, journalist (4/ 2000).**

# EGYPT

## Hosni Mubarak
## President

*(pronounced "HAHS-nee moo-BAR-ak")*

*"Our goal is to create an equal society, not a society of privilege and class distinctions. Social justice is the first rule for peace and stability in society."*

The Arab Republic of Egypt is located in North Africa but is commonly referred to as part of the Middle East. It is bounded at its northeastern tip by Israel, on the east by the Red Sea, on the south by Sudan, on the west by Libya, and on the north by the Mediterranean Sea. Even though the total area of Egypt is 1,002,000 sq km (386,900 sq mi), the cultivated and settled areas of the Nile Valley, delta, and oases, cover only about 35,580 sq km (13,740 sq mi). About 90% of the country is desert, and rainfall averages only 20.3 cm (eight in) per year.

The population of Egypt has been estimated at 67.3 million and is growing at a rate of almost 2% annually. The official language is Arabic although French and English are widely spoken. Islam is the primary religion (and the religion of the state) and is considered to be the faith of about 90% of the population. Approximately 7% of the Egyptian people are Coptic Christians, the remainder being Roman Catholics, Protestants, or Greek Orthodox, with a small number of Jews.

The Egyptian unit of currency is the pound. Egypt's major exports are crude and refined petroleum, as well as cotton. The per capita GDP has been estimated at $2,850 and is estimated to be growing at a rate of 5% annually.

## POLITICAL BACKGROUND

Part of the Ottoman Empire from 1517, Egypt became a British protectorate in 1914 and an independent monarchy in 1922. The Anglo-Egyptian Treaty of 1936 recognized full Egyptian sovereignty and provided for the gradual withdrawal of British troops. However, troop withdrawal was postponed when Italy invaded Egypt in 1940. After World War II, British forces did withdraw, with the exception of a military contingent in the Suez Canal Zone.

The monarchy was overthrown on 23 July 1952 in a bloodless military coup led by Colonel Abdul Nasser, and the country was declared a republic one year later. Egypt merged with Syria in 1958 to form the United Arab Republic. The former retained that name when Syria broke away from the union in 1961, finally re-adopting the name of Egypt in 1971. Under its present constitution, Egypt has a democratic-socialist system of government. The Islamic code is a principal source of legislation.

The president, who must be of Egyptian parentage and at least 40 years of age, is nominated by at least one-third of the members of the People's Assembly, approved by at least two-thirds, and elected by popular referendum. His term is

for six years, and he may be re-elected for subsequent terms. He has broad executive authority and may appoint one or more vice presidents, as well as all ministers. He also holds the power to dismiss these individuals.

The People's Assembly, elected for five years, is a legislative body which approves general policy, the budget, and the development plan. Under the state constitution, it has not less than 444 elected members, at least half of whom are workers or farmers. The president may appoint up to 10 additional members. Elections to the People's Assembly were held in November 1995 and are expected to be held again in 2000. The ruling National Democratic Party (NDP) took 72% of the seats in the People's Assembly.

A second legislative body, the Advisory Council, functions only as an advisory body. It held elections in 1995 and the NDP took 99% of the 264 seats. This near sweep was aided by a provision allowing the president to appoint 88 members to the Council. A date for the next election to the Advisory Council has not been determined.

In June 1977, the People's Assembly adopted a new law which permitted the formation of political parties for the first time since 1953. Presently, there are four opposition parties represented in the Assembly, but their representation is negligible compared to the overwhelming majority enjoyed by the NDP. All new parties must be approved by the government, and religious parties are illegal. Since the main source of opposition to the current government is the Muslim Brotherhood, an illegal religious organization, the real contest for power in Egypt takes place outside the party and legislative systems.

## PERSONAL BACKGROUND

Mohammed Hosni Mubarak was born on 4 May 1928 in the village of Kafr El-Meselha, in the Nile River Delta province of Menoufiya. He was one of five children born to an inspector in the Ministry of Justice. Mubarak received his early education at local elementary and secondary schools. Afterward, he enrolled in the National Military Academy, from which he graduated in 1949. He continued his military education, pursuing a two-year course at the Air Force Academy. From 1952 through 1959, he served as a flight instructor at the Academy. In 1964, Mubarak went to Moscow for a year of study at the elite Frunze General Staff Academy, the most prestigious military school in the former USSR. Upon his return to Egypt in 1965, he served as commander of several air force bases. He rose through the

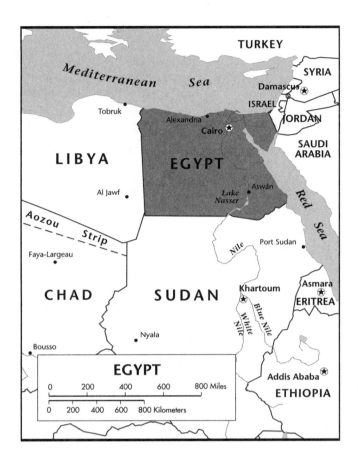

ranks rapidly, being promoted to commander of the Air Force Academy (1967), air force chief of staff (1969), and commander in chief of the air force and deputy minister of war (1972). Mubarak presently lives in a modest two-story house in suburban Heliopolis with his wife, Suzanne. They have two sons, Alaa and Gamal, and one grandson.

## RISE TO POWER

Mubarak acquired instant fame and the respect of then-president Anwar Sadat with his successful offensive against the Israeli forces on the first day of the October 1973 Arab-Israeli War. Pilots destroyed 90% of their targets within 20 minutes, thus minimizing Egyptian infantry casualties. After the UN-sponsored cease-fire in late October, Sadat dispatched Mubarak to every Arab country to explain the Egyptian government's determination to achieve a peaceful solution to the conflict.

Sadat named Mubarak vice president on 15 April 1975 and over the next few years entrusted him with several important diplomatic missions. Perhaps the most significant was Mubarak's involvement in negotiations with Israel. After Sadat's decision to accept the Camp David Peace Accords in 1978, which provided the foundation for an eventual settlement of the Arab-Israeli dispute, Egypt was practically ostracized from the Arab world. Despite the agreement, lingering conflicts between Israel and Egypt remained unresolved. Sadat sent Mubarak to Germany to solicit that government's help in settling the Arab-Israeli dispute. Later in the year, after Sadat had begun to doubt the possibility of ever resolving differences between his government and that of

Israeli Prime Minister Menahem Begin, Mubarak took part in meetings with the leaders of several Israeli opposition parties. He eventually took over the daily chores of running the government, freeing Sadat to pursue foreign policy interests. Mubarak was elected in 1980 to the vice chairmanship of the National Democratic Party (NDP), which secured his position as Sadat's heir apparent.

On 6 October 1981, Sadat was assassinated by a band of militant Islamic fundamentalists. The following day, the NDP nominated Mubarak as its presidential candidate, and the Egyptian parliament approved his immediate succession to the office, subject to confirmation by the voters. This was accomplished on 13 October when Mubarak was accepted by more than 98% of the electorate. Voters confirmed Mubarak's nomination for three subsequent six-year terms in 1987, 1993, and 1999.

## LEADERSHIP

As of 2000, Mubarak was Egypt's longest-serving modern leader, respected for his achievements in both domestic and foreign policy. In his 19 years in power, he had steered the nation through difficult economic times and largely eradicated the wave of Islamic fundamentalist violence that had threatened both Egypt's security and its lucrative tourism industry in the 1990s. He had also survived some 10 assassination attempts. As he embarked on his fourth term in office, there was considerable speculation about a political successor, a post for which no long-standing candidate had been groomed. (Mubarak had never named a vice president.) Some observers saw the appointment of Mubarak's son Gamal to a senior position in the ruling political party in February 2000 as an attempt to pave the way for political succession, in spite of previous disavowals of dynastic ambitions by Mubarak.

## DOMESTIC POLICY

First among Mubarak's domestic policy initiatives as president has been the campaign to quell Islamist opposition. In the wake of Sadat's assassination he ordered the arrest and imprisonment of more than 2,500 people. He continued to detain nearly all of the more than 1,500 prisoners taken a month earlier during Sadat's crackdown on critics of his regime. Through most of the 1990s, Islamist opposition to Mubarak's government remained his foremost domestic policy problem. During a 1995 visit to Addis Ababa, Mubarak survived an assassination attempt by Egyptian Islamists, allegedly supported by the government of neighboring Sudan. An extended crackdown on members of Islamist groups was implemented over several years, resulting in the detention of an estimated 20,000 persons by 1999. By 1997 the main opposition groups declared a ceasefire, but a terrorist attack on a tourist bus in Luxor and continued fighting in the southern part of the country suggested that the problem had not yet been resolved. In the late 1990s, the number of violent incidents decreased sharply. By 2000 observers considered the problem to be largely under control, and the government had released some 5,000 of the detainees arrested during the crackdown.

Mubarak is credited with bringing economic as well as political stability to Egypt during his long tenure as president. Since the early 1990s, the Mubarak government has embarked upon a program of structural reform. It has brought the inflation rate under control, reduced the budget deficit, and begun the process of selling off state-owned companies and reducing the degree of government regulation. It remains to be seen whether these reforms will achieve a growth rate sufficient to improve the standard of living in a country where the population grows by 1.2 million per year. Until recently the economy was held in check by a huge and inefficient public sector and excessive government regulation. Mubarak's economic policy is further complicated by rapidly growing cities that devour valuable farmland while outstripping the growth of basic services. It is the stated policy of the government to turn Egypt into a "tiger on the Nile." In other words, they wish to imitate the export-driven economic growth of the emerging economies of the Pacific Rim. There is still a long way to go, but Western business leaders are impressed by the direction Egypt is taking. Shortly after his reelection in September 1999, Mubarak replaced prime minister Kamal el-Ganzouri, in a move seen as a response to El-Ganzouri's perceived failure to deal effectively with economic issues, including privatization of the financial sector and exchange rate problems.

## FOREIGN POLICY

Upon taking over from Sadat, Mubarak reconfirmed his commitment to the Camp David Peace Accord and to the peace process with Israel. Although relations have occasionally been cool, Egypt remains one of only two Arab nations at peace with Israel and is a leading player in the effort to resolve differences between Israel and the Palestinian state. The 1993 Oslo agreement between Israel and the Palestinians led to an interim agreement which was negotiated in Egypt in 1995. Since then, on-again off-again negotiations have taken place in Egypt. Egyptian-Israeli relations were strained during the tenure of hardliner Benjamin Netanyahu as Israel's prime minister from 1996 to 1999, especially over the Israeli government's efforts to build housing for settlers at Har Homa outside Jerusalem. Since the election of Ehud Barak, the Egyptian and Israeli leaders have held talks as part of a wider effort at revitalizing the Middle East peace process.

Relations with the Sudan improved significantly in 1998 as the two nations agreed to cooperate on issues that raised security concerns.

## ADDRESS

Office of the President
Cairo, Egypt

## REFERENCES

"Beyond Mubarak." *Middle East Economic Digest,* 8 October 1999, p. 7.

CIA. The World Factbook, 1999. [Online] Available http://www.cia.gov (Accessed May 2000).

*Current Biography.* New York: H.W. Wilson Co., 1982.

"Egypt's Waiting Game." *The Economist,* 25 September 1999, p. 51.

*Europa World Yearbook.* London: Europa Publications Ltd., 1989; 1999.

*Financial Times,* 13 May 1997.

"Gamal Mubarak Gets Party Political Role." *Middle East Economic Digest,* 18 February 2000.

*The Guardian,* 7 October 1997.

*Jane's Intelligence Review,* 1 November 1997.

*New York Times,* 10 June 1990.

Paxton, John, ed. *Statesman's Yearbook, 1989.*

*Political Handbook of the World.* Binghamton, NY: CSA Publications, 1999.

"Where Does Egypt Fit in the World?" *The Economist,* 20 March 1999, p. 17.

**Profile researched and written by Erik O. Gilbert, University of Vermont (3/98; updated by Kathryn L. Green, Ph.D., California State University, San Bernardino, 5/2000).**

# EL SALVADOR

### Francisco Flores
### President
*(pronounced "fran-SIS-koh FLOR-es")*

*"The foremost and most urgent requirement of our government is to promote jobs. We must encourage all enterprises and businesses to create employment as the only alternative to neglect and poverty."*

The Republic of El Salvador, is located on the Pacific coast of Central America. It is the smallest and most densely populated of the five Central American republics and the only one without a coastline on the Caribbean Sea. It shares a long border with Honduras to the north and a shorter border with Guatemala to the west. The Gulf of Fonseca lies to its east and separates it from Nicaragua. The country's 21,393 sq km (8,260 sq mi) terrain is mostly mountainous, with a narrow belt of fertile coastal lowlands and central plateau, where nearly three-fourths of the nation's six million people live. Geologically it is located on one of the world's volcanic plates and has been subject to frequent and sometimes quite destructive earthquakes. The capital city of San Salvador has experienced earthquakes on 14 separate occasions.

Spanish is the official language, with a small percentage of the population speaking Nahuatl. Ethnically, almost all Salvadorans are mestizo; the Indian population is variously estimated at 5–10%. Although Roman Catholicism continues to be the dominant religious affiliation (75%) among Salvadorans, a growing percentage identify themselves with various Protestant and evangelical groups. An estimated one million Salvadorans considered themselves Protestant evangelicals. Illiteracy is high. About 50% of the population are illiterate, and another 25% are functionally illiterate. Life expectancy is 68 years for men and 75 years for women.

The Salvadoran unit of currency is the *colon*. Coffee production and export have dominated the economy for the last century. In 1998, revenues from the *maquila* industry were more than three times those from coffee sales, whose earnings have declined sharply in the last few years. The largest source of revenue into the country, however, is from remittances from Salvadorans living in the United States, currently running at $1.3 billion. El Salvador's primary trading partner is the US, followed by neighboring Guatemala. Inflation in 1998 was only about 4%. Per capita GDP has been estimated at $3,000. In the 1990s the economy expanded at an average annual rate of 2.3%.

## POLITICAL BACKGROUND
Since the 1930s, the military had been the primary source of authority within El Salvador. For 60 years its power over Salvadoran political life was nearly absolute. The armed forces operated with a high degree of independence and internal loyalty—a loyalty forged through the *tandas* (cohort) system of military education and promotion. This loyalty transcended even that given to the country's president. Since

the end of the 12-year civil war in 1992, the military has been drastically scaled down, largely purged of human rights abusers, and essentially removed from politics.

Even so, the transition to a broad-based democracy and thriving economy is far from being achieved. Corruption and violence, particularly against peasants, have been the hallmarks of Salvadoran society for centuries. The introduction of coffee into the country during the 19th century established the social structures that still exist today. Land has been, and continues to be, a primary issue. Land ownership has been concentrated in the hands of a few, with the consequence that the livelihood of the vast majority of Salvadorans has been subject to the whims of the wealthy landowners. Throughout the 20th century, an iron-fisted oligarchy—the so-called "fourteen families" that control coffee production—have dominated the Salvadoran economy and political system in concert with the military.

During the 1960s there was a small opening in Salvadoran political life, when middle class reformist politics (in particular the Christian Democrats) began to participate in the political process. This opening was abruptly shut in 1972, when the military stole the election from Jose Napoleon Duarte and Guillermo Ungo, who were sent into exile. Other moderates were systematically killed. Salvadoran society became increasingly polarized and anti-government guerrilla movements began to form. In 1980, these groups coalesced into the *Frente Farabundo Martí de Liberación Nacional* (FMLN), and civil war broke out. The horrors of this war were not confined to military clashes. The Salvadoran military had also formed clandestine "death squads" that indiscriminately tortured and killed. During the course of the 12-year war, more than 75,000 civilians—including mayors, union leaders, teachers, health care workers, priests, religious workers, and the country's archbishop were murdered largely, but not exclusively, by government security forces.

Over the 12-year period of civil strife, the United States poured nearly $6 billion in military aid into the country, and funded candidates, parties, and processes in a series of "demonstration" elections. By the mid-1980s, this aid made El Salvador the second highest per capita recipient of US aid in the world. For several years running, this aid equaled $1.5 million a day and constituted half of the entire budget of the Salvadoran government. United Nations-brokered negotiations led to the Peace Accords signed on 16 January 1992 in Chapultepec, Mexico.

El Salvador operates under a 1983 constitution, the Pact of Apaneca. Engineered by the US government, it was an attempt to establish common ground among El Salvador's ideologically disparate political parties, based on principles of representative democracy. The head of state is the president, elected independently of the Legislative Assembly to one five-year term. The national legislature is a unicameral Legislative Assembly, expanded from 60 to 84 members in 1991 in order to give smaller political parties more opportunity to gain access to the legislative process. The Assembly now consists of 64 locally and 20 nationally elected deputies simultaneously chosen every three years. The country is divided into 14 departments, which are subdivided into 262 municipalities. The municipalities elect mayors every two years.

Although seven political parties nominated candidates for the office of president in 1999, four are primary. The incumbent party is the Nationalist Republican Alliance (ARENA), a right-wing party founded in 1980 as a coalition of the military and the country's economic elite. It is well financed and highly organized. The leadership is well educated and bilingual. The former president, Armando Calderon Sol, represented a more moderate wing of the party.

The newest party, and ARENA's principal rival, is the Farabundo Marti National Liberation Front (FMLN), whose political base is primarily among the poor. Formerly the name of the leftist guerrillas, they kept their name after the peace accords were signed in 1992. Although the FMLN had been gaining popular support over the last five years, divisions surfaced during the nominating process and blunted its effectiveness. Some wanted to follow more radical, Marxist policies. Others were more moderate pragmatists who have taken on issues such as tax policy and public safety.

The Christian Democrats (PDC) is a centrist party based largely in the country's interior. However, during the 1980s, they became associated with widespread corruption and economic calamity. Their support has steadily dwindled. The United Democratic Center (CDU) is a left-of-center party of reform-minded members, based in the large urban centers, with ties to various labor and popular organizations. Except for ARENA, the organizational state of the political parties is rather poor.

## PERSONAL BACKGROUND

Francisco Guillermo Flores Perez was born in El Salvador's second largest city, Santa Ana, on 17 October 1959. He is the son of a well-known lawyer and an ethnographer. Unlike his party's last two presidents, who were conservative businessmen, Flores was previously a philosophy professor. Flores received his bachelor's degree in political science from Amherst College in Massachusetts and studied philosophy at World University, a small unaccredited institution in Ojai, California. In the early 1980s he visited India several times to study mysticism and philosophy under Hindu swami, Sri Sathya Sai Baba, who preaches tolerance, patriotism, and nonviolence. Despite this training, Flores considers himself to be a devout Catholic. During the late 1980s he lectured at the Central America University (UCA) and Jose Matias Delgado University.

Leftist guerrilas were responsible for the death of Flores' grandfather and father-in-law. But Flores did not participate in the civil war. Instead he attended college and graduate

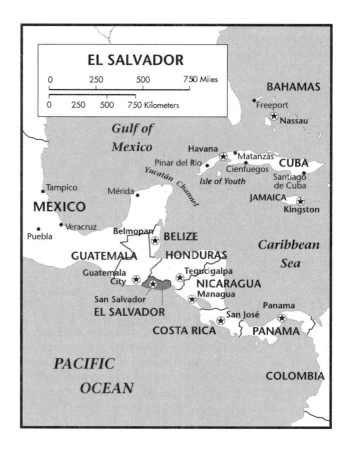

school, taught philosophy, and managed an irrigation project for a community of 300 families living adjacent to the cattle ranch and stud farm he had inherited from his grandfather. He joined the government in 1990 in ministerial and advisory positions before becoming elected to the National Assembly in 1994. By 1998, he had become head of his party's congressional delegation and the assembly's speaker. Known by the nickname of "Paco" or "Paquito," Flores is an expert horse tamer. His wife, Lourdes Rodriguez, is a schoolteacher. They have two children, an 11-year-old daughter, Gabriela, and a 7-year-old son, Juan Marcos.

## RISE TO POWER

As a member of El Salvador's National Assembly, Flores was known as "the peacemaker" and developed a reputation as a consensus builder. But he shocked his own party when he announced his candidacy months before other parties had decided on nominees. Though his party had been well known for its vehement anti-communist rhetoric in past elections, Flores avoided the polarizing rhetoric of his predecessors.

Instead he portrayed himself as a moderate centrist, and used a massive, costly media campaign to get across his message. In March 1999 he won by a landslide, garnering 52% of the vote. His closest rival was Facundo Guardado of the FMLN, who collected a mere 29% of the vote. Turnout, however, was low. Only about 1.2 million voters cast ballots out of three million eligible voters.

## LEADERSHIP

Flores, who became the youngest president in the Americas when he took his oath of office on 1 June 1999 wants to form a broad-based government, which he has dubbed the "New

Alliance." He is known to be an independent thinker and may find himself at odds within his own party, particularly with former president, Alfredo Cristiani, who has let it be known that he wants to influence the shape of the new government.

Flores will also have to contend with determined opposition from at least one faction within the FMLN. The FMLN had been gaining popular support during the last several years, winning the election in San Salvador's mayoral race and capturing nearly an equal number of legislative seats to those held by ARENA. In the current election, division surfaced between hardline socialists and moderates during the party's nominating process. FMLN candidate, Facundo Guardado, more moderate than some elements within his wing of the party, nonetheless indicated his lack of enthusiasm for working with Flores. His actions will also be closely followed by the Roman Catholic Church, which has been pressing the government to provide more security, better education, and improved health care.

## DOMESTIC POLICY
During the election campaign Flores stressed issues of poverty and crime. His administration faces some major challenges. First, he wants to raise the standard of living in a country where 50% of the population live below the poverty line and where unemployment officially stands at 7.2%, and underemployment is estimated at 31%. He hopes to provide loans to small and medium-sized businesses as well as modernize the country's infrastructure. He also promised to expand access to health, housing, and educational services and find ways to protect the environment. Both air and water pollution levels are alarmingly high in El Salvador. Flores is expected to continue the privatization program of public services begun during Calderon Sol's administration.

Flores has pledged to lower the country's rampant crime rate, which is the primary concern of most Salvadorans according to recent polls. Over the past five years, more than 7,000 people have died violently, one of the highest murder rates in Latin America. Flores has promised to crack down on organized crime, toughen penalties, and improve the prison system. He appointed Mauricio Sandoval, the former head of intelligence, to be his new national police chief. Finally, the country's arcane, byzantine voting system is especially daunting to the poor and a major source of dissatisfaction. The government, though recently enacting some electoral reforms, has been slow to implement them.

## FOREIGN POLICY
El Salvador has been dependent upon external support and world commodity prices for its economic stability and well-being throughout the 20th century. For 12 years its fate as a nation was intimately tied to the policies and politics of the United States. Since 1992, however, El Salvador's fortune has been rapidly de-linked from decisions made in Washington and increasingly bound to Wall Street, where the price of coffee is determined. Nonetheless, the hurricane-related destruction of much of Central America's agricultural-based economies will require substantial infusions of foreign aid, including debt relief.

Flores will continue to expand the Salvadoran economy, pursuing an aggressive strategy of export-led growth together with a strong program of boosting foreign investment and increasing Central American integration. He is expected to pursue full NAFTA parity for El Salvador, though the immediate prospects seem dim. Moreover, the region's economic troubles have resulted in a new wave of emigrants moving to the US in search of jobs and money to send home. The US has responded by aggressively deporting all undocumented Salvadorans.

## ADDRESS
President of the Republic of El Salvador
Presidential House
San Salvador, El Salvador

## REFERENCES
Agence France Presse, 31 May–1 June 1999.
Associated Press, 6–9 March 1999.
*Boston Globe,* 7–9 March 1999, 2 June 1999.
Economist Intelligence Unit. *Country Report,* 2nd Quarter, 1999.
*Latin American Weekly Report,* 16 February–25 May 1999.
*New York Times,* 8–9 March 1999.

**Profile researched and written by James L. McDonald, Senior International Policy Analyst, Bread for the World, Silver Spring, MD (9/99; revised by Patrizio Navia 4/2000).**

# EQUATORIAL GUINEA

Teodoro Obiang Nguema Mbasogo
President

(pronounced "tay-oh-DO-ro OH-bee-ong eng-GWAY-muh em-bah-SOH-go")

"This idea that there has been a climate of intimidation doesn't correspond to concrete reality."

The Republic of Equatorial Guinea (*La República de Guinea Ecuatorial*) is in west central Africa at latitude 2° north and longitude 10° east. The country's territory comprises the coastal enclave of Rio Muni, situated between the southwest corner of Cameroon and the northwest corner of Gabon; the island of Bioko, off the coast of Cameroon; and Annobon and Corisco in Corisco Bay. The total land area is 28,050 sq km (10,831 sq mi). The capital of Equatorial Guinea is Malabo on the island of Bioko. Bata is the principal city of Rio Muni. The country contains seven provinces: Pagalu, Bioko Norte, Bioko Sur, Centro Sur, Kie-Ntem, Litoral, and Wele-Nzas. Bioko and the smaller islands are of volcanic origin. In Rio Muni, a coastal plain rises to thickly forested hills in the interior. The climate is very hot and humid year-round.

Eighty percent of the country's population belongs to the Fang tribe. The Bubi account for about 15% of the population. A half dozen other ethnic groups, each speaking its own language, make up the remaining 5% of the population. A small European community, mostly Spanish, also lives there. Because of Equatorial Guinea's recent colonial history, the country's official language is Spanish. Fang and Pichinglis (Pidgin English) are the lingua franca. Minority languages include Benga, Bubi, Crioulo, Krio, Ngumba, Ngumbi, and Yasa. Three-fourths of the population practice Roman Catholicism, sometimes mingling it with pre-Christian traditions. About 20% of the population is animist. The population of Equatorial Guinea has been estimated at 466,000.

The vast majority of Equatoguineans still practice subsistence agriculture, raising bananas, manioc, yams, cassava, oil palm nuts, and livestock. Agriculture, forestry, and fisheries account for roughly one-half of GDP with coffee, timber, and cocoa being the primary export commodities. Export crop production has dropped dramatically since independence, however. Once known as the "Switzerland of Africa", cocoa production on Bioko has declined since the late 1960s. The country's precarious financial situation is expected to improve soon, as major new offshore oil deposits are phased into production. The country may also have untapped mineral resources, including alluvial gold, iron ore, manganese, titanium, and uranium. The unit of currency is the CFA *franc*. Per capita GDP has been estimated at US$1,500.

## POLITICAL BACKGROUND

Like its West African neighbors, Equatorial Guinea experienced a long history of colonial rule under a series of European powers. Portugal claimed Fernando Po in 1494, hoping to establish a trade base there. The settlers who came to the island found the growing of sugar cane more lucrative, however, and they developed a thriving plantation economy instead. By the late 16th century, the slave population had outgrown the capacity of the plantations, and the settlers started moving their operations to Brazil. Fernando Po became a holding port for slaves who were to be shipped to the New World. In 1781, the British Navy occupied the island, using it as a base for its antislavery patrol and as a settlement for liberated slaves. These slaves became known as "Fernandinos"; their descendants still populate the island today.

Spain acquired the rights to Fernando Po and Annobon Island in 1844 and later added Rio Muni, forming the colony of Spanish Guinea, as the territories were collectively known. Under Spanish rule, Fernando Po was once again developed as a plantation economy, this time worked by a contract labor force of Nigerian migrants. Cocoa and coffee exports made the Bubi and Fernandinos living on the islands relatively prosperous, but Rio Muni was neglected, and the Fang tribe was left to eke out a survival through subsistence farming and fishing.

When Spain finally granted Equatorial Guinea its independence on 12 October 1968, the country was heavily stratified along ethnic and regional lines. Thus in the first constitutional election, the Fang, determined to assert their numerical dominance, succeeded in electing Macías Nguema, a civil servant, as the country's first president. Nguema quickly surrounded himself with Fang supporters. Within a year, perceiving that their interests were dangerously threatened, the minority groups staged a coup. It failed, and Nguema's response was swift, far-reaching, and deadly. Unsure of himself and trusting no one, Nguema began what was to become a brutal reign of terror. The political murders, arrests, torture, beatings, atrocities, and corruption perpetrated by his regime eventually reached throughout the country, devastating even his own ethnic group. In a country gripped by fear and distrust, Nguema held power until 1979 when he was overthrown in a violent coup by his nephew, then-Lt. Colonel Teodoro Obiang Nguema Mbasogo. Macías Nguema fled but was soon arrested, tried, and convicted of genocide, murder, treason, violation of human rights, and misappropriation of

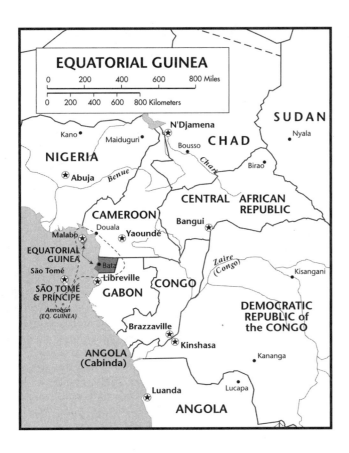

public funds. Nguema was executed by firing squad, along with six of his associates.

## PERSONAL BACKGROUND

Teodoro Obiang Nguema Mbasogo was born on 5 June 1942 in Acoa-Kam in the east-central Mongomo district of Rio Muni. He attended secondary school at Bata, completing his studies at evening school. In 1963 Obiang traveled to Spain to attend the Saragossa Military Academy. He graduated in 1965 with the rank of junior lieutenant and returned home to begin his military career. Obiang is married to Constancia de Obiang Nguema. They have several children.

## RISE TO POWER

Obiang's first assignment was as a territorial guard. He was soon promoted to the rank of lieutenant. As the nephew of then-president Macías Nguema, Obiang was given several important positions and promotions. He served as the military governor of Fernando Po and as director of the Playa Negra prison. In 1975 he was promoted to lieutenant colonel and became Nguema's aide-de-camp, a position he held until ousting his uncle from power.

In the spring of 1979, Macías Nguema had Obiang's brother executed. Obiang reportedly began planning his uncle's overthrow at this time. He evacuated his family and on 3 August 1979 set into motion the coup d'état that would place him in power.

## LEADERSHIP

Obiang Nguema's government is widely viewed as a continuation of the clan politics practiced by his predecessor, albeit in a less vicious form. It is generally believed that Obiang

personally carried out many of the repressive and expulsionary orders issued by Macías Nguema. Thus support for the Obiang regime has never extended far beyond its immediate beneficiaries.

For the first 10 years, Obiang ruled as chairman of the Supreme Military Council. Political activity was banned, but opposition groups were organized abroad and at home. Under pressure from international donors to effect political and economic reforms, Obiang's government has ostensibly been preparing for the transition to a multiparty democracy since 1982, but in fact, there have been no free elections in Equatorial Guinea since independence. The 1982 constitution provided for a return to civilian rule after a seven-year transition. Parliamentary elections were organized for August 1983 but opposition parties were not permitted to participate, and all 41 candidates seated were nominated by Obiang. In 1987 Obiang announced the formation of the government *Partido Democratico de Guinea Ecuatorial* (Democratic Party for Equatorial Guinea—PDGE), of which he was the head. At the end of the transition period presidential elections were held. Brig. Gen. (Ret.) Obiang Nguema ran uncontested and on 25 June 1989 won a new seven-year term.

Elections to the 80-seat House of People's Representatives held in 1993 were boycotted by the opposition as fraudulent and condemned by foreign observers. Municipal elections held on 17 September 1995 were preceded by widespread government use of arbitrary arrest, illegal detention, and beatings of opposition organizers and candidates. Opposition candidates stayed in the race, however, and on polling day, international observers declared that reports from polling stations indicated that the *Plataforma de la Oposicion Conjunta* (Joint Opposition Platform—POC) had won with 60% of the vote, and the ruling PDGE had received 25%. The government refused to release these results. Ten days later it announced that the PDGE had won a two to one majority of seats.

Opposition groups redoubled their efforts to campaign for the presidential election scheduled for June 1996. In a boldly unconstitutional move, Obiang announced in January 1996 that he was moving the date of the election up to 25 February. The government next decided to abandon the voter's poll that had been drawn up in 1995 with foreign donor participation. Finally, election procedures were changed to eliminate the possibility of a run-off. Eventually all but one opposition candidate, Secundino Oyono of the Social Democratic and Popular Convergence Party, withdrew from the race, charging fraud and intimidation. International observers agreed. The voting itself, which was witnessed by international observers, was fraught with irregularities. When the official results were announced, Obiang had been awarded 97.9% of the vote, and the four opposition candidates who had withdrawn shared the remaining 2.1%.

## DOMESTIC POLICY

This country of less than half a million people has an army, a navy, an air force, a rapid intervention force, and a national police force, all of which Obiang commands as chief of state. The constitution of 1991 guarantees citizens fundamental liberties, but in practice, Obiang rules Equatorial Guinea with an iron fist, and Equatoguineans have almost no political rights.

In the months preceding the 1995 municipal elections, the government released numerous political prisoners, including prominent opposition leader Severo Moto Nsa. The releases raised hopes among the opposition and international community for the possibility of genuine political reform. The optimism was short-lived. In mid-January 1996 political activist Genoveve Nchama was arrested after criticizing the government on a Spanish radio program. She was held in detention for several weeks and beaten. On 16 February 1996, several members of the POC were arrested, detained in custody for up to two days, and severely beaten. Roman Catholic priests were also reportedly arrested and tortured for opposing the regime.

In April, the 53-member UN Human Rights Commission adopted unanimously a resolution condemning Obiang's government for "grave and persistent" violations of human rights. Obiang met with opposition leaders on 18 March to co-opt them into participating in the new government but clearly failed to do so. Of the 40 members of government, only five positions went to junior members from minor parties that ultimately supported the president's reelection. The three key ministerial portfolios—interior and local government, foreign affairs and international cooperation, and mines and hydrocarbons—went to long-time supporters from Obiang's home town.

The prospects of newfound wealth from the discovery of oil-rich deposits near the maritime border with Nigeria virtually ensured that Obiang would employ all possible means to stay in power. By 1999, oil had become the country's major export, accounting for approximately 70% of the gross national product (GNP).

In March 1999, the second multiparty legislative elections in the country's history featured nearly 700 candidates representing 13 political parties. Obiang's party, PDGE, won 75 of the 80 seats. Members of the opposition parties argued that the elections were unfair, but international observers reported that the elections could stand.

When the Parliament opened in April, the five opposition candidates were away on what was reported to be official business in Spain. The next month, Obiang rejected a plan by the parliament of Spain to send a delegation to investigate alleged irregularities in the March legislative elections, insisting that the voting had been free and fair.

## FOREIGN POLICY

Soon after taking power, Obiang sought to reestablish relations with Spain, which had deteriorated during his predecessor's regime. As a measure of his success, Spain signed permanent agreements to provide economic and technical assistance. Obiang also moved to develop relations with France. In 1985 Equatorial Guinea joined the African Financial Community, switching currencies to the fully convertible CFA *franc*. Soon afterward he instituted a policy of compulsory study of the French language in the schools in an effort to make the country bilingual in Spanish and French. In the late 1980s, however, relations with the international community began to sour. Donors began linking development assistance to political and economic reform, a policy that Obiang viewed as a direct assault on his country's sovereignty. During both the 1993 and 1999 parliamentary elections, diplomatic relations with the West were severely strained or severed because of questions from outside the country about the progress of political reform.

As of 2000, Equatorial Guinea was involved in a number of territorial disputes with its neighbors, including Nigeria, Cameroon, and Gabon, because of offshore oil fields.

## ADDRESS

Oficina del Presidente
Malabo
República de Guinea Ecuatorial

## REFERENCES

Amnesty International News Service postings. 7 August 1995, 20 February 1996.

Derksen, Wilfried P.C.G. "Parliamentary Elections in Equatorial Guinea." *Parliamentary Elections Around the World*. 1995, 1999.

Economist Intelligence Unit. *Country Reports*, 1st quarter 1995–2nd quarter 1999.

"Economy: Turning the Corner." *Institutional Investor International Edition*, August 1999.

Fage, J. D. *A History of West Africa*. New York: Cambridge University Press, 1969.

Fouad, Ashraf. "Equatorial Guinea—on the Brink of an Oil Boom." *Reuters*, 25 February 1996.

Jackson, Robert H. and Carl G. Rosberg. *Personal Rule in Black Africa*. Berkeley: University of California Press, 1982.

Liniger-Goumaz, Max. *Historical Dictionary of Equatorial Guinea*. Metuchen, NJ: Scarecrow Press, 1988.

*MBendi Information Services*. "Equatorial Guinea: Country Profile." 1996.

Shaxson, Nicholas. "Equatorial Guinea President Says Poll Will Go On." *Reuters*, 23 February 1996.

———. "Polls Close in Chaotic Equatorial Guinea Election." *Reuters*, 25 February 1996.

US Department of State. "Equatorial Guinea Human Rights Practices, 1995." March 1996.

Young, Eric. "Equatorial Guinea." In *Africana: The Encyclopedia of the African and African American Experience*. Kwame Anthony Appiah and Henry Louis Gates, Jr., et al. New York: Basic Books, 1999.

**Profile researched and written by N. Lynn Graybeal, a researcher and consultant in political affairs (9/96; updated 3/2000).**

# ERITREA

## Isaias Afwerki
## President
*(pronounced "uh-ZAY-us aff-WER-kee")*

*"Men make history, and we have made an independent Eritrea."*

The State of Eritrea, a former province of Ethiopia, voted its own independence from that country in April 1993 in a United Nations-sponsored election. That election ended 30 years of civil war in the new nation, which borders on the Red Sea in the east, the Sudan in the west and north, and Ethiopia and the Red Sea in the south. Eritrea covers an area of 125,000 sq km (48,000 sq mi) and has a population of 3,985,000. Eritrea's land varies dramatically between highlands above 2,134 m (7,000 ft) and its surrounding lowlands which descend to sea level on the Red Sea coast in the east and the arid Sudan border in the west and north. Between the capital city, Asmara, and the Red Sea port at Massawa, the road descends 2,286 m (7,500 ft) in only 80 km (50 mi). Eritrea's climate, especially its rainfall, is erratic. Because Eritrea lies in the easternmost part of the African sahil, it frequently has been vulnerable to drought. Its major famines in the 1970s and 1980s have resulted from a combination of drought and its civil war with Ethiopia. Eritrea has few natural resources, though deposits of salt in its eastern lowlands have long been an important product for both animal and human consumption in the region. Its river valleys flowing west to the Nile basin are potential resources for irrigation agriculture.

Eritrea is a rich blend of cultures, religions, and languages. About half of its population are Ethiopian Orthodox Christians, and about half are Muslim. The dominant language is Tigrinya, a Semitic language. Other important languages include Afar, Bilen, Tigre, and Arabic. Most highlanders are farmers, while many lowlanders continue to be nomadic herders of camels and goats. Residents of towns generally are merchants or civil servants.

Much of Eritrea's economy has been shattered by the effects of the civil war and major famines caused by drought. Roads, factories, and water and irrigation systems have been damaged or destroyed. Per capita GNP of Eritrea is US$660, making it one of the poorest countries in Africa. The unit of currency is the *birr*.

## POLITICAL BACKGROUND

Eritrea's history derives from its position on the northern limits of the Ethiopian highlands. It formed part of the Axumite empire established in the 1st century AD. Over the course of its history, however, its strategic geographic location along the Red Sea coast has made it the object of numerous invasions by external powers who sought to control trade along the coast and in the interior. Along with the Ethiopian highlands, much of Eritrea converted to Christianity in the 4th century AD, though Islam spread in the lowlands beginning in the 7th century. Conflicts over religion and territory between Christian highlanders and Muslim lowlanders have characterized Eritrea's internal history. That history has also seen cooperation between the groups in trade and responses to outside invaders. The major external invaders have been the Ottoman Turks (16th century), Egypt (19th century), and Italy (late 19th century).

Italy controlled Eritrea as a formal colony from 1890 until 1941. During that period, Italy invested in building an industrial and transportation infrastructure to serve as a base for expansion of its empire to Ethiopia. Italians established Asmara as their capital and built large irrigation schemes, recruited Eritrean men into a colonial army, and attempted to shift Eritrean trade to Italy's benefit. In 1935, Italian dictator Benito Mussolini used Eritrea as a base for his invasion of Ethiopia. In 1936, Eritrea became a province of Italian East Africa which consisted of Eritrea, Ethiopia, and Italian Somaliland. Italian rule ended in 1941 with the defeat of Italian forces by the combined efforts of Allied troops and Ethiopian resistance fighters.

Between 1941 and 1952, Britain controlled Eritrea as a UN mandate. In 1952, the UN agreed to federate Eritrea to the Empire of Ethiopia, then ruled by Emperor Haile Sellassie. Eritrea retained its own parliament and control over its economy and local government. In 1962, the Ethiopian government forcibly annexed Eritrea as its fourteenth province. In that year a small resistance movement calling itself the Eritrean Liberation Front (ELF) started fighting in the western lowlands to reclaim Eritrea's independence. This movement gathered momentum after the 1974 Ethiopian revolution, led by a new group, the Eritrean Peoples' Liberation Front (EPLF). This group was dominated by highlanders and led by Isaias Afwerki.

The Eritrean war intensified as both sides sought a military solution, driving hundreds of thousands of refugees into the Sudan and also to Europe and North America. The EPLF organized its refugee community overseas to lend political support to its efforts inside Eritrea. In May 1991, the Ethiopian government under Mengistu Haile Mariam collapsed and withdrew its army from Asmara. The new government in Ethiopia declared itself amenable to an independent Eritrea and agreed to cooperate with the Eritrean government over access to the port of Assab. The EPLF entered Asmara and set up a provisional government in anticipation of the April 1993 elections. In those elections 99.8% of the voting public approved the referendum for independence and the formation of a new government under Isaias Afwerki. Eritrea officially became a nation on 24 May 1993, and Iasaias Afwerki became its first, and as of early 2000, only president.

The National Assembly has set the following goals: the drafting of a democratic constitution to guarantee the basic rights of all citizens and the establishment of an elected government.

## PERSONAL BACKGROUND

Afwerki was born on 2 February 1946 in Asmara, now the capital of Eritrea. He graduated from Prince Mekonnen Secondary School in Asmara, then attended the University of Addis Ababa in Ethiopia. In 1966, Afwerki was a second-year engineering student when he interrupted his university studies to join the Eritrean Liberation Front (ELF) as a combatant.

Despite his powerful role and his long leadership of the EPLF, Afwerki has kept a low profile in public life. Unlike many heads of state in Africa who have cultivated a cult of personality in their style of rule, few details are known about his background, and he is rarely photographed. He often attends official functions wearing jeans and sandals. His trademark is his simplicity. His struggle to build an unshakable unified Eritrean nationalism has gained him popularity among his people.

## RISE TO POWER

After leaving university in 1966, Afwerki served as Deputy Division Commander in the ELF (1967–70). In 1970, he and his group founded the Eritrean Popular Liberation Front (EPLF), which later became the dominant power in the history of the country. Until 1977, he held various leadership positions and in 1987, the Front in its Second Congress elected him as the organization's Secretary General.

During the civil war, Afwerki chose not to base himself and his leadership in Europe or North America. Instead, he remained within Eritrea (often at the stronghold of Naqfa) organizing guerilla warfare against the Ethiopian government troops. Overseas, his supporters waged an extremely effective campaign of political persuasion, winning international support, if not official recognition.

The EPLF has played a critical role throughout Eritrea's independence struggle. In 1988, the EPLF was able to force the Ethiopian army to withdraw its forces from Keren, Eritrea's second largest city, and several western lowlands. Under his leadership the EPLF won the war with Ethiopia in May 1991, and Eritrea gained independence. The government that took power in Ethiopia in May 1991 declared itself amenable to an independent Eritrea and agreed to cooperate with the Provisional Government of Eritrea (PGE) over access to the port of Assab.

## LEADERSHIP

In April 1993, the vote for Eritrean independence also included the election of Afwerki to the position of president and chairman of the National Assembly. Afwerki thus enjoys control over both the legislative and executive branches of Eritrea's government. He is the head of government and commander in chief of the army. Afwerki has the authority to nominate individuals to head various ministries, authorities,

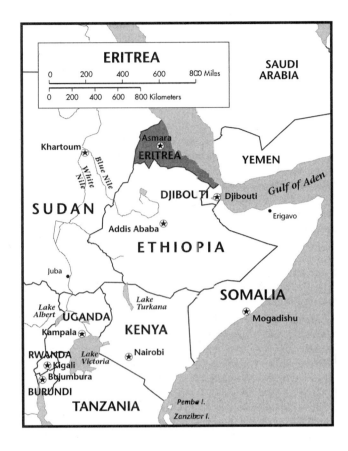

commissions, and offices—pending approval of the legislative body.

Afwerki states that he is dedicated to bringing democracy to Eritrea. Yet he has declared that democracy should be subservient to stability. Elections were promised for 1998 but did not take place. The border war with Ethiopia, ongoing as of early 2000, seemed to be the main obstacle to elections, although some complain about the lack of political openness in Eritrea. Although the opposition parties, most of which are remnants of the ELF, call Afwerki's government dictatorial, the great majority of the population does not seem to have complaints about his government. Afwerki, a Christian, has included Muslims in his cabinet. He has also declared his opposition to political parties based on religious or ethnic lines.

## DOMESTIC POLICY

Eritrea's leadership not only faces the problems of reconstructing a national economy but of building a nation. In 1996, a draft constitution, creating a free, multiparty was presented and ratified in a May 1997 referendum. Elections scheduled for May 1998 were not held due to outbreak of conflict with Ethiopia along the 938-km (620-mile) border).

Though it has major agricultural products of sorghum, cotton, left (a grain grown only in the Ethiopian highlands), and citrus fruits, Eritrea has historically been an importer of food from its neighbors. In the 21st century, rebuilding its industrial base and searching for foreign capital will be major focuses of government domestic policy.

The effects of war, however, have damaged Eritrea's ability to serve as the region's exporter and importer in the near future. Together with the threat of periodic droughts to agriculture, Eritrea's economy can expect to be dependent on international aid for some years to come. The economic policy of Eritrea is contained within an Emergency and Recovery Action Program that concentrates its efforts on transportation, agriculture, and industry—three areas which had historically been the basis for Eritrea's economy. Despite its socialist ideology during the war for independence, the government has pledged to pursue a mixed economy that encourages foreign investment and joint ventures.

## FOREIGN POLICY

Eritrea's economic and political future will reflect long-term trends of the past. Eritrea's history and its economic role in modern times have been a product of its strategic location astride routes of trade and communication leading from the Nile Valley to the Red Sea and the Arabian peninsula and from central Ethiopia to the port of Massawa. These routes have drawn external powers to the area, less for its resources than its geographical position. Historically, Eritrea has maintained an economy based partially on agriculture and partially on the export and import of goods. Its strategic position between the Red Sea, the Nile Valley, and central Ethiopia has allowed its merchant population to profit from the exchange of goods with those areas. As Ethiopia's northern neighbor, Eritrea will continue to re-export goods from its own ports to Ethiopia and Sudan.

The destruction and dislocation of three decades of war have meant that Eritrea's foreign policy in the early years of the 21st century will continue to focus primarily on securing foreign development assistance and addressing the difficult problems of repatriating 750,000 refugees. About 500,000 are in Sudan and the rest are in the Middle East, Persian Gulf, Europe, and North America. Of these refugees, the government has given priority to repatriating those in Sudan. Many refugees, including those in North America and Europe, have prospered in business, academia, and politics and now constitute an important body of wealth and opinion. Expatriate Eritreans form a large part of the private funds invested in the country's recovery and are a source of support for gaining bilateral aid from foreign governments and international agencies such as the World Bank.

## ADDRESS

Office of the President
Asmara, Eritrea

## REFERENCES

*Christian Science Monitor,* 21 June 1993, 30 April 1993.

*The Economist,* 20 March 1993.

Ellingson, Lloyd. "The Emergence of Political Parties in Eritrea, 1941–1950." *Journal of African History.*

Embassy of Eritrea. *Research and Information Papers,* September 1993.

Erlich, Haggai. *The Struggle over Eritrea, 1962–78: war and revolution in the Horn of Africa.* Stanford, CA: Hoover Institution Press, 1983.

———. *Ras Alula and the Scramble for Africa: A Political Biography: Ethiopia and Eritrea 1875–1897.* Lawrenceville, NJ: Red Sea Press, 1996.

Hammer, Joshua. "Back from the Ruins: Can This Be an African Nation that Works?" *Newsweek,* 26 February 1996, p. 40.

Killion, Tom. *Historical Dictionary of Eritrea.* Lanham, MD: Scarecrow Press, 1998.

*New York Times,* 24 April 1993.

Smyth, Frank. "So Much for Africa's 'New Leaders.'" *The New Republic,* 1 March 1999, p. 14.

Street, Jennie. "Spirit of Independence (Special Report: Eritrea—Fierce Will to Succeed)." *African Business,* April 1998, p. 16+.

Yohannes, Okbazghi. *Eritrea: A Pawn in World Politics.* Gainesville: University of Florida Press, 1991.

**Profile researched and written by James C. McCann, Boston University (1993; revised by Markos Ezra, Ph.D., Brown University 4/2000).**

# ESTONIA

Lennart Meri
President
*(pronounced "LEHN-art MEH-ree")*

*"Estonia's strength is our common sense, our aptitude for learning and our will to act."*

The Republic of Estonia lies on the shores of the Baltic Sea and the Gulfs of Riga and Finland, and borders Latvia and Russia. Total land area claimed by Estonia is 47,549 sq km (18,359 sq mi); area actually controlled by Estonia is 45,100 sq km (17,413 sq mi). (The disputed area was annexed by Russia in 1945.) Estonia's population has been estimated at 1.4 million. Estonians account for 61.5% of the republic's population, while Russians make up 30.3%. Ukrainians, Belarusians, and Finns account for most of the remainder. The official language is Estonian, which is a member of the Finno-Ugric family of languages, more similar to Finnish and Hungarian than Russian or English. No reliable recent figures regarding religious affiliation are available, but Estonians tend to be Lutherans while Russians tend to be Russian Orthodox.

The official currently is the *kroon*. Estonia's GDP has been estimated at US$7.8 billion. Estonia produces excavators, electrical engines, cotton cloth, and furniture. It is a net exporter of agricultural products. Leading exports are light industrial goods, foodstuffs, machinery, and petrochemicals. Top imports include machinery, light industrial goods, chemicals, and food. Estonia is the world's second-largest producer of shale oil.

## POLITICAL BACKGROUND

After centuries of foreign domination by Danes, Germans, Swedes, Poles, and Russians, Estonian leaders declared independence from the Russian empire on 24 February 1918. An unstable but democratic parliamentary system operated from 1919 until 1934 when acting President Konstantin Päts seized power and dissolved parliament. In 1940 the Soviet Union annexed Estonia, making it the Estonian Soviet Socialist Republic (Estonian SSR). The German army invaded Estonia in 1941, ruling it until 1945. It is estimated that 90,000 people, or 8% of the prewar population of Estonia, died in the course of the war. During Stalin's reign, 80,000 people were arrested or deported and 15,000 died in a guerrilla war of resistance.

Under Communism, Estonian culture and other forms of national expression were repressed, and large numbers of Russians settled in Estonia. Russified Estonians (some of whom spoke no Estonian), Russians, and others were brought in to rule Estonia. In the post-Stalin era, dissidents calling for observation of human rights or protesting the repression of the Estonian nation were harassed, arrested, exiled, and even killed.

Significant changes came after Mikhail Gorbachev became leader of the USSR. In fall 1987 the policies of *glasnost* (openness) and *perestroika* (restructuring) provided the opportunity to discuss openly various economic, environmental, and historical issues in Estonia for the first time. The Popular Front, an organization dedicated to bringing about progressive changes and unaffiliated with the Communist Party, was established in April 1988. Soon thereafter the government legalized the flag of independent Estonia and declared Estonian the official language of the republic. In November the Estonian parliament, the Supreme Soviet, interpreted the meaning of "sovereignty" in the republic's constitution in the broadest possible terms, provoking an angry attack from Gorbachev.

A constitutional amendment adopted in February 1990 stripped the Communist Party of its leading role in Estonian society. In March 1990 the Estonian Communist Party split into two factions, one supporting Moscow, the other declaring itself independent from Moscow. Also in March, 16 parties ran candidates for the 105 seats in the Estonian parliament. Estonian nationalists won an overwhelming majority. Arnold Rüütel was elected president by the new parliament.

When the coup d'etat against Mikhail Gorbachev began in Moscow in August 1991, the Estonian government immediately allied with Russian president, Boris Yeltsin. On 20 August, Estonia declared itself independent of the USSR; the following day the Russian Federation recognized Estonia as an independent state. The Communist Party of the Soviet Union and other organizations supporting the coup were outlawed. In September the Soviet Union recognized Estonian independence. The Estonians began to dismantle the Soviet secret police (KGB). The Soviet government agreed to withdraw all its troops from Estonian soil by the end of 1994.

In 1992, a constitutional assembly introduced amendments to the 1938 constitution. After the draft constitution was approved by popular referendum, it came into effect 3 July 1992. Elections for the new parliament and president were held on 20 September 1992.

On 5 March 1995, Estonia held its second parliamentary elections since achieving independence from the Soviet Union. The center-left Coalition Party/Rural Union alliance won an impressive victory, taking 41 seats in the 101-seat parliament.

## ESTONIA

The market-reform-oriented Estonian Reform Party-Liberals coalition won 19 seats. The center-left Estonian Center Party finished third with 16 seats. The rightist Pro Patria/Estonian National Independence Party group (now known as the Fatherland Union), fell to only eight seats. A coalition representing the Russian-speaking population, Our Home Is Estonia, won six seats. The Moderates won six seats, and the Rightists won five. On 5 April 1995, the parliament elected Coalition Party leader Tiit Vahi as prime minister of Estonia. He formed a government with the Center Party. After a wiretapping scandal, the Center Party was forced out in October 1995 and was replaced by the Reform Party. In November 1996 this coalition collapsed in turn, and the Coalition Party appeared headed back into coalition with the Center Party.

## PERSONAL BACKGROUND

Lennart Meri was born on 29 March 1929 in Tallinn. His father, Georg, served in the Estonian diplomatic service, rising to the post of minister to Germany from 1935 to 1938. His family was deported to Central Russia by the Soviet government in 1941. Lennart Meri returned to Tallinn in 1946. He graduated cum laude from Tartu University in 1953, majoring in history. Upon graduation from college, Meri became the director of the literature department of the Vanemuine Theatre in Tartu. He worked there until 1955 and also taught history at the Tartu Art School. From 1955 to 1961 he worked as an editor for Estonian Radio. During 1963–71 and 1976–78 he was an editor at the Tallinnfilm studio. Meri is the author of numerous award-winning

books, many of which have been translated into English, French, German, and Russian, and he has directed several films on the ethnic history of the Finno-Ugric peoples. He speaks English, Russian, German, French, and Finnish fluently, along with Estonian. He is married and has two adult sons from a previous marriage and a young daughter from his current marriage.

## RISE TO POWER

Meri became involved in politics in the Gorbachev era. During 1985–87 he was a senior official at the Estonian Writers' Union in charge of foreign relations. In 1988 Meri became active in some of the "informal groups" that formed under glasnost. He played a key role in the 1988 plenary session of the Estonian artistic unions, an event that shaped the early forces for change in Estonia. He became a prominent leader of the Popular Front of Estonia and the Estonian Heritage Society, both of which sought to reestablish Estonia's political independence. During 1989–90 he headed the non-governmental Estonian Institute.

In March 1990 Meri was elected to the Council of Estonia, the governing body of the Congress of Estonia. In April 1990 Meri was confirmed as Estonia's minister of foreign relations by the newly elected Supreme Council. In 1992 he was named ambassador to Finland, Estonia's most important ally.

In the 20 September 1992 national election, Arnold Rüütel received 43% of the votes cast for president; Meri received 29%; and US professor Rein Taagepera received 23%. Because no candidate received an outright majority, the election was thrown into the Riigikogu, the new parliament. Meri's party, Isamaa (Pro Patria), captured 29 of the 101 seats. Isamaa formed a right-wing coalition with the Moodukad (Moderates) and the Estonian National Independence Party (ERSP), totaling 51 seats and achieving control of the government. On 5 October 1992, the parliamentary deputies elected Meri as president of Estonia, with 59 votes to 31 for Arnold Rüütel. Meri ran for reelection as president of Estonia in August 1996. According to Estonia's constitution, the president is elected by a two-thirds majority in the Estonian parliament. If no candidate receives the required number of votes after three rounds of voting, an electoral college of members of parliament and local legislatures selects the president by a simple majority. On 26 and 27 August, Meri handily outscored his main opponent, Arnold Rüütel, in the three rounds of parliamentary voting but did not win a two-thirds majority. In the vote of the electoral college on 20 September Meri won a majority, beating Rüütel by a vote of 196 to 126 (with 44 abstentions and six invalid ballots) in the 374-member electoral college.

## LEADERSHIP

Meri was elected in 1992 in part because, unlike most post-Soviet leaders of his generation, he was never a member of the Communist party. Meri's more difficult path to reelection in 1996 was due in part to the defeat of the right-of-center coalition in the 1995 parliamentary elections. However, Meri lost support even among some right-of-center deputies who believed he overstepped his constitutional powers when he signed a troop withdrawal treaty with Russia in July 1996, allowing many Russian military retirees to stay in Estonia.

Meri was also dogged by unproven allegations that he had collaborated with the KGB in the Soviet period.

## DOMESTIC POLICY

Since independence Estonia has made dramatic economic progress by implementing a tough austerity program of balanced budgets, tight monetary policy, and the establishment of a strong currency. Inflation for 1995 was 29%, a sharp improvement over 1,069% in 1992. Estonia's currency, the *kroon*, is officially pegged at one-eighth of a German mark and must fluctuate within 3% of the German mark exchange rate established by the Bank of Estonia. Dependence on the former Soviet market has been reduced while trade with the West and foreign investments, especially from Finland and Scandinavia, have grown substantially. Privatization has also moved forward in Estonia. In early 1996 the head of Estonia's privatization agency declared that Estonia has "more or less finished" privatization, with only about 20 troubled large enterprises in state hands.

Estonia held its third general election in March 1999. There was a close race of 2,000 candidates for 101 seats in the Riigikogu, the Estonian parliament. The 55% voter turnout was lower than expected and down from the 70% turnout in the general election in 1995. Former Prime Minister Edgar Savisaar's Center Party won the largest number of votes and gained 28 seats, but a coalition of Reform, Fatherland, and Moderate parties won a narrow majority of 53 seats. The election represents a political shift to the center and right and has put into place a government dedicated to continued economic reform in spite of current setbacks.

Like Estonian society as a whole, Estonian politics are complicated by the question of how to integrate ethnic Russians (who comprise 20% of the electorate) into Estonian national life. One-third of Estonia's 1.4 million inhabitants are Russian-speakers, and some areas are predominantly Russian, such as the depressed industrial border town of Narva, which is 95% Russian. Not unexpectedly, relations between Estonians and ethnic Russians are often strained. The Estonian government has imposed strict citizenship examinations that require knowledge of the Estonian language, and Russians find these an obstacle to obtaining full Estonian citizenship. In January, Estonia let go 300 Russian-speaking policeman who failed the examination. Still, most ethnic Russians voted for Estonian rather than Russian parties in March 1999.

## FOREIGN POLICY

Estonia's foreign policy focuses on integration of the Baltic States into European and international institutions in order to protect itself against possible reemergence of a hostile and aggressive Russia. Estonia applied for European Union (EU) membership in 1995. The EU opened talks with Estonia on possible membership in March 1998 and announced in October 1999 that Estonia was close to meeting the economic requirements for membership in the EU and was one of twelve nations being considered for membership, which might be granted Estonia as early as 2003. The EU announced in March 1999 the committal of $60 billion over a seven-year period for building up the economies and infra-structures of prospective member countries in Central and Eastern Europe, Estonia among them; Germany, however, refuses to fund further spending in this direction.

Considering its geographical situation, Estonia has naturally developed strong economic ties with the Scandinavian countries. Scandinavian banks have sought aggressively to expand into the Baltics, where growing economies and underdeveloped markets make for prime investment territory. SwedBank gained a majority interest in Hansabank, the largest bank in Estonia and a preeminent Baltic financial institution. The banking industry is relatively nascent in Estonia due to its Soviet past, and as of 1999 total bank deposits in Estonia comprise only some 30% of its GDP. The country now has five commercial banks as the result of closures and mergers, including foreign mergers.

Relations between Estonia and its Scandinavian neighbors are not without tensions, however. Strong diplomatic, military, and economic ties between Finland and Estonia have been tested by wage disparities between the countries. Finnish dock workers have refused to unload ships of the Estonian Shipping Company (partly Norwegian-owned) because the Estonian ships have been transporting cargo between Denmark and Finland much more cheaply than could a Finnish ship due to the lower wages paid Estonian shipworkers. In 1999, Finnish sailors earned $2,400 a month whereas Estonian sailors were paid $600 a month, a high salary in Estonia. Estonia has presented its case to the EU in Brussels for adjudication, a move that will probably prove futile since the shipping trade falls outside the purview of European competition laws.

Russian-Estonian relations have been strained since Estonia's independence. The 31 August 1994 withdrawal of Russian troops resolved one key issue, but other issues remain, including the Russian-speaking minorities in the Baltic states, Estonia's desire to join NATO, and a border demarcation dispute. Estonia struggles to assert its new-found identity against the influence of its huge neighbor to the east. The Estonian town of Narva cut off water and sewage treatment it had provided to the Russian town of Ivangorod across the border after the latter failed to pay more than $1 million for services received. A 78-year-old man, a former member of the Soviet secret police, was convicted and given an eight-year suspended sentence for having ordered the deportation of over 20 families during the Stalinist era. For their part, Russian authorities expelled an Estonian man after he confessed to gathering secret information about the Russian air force for the intelligence wing of a militant group in Estonia. Yet the government in Estonia remains stable; according to Transparency International, a non-governmental group that monitors governmental corruption, Estonia is among the former Communist bloc nations least affected by government corruption.

## ADDRESS

Office of the President
Lossi plats 1A
Tallinn 200100
Estonia

## REFERENCES

Estonia. Office of the President. [Online] Available http:// www.president.ee (Accessed May 2000).

"Estonia's Latest Challenge." *The Economist,* 13 March 1999, vol. 350, no. 8110, p. 60.

Estonian Foreign Minister Information Office. [Online] Available http://www.vm.ee (Accessed October 1996).

Girnius, Saulius. "Meri Reelected Estonia's President." Open Media Research Institute Analytical Brief, 23 September 1996, OMRI Internet. [Online] Available http:// www.omri.cz. (Accessed December 1996).

Misiunas, Romuald, and Rein Taagepera. *The Baltic States: Years of Independence.* 1983.

*PlanEcon Review and Outlook for the Former Soviet Republics.* August 1996, pp. 57–67.

Woehrel, Steven. "The Baltic States: U.S. Policy Concerns." Congressional Research Service Report 96-584, 22 October 1996.

**Profile researched and written by Steven Woehrel, Specialist in European Affairs (12/96; updated 5/2000).**

# ETHIOPIA

## Meles Zenawi
## Prime Minister

*(pronounced "MELL-ez zeh-NAH-wee")*

*"We are now able to make the transition to a fully democratic government which will satisfy the
wishes of our peoples and their centuries-old longing for such a system."*

The Federal Democratic Republic of Ethiopia is situated in northeastern Africa. To the north lies Eritrea and the Red Sea; to the east, Djibouti and Somalia; to the south, Kenya; and to the west, Sudan. Its total area is 1.2 million sq km (42,000 sq mi) and consists of high plateaus, mountains, and dry lowland plains.

The population of Ethiopia has been estimated at 59,700,000. Ethnically, the country is comprised of 45% Oromo, 25% Amhara, 12% Tigre, and 9% Sidama, with the remainder made up of other groups. Religiously, about 40% of the population is Ethiopian Orthodox; about 40% is Muslim; and the remainder practice indigenous beliefs. Amharic is the official language; Tigrinya, Orominga, Arabic, and English are also spoken.

Ethiopia's economy is among the least developed in the world. Its per capita GDP has been estimated at $560. The chief source of livelihood is agriculture. About 90% of Ethiopians are subsistence farmers. Coffee is the country's primary cash crop; other exports include hides and skins, pulses (vegetables and legumes), and live animals. The Ethiopian unit of currency is the *birr.*

## POLITICAL BACKGROUND

Modern Ethiopia dates its political origin to 1896 when Emperor Menilik defeated the Italians at the famous battle of Adewa. Upon the death of Menilik, his cousin, Ras Tafari Markonnen, became the regent of Menilik's daughter. In 1930, Ras Tafari proclaimed himself Emperor Haile Selassie of Ethiopia. In 1974, Haile Selassie was deposed by a coup of leftist soldiers led by Mengistu Haile Mariam.

Under the constitution of 1987, Ethiopia became a socialist country based on Marxist-Leninist principles. The supreme power belonged to the president, Mengistu, who was also commander-in-chief of the armed forces and president of the Council of Ministers. The People's Democratic Republic of Ethiopia, as it was then called, became a one-party state, ruled by the Workers' Party of Ethiopia. Mengistu was responsible for the brutal death of thousands of people. His reign lasted from 1974 to 1991, and it was marked by the massive execution of intellectuals who were perceived to be enemies of the regime. Mengistu was widely regarded as a ruthless killer. According to the *New York Times* of 22 May 1991, "Even by the bloody standards of African power-grabbing during the era of Idi Amin of Uganda and Emperor Bokossa I of the Central African Republic, Colonel Mengistu was considered notorious." The

opposition to Mengistu was led by Eritreans, organized under the banner of the Eritrean People's Liberation Front and the leadership of the Tigray People's Liberation Front (TPLF).

Mengistu was also responsible for the destruction of traditional methods of agriculture and the introduction of Marxist-Leninist ideas of joint ownership of the tools of production and state ownership of all land. The famine which struck much of Africa in 1984 and 1985 created a food crisis in Ethiopia that the Mengistu regime could not resolve. This combination of famine and the loss of military support from the USSR proved too much for Mengistu to survive. In May 1991, when three factions of rebel forces converged on Addis Ababa, Mengistu fled the capital to Zimbabwe. One week later the rebel forces entered the capital and the demise of the Mengistu regime was complete.

In a weeklong conference convened 1–5 July 1991 in Addis Ababa, the new transitional government agreed to draft a constitution within two years. Political representation was distributed in proportion to the population of the nationalities. For example, the Ethiopian People's Revolutionary Democratic Front (EPRDF), a coalition of four parties, received 32 seats, and the Oromo Liberation Front, 12 seats. The rest of the groups received from one to three seats each. The Council of Representatives elected the transitional president, Meles Zenawi, who would appoint the prime minister. The Council of Representatives, with 87 members, exercised legislative functions and oversaw a Council of Ministers. The Council of Representatives was composed of 27 ethnic and political groups. It was decided that Eritrea should be given its independence through a national referendum held in mid-1993. In exchange, the Eritreans promised the EPRDF that Assab, an important port on the Red Sea in the north, which accommodates 70% of the country's trade, would be accessible to Ethiopians. Without Assab, Ethiopia would be landlocked.

In May and June 1995, Ethiopia's first multiparty elections were held across the country, and the members of the new Council of People's Representatives (parliament) were selected. On 22 August 1995, the newly elected parliament was sworn in for a five-year term, bringing to an end the transitional government that followed the overthrow of Mengistu Haile Mariam. During a four-day session, the Council of People's Representatives selected a new president, Negasso Gedda, an Oromo official of the Oromo Democratic Coalition; swore in the prime minister, Meles Zenawi; and adopted the new constitution.

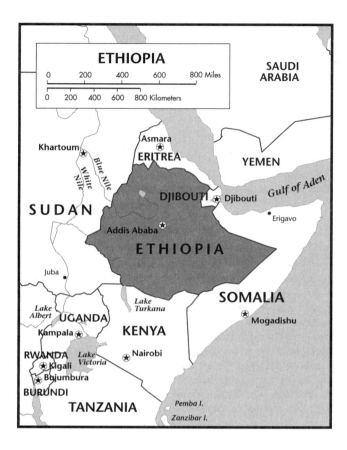

A democratic federal state structure was established, comprising nine states that are delineated on the basis of the settlement patterns, identity, language, and consent of the people concerned. The newly-named Federal Democratic Republic of Ethiopia has two houses: the Council of the People's Representatives (548 seats), which is the highest authority of the federal government; and the Council of Federation (155 seats), which has the power to interpret the constitution. The position of the head of state is purely honorary while executive power is held by the prime minister. It is the prime minister, elected from among the members of the Council of People's Representatives, who names the government ministers, members of the Central High Court, and the auditor general. He also monitors the execution of laws and decisions, presides over the Council of Ministers, controls the armed forces, and sets Ethiopia's foreign policy.

## PERSONAL BACKGROUND

Meles Zenawi was born on 8 May 1955 in the Tigrean town of Adwa. He attended secondary school in Addis Ababa at the General Wingate High School. Meles started his undergraduate studies at the Medical Facility of Addis Ababa University. He discontinued his studies in 1974 while a second-year student to join the TPLF, which spearheaded the popular struggle against the military dictatorship of the Mengistu regime. Meles has been described as an "energetic, wiry, hyperactive," cautious, and able leader. Meles' real name is Legesse Zenawi. His adopted name is taken from a hero who was executed in 1985 by the Mengistu regime. Meles speaks fluent Amharic and English besides his native language, Tigrinya. He is married and has two children. Meles holds an MBA from Open University, UK.

## RISE TO POWER

Meles became head of the TPLF in 1989. The TPLF was the main part of the EPRDF, of which Meles also became chairperson and, therefore, was responsible for the leadership of the Front. With the end of the Mengistu regime in 1991, Meles became president of the transitional government. On 23 August 1995, he was chosen to be prime minister of the newly established Federal Democratic Republic of Ethiopia. The following day, the new Cabinet of Ministers formed by Meles was endorsed by the parliament.

Second multi-party elections for Ethiopia will be held on 14 May 2000. Even with full opposition party participation, if the opposition gets their act together, Zenawi is widely expected to be reelected.

## LEADERSHIP

Meles told Parliament that he selected his cabinet on the basis of ability and dedication to implement the EPRDF's five-year development plan. The 17 members were carefully chosen from different ethnic groups and political affiliations. The new regime prides itself in establishing a government based on the recognition of "ethnicity" as a legitimate form of assigning rights and liberties. This concept was anathema to the previous regimes which were grounded on the uncontested right of the Amharas, who traced their ancestry to the Solomonic dynasty, to rule. As Prime Minister Meles stated, "Ethnic identity cannot simply be wiped away... It has always been part of life in Ethiopia and always will be. The best thing is to see it as a blessing, not a curse. We should not hide, or else it will break out in some hateful manner."

The political vision of the EPDRF began with strong Marxist-Leninist convictions. Over the years, the vision has evolved into a cautious embracing of democratic thought and free market principles. Meles is reputed to have favored multiparty elections with participation of all organizations in Ethiopia.

The US Department of State describes the human rights record of Zenawi's government in 1999 as generally poor but improving. Serious problems, such as extrajudicial killings by security forces, remained. Ethiopia has been criticized for the handling of Eritreans and Ethiopians of Eritrean origin since the outbreak of the border conflict in May 1998. More than 67,000 of them have left Ethiopia for Eritrea, most of them deported, and some 1,200 males are being held in internment camps.

## DOMESTIC POLICY

The newly founded Federal Democratic Republic of Ethiopia has announced a five-year plan of development. In his inaugural address to parliament on 23 August, Meles said, "In order to complete the difficult task given to it by the people of our country, the major task of the government of the Federal Democratic Republic of Ethiopia in the next five years will be to develop an action plan for development, peace, and democracy."

The new action plan emphasizes that peace is a political condition which without democracy and development cannot flourish. Furthermore, it stipulates that democracy must be institutionalized by constitutionally mandated articulations and specifications of citizen's rights and liberties. Toward this goal, the police force will be the backbone of democracy. Similarly, courts will be strengthened; human rights commissions will be established; and political parties will be encouraged to participate in the dissemination of political culture. In July 1995, the Ethiopian Council of Representatives of the transitional government allocated $1.6 billion for 1995–96. A total of $473 million would be secured from foreign aid, with the rest generated from local revenue. Most of this income comes from exporting coffee, pulses, and hides. During a visit to the US in October 1995, Meles told reporters that according to the World Bank, the economy is stabilizing; the marginal tax rates have been cut from 80% to 40%; and a privatization program is under way. In 1997 Meles announced that the country had registered an over-50% record increment in food production over a two-year period, enabling the country to attain national food self-sufficiency. Ethiopia continues to press on with the program of economic reform, but renewed fighting with Eritrea has increased military expenditure and dims future economic prospects. In December 1999 the customs authority introduced a 10% surtax on most imports to raise additional money for the war.

In response to escalating armed rebel insurgency, the Ethiopian military has had to intensify its military operations, especially against the Oromo Liberation Army (OLA—armed wing of the OLF), which have resulted in deaths of over 2,000 rebels and Ethiopian soldiers in battles between May and August 1999. Military forces also intensified operations against the Somali-based Al'Itthad terrorist organization, rebel elements of the Ogaden National Liberation Front, and Tokuchuma (another terrorist group operating in eastern Ethiopia), both in the country and southern Somalia and in Northern Kenya. Ethiopia accuses Eritrea and Somalia of financially supporting and training the OLF and Al'Ittihad.

## FOREIGN POLICY

Under Mengistu, Ethiopia maintained a strong military alliance with the Soviet Union, which resulted in about $12 billion in arms. When this alliance ended in December 1990, a casualty of the end of the Cold War rivalry, military assistance came to a halt. Before and after the flight of Mengistu, the US government played a key role in supporting the EPRDF's effort to enter the capital city of Addis Ababa. Although a US official attended the conference held in Addis Ababa only as an observer, Washington officials appeared to be involved in the pre-conference proceedings. Now that Meles has embraced democracy, the US government expects the foreign policy to be less ideological and more pragmatic. In return, the Ethiopian government will expect substantial economic and humanitarian aid from the US to relieve the food crisis and lead the country toward economic recovery. Ethiopia has since made considerable progress on the economic reform front and is considered a showcase for the World Bank and International Monetary Fund.

Since July 1991, the government of Ethiopia has effectively embraced peace with its neighbors as a beacon of its foreign policy. It played the role of peaceful mediator in the civil war in Somalia, in Rwanda, and in the conflicts between Eritrea and Yemen. Meles is the architect of this policy and has often emphasized the promotion of fraternal ties with Ethiopia's neighbors. The peace mission is strikingly consistent with the Organization of African Unity's (OAU) mission of promoting and protecting peace in the continent of Africa. Zenawi was elected chairman of the OAU in June 1995, the headquarters and secretariat of which are located in Addis Ababa.

In 1997 Diplomatic relations between Ethiopian and Sudan were at their lowest ebb since the attempted assassination of Egyptian President Hosni Mubarak in June 1995. Ethiopia accused Sudan of harboring some of the fundamentalists who tried to kill Mubarak as he arrived for the annual summit of the Organization of African Unity (OAU) on 26 June 1995. The relations were further strained amid Sudan's claims that Ethiopia was helping an alliance of Sudanese rebels who seized several towns. Despite massive war rhetoric and threats from Sudan, Zenawi exercised great restraint and refused to go to war with Sudan. Relations have since improved, somewhat. A territorial dispute with Somalia over Ogaden remains unresolved. Most of the southern half of the boundary with Somalia is a Provisional Administrative line.

Ethiopia is at war with Eritrea. The war started with the invasion and occupation of territory within northeastern Ethiopia by Eritrean soldiers in the first week of May 1998. In the fighting that followed, Ethiopia recaptured Badme, but fighting has continued, interspersed with periods of inactivity and diplomacy. Although reliable casualty figures are not available, analysts believe that tens of thousands have died in the war between neighbors over disputed boundaries. A USA-Rwanda peace plan proposed in early June 1998 failed; so have arbitration efforts by the OAU. An OAU framework agreement called on Eritrea to withdraw from Ethiopian territory occupied by force since May 1998, and Ethiopia to withdraw from Eritrean territory it occupied after retaking Badme in February 1999. Each country accuses the other of making impossible preconditions to implementing the framework agreement, while saying they accept it. March 2000 ended with no solution in sight to the stalemate, despite frantic peace efforts by the OAU and other nations.

## ADDRESS
Office of the Prime Minister
PO Box 1013
Addis Ababa, Ethiopia

## REFERENCES
*Africa Confidential,* various issues.
BBC Worldwide Monitoring, 15 August 1999, 17 September 1999.
*Deutsche Press-Agentur,* 24 August 1995.
"Ethiopia and Eritrea Fight in WWI-like Trench Battles." *International Journal on World Peace,* September 1999, p. 76.
Ethiopian TV, Addis Ababa, BBC Monitoring International Reports, as provided by BBC Worldwide Monitoring, 6 February 1997, 11 August 1999.
*New York Times,* various issues.
PanAfrican News Agency, 7 February 1997, 10 June 1999, 31 March 2000.
Reuters World Service, 26 July 1995, 20 August 1995, 19 August 1999.
Smyth, Frank. "So Much for Africa's 'new leaders.'" *The New Republic,* 1 March 1999, p. 14.
*Washington Times,* 22 October 1995.
*Washington Post (DC),* 2 September 1999.

**Profile researched and written Teodros Kiros, Boston University (1/96; updated by Leo Zulu, University of Illinois at Urbana-Champaign 4/2000).**

# FIJI

## Mahendra Chaudhry
## Prime Minister

*(pronounced "mah-HEN-drah CHAW-dree")*

*"We are here to govern for the benefit of everybody in the country and the focus and emphasis will be on the poor."*

The Republic of Fiji comprises 322 islands spread over 700,000 sq km (270,000 sq mi) of the southwest Pacific Ocean. Total land area is slightly more than 18,300 sq km (7,000 sq mi). The two largest islands are Viti Levu, with an area of 10,388 sq km (4,011 sq mi) and Vanua Levu, which has an area of 5,538 sq km (2,140 sq mi). Geographers consider Fiji the eastern border of Melanesia, but language and traditional culture are more closely linked to the Polynesian islands to the east. These connections are especially close to Tonga in the southeast. Fiji's other near neighbors are Vanuatu to the west and Samoa to the northeast.

Fiji has a multi-ethnic population, estimated to total some 813,000. About 52% are Fijians native to the islands while 43% are Indians or Indo Fijians, who are descended from laborers brought from India by the British to work on the sugar plantations in the late 1800s. The remaining 5% of Fiji's residents are Europeans, part-Europeans, Chinese, and other Pacific Islanders. English is the main language of business and government. It is widely spoken, along with native Fijian and varieties of Hindi. The main religions are Christianity and Hinduism. A minority of Indo-Fijians are Muslim.

Fiji has the most developed economy in the South Pacific. More than 75% of all households engage in crop production, livestock, forestry, or fishing. Sugar production dominates commercial agriculture, accounting for 40% of that sector. Tourism has been growing over the last decade and exceeds agriculture as a source of foreign exchange earnings. Fiji's per capita gross domestic product (GDP) has been estimated at US$6,700. The unit of currency is the Fijian dollar.

## POLITICAL BACKGROUND

Europeans entering the southwest Pacific in the late 19th century set in motion many changes among the islanders. Fijians attempted to create new forms of political organization out of what had been an array of often-warring chiefdoms. Increased numbers of Europeans and Americans settled in Fiji to pursue commercial and other interests. Conflicts among settlers, and between them and their Fijian hosts, presented a threat to the new political system. This led the ruling chiefs to seek British protection. In 1874, the chiefs signed a "Deed of Cession," making Fiji a British crown colony. This colonial status continued for nearly 96 years. Within five years of secession, the first group of laborers was imported from India to work on the emerging sugar planta-

tions. By 1916, when importation ceased, more than 60,000 men, women, and children had arrived in Fiji.

Many social changes, including increased militancy by Indo-Fijians, resulted in new elections in 1963. For the first time, all adults were given the right to vote. Two years later, two political parties had emerged as strong forces. The National Federation Party (NFP), associated with Indo-Fijians, called for independence and a common electoral roll rather than contests based on ethnicity. The Alliance Party, seen as the party of native Fijians, favored gradual political change and continued ethnic or communal voting. These parties continued to dominate national politics after Fiji achieved its independence in October 1970.

In 1985, Fiji's national politics changed forever with the formation of the Fiji Labor Party (FLP). The FLP boasted of its genuine multi-ethnic nature, dominated by younger, less conservative Fijians and Indo-Fijians, with close ties to labor unions. Though the FLP had been critical of NFP leadership, these two parties formed a coalition headed by native Fijian, Timoci Bavadra, to contest the 1987 general election. Although this coalition won 28 seats, its electoral victory was short-lived. On 14 May 1987, Sitiveni Rabuka, a lieutenant colonel in the Royal Fijian Military Forces, led a bloodless coup with the stated goal of restoring Fiji to the Fijians. A series of interim governments resulted in a second Rabuka-led coup in September 1987. After this action, Rabuka declared Fiji to be a republic and asked the former Alliance leader and prime minister, Kamisese Mara, to serve as prime minister of a new government. This government ruled Fiji from December 1987 until 1992.

In 1990, a new constitution was formally promulgated that was clearly designed to strengthen the political dominance of native Fijians. It created a new House of Representatives of 70 members: 37 Fijians, 27 Indo-Fijians, 5 general electors, and 1 Rotuman from an island of Polynesians in the archipelago. All voting was to be on a purely communal or ethnic basis—Fijians and Indo-Fijians could only vote for representatives of their own group. Electoral boundaries were redrawn so that only five of the Fijian electorates were in urban areas. This reduced the voting strength of urban Fijians who had supported the FLP in 1987. The constitution provoked considerable debate, and a number of new political parties were formed, including the *Soqosoqo ni Vakavulewa ni Taukei* (SVT) which claimed to represent native interests. In the 1992 general election, this party won 30 of the 37 Fijian seats but could only form a government in coalition with other parties. This party chose Rabuka as prime minister.

Political unrest that followed the 1987 coup had serious repercussions. Fiji lost its membership in the British Commonwealth of Nations. Many Indo-Fijians, including a number of educators, civil servants, and businessmen immigrated to other countries. Tourism suffered and the nation was the object of international criticism. In 1995, a Constitution Review Commission was established to create a system that could deal with these and other issues. This commission spent almost two years at its task and achieved a success that, in terms of positive response within Fiji and internationally, could not have been imagined a decade earlier. Its recommendations were unanimously adopted by parliament in July 1997.

The new constitution creates a system that avoids purely ethnic politics and at the same time takes account of the concerns of the native Fijian community. It specifies that the president must always be a native Fijian and gives considerable recognition to the Great Council of Chiefs. The Council not only nominates and participates in electing the president but also has responsibility for all matters relating to native Fijians. Parliament consists of two houses. The Lower, where all legislation must originate, has 71 members. Of these, 46 seats are communal: 23 for Fijians, 19 for Indians, 3 for General Electors, and 1 for Rotumans. The remaining 25 are "open" seats, contested on a common roll basis without any reference to ethnicity—either for the voters or for the candidates.

The president appoints as prime minister the member of parliament who commands the majority support in the Lower House. The Constitution also provides for mandatory power sharing in cabinet. Any party with more than 10% of the seats in the House (eight) can be invited to join cabinet in proportion to the number of seats it holds. The Upper House consists of 32 appointed members: 14 nominated by the Great Council of Chiefs, 9 by the prime minister, 8 by the leader of the opposition, and 1 by the Council of Rotuma. Parliament serves a maximum of four years after a general election though it can be dissolved by the president, acting on the advice of the prime minister. This system was in place for the 1999 general election.

## PERSONAL BACKGROUND

Mahendra Pal Chaudhry was born in Tavua, Ba (pronounced "mbah") province, on 2 September 1942. He is the grandson of Indian indentured laborers. His late father ran a bus and farm business in Ba. Chaudhry was educated at Tavua Indian School and Shri Vivekananda High School.

After working with his father, he was employed in the research unit of Emperor Gold Mines. In 1960, he became a civil servant in the auditor-general's office. He became the Lautoka branch secretary of the Fiji Public Service Association in 1968. Seven years later he resigned his civil service position to become a full-time union official.

In 1965, Chaudhry married Veer Mati, a dental therapist at the Colonial War Memorial Hospital in Suva. They have three children.

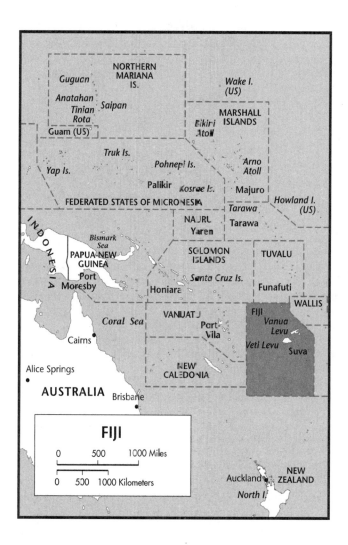

## RISE TO POWER

For more than two decades, Chaudhry has been associated with labor and farming organizations. In 1975, he became assistant secretary of the Fiji Trades Union Congress and served as national secretary from 1988 to 1992. In 1978, with Dr. Bavadra, he established the National Farmers Union to represent sugar cane growers and was elected to the Joint Committee of the Cane Growers Association two years later. His labor union connections led him to become a founding member of the FLP in 1985. He was elected to parliament in 1987 and served briefly as minister of finance and economic planning until the Bavadra government was deposed by Rabuka's coup. Along with others, he was held prisoner for six days after the coup.

The election results, which made Chaudhry the first Indo-Fijian prime minister in history, surprised almost everyone. Two factors are considered important. The first was the decision of Rabuka's SVT party to form a coalition with the NFP to contest the election. This alliance undermined the Fijian vs. Indian opposition of the past, as did the coalition of FLP with two smaller Fijian parties, Fiji Association Party (FAP) and Party of National Unity. The second factor was the use of the preferential ballot, in which voters must indicate not only their first choice, but also their order of preference for as many candidates as are in the running. In one electorate, the FLP candidate was chosen only after counting down to the sixth preference after running behind the FAP and SVT candidates when first choices were counted. Whatever the reason, the results amounted to a landslide for the Fiji Labor Party, as FLP candidates won 37 seats. Rabuka's SVT took only eight seats, and the once powerful NFP won no seats at all. Despite his absolute majority, Chaudhry maintained his coalition with FAP and the Party of National Unity. He chose 11 Fijians and only six Indians for his first cabinet. His two deputy prime ministers are Fijians, one from FLP and the other from FAP. Another noteworthy result is that almost 9% of the new House are women.

## LEADERSHIP

Chaudhry has been criticized for his abrasive or confrontational style as a union leader. His response has been that he cannot abide injustice. His willingness to acknowledge native Fijian interests in putting together his government suggests greater sensitivity than he had been given credit for. In fact, unsuccessful NFP leaders have been among his most severe post-election critics.

It is certain that the FLP won support by promising to improve the lives of ordinary citizens, regardless of ethnicity. Some observers doubt the ability of Chaudhry to fulfill all those commitments in view of present economic conditions; others feel that Fiji may be poised for new economic growth. Because of the unprecedented nature of his victory, Chaudhry must continue to pursue a truly multi-ethnic vision if unrest like that in the past is to be avoided.

## DOMESTIC POLICY

Chaudhry's domestic program initiatives reflect his populist and labor commitments. He intends to reverse the previous policy of privatizing such industries as forestry and civil aviation. One of his first acts was to reinstate union members who had been laid off from the Civil Aviation Authority. Foreign economists argue that privatization is inevitable if Fiji's economy is to grow. It remains to be seen whether Chaudhry's policy can succeed.

The most important domestic issue facing the new prime minister involves leases for sugar cane growers. Most of the growers are Indo-Fijians while the land is owned by native Fijians and managed on their behalf by a government agency, the Native Land Trust Board (NLTB). The Agricultural Landlords and Tenants Act (ALTA) is the legal structure for managing leases, most of which is to expire in 2000–01.

Growers want security of leases for the longest term possible while at least a few Fijian chiefs expressed their displeasure at Chaudhry's victory by announcing they would not renew any leases to Indians. Given the importance of sugar in the Fijian economy, a workable solution to this problem is vital.

## FOREIGN POLICY

The FLP emphasized domestic issues in its campaign, and significant foreign policy initiatives have yet to emerge. Fiji's first prime minister, Ratu Mara, was a towering figure in Pacific Island affairs for decades and still commands respect. Rabuka has surprised those who denounced him after the 1987 coups by emerging as something of a statesman in recent years. Despite his commoner origin, he was made a life member of the Great Council of Chiefs after the coup, and in 1999 was elected chairman of that group, defeating the paramount chief of western Fiji. In July 1999, he successfully negotiated a peace settlement of civil strife in the Solomon Islands.

Little in Chaudhry's background indicates an interest in international affairs although he succeeded in mobilizing overseas labor support in the aftermath of the coups. Fiji has a long-standing prominence in the Pacific Islands; Ratu Mara was instrumental in establishing the first regional organization, now the South Pacific Forum. The country is a member of the United Nations, the World Bank, and Asian Development Bank and recently was reinstated in the British Commonwealth. The new prime minister has inherited significant international ties; how he will build upon them remains to be seen.

## ADDRESS

Office of the Prime Minister
Government House
Suva, Fiji

## REFERENCES

Bank of Hawaii. *Fiji Economic Report.* Honolulu: September 1998.
*Fiji Times,* May–June 1999.
Lal, Brij V. *Broken Waves: A History of the Fiji Islands in the Twentieth Century.* Honolulu: University of Hawaii Press.
*Pacific Islands Monthly,* June 1999.

**Profile researched and written by Eugene Ogan, Professor Emeritus, University of Minnesota (9/99; updated 2/2000).**

# FINLAND

## Paavo Lipponen
### Prime Minister

*(pronounced "PAA-vo LIP-ponen")*

*"The government will move forward, sustained by the legacy of its predecessor. We can look to the future with optimism."*

The Republic of Finland lies in northern Europe, bordering on Norway to the far north, Sweden to the west, and Russia to the east. In area, Finland covers 338,145 sq km (130,559 sq mi); its western shores extend approximately 1,164 km (710 mi) along the Baltic Sea.

The total population has been estimated at about 5.2 million. Approximately 93% of the people are Finnish-speaking, with linguistic minorities (principally Swedish-speakers) making up the remaining 7%. Despite a history of language antagonism, both languages remain official. There is a small population of several thousand nomadic Saami (Lapps) in the far north.

Timber, paper, and other forestry-related products are major exports, but the metal, machine tool, and especially electronic industries are leading employers. Industry, construction, and transportation employ about one-third of the labor force, while agriculture, forestry, and fishing employ about 8%, and public and private services account for about 56% of total employment. Although Finland has significant mineral resources, its design and high technology sectors are currently more important. The Finnish currency is the *markka* (Fmk). The per capita GDP has been estimated at us$20,100.

## POLITICAL BACKGROUND

Russian expansion incorporated all of Finland into the Russian Empire as an autonomous grand duchy in 1809. Finland kept many of its political institutions and developed its own cultural and political consciousness under the Tsars. By the end of the 19th century Finnish nationalism was increasingly hostile to Russian autocracy, and the collapse of the Russian state in war and revolution paved the way to Finnish independence in 1917. A brief but extremely bloody civil war followed, in which socialist Reds supported by the Bolsheviks in Moscow were defeated by nationalist Whites.

A democratic constitution was adopted in 1919, and Finland was one of the few newly independent states in Eastern Europe to sustain democracy and repay its foreign debts throughout the inter-war period. Finnish rejection of Soviet demands for naval bases and other territorial concessions in southeastern Finland led to an invasion by Stalin's army in November 1939. Although its troops performed heroically, Finland was forced to cede most of the heavily populated Karelian Isthmus to the Soviet Union in March 1940. Seeking to recapture their lost territories, the Finns joined Nazi Germany as co-belligerents in attacking the USSR in June 1941 but were forced to sign an armistice in September 1944.

Under the 1947 peace treaty Finland ceded some 12% of its territory to the USSR, imprisoned several prominent politicians, reduced its armed forces, and undertook to pay heavy economic reparations. A Soviet naval base was established only 25 km (16 mi) from Helsinki. A separate Treaty of Friendship, Cooperation, and Mutual Assistance, concluded in 1948 under heavy Soviet pressure, obligated Finland to resist attacks on itself or the USSR and in effect precluded Finland from undertaking any significant foreign policy initiative without the Kremlin's approval. After 1955, when the Soviets withdrew from their Finnish base, Finland became an increasingly active member of the United Nations and Nordic Council, as well as various Western economic organizations. Despite Soviet pressure, the Finnish Communist Party steadily declined in influence. Finland's standing was further enhanced by the signing of the 1975 Helsinki treaty, which called for pan-European cooperation in security, economic, political, and human rights matters.

Finland's republican constitution combines a parliamentary system with a strong presidency. Legislative powers are vested in the *Eduskunta* (Parliament), a unicameral body of 200 members elected by proportional representation from 15 multi-member electoral districts. After the 1999 elections, nine parties are represented, but the five largest (and traditional) parties share 176 seats. The normal parliamentary term is four years, but the president may dissolve the assembly at any time. The president is elected directly in a two-stage vote. If no candidate gets a majority in the first round, a second round is held between the two candidates with the largest first round totals.

Finland's political system is more like the French than most other European parliamentary democracies because of the division of executive power between the president and the prime minister. The president is the constitutionally designated head of state who appoints the cabinet, serves as commander-in-chief of the armed forces, and, until recently, had primary responsibility for foreign policy. During the Cold War, Finnish presidents had a special role in reassuring the USSR of Finnish good intentions. Now foreign and security policy has become a shared responsibility between the president and the cabinet with recent prime ministers taking an active role in reasserting full Finnish independence. The prime minister has, however, served as the actual head of government, with strong influence on the country's day-to-

day affairs. Party leaders with the most seats in parliament select the prime minister in a complex bargaining process. Since 1945 no single party has ever held an absolute parliamentary majority, so all political decisions involve coalitions. The cabinet is composed of the heads of government ministries and has as its primary responsibility the preparation of governmental budgets and legislation and the administration of public policies. The prime minister and cabinet serve only so long as they enjoy the support of a working majority in parliament, and there have been frequent changes of government.

### PERSONAL BACKGROUND
Paavo Lipponen was born on 23 April 1941 in Turtola. He attended the University of Helsinki, where he edited the student newspaper *Ylioppilaslehti* between 1963 and 1965. During his student years Lipponen married Alia-Marja Nikupeteri. He completed his master's degree in political science in 1965. After graduation, he continued in journalism as a freelance reporter for the Finnish (state) Broadcasting Company (YLE) for the next two years.

### RISE TO POWER
In 1967, Lipponen became an employee of the Social Democratic Party (SDP) and worked first in its research and international affairs section and later as head of the political section. Between 1979 and 1982, he served as a special

political advisor (private secretary) for the Social Democratic prime minister. Lipponen served in the Finnish parliament between 1983 and 1987. He was also elected to the Helsinki City Council in 1985 and served in that capacity for the next ten years. Lipponen gained some valuable business experience as managing director of Viestintae Teema OY in 1988 and chairman of the supervisory board of Outokumpu OY in 1989–90. He also headed the Finnish Institute of International Affairs between 1989 and 1991.

Lipponen became leader of the SDP in 1993, as Finland's deep economic recession bottomed out. Although his predecessor, Ulf Sundqvist, had suffered a severe electoral defeat in 1991, the party was recovering in public opinion polls. Lipponen thus became heir-apparent to the premiership almost from the start of his tenure as SDP chief.

Lipponen conducted a vigorous campaign in the run-up to the March 1995 parliamentary election. Although Finland's economy was bouncing back from the depths of recession, recovery was still tentative, and unemployment exceeded 17% of the labor force. Voters clearly wanted a change. The outcome was the best showing of the SDP since World War II. The SDP won 28.3% of the vote and 63 seats (a gain of 15). Lipponen was asked to form a coalition government.

### LEADERSHIP
Lipponen's new government continued the Finnish tradition of broad coalitions. He formed a five-party government, called the "Rainbow Coalition," that stretched from the former Communist Leftist Alliance and the Green League through the Social Democrats and included the centrist Swedish People's Party and the moderate Conservative Party. Esko Aho's Center Party became the main opposition. The new coalition commanded 145 seats in the 200-seat Finnish parliament. With such political diversity, managing the coalition would be a severe test of Lipponen's political skills. Despite major disagreements on EU policy matters and the priorities of domestic economic reform, Lipponen kept the team together.

As the March 1999 elections approached, public opinion polls reflected a three-way dead heat between Lipponen's Social Democrats, his deputy prime minister and finance minister Sauli Niinisto's Conservative Party, and opposition leader Aho's Center Party. A cooling economy (caused by Russia's economic collapse in 1998), the opposition's plans for radical tax cuts, and controversy about EU policies dominated the campaign. The outcome was a setback for the Social Democrats, whose share of the votes declined from 28.3% in 1995 to 22.9% in 1999. The SDP parliamentary delegation declined from 63 to 51. The Conservatives advanced from 17.9% of the vote in 1995 (and 39 seats) to 21% in 1999 (and 46 seats). The three smaller coalition parties continued to share 42 seats among them. The opposition Centrists advanced modestly from 19.9% to 22.4% of the vote (gaining four seats for a total of 48). The SDP remained the largest parliamentary group, and Lipponen retained the right to renew his coalition, making it the longest-serving government in Finnish history.

### DOMESTIC POLICY
Lipponen made it clear that economic recovery, including tax reforms and employment measures, would continue to be the

government's highest domestic priority. Although his first government succeeded in cutting the 1995 unemployment rate nearly in half (to below 10% by conventional measurement), the goal for 2003 is "full employment" (which means not more than 5% unemployment). Moreover, the government intends to raise the average age of retirement (currently below 60 years). Reduction of public debt to below 50% of GDP is another goal, which will be aided by the planned sale of government shares in industry.

Economic growth with low inflation has been impressive under the Lipponen government. In 1997, GDP soared at a 5.5% annual rate while in 1998 the figure was about 4.7%. Growth in 1999 was projected to be a more modest 3.5% as Russian economic problems and German stagnation affect two of Finland's important foreign markets. Public finances have recovered, but Lipponen has refused to promise significant tax cuts until public debt is cut and structural budgetary deficits are removed. This was a central issue in the electoral campaign. The Conservatives, led by Finance Minister Niinisto, were more anxious to see tax relief for business, while the leftist parties (the Leftist Alliance and the Greens) pulled in the opposite direction. Hence Lipponen can balance domestic economic policy within his government without concern for parliamentary majorities.

Although Finnish politics has been historically free of scandals, Ulf Sundqvist, a former Social Democratic leader and minister in the first Lipponen government, resigned over financial misdeeds. Lipponen himself was not involved, but critics felt he had been less than candid during parliamentary debates. The Social Democrats received a boost in the spring 2000 presidential elections when Lipponen's Foreign Minister Tarja Halonen won in the run-off election. Lipponen was hailed by a number of European feminists and female politicians for taking advantage of a week's parental leave at the birth of his daughter in March 2000.

## FOREIGN POLICY

Between 1944 and 1990, democratic and capitalistic Finland lived in the shadow of the Soviet Union. This fact affected nearly every aspect of Finnish public life. Both the 1947 peace treaty and the 1948 Treaty of Friendship, Cooperation, and Mutual Assistance restrained domestic politics and gave Finnish presidents a special role in managing Finland's sensitive relations with the USSR. The collapse of the Soviet

state and empire directly affected Finland and its foreign policy, as evidenced by the severe economic recession, the renewed independence of Finland's Baltic neighbors, and the integration of Finland into the European Union in 1995. Politics can change quickly, but geography does not. Finland continues to pay close attention to its relations with the Russian Federation. Although fully part of the European Union and, since 1999, a member of the Economic and Monetary Union, Finland has resisted integration into exclusive European and Western defense arrangements. Emphasis remains on the United Nations and the inclusive Organization for European Security and Cooperation (founded in Helsinki in 1975). Relations with NATO are close but channeled through the Partnership for Peace. While the door to NATO remains open, the Lipponen government plans no significant changes in Finnish security policy.

Foreign policy is closely tied to the United Nations and the inclusive Organization of European Security and Cooperaiton, founded in Helsinki in 1975. Finland has been a consistent contributor of troops and resources to UN peace-keeping missions since 1956. During the Kosovo crisis of 1999, then-President Martti Ahtisaari drew on his vast diplomatic experience to promote communication and bargaining between NATO and Russia, as well as with Yugoslavia itself. Finland has urged moderation and pragmatism on the Baltic states, especially its nearest neighbor Estonia.

## ADDRESS

Office of the Prime Minister
Snellmaninkatu 1-A,
FIN-00170 Helsinki, Finland

## REFERENCES

*Agence France Presse*, 1998–99.

*Europe*, February 1998.

Finnish government. [Online] Available http://virtual.finland.fi (Accessed 5/2000).

Finnish government. [Online] Available http://www.vn.fi (Accessed 5/2000).

*Hilfe Country Report*, Quest Economic Database, 1999.

"Photo Finish. (Politics and Government in Finland)." *The Economist*, 27 March 1999, p. 54.

Profile researched and written by Eric S. Einhorn, University of Massachusetts, Amherst (9/99; updated 5/2000).

# FRANCE

## Jacques Chirac
## President

*(pronounced "ZHOCK sheer-ROCK")*

*"I would like all fellow citizens, more at ease about their future, to feel they are part of a collective destiny,...more patriotic and at the same time more European."*

The French Republic is the largest west European country, encompassing 551,670 sq km (220,668 sq mi), including the Mediterranean island of Corsica. It is bounded to the west by the Atlantic Ocean; to the north by the English Channel; to the east by Belgium, Luxembourg, Germany, Switzerland, and Italy; and to the south by the Mediterranean Sea and Spain. The Republic also includes overseas territories and departments. The capital is Paris.

The population of 59 million is overwhelmingly nominally Roman Catholic (90%); fewer than 2% are Protestant and Jewish; and recent immigration trends have created a Muslim community that is an estimated 8% of the total population. The language is French, which has several significant regional dialects; Breton and Basque are spoken as well by some.

The fourth-largest Western industrialized economy, France has a GDP of $1.32 trillion. Per capita income is $23,000. Inflation is low at 0.7%, but unemployment has reached 12% in the general population and stands at nearly twice that for younger workers. France is one of the world's leading producers and exporters of dairy products, wheat, and wine; industrial output includes aircraft and engines, electrical equipment, cosmetics, and pet-care products. The currency is the *franc*.

## POLITICAL BACKGROUND

France was one of the first nation-states and during the reign of Louis XIV (1643–1715) was the dominant European power. Financial overextension coupled with popular resentment of the privileged classes led to the French Revolution (1789–94). Despite advocacy of the ideals of republicanism and egalitarianism, the country reverted to monarchy or absolute rule four times: during the Empire of Napoleon, the Restoration of Louis XVIII, the reign of Louis-Philippe, and the Second Empire of Napoleon III. In 1870, at the close of the Franco-Prussian War, the Second Republic was established; it lasted until the military defeat of 1940. In July 1940, on the heels of the German invasion and occupation of France, the Third Republic was installed. Known as the Vichy Government, the leaders openly collaborated with the Nazis, in the hope of maintaining some semblance of French sovereignty. Liberated in 1944, France was briefly governed by a provisional government led by General Charles de Gaulle, who oversaw the creation of the Fourth Republic and the drafting and promulgation of a new constitution. The Fourth Republic was beset with successive cabinet crises and changes of government, primarily over the divisive issues of French colonial policy in Indochina and Algeria. In May 1958 the government collapsed under the weight of the Algerian conflict, and de Gaulle was called upon to head a new government in order to avert civil war. De Gaulle became prime minister in June 1958. The Fifth Republic was constitutionally established in September 1958, and de Gaulle was elected president in December of that year. Since de Gaulle's tenure ended in 1969, France has elected as president Georges Pompidou (Gaullist, 1969–74); Valéry Giscard d'Estaing (Independent Republican, 1974–81); Francois Mitterand (Socialist, 1981–95); and Jacques Chirac (1995–present).

Under the 1958 Constitution, executive power in France is held by the president, who since 1962 has been elected by direct popular vote for a seven-year term. Elections are provisionally structured in two rounds to provide a run-off if no candidate wins an outright majority in the first ballot. The president appoints a 47-member cabinet, headed by the prime minister, whom he also appoints. The president may submit questions to a national referendum and has the power to dissolve the National Assembly. Parliament is composed of the 577-member National Assembly, the members of which are directly elected every five years, and the Senate, one-third of whose 321 members are chosen every three years by an electoral college to serve nine-year terms. Legislative power lies with the National Assembly. Suffrage is universal, but non-compulsory at age 18.

## PERSONAL BACKGROUND

Jacques René Chirac was born in Paris on 29 November 1932 to Francois and Marie-Louise Chirac. He attended *Lycée Carnot*, an old established school. Although an unexceptional student, Jacques did well enough to transfer to the elite *Lycée Louis-le-Grand*. He graduated in 1950, taking a *baccalaureat* with honors. Chirac's education continued with his enrollment at *l'Institut d'Etudes Politiques* (IEP/Institute for Political Studies), a university that trained those interested in careers in politics and diplomacy. In the summer of 1953, Chirac studied at Harvard University. Having received his degree in political science from *IEP*, he planned to enter *l'Ecole Nationale d'Administration* (ENA/National School of Administration), another government service school. He was drafted into the army prior to enrollment. After a six-month course at officer's training school, Chirac volunteered for duty in Algeria, where France was engaged in a colonial war. Chirac was involved in a great deal of the fighting and was wounded in action. He won several awards, including the *Grand-Croix de la Légion d'Honneur*, the *Grand-Croix de l'Ordre National du Mérite*, and the *Croix de la Valoir Militaire*. His military service ended in 1957, whereupon he entered *ENA* in 1958 and graduated in 1959. Chirac and his wife, the former Bernadette Chodron de Courcel, have two daughters.

## RISE TO POWER

After completing his extensive education, Chirac immediately embarked upon a career of government service. He worked briefly as a civil servant in Algeria, after which he was employed as an auditor in the *Cour de Comptes* (similar to the US General Accounting Office). In April 1962, he joined the General Secretariat of the Council of Ministers and before year-end had been named to the staff of Prime Minister Georges Pompidou. In 1965, he became municipal counselor for his parents' hometown, Sainte-Féiéole. In 1967, he was elected deputy to the National Assembly for Corrèze. Also in 1967, Pompidou named Chirac to be under-secretary of state for social affairs and in the following year secretary of state for economic affairs and finance. Chirac continued in the same capacity under the new minister, Valéry Giscard d'Estaing, and was subsequently given responsibility for the budget. In 1973, he was appointed minister of agriculture and rural development. When Pompidou died in office, Chirac was instrumental in the victory of Giscard d'Estaing. In May 1974, he was repaid for that support when the president named him prime minister. Ideological differences later provoked a rift between the two men, and in April 1976 Chirac resigned as prime minister.

In December 1976, Chirac was elected president of *L'Union de Démocrates pour la République (RPR)*, the conservative political party of which he had been under-secretary since 1974. Chirac immediately changed the name to *Rassemblement pour la République*, which was evocative in name as well as ideology of the party of de Gaulle. Chirac soon became the driving force within the party and consequently a significant actor on the political right.

Despite his earlier opposition to the creation of the office of mayor of Paris, in 1977 Chirac declared himself a candidate for the post. He won the March elections, and the following year RPR candidates swept to victory in the parliamentary elections. His disputes with Giscard d'Estaing widening, in 1981 Chirac announced his intention to run for president. He finished third in the first-round balloting with only 16% of the vote. In the run-off, Chirac declined to endorse Giscard d'Estaing, and the victory went to the Socialist candidate, Francois Mitterand.

Although sidelined in the national political arena, Chirac retained his municipal level positions, continuing as mayor of Paris and gaining re-election to the National Assembly. In 1986, he returned to national prominence when a coalition of conservative candidates won a majority in the National Assembly. Mitterand appointed Chirac prime minister and asked him to form a government. "Cohabitation," as the arrangement between the Socialist Mitterand and the Conservative Chirac came to be called, helped establish Chirac as a national leader even as he remained mayor of Paris. Social and economic reverses eroded support for his policies. Though he campaigned again for the presidency in 1988, he

ultimately lost the election. Mitterand's reelection marked the end of cohabitation, and Chirac's tenure as prime minister came to an end. Chirac was re-elected deputy for Corrèze in June 1988 and as mayor of Paris in March 1989. He also continued as leader of RPR. Chirac was widely credited as a key to the passage of the Maastricht treaties on the European Union in the 1992 national referendum. The 1993 Treaty of Amsterdam paved the way to a strengthened European community in social policy and employment, influencing Chirac's approach to social policy-making as president of France.

In the months preceding the first round of voting in the 1995 presidential campaign, Chirac's place as front-runner among the nine candidates was well established. Therefore, his second-place finish on 23 April 1995 with only 20.4% of votes cast was surprising. That he finished behind Lionel Jospin, the Socialist candidate, was nothing short of astonishing. In the second round of voting on 7 May 1995, Chirac emerged victorious, with 52.6% of the vote; Jospin polled 47.4% in an unexpectedly strong finish.

## LEADERSHIP

Inaugurated on 18 May 1995 amid very little fanfare, Jacques Chirac became the fifth president of the Fifth Republic. Conservatives also control 80% of the seats in the National Assembly, 67% of the Senate, and 20 of 22 regional councils, as well as a large number of municipalities. Such ideological consensus is unprecedented in the history of the Fifth Republic, and brings with it the potential for enormous presidential power. The passage in July 1995 of a constitutional amendment granting the president greater power to present questions directly to the French people via referendum enhances that power further.

Chirac chose Alain Juppé as his prime minister, who served as budget minister during Chirac's 1986–88 government. Juppé brings a strong commitment to a united Europe, being largely credited with having persuaded Chirac to support the Maastricht treaties. His selection is a signal that moderate Gaullism will be the tone taken during Chirac's administration.

Chirac inherited a nation with great strengths and serious weaknesses that many analysts argue is at a critical juncture. The French economy is strong at home and abroad, but extraordinarily high unemployment hinders growth. The European Union has, with France's support, become more concrete. However, Chirac's support for the EU in the past has been lukewarm. Xenophobia runs rampant in some sectors, and ethnic violence has increased. As of 2000, it remained to be seen precisely how Chirac will use his mandate to address these issues.

## DOMESTIC POLICY

Chirac pledged throughout the 1995 presidential campaign that his number one priority would be to address the high unemployment plaguing the French economy and the poverty associated with it. In the heat of the campaign, Chirac promised an array of programs that would deal with the unemployment issue and spur job creation. At the same time, he promised to lower taxes and to cut the budget deficit. These could not be accomplished simultaneously, especially in an economy that has had zero growth rates in the early 1990s and was growing only slowly by the end of the decade. Chirac will continue the privatization of state-owned companies, which will in all likelihood lead to job losses. Pledges made during the campaign raised expectations in many sectors of French society, and when it became clear that Chirac could not deliver, tensions in the government grew. Chirac called for parliamentary elections in May 1997, ten months earlier than were required by law. Voters surprised Chirac by handing the Socialist Party control of the Parliament, pushing Chirac's center-right coalition out. Although presidential elections are not scheduled until May 2002, Chiraq's ability to deliver on his 1995 campaign plans was severely hampered following the elections. The legislature planned to phase in a reduction in the workweek from 39 to 35 hours by 2002 to help ease the unemployment problem.

## FOREIGN POLICY

France is a charter member of the United Nations and holds a permanent seat on the UN Security Council. France is a signatory to the North Atlantic Treaty, and for the first time since 1966, France participated in a NATO military peace-keeping mission in Bosnia-Herzegovinia, in 1997.

In the late-1990s, France was deeply enmeshed in the crisis in former Yugoslavia. It had the largest contingent of troops in the UN peace-keeping forces on the ground. France argued vociferously, both through diplomatic channels and publicly, for a more active role for other Western democracies.

France's relations with other countries are cordial. Especially in former colonial holdings, France participates in a wide range of social and humanitarian programs throughout the world. In 1996, development assistance amounted to .54% of the country's GDP and ranked first in the world in terms of development aid, half of which goes to Africa. France and the US share similar values and tend to enact similar policies on important issues. When conflicts arise, they are addressed in a spirit of close cooperation. In Europe, France is a significant power and has chosen to work closely with Germany in order to strengthen the institutions and influence of the European Union, economically as well as strategically. In January 1999, France joined with 10 other European nations in launching the euro.

Chirac has given no indication that he plans an abrupt shift in the direction of France's foreign relations. Yet, France's decision to proceed with nuclear testing in the South Pacific has provoked an outcry around the globe. Chirac claims that he wants to work towards a total ban on nuclear testing in conjunction with other nuclear powers, but national security may prevent such action.

## ADDRESS
Palais de l'Elyseé
5–57 rue du Faubourg Saint Honoré
77008 Paris, France

## REFERENCES
*Current History*, various issues 1988–2000
*The Economist*, various issues 1992–2000.
*New York Times*, various issues 1993–2000.
*Wall Street Journal*, various issues 2000.

**Profile researched and written by Alison Doherty Munro (8/95; updated by Mary Sugar 4/2000).**

# GABON

### Omar Bongo
### President
*(pronounced "oh-MAR bone-GOO")*

*"I urge the people of Gabon to look towards the future with hope."*

Gabon (formally known as the Gabonese Republic) lies on the Atlantic coast of Central Africa. It shares borders with Equatorial Guinea to the northwest, the Congo Republic to the east and south, and Cameroon to the north. Gabon's land area comprises some 267,667 sq km (103,347 sq mi). There is a narrow coastal plain with a hilly interior and savanna in the east and south. Some 77% of the land is heavily timbered. The main cities are Libreville, with 260,000 inhabitants, Port-Gentil, with 78,000, and Franceville with 23,000.

There are more than 40 distinct ethnic groups in Gabon. The largest of these include the Fang, Eshira, Bapounou, and Bateke. French is the official language though many Gabonese speak languages belonging to the Niger-Congo group.

In January 1956, petroleum was first produced in the Port-Gentil area, south of Libreville. Uranium was discovered in December 1956, and production began five years later. Other major sources of income include wood, cocoa, coffee, natural gas, and manganese. Gabon's population has been estimated at 1.2 million. Per capita GDP stands at $6,400. The national currency is the CFA *franc*.

## POLITICAL BACKGROUND
The French established colonial rule over the region in 1886. In 1910, the colony became part of the federation of French Equatorial Africa. Gabon became an independent nation in 1960 and established its first constitution the following year.

Gabon has a highly centralized political system with two main institutions, the presidency and the official political party, *Parti Democratique Gabonais* (PDG or Gabonese Democratic Party). The PDG was created in May 1968 after President Bongo dissolved all other political parties. The president of the republic is also the secretary-general (and as such the top official) of the PDG. In 1975, the constitution was revised, and the office of prime minister was created. In 1981, a second revision made the prime minister head of government and responsible to the president, the Central Committee of the PDG, and the legislature (National Assembly). The latter consists of 84 members elected by the people and 9 nominated by President Bongo. The president of the republic is elected by universal direct suffrage for a seven-year term. Were the president temporarily unable to perform his duties, his function would be taken over by a college comprising the prime minister, the president of the National Assembly, a member of the Political Bureau of the PDG, and a member of the government.

## PERSONAL BACKGROUND
Albert Bernard Bongo was born on 30 December 1935 at Lewal, in the Lekori prefecture of Haut-Ogodue province. He is from the Teke group, an ethnic group closely related to the Bateke of the Congo Republic. His father died when he was seven years old. The youngest of nine children, Bongo attended a public school in the Bacongo section of Brazzaville, in the Congo Republic, where he had relatives. He completed his secondary studies in commerce at the technical high school in Brazzaville. In 1958, Bongo obtained a position with the Post and Telegraphic Service. In 1959, he married Josephine Kama. The couple divorced in 1985, and Bongo remarried four years later. His second wife is Edith Sassou-Nguesso, the daughter of President Dennis Sassou-Nguesso of the Congo Republic. Bongo changed his given name to "Omar" in 1979 after converting to Islam.

## RISE TO POWER
Between July 1958 and October 1960, Bongo was second lieutenant in the French Army of the Air. During this time he earned his baccalaureate (high school diploma) at Brazzaville. While serving as a lieutenant, he was assigned to the Ministry of Foreign Affairs (1960–62). Bongo then served as assistant director of the president's cabinet for seven months and director of the cabinet until 1965. He was subsequently given responsibilities for information and tourism (1963–64) and for national defense (1964–65). In February 1965, a military coup d'etat overthrew President Leon Mba. However, France intervened militarily and restored Mba to power. In September 1965, Bongo was named minister delegate to the presidency, responsible for national defense and coordination. The following year, he was appointed vice president responsible for defense, planning, information, and tourism.

By this time President Mba was gravely ill. He advanced the date for presidential elections and established the post of vice president. In March 1967, national elections were held. Mba was re-elected president, and Bongo was elected vice president. On 28 November 1967, Leon Mba died, and Bongo succeeded to the presidency.

## LEADERSHIP
Bongo was formally elected president for the first time on 25 February 1973 when a new National Assembly was also chosen. He has subsequently won re-election in December

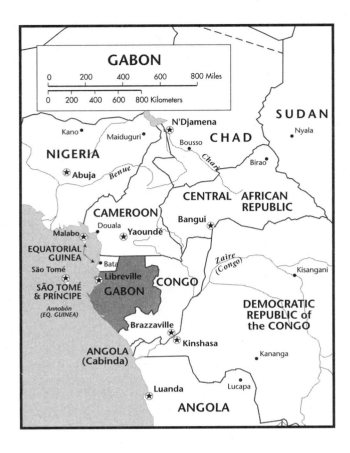

**GABON**

0    200    400    600    800 Miles

0    200    400    600    800 Kilometers

SUDAN

Kano    Maiduguri    N'Djamena    Nyala

NIGERIA    CHAD    Bousso

Abuja    Benue    Birao

CENTRAL    AFRICAN

CAMEROON    REPUBLIC

Douala    Yaoundé    Bangui

Malabo

EQUATORIAL    Zaire

GUINEA    Bata    (Congo)    Kisangani

São Tomé    Libreville

SÃO TOMÉ    GABON    CONGO

& PRÍNCIPE

Annobón    DEMOCRATIC

(EQ. GUINEA)    REPUBLIC of

Brazzaville    the CONGO

Kinshasa

ANGOLA    Kananga

(Cabinda)

Luanda    Lucapa

ANGOLA

1979, November 1986, December 1993, and most recently in December 1998.

As one of the world's longest-ruling heads of state, Bongo has proven himself to be a savvy politician. His rise to power in the early 1960s was swift and steady. Upon gaining the presidency in 1967, Bongo undertook to fight tribalism and regionalism, both of which he condemned as dangers to national unity, peace, and harmony. He praised inter-ethnic, inter-provincial marriages as vital to the emergence of a Gabonese national. He successfully forged strong relations with the French, particularly with the d'Estaing and Chirac governments. Throughout the 1970s and 1980s, his one-party political system was effectively unchallenged, with most opposition groups having been driven out of the country. To consolidate power, Bongo assumed direct responsibility for several ministries. The remaining 40 to 50 cabinet posts were reshuffled as many as three or four times a year—as both a means of rewarding supporters and of keeping potential opposition from gaining a foothold in the government. Members of the government and party leaders were required to take a loyalty oath to Bongo and to the party. Trade unions were consolidated into a single federation, which was affiliated with the PDG. Economically, Bongo favored a pragmatic liberal approach, in which the state has played an active role.

Personally, Bongo has lived a lifestyle of grandeur. He reportedly spent as much as US$300 million for a presidential palace that contains his residence and the executive offices. In addition, he spent vast sums of money to host a 1977 meeting of the Organization of African Unity.

When opposition demands for a multiparty system were backed by popular protest and international pressure in the early 1990s, Bongo responded with brutal force but also went to the bargaining table. Multiparty elections were held in 1993, and Bongo retained the presidency with a scant 50.7% of the vote. Popular protests ensued and were not quelled until Bongo agreed to French-mediated roundtable discussions with opposition groups in Paris. The talks resulted in the establishment of an independent electoral commission. Shortly before the 1998 elections, Bongo succeeded in stripping this commission of many of its powers and handing the duties over to the state-friendly Interior Ministry.

In December 1998, Bongo ran against a fragmented opposition of six candidates, including two rivals from the National Woodcutters Rally (RNB). He was reelected to another seven-year term with 67% of the vote. Pierre Mamboundou, the first runner-up (with 16% of the vote), contested the results and called for mass strikes. Bongo's vast financial resources, his dominance of the broadcast media, and his widespread patronage system gave him an enormous advantage over his opponents. Yet, public reaction was far less vocal than it had been in 1993. This suggests that Bongo should not face any immediate challenge to his leadership.

## DOMESTIC POLICY

Bongo is faced with a number of immediate domestic challenges. In particular, the collapse in prices for crude oil has resulted in plummeting revenues for Gabon. Further, there are fears that Gabon's oil reserves are running low, though the exploration of newly acquired offshore fields may offset these concerns. Also, the Asian economic crises of the past few years has resulted in substantially decreased demand for tropical hardwoods and oils, further reducing state revenues and income to the populace. The state-run lumber industry has been forced to lay off some 25% of its employees. This situation is particularly dangerous since most lumber workers live in the predominantly Fang northern region—a section of the country that has long been a center of opposition to Bongo's government. The potential for another devaluation in the CFA also threatens to cut the buying power of the Gabonese populace. Perhaps foreseeing such problems, Bongo ran for reelection in 1998 on a "realistic" platform that stressed the hard times that lay ahead. He has also stated that steps must be taken to diversify the economy in order to reduce the country's dependence on oil and timber exports.

In the late 1990s, Bongo has leaned more towards supply-side economics. In 1998, he privatized the Energy and Water Authority and suggested that the Post and Telecommunications Authority might soon be sold. Many observers doubt that he will be willing to privatize the OCTRA authority, which manages the Trans-Gabonese railway. Bongo is rumored to hold a major interest in this concern.

## FOREIGN POLICY

Bongo has consistently maintained close ties to France and was decidedly pro-Western during the Cold War. France and the US became less tolerant of authoritarian rulers after the collapse of the Soviet Union, and Bongo has seen a slight cooling of relations with the West. He has been forced to endure international criticism for alleged irregularities in the

1993 and 1998 elections. Furthermore, his government has faced harsh criticism in the French press for corruption. Bongo has even threatened to leave the CFA zone if the currency is devalued as France makes its transition to the Euro. Shortfalls in earnings have placed Gabon in danger of default on its nearly $4 billion debt. Such a default would likely lead to IMF-mandated austerity measures.

The spread of conflict in Central Africa has drawn Bongo into regional politics. As the son-in-law of Dennis Sassou-Nguesso and a close friend of Pascal Lissouba, Bongo was called upon to mediate between these leaders to end their bloody contest over rule in the Congo Republic. He earned accolades from the Organization for African Unity for his efforts. As a long-term friend of former Zairean dictator, Mobutu Sese-Seko, Bongo also found himself embroiled in the multi-state conflict being waged in the new Democratic Republic of the Congo (DRC). Gabon has sided with Angola and the Congo Republic in opposing Kabila's DRC government and in calling for an end to support for the rebels still operating in eastern Angola. In 1998, Bongo hosted a Francophone summit that called on African states to deny fly-over and landing rights to planes ferrying arms and supplies to the Angolan rebels.

In 1999, Gabon concentrated on sustaining bilateral relationships through presidential visits to the United States and Canada and receiving high-level delegations from Cote d'Ivoire and Morocco. Morocco and Gabon have long been security partners, the former providing soldiers for Bongo's private security detail for years.

## ADDRESS

Presidence de la Republique
Boite Postale 546
Libreville, Gabon

## REFERENCES

Alcardi, Marc de Saint Paul. *Gabon: The Development of a Nation.* 1989.
*Agence France-Presse,* 4 December 1998, 12 December 1998.
*The Economist,* 1 January 1999.
Gardinier, David. *Historical Dictionary of Gabon.* 1981.
*Jane's Foreign Report,* 26 November 1998.
*Jeune Afrique,* 5 June 1990.
*Marches Tropicaux et Mediterraneans,* 15 December 1989.
Pan African News Agency, 12 December 1998.
*Washington Post,* 7 December 1998.
*Washington Times,* 10 December 1998, 24 December 1998.
*Weekly Mail and Guardian,* 27 June 1997, 2 October 1998.

**Profile researched and written by Jonathan T. Reynolds, Livingstone College (6/99; updated 2/2000).**

# GAMBIA

## Yahya A.J.J. Jammeh
## President
### (pronounced "YAH-ya JA-may")

*"We will continue to work for closer cooperation throughout, particularly with our closest neighbors."*

The Republic of the Gambia is named after the River Gambia which flows the length of the country's territory, extending eastward about 470 km (292 mi). Nestled on the sides of the banks of the river, the Gambia's land area of 11,295 sq km (4,361 sq mi) measures only about 24 km (15 mi) in width for most of its length and 50 km (31 mi) at its widest point. The country is surrounded by Senegal on its northern, southern, and eastern borders, and the Atlantic Ocean to the west. The Gambia's population has been estimated at 1.3 million, with more than 63% living in rural areas. The principal ethnic groups are the Mandinka (39.6%), Fula (18.8%), and Wollof (14.6%). About 85% of the people are Islamic, and most of the remainder are Christian. English is the official language, but Mandinka, Fula, Wollof, Jola, Serahula, and Serere are also spoken. Agriculture, forestry, and fisheries provide employment and income for almost 85% of the population. Groundnuts are the most important cash crop though tourism is the major source of foreign exchange. The per capita GDP has been estimated at US$1,000, and the currency is the *dalasi*.

## POLITICAL BACKGROUND

Gambia was declared a British protectorate in 1888 and gained independence as a constitutional monarchy in the British commonwealth system in 1965. In April 1970, it became a republic with Dawda Jawara as president. In 1981, an attempted coup was successfully thwarted by the Senegalese army. This incident and Gambia's geographic position led to the establishment of the Senegambian Confederation in 1982. Another consequence of the attempted coup was the establishment for the first time of a Gambian army. The purpose of the Senegambian Confederation was to coordinate defense, foreign affairs, and economic policies (including a trade and customs union). However, Gambia's lucrative re-export trade over the porous borders with Senegal would have been adversely affected by a trade and customs union. The Confederation seemed to fuel fears of Senegalese domination. Its dissolution in 1989 strained relations between the two countries.

Gambia under Jawara was one of the few African countries that had maintained civilian rule since independence. However, its multi-party government with a unicameral legislature was dominated by the People's Progressive Party (PPP). Opposition parties claimed that they were prohibited from effectively challenging Jawara. He was re-elected to a fifth term in April 1992. After unrest developed in the Gambian army, President Jawara signed a defense agreement with Nigeria that allowed Nigerian officers to head the Gambian army. Despite the presence of Nigerian officers in Banjul, Lieutenant Yahya Jammeh and several other lieutenants succeeded in overthrowing the government in a bloodless coup on 22 July 1994, ending one of Africa's more competitive political systems since independence.

## PERSONAL BACKGROUND

Yahya Jammeh, of the Jola ethnic group, was born on 25 May 1965 in Kanilai, a village in the Foni Kansala district of the western division of Gambia. In 1983, he completed his education at the Gambia High School and joined the National Gendarmerie. He received an officer's commission in 1989 and served in the Presidential Guards in 1989 and 1990. Jammeh entered the Gambia National Army with the rank of lieutenant in 1992. He received four months of military police officer's training at Fort McClellan, Alabama, in 1993–94. During that time he was appointed an honorary citizen of the state of Georgia and honorary lieutenant colonel in the Alabama state militia. He is married to Tali Faal-Jammeh.

## RISE TO POWER

After the 1994 coup, an Armed Forces Provisional Ruling Council (AFPRC) was formed, with Jammeh as chairman. The AFPRC announced a 14-member government that was evenly split between military and civilian members. Upon seizing power, the AFPRC issued decrees that restricted the political rights of Gambians. Pre-emptive arrests of military personnel with the rank of captain or major were carried out. The domestic situation continued to deteriorate. Civilians who had been co-opted to serve in the AFPRC government were removed from office and placed under detention. Harassment of the press increased. On 24 October 1994, the AFPRC announced that the transition program to return the country to civilian rule would not be accomplished until the end of 1998. The international community found this timetable unacceptable, and the Gambia labor movement, the Teachers Union, and the Bar Association demanded a speedier return to civilian rule.

## LEADERSHIP

On 11 November 1994, there was an attempted coup led by Lieutenant Basiru Barrow. Rumors of as many as 50 deaths were reported. The United Kingdom, Denmark, and Sweden, in particular, warned their citizens against traveling to Gambia. This led to an estimated loss of 25% of tourist industry employment. Responding to pressure for a return to civilian rule, the AFPRC established a National Consultative Committee (NCC) to review the issue.

The AFPRC reluctantly accepted the Committee's recommendation that the transition period be reduced to two years. The Jammeh regime decreed that no new political parties could be formed until three months before the elections. The suspension of the constitution and the ban on political parties and political activities also remained in effect. The government decided that a draft constitution had to be submitted to a referendum before the ban on politics was lifted. However, the AFPRC had formed its own 22 July Movement, which manifested all of the features of a political party and was used to contest the elections from an incumbency position. Presidential elections were postponed from July to September 1996.

On 14 August 1996, the ban on political parties and political activities was lifted for all but three pre-coup parties. The People's Progressive Party (PPP) of former president Jawara, the National Convention Party (NCP), and the Gambian People's Party (GPP) were banned for their "participation in 30 years of misrule in the country." The Commonwealth expressed deep concern over the government's decision and indicated that unless the Jammeh regime rescinded it, the Commonwealth could not endorse such a flawed process. In September, the president of Gambia's independent electoral commission also called for the release of political detainees.

Having conducted political rallies and organized pre-party activities via the 22 July Movement over a two-year period, the regime's Alliance for Patriotic Re-Orientation and Construction (APRC) gained a significant advantage over the other parties. Jammeh and three civilian rivals contested the presidential elections on 26 September 1996 in a heavily flawed process. Jammeh officially took 56% of the vote, becoming Gambia's second elected president in 31 years of independence. He was inaugurated 18 October 1996. Elections for the National Assembly were held on 2 January 1997. The APRC took 33 of 45 contested seats, the United Democratic Party took seven seats, the National Reconciliation Party two seats, the PDOIS one seat, and independents took the remaining two seats.

## DOMESTIC POLICY

In January 1994, the 50% devaluation of the CFA *franc* hurt Gambia's re-export trade via Senegal, a trade which already had suffered from a Senegalese embargo. The re-export trade has been estimated at up to 60% of the goods imported into Banjul (the country's only port) and then re-exported by road across Senegal for purchase by other West African countries. Gambia's liberal policy on custom duties and bureaucratic requirements had made its port popular among international merchants exporting goods to the West African sub-region. However, Senegal maintained that it was not collecting the

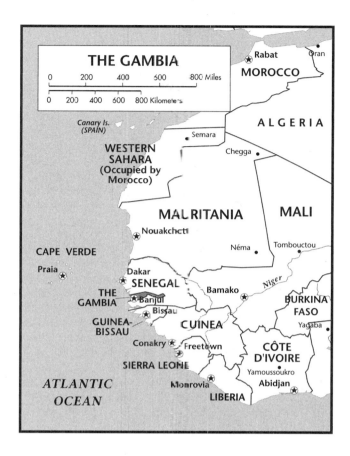

customs due on the re-exported goods, while Gambian merchants claimed that smuggling was carried out primarily by Senegalese. Gambia attempted, with limited success, to switch to coastal freighters and airfreight to avoid the adverse impact of Senegal's border closure. The military coup in July 1994 aggravated this situation further.

Following the 1994 coup, the European Union (EU) suspended all but humanitarian aid and funding for existing projects. The US suspended all assistance, as did the World Bank, which cut its assistance until a plan for returning Gambia to civilian rule was in place. Because development assistance constituted about 25.5% of Gambia's GNP, an estimated 20% of Gambia's labor force became unemployed. Over 10,000 workers lost their jobs in tourism, and considerable revenues in sales taxes, airport departure taxes, and income taxes were also lost. There was also considerable capital outflow as some established businesses moved their operations to the more stable neighboring Guinea-Bissau or Cape Verde. By reducing the transition timetable from four to two years, Jammeh was able to reinstate The Gambia in the donor countries' good graces.

Gambia turned in a solid economic performance in 1997, reducing its debt to US$430 million and increasing the real GDP by 4% (projected). Despite the flooding of 1999, cereals production was up 20%, and the government was estimating GDP growth of 4.2% in 1999. However, the IMF threatened to withhold further disbursement under the three-year enhanced structural adjustment facility (ESAF) dating from 1998 unless the government proceeded apace in selling off its hotels, telecommunications, and water and electricity utilities.

The peanut corporation (GGC), taken over by the government in January 1999, was a more immediate target of the IMF. Charges of embezzlement embarrassed the government, and the threat of smuggling the harvest into Senegal had serious implications for The Gambia's balance of payments.

An alleged coup attempt in January 2000 gave Jammeh an excuse to tighten his grip on state security and on military officers, promoting some and dismissing others. Jammeh is Jola, who make up only 10% of the population. The middle ranking and senior officers predominantly of the Mandinka and Fula ethnic groups have been removed.

## FOREIGN POLICY

During the first weeks of military rule Senegal distanced itself from the new regime, particularly as rumors developed of a Libyan connection within the AFPRC. Since then, President Jammeh has endeared himself to the Senegalese government by mediating the protracted Casamance (Senegal) secessionist movement led by members of the Jola ethnic group.

The Gambia gained international recognition by its membership in the Security Council as a non-permanent member for a two-year term, its first such appointment. Jammeh also became chairman of the Inter-state Committee on Drought in the Sahel (CILSS), a regional body established in the early 1980s to combat drought and famine in the semi-desert fringe bordering the Sahara in West Africa.

Gambia remains an active member of the Gambia River Basin Development organization, the Economic Community of West African States (ECOWAS), and the Organization of African Unity (OAU). Gambia was one of the few African countries that supported the US proposal for an All-African peace-keeping force to help resolve conflicts on the continent. In 1999, The Gambia sent 140 peacekeepers to Guinea-Bissau.

## ADDRESS
Office of the Chairman
State House
Banjul
Republic of the Gambia

## REFERENCES
Africa News Online. [Online] Available http://www.africanews.org/west/stories/1999_feat1.html (Accessed May 2000).
*Africa Report,* March/April 1994; January/February 1995.
*Africa Research Bulletin,* various issues.
*Africa South of the Sahara.* London: Europa Publications Ltd., 1999.
Africaonline. [Online] Available http://www.africa-online.com (Accessed May 2000).
Davidson, Basil. *African Civilization Revisited: From Antiquity to Modern Times.* Trenton, NJ: Africa World Press Inc., 1991.
Economist Intelligence Unit, Ltd. *EIU Country Reports.* 1999.
*The Gambia.* Banjul: Ministry of Tourism and Culture, 1995.
Gailey, Harry A. *Historical Dictionary of The Gambia.* Second Edition. *African Historical Dictionaries.* No. 4. Metuchen, NJ, and London: The Scarecrow Press, Inc., 1987.
Integrated Regional Information Network (IRIN). [Online] Available http://www.reliefweb.int/IRIN (Accessed May 2000).
Kandeh, Jimmy D. "What Does the 'Militariat' Do When it Rules?" *Review of African Political Economy,* September 1996, vol. 23, no. 69.
*West Africa,* 22–28, January 1996; 22–28 April 1996; 3–9 June 1996; 22–28 July 1996; 2–8 September 1996); 9–15 September 1996.
*World Bank Development Report: From Plan to Market.* Oxford: Oxford University Press, 1996.

**Profile researched and written by Mae C. King, Ph.D., Howard University (12/96; updated by Robert J. Groelsema 5/2000).**

# GEORGIA

## Eduard Shevardnadze
## President
*(pronounced "ed-WARD sheh-vard-NAHD-zeh")*

*"Only after we have shown the civilized world our determination to build a democratic society will the West begin actively to help us. The situation is grave. It is a question of saving this nation."*

Georgia borders Russia to the north, Armenia and Azerbaijan to the southeast, Turkey to the southwest, and the Black Sea to the west. Its land area is 65,201 sq km (26,872 sq mi). The capital of Georgia is Tbilisi ("tbee-LEE-see").

Georgia's population has been estimated at 5.1 million. A Soviet-era census reported that about 70% of the population was ethnically Georgian, 8% Armenian, 6% Russian, 6% Azerbaijani, 3% Ossetian, 2% Abkhazian, and the remainder were other. Abkhazians and Ajars have autonomous regions within Georgia despite the fact that they make up a minority of the population in the regions. The predominant church is the Georgian Orthodox Church.

The decline in Georgia's Gross Domestic Product (GDP) — some 80% over the period 1990–1994 — halted in 1995, with the economy growing 5.1% in 1998, led by the construction, oil, and services sectors. The World Bank reports, however, that GDP growth was set back late in 1998 as part of the fallout of the Russian financial crisis. Inflation also jumped late in 1998, but was a low 3.6% for the year. Budget deficits have been around 4–4.5% in 1995–99. Russia's 1998 financial crisis and the refusal of 90% of Georgians to pay taxes contributed in late 1998 to the substantial devaluation of the *lari*, price inflation for imports, and a nagging budget deficit that prevented the timely payment of pensions and state salaries. Shevardnadze reported in April 2000 that GDP growth was 4.4% in 1999, although budget deficits increased. Almost all housing and most small enterprises have been privatized, and over 80% of agricultural holdings and medium and large enterprises, though the slow registration of land titles has held back progress. Some port facilities and resource industries have been designated as strategic and the state will retain majority ownership. Exports are primarily agricultural goods that thrive in Georgia's Mediterranean climate, including tea and oranges. Georgia holds promise as a major north-south and east-west transit area. An "early oil" pipeline carrying about 100,000 barrels per day from Azerbaijan to Georgia's Black Sea port of Supsa (near Poti) opened in April 1999. Georgia is also a proposed route for a "main oil" pipeline (carrying larger volumes of oil) to the Turkish port of Ceyhan.

## POLITICAL BACKGROUND
The tribes that gave rise to the Georgian peoples first settled in the area between the 12th and 7th centuries BC, making them one of the oldest nations in the former Soviet Union. Georgia has endured waves of conquerors through its long

history: Romans, Iranians, Arabs, Turks, Mongols, and the hordes of Tamerlane. Fiercely independent, the Georgians managed to regain independence after each of these invasions. In the 19th century, Russia began a step-by-step conquest of Georgia, which it completed in 1878. Georgia gained its independence from the Czarist Empire in 1918. By 1921, Georgia gained recognition of its independence from 22 countries, including Soviet Russia. However, in February 1921 the Red Army invaded and conquered Georgia under the orders of Georgian Bolsheviks Sergo Ordzhonikidze and Joseph Stalin.

Despite Stalin's Georgian heritage and the fact that many of his henchmen in the security apparatus were Georgian, Georgia suffered as much as any region from Stalin's crimes, if not more. During the Khrushchev and Brezhnev periods, the Georgian leadership, which took bribes from the large private sector, was one of the most corrupt in the Soviet Union. A purge took place in the 1970s under the leadership of Georgian Interior Ministry chief and later republic Communist Party boss, Eduard Shevardnadze. *Perestroika* touched off Georgia's drive for independence, which received a decisive boost by the 9 April 1989 massacre of 20 peaceful demonstrators in Tbilisi by Soviet military forces. The massacre turned Georgians against the Communist Party. At the head of one of the opposition groups was former political prisoner, Zviad Gamsakhurdia, leader of the Round Table coalition of political parties. Gamsakhurdia's coalition decisively defeated the Communist Party in October 1990 elections to the Georgian Supreme Soviet. Gamsakhurdia was elected chairman of the legislature. He closed opposition newspapers, harassed and arrested opposition politicians, and installed his personal representatives throughout the country to ensure his decrees were carried out.

On 31 March 1991, a referendum on independence was endorsed by almost 80% of the electorate. Gamsakhurdia then proposed a formal declaration of independence, which was unanimously approved by the parliament on 9 April 1991. A month later, Gamsakhurdia was elected president of Georgia by 87% of the popular vote, partly because of the popularity of his defiant anti-Moscow stand but also because of his repression of the opposition.

Gamsakhurdia's increasing authoritarianism alienated many of his supporters, including his prime minister, Tenghiz Sigua. In addition, many were upset by Gamsakhurdia's behavior during the failed August 1991 coup when he first obeyed the instructions of the coup leaders before

condemning them as it became clear that the coup was collapsing. Sigua, Georgian National Guard commander, Tenghiz Kitovani, and other former Gamsakhurdia supporters joined to topple him, and after heavy fighting in Tbilisi, Gamsakhurdia in January 1992 was driven from the city. The opposition set up a "Military Council" chaired by Kitovani and Jaba Ioseliani, the commander of a paramilitary organization called *Mkhedrioni* (the horseman), dissolved the Georgian Supreme Soviet, and set up a provisional government, headed by Sigua. In an attempt to secure international acceptance in the wake of their takeover, the new leadership chose former Soviet foreign minister, Eduard Shevardnadze, as chairman of a new governing State Council on 11 March 1992.

## PERSONAL BACKGROUND

The son of a teacher, Eduard Amvroslyevich Shevardnadze was born on 25 January 1928 in the village of Mamati in western Georgia. His elder brother, Ippokrat, became a powerful Communist Party functionary and served as a mentor to Eduard. Shevardnadze's education was largely devoted to preparing him to join the Party apparatus. He studied at the Higher Communist Party School in Georgia and later earned a history degree from Kutaisi State Pedagogical Institute's correspondence school. He and his wife, Nanuli, have a son, Pata, a physicist, and a daughter, Monana. The Shevardnadzes have four grandchildren. Shevardnadze speaks Georgian and Russian.

People who have met Shevardnadze describe him as friendly, unpretentious, and often charming—yet meticulously polite and formal in public gatherings. Shevardnadze has also demonstrated ruthlessness in dealing with opponents, particularly when he was party chief in Georgia.

## RISE TO POWER

Shevardnadze's political career has had three stages. The first was his rise to the top of the Georgian Communist Party. He joined the party in 1948 and spent more than a decade in the Communist youth league, known as the *Komsomol*. In 1956, he became first secretary of the Georgian *Komsomol*. After holding various posts in the Communist Party apparatus in the early 1960s, Shevardnadze became Georgia's deputy minister of internal affairs in 1964 and minister of internal

affairs in 1965. In this position, he tried to fight rampant corruption in the republic. Georgian dissidents (including the former dissident Gamsakhurdia) bitterly note that the Georgian police imprisoned and tortured them during Shevardnadze's tenure. In 1972, Shevardnadze helped to engineer the dismissal of corrupt party leader Vasily Mzhavanadze and was elected to replace him. In his 13-year tenure as Georgia's leader, Shevardnadze conducted an expanded crackdown on corruption and introduced modest economic reforms that improved Georgia's economic performance. Shevardnadze became a member of the Soviet Communist Party Central Committee in 1976 and a non-voting member of the Soviet Politburo in 1978.

The second stage of Shevardnadze's career came when he was named USSR foreign minister on 1 July 1985, less than four months after Mikhail Gorbachev took power. This announcement came as a surprise to the international community since Shevardnadze had little previous foreign policy experience. Gorbachev and Shevardnadze had known each other since their tenure in the *Komsomol* in the 1950s. Gorbachev selected Shevardnadze in part because he saw in him many of his own qualities: pragmatism, energy, and a conviction that the Soviet system had become terribly corrupt and required radical reform. Shevardnadze launched the "new thinking" in Soviet foreign policy. This new pragmatic course aimed at reducing the Soviet Union's external burdens to allow domestic reform to succeed. The Soviet Union disengaged itself from costly foreign commitments, like the war in Afghanistan, and pursued a conciliatory line toward the West. After the collapse of the Soviet empire in Eastern Europe in 1989 and the reunification of Germany in 1990, Shevardnadze came under attack from conservatives who accused him of betraying the country. Frustrated by these charges, and by Gorbachev's shift toward a conservative domestic policy, Shevardnadze suddenly resigned as foreign minister in December 1990. In his resignation speech, he warned of a "coming dictatorship" in the Soviet Union if Gorbachev did not change course. After the failed Soviet coup in August 1991, which many saw as the fulfillment of Shevardnadze's warning, Gorbachev asked his old friend to resume his post as foreign minister. Shevardnadze at first refused, but in November 1991, he headed the foreign ministry for a few weeks before the dissolution of the Soviet Union in December 1991.

## LEADERSHIP

Shevardnadze's third career change might be viewed as a resumption of his first role as leader of Georgia. Because of his past as a Communist Party leader and KGB chief in Georgia, his initial opposition to Georgian independence and his inability to stop the Tbilisi massacre of 1989, Shevardnadze was anthema to many Georgians, especially those supporting Gamsakhurdia. The increasingly desperate situation in his country, he said, led him to accept the leadership of the State Council in March 1992 to rule until legislative elections could be held. This executive and legislative body was dissolved in October 1992 after the elections. Despite boycotts from nine electoral districts in Abkhazia, Mingrelia, and South Ossetia, and reported voter irregularities, a new unicameral legislature of 235 members was elected on 11 October 1992 in voting generally judged by international observers as "free and fair." The elections heralded the creation of a political system where the legislative chairman served as the highest official, and the presidency was abolished. The election law provided for the popular election of the chairman, who could not be a member of a political party. Shevardnadze, who ran uncontested, was elected speaker of the legislature, gaining 95% of the popular vote. After convening on 4 November, the new legislature granted Chairman Shevardnadze wide-ranging powers as head of state pending completion of a new constitution.

In November 1995, Shevardnadze was elected to the new post of president (re-created by the 1995 constitution), winning 74.3% of the vote in a six-man race. The voting was described by international observers as generally "free and fair," though violations were reported in Ajaria. He has been threatened by coup attempts and other civil disorder, but appeared successful in consolidating his power during 1995–96 by forcing most of his political opponents out of power.

Seven candidates were registered to run in Georgia's 9 April 2000 presidential election. The major challengers to Shevardnadze were Jumbar Patiashvili, former first secretary of the Georgian Communist Party (who ran in the 1995 presidential race), and Aslan Abashidze, Chairman of the Ajarian Supreme Council. Both challengers were leaders of the Revival Bloc that contested the 1999 legislative races. Abashidze did not actively campaign and withdrew from the race one day before the vote, alleging an unfair contest. Other speculation was that he withdrew in return for concessions from Shevardnadze on local power and finances. Voting did not take place in Abkhazia or South Ossetia. The Georgian Central Electoral Commission reported that Shevardnadze received 80% of 1.87 million votes, and Patiashvili received 17% (less than he received in 1995).

## DOMESTIC POLICY

Among Shevardnadze's early efforts to consolidate power and bring stability to Georgia, his greatest crisis was caused by military losses in Abkhazia in 1993–94. After Abkhazia's Supreme Soviet declared independence in July 1992, Georgia sent in troops to quell the secession. Shevardnadze had pursued peace talks with mediation by Russia's Foreign Ministry. In September 1993, the breaking of a ceasefire and heavy fighting caused Shevardnadze to fly to Abkhazia to take personal command, but the Abkhazians, with the aid of Chechens and other mercenaries (and connivance of some Russian military elements in Abkhazia), drove out all Georgian forces. Georgian and Abkhazian officials signed a Russian-brokered cease-fire in May 1994. As part of this agreement, Russian troops, formally acting as CIS "peacekeepers," were deployed in a security zone along the Inguri River which divides Abkhazia from Georgia. Shevardnadze stated in June 1997 that he had been forced to permit the CIS "peacekeepers" into Abkhazia because the UN had balked at sending a sizeable force. Another major crisis took place when Gamsakhurdia and his supporters launched an insurrection in the Mingrelian area of western Georgia and marched on Tbilisi. Shevardnadze appealed to Russia for assistance, and Russia's tank forces were instrumental in quelling the insurrection. As part of the price for Russia's military aid in defeating Gamsakhurdia, Georgia entered the CIS in 1993, and Shevardnadze signed the CIS Collective

Security Treaty, a Russian-Georgian Friendship Treaty, and border troop accords. (Russia's legislature has refused to ratify the latter.) Georgia's entrance into the CIS was regarded as anathema by many Georgians, though Shevardnadze stressed the "realism" of accommodating Russia at that time. In March 1995, the two sides signed a treaty granting Russia rights to four military bases through the year 2020. The Georgian legislature refused to ratify this basing accord. Although Shevardnadze initially viewed the basing agreement as a means to entice Russia to support Georgia's interests in settling the Abkhaz conflict, his government in the late 1990s called for removing the bases. Shevardnadze reportedly received strong US and Western support in pressuring Russia to close two of the bases by mid-2001 and to discuss closing the other two as part of the adaptation of the Conventional Armed Forces in Europe Treaty in November 1999. In January 1999, Georgia assumed full control over guarding its sea borders, and on 15 October 1999, the last Russian border troops left, except for some liaison officers.

As guided by Shevardnadze, a new constitution was approved by the legislature in August 1995. It reestablishes a strong presidency, though affirming a balance of executive and legislative powers more equitable than those in most other new constitutions approved by former Soviet republics. Under this constitution, voting for a new legislature took place simultaneously with the race for the re-created presidency on 5 November 1995. In the legislative race, only three of the 54 parties running received at least 5% of the party list vote required to win seats, though other parties won representation through constituency races. Shevardnadze's Citizens' Union Party won the largest bloc of seats, giving him major influence, though the legislature has at times opposed his policies. The election was judged "consistent with democratic norms" by international observers. Legislative elections were held most recently on 31 October 1999. Voting was by party lists (150 seats) and single-member constituencies (73 seats; 12 sitting members representing separatist Abkhaz districts were allowed to retain their seats). At the time of its convocation on 20 November 1999, the Citizens' Union Party held the largest bloc of seats, permitting it to claim the speakership and two of four deputy speakerships. Two other deputy speakers representing Abkhazia (the exiled government) and Ajaria marked a federal element.

In his presidential election manifesto, Shevardnadze stressed economic and social reforms. He called for eliminating poverty, creating a balanced budget, fighting corruption, eliminating wage and pension arrears, and reducing unemployment. He envisaged a five-year plan that would result in ample employment and a "normal" economy. His manifesto also called for the return of displaced ethnic Georgians to Abkhazia by 2005 and the restoration of Georgia's control over Abkhazia. After his re-election as president, Shevardnadze stated that he would deepen a process of national reconciliation of political factions by declaring an amnesty. In late April 2000 he stated that he might seek emergency powers or changes in the constitution to combat corruption and other economic problems.

## FOREIGN POLICY

Shevardnadze has sought good relations with both East and West in pursuit of security and reform aid, stating in April

2000 that "our main principle is state pragmatism....We are prepared to cooperate with all countries that help us resolve several fundamental problems...including our most important, burning issue, the settlement of the conflict in Abkhazia." Although Shevardnadze has attempted to maintain working political, economic, and security ties with Russia, he seeks close ties with the West and international organizations to maximize Georgia's independence. Relations with Russia deteriorated in late 1999 after it launched a new military campaign in its breakaway Chechnya region, which borders Georgia. Some fighting and refugees have spilled over Georgia's borders, and Russia has accused Georgia of aiding and abetting Chechen "terrorism." Russia's objectives toward Georgia include retaining some political, military, and economic influence in the South Caucasus region though its policies sometime seem contradictory and of limited success. Among its neighbors, Georgia has good relations with Armenia and Azerbaijan, though it has raised concerns about human rights conditions of ethnic Georgians residing in Azerbaijan, and Azerbaijan and Armenia have raised concerns about ethnic Azeris and Armenians in Georgia. Georgia has an ongoing interest in ties with about one million Georgians residing in Turkey and about 50,000 Georgians residing in Iran.

Shevardnadze assiduously pursued membership in the Council of Europe and the World Trade Organization as indicators of Georgia's progress in implementing Western-style reforms, resulting in admission to the Council of Europe in April 1999 and the World Trade Organization in October 1999. In April 2000, Shevardnadze hailed the support from the West, stating, "I can say without exaggeration that if it had not been for this support, including the financial and material support, we would not have survived and we would not have been able to build the independent Georgian state....The more we strengthen Georgian democracy, the more intensive the aid and support that we are receiving will become." His presidential election manifesto called for Georgia to seek entry into NATO by 2005.

## ADDRESS

Plekhanova 103
Tbilisi 880064, Georgia

## REFERENCES

*Plan Econ Report,* 17 March 1992.
*Problems of Communism,* November–December 1991.
*Radio Liberty Research Bulletin,* 3 July 1985, 17 January 1992.
*Washington Post,* 10 March 1992.

**Profile researched and written by Jim Nichol, Congressional Research Service (May 2000).**

# GERMANY

### Gerhard Schröder
### Chancellor
*(pronounced "SHROH-der",*

*"We want a new spirit in Germany, where people ask what they can do for their country."*

The Federal Republic of Germany comprises the former states of West Germany and East Germany, unified through a state treaty effective 3 October 1990. The country is situated in north central Europe and shares a border with Denmark to the north, Poland and the Czech Republic to the east, Switzerland and Austria to the south, and France, Belgium, the Netherlands, and Luxembourg to the west. The total area is 357,041 sq km (137,854 sq mi), with an estimated population of 82 million inhabitants. Berlin is the capital and largest city.

Germany is a culturally and ethnically homogenous nation, with German being the official language. The population is comprised primarily of ethnic Germans with approximately seven million non-ethnic German residents. The largest ethnic minorities consist of Turks, Yugoslavs, Italians, Greeks, and a small Slavic group. The country is predominantly Christian; in the north and east the majority is Protestant whereas in the south the majority is Roman Catholic.

Germany is a highly industrialized and urbanized country, with the largest economy in Europe. Its major exports are construction machinery, transport equipment, chemicals, iron and steel, textiles, fuels, and precision and optical equipment. The German currency is the *Deutsche mark* (DM).

## POLITICAL BACKGROUND

Upon defeat of the Nazi Reich in 1945, the country was divided into four occupied zones controlled by the US, Britain, France, and the Soviet Union. Similarly, Berlin was divided into four occupied sectors. In 1949, the American, British, and French leaders decided to unite their zones to form the Federal Republic of Germany (FDR), with Bonn as its capital. West Germany soon thereafter became integrated into the military and economic structures of the Western Alliance. The Soviet-occupied region became the German Democratic Republic (GDR), with East Berlin as its capital. East Germany entered the communist bloc comprised of the Soviet Union and other Central and Eastern European countries.

In 1989, following political upheavals in other communist Eastern European countries, popular protests erupted against the East German regime and its leader, Eric Honecker. A large number of East Germans fled to West Germany through neighboring countries. In an attempt to halt the exodus, East Germany closed its borders, setting off mass demonstrations in every major East German city. Without Soviet support, the

collapse of the communist regime appeared imminent, and on 9 November 1989, the Berlin Wall began to be dismantled. The West German chancellor, Helmut Kohl, championed appeals for the reunification of Germany and began talks to outline how the two countries would unify. On 3 October 1990, Germany became unified, and the first all-German elections took place the following December.

The Basic Law has been the constitution of West Germany since 1949 and continues to serve that purpose in the unified country. Germany is a federal state, with responsibilities divided between the federal government and the states (*Lander*). There are 16 *Lander* (10 from West Germany and six from East Germany). The head of state is the federal president (*Bundesprasident*), who is elected by a federal convention for a five-year term. The president serves primarily as a symbolic representative of the nation. In July 1999, Johannes Rau became the first Social Democratic president in 30 years.

Germany has a bicameral legislature consisting of the Federal Council (*Bundesrat*) and the National Assembly (*Bundestag*). Members of the *Bundesrat* (upper house) are appointed by states with no set terms and represent states' interests in policy areas that fall under joint federal-state jurisdiction. The *Bundesrat* has veto power only on legislative matters that concern the *Lande*. Legislative power rests primarily with the *Bundestag* (lower house). Members of the *Bundestag* are elected by universal suffrage to four-year terms, via a mixed direct and proportional electoral system, whereby representatives are elected by individual districts and chosen by party lists. Currently there are 669 seats in the *Bundestag*.

The major political parties in Germany and their respective number of seats following the 1998 election are: the center-left Social Democratic Party (SPD) with 298 seats; the center-right Christian Democratic Party (CDU) and its sister party in Bavaria, the Christian Social Union (CSU) with 245 seats; the liberal Free Democratic Party (FDP) with 44 seats; the Greens with 47 seats; and the Party of Democratic Socialism (PDS), the former East German Communist Party, entering the *Bundestag* for the first time with 35 seats.

The head of government is the chancellor (*Bundeskanzler*), who is elected from the *Bundestag* and is usually the head of the largest party or coalition. On 27 September 1998, Gerhard Schröder became chancellor-elect, ending Helmut Kohl's 16-year run as chancellor of Germany. In April 1999,

### GERMANY

0    100    200    300 Miles

0    100    200    300 Kilometers

Schröder married Doris Kopf, his fourth wife, in 1997. Kopf is a journalist from Bavaria, who assisted on Schröder's national election campaign. The Schröders have an apartment in Hannover.

## RISE TO POWER

Schröder's base of power has been his home state of Lower Saxony. He first made his name in German politics during the early 1970s as a leader of an anti-American, anti-nuclear youth group of the SPD. Upon completing his law training, Schröder became a member of the SPD Executive Committee for the Hannover constituency in 1977 and then the national chairman of the SPD Young Socialists the following year. In 1980, at the age of 36, he became a member of the *Bundestag*, representing the district of Hannover for six years. Schröder returned to Lower Saxony and served as chairman of the SPD Party Group and leader of the opposition in the Lower Saxony parliament from 1986 to 1990. He then focused on the premiership of Lower Saxony and won his party's nomination to run for premier in 1986. While he did not win that election, he won four years later and has been premier of Lower Saxony since that time.

In March 1998, Schröder won his third term as premier in a landslide victory. Many observers say that this success established Schröder as the most viable SPD candidate to challenge Helmut Kohl. In April, at the conference in Leipzig, Schröder won his party's nomination. On 27 September 1998, Schröder was able to defeat the longest-serving German chancellor since Otto von Bismarck.

## LEADERSHIP

As premier of Lower Saxony, Schröder achieved national prominence. But it has been his popularity with the general public, rather than his status within his party, that established him as a national leader. Observers have said that Schröder presents a new face to Germans, a modern alternative to a new generation, tired of 16 years of conservative rule. Critics have charged that the media-savvy, telegenic Schröder ran a "substance free" campaign, attempting to capture the mood of the electorate and avoiding any serious discussion of political goals and policies. Many within the SPD do not consider Schröder to be interested in a traditional leftist agenda. Rather, they view him as someone who is primarily interested in attaining power.

Schröder has advocated a moderate reformist agenda. He seeks practical solutions rather than ideological ones. His appeal for a "new center" echoes many of the themes of Britain's "New Labour." Adopting the slogan "We won't change everything—we'll just do things better," he has modeled himself after Tony Blair of the United Kingdom and Bill Clinton of the US.

Part of Schröder's effectiveness as a national leader arises from not being confined by the sentiments and policies of his party. He has built his national reputation by distancing himself from the party and by his willingness to cross party lines, which has not endeared him to the SPD leaders.

In 1999, Oskar Lafontaine resigned as chairman of the SPD and finance minister. Although he was highly regarded by the rank-and-file Social Democrats due to his leftist credentials, in the late 1990s he took the blame for the recession in Germany. Schröder named himself chairman of

he presided over the moving of the capital from Bonn back to Berlin.

## PERSONAL BACKGROUND

Gerhard Schröder was born in Mossenburg, a small town in Lower Saxony, on 7 April 1944. His birth occurred a few days before his father, a conscript in the German military, died on the eastern front in World War II. Schröder grew up in poverty; his widowed mother took cleaning jobs to raise the family. He had to leave school at the age of 14 to find a job. He worked as a hardware salesman before finishing secondary school. As a student, he proved himself an articulate speaker and an able debater. It was this struggle to get started in life, some observers say, that gave him a strong belief in the need for equal opportunity and propelled him into leftist politics.

Schröder took evening classes to get into college. With the support of the government, he studied law at Gottingen University during the turbulence of the late 1960s. During his college years, Schröder became involved in leftist politics. He led the Young Socialists, a youth organization of the Social Democratic Party in the district of Hannover, the state capital of Lower Saxony. He was a mainstream Marxist and demonstrated against the installation of US nuclear missiles in West Germany. In 1972, he continued his post-graduate judicial service training and received his law degree in 1976 at the age of 32. From 1976 until 1990, Schröder was employed as a lawyer in Hannover. Prior to the election, he served as a supervisory board member of Volkswagen AG and Norddeutsche Landesbank.

the SPD and named Hans Eichel finance minister. The party officially elected him chairman in December.

With 298 of 669 total seats in the *Bundestag*, the Social Democrats failed to gain a majority. Therefore, the SPD has entered into a coalition government, as is the usual case in German politics. Schröder's SPD has entered into a historic "Red-Green coalition." With the Greens' 47 seats, Schröder controls a majority of 21 seats. He named Joschka Fisher, the popular leader of the pragmatic wing (*realos*) of the Green Party, to be foreign minister and vice chancellor. Sharing power may provide another challenge to Schröder's leadership abilities. The radical wing of the Green Party (*fundis*) has been most vocal in advocating policies such as opposing NATO expansion, instituting steep "ecology taxes," and closing all of Germany's 20 nuclear power stations. These issues may strain the coalition partnership.

## DOMESTIC POLICY

The major issues that Schröder faces include unemployment, the overburdened welfare system, and the immigrant question. Germany's unemployment rate is currently 10.6% with four million unemployed workers. Schröder pledged that he would bring 100,000 unemployed youths into training programs. He also emphasized that a more flexible organization of work was needed and that business should invest and innovate their industries. In eastern Germany, unemployment rates are nearly double the national average, with one in five people of working age out of a job. Schröder has promised to foster reconciliation in a country still divided by economic inequalities. The Social Democrats and Greens agree on the need to bring together employers and labor unions to discuss a program to create jobs, perhaps through pledges of wage restraints from unions and pledges of jobs from employers. The cost of hiring a German worker is among the highest in the world.

While Schröder supports Germany's generous welfare state, he is searching for ways to adapt Germany's expensive welfare system to global competition and reduce the tax burden on citizens. Partly due to the high expenditures in eastern Germany after unification, and partly because of competition with other countries, Germany can no longer afford to maintain the restrictive labor laws, ample pensions, and generous health care system. Schröder has said that the welfare state has reached its limits and has emphasized the need to balance social compassion with fiscal prudence. Both the Green Party and the SPD seem united in a desire to preserve at least the foundations of the welfare system against more radical free-market reforms. Schröder hoped that appointment of Oskar Lafontaine as finance minister would aid in the defense of minimum social, ecological, and welfare standards against the deregulation that global markets tend to inspire, but in fact Lafontaine resigned when the economy lagged.

Under the Schröder government, immigration laws seem likely to change. The treatment of Germany's seven million immigrants has been a salient issue in past elections. Schröder pledged that his government "will make it possible to have dual citizenship," allowing many German-born children of immigrants to become citizens. The SPD has traditionally been more favorable toward integrating non-ethnic Germans. In 1999, the Schröder government changed the citizenship laws to allow people who have lived in Germany for eight years or longer to apply for citizenship (formerly open only to those whose parents were born in Germany).

## FOREIGN POLICY

As chancellor, Schröder must lead Germany through the final stages of European integration, including monetary union. He plans to continue German foreign policy on its present course, including a strong commitment to NATO, to the European Union, and to Russian economic development. As the region's strongest economic nation, Germany plays a crucial role in the process of European integration. While Germany supports European unification, it is no longer willing to be considered the "rich uncle" of the EU, especially given the economic demands of unification and the heavy investments made for Russian economic development. Germany has demanded that the rules be rewritten for a more equitable distribution of payments among EU members.

Schröder must preside over a Germany that is contemplating a larger, more independent role in international affairs. While the German constitution bans deploying troops outside of the NATO area, amendments have allowed the use of German troops for UN peacekeeping and humanitarian operations in the Balkans and in Somalia. Schröder expressed support for greater German participation in international operations, saying that he would intervene in the embattled Serbian province of Kosovo if the UN remained silent and other European countries wanted to act.

## ADDRESS

Bundeskanzler
Adenauerallee 141
5300 Bonn 1, Germany

## REFERENCES

*Christian Science Monitor*, 10–30 September 1998.

German Information Agency. *The Week in Germany*, 24 April 1998; 11 September 1998.

"Eyes on the Prize: Germany's Chancellor Talks About the Need for Social and Economic Change and His Country's Central Role in Building the New Europe." *Time International*, 15 November 1999, p. 30+.

"Germany Is Leading—In the Wrong Direction." *Business Week*, 13 December 1999, p. 66.

*Manchester Guardian Weekly*, 4 October 1998.

*New York Times*, 21–28 September 1998.

**Profile researched and written by S. Martin Hwang, Binghamton University (12/98; revised 6/2000).**

# GHANA

**Jerry Rawlings**
**President**

*(pronounced "JER-ee RAW-lings")*

*"Democracy and elections did not drop down from the sky...*
*They were a stage in a long process. After all, what is democracy*
*if the people at the grassroots are not empowered to make decisions affecting themselves?"*

The Republic of Ghana occupies 238,540 sq km (92,100 sq mi) of territory in Western Africa. The capital is Accra, located on the southern coast. Its southern boundary is the Gulf of Guinea in the Atlantic Ocean; to the east it is bordered by Togo; to the north by Burkina Faso; and to the west by Cote d'Ivoire (Ivory Coast). It is inhabited by 18.9 million people, 99% being black African, from the Akan, Moshi-Dagomba, Ewe, and Ga peoples. Fewer than 1% of the population are of European or other non-African extraction. English is the official language of government and business, although as many as 75 African languages and dialects are spoken as well. Approximately 43% of Ghanaians profess Christian beliefs and 30% are Muslim. However, 38% adhere to indigenous religious practices, indicating that a significant proportion have adopted new religions without discarding traditional systems.

The Ghanaian economy is heavily reliant on agriculture and mineral extraction. Chief exports include cocoa, timber and gold. Per capita GDP currently stands at US$1,800. The currency of Ghana is the *cedi*. Unemployment stands at 20% and underemployment is also problematic.

## POLITICAL BACKGROUND

Ghana has experienced four coups and three republics since it was granted independence from Britain in 1957. The failure of each regime is usually linked to difficult economic conditions and official corruption. The regime of Kwame Nkrumah, the new nation's first prime minister, was marked by increasing levels of authoritarian rule coupled with growing financial mismanagement and economic decline. In 1964 the army and police staged a successful coup d'etat, and overthrew the Nkrumah government. A new government was established, headed by the National Liberation Council. The second republic was instaurated in 1969, after parliamentary elections gave a majority to the Progress Party, led by Kofi Busia. In response to increasing public discontent with the economy, the military once again seized power. The new government organized itself as the National Redemption Council and was headed first by I.K. Acheampong and later by Frederick Akuffo. Neither leader was able to improve the economic situation or to rid the regime of endemic corruption. On 4 June 1979, the Akuffo government was overthrown in a violent coup by a group of junior military officers. The leaders formed the Armed Forces Revolutionary Council (AFRC), with Flight Lieutenant Jerry Rawlings as its chairman.

## PERSONAL BACKGROUND

Jerry John Rawlings was born in Accra on 22 June 1947, the son of John Rawlings, a Scottish retail chemist and Victoria Agbotui, a Ghanaian of the minority Ewe ethnic group. He was educated at Achimoto College, Ghana's leading secondary school, after which he entered the military academy at Teshie. Attracted at first by the security of a military career, Rawlings found that it also provided an outlet for his growing interest in politics. Commissioned a second lieutenant in 1969, Rawlings volunteered to serve in a squadron of jet fighters which had a training fatality rate of 50%. He proved himself a superior pilot and was awarded trophies for his skills in airborne maneuvers. In 1978 he was promoted to the rank of Flight Lieutenant.

Jerry Rawlings has been married since 1977 to Nana Konadu Agyeman; the couple has one son and three daughters. To keep up appearances, Rawlings and his wife were living together in 1999, though speculation was that their marriage had all but dissolved. With political ambitions of her own and a Machiavellian temperament, Nana Konadu Agyeman has been cited as a possible successor to Rawlings. Tall and good-looking, Rawlings tends to cut a dashing appearance in public. His choice of recreational activities includes flying, swimming, marksmanship, and reading.

## RISE TO POWER

During his military career, Rawlings developed a passion for politics and a deep-seated moral outrage at the rapacious corruption of senior officers. Even after the Acheampong regime was overthrown, Rawlings wanted to ensure that those most responsible for the economic mismanagement would not be allowed simply to retire and live off the spoils of their corruption. Thus on 15 May 1979 Rawlings staged an unsuccessful coup against the Akuffo government. He was court martialed for the attempt, and during the trial he attacked the military for its ineptitude and corruption. A complete unknown at the time of the failed coup, by the end of the trial Rawlings was being applauded daily for his outspoken stand against the military. On 4 June 1979 Rawlings was freed from jail by a group of junior officers. Later that day, after a brief but violent struggle, the group ousted Akuffo and seized power in the capital.

Rawlings created the Armed Forces Revolutionary Council (AFRC) and immediately introduced policies aimed at ridding the government of corruption. He also promised that elections would be held as scheduled on June 18, although the return to civilian rule would be postponed until the fall, in order for some of the anti-corruption measures to take effect. Rawlings orchestrated trials by secret tribunal of former heads of state, who were convicted of squandering government funds, economic sabotage, and amassing wealth by abuse of power; all were summarily executed. Rawlings kept his pledge that the AFRC was a temporary government, and elections were held as scheduled later in the month. In a runoff election on 10 July 1979, Dr. Hilla Limann was elected president, and was inaugurated on 24 September 1979, when Rawlings made good his promise to relinquish power.

The political and economic circumstances in which Limann came to power were such that there were no easy answers to any of Ghana's many problems. The economy was in shambles, with 80% inflation, cocoa production at a record low point, and industry functioning at 25% of capacity. Politically, Limann was not well-known and was overshadowed by the charismatic Rawlings. Trying to defuse the situation, Limann dispatched the members of the AFRC to posts abroad, and retired Rawlings from military service, on the grounds that a former head of state could not properly return to service as a junior officer. Retirement gave Rawlings the leisure to engage full-time in political activity, and his home in Accra was soon the unofficial headquarters of the opposition. In 1980 Rawlings was arrested on suspicion of plotting a coup and spent a short time in jail. Despite several small steps aimed a economic recovery, Limann did not have the political will or popular support necessary to enact the difficult measures required to improve Ghana's economy. By 1981, inflation had climbed to over 100% and factory utilization had fallen to 20%. On 31 December 1981, citing Limann's direction down the road of economic ruin, Rawlings once again seized power.

The seven-member Provisional National Defense Council (PNDC) promptly suspended the constitution, dissolved the legislature, banned political parties, and imposed a dusk-to-dawn curfew. Notable in this takeover was the lack of a promise by Rawlings to quickly return power to civilians.

## LEADERSHIP
The PNDC was notably different from Ghana's previous military regimes both for its tenure and for its violence. Merchants were required to lower prices on goods, the order often coming at gunpoint; those who failed to comply were publicly flogged and their stalls and merchandise destroyed. Military personnel who failed to support the coup were executed and there were reports that hundreds of civilians died as well.

Although still intent of ridding Ghanaian politics of corruption, Rawlings appeared not to have any other concrete plan to address the nation's problems. His rhetoric became more populist and anti-Western than previously and he promised a radical regime. Broad changes were proposed for the judiciary, and Rawlings ordered the formation of workers' councils and people's defense committees in an attempt to mobilize the masses to his cause.

The PNDC received enthusiastic initial support, but by 1984 the lack of economic progress was generating popular discontent. Several attempted coups were reported between 1984 and 1987. District-level elections scheduled for mid-1987 were postponed until late 1988 and the ban on political

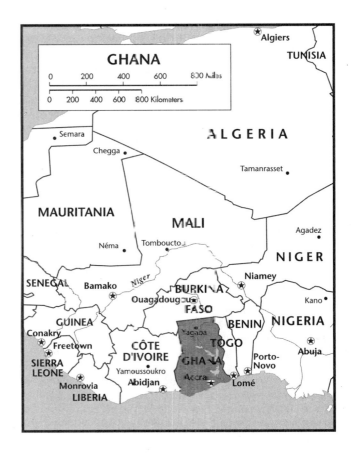

parties remained in effect. The elections took place between December 1988 and February 1989, after extensive reorganization of the country at the district level, and with one-third of the seats reserved for PNDC appointees.

Under pressure from Western donor nations, Rawlings announced in July 1990 the formation of a National Commission for Democracy, whose task it would be to determine the political future of the country. In December 1990 Rawlings proposed the introduction of a new constitution by the end of 1991. The NCD presented its recommendations in March 1991, and these included the election of an executive president for a fixed term, the establishment of a legislature and the creation of the post of prime minister. In May the PNDC endorsed the recommendations as well as the return to a multi-party system, although the ban on political associations was reiterated in no uncertain terms. Later that month the PNDC announced the creation of a 260-member consultative assembly whose purpose was to present a new constitution to the government by the end of the year. In August Rawlings announced that presidential and legislative elections would take place in late 1992. The new constitution, which provided for a president elected to a four-year term by universal suffrage, was presented at the end of March 1992. A national referendum in April 1992, brought about the adoption of the new constitution.

Elections were held in November 1992, and Rawlings was elected. Opposition leaders were distressed not only by the results, but by the amount of fraud they claim was perpetrated by Rawlings' National Democratic Congress (NDC). As a result, they boycotted the second round in which voters elected parliamentary representatives. NDC candidates won

198 of the 200 legislative seats; the remaining two were won by independent candidates. The government of Ghana's Fourth Republic was inaugurated in January 1993.

The 1996 elections again represented a contest between the overwhelming organization of Rawlings and the NDC and a disorganized and contentious opposition. Having learned the lesson in 1992 that a fragmented opposition rarely attains electoral success, the New Patriotic Party (NPP) and the People's Convention Party (PCP) created the Great Alliance and backed one candidate, John Kufour. Edward Mahama of the Peoples National Convention (PNC) was also a candidate. This was a hotly-contested election, and voters turned out in large numbers—76.8% of eligible voters cast ballots. When the votes were tallied Rawlings had been reelected with 57.2% of votes cast. The Parliamentary elections were held the same day: of the 200 seats, Rawlings' NDC won 130, the NPP won 59, and the PNC won one.

Rawlings has stated publicly that he will stand down freely upon the completion of his second term in December 2000. The Constitution prohibits a third term. While there is speculation that he may do otherwise, and members of his own party may not want him to do so, he appears ready to take on other responsibilities, perhaps as one of Africa's new elder statesmen. If he does leave on schedule, his legacy of having led Ghana into the early stages of democratization and decentralization may well overshadow his past transgressions.

## DOMESTIC POLICY

Domestically, Rawlings has faced two principal challenges to his continuation in power. In the early 1980s there were frequent reports of attempted coups against the regime. Rawlings responded brutally whenever he was confronted by such a threat to his authority: conspirators were jailed or executed, all political opposition was banned. As he has maintained himself in power, Rawlings' authority has been challenged with decreasing frequency, and those challenges have recently been coming through more acceptable channels.

The other issue with which Rawlings has dealt is the economy. Vowing to set Ghana on a revolutionary road, and peppering his speeches with fiery radical slogans and promises, Rawlings' first attempts at economic reforms were disastrous. By 1983 the economy was shrinking at an annual rate of 6%, inflation was above 100%, exports had collapsed, and in some areas of the country there was famine. Although he continued to espouse revolutionary change in his public pronouncements, Rawlings altered the economic course he had set for Ghana and adopted free-market policies. These were largely a success: inflation fell to 10% by the early 1990s and growth was about 5% annually. Unfortunately, Rawlings elected to use public resources to ensure his victory in the 1992 elections, and bowed to the demands of special interests: the result was to unravel much of the economic progress which had been made during the previous decade. After the election, Rawlings returned to more prudent economic management and things once again began to improve.

During the 1996 campaign, Rawlings refrained from repeating his behavior of four years earlier.

Despite low real GDP growth in 1999 (est. 3%), annual inflation at 14%, and a sliding CEDI, donors and foreign business partners remained bullish on Ghana, largely because of Rawlings' compelling personality and perceived personal commitment to ridding the country of corruption. In May, at the Accra Economic Summit, business and public sector leaders gathered for an African-American summit in Accra to explore business links. In June, Japan announced the donation of US$16.5 million for importing machinery, spare parts, and industrial materials. The EU provided financing for rural roads an electrification in the amount of 66 million Euros. The US firm, CMS Energy Corporation, announced that its subsidiary, CMS Generation, and its Ghanaian partner, the Volta River Authority (VRA), signed a US$44 million engineering, procurement, and constructions contract with Black and Veatch to build a 110 megawatt electric generating unit in Ghana.

## FOREIGN POLICY

Ghana is an active member of the UN, as well as the Non-Aligned Movement, the Organization of African Unity and the Economic Community of West African States. Ghana as a rule adopted positions taken by the Non-Aligned Movement and OAU on issues which did not affect it directly. Ghanaian troops are frequently members of UN peacekeeping forces, and have been part of ECOWAS' ECOMOG peacekeeping forces in Liberia and Sierra Leone. Rawlings' government maintains close ties with Cuba, Libya, and other ideologically similar countries. However, ideology is not a condition for favorable diplomatic relations and Ghana seeks friendly relations with all countries.

US-Ghanaian relations at the official level have suffered strains intermittently since Rawlings' takeover in 1979. The Rawlings government on several occasions publicly accused the US of sympathizing with the opposition. The nadir was reached in 1983 when the US froze development aid in response to false accusations. Although relations warmed somewhat the following year, 1985 saw yet another low point after another series of allegations against the US. The 1990s have seen a genuine effort on the parts of both countries to effect a warming in bilateral relations capped by Rawlings' visit to Washington in February 1999.

In 1999, Ghana concluded a number of important regional deals. It joined forces with South Africa to oppose the IMF and Britain's gold sales, which would severely depress the sector in both countries. With a high powered delegation from neighbor Côte d'Ivoire, it established an ad-hoc technical committee to develop strategies for cocoa marketing. The government also signed a memo of understanding with Nigeria, Benin, Togo and Chevron and Shell on the US$400 million Nigerian gas pipeline.

## ADDRESS

Office of the President
PO Box 1627
Accra, Ghana

## REFERENCES

Africa News Online. [Online] Available http://www.africanews.org/west/stories/1999_feat1.html
Africa Online. [Online] Available http://www.africa-online.com
*Africa Report,* March–April 1994.

*Africa Today,* Fall 1995.

*African Affairs,* April 1995.

*Africa South of the Sahara.* Europa Publishers, 1999.

*EIU Country Reports.* Economist Intelligence Unit Ltd., 1999.

Integrated Regional Information Network (IRIN). [Online] Available http://www.reliefweb.int/IRIN

*Journal of Black Studies,* March 1994.

*Journal of Modern African Studies,* vol. 34, no. 2.

*Panafrican News Agency,* 7–13 December 1996.

U.S. Department of State. *1995 Country Reports on Economic Policy and Trade Practices: Ghana.*

_____. *FY 1997 Country Commercial Guide: Ghana.*

_____. *Ghana Country Report on Human Rights Practices for 1996.*

**Profile researched and written by Alison Doherty Munro (4/97; updated by Robert J. Groelsema, 5/00).**

# GREECE

## Costas Simitis
## Prime Minister

*(pronounced "CUSS-tohs seh-MEE-tees")*

*"Our task is to link the past experience with the necessary renovation."*

Greece, known officially as the Hellenic Republic, is located in the southern tip of the Balkan Peninsula. Greece consists of the mainland and numerous islands, both on the Ionian and Aegean Seas, covering a total size of 131,957 sq km (51,146 sq mi). The population has been estimated at 10.7 million. The two largest cities are Athens and Salonika. The population of the Hellenic Republic is composed primarily of Greeks but also includes minority groups of Muslim Turks and others. The vast majority of the Greek population (98%) belong to the official Eastern Orthodox Church.

Greece's economy is primarily agricultural. However, tourism and shipping are also among the most important activities that contribute to foreign exchange earnings. Other industries include textiles, food, and tobacco processing, chemicals, mining, and petroleum. Principal Greek exports are textiles, cement, chemicals, basic metals, fruits, vegetables, olives, and oil. Major import items are petroleum, machinery, and transport equipment, iron and steel, plastic materials, and meat. The Greek currency is the *drachma*.

## POLITICAL BACKGROUND

Twentieth-century Greek history records repeated confrontations with its neighbor Turkey (the successor of the Ottoman Empire). Greece gained its independence from the Ottoman Empire in 1830 after a prolonged war of liberation with substantive help from Great Britain, France, and Russia. Territorial disputes with the Ottoman Empire over the disposition of the Balkan territories brought about a succession of Balkan Wars (1912–13). After these wars were concluded, Greece significantly increased the size of its territories at the Ottoman Empire's expense.

After World War I, Greece occupied western Anatolia following the defeat of the Ottoman Empire. The occupation, though, resulted in Greece's military defeat and a massive exchange of populations between Turkey and Greece. In total, about 1.5 million refugees came to Greece, and about 800,000 Turks were transferred from Greece to Turkey by 1922. Also, Greece and Bulgaria agreed to an exchange of their ethnic minorities; about 92,000 Bulgarians left Greece for Bulgaria, and 46,000 Greeks emigrated from Bulgaria to Greece.

From 1925 to 1935, Greece was a republic. After the restoration of the monarchy, a right-wing dictatorship was established by Ioannis Metaxas. In October 1940, however, Greece was attacked by the Italians, and after April 1941 the German occupation forces controlled political power in the country. The Greek monarchy was returned to power in

1946, after the end of Axis occupation during the Second World War. The civil war between the royalists and Communists that erupted during this period ended when Communists were defeated with British and US military assistance in 1949.

In 1964 a center-left coalition called the Center Union led by George Papandreou gained a parliamentary majority, ending the long period of successive conservative governments of 1949–64. This new era was marked by continual political crises as the country remained ideologically polarized between left and right, leading to the establishment of a military junta in 1967.

Political difficulties, the disputes with Turkey, and growing inflation laid the groundwork for transition to civilian rule. In the 1974 parliamentary elections, Constantine Karamanlis was confirmed as the prime minister. Karamanlis, the leader of the center-right New Democracy (ND), further expanded his political influence following the 1977 elections, in which his party gained a substantial victory.

In the 1981 general election, Andreas Papandreou's left-wing Panhellenic Socialist Movement (PASOK) won a clear victory. Papandreou was reelected in 1985. His party lost power in 1989 because of highly-publicized scandals. After four years in opposition, PASOK returned to the government, again headed by Papandreou, in the elections of October 1993. Illness forced his resignation on 15 January 1996, and Costas Simitis was sworn in as his replacement. Hoping to achieve a broad mandate from voters, he called for legislative elections on 22 September. His Panhellenic Socialist Movement won 41.5% of the vote—giving him a comfortable majority in parliament. Under Simitis's leadership, PASOK won reelection on 9 April 2000 with 43.8% of the vote.

Despite significant military influence in the past, Greece is now a parliamentary democracy with a 300-member national assembly. Political power rests largely with the premier while the president fills a mainly ceremonial role. Following the 9 April elections, the major political parties represented in parliament are PASOK (158 seats) and ND (125 seats). The remainder of seats are held by the Greek Communist Party (KKE) and Coalition of the Left and Progress (SYN).

## PERSONAL BACKGROUND

Costas Simitis was born in Athens on 26 January 1936. He is the son of George Simitis, an attorney and professor. He is married to Fani Arkadiou and has two children.

Simitis was trained in Germany and Britain. He studied law and economics at the University of Marburg in the

Federal Republic of Germany between 1954 and 1959. He gained his *Doctor Juri* (PhD) from the University of Marburg in 1959. During 1961 and 1963, he studied at the London School of Economics and Political Science.

Since 1961 he worked as an attorney and taught commercial law at several universities. In 1971 he was assistant professor at the University of Konstanz in Germany. He served as a full professor of commercial law and civil law at the Justus Liebig University in Giessen during 1971–75. Since 1977 he has taught commercial law at the Pantions University of Political Sciences. He is the author of several books on political science and law and has also published numerous articles in law reviews.

In 1965 he was one of the founders of the Alexandros Papanastasiou Society (Society for Political Research and Studies). During 1967–69 he undertook clandestine actions against the junta but avoided arrest by escaping abroad. In 1970 he served as a member of the National Council of the Panhellenic Liberation Movement (PAK). During 1969–74 he stayed in Germany and participated in public meetings in opposition to the Greek dictatorship.

On 3 September 1974, the PASOK (Panhellenic Socialist Movement) was founded. Simitis was one of the founding members and served on the central and the executive committees. He served as minister of agriculture between October 1981 and 1985, and minister of national economy from June 1985 to October 1987. He was elected to parliament four times since 1985. From June 1989 to November 1989, he was minister of education. After the October 1993 elections, he became minister of industry, energy, technology, and commerce.

## RISE TO POWER

Although Simitis undertook many posts in every Papandreou government, he remained a largely unpublicized and silent figure. Yet, he was critical of his leader's fervent style and excessively populist policies. Simitis was opposed to Papandreou's anti-European Union and anti-American rhetoric. He favored a modernization of PASOK and espoused more moderate policies in foreign affairs. His resignation in September 1995 from the Papandreou government, over economic policy differences, increased his visibility as a leading anti-Papandreou dissident.

When Papandreou fell ill and was admitted to the hospital, Simitis and others within PASOK who had argued for changes within the party found a favorable environment for advancing their reformist vision. Although Papandreou was reluctant to relinquish power to this reformist wing, Simitis was elected by PASOK deputies as party leader and prime minister on 22 January 1996. He defeated acting Prime Minister Akis Tsokhatzopoulos in the second round of voting at the party convention. He also eliminated his other rivals, Defense Minister Gerosimos Arsenis and former Deputy Prime Minister Yannis Haralambopoulos. Simitis's success marked a victory for the reformist wing and may usher in a period of party changes within PASOK.

## LEADERSHIP

The qualities which make Simitis a strong leader include his ability to form consensus among the factionalized PASOK and his moderate style. After coming to power Simitis

pursued a policy of compromise and moderation vis-à-vis his former opponents in PASOK. He carefully avoids confrontation, seeks dialogue, and tries to present himself as a pragmatic and realistic leader.

Simitis's success as a leader was dependent upon his ability to reform PASOK. To do so he had to placate both ex-Papandreou followers and the more conservative elements in the party. While the ideological gap was quite large, Simitis has already demonstrated his leadership skills.

First, he has offered ministerial positions to both factions of PASOK. His chief rival, Akis Tsokhatzopoulos, for example, was given the important position of minister of defense. Another rival, Gerasimos Arsenis, became minister of education. George Papandreou, the former prime minister's son, was also given a cabinet position. Clearly Simitis is trying to maintain unity in his party, while simultaneously moving it closer to the center of the political spectrum.

Simitis has carefully implemented a policy of reform, thus undermining the main opposition party's (New Democracy) platform. He has revamped his party's policies so that PASOK and New Democracy now agree on many major issues facing the country. By doing this, Simitis has effectively undercut ND's potential ammunition against his party.

Although lacking Andreas Papandreou's fervent charisma, the new leader of Greece smoothly transformed the political balance, both within PASOK and Greek politics at large, by shifting power to the reformist side. As a man uncomfortable with public attention, Simitis has managed to avoid the disruptive factional tensions that had long haunted PASOK.

## DOMESTIC POLICY

Although Andreas Papandreou and Simitis were members of the same political party, the election of Simitis signaled major domestic and foreign policy changes. During the first months Simitis pursued reforms that contradicted Papandreou's socialist vision. Simitis and his associates, while still professing socialist ideals, adopted pro-Western and pro-market policies. Late Premier Andreas Papandreou's son, George Papandreou, stated that the new policies reflect "the liberal American tradition."

The Greek economy experienced marked difficulty in the early 1990s. Simitis responded by sharply reducing government spending to control the deficit and inflation. By the end of 1998, inflation had been reduced to 4%. Furthermore, the economy is now showing signs of growth. The new government also improved tax collection by imposing a net worth tax.

Simitis's economic policies emphasize austerity, monetary rigor, and privatization. He favors austerity measures to bring Greece's economy in line with those of its European Union partners. He also wants to partially privatize the national telecommunications company and the national petroleum corporation, and to push for the compilation of EU-funded public works. He has promised to reduce red tape in order to attract more foreign investors.

Simitis also hopes to sweep away the sprawling and inefficient bureaucracy and replace it with meritocracy. He tackled the patronage system by cutting unnecessary jobs in the civil service and public sectors and ordered his economic minister to eliminate at least 15,000 civil service jobs over the next three years and make deep cuts in local government spending.

## FOREIGN POLICY

Simitis's tight economic policy stems from his eagerness to bring Greece closer to NATO and the European Union (EU). Since coming to power Simitis has visited the nations of Western Europe and the US to improve relations. Contrary to Papandreou's anti-NATO, anti-EU views, Simitis aims to meet Maastricht targets by the end of the decade and participate in the European monetary union by 2002. He believes that Papandreou's policies created an economy that could not meet the demands of the European Union standards. His policies emphasize Greece's obligations—reducing inflation, unemployment, and the budget deficit. He seeks to harmonize the Greek economy with that of other EU countries, which is the cornerstone of his foreign policy.

Concern over Turkish actions in the region has prompted Simitis to pursue a pragmatic approach to regional affairs. A top priority is dealing calmly with Turkey. After serving in the office for barely a month Simitis had to deal with a dispute over two islets in the Aegean Sea, which brought Greece and Turkey close to war. His capable handling of this dispute without resorting to harsh means sent a positive signal to the international community. He adeptly managed the crisis through negotiation, much to the anger of opposition politicians. He hopes to solve the long-standing conflict with Turkey through mediation in the international court at the Hague.

Simitis seeks closer ties with the former Yugoslav Republic of Macedonia. In the past Greece also mishandled relations with Bulgaria and Albania. The Simitis government stresses the importance of improving relations with its Balkan neighbors through diplomatic and legal channels instead of resorting to inflammatory rhetoric. If peace in the region is sustained, Greece hopes to prosper as a major trading partner in the region.

Simitis's third year in power provided the moderate leader with his most serious challenges in foreign relations. That February, relations with Turkey reached a new low following the capture of Kurdish terrorist leader Abdulah Ocalan by elements of the Turkish secret services in Nairobi, Kenya. Ocalan had taken refuge in the Greek embassy and was on his way to the airport—and presumably an asylum granting country—when he was apprehended. His capture led to Turkish charges that Greece was a state sponsor of terrorism. In the wake of the fiasco, Simitis fired his outspoken foreign minister, Theodoros Pangalos, and replaced him with George Papandreou. The American-born younger Papandreou pursued a more amiable approach in his dealings with Western diplomats. The outbreak of the Kosovo war the following month demonstrated an outpouring of popular anti-NATO sentiment among the Greek population. Nevertheless, Simitis succeeded in walking a diplomatic tightrope by offering logistical support to its NATO allies without actually participating in a combat role.

In late summer, however, relations with Turkey underwent a drastic improvement following earthquakes in the two countries. In August, a devastaking quake killed over 20,000 Turkish citizens. In response, Simitis offered Greek humanitarian assistance which was gladly accepted by the stricken neighbor. A smaller quake in Greece the following month killed more than 100, and Turkey reciprocated the gesture. Following these twin tragedies, the Simitis government proceeded to reach agreement with Turkey in several areas of mutual interest, including trade and the fight against terrorism. Central to these efforts at Greek-Turkish reconciliation was the personal rapport that developed between George Papandreou and his Turkish counterpart Ismail Cem.

## ADDRESS

Office of the Prime Minister
Greek Parliament Building, Constitutional Square
Athens
Greece

## REFERENCES

Banks, Arthur, Alan Day, and Thomas Muller, eds. *Political Handbook of the World, 1995–1996.*
*Christian Science Monitor,* 11 July 1996.
*The Economist,* 27 January 1996; 24 February 1996.
*Financial Times,* 25 September 1996.
*Keesing's Record of World Events,* January 1996.
*Le Monde,* 26 September 1996.
*Washington Post,* 23 September 1996.

**Profile researched and written by Ayse Betül Çelik and Volkan Aytar, Binghamton University (10/96; updated by Terry Netos 6/2000).**

# GRENADA

### Keith Mitchell
### Prime Minister

*(pronounced "KEETH MITCH-el")*

*"Equal opportunity for all irrespective of class, creed or gender....We must value all, look down on none, and support each other in our effort to make this beautiful country the very best it can be."*

Grenada is the most southerly of the Windward chain of West Indian islands. To its south is Trinidad and Tobago, and to its north is the island of St. Vincent. The total area of the country is 345 sq km (about 130 sq mi).

Grenada's estimated population of 97,000 is 90% African, with a white or mixed minority and a small number of persons of Portuguese and East Indian origin. The main religion is Roman Catholicism. English is the official language of the country although a French patois used to be widely spoken and is still spoken by older segments of the population.

Grenada is known as the "Spice Island" because it is a major world exporter of an assortment of spices, including nutmeg and mace. Bananas and cocoa are the other main exports, supplemented by other fresh fruits and vegetables and some light manufactures. Tourism is also an important income earner for the country. Per capita GDP has been estimated at US$3,500. The unit of currency is the EC (Eastern Caribbean) dollar.

## POLITICAL BACKGROUND

Anglo-French rivalry during the 18th century was reflected in Grenada's numerous changes of ownership between Britain and France. In 1763, the island was ceded to Britain. It became a crown colony with limited self-government in 1877. Universal suffrage was introduced after World War II, largely as a result of pressure from labor groups. In 1967, full internal self-government was granted to Grenada and other Eastern Caribbean islands under a specially-devised status that made these nations "Associated States" of Britain. Under this arrangement, Britain was responsible for external affairs and defense. In 1974, despite widespread social unrest and opposition to the prevailing leadership, Britain granted independence to Grenada. Two main political parties had emerged after World War II: the working class-oriented Grenada United Labor Party (GULP) led by labor organizer Eric Gairy; and the Grenada National Party (GNP), which appealed to the middle and upper classes. GULP dominated the political scene until 1979 when its autocratic leader was removed in a coup staged by the socialist and youth-oriented New Jewel Movement (NJM). The NJM's People's Revolutionary Government (PRG) lasted until 1983 when internal factionalism led to the execution of its leader, Maurice Bishop, and several colleagues. After an appeal by the neighboring Eastern Caribbean states, the US sent troops to restore order, paving the way for elections in 1984.

Until 1979, Grenada had been a parliamentary democracy, patterned along the lines of the British Westminster system. The PRG replaced this with rule by a Political Bureau supported by parish councils. In 1984, the former constitution was restored. The legislature is bicameral, and the head of government (prime minister) is the leader of the majority party in parliament. The head of state (governor general) performs mainly ceremonial and procedural duties. The country has retained its links with the British Commonwealth and the British monarchy. Between 1984 and 1995, Grenada's former two-party system was replaced by a vigorous multiparty democracy that engendered unstable coalition governments. This was changed in June 1995 when the New National Party (NNP) won a majority of eight (out of 15) seats in the House of Assembly. The opposition was formed by the National Democratic Congress (NDC), holding five parliamentary seats, and the Grenada United Labor Party (GULP) with two seats. The NNP leader, Keith Mitchell, became prime minister In December 1998, the country's foreign minister, Raphael Fletcher, resigned from the government, citing concerns about governmental integrity and disenchantment with the prime minister's leadership style. His resignation was preceded by an unsuccessful vote of no confidence brought by the opposition. Fletcher's resignation left the government without a parliamentary majority, and fresh elections were called as required by the constitution. In January 1999, the NNP, led by Mitchell, was returned to power, sweeping all 15 parliamentary seats. Five parties and two independent parties contested the results. The NNP gained 62.2% of the vote while its nearest rival gained only 24.9%. As a result, there is no formal parliamentary opposition in Grenada.

## PERSONAL BACKGROUND

Keith Mitchell was born in St. George's, the capital city of Grenada. He attended primary and secondary school in Grenada. Mitchell was active in sports, representing Grenada as captain of the cricket team and leading the Windward/Leeward Islands combined youth team. In 1968, he attended the University of the West Indies Barbados (Cave Hill) campus, on a government scholarship. There he studied mathematics and chemistry, graduating with a bachelor's degree in 1971. Mitchell returned to Grenada to teach, then won a Howard University scholarship to study for a Master of Science degree in mathematics. He attended American University on scholarship and graduated in 1979 with a PhD in mathematics and statistics. Between 1977 and 1983,

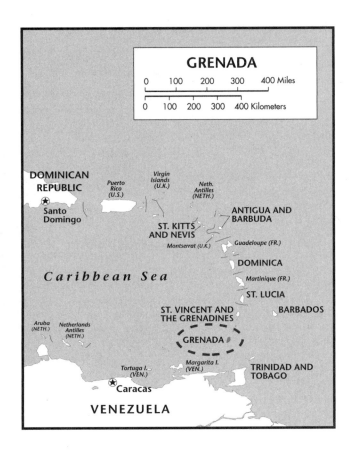

**GRENADA**

0　100　200　300　400 Miles

0　100　200　300　400 Kilometers

DOMINICAN REPUBLIC

★ Santo Domingo

Puerto Rico (U.S.)

Virgin Islands (U.K.)

Neth. Antilles (NETH.)

ANTIGUA AND BARBUDA

ST. KITTS AND NEVIS

Montserrat (U.K.)

Guadeloupe (FR.)

*Caribbean Sea*

DOMINICA

Martinique (FR.)

ST. LUCIA

ST. VINCENT AND THE GRENADINES

BARBADOS

Aruba (NETH.)

Netherlands Antilles (NETH.)

GRENADA

Tortuga I. (VEN.)

Margarita I. (VEN.)

TRINIDAD AND TOBAGO

★ Caracas

**VENEZUELA**

Mitchell taught at Howard University. He also started his own consulting firm in Washington and subsequently worked for various international organizations and US government agencies. Mitchell is married to the former Marietta Cummins and has one son.

## RISE TO POWER

Mitchell's entry into politics was facilitated by Grenada's post-revolutionary return to democratic rule in 1983. Like other exiles and immigrants, Mitchell returned from the US to join in the democratic rebirth. He became a member of the New National Party (NNP), a coalition of center-right parties at the core of which was the old opposition party, the GNP. The NNP coalition, promoted by several Eastern Caribbean leaders and, indirectly, by the US, was successful in gaining power. Mitchell was put in charge of the ministries of Works, Communications, Public Utilities, Civil Aviation, and Energy. His base of support was in the black working classes.

By 1987, the NNP coalition had collapsed as a result of internal differences over leadership style and policy. The most important coalition partners left to form the National Democratic Congress (NDC, formerly National Democratic Party). Mitchell used the opportunity to express his own dissatisfaction with the aging and authoritarian leadership of Blaize, who had been the GNP leader and was given the leadership of the NNP coalition. Beyond personal ambition and personality differences, Mitchell opposed the government's fiscal policy, restrictions on militant groups, and failure to alleviate youth unemployment.

In 1989, Mitchell mounted a challenge to Blaize's leadership and succeeded in being elected to head the NNP.

This created an unusual situation. Blaize was no longer the leader of the majority party in parliament but still continued to rule as prime minister. In July 1989, Blaize dismissed Mitchell from the cabinet and moved to form his own party, The National Party (TNP). Mitchell, deprived of a majority in parliament, was unable to carry through with a proposed no-confidence vote intended to oust Blaize from the prime ministership. Blaize remained as prime minister until his death in December 1989.

Mitchell entered the 1990 elections plagued by broad allegations of corruption (which were never proven although a commission of inquiry was set up), and by some popular dissatisfaction over his aggressive removal of Blaize. At the same time, the NNP/TNP administration had not demonstrated an ability to solve the country's economic problems. Thus it was not surprising that the election was won by the NDC, which formed the government in coalition with the TNP. Mitchell's party won only 2 seats and formed the opposition, along with Gairy's GULP.

The NDC proved to be no better that the NNP at improving the economy. In particular, despite overall statistical growth in the economy, unemployment rose considerably; foreign investment did not bring major expected rewards; tourism declined; and the agricultural sector suffered various setbacks. In 1995, Mitchell harnessed the discontent not only of the working class but also the heavily taxed middle classes. He promised a repeal of the national income tax and promised jobs and other programs for the large number of unemployed young people. Mitchell was careful not to make any excessive promises. His success was attributed to his appeal to moderation and to national unity at a time of national and regional economic uncertainty.

In the period before the 1998 election, Mitchell's government was accused by the opposition of a lack of accountability and transparency in government, and an excessive focus on expensive large projects that did little to lower the high unemployment rate. Mitchell was able to successfully counter these accusations by emphasizing that rumors of corruption were completely unsubstantiated and by outlining the benefits that his government's projects had brought to the people of Grenada. Beyond these policy issues, Mitchell's overwhelming success in the 1998 elections was premised on the promise of continuing domestic stability and investor confidence. In contrast, the agreement that joined the GULP and United Labor Party was seen as an opportunistic and unstable alliance of ambitious individuals that would inevitably end in post-electoral squabbling. Mitchell also benefited from accusations against Fletcher of improper use of travel monies while in government and similar accusations of impropriety against the daughter of former prime minister, Eric Gairy. Finally, Mitchell's success was attributable to popular respect for his leadership and willingness to allow him more time to complete his promising public policy agenda.

In January 1999, Mitchell's ruling New National Party became the first in Grenada to win two successive terms since 1984 when parliamentary democracy was restored in the three southern Caribbean islands which make up the nation.

The party, which held a slim eight–seven majority in Parliament, captured all 15 seats in the January elections despite defections by two of Mitchell's top aides and accusations of corruption in his government. Mitchell was accused of irregularities in awarding public works contracts and negotiating with foreign investors with questionable credentials. He was forced to call elections 18 months ahead of schedule when a member of his party and parliament resigned, leaving his government in the minority. Turnout was low, with only 56.4% of registered voters casting ballots. Opponents complained that they only had six weeks to campaign, which gave Mitchell an advantage. Mitchell has been credited with stimulating the economy and attracting investment. The Organization of American States, which monitored the elections and called them fair, later said Grenada should consider campaign finance reform, as opponents claimed they could not compete against the better-funded NNP.

## LEADERSHIP

Mitchell is generally viewed as an astute and competent leader who has brought some political unity to Grenada. He has praised the contributions of the TNP and the GULP (under Eric Gairy) and has also lauded the social contributions of the PRG. In the wake of his overwhelming victory at the polls, he exhibited a statesman-like humility. On the other hand, relations with the NDC are cool, given policy differences, and there has long been personal animosity between Mitchell and Democratic Labor Party leader Francis Alexis. The death of Gairy and the fact that the GULP allied with Alexis during the 1998 election has soured relations between Mitchell and that party. In general, political divisions among the elite appear to have been heightened in recent years.

## DOMESTIC POLICY

In its first term, the NNP government vowed to promote job creation and job training, as well as entrepreneurial activity, especially at the level of small business. Instead, the focus has been on the creation of needed infrastructural development (roads and water projects) and on major construction projects, including a fisheries complex, a vendors mall, and school rehabilitation projects. More visible and much-criticized projects, such as the erection of an expensive national stadium and the construction of major hotels, have also been undertaken. Concerns have been expressed about the government's weak commitment to small business, despite the initiation of a micro-enterprise project. Related to this is the downturn in light manufacturing, which has suffered from regional competition. Tourism has grown only modestly and the impact of new hotel development on employment and on the local agricultural and handicraft sectors remains unclear. Although the government correctly boasts that unemployment has been cut in half (to about 14%), it is still high. Moreover, the rural sectors have suffered as agriculture continues to experience downturns. A mealy bug infestation that plagued fruit production for many years has finally been brought under control. However, the banana and cocoa industries have been depressed by quality issues and lack of financial resources, as well as uncertainties affecting the continuation of the important European banana regime. Thus the government urgently needs to initiate activities to help those sectors that do not perceive themselves as benefiting from macro planning and restructuring. Finally, one of the NNP's early promises was to remove the personal income tax for most residents in order to stimulate growth. The abolition of income taxes has indeed been accomplished but has resulted in increased reliance on international trade taxes. There is concern that this will lead to increased government debt. On the other hand, the government has been cautiously successful in increasing compliance with regard to tax collection on goods and services and non-personal income.

## FOREIGN POLICY

The Mitchell government has a strong base of support among immigrants in North America who have contributed to revenues through remittances and investments. The prime minister, himself a graduate of US educational institutions, has promoted close relations with these expatriate sectors, as well as with the governments of the United States and Canada. A major focus has been on increasing educational and technical exchanges between Grenada and the United States. Grenada has also been cooperating closely with the US in narcotics interdiction efforts.

As a small country, Grenada's main arena of action is naturally regional. Mitchell has upgraded his country's presence in Caribbean Community (CARICOM) affairs. He has aggressively promoted implementation of the single market economy, a key aspect of regional economic integration. As chairman of CARICOM in 1997, Mitchell played a key role in resolving ethno-political instability that occurred in Guyana after general elections in December 1997. Mitchell and two other CARICOM leaders succeeded in brokering an agreement between the African and East Indian political elements. He has also been supportive of the Association of Caribbean States (ACS), a grouping that brings CARICOM nations together with their Central American and northern South American counterparts for the purposes of functional cooperation and future free trade. Through the ACS, Mitchell hopes that Grenada will be able to take advantage of the technological development of larger regional countries, such as Mexico. Under the Mitchell government, Grenada has pursued particularly cordial relations with Cuba. Mitchell believes that Grenada can learn from Cuba in technological areas and that Cuba can learn about the building of democratic institutions from Grenada and the other Caribbean countries. With this in mind, he has visited Cuba a number of times, and Cuban president Fidel Castro paid a reciprocal visit to Grenada in 1998.

## ADDRESS

Prime Minister's Office, Botanical Gardens, Tanteen, St. George's, Grenada

## REFERENCES

Caribbean Development Bank. *Annual Report 1997*. St. Michael, Barbados: 1998.

Caribbean Development Bank. *Caribbean Studies Newsletter*, Winter/Spring 1990.

*Caribbean Week*, various issues.

*Grenadian Voice*, various issues.

*Latin America and Caribbean Contemporary Record*. New York: Holmes and Meier, 1981–82.

*Oxford Companion to Politics of the World*. New York: Oxford University Press, 1999.

*Trinidad Express*, 20 August 1995.

**Profile researched and written by Jacqueline Anne Braveboy-Wagner, Graduate School and University Center, City University of New York (6/99; updated 2/2000).**

# GUATEMALA

## Alfonso Portillo Cabrera
### President
*(pronounced "al-FOHN-soh poor-TEE-oh ca-BRAR-ah")*

*"I have rejected the intervention of the state in the economy, the class struggle, the dictatorship of the proletariat. That was an era of romanticism in my life."*

Guatemala lies between Mexico to its north, El Salvador to its south, Honduras to the southeast, and Belize to the east. Guatemala's territory, comprising 108,890 sq km (42,042 sq mi), touches both the Pacific Ocean and Caribbean Sea. Geographically, the country is divided into three regions. The Northern Plain, sparsely populated and covered largely by tropical rain forests, is the site of many ancient Mayan ruins, most notably Tikal. The Central Highlands, where most of Guatemala's 12.3 million people live, is a region dominated by a chain of mountains with many volcanoes, some of which are active. The beauty and climate of this region has given Guatemala the nickname "Land of Eternal Spring." The Pacific Lowland, a thin strip of land along Guatemala's 241 km (150 mi) of hot and humid southern coast, is largely farmland owned by a few families who grow sugar cane, bananas and cotton or raise cattle for agroexport. Guatemala City is the capital. Guatemala, with the largest population in Central America, is further distinguished by its large indigenous population, descendants of the Mayans, who compose over half the country's total population. The Mayans belong to 22 language and ethnic groups. The remainder of the population (40–45%) is known as *ladino*, because they have mixed blood ancestrally and have abandoned the dress and customs of the indigenous culture. Although Spanish is the official language, many Indians speak only their own. While Roman Catholicism is the predominant religion, about one-third of the population is now affiliated with evangelical and Pentecostal churches. Many Mayans also continue to follow their ancient religious beliefs and practices, codified in their sacred writings, the *Popul Vuh*. Forty-five percent of the population is under 15 years of age and only 3% over age 65. Life expectancy among indigenous men is 47 years, compared to 64 for *ladinos*.

In this agrarian country, just 2% of the population owns 70% of the land. While the agricultural sector employs nearly 60% of the labor force and supplies two-thirds of exports, it accounts for only 26% of GDP ($12 billion in 1994). Growth in the agricultural sector has been due to large-scale agribusiness concerns growing crops such as coffee, sugar, fruits and vegetables for export. Ironically, Guatemala is a food importer. The manufacturing sector is also divided into two components, a large traditional sector focused on such products as food, beverages, and tobacco, and a small but rapidly expanding enclave sector of assembly-plants (*maquiladoras*) specializing in clothing and electronics. A large amount of Guatemala's trade occurs with the United States, Mexico and the other Central American countries, especially El Salvador. The unit of currency is the *quetzal*. The per capita GDP has been estimated at $1,180. More than 75% of Guatemalans live in poverty. About one in three Guatemalan children suffers from malnutrition; among the indigenous populations, three of every four children are seriously malnourished.

## POLITICAL BACKGROUND

Guatemala was the center of a great and thriving Mayan civilization between AD 250 and 900. However, by the time the Spanish arrived in the 16th century, the indigenous population had abandoned their great centers, dispersed into the central highlands, and organized themselves in *ejidos*, a communal village-based landowning system engaged in subsistence agriculture. After the Spanish conquest, Guatemala became the regional administrative seat and monopolized Central American trade with Spain. In the 1820s, as Spain's already weak presence in the region gave way to the movement for political independence, the hacienda system was the dominant political force. Although Guatemala established itself as a separate republic in 1839, the governmental system was weak. Essentially the country was governed by local elites, landowners and merchants operating a kind of feudal system, which minimized the role of the state except for the purpose of raising an army to control the Indian population and harness its labor for the development of commercial enterprises. The introduction of coffee in the 1870s, coinciding with the rise of the Liberal movement and the reign of one of Guatemala's most notorious dictators, Justo Barrios (1873–85), reinforced this structure. For the most part, Guatemala's political history has been one of authoritarian governments controlled by the military, responsive to the landed elites, and hostile to the indigenous population. The most notable exception was the period from 1944–54, when two democratically elected leaders, José Arévelo and Jacobo Arbenz, brought an era of political openness and reform. Arévélo was a populist, whose six-year term saw the emergence of urban trade unions and the promulgation of pro-labor laws, a flowering of political freedoms and parties, and the institution of a social security system. Arbenz, a military leader who was nonetheless drawn to the promises of Marxism, sought to transform Guatemala through a program of nationalist economic development and agrarian reform. He was overthrown in 1954 by a CIA-orchestrated coup which brought the military back into control of the country's government for the next 30 years.

From 1960 to 1996, a brutal civil war, pitting the Guatemalan army against a rural-based guerrilla insurgency, terrorized the country. The repression of the population escalated beginning in 1978 with the reign of General Lucas García, when the army, according to its own estimates, destroyed 441 villages over a two-year period, and the violence moved into urban areas including the capital. The repression peaked in the early 1980s with the accession of General Efraín Ríos Montt, whose 18-month rule began and ended with coups. All told, more than 150,000 peasants were killed, 45,000 disappeared, 500,000 were internally displaced, and another 100,000 became refugees. A Historical Clarification Commission accused the military of genocide in a 3,600-page report in 1999, saying that most crimes were committed by the military. During a visit that year, President Bill Clinton expressed regret for US support for the Guatemalan army during the conflict.

In 1982 four guerrilla organizations joined forces to form the Guatemalan National Revolutionary Unity Party (URNG), the chief political arm of the country's leftist opposition. During the late 1980s, Guatemala experienced a transition to democracy of sorts. Since 1985 there have been four "free and fair" elections for new civilian leaders. However, there were few substantive changes in political practice or social policy. The military remained the power behind the throne, and repression persisted well after the signing of a peace accord in December 1996.

When Vinicio Cerezo, a Christian Democrat, took office as Guatemala's newly-elected civilian president in January 1986, he was faced with high unemployment, inflation running at 40%, and a foreign debt of $2.5 billion. While he had won over two-thirds of the votes cast in the December run-off election, it was clear where his real support lay. During the campaign he had assured both the oligarchy and the military that he would not press for banking or land reforms and would stay clear of anything that would scare away foreign capital. Cerezo seemed committed solely to maintaining himself in office. Despite his weathering of several unsuccessful coup attempts, Cerezo's hold on the presidency was tenuous.

In January 1991, Jorge Serrano became the second civilian elected president of Guatemala. Serrano, a businessman and university professor, had been chosen by a newly organized political party, the Solidarity Action Movement (MAS), and had campaigned on a populist platform. His New Right coalition hoped to achieve modernization and long-term stability through neo-liberal economic policies coupled with new approaches for diffusing social tensions. But in May 1993, Serrano had grown frustrated by his inability to enact his agenda. Following the example of President Fujimori in Peru, he tried to seize absolute power by suspending the constitution, but was rebuffed by the military and fled the country. The legislature then elected human rights ombudsman Ramiro de Leon Carpio to complete his term. Negotiations between the army and the URNG, with mediation by the Catholic church, began in 1991. In late 1994, after a long impasse, a new round of talks began, this time mediated by the United Nations.

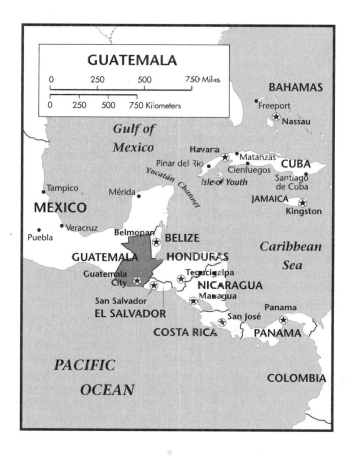

In November 1995, Álvaro Arzú, candidate of the National Advancement Party (PAN) won 46% of the vote, beating 18 other candidates but falling short of the 50% needed for victory. In the run-off on 7 January 1996, Arzú faced Alfonso Portillo from the right-wing Guatemalan Republican Front (FRG). Portillo was the hand-picked stand-in for the former dictator Rios Montt, who would have run but was barred because of his role in the overthrow of Lucas García in 1982. Although Portillo received only 20% of the vote in November, the January election was a cliffhanger. Arzú beat Portillo by just 30,000 votes. Only 37% of the country's 3.5 million registered voters went to the polls. Arzú accomplished what other presidents could not. Politically isolated from the world community, Arzú was forced to negotiate an end to the civil war. With United Nations assistance, Arzú and the URNG signed a peace treaty that ended the war in December 1996. Yet, Arzú was unable to curb an alarming wave of robberies, kidnappings, and killings— including the murders of prominent human rights workers and advocates—that followed the end of hostilities between the army and leftist guerrillas. He was also unable to completely institute terms of the 1996 peace accord. Guatemalans had become disenchanted with the PAN by 1999. Portillo, in the meantime, had been building support with a populist campaign that promised law and order. Thanks to a well-managed campaign and relentless attacks against the PAN, and despite revelations that he had killed two men in Mexico in 1982, Portillo won the presidency with 68.3% of the vote. He was 48 when he took office in January 2000.

## PERSONAL BACKGROUND

Portillo is the son of a rural teacher. During his youth, he was sympathetic to the leftist forces fighting in his country. Later, he described his leftist sympathies as youthful indiscretions, and came to describe himself as a social democrat. A lawyer and economist, he has been a university professor, both in Guatemala and abroad. He favors the death penalty to combat high crime levels in his country. One of the most violent episodes in his private life became a major symbol in his populist law and order presidential campaign in 1999. During the campaign, Portillo was forced to admit that he killed two men during a confrontation in the Mexican state of Guerrero and fled the country to avoid prosecution in 1982. Portillo, a law professor at the Guerrero Autonomous University of Mexico at the time, said he fled because he feared he would be prosecuted unjustly. Instead of being reviled for the killings, many Guatemalans admired him for his act. One of his most prominent ads for his campaign proclaimed: "Portillo. If he can defend himself, he can defend you and your family."

## RISE TO POWER

Portillo has behaved like a political chameleon, moving from the left to the far right with little damage to his reputation. Sympathy for the left, he explained, was rooted in youthful romanticism. Later, he came to describe himself as a social democrat sensitive to the needs of the poor. But it was his alliance with the far right that brought him to power. In 1995, former dictator Efraín Ríos Montt (1982–83) invited Portillo to join his Guatemalan Republican Front (FRG). At the time, Portillo was a Christian Democrat. Montt had been barred from running for the presidency because of his role as former dictator, and he needed a presidential candidate to represent his party. Portillo did well in the first round of the presidential election, receiving 20% of the vote. In the January 1996 runoff election, Alvaro Arzú beat Portillo by just 30,000 votes. Portillo remained a member of the FRG, and campaigned vigorously for the 1999 contest. During the 1990s, Montt, secretary-general of the FRG, had come increasingly under criticism for violation of human rights during his dictatorship. The country's Historical Clarification Commission in 1999 said the military had committed acts of genocide during Montt's rule. Yet, among many Guatemalans, Montt had wide appeal and was seen as someone who was committed to order. Portillo could not escape Montt's shadow even though he was portrayed as leading the more liberal faction of the FRG party. Portillo insisted he was not Montt's puppet and would not fall under his influence if elected president. With a populist law and order campaign, and relentless attacks against PAN, Portillo became the candidate to beat in the November 1999 election. But Portillo, and PAN candidate Oscar Berger, a businessman and former Guatemala City mayor, failed to get 50% of the vote, forcing a runoff election a month later. Rather than being hurt by his ties to Montt and the Mexico murders, support for Portillo only grew. In the December runoff election, Portillo received nearly 69% of the vote. He was inaugurated in January 2000.

## LEADERSHIP

Portillo has been described as a charismatic and populist leader. While he may be considered a member of the political elite, Portillo gained support from the country's lower classes by constantly attacking and criticizing the elitism of the PAN. In heavy-handed speeches, he said the PAN was corrupt and exclusionary. He built most of his support with promises to end the crime wave that started during the Arzú administration. Having killed two men to defend himself in Mexico, Portillo came to be seen as a tough and fearless leader. Since his inauguration, he has sought to distance himself from Montt, who was expected to heavily influence the presidency. Montt is president of Congress and leader of the FRG, which controls Congress with 63 of 113 seats. Portillo has claimed that Montt's influence is simply a myth, but it is clear he will need him and his votes in Congress to run the government. Most FRG congressmen are considered loyal to Montt. Portillo is expected to deal with him carefully, especially after Nobel Peace laureate Rigoberta Menchu filed a human rights case against the former general in a Spanish court in March 2000. After taking office on 14 January 2000, Portillo appointed his closest colleagues to about half of the cabinet posts. The rest, including the vice presidency and the ministry of economy and trade, went to allies of Montt. Portillo surprised some critics by naming two prominent human rights activists to his cabinet. Otilia Lux de Cotí, a former member of the Historical Clarification Commission, was named minister of culture. Edgar Gutierrez, a journalist and coordinator for the Catholic Church's Recovery of Historic Memory, a report on the civil war, was named secretary in charge of the president's office for strategic affairs. To assuage fears that he is not a puppet of the army, Portillo had promised to clarify the unsolved 1998 murder of Bishop Juan Jose Gerardi. He was killed two days after he published a 1,400-page report that blamed the army and its allies for 90% of the civil war's crimes. The Arzú government had been criticized for protecting the killers. With Portillo in office, the government reported the arrest of three military officers charged in the killing.

## DOMESTIC POLICY

One of Portillo's greatest challenges is to reassure Guatemalans—and the international community—that he remains committed to the peace process. The December 1996 accord, signed by the Arzú administration and leftist forces, was not fully enacted and remains a delicate matter in Guatemala. In a 1999 plebiscite, Guatemalans voted down key constitutional reforms that would have expanded and protected the rights of indigenous peoples. Portillo vowed to wrap up the peace accord and move the country toward reconciliation. He has often spoken of a governability pact to address national problems. But that would mean a closer alliance with the PAN and the leftist Alianza Nueva Nación. The leftist coalition said it would support a pact only if it was based on the peace accord. PAN has been stung by constant criticism from Portillo and may be unlikely to support any pact with the government. On the economic front, Portillo has promised to enact a series of economic policy initiatives to pull Guatemala from an economic crisis and restore stability.

## FOREIGN POLICY

Several nations, including the United States, have told Guatemala they will release hundreds of millions of dollars in economic aid only if the Central American nation continues to institute terms of the December 1996 peace accord approved by the Arzú administration. The Arzú government only approved 30% or so of laws required by the peace accord. Portillo assured the international community that he would work to ensure the full implementation of the accord. Portillo is under pressure to reach national reconciliation and press for investigations of human rights abuses. International donors are expected to continue to pressure the government to comply with electoral law reform, justice system reform, and decentralization of government. Portillo also will remain under pressure to promote human rights, and improve the rights and social conditions of the country's indigenous peoples. In March 2000, the Portillo government accepted "institutional responsibility" for 44 of 155 cases of human rights violations being heard by the Organization of American States. Human rights organizations feared the Portillo government was only trying to enhance its image by taking responsibility but would do nothing for the families of victims. The government also will have to deal with Spain, which accepted a human rights case filed by Nobel laureate Rigoberta Menchú against Montt and others.

Much like Arzú, Portillo wants to continue to open the country's economy and bring Guatemala into the North American Free Trade Agreement (NAFTA). Portillo also is expected to continue to encourage greater economic cooperation among the Central American countries. During the first four months of his presidency, he traveled extensively through Central America to improve relations with neighbors.

## ADDRESS

Presidente de la Republica de Guatemala
Palacio Nacional
Guatemala, Guatemala

## REFERENCES

*The Economist Country Report: Guatemala.* First Quarter 2000.
*The Economist,* various issues.
"Guatemala's Precarious Peace." *Current History,* February 2000, p. 78.
*The New York Times,* various issues.
*Los Angeles Times,* various issues.
*Washington Post,* various issues.

**Profile researched and written by Ignacio Lobos, journalist (5/2000).**

# GUINEA

## Lansana Conté
### President
*(pronounced "lahn-SAH-nah KOAN-tay")*

*"It is you—the farmers, craftsmen and industrial workers who make up the riches of this nation. It is the role of Guinean men and women to build or develop their business."*

The Republic of Guinea is located on the west coast of Africa. It is bordered, clockwise from the northwest, by Guinea-Bissau, Senegal, Mali, Côte d'Ivoire, Liberia, Sierra Leone, and the Atlantic Ocean. Its area is 245,857 sq km (94,926 sq mi), and its population is estimated to be 7.6 million. Conakry, the capital, is the largest city, followed by Kankan. Guinea gained its independence from France in 1958. The official language is French, although Malinke, Fula, Susu, and Forester languages are also widely spoken. In terms of ethnicity, the Fulani make up 36% of the population, the Malinke 24%, the Susu 20%, with Forester and other groups making up the remainder. Ethnic sensitivities run deep in Guinea and are the basis for economic and political stratification. The Islamic religion is practiced by 90% of the people in Guinea while 10% practice Christianity. Thirty percent of the total population overlay their religious beliefs with traditional animist religions. The currency is the Guinea *franc*. The per capita GDP is estimated at US$1,180. Guinea's major exports are bauxite and peanuts.

## POLITICAL BACKGROUND

The constitution of the People's Republic of Guinea was established in May 1982, suspended by the Military Committee for National Recovery (CMRN) following a coup in 1984, rewritten by a presidential task in the late 1980s, and passed in a national referendum in December 1990. Conté's Transitional Council for National Recovery (CTRN) wrote the organic laws in lieu of a legislature up to 1995. The Constitution gives disproportionate powers to the president, who, despite the presence of a National Assembly, rules largely by decree. The president is also commander in chief of the armed forces, appoints judges, cabinet ministers, governors, prefects, and other mid- to senior-level officials in the public bureaucracy.

Guinea's political system has evolved dramatically since Sékou Touré's socialist party-state of the First Republic. The CMRN banned the PDG following the April 1984 takeover, and President Conté and his government engineered Guinea's transition towards a democratic multi-party system of government with republican institutions. These institutions are mostly in place, but Guinea's electronic broadcast media are state-run, and the separation of powers is more theoretical than real. Because no effective system of checks and balances exists, real power belongs to the Executive Branch.

## PERSONAL BACKGROUND

General Lansana Conté was born in Dubreka in 1934. His roots lie in the less-privileged segment of both Guinean society and the Guinean army. Like Sékou Touré, his education was mainly experiential. Despite his Russian military training, Conté espouses no particular ideology or doctrine. His adversaries concede his penchant for hard work, loyalty, discipline, and traditional folk values. He is taciturn, stays out of the limelight, and prefers spending time on his expansive farm near Dubreka. He officially has two wives, one of whom is a former Miss Guinea. He resides on the grounds of Camp Samory, in Kaloum near downtown Conakry. Conté is Guinea's only active military General, and he holds an honorary doctorate degree from Central State University in Cincinnati, Ohio. His chain-smoking habit and diabetes have raised concerns about his health.

## RISE TO POWER

Lansana Conté succeeded Sékou Touré in the wake of a bloodless coup staged by middle- and low-ranking military officers on 3 April 1984. Touré died on 26 March in Cleveland, Ohio, undergoing heart surgery. Then Colonel Conté had been Touré's personal bodyguard and had witnessed the unvarnished exercise of power for many years as Touré's confidante. Indeed, one popular rumor tells how Conté carried Touré upon his back during long processions in Mecca while on pilgrimage. Thus he became the CMRN's choice to put Guinea's "bloody and ruthless dictatorship" to rest.

Following the coup, the CMRN banned the PDG, suspended the 1982 constitution, and prepared to follow liberal economic and political paths. The CMRN reduced the state's role and encouraged the private sector in the economy, promised reductions in the over-sized civil service, and released 1,000 political prisoners. The CMRN also set out to develop closer relations with the West, particularly France. To make the necessary changes, the CMRN needed to gain the confidence of the people.

Opportunism and factionalism soon divided the CMRN. A power struggle evolved between Conté and his Prime Minister, Colonel Diarra Traoré, a Malinke. After being demoted to Minister of Education, Traoré staged an aborted coup in July 1985 while Conté was attending an OAU summit in Lomé. In the aftermath of the coup, Conté consolidated his power. He condoned reprisals not only against the mutineers, but also against the Malinke generally. Shops were

# GUINEA-BISSAU

## Koumba Yala
### President
*(pronounced "KOOM-bah YAY-lah")*

*"I am appealing to all the people, the main stakeholders of change in the country. The national reconciliation process has to succeed because we are compelled to shoulder our responsibilities of developing our country."*

Officially known as the Republic of Guinea-Bissau and formerly known as Portuguese Guinea until its independence from Portugal in 1974, Guinea-Bissau is situated on the west coast of Africa. To the north is Senegal; to the east and south is the Republic of Guinea; and to the west is the Atlantic Ocean. Its total area is 36,125 sq km (13,948 sq mi) and includes the offshore Bijagós Islands. The population has been estimated at 1.2 million. The Guinean unit of currency is the Guinea *peso* (GP). Portuguese is the official language although Creole and Balanti are widely used. Ethnically, Guinea-Bissau's population is 99% African and includes 33% Balanti, 22% Fulani/Fula, 14% Mandyako, 13% Malinke/Mandingo, 7% Pepel, and 1% European and bi-racial. Guinea-Bissau's religion is 65% animist, 30% Muslim, and 5% Christian, mainly Roman Catholic. While Guinea-Bissau's primary export is cashew nuts, other exports include peanuts, fish products, palm nuts, timber, and cotton.

## POLITICAL BACKGROUND
Until 1991, Guinea-Bissau had a one-party republican form of government. A constitution adopted in 1984 created a 150-member National People's Assembly, whose members were drawn from the eight regional councils. All members of the regional councils had to be at least 21 years old and nominated by the *Partido Africano de Independencia de Guiné e Cabo Verde* (PAIGC). The National People's Assembly elected a 15-member Council of State. The president of the Council was head of state, commander in chief of the armed forces, and the secretary-general of the PAIGC. The Constitution was amended 4 May 1991, revised February and June 1993, in 1996, and again in 1999.

Among the leaders in the struggle for independence were Amilcar Cabral, Luis Cabral, and João Bernardo Vieira. They formed the PAIGC in 1956 and by 1959 had called for an all-out struggle to win independence. By 1963, a large-scale guerrilla war had broken out in the territory. Amilcar Cabral was assassinated in Conakry (Guinea) in 1973, but the Portuguese coup in 1974 led to an agreement and shortly thereafter to independence on 10 September 1974. Luis Cabral, Amilcar's brother, led the new government as head of the PAIGC. In 1980, perceptions that Cape Verdeans were controlling the country led to a coup d'etat by Joao Bernardo "Nino" Vieira. Vieira survived numerous coup attempts until he agreed to hold a national conference in 1990.

In October 1990, 350 representatives of the PAIGC, government, civil society, and private organizations met to discuss the rules for advancing political reform and democratization in Guinea-Bissau. In May 1991, the National Assembly voted to end single-party rule. Free and fair multi-party elections occurred in July 1994. In June 1998, a coup triggered an 11-month civil war, which Guinean and Senegalese troops quelled at Vieira's request. Renegade troops led by General Ansumane Mane ousted Vieira in April–May 1999, paving the way for an interim government and the next rounds of legislative and presidential elections held in November 1999 and January 2000.

General Mane and the junta promised to stay out of politics once a new civilian government was elected, but two weeks before the elections a "Magna Carta" was published demanding a 10-year role for the junta. The military has repeated its commitment to return to the barracks after the elections, but soldier and veteran benefits is a continuing concern.

## PERSONAL BACKGROUND
Koumba Yala is a graduate in philosophy and law from Lisbon's Classic University. He speaks several languages. He is a member of the Balante ethnic group, which is the predominate group in the southwest, and was opposed to Vieira. A former teacher, he joined the PAIGC and then broke with it to challenge President Vieira in the country's first multi-party elections in 1994. Indeed, his courage as leader of the Social Renewal Party, *Partido da Renovacao Social* (PRS), brought him wide public notice. He is considered a good speaker and a man of the people but has also been criticized as mercurial and authoritarian. In December 1999, during the runoff campaign, Yala was outside the country receiving medical treatment in Portugal but returned in time to stage a well-executed campaign.

## RISE TO POWER
Koumba Yala is a product of Bissau democratization, which was a reaction to the sometimes well-intentioned, but corrupt and inept, PAIGC regimes, dating back to 1974. Luis Cabral, Guinea-Bissau's first president, was widely perceived as having mismanaged the economy. His regime squandered state resources on inappropriate large-scale development projects while periodic droughts and neglect of the agriculture resulted in scarcity of rice, the staple food of Guinea-Bissau. Hence, the 1980 ousting of Cabral became known as the "rice coup." Global recession and declining terms of trade added to Guinea-Bissau's dependency on

donors. This dependency stemmed in no small part to the colonial experience and war of liberation, which left Guinea-Bissau with little capacity, almost no infrastructure or industry, and an undereducated population.

Cabral's policies angered the military and served as the catalyst or spark for the coup. As part of the demobilization scheme following the war for independence, Cabral planned to ship ex-soldiers to farms in remote parts of the country. He also attempted to introduce a new ranking system for the military. Both of these plans proved to be unpopular with the uniformed forces. Cabral also proposed constitutional changes, which would lead to the unification of Guinea-Bissau with Cape Verde and strengthen the power of the president at the expense of the Prime Minister. These changes angered black Guineans who feared domination by the mixed-race and better-educated Cape Verdeans, which included President Cabral.

A relatively bloodless coup led by Major Vieira on 15 November 1980 cost the lives of two senior government officials. Several government officials were abroad, and President Cabral was vacationing at his home in the Bijagós Islands, where he was placed under house arrest. Cabral was later exiled to Cuba after Vieira and his forces discovered the bodies of more than 500 political prisoners who had been executed during Cabral's six-year reign. (Cabral was allowed to return to Guinea-Bissau December 1999). Many Guineans welcomed the coup and celebrated the promise of better living conditions.

Although President Vieira was a reluctant champion of political reform, the advent of democracy across Africa gave him few options. The constitution underwent extensive amendment, a national conference to determine the country's future took place, and opposition parties were authorized. In Guinea-Bissau's first multi-party elections in July and August 1994, President Vieira narrowly beat a former PAIGC member, Koumba Yala, 52% to 48%. The vote was considered reasonably free and fair despite Yala's protestations.

In March 1998, an independent electoral commission was established. Vieira's fall in April–May 1999 and his subsequent exile ushered in an interim government led by Malam Bacai Sanha. A second set of multi-party elections for the National Assembly and presidency, in which 12 candidates competed, were organized. In the 28 November round, Koumba Yala scored 38.5% to Sanha's 23.4%. In the 16 January run-off, he swept 72% of the vote. In the Assembly elections, Yala's PRS party took 38 of 102 seats. The *Resistencia da Guine-Bissau-Movimento Bafata* took 28 while the PAIGC managed 24 seats. Five other parties captured the remaining 12 seats.

## LEADERSHIP

The 92% voter turnout indicated wide popular support for Yala. Indeed, he was part of a two-hour televised and radio-broadcast political debate with Mr. Sanha, a first for Africa. Since his inauguration on 16 February, Yala has affirmed that the provision of health and education programs, as well as the revitalization of the agriculture sector, would be among the priorities for his government. He also pledged to fight corruption, a consistent plague in the past. He intends as well to build a freer society, in his mind part of the foundation for good governance and democracy.

## DOMESTIC POLICY

Yala's leadership will be tested by major social, economic, and political obstacles. Guinea-Bissau is one of the 15 poorest countries in the world. Civil servants, health workers, and teachers staged strikes in the weeks leading up to the elections to protest nine months of salary payments in arrears. Unpaid workers in the electric and water utility cut off power and water to the capital city for almost a week while on strike. Similar protests are likely to occur again. To appease disgruntled military leaders, Yala offered the military junta five cabinet posts. General Mane has pledged to stay out of politics and he turned down the prime minister's offer to advise the president. The second in command, Colonel Verissimo Correia Seabre, has refused to accept his appointment as Defense Minister. Some 90 war prisoners have yet to stand trial.

Despite these challenges, Yala is benefiting from strong international support. The IMF has released US$2 million in assistance, and the World Bank is planning to distribute an economic recovery and rehabilitation credit worth US$25 million by mid-2000. The EU has started to release some of the US$38 million it pledged for the post-war reconstruction program. According to the IMF, real GDP grew by 8.7% in 1999, stemming from reconstruction and a resumption of exports of cashews, the country's main source of foreign exchange earnings.

## FOREIGN POLICY

In the early going, it appears that President Yala will enjoy considerable international support. Local and foreign dignitaries, including the presidents of Cape Verde and The Gambia, as well as the Portuguese foreign minister, attended his inaugural ceremony. Former President Vieira, in exile, congratulated him by letter.

Guinea-Bissau traditionally has maintained its closest relations with Portugal, for better and for worse. Since joining the West African Monetary Union (WAMU/UEMOA) and becoming part of the CFA zone in March 1997, the French connection has become more important. Under Vieira, ties were established with Taiwan and Morocco.

Aside from currying favor with Western donors, Yala is likely to build strong relationships with neighbors in the region, including Cape Verde, Guinea, and Senegal. Yala should benefit from Guinea-Bissau's mediation in the peace negotiations between the Senegalese government and the Casamance separatists. The sporadic attacks along the border, however, indicate that this long-festering sore has not yet mended.

## ADDRESS

Conselho de Estado
Bissau, Guinea-Bissau

## REFERENCES

*Africa Confidential*, various issues.

Africa News Online. [Online] Available http:// www.africanews.org/west/stories/1999_feat1.html (Accessed June 2000).

*Africa Report*, various issues.

*The Africa Review*, various issues.

Africaonline. [Online] Available http://www.africa-online.com (Accessed June 2000).

Economist Intelligence Unit. *EIU Country Reports*. 1 April 2000.

"Guinea-Bissau: President Sworn In." *The New York Times*, 18 February 2000, p. A6.

Integrated Regional Information Network (IRIN). [Online] Available http://www.reliefweb.int/IRIN (Accessed June 2000).

*Review of African Political Economy*, May–September 1981.

*West Africa*, various issues.

**Profile researched and written by Robert J. Groelsema (6/2000).**

# GUYANA

## Bharrat Jagdeo
## President

*(pronounced "bar-RAHT JAG-day-oh")*

*"I know that there are tens of thousands of patriotic Guyanese from all walks of life who are prepared to put their shoulders to the wheel to build a happy tomorrow."*

The Republic of Guyana is situated on the northeastern shoulder of South America. The only English-speaking country on the continent, it is bound on the west by Venezuela, on the east by Suriname, and on the south and southwest by Brazil. Guyana occupies an area of approximately 215,000 sq km (83,000 sq mi). Its capital city and major port, Georgetown, is on the Atlantic coast.

The population of Guyana is estimated at 705,000. Its racial composition includes East Indians (49%), Africans (32%), Amerindians (6%), Chinese and European (1%), and mixed races (12%). Both the Afro-Guyanese and the Indo-Guyanese were brought to the country by the Europeans to work on sugar plantations. The Afro-Guyanese arrived as slaves. The Indo-Guyanese, Chinese, and Portuguese came after slavery had been abolished and worked as indentured servants. The official language is English although derivatives of Hindu, Hindustani, Portuguese, and Africanisms exist as well. Among Amerindians, the Warrau, Arawak, and Carib languages are spoken. The major religions are Christianity, Hinduism, and Islam.

The economy is based primarily on exporting bauxite, alumina, sugar, rice, timber, rum, and shrimp. Agricultural activity is concentrated along the coastal belt where most of the population resides. Extensive timber resources in the tropical hinterland remain largely untouched. The local currency is the Guyana dollar.

## POLITICAL BACKGROUND

Guyana was the first country in the New World to be explored by non-Iberians. It was originally divided into three Dutch colonies: Essequibo, Demerara, and Berbice. Following a war between Britain and the Netherlands in 1803, the British captured the colonies, which were ceded to them by the Dutch 11 years later. The three colonies were united to form the colony of British Guyana in 1831. That colony remained under British control until 26 May 1966 when Guyana gained its independence.

In 1980, the Guyanese government adopted a constitution that established the country as a cooperative republic within the Commonwealth. Under this new constitution, the president is the head of state and is elected for a five-year term on the basis of parliamentary elections. The prime minister is the head of government and leader of the majority party in the National Assembly. The National Assembly has 65 members, 53 of whom are elected by a system of proportional representation, with each voter casting his vote in favor of a list rather than a specific candidate. There are also 12 members delegated to the House of Assembly by the local government councils. The president, from among opposition members of the Assembly, appoints a leader of the opposition.

Currently, Guyana has two major political parties. The People's Progressive Party/Civic (PPP/Civic) is a socialist party led by Bharrat Jagdeo. The People's National Congress (PNC) is a socialist/populist party, headed by Hugh Desmond Hoyte. There are also three minor parties: the Guyana Labour Party, The United Force, and The Working People's Alliance (WPA).

The PPP was launched on 1 January 1950 with Cheddi Jagan as its leader, Linden Burnham as its chairman, and Janet Jagan as its secretary. In 1953, the first general elections under adult suffrage were held. The PPP won 18 of the 24 seats in the parliament. However the PPP faced a hurdle when, in 1955, Burnham and his supporters split the party. The major reason for this was that Burnham wanted to be leader of the PPP. In 1957, he launched his own party, the PNC, but was defeated in the general elections, which were held that year. The PPP continued to be victorious in the general elections of 1961 and 1964.

Corruption, violence, and fraud marred the electoral system after 1964. The PPP lost the 1968 election to the PNC—who captured 56% of the vote. In the elections of 1973, 1980, and 1985, the PPP and the WPA accused the PNC of electoral fraud and corruption. The popular and charismatic leader of the WPA, Walter Rodney, was allegedly assassinated in 1980 for his opposition to the policies of the PNC.

In October 1992, free and fair elections were held. The PPP/Civic emerged victorious, having received 54% of the vote. Jagan was once again reinstated as president. However, the PPP suffered a great loss when he died five years later. In the 1997 general elections, Janet Jagan, widow of the former president, led the PPP to victory once again—capturing 29 of the 53 elected seats in the House of Assembly. Her government included Sam Hinds as prime minister and Bharrat Jagdeo as vice president. Health problems forced Jagan's resignation. On 11 August 1999, Jagdeo was sworn in as the sixth president of the Republic of Guyana.

## PERSONAL BACKGROUND

Bharrat Jagdeo was born at Unity Village, East Coast Demerara on 23 January 1964. "Bharrat" means India in Hindi. His mother gave him this name in honor of his ancestral homeland. Jagdeo is from a simple, working-class family. His father was a railroad worker. His mother, a housewife and farmer, had the task of raising her six children. Jagdeo attended the Gibson Primary School and then proceeded to the Mahaica Multilateral School for his secondary education. He was successful in the Caribbean Examination Council (CXC) and the General Certificate of Education (Advanced Level) examinations. He then returned to his local primary school for a short teaching stint. In 1984, Jagdeo was awarded a scholarship to pursue studies in Moscow. He graduated from Moscow's Patrice Lumumba University in 1990 with a Master of Science degree in economics. Shortly after completing his studies, Jagdeo returned to Guyana and began working for the government. Jagdeo and his wife, Vashnie, were married in 1998.

## RISE TO POWER

Jagdeo held various government finance and banking positions in the early 1990s. From 1992 until 1999, he served as director of the Guyana Water Authority, the Caribbean Development Bank, and the National Bank of Industry and Commerce. He was also Guyana's governor on the World Bank. Jagdeo represented Guyana at international meetings of the World Bank, the Inter-American Development Bank, and the International Monetary Fund (IMF). He worked as an economic planner in the State Planning Secretariat. Following this assignment, Jagdeo was appointed special advisor to the minister of finance. In October 1993, he was named junior minister of finance, rising to senior minister two years later. Jagdeo was a member of the Progressive Youth Organization (PYO). He is currently a member of the Central Committee and executive member of the PPP.

## LEADERSHIP

Guyana's economy had been experiencing deterioration since the late 1970s. The per-capita income is now under US$350, making Guyana one of the poorest nations in the Western Hemisphere. However, since his appointment as senior minister of finance, Jagdeo has been responsible for the success of Guyana's campaign for debt relief. He has single-handedly steered the Ministry of Finance and played a major role in improving the economy. By 1996, Guyana had posted its fifth straight year of economic growth of 5% or higher. This was due to increases in gold and bauxite mining and sugar production.

As minister of finance, Jagdeo was given the task of coordinating efforts to craft a National Development Strategy. He was able to bring together more than 200 local professionals and hundreds from across the nation to plan Guyana's future development. His ability to do this demonstrated his leadership capacity, and the success of his efforts continues to be acknowledged. He was also able to reduce the stock of debt by US$700 million and has successfully negotiated grants and loans totaling $300 million.

As president, Jagdeo continues to face the overwhelming challenge of steering Guyana further away from economic turmoil and financial devastation. With the exchange rate at its current high, Jagdeo will have to implement more "life-saving" policies to pull the nation out of the economic doldrums. Over the years, Jagdeo has been described as a "go-getter," a hands on minister who opposes corruption and

advocates clean and honest governance. Based on his recent success as a young and talented minister, it is expected that he will achieve great success. As the former president, Janet Jagan stated, "there is more hope for a bright future with Bharrat Jagdeo at the helm."

## DOMESTIC POLICY

Guyana has a history of economic deterioration resulting from the implementation of economic policies which did more to increase international debt than to improve the conditions for social and economic growth. Guyana's per capita income is now under US$350, and it remains one of the poorest nations in the world. The country has also been confronted with rapid devaluation and, as a result of political corruption, has received negative publicity abroad. Consequently, during the 1980s and early 1990s, business suffered tremendously. When the PPP/Civic won the elections in 1992, many businesses breathed a sigh of relief. They viewed this government as bringing new hope for economic survival.

As minister of finance, Jagdeo sought to remove the country from the international club of debt-ridden nations. Guyana was able to honor huge international debts with as much as 90 cents from each dollar earned by earmarking export income for payment of foreign debt. According to the Caribbean Development Bank Report, GDP grew by 7.9% by 1996, which was in line with the rates achieved over 1992–1994. They praised Guyana for this economic growth as it was the highest in the region and the highest among the bank's borrowing member countries. Inflation also decreased from 8.1% in 1995 to 4.5% in 1996. The rate of inflation has seen further reduction and now stands at 4.1% (1998).

Current revenue has also increased by 16%, from Guy$29.5b in 1996 to Guy$34.2b in 1997. This resulted from increased economic activity and improved tax collections and compliance. Output in the mining sector has seen an increase of 15.3% (1997), especially due to increases in such areas as gold, bauxite, and diamond production. Sugar production increased from 247,000 tons in 1992 to 280,000 in 1996. Rice production increased from 168,300 tons to 320,000 over the same period. The agricultural sector as a whole rose by 7.7% during the same time. During its years in office, the PPP/Civic has been able to preside over this amazing economic revival.

The stable macroeconomic environment and the overhauling of social, economic, and physical infrastructure has revived business interests. Both local and foreign investors are now ready to grasp the opportunities created by the government. As president, Jagdeo has made it clear that he intends to build partnerships with "the major players of the Guyanese society." These "major players" are the private sector, the labor movement, civic society, and the political opposition. These partnerships, Jagdeo feels, will help to accelerate his goal of satisfying the needs and aspirations of the Guyanese people. The rate of unemployment currently stands at 12%. In light of this, Jagdeo intends to focus on job creation. The government's macroeconomic policy will continue with specific focus given to housing, education, and health care. Jagdeo recognizes that continued economic recovery will depend, in the short term, on the continued exploitation of minerals, fishery, and forestry resources and on continued primary production. As Jagdeo continues rebuilding the economy, he hopes to achieve growth and, at the same time, use the wealth created to enhance the well being of his people.

## FOREIGN POLICY

Jagdeo intends to deepen friendly ties with neighboring states—Brazil, Suriname, and Venezuela. He also aims to quicken the process of political and economic union within the Caribbean Community (CARICOM) and recognizes the need to maintain close ties with the international community. To that end, he hopes to strengthen relations with the United States, Canada, Britain, India, and China.

Although the economic indicators in Guyana have been impressive, foreign investment has come mainly from outside the Caribbean region. Asian-based logging companies have taken an interest in Guyana's forestry sector while American and Canadian groups are heading towards the mining and other extractive industries. Caribbean interest has been limited to Trinidad and Tobago, Barbados, and Jamaica. To encourage other Caribbean countries to invest in Guyana, Jagdeo intends to develop attractive investment and incentive packages.

## ADDRESS

Office of the President
New Garden Street and South Road
Georgetown, Guyana

## REFERENCES

*Caribbean's Top 100 Public Companies 1997–98.*
Central Intelligence Agency. *The World Factbook 1999.* [Online] Available http://www.cia.gov/ (Accessed February 2000).
*Daily Gleaner,* various issues.
*Mirror,* various issues.

**Profile researched and written by Ian and Rachael Boxill, University of the West Indies, Mona, Jamaica (12/99; updated 2/2000).**

# HAITI

### René Préval
### President
(pronounced "ra-NAY pray-VAL")

*"The country belongs to all of us. Together we will save it. The choices won't be easy.
I'll say it from the beginning of the game."*

The Republic of Haiti occupies the western third of the Caribbean island of Hispaniola, with a total area of 27,750 sq km (10,714 sq mi). The capital is Port-au-Prince, located in the southeastern region of the country. Haiti shares the island with the neighboring Dominican Republic. Cuba lies about 80 km (50 mi) to the west; the Bahamas are to the north. The population has been estimated at 6.9 million. Ninety-five percent of Haitians are of African descent; the other 5% are mixed African-Caucasian. Haiti is one of the world's most densely populated countries, with approximately 250 people per sq km (650 per sq mi); 70% of Haitians live in rural areas. Catholicism, the state religion, comprises 80% of the population, while Protestantism makes up 10%. Voodoo practice is widespread, and most Haitians see no conflict between religious faith and voodoo rituals and rites. The official languages are French, spoken by only about 10% of the people, and Creole, which is spoken universally. Only 20% of Haiti's territory is arable land; with nearly 75% of Haitians engaged in subsistence farming, the pressures on the land have been enormous and devastating: deforestation and soil erosion have combined to diminish agricultural productivity to the point where Haiti cannot feed itself, relying instead on food imports and feeding programs for most of its people. Fewer than 10% of Haitians are employed in what little manufacturing takes place in the country. 60% of the work force is unemployed. Large-scale emigration of skilled workers has left Haiti with a potential work force with little or no education and few skills. Coffee, cocoa, mangoes, and essential oils make up the bulk of Haiti's exports, most of which are destined for the United States (75%). Per capita GDP has been estimated at $1,300. Inflation is 8%. Haiti's income distribution is among the most skewed in the world, with 90% of wealth controlled by less than 10% of the population. Haiti is the poorest country in the Western Hemisphere and among the poorest in the world. The currency is the *gourde*.

## POLITICAL BACKGROUND

Haiti was colonized in 1659 by the French, who developed large sugar plantations utilizing slave labor from Africa. The years between 1659 and 1791 are the only period of political stability Haiti has known. From 1791 through 1803, the country experienced a slave rebellion that culminated in the slaves' victory over Napoleon's army and the establishment in 1804 of the independent state of Haiti, ruled by Dessalines, who declared himself emperor. The remainder of the 19th century was marked by frequent and often violent shifts in political power, with 22 changes of government during the period 1843–1915. Much of the conflict arose from the ethnic hierarchy, which remained essentially unchanged from Haiti's colonial period. Although Haitians of African descent made up the vast majority of the population, political power was concentrated in the hands of mulattos and light-skinned descendants of European landholders, which created extraordinary social tensions. After an extended period of heightened conflict and bloodletting between the two segments of society, the US occupied Haiti in 1915 and ruled the country until 1934. A succession of leaders followed the US departure, including the first black president of the republic, Dusmarsais Estime, in 1946. Two subsequent regimes were overthrown before 1957, and six held power that year before François Duvalier, a much beloved country physician, was elected president.

Despite a promising start, characterized by significant popular support, Duvalier (known popularly as "Papa Doc") quickly assumed dictatorial powers, declaring himself President-for-Life, and unleashed what would become a 30-year reign of terror led first by himself and then by his son, Jean-Claude "Baby Doc," who succeeded to the presidency in April 1971 when his father died. Both Duvaliers used the *Tontons Macoutes*, a loyal private militia to control the nation and to crush opposition. Nevertheless, the 1970s and 1980s were characterized by intensifying public protest, despite increasing government repression. In 1985, in a last-ditch attempt to control the political forces sweeping Haiti, Baby Doc announced a series of constitutional reforms that would open the political process. Public opposition continued unabated, and Duvalier responded in January 1986 with the imposition of a state of siege and the declaration of martial law. On 7 February 1986, finally bowing to intense pressure both at home and abroad, Jean-Claude Duvalier and his family fled Haiti for exile in France. A series of unstable provisional military governments followed until March 1990 when Ertha Pascal Trouillot, a supreme court judge, was named head of yet another interim government. Trouillot was committed to democratic elections that had been promised and subsequently canceled by military leaders in the post-Duvalier period. These elections took place in December 1990 when Jean-Bertrand Aristide, a former priest, was elected president of the Republic of Haiti with 67.5% of the vote. Aristide was overthrown in a military coup on 30 September 1991. The junta remained in power until October

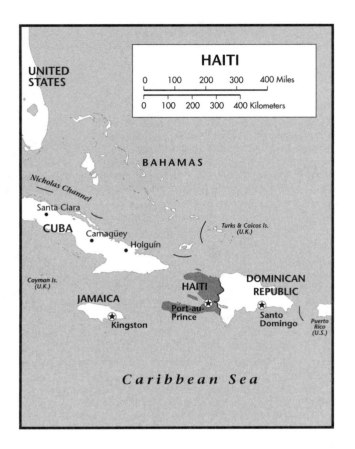

1994 when 20,000 US troops came to prepare for Aristide's return.

Under the Constitution approved by referendum in March 1987, the national government is comprised of several elements, all of which are intended to exert checks and balances on each other, thereby preventing any one element from acquiring overwhelming power. The legislature is bicameral, consisting of an 83-member Chamber of Deputies and a 27-member Senate. The executive power is held by the president, elected to a single five-year term, and the prime minister, chosen by the president from the majority party in the legislature, subject to the approval of that body. The Constitution explicitly bans former Duvalierists from elective office for 10 years. The voting age is 18, and suffrage is universal.

## PERSONAL BACKGROUND

René Préval is 52 years old. He comes from an urban middle-class background. His father was a government minister in the early 1950s, but the family was forced into exile in 1963 during the Duvalier dictatorship. Préval attended university in Belgium during that exile and later lived for five years in New York City. He returned to Haiti in 1982 and opened a bakery. His personal life is largely unknown, and even many Haitians regard Préval as a shadowy and secretive figure; in fact, there is not even agreement as to the president's age. He has a reputation as a man of the left who is suspicious of private enterprise, and some in the United States regard Préval as a dangerous radical.

## RISE TO POWER

Préval met Jean-Bertrand Aristide during the 1980s and quickly became a close personal friend and confidante. He was a behind-the-scenes advisor to Aristide during his presidential campaign. When Aristide was elected to the presidency, he chose Préval as his first prime minister. Together the two men envisioned a social transformation on a grand scale, based on redistributing the nation's wealth to the poor masses. When the Aristide government was overthrown in 1991, Préval accompanied the president into exile. When Aristide was returned to power, Préval was not given a cabinet post, due in large part to lingering American distrust. Instead, he became an informal advisor to the president, who named Préval director of the Foundation for Economic and Social Assistance, supervising and financing development projects; this position was essentially a patronage operation for the president. Although Préval has never held elected office, his close association with Aristide made him the front-runner in the 1995 presidential campaign. Préval emphasized that relationship while he campaigned and left largely unexplored his positions and plans. One curious development in the campaign was Aristide's seeming reluctance to endorse Préval's candidacy. Préval was thought to be Aristide's choice for the Lavalas candidacy; however, it was not until 15 December that the president formally endorsed Préval.

The 1995 presidential field was made up of 14 candidates. Préval was the front-runner from the moment he entered the race, simply by virtue of being the candidate of Aristide's Lavalas movement. In contrast to the chaotic June 1995 elections, the 17 December 1995 presidential election occurred peacefully and without incident, and was declared to be the first truly open and honest election in Haiti's history. Unlike the 1990 election, when Haitians voted in large numbers, only 28% of Haiti's registered voters participated in the 1995 presidential election. Préval won 87.9% of the vote; the runner-up received 2.5%.

## LEADERSHIP

On 7 February 1996, exactly 10 years after Baby Doc Duvalier fled Haiti, René Préval accepted the presidential sash from President Jean-Bertrand Aristide. Then he stated to the assembled crowd, "Today an elected president hands over power to another elected president. No Haitians before you have had the privilege of witnessing this in our history." Within two weeks, Préval named as his prime minister Rony Smarth, an agricultural economist whom Préval has known for at least 10 years. This choice is indicative of Préval's determination to address Haiti's declining agricultural production: valued at $120 million in 1991, it plummeted to approximately $75 million in 1995. Elections held in June 1995 gave Lavalas 80% of the 110 seats in the National Assembly and Senate. However, this majority is far from a rubber stamp for presidential policies: even under Aristide, Parliament argued for months about the 1996 budget and failed repeatedly to adopt IMF economic guidelines, thus jeopardizing 65% of the nation's $760 million budget.

Even before assuming office, Préval addressed two issues critical to Haiti's future. He asked UN troops, scheduled to leave Haiti on 29 February 1996, to extend the peacekeeping mission until the end of August. US troop commitments ended as scheduled at the end of February. In January 1996, the president also resumed negotiations with the IMF and World Bank, broken off in October 1995, in an attempt to free up millions of dollars in aid that had been frozen due to Haiti's lack of compliance with required austerity measures. In his inaugural address, Préval stressed his commitment to creating jobs, to lowering the cost of living and to ending the street violence that has been on the increase since autumn of 1995. However, he also made it clear that these changes would not occur overnight.

## DOMESTIC POLICY

Préval made clear in his inaugural address that economic recovery was of paramount importance. The Haitian economy, never strong to begin with, was decimated under the military regime during the early 1990s due to widespread corruption and mismanagement and the effects of the economic sanctions imposed by the international community. There has been no substantial improvement since the end of the dictatorship, and many experts agree that it will be several years until economic production reaches pre-coup levels. In the meantime, many Haitians are malnourished, unemployed, and without real hope of a better life in the foreseeable future. The president needs to create jobs, to increase agricultural production, and to restore hope to Haiti's impoverished masses. One crucial element of Préval's plan must include the adoption of IMF economic guidelines, which include widespread privatization of industry and economic austerity measures designed to further reduce inflation. Sixty-five percent of Haiti's budget comes from foreign donors and is contingent upon the adoption of these measures. As of 1999, seven state-owned companies, including Teleco, the telephone company, were set to be privatized.

Haitians have experienced continual chaos since Prime Minister Rosny Smarth resigned in 1997 to protest electoral fraud. Elections, last held in 1997, have been repeatedly postponed, and with no budget and no functioning parliament the country has lacked a government. In January 1999, President Rene Preval installed by decree former Education Minister Jacques-Eduard Alexis as prime minister when he also dissolved parliament by declaring legislative terms expired. Since there had been no new elections, he also began replacing many mayors and other officials. The Haitian Supreme Court refused to rule in the dispute between Preval and legislators over the length of legislative terms. In March 1999, Preval created a new 15-member cabinet by decree. The United States released $3.5 million to Haiti for the creation of voter registration cards as a step towards less fraudulent elections. Former President Jean-Bertrand Aristide announced that his party would participate in the elections, the date for which was set as 19 March 2000. Political unrest grew, and violence escalated throughout the year. President Preval's sister was wounded, and members of the opposition party, Organization of People in Struggle (OPL), were repeatedly attacked, some killed. Election offices were burned; street violence and demonstrations increased. As a result of escalating violence, elections were once again postponed, set this time for 21 May 2000. However, both foreign and Haitian analysts say that the odds of the elections actually being held as scheduled are little less than even.

## FOREIGN POLICY

Haiti is one of the original members of the United Nations and participates in many of its specialized agencies. The country maintains diplomatic relations with most European and Latin American countries, although most do not maintain embassies in Haiti. Out of pure self-interest, Préval must remain on friendly terms with donor countries, which include Canada, France, Germany, and Japan, as well as the US. These are also the countries that are likely sources of foreign economic investment.

In 1998, Haitians, already the poorest people in the Americas, saw their economy suffer from the forces of nature, as well as their own politicians. A hurricane devastated the economy, damaging rice crops and leaving hundreds dead. The United States and the European Union offered recovery assistance, but most other foreign aid has been suspended since the country has lacked a government and a budget since 1997.

Drug-running has grown. Since 1999, Haitian police have been attempting to close down a network that carries drugs from Colombia through Haiti to the United States and other destinations. Six of the police themselves were detained on suspicion of theft. They were believed to have stolen the majority of a haul of cocaine that was discovered in a boat headed for Miami. US government officials estimate 20% of drugs now reaching the country pass through Haiti. The national police of Haiti decided to intensify the fight on drug trafficking as a means of lowering crime in general, in hopes of improving the environment for the upcoming elections.

Defense officials announced the closing of the United States' permanent camp in Haiti and the gradual withdrawal of US troops. The US military presence will be reduced to specific humanitarian missions in the future. They are already engaged in road building and repair and medical care. A series of humanitarian visits will begin as part of the "New Horizons" program in the Caribbean region.

## ADDRESS

National Palace
Port-au-Prince
Haiti

## REFERENCES

*Boston Globe*, various issues.
*Christian Science Monitor*, various issues.
Constable, Pamela. "A Fresh Start for Haiti." *Current History*, February 1996, pp. 65–69.
*Current History*, various issues, 1999.
*The Economist*, various issues, 1995–96, 1999.
*Foreign Affairs*, various issues, 1994–95.
*Latin American Weekly Reports*, various issues, 1994–96.
*New York Times*, various issues, November 1995–March 1996.

**Profile written and researched by Alison Doherty-Munro, independent researcher (3/96; updated 4/2000).**

# HONDURAS

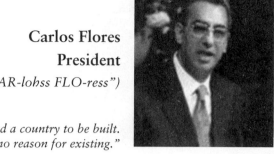

## Carlos Flores
## President
*(pronounced "CAR-lohss FLO-ress")*

*"There is a world to be conquered and a country to be built. Without the youth of this nation, the New Agenda has no reason for existing."*

The Republic of Honduras is bounded on the north by the Caribbean Sea, on the west by Guatemala, on the southwest by El Salvador, and on the southeast by Nicaragua. The northern coast measures 820 km (509 mi). In the south there is limited access to the Pacific Ocean through the Choluteca River and the Gulf of Fonseca. More than 75% of the country is mountainous, with the highest mountain reaching 2,800 m (9,200 ft). Most urban settlements and agricultural production are located in a large northern lowlands area and a smaller southern lowlands region. At 112,492 sq km (43,433 sq mi) and with a population of 6 million, Honduras is the third-largest Central American country in area and population.

More than 90% of the population is mestizo (mixed Indian and European), with the remainder divided among Indians, blacks, and whites. The rapid population growth rate of 2.24% per year has helped increase economic problems. Despite a high infant mortality rate of 40.84 deaths per 1,000 live births, the population is expected to double in 20 years. The 1999 fertility rate was 3.97 children per woman. Life expectancy remains low at 64.68 years. Some progress in literacy has been made in recent years. In 1999, an estimated 72.7% of all Hondurans aged 15 and over were literate. Although Spanish is the official language, several indigenous dialects are also spoken in scattered areas. Roman Catholics make up 97% of the population and, although there is an official separation between church and state, Catholics hold political and economic power. A small but growing Protestant minority, heavily financed by US-based churches, has begun to emerge in recent years, mainly in urban areas.

The economy is based on tropical agriculture. Almost two-thirds of the labor force is employed in agriculture, and more than two-thirds of the exports come from agricultural crops such as bananas, coffee, and citrus. Manufacturing, especially the textile industry, has also grown in recent years. With low productivity, low wages, and unskilled labor, the manufacturing industry (10% of the workforce) is characterized by sweatshops and poor working conditions for many women and children. The economy shrank in 1999 by 4.5%, one of the worst recessions in recent years. Per capita GDP amounted to $740, which places Honduras among the poorest countries in the hemisphere. With an annual inflation rate of 26%, and a foreign debt of $4.1 billion, the economy is unable to meet the urgent needs of its growing poor and young population. Some 50% of Honduras live below the poverty line, and unemployment and underemployment affect 30% of the population. The unit of currency is the *lempira*.

## POLITICAL BACKGROUND

In the pre-Colombian period, parts of the region were occupied by the Maya civilization. Christopher Columbus reached Honduras in 1502, but permanent European settlement did not begin until 1522 when the first Spanish governor was appointed. The indigenous population reacted and fought the Spaniards. The discovery of silver in 1570 brought renewed economic activity to the area and an increase in population. However, Honduras remained a small and unimportant province of the Captaincy of Guatemala during the colonial period.

Honduras declared independence in 1821 and withdrew from the Central American Federation in 1838. Conservative landowners held political power until 1876 when Liberals gained the presidency and adopted a new constitution. At the turn of the century, political unrest and instability threatened the economic interests of American landowners, particularly the United Fruit Company, and the US sent troops to protect investments in banana production. In 1932, with the election of general Tiburcio Carías, unrest came to an end. Carías became a dictator and governed with widespread repression until his fall in 1949. Heavy American intervention secured banana production but brought little support for democratic forces in the country. For the most part, military strongmen ruled the country from 1949 to 1981. In 1981 a civilian government was elected to office, but the military remained strong.

There have been four democratically elected presidents in Honduras since 1982. The two leading political parties are the right wing Liberal Party and the pro-military National Party. The left was heavily repressed during the military governments and has since been unable to organize and succeed in elections. Liberals Roberto Suazo (1981–85) and José Azcona (1985–89) are credited with restoring civilian rule and limiting the power of the military. National Party leader, Rafael Callejas (1989–93), successfully managed to distance himself from the military and won the election of 1989. Yet, his economic plan brought increased poverty and was not able to improve the economy. In 1993, Liberal Party candidate, Carlos Roberto Reina was elected to the presidency. He attempted to bring to trial known human rights violators among military officers and tried to foster economic growth. Reina successfully amended the constitution to reduce the power of the military and abolish mandatory military service. His "moral revolution" concentrated on fighting corruption. Many high government officials were sent to jail, including some of Reina's personal friends. He was less successful in his efforts to improve the economy. While inflation was brought under control, it remained moderately high (20% in 1996). Though the economy had grown at the moderate rate of 4% in recent years, this was not sufficient to meet the urgent demands of the rural and urban poor. Since the Honduran constitution contains no provisions for reelection, Reina was prevented from seeking a second term in 1997. Instead, the Liberal Party chose Carlos Flores as their candidate. On 30 November 1997 Flores succeeded in defeating the National Party's candidate and began his four-year term as president on 27 January. His victory represents the fifth consecutive transfer of power between civilians since the last military dictatorship ended in 1982.

The constitution is based on a separation of powers between three branches of government. A strong presidency is filled by national elections every four years. The National Congress, a unicameral body, is elected by proportional representation every four years. The judiciary, headed by the Supreme Court, is appointed by the legislature. There is universal adult suffrage, and all parties may participate in political life.

## PERSONAL BACKGROUND

Carlos Roberto Flores Facussé was born on 1 March 1950 in Tegucigalpa, the capital of Honduras. The son of successful entrepreneurs, Flores was educated in private schools in Honduras and then attended college in the US. He received a bachelor of science degree in industrial engineering from Louisiana State University and went on to study international economics and finance as a graduate student. In 1974 he married Mary Carol Flakes, an American citizen. Flores and his wife settled in Honduras and joined his father in family business ventures. In 1979, Flores and his father started a newspaper, *La Tribuna*, which soon became a leading newspaper in the country.

## RISE TO POWER

In 1982, Flores was elected to Congress as a Liberal Party candidate. He served as minister for the presidency in the administration of President Roberto Suazo Córdoba (1982–86) but was dismissed in 1984. Reelected to Congress in 1985, Flores worked toward becoming the presidential nominee of his party in 1989. He lost the election to Rafael Callejas in the Liberal Party's only electoral defeat since the restoration of democracy in 1982. After his defeat, Flores prepared to return to Congress. He concentrated on increasing his financial power through the family businesses and his political power through the newspaper. He was reelected to Congress in 1993 and became the leader of his party and president of the legislature, the second most powerful position in the Honduran government.

With the political support of former president Suazo, Flores vied for the presidency again in 1997. He secured his party's nomination but distanced himself from the Reina administration. He successfully portrayed himself as an opposition candidate from the same party as the incumbent

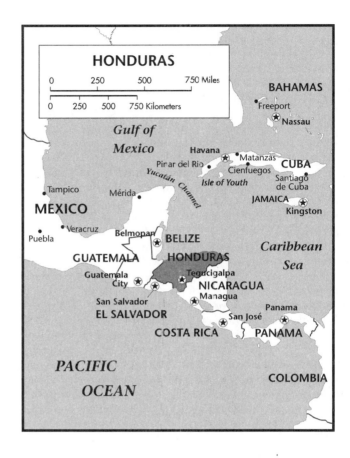

president. Flores was able to capitalize on his record as president of Congress and on the poor economic performance of the Reina administration. In the presidential elections, the National Party's candidate was Nora Gunera de Melgar, the widow of a former military leader and first woman to be nominated to the Honduran presidency. The campaign was characterized by Melgar's refusal to debate Flores in a nationally televised debate and by an airplane accident that nearly cost Flores his life. After the accident, Flores experienced a resurgence in his level of support and gained a commanding lead which lasted until election day. Although abstention levels were high (30%), Flores secured 53% of the vote to Melgar's 42.5%. In order to assure that the election would be fair, voters were required to produce identification cards. Some questions were raised about possible electoral fraud by the government, but all losing candidates accepted the final results and praised the democratic process. The two major political parties, the traditionally conservative Liberal Party and the former pro-military, turned centrist, National Party have traditionally gathered an overwhelming majority of votes. In 1997, however, the Christian Democratic Party and a leftist party successfully bid for seats in the legislature.

## LEADERSHIP

Flores has fiercely criticized the economic policies of Reina and has promised to take measures to reduce poverty levels. More than 75% of all households in the country live below the poverty line and about 47% of all Hondurans subsist on a daily income of less than $1. Flores has suggested the "New Agenda" as the centerpiece of his administration. This optimistic plan calls on Hondurans to recover the faith and initiate a search for a more prosperous future. The "New Agenda" proposes 10 central themes for the next four years to increase growth, reduce unemployment, and stabilize the economy.

## DOMESTIC POLICY

Under the "New Agenda," Flores promised to promote education for low income families by creating scholarships and developing partnerships with the private sector, to adjust salaries in order to keep pace with inflation, and to fight domestic violence and set up nurseries for working mothers. He has committed himself to the development of a mixed private and public pension system. However, it is unlikely he will achieve much of what he has promised. The tax system needs to be revamped but Flores is unwilling or unable to carry out tax reform. Without an effective tax system, resources to promote education, health, and pension reform will be wanting. Wage increases will need to be accompanied by increases in productivity in order to prevent inflation. Without investing in education, health, and infrastructure, it is unlikely that productivity will increase. Foreign debt renegotiation, subsidies and low interest loans from industrialized countries, an increase in the tax base, and foreign investments will be needed in order to generate the revenues required to develop a pension system and provide greater opportunities for women who want to enter the work force.

It is unlikely that Flores will continue to prosecute military personnel involved in human rights violations during the 1980s. However, he is expected to continue the campaign against corruption initiated by Reina. The Flores government will also attempt to attract foreign investors by privatizing some state enterprises and providing access to the country's natural resources. He has pledged to promote sustainable development while protecting the country's rich ecological diversity.

The most recent economic crisis that hit the country in late 1998 caused a deep contraction in the economy. Unemployment increased and the government's ailing budget was overwhelmed by the increase in poverty and unemployment. President Flores' popularity has fallen but no opposition leader has been able to emerge as a serious contender for power in that country.

## FOREIGN POLICY

Although the Honduran government has never been a key player in international affairs, support for the Nicaraguan Contras in the 1980s gained it a reputation for being a puppet of the most conservative political forces of the US. The Honduran army trained and supported Nicaraguan rebels who opposed the Sandinista government. Since the Central American wars ended in 1989, Honduras has attempted to distance itself from the US on some issues while remaining a strong ally to its major trading partner. It is unlikely that the situation will change with Flores. Honduras is expected to continue its support for the embargo against Cuba and will not take an active role in the effort to create a free trade market in Central America.

Perhaps the only area where Honduras has shown some political independence is in its continuous effort to develop economic ties with Taiwan. Despite China's opposition, Honduras has been the most enthusiastic supporter of Taiwan in the hemisphere. In return, Taiwan has encouraged investment in the country and has made low interest loans to the government. It is unlikely that Flores will attempt to alter this close relationship with Taiwan.

## ADDRESS

Casa Presidencial
6a Avenida 1a Calle
Tegucigalpa, Honduras

## REFERENCES

*CIA World Fact Book.* [Online] Available http://www.odci.gov/cia/publications/nsolo/factbook/ho.htm (Accessed April 2000).

CNN. [Online] Available http://cnn.com (Accessed December 1997).

*El País.* [Online] Available http://www.elpais.es/ (Accessed December 1997).

*Encyclopedia Britannica.* [Online] Available http://www.eb.com (Accessed April 2000).

*La Prensa de Honduras,* 8 September–3 December 1997.

*La Tribuna de Honduras,* 29 November–1 December 1997.

MacEoin, Gary. "Honduras: Corruption Hinders Hurricane Recovery." *National Catholic Reporter,* 30 April 1999, p. 6.

Noticias Nacionales. [Online] Available http://www.hondutel.hn/dtiempo/nacional.htm (Accessed April 2000).

**Profile researched and written by Patricio Navia, New York University (3/98; updated 4/2000).**

# HUNGARY

## Viktor Orban
## Prime Minister

*(pronounced "VIK-tor OR-ban")*

*"This will be a government of freedom, order, economic growth, solidarity, and cooperation with the member countries of the European Union."*

The Republic of Hungary lies in the Carpathian Basin in the heart of central Europe. To Hungary's west lies Austria; to the north, Slovakia; to the east, Ukraine and Romania; and to the south, Serbia, Croatia, and Slovenia. Hungary's area is approximately 93,010 sq km (35,919 sq mi).

Hungary has about 10.2 million inhabitants, of which approximately 92% are Hungarian, 4% are Romany (Gypsy), and about 2% are German. The capital is Budapest, with a population of about 2 million. About 67% of the population is Roman Catholic; some 20% are Calvinist; and 5% are Lutheran. The principal language is Hungarian, a Finno-Ugric language, spoken by about 98% of the people.

The national currency is the *forint*. Hungary's primary industries include machinery, transportation equipment, textiles, and pharmaceuticals. It also produces many agricultural goods such as meats and produce.

## POLITICAL BACKGROUND
Hungary's history has been one of conquest and invasion, drastically shifting borders, and widely divergent political systems. The Kingdom of Hungary was invaded by the Ottoman empire in the 16th century. Hungary was later incorporated into the Austrian Habsburg monarchy, which in 1867 ceded much autonomy to Hungary in a dual Austro-Hungarian empire. After World War I, the Austro-Hungarian monarchy collapsed, and many successor states emerged. Hungary lost about two-thirds of its former territory as a result of the 1920 Trianon peace treaty. In World War II, Hungary allied with Nazi Germany and during this time regained much of its former territory at the expense of Czechoslovakia and Romania, but the Trianon borders were essentially restored after the war. With support from the Soviet Union, the Hungarian Communist Party imposed a one-party system, and the People's Republic of Hungary was declared in 1949. A popular uprising against communist rule in 1956 was crushed by invading Warsaw Pact forces. Communist leader Janos Kadar, who ruled from 1956 to 1989, embarked on cautious liberalization and economic reform policies during his tenure.

In 1989, the year of East European revolutions, Hungary gradually but systematically moved toward a multiparty democracy. A peaceful transition from communism to democracy was confirmed in the first freely contested elections in 1990. The conservative Hungarian Democratic Forum (MDF) won 43% of the vote and led a noncommunist coalition government with Jozef Antall as prime minister. Unlike the other new democracies, Hungary faced no early elections or toppled governments for four years and appeared to many observers to be an island of stability in the region. The process of economic transformation, however, incurred considerable costs, leading to recession, rising unemployment, and declining output. New elections in 1994 returned the former Communist Party to power. The Hungarian Socialist Party won a majority of seats in parliament, Though able to govern alone, the Socialists worked out a coalition agreement with the liberal Alliance of Free Democrats. Gyula Horn of the Socialist Party became prime minister. Strains in the coalition became evident in late 1994 and early 1995 due to differences over economic policy and privatization. After months of delay, in March 1995 the Horn government launched sweeping economic reforms designed to stabilize the economy and reduce the country's foreign debt and budget deficit. The austerity measures were hugely unpopular but contributed to a significant economic turnaround. GDP growth in Hungary reached 4% in 1997.

Leading up to the next elections on 10 and 24 May 1998, the Hungarian Socialist Party and the opposition Federation of Young Democrats-Hungarian Civic Party (Fidesz) led in opinion polls. In the first round, the Socialists won 32.2% of the vote, and the Fidesz-Hungarian Civic Party won 28.2%. After the second round, the Fidesz-Hungarian Civic Party surged ahead, signaling a shift in power back to the right. The Fidesz-Hungarian Civic Party ended up with the largest share of parliamentary seats, 148 out of a total of 386, but short of a majority. The Socialists won 134 seats and its coalition partner Free Democrats won 24, a substantial loss from the last elections. Also winning seats were the populist Independent Smallholders Party (48), the Hungarian Democratic Forum (17), and for the first time, the far-right Hungarian Party for Justice and Life (14). Fidesz concluded negotiations on forming a ruling coalition with the Hungarian Democratic Forum and the Independent Smallholders Party; altogether the coalition commands 213 of 386 seats in parliament. President Goncz designated Fidesz leader, Viktor Orban, to be prime minister of a center-right government on 18 June. Parliament approved Orban's nomination and the coalition government on 6 July by a vote of 222 to 119.

## PERSONAL BACKGROUND
Viktor Orban was born on 31 May 1963 in Szekesfehervar, a farming village west of the capital, Budapest. He studied law at the Eotvos Lorand University in Budapest and was active in promoting democratic reforms. One year after graduation

**HUNGARY**

opposition during the tenure of the Socialist Horn government from 1994 to 1998. During these years, Orban worked to transform the party from an activist youth movement to a mainstream party ready to assume power and represent all Hungarians. His detractors have accused him of having an autocratic leadership style; however, his efforts succeeded in consolidating the center-right of the political spectrum. Prior to the 1998 vote, Orban secured an agreement with the Hungarian Democratic Forum, now a coalition partner. After the vote, Orban worked out a deal with the Independent Smallholders Union, led by the charismatic and populist, Jozsef Torgyan. As some observers predicted, the Smallholders have assertively championed the interests of their rural agrarian membership, attempting to ban dairy imports and going beyond the allotted agriculture budget. However, Prime Minister Orban has been accommodating, at least partly because he needs the Smallholders' support to hold his coalition together.

## DOMESTIC POLICY
The Orban government has effected no drastic changes in domestic policy, even with the shift from a socialist to a liberal-conservative government. Political priorities outlined by Orban include a concerted crackdown on crime and violence with a stronger police force, tougher criminal laws, and laws against illegal immigration. Other priorities of his government include improvements in the higher education system and the social security system, as well as incentives for small and medium-sized enterprises.

## FOREIGN POLICY
Under the Orban government, Hungary continued its progress toward the longstanding goal of becoming fully integrated into European institutions. In July 1997, NATO invited Hungary, along with Poland and the Czech Republic, to join the North Atlantic alliance, and all three nations became full members of NATO in March 1999. Accession negotiations with the European Union, begun in March 1998, continued, with a projected admission date of 2004. Orban has indicated that his government will seek to augment or even renegotiate bilateral treaties with Slovakia and Romania, securing the rights of ethnic Hungarians living abroad. In late 1999 and early 2000 Orban drew unfavorable attention abroad for his failure to denounce the entry of Jorg Haider's right-wing Freedom Party into the governing coalition of neighboring Austria.

## ADDRESS
Office of the Prime Minister
Kussuth Square, Kussuth Street 1–3
Budapest, Hungary 1054

## REFERENCES
Brown, J.F. *Surge to Freedom*. Duke University Press, 1991.
*Budapest Sun*. [Online] Available http://www.budapestsun.com/ (Accessed November 1999).
*Financial Times*, 8 May 1998.
*Foreign Broadcast Information Service*, various issues.
Sugar, Peter. F. *A History of Hungary*. Bloomington: Indiana University Press, 1990.
*Washington Post*, 26 May 1998.

**Profile researched and written by Julie Kim, Congressional Research Service (9/98; updated 5/2000).**

(1987) he became a co-founder of a new anti-Communist party, (renamed the Federation of Young Democrats-Hungarian Civic Party in 1995 and also known as Fidesz ). In 1989, he won a one-year scholarship to study liberal philosophy and civil society at Oxford University in the United Kingdom. But he returned from Britain after just three months, in order to participate with Fidesz in Hungary's first freely contested elections in 1990. Orban is married and has three children.

## RISE TO POWER
Though only 35 years old at the time of his election, Orban has achieved a steady rise to national prominence. Orban became widely known in June 1989 when he provocatively called for the withdrawal of Soviet troops at a ceremonial reburial of Imre Nagy, Hungary's leader during the 1956 revolution. Orban was elected to parliament from the party list of the Young Democrats in 1990 and again in 1994. He chaired the party's parliamentary group from 1990 to 1993. In April 1993, Orban became party chairman and remained at the top leadership of Fidesz through the 1998 election. In parliament, he also chaired the committee on European integration since 1994. After Fidesz performed poorly in the 1994 elections, winning only 6% of the vote, Orban spent the next years working to broaden the party's appeal and to cooperate with other conservative parties.

## LEADERSHIP
Since its founding in 1988, Fidesz has consistently remained one of the most popular political parties in Hungary, with Orban as its most prominent politician. Orban was a leader of the party's parliamentary group in its early opposition years. He then led the entire party as it remained in

# ICELAND

## David Oddsson
## Prime Minister

*(pronounced "ODD-suhn")*

*"The events that took place in Europe less than a decade ago radically transformed the political landscape in the continent. If we fail to seize this magnificent opportunity to consolidate democracy throughout the continent, generations to come will be astonished and shocked at our performance."*

The Republic of Iceland occupies an island in the North Atlantic, just touching the Arctic Circle. To the northwest is Greenland, to the east is Norway and to the south is the United Kingdom. Iceland covers an area of 103,000 sq km (39,679 sq mi) and has a population of 273,000. The per capita GNP is estimated to be $22,400. The Icelandic unit of currency is the *krona* (plural: *kronur*). Icelandic is the primary language, although English is widely taught. Ethnically, the population is almost exclusively Icelandic, a mixture of Norwegian and Celtic heritage. Iceland's religion is 95% Evangelical Lutheran, 3% other Protestant and Roman Catholic denominations, and 2% with no affiliation. Iceland's major exports include fish and fish products, other animal products, aluminum, and diatomite.

## POLITICAL BACKGROUND

Iceland boasts of having the world's oldest democratic body. The parliament, or *Althing*, was originally established in 930 AD. From the 14th century until it declared its independence on 17 June 1944, Iceland was under Danish control.

As of 2000, Iceland has a parliamentary form of government. The *Althing* is a bicameral parliament with 63 members; 49 are chosen proportionally from eight districts, and the remainder are selected to make the total number of representatives proportional to the national vote totals for each party. Parliamentary elections are held every four years; the most recent election was held in May 1999. De facto executive power is held by the prime minister, who is appointed by the president from the majority party or coalition of parties. Five different parties held seats in the *Althing* after the 1999 election.

The prime minister wields effective executive power in Iceland. Iceland also has a president, whose power is largely ceremonial. In addition to appointing the prime minister, the president also has the power to dissolve the *Althing*. While the prime minister exercises most executive power and serves as head of government, the president is the formal head of state. The presidential term lasts four years; the parliamentary elections are held every five years. The current president is Olaf Ragnar Girmsson who succeeded Vigdis Finnbogadottir in 1996. When Finnbogadottir was first elected in 1980, she became the first democratically elected female head of state in the world. David Oddsson first became prime minister in a coalition government in 1991,

and has managed to retain the position after parliamentary elections in 1995 and 1999.

## PERSONAL BACKGROUND

David Oddsson was born on 17 January 1948 in Reykjavik, Iceland to Oddur Olafsson, a medical doctor, and Ingibjorg Kristin Ludviksdottir, a bank department chief. He was educated in Iceland, and graduated from Reykjavik Higher Secondary Grammar School in 1970. He attended the University of Iceland and received a degree in law in 1976.

While attending college, he held several jobs. From 1970 to 1972, he worked as chief clerk at Reykjavik Theatre. Oddsson continues to be a comic playwright in his spare time. He was a parliamentary reporter for *Morgunbladid*, Iceland's biggest newspaper, from 1973 to 1974. And he held a position at *Almenna bokafelagid* (Book Publishers and Book Club) from 1975 to 1976. In 1970, Oddsson married Asgridur Thoracensen.

From 1968 to 1975, Oddsson produced several radio programs for the Iceland State Broadcasting Service. He has co-written two plays and authored two television dramas. His plays have been broadcast in other Nordic countries. He has also written two political books, namely *Sjalfstaedisstefnan* (The Independence Movement), published in 1981, and *Eistland: Smapjod undir oki erlends voids* (Estonia, a Small Nation under the Yoke of a Foreign Power), published in 1973. It was under Oddsson's leadership that Iceland became the first country to recognize Estonia's independence in 1991.

## RISE TO POWER

Oddsson's political career began in 1974 when he became a member of the Reykjavik City Council. In 1976 he became office manager of the Reykjavik Health Insurance Fund; and in 1978 he was promoted to managing director. He became a member of the Executive Committee of the Reykjavik City Council in 1980; and in 1982 he became chairman after being elected city mayor of Reykjavik. He has also served on the boards or committees of numerous other organizations.

His affiliation with the Independence Party (IP) dates back to his college days. From 1973 to 1975 he served on the Board of Directors of the Independence Party Youth Federation. In 1979 he became a member of the Executive Committee of the Independence Party. In 1989 he was elected to the position of vice chairman of the Independence Party; and in March 1991, he was elected chairman.

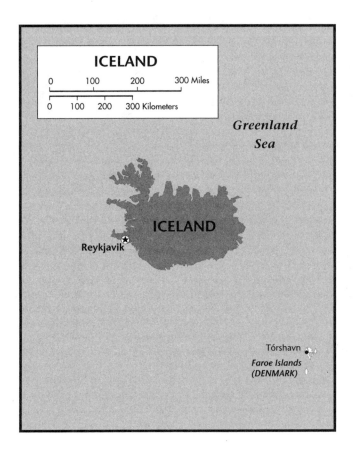

Oddsson's appointment as prime minister came on the heels of his first election to the *Althing*. He was officially sworn in as prime minister on 30 April 1991 in a coalition government with the left. Oddsson held onto the prime ministership in a center-right coalition in the 1995 election; this center-right coalition continues to hold power after the May 1999 election when Oddsson's Independence Party increased its share of the popular vote from 37.1% to 40.7%. The coalition partner, the centrist Progressive Party, fared worse in the 1999 elections when its share of the popular vote fell from 23.3% to 18.4%. The parties of the opposition left, which ran a single platform in the election, gained only 26.8% of the vote. Oddsson's electoral success is attributable to his economic record. The country has had nearly five years of 5% GDP growth, continued low inflation, and an enviable unemployment rate of just 2.5%. The government budget is in surplus, and public debt is falling. Ten years prior inflation was raging at 25% and more.

## LEADERSHIP

As a member of the Independence Party and politician in the capital city Reykjavik, Oddsson has been very popular. As mayor, he established a reputation for dynamic and uncompromising leadership. Oddsson differs from many Icelanders in never having lived abroad and he is ill at ease in expressing himself in foreign languages. At home, he has been called a master politician for his pragmatic approach in dealing with coalition partners from the center as well as the left in earlier coalitions. The Independence Party is a conservative party that adheres to Iceland's continuing membership in NATO and the retention of the existing US base in Iceland. It also favors Iceland's participation in the European Economic Area (EEA), but has rejected full membership to maintain autonomy over Icelandic maritime resources.

## DOMESTIC POLICY

Oddsson's continued popularity has been attributed to his astute handling of Iceland's economic situation. Prime Minister Oddsson's biggest challenge was to bring Iceland out of its economic recession. The austerity measures instituted by the previous Prime Minister Hermannsson were very unpopular. Yet trimming the Icelandic welfare state has continued under Oddsson. The retirement age was increased from 65 to 67, with further increases in age eligibility on the horizon. With nearly 75% of export earnings coming from the fishing industry, fluctuating world fish prices make the Icelandic economy particularly vulnerable. Negotiations with the European Union under the EEA on access to the EU's markets for Icelandic fish products has been instrumental in fostering economic growth, as has diversification into nascent technological industries. Under the EEA, Iceland has had to liberalize many areas of the economy, from telecoms to banking (but not fisheries and food sectors). Current policies of the Oddsson government have resulted in Icelander's buying power increasing four times faster than the OECD average during the period of 1995–1999.

## FOREIGN POLICY

Based on Prime Minister Oddsson's affiliation with the Independence Party of Iceland, he is expected to continue Iceland's membership in NATO. Relations with Europe and especially the European Union are expected to remain strong. While surveys in 1999 show a majority of Icelanders favoring negotiations on EU membership, no party has put the issue high on their agenda. The question of full EU membership hinges upon Iceland extending fishing rights within their own fishing zone to other EU member-states; this is seen as impossible, as the fisheries are the cornerstone of the Icelandic economy.

Perhaps more than the other Nordic countries, Iceland's foreign policy agenda is as heavily oriented toward the United States as it is Europe. Iceland maintains very friendly relations with the US, and this warm relationship has expanded under Oddsson's leadership. While Oddsson's support for maintaining the US military base in Iceland and signing a US-Icelandic security agreement separate from NATO were contentious 10 years ago, these policies have subsequently garnered widespread support among Icelanders.

Iceland's relations with the USSR became strained under the previous prime minister's government when the *Althing* voted in February 1991 to establish diplomatic relations with the Baltic states which were seeking independence. The USSR recalled its ambassador to Iceland in protest and accused Iceland of interfering in the USSR's internal affairs. In August 1991, Oddsson's government was the first to officially recognize the sovereignty of Lithuania, Latvia, and Estonia.

## ADDRESS

Office of the Prime Minister
Stjoharradshusid v/Lkaejartorg
150 Reykjavik, Iceland

## REFERENCES

Council of Europe. [Online] Available http://www.coe.fr/
    summit/discours/eislanmde.htm (Accessed 6/00).
*Curriculum Vita for David Oddsson*, Icelandic Embassy.
Facts on File
*New York Times*, 22 April 1991.
*Agence France Presse*, 5 May 1999.

*Financial Times*, 10 May 1999.
*Financial Times*, 7 May 1999.
*CIA World Fact Book*, 1999.

Profile researched and updated by Dr. Katie Verlin Laatikainen, Wilkes University (5/2000; sections contributed by Lawrence Marcus, Washington University 8/91).

# INDIA

### Atal Behari Vajpayee
### Prime Minister
*(pronounced "AH-tahl beh-HAH-ree vaj-PAY-ee")*

*"Our goal is the good of India, to endeavor to take our country to its rightful place
in the community of nations; above all, to bring peace, unity, well-being,
and prosperity in the lives of all citizens of our country."*

India dominates the southern part of the Asian continent, with an area of 3,287,590 sq km (1,269,346 sq mi). It is bordered to the northwest by Pakistan and to the north–northeast by China, Nepal, Bhutan, Bangladesh, and Myanmar. The country's geography can be divided into three main regions: Himalayan Mountains, the Indo-Gangetic Plains, and the Deccan Plateau.

India's population has been estimated at more than one billion, second only to China. Approximately 73% of the people live in rural areas, but there are nearly 30 urban centers, each with more than a million people. The country's population density is 283 persons per sq km (733 per sq mi). India's people are ethnically and culturally diverse. The two main ethnic groups are Indo-Aryans and Dravidians. While nearly 600 languages and dialects are spoken in India, only 17 are recognized as official languages. Hindi is most widely spoken in the northern and central regions of the country. It is also the official language of the central government. Many educated Indians speak English, an "associate" official language. An overwhelming majority of Indians belong to the Hindu faith (83%). Muslims constitute the largest minority religion (11%). Hindu society is divided into castes, which are hierarchically grouped according to traditional occupation and religious purity. Membership is determined by birth, and a person's social status usually depends on caste considerations.

The unit of currency is the Indian *rupee*. The country's largest trading partners are the European Union and the US. Its chief exports are textile goods, precious stones, engineering goods, and leather goods.

## POLITICAL BACKGROUND

India achieved independence from British colonial rule on 15 August 1947 after a bitter sectarian struggle that led to Muslim-majority areas in the northwest and northeast of British India forming the separate country of Pakistan. The Union of India is the world's most populous democracy, organized as a federal republic of 26 states and six centrally administered territories.

India is governed under a constitution, promulgated on 26 January 1950, which provides for a parliamentary form of government, guarantees the basic rights of citizens, prohibits discrimination on the basis of religion, caste, sex, or place of birth, and demarcates the areas of jurisdiction of the union and state governments. The constitution also provides for an independent judiciary consisting of a single integrated system of courts, with a supreme court at the top, to administer union and state laws.

The government's legislative and executive powers are vested in a parliament that is comprised of two houses: the *Rajya Sabha* (Council of States), which is the upper house, and the *Lok Sabha* (House of the People), the lower house. The president of parliament appoints the leader of the majority party to form and head the cabinet as prime minister. Real executive power, therefore, resides in the cabinet. However, if parliament withdraws support from the cabinet, the president can either dismiss the prime minister or dissolve the *Lok Sabha* and call for new elections.

India's main political parties are the Congress Party, the Bharatiya Janata Party (BJP), and the United Front (UF), a loose coalition of leftist and regional parties. Since independence, Congress has ruled almost continuously as the majority party. However, the 1996 elections resulted in a hung parliament, from which the BJP emerged as the largest single party. The BJP formed a government that lacked parliamentary support and lasted only 13 days. A minority UF government, backed by Congress, was then sworn in. Dependent on Congress for survival, the government of I. K. Gujral fell in November 1997 when Congress withdrew support. Existing political alignments precluded a new government, prompting President Narayanan to dissolve the *Lok Sabha*. New elections in early 1998 again delivered an inconclusive verdict. But the BJP mustered enough support to lead a coalition government. This government collapsed in April 1999, but in elections held in September–October of that year, the BJP was again able to gather enough support to form a government at the head of a coalition known as the National Democratic Alliance.

## PERSONAL BACKGROUND

Atal Behari Vajpayee was born on 25 December 1926 in the Central Indian town of Gwalior. As a teenager he joined the *Rashtriya Swayamsevak Sangh* (RSS), a Hindu revivalist organization, and participated in the independence movement. In 1942, he was briefly imprisoned by British colonial authorities. After graduating from Laximbai College in Gwalior, Vajpayee earned an MA in political science from Dayanand Anglo-Vedic College in Kanpur. When India achieved independence, he gave up studies for a law degree to devote more time to the RSS as a journalist and social worker, editing and writing for the organization's publications. In 1951, Vajpayee helped establish the *Jana Sangh*, a conservative political party strongly influenced by Hindu nationalist ideology. Six years later he was elected to the *Lok Sabha*.

Considered an erudite politician with a cosmopolitan outlook, Vajpayee is a noted orator, a published poet, and the author of several books, including one on Indian foreign policy. He has served on various government committees and traveled abroad extensively on parliamentary and diplomatic missions. As a reform-minded social activist, he has championed Indian cultural values, women's rights, and the eradication of the caste system. In 1992, Vajpayee was awarded India's second-highest civilian honor, the *Padma Vibhushan* and, in 1994, was named "Best Parliamentarian." He also holds an honorary PhD from Kanpur University.

Though charismatic in public, Vajpayee is described as privately reserved and reclusive. Never married, he lives in New Delhi with an adopted family—Namita, daughter of an old friend and her husband, Ranjan. He also enjoys the company of adopted granddaughter Neharika. A cultivated man, Vajpayee is fond of reading, writing, the arts, and good cuisine.

## RISE TO POWER

A political veteran, Vajpayee spent his first 20 years in parliament leading the opposition *Jana Sangh* and building a reputation as a forceful and articulate critic of the ruling Congress Party. In 1975, Vajpayee was among a group of dissident politicians jailed under the state of emergency declared by Prime Minister Indira Gandhi. In 1977, the *Jana Sangh* merged with other anti-Congress forces to form the Janata Party. Elections held that year swept the Janata Party into power, and Vajpayee became the new government's minister for external affairs. However, divisions within the Janata Party caused this government's collapse in 1980, and the Congress Party was returned to power. Rather than resurrect the now disbanded *Jana Sangh*, Vajpayee helped found a new party (the BJP), aimed at continuing the nationalist legacy of its predecessor.

As the BJP's first president (1980–86), Vajpayee downplayed the party's ideological ties to the more extremist Hindu nationalism of the RSS. His efforts failed to resonate with voters. The BJP fared poorly in the 1984 elections, and Vajpayee lost his seat in the *Lok Sabha*. In 1986, Vajpayee won a seat in the *Rajya Sabha* and became the leader of his party's small parliamentary delegation. But hardliners had taken over the BJP and embraced a highly controversial agenda emphasizing the paramount importance of Hindu culture, values, and traditions in India. Critics accused the BJP of fomenting communal and ethnic strife and abandoning the Constitution's principle of secularism. Nonetheless, this strategy successfully galvanized support among upper-caste Hindus in the north and, in the 1991 elections, the BJP emerged as the major opposition in parliament. Vajpayee was among the 120 BJP members elected to the *Lok Sabha* that year. In 1992, however, the BJP was put on the defensive when militants affiliated with the party demolished a mosque in Ayodhya, sparking violent Hindu-Muslim riots across India.

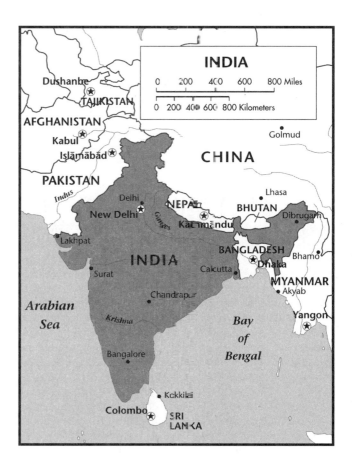

In the run-up to the 1996 elections, Vajpayee ran as the BJP's prime ministerial candidate. He denounced the Ayodhya incident, and many observers interpreted his selection as the BJP's attempt to present a less confrontational face to voters, in hopes of broadening the party's appeal. The elections unseated the ruling Congress Party, and Vajpayee became prime minister of a short-lived BJP government. The "secular" Congress-UF axis, which ousted Vajpayee's government, did not endure, and the ensuing parliamentary impasse forced new elections. Seizing its opportunity, the BJP formed electoral alliances with a heterogeneous group of smaller parties to increase its chances of a parliamentary majority and promised voters a stable government. Buoyed by the UF's weak showing at the polls, the BJP and its allies came within striking distance of a majority in the new *Lok Sabha*. After intense maneuvers, the BJP gained the additional support needed to form a government. On 19 March 1998, Vajpayee was sworn in as the nation's third prime minister in a year. Ten days later his government won parliament's vote of confidence, although only by a margin of 13 votes. With such a slim majority, Vajpayee's government was always subject to pressure from his coalition allies. It required all of the prime minister's considerable political skills to hold the coalition together. In April 1999, however, the AIDMK withdrew its support from the government. On 17 April, Vajpayee lost a parliamentary vote of confidence by a single vote, and he resigned as prime minister. As Congress was unable to form a coalition government, parliament was dissolved, and new elections scheduled for the fall of 1999.

During the summer, Sonja Gandhi, widow of former prime minister Rajiv Gandhi, entered the political arena, actively campaigning for Congress. Her involvement, however, did little to boost Congress in the polls. Vajpayee emerged from the September–October elections in a strong position, with the BJP and its allies controlling 298 seats in the *Lok Sabha*. Vajpayee was sworn in as prime minister on 14 October 1999 as head of the National Democratic Alliance (NDA) government. He became the first Indian leader in several years to have a working majority in parliament.

## LEADERSHIP

Considered an honest and capable man, Vajpayee is one of the country's most admired public figures. Many voters, otherwise suspicious of the BJP, appear to trust Vajpayee's responsible, flexible, and pragmatic political style. They regard him as best suited for the prime ministership. Vajpayee has revealed his preference for achieving consensus on major issues. Striking a conciliatory and reassuring tone, he has called for cooperation and expressed sensitivity to the concerns of India's ethnic and religious minorities. He has also rejected suggestions that he is a figurehead manipulated by RSS ideologues. Vajpayee's personal popularity is his greatest asset, but it may not provide him sufficient leverage against recalcitrant allies and unreconstructed hardliners in the BJP.

Vajpayee leads a patchwork coalition whose members have disparate and contradictory interests. To gain support, Vajpayee has made significant concessions and compromises—abandoning the BJP's cherished but contentious objectives. He has also awarded coalition partners plum ministerial portfolios and included consideration of their pet issues among the government's listed priorities. Vajpayee remains susceptible to pressures from allies and to resistance from disgruntled BJP hardliners. However, with his 1999 election victory, he no longer has to deal with a slim majority in parliament and depend on the political calculations of a handful of MPs who, though allies, do not share the BJP's philosophy. Although still having to deal with a coalition (in which the BJP has a smaller share than in the previous government), Vajpayee is in a relatively stronger position. The main parliamentary opposition, Congress and the UF, is in disarray and unable to offer a credible alternative to the NDA government. Following years of instability, the Indian electorate has given Vajpayee the opportunity to show that he is the right man to lead the country into the new millennium.

## DOMESTIC POLICY

India is one of the world's poorest countries although its GNP (measured in purchasing power parity terms) is the fifth largest. Vast sections of the populace remain impoverished even after substantial progress towards reducing malnutrition and mortality rates. Vajpayee's government has set out its plan to deal with the country's endemic social and economic ills in its "Agenda for a Proud, Prosperous India." The main thrust of this program lies in speeding up economic reforms. Some unpopular—but necessary—decisions have already been made. The price of diesel fuel, for instance, has been increased 35% to bring it in line with international levels. The government also plans cuts in spending. The May 2000 budget included reductions in food and fertilizer subsidies,

which led to protest marches by the opposition. However, Vajpayee pledges to press ahead with his economic initiatives, which include privatization, financial reforms, encouraging foreign investment, and liberalizing trade restrictions. Such policies were generally well received in the country (the Bombay Stock Exchange reached record highs the week after Vajpayee's election victory).

Other priorities for the government include reducing unemployment and providing all people with basic necessities, such as safe water, health care, and education facilities.

Internal security remains a major concern, with Kashmir high on the government's agenda. Vajpayee has promised to stamp out terrorism, as well protect ethnic and religious minorities from violence. He has also promised to target corruption and introduce electoral reforms to eliminate the undue political influence wielded by wealthy elites in the country.

## FOREIGN POLICY

India's relations with Pakistan, the Kashmir problem, and nuclear policy are at the head of Vajpayee's foreign agenda. Vajpayee was prime minister when India tested several nuclear devices in May 1998, and India clearly has the means to deliver nuclear warheads with medium-range missiles in any regional conflict. With Pakistan similarly armed, there is heightened concern of a potential nuclear conflict in South Asia. India and Pakistan have fought three wars since the countries achieved their independence and are engaged in a low-level conflict in Kashmir. However, Vajpayee has pledged to improve Indo-Pakistan relations. India now appears willing to consider signing the Comprehensive Test Ban Treaty, a change from its earlier position and a source of friction with the US. Yet, Vajpayee has dealt with Pakistani aggression with unexpected firmness. His handling of Pakistan's invasion of Kargil in the summer of 1999 increased his stature on the Indian political scene. Concerns that the BJP's historically chauvinistic attitude in foreign affairs might influence foreign policy have eased as Vajpayee has moved his party towards a more centrist position.

Vajpayee is also committed to improving relations with India's other neighbors in the region. In January 1999, India renewed its bilateral Transit Treaty with Nepal, which governs trade across the India-Nepal border and gives landlocked Nepal transit rights through Indian territory. April 2000 saw talks with China over border issues in the Jammu, Kashmir, and Ladakh region. After some initial hesitation, India responded positively to Sri Lanka's appeal in May 2000 for assistance in case an evacuation of government troops surrounded by Tamils in northern Sri Lanka became necessary. Outside the region, Vajpayee is expected to work to improve India's relations with the US and to maintain India's non-aligned position in international affairs. India actively participates in regional and international organizations, such as SAARC, the Commonwealth, and the UN.

## ADDRESS

Office of the Prime Minister
South Block
New Delhi 110011, India

## REFERENCES

Bharatiya Janata Party Official Web Site. [Online] Available http://www.bjp.org (Accessed June 2000).

*The Economist*, 29 November 1997; 4 April 1998; 4 September 1999; October 9 1999.

*EIU Country Reports: India and Nepal.* London: The Economist Intelligence Unit Ltd., 1998.

*Europa World Yearbook.* London: Europa Publications, 1999.

*Far Eastern Economic Review,* 2 April 1998.

*Frontline,* 21 March–25 April 1998.

*The Hindu,* November 1997–April 1998.

*India Today,* 30 March 1998.

*New York Times,* 19 March 1998.

Vajpayee, Atal Behari. "India's Commitment to Excellence." *Presidents and Prime Ministers,* September 1999.

**Profile researched and written by Taufiq Rashid, Indiana University (9/98; updated by Deryck Lodrick, University of California 6/2000).**

# INDONESIA

## Abdurrahman Wahid
## President
*(pronounced "ahb-derr-RAH-mun wah-HEED")*

*"What happened in Aceh was caused by unfair treatment…by the violations of human rights."*

With a population of nearly 216 million people, the Republic of Indonesia is the fourth-most populous country in the world. It consists of a 13,000-island archipelago that is stretched out over 1,948,000 sq km (740,100 sq mi) in Southeast Asia, at the point where the Indian Ocean, Pacific Ocean, and the South China Sea meet. It shares the island of Borneo with Malaysia and Brunei, shares New Guinea with Papua New Guinea, and lies north–northwest of Australia and south of the Philippines. The densely populated island of Java, traditionally the cultural center of the region, holds almost two-thirds of the population. The islands of Timor, Irian Jaya, and Sumatra contain secessionist movements seeking self-determination. There are more than 13,000 islands, with at least 300 ethnic groups speaking 200 different languages.

Indonesia is an religiously diverse nation, with 88% of the population adhering to the Islamic faith and 8% professing Christianity. In fact, it is the most populous Muslim country in the world. The country is ethnically fractionalized, with the major ethnic groups including the Javanese (45%); the Sundanese (14%); Madurese (7.5%); and coastal Malays (7.5%). Bahassa Indonesia, based on the language of traders in the region and developed during colonial rule, is the official language.

The literary rate in Indonesia is 83.8%, and the GDP per capita is $2,830, purchasing power parity, with services constituting over 40% of the country's economic activity. Its major exports include textiles and garments, gas, electrical appliances, and wood and wood products. Major trading partners are Japan, EU, Singapore, and the United States. The capital and largest city, Jakarta has a population of more than 10 million inhabitants. The currency is the *rupiah*.

## POLITICAL BACKGROUND

Two presidents have dominated Indonesia, a former Dutch colony, since winning independence after World War II: Sukarno and Suharto. Both men were dominant political figures during their rule. Sukarno, the main political leader for independence and Indonesia's first president, unified the nation through his *pancasila* or five bases: 1) belief in one God; 2) internationalism and concern for humanity; 3) national unity; 4) the sovereignty of the people; and 5) social justice. These principles have provided a common rallying point for the diverse religious, cultural, political, and ethnic groups that populate Indonesia.

Suharto gained power when Sukarno lost popular support as he turned more radical and confrontational. In September 1965, under mysterious circumstances, six senior generals were kidnapped and assassinated when the powerful Communist Party of Indonesia (PKI) made a hasty attempt to take power, and the military responded swiftly and brutally. Hundreds of thousands of people (mainly PKI supporters, peasants, and ethnic Chinese) were killed during the violence surrounding the military's crackdown. As the newly appointed "commander for the restoration of security and order," Suharto oversaw the military's response.

The decisive victory of the military boosted Suharto's power. Formal titles bestowed over the next few years provided evidence of his de facto control of the government. He was granted certain executive powers in 1966, was named acting president in 1967, and was elected president by the People's Consultative Assembly in 1968. With each step, the new leadership tried to push the still-powerful Sukarno aside without appearing to disrupt the continuity of the government. By 1970, when Sukarno died, the transition from Sukarno's Guided Democracy to Suharto's "New Order" was already complete. When secessionist movements gained strength in the 1990s and the economy faced its major crisis in 1997, Suharto was forced to resign. Immediately following his resignation he announced that Vice President Habibie would assume the presidency. In 1999, Wahid was selected as president by the Peoples Consultative Assembly.

The Constitution gives broad power to the president, who is both head of state and chief executive. The presidential term is five years with no limits on re-election. The president is elected by the People's Consultative Assembly, which he heads. The Assembly consists of 1,000 members, with some elected and some chosen as regional delegates or as representatives of professional groups, political organizations, or the armed forces of Indonesia (ABRI) and includes the 500 members of the House of Representatives, who are selected proportionate to the general election results. Presently there are 425 members representing parties and 75 seats reserved for the military and police. *Golkar*, a large umbrella party with a nationalist orientation, is the government party and dominated the country until the last general election in 1999. A number of decrees introduced in the late 1990s curbed the power of the president and the military, introduced the secret ballot, and provided legislative checks on the bureaucracy. Several opposition leaders who gained prominence in the 1990s include Megawati Sukarnoputri, the daughter of Sukarno, and Amien Rais, an Islamist reformer.

## PERSONAL BACKGROUND

Abdurrahman Wahid was born in 1940 in the rural province of Jombang, East Java, to a family long steeped in religious activism and politics. His grandfathers, both of whom were religious leaders, founded the Nahdlatul Ulama (NU), or the Revival of the Religious Scholars, a traditional Islamic organization, in 1926. Wahid spent his early years studying the Koran and preparing for a life of religious service.

In 1964, Wahid enrolled at the renowned Al-Azhar Islamic University in Cairo. Unlike many students, Wahid was more interested in the practical aspects of the Islamic faith, rather than the stultifying atmosphere of an Islamic university. He took to the streets of Cairo, joined political discussion groups, and used the public library to obtain a well-rounded liberal arts education. After spending four years in Cairo, he went to Baghdad to study Arabic and European philosophy. He developed a passionate love of classical European music, cinema, and literature. Having traveled extensively in Europe, Wahid developed an appreciation for Russian and French classics, in particular Dostoevsky, Tolstoy, Balzac, Zola, and Flaubert.

Upon returning to Indonesia in 1971, Wahid became a lecturer at a small university in East Java while becoming a political activist through the NU organization. He developed a reputation as a brilliant scholar, yet practical in approach for resolving problems as they emerged. In 1984, he was elected chairman of the NU, which by that time had become a major organization with a membership exceeding 30 million.

Wahid's health is a major concern. Over the past two years, he suffered two strokes and is effectively blind. While laser surgery in the United States improved his ability to distinguish white and black, a personal assistant must read to him and tell him where he needs to sign. While doctors say that his health is otherwise good, he is assisted when standing up or walking. In Indonesia, he is affectionately known as "*Dus Gur.*" *Dus* is an Islamic honorific and *Gur* is a syllabic from his given name. In his leisure time, Wahid is a fan of soccer, Western classical music, and literature.

## RISE TO POWER

Wahid's power base consists of his leadership in the NU. Since the early 1980s, he was seen as a critic of Suharto's authoritarianism. He repeatedly spoke out about issues of human rights, social equality, and racial tolerance. He resisted Golkar's pressure to weaken and subsume the NU under its auspices.

In 1994, Wahid refused to support Suharto's sixth consecutive term for the presidency and refused to join the government-backed Association of Muslim Intellectuals. He became increasingly critical of Suharto's embrace of religion for the sake of increasing political legitimacy. Instead, Wahid called for a separation between religion and state. Suharto responded by orchestrating the ouster of Wahid as chairman of NU. However, Wahid was reelected by a narrow margin. Despite strained relations with Suharto's Golkar, he supported the party in 1997 elections. However, in 1998, he organized the National Awakening Party (PKB), based on the principles of moderation, tolerance, and harmony. Then in 1999, even though he was one of three candidates for the presidency, he made it public that he would be more than willing to step down in favor of Megawati Sukarnoputri, the

daughter of Suharto and leader of the main opposition party, the Indonesian Democratic Party. Before the voting in the People's Consultative Assembly in October 1999, Wahid's shrewd political maneuvers won him the support of Golkar and his own party, thereby defeating Megawati for the presidency. The irate Megawati urged to followers to remain calm and assumed the position of vice president.

## LEADERSHIP

Wahid once joked that Sukarno was crazy about women; Suharto was crazy about money; and BJ Habibie was just plain crazy. Then he quipped that in his case, it was the people who elected him that were crazy. Such is the humor of the enigmatic Wahid. Having observed the ethnic conflict in Indonesia in 1965, after the failed coup against Sukarno, Wahid resolved that ethnic tolerance was necessary for the survival of the country. He was shaken by the banality of what human beings could do to each other. To those critics who say that he is not Muslim enough, he states, "Those who say that I am not Islamic enough should reread their Koran. Islam is about inclusion, tolerance, community."

Some critics believe that Wahid is senile and affected by the two strokes he suffered. Most believe that he should not be underestimated and that Wahid has a unpredictable and unorthodox approach to political issues, which allows him to think and operate outside the established parameters. A few believe that he possesses Rasputin-like characteristics. What most people seem to agree on is that Wahid is a shrewd political leader whose personal ethics are beyond reproach.

Wahid is a consensus-oriented leader who will work with the military and secessionist movements to create solutions to problems. He has a good sense of humor and looks at politics as acting from behind the scenes, piecing together the parts of a puzzle like a sleuth. His main message is one of reconciliation, the protection of human rights, and ethnic tolerance. He bases his belief on a tolerant brand of Islam, known as "secular Islam," which views people who do good deeds as servants of God even if those people do not believe in the existence of God. Wahid will have to convince critics and supporters that his health is not a major concern and that he is the leader who can reform Indonesia's economic and political system, without alienating powerful interest groups, such as ethnic minorities, the army, and religious fundamentalists.

## DOMESTIC POLICY

Indonesia avoided the worst mistakes that many oil-exporting countries made in the 1970s. However, top government officials and military officers benefited personally from government contracts and monopolies. Despite the government heavily investing in rural development and education, only a slight increase in the standard of living was achieved for many Indonesians. When oil prices plummeted in the mid-1980s, Indonesia's economy received a severe shock, and the government cut spending sharply. The loss of oil revenues exposed Indonesian dependence on oil exports, and inspired economic deregulation and attempts to develop other exports. That effort was successful. The economy recovered from crisis and went on to thrive in the 1990s. As the country opened itself to foreign investment and steadily deregulated its economy, growth in industry, transport, and tourism spearheaded an expansion that averaged 7% per annum between 1991 and 1996.

Indonesia's economic prospects took a turn for the worse in the fall of 1997 as an Asia-wide economic crisis struck Hong Kong, Thailand, South Korea, and Indonesia. The *rupiah's* value declined as much as 90%, and foreign investors fled the nation. The crisis resulted in the flight of foreign investment, food riots, inflation, and an International Monetary Fund (IMF) bailout that many Indonesians think infringes on their national sovereignty.

Dealing with this crisis will be Wahid's biggest challenge. His predecessor, B.J. Habibie, negotiated an IMF-brokered recovery plan to begin the process of dismantling the edifice of "crony capitalism" erected by his predecessor. State-owned companies have moved to sever their ties with businesses owned by the Suharto family. However, economic volatility continues. Recently, massive demonstrations broke out in the capital in response to the government's adherence to IMF conditionality that would have dramatically increased gasoline prices. Wahid will likely renegotiate some of the IMF-dictated terms.

Another major area of domestic concern is ethnic conflict and its impact on national unity. Given the ethnic diversity and the logistics of governing 13,000 islands, Wahid must address smoldering grievances developed over many years of human rights abuse and economic exploitation of the hinterlands by Jakarta. The economic situation contributes to ethnic and social divisions. Indonesia's economic crisis brought to the forefront social division that was less apparent during more prosperous times. During the protests and rioting that preceded Suharto's fall from power, ethnic Chinese were singled out by looters. Though a minority of the population, they control a large part of the economy.

Wahid is known for his conciliatory approach toward ethnic minorities. Recently, he allowed the Chinese to celebrate the Chinese Lunar New Year for the first time, lifting a ban on its public celebration. Publicly he stated that the Chinese were an integral part of Indonesia's economy and national life. Furthermore, while Wahid is a devout Muslim, he is also a secularist who understands the danger in instituting Islamic government. Therefore, he has the support of Christians and other religious minorities. He moved swiftly to reach a cessation of hostilities with the Aceh People's Movement in Sumatra and continues to work with the UN peacekeeping forces in East Timor. To do this, he successfully weakened the role of the military in decision-making by dismissing General Wiranto, who is widely believed to have orchestrated the violence in East Timor. At the same time, Wahid has the military's support. Even in the case of General Wiranto, he promised amnesty even if charges are eventually brought up against him. Wahid urges moderation, patience, and tolerance in dealing with domestic issues.

## FOREIGN POLICY

The debacle over East Timor and Aceh created a public relations nightmare for Indonesia. As the abuse of human rights became public and with accounts internationally distributed, Indonesian authorities experienced international disapproval. Meanwhile, throughout 1998, the Indonesian economy worsened. It appears that the worst is over in both of these situations.

The agreement on Aceh and the deployment of UN forces to East Timor coupled with Wahid's admission that the government abused human rights during the Suharto years improved relations with the international community. Wahid moved to remove Wiranto from the government, signaling a commitment to institutionalizing democracy. The international community believes that a democratic and politically stable Indonesia is necessary to the security of the region.

Wahid's internal reforms brought about an increase in international good will. He has spent the first three months in office traveling abroad to seek recognition for Indonesia's unique economic problems. While foreign investors have not flocked backed to Indonesia's domestic market and the International Monetary Fund plays a major role in stabilizing the economy, Wahid's calm approach in addressing these problems promotes foreign confidence in his administration. Australia, Indonesia's most important neighbor, has publicly come out to support Wahid and his domestic political and economic reforms. In the future, Wahid will be working with international creditors to develop a long-range plan for Indonesia's economic growth. Furthermore, with Indonesia completing a transition to democracy, ASEAN leaders can look forward to greater international respected for Indonesia. Democracy in Indonesia is a positive development for both the country and the entire region.

## ADDRESS

Office of the President
Bina Graha, Jl. Veteran 17
Istana Merdeka
Jakarta, Indonesia 10110

## REFERENCES

*The Age* (Australia), 26 January, 2000.
*BBC News*, 2 September, 1999; 14 February 2000.
Embassy of Indonesia, Ottawa, Canada. [Online] Available http://www.prica.org/ (Accessed June 2000).
*The Guardian Observer*, 20 October 1999.
*Sydney Morning Herald*, 15 February 2000; 15 June 2000.
*The Times of India*, 29 March 2000.
*Washington Post*, 3 June 2000.

**Profile researched and written by Robert Compton, Jr., Western Kentucky University (6/2000).**

# IRAN

## Mohammed Khatami
## President
*(pronounced "mow-HAH-muhd kah-TAW-mee")*

*"Let me declare my belief clearly...when we speak of freedom we mean the freedom of the opposition. It is no freedom if only the people who agree with those in power and with their ways and means are free."*

The Islamic Republic of Iran is bordered on the north by the Caspian Sea and the central Asian republics of Azerbaijan and Turkmenistan, on the east by Afghanistan and Pakistan, on the south by the Persian Gulf, and on the west by Iraq and Turkey. Iran has an area of 1,648,000 sq km (636,290 sq mi).

The population is estimated to be 65 million, with an annual growth rate of about 1%. Persian, which belongs to the Indo-European family of languages, is Iran's official language, with Kurdish, Baluchi, Luri, Armenian, Azeri Turkish, and Arabic being the other principal tongues in this multi-ethnic country. Shiite Muslims comprise 93% of the population while Sunni Muslims, Zoroastrians, Christians, Jews, and the Bahai's constitute Iran's minorities.

The Iranian currency is the *rial*. The per capita GDP has been estimated at US$5,000. Iran's primary export is crude petroleum. Its major trading partners are Japan, Germany, Spain, United Arab Emirates, Greece, the UK, Italy, and France.

## POLITICAL BACKGROUND

In 1979 the dictatorial regime of Shah Muhammad Reza Pahlavi was forced to relinquish power. In its place, Iran was transformed into an Islamic republic, led by Ayatollah Ruhollah Khomeini until his death in 1989.

The Iranian political system is based on the 1979 constitution and principle of *shariah,* or Islamic law. Ultimate authority is vested in the Wali Faqih, a spiritual leader appointed by the Shiite clergy who reflects the will of God. An elected president is the chief executive and reflects the will of the people. The 270-member Islamic Consultative Assembly (*Majlis Shura-ye Islami,* commonly referred to as the *Majlis*) constitutes the legislative branch of government. All candidates for the Majlis must be recommended to the voters by legitimate Islamic political groups and approved by an Islamic screening committee. All legislation from the Majlis must be approved by the 12-member Council of Guardians, appointed by the religious leader and the Supreme Judicial Council. But the Council of Guardians can be bypassed by a resolution of the Expediency Council. This discretionary council, whose members are elected by the supreme leader, rules on legal and theological disputes between the Majlis and Council of Guardians. It is charged with ruling in the best interest of the country by establishing a balance between different interpretations of the tenets of Islamic law.

The president, elected for four years by popular vote, is the head of the cabinet and the civilian part of the executive branch. Thus, the government combines the authority of the supreme Shiite jurisconsult with the elected president and parliament, producing a complex system of religio-juridical checks and balances. The entire system is based on a balance of power between the different factions of the ruling clerics. The supreme leader (Ali Khamenei) represents the conservatives, but the Majlis speaker, Mehdi Karubi of the Militant Clerics' Association (elected speaker unopposed in May 2000), represents the reformist coalition.

## PERSONAL BACKGROUND

Mohammed Khatami was born in 1943 in the southwestern town of Ardakan, in the Iranian province of Yazd. His father was a prominent religious scholar who was appointed prayer leader of Yazd by Ayatollah Khomeini following the 1979 revolution. After finishing his theological studies at Qom and Isfahan, Mohammed Khatami received a master's degree in philosophy and education from Isfahan University.

Khatami is widely regarded as an honest and virtuous cleric. He lives modestly in a yellow-brick townhouse in northern Tehran and drives an Iranian-made car. He is married and has one son and two daughters. Khatami is well connected to important clerical families through marriage. He wears a black turban, indicating direct descent from the prophet Mohammad. This enhances Khatami's charismatic appeal along with his reputation as a liberal-minded cleric. The contrast between Khatami and the hard-line clerics who dominated Iran's political establishment until 2000 is such that some Iranians referred to him half-jokingly as Ayatollah Gorbachev, after the leader of the former Soviet Union who opened that country to the West in the late 1980s.

Khatami speaks Arabic, German, and some English. He reads a great deal and has published several books on subjects such as the relationship between Islam and the modern world. His hobbies include hiking and table tennis.

## RISE TO POWER

During the 1960s and 1970s, Khatami became involved in the activities of the Militant Clerics Association, which rallied opposition to the Shah. Through political pamphleteering he supported the efforts of Ayatollah Ruhollah Khomeini, who was then living in exile. He developed a close friendship with Khomeini's son, Ahmad, who would later provide helpful support in resolving post-revolutionary factional disputes.

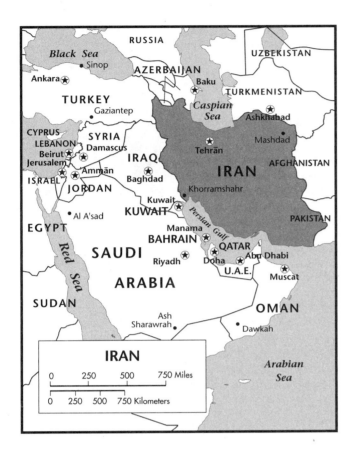

In the late 1970s, Khatami came to the attention of Ayatollah Mohammad Beheshti, chief ideologue of the Islamic Republican Party and a key tactician of the revolution. Beheshti appointed him to run the Islamic Center of Hamburg (Germany) to help mobilize expatriate Iranians against the Pahlavi regime.

After the revolution he returned to Iran and took over Kayhan Institute, the largest publishing house in Iran. In 1980 he was elected to the first Majlis and in 1982 became minister of culture and Islamic guidance, with responsibility for overseeing Iranian films, publishing, and mass media. Khatami held this position for more than a decade, and his policies heralded a new era of cultural development in post-revolutionary Iran. He became known as a harbinger of tolerance by easing censorship regulations and promoting the publication of many independent journals and book titles. His policies encouraged creativity in the areas of classical music, film, and fiction. The Iranian film industry flourished, receiving much critical acclaim at international festivals over the past two decades. In 1992, Khatami was forced to resign under pressure from conservative clerics who considered his policies too permissive. Between 1992 and 1997 he served as a cultural adviser to President Rafsanjani while heading Iran's national library.

Khatami announced his decision to run for the presidency in January 1997 after consultation with government leaders. In order to qualify, all presidential candidates were screened for ideological purity by the Council of Guardians. This group rejected all but four of 238 presidential hopefuls. Khatami was favored by both radical and pragmatic factions of revolutionary clerics since they wanted to contain the

power of conservatives, who at that time enjoyed a majority within the Majlis. While both factions have different views on economic policy, they agreed with Khatami on the need for a more open society. Many Iranians feared that the conservative religious establishment would resort to fraud in order to prevent Khatami from winning the election, but popular support for Khatami was so overwhelming that his opponents had no choice but to let the election proceed without interference. The result was a landslide victory for Khatami on 23 May 1997 in Iran's first freely contested presidential election since 1980. With an estimated 94% of eligible voters casting ballots, Khatami received 69% of the total vote.

## LEADERSHIP

Khatami supporters include secular intellectuals, reform-minded technocrats, youth, and women. This constituency expects him to fulfill campaign promises by allowing more personal freedom, making economic changes that will cut the power of state-backed monopolies, and creating a more flexible Islamic regime. They voted overwhelmingly for reformist candidates for the Majlis in the 2000 election. (The average age of representatives elected to the sixth parliament is significantly lower than that of the fifth parliament.

Conversant in Western philosophy and history, Khatami has shown a special interest in the value of Enlightenment and Civil Religion as reflected in the writings of Immanuel Kant and Alexis de Toqueville. He favors a more objective understanding of the West by encouraging a dialogue on intellectual and strategic issues. As minister of culture, Khatami implemented policies aimed at creating a more open society. During his barnstorming campaign he was able to generate broad interest and excitement over his relatively liberal agenda by focusing on the issues of free expression, civil rights, and diversity of attitudes. Moreover, he challenged the notion that politics should be monopolized by a specific group. Since taking office, Khatami has defied hard-line opponents by selecting moderates and women for his cabinet. His choices reflect a determination to honor campaign pledges. On 20 August 1997, a major hurdle was cleared when the conservative-dominated parliament approved his cabinet, to the surprise of most observers. Achieving this victory was the first sign of Khatami's negotiation skills in dealing with hard-line legislative opponents. Three years later, in May 2000, the conservative parliament held its last meeting in the Tehran as the newly elected parliament prepared to take over. When taking their seats in the Majlis, all representatives must, according to the 1979 constitution, swear allegiance to the 1979 Islamic Revolution. The reformist coalition, seated in late May 2000, controlled about 80% of the seats following the February and May 2000 elections. Supporters of President Khatami—Mehdi Karubi and Majid Ansari—were elected speaker and deputy speaker while Behzad Nabavi and Mohammad-Reza Khatami (President Khatami's younger brother) were elected first and second deputy speakers.

## DOMESTIC POLICY

Khatami is committed to social and political reform, and his very election was the result of the desire for social reform in Iran. Above all, he interprets Islam in terms of pluralism and openness. Protecting civil liberties and establishing the rule of law constitute two major pillars of his social and cultural agenda. Khatami's reform programs, while receiving popular support, came under fire from conservatives, who closed a number of liberal newspapers in early 1999. By early 2000, the Khatami government had enacted greater press freedom, and newspapers played a key role in the public debate on the role of religion in politics leading up to the parliamentary elections.

As of 2000, political parties were not officially sanctioned, having been effectively outlawed since the 1979 revolution. However, the Khatami government had been successful in curbing the police and religious militia, easing the enforcement of Iran's strict social code.

Khatami's economic policies follow the previous government's commitment to industrialization. The government's first five-year plan was begun after the Persian Gulf War and was responsible for the creation of hundreds of industrial and infrastructure projects. Because his views are similar to those of the outgoing president, Ali Akbar Hashemi Rafsanjani, he initially had in Rafsanjani a powerful ally in his struggle against the conservatives. Rafsanjani ran for parliament in the 2000 election and was soundly defeated. Even after his defeat, Rafsanjani continued to hold the influential position of chairman of the Expediency Council.

Khatami advocates a modified version of the market-oriented economy, buttressed by domestic production. He has sought to address the problems of a rising cost of living, inflation, and a tight job market by curbing the power of state-supported monopolies and expanding economic ties with Western countries. In financing his development plans, Khatami faces the liability of Iran's dependence on oil revenues (which are subject to fluctuations in global prices) for about 80% of foreign exchange income. Corruption and bureaucratic hurdles are further challenges he needs to deal with in order to attract foreign and local investors. Khatami maintains that no country can achieve social justice without having a sound economic development plan.

## FOREIGN POLICY

In his inaugural address, Khatami stressed that his foreign policy objectives would be based on three principles: wisdom, integrity, and expediency in pursuing peace and security. He also expressed his hope to establish a dialogue between Islam and other civilizations in an effort to achieve detente with the outside world. As of 2000, he faced pressure to actually deliver on these goals and objectives.

In the 1980s and 1990s, relations with Europe had been strained because of Iranian government insistence on its right to eliminate political opponents who seek refuge in Europe. Yet, despite this source of tension, trade with European countries has flourished since 1992. Khatami has indicated an interest in easing tensions and improving commercial ties with European nations. As a step toward meeting those objectives, Khatami made state visits to Italy, the Vatican, and France in 1999.

The Khatami government favors greater cooperation with Arab states in the region as well. In November 1997, Iran hosted the Islamic Conference summit meeting, and in 1999 Khatami made official visits to Syria and Saudi Arabia. Khatami had pledged particular attention to the improvement of relations with states in the Persian Gulf region.

Regarding US-Iranian relations, Khatami has stated that the key is in America's hands, citing the 1995 Clinton administration decision to cut off all dealings with Iran. The Iran Sanctions Act specified that any non-American firm investing over US$40 million a year in Iranian oil or gas would be punished. Sanctions were intended to continue until Iran stopped sponsoring terrorism, undermining the Arab-Israeli peace process, and trying to develop weapons of mass destruction. In late July 1997 the Clinton administration decided not to oppose construction of a pipeline that would carry Iran's natural gas from Turkmenistan to Turkey. Though this decision appears to violate the spirit of sanctions, senior aides deny that any softening of its position is intended.

Khatami is careful to avoid any suggestion of openness to the West. He has said nothing publicly to distance himself from the anti-US policies of the supreme leader, Ayatollah Khamenei. The future of US-Iranian relations may depend upon how and when the ruling clerics will find it expedient to change their position. Khatami's role will be to facilitate such a change.

## ADDRESS

Office of the President
Tehran, Iran

## REFERENCES

*The Economist*, 2 August 1997.

*Facts on File World News Digest*, 29 May 1997.

Iranian Government Appointments. BBC News, 17 June 2000. [Online] Available http://news6.thdo.bbc.co.uk/hi/english/world/middle%5Feast/newsid%5F795000/795114.stm (Accessed June 2000).

*Middle East Economic Digest*, 8 August 1997.

*Middle East International*, 30 May 1997.

Mohammed Khatami, President of the Islamic Republic of Iran. [Online] Available http://www.persia.org/khatami/index.html (Accessed June 2000).

*New York Times*, 23 May–21 August 1997.

"The Oath." *Washington Post*, 27 February 2000, p. B-4.

Presidency of the Islamic Republic of Iran. [Online] Available http://www.president.ir/ (Accessed June 2000).

*Washington Post*, 23 May–3 August 1997.

**Profile researched and written by Touraj Noroozi, University of Utah (7/97; updated 6/2000).**

# IRAQ

### Saddam Hussein
### President

*(pronounced "sah-DAHM hoo-SANE")*

*"We have neither the desire nor the intention to commit aggression against anyone, but we must say that we have the determination and the will to retaliate against any aggression."*

The Republic of Iraq (al-Jumhuriyah al-Iraqiyah) is a landlocked country, except for its 58 km (36 mi) coastline at the Persian Gulf. Iraq is bounded by Iran, Kuwait, Saudi Arabia, Jordan, Syria, and Turkey. Its total area, excluding the Iraqi-Saudi Arabia Neutral Zone, is 438,317 sq km (169,235 sq mi).

The population of Iraq was estimated to be 22.4 million in 1995. About 75–80% of the people are Arabs; 15–20% Kurds; and 5% Turkomans, Armenians, Persians, and other smaller ethnic groups. Almost 97% of the population is Muslim (60–65% Shiite, 32–37% Sunni), and the remainder consists of various Christian sects, the Yazidis and Sabeans communities. While Arabic and Kurdish are the official languages of Iraq, Kurdish is the official language in the Kurdish regions. The Iraqi unit of currency is the *dinar*. Per capita GDP has been estimated at $2,400. Iraq's main natural resource and export is oil. The main imports are foodstuffs, machinery, capital equipment, motor vehicles, and consumer goods. Iraq's major trading partners, prior to August 1990, were the US, Japan, Brazil, Germany, the UK, Turkey, and the USSR.

## POLITICAL BACKGROUND

Iraq was a British mandate under the League of Nations from 1920 until 13 October 1932 when it became a sovereign and an independent state. Following the military coup of July 1958, which overthrew the monarchy, Iraq was declared a republic and has since been governed by various constitutions. According to the 1970 constitution and its 1973 amendments, the Revolutionary Command Council (RCC) is the supreme organ of the state. A simple majority elects its members from the Regional Command of the Socialist Arab Baath Party. The RCC oversees foreign as well as domestic policies, declares war, concludes peace, and ratifies treaties. It elects the president and the vice president by a two-thirds majority. The president of the country is concurrently the chairman of the RCC. The president is responsible to the RCC, but the constitution does not spell out his term of office. The president is the commander-in-chief of the armed forces, nominates members of the council of ministers, and appoints Iraq's diplomatic representatives abroad. The vice president and minister are responsible to the president.

The constitution contains provisions for an Assembly with responsibility to consider bills suggested by the RCC or the Assembly members. No National Assembly existed in Iraq between the 1958 revolution and June 1980 when the first National Assembly was elected. The election for the third National Assembly was on 1 April 1989, in which the Baath Party candidates succeeded in capturing more than 50% of the 250 seats. The legislative election for the fourth National Assembly was held in March 1996. Only members and non-partisan supporters of the Baath Party were allowed to run in the election for the fifth National Assembly held 27 March 2000.

The constitution also specifies that "the area whose majority of its population is Kurdish shall enjoy autonomy in accordance with what is defined by the law." Since 1976, of 18 provincial governments, three have been designated as Kurdish autonomous regions. Elections for the Kurdish legislative council were held in 1980, 1986, and 1992. Although the National Assembly has been operative, real power still resides with the RCC. The government announced the details of a new, permanent constitution in March 1989, which proposed the abolition of the RCC and the assumption of its duties by the National Assembly and a 50-member consultative assembly. The permanent constitution is to be approved by a national referendum.

## PERSONAL BACKGROUND

Saddam Hussein was born on 28 April 1937 in a village near Takrit, about 162 km (100 mi) north of Baghdad. He attended primary school in Takrit and then went to al-Karh Secondary School in Baghdad. Saddam Hussein graduated from al-Qasr Al-Aini Secondary School in Cairo in 1961 and entered the University of Cairo Law School in the fall of 1962. He returned to Iraq after the overthrow of Abdul Karim Qasim in 1963 and resumed his legal studies at Baghdad's al-Mustansiriyah University. However, his political activities and subsequent imprisonment interrupted his education. He married Sajida Khairallah Talfah in 1963 and has two sons and two daughters.

## RISE TO POWER

Saddam Hussein's rise to power was a long and risky affair. He has been involved in coups and assassinations and has escaped several attempts against his life as well. He participated in an abortive coup attempt against King Faisal in late 1956 and became a member of the Baath Party in 1957. On 14 July 1958, General Abdul Karim Qasim and Colonel Abdul Salem Arif overthrew the Hashemite Kingdom in a military coup. Within the Qasim regime political differences subsequently emerged among the Communists, the Nationalists, and the Baathists over Iraq's relations with the United Arab Emirates and the union of Egypt and Syria. When the Baathists decided to get rid of Qasim in October 1959, Saddam Hussein was one of the men chosen for the assassination. Qasim was shot but only wounded. Most of the participants were arrested, but Saddam Hussein successfully fled to Syria. He was tried and sentenced to death in absentia for the attempted assassination. In 1962 Saddam Hussein moved to Egypt and joined the Cairo branch of the Baath Party.

On 8 February 1963, a military coup carried out by the Baath Party and Nationalist army officers overthrew the government of Qasim. Abdul Salem Arif, who had been sentenced to death by Qasim in January 1959, became the prime minister. Following this coup, Saddam Hussein returned to Baghdad and actively participated in the Baath Party. When political disagreements arose between Baathists and Arif, Prime Minister Arif staged a military coup against the Baath Party in November 1963 and declared it illegal. Thereafter, Saddam Hussein went underground but was arrested in 1964 and spent two years in prison. After escaping, he fled into hiding again and was named deputy secretary of regional leadership for the Baath Party in 1966.

When Arif was killed in a helicopter crash in April 1966, his brother Abdul Rahman Arif became the president. A group of Baathist officers under Hassan al-Bakr organized a military coup on 17 July 1968 and deposed Abdul Rahman Arif. Al-Bakr then became the president and the chairman of RCC. Saddam Hussein, who took an active role in organizing the coup, was elected acting deputy chairman of the RCC from November 1969 until July 1979. Finally, on 16 July, President al-Bakr announced his resignation from both the Baath Party and the government because of health reasons. He relinquished the presidency to Saddam Hussein, who became chairman of the RCC, prime minister, and secretary of the Baath Party.

## LEADERSHIP

Saddam Hussein has been characterized by his supporters as a struggler, a thinker, a pragmatist, and an organizer. By opponents he is thought to be an autocrat, a dictator, a despot, and a ruthless man. Both the Iran-Iraq War and the Persian Gulf War have influenced the sources of Saddam Hussein's support and opposition. His ambition to become a regional leader, along with his fear of the impact of the Islamic revolution, motivated his decision to invade Iran in September 1980. He used the war to generate internal as well as external support for his regime and to weaken opposition forces in Iraq.

Saddam Hussein derives most of his support from members of the Baath Party, the RCC, the council of ministers, the armed forces, and intelligence organizations. Throughout the years, actual and potential opponents have been systematically purged from these institutions and were replaced by loyalists. Learning from the experience of military coups in the 1960s, Saddam Hussein has paid close attention to the loyalties of senior military officers and the political control of the military forces by the Baath Party. He has placed relatives and members of his clan from Takrit in a number of sensitive positions in the military. Surveillance and intimidation have been accompanied by material incentives.

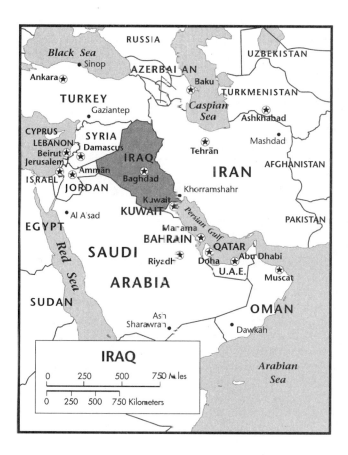

Despite such inducements and control, opposition to Saddam Hussein by the military cannot be ruled out, and coup attempts by senior army officers were reported in 1989 and 1995.

Opposition to Saddam Hussein comes from disparate Kurdish, Communist, and Shiite organizations. These forces are internally divided and often antagonistic toward one another. The government has tried to coerce, intimidate, and appease the opposition. Kurdish and Shiite opposition intensified during the course of the Iran-Iraq War. In November 1980, the Iraqi Communist Party (ICP), the Unified Socialist Party of Kurdistan (USPK), and the Democratic Party of Kurdistan (DPK) formed the Democratic Iraqi Front. Around the same time, a National Pan-Arab Democratic Front, composed of different groups, including the Patriotic Union of Kurdistan (PUK) and Baath, as well as ICP dissidents, was formed in Syria. In November 1982, the Shiite opposition established the Supreme Council of the Islamic Revolution of Iraq for the purpose of overthrowing Saddam Hussein's government. In May 1988, the DPK and the PUK announced that a coalition of six organizations had been formed to continue the struggle for Kurdish self-determination. Moreover, a coalition of opposition groups created the Iraqi National Congress in October 1992 to overthrow Saddam Hussein. Some of these opposition forces have been encouraged or supported by Iran and Syria, but they remain weak and divided.

Despite the scarcity of food, educational supplies, and other basic necessities caused by nine years of international trade sanctions against his country, Hussein celebrated his sixty-third birthday in 1999 with the unveiling of a large mural depicting himself as Nebuchadnezzar, the ruler of ancient Babylon. Supporters paraded as part of the birthday celebration, carrying banners that proclaimed, "With your birth Iraq was reborn."

## DOMESTIC POLICY

In August 1990, Iraq invaded Kuwait after a lengthy dispute regarding territory, debt repayment, and petroleum production quotas. The United Nations imposed sanctions on Iraq. After Saddam Hussein refused to withdraw his troops by the UN-specified deadline of 15 January 1991, a multinational force led by the US began "Operation Desert Storm"— a series of air strikes on Baghdad followed by a ground offensive to liberate Kuwait. Defeated in a few short weeks, Saddam Hussein withdrew his forces from Kuwait and accepted UN Security Council Resolution 687, which indicated the terms for a ceasefire, war reparation, and conditions for the lifting of sanctions against Iraq. Devastation resulting from Allied bombing, and the UN sanctions have led to a deterioration of economic conditions: hyper-inflation, the devaluation of the Iraqi currency, the rise of unemployment, and the decline of agricultural production. Most of the industrial development projects requiring foreign participation have been suspended, and political opposition has been intensified.

Since the end of the Gulf War, the Iraqi government has been concerned with the reconstruction of its damaged infrastructure and restoration of its industrial production. In May 1991, new rules were approved to encourage greater Arab investment. The Iraqi government has provided incentives for farmers to enhance agricultural output. Saddam Hussein has adopted various policies to retain or enhance his political power. Through these measures he expects to attract the support and loyalties of a broader spectrum of the population, as well as to weaken political opposition to his regime. An uprising by the Shiite population of southern Iraq and a revolt by Kurdish guerillas in the northern provinces were crushed by the armed forces loyal to the government in 1991. In an effort to counter the economic crisis, Saddam Hussein dismissed the ministers of finance and agriculture and assumed the post of prime minister in May 1994.

Unsuccessful coup attempts prompted a reorganization of the armed forces and resulted in the appointment of a new chief of the general staff in April 1995. Two high-ranking government officials (and sons in-law of the President) defected to Jordan in August 1995 and appealed to the Iraqi army to overthrow Saddam Hussein. He responded by organizing a national referendum to approve the renewal of his presidency for seven more years. The result was a 99.96% endorsement. The international community reacted with incredulity to this degree of support. In February 1996, the two defectors returned to Iraq and were assassinated by forces loyal to the President. He remains concerned about domestic threats.

## FOREIGN POLICY

Since 1980 Iraq's foreign policy has been influenced by Saddam Hussein's invasion of Iran and Kuwait. Though the Iran-Iraq War ended in August 1988, antagonism has persisted between these two nations. The question of war

reparation, the repatriation of prisoners of war, and other issues have remained unresolved. The invasion of Kuwait changed Iraq's relations with the Arab world. Egypt, Saudi Arabia, Syria, Oman, Qatar, the United Arab Emirate, and Morocco were among the countries that supported Kuwait in the UN coalition. Since the Gulf War, Iraq's relations with Jordan have deteriorated because King Hussein of Jordan has been supportive of political opposition within Iraq and has sought to restore his relations with the US, Saudi Arabia, and Kuwait. The Iraqi government has tried to improve relations with Syria, but the longstanding differences between the two regimes prevent any significant change. Iraq severed its diplomatic relations with Egypt and Saudi Arabia in February 1991. Egypt has since softened its position toward Iraq. In return, Iraq's foreign minister visited Cairo in July 1995; the Egyptian trade center was reopened in Baghdad; and Egyptian workers were allowed to return to Iraq.

The main focus of Saddam Hussein's foreign policy will be an effort to end the UN economic sanctions. In 1999, the ninth anniversary of the sanctions, the Iraqi government issued a statement describing the sanctions as criminal. A number of UN-member nations, including Russia, France, China, and Turkey, are in favor of easing the UN sanctions on Iraq. By contrast, the US and Britain insist on prolonging the sanctions and may continue to do so until Saddam Hussein is deposed. Their view is that Iraq must fully comply with all UN Security Council resolutions, including those that relate to human rights abuses and weapons inspection. The UN weapons inspector assigned to Iraq resigned in 1999, frustrated over lack of cooperation by the Iraqi government and lack of aggressiveness by the UN and United States in enforcing weapons inspection procedures.

## ADDRESS

Office of the President
Baghdad, Iraq

## REFERENCES

Amin, Rula. "Amid Isolation, Iraq's Educational System Deteriorates." CNN Online, 14 October 1999. [Online] Available http://www.cnn.com/WORLD/meast/9910/14/iraq.schools/ (Accessed June 2000).

*Current History,* January 1996, pp. 10–15.

Hiro, Dilip. *Dictionary of the Middle East.* New York: St. Martin's Press, 1996.

*Journal of South Asian and Middle Eastern Studies,* Spring 1996, pp. 1–20.

Karsh, Efraim and Inari Rautsi. *Saddam Hussein: A Political Biography.* New York: The Free Press, 1991.

*The Middle East and North Africa, 1997.* 43rd ed. London: Europa Publications Ltd., 1996.

"UN Arms Inspector Says Iraq Still Not Cooperating." CNN Online, 2 June 2000. [Online] Available http://www.cnn.com/2000/WORLD/meast/06/02/iraq.inspectors/ (Accessed June 2000).

"Why Bombs Are Falling in Iraq." *The Economist,* 6 March 1999.

*The World of Information Middle East Review 1997.* Saffron Walden, England: Walden Publishing Ltd., 1997.

**Profile researched and written by Ahmad Sheikhzadeh, Columbia University (6/97; revised 6/2000).**

# IRELAND

**Bertie Ahern**
**Prime Minister**
*(pronounced "BURR-tee ah-HERN")*

*"The people of Ireland want to see our country modernized,*
*but they want to see it modernized in a way that's consistent with their own beliefs."*

The Republic of Ireland is situated on a small island in the Atlantic Ocean, located approximately 80 km (50 mi) to the west of Great Britain. The two countries are separated by the North Channel, the Irish Sea, and the St. George's Channel. Covering a total area of 70,282 sq km (27,136 sq mi), the republic encompasses all but the six northeastern counties.

The first official language of the country is Irish, but its use is not as widespread as English, which is spoken universally. Ireland is overwhelmingly Roman Catholic (95%). The largest city and capital, Dublin, is home to almost one-third of the country's 3.6 million people.

Economic growth has been exceptionally strong since the mid-1990s, averaging around 7% annually, and was forecast to rise to over 8% in 2000. GDP per head of the population rose from US$12,884 to US$22,980 in less than 10 years. Rising import prices and a real estate bubble threaten to increase inflation to 4.9% in 2000. Unemployment fell to 5% in 2000, down from 16% in 1993. The Irish economy is in danger of overheating in 2000.

Ireland joined the European economic and monetary union in 1999; currency is the Irish *punt* (pound).

## POLITICAL BACKGROUND
From 1800 to 1921, the whole of Ireland was a part of the United Kingdom of Great Britain and Ireland. However, a Catholic independence movement had demanded for decades that the union between Britain and Ireland be dissolved. The movement was opposed mostly in the northeast where a large Protestant community was determined to maintain its political ties with Britain.

In 1920, the British Parliament passed an act that divided Ireland into Northern Ireland, consisting of six counties, and Southern Ireland, consisting of 26 counties. Both were to maintain separate parliaments that would remain under the supremacy of the British. This political arrangement proved unworkable, and in 1921 the South was granted home rule by Britain. It became known as the Irish Free State and held dominion status in the British Commonwealth. The North, with a Protestant majority, maintained its traditional ties to Britain. In 1937, the Irish Free State achieved full sovereignty within the Commonwealth, and in 1949 it became a republic. The republic has always been regarded by a majority of its citizens as the legitimate government of the entire island. Since the 1970s several outlawed paramilitary groups have fought both for and against uniting the island by force. The largest and best-known of these groups has been the Irish

Republican Army (IRA), whose continual campaign of bombing and terror to remove the British from the North has contributed significantly to what many people call "the troubles."

Ireland is a parliamentary republic. While the president is the head of state, the prime minister is the head of government. The legislature is divided into two houses, the Dail (House of Representatives) and the Seanad (Senate). The Dail consists of 166 members, elected by citizens over the age of 18 for five years under a system of proportional representation. The Seanad has 60 members. The Dail is the more powerful of the two houses; the Seanad may only consider and amend, but may not veto, bills sent to it by the Dail.

The prime minister is the leader of the party, or coalition of parties, that wins the most seats in the Dail. The major parties are Fianna Fail, which is led by current Prime Minister Bertie Ahern, and Fine Gael. While many observers of Irish politics tend to regard Fine Gael as more moderate on the issue of Irish reunification, in practice there has been little difference between the policies of the two parties. The system of proportional representation, which encourages the formation of smaller parties, makes it difficult for any party to win an outright majority in the Dail. As a result, governments are often short lived and based on coalitions between parties and/or independent legislators.

## PERSONAL BACKGROUND
Bertie (short for Bartholomew) Ahern was born on 12 September 1951 in Dublin. His father was a farmer who joined the Irish Republican Army during the 1919–21 war for independence. Ahern grew up in a working-class neighborhood on the north side of the city and later attended University College Dublin, where he received a degree in accounting. He was first elected to the Dail in 1977, serving as a member for the Dublin Finglas constituency. Over the next five years he served in a variety of lower-level ministerial posts. In 1982, he was became his party's chief whip and its parliamentary leader in the political opposition. During this time he also served for a year as Dublin's lord mayor. When Fianna Fail returned to power in 1987, Ahern received his first cabinet post as the minister of labor. Four years later he was named finance minister.

## RISE TO POWER
Ahern was elected leader of Fianna Fail in November 1994 when a scandal in the government forced Albert Reynolds to

## IRELAND

0    100    200    300 Miles

0   100   200   300 Kilometers

*Shetland Islands*

*Orkney Islands*

*Outer Hebrides*

UNITED KINGDOM

*North Sea*

IRELAND

Belfast

*Isle of Man (UK)*

Newcastle upon Tyne

Dublin

*Irish Sea*

Liverpool

Cardiff

*Thames*  London

ATLANTIC OCEAN

*English Channel*  FRANCE

*Guernsey (UK)*
*Jersey (UK)*

Le Havre

resign. Though Reynolds left office, his party's coalition government continued to hold a majority in the Dail, and Ahern, as party leader, was set to assume the office of prime minister. However, the scandal left the coalition divided. Reynold's major partner in the government, Dick Spring of the Labor Party, withdrew his support from Fianna Fail and threw it behind John Bruton and the Fine Gael Party, who then formed the new government. Since Bruton came to power more than two years after the most recent election, he was forced to call another one in 1997. This not only gave Bruton a short tenure in office before having to face the voters, it also gave Ahern a relatively quick chance to face Bruton head-on in an election.

In the 6 June vote, no party won an outright majority of at least 84 seats in the Dail. Fianna Fail won 77, and its coalition partner, the Progressive Democrats, won only four. This left Ahern still a few seats short of a majority but well ahead of the opposition's Rainbow Coalition of Fine Gael, Labour, and the Democratic Left, who combined for only 75 seats. However, it took Ahern the better part of a month to bring together a parliamentary majority. On 26 June 1997, Bertie Ahern was finally elected by a vote of 85 to 78, becoming the youngest prime minister in the history of the Irish Republic.

The coalition of Fianna Fail and Progressive Democrats was dogged by political controversy in 1998 and 1999. Two tribunals established to examine allegations of financial impropriety have exonerated the current leadership. But Charles Haughey, a former prime minister and close ally of Ahern, was convicted of taking bribes for personal use and misusing party funds.

A second important development is the merger of the Labour party and the Democratic Left. The new party will be called Labour party and is more likely to provide a genuine center-left alternative to the governing coalition.

## LEADERSHIP

Ahern comes to power supported in the Dail by two political parties and a handful of independents as his own party did not receive a numerical majority. Keeping this governing coalition together for a full five-year term may not be an easy task. However, Ireland has had minority governments in the past that have worked very well. Moreover, Ahern is regarded as an able politician. He is more popular than his own party and has maintained high approval ratings. He is considered to be very personable. Ahern is noted for his abilities as a conciliator and a negotiator, liking to hear all shades of opinion before making decisions. Yet once he does make a decision, he shows what those who know him call a steely resolve.

Ahern has displayed this resolve in several areas. During the campaign and early in his term, he spoke of the need to crack down on crime, especially on drug-related violent crime, which has increasingly plagued Ireland in the past few years. Promoting a zero-tolerance policy, Ahern has withstood criticism, saying that he rejects the notion that there can be an acceptable or tolerable level of crime. Ahern has also set very clear terms for dealing with the IRA. Though soon after his election a ceasefire was declared, Ahern had previously stated that he would refuse to allow Sinn Fein to have any role in negotiations until the IRA refrained from violence. In spite of his precarious parliamentary position, few believe that Ahern will be swayed in negotiations by threats from strongly nationalist deputies on whom he has to rely for votes.

## DOMESTIC POLICY

Low corporate taxes, generous state subsidies, and a skilled workforce attracted large flows of investment capital from abroad, especially in the new information technology sectors. A shortage of skilled personnel has emerged, and the government advertises jobs in US cities with large Irish populations, thereby revising Ireland's historic population patterns. Instead of large outflows of people seeking jobs and better livelihood abroad, the government of Ahern has faced an inflow of people seeking economic opportunities. In addition, Ireland has become attractive to asylum seekers. The influx of more than 100 new economic and political refugees a week has exhausted all the country's emergency shelters. In response, Ahern has taken to providing them with shelter in bed-and-breakfast inns and small hotels.

Ahern has also spurred the privatization of semi-state bodies, and Ireland is on its way to becoming a nation of shareholders.

Strong growth leads to price pressures and rising inflation. To cool off the economy, the government, employers, and unions signed a wage pact in early 2000, holding down pay increases to 15% stretched over 33 months. In return, the government pledged to cut taxes and increase spending on social welfare.

## FOREIGN POLICY

In the area of foreign policy, one issue looms above all others: continuing the peace process begun by his predecessors with great Britain, Northern Ireland, and Sinn Fein over the future of the North and its relationship with Britain and Ireland. Soon after Ahern's triumph in the Dail, the IRA announced that it would begin a new ceasefire, eschewing the use of violence to achieve the aim of reunifying all Ireland. In response to this, Ahern made a conciliatory move, approving the early release of several IRA prisoners. He also met with British prime minister, Tony Blair, to discuss the peace process and outline their next steps. The result of that meeting was a peace agreement (Good Friday Agreement) with the UK in which Ireland pledged to amend Articles 2 and 3 of the Irish constitution, which lay claim to the territory in the North. In return, the UK promised to amend the Government of Ireland Act. The constitutional amendments were accepted by 94.4% of the Irish electorate in a referendum on 22 May 1998.

Since the signing of the Good Friday Agreement, the peace process has experienced many highs and lows. Lack of confidence led to a cautious implementation of some provisions of the agreements. But one major stumbling bloc has been the fashion in which the IRA would disarm itself. Hardline voices in the Ulster Unionists, always suspicious of the IRA, refused to enter into any power-sharing arrangements with Sinn Fein (the political arm of the IRA) until the military branch has surrendered all its weapons. Blair and Ahern kept the peace process alive, and the IRA announced in May 2000 that it would allow foreign observers to inspect the contents of arms dumps to ensure that no weapons had been removed. In turn, the Ulster Unionists, under considerable outside pressures, agreed to go back into government with the IRA and revived the joint government with the Catholic minority on 29 May 2000.

In addition to the problems with Northern Ireland, Ahern is expected to devote a great deal of attention to strengthening Ireland's ties to the rest of Europe and to shed Ireland's traditional isolationism from Europe on defense matters. Ahern declared Ireland's intention to join the Partnership of Peace initiative. The government also expressed support for the NATO campaign against Serbia although Ireland remained officially neutral.

## ADDRESS
Office of the Prime Minister
Government Buildings
Upper Merion St.
Dublin 2, Ireland

## REFERENCES
*Barclays Bank Country Report*, 28 March 2000.
*The Economist*, various issues.
*Europe Review World of Information*, 11 November 1999.
*Irish Times.* [Online] Available http://www.irishtimes.ie (Accessed May 2000).

**Profile researched and written by David Bernell, Johns Hopkins University (8/97; updated 5/2000).**

# ISRAEL

### Ehud Barak
### Prime Minister

*(pronounced "eh-HUD bah-ROCK")*

*"In order to bring peace and security to the State of Israel,
we first need to bring about peace among ourselves, and I intend to achieve this."*

The State of Israel is located on the eastern coast of the Mediterranean Sea, bounded by Lebanon to the north, Syria to the northeast, Jordan to the east and southeast, and Egypt to the southwest. An 18 km (11 mi) strip of coastline along the Gulf of Aqaba gives Israel access to the Red Sea. Israel's boundaries were determined initially by armistice lines set following the country's war of independence in 1949; the area within these lines (the so-called "Green Line") is 22,770 sq km (7,922 sq mi).

In 1967, following war with Egypt, Syria, and Jordan, Israel acquired control of territories beyond the Green Line, including the Sinai Peninsula and Gaza Strip from Egypt, the West Bank from Jordan, and the Golan Heights from Syria. Eastern Jerusalem had been under Jordanian control between 1948 and 1967 but was annexed by Israel immediately thereafter. The Sinai Peninsula was returned to Egypt in 1982. Israel entered into an agreement with the Palestine Liberation Organization (PLO) in 1993–94. An autonomous Palestinian Authority would assume gradual control over domestic affairs in large areas of the West Bank and Gaza Strip, pending determination of the final status of those territories in negotiations between Israel and an elected Palestinian Council. Meanwhile Israel retains responsibility for some 170,000 Jews living in these territories. In addition Israel maintains full control of the Golan Heights.

The population of Israel has been estimated at 5.7 million. This figure included more than four million Jews living anywhere under Israeli jurisdiction (including the West Bank, Gaza Strip, and the Golan Heights) and about 1.2 million non-Jews (including Muslims, Christians, Druze, and members of other religious groups). An additional 1.7 million non-Jews inhabited the West Bank, and more than one million lived in the Gaza Strip. The official languages of Israel are Hebrew and Arabic.

Israel has a market economy. Because of limited natural resources, Israel must import much of its food, fuel, and raw materials. Its historically tense relations with its neighbors have necessitated the importation of much military equipment. Exports include textiles, fruits (especially citrus), polished diamonds, pharmaceuticals, and advanced electronic equipment. Tourism is also a major source of revenue. Israel's per capita GDP has been estimated at $18,100. The monetary unit is the new Israeli *shekel*.

## POLITICAL BACKGROUND

United Nations General Assembly Resolution 181 of 29 November 1947 called for the partition of the British mandated territory of Palestine into a Jewish and a Palestinian Arab state. The Jews in the territory accepted the resolution; the Arabs did not. On 14 May 1948, when the last British troops left the country, Jewish leaders proclaimed an independent State of Israel while local Arabs joined with the armies of five Arab countries in an effort to destroy the new Jewish entity. Israel defended itself successfully and in consequence of the 1949 armistice agreements extended its control to the area within the Green Line. Transjordan annexed the West Bank, and Egypt administered the Gaza Strip; the Palestinian Arab state never came into existence. Many Palestinian Arabs fled the country during the 1948 war and were prevented from returning afterwards.

In its Proclamation of Independence, Israel defined one of its missions to be the ingathering of Jews from throughout the world to their historic homeland. In the first years after the state was established, more than a million Jews, survivors of the Nazi Holocaust and refugees from Arab countries, came to settle in the new Jewish state. Israel faced the difficult task of integrating so many people of widely divergent backgrounds into a single society while at the same time defending itself against neighbors who did not recognize its legitimacy.

Israel's leaders chose to accomplish these tasks through a multiparty parliamentary democracy. At least once every four years, citizens over 18 years of age cast a ballot for one of the country's numerous political parties vying for seats in the 120-member *Knesset* (parliament). The seats are allocated in proportion to the number of votes received by each party. In May 1999, 15 parties won *Knesset* seats. The party that received the largest number of votes, the One Israel Party, was awarded 26 seats.

Reform legislation introduced in the 1990s decreed that, instead of being chosen by the *Knesset*, the prime minister would be elected directly by the voters. In the 1999 elections, Ehud Barak, leader of One Israel, challenged the incumbent prime minister, Benjamin Netanyahu of the *Likud* (Unity) Party. In what was considered a landslide victory, Barak received 1.8 million votes (56.1%) to Netanyahu's 1.4 million (43.9%). Nevertheless, because his party did not receive a majority of *Knesset* seats, the new prime minister will have to preside over a coalition government.

## PERSONAL BACKGROUND

Ehud Barak (originally Brog) was born on 12 February 1942 on Kibbutz Mishmar Hasharon, a small collective farm in a part of British-controlled Palestine that is now northern Israel. Early in his military service, which began in 1959, he decided to make the army his career. He rose quickly through the ranks, becoming the most decorated soldier in Israeli history and serving as commander of an elite commando unit, head of planning, head of military intelligence, commander of the central region, and (from 1991 until 1994) chief of staff. During his term of duty he also earned bachelors degrees in physics and mathematics from the Hebrew University of Jerusalem and a masters degree in systems analysis from Stanford University. He is generally regarded as a person of keen intelligence.

Barak was chief of staff when the initial Israel-PLO negotiations were concluded. Although hesitant about some of their ramifications, he assumed a central role in implementing their military aspects. He also participated in negotiations with Syria over a possible Israeli withdrawal from the Golan Heights in exchange for peace, and he helped formulate the peace agreement signed with Jordan in 1994. Such intensive involvement in political matters was unusual for a military figure. Barak was criticized for his involvement by *Likud* and other opposition leaders.

## RISE TO POWER

In July 1995, Barak accepted Prime Minister Yitzhak Rabin's invitation to join his government as minister of the interior. In doing so, he immediately became a central figure in Rabin's Labor Party. Four months later Rabin was assassinated by an opponent of the Israel-PLO agreements. Foreign Minister Shimon Peres became acting prime minister in Rabin's stead, and Barak took over the foreign ministry.

New elections were set for May 1996. In preparation for the elections the Labor Party placed Barak in the second position on its *Knesset* list, immediately behind Peres. Labor was evidently worried by the widespread perception of Peres (who had no military background) as an idealist whose eagerness for a peace settlement might induce him to make unacceptable compromises on security issues where Rabin, himself a former military hero, was likely to hold firm. Barak thus began to assume the mantle of Rabin's true heir—a hard-nosed realist who could be counted upon to pursue peace with a soldier's eye for Israel's strategic defense needs. He continued to cultivate this image following the defeat of Peres by Netanyahu. It, no doubt, helped him take over the leadership of Labor in June 1997 and to head the opposition to the Netanyahu government.

Netanyahu had opposed the Israel-PLO agreements, although as prime minister he pledged to honor them. Even as he and members of his government continued to meet with PLO representatives, however, his lack of enthusiasm for the agreements was palpable. He delayed acting according to the timetable the agreements had initially set out. As a result he was subjected to intense diplomatic pressure from the US, culminating in his reluctant signing of the Wye accord in October 1998, in which he agreed to enlarge the West Bank areas where the Palestinian Authority exercised control. His coalition government, however, contained many elements unalterably opposed to transferring any authority in the West

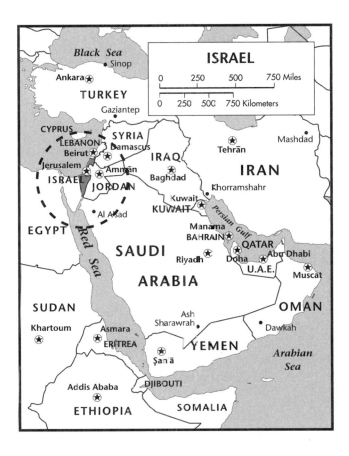

Bank to an autonomous Arab leadership. Under pressure from them, Netanyahu soon suspended implementation of the Wye agreements. This move, in turn, displeased other members of his coalition. Finally, in December 1998, Netanyahu reluctantly concluded that his government could not hold together. The *Knesset* was dissolved and new elections called. Barak prepared to lead his first political campaign.

Initially Barak did not make an attractive candidate, largely because of a personality many perceived as aloof. During early 1999 there seemed to be strong grassroots support for a centrist alternative to both Barak and Netanyahu. Initially attention centered on another former chief of staff, Amnon Lipkin-Shahak; later on Netanyahu's former defense minister, retired general Yitzhak Mordechai. Early polls showed either alternative candidate likely to obtain a plurality in the elections and force a runoff. Barak, however, managed to overcome the centrist challenge. He ran his campaign on the theme of national unity, as one who could ease the social and cultural tensions that had increasingly fragmented the Israeli body politic. Endeavoring to broaden the traditional base of Labor support, he forged alliances with leaders of certain socially disadvantaged communities who had tended to vote *Likud,* as well as with moderate religious elements from whom the predominantly secular Labor Party had become alienated in recent years. These alliances were reflected in the abandonment of the Labor label. The formation of the new One Israel Party helped Barak preempt the centrists' claim to represent a new way of doing politics. In the end, the centrist candidate for prime minister (Mordechai) withdrew from the race; his party received only six *Knesset* seats.

Another factor that helped Barak was the poor performance of the Israeli economy during Netanyahu's term. Netanyahu's government had pursued aggressive free-market economic policies, but by late 1998 GDP growth had fallen to 1.5%, with 12% unemployment and 10% inflation. Departing from a traditional Labor position, Barak blamed these developments not on the free market itself but on the Netanyahu government's ideologically-driven spending on projects for Jews living beyond the Green Line at the expense of investment in the economic infrastructure. His campaign pledge to "establish a just society with mutual responsibility and social sensitivity [in which] a free market and wise government investments will enable many people to break out of the cycle of poverty" evidently resonated with many who had long shunned Labor for its socialist rhetoric.

## LEADERSHIP

Within the first year of his tenure as prime minister, Barak established himself as a pragmatist and a man of action, taking significant strides toward stabilizing relations with Israel's Middle East neighbors through negotiations with the Palestinians and with Syria and earning praise from his foreign counterparts for being straightforward and honest. During the election campaign he had presented himself as a competent professional manager whose military experience had taught him to be a team player and to lead by example. Opponents, however, have claimed that he tends not to consult widely before making decisions, leading more by command than by persuasion or negotiation. They have also called repeated attention to the one blemish in his military record, an incident in 1992 when he was said to have abandoned soldiers wounded during a training exercise. An independent investigation determined that he did not act improperly, but some adversaries continue to use this episode to cast doubt upon his leadership abilities.

An early clue to Barak's leadership style as prime minister came with his naming of several former generals to key advisory posts. In this regard he appears to be following Netanyahu's practice of establishing American-style expert advisory councils parallel to government ministries, although Netanyahu tended to be suspicious of the military elite, to whom Barak is close.

## DOMESTIC POLICY

Although discontent with the stagnant Israeli economy played a significant role in Barak's election, his reputation for leadership has initially rested primarily on his accomplishments in the area of foreign relations. As of 2000, Israel continued to be plagued by slow economic growth and high unemployment, and critics on the left criticized social spending in the proposed national budget as inadequate, likening Barak's economic policies to those of "new liberal"

centrist leaders in other countries, including Bill Clinton, Tony Blair, and Lionel Jospin.

Barak's campaign platform introduced the concept of a "solidarity state," in which "government intervention is justified only in the areas where a market economy cannot bring about the targeted social and economic results," including "security, education and health, a fair distribution of income, [and] physical infrastructures." It spoke in particular of guaranteeing free education to preschoolers and university students and also emphasized attention to the rights, needs, and status of women and minorities. One specific proposal called for ending military service exemptions for students in Jewish religious academies—a plan certain to bring him into conflict with some of the country's religious parties, which grew in strength in the last election. Indeed, relations between the state and the religious establishment will likely be one of the most difficult issues with which the Barak government will have to wrestle.

## FOREIGN POLICY

In his first year as prime minister, Barak carried out his campaign promise to renew the peace process that Netanyahu had effectively suspended. He resumed negotiations with Palestinian leader Yassir Arafat over Israeli withdrawal from the West Bank, extending the Wye accord and working out new terms for withdrawal. In addition, he pledged Israeli withdrawal from south Lebanon during the year 2000 and, at the end of 1999, resumed peace talks with Syria, which had been broken off four years earlier. Observers considered it of utmost importance for Barak to reach permanent agreements with Arafat and with Syrian leader Hafez el Assad while the two aging leaders were still in power and could wield the authority to win acceptance of such agreements by their constituents.

## ADDRESS

Office of the Prime Minister
Jerusalem, Israel

## REFERENCES

*Ehud Barak.* [Online] Available http://www.ehudbarak.co.il (Accessed September 1999).

*Haaretz* (Hebrew-language daily newspaper), May–June 1999.

Israeli Foreign Ministry. [Online] Available http://www.israel-mfa.gov.il (Accessed September 1999).

*Knesset.* [Online] Available http://www1.knesset.gov.il/elections/pm (Accessed September 1999).

*Maariv* (Hebrew-language daily newspaper), May–June 1999.

State of Israel, Central Bureau of Statistics. *Statistical Abstract of Israel.* 1998.

*Yediot Aharonot* (Hebrew-language daily newspaper), May–June 1999.

**Profile researched and written by David Engel, New York University (9/99; updated 5/2000).**

# ITALY

### Giuliano Amato
### Prime Minister
*(pronounced "joo-lee-AHN-o ah-MAH-toe")*

*"The world is changing; the economy is changing; jobs are changing. We must all innovate."*

The Italian Republic, a southern European peninsula, is bordered on the north by Switzerland and Austria, on the northeast by Slovenia, and on the northwest by France and Monaco. Included in the Italian Republic are the islands of Sicily and Sardinia, as well as smaller groups of islands in the Mediterranean Sea. Encompassing a land area of 301,277 sq km (116,323 sq mi), Italy has a population of approximately 57 million.

Although most of the population is Italian, there are significant minority groups, such as the South Tyrolians, the Slovenes, and Croatians. While Italian is the official language, French, German, and Slavic dialects can be heard in various regions of the country. Approximately 95% of the population are Roman Catholic. The remainder are Protestant, Moslem, and Jewish minorities.

The Italian *lira* is the official currency. Italy's per capita GDP is approximately US$20,800. Major exports include textiles, wearing apparel, metals, transportation equipment, chemicals, and food products.

## POLITICAL BACKGROUND

Italy achieved political unity as a nation in 1861 under the Royal House of Savoy. The republican form of government was adopted in 1946. There have been two republics in postwar Italy, beginning in June 1946 and April 1994, respectively. According to the constitution, power is shared between executive, legislative, and judicial branches. The popularly elected bicameral parliament consists of a 315-member Senate and a 630-member Chamber of Deputies, both elected to five-year terms. Parliament is subject to dissolution by the president or by a vote of non-confidence when a new government cannot be formed. Twenty-one national parties presently dominate Italian politics.

The prime minister is nominated by the president of the Republic (Oscar Luigi Scalfaro) and forms a government and political agenda that must be approved by both chambers of parliament. The prime minister is the head of government and must retain the confidence of parliament, either through governing majorities or benign political consent. The prime minister's power has been limited in the past by divisions among the many political factions within Parliament. Italy has had 58 governments since 1945. The current prime minister is Giuliano Amato, who arrived at the job on 21 April 2000 after being appointed by President Carlo Azeglio Ciampi.

## PERSONAL BACKGROUND

Giuliano Amato was born on 13 May 1938 in Turin, the home of Fiat. He majored in law at the prestigious Normale University in Pisa and received a Master's degree in Comparative Law from Columbia University in 1962. From 1964 to 1969, he taught law at the university of Rome, moved to Perugia and then Florence, and returned to Rome in 1975 to take up a post in comparative and constitutional law. He has written books and articles on the economic and public institutions, personal liberties, federalism, and comparative government.

Amato is known for his wit and imagination and is considered one of Italy's cleverest politicians. He speaks excellent English and is master of complex legal and economic matters thanks to his long years in academia. His interests, moreover, are far-ranging, and he can talk about almost anything. His nickname is "Subtle Doctor" for his ability to see the fine points of an argument.

He is married and has a son and daughter.

## RISE TO POWER

Amato joined the Socialist party at age 20 in 1958 and became a member of its central committee in 1978. He was first elected to parliament in 1983—at the time of Bettino Craxi's leadership. Craxi aimed to purge the Socialists of their Marxism and to enlarge the party's appeal among the urban middle class. In this project, Amato was a close partner of Craxi, who appointed him as cabinet chief from 1983 to 1987. He was re-elected to parliament in 1987 and served as deputy premier. From 1987 to 1989, Amato was treasury minister. In 1992, he was back in parliament and later that year served briefly as prime minister. During his short stint as prime minister (a total of 10 months) he led Italy through a dire financial crisis as it rebounded from the embarrassment of the *lira* being forced out of the European Monetary System. He enacted the first and deepest of a string of austerity budgets, known as the "blood and tears" budget, that prepared Italy for joining European Monetary Union in 1999.

Amato was number two in the Socialist party and a close ally of Craxi, who died in Tunisia in January 2000—a fugitive from Italian justice. Craxi is best known for having been one of Italy's most corrupt politicians. His basic flaw was that he tolerated systematic embezzlement to pay for party campaigns, lavish party conferences, and the good life for himself and his lieutenants. In 1992, major judicial investiga-

251

not the issue for most voters because after years of sluggish growth the economy finally turned a corner and was said to head for a healthy 3% growth in 2000. Voters had also little to complain about the pace of structural reforms. On one hand, the government of D'Alema continued to squeeze spending on hospitals and schools and did not lower Italy's high tax rate. On the other, deregulation and liberalization have made little progress, and reforms of administration, the tax system, or health care have not been undertaken. Mainly, the left lost the regional election for two extraneous reasons. The coalition consists of 12 squabbling parties. D'Alema, for his part, is a dour sort of fellow and does not appeal to voters emotionally. The second reason is illegal immigration. The right ran on an anti-immigration platform and accused the left of being soft on crime, asylum seekers, and illegal immigration.

Because of his administrative and technocratic skills, the feuding coalition partners appointed him to lead them for the next eleven months or until the next election.

## LEADERSHIP

The first test of Amato's leadership was the long-awaited referendum to reform the electoral system. Over the past seven years, attempts have been made to inject stability into a political system by changing its electoral laws. In 1995, Italy moved away from the old system of proportional representation and adopted a first-past-the-post-system for the election of 75% of the seats in the chamber of deputies. The May 2000 referendum asked voters to scrap the remaining 25 percent of the seats elected on the basis of direct proportional representation. For the referendum to pass, 50% of eligible voters had to take part. Amato was silent on how voters should chose, realizing that the scrapping of proportional representation would not give Italy a stable political system. On 21 May 2000, only about 32% of the voters bothered to cast a ballot, thereby invalidating the whole referendum, which consisted of seven questions.

The low turnout was a political fiasco for Amato, who had hoped that a favorable vote would give him strong public backing for electoral reforms that previous center-left governments had not been able to pass in a parliament with some 40-plus parties. Most Italians seem to favor a reform of the electoral system but political fatigue, confusion, and disaffection against the country's political establishment kept many voters home.

## DOMESTIC POLICY

Amato has limited room to maneuver, and his coalition enjoys a slim majority in parliament. The budget for 2001 includes some small reforms, but the government does not have the votes to push for cuts in pensions and social security allowances. At the same time, the 2001 budget did not contain tax increases for the first time in years as the EMU-imposed fiscal constraints are slowly relaxed. The public deficit was down to 1.9% of GDP in 2000.

The next election will be held in April 2001, if not sooner. Likely, Amato will not try to introduce controversial reforms, such as cuts in social spending, during his short term as leader. He is on record, however, as favoring drastic reforms of the pension system and encouraging private pension provisions. A reform of the pension system is needed as Italy has

tions in the financial affairs of the Socialist party uncovered massive corruption, bribery, and fraud. Craxi was forced to resign, fled to Tunisia, and the Socialist party fell apart. Considering Amato's closeness to Craxi, his political career could have ended right then and there. Cannily, however, Amato put himself forward as a caretaker prime minister in 1992 and distanced himself from his mentor. In 1993, he declared that Craxi was gone politically, and he apologized for not doing more to stop the rot in the party. Craxi never forgave Amato.

After his 10-month stint as prime minister (1992–93), he returned to academia and headed the Aspen Institute Italia. He rejoined public life as Italy's first anti-trust chief from November 1994 to November 1997, during which time he handed down a string of tough competition rulings. He then went back to academic life at the European University in Florence before returning to the fray as reform chief under D'Alema in 1998–99. He was again treasury minister in the second D'Alema government (1999–2000) until his appointment as prime minister.

Since the collapse of the Socialist party in the wake of the financial scandals of its former leader, Amato has been unaffiliated with any party and has no personal base. He joined the center-left coalition as an individual and was appointed as prime minister by the fractious coalition partly because he was not beholden to any particular political faction.

The second D'Alema government fell after a severe drubbing in regional elections, in which the left won only seven out of the 15 regions while the right, under the leadership of Silvio Berlusconi, won eight regions. Policy was one of the lowest birth rates and a rapidly aging population. Generous rules and allowance will stretch the system to its limits if no changes are undertaken in the next few years. The coalition itself is divided on some key issues, and Amato is in no position to enforce unity among 12 discordant groups of Greens, Socialists, Catholics, ex-Communists, and disciples of former prime minister Romano Prodi who went to Brussels to run the European Commission in 1999. Trade unionists, unreconstructed Communists, and old-fashioned Catholics want Italians to have jobs for life, generous state pensions, and extensive public health service. The "new left" represented by Amato, many Democrats of the Left (former Communists), and plain Democrats (a small group of liberals who are affiliated with the Prodi bloc) want to sell off state assets, liberalize the service sector, and loosen the job market. Because Amato is not really the leader of the coalition, he is merely the prime minister they back; his hands are tied.

## FOREIGN POLICY

Amato has been a firm supporter of continued Italian integration into a united Europe. The reappointment of Lamberto Dini as foreign minister signaled a continuation of pro-Western, pro-NATO, and pro-UN policies. Concern about illegal immigration means that Italy is concerned about the reconstruction of the former Yugoslavia and Albania.

Italy has more than 10,000 troops involved in peacekeeping abroad. The most significant presence is in Kosovo, where Italy is in charge of one of the five military sectors. It also has a large contingent in Bosnia.

Italy continues to support institutional reforms of the European Union in order to bring about greater transparency and effectiveness. Reform of the Commission and voting procedures in the Council are also needed to prepare for the next round of enlargement to the East.

## ADDRESS
Piazza Colonna, 370
00187 Rome, Italy

## REFERENCES
*The Economist,* various issues.
*Financial Times,* various issues.
Gundle, Stephen and Simon Parker. *The New Italian Republic.* London: Routledge Press, 1996.
*Hilfe Country Report,* 30 March 2000.
*New York Times,* 22 May 2000.

**Profile researched and written by Joseph A. Bongiorno, St. John's University (3/99; updated 5/2000).**

# JAMAICA

**Percival James Patterson**
**Prime Minister**
*(pronounced "PURR-sih-vull JAYMZ PAT-er-son")*

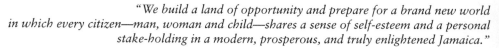

*"We build a land of opportunity and prepare for a brand new world
in which every citizen—man, woman and child—shares a sense of self-esteem and a personal
stake-holding in a modern, prosperous, and truly enlightened Jamaica."*

With an area of 10,992 sq km (4,244 sq mi) and a population of approximately 2.6 million people, Jamaica is the third-largest of the Caribbean islands. It lies 145 km (90 mi) south of Cuba and 161 km (100 mi) west of Haiti.

Like other islands in the region, European settlers imported African slaves to work on the sugar plantations. The descendants of these slaves now comprise about 90% of the population. The remainder are descendants of Europeans, East Indians, Chinese, Syrians, and Lebanese. The official language is English although a local Jamaican dialect is widely spoken. The major religion is Christianity.

The national currency is the Jamaican dollar. Jamaica's major exports include bauxite, alumina, sugar, bananas, processed foodstuffs, and garments. The country also has one of the largest tourist industries in the Caribbean.

## POLITICAL BACKGROUND

According to historical records, the country was first settled by the Ciboneys who migrated from Florida and later the Amerindian people who sailed from the Orinco region of South America. In 1509, Spaniards established the first European settlement. After 161 years of Spanish domination, the island was captured by the British in 1655.

Jamaica won its independence from Britain in 1962 and enjoys a democratic form of government. It functions through a governor general, appointed by Queen Elizabeth II of Britain and a prime minister, who normally leads the majority party. A bicameral legislature is made up of 60 elected members of the House of Representatives and 21 members in the Senate. Members are nominated by the government and the opposition parties and are appointed by the governor general.

Jamaica's political life is dominated by three political parties: the Jamaica Labour Party (JLP), the People's National Party (PNP), and the newly-formed National Democratic Movement (NDM). Both the JLP and the PNP evolved from the trade union movement, which developed in the 1930s throughout the English-speaking Caribbean. To date both parties get substantial support from their affiliated trade unions. The NDM was formed in 1995 as a result of party conflicts between the leader of the JLP, Edward Seaga, and former party chairman, Bruce Golding.

Under the Jamaican constitution, general elections are held every five years or when parliament is dissolved. Provision is also made for the election of a local government for each of the 13 parishes. The prime minister must be an elected official. The voting age is 18 years.

## PERSONAL BACKGROUND

Percival James (know as P.J.) Patterson was born in 1935. His father was a farmer and his mother a primary school teacher. Patterson was educated at Somerton Primary School and won a scholarship to attend Calabar High School. He graduated in 1953 and went on to the University of the West Indies (UWI), earning a bachelor of arts degree (with honors) in English in 1959. He studied law at the London School of Economics, where he was awarded the Leverhume Scholarship and the Sir Hughes Parry prize for excellence in the law of contracts. He graduated from the London School of Economics in 1963 with a bachelor of law degree. Upon completion of his studies, Patterson was called to the Middle Temple and Jamaican Bars. He is divorced and has two children.

Patterson's political activity began at the UWI, where he was a founding member of the Political Club. As president, he presided over the first political address given in the Caribbean by the late Eric Williams, a scholar, regionalist, and founder of the Trinidad and Tobago's People's National Movement (PNM). In 1955, he made further contacts with prominent leaders of the PNM and made his first appearance on a political platform during an election campaign. On graduating from UWI, he joined the PNP's organizing staff, serving a number of rural parishes.

## RISE TO POWER

Patterson has enjoyed a long and distinguished period of service with the PNP and as a government official before becoming prime minister. He was party organizer from 1958 until 1960 and also served as a member of the PNP's Constituency Executive, National Executive Council, and Party Executive. He was campaign director for the general elections of 1972, 1976, and 1989. From 1969 until 1982 he served as the party's vice president and has been its chairman since 1983.

Patterson's first experience as a government official was as senator from 1967 until 1970. He served as the opposition leader from 1969 until 1970 and was then elected to the House of Representatives as a member from the rural parish of South East Westmoreland. He held that seat for the next 10 years and was reelected in 1989. Following the PNP's victory at the polls in 1972, he was given his first ministerial post as minister of industry, foreign trade, and tourism. In

1979, he was appointed deputy prime minister and minister of foreign affairs and foreign trade, a position which he held until 1980 when the PNP lost the general elections to the JLP.

During the socialist era of the 1970s Patterson played a key role in the construction of policies aimed at transforming Jamaica's political and economic system. Further, between 1990 and 1991 he was responsible for preparing the Five-Year Development Plan, establishing a National Planning Council, and assuming leadership of the National Productivity Council.

Following the PNP's electoral victory of 1989, he was once again appointed to the position of deputy prime minister and minister of development, planning, and production. Between November 1990 and December 1991, Patterson held the portfolio of minister of finance and planning. In January of 1992, he was forced to resign as deputy prime minister because of his involvement in a perceived conflict of interest controversy. The government provided import tax waivers worth US$1.47 million for a senior PNP official. Although acknowledging that he had erred in not consulting with cabinet members, he has insisted that he never profited personally from the affair. Following the resignation of Prime Minister Michael Manley due to poor health, Patterson won the election as party leader of the PNP and was sworn in on 30 March 1992 as Jamaica's sixth prime minister since its independence from Britain.

Patterson returned to office following national elections that were held in March 1993. He served as prime minister and member of parliament for a further four years, until December 1997 elections. In a landslide victory, his PNP won a third term, making this the first time in Jamaican history that a political party has won three consecutive elections.

## LEADERSHIP
Patterson is well known for his international accomplishments. He represented Jamaica at the Conference on Economic Cooperation in Paris from 1976 until 1977, Commonwealth summit conferences, meetings of the Nonaligned Movement, and the Group of 77. He is widely acknowledged to be one of the chief architects of the LOME Convention and has utilized his legal skill in leading successful negotiations between the African Caribbean and Pacific (ACP) countries. He is also known to be one of the key players in the evolution of the Caribbean Free Trade Association (CARIFTA) into the Caribbean Community (CARICOM). Patterson is now the chairman of this body and his goal for the region is to achieve a single market economy before the end of this century.

As prime minister, he spearheaded the ending of an 18-year borrowing relationship with the International Monetary Fund (IMF), creating a platform for Jamaica to gain control over its economic affairs. He has introduced a national industrial policy and a national land and shelter policy. Patterson also introduced the "Operation Pride" program, which assists in the country's housing needs. His administration established several programs for the young and the elderly, including the National Youth Service, Special Training and Empowerment Program, (STEP), and the Jamaica Drugs for the Elderly Program.

Although Patterson is not as charismatic as his predecessor, Michael Manley, he has gained popularity because of

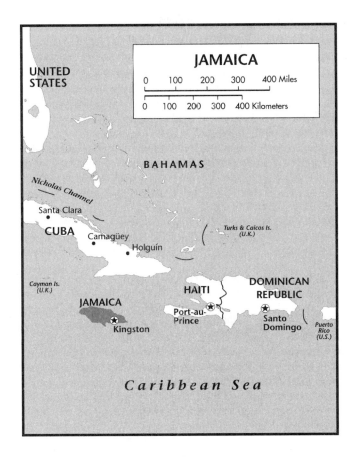

his international achievements, his administrative skills, and his professed intention to create strong moral principles in all aspects of national life. His historic victory at the polls in 1997 demonstrates that he has moved out of the shadow of Michael Manley and is no longer perceived as simply a manager. He is now viewed as a man of the people, who has made vigorous attempts to understand all classes of society through face-to-face public discussions.

## DOMESTIC POLICY
The Jamaican economy has been in turmoil since the early 1990s as a result of decreases in manufacturing output and the closure of several financial organizations. Per capita GDP has been estimated at US$3,300. The major economic concerns of the PNP have been to stabilize the Jamaican dollar and reduce inflation.

Several banks and insurance companies have had to close because of the inability of major customers to repay loans and because of the collapse of the real estate market where most of their investments were placed. The major problem that the Patterson government now faces is paying out large sums to keep financial institutions from collapsing. The controversial Financial Sector Adjustment Company (FINSAC) was established in January 1997 to rehabilitate troubled institutions and restore calm to the Jamaican financial system. To date, FINSAC has taken over the management of several banks to prevent further losses to investors.

The manufacturing sector has also experienced severe difficulties. Several international as well as local companies have had to terminate operations in Jamaica because of high import duties, high interest rates, competition from cheap imports, and an erosion of the country's export competitiveness. The government hopes to encourage new investment by eliminating import duties on non-competing raw materials and capital equipment, and by providing trade financing through the Ex-Im Bank. New investment will not only help to strengthen the economy, but also provide much needed employment opportunities.

The Rural Agricultural Development Authority (RADA) was established to provide support for small farmers and to encourage improved technology in the agricultural sector. The Patterson government also seeks to improve Jamaica's international competitiveness in agriculture through more effective marketing, and by developing the research field to improve quality and productivity. Although the tourist industry grew by US$46.8 million in 1997, new schemes have been introduced to increase visitor arrivals.

Patterson has favored the expansion of domestic telecommunications and has facilitated major investments to ensure continued growth and development in information technology. His goals in the new millennium include the following: to create a national information infrastructure to optimize the potential benefits of new technologies; to ensure that all schools, libraries, museums, and voluntary organizations are positioned to utilize this new infrastructure; and to structure the regulatory framework to reflect the realities of an open and competitive economy, driven by technological advances.

In 1999 crime and violence swept through Jamaica. In April riots broke out as Patterson announced gasoline prices would rise by 30%. As the nation decried the violence, army troops were called to pacify rioters in Kingston, where soldiers set up military outposts in the neighborhoods, and began helicopter patrols during the night in July. A dusk-to-dawn curfew was imposed in some areas, and military patrols were allowed to conduct searches for weapons and drugs. In the meantime, the government was having problems with its police force, which began an unofficial strike over a pay dispute in July, with officers calling in sick. In their increasing role, soldiers guarded the country's jails when guards went on strike. The union representing 7,100 police officers finally accepted a 24% raise, easing some of the tensions. In September, to answer criticism against police violence, the government announced it had disciplined more than 1,000 officers and fired 29.

## FOREIGN POLICY

Patterson's interest in regional cooperation is evident from his role as chairman of CARICOM. He continues to stress the importance of a single market economy and free trade area of the Americas and supports the development of regional institutions such as the Caribbean Development Bank (CDB) and The University of the West Indies (UWI).

Patterson seeks to widen linkages with traditional partners, North America and Europe. He is also working to ensure that NAFTA takes full account of the needs of Caribbean countries, and hopes to gain access to the US markets on the basis of parity. Patterson has also increased links with Africa in order to pursue trade and cultural exchanges. Visits from Nelson Mandela and various other African heads-of-state have also helped to expand trading relationships.

## ADDRESS

Office of the Prime Minister
1 Devon Road
Kingston 10, Jamaica

## REFERENCES

*Caribbean Development Bank: Annual Report.* St. Michael, Barbados: Caribbean Development Bank, 1995.
*The Caribbean's Top 100 Public Companies 97–98.* St. Michael, Barbados: Tim Forsythe, 1997.
*Encyclopaedia of the Third World.* 4th edition. Oxford: Facts on File, 1992.
*Highlights of the Manifesto of the People's National Party.* Kingston, Jamaica: The Gleaner Co., 1997.
*Jamaica News,* April 1992.
*Jamaican Weekly Gleaner,* January 1997–February 1998.
*The Miami Herald,* various issues, 1999.
*The New York Times,* various issues, 1999.

**Profile researched and written by Rachael and Ian Boxill, University of the West Indies, Jamaica (6/98; updated 5/2000).**

# JAPAN

### Yoshiro Mori
### Prime Minister
*(pronounced "yoh-SHEE-roh moh-REE")*

*"I will strive to make it possible for the LDP, as a party and as a member of the ruling coalition, to gain the overwhelming confidence and support of the people in our struggle for victory."*

Japan is an East Asian nation consisting of four main islands: Honshu, Hokkaido, Shikoku, and Kyushu. Its neighbors consist of Russia, the People's Republic of China, South Korea, and North Korea. Japan is a mountainous country where most of its 126.2 million residents live along the eastern coastline on the island of Honshu. Severe winters are common for residents on the western coastline, especially in northern Honshu. Japan's population density is 867.7 people per square mile. Tokyo, the political and financial capital, has a metropolitan area population of 27 million. It is located centrally in the western coast of Honshu.

Japan is a highly secular and advanced industrial nation with a rich cultural and religious tradition. Primary religious affiliations include Shintoism (39.5%), Buddhism (38.3%), and Christianity (3.8%), with many Japanese believing in more than one religion. Shinto, a native Japanese religion based on shamanism, emphasizes the worship of nature and the honoring of ancestors. Although Japan currently has no official religion, Shinto was the state religion prior to the end of World War II. Buddhism became an integral part of the nation's custom and cultural life since its importation from ancient China. The Japanese place a high priority on education and enjoy a 99% literacy rate. Newspaper circulation (576 per 1000 people) is twice that of the US. Life expectancy is 77.02 years for males and 83.35 years for females.

The Japanese economy is highly dependent on international trade for obtaining natural resources and for exporting finished industrial and consumer goods. The US is Japan's major trading partner, accounting for 22% of its imports and 27% of its exports. Japan also has extensive trading relations throughout East and Southeast Asia. The monetary unit is the *yen*. Per capita GDP has been estimated at $23,100.

## POLITICAL BACKGROUND
During the Tokugawa Period, prior to the Meiji Restoration in 1868, Japan isolated itself from the rest of the world. During that time, Japan experienced cultural, social, and political development, which underscores the country's major differences with its neighbors to this day. The drafting of the Meiji Constitution in 1889 created the initial framework for parliamentary government.

After World War II, Japan underwent an American-led occupation, which democratized and secularized the nation. Political transformation during that period included the introduction of universal suffrage, the creation of a constitutional monarchy, and a purge of the economic and political elite

responsible for Japan's aggression before and during World War II. The present constitution, dubbed the "MacArthur Constitution" (after US General Douglas MacArthur), was promulgated in 1947 during the US occupation of Japan and has never been formally amended despite its foreign origins.

According to the Constitution, the national legislature is the supreme organ of the state. The bicameral legislature, or Diet, is composed of the House of Councilors (HC) and the more powerful House of Representatives (HR). The 500 members of the HR are elected to four-year terms through a modified proportional representation system, in which 300 members are chosen from single-member districts, and 200 are chosen proportionally in 11 electoral districts. The 252 HC members serve six-year terms, with one-half of the members up for election every three years. Every three years, 50 HC members are elected from the nation at-large, and 76 are chosen from prefectural districts of varying size. The HR is responsible for the budget and other legislation, with the HC able to veto budgetary legislation approved in the HR, but the HR can override the veto. Two-thirds majorities in both houses are necessary to amend the Constitution.

Political turmoil characterizes Japanese politics since the Liberal Democratic Party's (LDP) disintegration in 1992 and its loss of parliamentary majority in the 1993 elections. In 1996, the LDP captured 239 seats with the now disbanded New Frontier Party garnering 156 seats. Since that time, the repeated exodus and return of party members kept the LDP's strength in a state of flux. The HC elections on 12 July 1998 resulted in the LDP's loss of 15 of 118 seats and prompted the resignation of Prime Minister Ryutaro Hashimoto. The Diet selected Keizo Obuchi to be the new Prime Minister of Japan, but he passed away in April 2000 after a stroke and coma. His successor, Yoshiro Mori, governs through a coalition with the Komei Party and the Honshu-to, a new party consisting of remaining Liberal Party members. Elections are scheduled for June 2000.

## PERSONAL BACKGROUND
Yoshiro Mori was born on 14 July 1937 in Ishikawa prefecture in the sparsely populated western Honshu. While both his father and grandfather were distinguished members of the community, sorrow and loneliness surrounded Mori's childhood. In 1937, his father was sent abroad in the Imperial Army, and his mother passed away shortly thereafter. His grandparents raised him until his father returned from abroad at the end of World War II. During his high school years, he

## JAPAN

was active in sports, and his classmates admired his large physique. He played on the school's rugby team and became the star of his school.

After graduating from high school, Mori chose to attend the renowned Waseda University, majoring in commerce. Initially playing rugby at Waseda, Mori's health deteriorated, and he had to resign from the team. Unable to play rugby, the depressed Mori met Yokoyama, the former head of the Japanese Electrical, Electronic, and Information Union and decided to join the Waseda debate club. This was where he met Obuchi, the deceased prime minister and Aoki, the LDP Chief Cabinet Secretary. He was also arrested during his time at Waseda for soliciting prostitution.

After graduating from Waseda, Mori became a reporter for the Sankei Newspaper in Tokyo. In 1969, he was elected to the House of Representatives representing the First Ishikawa District, a position he held until 1996. In 1996, he was elected from the Second Ishikawa District. As a representative, he was instrumental for developing a bullet train route directly to Kanazawa, at a cost of US$14 billion to the taxpayers.

Mori remains a sports enthusiast, especially for baseball, and during his tenure as an LDP elder statesman, he successfully recruited a wrestler, an Olympic skater, and a soccer player to run for office successfully. He is married to Chieko, and they have two children, a son and a daughter.

## RISE TO POWER

Like many Japanese politicians, Mori's political fortunes derive from the internal workings of LDP factional politics. He is currently head of the large faction, formerly the Mitsuzuka grouping, which has traditionally played an important role in selecting the prime minister and the more important cabinet portfolios. The Obuchi faction is the primary rival faction of the Mori camp. His success as a politician closely mirrors his service to the LDP and his faction.

Since his initial election in 1969 to the House of Representatives (HR), Mori has continued to win reelection. His consistency at the polls has allowed him to advance within the party hierarchy by assuming increasingly important party and government positions. He is viewed as a conservative and consensus-oriented politician. From 1975 to 1976, Mori became deputy director-general of the prime minister's office under Prime Minister Miki. In 1977–78, he was the deputy chief cabinet secretary, serving as the right-hand man to the cabinet secretary, who assists the prime minister in the day-to-day affairs of the cabinet. From 1978 to 1981, Mori became the director of the Education division of the Policy Research Council. The Policy Research Council worked with bureaucrats to craft future legislation.

Mori was active within the LDP during the years 1978 to 1985, holding intermittently the position of deputy secretary-general of the party. During that time, he was also the chairman of the Committee on Finance. He received his first cabinet-level position in 1983 as minister of education under the Nakasone administration. During 1984–87, he was chairman of the Special Committee on Education Reform in the Policy Research Council of the LDP. From 1989 to 1991, Mori again held important positions with the Policy Research Council dealing with educational issues.

During the 1990s, Mori continued to move up the LDP hierarchy. In 1991, he became the chairman of the powerful Standing Committee on Rules and Administration in the HR, as well as chairman of the Policy Research Council. In 1992–93, he became minister for international trade and industry (MITI) in the Miyazawa government. This position is viewed as a precursor to the prime ministership. From 1993 to 1995 and again from 1998 to 2000, Mori assumed the position of secretary-general of the LDP, making him one of the most powerful party politicians. In 1995–96, he was minister of construction, a highly coveted position for doling out government funds and soliciting campaign contributions. In April 2000, Mori was installed as LDP party president and prime minister. He was selected by the HR to become prime minister by securing 335 of 488 votes cast.

## LEADERSHIP

The June 2000 elections are key to the survival of the Mori government. The death of Keizo Obuchi sent shock waves throughout Japanese political circle because few had expected him to suddenly pass away. While Obuchi lacked charisma, he successfully maintained the stability of the coalition by holding his own party together and by successfully appealing to the Liberal Party and the Komeito to remain coalition members. However, at the beginning of 2000, Obuchi came under increased pressure, and many Liberal Party members left the coalition government.

Mori is largely viewed as a traditional politician who excels at building coalitions and consensus within his party. Many people expect that he will not attempt to reform

Japanese politics, but rather work within the constraints dealt him.

One of his major problems is his connection to past scandals, including the Recruit Scandal in 1988 in which he accepted 30,000 of Recruit stock prior to issuance. He is also implicated in 1992 and 1997 scandals but emerged relatively unscathed. Recently he made disparaging comments about urban residents of Osaka and people with AIDS. He commented in February that all Americans bought guns in preparation for Y2K power failure because gangs and murderers would run amok. His major asset is his health, appearing to be much more vigorous in his speech and movements than his predecessor, Obuchi.

Upon being elected prime minister, Mori dissolved the HR on 2 June, calling for elections. His strategy is to use the "sympathy vote" from Obuchi's death as a way of increasing the power of the LDP in the HR. However, Mori's popularity has so far been low, and it is uncertain whether the LDP could significantly improve in the polls. The LDP needs to acquire as close as possible to the 251-seat majority, so it will be in a position of strength when inviting prospective coalition partners. Mori needs to show that he is more than just a caretaker for the next prime minister. Nonetheless, political insiders expect Koichi Kato to emerge as eventual prime minister sometime after the election.

## DOMESTIC POLICY

Over the past two years, it appears that the Japanese economy started to experience anemic economic growth. Projections for 2000 suggest a 0.5% GDP increase. Despite such poor economic performance, this positive gain represents a significant change from the past two years when Japan experienced negative growth. In part, Obuchi's aggressive deficit spending could be credited with the growth of the economy. At no time in post-World War II history has Japan's national debt been greater, thanks to years of fiscal stimuli.

Mori's primary domestic policy remains economic. His major domestic priority is to rekindle growth in the stagnant Japanese economy, which has been in a slump since the early 1990s. The business community expects action from the government, and Mori has close ties to small- and medium-sized firms. In 1999, Mori was a member of a political group that lobbied government for regulatory protection. It is unlikely that he will liberalize the Japanese economy. Instead, it is likely that he will resort to increased government spending. Mori must refrain from such a move if he is to

successfully plant the seeds for long-term economic growth. Failure to do this will result in investor lack of confidence in the Japanese economy.

## FOREIGN POLICY

Since World War II, Japan has maintained a pro-Western foreign policy. In fact, Japan remains a cornerstone of US efforts to maintain political stability in Asia. Despite hopes that Japan would lead the rest of Asia out of Asian crisis, the opposite occurred. Because domestic demand continues to remain weak, Japan resorted to increasing exports to boost its economy, much to the disappointment of Asian and Western leaders. Japan, once again, failed to exercise leadership within the global economy. However, it is vital for Japan to continue and accelerate economic liberalization if it wants to regain the faith of its neighbors and the Group of Eight (G-8). Such enlightened self-interest seems to evade Mori, who is content with adhering to economic policies of the 1970s and 1980s.

Mori's major test, assuming that he successfully navigates the upcoming elections, will be the G-8 Summit scheduled for July 2000 in Okinawa. Mori has limited international experience, so he will require on-the-job training to hone his diplomatic skills. Unfortunately, he lashed out at Okinawan teachers recently by calling them communist-controlled subversives, setting the stage for potentially serious protests during the meeting. Mori will continue to maintain close security relations with the US through the continued maintenance of American bases on Japanese soil.

## ADDRESS

Prime Minister's Office
106 Nagata-cho
Chiyoda-ku, Tokyo
Japan

## REFERENCES

*Asia Now,* 17 April 2000, vol. 155, no. 15.
*The Economist,* 8–14 April 2000, pp. 39–40.
*Far Eastern Economic Review,* 13 April 2000.
Prime Minister's Office. [Online] Available http://www.kantei.go.jp. (Accessed June 2000).
*Profile of Foreign Minister Mori Yoshiro.* Liberal Democratic Party. [Online] Available http://www.jimin.otr.jp/english/e-staff/mori-yo.html (Accessed June 2000).
*The Weekly Post,* 15–21 May 2000.

**Profile researched and written by Robert W. Compton, Western Kentucky University (6/2000).**

# JORDAN

## Abdullah II
## King
*(pronounced "ab-DOO-lah")*

*"Democracy is a learning experience. Down the line you will see a shift of responsibility as institutions mature."*

The Hashemite Kingdom of Jordan is a landlocked country, except for its 26 km (16 mi) coastline along the Gulf of Aqaba, which provides access to the Red Sea. Its area occupies 91,880 sq km (35,475 sq mi), bordered on the north by Syria, northeast by Iraq, east and south by Saudi Arabia, and on the west by Israel. Amman, Jordan's capital, is also the country's largest city. The estimated population is nearly 4.6 million, almost evenly divided between native Jordanian Arabs and Palestinian Arabs; most of the latter came as refugees from Israeli-held lands west of the Jordan River. The overwhelming majority of the people are Sunni Muslims. Christians constitute about 5% of the population. Arabic is the official language, and Islam is the state religion.

Jordan's developing economy is highly dependent on foreign aid, as well as on oil imports from neighboring Saudi Arabia and Iraq to meet its energy needs. The country's primary exports are agricultural products and phosphate rock. Jordan's currency is the *dinar*.

## POLITICAL BACKGROUND

For four centuries, the territory constituting present-day Jordan was part of the Turkish Ottoman Empire. Liberated from Turkish rule in 1918, this area became part of British-administered Palestine under a League of Nations' mandate. In 1921, the British divided the mandate. Land east of the Jordan River was designated as Transjordan and given nominal self-rule as an emirate under Abdullah ibn Hussein. Transjordan became a fully independent state in 1946, and Abdullah was proclaimed king. In 1948, Transjordan joined other Arab countries in a war against the newly created state of Israel. During this conflict, the Transjordanian army crossed the Jordan and occupied parts of the river's West Bank and the old city of Jerusalem. In 1950, the Arab-held West Bank was formally annexed by Transjordan, and the kingdom was renamed Jordan. Following Abdullah's assassination in 1951, his son Talal became king. Talal, who suffered from schizophrenia, was deposed by the Jordanian parliament in 1952. His 17-year-old son, Hussein, assumed the full powers of the monarchy on 2 May 1953.

In the early 1960s, friction between Jordan and Israel grew over rights to the waters of the Jordan River and over problems posed by displaced Palestinian refugees. In 1964, the Palestine Liberation Organization (PLO) formed, vowing to restore Arab claims to the territory now constituting Israel. The PLO's use of Jordan to launch raids into Israel provoked reprisals against the kingdom, further increasing tensions in the region. In 1966, Jordan withdrew its support of the guerillas, prompting the PLO to urge the overthrow of King Hussein. The 1967 war between Israel and its Arab neighbors proved disastrous for Jordan, which lost control of the West Bank and East Jerusalem. By 1970, a growing PLO military presence in Jordan had begun to threaten the government's authority. In September of that year, clashes erupted between the Jordanian army and the PLO forces, resulting in a defeat for the guerillas and the expulsion of PLO fighters. Jordan did not participate in the 1973 Arab-Israeli war. In 1974, under pressure from other Arab nations, King Hussein recognized the PLO as the sole representative of West Bank Palestinians. On 31 July 1988, he severed Jordan's legal and administrative links with the West Bank, effectively relinquishing Jordanian claims to the territory.

Jordan's 1951 constitution established a limited monarchy with a parliamentary form of government. In practice, the monarch has preponderant powers as chief executive and head of state. He is the commander-in-chief of the armed forces and is vested with the power to declare war, conclude peace, and sign treaties. He appoints a prime minister who forms the cabinet. The prime minister and members of the cabinet are responsible to parliament but serve at the king's discretion. The legislative body is the National Assembly. It consists of the Senate (whose 30 members are appointed by the king) and the Chamber of Deputies (whose 80 members are popularly elected to four-year terms). The king has the right to dissolve the National Assembly and postpone general elections indefinitely. A ban imposed on political parties in 1963 was not lifted until 1992. However, candidates belonging to organized opposition groups, like the Muslim Brotherhood, and independent Islamic candidates displayed significant strength in the 1989 general elections.

In the early 1990s, new restrictions were placed on the media, and political freedoms curtailed. Electoral laws were also changed to favor pro-monarchy candidates at the polls. Subsequently, the 1993 and 1997 general elections returned parliaments friendly to the throne. Following tradition, Jordan's constitution designates the king's eldest son be crown prince and heir to the throne. In 1965, the constitution was altered to allow the king to name his younger brother, Hassan bin Talal, to the post.

Under the leadership of King Hussein, Jordan emerged as a modern state. However, the country's political institutions are feeble, and democratic rights and freedoms are restricted. The monarchy draws its main support from East Bank Jordanians and the Bedouin desert tribes. Wealthier and moderate Palestinians also tend to be supportive.

## PERSONAL BACKGROUND

Abdullah bin Hussein al-Hashem was born in Amman on 30 January 1962 to King Hussein and his second wife, British-born Antoinette Gardiner. Educated abroad, Abdullah's early schooling was at Saint Edmunds and at Harrow in Britain. He also attended Deerfield Academy in Massachusetts. Abdullah's post-secondary education includes military training at the elite Sandhurst Military Academy, a diploma in international politics from Oxford University, and a year's study at Georgetown University in Washington, DC.

Returning to Jordan in 1984, Abdullah became an officer in the Jordanian army. On 10 June 1993, he married Rania Yassin, a Kuwaiti-born Palestinian with family roots in the West Bank town of Tulkarm. They have two young children: a son, Hussein, and a daughter, Iman.

An athletic and easygoing man, Abdullah is an accomplished marksman and a licensed pilot. His interests include scuba diving, parachuting, and auto racing. He also collects antique weaponry and is a fan of the television show, *Star Trek*.

## RISE TO POWER

Hussein's 45-year reign was turbulent. He weathered numerous threats to his life and to his kingdom's survival. Aware of the personal risks he faced, Hussein decided to appoint an adult heir to his throne in 1965, replacing three-year-old Crown Prince Abdullah. This decision was also motivated by concerns that conservative-minded Jordanians would not accept Abdullah as king because of his mixed Anglo-Arab parentage.

Relieved of the burden and responsibilities of being crown prince, Abdullah grew up away from the public eye. He joined the Jordanian army and pursued a military career, the early years of which were spent in remote desert bases. Expected to become the army's chief of staff, Abdullah rapidly rose to the rank of brigadier-general. In May 1998, he was promoted to major-general and placed in command of the elite Special Forces responsible for internal security and counter-terrorism.

In 1992, Hussein had been successfully treated for a cancerous kidney. In mid-1998, he became ill with Non-Hodgkin's lymphoma. After six months of medical treatment in the United States, Hussein returned to Jordan in January 1999, apparently cured. In a surprise move, he dismissed Hassan as crown prince and named Abdullah to be his successor. The dismissal was reportedly prompted by the king's displeasure with Hassan's performance as regent during his absence abroad. Some accounts suggest that Hussein had long contemplated replacing his brother in order to restore the line of succession to his children. Shortly after appointing Abdullah as crown prince, Hussein flew back to the US for further cancer treatment. His condition proved to be terminal, and the comatose monarch was flown back to Jordan. Hussein died on 7 February 1999, and the cabinet immediately proclaimed Abdullah to be the new king.

## LEADERSHIP

Hussein was regarded as a firm but tolerant ruler who inspired confidence in Jordan's stability and symbolized national unity. Abdullah is largely unknown to most of his people and is seen as a political novice, unseasoned in the rough-and-tumble of Middle Eastern statecraft. Though he

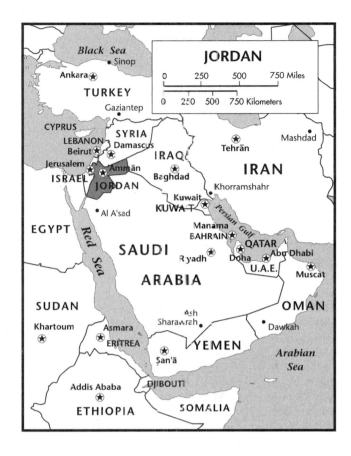

lacks Hussein's stature and experience, Abdullah is said to have inherited many of his father's personal qualities. Indeed, his energy, character, and common touch have reassured those concerned about the transition. Beyond expressing a desire to continue his father's legacy, Abdullah has yet to articulate his own vision for the country's future. Most observers believe that his inexperience will force Abdullah to rely on advisors and may inhibit the bold steps needed to deal with the challenges he is likely to face.

Daunting tests await Abdullah's promised inclusive leadership style. A delicate balancing act will be required to deal with the country's large Palestinian population, its economic woes, and calls for greater democratization. The rapprochement with Israel has grown increasingly unpopular among many Jordanians, especially those of Palestinian origin. Abdullah has pledged his commitment to peace with Israel. However, Palestinian intentions to declare statehood for West Bank territories under their control could provoke Israeli retaliation and result in violence, threatening the kingdom's stability. Abdullah has rejected Palestinian President Arafat's offer to federate these territories with Jordan and has urged him to delay the declaration of statehood. On the economic front, Abdullah aims to further liberalize Jordan's economy through market-oriented reforms. He is expected to face strong opposition from the Muslim Brotherhood, other Islamist parties, and leftists.

Most analysts anticipate that Abdullah will take steps to consolidate his authority first and then proceed gradually on political reforms. Despite calls for lifting restrictive media and electoral laws and dissolving what is widely regarded as a "rubber stamp" parliament, no immediate moves towards political liberalization are foreseen. Abdullah has quickly moved to establish his control of the government and military by replacing Hassan loyalists. A new cabinet has been formed, but the palace holds real power.

Rumored royal family tensions, stemming from Hassan's abrupt dismissal, are officially discounted. Hassan has pledged fealty to the new king. Respecting his father's wishes, Abdullah has appointed his half-brother, Hamzeh, to be the new crown prince. This choice has received universal praise.

In June 2000, King Abdullah implemented his first major government shakeup, replacing Prime Minister Abdul-Raouf al-Rawabdeh with the more progressive Ali Abu al-Ragheb, a former minister of commerce and industry. A new cabinet was appointed as well. Al-Rawabdeh had been the target of widespread criticism for alleged nepotism and corruption.

## DOMESTIC POLICY

Jordan has a small, underdeveloped economy and few natural resources. Nearly one-third of its people live in poverty, and recent estimates place the unemployment rate at around 15%. Declining oil prices in the 1980s led to a drastic cut in hard currency inflows and contributed to the country's rising foreign debts, which are now approximately US$8 billion. In the late 1980s, difficulties with debt servicing sparked a currency crisis, forcing adoption of an IMF structural adjustment program. The government introduced reforms to reduce the role of government in the economy, including privatization of public enterprises. These reforms resulted in tax increases, reduced public spending, and higher prices on staple products. Economic distress was compounded by fallout from the Iraqi invasion of Kuwait. The subsequent Gulf War and UN sanctions against Iraq deprived Jordan of a principal trading partner and oil supplier. Moreover, the country had to cope with an influx of refugees from Iraq and Jordanians of Palestinian origin who were expelled from Kuwait. The potential for social upheaval caused by economic strains is given as one justification for the government's clampdown on political dissent in the early 1990s. However, widespread unrest did not materialize, partly due to the generosity of Western aid donors who provided stopgap financing to alleviate the country's fiscal crisis.

After about six months in office, Abdullah recalled the parliament from its summer recess for the purpose of acting on legislation. By September, amendments to existing laws were passed to list restrictions on some forms of freedom of the press.

Abdullah considers the continuity of reform essential to solve Jordan's economic problems. Consequently, he has appointed seasoned pro-reform figures to key economic policy posts. Observers are keenly watching how Abdullah will respond to IMF calls for more progress on privatization and to domestic pressures for tax relief and against further cuts in subsidies.

## FOREIGN POLICY

Though small and weak, Jordan is considered pivotal in the geopolitics of settling the region's protracted conflicts. Under the leadership of Hussein, Jordan became a bastion of the moderate Arab camp and followed a generally pro-Western foreign policy. Jordan's vulnerability in the region required an alignment with the West in order to blunt perceived threats to its survival. Attempts to forge friendly relations with its neighbors have been complicated by the vicissitudes of the broader Arab-Israeli conflict. Jordan is home to a sizeable Palestinian population. In its quest for peace with Israel, Jordan must balance its own security needs with Palestinian aspirations for a separate homeland.

For many years, Hussein vied with the PLO for Palestinians' loyalty. In the mid-1980s, he tried to subordinate the PLO to his own peace process, but opposition from Palestinians and other Arab countries forced him to acknowledge the PLO's claim to be the Palestinians' sole representative in any future peace talks.

Jordan played a significant role in the 1991 secret negotiations between Israel and the PLO that led to the Oslo Accords of 1993, which produced a declaration of principles regarding Palestinian self-rule in Israeli-held territories. Relations between Jordan and Israel warmed, and in 1994 the two countries formally ended their state of war. Abdullah affirmed his government's commitment to the peace process in the Middle East and to the founding of a Palestinian state. During his first year in office, he traveled extensively throughout the region, restored diplomatic relations with Kuwait, and made great strides in improving relations with Syria.

Relations with Saudi Arabia, Syria, and Iraq are high on Abdullah's diplomatic agenda. Saudi Arabia was harshly critical of Jordan's tilt towards Iraq during the Gulf Crisis. Since then, the two kingdoms have slowly reconciled their differences. Many analysts see Iraq and Syria presenting Abdullah with his greatest external challenge. Both countries disapprove of Jordan's peace with Israel and may capitalize on popular Jordanian disillusionment to undermine Abdullah. In 1995, Hussein distanced himself from the Iraqi regime and called for its replacement. Abdullah appears to share this view, but in November 1999, he called for lifting of sanctions against the people of Iraq and Sudan. The Jordanian public opposes active support for efforts to remove the Iraqi regime and may warm to the humanitarian aspects of lifing the economic sanctions. Jordan's diplomatic and military partnership with the US is expected to continue.

## ADDRESS

Royal Palace
Amman, Jordan

## REFERENCES

*The Economist*, 13 February 1999.

*EIU Country Profile: Jordan 1998*. The Economist Intelligence Unit Ltd., 1998.

*EIU Country Reports: Jordan*. The Economist Intelligence Unit Ltd., 1998.

Goldberg, Jeffrey. "Learning How to Be King." *New York Times*, 6 February 2000, Sunday Magazine.

*Jerusalem Post*, 7 February–5 March 1999.

*Middle East*, March 1999.

*New York Times*, 26 January–8 February 1999.

**Profile researched and written by Taufiq Rashid, Indiana University (6/99; updated 6/2000).**

# KAZAKHSTAN

## Nursultan Nazarbayev
### President
*(pronounced "nor-sool-TAN nah-zahr-BAI-eff")*

*"The path from totalitarianism to democracy lies through enlightened authoritarianism."*

The Republic of Kazakhstan is located in the heart of the Eurasian landmass. Covering 2.7 million sq km (1,059,750 sq mi), the land area is 12% of the former Soviet Union. Kazakhstan is the second-largest of the former Soviet republics, after the Russian Republic. It is about four times the size of Texas.

Kazakhstan is one of the most populous of the Central Asian states, with an estimated population of 16.8 million. In 1995, the Kazakh legislature endorsed moving the nation's administrative capital to a windswept small town in northern Kazakhstan, renamed Astana, in a bid to strengthen control over areas heavily populated by ethnic Russians. Officials reported in December 1998 that ethnic Russians constitute 31.4% (4.9 million) of the population and Kazakhs over 50%. There are more than 100 other small ethnic communities. Kazakhs are divided by tribes called hordes. The Great Horde occupies southeastern Kazakhstan; the Middle Horde occupies the center and north of the country; the Little Horde can be found in the west. Horde identity has been reasserting itself, with the Great Horde dominating the government. Because of earlier immigration by Russians and deported nationalities, and the death of Kazakhs during collectivization and purges, Kazakhs became an ethnic minority. Recent immigration of Kazakhs from Mongolia and elsewhere, a relatively high Kazakh birthrate, and the departure of other ethnic groups have restored the Kazakhs as a majority of the population. Kazakhs are traditionally Sunni Muslims while the Russians tend to be Orthodox Christians. Official languages for government business include Kazakh (a Turkic language) and Russian, though Russian is increasingly discouraged. Few ethnic Russians have endeavored to learn Kazakh although many have lived in the region for several generations. Kazak-Russian ethnic tensions have not yet grown into broader conflict, but a more nationalistic Kazakh government could fuel separatism in the Russian-dominated north.

Kazakhstan introduced its own currency, the *tenge,* in 1992. Gross domestic product has been estimated at $52.9 billion, and per capita GDP at about $3,100. There is widespread poverty.

## POLITICAL BACKGROUND
The Kazakh nation emerged in the 15th century from Turkic Moslem peoples and Mongols living in the area of modern Kazakhstan. Contact with Russia began in the 16th century. By the 19th century, vast areas of the steppes had been taken over by Russian and other settlers. After the Russian revolution in 1917, Kazakhstan declared itself independent but came under Bolshevik power in 1919. It became a separate republic within the Soviet Union in 1936. During Stalin's forced collectivization campaign in the 1930s, as much as one-third of the population perished. There were major boosts in industrialization during World War II and in grain and livestock production during the "Virgin Lands" campaign of the 1950s, but these also resulted in environmental degradation and human suffering. In December 1991, Kazakhstan and other Central Asian states insisted on being included in the newly formed Commonwealth of Independent States (CIS). In joining the CIS, Kazakhstan hoped to maintain economic links with the Slavic republics and assuage its large Russian minority.

## PERSONAL BACKGROUND
Born in 1940 to a family of mountain shepherds, Nursultan Abishevich Nazarbayev joined the Communist Party when he was 22 years old. He received a technical degree in metallurgy in 1967, a doctor's degree at the Russian Academy of Management in 1992, and a correspondence degree from the Soviet Communist Party Higher Party School. He worked as a technician and later as an economist at the Karaganda Metallurgical Combine from 1960 until 1969. Nazarbayev then moved into Komsomol and Communist Party work in 1969. He served as the second secretary of the local Communist Party committee in Karaganda from 1973 until 1977. In 1977, he became a secretary of the Karaganda Regional Committee of the Kazakh Communist Party (KCP). In 1979, he became a secretary of the KCP Central Committee, with broad responsibility for industrial management. From 1984 to 1989, he was chairman of the Kazakh Council of Ministers (Prime Minister). He and his wife, Sara Alpysovna, have three daughters and three grandchildren. Nazarbayev enjoys playing tennis.

## RISE TO POWER
In 1986, riots broke out in Almaty, and other Kazakh cities after Soviet leader Mikhail Gorbachev replaced an ethnic Kazakh with an ethnic Russian as KCP leader. Correcting this error, Gorbachev appointed an ethnic Kazakh—Nursultan Nazarbayev—to head the KCP in 1989. Nazarbayev was also elected chairman of the presidium of the Kazakh Supreme Soviet in 1989, and after a newly elected legislature convened in April 1990, he had it elect him to the newly created post of

president of Kazakhstan. Following the failed coup against Gorbachev launched by hard-line Soviet Communist Party officials, Nazarbayev resigned as first secretary and member of the KCP. He was reelected president in an unopposed popular vote in December 1991. He orchestrated a call by a popular body he created (the People's Assembly) to hold an April 1995 referendum on extending his rule until the year 2000. The extension was approved by over 93% of voters.

## LEADERSHIP

Nazarbayev has proven to be an astute politician who has prevented ethnic tensions from threatening the integrity of Kazakhstan and has protected the nation's independence by cooperating with Russia on some issues and quietly circumventing it on others. He has allowed some opposition parties and media to operate, but has controlled them through use of a law outlawing threats to the "honor and dignity" of the president and other means. In an interview in April 2000, he called for ethnic Kazakhs to "respect other ethnic peoples," including foreigners, so that Kazakhs may be considered "intelligent and developed people" in the global economy. He particularly warned against ethnocentrism against Russians residing in Kazakhstan, since Russian-Kazakh ethnic conflict could tear Kazakhstan apart, and accused much of the political opposition of fomenting ethnic discord. Instead, he urged "ethnic Kazakh unity" to ensure political stability, since "Kazakhstan is for the ethnic Kazakhs." He also dismissed political liberalization, stating, "let no one think that [I] will allow everyone to do whatever they want. I will not allow that. People trusted me and elected me as their president in order to bring order to the state." He also stated that the opposition seemed to prefer state socialism since they criticized his economic reforms. Nazarbayev asserted that he had opened the economy and carried out privatization, and

that the economy had recently stabilized. He concluded that his political and economic reforms had created an independent Kazakhstan, where Kazakhs "are slowly getting rid of the psychology of a slave....We and I have organized all this."

In 1993, the Supreme Soviet (or Supreme *Kenges*) approved a new constitution. An election was held the following year to a new unicameral legislature of 177 members. This election was judged by international observers to not be free and fair. The Kazakh Constitutional Court ruled in early 1995 that the election was invalid. Nazarbayev supported this decision, since the legislature had balked at approving his policies. Dissolving the legislature, he assumed legislative powers and ruled by decree for the rest of the year. A new constitution, approved by a questionable referendum in August 1995, increased the powers of the presidency and reduced those of the legislature. Less emphasis was given to the protection of human rights. While the president was given broad powers to dissolve the legislature, he could only be removed for disability or high treason. The independence of the judiciary was also constrained by replacing an earlier Constitutional Court with a Constitutional Council, mostly controlled by the president. The 327-member People's Assembly, created by Nazarbayev and composed of various cultural and ethnic leaders, acted as a propaganda forum for the president.

Legislative elections, held on 5 and 9 December 1995, were judged by international observers to be largely fair although some problems were evident. An onerous fee was required to register as a candidate and voter turnout rates were inflated. The 47 deputies of the Senate were indirectly elected by regional legislatures, except for seven appointed by Nazarbayev. Deputies to the 67-member lower chamber (the *Majlis*) were directly elected by district. The two opposition parties alleged government harassment and voting irregularities. Most deputies who won election were formally unaffiliated, though the nomination process was heavily weighted toward pro-Nazarbayev candidates.

In October 1998, Nazarbayev orchestrated changes to the constitution allowing him to advance the timetable for the presidential race by one year to 10 January 1999. The official reasons given for changing the date were increased economic uncertainty following the August 1998 Russian currency devaluation and the need to get the election out of the way before addressing the economy. A more pressing reason might have been concern about the widening political disenchantment with Nazarbayev as the economy worsened.

The Kazakh Central Electoral Commission and Supreme Court ruled in November 1998 that Nazarbayev's main opponent, the popular former prime minister Akezhan Kazhegeldin, was ineligible to run in the presidential race, because of his earlier participation in an "unauthorized" public meeting. Three candidates were registered besides Nazarbayev, two of whom were Nazarbayev supporters and only one, Serikibolsyn Abdildin (head of the Communist Party), a true opposition candidate. Onerous registration requirements included a $30,000 deposit (forfeited by the losers) and 170,000 signatures gathered in at least 11 of 16 regions. Campaigning by the minor candidates was impaired by their lack of funds, while Nazarbayev was given extensive coverage by state-owned and private media. The Kazakh

Central Electoral Commission reported on 16 January 1999 that Nazarbayev had won the 10 January presidential race with 79.8% of about seven million votes cast. The Organization for Security and Cooperation in Europe (OSCE), critical of the run-up to the election, sent only token monitors, and declared on 11 January that "the electoral process...was far removed from the standards which the Republic of Kazakhstan has pledged to follow as an OSCE member state." Human Rights Watch on 5 January also characterized the electoral campaign as being "blatantly unfair." Nazarbayev was inaugurated on 20 January 1999 for a seven-year term.

## DOMESTIC POLICY

During his presidential campaign, Nazarbayev pledged to continue his existing domestic policies and to keep most government officials in place. Picking up a campaign theme used by Abdildin, he also pledged to work to improve people's living standards. In line with these pledges, Nazarbayev reappointed his previous prime minister, Nurlan Balgimbayev, and much of the cabinet. In his inaugural address, he stated that "the first task is the people's prosperity. The second task is to develop democracy in the country." He promised that the fruits of the reforms he has been carrying out will soon be seen on people's tables and in their pockets. He also argued that the vote showed that Kazakhs wanted his leadership during the economic downturn.

Nazarbayev hailed the democratic character of the election, stating that it was "the first time a presidential election was held in the country with a choice of candidates. It will go down in Kazakh history as the day Kazakhstan started along the road of democratization." He also stressed that the election meant that Kazakhs, "particularly ethnic Kazakhs...want to say farewell to totalitarianism." Nazarbayev pledged that the 1999 legislative elections will be democratic. However, he added that full democratization would take some time to develop. "In conditions of severe crisis...at a time when people do not have such elementary things as a roof over their heads, or enough food, clothes, or work...I think the authorities ought to be strong, right now. I am not saying that this ought to be preserved for all eternity. Right now, the reforms must be carried out from above. Order must be brought from above. It is my personal view and, of course, people can take issue with it, but I think that both Kazakhstan and Russia ought to have strong presidential power."

Nazarbayev has claimed that the high number of votes he received meant that most ethnic groups had supported him. His policy has been to appeal to both Kazakh nationalists and to ethnic Russians. In a speech delivered to the legislature on 21 January 1999, Nazarbayev stated that ethnic accord should be taken as "the absolute truth," and that maintaining independence and ensuring the rights of all citizens was possible only in conditions of ethnic harmony. He called for former Kazakhstani residents to "come back to our common homeland, our doors are open, and we hope that together, we can become stronger." While calling for ethnic harmony, he nonetheless stressed that "it is impossible to refuse to safeguard the ethnic interests of the Kazakh people, who account for the majority of the country's population." He declared that Kazakhstan's ethnic policy encompasses the "targeted development of the Kazakh cultural nucleus, while at the same time creating conditions for the development of other groups."

## FOREIGN POLICY

Nazarbayev has stated that the geographic location of Kazakhstan and its ethnic makeup dictate its "multipolar orientation toward both the West and the East." Kazakhstan has railway and air links with China and extensive trade ties with Xinjiang Province, where many ethnic Kazakhs and Uighurs reside. Nazarbayev has visited Turkey and Iran. The Kazakh legislature ratified the Lisbon protocol, the START Treaty, and the Conventional Armed Forces in Europe (CFE) Treaty in 1992. The following year, it voted to ratify the Nuclear Nonproliferation Treaty. In April 1995, the last of approximately 1,040 nuclear warheads were removed from SS-18 missiles in Kazakhstan and transferred to Russia, allowing Kazakhstan to announce that it had become a nuclear weapons-free state. In 1995, Kazakhstan joined a customs union formed by Russia and Belarus, which was reaffirmed in an accord on "deeper integration" signed in 1996. The economic crisis in Russia, however, has led Kazakhstan and Russia to levy high tariffs on each other's trade goods, vitiating the customs pact. In an interview soon after his inaugural address, Nazarbayev called for tariffs to be equitably applied within the customs union. While criticizing Russian tariff policies, he nonetheless emphasized that Kazakhstan considered itself a "friend of Russia." He stressed that Kazakhstan would renew its commitment to the CIS Collective Security Treaty because "Russia remains the strongest country among us in military and defense terms," and so is best able to assist Kazakhstan.

## ADDRESS

Office of the President
Government of the Republic of Kazakhstan
Krasnyy Yar
Astana, Kazakhstan

## REFERENCES

Foreign Broadcast Information Service. *Central Eurasia: Daily Report*, 1 October 1998–30 January 1999.
Jamestown Foundation. *Monitor*, 4–22 January 1999.
Kazakh Presidental Election. [Online] Available http://www.eurasia.org.ru (Accessed May 5, 2000).
Radio Free Europe/Radio Liberty. *Newsline*, 4–22 January 1999.
Reuters. 4–21 January 1999.
*Turkestan Newsletter*, 8 January–1 February 1999.
US Department of State. *Kazakhstan Country Report on Human Rights Practices for 1998*. 26 February 1999.

**Profile researched and written by Jim Nichol, Library of Congress (5/2000).**

# KENYA

## Daniel arap Moi
## President
*(pronounced "DAN-yell air-ap MOY")*

*"My next government will be more sensitive to the needs and aspirations of the people. I now appeal to all Kenyans to quickly close ranks and open a new chapter that is devoid of hate, fear, and confrontation."*

The Republic of Kenya is situated on Africa's east coast. It is bordered to the northeast by Somalia, to the north by Ethiopia, to the northwest by Sudan, to the west by Uganda, and to the south by Tanzania. The capital city is Nairobi. Its total area is 582,646 sq km (224,960 sq mi). Because the northern part of the country is virtually without water, approximately 85% of Kenya's population live in the southern highlands bordering Lake Victoria and Tanzania.

The African population is comprised of many ethnic groups. The non-African population is comprised primarily of Europeans (especially English), Asians (Indians and Pakistanis), and Arabs. English and Kiswahili are Kenya's official languages. The majority of Kenyans are Christian, but a shrinking number still adhere to traditional beliefs. There is also a growing Muslim population.

Nearly 80% of the people are involved in agricultural activity. Much of Kenyan industry is also agriculturally related although diversification has begun. Landlessness is a problem for many Kenyans. The urban unemployment rate is 35%. Export crops include coffee, tea, sisal, sugar, and horticultural products. Tourism also plays an important part in the economy. The monetary unit is the Kenya *shilling*. The per capita GDP has been estimated at US$1,550.

## POLITICAL BACKGROUND
Kenya gained independence from Great Britain in 1963 and joined the British Commonwealth the following year. The country adopted a republican form of government and switched from a parliamentary to a presidential system. Jomo Kenyatta, leader of the Kenya African National Union (KANU), was the country's first leader. He remained president until his death in 1978.

The Kenyan constitution provides for a president, elected to a five-year term and eligible for re-election. The vice-president is appointed by the president. The legislature is the unicameral National Assembly. Its 210 members are elected by universal suffrage for five-year terms. Twelve members are appointed by the president. The cabinet is a 33-member body appointed by the president. The president, vice-president, and ministers must all be members of the National Assembly.

KANU has been the only political party allowed in Kenya since 1969. Despite being a one-party state, Kenyan elections were vigorously contested by multiple candidates. Through much of the 1970s and early 1980s, parliamentary debate was open and robust. Power was gradually consolidated in KANU and its leadership. By the early 1980s, debate in the legislature had virtually ceased to exist and democracy within KANU was seriously limited. Any opposition to the government was considered a capital offense.

The early 1990s saw a partial re-emergence of democracy in Kenya when the 1992 election was opened to other political parties. Dozens of opposition parties sought to register. Debate, often heated, returned to parliament and enlightened civil society. The government, however, retained the right to refuse the registration of parties it deemed unsuitable (i.e., a significant threat to KANU's electoral success) and used repressive laws regulating public assembly to restrict effective political action. KANU's success at the polls was virtually assured due to a splintered opposition and election laws favoring KANU. Prior to the 1997 elections, the government reformed the electoral process again and eliminated some of the most oppressive laws concerning public assembly and speech. At the time of the December 1997 elections, there were 26 registered parties in Kenya. Ten parties won parliamentary seats. The period after the 1997 elections was dominated by mounting internal and external pressure for a participatory review of the 1963 constitution to, among other things, curtail the powers of the president and introduce a bill of rights.

## PERSONAL BACKGROUND
Torotich arap (son of) Moi was born in 1924 in the village of Kuriengwo (some sources say Sacho) in the Baringo district of the Rift Valley Province in western Kenya. His family were farmers and members of the Tugen sub-group of the Kalenjin people, an African minority in Kenya. He took the name Daniel when he was baptized by Christian missionaries as a schoolboy.

Moi attended the African Mission School in Karbatonjo and, with the encouragement of his teachers, continued his education in Kapsabet, Baringo's district headquarters. There, he attended the African Inland Mission School, the Government African School, and Kapsabet Teacher Training College. He became a teacher in 1945 and later a school administrator.

Like many Kenyan government officials, Moi is a successful businessman. He has extensive land holdings and owns the East African International Harvester distributorship and Kobil, a company he formed by merging the Kenya Oil Company and Mobil Oil, Kenya. He also owns substantial real estate in Nairobi. Moi is a father of two girls and five boys. He divorced his wife, Lena, in 1976 after 25 years of marriage on grounds of her adultery. He has never remarried. Moi tries to maintain a quiet private life. He is perceived by some to be puritanical because he neither drinks alcohol nor smokes.

## RISE TO POWER

Moi began his political career while Kenya was still under British control. In October 1955, he was named by the British district council to fill the vacant Rift Valley seat in the Kenya Legislative Council. In 1957, the first election in which blacks were allowed to vote, he was one of eight blacks elected to the Legislative Council. Moi has served in the Kenyan legislature ever since. He holds the record for longest political service to Kenya.

In 1960, Moi was a delegate to the Lancaster House Conference in London, which drafted the new Kenyan constitution. He was elected assistant treasurer of KANU later that year. Because KANU was dominated by the Kikuyu and Luo tribes, Moi and several leaders of other small minorities withdrew from KANU and founded the Kenya African Democratic Union (KADU), of which he served briefly as chairman. In 1961, as a KADU member of the Legislative Council, Moi served for several months as parliamentary secretary to the Ministry of Education, and in December he was named minister of education. In 1962, he became minister for local government and participated in a series of conferences designed to prepare Kenya for independence. He fought successfully for the creation of a federal system insuring regional autonomy and protection of minority rights.

After the 1963 departure of the British and the dissolution of KADU, Moi joined Kenyatta's government. He was made minister of home affairs, putting him in charge of Kenya's national police force and making him responsible for national security. He was elected vice-chairman of KANU in the Rift Valley Province. Still retaining his Ministry position, Moi was named vice-president of Kenya and vice-chairman of the KANU Parliamentary Group in January 1967.

On 22 August 1978, Kenyatta died and Moi became the interim president of Kenya. Six weeks later, he was designated president and was inaugurated on 14 October. In 1979, Moi was elected to a regular five-year term. He ran unopposed in 1983 and 1988. When multi-party politics were reintroduced in 1992, Moi won the presidency with 36% of the vote and again in December 1997 with 40% of the vote. The next election was scheduled for early in 2003.

## LEADERSHIP

As president, Moi at first appeared intent on strengthening the democracy which Kenya had created within the confines of a one-party state. His first two years in office signaled an openness in government unheard of in Kenyatta's time. Moi released all political prisoners by 1980, making Kenya the only African country with none. Newspapers were now free to cover and debate the political issues of the day. Unpopular politicians, who had retained their seats under Kenyatta, found themselves turned out of the National Assembly in the 1979 elections. Moi declared war on corruption, advocated a national program of land reform, and called for a free milk program for schoolchildren. Most significantly, it even appeared possible that a second party would be tolerated.

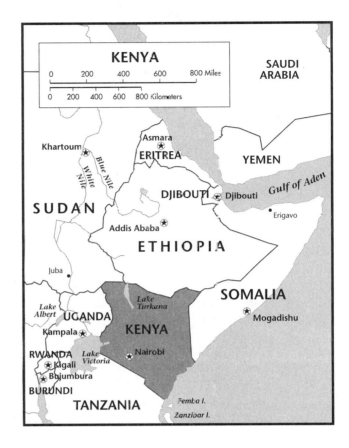

Kenya appeared to be on the road to a full and vigorous democracy.

In 1981, Moi altered his approach. Until then he had been trying to build a solid base of popular support to sustain his power. Afterward, he began to rely more and more on an increasingly corrupt elite. As popular dissent rose, Moi clamped down on Kenyan society. He continued to consolidate power, demanding loyalty from the party, parliament, and his ministers. KANU became increasingly important in setting government policy. Corruption had once again become a fact of life as Moi placed his own people in government positions. It gradually spread and reached new levels. As of 2000, Moi is considered to be one of the most corrupt leaders in Africa

Because there are no conflict-of-interest laws in Kenya, politicians are free to use their positions to enhance their business and commercial interests. Moi has used his presidency to great advantage. He bought the Kenya Oil Company and Mobil Oil, Kenya, and consolidated the two. He also owns so many buildings in Nairobi that it is easier to list those he does not own.

In 1986, Moi officially reduced the National Assembly to an advisory capacity and KANU became the premier decision-making body in Kenya. He also eliminated the tenure of both the attorney general and controller general and made them simply two more political appointments under his control. For about a decade there was no longer an independent office to investigate the government for any kind of misconduct. A Kenya Anti-Corruption Authority has since been instituted to fight corruption. The secret police were granted broad discretionary powers to quash any opposition.

With the many security arms of his government, Moi governs Kenya effectively as a police state. Political prisoners are no longer a thing of the past. Many people have been detained and about 100 are imprisoned at any given time. There have been numerous reports by detainees of torture and deaths resulting from it. While the government denies these reports, the evidence overwhelmingly supports the allegations. As of 2000, Moi continued to arrest his political opponents and journalists on flimsy charges based on archaic and oppressive sections of the 1963 constitution.

Most analysts agree that Moi's policies and activities stem largely from greed. The way in which he consolidated power actually weakened his position. For close to a year-and-a-half after his 1997 reelection, Moi refused to appoint a vice president as required by the constitution. Finally, he bowed to intense pressure including two legal suites, renaming Professor George Saitoti as Vice President in early April 1999. Moi failed to eradicate the opposition, despite years of trying to do so. Dissent, once the purview of students, intellectuals, and politicians, has now spread to the general public—often leading to violent clashes between the population and the government, particularly during the lead up to the 1997 elections and following on from them. Although Kenya is divided as to who should lead the process, the widespread dissent has been harnessed into an unprecedented unity of purpose aimed at an overhaul of the country's 37-year-old constitution into one commensurate with the current democratic, social, and economic needs of the country.

For a variety of reasons, not least of which has been the economic pressure put on the government by Western donor nations, Moi is poised to leave the presidency in 2003. As of 2000, observers are still hopeful that Moi will end his presidency having been pressured to return the government to the democratic principles and institutions he was instrumental in destroying earlier in his tenure.

## DOMESTIC POLICY
During the late 1990s, Kenya was just beginning to recover from an economic decline of the mid 1970s. Although some of its problems can be attributed to worldwide conditions over which Kenya had no control, many are a direct result of the widespread corruption within the government. Short-sighted and inappropriate economic policies added to the problems until the economy bottomed out in 1993 with inflation at 100%, a record-high budget deficit, and agricultural production contracting at an annual rate of 3.9%.

With the participation of the IMF and World Bank, liberalization policies undertaken since 1993 have begun to take hold. The GDP is growing again; inflation has been reduced; and government-owned industries have been privatized. However, Kenya's refusal to meet IMF guidelines in July 1997 has slowed recovery, leading to the suspension of a significant amount of international aid. In November 1999, Kenya relented and reestablished normal relations with the IMF, whose board voted to resume aid effective 20 January 2000. This creates hope for new aid flows and some level of economic recovery. Although its economy is among the most advanced on the African continent, Kenya is among the poorest of African nations. Years of corruption, mismanagement, and an insupportably high population growth rate have negated any advantage this might have brought.

As of 1999, two years into Moi's fifth term, Kenya was faced with rising inflation, persistently high unemployment, and a decimated infrastructure. Poverty was the norm for the majority of Kenyans, and HIV/AIDS was exacting a heavy toll on the population and threatened to reverse the little economic gain achieved. The potential for economic recovery existed, with Nairobi serving as an East African commercial hub, and the presence of many international companies in the country. In November 1999 Kenya, Tanzania, and Uganda signed a treaty reestablishing an East African Common Market that was expected to boost trade and investment among the three sister countries. Kenya was downsizing its bloated civil service as one measure to reduce public expenditure. As the developed nations of the West take interest in Africa in 2000, careful and pragmatic policy choices by Moi could lead to a sustainable economic recovery. Basic services need to be restored; the budget deficit must be reduced; population growth must be slowed; and corruption must be eliminated from the national government.

## FOREIGN POLICY
Kenya's relations with neighboring countries are generally cordial. Past tensions with Tanzania and Uganda have eased, leading to a revival of the East African Community (EAC), whose attempts at economic cooperation ceased in the 1970s. Kenya generally follows a policy of non-intervention with other African nations, although charges have been made that Kenya hosts rebels from neighboring countries. Although relations with some of these countries have broken off in the past, it is more likely that discrete disputes will be handled within diplomatic bounds. Kenya has at times played a role in conflict resolution in the East African region, and serves as a major host for refugees from the turmoil in Somalia.

Britain maintains close relations with Kenya. It is a major trading partner and source of foreign economic assistance, although it suspended financial aid in 1995 due to Kenya's human rights record. With Kenya's reestablishment of relations with the IMF in January 2000, Britain and other western donors are considering resumption of aid to Kenya, at the same time keeping a keen interest in the constitutional and economic review processes.

US-Kenya relations have been cordial since independence despite US concerns over human rights abuses. More than 6,000 US citizens live in Kenya, and some 35,000 visit each year. The US is a significant source of economic assistance, and its businesses also play a part in the Kenyan economy. In early 1998, President Clinton made Africa a priority of his international agenda. This will likely result in increased business investment in the country. In August 1998, Kenya fell victim to a terrorist attack aimed at the US, widely believed to have been masterminded by Osama bin Laden, a Saudi Arabian terrorist operating from Afghanistan. The American Embassy in Nairobi was bombed, and 257 people were killed, including 12 Americans. This event has not affected US-Kenya relations.

## ADDRESS
Office of the President
P.O. Box 30510
Nairobi, Kenya

## REFERENCES

*Africa Report*, May/June 1995.

*AfricaOnline News Stands Weekly Review*, 9–16 January 1998.

*Boston Globe*, 24 August 1997–1 February 1998.

Central Intelligence Agency. *The World Factbook 1999*. [Online] Available http://www.cia.gov/publications/factbook/ke.html (Accessed April 2000).

*Daily Nation, Nairobi*. BBC Monitoring International Reports, as provided by BBC Worldwide Monitoring, 3 April 1999, 21 February 2000, 16 March 2000.

*The Economist*, 1 March 1997–17 January 1998.

*Kenya Broadcasting Corporation TV, Nairobi*. BBC Monitoring International Reports, as provided by BBC Worldwide Monitoring, 20 December 1999.

*KTN TV, Nairobi*. BBC Monitoring International Reports, as provided by BBC Worldwide Monitoring, 3 October 1998.

*National Interest*, Winter 1995.

*New York Times*, July 1997–January 1998.

*Panafrican News Agency*, 29 December 1997.

**Profile researched and written by Alison Doherty Munro, independent researcher (6/98; updated by Leo Zulu, University of Illinois at Urbana-Champaign 4/2000).**

# KIRIBATI

## Teburoro Tito
## President
*(pronounced "teh-BOO-roar-o TEA-toe")*

*"As people become more politically aware, it will be much more difficult for politicians to stand up and make promises. A better pattern of governing will develop, which will reflect the fundamental values of Kiribati culture."*

The Republic of Kiribati consists of 33 coral atolls of three groups (Gilbert group, Phoenix Islands, and Line Islands), scattered over 7,770,000 sq km (3,000,000 sq mi) of the central Pacific Ocean. Its neighbors are Nauru to the west; Samoa, Tuvalu, and Tokelau Islands to the south. Formerly part of a British Crown Colony known as Gilbert and Ellice Islands, Kiribati's land mass, 717 sq km (277 sq mi), is about the size of New York City; its population has been estimated at 86,000. Except Banaba (Ocean Island), all islands are low-lying atolls composed of coral sand and rock fragments subject to erratic rainfall. Water is as precious as gasoline. Kiribati is the only country that sits on the international date line. Its capital, largest city, and principal port is Bairiki in southern Tarawa, with a population of 25,154.

Kiribati is a nation that was heavily influenced by American and British missionaries. According to estimates, 41% of the people are Protestant (Kiribati Protestant Church); 53% are Catholic; and 6% other. About 96% of the population is I-Kiribati (Gilbertese) Micronesian, speaking English and I-Kiribati. Approximately 70% of the population under age 30.

Phosphate mining was the major economic activity of Kiribati before independence, but most deposits were depleted shortly afterwards. Lacking fertile soil, the economy and government of Kiribati are assisted by large sums of foreign aid ($142 million) to fund development projects according to the 1987–91 National Development Plan. Like many South Pacific nations, Kiribati suffers from a massive trade imbalance with an import-to-export ratio of six to one. Its primary exports are copra (dried coconut meat), fish, seaweed, and postage stamps; primary imports are food and fuel. Recently, expanding commercial fishing in Kiritimati and licensing of foreign fishing vessels also provide some income. About 2,500 I-Kiribati work overseas, primarily on Nauru in phosphate mines, and their remittances are an important source of income. Major trading partners are Fiji, the US, Australia, and Denmark. The monetary unit is the Australian dollar. Kiribati's per capita GDP has been estimated at $800.

## POLITICAL BACKGROUND

Formerly a part of the British Crown Colony of Gilbert and Ellice Islands, Kiribati became internally autonomous in 1977. It became an independent nation within the British Commonwealth in 1979. Kiribati was separated from Ellice Islands (now Tuvalu) in 1975 based on a postal vote in 1974 in which most of the Ellice people sought separation from the Gilbert Islands. The 1979 Treaty of Friendship between the US and Kiribati led to the former's recognition of sovereignty over various disputed islands in the Phoenix and Line groups. In return, the Kiribati government must consult with the US if a third party is allowed access to the islands for military purposes. Furthermore, the US has the right to construct facilities on the islands. Kiribati's independence also provided for the inclusion of Banaba, a former phosphate-mining center, as a part of the new nation despite the contrary wishes of its native residents.

The constitution of Kiribati developed from a convention held at Bairiki on Tarawa in May 1977, involving 200 men and women representing all the islands and various interest groups. A sense of egalitarianism and communitarianism, and a suspicion of central authority have long been part of the Kiribati political culture. The resulting complex political system built in safeguards to curtail the abuse of power. A constitutional review committee was appointed in 1994 to prepare for a constitutional convention in 1996.

Kiribati has a unicameral legislature, the National Assembly, known as the *Maneaba Ni Maungatabu*. In traditional I-Kiribati culture, the *Maneaba*, found at the center of the village, was the cultural and social center of village life. All villages have the *Maneaba* to this day; it is the place where information is passed on, ideas are discussed, and consensus is reached. Therefore, the National Assembly embodies that spirit. It includes 39 members, who are popularly elected to four-year terms by universal suffrage from each island based on population. If no candidate receives a majority of the votes, a runoff election must be held. A district with a population of 300 to 2,000 has one representative; over 2,000 but less than 4,000 has two; over 4,000 residents, three representatives. Additionally, two members, one appointed for the Banaban community in Rabi Island (Fiji) and the attorney general, ex officio, are represented. Each member of the *Maneaba Ni Maungatabu* serves unofficially as a social worker and welfare officer, a messenger and interpreter of the laws of Kiribati and is an ex officio member of the island council of his or her district.

The head of state and government is the president or *beretitenti*. He is elected by universal suffrage from a list of at least three but no more than four members provided by the National Assembly. In the event that there are more than four candidates nominated for the election from the National Assembly, secret balloting based on preferential voting is conducted. Each member of the National Assembly ranks his or her preferences from one to four, with four votes for the most preferred. After the preference ballots are counted, the top four candidates are nominated for the election. There is no runoff presidential election. The president has the power to dissolve the assembly and call for general elections, and to govern with an appointed cabinet. While the constitution stipulates that the president cannot serve more than three-year terms, the rule was set aside for President Tabai, Kiribati's first president. After a presidential no-confidence vote, the president must resign, and the Council of State (composed of the chair of the Public Service Commission, the chief justice, and the speaker of the national assembly) assumes the functions of a transitional executive until the new president is elected. While traditional Kiribati politics are party-free, two major political groups resembling parties have emerged: the Christian Democratic Union Party and the Liberal Party of Independents. Kiribati's defense force was abolished in 1978 by then-president Tabai.

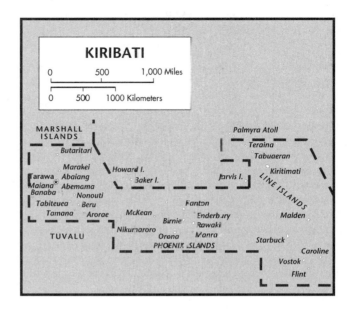

## PERSONAL BACKGROUND

Teburoro Tito was born on 25 August 1953 at Tabiteaua North (a northern island of the Gilbert group). He started his primary education at St. Patrick School in 1959 and left in 1966 to relocate to Tabwiroa, Abaiong (a southern island of the Gilbert group). There he began attending St. Joseph's College and graduated in 1969 with a Colony Junior Certificate. He continued his secondary education at King George V (Government Secondary School). After graduating from secondary school in 1970, Tito received a government scholarship in 1971 to study at the University of the South Pacific (USP) in Suva, Fiji. He graduated in 1977 with a Bachelor of Science degree, majoring in organic chemistry and ecology, and a graduate certificate in education. Tito was an active member of the student body and, in 1976, he became president of the USP Students Association. In 1977, he became student coordinator for the University of the South Pacific Students Association, remaining in Suva until 1980. Since his return to Kiribati, he has resided in South Tarawa. In 1981, he attended the Papua New Guinea Administrative College to study statistics.

Tito is an avid sportsman, particularly when it comes to soccer. He served as the chairman of the Kiribati Football Association from 1980 to 1994. He is married to Nei Keina Tito and has one child.

## RISE TO POWER

Teburoro Tito joined the Kiribati civil service upon his return. He became the scholarship officer with the Ministry of Education (1980–82) and senior education officer responsible for secondary and tertiary schools in January 1983 During that time, Tito represented the Kiribati government at educational meetings and conferences abroad.

Tito's national political career began in 1987 when he was elected to the National Assembly representing the South Tarawa district. He quickly established himself as a leader of the opposition. Also in 1987, he was nominated for the presidential election by the National Assembly and came in second in a three-way race with 42.7% of the vote. In 1989, he became the opposition leader upon Harry Tong's decision to step down. As the opposition leader, he was an outspoken

critic of the Tabai government's inefficiency and mismanagement. He charged that the qualitative decline of democracy and the government's lack of efficiency were the major reasons for the government's inability to live up to people's expectations. During his first term as a member of the National Assembly, Tito became a member of the Public Accounts Committee and the Commonwealth Parliamentary Association for the Pacific region. In 1991, Tito was reelected to the National Assembly.

On 24 May 1994, President Teannaki (who succeeded Tabai in 1991) was forced to resign after the opposition passed a no-confidence vote. The Teannaki government was accused of financial misuse of travel funds. Executive power was transferred to the Council of State until elections were conducted on 30 September 1994. Tito was elected the third president with 10,834 votes; his three other competitors had less than 4,000 votes each. In November 1998, Tito was reelected, winning 52% of the vote. The next election was scheduled for November 2002.

## LEADERSHIP

Tito has held government positions since the early 1980s, including seven years as a member of the National Assembly. The foundation of his leadership is his Christian Democratic Unity Party (CDUP), which has 13 of the 39 total seats. Seven belong to the opposition Gilbertese National Progressive Party, and 19 are independents.

Tito is widely respected for his articulate speaking style and his forthright style of questioning. In the past, Tito has criticized Kiribati politics as one dominated by elites. He has often spoken about the need to have a long-term vision of democracy for his country. While his direct manner has made him popular among many I-Kiribati, some more traditional politicians dislike his modern style. They have complained that the spirit of Kiribati politics is not one of confrontation but one of consensus decision making. While in the past Tito has criticized civil servants for their inefficiency, he needs their cooperation if he wants to develop the social and economic potential of his country. He has often said that it is important for politicians to be committed to the long-term future of the country rather than to seek re-election. His vision for the country is self-sufficiency and a stronger democracy with more active participation on the part of the I-Kiribati.

## DOMESTIC POLICY

Since Kiribati is a young nation-state, Tito believes in the importance of nation-building. The development of Kiribati's economy is the most important domestic policy issue. National integration is also an important aspect of Tito's nation-building. In the past, Kiribati's economy and government suffers from a lack of self-sufficiency because of its limited size and resources. In 1999, Tito made a plea to the international community for aid in coping with a serious drought. Foreign aid has always been a major component of the government's budget. Furthermore, Kiribati has a long history of protracted trade deficits, which must be covered by foreign aid. Tito's long-term strategy is to develop the economy by focusing on tourism and fishing.

Tourism is one area that Tito believes could provide foreign earnings to improve the living standards of the I-Kiribati. In 1999, Kiribati spent heavily to promote its islands as millennium tourist destinations, renaming one Caroline Island Millennium Island, and claiming that it would be the first place on earth to see the 21st century. Besides tourism, Tito seeks to attract foreign investment into commercial fishing. Tito has proposed the construction of more international airports to improve on the accessibility of the many islands. The upgrading of ports and shipyards so that exports and imports can be managed more efficiently is also on his policy agenda.

Tarawa, where the capital is located, is suffering from an expanding population and urbanization. To alleviate this problem, he has suggested the construction of additional roads. Kiribati is increasingly threatened by water shortages and waste pollution as the population grows. In particular, by 1999 a potable water shortage had reached crisis levels as animal and human effluents contaminate limited water supplies. In addition, the country claims to have lost two islands due to rising sea levels and reports that whole villages must be moved inland from coastal regions. Tito must balance the need for economic development and concern for the fragile ecosystem of the region. A month after taking office, Tito established two new ministries to manage these problems: the Ministry of Environment and Social Devel-opment and the Ministry of Communications, Industry, and Tourism.

## FOREIGN POLICY

Kiribati is concerned about a variety of issues that affect Pacific island-states. In particular Kiribati has expressed concern regarding French nuclear testing in the area, the prospects of long-term increase in the elevation of the sea level, global warming due to greenhouse gases, and the economic viability of micro-states. Tito's government seeks foreign investment, especially in the commercial fishing area and tourism.

Other issues that the Tito government is pursuing include a call for international action to reduce greenhouse gas emissions and compensation for I-Kiribati families who suffered personal and property losses caused by Japanese soldiers on Banaba during World War II. Tito claims to possess a copy of the British-commissioned survey of damage and lives lost during World War II that will be used as the starting point for negotiations. As of 2000, Kiribati did not maintain an embassy in the US. In 1999, along with Tonga and Nauru, the country entered into membership in the United Nations (UN).

## ADDRESS

Office of President
P.O. Box 68
Bairiki, Tarawa
Republic of Kiribati

## REFERENCES

Banks, Arthur. *Political Handbook of the World, 1995–96.*
*Bio-Data of H.E. the Honorable Teburoro Tito: Beretitenti of the Republic of Kiribati.* National Archives and Library of Kiribati, 1994.
"New Meaning to the Term Down Under. (The Tiny Islands of Kiribati, Tuvalu And Nauru Are Pressuring Australia to Reduce Greenhouse Gas Emissions.)" *The Economist (US),* 27 September 1999, p. 41.
*Pacific Report,* 3 October 1994, 15 November 1994.
"UN Admits Three New Members, General Assembly Opens." Associated Press, 15 September 1999.
Van Trease, Howard, ed. *Atoll Politics: The Republic of Kiribati.* 1993.

Profile researched and written by Robert W. Compton, Jr., Binghamton University (SUNY) and State University College at Oneonta (2/96; updated 3/2000).

# KOREA
## DEMOCRATIC PEOPLE'S REPUBLIC OF

### Kim Jong Il
### National Defense Commission Chairman
*(pronounced "kim jung ILL")*

*"Ideology, technology, and culture—all according to the demands of juche [self-reliance]."*

The Democratic People's Republic of Korea is located on the northern half of the Korean peninsula. It is bordered by the People's Republic of China to the northwest, Russia to the northeast, and South Korea to the southeast. The 38th Parallel has divided North and South Korea since the end of the Korean War (1953).

The total area is 120,538 sq km (46,540 sq mi), and the population has been estimated at 21.4 million. The population is ethnically homogeneous, and the official language is Korean. The state is officially atheist. The capital and largest city is Pyongyang (two million), with Chongjin and Kaesong being the other major cities.

The Soviet style command economy is at least 90% state controlled, with agriculture totally collectivized. The GDP per capita has been estimated at US$1,000. The currency unit is the *won*. The currency is not convertible and most trade is conducted by barter. Minerals, coal, rice, marine products, silk, and cement are North Korea's major exports.

## POLITICAL BACKGROUND

After the end of World War II, Korea was liberated from Japanese colonialism with the US controlling the southern zone and the Soviet Union the north. The People's Democratic Republic was organized on 9 September 1948, under the leadership of Kim Il Sung, known as the Great Leader in response to the establishment of South Korea. The two Koreas have maintained a hostile relationship from the beginning, with the North assisted by communist states and the South protected by US troops stationed there. Even though both sides wanted unification, suspicion and hostilities grew. In 1950, North Korea invaded South Korea, only to be opposed by a UN force led primarily by the US. An armistice was signed and borders were re-established at Panmunjom, the 38th Parallel. The heavily fortified borders still stand to this day, with troops from both sides on intense guard for the resumption of hostilities.

The communist state of North Korea is one of the few remaining authoritarian regimes in the post-Cold War world. Political authority is in the hands of the party, the military, and the bureaucracy with membership frequently overlapping. North Korea, a one party state, is dominated by the Korean Workers' Party (KWP). Under changes made in 1998 to the reformed 1972 constitution, the post of president, formerly held by Kim Il-sung, was abolished, and executive authority was vested in the nation's current leader, Kim Jong-il, who is chairman of the National Defense Commission.

North Korea has a unicameral legislature, the Supreme People's Assembly, that meets for a few days annually. It has 687 members elected from party-approved nominees for five-year terms. Although it is nominally the highest organ of state power, policy rarely emanates from this body. Rather, assembly business is handled by a Presidium created in 1998. In addition, a small cabinet, replacing the former Administration Council, functions as an administrative and executive arm of the SPA.

The KWP actually controls power in North Korea through a system of overlapping membership in the party, executive, and legislative posts. The Party Congress meets infrequently. It elects the Party Central Committee, which in turn selects the Politburo. A Presidium presides over the Politburo. Together, the two control the party bureaucracy and the various party organs. The general secretary, chosen by the Party Central Committee, heads the party.

## PERSONAL BACKGROUND

Little is known with certainty about Kim Jong Il. Western, South Korean, and North Korean accounts vary widely. North Korean and South Korean propaganda have deliberately reconstructed the personal background of Kim Jong Il to serve their own political interests. At home he is a demigod, abroad a playboy terrorist with a passion for films.

His father, Kim Il Sung, was an anti-Japanese guerilla fighter during World War II who fled to the Soviet Union when the Japanese crushed the Korean resistance force. During exile, Kim Jong Il was born in February 1942 in a Soviet camp near Khaborovsk, Siberia. According to Western sources, the early childhood of Kim Jong Il was filled with difficult circumstances. During the first years of his life, he was cared for by a Russian kitchen maid and was often away from his parents who were involved with resisting the Japanese occupation of Korea. His mother died in 1949.

Kim Jong Il attended kindergarten at Namsan Elementary School in Pyongyang. During the Korean War (1950-53), he spent his life in Manchuria. As a fourth grader, he attended the elite Mangyongdae School for Children of Revolutionaries. In 1953, he studied at No. 4 Pyongyang Primary School. It appears that he spent some period of his latter high school years studying in Romania and East Germany.

His father wanted him to obtain a university education in Eastern Europe, but Kim Jong Il decided to attend Kim Il

Sung University in Pyongyang. He graduated on 18 May 1964 with a degree in political economy. His thesis was an analysis of his father's ideas on the socialist rural question. He later attended aviation school in East Germany. After graduation, Kim Jong Il started to work for the Korean People's Party. He built up a strong base of friendship during his university career and early years working with the party.

Kim Jong Il has led a reclusive lifestyle, rarely speaking in public. The public had not heard his voice until 1992, and the domestic press rarely mentioned his name. Some consider him to be shy but ostentatious in lifestyle. His hobbies include videos, computers, and theater. He is thought to be married with two children. His brother died in a 1947 drowning accident, and the whereabouts of his sister, Kim Kyong Hui, is unknown.

## RISE TO POWER

Kim Jong Il's rise to power is attributed to his lifetime association with his father. He has been carefully groomed for power over the past two decades. His rise to power was carefully orchestrated as he took on more responsibility. His father, Kim Il Sung, orchestrated a plan for the first dynastic succession in Communist history.

After graduating from Kim Il Sung University, Kim Jong Il found employment with the Department of Organization and Guidance of the Central Committee of the Korean Worker's Party as the section chief to the deputy director. He worked closely with the artistic and performing community and is credited with the production of films and stage plays. In 1970, he was promoted to the director of Culture and Arts and deputy director of the Department of Propaganda and

Agitation. At the seventh plenum of the Fifth Central Committee in 1973, he was appointed secretary in charge of organization, propaganda, and agitation. At the conclusion of the Sixth Party Congress in October 1980, he held the following positions: member of the Presidium of the Political Bureau of the Central Committee, secretary of the Central Committee, and member of the Military Committee. It was at this Congress that he was designated heir.

Throughout the 1970s to the mid-1980s, Kim Jong Il increased his activities at home and abroad. In 1973, he initiated a Chinese-style Cultural Revolution. The Three Revolution Brigade, under his direction, led the purge of veteran party leaders and shake-up of the bureaucracy. He extolled his father's ideology of *juche*—persistent self-reliance. By being loyal to his father, he built up his own cult of personality. His pictures were hung in schools and sold in department stores and his birthday came to be celebrated. From the fall of 1975, Kim Jong Il's role as the leader of the party was embodied in a mysterious term, party center. This term came to be used in conjunction with various pronouncements in the North Korean media to support his absolute authority and to obey unconditionally the directives of the great leader's successor.

Western sources have attributed the 1973 kidnapping of a South Korean movie director and his wife, the 1976 axe murder of two American soldiers at Panmunjom, the 1983 bombing attack on South Korean officials in Rangoon, and the 1987 downing of the Korean Airlines flight to Kim Jong-il. The North Korean media, on the contrary, state that he is a great thinker and theoretician, skillful politician, boundlessly benevolent teacher, and great leader of the century. As the senior Kim went into semi-retirement, Kim Jong Il made frequent tours of the country, encouraging citizens while he promoted his own cult of the personality. While North Korean accounts of Kim Jong Il's rise to power are unlikely to be accurate, Western accounts of a master terrorist may not be totally accurate either.

## LEADERSHIP

Kim Jong Il became the de facto leader of North Korea upon the death of his father, Kim Il Sung, on 8 July 1994. The world watched as the succession mechanism put in place over the last 20 years operated with relative smoothness, making him the first leader to become the head of a Communist country through dynastic succession. Over the next four years, he slowly consolidated his power, replacing many of his father's appointees with younger officials. While the "Dear Leader," as he is called, did not have the charisma or energy of his father, he appeared to have the support of North Korean citizens. This support had been built up through many years of orchestrated propaganda and loyalty to his father.

After a three-year trial period, North Korea's ruling party cleared the way for Kim Jong Il to assume the post of general secretary of the ruling Korean Workers' Party on 8 October 1997. Analysts observed a notable increase in the praises heaped on Kim once the mourning period for his father ended in July 1997. On 5 September 1998, Kim's position as leader of his country was made official by the Supreme People's Assembly; however, instead altogether in tribute to Kim Il-sung, leaving Kim Jong-il with the title of chairman of the

National Defense Commission, a position that by default became the highest in the land. The move to elevate him came as an acute food crisis engulfed the country after three years of alternating floods and drought, making it certain that his leadership abilities would be put to the test over the coming months and years.

## DOMESTIC POLICY

North Korea continues to be organized as a Stalinist state with high levels of repression and centralized economic control. The collapse of the Soviet bloc, Western pressure, and the monumental economic success of South Korea have left North Korea isolated. Piecemeal domestic changes have occurred in recent years. It is said that a younger generation of Chinese-trained officers seek a military backed industrialization program, and a new generation of party officials would like to stimulate the economy by introducing reforms that would deviate from *juche*. However, in spite of a dire need for foreign investment and technology, the government of Kim Jong-il fears that greater openness could lead to its downfall, as occurred in the Soviet Union. North Korean officials want to improve the economy without losing their monopoly on power. Therefore, reform is likely to be carefully orchestrated, with tight party control. Future economic reform will likely be based on the Chinese model.

The economy of North Korea continues to reel from the collapse of trade with the former eastern bloc. The nation's economy is estimated to have shrunk by one-third in the 1990s. Extensive flood damage has forced this fiercely xenophobic nation to request international aid. Humanitarian agencies estimate that food shortages have killed hundreds of thousands and left many more, including large numbers of children, malnourished and in danger of dying. Many governments are reluctant to send aid unless they can be sure that it reaches the starving people and is not diverted to military storehouses. But the North Korean government is distrustful of foreigners and limits the amount of monitoring that is allowed.

## FOREIGN POLICY

Kim Il Sung's *juche* policy and the purported terrorist activities of the regime consolidated North Korea's image as a pariah state. In the past, North Korea was able to rely on the People's Republic of China and the Soviet Union for economic and political support. Those days are long gone. China's support for North Korea has weakened considerably, and Russia has dramatically cut back aid as it deals with its own economic morass. After consolidating his power for several years, Kim, who has never traveled outside the Communist world, now appears to have greater authority to oversee a gradual opening-up of his country and develop ties with the US. In a major essay published in August 1997, he gave the clearest indication that more flexible policies may be possible. Kim indicated that improving relations with South Korea was a major foreign policy objective. He hopes to put into effect some long-frozen accords between the two Koreas

and expressed a willingness to negotiate with the South. Kim also wants to improve relations with Japan and the US. "We have no intention to regard the United States as our eternal sworn enemy," he wrote. An active program of diplomatic rapprochement initiated by Kim in 1999 has begun to show tangible results. By the spring of 2000 normalization talks with Japan were under way, and a summit meeting with South Korea was scheduled for mid-June.

A major foreign policy issue faced by North Korea is the future of its nuclear weapons program. North Korea has been developing these weapons in secret for some time, and Western intelligence suspects that it may have up to five bombs. In 1994 the US proposed that North Korea's existing atomic power reactors be replaced by two light-water reactors, believed to be less easily adapted to the production of nuclear weaponry. The US agreed to establish a consortium to finance and supply these reactors and donate 500,000 metric tons of heavy fuel oil until they are built. After several years of negotiations, final protocols to this agreement were signed in January 1997, with construction scheduled to begin at the end of the year. In order to monitor compliance, North Korea agreed to allow inspection of its nuclear facilities by the International International Atomic Energy Agency. However, as of 1999, IAEA monitors were still denied access to certain laboratory sites. North Korea had also elicited international protest in August 1998, when it was suspected of having launched a ballistic missile over Japan and into the Pacific, a charge it denied, claiming that what had been fired was actually a satellite launcher.

## ADDRESS
Office of the General Secretary
Pyongyang
Democratic People's Republic of Korea

## REFERENCES
"The Accession: North Korea." *The Economist*, 12 September 1998, p. 43.

An. Tai Sung. *North Korea in Transition*. 1993.

*Asian Survey*, 1994.

*The Economist*, 4 October 1997.

*Europa World Yearbook 1997*. London: Europa Publications Ltd., 1997.

*Far Eastern Economic Review*, 21 July 1994.

*Financial Times*, 11 July 1994.

*New York Times*, 23 September–9 October 1997.

*Nikkei Weekly*, 11 July 1994.

"North Korea: Why It's Suddenly Ready to Come in from the Cold." *Business Week*, 24 April 2000.

*Political Handbook of the World*. NY: CSA Publications, 1999.

"Stubbornly Starving." *Scholastic Update*, 21 September 1998, p. 7.

Suh, Dae-Sook. *Kim Il Sung: The North Korean Leader*. 1988.

**Profile researched and written by Robert W. Compton, Jr., Binghamton University (SUNY) (8/94; updated 10/97 and 5/2000).**

# KOREA
## REPUBLIC OF

### Kim Dae Jung
### President
*(pronounced "kim die zhung")*

*"I will open a new age of democratic order that respects market mechanisms and competition."*

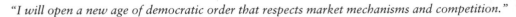

The East Asian nation of South Korea shares the Korean Peninsula with North Korea. Its topography consists of mountainous terrain to the north and east and plains to the south and east. The western and southern coasts are deeply indented with many harbors and islands. The total area is 99,147 sq km (38,375 sq mi).

South Korea's population is estimated at 46.8 million. Its people are ethnically homogeneous, with the exception of some Chinese. Most Koreans live in the south and around Seoul, the capital and largest city of 10.7 million inhabitants. Other major cities are Pusan (3.8 million) and Taegu (2.2 million). South Korea possesses a literacy rate exceeding 98%. The official language is Korean. The primary religions are Christianity (49%) and Buddhism (18%).

The recent entry of South Korea into the prestigious OECD (Organization for Economic Cooperation and Development) demonstrates the highly modernized condition of its economy. Its meteoric rise over the past 30 years has made South Korea the world's eleventh largest economy, with a per capita GDP of US$13,000. Primary exports are consumer electronics, automobiles, chemicals, ships, and textiles. South Korea's primary trading partners are Japan and the US. The national currency is the *won*.

## POLITICAL BACKGROUND

Korea possesses a unique and ancient cultural history. It was a Chinese vassal state for many centuries. In 1910, Japan annexed Korea and, until 1945, ruthlessly ran the country as a colony. The northern area became an industrial center economically integrated into Manchuria while the south remained largely agricultural. After Japan's defeat in World War II, the northern part of the peninsula was occupied by the Soviets with the Americans occupying the south. In 1948, the Soviets assisted in establishing the Democratic People's Republic of Korea (DPRK). The Americans, under the auspices of the UN, organized elections for South Korea. Both Soviet and American troops left the Korean peninsula by 1949. DPRK forces attacked the south and sought to unify the nation in 1950. Relative peace was not established until North Korean forces, backed by their Communist allies, were driven north of the 38th parallel by UN forces. The armistice on 21 June 1953 established a military demarcation line and demilitarized zone around the 38th parallel, which remains the border between North and South Korea today.

Military regimes controlled Korean politics from 1948 through the 1980s. Syngman Rhee ruled the nation with an iron fist from 1948 to 1960 and established the precedent for successive military rule. After a short democratic interlude, Park Chung Hee and four other military officers seized power in 1961. After Park's assassination in 1979, Chun Doo Hwan (1980–87) and Roh Tae Woo (1987–92) continued the military line of succession. Roh Tae Woo, however, began to move the nation toward democracy. By institutionalizing his political party, the Democratic Liberal Party (DLP), he began moving away from centralized presidential leadership. In the December 1992 elections, Kim Young Sam became the first non-military candidate to become president.

The 1988 Korean constitution provides for a strong popularly elected president and a unicameral legislature, the 299-member National Assembly. The president is elected for a five-year term, and legislators serve for four years. Upon election, the president is responsible for appointing the prime minister, who serves upon legislative confirmation. While the president lacks the power to dissolve the legislature, he selects his cabinet members from the members of a State Council consisting of elected legislators. He also serves as the head of his party. Based on 1996 legislative elections, the Grand National Party (then called the New Korea Party) had 139 seats and Kim Dae Jung's National Congress for New Politics (NCNP) held 79 seats. Kim's strategic alliance with Kim Jong Pil's conservative United Liberal Democrats (with 50 seats) made his 1997 presidential victory possible. Kim's party changed its name to the New Millennium Party in preparation for the 2000 general election.

## PERSONAL BACKGROUND

Kim Dae Jung was born in South Cholla Province around December 1925. Born to a farmer in the country's most backward province, his family delayed registering his birth, prompting present debate about his precise age. He graduated from Mokpo Commercial High School in 1943. During the 1950s, he became president of the Mokpo Daily News and also operated a shipping business. He attended Konguk University, as well as Korea and Kyunghee Universities in the 1960s. In 1970, he completed his studies, earning a master's degree in economics from Kyunghee University. During the 1950s and 1960s, he polished his oratory skills and became an outspoken critic of Korea's authoritarian political and economic system.

An avid student of Western history and literature, many organizations and universities throughout the world have awarded Kim numerous honorary doctorates. He was nominated for the Nobel Peace Prize 11 times. Kim has published many books and monographs, some of which were translated into English. A devout Roman Catholic, he also enjoys calligraphy during his leisure time. Kim is married to Lee Hee Ho, his second wife. He has three children, two by his first wife.

## RISE TO POWER

First elected to the National Assembly in 1960, he briefly served as a spokesman for the democratic prime minister, Chang Myon. Kim became a spokesman for the Democratic Party in 1963 and served as a member of its finance committee. Reelected in 1965, he became a spokesman for the new Masses Party and then for the New Democratic Party in 1967. As President Park's authoritarianism increased, Kim's popularity in Cholla increased. Over the next three decades, Kim became the major Korean dissident who continually challenged the ruling conservatives in public and at the polls.

The 1971 presidential elections pitted Kim against Park. Kim accused the ruling elite of crushing democratic institutions to prolong authoritarian rule and called for greater political and economic liberalization. He won the sympathy of students and the working class, particularly from Cholla, but gained the disdain of military leaders and big business interests. Kim lost the election but was able to obtain 46% of the popular vote. Pro-democracy observers declared the election to be highly irregular. However, it established Kim as a national and international figure who risked his life to combat authoritarianism.

Throughout his political career Kim has faced numerous challenges including assassination attempts, kidnaping, torture, imprisonment, house arrest, and other forms of harassment. These experiences strengthened his will, allowing Kim to develop his political philosophy and understanding of human nature and Korean society. In 1976, a group of religious leaders, professors, and students signed a statement urging Park to step down. Riots followed in protest against the arrest of dissident leaders, including Kim. He was later sentenced to an eight-year prison term for advocating the overthrow of the government. Kim was ultimately released, but re-arrested in 1980 and sentenced to death by hanging. This brought an immediate outcry from the international community, which led to his release in 1982. Kim arrived in the US for medical treatment and became a research fellow at Harvard University in 1983.

Several factors facilitated Kim's rise to power. The political climate within Korea was undergoing a gradual liberalization. This process had begun after the 1979 assassination of Park Chung Hee. Furthermore, faced with corruption charges and human rights abuses, both former presidents Roh Tae Woo and Chun Doo Hwan were arrested, charged, and sentenced. This negative image of the ruling party became stronger as additional scandals came to light, and citizens began to challenge the authority of the ruling elites. In many ways, Kim no longer appeared to be a radical. Instead he was viewed by many as an astute observer of contemporary Korean politics.

The economic crisis that swept through Asia, beginning in the summer of 1997, severely infected the South Korean economy. By December, the economy teetered on the verge of

bankruptcy as the stock market crashed. The currency was devalued, and corporations were unable to pay their debts. Talks of an IMF bailout made people realize that the Korean political and economic elites abused their positions of power and should be held accountable for the economy's desperate condition. The US$60 billion in anticipated IMF loans would require massive economic reorganization and hardship for average Koreans. Kim benefitted from the people's anger, capturing 40.3% of the vote on 18 December 1997. His main opponent, Lee Hoi Chang, a former judge, obtained 38.7%; a third party candidate obtained 19.2%. The fact that Kim did not need a majority of votes to win and was able to gain the support of opposition leader, Kim Jong Pil, contributed to his narrow victory.

## LEADERSHIP

Having endured political persecution and then being democratically elected, Kim has earned the moral authority to govern, something many of his predecessors lacked. He is considered incorrigible, charismatic, politically astute, and courageous. His speeches are known for their dynamic quality and passion. Clearly, he has the courage and ability to mobilize public opinion in this crucial stage in Korean history. Untainted by the previous regime's corruption, Kim can legitimately undertake campaign finance reform and much needed economic reform. His recent pardons of Chun and Roh brought criticism from some supporters but represent the first attempt at healing national political divisions.

Kim's political base consists of students, small shopkeepers, intellectuals, unions, and residents of his native

Cholla province. Yet, his strategic alliance with Kim Jong Pil may handcuff his attempts at further political and economic liberalization. In addition, many groups distrust his leftist orientation—particularly the bureaucracy, large corporations (known as chaebols), and the military. His critics contend that he will be unable to manage the economy during these tumultuous times. Kim's powerful economic ally, Park Tae Joon of POSCO Steel, allays fears that the new president might promote socialism. Other critics claim that Kim has the same authoritarian instincts as his predecessors and will resort to punishing enemies and rewarding friends. In this context, his pardoning of the former presidents can be viewed as an effort to achieve national reconciliation. In the April 2000 general election, Kim's party, the New Millenium Party, also known as the Democratic Party, failed to secure a majority of the seats by capturing only 115 seats. The GNP and the United Liberal Democrats (ULD), captured 133 and 17 seats, respectively. Therfore, Kim's party does not possess the ability to govern on its own.

## DOMESTIC POLICY

A major domestic issue that Kim must address is how to redefine the relations between government and business. In the past, close ties between the public and private sectors assisted chaebols in evading economic accountability. The government protected their inefficient ways and encouraged loans without regard to profitability. The chaebols, in return, supported military involvement in politics and, more recently, funneled large sums of cash into political campaigns. Such a system undermined Korea's young democracy and stifled new and smaller corporations from emerging. Many economic and political analysts point to these factors as the root cause of the recent economic turmoil. Kim must change the conditions that gave rise to the current crisis by restraining the economic and political influence of the chaebols and by rewriting the existing laws on campaign finance. At the same time he needs to relieve the concerns of the chaebols about his ability to manage a complex economy while maintaining cordial relations with labor unions. Without the cooperation of the chaebols, economic revitalization would prove next to impossible. Since taking office, Kim's reform efforts have merited a moderate level of international praise. However, much more needs to be done to fully implement the economic reforms necessary to continue the growth over the past two years.

A second issue facing Kim is how to achieve national political reconciliation. Some supporters in Cholla want him to deal harshly with those who repressed their political and economic rights. If Kim fails to address their concerns, he may jeopardize his base constituency. Additionally, a large number of political dissidents are still held as political prisoners. It remains to be seen if he will release them and how the conservatives will react.

## FOREIGN POLICY

Kim's major foreign policy issue is how to restore international faith in the Korean economy. He needs to convince foreign governments and corporations that he is willing to undertake the IMF-imposed sanctions. At the same time, he needs to maintain domestic tranquility so that foreign investment will increase. The currency devaluation will likely increase exports but raise the costs of imports into his country. South Korea in 1999 and 2000 successfully increased its exports, but many Korean firms still face the daunting task of repaying years of accumulated debt. While Kim successfully negotiated with the IMF and international lenders for flexibility in interest payments and the country was able to repay most of the loans, further reforms will be necessary to make the country even more productive.

Another foreign policy issue that has brought much criticism is Kim's attempt at reconciliation with North Korea. In the past, the two countries severed ties completely during the Korean War and have not allowed family members to contact one another or even exchange mail. Kim has pressed for reunions with separated family members and plans to open the airways, allowing citizens access to North Korean radio. He will even permit private companies to invest in the North. In June 2000, Kim Dae Jung held a much publicized summit with his counterpart, Kim Jong Il. Many believe that the meeting reduced mutual suspicions and established the groundwork for an era of cooperation on humanitarian and economic issues.

## ADDRESS

Office of the President
Chong Wa Dae (The Blue House)
1 Sejong-no
Chongnu-ku
Seoul, Republic of Korea

## REFERENCES

*Current Biography Yearbook, 1985.* New York: H.W. Wilson, 1986.
*The Economist,* 13 December 1997–3 January 1998.
*Far Eastern Economic Review,* 11 December 1997; 8 January 1998; 22 June 2000.
*Financial Times,* 19–31 December 1997.
*International Who's Who, 1997–98.* London: Europa Publications Ltd., 1997.
*The Korea Herald.* [Online] Available http://www.korea-herald.co.kr (Accessed October 1999).
*Korea Times.* [Online] Available http://www.koreatimes.co.kr (Accessed October 1999).
Nahm, Andrew. *Historical Dictionary of the Republic of Korea.* Metuchen, NJ: Scarecrow Press, 1993.
*New York Times,* 19 December 1997; 12 October 1999.
*Political Handbook of the World.* Binghamton, NY: C.S.A. Publications, 1997.
*Washington Post,* 19–28 December 1997.

**Profile researched and written by Robert W. Compton, Jr., Western Kentucky University (SUNY) (6/98; updated 6/2000).**

# KUWAIT

## Jabir III
### Emir
*(pronounced "JAH-beer")*

*"We, in Kuwait, are in the forefront of the community of nations to condemn terrorism."*

The State of Kuwait is located at the head of the Persian Arabian Gulf, surrounded on the north and west by Iraq, and on the south by Saudi Arabia. Its area is 17,818 sq km (6,880 sq mi), including its share of the neutral zone jointly controlled with Saudi Arabia. Its territory is mainly flat desert with a few oases.

Kuwait's population has been estimated at about 1,991,000, of which 41% are native Kuwaitis, and the rest are expatriate workers. Expatriates (including Palestinians, Indians, and Iranians) meet about 81% of the country's manpower needs. The majority of native Kuwaitis are Sunni Arab Muslim. However, 30% of the total population is believed to be Shia.

The *dinar* is Kuwait's official currency. Kuwait's economy, which was traditionally based on pearling and trading, is now mainly dependent on oil, which in 1995 accounted for 94% of the government revenues. It has the third-largest oil reserves in the world, estimated in 1996 at about 94,000m barrels. Largely owing to its oil reserves, Kuwait has one of the highest per capita incomes in the world, which has been estimated to be $22,700. Its major trading partners are Japan, the US, Germany, the UK, France, Italy, and Saudi Arabia.

## POLITICAL BACKGROUND
Kuwait emerged as a semi-autonomous political entity in the late 18th century when the leading families of the Bani Utab section of the Anazah tribe led by the Sabah family settled there. Its independence was secured from the Ottoman Empire when Sheikh Mubarak negotiated a treaty with the British in 1899, giving the British control over Kuwait's foreign policy. Complete independence from the British was secured in 1961.

Kuwait became a semi-constitutional monarchy ruled by the emir from the Sabah family. Its constitution, promulgated on 11 November 1962, declared Kuwait to be an Arab state, with Islam as the state religion and *shariah* (Islamic jurisprudence or system of law), the source of legislation. The constitution defines the political system as "democratic, under which sovereignty resides in the people, the source of all powers." The constitution lays the basis of the extensive welfare system by obliging the state to care for the young, sick, old, and handicapped and to promote education and provide for public health. Executive power resides in the emir who exercises it through a Council of Ministers. The emir is always selected from the Mubarak line of the ruling Sabah family. The emir appoints the prime minister after traditional consultations and appoints and dismisses ministers on the recommendation of the prime minister.

The emir shares legislative powers with the *Majlis al-Umma* (National Assembly), a 50-member body serving four-year terms. Until 1996, suffrage was limited to males over 21 who were born in Kuwait, or who had lived in Kuwait since 1920, and their male descendants at age 21. Legislation enacted in 1994 provided voting rights for Kuwaiti-born literate males over the age of 21 who have been naturalized for more than 30 years; those who qualified voted for the first time in 1996. Expatriates, servicemen, police, and women are not permitted to vote. In the 1996 elections, only about 10% of all citizens were eligible to vote. Political parties are not permitted. However, there are loose political groupings based on political orientation, such as Arab nationalists, pro-Islamic activists (Islamic Social Reform Society), and Shias. While Kuwait is the only Arab Gulf petromonarchy to have a elected legislature, the democratic experience has not been smooth. The first National Assembly was elected in 1963. Since then the emir dissolved the Assembly three times: in 1976, in 1986 (after which it remained suspended until the elections of 1992), and in 1999. In elections that followed the 1999 suspension, pro-government politicians dropped from 30 seats to 14 while liberal candidates won 16 seats, and Islamists won 20. Turnout was high, with an estimated 80% of those eligible casting ballots.

## PERSONAL BACKGROUND
Jabir al-Ahmad al-Sabah (Jabir III) was born on 29 June 1926 in Kuwait City. He is the third son of Sheikh Ahmad al-Jabir, who ruled Kuwait from 1921 to 1950. While his father is from the al-Jabir line, his mother is from the al-Salim line of the al-Sabah family. He received his education at Mubarakiya School and later was tutored privately in English, Arabic literature, religion, and basic sciences.

## RISE TO POWER
Jabir began his career as the head of public security at Ahmadi (the oil-producing region of Kuwait) from 1949 to 1959. He also represented the ruler in dealings with the oil companies. In 1959 he was appointed to head the finance department. Under his direction, budgetary controls were extended to all government departments, and the Kuwait Fund for Arab Economic Development was established. Jabir was also involved in negotiations which led to the establishment of the Organization of Petroleum Exporting

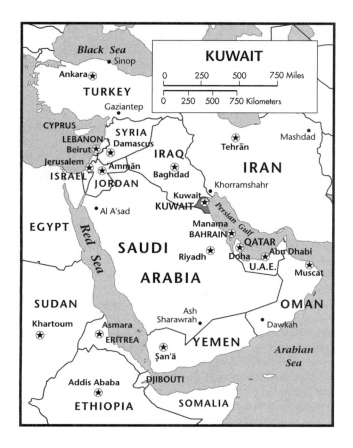

Countries (OPEC) in 1960. Even though he was not the foreign minister, he led the Kuwaiti delegation to the Arab League Council meeting in Cairo in 1961 and traveled to other Arab capitals to secure Arab support for Kuwaiti independence (declared in June 1961 and promulgated in November 1962) and assistance against Iraqi threats. In 1962, he became the minister for finance and economy when the finance department was upgraded to a ministry after independence. Jabir marked himself as a competent leader and administrator while he served as finance minister and was in charge of oil negotiations. He implemented the policies of Emir Abdullah to redistribute the oil income through a land compensation plan.

He was appointed deputy prime minister in January 1963 and prime minister in November 1965, on the accession of Sabah III as emir. When Emir Sabah al-Salim became stricken with ill health, Jabir exercised his powers as prime minister in running day-to-day government operations. On the death of Emir Sabah in 1977, Jabir became the new emir. The fact that Jabir is closely related to his mother's Salim side of the Sabah family and his father's Jabir side made him acceptable to both branches of the family.

## LEADERSHIP

The Sabah leadership has been an integral part of the Kuwaiti state since its inception. The family regulates and controls the government and receives a salary from the state. The Sabah family has been compared to a corporation: an organization with policies, plans, and a hierarchy of its own. While the emir is the head of state within what can be called the corporate structure of the Sabah family, he does not neces-

sarily have a monopoly on power. Rather, decisions are often made by a family council, which meets regularly to discuss important issues.

Kuwait's Sabah family has been more successful than neighboring Gulf petromonarchies in settling intra-family disputes in a peaceful manner. Since the discovery of oil, Sabah influence has increased as tribes and merchants have come to rely on the state. The military is firmly controlled by the Sabah family, whose members are dominant in the higher echelons of the armed forces. In the 1980s the Shias emerged as a threat to the regime as a result of the Iranian revolution and the Kuwaiti support of Iraq in its war with Iran. Kuwait was a frequent target of terrorist attacks, including an assassination attempt on Jabir's life in May 1985. Sabah members have successfully survived these threats and have in fact acquired the sympathy of the Kuwaiti public. The challenge Jabir and the Sabah family face is to allow political participation in government decision-making without letting power slip entirely from their hands. While this may not be easy, the family has shown an ability to survive challenges in the past.

## DOMESTIC POLICY

Kuwait has prudently followed the policy of investing its oil income for the post-oil future. It has made substantial investments in the West in stocks, real estate, and downstream hydrocarbon activities. Kuwait is a highly developed welfare state that provides free education to all citizens and some foreigners from preschool to university levels. Seventy percent of Kuwaitis and 75% of foreigners living in the country are literate. Its extensive national comprehensive health care system with one physician for 619 residents is one of the best in the world. Local telephone calls are free, and housing is heavily subsidized. There is no personal income tax.

Jabir has continued the welfare policies of his predecessors which he helped formulate. Under his rule, Kuwait faced a major economic crisis in the collapse of the Souq al Manekh (unregulated securities market) which produced serious economic and political repercussions for Kuwait. Attempts to resolve this crisis led to disagreement between the National Assembly and Emir Sabah. The emir supported the policy of paying off the investor's debts from public funds while the National Assembly strongly opposed such measures, fearing possible corruption and the creation of a bad precedent for the use of public funds. Because of the conflict, the minister of finance and the governor of the Central Bank both resigned and were replaced by members of the Sabah family. The emir's policies prevailed and further strengthened the ruling family. Thus the old system of benevolence prevailed over the institutionalized path of policy-making.

Another major domestic concern has been the Iranian influence over the Shiite minority. While the Shia merchant community has existed for a long time and has financial commitment to the country, a rash of terrorist attacks and discovery of a plot to overthrow the royal family in June 1989 led to severe measures to curb subversion. The Kuwaiti government has consistently refused to consider releasing Shiites in its prisons even when the US government was willing to consider such arrangements in 1987.

Violent crime and threats from foreigners have underscored the vulnerability of the Kuwaiti population as a minority in its own country. This situation has led to a program of "Kuwaitization" of the population. The objective is to achieve a majority of Kuwaitis in the population by the beginning of the next century. The Kuwaiti government has been successful in reducing the expatriate element in the public sector by shifting government jobs to native Kuwaitis. However, the private sector is still dominated by foreign expatriates.

The emir proposed legislation to allow women to vote and run for the National Assembly in 2003. Liberals and others support the proposal while conservative Islamic politicans oppose it, describing it as a Western-influenced move to erode Kuwaiti society.

## FOREIGN POLICY

Though Jabir did not serve as Kuwaiti foreign minister, he played an active role in setting foreign policy after independence. Kuwait's oil wealth and its geographical position have made it vulnerable to external threats. In 1962 Iraq claimed the total territory of Kuwait as its province just when Kuwait became independent. In the 1980s, Iran threatened to retaliate when Kuwait supported Iraq in the Gulf War.

Kuwait has also used its wealth to reduce foreign threats. For example, it has acquired the goodwill of Arab and Third World countries by its generous financial aid. As a member of the Arab League, Kuwait has supported Arab causes both diplomatically and financially. It has been a strong supporter of Palestinian nationalism and one of the main financial contributors to the Palestinian Liberation Organization (PLO). This move, of course, has also had the effect of placating the large Palestinian community in Kuwait. As an oil exporter, Kuwait has been active in OPEC and Organization of Arab Oil Exporting Countries (OAPEC) from the beginning.

In July 1990, President Saddam Hussein of Iraq criticized Kuwait for disregarding the petroleum production quotas that had been stipulated by OPEC, which led to a decline in world oil prices. He further accused Kuwait of having stolen Iraqi petroleum reserves by drilling oil wells in disputed territory. His demands for the return of land claimed by Iraq and financial compensation were denied. In response, some 100,000 Iraqi troops invaded Kuwait on 2 August 1990. Saddam announced the formal annexation of Kuwait, despite condemnation from the UN Security Council. After diplomatic efforts failed to resolve this crisis, a US-led multinational force launched a military campaign to liberate Kuwait on 17 January 1991. Within days after the deployment of ground forces the Iraqi government agreed to a cease-fire.

Since the 1991 liberation, Kuwait has actively pursued defense cooperation agreements with its allies. In March 1997 Kuwait announced the creation of a National Security Council to promote national security and ensure territorial integrity. In 1999, Kuwait took tentative steps to improve relations with Jordan and Yemen, which had been strained since since 1991 when the two countries appeared to side with Iraq in its invasion of Kuwait. Iraq issued threats against Kuwait and Saudi Arabia for their friendly relations with the West.

## ADDRESS

Seif Palace
Emiry Diwan
Kuwait

## REFERENCES

"A Bolder Kuwait." *The Economist*, 10 July 1999.
*Current Biography Yearbook*. New York: H.W. Wilson Co., 1988.
*Europa World Year Book*. London: Europa Publications Ltd., 1997.
"Kuwait: An Unholy Row." *The Economist*, 8 May 1999, p. 48.
*New York Times*, various issues.
Rush, Alan. *Al-Sabah: History and Genealogy of Kuwait's Ruling Family*. 1987.
"Women's Day in Kuwait." *The Economist*, 22 May 1999.
Zahlan, Rosemarie Said. *The Making of the Modern Gulf States*. 1989.

**Profile researched and written by Bashir Ahmed (7/90; updated 3/2000).**

# KYRGYZSTAN

### Askar Akayevich Akayev
### President
*(pronounced "AS-kar ah-KAH-yeff")*

*"Our main policy [is] to discover the interests of different social, national, and age groups and to create conditions for their fulfillment. Not to be a benefactor, not to patronize, but to open up scope for their own actions, for creativity and initiative."*

Kyrgyzstan (pronounced "KIR-gih-stan") borders Kazakhstan to the north, Uzbekistan to the east, and Tajikistan and China to the south and west. It has a total land size of 198,500 sq km (76,640 sq mi). The population has been estimated at 4.5 million. The Soviet-era 1989 census listed a population of 7.3 million, of which 52.4% were ethnic Kyrgyz, 21.5% Russian, 12.9% Uzbek, 2.5% Ukrainian, 2.4% German, and several other nationalities. The Russian government in late 1999 estimated that about 650,000 Russians remained in Kyrgyzstan. The Kyrgyz language, a Turkic language, is spoken by virtually all Kyrgyz; about 57% of Kyrgyz also speak Russian fluently. The Kyrgyz and Uzbeks are mostly Sunni Muslim while the Russians, Ukrainians, and Germans are Christian.

Kyrgyzstan's official currency is the *som*. Per capita GDP has been estimated at about $2,200. Poverty is widespread. Kyrgyzstan is the least urbanized of the former Soviet republics; most Kyrgyz reside in rural areas and are employed in agriculture. A mountainous country, only about 7% of the land is arable while 43% is pasture and hay land used to raise sheep and goats. Kyrgyzstan is a sizeable producer of wool, and it also produces cotton and tobacco. It has significant mineral reserves of antimony and mercury. The capital of Kyrgyzstan is Bishkek (formerly Frunze).

## POLITICAL BACKGROUND

In the 10th century, nomadic Kyrgyz tribes began to migrate south from the region of the Yenisey River in Siberia to present-day Kyrgyzstan. This migration accelerated in the 13th century as invading Mongols pushed them south. The Kyrgyz were overrun in the 17th century by the Kalmyks, in the 18th century by the Manchus, and in the 19th century by the Uzbek Kokand Khanate.

The Russians moved into the area in the mid-19th century and by 1867 the Kyrgyz were assimilated into the Russian empire as part of Russian Turkestan. After the Bolsheviks defeated local opposition forces in 1919, Kyrgyzstan was made part of the new Turkestan Autonomous Republic. In 1924, the Kara-Kyrgyz Autonomous Oblast (region) was established, renamed the Kyrgyz Autonomous Republic in 1926. In 1936, Stalin upgraded the status of Kyrgyzstan to that of a union republic. While some local self-rule was allowed in the 1920s, by the early 1930s Stalin had begun a process of Russification in Kyrgyzstan, including massive purges of local cadres and forced collectivization of the

largely nomadic society. For many decades, Russians remained disproportionately represented and very influential in the Communist Party leadership of Kyrgyzstan.

The Communist Party of Kyrgyzstan was largely discredited in 1990 and 1991 for opposing sovereignty, democratization, freedom of the press, and market reforms. The long-time Kyrgyz Communist Party leader, Absamat Masaliyev, was rejected by a nationalist and reformist bloc of deputies in the Kyrgyz Supreme Soviet in his bid to become president in October 1990. He later resigned from the party leadership. Instead, the deputies narrowly elected Akayev to the newly created post of president. In December 1990, the Kyrgyz Supreme Soviet passed a declaration on state sovereignty, the last Soviet republic to make such a declaration because of Masaliyev's opposition, and changed the republic's name to Kyrgyzstan.

Akayev resolutely opposed the August 1991 Soviet coup attempt against Gorbachev, in contrast to other Central Asian leaders who actively or tacitly supported the coup. After the coup attempt, the Kyrgyz Supreme Soviet declared Kyrgyzstan an independent democratic state and scheduled direct presidential elections for October 1991. With the breakup of the Soviet Union at the end of 1991, Kyrgyzstan joined most other former Soviet republics in the Commonwealth of Independent States (CIS) on 21 December 1991.

## PERSONAL BACKGROUND

Askar Akayevich Akayev was born to a farm family on 10 November 1944 in the village of Kyzyl-Bairak and is an ethnic Kyrgyz. He grew up in Kyrgyzstan, working in industry before moving to St. Petersburg (formerly Leningrad), where he received advanced and postdoctoral degrees in optical physics at the Institute of Precision Mechanics and Optics. In 1981 he joined the Communist Party. He speaks Kyrgyz and Russian. His wife Mairamkul is also a scientist; they have two daughters and two sons.

## RISE TO POWER

In 1976, Akayev returned to Kyrgyzstan to work as a scientist and teacher in the field of quantum optics. In 1986 he was summoned to Moscow to serve in the Soviet Central Committee Department on Science and Education. He was elected vice president of the Kyrgyz Academy of Sciences in 1987 and in 1989 became its president. In 1989 he was elected by the constituents of the Naukatsk district to the newly created USSR Congress of People's Deputies and subsequently selected to serve in the Soviet of Nationalities of the USSR Supreme Soviet, where he was a member of the Constitutional Oversight Commission and the committee on economic reform. As a legislator, he travelled extensively, meeting with constituents and came to the conclusion that he would shift his career from science to politics in order to contribute to the betterment of Kyrgyzstan. In a significant speech at the Congress of People's Deputies in December 1989, he called for marketization to improve the Soviet economy.

In the summer of 1990, ethnic tensions in the Osh region led to mass demonstrations in Bishkek against Communist Party rule, with demands for the ouster of the Communist Party leader Masaliyev. When the Kyrgyz Supreme Soviet convened in October 1990, deputies aligned in a democratic bloc narrowly defeated Masaliyev's bid to become president; Akayev's supporters urged him to quickly return to Kyrgyzstan from his legislative duties in Moscow, and after repeated voting elected him to the newly created post. In an uncontested direct popular election held in October 1991, he was re-elected president, winning 95% of the vote. In the face of growing legislative and regional opposition to his rule, Akayev held a popular referendum in January 1994 on whether he should finish out his term, winning support from 96.2% of the voters to continue his reforms. He was re-elected president in December 1995, winning 72% of the vote in a three-way race. In July 1998, Akayev hailed a Constitutional Court decision permitting him to run for a third term in the year 2000.

## LEADERSHIP

Akayev's popularity has remained high despite the economic and political turmoil of the 1990s. Akayev has been effective at personally explaining unpopular policies to groups and organizations and listening and acting on their views, defusing discontent. Although Akayev advocates a "strong executive power" in Kyrgyzstan in order to control ethnic and social tensions, he has also advocated marketization.

In September 1995, Akayev's supporters submitted a petition signed by 1.2 million (52% of the voting age population) urging the legislature to approve a referendum extending Akayev's term to the year 2001. After contentious debate, the legislature rejected holding a referendum, and Akayev instead announced that a presidential election would be held on 24 December 1995. Thirteen candidates were registered, but 10 were disqualified, leaving Akayev, Masaliyev, and former speaker Medetken Sherimkulov. Akayev won re-election to a five-year term, receiving 72% of the vote in a race deemed generally "free and fair" by international observers, though questions were raised about the disqualifications. In July 1998, Akayev hailed a Constitutional Court decision permitting him to run for a third term in the year 2000.

## DOMESTIC POLICY

Akayev has declared that his primary goals are a modernized economy and maintenance of ethnic harmony. Economic priorities are meeting food supply needs, full employment, and the training and retraining of youth. Foreign assistance has been a significant factor in Kyrgyzstan's budget, but

Akayev hopes that his economic reforms will permit Kyrgyzstan to rely less on such aid after the year 2000. Kyrgyz GDP stopped declining in 1995 and grew 1.8% in 1998, led by increases in agricultural and industrial production (the latter including mining, food processing, and textiles). The Russian financial crisis and declining world gold prices harmed the Kyrgyz economy in late 1998, contributing to reduced Kyrgyz exports to Russia, increased budget deficits and a budget cut, increased inflation, and the devaluation of the *som*. Akayev reported in late 1999, however, that GDP had rebounded by 3.5%, fueled by agricultural production, though industrial production continued to decline. He stated that efforts to combat terrorism in southern Kyrgyzstan had cost several million dollars, harming economic recovery. He has been vulnerable to criticism of widespread corruption in his government and of not being able to bring increasing crime under control. Akayev has championed privatization although his legislature and most of the public have appeared to oppose it. In October 1998, nonetheless, Akayev cleverly received public approval for private ownership of land within five years by bundling the proposal with other referendum proposals. Privatization has proceeded further in Kyrgyzstan than in the rest of Central Asia. A majority of state industries and most housing and retail outlets have been at least nominally privatized. To encourage agricultural privatization, Akayev has set up agricultural committees throughout Kyrgyzstan with powers to abolish bankrupt state and collective farms, boost production, and distribute land to those who want a private farm. Kyrgyzstan's admission into the World Trade Organization (WTO) in late 1998 was a major accomplishment of his presidency. At the OSCE Summit in November 1999, Akayev called for the OSCE to foster greater international economic cooperation, since "economic stability secures peace and political stability."

A new constitution was approved in 1993, establishing a democratic presidential system with separation of powers and expansive human rights guarantees. In September 1994, Akayev decreed an October referendum to approve amendments to the constitution, including provisions revamping the legislative system to weaken it relative to the presidency. He argued that legislative and other provisions of the May 1993 constitution were too "idealistic" since the "people are not prepared for democracy," and a "transitional period" was needed. Akayev spearheaded another referendum to be held in February 1996 to further alter the constitution. These changes gave Akayev greater powers to veto legislation, dissolve the legislature, and appoint all ministers without legislative confirmation, while making impeachment more difficult, along the lines of the Russian Constitution. Moving further to weaken the legislature, Akayev spearheaded a third referendum in October 1998 to again amend the constitution. These amendments sharply restricted the legislature's influence over bills involving the budget or other expenditures and limited a legislator's immunity from removal and prosecution. They also provided for private land ownership and reaffirmed freedom of the press.

Akayev has said that he supports democratization and the adherence to human rights commitments Kyrgyzstan made when it joined the Organization for Security and Cooperation in Europe in 1992. Compared to other Central Asian states, many observers stress, Kyrgyzstan has a less objectionable human rights record. According to the State Department's *Country Reports on Human Rights Practices for 1999*, the Kyrgyz government generally respected the human rights of its citizens, but there were problems with freedom of speech and the press, due process for the accused, religious freedom, ethnic discrimination, and electoral irregularities. There are cases of police brutality and arbitrary arrest, and apparent politically-motivated arrests. Citizens have only a limited ability to peaceably change their government since elections and referenda have involved "irregular" procedures. There are independent newspapers, magazines, and radio stations, and some independent television broadcasts though the government can influence the media through subsidies. Laws making libel a criminal offense have been used to arrest reporters and silence dissent.

The Akayev government appeared to move toward authoritarianism when flawed legislative elections were held in February–March 2000. Election monitors from the Organization for Security and Cooperation in Europe who observed this race concluded that it was not "free and fair," pointing to problems such as the disqualification of prominent opposition parties and candidates, the pro-government composition of electoral boards, government harassment of opposition candidates, and irregularities in vote-counting. Akayev rejected these assessments as overlooking Kyrgyzstan's democratic and economic accomplishments. Among the problems, opposition Dignity Party head Feliks

Kulov received more votes than his opponents in the first round of the February 2000 legislative race but was heavily defeated in the second round through apparent legerdemain, according to the OSCE. Kulov was later arrested and accused of committing crimes several years ago.

Akayev initially supported a unified Commonwealth of Independent States (CIS) armed forces and preferred that Kyrgyzstan not incur the expense of maintaining its own armed forces. However, faced with the emergence of individual armed forces in the new states of the former Soviet Union, he formed a Kyrgyz armed forces in 1992 that numbered about 12,200 ground troops in 1998 (*The Military Balance*). Most of the troops are ethnic Kyrgyz conscripts though some officers are Russians. Kyrgyzstan had about 5,000 border troops in 1998. Several hundred Russian border troops (most reportedly were Kyrgyz citizens) guarded the Chinese border for most of the 1990s, but Russia handed over border control to Kyrgyzstan in August 1999.

That same month, Akayev's leadership was severely tested by an armed incursion by Tajik and Uzbek guerrillas into southern Kyrgyzstan. These guerrillas aimed to create an Islamic state in southern Kyrgyzstan as a base to launch attacks into Uzbekistan. Akayev's military, police, and border forces initially appeared unequal to defeating the guerrillas, and Akayev appealed to the Commonwealth of Independent States (CIS) for assistance. Russia agreed to send military equipment while Uzbekistan launched air strikes and border assaults. Akayev announced in October 1999 that the guerrillas had been driven out of Kyrgyzstan. Uzbek President Islam Karimov criticized Akayev of laxity in combating the guerrillas while Akayev criticized Karimov's forces of not always consulting with Kyrgyzstan before launching attacks against guerrillas.

## FOREIGN POLICY

Kyrgyzstan endeavors to establish broad-ranging ties with all nations of the world, particularly border states. Akayev has stressed close relations with Russia. Reasons include hoped-for economic and trade benefits and security ties to alleviate residual concerns about Chinese and Uzbek intentions. Akayev and Yeltsin signed a Friendship and Cooperation Treaty in 1992, and Akayev gave early support to the 1992 CIS Collective Security Treaty, which called for mutual military assistance in case one of the signatories is attacked. Akayev has urged that the CIS cooperate on economic and security matters. Kyrgyzstan has signed a customs union agreement with Belarus, Russia, and Kazakhstan (Tajikistan joined in 1998), but the union remains moribund. In 1994, Kyrgyzstan joined Kazakhstan and Uzbekistan in a "Central Asian Economic Community" that includes a bank, a peacekeeping battalion, and mutual defense assurances (Tajikistan joined in 1998), but it has been buffeted by regional economic problems. Kyrgyzstan's relations with Uzbekistan are mercurial. The two have trade disputes, and Uzbekistan has criticized Kyrgyzstan for providing refuge to some Uzbek dissidents and for purportedly permitting terrorist groups to "escape" Kyrgyzstan in October 1999 (see below). Akayev's March 1999 foreign policy concept called for close relations with ancient "silk road" route countries, including China, former Soviet republics, and Turkey, Iran, India, and Pakistan. Kyrgyzstan has also pursued good relations with Western states in its search for aid. Akayev has stressed that landlocked Kyrgyzstan must rely on its neighbors for access to world markets. Cultivating good ties with China, Akayev joined leaders from Russia, Kazakhstan, and Tajikistan in 1996 and 1997 in signing agreements with China on demarcating and demilitarizing the former Soviet-Chinese border. Kyrgyzstan hosted a meeting of this "Shanghai Five" in August 1999. Kyrgyzstan and China have essentially completed border demarcation.

## ADDRESS

Office of the President
Bishkek
Ulitsa Kirova 205
Kyrgystan

## REFERENCES

*FBIS Daily Report: Central Eurasia,* various issues.
*New York Times,* various issues.
*RFE/RL Research Report,* various issues.

**Profile researched and written by Jim Nichol, Library of Congress (5/2000).**

# LAOS

## Khamtay Siphandone
## President

*(pronounced "KAM-tie SEE-pan-don")*

*"We must put a stop to exploitive business practices, such as indisciminate logging of our forests."*

The Lao People's Democratic Republic (Lao PDR) is a landlocked nation, which lies between Vietnam and Thailand and also borders Cambodia, China, and Myanmar. With an estimated area of 236,000 sq km (91,120 sq mi), Laos is made up of 89% mountainous terrain and dominated by tropical forests and jungles.

The population of 5.4 million people is comprised of three major ethnic groups: 63.4% Lao-Lum (valley lowland Lao), 23.8% Lao Theung (Lao living on mountain slopes), and 10.1% Lao-Sung (mountaintop Lao). Approximately 65% of the Lao people are Buddhist, and 33% are animists. The national language is Lao, while some older government officials still speak French. Other officials may speak English or languages such as Russian, Vietnamese, German, or Czech.

The unit of currency is the *kip*. The Lao economy ranks among the poorest in the world, with a per capita GDP of about US$1,260.

Laos also has one of the highest death rates in the world, with poor health conditions in many of the remote areas of the country. The economy is principally agricultural, with 80% of the population engaged in subsistence farming of rice, maize, tobacco, cotton, sugar cane, fruits, and coffee. Lao and US authorities are working closely together to eliminate remnants of opium production and trade. With the opening of the economy in 1986, Lao exports have steadily increased. Major exports include timber, coffee, tin, various minerals, electricity, light manufacturing products, and handicrafts.

## POLITICAL BACKGROUND

Like its neighbors, Vietnam and Cambodia, Laos was subjugated to French colonialism in the late 19th century. The French saw Laos primarily as an extension of their Vietnam colony. After a period of Japanese occupation during World War II, and the conclusion of the first "Indochina" war, Laos gained its independence in 1953. Gradually Laos was drawn into the vortex of the Cold War, and a struggle developed between the Communist faction, called the *Pathet Lao*, and the pro-Western regime of the Royal Lao government. In 1957, 1962, and again in 1973, there were unsuccessful attempts to form coalition governments. Throughout the 1960s and early 1970s, the Royal Lao government received substantial financial and military assistance from the US, making Laos a hyper dependent country. Politics during this period were characterized by chaos, significant in-fighting among rival factions, and numerous military coups. US military assistance was part of the "secret war in Laos"

orchestrated by the CIA through front organizations such as Air America. It was not until 1973 that a cease-fire agreement was signed between the *Pathet Lao* and the government forces of Prince Souvanna Phouma.

The 1975 victories of communist forces in Vietnam and Cambodia motivated the *Pathet Lao* to undertake an offensive of its own, eventually seizing all major Laotian cities, including the capital of Vientiane. Basic control was consolidated by August, and on 2 December 1975, the *Pathet Lao* established the Lao People's Democratic Republic, terminated the coalition government, and abolished the monarchy. Important military and civilian officials were sent to "re-education" camps. Those involved in the "secret war" and closely associated with the US government or CIA suffered the most in such camps.

In the Lao People's Democratic Republic, the National Assembly officially acts as a principal law-making body. With a membership of 99, it determines major national laws and appoints the Council of Ministers and president. Assembly members are elected from the various areas of the country. There are 12 ministries, including education, interior, finance, and agriculture. The Council of Ministers is led by its chairperson, who also assumes the title of premier. Under the premier there are five vice-premiers. They assist the premier in five key realms of government: economy; health, education and culture; defense; foreign affairs; and national development planning.

Any discussion of Lao politics would be incomplete without describing the critically important role of the Lao Communist Party, the country's only legal political group, known formally as the Lao People's Revolutionary Party (LPRP). It dominates Lao politics, and opportunities for advancement are highly dependent on one's ranking within the party. Unlike the money politics of many neighboring countries, political success in Laos is highly dependent upon loyalty to the party and its ideology. Under this system, minorities and those of humble background have been able to attain high ranking positions in the party.

## PERSONAL BACKGROUND

Khamtay Siphandone was born in the southern province of Champasak in 1924. Little is known about his early years although evidence suggests a rather humble background. During World War II Khamtay spent some time in India. At the end of the war he returned to Laos and was employed as a postal worker in the south.

## RISE TO POWER

Khamtay's involvement in Lao politics started as early as 1945. Driven by a strong sense of nationalism, he participated in *Lao Issara* (Free Laos), a movement opposed to French colonialism. During the nationalistic struggle that ensued, a split occurred between anti-Western and royalist factions. Khamtay sided with the leftist, anti-Western faction led by Prince Souphanouvong and Kaysone Phomvihane, and was soon entrusted with major military affairs of the LPRP. In 1954, Khamtay was appointed chief of staff of the Lao People's Liberation Army (LPLA) and later became its commander in chief.

During the 1960s and 1970s, primarily as the result of his military role and loyalty to the *Pathet Lao* leaders, Khamtay climbed to the upper echelon of the party hierarchy.

In 1972, he was appointed a member of the party's Central Committee. By December 1975, when the *Pathet Lao* had consolidated its control of the country, Khamtay was named minister of defense. In subsequent years, he gained even greater political power, eventually surpassing Prince Souphanouvong. In 1988, Khamtay was appointed secretary of the LPRP and positioned himself to become the successor to President Kaysone—the highest ranking Lao politician. The army's success in a border war with Thailand further enhanced his national stature.

On 15 August 1991, the National Assembly approved Khamtay Siphandone as the new prime minister, succeeding Kaysone Phomvihane, who then became the nation's president. Khamtay's promotion was, in part, due to his long-term loyalty to the powerful Kaysone—a revolutionary hero in Laos. Khamtay and Kaysone were close partners since the 1940s, dating back to their involvement in the anti-colonial struggle. In 1986, Kaysone introduced the New Economic Mechanism policy to allow free market forces to operate in the economy. This important new policy directive was enthusiastically endorsed by Khamtay, who played a major role in its implementation.

## LEADERSHIP

Khamtay's 1998 promotion to the presidency, following December 1997 national elections, represented the second major shift in Lao politics in 23 years. The first occurred in 1991 when Khamtay was promoted to the premiership and Kaysone became president. After the 1991 shake-up, many "old-guard" politicians voluntarily retired and have since died, although hard liners continue to exert influence within the government.

A key and surprising element in the 1998 shake-up was the elevation of Sisavat Keobounphan to the premiership. Sisavat was born in 1928 in the remote northeastern province of Huaphanh. During the 1991–95 period, he gained valuable international experience while serving as minister of agriculture and forestry. Among the nine politburo members, his rank was number eight. This was primarily as a result of his readmission to the politburo after having been dropped in 1991. Thus, assuming the premiership and becoming the potential successor to Khamtay represented an extremely impressive political comeback for Sisavat. Strong military credentials were a major factor in his promotion. In 1938, Sisavat played an important role as the military strategist in the border war with Thailand and the negotiator of a

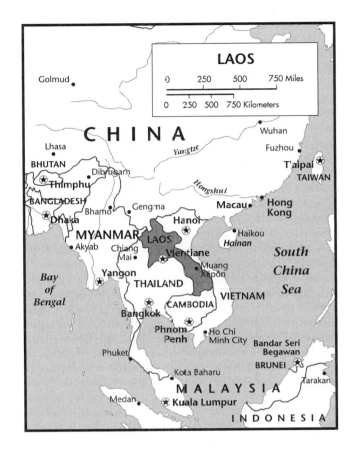

successful peace settlement that ended the conflict. He is described as an outgoing, warm person who is practical, decisive, and determined. Sisavat is generally considered to be a conservative leader.

Superficially, it may seem that the changes taking place in Laos mirror those which occurred in Eastern Europe in the late 1980s and early 1990s. Actual political conditions are different in many respects. The success of communism in Laos was primarily as a force of nationalism—to restore national unity, culture, and political independence after decades of revolutionary struggle; while in Eastern Europe communism was "imposed and installed" by the former USSR. Unlike Eastern Europe, a one-party system remains an integral aspect of the political structure. The Lao leaders have looked to countries such as Singapore, with stable authoritarian governments, as potential models, rather than what they perceived as "chaotic" multiparty systems in countries such as Thailand and Cambodia. Thus, a major challenge for the current leadership is to foster and preserve the distinct political culture of Laos, which involves a fascinating blend of Marxism, free market mechanisms, and strong Buddhist traditions.

## DOMESTIC POLICY

Introduction of the New Economic Mechanism in 1986 and the adoption of the first constitution of the Lao PDR in 1991 reflected the reform of Laos' political and economic system. The constitution represented an important watershed in the country's economic and political life. In the economic realm, it legally recognized the shift from a planned to a market economy with significant liberalization. The constitution vows "to protect private property of national and international capitalists." The implementation of a clear legal framework was seen as essential to attract critically needed international investment. The new constitution and subsequent laws led to a dramatic increase in foreign investment in the 1990s. Party leadership has frequently pulled back from completely endorsing economic reform. The 1999 sacking of high level finance officials associated with a free market appeared to indicate confusion within the government about which economic course to pursue.

On the political front, the constitution confirmed the absolute power of the Lao People's Revolutionary Party. The LPRP is normally referred to simply as "the party." With the promulgation of the 1991 constitution, the hammer and sickle were removed from the Lao national symbol and replaced by the famous That Luang Buddhist temple, now the symbol of the nation.

The party determines fundamental policy in Laos, and the National Assembly debates laws to implement party policies. The constitution designates the country as a "people's democratic republic." Its democratic dimension is not in the area of Western style political liberty and pluralism but in an emphasis on equality and political mobility. Members of ethnic minorities serve in the politburo. Under the new system, the appointed Supreme People's Assembly was replaced by an elected National Assembly. Eligible voters are those 18 years and older. Party membership is not required to compete for seats though most candidates and those elected are, in fact, party members. Each member of the National Assembly serves for five years.

The liberalization of the economy brought new problems related to influence-peddling and growing corruption. Forest depletion has resulted from increased logging, legal and illegal, for exports to Thailand and other parts of Asia. An August 1991 decree attempted to address this problem by banning many types of logging activity, and efforts have been made to restrict timber exports. To deal with the problem of corruption, an Anti-Corruption Commission was established in 1993, reporting directly to the prime minister. As of 2000, this group had recovered a significant amount of money earned illegally and had the authority to remove and punish corrupt officials. However, crime, smuggling, and corruption have continued to be on the rise into 2000.

The Khamtay and Sisavat government continued to face several major domestic challenges. It has been slow to react to the effects of the economic crisis in neighboring Thailand and compensate for reduced investment flows. To be successful it must ensure that rapid economic development is sustainable, with controls on environmental and social damage. Khamtay, expected to be in office until 2003, remains a secretive, authoritarian leader, operating within a political system which lacks transparency and accountability. The governed have been slower to stir in Laos than in other Asian nations, but may not be as docile in the new decade.

## FOREIGN POLICY

Lao foreign policy was dramatically redefined in the 1990s after the collapse of the former USSR. Laos now has one of the most open foreign policies in the world and is basically on good terms with every nation. It has, for example, established diplomatic relations with both North and South Korea. In July 1997, Laos became a formal member of the Association of Southeast Asian Nations (ASEAN). Though membership places a financial burden on the country, it should help to facilitate expanded and diversified trade and foreign investment. As of 2000, Laos appears to be grouped in a bloc of underdeveloped, authoritarian states within ASEAN (with Cambodia, Burma and Vietnam). Vietnam is still perceived as Laos's "elder brother" in guiding its foreign policy, if not its economic relationships.

In the 1980s foreign aid was received primarily from the USSR and Eastern bloc countries. Since then Laos has successfully diversified its sources of foreign aid and technical assistance. The major donor is currently Japan, but substantial aid is also received from the World Bank, Asian Development Bank, Australia, the Nordic countries, Switzerland, France, and Germany. The historic bridge across the Mekong River, which opened in April 1994, was financed by Australia.

Since the border war of early 1988, Lao-Thai relations have improved significantly, and Thailand is now the country's major trade partner and largest foreign investor. The improved nature of this relationship is reflected in visits of Laotian leaders to Thailand and the frequent visits of the Crown Princess of Thailand to Laos. However, the exploitive nature of Laos' growing economic dependence on Thailand has been a serious concern, and key political figures have been demoted because of their perceived closeness to Thai interests. China has come to nearly rival Thailand as a trading partner and has assisted in infrastructure development to facilitate transport of goods northward through Laos to its Yunnan border.

## ADDRESS

Office of the President
Vientiane, Lao PDR

## REFERENCES

*Asiaweek,* 24 December 1999.

*Bangkok Post,* 13 December 1995, 25 February 1998.

Leifer, Michael. *Dictionary of the Modern Politics of South-East Asia.* London: Routledge, 1996.

*The Nation,* 23–25 February 1998.

*Results from the Population Census: 1995.* Vientiane: State Planning Committee and National Statistical Centre, April 1997.

Stuart-Fox, Martin. *Buddhist Kingdom, Marxist State: The Making of Modern Laos.* Bangkok: 1996.

Stuart-Fox, Martin. *A History of Laos.* Cambridge: Cambridge University Press, 1997.

Stuart-Fox, Martin and Mary Kooyman. *Historical Dictionary of Laos.* Metuchen, NJ: Scarecrow Press, 1992.

**Profile researched and written by Gerald Fry, University of Oregon (6/98; updated 3/2000).**

# LATVIA

### Vaira Vike-Freiberga
### President

*(pronounced "VAHY-rah VEE-ke FRAY-behr-guh")*

*"We are the inheritors of our past, but we are not slaves who should live in the shadow of our past. We are the builders of our own future."*

The Republic of Latvia borders on the Baltic Sea, the Gulf of Riga, Estonia, Lithuania, Russia, and Belarus. A total land area of 63,688 sq km (24,590 sq mi) makes Latvia comparable in size to West Virginia.

The population has been estimated at 2.4 million people, of whom 56% are Latvians and 31% Russians; the remaining 13% are chiefly Belarusians, Ukrainians, Poles, and Lithuanians. The official language is Latvian. Most Latvians are Lutherans, but some are Roman Catholics or Baptists. Ethnic Russians generally belong to the Orthodox faith. Only a handful of Jewish congregations remain in existence.

The official currency is the *lats*. Per capita GDP has been estimated at $4,100. Latvia produces farm equipment, railroad cars, radios, telephone equipment, hosiery, washing machines, fish, and other foodstuffs. It exports machinery, agricultural products, light industrial goods, and chemicals. Its service sector has grown dramatically in recent years, now accounting for a majority of economic activity.

## POLITICAL BACKGROUND

Latvia declared independence in November 1918 with the collapse of central authority in Russia and the defeat of the German army. In 1940, Latvia again fell under Russian rule, as the Union of Soviet Socialist Republics (USSR) annexed the country. The Republic of Latvia ceased to exist and was replaced by the Latvian Soviet Socialist Republic, a constituent union-republic of the USSR. The army of Nazi Germany invaded Latvia in 1941 and occupied it until 1945. These two brutal occupations resulted in the death of 180,000 people, or 9% of the pre-World War II Latvian population. To consolidate Soviet authority, Stalin deported or arrested 100,000 more people; 25,000 died in a war of resistance against the Soviet Union.

Under Communism, Latvian culture and other forms of national expression were repressed. Russified Latvians (some of whom spoke no Latvian), Russians, and others were dispatched to rule Latvia. In the post-Stalin era, dissidents who called for observance of human rights or religious rights, or who protested the repression of the Latvian nation were harassed, arrested, imprisoned, and sometimes killed.

Mikhail Gorbachev relaxed the controls on Soviet society, and many Latvians leaped at the opportunity. Various groups seeking greater local control sprang up. The most important of these groups, the Popular Front of Latvia (PFL) was formed in October 1988, marking a watershed in Latvian history. This broad-based movement provided organizational

strength to harness the discontent with Soviet rule pervasive among Latvians and others.

A PFL slate of moderate nationalists won three-fourths of the Latvian SSR's seats in the USSR's newly created legislature in the March 1989 elections. The PFL grew increasingly radical in 1989, finally declaring itself in favor of eventual independence from the USSR. Throughout 1989 and 1990, in mass demonstrations and behind-the-scenes diplomacy, Latvian leaders pursued independence.

During the hard-line coup of August 1991 in Moscow the leadership of Latvia quickly declared its opposition to the coup and support for Russian president, Boris Yeltsin. The Latvian government declared the country independent on 21 August, insisting that the coup proved that there was no alternative. Once the Soviet Union crumbled, countries around the world recognized Latvia's independence.

In preparation for electing a new, post-independence legislature, the Supreme Council passed a citizenship law, but left key issues unresolved. Because of the fear of Russian domination and the fact that Latvians barely made up a majority of the country's population, Latvian leaders sought to write a citizenship law that ensured ethnic Latvian control over the fate of Latvia, while respecting the rights of others. Thus, the law they passed automatically granted citizenship to those who were citizens in 1940 and to their descendants. Others would be eligible for citizenship if they demonstrated proficiency in the Latvian language and if they have been residents for at least several years. The legislature did not, however, provide for a naturalization process, thereby leaving one-quarter of the population without citizenship.

Because of the difficulty involved in deciding on a citizenship law, elections for Latvia's first post-Soviet *Saeima* (parliament) did not take place until June 1993. The results indicated that many voters supported the status quo and hoped to see a moderately paced transition in the economic realm.

Latvia elected a new *Saeima* in Fall 1995. Latvia's voters showed themselves clearly divided, electing a parliament so evenly divided on core issues that selecting a government took months. Conservatives favored closer ties with the West and opposed weakening the citizenship laws. Liberals argued for improving relations with Russia and easing naturalization rules. This situation left two extremist parties—one on the left and one on the right—holding the balance of power at the margins. Just before Christmas the parliament approved a broad-based coalition cabinet. Andris Shkele, a businessman

and former government official, agreed to lead a cabinet that included every party in the *Saeima*, except the extremist Socialists and People's Movement.

Shkele proved an effective leader. He forced through the unpopular spending cuts and tax increases that were necessary to balance the budget. He accelerated economic reform. His abrasive style and unpopular policies, however, forced him to resign in January 1997. The president renominated Shkele, and he won with overwhelming support in the *Saeima*. He continued as prime minister until his coalition collapsed in July 1997.

Latvia's economy suffered terribly in 1998. Russian purchases of Latvian goods and services declined precipitously, causing Latvia's economy to contract, increasing the trade imbalance and increasing the unemployment rate. In June 1998 the *Saeima*, acting at the behest of the European Union, approved amendments to the citizenship law, easing requirements for obtaining citizenship.

At the same time, parliamentary elections resulted in Shkele's People's Party winning a plurality of the vote. Because Shkele was so reviled by other politicians, however, three smaller parties, with the acquiescence of a left-wing party, were able to form a minority government without Shkele in November 1998. A new president was elected by the *Saeima* on 17 June 1999. Vaira Vike-Freiberga was inaugurated as Latvia's first female president on 8 July 1999.

## PERSONAL BACKGROUND

Vike-Freiberga was born in the Latvian city of Riga on 1 December 1937. During World War II, she fled with her family to refugee camps in Germany. After the war the family

emigrated to Morocco and, in 1954, to Canada. Vike-Freiberga earned bachelor's and master's degrees in psychology from the University of Toronto. She went on to receive a PhD in experimental psychology in 1965 from McGill University in Montreal.

Vike-Freiberga is fluent in Latvian, French, English, German, and Spanish. From 1965 until 1998 she was a professor of psychology at the University of Montreal. She lectured on psychopharmacology, psycholinguistics, theory of science, and experimental methods. Vike-Freiberga has published numerous professional articles and books. She is best known among Latvians for her studies of the poetic character and structure of Latvian folksongs.

In 1998, Vike-Freiberga assumed leadership of the Latvian Institute, a private non-profit group that promotes Latvian culture and interests in the international community. She has headed various professional societies and has received numerous awards from Western, as well as Latvian, organizations.

She is married to Imants Freibergs, who teaches computer science at the University of Quebec at Montreal. They have a daughter, Indra, and a son, Karlis.

## RISE TO POWER

Latvia's president is elected by the *Saeima*. Of the 100 deputies, 51 votes are required for election. Vike-Freiberga emerged as the surprise winner, with 53 votes. She won after a 14-hour marathon session in the seventh round of balloting. None of the initial candidates proved capable of finding support outside their own parties in the first five ballots. Even as candidates dropped out of the race, many parties chose to abstain or vote against all candidates rather than support the remaining ones. After the fifth round, all the original candidates had withdrawn. Vike-Freiberga's victory came after the center-right People's Party, the right-wing Fatherland and Freedom/LNNK Party, and the left-wing Social Democratic Party joined together to support her candidacy.

## LEADERSHIP

Vike-Freiberga is the first woman to be elected president in any of the former Soviet republics. She is accustomed to being a maverick. As an immigrant and a woman, she knows what it means to be outside the mainstream. As a professor at a French-speaking university, she knows the challenges faced by linguistic minorities. Furthermore, her desire to maintain close ties to Latvia and Latvians during the Soviet era and her criticism of the authoritarian tendencies of some emigre Latvians resulted in her being labeled a leftist by conservative emigres. She seems prepared to tackle the challenges of being a Westerner and a woman leading a post-Soviet society in which women are often treated patronizingly.

Two major issues demanded her immediate attention. First, the *Saeima* overwhelmingly approved a new language law, which Western and Russian leaders criticized for the restrictions it placed on the use of languages other than Latvian in business affairs. Yielding to Western pressure, Vike-Freiberga returned the law to the legislature for review, recommending that the offending sections be amended. Both Western and Russian leaders applauded the decision while Latvian politicians and the public were divided.

On 5 July 1999, her government resigned as the parliamentary coalition was breaking up. Vike-Freiberga nominated Shkele to form a new government, which was approved by the *Saeima* on 16 July. As prime minister, he is being called upon to balance the budget and pull Latvia out of its economic slump. An entrepreneur and former deputy agriculture minister, Shkele has proven himself an effective leader and commands the respect of many politicians, though not much affection.

## DOMESTIC POLICY

Debate over the citizenship issue has abated somewhat since the rules on naturalization were passed. Many non-Latvian residents eligible for citizenship, however, denounce the pace at which naturalization is proceeding. Conservative groups, on the other hand, have failed in their attempts to slow the process even more. The issue retains its resonance among a large segment of the population. The 1999 amendments to the language law stirred up the issue once again.

Latvia's economy had been growing steadily until Russia's economy collapsed in 1998. The decline in trade with Russia caused the economy to contract. In the long term, Latvia faces a problem in imports growing much more quickly than exports. The Russian crisis also scared away potential foreign investors. The unemployment rate grew to 10% by March 1999 as a result of privatization and the economic contraction. Inflation has been tamed, however, falling to 2.3% annually in the first quarter of 1999.

## FOREIGN POLICY

Because of its size and location, Latvia places great faith in multilateral organizations to preserve its independence and increase its prosperity. It is a member of the United Nations, the International Monetary Fund, the World Bank, the Council of Europe, the Organization for Security and Cooperation in Europe, and the Nordic Council. Latvia was one of the founding members of the Council of Baltic Sea States. Close economic and political cooperation with the West, particularly the Scandinavian countries, is a major goal. Long-term policy goals shared by all major political parties include full membership in the European Union (EU) and NATO. The EU announced in October 1999 that Latvia was one of six nations newly added to the EU's list of candidates for membership. Latvia could join the EU as early as 2003.

Russia will always have a significant influence on Latvia by virtue of its political, economic, and military presence. Although Russia completed its troop withdrawal in August 1994, relations between the two nations remain strained. Despite repeated findings by impartial investigations that the human rights of ethnic Russians are not being violated, the Russian government continues to accuse Latvia of committing such violations. The repeated accusations have tarnished Latvia's international reputation. The two countries signed a border treaty in October 1997 once Latvia dropped its claim to land annexed by the USSR in 1944. However, that treaty has not been ratified by the Russian parliament and thus not yet implemented. An additional oil pipeline between Russia and Latvia is planned, but building has not yet begun.

Latvian governments in the post-Soviet era have consistently sought admission to NATO. Russian leaders object strenuously, however, and Western leaders fear offending Russia. Thus, it appears that all of the former Soviet republics, including Latvia, face difficulty in receiving an invitation to join. Until that happens, Latvia will have to rely on Western rhetoric and its own devices to ensure its security.

The three Baltic states have not continued to cooperate as they did in their struggle to leave the Soviet Union. They have not coordinated their foreign policies to a beneficial degree and have fallen into disputes amongst themselves. Latvia and Estonia have quarreled over fishing rights in the Baltic Sea. While a significant sea border dispute between Lithuania and Latvia has been resolved, questions about possible oil exploration rights remain.

There have, however, been some areas of cooperation. In 1993, all three Baltic States signed a free trade agreement, abolishing tariffs on most non-agricultural goods and establishing common customs and visa regulations. In 1994, the three countries declared a free trade area for industrial goods effective in the Baltic States.

## ADDRESS

The President
Pils laukums 3
Riga LV-1900, Latvia

## REFERENCES

*Baltic Economies—The Quarter in Review*, February 1999, 12 May 1999.

Central Statistical Bureau of Latvia. [Online] Available http://www.csb.lv (Accessed May 2000).

Chancery of the President. [Online] Available http://www.president.lv (Accessed May 2000).

*Christian Science Monitor*, 7 July 1999.

Dreifelds, Juris. *Latvia in Transition*. Cambridge: Cambridge University Press, 1996.

Latvian Institute. [Online] Available http://www.latinst.lv (Accessed May 2000).

*Montreal Gazette*, 19 June 1999.

Parliament. [Online] Available http://www.saeima.lanet.lv (Accessed May 2000).

Plakans, Andrejs. *The Latvians: A Short History*. Stanford: Hoover Institution Press, 1995.

**Profile researched and written by Andrejs Penikis, Columbia University (12/99; updated 5/2000).**

# LEBANON

### Emile Lahoud
### President
*(pronounced "AYE-meel LA-hood")*

*"I have few promises, many tasks, and much hope. I will try my best to be the example in every aspect called for by duty, requested by the law, and made inevitable by responsibility."*

The Republic of Lebanon is located in the Middle East, bordered on the north and east by Syria and on the west by the Mediterranean Sea. Lebanon's area is 10,452 sq km (4,036 sq mi). The population has been estimated at around 3.6 million. Arabs are the predominant ethnic group. Armenians, Assyrians, and Kurds constitute small minorities. Nearly all Lebanese are Muslims or Christians. Most of the Muslims, who comprise 60% of the population, belong to either the Sunni or Shia sects. In the 1980s, the Shia became the largest single religious group. The majority of Lebanon's Christians belong to the Maronite Church, an eastern branch of Roman Catholicism. Arabic is the official language, but French and English are widely used as second languages.

Lebanon's service-oriented economy depends on banking, trade, and finance as the chief sources of income. The agricultural and manufacturing sectors, though smaller, are important as producers of exports. After the devastation of several years of civil war, the economy has recovered robustly. GDP has been estimated at $15.8 billion, more than doubling in size since 1993. The Lebanese unit of currency is the pound.

## POLITICAL BACKGROUND

Lebanon's constitution, promulgated in 1943, vests legislative powers in a unicameral legislature, the *Majlis al-Nuwab* or National Assembly, whose members are elected to four-year terms. The constitution also mandates an executive branch and an independent judiciary. The president of the republic and a prime minister head the executive branch and collaborate to form a government. Members of the National Assembly elect the president for a single six-year term. The president, in consultation with the speaker and members of the Assembly, appoints a prime minister and a cabinet who are responsible to the Assembly. An unwritten agreement, reached in 1943, provides the formula for power sharing between the Muslim and Christian communities. The president is always a Maronite Christian, the prime minister a Sunni Muslim, and the speaker of the Assembly a Shia Muslim. Cabinet portfolios are allocated proportionate to the different religious groups' representation in the National Assembly. Political parties in Lebanon are identified with particular religious affiliations, and attempts to form national parties have generally failed.

Constitutional reforms enacted in 1990 granted greater political power to Lebanon's Muslim majority. The 128-seat Assembly and cabinet portfolios are now equally divided among Muslims and Christians. Moreover, the powers of the president have been significantly reduced in favor of the cabinet and prime minister, who serves as the head of the government. The new constitutional division of power among the president, prime minister, and parliamentary speaker is seen as creating a semi-official ruling "troika."

These reforms follow several years of civil strife that erupted in the 1970s. The conflict was caused by the problems created by a large Palestinian refugee presence in the country and the emergence of a Muslim majority demanding a greater voice in the constitutional order. From 1975 to 1990, a civil war wracked the country, pitting Lebanon's Muslims and their Palestinian allies against the Christians. During this period, the country endured foreign military interventions and disruption of normal governance as rival militias, representing religious factions, battled for control. A Syrian-dominated Arab Deterrent Force arrived in 1976 but failed to impose a lasting settlement.

In 1982, an Israeli invasion forced Palestinian guerillas from their strongholds in Lebanon. An incomplete withdrawal left a 15 km (9 mi) strip of southern Lebanese territory under Israeli occupation. In September 1988, a divided assembly failed to choose a replacement for outgoing president, Amin Gemayel. When his term expired, Gemayel appointed the Maronite army commander, General Michel Aoun, to head an interim military government. Claiming this government violated the 1943 agreement, the Muslim prime minister, Selim al-Hoss, declared his government the only legitimate authority. In March 1989, Lebanese troops loyal to Aoun clashed with Syrian forces. Urgent mediation efforts by Arab countries followed. A "charter of national reconciliation" was proposed to end the civil war. Members of the assembly then met in Taif, Saudi Arabia, to approve this charter. The Taif agreement called for constitutional changes, the disbanding of militias and reconstituting the factionalized Lebanese army into a unified force capable of maintaining internal security. In November 1989, the assembly ratified this agreement and elected a new Maronite president, Reni Mouwad. Aoun, who opposed the agreement because it did not stipulate the withdrawal of Syrian forces from Lebanon, declared himself president. Mouwad was soon assassinated and the assembly elected Elias Hrawi as his successor. The Taif accords opened deep fissures in Christian ranks. Violence between the Aoun-led "rejectionists" and "accommodationists" eventually resulted in Aoun's defeat in 1990 by joint Syrian-Lebanese military action.

Lebanon's return to relative normalcy is credited to the Taif accord. Most militias have been disbanded and the Lebanese army has successfully reasserted the government's authority. The improved political and security climate has buoyed investor confidence. However, the Syrian-dominated order has not yet consolidated support among the Maronite community, which remains uneasy with its diminished political power and Syria's role in Lebanon.

The first legislative elections in 20 years were held in 1992. Rafik Hariri was appointed prime minister. In 1995, Hariri resigned after a dispute with Assembly speaker, Nabih Berri, over a constitutional amendment allowing President Hrawi to serve a second term. A Syrian-backed compromise cleared the way for Hariri's reappointment as prime minister and passage of a constitutional amendment extending Hrawi's term for three years. On 15 October 1998, the National Assembly unanimously elected Emile Lahoud to succeed Hrawi as president.

## PERSONAL BACKGROUND

Emile Lahoud was born on 10 January 1936 to Jamil Lahoud and Adrinei Bajakian in the Christian enclave of Baabdat. He completed his secondary education at Broummana High School and then entered the Military College as a student officer in 1956. A year later, he left for Great Britain to attend the prestigious Dartmouth Naval Academy. Upon graduating, Lahoud received his commission as an officer in the Lebanese navy.

Lahoud comes from a prominent Maronite family, with a history of public service. His father, Jamil Lahoud, helped to build Lebanon's army and later served in the National Assembly, and as minister for social and labor affairs. In 1970, he ran unsuccessfully for president.

Lahoud is described as an austere "workaholic" who shuns the spotlight. He is said to believe in maintaining high standards of professional conduct and respect for the law. As a military officer, Lahoud earned a reputation for eschewing political or sectarian partisanship.

Married to Andrie Amadounian since 1967, Lahoud has two sons and a daughter. He is fluent in Arabic, French, English, and also speaks Armenian. Lahoud is technically oriented, reads avidly, and is well informed on international issues. Athletically inclined, he enjoys swimming, diving, and fast cars.

## RISE TO POWER

Lahoud began his military career as a naval officer, commanding patrol boats and landing vessels. In 1970, he was transferred to the fourth army division as transportation chief. Three years later, Lahoud was assigned to the army command in Yarze. In 1980, he was promoted to colonel and appointed army personnel director. In 1983, Lahoud became chief of military affairs in the Ministry of National Defense. Promoted to major-general in 1985, he briefly served as a deputy to General Aoun, the army commander. Aoun's decision to launch a "liberation war" against Syrian forces in Lebanon in 1989 prompted Lahoud to resign from his official duties. Reportedly dismayed by Aoun's ill-conceived actions, and by the disintegration of Lebanon's army into hostile sectarian camps, Lahoud retreated into private life. Later that year, he was called back to service.

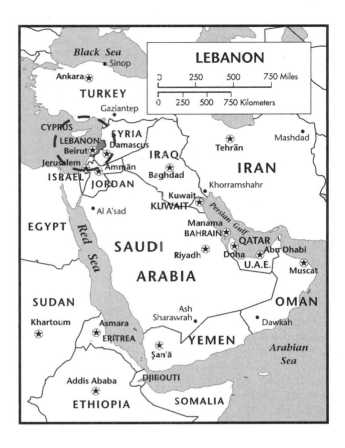

In November 1989, the government of Prime Minister Salim al-Hoss made Lahoud a general and appointed him army commander. He was charged with the task of rebuilding Lebanon's fragmented army. By all accounts, Lahoud successfully accomplished a task many thought impossible. He built an integrated, well-trained military force and ended political and religious interference in its ranks. Most analysts credit Lahoud's record of achievement as army commander for his subsequent elevation to the presidency.

By early 1998, it was unclear whether Hrawi's term, due to expire in October, would again be renewed. He had proven to be a weak leader, and his standing among Maronites was low. Other declared candidates seemed unlikely to win Syria's approval. Lahoud's name surfaced as a potential successor who would be acceptable to the Syrians and have credibility in the Maronite community. His reputation for political neutrality was a further asset. In an early October meeting between Hrawi and Syrian President Hafiz al-Assad, Lahoud was confirmed as Hrawi's preferred replacement. However, certain constitutional obstacles remained. On 13 October, the Assembly introduced a unique amendment to the constitutional clause requiring senior public servants to leave office two years before running for president. Two days later, Lahoud was unanimously elected president by the National Assembly. On 24 November 1998, he was sworn in as Lebanon's eleventh president. The election represented the country's first peaceful transition of power in nearly 30 years.

## LEADERSHIP

Lahoud is regarded as a capable and honest administrator. He enjoys broad public and parliamentary support. Perhaps more importantly, he is supported by Syria. Consequently,

Lahoud can claim a firm mandate for implementing much-needed reforms, tackling the problems of widespread corruption and entrenched sectarianism that plague Lebanon's public administration. Lahoud is also expected to provide a stronger voice for the Maronite community, which has felt increasingly marginalized in the country's new political order. Several prominent Maronites have welcomed Lahoud's election. Others have dismissed him as Syria's Lebanese satrap. Clearly, Lahoud's ability to fulfill his mandate depends on his influence in the ruling troika and will be constrained by the need to consider the interests of the country's religious communities and Syria. Forming a new government presented Lahoud with his first leadership test.

In the previous government, Prime Minister Hariri was the dominant figure in the troika leadership but was often at odds with Hrawi and Speaker Berri. These disputes, resolved only after Syrian mediation, underscored perceptions that the troika system created stalemates in leadership and hindered effective government. The troika's shortcomings may have helped strengthen Lahoud's hand and restored some of the presidency's old clout. Lahoud's cabinet choices suggest that he will exercise more influence in the new government than his predecessor. Hints of this shift were evident in the run-up to naming the cabinet when Lahoud and Hariri disagreed on the cabinet's composition. After consultations with Assembly members, Lahoud reappointed Hariri as premier. Hariri refused the offer, even though a clear majority in the Assembly backed his selection. Hariri accused the president of a constitutional breach, violating the Taif accord. He claimed that some assembly members had delegated Lahoud to choose the prime minister on their behalf, granting the president unconstitutional authority. Arguably, Hariri's decision may have been prompted by recognition of new limits on his influence. On 1 December 1998, Lahoud appointed Salim al-Hoss to be the new prime minister and head of a reform-minded cabinet. This veteran politician had been a frequent critic of Hariri. Lahoud's assertiveness has been welcomed in most quarters.

## DOMESTIC POLICY
Since the civil war ended, Lebanon's reconstruction has been the government's top priority. Hariri's administration emphasized economic infrastructure development, embarking on ambitious building and public works projects. To fund this effort, the government borrowed heavily and ran up huge deficits. Rapid economic growth followed, but critics note its uneven benefits that favored the wealthy minority at the expense of the poor. Hariri's programs also enlarged the bureaucracy in which nepotism and corruption were endemic.

Economic and administrative reforms spearhead the new government's plans. While the details are not firm, early rhetoric signals a reoriented economic strategy emphasizing the productive sectors, such as agriculture and manufacturing. There are few alternatives for dealing with the mushrooming public debt and fiscal deficits. Higher taxes coupled with improved collections, privatization of profitable state-owned enterprises, and restructuring of public utilities are being considered. Lahoud may cancel some planned public works projects. To get the budget under control and increase the bureaucracy's accountability, the government is also weighing several options, including merging or terminating some government agencies. A shake-up of the civil service is anticipated: patronage will be abolished and several high-ranking officers are expected to lose their jobs. The Hoss cabinet has lifted a four-year ban on public demonstrations and will proceed with electoral law reforms.

The Hoss government's 1999 budget projected increased spending of $5.5 billion and revenues of $3.4 billion. Higher taxes, privatization of loss-making public enterprises, and improved revenue collection are measures proposed to combat the deficit. Analysts, however, view the budget doing little to ease the fiscal deficit, which has grown to 15% of GDP. In November 1999, the government admitted it would not meet its deficit reduction target.

## FOREIGN POLICY
Observers anticipate little change in Lebanon's external policies under Lahoud. Since the passage of the Taif accord, Lebanon and Syria have moved closer, formalizing mutual security ties. Moreover, it is clear that Syrian troops will remain in Lebanon until a comprehensive peace treaty between Israel and Syria is reached. In public statements, Lahoud has supported resistance against Israel's occupation of a so-called "security zone" in southern Lebanon. He rejected a separate peace with Israel and reiterated his commitment to a coordinated Syrian-Lebanese stance on negotiations that include an Israeli pullout from Syria's Golan Heights. These remarks suggest that the new government will not be more responsive to Israel's 1998 offer of a conditional withdrawal from occupied Lebanese territory.

Lebanon's security and stability highlighted problems facing the new government in 1999. Even though a consensus in Israel favored an Israeli withdrawal from the "security zone," the cycle of attacks and reprisals continued in the area throughout the year. Early in the year, retaliatory Israeli air strikes against Hezballah strongholds occurred. The clashes escalated after a guerrilla ambush killed an Israeli general. The government rejected an Israeli demand to disarm the guerrillas. Prime Minister Hoss also denied reports alleging secret peace talks with Israel, which has sought security guarantees from Lebanon in exchange for withdrawal from the "security zone." Aware of Syrian interests, the Hoss government has insisted that it will not strike a separate deal, and that the Israeli withdrawal occurs only within the framework of a comprehensive peace settlement involving Syria. The new Barak government in Israel has committed to pull out of this zone by July 2000, indicating it will do so even if no agreement is reached.

## ADDRESS
Palais de Baabda, Beirut, Lebanon

## REFERENCES
*Al-Ahram Weekly*, 22–28 October 1998.

*Daily Star*, July 1998–January 1999.

*EIU Country Profile: Lebanon, 1998–1999*. London: The Economist Intelligence Unit, Ltd., 1998.

*Europa World Yearbook*. London: Europa Publications Ltd., 1998.

*Middle East*, December 1998.

*Middle East Policy*, October 1998.

**Profile researched and written by Taufiq Rashid, Indiana University (3/99; updated 5/2000).**

# LESOTHO

### Pakalitha Mosisili
### Prime Minister
*(pronounced "PAK-a-leeth-a mo-see-SEE-lee")*

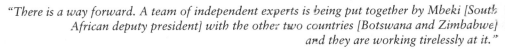

*"There is a way forward. A team of independent experts is being put together by Mbeki [South African deputy president] with the other two countries [Botswana and Zimbabwe] and they are working tirelessly at it."*

The Kingdom of Lesotho (pronounced "leh-SOO-too") is a landlocked enclave of 30,355 sq km (11,720 sq mi), surrounded by the Republic of South Africa. It is a country of rugged mountainous terrain, dissected by deep river valleys at elevations of 8,100 to 17,700 m (approximately 5,000 to 11,000 ft) above sea level.

Most Basotho, as the people of Lesotho are called, are of southern Sotho origin and speak Sesotho, a Bantu language. English is the second official language, but many Basotho are also fluent in other southern African languages or Afrikaans. Europeans, Asians, and people of mixed origins constitute less than 1% of Lesotho's citizens.

Over 80% of Lesotho's two million people engage in subsistence farming, but agriculture accounts for just 20% of GDP, and basic foodstuffs must be imported. Most of Lesotho's arable land is in the west of the country, with high population densities reaching 200 per sq km. The result of the geographic constraints, combined with the growing population and periodic droughts, has been land shortage, soil erosion, and falling agricultural productivity. Maize is the staple crop. Sorghum, beans, dry peas, oats, and sunflower oil are also cultivated. Summer wheat is the only export crop for Lesotho, most going to South Africa. Cattle exports, along with wool and mohair, also contribute to the agricultural earnings of the country though this sector of the economy is underexploited.

Lesotho's major export continues to be laborers to South African mines, farms, and industry. Up to 60% of annual household income is derived from migrant remittances. Migrant workers made up an estimated 60% of the male work force in 1996 in South Africa. The remittances of these workers represent 45% of Lesotho's gross national product. Water export to South Africa from the Lesotho Highlands Water Project (LHWP) is achieving greater and greater importance in the country's earnings. Revenue from Lesotho's customs and monetary union with South Africa (the Southern African Customs Union) also constitutes a substantial portion of government income. In addition, foreign aid from international donors has also been a vital source of sustenance. With no exploitable mineral resources and only small-scale industries, Lesotho seeks to attract tourists with its casinos and spectacular mountains, which offer winter snow and skiing. Lesotho's unit of currency is the *loti.*

## POLITICAL BACKGROUND

Lesotho coalesced in the early 19th century under the leadership of a shrewd diplomat and warrior, Moshoeshoe I, from remnants of peoples displaced by an expanding Zulu kingdom. The nation became known as Basutoland when it accepted British protection in 1868. Colonial rule prevented the country from incorporation within South Africa but left it economically destitute and politically unstable. With its most fertile land lost to the Orange Free State province of South Africa, the Basotho were compelled to eke out a living in the rugged mountainous terrain. Excessive plowing and grazing, torrential rains, and protracted droughts caused serious erosion and rapid deterioration of the arable land.

Independence from British colonial rule was not gained until 1966. Since then Lesotho has experienced a chaotic governing situation. The 1966 constitution took the form of a parliamentary system with a constitutional monarch, Moshoeshoe II, serving as head of state. It provided for an independent judiciary and public service commission and included a comprehensive Bill of Rights. Executive power resided in the elected prime minister, Leabua Jonathan, and a cabinet staffed by the conservative Basotho National Party (BNP), which won the 1965 pre-independence election. Strong parliamentary opposition came from Ntsu Mokhele's Basutoland Congress Party (BCP) and the royalist Marematlou Freedom Party (MFP). Despite losing the 1970 election, Leabua Jonathan remained in power with support from the paramilitary police unit and the South African government. Jonathan's civilian rule by decree persisted until 1986.

Worsening civil strife, a mutiny over pay and conditions of service in the paramilitary force, South African commando raids on African National Congress installations in the capital city of Maseru, and a South African economic embargo precipitated the seizure of power by Metsing Lekhanya in 1986. Acting with the approval of the South African government and buoyed by popular disgust with the old regime, Lekhanya replaced the civilian autocracy with a military dictatorship disguised as a coalition regime with the independent-minded monarch Moshoeshoe II. A six-member military council presided over a council of ministers, which included 15 civilian politicians drawn from various partisan backgrounds and three military officers.

Lekhanya's popularity and credibility were gradually undermined by his own actions and by changes in the regional environment beyond his control. Rapid reform in

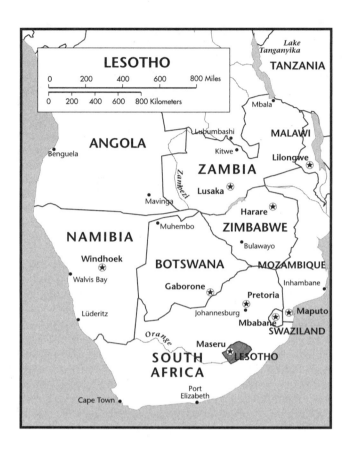

South Africa after the release of Nelson Mandela made foreign aid donors more willing to require democratization as a condition for further assistance. Having promised to return Lesotho to civilian rule, Lekhanya could no longer suppress popular criticism and dissent from an outspoken popular press. Controversy raged around Lekhanya's dethroning of Moshoeshoe II and installing the 27-year-old heir Letsie III with only ceremonial duties.

In 1991, Lekhanya was forced to resign at gunpoint by soldiers who had been unsuccessful in their attempts to gain wage increases. Colonel Phisoana Ramamema, the least visible member of the ruling junta, was thrust into power. He presided over a process of constitutional and economic restructuring that permitted the return of Lesotho to civilian rule with a small budget surplus.

Elections in 1993 brought Ntsu Mokhele to power. The BCP won all 65 seats in the national assembly. In August 1994, King Letsie III announced the suspension of the constitution and the dissolution of the Mokhele government. Opposition to this move was widespread and daily affairs came to a standstill. Representatives from Botswana, South Africa, and Zimbabwe were called upon to resolve this crisis. Their plan resulted in the reinstatement of the Mokhele government, the abdication of Letsie III (who assumed the role of crown prince), and the reinstatement of King Moshoeshoe. Although Letsie III was returned to the throne after the death of Moshoeshoe in a 1996 auto accident, he pledged not to involve the monarchy in political life. In 1998, the ailing Mokhele announced his retirement, paving the way for his deputy, Pakalitha Mosisili, to assume leadership.

## PERSONAL BACKGROUND
Bethuel Pakalitha Mosisili was born on 14 March 1945 at Qacha's Nek, Lesotho. He is an educator with B.A., M.A. and M.Ed. degrees in linguistics and education. For more than 10 years, Mosisili was a lecturer at the University of Lesotho (1972–83). He also taught at three South African universities: University of Fort Hare (1983–84), University of Transkei (1985–88), and University of Zululand (1989–93). In addition to his university teaching positions, Mosisili acted as external examiner in African languages and pedagogy for various universities. He maintains active membership in several academic associations, including the Lesotho Educational Research Foundation, African Languages Association of Southern Africa, and the Southern African Pedagogical Society. He is married and has two daughters and two sons.

## RISE TO POWER
Mosisili joined the Basotholand Congress Party of Ntsu Mokhele in 1967 and remained an active party member for the next 30 years. In 1993, he was elected to parliament, representing his birthplace, Qacha's Nek. From 1993 until 1995 Mosisili held the minister of education portfolio. In February 1995 he was promoted to the post of deputy prime minister. Fearing a defeat in upcoming BCP elections, Mokhele led a mass walkout in 1995 and formed the Lesotho Congress for Democracy (LCD). A majority of the BCP MPs followed Mokhele, including Mosisili, who was named deputy leader of the new political party. He became heir-apparent to the aging Mokhele and held three ministerial portfolios (deputy prime minister, minister of home affairs, and minister of local government) from 1995 until 1998. When Prime Minister Mokhele announced his unexpected retirement from public life, the way was clear for Mosisili to assume leadership of the LCD. His party scored a landslide victory in elections held on 23 May 1998, winning 79 of 80 seats in parliament. Mosisili was sworn in as the new prime minister.

## LEADERSHIP
The country's political, economic, and social woes are enormous. The most immediate concern faced by Mosisili on taking office was the crisis created by his party's victory in the May 1998 elections. Allegations of vote rigging led to mass demonstrations. In response, Mosisili agreed to the appointment of a regional committee to investigate these charges. The South African deputy president, Thabo Mbeki, led an investigative team which reported "serious concerns" about the voting but did not recommend that the election be invalidated. Demonstrators and opposition party leaders indicated that they did not accept the Mbeki mediation effort. Instead, they called for the immediate removal of Mosisili and the formation of a new unity government.

As protests grew increasingly violent and the Mosisili government appeared to be losing control of its military, South African troops were asked to restore order. With little public support, the intervention proved more difficult than expected. The troops met fierce resistance from Lesotho's mutinous army, resulting in 60 deaths and over $150 million in property damage. Nine days after the South African invasion began, government and opposition parties sat down at the negotiating table and agreed to hold new elections within 18 months. A Transitional Executive Committee was created to oversee preparations for new elections and to restructure Lesotho's Independent Electoral Commission.

Parliamentary elections were set for April 2000. Lesotho's Interim Political Authority (IPA) announced in May 1993 that the number of seats in the kingdom's parliament would be increased by 50 to 130 for the upcoming 2000 elections. The Mosisili government remained in control until elections are held.

## DOMESTIC POLICY

Lesotho is one of the world's least developed countries. The country's per capita GDP has been estimated at US$2,400. The Lesotho Highlands Water Project (LHWP) increasingly dominates government planning and revenue calculations. Spending on construction for this project has resulted in increasing customs revenues. These revenues now amount to US$40 million per year. As Korinna Horta, an environmental economist with the Environmental Defense Fund, states: "The LHWP is likely to overwhelm Lesotho and determine its political economy for generations to come. The sheer size of the project diverts attention from any other possible development programs for Lesotho." In July 1998, the World Bank approved construction of the Mohale Dam, the second of five dams to be constructed. The project has created great consternation in many quarters as it emphasizes a supply response to South Africa's water concerns rather than conservation efforts. Within Lesotho, thousands of people have been displaced by the Katse Dam, and there has been little success in creating new incomes for these families.

Unemployment hovers consistently around 50%. Government response has come in the form of increased attention to tourism and focus on education for its citizenry. Despite the poor quality of most of Lesotho for arable cultivation, over 80% of the population depends on agriculture for subsistence. Drought, soil erosion, insecure land tenure, and poor farming practices have led to a sharp drop in revenue.

Lesotho enjoys a high literacy rate, and its laborers have an excellent reputation in South Africa. The government has attempted to use these advantages to attract manufacturing capital, combined with tax inducements and duty-free access to the EU and SACU markets. Attempts have also been made to encourage South African firms to relocate by offering various incentives to do so. The result of these efforts led to an annual average growth rate in the industrial sector of 13.8% in 1985–95 and an increase in manufacturing's contribution to GDP from 6% in 1986 to 16.4% in 1995. Tourism earnings have also increased.

## FOREIGN POLICY

External affairs will always be dominated by Lesotho's relationship with the Republic of South Africa. Geography alone requires this domination as the country is surrounded on all sides by the Republic. Still poorly developed in transportation infrastructure, Lesotho has relied heavily on South African road and railway outlets. The Lesotho Highlands Water Project, negotiated in 1980 and officially signed in 1986, has drawn the two countries closer together. Diplomatic relations at the ambassadorial level were established in May 1992. During the South African apartheid era, sharp tensions were inevitable. This situation ended when the apartheid system was dismantled in 1994 with the election of Nelson Mandela to the South African presidency. Problems continue over cross-border cattle thefts and unresolved land claims in South Africa's Orange Free State.

In late 1995, South Africa announced a new policy of granting permanent residency rights to migrant workers. This policy change could have a very negative impact on Lesotho's revenue figures. The compulsory Lesotho Deferred Payment Scheme, set up in 1974, initially gave the Lesotho government access to 60% of migrant laborers' wages (this was reduced to 20% in 1990) in a general account deposited every month in Lesotho Bank. This money is then available for the government's short-term use until the worker returns. The scheme is currently under study, with the National Union of Miners calling for its abolition, and will in all likelihood be phased out in the near future, a further blow to Lesotho government revenues. As 1998 came to a close, the question remained as to what the long-term effects of the South African intervention would be.

At the outset of 1999, Lesotho's opposition alliance was unhappy with the overstay of the peacekeeping forces and requested the United Nations intervene to get the South African and Botswana troops out of Lesotho. South Africa's military intelligence and other foreign soldiers were openly warned to leave the country by the end of July or face "elimination." The warnings were seemingly heeded as South Africa and Botswana began withdrawing their forces in April.

## ADDRESS

Prime Minister's Office
P.O. Box 527
Maseru 100, Lesotho

## REFERENCES

Africa News Online. [Online] Available http://www.africanews.org/south/lesotho (Accessed June 1998, August 1998, and April 2000).

*Africa South of the Sahara*. 27th ed. London: Europa Publications Ltd., 1997.

*Electronic Mail and Guardian*. [Online] Available http://www.mg.co.za/mg/news. (Accessed June 1998, August 1998, and April 2000).

*Lesotho's Long Journey: Hard Choices at the Crossroads*. Maseru, Lesotho: Sechaba Consultants, 1995.

Profile researched and written by Kathryn Green, California State University, San Bernardino (12/98; updated by Ezekiel Kalipeni, University of Illinois 3/2000)

# LIBERIA

## Charles Taylor
### President
*(pronounced "CHAR-els TAY-lor")*

*"We are one people with one purpose, with one country.
Let us join hands and together build this country for our children."*

The Republic of Liberia is located on the Atlantic coast of the African continent and is bordered to the northwest by Sierra Leone, to the north by Guinea, and to the east by Cote d'Ivoire. It occupies a total area of 111,370 sq km (43,000 sq mi).

Liberia is home to nearly 3 million people. Some 500,000 refugees continue to live in neighboring countries. Over 95% of the population is ethnically indigenous African, drawn from more than two dozen groups; the remaining 5% are Americo-Liberians, descended from 19th century American settlers who founded a colony near what is now the capital of Monrovia. English is the official language and is spoken by approximately 20% of the population. In terms of religion, the majority of Liberians profess traditional African beliefs; however approximately 20% are Muslim and 10% are Christian.

The economy has been decimated by a seven-year civil war, and most statistics are either outdated or unreliable. Exports include iron ore, rubber, timber, and coffee. Liberia has also become a transshipment point for illicit drugs. Inflation in 1994 was estimated at 50%; in 1996 it ran at 100%, but no annual indicators were available for measure in 1997–98. The official currency is the Liberian dollar, which is officially linked at parity to the US dollar. The approximated per capita income is us$1,000.

## POLITICAL BACKGROUND

The Republic of Liberia has its origins in a 19th century effort to create a colony in Africa for the increasing numbers of freed American slaves, coupled with missionary desires to gain a foothold in the region. In 1822 a settlement was established near what is now Monrovia. As more settlers arrived the territory grew, both through annexation of neighboring settlements and through the subjugation of indigenous peoples. The Free and Independent Republic of Liberia was declared on 26 July 1847.

The Liberian government has historically been patterned after that of the United States, and its Constitution echoes that of the US as well. The country's president is elected to a renewable six-year term by universal suffrage. Its legislature is the bicameral National Assembly, which is composed of a 26-member Senate and 64-member House of Representatives.

One of the most notable characteristics of the Liberian state prior to 1980 was its basis of privilege. Political and economic power was wielded by the minority elite Americo-Liberians, about 50 extended families, who were directly descended from the former American slave settlers. The introduction of universal suffrage in the 1940s did little to shift the balance of power, since few of the newly enfranchised bothered to vote.

The "evolution of privilege," as coined by the late Professor J. Gus Liebenow, received its wake up call from William Tubman, True Whig candidate elected president in 1944. Until his death in 1971, Tubman introduced reforms intended to eliminate social and economic discrimination against indigenous Liberians. Tubman was succeeded by his vice president, William Tolbert. Tolbert held office until 1980, amid increasing pressure from indigenous Liberians to speed up the pace of reforms. In 1978 the Progressive Alliance of Liberia was formed, representing the first significant opposition to the government. In April 1979 riots and looting broke out in response to a government plan to increase the retail price of rice. The now infamous rice riots led to Tolbert's assumption of emergency powers. In April 1980, Tolbert was assassinated in a coup led by Master Sergeant Samuel Doe. On assuming power as chairman of the People's Redemption Council (PRC), Doe suspended the Constitution and proscribed all political parties.

Thus began a decade of political and institutional upheaval in Liberia. Sergeant Doe, an illiterate career soldier, unleashed a reign of terror, during which summary executions became routine. In 1981, a commission was appointed to draft a new constitution, and it was announced that a return to civilian rule would occur by 1986. In July 1984 the new Constitution was approved by 78% of registered voters. In the same month Doe dissolved the PRC and appointed an interim national assembly. In August, Doe founded the National Democratic Party of Liberia (NDPL) and announced his candidacy for the presidency. He also lifted the ban on political parties.

By 1985, almost a dozen political parties had been created, but experienced significant legal obstacles in attempting to complete the registration process for the upcoming elections. Elections took place in October after a fractious campaign where opposition leaders were detained, and opposition parties proscribed. Doe won the election with 50.9% of the vote, but the NDPL won 22 of the 26 Senate seats and 51 of the 64 seats in the House of Representatives. The elections were widely regarded as fraudulent, and several analysts consider them to have been the catalyst for the violence that followed.

Doe's tenure was marked by violence, brutality, and uncontrolled opposition to his chaotic policies. Prior to his inauguration, Doe was the target of an attempted coup. Subsequent fighting between government and rebel forces led to at least 600 deaths. Opposition leaders were once more detained and others deemed likely to be critical of the government were banned. Throughout the late 1980s, the Doe administration continued to operate in an increasingly tenuous atmosphere in the face of mounting unpopularity.

On 24 December 1989, an armed insurrection began in the northeastern border region of Nimba County. The rebels were members of the previously unknown National Patriotic Front of Liberia (NPFL), an opposition group led by Charles Taylor, a former government official in the Doe administration.

## PERSONAL BACKGROUND

Charles McArthur Taylor was born in Liberia in 1948, the son of an American father and Liberian mother. Through his mother's side of the family, Taylor is Americo-Liberian. The family lived until recently in Clay-Ashland, a town just outside the capital. Taylor attended Bentley College in Waltham, Massachusetts, graduating with a bachelor's degree in economics in 1977. He then moved to nearby Boston where he worked as a mechanic.

Despite his Americo-Liberian lineage, Taylor's political sympathies have long been with the indigenous people of Liberia. During his college years he organized other exiled Liberians to oppose the Tolbert government, which was dominated by the politically powerful descendants of the first American settlers. He was thrilled when Samuel Doe took power in a coup, despite the vicious nature of his regime. Taylor returned to Liberia shortly after Tolbert's assassination in 1980 and joined Doe's administration. He headed the General Services Agency, whose principal function was the allocation of funds to government ministries, and was appointed a personal advisor to the President.

Taylor remained in Liberia until 1983 when he fled to the US amid allegations of corruption. The Liberian government charged that Taylor had embezzled US$900,000 from the government and they sought his extradition. A Boston court ruled that there was evidence to support the allegations, and Taylor was held in the Plymouth House of Corrections awaiting extradition to Liberia. In 1985, Taylor escaped from jail and fled to parts unknown, although there are some indications that he spent a large part of the next five years in Libya, as the guest of Colonel Muammar al-Qadhafi.

## RISE TO POWER

From 1985–89, Taylor established his leadership of the NPFL and prepared his Christmas Eve invasion, which subsequently launched a seven-year civil war. He established NPFL headquarters at Gbarnga, near the Liberian border with Guinea, and consolidated his control over the country. He created a new currency and banking system, developed an international airfield, and reestablished exports of diamonds, gold, rubber, and timber—in effect, he established a country within a country with himself as its warlord.

Throughout the early part of 1990, Taylor had the support not only of the majority of Liberians, but of the United States

as well. The US was a staunch ally, despite legitimate concerns about gross human rights abuses. Taylor appeared to be a preferable alternative to Samuel Doe; he was well-spoken and articulate, repeatedly expressed a commitment to democratic ideals, and stated his intention to hold elections and permit vigorous opposition.

By late July 1990, however, support for Taylor was evaporating both at home and abroad. When his troops entered Monrovia in July, Taylor claimed executive authority, but was immediately challenged by a faction within the NPFL, led by Prince Yormie Johnson. Johnson's troops quickly captured parts of the capital. While Taylor's control over the rest of the country remained unchallenged, he was unable to gain control over Monrovia. The Economic Community of West African States (ECOWAS) repeatedly attempted to negotiate a ceasefire without success, and in late August the ECOWAS Monitoring Group (ECOMOG) was dispatched to enforce peace in the capital. Doe and Johnson had agreed to accept ECOMOG troops but Taylor greeted their arrival with armed opposition.

On 30 August 1990, exiled opposition leaders met in Gambia, and elected Amos Sawyer to be the leader of an Interim Government of National Unity. The pitched battle for Monrovia nonetheless continued and on September 10, after being captured by Johnson's rebels, Samuel Doe was executed.

Taylor rejected the authority of President Sawyer, as well as any proposal that would require power-sharing with the opposition. His tactics for maintaining his position became increasingly brutal as the conflict escalated. Despite numerous ECOWAS-brokered ceasefires, the increasing involvement of ECOMOG troops in the conflict, and a popular desire to end the fighting, Monrovia remained essentially under siege.

Throughout numerous setbacks to peace, the international community insisted upon elections and a reinvigoration of civil society. Only when it became obvious that Taylor would not achieve his objectives militarily, did he accept the ballot box alternative.

Presidential and legislative elections were held on 19 July 1997. Taylor transformed the NPFL into the NPP (National Patriotic Party), and orchestrated an effective, well-financed campaign. Weary of war, 85% of registered voters turned out to give Taylor a lop-sided victory. Taylor was officially declared the victor on July 24 with 75% of the vote. The elections were closely monitored by international observers and found to be generally free and fair.

## LEADERSHIP

Even before his official inauguration, Taylor began the process of forming a government. Declaring that he needed the talents of his former rivals in order to pursue reconstruction of the war-ravaged country, Taylor pledged to include some opposition leaders in his administration.

Unfortunately, very little in Taylor's past behavior indicated that he would govern by consensus. With the help of his official advisors and his kitchen cabinet of family members and NPP cohorts, Taylor has used his executive authority to push through his agenda for the country. He bullies his opponents, and without a system of functional checks and balances in place, few individuals or institutions are his match.

However, Taylor's power is not monolith. In November 1999, NPP members of the House of Representatives ordered an immediate halt to the demolition of a large barracks in Monrovia, citing the unconstitutionality of the decision to grant the building to a high-profile charity. The bill to authorize the demolition had not passed through the National Assembly. Then, in March 2000, buckling under pressure from Catholic Archbishop Michael Francis, the winner of the 1999 Robert Kennedy Human Rights award, Taylor allowed Radio Veritas to resume broadcasting. In January, police had closed Veritas and Star Radio, Liberia's only non-commercial privately held news and information stations. Future challenges to his authority may come from within the NPP, perhaps discontented members who resent the concentration of power in the hands of a few confidantes.

President Taylor's awareness of his dubious popularity may be seen in his retention of Cohen and Woods, International, a Washington-based public relations firm run by former Assistant Secretary of State for Africa, Herman (Hank) Cohen. The firm may have helped persuade a US court in Massachusetts to drop criminal charges against Taylor, and to allow him to address the UN General Assembly in September 1999. Image notwithstanding, a political force to unseat Taylor, the New Democratic Alternative of Liberia, was launched in 1999 on both sides of the Atlantic.

## DOMESTIC POLICY

Since 1997, four domestic priorities were driving Taylor's policy: rehabilitation of the social sector, rebuilding the basic infrastructure of the country, restarting the economy, and restoring peace and order. None of these were achievable without significant donor participation.

During the war, social infrastructure was disrupted or destroyed. Nearly 150,000 Liberians were killed, 500,000 sought refuge in neighboring countries or fled into exile abroad, and several hundred thousand were displaced from their homes but remained within the country. From 1997 to 1999, donors helped resettle more than one million internally displaced persons and refugees in their home areas. Donor-led revitalization of the agriculture sector, improvements in basic education and health services, and vocational training for ex-combatants were important to achieving resettlement.

Due to years of neglect and to the war, Liberia's infrastructure is essentially non-existent. Roads are in disrepair, and electric power lines are still down. Aside from privately owned generators, Monrovia was still without power in May 2000. Indeed, Taylor declared that restoring electricity to Monrovia was not a priority. Despite his intransigence, hundreds of schools, clinics, four hospitals, dozens of market buildings, and several hundred bridges, latrines, and water wells have been renovated.

By May 2000, Taylor had provided no clear vision of his government's economic recovery program. Observers alleged that the most lucrative contracts in gold, diamonds, and lumber were being awarded to friends of senior ruling party officials. After 41 years of nominal operations, the Bong Mining Company about 50 miles north of Monrovia closed down. One bright spot was the June 1999 signing of a new concession agreement between the Liberian government and Firestone/Bridgestone Rubber Plantation.

Although Liberia was nominally at peace in 2000, a state of insecurity prevailed, and a cessation of hostilities had not yet occurred. Dissidents controlled areas of Lofa County in the Forest Region, and incidents of violence were commonplace. Since 1998, a Lutheran World Services warehouse was looted, UNHCR vehicles were looted by armed bandits, several Western aid workers were abducted, and the state security service (SSS) harassed and intimidated press critics and political opponents. Local elections were delayed presumably due to lack of funds.

## FOREIGN POLICY

Liberia is a member of the United Nations, the Mano River Union comprising Guinea and Sierra Leone, and ECOWAS. Relations with Guinea and Sierra Leone have been strained because of cross-border attacks, Taylor's alleged support for the RUF, and refugee flows. Liberia ended its dependence on the regional peacekeeping force, ECOMOG, when the last of the forces left in October 1999.

Historically, US-Liberian relations have been close, but they were strained following a shooting incident in front of the US Embassy in Monrovia in September 1998. Beginning 29 July 2000, Liberia will be subject to sanctions under the Brooke-Alexander Amendment for failing to meet payments on its US bilateral debt. These sanctions will prevent any bilateral US assistance to aid the Liberian government directly. It does not prevent humanitarian assistance or aid to NGOs and civil society groups.

**ADDRESS**

Executive Mansion
P.O. Box 10–9001
Capitol Hill
1000 Monrovia 10, Liberia

**REFERENCES**

Africa News Online. [Online] Available http://www.africanews.org/west/stories/1999_feat1.html (Accessed 5/00).

AfricaOnline. [Online] Available http://www.africa-online.com (Accessed 5/00).

*Africa Report,* March–December 1994.

"Liberia." *Africa South of the Sahara,* Europa Publishers, 1999.

*American Heritage,* December 1995.

*Boston Globe,* 21 July–3 August 1997.

*Commonweal,* 1 June 1996.

*Current History,* May 1996.

*The Economist,* 3 September 1994–26 July 1997.

*EIU Country Reports.* Economist Intelligence Unit Ltd, 1999.

Integrated Regional Information Network (IRIN). [Online] Available http://www.reliefweb.int/IRIN (Accessed 5/00).

*Journal of Democracy,* July 1995.

Liebenow, J. Gus. *Liberia: The Quest for Democracy.* Bloomington: Indiana University Press, 1985.

*MacLean's,* 27 May 1996.

*New Republic,* 13 May 1996.

*New York Times,* 14 April 1992.

*Newsweek,* 24 April 1996.

*UN Chronicle,* December 1995–Summer 1996.

*US Department of State Dispatch,* 16 October 1995.

**Profile researched and written by Alison Doherty Munro (10/97; Updated by Robert J. Groelsema (5/00).**

# LIBYA

## Mu'ammar Al Qadhafi
### Head of State
*(pronounced "moh-AH-mar al guh-DAH-fee")*

*"The instrument of government is the prime political problem which faces human communities."*

Officially known as the Socialist People's Libyan Arab Jamahiriya, Libya is situated in the north of Africa. It is bordered by the Mediterranean Sea to the north, Egypt to the east, Sudan to the southeast, Chad and Niger to the south, and Algeria and Tunisia to the west. Much of Libya's land area is desert, part of the Sahara, with a few scattered oases throughout. Libya's capital is Tripoli, part of the northwestern region called Tripolitania. The other major city of the country is Benghazi, on the Cyrenaica peninsula in the northeast of the country and bordering the Mediterranean Sea, as does Tripoli. Libya's total surface area is 1,760,000 sq km (679,360 sq mi). The population has been estimated at 4,993,000, with an annual growth rate of 2.4%. The Libyan currency is the *dinar*. Per capita GDP has been estimated at $6,700. There is a negative GDP growth rate, an inflation rate of 24.2%, and an unemployment rate of 30%. Arabic is the official language, and ethnically, Arabic-speaking Sunni Muslims of mixed Arab and Berber ancestry make up well over 90% of the indigenous population. The remaining groups are Berber, Tawariq, sub-Saharan Africans, and small but long-settled Greek and Maltese communities. Libya's primary export is crude petroleum. Its major trading partners are Italy, Germany, Spain, France, the United Kingdom, and Greece.

## POLITICAL BACKGROUND

The coastal areas of Libya were part of the Ottoman Empire for several hundred years before the Islamic Sanusiya movement formed in the 19th century and became the major pole of resistance to the Italians, whose conquest began in 1911. It was not until the 1930s, however, under Mussolini, that the Italians completed their conquest of Libya with very repressive policies to solidify their control. Resistance to them ended with the capture, trial, and hanging of Omar Mukhtar, the leader of the resistance, while the head of the Sanusiya order took refuge in Egypt under British protection. Italian colonial policy consisted of heavy subsidies to Italian colonists, whose numbers had reached 110,000 by 1940. During World War II Libya was a major battleground between British, German, and Italian armies. After the war, due to much indecision on the part of the victorious Allied powers, the future of Libya was laid at the feet of the United Nations, which voted in 1951 for an independent Libyan monarchy under the Grand Sanusi, Idris, and uniting the three provinces of Cyrenaica, the Fezzan (the vast Saharan central portion of the country), and Tripolitania. The constitutional monarchy existed from 1951 to 1969.

During that period the agreement with the United States and Britain for operation of Wheelus Field, a strategically important military base, and other air bases for Britian provided the major source of employment for Libya's population. The monarchy was conservative and distrustful of the political process. Political parties were soon banned after its establishment. Women were not granted the right to vote until 1963.

On 1 September 1969, a group of young army officers, influenced by the neighboring Egyptian revolutionary government and doctrines of Jamal Abd Al Nasir, deposed King Idris when he was out of the country for medical treatment and proclaimed a Libyan Arab Republic. The coup was led by Capt. Muammar Muhammad al-Qadhafi.

Qadhafi established a very deliberate policy of change, including closure of Wheelus and the British bases to outside control and various attempts to forge Arab unity pacts and unions with other Arab governments. The 1977 Libyan constitution incorporates a blend of Islamic and socialist theories espoused in Qadhafi's *Green Book* and his *Third Universal Theory*. The direct people's authority constitutes the political order while the social system is governed by the *Holy Quran*. Political institutions are represented by people's congresses, committees, trade unions, and vocational syndicates.

Qadhafi is the de facto head of state and ultimate decision maker. Nominally, however, Libya is headed by the secretary of the General People's Congress and run by the secretary of the General People's Committee.

The General People's Committee is the executive branch of government, with people's committees acting as ministries. The administration is run by secretaries who are responsible for carrying out government policies. The General People's Congress, on the other hand, is the legislative branch of government. It convenes biannually, and delegates are elected by popular committees and congresses at local and regional levels. Libya has no political parties.

## PERSONAL BACKGROUND

Mu'ammar Al Qadhafi was born in 1942 in the region of Sirte, on the Mediterranean coast of Libya. He was the only surviving son and the youngest child of a poor family belonging to the Qadhadhifa, an Arabized Berber tribe. In 1952, after an initial religious education, he was sent to a secular elementary school in Sirte, where his schoolmates taunted him for being nothing more than a poor bedouin. Four years later he moved with his family to the Fezzan province, where he attended the Seb'a Preparatory School. The five years Qadhafi spent at Seb'a, between 1956 and 1961, were his politically formative years. Major economic and political changes were taking place in neighboring Egypt where the charismatic Jamal Abd Al Nasir had established himself as the champion of Arab unity. Nasir's leadership had a profound impact on Qadhafi. Inspired by Nasirism, he created the first Command Committee, composed of many of those who would later become members of Libya's Revolutionary Command Council (RCC). Qadhafi was expelled from school in 1961 for his political activities. Qadhafi and his family left Seb'a and moved on to Misrata, in Tripolitania, where he completed his secondary education and prepared to enter college. In Misrata, he re-established contact with many of his childhood friends from Sirte, with whom he promptly began talking about a new order in Libya. After graduation in 1963, Qadhafi and two of his closest friends joined the military academy in Benghazi. There they created the nucleus of the Free Unionist Officers Movement, which was an organization aiming at overthrowing the Sanusi monarchy and taking over power in the country.

## RISE TO POWER

After graduating from the Military Academy in 1965, Qadhafi was sent to Britain to attend an army school at Bavington Hythe in Beaconfield, where he took a six-month signals course. On his return to Libya he enrolled at the University of Benghazi and majored in history. He never completed his studies but was commissioned in 1966 to the signals corps of the Libyan army and posted at the barracks outside Benghazi. Three years later, on 1 September 1969, the new order in Libya first conceived in Misrata was realized when the Free Unionist Officers carried out a coup d'etat and proclaimed the Libyan Arab Republic. On 13 September, Qadhafi was appointed president of the Revolutionary Command Council.

## LEADERSHIP

In September 1999, Qadhafi celebrated 30 years as the head of the Libyan government. Commentators have described Qadhafi's policies during these years in power as "revolutionary," "idiosyncratic," and "confused." Qadhafi's first years in power were remarkable for his persistent, if unsuccessful, attempts to bring about the union of Libya with other Arab countries, notably Egypt, Syria, and Tunisia, among others. All of these attempts, however, remained fruitless, despite Qadhafi's enthusiasm for union.

Failing to achieve the hoped-for political mergers, Qadhafi adopted a new course, that of natural socialism. In May 1973, he presented his political philosophy in his *Third International Theory,* an alternative to "capitalist materialism and communist atheism." His principles comprised an unusual blend of Islamic fundamentalism and socialism, the application of which went through several phases. The first, between 1969 and 1973, was characterized by the twin process of nationalization and Libyanization. Subsidiaries of international oil companies operating in Libya were nation-

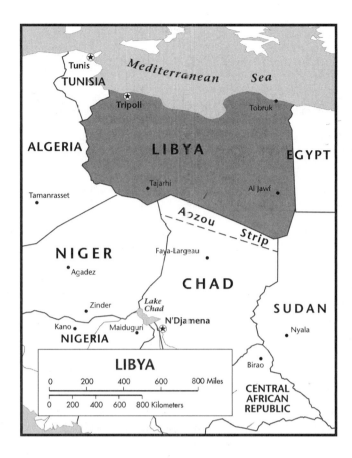

alized; branches of foreign banks were put in Libyan hands; and foreign property was taken over by the state.

During the second phase, 1973 to 1975, Qadhafi concentrated on building a power base for his regime by redistributing some of the country's oil wealth among the largest possible number of Libyans and providing them with much-needed social services. Industry received a big boost, and many new plants and factories were opened between 1973 and 1975.

*The Green Book,* meanwhile of which the first volume, *The Solution to the Problem of Democracy,* had appeared in 1976, heralded more drastic economic policies. Workers were encouraged to take over and administer industrial and commercial enterprises. Tenants became owners of their homes, paying mortgages to the state rather than rent to the landlords. Public corporations replaced the private sector in foreign trade, and large government cooperatives became substitutes for small retail traders.

On 2 March 1979, Qadhafi, stressing the need to separate the state apparatus from revolutionary action, claimed to abandon all official posts, remaining only the "leader, theoretician, and symbol" of the revolution. The people would henceforth "exercise and consolidate all power" in conformity with direct democracy as defined in *The Green Book.*

The phase between 1980 and 1987 was a very difficult one for the Libyan leader. The fall in oil prices and the imposition of economic sanctions on Libya by the US and other Western powers for his alleged involvement with international terrorist groups further eroded Libya's economy. It became indebted, had to freeze or cancel many of its industrial and housing projects, and by the mid-1980s resorted to expelling tens of thousands of foreign workers, whom it could no longer employ or pay. Black-marketeering flourished as Libyans found ways to circumvent the state's Draconian economic measures. The smuggling of subsidized products such as rice, oil, and tea from Libya to neighboring states where they were sold for higher prices further exacerbated existing shortages.

By 1988, Qadhafi had to face the fact that his policies had failed. They had led neither to the development of the economy nor to the creation of a political base for the regime. There was strong opposition to his policies at all levels of society, and the 1980s witnessed more attempts at overthrowing him than at any other time to that point. To survive politically Qadhafi began to change course. In 1988–89, he set free a number of political prisoners and invited members of the Libyan opposition living abroad to come home, promising to return their confiscated property. Shopkeepers were also gradually allowed to open up their stores and sell their products on the market.

In the 1990s Qadhafi has faced continued coup attempts. He faces growing unrest in the armed forces, the alienation of tribal support, and an increasingly militant Islamist sector of the population, though it is split among several groups that are not united. His refusal to extradite two officers of his intelligence service for trial in the 1988 Lockerbie Pam Am bombing hurt the economy. Two separate UN resolutions, Resolutions 748 and 883 in 1992 and 1993, condemned his decision and placed increasing levels of sanctions against Libya. The United States placed further economic sanctions beyond those assessed by the UN. However, Western European dependence on the low-sulfur crude oil of Libya did not affect this most important sector of the Libyan economy. In addition, various African and Arab states (and the Vatican) began to call for the removal of the sanctions and to engage in economic and diplomatic relations with the regime years before Qadhafi's 1998 decision. His reversal regarding extradition in August 1998 (though months of negotiating over the details came after this decision) came after years of negotiations and an agreement to hold the trial in Netherlands under Scottish judges but with UN supervision. It remains to be seen how well he will be able to regroup from these years of economic and diplomatic sanctions from the part of the western world.

## DOMESTIC POLICY

Libya's petroleum industry remains the backbone of the economy in terms of export. However, the 1990s have seen an economic downturn that has greatly reduced the per capita income, led to black marketeering, and produced increasing charges of corruption in the public sector. The petroleum industry only provides 10% of the employment for Libya's population, so agriculture is considered by the regime to be vitally important for alleviating unemployment. Libya is a major food importer, and though the regime has a goal of food self-sufficiency, the likelihood of achieving this goal is a far off one indeed. The success of the "Great Manmade River" project, announced in 1983 and officially instituted in 1991, to bring water from underground lakes in the Sahara is an important component in achieving this goal. Until then,

animal husbandry will remain the most important sector of agriculture in Libya.

In 1994 a recognition of the growing importance of Islamic fundamentalist strains in the Arab world led to the passage of new laws instituting Shari'ah (Islamic law) in family law and certain criminal proceedings. However, Qadhafi is a firm believer in the Islamic basis of women's rights and other progressive social changes that he has instituted. These will make a continuing contest with Islamic fundamentalists almost inevitable. Among the Islamist groups that have been noted are the Militant Islamic Group, the Islamic Martyrs' Movement, Libya Islamic Group, and Supporters of God. Observers believe these groups represent a real threat to Qadhafi's government, but information on them remains sparse. In 1997 the General People's Committee adopted the "Charter of Honor," imposing collective punishment on family and tribal members of Libyans convicted of serious crimes against state order. The charter is directed against opposition groups, both Islamist and other political groups mainly living in exile outside the country.

## FOREIGN POLICY

Qadhafi's decision to finally allow the extradition of the Lockerbie bombing suspects will undoubtedly brighten his relations with most western powers. The UN Security council suspended the 1992 sanctions imposed but continued to insist on progress reports regarding Libya's involvement with international terrorism and compensation for the victims of the Pan Am bombing should the Lockerbie suspects be found guilty at trial. Britain resumed full diplomatic relations with Libya in July 1999, ending 15 years of broken official contact. However, there are few signs that the US will alter its attitude towards Libya and fully suspend the trade and financial sanctions imposed upon it. Washington still accuses the Libyan regime of supporting international terrorism. In January 1999, Libyan courts issued arrest warrants against US officials accused of involvement in the 1986 air strikes against Libya.

Relations with Italy, Libya's former colonial ruler, meanwhile, remain strong despite Qadhafi's demands that Rome pay Tripoli a large indemnity for what he labeled as one of the darkest chapters in Libyan history. Libya is Italy's largest oil supplier.

Egypt considers Qadhafi's government as an important force against Islamist groups in the region. Though trying to maintain good relations with his Arab neighbors, Qadhafi has turned in recent years away from the Arab world towards an identification of Libya with the African continent. In early 1998 he initiated formation of an economic and cultural organization, the Community of the Sahel-Sharan States (COMESSA), which included the countries of Burkina Faso, Chad, Mali, Niger, and Sudan. In December 1998, the state-controlled radio changed its name from "Voice of the Greater Arab Homeland" to "Voice of Africa." He has even gone so far as to suggest that Libya should become a "Black" country and has urged Libyans to marry Black Africans. He has received many sub-Saharan African leaders for official visits to Tripoli and is active in mediation efforts in various conflicts on the continent.

## ADDRESS
Office of the Secretary of Information & Culture
Tripoli, Libya

## REFERENCES

Adams, Michael, ed., *The Middle East*, 1988.

*Guardian* newspaper Pan Am Lockerbie bombing trial site. [Online] Available http://www.guardianunlimited.co.uk/ Lockerbie/ (Accessed June 2000).

*Libya: A Country Study,* 1988.

*Middle East and North Africa.* 46th ed. London: Europa Publications, 1999.

Spencer, William. *The Middle East.* 8th ed. Dushkin/ McGraw-Hill, 2000.

St. John, Ronald Brace. *Qadhafi's World Design.* 1987.

Wright, John. *Libya: A Modern History.* 1982.

**Profile researched and written by Kathryn Green (6/2000).**

# LIECHTENSTEIN

## Hans Adam II
## Prince
*(pronounced "HANS A-dam")*

*"A reigning prince should look at long-range projects and concentrate on guidelines, but leave the day-to-day management to the government."*

Located along the Rhine River in the Alps mountain range, the Principality of Liechtenstein (*Fürstentum Liechtenstein*) is bordered in the east and north by Austria and to the south and west by Switzerland. Liechtenstein is one of the smallest countries in the world with an area of only 160 sq km (61.8 sq. mi.). The capital is Vaduz. Liechtenstein's population is estimated at 32,057, about a third of whom were actually citizens of other countries. The native population is descended almost entirely from an ancient Germanic tribe, the Alemanni, and comprises 64.2% of the total. Other major nationalities represented in Liechtenstein are Swiss (15.9%), Austrian (7.8%), and German (3.7%). The country's official languages is German, though most people speak the local Alemannic dialect. Religious affiliations in the country are Roman Catholic (87.4%), Protestant (8.3%), and others (4.3%).

The per capita GNP, which in 1984 was US$23,000, and living standards in Liechtenstein are among the highest in the world, largely because of the country's prosperous banking and manufacturing industries. Liechtenstein's major exports are machinery and transport equipment, hardware, chemical products, textiles, and ceramic. Other important sources of income are tourism, philately, and corporate taxes. Tourist arrivals in 1988 reached 75,682, nearly three times the resident population. Sales of Liechtenstein postage stamps to collectors worldwide make up nearly 10% of annual government revenues. Almost a third of total revenue is derived from more than 50,000 foreign companies registered in Liechtenstein, mainly for tax purposes, and from premiums on foreign insures. Through a treaty with Switzerland, the Swiss franc serves as the nation's currency.

## POLITICAL BACKGROUND

Liechtenstein is the last surviving monarchy of the Holy Roman Empire and owes its existence to the will of its ruling family. From its origins in the 12th century, the House of Liechtenstein played a prominent role in the history of imperial Austria, providing numerous politicians, generals, and diplomats. Raised to princely rank in reward for its services, the family sought one further distinction, its own sovereign territory.

Prince Hans Adam von Liechtenstein bought the *Reichsherrshaft* of Schellenberg in 1699 and the *Grafschaft Vaduz* in 1712 from the Counts von Hohenems. On 23 January 1719, these two territories were combined by imperial edict to form the *Reichsfüstentum Liechtenstein*, thereby fulfilling the family's ambitions. The historical components of the principality are still reflected in the two voting districts of today.

Although the major landholdings of the House of Liechtenstein were expropriated by Communist regimes in Czechoslovakia and Hungary after World War II, the family still owns large estates in Austria which have more land than the principality itself. In addition to other properties in Texas and Arkansas, the family owns the largest vineyards in Liechtenstein, a world-renowned art gallery in Vaduz, and one of the country's three banks. The value of the art holdings at the death of Prince Franz Josef II in 1989 was estimated at US$150 million. The family's total wealth has been estimated to worth up to US$3 billion, among the largest fortunes in Europe.

The principality is a constitutional monarchy with succession through the male line. The constitutions dates from 5 October 1921, and divides power between the ruling prince and the people. The prince is head of state with powers to call and dissolve the Diet (parliament) and to appoint the head of government, though this traditionally means following the wishes of a majority of the Diet. All legislation must be approved by the prince to become law. The prince also represents his country in foreign affairs, with the proviso that treaties must be approved by the Diet. Unlike most other Europeans monarchs, the princes of Liechtenstein remain more than mere figureheads. Their personal power coexists with the democratic rights of their subjects.

The unicameral Diet was expanded from 15 to 25 members by referendum in 1988. Members are elected by proportional representation and serve four-year terms. The people also have the right of initiative and referendum. Citizens over the age of 20 have the right to vote. Women could not vote until approval of female suffrage in a referendum on 1 July 1984, after two previous referenda had been defeated by the country's male voters. The 1986 elections were the first in which women could participate in politics and saw the first woman elected to the Diet.

The highest body of the government is the five-member Collegial Board, which functions as a cabinet. The Board is chaired by the head of government, also the leader of the majority party in the Diet. The deputy head of government is from the second party. The three other government councilors are split between the parties. The coalition arrangement has lasted since 1938, when a coalition was first formed because of the mounting threat from Nazi Germany (neighboring

ıst been absorbed in the *Anschluss*) and a small
nt was operating in Liechtenstein.

cal parties have dominated the government of
ıtenstein. They are the Patriotic Union Party
Progressive Citizen's Party (FBPL). The VU and
istinguishable in philosophy and both support
. The motto of both parties is "Faith in God.
atherland." From 1928 to 1970 the FBPL was
party. The VU held the majority from 1970 to
the FBPL regained the advantage. From 1978
997 elections, the VU held the majority. Results
ection gave the VU 13 seats, the FBPL 10 seats.
List (FL) party, two seats. Since 1993, the head
t has been Mario Frick (VU); Michael Ritter has
deputy head of government since 1997.

## L BACKGROUND

Adam Pius was born on 15 February 1945, to
osef II and Princess Gina. Reflecting the Liecht-
family's Roman Catholic faith and connections,
was named the boy's godfather. According to
ish that he be brought up in contact with his
future subjects, Hans Adam attended public school and
participated in a local boy scout troup in Vaduz before
moving on to the Catholic Schotten Gymnasium in Vienna,
Austria (1956–60). He completed his secondary education in
Switzerland at Zuoz. After working in a London bank for a
brief period, Hans Adam completed his education at St.
Gallen University in Switzerland where he received a degree
in economics in 1969.

Hans Adam spent many years in the management of his
family's extensive fortune. Taking control in 1969, he reorganized the holdings of the Prince of Liechtenstein Foundation
in 1970. The prince brought in professional managers to help
oversee the foundation's growth. In 1981, Christian Norgen,
a Swedish banker, was appointed executive head of the
foundation and chairman of the Bank in Liechtenstein in an
effort to internationalize the family's holdings. The bank has
expanded rapidly in recent years and has opened branches or
subsidiaries in several world financial centers: London,
Zurich, New York, Frankfurt, Hong Kong, Buenos Aires, and
Rio de Janeiro.

On 30 July 1967, Hans Adam married Countess Marie
Aglaë Kinsky von Wichinitz und Tettau (born in Prague on 14
April 1940) at St. Florian parish church in Vaduz. Princess
Marie Aglaë comes from an old Austrian noble family which
left Czechoslovakia for West Germany at the end of World
War II. The wedding was attended by various European
royalty, including Queen Anne-Marie of Greece, former
Empress Zita of Austria-Hungary and her son Otto von
Habsburg, and the pretender to the French throne, the Count
of Paris. The Prince and Princess have three sons—Prince
Alois (born 11 June 1968), Prince Maximilian (born 16 May
1969), Prince Constantin (born 15 March 1972), and a
daughter—Princess Tatjana (born 10 April 1973).

## RISE TO POWER

Two events marked Hans Adam's assumption of the formal
rights and duties of a sovereign prince of Liechtenstein. On 4
July 1983, Prince Franz Josef II announced his intention of

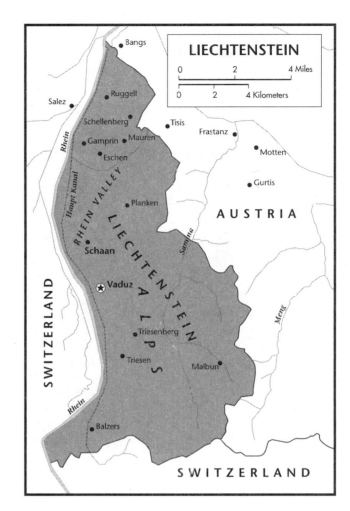

turning executive power over to his son. This was accomplished in a formal ceremony on 26 August 1984.

At the death of his father on 13 November 1989, Hans
Adam became the thirteenth ruling prince of Liechtenstein, as
Prince Hans-Adam II. His mother had died only a month
previously. The prince's official title is His Serene Highness
Prince Hans-Adam Pius von und zu Liechtenstein, Duke of
Troppau and of Jagerndorf, Court of Reitburg.

## LEADERSHIP

Because Hans Adam's position is based on hereditary rights,
he does not engage in politics in the manner of an elected
official. Thus, he is free to offer guidance to Liechtenstein's
voters on a non-partisan basis. By all accounts, the prince's
unpretentious personal style is quite popular with his
subjects.

## DOMESTIC POLICY

One of Hans Adam's major goals for many years was to
secure voting rights for women. The referendum approving
female suffrage coincided with the prince's assumption of
executive power and was seen as a victory for his position. At
the same time, the prince identified two other priorities for
his country. The first of these was the introduction of a new
code of criminal law to replace the existing one based on 19th
century Austrian law. He also sought reform of the tax code,
including introduction of an income tax.

In order to preserve the country's economic prosperity, Hans Adam believes that Liechtenstein must continue to rely on a diversified, highly industrialized and technological business mix, especially in light of the limited labor supply.

## FOREIGN POLICY

For most of the last century, the emphasis of Liechtenstein's foreign policy has been on neutrality. The country's last foreign involvement was in 1866, when Liechtenstein sent 80 men to patrol the Austrian border with Italy under its obligation to the German Confederation. The army was disbanded in 1868, shortly after the Confederation broke up. Although neutral in both world wars, Liechtenstein's economic links with Austria made it a target of Allied embargoes each time.

Liechtenstein's closet international association is with Switzerland, a relationship which dates to the Customs Union Agreement signed in 1923. Liechtenstein is represented abroad by Switzerland, but diplomatic decisions affecting Liechtenstein cannot be made legally without its consent. As a recognized sovereign state, Liechtenstein belongs to the Council of Europe, International Telecommunication Satellite Organization (INTELSAT), the European Free Trade Association, and several specialized UN organizations. Liechtenstein participated in the Helsinki Convention in 1974 and the follow-up conferences.

Prince Hans-Adam's goal—to persuade his countrymen to join the UN—was realized in 1990. The prince had argued that "UN membership would give us that extra bit of legitimacy as a national entity." Because of Liechtenstein's close relationship with Switzerland, the Swiss decision not to enter the UN hampered efforts to promote Liechtenstein's entry. In 1996, Hans-Adam took his goal of international participation a step further, when he led his country in a vote to approve entry into the European Economic Area (EEA).

## ADDRESS

Schloss Vaduz
9490 Vaduz
Liechtenstein

## REFERENCES

Agnihotri, Newal K. "Liechtenstein: A Focus on Humanity." *Presidents and Prime Ministers,* September 1998, p. 13.

*The Christian Science Monitor,* 13 June 1984.

*The Economist,* various issues.

*Financial Times,* 24 August 1984.

Lappen, Alyssa A. "A Royal." *Institutional Investor,* July 1998, p. 61.

*National Geographic,* February 1981.

*The New York Times,* various issues.

Stewart, Jules. "So Far But No Further. (Liechtenstein's decision to join European Economic Area)." *Euromoney,* July 1996, p. 150.

**Profile researched and written by Douglas Warfel (7/90; updated 3/2000).**

# LITHUANIA

### Valdas Adamkus
### President

*(pronounced "VAHL-dahs ah-DAHM-koohs")*

*"I shall do my utmost for Lithuania to become a full-fledged member
of the European and the Euro-Atlantic community during my term of office."*

The Republic of Lithuania borders the Baltic Sea, Latvia, Poland, Belarus, and Russia's Kaliningrad oblast. It has a total land area of 65,201 sq km (25,174 sq mi). The population has been estimated at 3.6 million, of whom 80% were ethnic Lithuanians, 8% Russians, and 7% Poles. The remainder consisted mostly of Belarussians and Ukrainians. The official language is Lithuanian. Most Lithuanians and Poles are Roman Catholics while Russians subscribe to the Russian Orthodox faith.

The official currency is the *litas* (LTLt). With the political upheavals of the late Soviet period and the dislocations resulting from the transition to capitalism, the economy suffered an initial decline. It has since rebounded, with per capita GDP estimated at US$4,900. Lithuania produces machine tools, electrical engines, hosiery, televisions, refrigerators, butter, and other agricultural products.

## POLITICAL BACKGROUND

In the 14th century Lithuania expanded to the East, defeating Slavic tribes in the process. When Prince Jogaila married Jadwyga of Poland, the two realms merged, creating a dominant power in Eastern Europe. This Polish-Lithuanian state eventually declined and, in the 18th century, fell under Russian domination.

With the Russian Empire crumbling, Lithuania declared its independence on 16 February 1918. Parliamentary democracy lasted only until 1926 when Antanas Smetona seized power. The country was plagued with strained relations with neighboring Poland, which seized and held the capital city of Vilnius throughout the interwar years.

In 1940, Lithuania was annexed by the Soviet Union. World War II was devastating for the country—leaving 280,000 people, or 9% of the pre-war population, dead. After the war, 260,000 people were deported or arrested, and 50,000 died in the guerilla war against Soviet authority. Under Soviet rule Lithuania's economy was industrialized, though not as rapidly as Estonia and Latvia. After Stalin's death the range of freedoms was expanded, though tight controls remained. Open displays of nationalism were prohibited, but they appeared in veiled forms in art, music, and literature.

Changes to the Soviet system, introduced by Mikhail Gorbachev, gradually took hold in Lithuania. Significant change began in December 1987 when members of the Writers Union criticized the slow pace of implementing Gorbachev's policies of *glasnost* (openness) and *perestroika* (restructuring) in Lithuania. A political organization independent of the Communist Party (called *Sajudis*) emerged in May 1988 and initially espoused moderate views. Under pressure from Moscow, the Communist Party granted some concessions on nationalist demands, permitting display of Lithuania's flag and the singing of the national anthem. As the result of a public outcry over police attacks on demonstrators, the reform-minded Algirdas Brazauskas replaced a conservative as first secretary of the Communist Party of Lithuania.

In February 1989, *Sajudis* declared that Lithuania had been forcibly annexed by the Soviet Union and that the group's ultimate goal was to achieve independence. Conservative Communist leaders threatened to crack down on *Sajudis* but backed down in the face of mass protests. *Sajudis* candidates fared well in elections to the Congress of People's Deputies, the newly created Soviet legislative body. Their candidates won in 36 of the 40 districts in which they ran. The Lithuanian Supreme Soviet amended the constitution to give precedence to Lithuanian laws over Soviet laws. Relations with Moscow deteriorated further in August when Lithuanians joined Estonians and Latvians to demand revocation of the Molotov-Ribbentrop pact. The Communist Party of the Soviet Union harshly condemned the action and the general mood in the Baltics. The Lithuanian parliament declared the annexation of Lithuania invalid and stripped the Communist Party of its guaranteed monopoly of power. This triggered a split in the Communist Party of Lithuania, leaving a majority faction (led by Brazauskas), which declared itself independent of Moscow, and a minority faction loyal to Moscow.

In February 1990, *Sajudis* and the Communist Party faced off in the first multi-party elections in modern Soviet history. *Sajudis* captured an overwhelming majority of parliamentary seats. On 11 March, the Lithuanian Supreme Soviet elected Vytautas Landsbergis president. That same day parliament formally declared Lithuania to be an independent nation. Gorbachev rejected the action, insisting that separation must be negotiated. In April he ordered an economic blockade of Lithuania, cutting off all oil supplies and reducing natural gas flow to one-quarter of the normal level. The blockade ended on 30 June after the Lithuanian parliament voted to freeze the declaration of independence for 100 days in order to permit negotiations between Moscow and Estonia, Latvia, and Lithuania.

Soviet hardliners took control of many Lithuanian government buildings in January 1991. The conflict reached alarming levels when Soviet troops stormed the Lithuanian

television building, killing 14 and injuring 140. In a March referendum, 90% of voters favored leaving the Soviet Union. It appeared that the Soviet government was intent upon intimidating the other republics by grinding Lithuania into submission.

Everything changed drastically with the failed coup attempt against Gorbachev in August 1991. Hardline forces within the Soviet government were severely weakened and unable to continue their campaign. Lithuania quickly outlawed its Communist Party and began to dismantle the Soviet secret police. One month later, the Soviet Union recognized Lithuanian independence and agreed to withdraw all troops by the end of 1994.

After gaining independence, Lithuania suffered from many problems faced by new states. The political situation was unsteady, with top government posts changing hands as power ebbed and flowed. The deteriorating economic situation put intense popular pressure on the post-Soviet government, composed largely of inexperienced people. Popular discontent with the government and growing political apathy were evident in a May 1992 referendum whereby Landsbergis attempted to increase the powers of his office. Although a majority voted for the constitutional change, voter turnout was so low that the results were not considered valid. In October 1992, Lithuanians again went to the polls to elect a new parliament, the *Seimas*. The Lithuanian Democratic Labor Party (LDLP), a successor to the Brazauskas's independent Communist Party showed surprising strength, trouncing the *Sajudis* coalition and the Christian Democrat (CD) coalition. The LDLP captured more

than half of the seats in the *Seimas* while *Sajudis* and the CD coalition controlled only one-third. Under the LDLP, the pace of economic reform slowed. The new parliament elected LDLP chairman Brazauskas to serve as interim president. The provision for direct election of the president was included in a new constitution, which was approved by voters at this same time. Under the new constitution, the president was given power to appoint the prime minister and cabinet, subject to parliamentary approval.

As presidential elections approached Brazauskas's popularity was evident. In January 1993, Landsbergis pulled out of the presidential race, and Brazauskas was elected with 60% of the vote. Polls indicated that the vast majority of ethnic Russians and Poles, and many Lithuanians living in rural areas, supported Brazauskas. Throughout 1993 and 1994 the economic situation continued to decline; criminal activity and political bickering increased. Conservatives, charging that LDLP leaders were profiting from the privatization program, failed in attempting to halt it. Lithuania's two largest banks collapsed in December 1995. The prime minister and interior minister were forced to resign when it became known that they withdrew funds from the banks days before the government took them over. Others sought to distance themselves from the scandal by resigning from the LDLP.

By 1996, the Conservative Party, formed from a core group of *Sajudis* leaders, enjoyed greater popular support. In *Seimas* elections, conservatives won nearly half of the seats. Thus, with their CD coalition partners, they controlled the parliament. In 1997, Conservatives won one-third of contested seats in local elections. In 1998, Valdas Adamkus, returning to his homeland after living in the US for more than 30 years, was elected president of Lithuania.

## PERSONAL BACKGROUND
Valdas Adamkus was born in Kaunas, the former capital of Lithuania, on 3 November 1926. During World War II, he joined a resistance movement for Lithuanian independence and published an underground newspaper for youth. When the Soviet army reinvaded Lithuania in 1944, Adamkus fled with his parents to Germany. He returned to join the resistance forces and fought the Red Army in western Lithuania. He returned to Germany soon thereafter, completed high school, and studied at the University of Munich.

In 1949, Adamkus emigrated to the US, where he continued to participate in Lithaunian affairs. He co-founded an organization for liberal-minded émigrés, which was regarded as unsavory by the more conservative mainstream émigré groups. While living in Chicago, he began working in an auto factory and later became a draftsman. For a time he served in US military intelligence. In 1960, he earned a bachelor's degree in civil engineering from the Illinois Institute of Technology.

Adamkus began working for the US Environmental Protection Agency (EPA) in 1970 and rose steadily through the ranks. He retired from federal service as chief of the EPA's Chicago regional office in June 1997. Widely respected for his integrity and commitment to the environment, Adamkus gained some renown for testifying before Congress that reports from his office had been altered to downplay environmental hazards.

## RISE TO POWER

Adamkus began regularly visiting Lithuania and the rest of the Soviet Union in 1972. In his official capacity, he played an important role in coordinating US environmental policy in Eastern Europe. In his unofficial capacity, he often distributed banned literature from the West. During this time he achieved a high profile in Lithuania. As restrictions eased in the late 1980s, he became more active in environmental affairs in the Baltics. In 1993, he managed the unsuccessful presidential campaign of his friend and fellow émigré, Stasys Lozoraitis. He also campaigned for candidates of the center-right in the 1996 legislative elections.

In 1997, following his retirement from the EPA, Adamkus and his wife moved back to Lithuania. The Lithuanian Center Union party nominated him to run for the city council in Siauliai, Lithuania's fourth-largest city. This same party later nominated him as its presidential candidate, though he had to go to court to override a residency requirement. In the first round of voting, Adamkus won 28% of the vote, well behind top vote-getter Arturas Paulauskas but ahead of third-place finisher Landsbergis. Since no candidate received a majority of votes, a runoff election was scheduled for 4 January 1998. Adamkus garnered 50.4% of the vote—a margin of 14,000 votes out of two million cast. The day before being sworn in as president, Adamkus renounced his US citizenship to comply with Lithuanian law.

## LEADERSHIP

As of 1999, Adamkus remained the most popular political figure in Lithuania. In contrast to the luxuries enjoyed by the ruling elite of the government that was voted out of office in 1996, Adamkus was admired for his integrity and down-to-earth lifestyle. He noted in his inaugural address in 1998, "I am convinced that progress...can be achieved only through fostering and establishing a standard of morality...by which one is answerable for his words and actions. "

## DOMESTIC POLICY

In his inaugural address, Adamkus stressed financial stability, education, health care, economic reform, and public safety as the domestic issues requiring the most attention. He added that the issues of religious and ethnic tolerance need to be addressed and that the city of Vilnius needs to be renewed. The first major policy initiative of the administration was to propose a reorganization of the government, reducing the number of ministries from 17 to 13. Administrative, social, and economic reform has remained a major focus of his presidency. In his 20 April 2000 state of the union address, he declared that the country's economic difficulties following Russia's 1998 economic crisis could have been lessened if key reforms, such as antitrust programs and energy industry restructuring, had not been delayed.

The economic dislocations and hardships resulting from the economic transition have been a major national problem. As of 2000, unemployment stood at a post-Soviet high of 11%, and President Adamkus criticized the government for failing to take effective action to reduce the nation's large budget deficit.

Given his long career with the Environmental Protection Agency in the United States during the years he lived there, Adamkus has taken a strong interest in Lithuania's recuperation from the environmental damage wrought during the Soviet era. He has worked to promote awareness of the environment and used his expertise to assist those charged with implementing the country's environmental policy, including a newly established Environmental Protection Department.

## FOREIGN POLICY

A major goal of Adamkus's presidency has been the continuation of Lithuania's efforts to integrate itself with the West. In his 2000 state of the union address, he emphasized once again the importance of membership in NATO and the European Union to Lithuania's economic and political future. In October 1999, the EU announced that it was considering Lithuania for membership by 2003.

Relations with Russia have remained of primary importance. Because citizenship was granted to virtually all Russians living in Lithuania, relations with Russia have been better than those of Estonia and Latvia. In 1993, the last Russian troops left Lithuania. Still, the Russian government opposes Lithuanian membership in NATO. Brazauskas was the first Baltic president to visit Russia, signing a border treaty in Moscow in October 1997. Russia is Lithuania's chief trading partner. Despite his Western background, Adamkus has repeatedly stated that maintaining good relations with Russia is a priority for his government.

Lithuania continues to cultivate strong relations with Estonia and Latvia. The Baltic States have maintained a free trade agreement since 1994. One issue that has caused some recent strain with Latvia has been the plan to develop Latvian oil reserves in contested waters of the Baltic Sea.

## ADDRESS

Office of the President
Gedimino 53
232026
Vilnius, Lithuania

## REFERENCES

*Analysis of Current Events*, February 1998.

*Baltic Times*, 13 November 1997–11 March 1998.

*Chicago Tribune*, 5 January 1998.

*Europa World Year Book 1997*. London: Europa Publications Ltd., 1997.

*Europa World Year Book 1999*. London: Europa Publications Ltd., 1999.

*Keesing's Record of World Events*, 1997.

"Lithuania: Westward Ho!" *The Economist*, 8 January 2000, p. 50.

*Los Angeles Times*, 9 February 1998.

Misiunas, Romuald and Rein Taagepera. *The Baltic States: Years of Dependence 1940–1990*. Berkeley: University of California Press, 1993.

Official parliamentary website. [Online] Available http://www.lrs.lt (Accessed June 1998).

*Political Handbook of the World*. Ed. Arthur Banks and Thomas Muller. Binghamton, NY: CSA Publications, 1999.

"Prodigal President." *People Weekly*, 29 June 1998, p. 129.

*Washington Post*, 16 January 1998.

*Weekly Baltic News*, 21–29 May 2000.

**Profile researched and written by Andrejs Penikis, Columbia University (6/98; updated 6/2000).**

# LUXEMBOURG

### Jean-Claude Juncker
### Prime Minister
*(pronounced "zhan-claud YUN-ker")*

*"I think there can be no Luxembourg view, because in the Union people should practice dual patriotism. To us this means a Luxembourg and a European patriotism."*

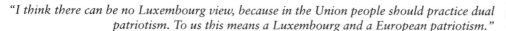

The Grand Duchy of Luxembourg is one of the smallest countries in Western Europe, encompassing only 2,586 sq km (999 sq mi). Wedged among three countries, Germany to the east, Belgium to the north and west, and France to the south, Luxembourg's geographic location provides its inhabitants with the advantage of having prosperous neighbors that help to fuel its economy. With a population estimated at 429,080 Luxembourg is quite densely populated. The capital is Luxembourg-Ville (Lutzelburg).

Since 1985 the official language has been Letzeburgish, a German dialect with French flavoring, but both French and German are used: French in government offices and German in commercial enterprises and the press. Students are taught in both French and German in school. About 95% of its population is Roman Catholic.

The economy is strong and provides Luxembourgers with annual per capita GDP of US$32,700, the highest of any of the European Union (EU) countries. Steel and chemicals are important industries, and they provide many of Luxembourg's principal exports: base metals and manufactures, machinery and transport equipment, rubber, plastics, as well as textiles and clothing, stone ceramics, and glassware. Most trade occurs with other EU countries. Since the 1970s, international finance and insurance have gained a dominant position in the economy. The currency is the Luxembourg *franc*. The Belgian *franc* is also legal tender. Inflation is low, hovering around 2%; and unemployment stands at less than 2%.

## POLITICAL BACKGROUND

In the medieval era, Luxembourg was one of many small principalities in Western Europe. For centuries, it successfully fended off efforts by its larger neighbors to absorb it. It succumbed to invasion by Nazi armies in 1940, regaining it independence in 1944, only after heavy fighting between US and German forces. Many American war dead, including General George S. Patton, are buried in US military cemeteries in the country. Constraints of size and location have been factors in the many cooperative agreements in which Luxembourg participates, and the country has cooperated in post-World War II moves toward European integration. A customs union was established with Belgium in 1921, which was interrupted only during the German occupation of 1940–44. Luxembourg was a founding member of NATO in 1949, and was an original member of the European Coal and Steel Community (forerunner to the

European Community, now the European Union). The Benelux Economic Union was negotiated in 1948, became effective in 1960 and in 1970, established Belgium, the Netherlands and Luxembourg as a single customs union. Membership in such institutions reflects an impulse to mesh the country's future with that of other Western democratic governments.

Luxembourg has been governed by coalitions since the 1920s, with the exception of Nazi rule during the war. Luxembourg's small size allow citizens to be familiar with the social, economic and political currents of each section of the country. In such circumstances, consensus-building is both important and possible, and coalition governments generally reflect an effort to forge consensus. Since World War II, the *Parti Chretien Social* (PCS or Christian Socialist Party), a centrist party, has led all coalitions except one. For a brief period (1974–79), the *Parti Ouvrier Socialiste Luxembourgeois* (POSL or Socialist Workers Party) led a coalition with the *Parti Democratique* (PD or Liberals) ) as their junior partners. Since April 1994, the PCS had been the senior partner in coalition with the POSL. Jacques Santer was the leader of this coalition until January 1995, when he became president of the European Commission, the key administrative body of the European Union.

Luxembourg is a hereditary constitutional monarch, and Grand Duke Jean, who came to the throne in 1964, is the head of state. His duties are primarily ceremonial. The unicameral legislature, the 60-member Chamber of Deputies, which is elected every five years, is the true instrument that gives legitimacy to any government. The voting age is 18, and all voters are required by law to vote. Executive power is vested in the Grand Duke, but is generally exercised by the Council of Ministers under the leadership of the president of the government, also known as the prime minister.

## PERSONAL BACKGROUND

Jean-Claude Juncker was born on 9 December 1954, in Redange-sur-Attert, Luxembourg. He was one of seven children in a working-class family. His father worked in a steel plant and was active in union affairs. Juncker excelled in school and attributes his work ethic to his father. In 1979, Juncker earned a law degree from the University of Strasbourg, but practiced law only briefly before entering politics. He is fluent in French and German. Juncker is married; he and his wife have no children.

## RISE TO POWER

In 1979, upon his graduation from law school, Juncker became president of the Christian Social Youth Organization, which is an arm of the PCS. Party leaders quickly noticed his talent for organization and willingness to make decisions. When he was 25, they made him parliamentary secretary of the PCS, a position that allowed him to see the workings of the party from the inside and to come to know its leaders well. In 1984, Juncker was elected to the Chamber of Deputies, and in that same year, at age 29, he became minister of labor. Although trained in law, he excelled in analysis of economic and financial problems, and gained a reputation for intelligence, energy, and directness. His straightforward manner and practical approach to problem-solving won him allies in the business as well as the political community. A succession of important government positions followed.

He was re-elected to the Chamber of Deputies in 1989, and was appointed to head both the labor and the finance ministries by Prime Minister Santer. He was re-appointed to these same posts after the PCS's electoral victory of 1994. In 1990, Juncker was elected president of the PCS. This administrative position allowed him to consolidate his political base and to direct the development of party policies on all issues of importance. Jean-Claude Juncker replaced Jacques Santer as prime minister on 26 January 1995, becoming the youngest head of government of any EU state. Jean-Claude Juncker, leader of the PCS, survived the 1999 election by joining forces with the Democratic Party (DP).

## LEADERSHIP

Juncker has demonstrated a commitment to maintaining Luxembourg's important position in international finance. At the same time, he remains faithful to his country's tradition of cooperation with its neighbors. The European Union is the focal point for Luxembourg's political and economic future. In his view, the more closely Luxembourg works with its neighbors, the more secure will be the future of the country. Close coordination with the European Union means surrendering a measure of sovereignty. Some of the larger EU countries, such as Britain, have resisted the trend towards a stronger European Union. Juncker, however, has unambiguously cast Luxembourg's lot with the European Union. While a minister in Santer's government, he strongly supported endorsement of the Maastricht Treaty, which calls for closer coordination of economic and political policies among EU states. The Chamber of Deputies agreed to the Maastricht Treaty in 1992. Among the treaty's requirements is the commitment by the EU members to the European Monetary Union (EMU), meaning that one currency for all EU states will be adopted in order to smooth the flow of trade and eliminate the need for currency exchange. Strict qualifying stipulations, or "convergence criteria," were issued by the EU for entry into the EMU. Those stipulations required that a state should keep inflation low, that its budget deficit be modest, and that its overall debt be confined to certain limits. As finance minister at the time of agreement to meet these EMU guidelines, and later as prime minister, Juncker was responsible for shaping relevant government policy. To nobody's surprise, Luxembourg joined EMU in 1999 and the Luxembourg franc was fixed to the euro at 40.33. The franc will be phased out in 2002.

Juncker had also occupied positions in international institutions that are important to Luxembourg's position as a center of finance and enhance his country's image in the international community. Since 1989, he has been a governor of the World Bank, providing him with a detailed understanding of the international economy. In February 1995, he was named a governor of the International Monetary Fund (IMF), where he is able to follow and influence monetary and fiscal policy in a large number of nations around the world. The vantage points of the World Bank and IMF provide Juncker with the opportunity to gain insight into world trade, the financial viability of various countries, and the borrowing needs of nations seeking to develop further their resources and industries.

## DOMESTIC POLICY

Luxembourg's domestic economic policy is closely tied to developments in the European Union because most of the country's trade and investments are with other EU states. ARBED, Luxembourg's principal steel making company, saw its profitability fall sharply in the 1970s with the worldwide decline in steel prices. The company was forced to eliminate many of its 27,000 workers. Through restructuring and specialization in customized metals, ARBED has bounced back into profitability, and is now Europe's third largest steel company. Nevertheless, employment at the company remains low. It had dropped to 8,000 workers by 1999.

With the decline of the steel industry, the government sought to capitalize on Luxembourg's strengths in developing new, viable industries. The country enjoys a central location and high educational standards. Luxembourg's leaders decided in the 1970s to make a concerted effort to develop a service economy, concentrating upon finance, banking, and insurance. Juncker, as prime minister, continued this trend. Luxembourg has low taxes, by European standards, on bank accounts and mutual funds; this draws investments from wealthy but more heavily-taxed neighbors, such as France and Germany.

Luxembourg has also had strong confidentiality laws to protect investors from inquiry about their holdings. For a period of time, the laws attracted money from drug cartels, which have sent money there in order to conceal its source, then re-invest it in legitimate enterprises. The Juncker government has supported changes in Luxembourg's confidentiality laws so that judicial investigators may learn the source of investments in order to prevent criminals from profiting by using the country's banking system.

Luxembourg's economy has adjusted from the difficult days of the 1970s to become one of Europe's strongest. Growth rates have been among the highest in the European Union, averaging around 5% in 1998 and 1999. Unemployment was only 1.6%, the lowest in the European Union. Its economy shifted from dependence on steel to an emphasis on services, notably finance and telecommunications. Luxembourg is now among the world's top ten financial centers and the financial sector employs approximately 10% of the workforce (20,000 people) and accounts for around one fifth of national income.

Some Luxembourgers believe that the country's economic wealth has led to an unwanted influx of foreign workers. The EU requires that each member state open its borders and employment to citizens of other EU states. The result has been that wealthy EU states, such as Luxembourg, attract workers from poor EU states where unemployment is high. Many of these workers take low-wage jobs and send their earnings back to their country of origin. There is little evidence as yet that they displace Luxemburgers from jobs. Nonetheless, the presence of large numbers of foreign workers—one estimate places the figure the high as 30% of the population in 1994—brings a clash of cultures. A challenge for the Juncker government will be to insure that native Luxemburgers and foreign workers live in harmony.

## FOREIGN POLICY

The Juncker government has strongly endorsed the Maastricht Treaty's call for an EU common foreign and security policy. Luxembourg's armed forces are minimal. Nonetheless, it has endorsed the French-German effort to build a "Eurocorps," or nascent European army for the EU. Its support for the Eurocorps will be primarily through funding, rather than through supplying combat personnel. At the same time, Luxembourg remains a member of NATO, and allows other allies to maintain on its soil supply depots that would be of critical importance in time of conflict. Despite its small size, Luxembourg was among the few nations to send troops to the former Yugoslavia in the UN Protection Force. The European Union, however remains at the core of Luxembourg's foreign policy. Challenges to Luxembourg's influence in the EU are on the horizon. The EU is likely to expand in the coming decade, and voting procedures within its governing institutions may change in order to prevent the organization from becoming unwieldy. Power may shift to the larger, more powerful, EU states. This could mean, for example, that the current practice of giving each country a veto over key decisions will be altered, a change that could adversely affect small states such as Luxembourg. Maintaining Luxembourg's economic vitality and its political influence in EU councils will be a primary task for the Juncker government.

## ADDRESS

Office of the Prime Minister
Hotel de Bourgogne
4, rue de la Congregation
2910 Luxembourg

## REFERENCES

*Bulletin of Information and Documentation.* Luxembourg Government Press and Information Service, 1994.

*Janet Matthews Information Services. CIRCA,* 10 February 2000.

*Janet Matthews Information Services. Barclays Bank Country Report,* February 29, 2000.

*Financial Times,* Special section on Luxembourg. 19 October 1994.

Foreign Broadcast Information Service-WEU-95-101, 26 January 1995; 25 May 1995.

*Wall Street Journal,* 31 March 1994.

*West European Politics,* January 1995.

**Profile researched and written by Paul E. Gallis, Congressional Research Service (6/95; revised 3/2000).**

# MACEDONIA

## Boris Trajkovski
### President

*(pronounced "BAH-riss try-KOFF-ski")*

*"I believe that we will succeed in making Macedonia a stable and prosperous democratic country with a high level of respect for human rights and freedoms and a high standard of living for all citizens."*

The Republic of Macedonia spans 25,713 sq km (9,928 sq mi) and is surrounded by Yugoslavia (now comprised of Serbia and Montenegro) to the north, Albania to the west, Bulgaria to the east and Greece to the south. The capital is Skopje, (pronounced "SKOPE-jeh") situated on the Vardar River. The population is estimated at 2.02 million, and breaks down as 64.6% Macedonian, 21% Albanian, 4.8% Turkish, 2.7% Roma (Gypsies), 2.2% Serbs, and about 4% others. The Macedonian Orthodox religion, likened to Eastern Orthodox teachings, is practiced by the vast majority of Macedonians. Situated at a strategic crossroads in the Balkan peninsula, geographic Macedonia has been subject to conquest and territorial disputes for centuries. In the 4th century BC, Alexander the Great established control over the territory of Greece and Macedonia. Macedonia was invaded by Slavic tribes in the 6th and 7th centuries AD. The Ottoman Turks conquered Macedonia in the 14th century and remained in control of the territory for over five centuries. Macedonia was wrested from Turkey in the Balkan Wars of 1913 and was divided among Serbia, Greece, and Bulgaria. After World War I, Macedonia was again partitioned. The Yugoslav part of Macedonia became incorporated into Serbia. After World War II, Macedonia was reconstituted by Marshal Tito as a constituent Yugoslav state, one of six equal federal republics. Tito permitted and promoted the development of a Macedonian culture, language, and nationality within Yugoslavia but distinct from either Serbia or Bulgaria.

Within Yugoslavia, the Republic of Macedonia was the poorest of the six Yugoslav republics, and contributed only about 6% of overall GNP. Its main industries are agriculture, textiles, and minerals which were mainly geared for markets in the other Yugoslav republics. A new Macedonian currency, the *denar*, was launched at the end of 1992.

## POLITICAL BACKGROUND
Ten years after the death of Tito, all six Yugoslav republics held multi-party elections in 1990. Elections in the Republic of Macedonia were held in November–December 1990. Nine parties won seats in the legislature, but no single party managed to secure a parliamentary majority. Out of 120 seats, the Internal Macedonian Revolutionary Organization-Democratic Party for Macedonian National Unity (IMRO-DPMNU) won 37 seats; the League of Communists of Macedonia-Party for Democratic Transformation (LCM-PDT, since renamed the Social Democratic Alliance)

won 31 seats; the Albanian Party for Democratic Prosperity (PDP) won 25 seats; the Alliance of Reform Forces for Macedonia (ARFM, since renamed the Liberal Party of Macedonia) won 17 seats; the Socialist Party won five seats; the Independent Party won three seats; and the remaining two seats were split between the IMRO-Democratic Party and the Party for the Emancipation of the Roma. The new legislature passed a declaration of sovereignty in January 1991, but coalition talks after the elections on forming a new government were unsuccessful. In March 1991, the National Assembly approved a so-called Government of Experts of mostly unaffiliated ministers headed by Nikola Kljusev.

Unlike the northern Yugoslav republics of Slovenia and Croatia, Macedonia originally had no interest in breaking away from the Yugoslav federation. As tensions flared up between Serbia, Slovenia and Croatia in June 1991, Macedonia at first favored a new "community of sovereign republics." Macedonia's position on independence shifted later that year. On 8 September 1991, Macedonia held a public referendum on independence, which resulted in a large majority (excluding most ethnic Albanians) in favor of independence. The National Assembly thereafter declared independence on September 9, and adopted a new constitution on 17 November 1991, establishing the republic as a sovereign, independent, democratic, and social state. In keeping with European Community conditions for recognition, amendments were added to the constitution in January 1992 that renounced any territorial claims or interference in the internal affairs of other states.

## PERSONAL BACKGROUND
Boris Trajkovski was born on 25 June 1956, in Strumica. In 1980 he received a law degree from the University of St. Cyril and Methodius in Skopje, afterward specializing in commercial and employment law. Until 1997, he headed the legal department of the Sloboda construction company in Skopje. He has also been a member of the Macedonia America Friendship Association, and he served as leader of the United Methodist Church's youth branch in the former Yugoslavia for 12 years. Trajkovski is married and has two children.

## RISE TO POWER
Trajkovski's rise to power has been extremely rapid. He first entered politics in 1997, when he was the top official in the mayor's office in the Kisela Voda Municipality (1997–98). In

society and nationwide policies to strengthen the family and its values.

## DOMESTIC POLICY

President Trajkovski has identified the stability and territorial integrity of Macedonia as his first priority. He has noted the need for Macedonia's military to be both technologically prepared and highly mobile to meet any challenge that may arise in the volatile Balkan area. He has also identified ethnic tolerance as the major road to internal stability.

The poorest republic in Yugoslavia during the Communist era, Macedonia has enjoyed a modest recovery in the 1990s as its agricultural sector has expanded and privatization has begun. However, high unemployment and increasing poverty remain problems. In the area of economic development, Trajkovski has cited increased exports and the attraction of foreign investment as priorities. He is a strong advocate of European integration and is committed to cooperation with international organizations including the World Trade Organization, to which Macedonia has applied for membership, and the European Union, which it would like to eventually join as well.

## FOREIGN POLICY

Macedonia's primary foreign policy concerns under President Gligorov were the extended dispute with Greece over international recognition, which lasted until the mid-1990s, and fears that ongoing conflicts in other parts of the former Yugoslavia would spread to Macedonia. President Trajkovski has voiced his intention of pursuing stability in the region by fostering friendly relations with neighboring states including Greece, Bulgaria, Albania, and the Federal Republic of Yugoslavia while also encouraging the development of democracy and respect for human rights. He regards EU membership as a strategic goal.

## ADDRESS

Office of the President
Republic of Macedonia
11 Oktomvri bb
91000 Skopje, Macedonia

1999 he served as deputy minister of foreign affairs. He has also been chairman of the ruling VMRO-DPMNE party's foreign relations commission and served as the chief political adviser on foreign policy to Prime Minister Georgievski. In the fall of 1999, Trajkovski ran for the presidency as the VMRO-DPMNE candidate. He was elected in November 1999 and sworn into office in December. The opposition Social Democratic Union charged electoral fraud, and OSCE observers noted some irregularities, primarily in majority-Albanian areas. However, they termed the overall election process fair and legitimate.

## LEADERSHIP

The election of Boris Trajkovski, who was born after World War II, to the presidency brings a new generation of political leadership to Macedonia. However, Trajkovski can be expected to continue the political moderation and emphasis on stability of his predecessor, Kiro Gligorov. As president of Macedonia, Gligorov made numerous attempts to moderate increasing tensions among the Yugoslav republics and proposed compromise solutions for Yugoslavia that would create a community of sovereign republics.

Like Gligorov, Trajkovski can be expected to work toward defusing potentially destabilizing ethnic tensions in Macedonia, especially those centered around Macedonia's Albanian population. In his inaugural address, he stated, "I will not allow ethnic hatred, chauvinism, and intolerance to destroy the stability of the country." During the campaign and following the election, Trajkovski also emphasized his belief in the importance of the family as the cornerstone of

## REFERENCES

Banks, Arthur and Thomas Muller, eds. *Political Handbook of the World*. Binghamton, NY: CSA Publications, 1999.

Clissold, Stephen, ed. *A Short History of Yugoslavia*. Cambridge University Press, 1966.

Constitution of the Federal Republic of Macedonia. Skopje, 1991.

Cviic, Christopher. *Remaking the Balkans*. New York: Council on Foreign Relations Press, 1991.

*The Economist*, 23 May 1992

*The Economist Intelligence Unit*, No. 2, 1992.

*Financial Times*, 6 February, 16 June, 8 July, and 24 August 1992.

*FBIS Daily Reports, East Europe*, 4 May, 11 & 24 June and 17 July 1992.

Jelavich, Barbara. *History of Balkans, 20th Century*. Cambridge University Press, 1983.

Kaplan, Robert D. "History's Cauldron," *The Atlantic Monthly*, June 1991.

Macedonia FAQ. [Online] Available http://www.erc.msstate.edu/~vkire/faq/politics/boris.trajkovski.html (Accessed 5/00).

Macedonia Ministry of Information. Press Release on the Presidential Campaign. 1 Oct. 1999

"Macedonia Reshuffles Government." *Reuters*, 27 December 1999.

*Macedonian Herald*, January 2000.

*New York Times*, 28 March, 5 & 17 April 1992.

*Radio Free Europe/Radio Liberty Research Reports*, various issues.

"Serious Irregularities in Macedonian Election." BBC News, 15 November 1999.

*Washington Post*, 9 June 1992.

Profile researched and written by Rosalie Wieder (5/2000); sections adapted from contributions by Julie Kim, Analyst in European Affairs, Library of Congress, (9/92).

# MADAGASCAR

### Didier Ratsiraka
### President

*(pronounced "DEE-dyay raht-suh-RAH-kuh")*

*"I will be the candidate if the people want me again."*

The Democratic Republic of Madagascar is located in the Indian Ocean, approximately 386 km (240 mi) off the southeast coast of Africa. It is the fourth-largest island in the world, covering an area of 587,041 sq km (226,657 sq mi). The central region of the island is dominated by a mountainous plateau, partly volcanic in origin. The elevation reaches 2,876 m (9,436 ft) atop Mount Maromokotro in the north. A narrow coastal plain is found in the east while a wider plain covers the west coast. The south is an extremely arid desert region.

The population of Madagascar, estimated at 14.9 million people, is ethnically diverse. The two major groups are the Mérinas (Hova) of Indonesian descent and peoples of African descent. Other smaller groups include Indians, Pakistanis, Comorans, French, Chinese, and people of Arab origin. Approximately 55% of the population hold traditional religious beliefs while about 36% are classified as Christians (with Protestants predominantly represented on the plateau and Roman Catholics in the coastal areas). About 9% are Muslim. The two official languages are Malagasy (of Malayo-Indonesian origin) and French.

The unit of currency is the Malagasy *franc*. Per capita GDP has been estimated at US$730. This makes Madagascar one of the world's poorest nations. Agriculture dominates the economy and contributes more than 60% of export earnings. Madagascar is the world's leading supplier of vanilla, but coffee is the country's major export crop. Other food crops include rice, bananas, beans, cassava, corn, sweet potatoes, cloves, peanuts, and yams. The primary industrial activities are mineral extraction and light manufacturing (mainly food processing). Automobile assembly and petroleum refining are expected to grow in importance. While France is the principal trading partner, other partners include Germany, Japan, Italy, and the US.

## POLITICAL BACKGROUND

During the 18th and 19th centuries Madagascar was ruled by the Mérina monarchy. After a short period of British influence, the French gained control by 1896. The country voted to become an independent republic within the French community in 1958 and established a Western-style democratic constitution the following year. Full political independence was gained in 1960.

The first republic of Madagascar was led by Philibert Tsiranana until 1972. His government was overthrown in a national uprising protesting continued French influence.

President Tsiranana was followed by General Ramanantsoa. Unable to satisfy the growing nationalist opposition, General Ramanantsoa resigned in 1975, and his successor, Colonel Ratsimandrava, was assassinated after only six days in office. Lieutenant Colonel Didier Ratsiraka formed a new government in June 1975. In December of that same year he won his first seven-year term as president. He was reelected to a second term in 1989. Chronic food shortages and student riots led to the growth of opposition parties, including Albert Zafy's Union Nationale des Democrates Chretiens (UNDC). Ratsiraka served three terms before he lost the 1993 elections to Albert Zafy. Less than five years later, on 29 December 1996, Ratsiraka regained the trust of the Malagasy people and was returned to office.

A new constitution, introduced in 1992, provides for a unitary state with a bicameral legislature (Senate not yet established). The president has limited powers and is directly elected for a four-year term, reduced from seven years previously. A constitutional referendum in 1998 passed narrowly, giving the executive greater powers. The executive appoints a prime minister from a list of candidates nominated by the National Assembly. The prime minister appoints the Council of Ministers. The legislative branch consists of a (future) Senate and a National Assembly. Two-thirds of the members of the Senate are selected by an electoral college for a four-year term, and the remaining one-third are appointed by the president. Deputies, who are members of the National Assembly, are elected for four years by universal suffrage under a system of proportional representation.

## PERSONAL BACKGROUND

Didier Ratsiraka was born on 4 November 1936 in the small village of Vatomandry. He was a member of one of the coastal tribes on the island that had historically been among the poorest in the country and whose members opposed the traditional domination by the Merinas of the high plateau. He attended primary school in Madagascar and went to high school in Paris. After graduating from the French Naval Officers' School, he served with the French navy. He was commissioned a captain and from 1970 to 1972 served as Madagascar's military attaché to France.

## RISE TO POWER

Although Madagascar gained its independence in 1960, French military and economic policies continued to dominate. Nationalists, whose roots predated independence, encouraged a rebellion in the southern part of the country in 1972. The rebellion spread to the cities, leading to the resignation of President Philibert Tsiranana. A combination of poor economic development, long-standing ethnic rivalries, and a continuing French naval and military presence led to the formation of a new government under military domination. Ratsiraka, because of his close ties with the rebellious officers who took power, was appointed minister of foreign affairs in 1972, a position he held until 1974. As foreign minister, Ratsiraka renegotiated a cooperation agreement with France that resulted in removal of French military bases. This achievement, along with Ratsiraka's nationalist leanings, made him highly popular throughout the country.

However, the new government proved unable to reconcile the opposing ideologies between moderates who wanted to maintain close ties with the West and radicals who demanded a socialist government. In 1975, the leader of the radical faction gained power but was assassinated within six days of being sworn in as president. In his place, a provisional 18-man military directorate took power and suppressed all internal opposition. Finally, in June of that year, Ratsiraka formed a new interim government with himself as president. In the December 1975 election, Ratsiraka won an overwhelming victory that gave him a seven-year term as president.

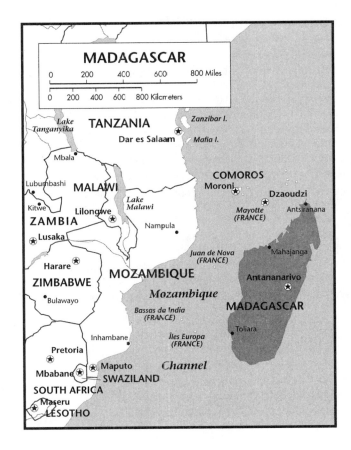

## LEADERSHIP

Despite frequent popular uprisings, Ratsiraka ruled Madagascar with almost absolute power for sixteen years. His leadership was influenced by Marxist ideology, which he acquired during his extensive trips as a military officer to socialist countries. With the collapse of communism and the Soviet Union in 1990 and the limitations imposed on presidential power by the 1992 constitution, Ratsiraka was forced to adapt. Though suffering a major electoral defeat in 1993, he benefited from the perceived incompetence of his successor and returned to power in 1997.

Ratsiraka is a skillful politician who commands significant loyalty from technocrats and business people. Ratsiraka has also enjoyed unwavering support among coastal peoples. However, his detractors have criticized him for benefiting unfairly from the wealth he and his family accumulated during his 16 years in power.

Madagascar remains one of the poorest countries in the world and faces serious threats to its fragile environment. The challenge before President Ratsiraka is to respond more effectively to the high expectations of the impoverished Malagasy people. He also must build a consensus in an increasingly polarized society where decentralized government could divide Malagasy further. His narrow margin of victory in the 1996 election gave him a tenuous mandate that he was able to strengthen through the passage of his constitutional referendum in 1998.

## DOMESTIC POLICY

Madagascar's economy declined in the mid-1970s following nationalization. The agricultural sector, which employed more than 75% of the labor force, was neglected in favor of industrialization through import substitution. This policy, along with unfavorable terms of trade, resulted in heavy external borrowing and deterioration of the balance of

payments. High inflation further eroded the purchasing power of the Malagasy *franc*. Real GDP dropped about 11% between 1980 and 1982.

Under increasing internal and external pressures for policy reforms, Ratsiraka's government negotiated a stabilization program with the International Monetary Fund and structural adjustment programs with the World Bank, the first steps in a series toward market-oriented policies. He removed price controls, liberalized trade, and adjusted the exchange rate of the *franc*. Despite modest growth and financial stability between 1983 and 1987, Ratsiraka's popularity continued to decline.

Since his re-election in December 1996, President Ratsiraka has faced difficult financial and political prospects. He has renegotiated with the IMF and World Bank, securing lending commitments through 1999, but assistance is contingent on privatizing parastatals such as Air Madagascar. Ratsiraka expects some debt relief from the Paris Club of government creditors. The price of oil, having risen from US$10 a barrel in January 1999 to US$30 a barrel in March 2000, continues to fuel inflation, and the Malagasy *franc* depreciated 6% against the Euro in 1999. Severe flooding displaced some 600,000 people in February and March 2000, disrupting economic growth and adding to the government's burdens.

Politically, Ratsiraka's main challenge is to handle the autonomous province issue with aplomb. He has promised to hold provincial elections in 2000, but many Malagasy fear that autonomy will hasten the end of Madagascar's long-standing political and social unity.

## FOREIGN POLICY

Madagascar's foreign policy shifted dramatically in 1973 in favor of closer economic ties with communist countries, in particular China and the former Soviet Union. As a result, Madagascar withdrew from the Franc Zone and the Francophone Common African and Malagasy Organization (OCAM). Despite its tilt to the east, Madagascar supported the non-aligned movement and African liberation movements. Relations with South Africa, which had deteriorated in protest against apartheid, improved after 1994.

In the 1980s, Ratsiraka returned to the West for development aid. Analysts now consider that Madagascar's future is linked closely with that of her southern African neighbors and that she would stand to gain by joining the Southern African Development Community (SADC). Madagascar has been a member of the Common Market for Eastern and Southern Africa (COMESA); however, Ratsiraka appears to be reluctant to join SADC's South African- and hence, Anglophone-dominated financial and technical community.

## ADDRESS

President of the Republic

Antananarivo, Madagascar

## REFERENCES

*Africa Confidential*, 13 December 1996.

Africa News Online. [Online] Available http://www.africanews.org/west/stories/1999_feat1.html (Accessed June 2000).

*African Development Indicators* 1996. Washington, DC: World Bank, 1996.

Africaonline. [Online] Available http://www.africa-online.com (Accessed June 2000).

Banks, Arthur S., Alan Day, and Thomas Muller. *Political Handbook of the World, 1995–96*. Binghamton, NY: CSA Publications, 1995.

Central Intelligence Agency. *The World Factbook 1999*.

Economist Intelligence Unit. *EIU Country Reports,* 3 March 2000.

*The Economist,* 22 March 1997.

Integrated Regional Information Network (IRIN). [Online] Available http://www.reliefweb.int/IRIN (Accessed June 2000).

*International Financial Statistics.* Washington, DC: International Monetary Fund, 1997.

*Jeune Afrique,* 25 September 1996–21 January 1997.

US Department of State. *1999 Country Reports on Human Rights Practices.* [Online] Available http://www.state.gov/www/global/human_rights/1999_hrp_report/madasc.html (Accessed June 2000).

*World Development Indicators (CD-ROM).* Washington, DC: World Bank, 1995.

**Profile researched and written by R. Charles Sebuharara, Binghamton University (7/97; updated by Robert J. Groelsema 6/2000).**

# MALAWI

**Bakili Muluzi**
**President**

*(pronounced "ba-KIH-ree moo-LOO-zee")*

*"There is evidence that countries that embrace democracy experience economic growth."*

The landlocked Republic of Malawi, formerly called Nyasaland, became an independent nation on 6 July 1964, and a republic in 1966. Malawi's neighbors include Tanzania to the northeast, Mozambique to the west and southwest, and Zambia to the east and northeast. The 360-mile Lake Malawi also borders the northeastern side of the country. Malawi has an area of 118,484 sq km (45,747 sq mi) and a population of 10 million. The country's topography consists of fertile plateaus and a mountain range lining the Rift Valley, which stretches from north to south. The climate is semi-tropical. Malawi's major cities include Lilongwe (pop. 395,000) and the former capital, Blantyre (pop. 446,800).

The major ethnic groups include the Chewa, the Mang'anja, the Tumbuka, the Yao, and the Lomwe. Most Malawians are Christians (75%), with Islam and traditional African beliefs also widely practiced. While English is the official language, African languages (primarily Chichewa) are also widely spoken. Malawi's economy is based primarily on subsistence farming and cash-crop agriculture. The southern portion of the country possesses large agricultural estates while agriculture in the north consists of family farms. The fertile land allowed Malawi's economy to profit from cash-crop production and agricultural processing in the 1960s and 1970s. However, by the 1980s, smaller farms suffered from soil depletion and overcrowding, reducing agricultural surplus for sale abroad. During the 1990s, a series of droughts and an influx of refugees from war-torn Mozambique further aggravated the weak economy. Malawi's major exports include tea, tobacco, peanuts, sugar, cotton, and corn. Its principal trading partners are South Africa, United Kingdom, and Japan. As one of the world's poorest countries, Malawi receives significant foreign aid. Its per capita gross domestic product was US$940 in 1997. The national currency is the *kwacha*.

## POLITICAL BACKGROUND

The trading kingdoms established in the Malawi region during the 1500s endured until British traders arrived in the area in 1859. In 1891, Malawi became the British protectorate of Nyasaland. In 1953, Nyasaland joined with Northern and Southern Rhodesia to form the Federation of Rhodesia and Nyasaland. However, internal opposition led by nationalist leaders, including Hastings Kamuzu Banda, forced the dissolution of federation in 1963 and the establishment of the independent nation of Malawi in July 1964.

Declared a republic in 1966, Malawi was governed as a one-party state under President Banda until 1994. The Malawi Congress Party (MCP), formed by Banda, governed the country through coercion and repression. In 1971, Banda was declared president-for-life. He once said, "One leader, one party, one government and no nonsense about it." Malawi entered a period of political stability and repression, with many dissidents fleeing the secret police and the paramilitary militia, Malawi Young Pioneers of the MCP. Significant support for Banda came from owners of large agricultural estates and agricultural processors who benefited from low state prices. Peasant farmers, who were unable to subsist on the land, became expatriate laborers in South Africa and other African countries. By 1985, 86% of rural households farmed less than 5% of the land.

By 1992, significant pressures for democratization and an end to repression came from the international aid community. The Catholic Church criticized the repressive government in an open letter. Despite the affirmation of one-party rule by the National Assembly, mass protests took place in May 1992, one month before another uncontested election. Banda, realizing his decreasing popularity and declining health, called for a national referendum on one-party rule. On 15 June 1993, 63.5% of Malawians who cast their ballot voted in favor of ending one-party rule.

On 22 July 1993, the National Assembly reformed the constitution by repealing articles that called for a one-party state and declared an amnesty for political exiles. Two months later, Banda underwent brain surgery. A provisional government, consisting of a three-member Presidential Council, began preparations for multiparty elections despite protest from opposition leaders, who preferred a transition led by a neutral team. In November, the National Assembly voted to end Banda's lifetime appointment. Presidential elections held on 17 May 1994, featured four candidates, including Banda. The winner was Bakili Muluzi of the United Democratic Front (UDF). Muluzi assumed the presidency and was subsequently reelected in June 1999.

Malawi has now become a multiparty democracy. The 192 members of the National Assembly are elected in single-member districts along with the president, who is elected nationally. All serve five year terms. The three major political parties are United Democratic Front (UDF), the Malawi Congress Party (MCP), and the Alliance for Democracy (AFORD). The cabinet and the vice president assist the president in the day-to-day operations of the country. In

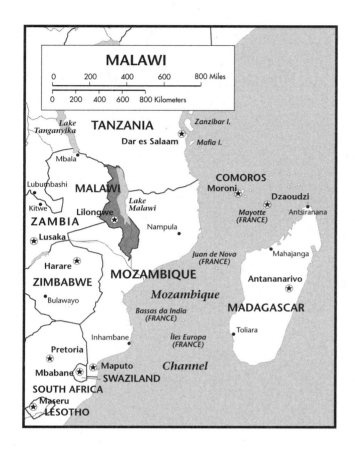

addition to the national government, there are 24 local government districts and three sub-districts.

## PERSONAL BACKGROUND

Bakili Muluzi was born in the Machinga district of southern Malawi on 17 March 1943. After graduating from primary and secondary school in Malawi, he attended Thirsted Technical College in Denmark and Huddersfield College of Education in the United Kingdom. Upon his return to Malawi, Muluzi became a clerk in the colonial service of Nyasaland. By 1968, he had become the government's court clerk.

When Muluzi was principal of Nasawa Technical College in 1973, Banda appointed him to parliament. Muluzi rose rapidly within the ranks of the Malawi Congress Party (MCP), eventually holding important positions in the party and government. However, he returned to private life in 1982 and established a profitable transportation and agricultural business. In 1992, he became a founding member of the United Democratic Front (UDF).

Muluzi is a devout Muslim who has significant political support from southern portions of the country. He has seven children, two from his estranged first wife, Anne, and the other four from his second wife, Patricia Shanila Fukula. On 15 March 1999 Muluzi announced officially the separation from his first wife of 30 years, Anne, who also served as the First Lady. Up until their separation in March 1999, Muluzi lived with Anne in the State House in Blantyre while the second wife, Patricia, resided at another of Muluzi's official residences in the former colonial capital of Zomba, some 70 kilometers northeast of Blantyre. On 9 October 1999, Muluzi

married his second wife, Patricia, in a lavish ceremony to make her the official First Lady. Muluzi was heavily criticized in the media for his insensitivity in blowing thousands of dollars from public coffers on a private ceremony to host several heads of state who attended the wedding while the majority of Malawians live in abject poverty and suffering.

## RISE TO POWER

Muluzi was second-in-command in the Banda government and secretary general of the MCP for nine years. He left the cabinet in 1982, having lost the support of Banda. From 1982 to 1992, Muluzi supported the opposition by heading the United Democratic Front (UDF), which at that time was a pressure group agitating for a multiparty system.

When the UDF became a political party in 1992, Muluzi was a founding member. The one-party system was abolished in 1993, and Muluzi began to prepare the UDF for parliamentary and presidential elections. He ran on a platform of reforming the Malawian political system by embracing democracy and alleviating poverty and illiteracy through increased social services.

Muluzi became president on 21 May 1994, having defeated Hastings Banda (MCP) and Chakufwa Chihana (AFORD) by obtaining 47.3% of the total vote. Banda, the runner-up and former president, received 33.6%. Despite having participated in the Banda government and having been accused of embezzling funds in 1968 as court clerk, Muluzi ran a campaign advocating change as an outsider. Most of Muluzi's support came from the south while the north strongly opposed him. He formed a coalition government with AFORD to obtain a governing majority in the National Assembly.

## LEADERSHIP

Upon becoming president, Muluzi commissioned a panel of inquiry to investigate the murder of four politicians during the Banda years. While the findings of the inquiry led to the arrest of six former officials, including Banda, the High and Supreme Court of Appeal acquitted all six, leading Muluzi to criticize the court. His power was weakened significantly in 1995 when allegations swirled that, as secretary-general of MCP under Banda, he should be held responsible for the actions of the party. In 1996, Banda apologized to the nation for the "pain and suffering" that occurred while he was president. Muluzi's first term focused on bringing about national healing and creating a climate in which the government's institutions could function democratically. He continued to actively seek foreign investment and aid.

In the 17 June 1999, elections, Muluzi and the UDF emerged victorious in an election marred by allegations of fraud. Muluzi obtain 52.4% of the vote while Gwanda Chakuamba, his main challenger and a candidate backed by the MCP and AFORD, received 45.2%. In the National Assembly, UDF obtained 93 seats, while MCP and AFORD secured 95 seats, with four non-partisans also being elected. Again, Muluzi's government lacked a legislative majority.

Muluzi's support remains confined to the densely populated south in a country where affiliations still determine voting patterns and political loyalties. Northerners continue to support AFORD, while those from the central region support MCP, and most of the southerners support the UDF.

As president, Muluzi needs to show that he is capable of transcending the regionalism and past political rivalries which have made governing acrimonious. Opposition parties demanded that the elections be annulled due to fraud and decided to take Muluzi and UDF to court. Protests and riots occurred in the northern region of the country.

During the election campaign, Muluzi promised that cabinet members who failed to retain their legislative seats would be excluded from the new government. When he announced his cabinet of 30 ministers and deputy ministers on 28 June 1999, it included two members who had lost their seats in parliamentary elections. Muluzi also failed to increase the representation of women in the cabinet, with only four being appointed. Three of Muluzi's lieutenants, Sam Mpasu, the UDF's secretary general and former information minister, Dumbo Lemani, sports minister, and Joseph Kubwalo of the Defense Ministry were dropped from the cabinet. These changes reflect Muluzi's attempt to strengthen his control over the cabinet and party by eliminating potential challengers to his authority.

Muluzi's government is three seats short of a majority in the National Assembly despite last minute defections by several AFORD and MCP politicians. The AFORD/MCP alliance remains a major threat to Muluzi's power. A united opposition is likely to make the upcoming passage of legislation, especially the budget, difficult. Thus far, Muluzi has refused to create a grand coalition to govern the country. The opposition has boycotted inaugural ceremonies. If he is to be effective, Muluzi needs to demonstrate his ability to bring the opposition into a cooperative framework with UDF.

## DOMESTIC POLICY

Malawi faces major domestic problems—AIDS, crime, environmental degradation, and national disunity. During protests over Muluzi's election, a number of mosques were destroyed and set ablaze. Malawi is a poor country that is religiously and ethnically divided. Muluzi's government must ensure that the national budget priorities reflect regionally balanced spending. If not, conflict in northern and central regions will weaken the government.

Muluzi is likely to continue development of the tourist industry and agricultural processing. In particular, the government will continue its privatization program and encourage private investment in Malawi's infrastructure, especially electricity generation and telecommunications. Because the country's economy is dependent on agriculture, it remains vulnerable to severe dislocations caused by occasional drought. In the past, international donors and the International Monetary Fund (IMF) aided Malawi. If Muluzi expects similar action in the future, he will have to maintain reforms and control spending. During the elections, he promised that the government would improve the delivery of clean water and provide free fertilizer and seeds for the subsistence farmers. He also promised to purchase more vehicles and train additional police officers to stem a flood of armed robberies as imported Russian automatic weapons have become increasingly common.

## FOREIGN POLICY

Malawi's foreign policy is centered on maintaining cordial relations with its neighbors and its Western trading partners. Following the June 1999 elections, President Clinton praised Muluzi for strengthening Malawi's democracy. The end of Mozambique's civil war will benefit Malawi as refugees leave and economic links are re-established. Because Malawi is a land-locked nation, the opening of the railroad line from Salima to Beira (in Mozambique) will lessen the burden of transportation costs for imports and exports.

As a member of the Organization for African Unity (OAU) and the South African Development Community (SADC), Malawi will benefit from the end of apartheid in South Africa with increased aid and trade. However, Malawi faces the flood of cheap foreign imports from Zimbabwe and South Africa, which negatively impacts domestic producers and could fuel a balance-of-payments problem. Negotiations are currently underway to create a duty free economic zone in southern Africa, involving Malawi and its neighbors. Muluzi needs to continue to campaign abroad for increased investment and aid in order to maintain the country's economic foundation. In early 1999, he visited Libya to seek economic assistance, which is necessary given the West's declining interest in sub-Saharan Africa since the end of the Cold War.

## ADDRESS

Office of the President
Private Bag 301
Capital City
Lilongwe 3, Malawi

## REFERENCES

*Africa.* Seventh Edition, Dushkin-McGraw-Hill, 1997.

Africa News. [Online] Available http://www.africanews.org. (Accessed 24–25 June 1999).

Banks, Arthur and Thomas Muller. *Political Handbook of the World.* CSA Publications, 1998.

BBC News, 18–21 June 1999.

Panafrican News Agency, March–July 1999.

Tenthani, Raphael. "Muluzi Denies Using Public Money on Wedding." *PanAfrican News Agency,* October 13, 1999.

Tenthani, Raphael. "Malawi To Have New First Lady." *PanAfrican News Agency,* September 11, 1999.

**Profile researched and written by Robert W. Compton, Jr., Western Kentucky University (12/99; updated 3/2000).**

# MALAYSIA

## Mahathir Mohamad
## Prime Minister
*(pronounced "ma-hah-TEER mo-HAH-med")*

*"I'll be here for as long as the people want me."*

Malaysia is one of the most divided countries on the face of the globe. Its nearly 21.4 million people come from a multitude of ethnic and religious backgrounds and are spread out over 329,757 sq km (127,584 sq mi). Malaysia is divided by the South China Sea into West Malaysia (the 11 states on the narrow Malay peninsula that stretches south from the Asian continent) and East Malaysia (the states of Sarawak and Sabah on the northern part of the island of Borneo). Western Malaysia borders its continental neighbor Thailand to the north on the peninsula and the island city-state Singapore on the southern tip of the peninsula. Its sits across from the Indonesian island of Sumatra on the eastern side of the narrow and strategically valuable Strait of Malacca (through which passes much of the world's oil from the Middle East on its way to Japan and the US). The capital, Kuala Lumpur, is situated near the strait on the western side of the peninsula. Eastern Malaysia borders the Indonesian states to the south on the island of Borneo and sits wrapped around the tiny and yet oil-wealthy Sultanate of Brunei on the north coast of the island.

As with many former British colonies in Asia and Eastern Africa, Malaysia has a large indigenous ethnic population supplemented by a healthy number of races from the other parts of the Empire. Malaysia is some 60% Malay and other indigenous ethnic groups, with a significant number of Chinese (30%) and Indians (8%) mainly descended from traders and tin mine workers who emigrated to Malaysia in the 18th and 19th centuries. Malay is the state language. Some 52% of the population, mainly Malay, are Muslims (the state religion is Islam); 17% are Buddhist; 12% Chinese folk-religionist/Taoist; 7% Hindu; 6% Christian; and the remaining 6% practice local religions. The Malaysian unit of currency is the *ringgit*.

Like many developing nations, Malaysia suffers from a large foreign debt (US$2.3 billion); however, it also does a healthy business in exports of petroleum, timber, rubber, and palm oil. The per capita GDP has been estimated at US$940.

## POLITICAL BACKGROUND

The different states of the Federation of Malaysia became independent from the UK and Singapore at different times: the 11 Malay peninsular states in 1957 and the Borneo states of Sabah and Sarawak in 1963. The predominantly Chinese island-city of Singapore split off from Malaysia in 1965. Malaysia is an independent member of the Commonwealth.

The supreme head of state or king, the *Yang di-Pertuan Agong*, is elected every five years by the nine hereditary Malay rulers of Western Malaysia. At election time, each state ruler is asked whether or not he wishes to run for the kingship. If there is only one candidate, he becomes king if he receives at least five affirmative votes from the other rulers; otherwise, a new candidate is sought. When there is more than one candidate, the ballots are taken in the order of a rotation system. The ruler of the last of the nine states to be represented in the kingship since independence, Sultan Azlan Shah, was elected in March 1989.

As in most parliamentary systems, political power resides in the Cabinet, headed by the prime minister. The King appoints the Cabinet from the 177-member House of Representatives, or *Dewan Rakyat*, whose representatives are elected by universal adult suffrage every five years. The other half of the Malaysian bicameral legislature is the 69-member Senate, or *Dewan Negara,* comprising two members elected by the legislatures of each of the states, and the remaining 43 senators appointed by the king, all for six-year terms. Political parties have mainly been formed along ethnic and religious divisions. Since independence, the Malaysian government has been controlled by a multi-racial coalition of political parties called the National Front, or *Barisan Nasional,* of which Prime Minister Mahathir's party, the Untied Malays National Organization (UNMO), is the largest partner.

## PERSONAL BACKGROUND

Mahathir Mohamad, the only commoner to be Malaysia's prime minister, was born on 20 December 1925 in Alor Setar in the state of Kedah in northern Western Malaysia. He attended the Islamic Malay schools as a boy and graduated from Sultan Abdul Hamid College in Alor Setar. He obtained his medical degree from the University of Malaya in Singapore and served as an army medical officer in his hometown, Kedah, Langawi, and Perlis before entering private practice in 1957.

A practicing Muslim, Mahathir does not drink or smoke. Popularly known as a workaholic, he is devoted to his political work. His debate skills are reported to be exceptional, though he is known as a leader who does not like to negotiate. Remarking on his medical background, a political opponent commenting on the intra-UMNO strife in 1987 said that Mahathir "will not think of negotiating his way out of a problem the way his predecessors, with their legal backgrounds, would have done. The medical solution is to cut out the cancer." He married Dr. Siti Hasmah binti Haji Mohd Ali in 1956, and they have three sons and two daughters.

## RISE TO POWER

After seven years of private medical practice, Mahathir saw his political career launched on a high and rapidly rising trajectory by not only winning a seat in the House of Representatives as the UMNO candidate from Kota Setar Selatan, but also being elected by his peers to the elite policy-making group of UMNO, the Supreme Council. He soon gained national and international attention by leading a small, radically nationalistic movement to take greater economic and political power away from the wealthy Chinese minority and give it to the relatively poor Malay majority of the population. He strongly criticized his party for not addressing this problem and wrote a book in 1969 called *The Malay Dilemma,* in which he called for greater Malay cultural awareness, strength, and unity. Because these were radical views in early 1969, the UMNO leadership banned his book and expelled him from the party.

In May 1969, ethnic riots rocked Kuala Lumpur and saw hundreds of Chinese killed by Malay mobs. For the next few years, while Mahathir was a chief administrator for the University of Malaya, the ruling *Barisan* coalition suspended parliamentary rule and instituted radical economic and political reform programs, much like those Mahathir had called for in his book, to lessen racial strife. The result was the 1971 New Economic Policy that saw the establishment of a national trust and a series of laws intended to promote government investment in *Bumiputra* ("Sons of the Soil," or Malay and other native ethnic groups) enterprises. The main goal was to have the *Bumiputra* increase their ownership of the nation's total commercial and industrial activities from the 4% they owned in 1970 to 30% in 1990.

Not surprisingly, Mahathir was brought back into UMNO and its Supreme Council in 1972. He was named a senator in 1973 and a year later was elected to the House. Back on the fast track to political success, he was soon made minister of education and in 1976 was elected by the party to the deputy premiership in the government of Prime Minister Hussein Onn, a position from which the premiership was just a matter of time.

## LEADERSHIP

In June 1981 Mahathir became prime minister, minister of home affairs, and minister of justice after Hussein Onn stepped down for health reasons and turned over the leadership of UMNO and the ruling *Barisan* coalition. Confident of his abilities and bolstered by popularity resulting from his "clean, efficient, smooth government" campaign, Mahathir called an early general election in April 1982 and won a landslide victory for UMNO in the House. Indeed, Mahathir's popularity returned the *Barisan* coalition to a 148-seat majority in the House in the 1986 federal and state elections and also gave it an absolute majority in simultaneous elections in all 11 peninsular Malay state assemblies.

In 1987 Mahathir faced a crisis in the party when Deputy Prime Minister Musa Hitam and former Minister of Trade and Industry Tengku Tan Sri Razaleigh Hamzah challenged

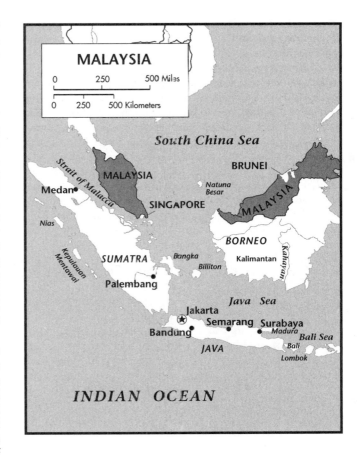

his leadership of the party in the intra-party elections. Mahathir won a bare majority of the party's leadership, but questionable campaign practices led to the party's being declared illegal by the High Court. Mahathir re-registered the party in March 1988 as UMNO *(Baru)* and forced his opponents out of the party in doing so. Meanwhile, Mahathir had cracked down on opposition outside the party by invoking the Internal Security Act in October 1987 and ordering the arrest of some 106 political opponents, Islamic fundamentalists and Chinese nationalists, and by closing four newspapers.

In 1983 Mahathir took on the nation's sultans in a constitutional battle whereby he tried to limit the powers of the royalty within their home states and to remove the power of the king to veto government legislation passed by the House. After a year-long heated battle, Mahathir won the power of a parliamentary override of the king's veto, but the king kept the veto and the power to declare national emergencies. In the process of taking on the popular royalty, Mahathir lost some of his approval.

In the 1990s, after undergoing heart surgery, Mahathir became concerned with the future leadership of UMNO *(Baru)* and named first Ghafar Baba and then, in 1993, Anwar Ibrahim as his chosen successor, under the title of UMNO deputy president. By 1998, however, Mahathir's relations with Anwar became strained when the two men disagreed on economic policy in the wake of the Asian economic crisis that had begun the previous year. In addition to removing Anwar from his post, Mahathir had him arrested and charged with corruption and sexual misconduct. In 1999, Anwar was sentenced to six years in prison while Mahathir's

National Front coalition retained its parliamentary majority in national elections.

While credited with much of the nation's economic progress over the past two decades, Mahathir has been widely criticized for the authoritarian grip with which he has kept his UMNO party in power. During his tenure in office, Prime Minister Mahathir has cracked down on political opposition both inside and outside the party and government by closing newspapers, arresting or detaining opposition leaders, and seeking to make the judiciary more dependent on the government. On his advice, parliament has enacted laws restricting the interpretive powers of the courts. In 1988 he persuaded the former king, Sultan Mahmood, to endorse a tribunal which then dismissed the Lord President and two justices of the Supreme Court.

## DOMESTIC POLICY

Mahathir's economic policies have been both successful and popular. He has consistently taken a nationalist approach to the economy, encouraging Malaysian self-reliance and blaming foreign powers and institutions for the nation's problems. Under his leadership, the New Economic Policy goal of increasing Malaysian ownership of the nation's enterprises has been achieved, and a majority of Malaysian industry is now domestically owned. Malaysia has become less dependent on income from traditional resources as manufactured goods have accounted for a rising share of all exports. When the country fell into recession following the Asian economic crisis of 1997, Mahathir overturned austerity measures and financial reforms introduced by deputy minister Anwar Ibrahim and imposed currency controls. The nation's recession was officially declared over by August 1999.

## FOREIGN POLICY

Mahathir's foreign policy has been molded by his anti-colonial beliefs and by his strict leadership. He has increased ties with other Asian nations, making Malaysia a senior member of Association of South East Asian Nations (ASEAN), and has improved ties with traditional opponents Indonesia, the Philippines, and Singapore. He has called for a "Look East" orientation among Malaysians to model themselves on the work ethic and success of the South Koreans and Japanese. Although he is the leader of a Muslim nation with strong ties to the Middle East, he is hostile to

Islamic fundamentalism. Some of his foreign policies have earned him a bad reputation in Western nations. For example, he banned the *New York Times* and the *Wall Street Journal,* which he denounced as "Zionist" for printing unfavorable editorials.

In the late 1990s, regional cooperation remained central to Malaysian foreign policy although relations with Singapore were strained at times over immigration and customs policies and the currency controls imposed by Mahathir in response to the Asian economic crisis. Controversy over the government's treatment of Mahathir's deposed protégé, Anwar Ibrahim, spilled over to the foreign arena to become an issue at the 1998 APEC (Asian Pacific Economic Cooperations) meeting hosted by Malaysia, at which it was raised by representatives of several nations, including US vice president Al Gore. Malaysia maintained cordial relations with the European Union, the United States, and Japan and began a two-year tenure as a temporary member of the UN Security Council in January 1999.

## ADDRESS

Office of the Prime Minister
Jalan Dato Onn
Kuala Lumpur, Malaysia

## REFERENCES

*Asiaweek,* various issues.
Banks, Arthur and Thomas Muller, eds. *Political Handbook of the World.* CSA Publications, 1998.
*Current Biography,* August 1988.
*Encyclopedia Britannica Book of the Year.* 1989.
*Far Eastern Economic Review,* 14 May 1987.
*Keesing's Record of World Events.* 1969.
"Malaysia: Inside the New Politics." *The Economist,* 8 April 2000, p. 42.
"Malaysia: Mahathir's Worries." *The Economist,* 20 May 2000, p. 54.
"Malaysia's Sham Elections." *Asian Wall Street Journal,* 26 November 1999.
"Vengeance Is Mahathir's: Another Crackdown on the Opposition in Malaysia." *The Economist,* 22 January 2000, p. 19.

**Profile researched and written by Steve Lewis (7/90; updated 6/2000).**

# MALDIVES

## Maumoon Abdul Gayoom
### President
*(pronounced "moh-MOON ab-DOOL gay-YOOM")*

*"We may lack in numbers; we may lack in material wealth; we may lack in technological advancement; in fact, we may lack in many of the material criteria by which progress is measured in the present day world. But, my country, the Republic of Maldives does not lack the courage to speak out freely according to its own convictions."*

The Republic of Maldives (pronounced "MALL-deeves") comprises a chain of 1,200 small islands extending north to south for 764 km (475 mi) and 207 km (129 mi) east to west in the Indian Ocean. Cape Comorin, India's southernmost extremity, 482 km (300 mi) to the northeast, and Sri Lanka, 644 km (400 mi) across the Laccadive Sea to the east are the nearest land masses. The islands have a combined area of 298 sq km (115 sq mi), yet only one-sixth of the islands are inhabited, and some are as small as football fields. The population is estimated at 300,220. The unit of currency is the Maldivian rufiyaa. Dhivehi, which is related to Sinhala, is the official language. With a traditional culture and closely knit society, Maldives is comprised of South Indian, Sinhalese, Dravidian, and Arab ethnic groups. Islam is the state religion; most Maldivians belong to the Sunni sect. Processed and raw fish make up 95% of the country's exports although shipping and tourism have increased in importance.

## POLITICAL BACKGROUND

Formerly a British colony ruled by a traditional Islamic sultanate, the Maldives gained independence from the UK in 1965. In a 1968 national referendum, the traditional Maldivian sultanate was replaced with a republican form of government. Sovereign and executive power is held by the president. The constitution of 1968 created a unicameral 48-member assembly, known as the Majlis, whose members serve five-year terms. Eight members are appointed by the president, and 40 are popularly elected. This assembly in turn designates the presidential candidate; if the candidate receives a majority of the popular vote in a national referendum, he becomes president for a five-year term. The president holds the highest political and religious authority. He is charged with appointing judges who will interpret Muslim beliefs in the adjudication of civil and criminal cases; thus, Maldivian courts are not independent of the executive branch. Along with an 11-member Cabinet and a 15-member Special Consultative Council (of economic advisors), the president also appoints 20 atoll (island group) chiefs to handle local political affairs. Political parties do not exist. Rather, because of the scarcity of trained manpower and the existence of traditional familial networks, Maldivian politics depends upon competition among a close-knit elite. Universal adult suffrage is guaranteed by the constitution. Women were granted the right to vote in 1952.

## PERSONAL BACKGROUND

An avid sportsman who likes cricket and badminton, Maumoon Abdul Gayoom was born on 29 December 1937 to a prominent Maldivian family. He was educated at Al-Azhar University in Cairo where he obtained a post-graduate degree in Islamic history and philosophy. His early career in academia began as research assistant at the American University in Cairo. He taught at Ahmadu Bello University in Nigeria before returning to teach at school in the Maldives in 1971. Soon recruited into government service, Gayoom held the positions of under secretary to the prime minister, deputy ambassador to Sri Lanka, Maldives' first permanent representative to the UN, and deputy transportation minister before becoming president in 1978. He is married to Nareena Ibrahim; they have two sons and two daughters.

## RISE TO POWER

Gayoom was acting transport minister in President Ibrahim Nasir's administration when the Maldivian Assembly nominated him to succeed Nasir in 1978. Ibrahim Nasir, prime minister since 1957 and president since 1968, earned a reputation for autocratic leadership; Gayoom was once banished for criticizing him. Amidst signs of declining support from the political elite and because of public demonstrations over rising food prices and his exile of the popular Prime Minister Ahmed Zaki, Nasir announced his intention to resign in 1978. Soon thereafter, Gayoom's nomination by the Assembly was approved by a majority of the popular vote. Gayoom began his first five-year term of office in 1978, was re-elected in 1983, 1988, 1993, and, since there were no other candidates, again in 1998.

## LEADERSHIP

As opposed to his predecessor's style of removing dissenters from political office, Gayoom's leadership style has been to tolerate dissent in order to develop a basis of political legitimacy. He was responsible for a 1979 amendment to the constitution that grants members of the Assembly parliamentary immunity for any stand they take. Gayoom also wants political parties to be legalized in the new constitution currently under review. In order to unify the country, he has held public meetings, led mass prayers, held numerous press conferences, and traveled around the country, especially to the poorer atolls. He has maintained an untarnished image and is respected as an experienced administrator, diplomat,

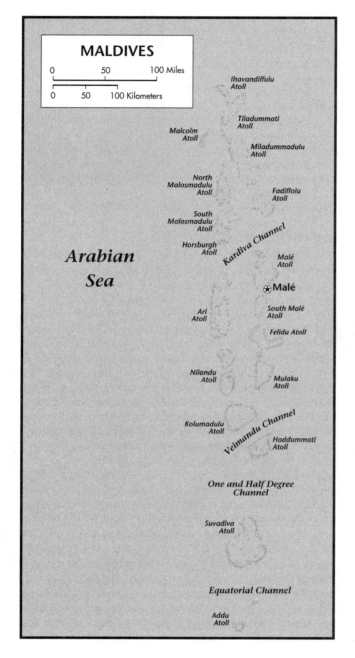

considering turning the national security service into a fighting force and installing radar equipment to guard the coastline in order to prevent the likelihood of another coup.

## DOMESTIC POLICY

Gayoom has tried to transform the Maldivian economy by encouraging development. With its scrub and dense tropical vegetation, the Maldives lacks mineral resources and must import even basic foodstuffs. Gayoom's policies are directed at improving transportation, communication, and small-scale industry among the 20 atoll groups. Fish product processing has been added to fishing as a mainstay of the economy; 80% of the population is involved in some aspect of the fishing industry. Emphasis has also been given to the development of tourism; Maldives hopes to continue to earn foreign currency through the appeal of its idyllic beaches. However, the industry is carefully regulated; no more than one resort may be built per island and an attempt is made to prevent tourists from influencing traditional Maldivian mores although this may change as increasing numbers of Maldivians are employed on tourist resort islands. Private sector services, which the growth of tourism supports, have provided new jobs in the banking, airline, and construction industry. It is somewhat ironic that the very industry supporting the islands has caused much of the pollution that is destroying them, with airplane emissions contributing the majority of the toxic pollutants causing global warming. The rise in water temperature of two or three degrees has caused, in some parts, more than 90% of the coral to die and lose color, and many reefs are now devoid of fish.

Lack of trained manpower remains the most crucial development problem for Gayoom. Under Gayoom's administration, the Maldives National Ship Management Limited, a government-provided service for exporters (and importers) who must ship goods to the nearest trading center, Sri Lanka, has encouraged the export of fish products, handicrafts, and clothing. However, the Maldives remains in the UN's ranking among the 20 poorest countries in the world. Gayoom intends to devote more government revenue to basic development needs, such as an improved water system and electricity as only the island of Malé has such facilities now. As of 1999, Gayoum has promised to fix the housing and land crisis by creating a new island, but he has not said how this is to be done.

## FOREIGN POLICY

President Gayoom has maintained an energetic and non-aligned foreign policy through a series of initiatives to consolidate relationships with historical allies like India, Sri Lanka, and Arab states. Gayoom wants the Indian Ocean declared a "Zone of Peace" and has not rented Gan Island, which was once a British base, to either superpower despite offers made in recent years. During Gayoom's administration, Maldives has increased its participation in international organization. It became a full member of the South Asian Association for Regional Cooperation in 1985. Gayoom negotiated a US$17 million developmental aid grant from India in 1986. Maldives is a member of the UN, the Islamic League, the Asian Development Bank, and the Colombo Plan. While it is Gayoom's goal to be free of dependent relationships, his country's underdeveloped status and vulnerability to invasion

and academic. All of those actions have greatly increased his popularity among the citizens.

Despite his popularity, however, he has faced three separate coup attempts: in 1980, 1983, and 1988. It has been alleged that former President Nasir has played a part in all three attempts; after the 1980 attempt a commission was formed which revealed that Nasir embezzled property from the government and unfairly taxed fishermen. Nasir had meanwhile moved to Singapore and never faced charges, so his property and resort investment holdings were nationalized. Gayoom relied on a contingent of troops sent by India to put down the 1988 attempted coup, which was carried out by Sri Lankan members of the terrorist organization Tamil Eelam, who had been promised a tourist resort in the Maldives and use of the capital Malé for gun-running. Because Maldives has no army and no prison, Gayoom is necessitate a close relationship with India. Furthermore, it will continue to rely on petroleum and consumer goods imported from Japan, Western Europe, and Thailand.

In March 1999, British Deputy Prime Minister John Prescott gave a grant of a half-million dollars for coral preservation to South Asia during a visit to the Maldives, but the problem is truly global—pollution from western industry causes the warming effect around the world. Individual, small South Asian countries like Maldives do not really have the clout to change environmental regulations, but together they make a force to be reckoned with. In 1985, Maldives, Nepal, India, Pakistan, Bangladesh, Sri Lanka and Bhutan gathered for the first SAARC meeting. This group of South Asian countries has formed more than an economic alliance, becoming by the 1990s a regional organization that also discusses political issues. The October 1999 coup d'état in Pakistan by Laskar-e-Taiba, a militant Islamic group from India's Kashmir region, and the three-year battle in Nepal with Maoist rebels from Tibet which has killed 900 people, are two large conflicts that affect Maldives and the rest of South Asia. Although the more pressing concern to the Republic of Maldives is its sinking islands, political stability in South Asia would increase the islands' chances of survival.

## ADDRESS
Office of the President
Marine Drive
Malé 20-05
Maldives

## REFERENCES
*The Economist,* various issues.
Heyerdahl, Thor. *The Maldives Mystery,* 1986.
*The New York Times,* various issues.
Phadnis, Urmila and Luithui, Ela Dutt. *Maldives: Winds of Change in an Atoll State.* 1985.

**Profile researched and written by Elizabeth Gittelman (7/90; updated 5/2000).**

# MALI

## Alpha Oumar Konaré
## President

*(pronounced "AL-fa OO-mar ko-na-REH")*

*"It is now imperative that we continue exploring all avenues likely to foster consensus among political and social stakeholders so that public life can regain its serenity and vitality; in this way, the citizens' confidence in our democratic and republican values can be further enhanced."*

The Republic of Mali, formerly the French Soudan, is a landlocked nation in West Africa. The mighty Niger River and its tributaries run through much of the southern half of the country, but the northern half is made up of the Sahara and Sahel region bordering the desert. Its neighbors are Algeria, Niger, Burkina Faso, Côte d'Ivoire, Guinea, Senegal, and Mauritania. The country takes its name from the ancient West African empire of Mali that was at its height in the 14th century, controlling much of the savanna area of West Africa. The Republic of Mali has an area of 1,240,192 sq km (478,841 sq mi) and is divided administratively into eight regions.

Mali has a population of approximately 10.4 million. Despite a high infant mortality rate of 119 deaths per 1,000 live births, the country has experienced a 3.01% population growth rate. Life expectancy is 46 years for males and 48.96 years for females. Its literacy rate is 31%. The official language is French, but the Bambara language is spoken by a majority of the population, with other major languages being Fulfulde, Sonrai, Tamashek, Soninke, and Senufo. Approximately 90% of the people profess to be Muslims, with the remaining 10% favoring traditional beliefs or various denominations of Christianity.

The currency unit is the CFA *franc*. Per capita GDP has been estimated at US$790, making Mali one of the poorest countries in the world. The main exports are raw cotton and cotton products (accounting for approximately 50% of export totals), cattle, and gold, with major trading partners being France, Côte d'Ivoire, and Senegal.

## POLITICAL BACKGROUND

Colonized by the French and part of the French West African Federation, Mali was known as the French Soudan. For approximately one year the Soudan formed a federation with Senegal. This federation was dissolved, and the Soudan gained its independence as the Republic of Mali in September of 1960 under President Modibo Keita. In 1968, Lt. Moussa Traoré, at the head of the Military Committee of National Liberation (CMLN), deposed Keita in a coup d'état and suspended the constitution. In 1974, under a new constitution, a 137-member National Assembly was created and Mali became officially a one-party state under the Democratic Union of the Malian People (UDPM). In 1979, Traoré was elected president in a tightly controlled election and re-elected in 1985.

Though relatively stable compared to some neighboring countries, Mali's bleak economic picture continued to fade under Traoré's increasingly corrupt and unyielding dictatorship. He imprisoned former political rivals; Keita died in prison in 1977. As multi-party democratic yearnings swept the continent in the late 1980s, Traoré was unwilling to yield any power. Repeated calls for political party formation outside of the UDPM met with firm resistance. Tensions between politically resistant groups calling for reform and the government continued throughout the fall of 1990 and into the spring of 1991, leading to several days of bloodshed in Bamako and other regional capitals. When it became obvious that Traoré was not going to yield, a group of army officers, led by Amadou Toumany Touré, deposed Traoré on 25–26 March 1991. They dissolved the government and the UDPM, suspended the constitution, and eventually set up a Transitional Committee for the Welfare of the People (Comité de Transition pour le Salut du Peuple, CTSP) with a 25-member cabinet.

Touré remained as interim head of state until municipal, legislative, and presidential elections were held in the winter and spring of 1992. Alpha Oumar Komaré emerged as the winner on 26 April 1992, becoming Mali's first democratically elected president.

## PERSONAL BACKGROUND

Alpha Oumar Konaré was born on 2 February 1946 in Kayes. In 1968 he led a student strike, protesting the coup d'état of Moussa Traoré. The following year he was named valedictorian of his class at the Ecole Normale Supérieure in Bamako, majoring in history and geography. In 1975 he defended his doctoral thesis in history at the University of Varsovie in Poland.

Konaré has been active in numerous international organizations. He has served as president of the West African Association of Archaeologists, a member of the Administrative Council of the World Center of Islamic Education in Mecca, a consultant with UNESCO, with the African Cultural Institute, and with the French Agency for Cultural and Technical Cooperation (ACCT), and has served as the first African president of the International Museums Council.

## RISE TO POWER

In 1978 Konaré was appointed minister of youth, arts, and culture. He resigned from this post two years later in protest against the repressive policies of the Traoré government.

Following that resignation he was employed at a government-financed research institute in Bamako. During this period he created the Jamana cultural cooperative. In 1986, he was involved with the founding of the National Democratic and Popular Front (FNDP), a group organized to coordinate activities of clandestine political opposition groups. Three years later he started the independent newspaper *Les Echos* and co-founded the Alliance for Democracy in Mali (ADEMA)—the group responsible for organizing 1990–91 anti-government demonstrations.

ADEMA was eventually transformed into a political party, winning a full majority of legislative seats in the 1992 general election. Starting with a field of nine presidential candidates, a runoff election was held on 26 April, leading to the election of Konaré with 69% of the vote. A disappointing 21% of the eligible voters actually cast their ballots. Election results gave Konaré's party 76 out of 116 National Assembly seats. Concern over the large majority of seats controlled by ADEMA led to the founding of a Front for the Safeguard of Democracy in Mali (FSD) by 13 of the approximately 50 political parties then said to exist in the country.

As the five-year terms of the legislature and presidency neared their completion, new legislative elections were set for April 1997. The Constitutional Court annulled a first round of legislative elections due to serious irregularities, such as a lack of certified electoral lists. Presidential elections scheduled for May were allowed to proceed even though nine opposition parties declared a boycott. Konaré urged opposition leaders to contest the elections, but only one candidate agreed to do so. In the 11 May elections, Konaré garnered 95.9% of the vote in what observers declared overall free and fair elections despite administrative flaws. Only 1.1 million votes were cast, a low turnout of 28%. Konaré took the oath of office for his second term on 8 June 1997.

## LEADERSHIP

Konaré believes in negotiation and compromise and therefore enjoys a reputation in the US and elsewhere as one of the few truly democratic African leaders to have emerged in the past decade. On the whole, he is personally popular, but there is rising disgruntlement within Mali over the one-party (ADEMA) control of the government. Opposition parties, with no nationwide organizations that can rival ADEMA's and plagued by unending personal infighting, seem incapable of winning a national-level election. They prefer to play politics by other means, alleging that the one-party state is back and that a fair election can be held only under a government of national unity—presumably including them. The opposition, therefore, has refused to recognize presidential and parliamentary election results. This position has provoked serious disruption from political opposition and student groups. Though Konaré has had some success in past negotiations with the students, opposition was rekindled in May 1997.

The rising unrest led to the arrest of several opposition party leaders who were charged with endangering state security. Their supporters had vandalized private property in protest at Konaré's inauguration, despite the boycotted May election. The following week the detainees were released on bail following pressure from religious and civil society

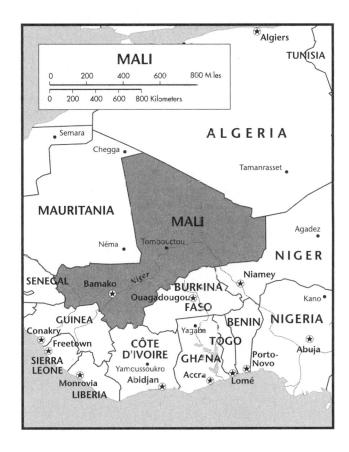

leaders. Violence erupted again during the first round of legislative elections on 20 July. A mayoral office and the ADEMA headquarters were burned. Two members of a political opposition group were killed in election-day violence.

On 6 August, Konaré began consultative meetings with various groups to address his serious concerns about the political stability of Mali. Three days later a police officer was killed at a political rally, leading to the arrest of several opposition politicians. On 11 August, approximately 15 journalists were detained by police at a press conference of an opposition leader and allegedly beaten for several hours before being released. These actions brought swift condemnation from an international group, the Committee to Protect Journalists.

The 1998 elections for urban councils and mayorships and the 1999 elections for councils in the 682 rural communes gave Malians a new avenue for political participation. Further, the prospect of Konaré as a lame duck in his second term alleviated some of the pressure on the president and ADEMA to engage the opposition in dialogue and consultation without further violence.

## DOMESTIC POLICY

Mali's sluggish economy and high population growth rates present a serious concern. Mali has a significant rural population, estimated at about 70%. Severe drought in the 1970s and 1980s pushed many of the pastoral people to either move into the towns or seek refuge in neighboring countries. Thus two of the administrative districts, Gao and Timbuktu, have seen significant depopulation in recent years. An estimated three million Malians live abroad, the majority in Côte d'Ivoire, Senegal, and France. There is little employment opportunity in Mali itself.

Yet, there are some signs that progress is being made. When Konaré was first elected in 1992, he was faced with the legacy of 23 years of corruption and mismanagement. The treasury was empty. Five years later Mali was praised by the IMF and World Bank as a case of successful structural adjustment in extremely difficult circumstances. Cotton production is booming: Mali is now second only to Egypt among African producers. Also, it will soon be Africa's third-largest gold producer.

The Malian people had very high expectations of the Konaré government, despite the fact that he did not make major promises. In his inaugural speech he only emphasized unity and hard work. Konaré received credit for resolving a dispute with the Tuareg, a northern ethnic group, and restoring relative calm in 1996. An agreement was accepted and formalized at Timbuktu on 27 March 1996. This peace effort has been quite successful, and in January 2000, an additional 1,000 Tuareg returned to northern Mali from their refuge in Niger.

Konaré's domestic policy has emphasized economic and political liberalization, peaceful dispute resolution, and decentralization. During his first term in office there was a large expansion of civil society through new, non-governmental organizations that are helping to set government policy. In his second term, he successfully championed Mali's first local elections, which promise to devolve considerable political and public administrative authority to the regions, circles (counties), and communes (townships).

Konaré also has managed to find innovative ways to cultivate participation in government affairs. *The Espace d'Interpellation Démocratique* (EID), or Forum for Democratic Consultation, is a means of modernizing the ancient tradition of palaver, at which ordinary citizens bring grievances directly to the attention of their chief. These days are held on the banks of the Niger in Bamako and have obtained much popular acclaim.

## FOREIGN POLICY

Mali's external relations in recent years have been dominated by the refugee problem created by the now-resolved Tuareg rebellion. Adjoining countries have been concerned about border security, as has the Malian government. Relations with Guinea were briefly strained when a Guinean army officer sought refuge in the Malian embassy, following an alleged coup attempt in 1995. The Malian government agreed to return the army officer to Guinea when they received assurances that his rights would be protected.

Relations with France were strained in 1996 when the French undertook forced repatriation of African immigrants in somewhat questionable legal proceedings. France is gradually dismantling some of its formal military and institutional ties with its former colonies but nevertheless remains a major donor. In 1999, French Minister for Cooperation and Francophonie Charles Josselin visited Mali. France contributed some $5 million toward social programs and $3 million to the energy sector.

Mali's efforts to democratize, decentralize, liberalize the economy, and play regional peacemaker have earned it the support of international donors. Mali received commitments for US$63.06 million from the International Monetary Fund (IMF) to support economic reforms, and US Secretary of State Madeleine Albright's visit in October 1999 affirmed Mali's favored position.

One measure of Mali's foreign policy prominence is Konaré's respected international stature. In November 1999 he became chair of West Africa's interstate regional organization, ECOWAS, and chair of the West Africa Monetary Union (WAMU or UEMOA). Further, Konaré has used his good offices to interdict the flow of illicit small arms into the region. Based on this record, and assuming a peaceful transfer of power at the ballot box in 2002, Konaré will retire a relatively young "elder" statesman of Africa.

## ADDRESS

Office of the President
BP 1463
Bamako, Mali

## REFERENCES

Africa News Online. [Online] Available http://www.africanews.org (Accessed June 2000).

*Africa South of the Sahara.* London: Europa Publications Ltd., 1999.

Africaonline. [Online] Available http://www.africa-online.com (Accessed June 2000).

Economist Intelligence Unit, Ltd. *EIU Country Reports.* London: 1999.

*Election Watch,* 1997.

*Electoral Studies,* 1994.

IRIN Online. [Online] Available http://www.reliefweb.int/IRIN (Accessed June 2000).

*Jeune Afrique,* May–July 1997.

*Le Monde Diplomatique,* August–November 1996.

*Le Nouvel Afrique Asie,* July–August 1997.

*Les Echos,* April–July 1997.

*New York Times,* 25 July 1997.

*Review of African Political Economy,* 1997.

USAID Congressional Presentation FY 1997. [Online] Available http://www.info.usaid.gov/pubs/cp97/countries.ml.htm (Accessed June 2000).

**Profile researched and written by Kathryn L. Green, California State University, San Bernardino (8/97; updated 6/2000).**

# MALTA

### Eddie Fenech-Adami
### Prime Minister
*(pronounced "FEH-nick an-DAH-mee")*

*"We must regain the time we lost during the last two years."*

The Republic of Malta is an island nation situated in the central Mediterranean Sea between Sicily and the North African mainland. It comprises an archipelago of three main islands: Malta, Gozo, and Comino. Also parts of Maltese territory are two small uninhabited islands: Cominotto and Filfla. The islands comprise a total area of 316 sq km (122 sq mi). They are a rocky formation rising from east to northeast to a height of 240 m (786 ft), with clefts that form deep harbors, bays, creeks, and rocky coves. The capital city is Valletta.

Malta's population is estimated at 381,603. With 1,208 residents per square kilometer, Malta is one of the most densely populated countries in the world. This high population density and unemployment have led to significant emigration in recent years. Most Maltese are believed to be descended from the ancient Carthaginians, but there are considerable elements of Italian and other Mediterranean stock as well. Other ethnic groups include Arabs, Sicilians, Normans, Spaniards, Italians, and English. Maltese is the national language and the language of the courts. Maltese and English are both official languages, while some Italian is spoken as well. The population is 98% Roman Catholic.

Malta has few natural resources, besides limestone. Agriculture is limited by the rocky nature of the islands, and most food must be imported. Industrial raw materials are lacking and also must be imported. Malta's economy relies on light industry, tourism, and other service industries, in addition to shipbuilding, maintenance, and repairs. Exports include clothing, semiconductors, textiles, furniture, leather, rubber, and plastic products. The Maltese *lira* is the official unit of currency. The per capita GNP is US$13,000.

## POLITICAL BACKGROUND

The strategic importance of Malta was recognized in the time of the Phoenicians, whose occupation was followed by that of the Greeks, the Carthaginians, and the Romans. The apostle Paul was shipwrecked at Malta in AD 58, and the islanders were converted to Christianity within two years. With the official split of the Roman Empire in 395, Malta was assigned to Byzantium, and in 870 it fell under the domination of the Saracens. In 1090, it was taken by Count Roger of Normandy, and thereafter was controlled by the rulers of Sicily. The Emperor Charles V granted it in 1530 to the Knights of St. John, who had been driven from Rhodes by the Turks. The Knights surrendered Malta to Napoleon in 1798. Two years later, the British ousted the French garrison, with

the aid of a revolt by the Maltese people. British possession was confirmed in 1814 by the Treaty of Paris. During most of the 19th and half of the 20th centuries, a British military governor ruled the colony. While substantial self-government was restored in 1947, it was not until 1964 that Malta became a sovereign and independent nation within the Commonwealth.

Malta is a parliamentary democracy in which the president, Ugo Mifsud Bonnici, is the head of state. A constitution was adopted in 1964, revised in 1974, and amended in 1987. The president appoints as prime minister the leader of the party with a majority of seats in Parliament. Together, the president and prime minister appoint other ministers to complete the cabinet. Actual political power is in the hands of the prime minister. The 65 members of the unicameral Parliament and its prime minister are elected on the basis of a complicated system of proportional representation and majority vote. In 1996, the government approved several constitutional amendments that have, in effect, guaranteed only a two-party presence in Parliament. Presently, there are three active factions in Maltese politics: the Nationalist Party, the Labor Party, and the Democratic Alternative (Green Party). The Democratic Alternative presently holds no seats in Parliament. The legal voting age is 18.

## PERSONAL BACKGROUND

Edward (Eddie) Fenech-Adami was born in Birkirkara on 7 February 1934. He received his Bachelor of Arts degree in economics, philosophy, and classics at St. Aloysius College (Malta) in 1955. By the age of 24, he had graduated with a doctor of laws degree from the Royal University of Malta. After passing the bar in 1959, he entered legal practice with Ganado and Associates in Valletta. He edited a weekly publication entitled *Il Poplu* from 1962 until 1969.

Fenech-Adami is known to be quiet-mannered and has a reputation for modesty and moderation. For example, during the events of "Black Monday," when Labor extremists terrorized the Nationalist Club and Fenech-Adami's family in their own home, he reacted by holding a Nationalist Party mass meeting where he told members not to retaliate violently.

## RISE TO POWER

In 1961, Fenech-Adami became involved with the Nationalist (Christian Democratic) Party and was assistant general secretary from 1962 to 1975. By the age of 43, he had

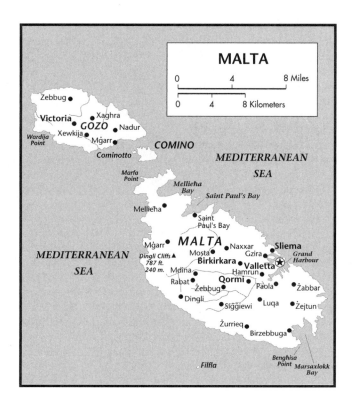

become the leader of the Nationalist Party. In 1979, he became the vice president of the European Union of Christian Democrats. He took the seat of a deceased Nationalist Member of Parliament (MP) in 1969 and was first elected on his own in 1971. He was the Nationalist Party's spokesman for Labor and Social Services between 1971 and 1977. Serving in Parliament as the leader of opposition from 1983 to 1987, he rallied support for his appointment as prime minister in 1987 and again in 1998.

## LEADERSHIP

During his first administration, from 1987 until 1996, Fenech-Adami followed consistent domestic policies that were aimed at reforming economic and governmental institutions previously controlled by the opposing Labor Party for 16 years. One of his initial programs was to shift the economy away from the socialist controls of the Labor Party by giving more freedom to the private sector. At the same time, he promised to expand various social welfare programs, assuming that the economy would grow at an annual rate of 10%.

Fenech-Adami also formulated policies that gave incentives to local and foreign enterprises in order to increase investment in Malta's economy. These included tax advantages and guarantees of secrecy to use the island as an offshore financial and trading center. A new emphasis was placed on tourism, financial services, and shipping registration. In other areas, Fenech-Adami sought prosecution for corruption and attempted to uncover pro-Libyan terrorist groups operating within Malta. Infrastructure improvements were instituted for the national airport, power stations, desalination plants, and telecommunications system.

By the early 1990s, Fenech-Adami began to direct his governmental policies toward fully integrating Malta into the European Union (EU). They included the removal of Maltese customs duties with the EU nations. This action caused a decrease in overall national revenue. In order to retain a balanced budget, Fenech-Adami and his party-led Parliament adopted a controversial value-added tax (VAT) which amounted to a 15% increase on virtually all consumer goods that would substitute for the loss of tariff income.

Although the removal of customs duties was a necessary prerequisite for final EU membership application, it caused anger amongst many Maltese and brought into question whether it was economically feasible for Malta to join the EU. Moreover, Fenech-Adami's pro-Western and European policies seemed to have compromised Malta's traditional policies of neutrality. The 1996 national election, seen by many as a referendum on Fenech-Adami's policies, resulted in a loss for the Nationalist Party. Alfred Sant's Labor Party had unexpectedly gained 52% of the electorate's support. After conceding defeat, Fenech-Adami ceded his post as prime minister and returned to Parliament as leader of the opposition.

Sant attempted to reverse most of Fenech-Adami's policies, including withdrawing application for EU membership. Yet, in other respects, some of Sant's "New Labor" policies were more conservative than those of the previous government. Strict austerity measures adopted by the Sant government included more indirect taxes, higher utility rates, and budget cutting measures. Many perceived these measures as conflicting with campaign promises to reduce the cost of living in Malta. Moreover, the effect of withdrawing EU membership application and reverting to a more neutralist foreign policy led to a greater isolation of Malta within the Western European and Mediterranean communities. In response to Sant's policies, an ideological difference developed amongst Labor Party members. The more socialist-minded followers of former prime minister, Dom Mintoff, withdrew their political support from Sant. That left the prime minister with only a one-seat majority in Parliament. In an attempt to reaffirm his 1996 electoral mandate and gain more seats in Parliament with other like-minded Laborites, Sant decided to call for new general elections for 5 September 1998.

In response to Sant's call for new elections, Fenech-Adami undertook to lead his Nationalist Party's electoral campaign to regain control of the government under the slogan, "Prosperity, Confidence, Direction." Fenech-Adami and the Nationalists claimed that the Labor Government no longer had a social conscience, as demonstrated by its recent austerity measures. At times during the campaign, it seemed that the National Party was campaigning more like the former Mintoff-led Labor against the Labor Party itself. Ironically, the main issue of the election was the same as that which led to Fenech-Adami's loss of power in the previous election—whether Malta could pursue its EU membership without sacrificing its standard of living. For the first time in Malta's electoral history, ideology took second place to the greater question of whether Malta should join the European Union. By a popular margin vote of 12,817 and a percentage differential of 51.81% to 46.97%, the Nationalists had regained power in the Parliament and premiership. On 6 September 1998, Fenech-Adami was once again sworn in as prime minister.

## DOMESTIC POLICY

Upon taking office in 1998, Fenech-Adami began to reimplement his former policies and reappoint many of his former cabinet ministers. He is expected to pursue a policy favorable to the private sector. This should include promotion of tourism, foreign investment, deregulation, privatization, and a lessening of excise and indirect taxes. In addition, he will continue to fight corruption and further improve the nation's infrastructure. Fenech Adami's goal is to transform his country into the financial center of the Mediterranean.

## FOREIGN POLICY

As in his previous administration, Fenech-Adami continues to follow a pro-Western, pro-European foreign policy. Although technically still neutral, Fenech-Adami's Malta plans to increase its support of international organizations and programs such as the United Nations and Partnership For Peace.

However, the major foreign policy objective of Fenech-Adami is to achieve Malta's entrance into the European Union in order to better integrate his nation politically and economically with the rest of Europe. Upon returning to office, he immediately took steps to reactivate Malta's EU membership application. If approved, Malta would become a full member of that organization by the year 2003.

## ADDRESS

Auberge de Castille
Valletta, Malta

## REFERENCES

BBC News. [Online] http://www.news.bbc.co.uk/hi/english/world/europe/newsid-1650
*CIA World Factbook.* 1998–99.
*Il Manifesto.* 8 September 1998.
*Malta Independent.* 4 September 1998.
Malta Election 1998. [Online] www.maltanetworkre-sources.com/mnr/elections.html

**Profile researched and written by Joseph A. Bongiorno, St. John's University, NY (12/98 updated 6/2000).**

# MARSHALL ISLANDS

### Kessai H. Note
### President
*(pronounced "KESS-eye NOTE")*

*"We will restructure, rebuild, and restore the integrity of the country's institutions. We will advocate discipline and transparency in all sectors of government."*

The Republic of the Marshall Islands (RMI) comprises 29 coral atolls (19 inhabited) and five coral pinnacles (four inhabited). These islands form two roughly parallel chains called *Ratak* (Sunrise) and *Ralik* (Sunset), located between 160° and 173° east longitude, and between 4° and 20° north latitude. Though the Marshall Islands spread over 1.95 million sq km (718,000 sq mi) of eastern Pacific Ocean, the combined land mass is just under 180 sq km (69.5 sq mi). Typhoons are not uncommon during the winter months, and can wreak havoc on these low islands.

The population is estimated at 65,500, with heavy concentrations in the capital, Majuro, and on Ebeye in Kwajalein Atoll. Under the Compact of Free Association, concluded in 1986, Marshallese have free entry to the United States and small communities are to be found there, especially in Hawaii and California where young Marshallese may pursue higher education. The Marshallese language is part of the Micronesian family of Oceanic Austronesian languages. There were probably a number of distinct dialects in the past, but only two (Ratak and Ralik) are spoken today. English is the official language of government and commerce. Three centuries of contact with the outside world have produced notable ethnic mixing, which has continued to the present.

## POLITICAL BACKGROUND

Spanish explorers first contacted the islands in the 16th century, but they were named after the British explorer, Captain John Marshall, who charted the area in 1788. The islands were largely ignored until the early 1800s. At that time, whaling ships began more frequent visits for water and refreshment, and in 1852 American missionaries moved from Hawaii to establish stations there. The Protestant mission legacy remains strong today. Later in the 19th century, the demand for coconut oil and copra (the dried meat of the coconut), brought the Marshalls into a new kind of economy. German trading interests became predominant, resulting in the establishment of a protectorate in 1885. When Germany lost World War I, Japan was given the Marshall Islands and other Pacific islands as a mandate of the League of Nations.

The Japanese have been described as the only committed colonizers of the Marshall Islands, which was one of six districts of Japanese administration. Copra production and education were expanded during the early years, but in the 1930s Japanese preparations for war became a high priority. World War II had a terrible impact on the islands as fighting killed many of the local population while bombing devastated

the landscape. When the Americans established military control in 1944, they found the Marshall Islands to be of strategic importance. For a half-century, this perspective has shaped the political changes which are now clearly visible in the modern RMI.

In 1947 the UN established the Trust Territory of the Pacific Islands (TTPI), including most of the Micronesian islands. The US was given authority for administration and charged with responsibility for islanders' welfare. America's special interest in the Marshalls became clear when nuclear tests were carried out from 1946 to 1956 at Bikini and Enewetak atolls. These tests meant relocation of whole island populations. Except for such military activities, little was done to develop the islands in more constructive ways until the 1960s. In 1961 the first UN visiting mission was critical of US administration in TTPI, and a 1962 polio epidemic in the Marshalls drew further attention to islanders' needs. As a result of these and other developments, American appropriations for the Territory as a whole went from US$7.5 million to over US$100 million by 1978. Other significant developments included the formation of the Congress of Micronesia, a Territory-wide legislature, to press the US on issues of importance to islanders. In 1966 large numbers of Peace Corps volunteers entered the Territory and other social programs associated with President Johnson's "Great Society" were introduced.

In 1979 the Marshall Islands chose to form their own constitutional government, reflecting their special relationship with the US. Marshallese were reluctant to share with the rest of TTPI the large sums of money they were receiving from the American government. In addition to various kinds of compensation for past nuclear testing, the US had, since 1959, been leasing Kwajalein Atoll to test missile guidance and anti-ballistic missile defense systems. As other parts of the TTPI chose separate constitutional arrangements, negotiations began with the goal of ending US administration.

These negotiations eventually produced the Compact of Free Association (CFA) that defined America's relationship with the three new nations—the Republic of the Marshall Islands, the Federated States of Micronesia, and the Republic of Palau—that had formerly been part of TTPI. In 1983 59% of Marshallese voted in favor of CFA in plebiscites held in these three states and the Compact became effective in 1986. The Compact is a complicated document and still subject to interpretation. What is significant for the Marshallese are the special financial arrangements connected to nuclear and conventional missile testing. There is very little economic base other than these payments, which have begun to decrease now that the Cold War has ended. RMI uses the US dollar as currency, and the largest cash employers are the government, followed by the commercial and retail sectors.

The Republic of the Marshall Islands is governed by a legislature (*Nitijela*) of 33 members who are elected by universal adult suffrage for two-year terms. The *Nitijela* in turn elects the president, who appoints his cabinet. There is also a council of *iroij* (chiefs), a consultative body. However, RMI politics have been dominated by *iroij* and *iroijlaplap* (paramount chiefs) whose conflicting interests have been more significant than any party affiliations. Amata Kabua, the first president, was *iroijlaplap* of Majuro. His successor and cousin, Imata Kabua, held a comparable title for Kwajalein. Long-standing conflicts between chiefs in different parts of the islands have been regularly reflected in 60%–40% divisions on such matters as the CFA plebiscite.

In late 1999 and early 2000 two major political changes took place. For the first time, an opposition party, the newly formed United Democratic Party (UDP), gained a majority in parliament, in the November elections. Then in January 2000, Kessai Note, the Speaker of the *Nitijela,* was elected to the presidency, becoming the first president of the Marshall Islands who is a commoner (i.e., not a traditional chief).

## PERSONAL BACKGROUND

Kessai H. Note was born on 7 August 1950 at Airok on Ailinglaplap Atoll in the central Marshall Islands. He graduated from Marshall Islands High School and received a degree in agriculture from Vudal College in Papua New Guinea. He entered public service the same year, taking a position as an agricultural economist with the Division of Agriculture.

Note was active in the Marshall Islands' drive for independence between 1976 and 1979 and has played a prominent role in government in the two decades since independence was achieved. In addition to serving in the parliament and cabinet, he has been a key player at the nation's constitutional conventions, as well as serving on the boards of the Marshall Islands Community Action Agency and the National Telecommunications Authority, and on the Foreign Investment Board. He has also served as president of the Marshall Islands Sport Council and vice chairman of the board of Air Marshall Islands.

Note is married to Mary Neimoj Yamamura and has five children and five grandchildren. Among his hobbies are fishing, tennis, and gardening.

## RISE TO POWER

Note began his political career in the late 1970s as a young activist in his homeland's drive for the independence. During this period, he was a delegate to its first constitutional convention. In 1979, when independence was won, Note was elected to its first *Nitijela* and appointed to the cabinet, where he served as Minister of Resources and Development. He remained a cabinet member for eight years, also serving as Minister of the Interior and Minister of Transportation and Communications.

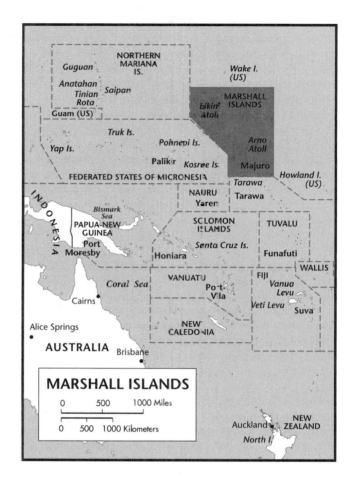

In 1988, Note was elected Speaker of the *Nitijela*, a post he held for 12 years. During this period he was also president of two constitutional conventions, in 1990 and 1995. Some of his actions as Speaker of the *Nitijela* were challenged in court by former president Imata Kabua and two of his top cabinet ministers, but both the High Court and the Supreme Court decided in favored of Note in each case. Note was elected president by the *Nitijela* in January 2000 after Kabua declined to run again following an electoral shake-up in November.

## LEADERSHIP

With the election of the first commoner to the Marshall Islands presidency since independence in 1979, it is expected that Kessai Note will introduce a different style of leadership, one not driven by local interests. Also unprecedented is Note's association with the newly formed, reformist United Democratic Party, which scored a stunning upset over the government party in the November 1999 elections. Voicing his intention to end the corruption that characterized the previous administration, Note has used the terms "credible," "accountable," and "transparent" to characterize the type of government he intends to lead.

## DOMESTIC POLICY

The greatest domestic challenge facing Kessai Note is to create a viable economy. The RMI shares certain problems with other island nations, including a young and rapidly growing population, unplanned urban growth, and a large public service sector that has been accused by the media of nepotism and financial mismanagement. World prices for copra, the primary export crop, declined in the 1980s, creating a serious trade imbalance. At the same time, shifting American policy in the post-Cold War era has diminished the strategic interests that directed attention, and funds, to the Marshalls, while the government remains dependent on US aid for over 80% of its revenue.

The Marshall Islands has begun an economic reform program, with the aid of the Asian Development Bank and other organizations. Since 1996, the country has reduced the size of the service sector, eliminated some utility subsidies, and attempted to increase revenues from fisheries and tourism. Note has pledged to continue economic restructuring and reform, even if doing so creates some short-term difficulties, in order to bring needed long-term growth. He also intends to continue the former government's support for the private sector.

The platform of the United Democratic Party (UDP), of which Note is a member, also opposes executive and legislative interference with the judiciary, which has resulted in the impeachment or resignation of four chief justices in an eight-year period.

## FOREIGN POLICY

In view of the RMI's dependence on financial aid in various forms from the US, domestic and foreign policy are hard to separate. Furthermore many of the conditions affecting RMI-US relations, such as the global and regional political situation, are beyond the control of the RMI or its elected officials. However, Note has expressed his desire for the continuation of the close relationship between his country and the US.

He has also expressed his intention of continuing the diplomatic ties inaugurated with Taiwan by the previous government in 1998, a relationship that had already resulted in more than US$10 million in aid for the RMI in 1999, plus funds for various infrastructure and construction projects. Note has stated that the previous government kept some aspects of the Taiwan-RMI relationship secret and has declared his intention of keeping the relationship open and transparent.

## ADDRESS

Kessai Note
President
Capitol Building
Majuro, MH 96960
Republic of the Marshall Islands

## REFERENCES

Banks, Arthur and Thomas Muller, eds. *Political Handbook of the World*. Binghamton, NY: CSA Publications, 1999.

"Kessai H. Note Elected President of the Marshall Islands." *Pacific Islands Report,* 3 January 2000.

Marshall Islands Embassy. Biographical information. Washington, D.C., June 2000.

"Marshall Islands President Kessai Note's Promise: Discipline and Transparency in All Government Sectors." *Pacific Islands Report,* 14 January 2000.

*Pacific Islands Monthly,* February 2000.

**Profile researched and written by Rosalie Wieder (6/00).**

# MAURITANIA

## Maaouya Ould Sid'Ahmed Taya
### President
*(pronounced "ma-OH-ya OOD sid-AH-med TAH-ya")*

*"I am glad to hail the increasing trust which our country enjoys with our partners in development and which has given us the opportunity to be the first country to benefit from the initiative to reduce debts."*

The Islamic Republic of Mauritania is bordered on the northwest by the Western Sahara, on the north by Morocco, on the east and southeast by Mali, and on the south by Senegal. Its total area is 1,030,700 sq km (297,950 sq mi). Two-thirds of the country is desert.

Mauritania's population has been estimated at 2.6 million, with an annual population growth rate estimated at 2.99%. The population density of Mauritania, the lowest in West Africa, is averaged at about two per sq km. Two-thirds of the people are Moors, comprised of the dominant *Bidan* ("white") Moors and the *Harratin* ("black") Moors, though the color terminology can be misleading. Both of these groups were traditionally nomadic. The *Harratin* are considered to be of servile origin, with official emancipation legislation not having been passed until 1980. The black African population (approximately one-third of the total) is made up of Fulbe (20%) and Wolof (12%). They are mainly sedentary cultivators and live in the southern zone of the country. Islam is the official religion of Mauritania. The official language is Arabic (declared so in the 1991 constitution), with Fulfulde, Wolof, and Soninke also widely spoken and recognized. French is frequently used for international commercial dealings.

The country has undergone intensive urbanization since the early 1970s, due primarily to drought conditions and an expanding desert. There has been a corresponding decline in nomadism—falling from 83% (1963) to 12% (1988). In a year of abundant rainfall, the Sahelian region to the south can support millet and sorghum crops as well as grazing for sheep, goats, and cattle. Camels graze primarily in the drier areas to the north. Millet and dates are also cultivated in some desert oases while salt deposits are harvested in Saharan zones. Per capita GDP has been estimated at $1,890. The monetary unit is the *ouguiya*.

## POLITICAL BACKGROUND

Mauritania gained independence from France in November 1960 and elected Moktar Ould Daddah as president. By 1964, he succeeded in merging all former political parties with his own, to form the *Parti du Peuple Mauritanien* (PPM), and declared Mauritania to be a one-party state. The political system became highly centralized and controlled by the president. The Ould Daddah regime attempted to strengthen the country's independence from France and foreign economic control. Iron-ore mines were nationalized in 1974, and a Mauritanian currency (the *ouguiya*) was introduced.

Until the early 1980s, the Western Sahara dominated Mauritanian politics and foreign affairs. In the early years of Ould Daddah's presidency, Morocco made territorial claims on both Mauritania and the Western Sahara. By 1969, however, Morocco finally recognized Mauritania as an independent state. In the mid-1970s, an agreement was concluded with Spain and Morocco, dividing the Spanish Sahara between the two African countries and ignoring an International Court of Justice ruling that the peoples of the Western Sahara should determine their own fate. In attempting to enforce this agreement, Moroccan and Mauritanian forces met strong resistance from the Western Saharan Polisario Front, supported by Algeria. This resulted in the bloodless military coup of July 1978, in which Mustapha Salek was installed as president. Salek, as head of the Military Committee for National Recovery, outlawed all political parties, including the PPM. He resigned in June 1979 due to shifts within the Military Committee.

Mohamed Khouna Ould Haidalla became prime minister in May 1979. Three months later an agreement was formalized with the Polisario withdrawing all Mauritanian claims to the Western Sahara. In 1980, Haidalla became president and dismissed members of the Military Committee who had been in charge of the government since the 1978 coup. Haidalla formed a civilian government and drafted a constitution providing for a multi-party system.

## PERSONAL BACKGROUND

Maaouya Ould Sid'Ahmed Taya was born in 1943 in the region of Atar. He joined the army as a young man and became aide to the first Mauritanian president, Moktar Daddah. Taya served as commander of the northern region during the Sahara war with the Polisario guerillas in 1976. After the coup that removed Daddah from power, he became a member of the ruling Military Council and minister of defense under President Mustapha Salek. Taya is a Muslim.

## RISE TO POWER

As army chief of staff, Taya replaced the civilian prime minister under President Haidalla in 1981. The draft constitution, providing for a civilian multi-party system, was abandoned. Haidalla proved unable to bring the country out of its economic doldrums. Reports of extravagance and corruption were widespread. In 1983, Taya deposed Haidalla

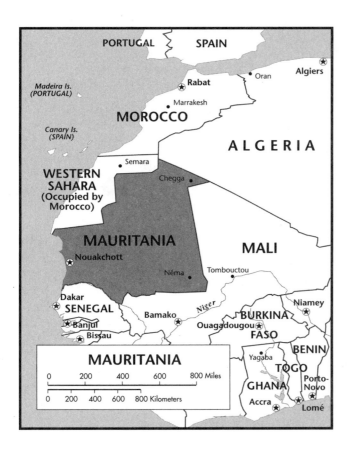

in a bloodless coup and has continued to maintain power since that time.

## LEADERSHIP

Taya's leadership has been plagued by problems involving human rights, press censorship, ethnic unrest, and setbacks in the democratization process. Human rights groups, as well as the US State Department, have criticized the Taya regime for failure to eliminate slavery, an inequitable judicial system, unacceptable prison conditions, press censorship, and poor treatment of dark-skinned Mauritanians. Serious discord developed between France and Mauritania in 1999 regarding the arrest in France of a Mauritanian army officer in July 1999 for allegations of torture in a prison in Nouakchott in 1990 and 1991.

Taya has attempted to follow the democratization process that has swept West Africa since 1990, though there are signs of increasing opposition to his rule. Amid claims of election rigging, a new constitution was approved in July 1991 that gave the president extensive powers and put no term limits on his service. Presidential elections were held in January 1992. As a candidate of the pro-government Democratic and Social Republic Party (DSRP), Taya was elected with 62.7% of the votes cast. His first democratically elected government included representatives from all major groups in the population. Multi-party municipal elections were held in 1994, and the DSRP won control of 172 of the nation's 208 administrative districts.

Presidential elections were held on 12 December 1997. Main opposition parties claimed that campaign conditions favored the reelection of Taya to a second six-year term, and

called for a boycott of the elections. Kane Amadou Moctar, the first black African ever to run for the presidency, presented himself as a non-aligned candidate with a platform promising to fight slavery, assist the return of Mauritanian refugees from Senegal, and reform the fisheries policy. The elections took place without incident and Taya was declared the winner, taking 90% of the votes. Turnout was estimated at 70%, despite the opposition boycott. Moctar received less than 1% of the vote. Opposition leaders described the poll as a "masquerade," citing reports of widespread irregularities that included children casting ballots.

Elections were held in April 1998 for 18 of the Senate's 56 seats. The DSRP won 17 of the 18 contested seats, with an independent gaining the remaining seat. In January 1999 the DSRP again won most of the 208 districts contested in municipal elections, though it is estimated that only 16% of the registered voters went to the polls.

## DOMESTIC POLICY

The state of the economy is critical to achieving political stability in Mauritania. As a country whose people depend for their living on agriculture, Mauritania had been faced with a persistent drought. Herding accounts for more than three times the contribution to the GDP of crop cultivation. In the mid-to-late 1980s, as the drought ended, the agricultural sector of the economy recovered, and GDP growth accelerated to 4.2%. In 1990, the GDP declined again, caused by the dispute with Senegal and the withdrawal of Middle Eastern aid due to Mauritania's support of Iraq in the Gulf War. By 1993, the GDP had grown by 4.9%, due to economic adjustments undertaken by the government. A further blow was dealt to Mauritania and many other West African nations in the rainy season of 1999 when flooding from rains that were heavier than the region had seen in 30 years decimated areas of Mauritania, submerging farmlands and destroying infrastructures. The mining sector grew quickly in the 1960s and 1970s and has now replaced agriculture in terms of contribution to the GDP. In 1994, only 20% of the GDP was agricultural products, despite the fact that over 62% of the population was employed in that sector. Continued mineral exploration may prove to be a saving grace for Mauritania's economy, at least for the short term, with promising reserves now known for gypsum, gold, tungsten, iron, petroleum, phosphates, diamonds, and uranium.

A major positive development in the economy of the 1980s and 1990s was the growth in the fishing sector. From 1983 until 1992, Mauritania insisted that all fish landing in their waters be processed in Mauritania and sold through the state fishing company. These provisions made the fishing sector an increasingly important part of the Mauritanian economy. That prosperity has been compromised, however, by over-exploitation, a decline in the Mauritanian fishing fleet (with only 60% now considered operational), and disputes with neighboring Senegal.

Mauritania's chronic budget deficit has been a constant constraint on the government. These deficits have been financed by external funds, and government attempts to find new currency sources have led to domestic instability. In 1988, the World Bank classified Mauritania as "debt-distressed," allowing debt restructuring and loan repayment cancellations. In 1992, the Mauritanian currency was devalued, provoking further difficulties for the population. The economy remains extremely fragile and threatens any political stability that could be maintained. In the summer of 1995, the government imposed a new Value Added Tax (VAT), which included an additional 5% on food products and 14% on industrial products. As a result, bread prices rose 25%, and the population rioted. Government measures were adopted to control the prices of essential consumer goods. At the end of 1998, Mauritania reached a three-year agreement with the World Bank for rescheduling its external debt in return for further privatization and currency controls. This agreement was enhanced in February 2000 by the World Bank and the International Monetary Fund agreeing to a debt reduction package that would amount to about 40% of the total debt outstanding at the end of 1998. Mauritania has an active Ba'ath party and periodically seeks agreements and aid from non-Western, Islamic/Arab states. The government reins in these ties, however, when fears of foreign involvement in internal Mauritanian politics develop.

The slavery issue continues to shadow Mauritania in its dealings in the international community. Since 1981, when slavery was officially abolished for the fourth time, it has been illegal to refer to slavery in Mauritania. Yet reports of its continuance in the country are frequent, by both internal and external human rights organizations. Arrests of lawyers and opposition figures over the issue continued in 1998 and 1999. In November 1998 Anti-Slavery International, a London-based human rights group, presented an anti-slavery award to Cheik Saad Bouk Kamara [Sadibou Camara] of the Mauritanian Human Rights Association, further highlighting the problem to the world community. In addition, the Opposition Parties Front (FPO), led by Ahmed Ould Daddah, in April and May 2000 led a series of demonstrations with following arrests that gave cause for great concern regarding the political stability of the government.

## FOREIGN POLICY

Diplomatic relations between Senegal and Mauritania were broken following ethnic disturbances in 1989. Relations were normalized in 1992, but the refugee question remains to be resolved and is greatly exacerbated by claims of racism against Mauritania. Members of the Mauritanian Association of Refugees in Senegal are not convinced that they will be safe and have called on the UN High Commissioner for Refugees to resume deliveries of medical and food aid. Complicating the refugee situation is the presence of Mauritanian refugees in Mali. The Taya government claims that some of these people were launching raids against Mauritania.

In January 1998, following a restructuring of the Organization for the Development of the Senegal River, Mauritania lost several key posts. The high commissioner was arrested for treason because he had agreed to this restructuring plan. The organization was deadlocked for the first time since its formation in 1972. Dam construction and water flow control of this important river is essential for the Mauritanian food supply.

Fisheries have also become a major issue between Senegal and Mauritania. The 1983 fishing convention has not been followed since the 1989–92 war between them. Following the 1998 presidential election, the fisheries minister announced that Mauritania and Senegal soon would begin renegotiating the 1983 fishing convention and that seized Senegalese fishing boats would be returned by the Mauritanian coast guard. A favorable treaty could give a needed boost to the Mauritanian fishing industry that has experienced steep decline in recent years.

Mauritania has pursued regional agreements with its neighbors, in an effort to reduce cross-border strife. Despite concerns about refugees, control of the Senegal River, and the fishing convention, an agreement was reached with Mali and Senegal in 1995. They agreed to cooperate over border issues, political extremism, arms smuggling, and drug trafficking. In the same year, a joint agreement was reached with Algeria for bilateral relations to combat "all manifestations of terrorism." In February 1995, the Taya government met with NATO member states Morocco, Tunisia, Egypt, and Israel for coordination of responses to Islamic fundamentalist organizations and weapons proliferation.

The Taya government sought to repair relations with the Gulf states, who had been angered by its support of Iraq in the Gulf War. This was followed in April 1994 by a joint communique in which Mauritania recognized Kuwait's borders. These events have led to a perceived loss of influence for Iraqi sympathizers and the Mauritanian Ba'ath Party. In 1998 and 1999 renewed relations with Israel, including allegations of an Israeli-Mauritanian agreement to store Israeli nuclear waste in Mauritania's desert, caused outrage in the Islamic world, with denials of the deal on the part of the Taya government. Taya and his ministers remained active, however, in diplomatic and economic partnership trips with various Maghrib and Arab world governments.

## ADDRESS

President of the Republic
B.P. 184
Nouakchott
Islamic Republic of Mauritania

## REFERENCES

Africa News Online. [Online] Available http://www.africanews.org/west/mauritania (Accessed June 2000).

*Africa South of the Sahara.* 29th ed. London: Europa Publications Ltd., 2000.

*Christian Science Monitor,* 10 May 1996–9 September 1997.

Embassy of the Islamic Republic of Mauritania. [Online] Available http://embassy.org/mauritania/ (Accessed June 2000).

US Department of State. *Mauritania Country Report on Human Rights Practices for 1996,* 30 January 1997.

**Profile researched and written by Kathryn L. Green, California State University, San Bernardino (6/98; updated 6/2000).**

# MAURITIUS

## Navinchandra Ramgoolam
### Prime Minister
*(pronounced "nah-veen-CHAN-drah ram-goo-LAHM")*

*"I want to make Mauritius the tiger of the Indian Ocean."*

The Republic of Mauritius lies in the Indian Ocean approximately 800 km (497 mi) east of Madagascar. It is comprised of the volcanic island of Mauritius as well as the Rodrigues, the Agalega islands, and the Cargados Carajos shoals. In total, the territory covers 2,040 sq km (788 sq mi) and has an estimated population of 1,182,212. Like other previously uninhabited islands in the Indian Ocean, the diverse population of Mauritius is the result of successive waves of explorers, colonists, traders, and workers who have settled there.

When the British abolished slavery in 1835, the sugar plantations—a mainstay of the Mauritian economy—could no longer rely on sources of imported labor from the Comoros, Madagascar and the East African coast. To compensate for the loss of workers, enormous numbers of indentured laborers were brought from India to Mauritius to work the cane fields and man the sugar mills. These workers came from different regions of the Indian subcontinent and brought their respective languages and religious practices. By 1860, they comprised the largest single ethnic group in the country.

Today, Mauritius is primarily made up of descendants from India (68%), Africa and Madagascar (26%), Europe (3%), and China (3%). Approximately 42% of the population lives in the urban center of the main island. The major religions are Hinduism, Islam, and Christianity. The official languages are English and French, with "Creole", Hindi, and other languages—such as Bhojpuri, Urdu and Chinese—in use. The official currency is the *rupee*. The per capita GNP is estimated at US$10,000, which is a very high average for a sub-Saharan African country. The literacy rate in 1998 was 87%, while population growth between 1992 and 1998 was 1.1% (compare with sub-Saharan Africa's 2.6%)

The economy of Mauritius was originally based on sugar and this crop still claims 80% of the arable land. In recent decades the country has significantly diversified and expanded its economy into manufacturing (textiles, electronics and software), other agricultural products (such as tea), and tourism. Offshore banking facilities were begun in 1989. The country supports an independent press with publications in several languages. Today, Mauritius is considered to be one of the most successful economies in all of Africa.

## POLITICAL BACKGROUND

Mauritius was known to early Arab traders traversing the Indian Ocean. The first Europeans to visit the main island were the Portuguese, who used its natural resources to replenish their ships on the way to their colonies in Goa and Malacca. Accounts of the island at this time refer to the large ebony forests and the *dodo* bird, both of which have disappeared due to extended human development of the land. The Dutch established a colony in 1598 and named the island after their own Prince Maurice of Nassau. They introduced sugar and slaves (primarily from Madagascar) but eventually abandoned the colony. In 1715 the French claimed the island and renamed it Isle de France. The economy of this colony was also based on sugar and was governed by the French East India Company. In 1810 the British captured the island, renamed it Mauritius, and confirmed their sovereignty in the Treaty of Paris. The British colony continued the tradition of sugar production but with the abolishment of slavery in 1835, planters began importing Indian and Chinese indentured laborers to work in the cane fields.

In 1968 Mauritius achieved its independence and set up a parliamentary democracy with sovereign control under Queen Elizabeth II. A governor general served as head of state and appointed the prime minister. In 1992 the constitution was amended and Mauritius became a republic within the British Commonwealth. The current chief of state is a Mauritian-born president with political power held by the parliament and the prime minister. The National Assembly holds legislative authority and consists of 60 representatives originating from 20 districts, each given three seats. In addition, two representatives are elected on the island of Rodrigues and four members are chosen to represent ethnic or underrepresented parties who have lost in the general election. Parliamentary elections are held every five years. The prime minister and Council of Ministers, made up of the leader of the majority party and 24 other ministers, hold executive power. The highest judicial authority is held by the Supreme Court, which consists of a chief justice and five other judges. At the local level, government consists of nine administrative divisions made up of municipal, town, and village councils. Universal suffrage is mandated for all citizens over the age of 18.

## PERSONAL BACKGROUND

Born on 14 July 1947, Navinchandra Ramgoolam is the son of Sir Seewoosagur Ramgoolam, the nation's first prime minister. He originally studied medicine at the Royal College of Surgeons in Dublin, Ireland. His medical training continued in vascular and general surgery at St. Laurence's Hospital and Monaghan County Hospital in Northern Ireland. He subsequently became the resident medical officer in Port Louis, Mauritius. Ramgoolam also studied law at the London School of Economics and received a degree in 1993. He is married and has no children.

## RISE TO POWER

Ramgoolam began his political career with the *Parti Travailliste* (Labor Party) in 1991 and was elected leader of the opposition. On 20 December 1995 he won a landslide victory, becoming the third prime minister of Mauritius since its independence.

His alliance of opposition parties, combining the Labor Party and the Mouvement Militant Mauricien (Mauritian Militant Movement—MMM), won 65.2% of the vote and all 60 of the seats in parliament allotted to the main island. His victory ended the 13-year tenure of Prime Minister Anerood Jugnauth. Ramgoolam's running mate, as deputy prime minister, was Paul Berenger. Berenger had served in both of the former prime ministers' cabinets and most recently was responsible for the portfolio of foreign affairs and international regional cooperation under Sir Aneerood Jugnauth.

In June 1997, Ramgoolam fired Berenger from the positions of vice-premier and Minister of Foreign Affairs. In protest, seven ministers who belonged to the MMM resigned. Only the Minister of Transport, Rashid Beebeejaun chose to remain in the cabinet as an independent candidate. His six colleagues and other elected MMM candidates joined the parliamentary opposition group. This precipitated a cabinet reshuffle, the second since Ramgoolam took power in 1995. Kailash Purryag, Vice President of the Mauritius Labour Party, has since filled Berenger's post(s). A similar incident had happened in 1983 when Navin's father, Sir Seewoosagur Ramgoolam, was the premier; 11 MMM ministers resigned, leading to new elections and Sir Seewoosagur's defeat.

## LEADERSHIP

Ramgoolam's campaign for the 1995 election focused on providing a fresh face after the 13-year reign of Prime Minister Jugnauth. He stressed two issues: putting an end to corruption and creating unity. Charges of widespread corruption in Jugnauth's government had been in circulation for some time and Ramgoolam promised reform. Also, language has long been a contested issue in the multicultural nation of Mauritius. Jugnauth had proposed that each student qualify in at least one oriental language as well as English and French. Ramgoolam opposed this idea, preferring to stress one national language.

Indeed Ramgoolam has maintained remarkable racial stability since the ethnic clashes between Creoles and Muslims in 1968. On visiting the island nation in September 1998, President Nelson Mandela of South Africa was to remark that Mauritius served as a role model of racial harmony for his own country.

Ramgoolam has vigorously promoted democracy and the rule of law, and taken a wholesome approach to sustainable development. Mauritius was in 1999 ranked with Botswana as the only consolidated democracies in the 14-member state

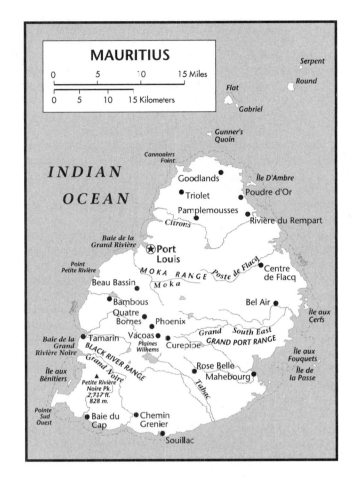

Southern Africa Development Community (SADC) by Anthoni van Nieuwkerk, research Director of the Johannesburg-based Institute for Global Dialogue. The durability of these democracies, Nieuwkerk says, depends on their ability to overcome the enemies of democracy: unemployment, poverty, corruption and social decay.

## DOMESTIC POLICY

Ramgoolam's government was elected as a coalition and maintaining this diverse entity is proving to be one of his most difficult challenges. He is faced with the problem of creating policies that will maintain economic growth while at the same time addressing some of the social and economic inequities. One of his most important campaign pledges was to end government corruption. Unfortunately, in August of 1996 his finance minister was forced to resign, faced with charges of falsely enhancing the 1995/96 deficits for the annual budget. This development increased stress within the coalition government and shook public confidence.

During his campaign, Ramgoolam pledged to continue economic development while expanding social welfare programs, such as public housing. As of 2000, the country has a remarkably low unemployment rate and has had to import workers from other countries. Most citizens, however, would like to see these benefits be more evenly distributed.

In 1995, one of the most pressing problems facing the new government was how to deal with the bloated civil service that places a strain on public coffers. The previous administration had promised a 15% raise in salaries for civil servants.

Ramgoolam stated that this will not be possible. The government does not have funds for such a raise and, in fact, would like to reduce the number of entrenched bureaucrats and replace them with younger workers. A commission for reform of the public sector was established, but making changes on this issue is difficult. In order to maintain his coalition, Ramgoolam cannot afford to anger the powerful civil service.

Another great challenge is how to expand the agricultural sector. As of the late 1990s, sugar exports, which accounted for 25% of the foreign exchange, were under their quotas in the EC and US markets. The gravity of this problem was brought to bear in 1999 when prolonged drought from the end of 1998 to 1999 was expected to cause a loss in sugar production of 300,000 tonnes valued at us$160 million. This was a contributing factor to a 79% increase in trade deficit over 1998 figures. Also, Mauritian sugar prices are as much as 20% higher than other competitors worldwide. As of 2000, Ramgoolam's government was considering two strategies to counter the current imbalance: first, a gradual conversion of land used for tea, which is less profitable, into land for sugar cultivation; and second, some kind of land reform. One of the largest obstacles to agricultural expansion is that the majority of farmers are working small plots. Of the 35,000 registered farmers, less than 20% can be considered to be full time agriculturists. The government wants to change the structure of agricultural production to make it more profitable and competitive with world markets. It also hopes to encourage increased production of profitable crops, such as tropical flowers.

The government would like to move further along the path of industrialization, expanding trade and manufacturing relationships worldwide. To this end the government doubled expenditures on research and development from 0.28% of GDP in 1995 to 0.44% in 1999. Policies that foster foreign investment are being encouraged by Ramgoolam's administration. There are also efforts to expand the important textile industry and encourage investments in electronics, software and assembly plants. Exports from the exports processing zones (EPZ), which are on the decline in many African countries, rose by 11%.

During the 1980s and 1990s, tourism grew to be an important part of the economy. In 1999, some 578,100 tourists visited Mauritius, representing a 3.5% increase over 1998. These numbers help to bring in foreign exchange and provide numerous jobs. This is partly a result of the government's efforts encouraging more frequent and less costly international flights in response the shrinking number of tourists coming from Europe. Mauritius started the year 2000 with a top-four tourist destination ranking in Africa, according to the African Travel International Congress. These development strategies are paying off for Mauritius. From 1988 to 1998, per capita GNP growth has been of the order of 5% to 6%.

The Ramgoolam government is also promoting investment in environmental preservation, to be guided by a new 10-year environmental management program unveiled in 1999, expansion of economic markets and infrastructure. Looking to the future, Ramgoolam has said that he would like to reinvest in the infrastructure of health care facilities and education.

The government generally respects the human rights of its citizens. Judicial inquiries however, are underway, for the death in police custody of a popular reggae musician in February 1999, and eight other detainees found dead in their cells between January 1998 and February 1999. The death of the musician sparked off a three-day riot that left three protesters and a policeman dead, over 100 people wounded, and some us$50 million in damage. It was only the intervention of the president and religious and social leaders that helped to quell the tensions and prevent a further degeneration into ethnic violence. In the wake of the violence, the government sacked the head of the Special Mobile Force, an elite anti-riot police unit.

## FOREIGN POLICY

Ramgoolam has stated, "we want Mauritius to enter the third millennium as a really modern state." To achieve this, his government is stressing external trade relationships and opportunities for foreign investment in his country. As an island with few natural resources beyond sugar, Mauritius is striving to link itself to other manufacturing markets and capitalize on opportunities to expand its existing exports. To this end, it belongs to the Commonwealth of Nations, African Caribbean Pacific grouping (ACP); the Southern African Development Community (SADC), and the Indian Ocean Commission (COMESA). Mauritius in 1999 ratified a trade protocol that was designed to make SADC a free trade zone within six years of its signing. Mauritius's development into an important center for offshore banking is helping to facilitate relations with Europe, Asia, and North America. Mauritius continues to carry out a nonaligned foreign policy and is a member of the UN, the Organization of African Unity (OAU), and the Nonaligned Movement (NAM).

Mauritius pursues a policy of peaceful co-existence with its neighbors, and is part of an OAU-led peace initiative in the Comoros Islands to quell fighting with secessionist rebels on Anjouan Island.

## ADDRESS

Office of the Prime Minister
Hotel du Gouvernement
Port Louis, Mauritius

## REFERENCES

*Africa Information Afrique,* 15 June 1999.
Agence France-Presse, 25 February 1999.
Central Intelligence Agency [Online] http://www.cia.gov/cia/ publications/factbook/mp.html
*EIU Country Profile,* London: The Economist Intelligence Unit Ltd., 1990–91, 2nd and 3rd quarters, 1996.
*New York Times,* various issues.
*PanAfrican News Agency,* as provided by PanAfrican News Agency, 3 July 1997; 12 September 1998; 26 February 1999; 24 June 1999; 20 July 1999; 26 September 1999; 1 February 2000; 7 March 2000; 29 March 2000.
*Reuters,* 23 December 1999.
U.S. Department of State. Background Notes: Mauritius, 1992.
World Bank [Online] http://www.worldbank.org/data/ countrydata/countrydata.html

**Profile researched and written by Wendy Walker (12/96; updated by Leo Zulu, University of Illinois at Urbana-Campaign 4/2000).**

# MEXICO

## Ernesto Zedillo
## President
*(pronounced "air-NEH-sto zeh-DEE-yo")*

*"The July 2000 elections will confirm that Mexico is a democratic nation."*

The United States of Mexico is the largest country of Middle America. Situated between the Gulf of Mexico to the east and the Pacific Ocean to the west, it has as neighbors the United States to the north, and Guatemala and Belize to the south and southeast. Mexico's total area is 1,980,000 sq km (764,478 sq mi), and the population is estimated at 100.2 million. The capital and largest city is Mexico City with more than 9 million inhabitants (20 million in the greater metropolitan area).

The Mexican unit of currency is the *peso*. Spanish is the official language but large groups speak Native American languages. Agriculture is the main employer, with petroleum and petroleum products being the largest industry. Leading exports are vegetables, fruits, coffee, gold, zinc, and oil. Tourism is considered a major foreign currency earner, as is the finishing of manufactured products in border towns for re-export to the US and elsewhere. Brewing and automobile exports are advancing rapidly. The US takes about 83% of Mexico's exports followed by Canada and Spain. The US is also Mexico's main supplier of imports. Mexico's foreign trade deficit for 1994 was about US$28 billion, a slight increase over 1993. The per capita GNP is US$8,300.

## POLITICAL BACKGROUND
Mexico was one of Spain's richest colonies thanks to its silver mines. Following the wars of independence (1810–24), the new nation went through years of turbulence and dislocation. Growth began under the dictatorship of Porfirio Diaz (1876–1910) but fell during the chaotic years of the Mexican Revolution (1910–17). Since then, Mexico has struggled with the problems of modernization and economic growth.

Mexico is a federal republic, governed according to the constitution promulgated at the end of the revolution in 1917. The presidency is very powerful. The president is elected for a six-year term and cannot be re-elected. The legislature is the bicameral National Congress. The 96 senators, two from each state and two from the federal district (basically Mexico City) also serve six-year terms; half of them are elected every three years. The Chamber of Deputies has 500 members, of whom 300 are elected directly from single-member constituencies and 200 by proportional allocation.

Since 1929, the ruling party has been the *Partido Revolucionario Institucional* (PRI). It claims descent from the time of the Mexican Revolution. The PRI regimes have believed in a nationalistic government policy and a central guiding role for the state. In foreign policy, the PRI has emphasized a non-interventionist position and independence from US policy. Under President Carlos Salinas, the Mexican government departed radically from former policies in favor of privatization and a free market approach. Salinas pushed through the North American Free Trade Agreement (NAFTA) which began on 1 January 1993, confronted the unions and management of the national petroleum industry (PEMEX), and caused considerable debate by legislating the sale of village communal lands (*ejidos*). The rewriting of history textbooks for schools in favor of a free market interpretation of Mexican history provoked argument within the party. Salinas surrounded himself with economists and technocrats, many of whom obtained their doctorates at top US universities. Ernesto Zedillo continued free-market policies during his presidency. By the year 2000, some political experts say the PRI continued to be deeply divided between traditionalists (dinosaurs), who prefer the party's old policies and monopoly of power, and the ruling technocrats or modernizers, who advocate free enterprise, less state control, and a more open political system.

There are two main opposition parties. The *Partido Accion Nacional* (PAN), founded in 1939, has generally been to the right of the PRI, and draws much of its support from the northern part of the country and the urban middle classes. It typically looks back to an older traditional Mexico and to closer ties with the Catholic Church. The *Partido Revolucionario Democratico* is a coalition of left and center groups which came together to support the presidential candidacy of Cuauhtémoc Cárdenas, son of the famous President Lazaro Cárdenas. In general, the party harks back to the Mexican Revolution and to more radical politics than the PRI which, it claims, has abandoned revolutionary principles.

## PERSONAL BACKGROUND
Ernesto Zedillo Ponce de Leon was born 27 December 1951, in Mexico City, the second of six children. When he was three, his family moved to Mexicali. All the children worked to help their father, who was an electrician, and mother, who held various jobs. At the age of 14, Zedillo joined his brother in Mexico City to obtain a secondary education. In 1969, he began his university studies, majoring in economics. He became part of a group of young economists, many of whom were foreign trained. He joined the PRI in 1971 and obtained his degree in 1972. In 1973, he won a scholarship to study at the University of Bradford (England). The following year, he obtained a Mexican national fellowship to study at Yale,

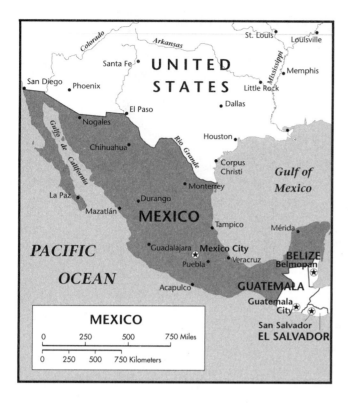

where he earned both his MA and PhD degree (1978) in economics. He returned to Mexico to work in the *Banco de Mexico*, then the nation's central bank.

In 1987, Zedillo moved into central government and was appointed under secretary of planning and budget. When President Salinas took office in December 1988 he appointed Zedillo, who had worked in his campaign, as secretary for programming and budget. In this capacity, Zedillo designed Salinas' National Development Plan, a radical change to a free market economy and privatization of industry. Zedillo was also a major negotiator of the PACTO Social, an agreement with business and labor, which the government claimed would halt inflation and bring economic stability. Critics of Zedillo note that his forecasts for growth, from 1989 to 1994, have failed.

On 7 January 1992 Salinas appointed Zedillo secretary of education. There, he decentralized the educational system, changed the pattern of teacher advancement, and ran into controversy when he attempted to revise the nation's basic textbooks.

Luis Donaldo Colosio was chosen as the PRI presidential candidate on 19 November 1993, and selected Zedillo as his campaign manager. It was reported that Zedillo was preparing himself for a presidential campaign in the year 2000. Colosio was assassinated while campaigning in Tijuana on 23 March 1994, and six days later the National Executive Committee of the PRI named Zedillo as its presidential candidate. Zedillo is married to Nilda Patricia Velasco Nuñez, also an economist. They have five children.

## RISE TO POWER

For Mexico, the PRI, and the Salinas government, 1994 was a turbulent year. On January 1, a rebellion broke out in the southern border state of Chiapas, the poorest in the nation. Negotiations between the rebel Zapatista Liberation Front and the Mexican government continued all year, with sporadic outbreaks of rural violence in the state and a hotly contested gubernatorial election.

The PRI celebrated its 65th birthday in early March, but on March 23 its candidate for president, Luis Donaldo Colosio, was assassinated. On March 29, the ruling PRI named Zedillo to replace him as the party's presidential candidate for the August 21 elections. At first his campaign went badly. Rumors about the Colosio murder and divisions within the PRI over Zedillo's candidacy placed him in a difficult position. Many also saw him as a poor campaigner and a diffident public speaker. Salinas had promised strenuous and costly procedures to obtain an open and fraud-free election, but the PRD candidate Cuauhtémoc Cárdenas, who claimed that he had defeated Salinas in 1988 and had been denied victory because of PRI fraud, warned that the same thing might happen again. In the early stages of the campaign the PAN candidate Diego Fernandez de Cevallos proved especially dynamic and moved ahead in the polls. In the first ever presidential debate, 12 May 1994, most believed that Fernandez was the clear winner. To make matters worse for Zedillo, on June 12 the Zapatista rebels in Chiapas rejected the government's peace proposals. It appeared then that Zedillo's candidacy was in trouble.

By July, Zedillo's campaign and his standing in the polls had both improved. Cárdenas and his party troubled some groups, who associated the PRD with instability and the revolt in Chiapas. The Fernandez campaign was seen as having become lackadaisical, fomenting new rumors that he and his party were too close to the PRI and had "cut a deal." The PRI campaign emphasized continuity, and played on the people's fears of political and economic instability.

The national elections took place on 21 August 1994. International observers, invited in large numbers for the first time, believed that the elections, while flawed in many places, were basically open. National newspapers wrote that while illegalities may have affected the congressional and state races, they had not been sufficient to change the results of the presidential elections. Cárdenas at first refused to recognize the result and denounced what he considered to be another PRI usurpation of power. The Zapatista rebels also denounced the elections as fraudulent, especially the governor's election in Chiapas.

Official tabulation declared Zedillo to be the winner with 50.18% of the vote. PAN candidate Fernandez de Cevallos received 26.69% of the vote, and Cárdenas of the PRD received 17.08%. The PRI also won easily in other races. It elected 300 of the 500 deputies and 64 of the 96 senators. About 73% of the eligible electorate voted, a huge increase in participation.

## LEADERSHIP

As Zedillo neared the end of his term in 2000, political analysts and historians attempted to determine his legacy. When he was inaugurated on 1 December 1994, Zedillo promised to distance his presidency from the PRI. He had often seemed uncomfortable by his authoritarian party's hold on power. He was also under great pressure to democratize the country's political system. While no other party had held the presidency in more than 70 years, the PAN and PRD had grown in strength and were demanding significant democratic reforms from the PRI. In the 1997 elections, the PRI lost its majority in the lower house of Congress for the first time in more than six decades; a PRD candidate was elected mayor of Mexico City; and the PAN and PRD had captured important governorships around the country.

Zedillo faced problems within his own party, where old party loyalists (popularly known as dinosaurs) resisted democratic and economic reforms. In March 1999, Zedillo made one of his most important and decisive moves to help celebrate the PRI's 70th anniversary: he got rid of the "*dedazo.*" Within the authoritarian regime of the PRI, Mexican presidents personally picked their successors from the party ranks, a practice that came to be known as the *dedazo* or roughly pointing a presidential finger at the new candidate. Zedillo replaced the *dedazo* with a presidential primary. Outside the party, Zedillo continued to openly call for democratic reforms. The 1997 elections were held under the auspices of the reformed Federal Electoral Institute (IFE). While there were some irregularities in the elections, they were generally seen as free and fair. The IFE was considered a completely independent body from political parties as the country prepared for the 2 July 2000 presidential election.

With Zedillo nearing his term, he faced the grim possibility of handing power to an opposite party. The PRI for the first time faced the possibility of losing the nation's top office. Francisco Labastida Ochoa, a PRI loyalist and Zedillo associate, led some presidential polls in early 2000. Zedillo had been criticized for backing Labastida, and ensuring his candidacy, despite claims of democratic reforms within the party. PAN candidate Vicente Fox Quesada made a remarkable jump in the polls in early 2000. Yet some political analysts believed Quesada would have to strike a political compromise with PRD candidate Cuauhtémoc Cárdenas to win the election. Cárdenas, running for a third time, was fading in the polls in early 2000.

Starting in the 1970s, economic crisis had quickly followed transfer of presidential powers. In early 2000, Zedillo confidently guaranteed a smooth transfer of power without the debilitating economic problems of the past, no matter who would become the country's next president. He already had promised to insure a "climate of freedom" during the elections, and said he would prevent any government funds from illegally seeping into political campaigns.

Zedillo was well aware of what had happened to the man he replaced in office. At first widely popular, former President Carlos Salinas de Gortari left the country in 1995, when he was being vilified for hurting the country's economy. In a more democratized Mexico, accusations against top government officials were no longer easily dismissed. Zedillo has often said, if indirectly, that he wants to be remembered for his democratic reforms.

When Zedillo was inaugurated in December 1994, he was forced to immediately pay attention to an escalating political and economic crisis. Three months earlier, Jose Francisco Ruiz Massieu, the secretary general of the PRI, was assassinated in Mexico City. It was widely believed that divisions within the party and drug trafficking both figured in his murder. After a stormy investigation, the prosecutor resigned on 23 November 1994, charging that leading party members

had hindered his investigation. Zedillo, who was in the US at the time, assigned a new prosecutor and promised to widen the investigation and punish the guilty. In January 1999, Raul Salinas de Gortari, the multi-millionaire brother of former President Salinas, was sentenced to 50 years for planning the murder of Ruiz Massieu, his brother-in-law. In September 1999, Mario Ruiz Massieu, Jose Francisco's brother and former top drug prosecutor, died from an apparent suicide in New Jersey. Mexican authorities had accused Mario of money laundering and protecting drug traffickers. In a suicide note, Mario blamed President Zedillo and his administration for driving him to his death. Zedillo rejected the charges.

During Zedillo's first year in office, Mexico was shocked by a huge financial scandal. Members of the financial conglomerate known as the *Grupo Havre*, some with close ties to the PRI, absconded with large sums, leaving deficits of millions of dollars. Zedillo's top priority was the economy. On the eve of his inauguration, he announced his cabinet. It contained one non-party member, but more significantly at least 10 of the 25 ministers were economists. Zedillo would closely follow Salinas' free market and pro-business policies, culminating in a free-trade agreement with the European Union, signed in March 2000. Zedillo has been credited with lowering inflation, and producing steady growth, with a 3.3% growth forecast for 2000.

## DOMESTIC POLICY

Zedillo had pledged to overhaul Mexico's notoriously corrupt and inefficient justice system. He promised to reform the economy, and he has been more successful in that area. Zedillo has acknowledged that social and political changes have been slow, and the country, which was expected to grow to 100 million by 2000, will continue to face many problems. The next president will inherit a debilitating crime and illegal drug trade problem that affects the entire nation. "Crime is a problem of extraordinary dimensions," Zedillo said.

Economic reforms have failed to close the gap between rich and poor, and political unrest continued in the states of Chiapas, Guerrero and Oaxaca. Zedillo visited Chiapas more than a dozen times, failing to reach agreement with the rebels. While he continued to assert that rebel leaders were intransigent, Zedillo took credit for improving social conditions in that state.

Democratizing the country's institutions, including his own party, were part of Zedillo's domestic policy. When he took office in 1994, Zedillo said few people believed he would get rid of the *dedazo*, a practice that allowed presidents to choose their own successors. Under Zedillo, major electoral reforms took place in 1996, leading to a completely independent Federal Electoral Institute. One of the major reforms allowed public financing for all legally registered political parties. Yet, Zedillo has acknowledged that democracy does not permeate many of the nation's institutions, and more needs to be done to ensure that democracy is firmly established in the country.

## FOREIGN POLICY

In the weeks after his inauguration Zedillo emphasized foreign policy. At the meeting of hemispheric leaders in Miami in mid-December he spoke of closer economic integration in the Americas, and of extending NAFTA. He also criticized US immigration policies and Proposition 187, an anti-immigrant initiative passed by California voters in November 1994.

The devaluation of the *peso* and subsequent economic insecurity forced Zedillo to turn to the international community for help. Both Japan and Europe offered loans, but the main financial support came from the United States. Under Zedillo, Mexico aggressively pursued economic agreements with other nations. In 2000, it signed a major agreement with the European Union. It also signed an economic agreement with Israel. Zedillo's strategy was to decrease Mexico's dependence on the United States.

## ADDRESS

Office of the President

Palacio Nacional

Mexico 1

Distrito Federal, Mexico

## REFERENCES

*Christian Science Monitor,* 1 December 1994.

*Ernesto Zedillo: Architect of a Modern Mexico.* Mexico: Institutional Revolutionary Party, 1994.

*Jornada* (Mexico City) 28 August 1994.

*Miami Herald,* 25 August 1994; 21 November 1994.

*New York Review of Books,* 17 November 1994.

*New York Times,* 7 December 1994; 25 October 1999; 31 March 2000.

Office of the Mexican President. [Online] Available http://www.world.presidencia.gob.mx (accessed April 24, 2000).

*Proceso* (Mexico City), various issues.

Purcell, Susan Kaufman and Luis Rubio, eds. *Mexico Under Zedillo.* Boulder, CO: Lynne Rienner Publishing, 1998.

"An Uneasy Waiting Game for Mexico, and Marcos." *The Economist,* 8 January 2000, p. 34.

"Zedillo Ponce de Leon, Ernesto." *Current Biography,* April 1996, p. 56.

**Profile researched and written by Murdo J. MacLeod, University of Florida (1/95; revised by Ignacio Lobos 4/2000).**

# MICRONESIA
## FEDERATED STATES OF

### Leo A. Falcam
### President
*(pronounced "LEE-oh fahl-KAHM")*

*"We as a nation must concentrate over the next four years (on) the recognition and protection of our cultural values, building our economy with a true determination to work together, and a strong commitment to effective international relations."*

The Federated States of Micronesia (FSM) consists of 607 islands lying in a broad eastward sweep across 2.5 million sq km (965,250 sq mi) of the Western Pacific Ocean, between the equator and 14 degrees south latitude. These are part of an archipelago that originally appeared on European maps as the Caroline Islands. (Another Caroline Island group now constitutes the Republic of Palau.) Total land area is only 701.4 sq km (270.8 sq mi), with an additional 7,189 sq km (2,776 sq mi) of lagoons. About 65 of the islands are inhabited. Islands within the FSM are of two basic geologic types: large, mountainous islands of volcanic origin and small coral atolls. The high islands are beautifully endowed with forested mountains and reefs providing world-class diving sites. FSM is made up of four states: Pohnpei, Yap, Chuuk (formerly Truk), and Kosrae. The first three consist of several islands and islets; Kosrae, the smallest state, of just five closely situated islands.

The people of FSM are classified as Micronesian, with the exception of the inhabitants of Kapingamarangi and Nukuoro atolls in Pohnpei state, who are of Polynesian origin. Eight major indigenous languages are spoken in the nation, reflecting the cultural diversity of the people. English is the official language of government and is taught in the schools. In addition, many older people are familiar with Japanese as a result of the Japanese administrative era from 1914 through World War II. The total population is estimated at 131,500. Almost half of these people lived in Chuuk state, a third in Pohnpei, a little over 10% in Yap, and less than 8% in Kosrae. As in many Pacific Island nations, FSM population is growing rapidly, averaging about 3% per year since the 1950s. However, about 2% of FSM population leaves for the US every year. There are growing communities of Micronesians in Hawaii and California. Overall the FSM population remains rural. Less than one-third are found in the urbanized areas.

Although FSM has a well-established money economy and a relatively high GNP compared to many Pacific Island nations, for some five decades the country has been a consumption economy funded by the US. By 2001 the US will have invested nearly US$3 billion in FSM. Most of this money is not foreign aid as usually understood, but constitutes rental payments that provide the US with exclusive access to the area's waterways for military use. Together with grants and other aid, total US payments amount to about US$1,000 per capita annually. This money has not been used to create productive resources, but rather to expand the size and gener-osity of FSM's government. Beyond US payments, fisheries dominate the domestic productive economy and offer great potential for expansion. The country has an Exclusive Economic Zone (EEZ) of 322 km (200 mi) rich in marine resources. Fishing by local people is mostly for subsistence; nearly all commercial fishing within the EEZ is conducted by foreign fleets. These fleets pay access fees that amounted to more than US$13 million in 1991. Observers have suggested that a fish processing plant could be built in Chuuk that would alleviate that state's high rate of unemployment and underemployment. The country's main agricultural crop, especially important in outer islands, is copra (dried coconut meat). Copra production has suffered from low prices in world markets, dropping from 8,500 tons in 1979 to a mere 200 in 1992, though some recovery has taken place more recently. Although FSM's rural population continues to provide for some of their basic needs through gardening and fishing, the significance of this subsistence sector to the overall economy is open to question. More than 23,000 tourists came to FSM in 1990, about 60% from the US and 25% from Japan. Tourism suffers because of FSM's distance from mass markets, 4,023 km (2,500 mi) from Honolulu and 3,572 km (2,220 mi) from Tokyo. There is potential for eco-tourism as a revenue source if the presently inadequate stock of hotels and other accommodations can be expanded. The currency used in FSM is the US dollar. The per capita GNP is $1,760.

## POLITICAL BACKGROUND

The Caroline Islands had a complicated colonial history, administered successively by Spain, Germany, and Japan. Some of the bloodiest battles in World War II were fought here as Allied troops attacked Japanese bases. After the war, the Carolines were included in the UN Trust Territory of the Pacific (TTPI) created with the US as administering authority in 1947. A long series of negotiations began in the 1970s to bring the TTPI to political independence. In this process, four Caroline Island groups decided to remain in a confederation, separate from Palau. In July 1978, voters on these islands ratified a constitution that was the founding document of the Federated States of Micronesia. After national elections, the present national and state governments were installed, and the constitution took effect in May 1979. The governments of the FSM and the US executed a Compact of Free Association, which was approved in June 1983 and signed into effect in November 1986. Provisions of the Compact include US rental

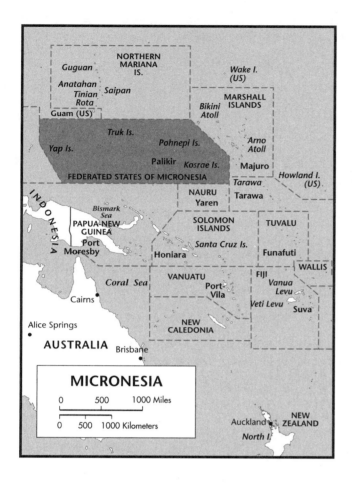

MICRONESIA

0      500      1000 Miles

0      500     1000 Kilometers

payments and free immigration access of FSM citizens to the US. The Compact will end in 2001. Either side may initiate termination or renewal.

This history, combined with a general distrust of centralized authority on the part of islanders, has produced a political structure that is distinctive for a nation of such small size. Three levels of government operate in FSM: national, state, and municipal. In addition, traditional governance exercised by local leaders continues to play a major role. The national constitution delineates executive, legislative, and judicial branches, but each state also has its own constitution, differing in some detail from the others. At the national level, the executive branch is headed by a president who is both chief executive and head of state. He and his vice president must be from different states within the federation. They are chosen from among the members of the FSM Congress by majority vote of that body and must then resign their congressional seats, which are filled by special election. They cannot serve more than two consecutive terms of four years each.

FSM's Congress is a unicameral body of 14 senators, but the constitution provides for two kinds of members, with different terms of office. One member is elected at large from each state for a four-year term. Ten members are elected for two-year terms from congressional districts within each state that are based on population. There must be at least one such district in each state, and Congress must reapportion itself into districts at least every 10 years. Among the senators elected to two-year terms in 1997, there was one from

Kosrae, one from Yap, three from Pohnpei, and five from Chuuk. Any citizen 18 years of age may vote, but a member of Congress must be at least 30 years old.

There are no political parties based on ideological lines. Rather, voting often follows family, clan, and island allegiances. Frequently, a local chief may "instruct" his people to vote in a certain way, creating bloc voting on many candidates and issues. In the 1999 elections for two-year terms, all 10 incumbents were returned to Congress; one ran unopposed in Chuuk, and all three were unopposed in Pohnpei. The four At-Large seats were taken by incumbents, except for the Pohnpei seat, which was taken from Resio S. Moses by Vice President Leo A. Falcam. Former President Jacob Nena won the At-Large seat in Kosrae.

## PERSONAL BACKGROUND

President Leo A. Falcam was born on 20 November 1935, in Pohnpei. He graduated from the University of Hawai'i with a Bachelor's degree in Sociology as the first East-West Center Grantee from the FSM. He pursued his Graduate Studies at the Woodrow Wilson School of Public and International Affairs at Princeton University, New Jersey. Afterwards, he was Delegate and Chairman of the Pohnpei Delegation to the 1975 Micronesian Constitutional Convention and was elected as one of the Convention's Vice Presidents. He served as Political Affairs and Executive Officer of the High Commissioner's staff in the former Trust Territory Government. He also was Assistant District Administrator and later District Administrator for the State of Pohnpei. President Falcam served as the first Liaison Officer for the Government of Micronesia in Washington D.C., Chairman of the Pohnpei Constitutional Convention from 1983 to 1984, first FSM Postmaster General, President and Board Member of the Bank of the FSM and also was member of the Board of Trustees and Peace Foundation of the Ponape Agriculture and Trade School. He was elected to the 5th FSM Congress At-Large in 1987 and, as a seasoned public servant, he served in numerous posts, including as Vice Chairman of the Committees on Judiciary and Government Operations, a member of the Committee on Health, Education and Social Affairs, and External Affairs during the 6th, 7th, 8th, 9th, 10th, and 11th FSM Congresses. His wife's name is Iris.

## RISE TO POWER

Falcam has been active in politics since the negotiations that led to the establishment of FSM. He represented Pohnpei in the constitutional conventions of the 1970s and became the District Administrator of that state. From 1983 to 1984 he served as the first Liaison Officer for Micronesia in the US. He worked in various capacities for the government in the areas of: mail service, banking, and agriculture and trade. In 1987, Falcam was elected to a four-year term in Congress from the open electorate of Pohnpei. He continued to operate in the political world of FSM to varying degrees during the 6th through the 11th Congresses.

Under the FSM constitution, former president Jacob Nena had to stand for election as Kosrae's four-year senator in 1999 in order to be a candidate for reelection as president. The former president won his At-Large senatorial seat, with hopes of retaining the FSM presidency. The Pohnpei seat that Falcam won, was the only place where the incumbent lost the race. Resio Moses, Falcam's running mate, was charged with broadcasting his campaign speech on a local radio station during the elections without permission from the National Election Commissioner (NEC). Falcam won the Pohnpei At-Large Congressional seat with twice the votes of his opponent.

Falcam went on to win the presidency against Nena, and was inaugurated the fifth president of FSM on 21 July 1999.

## LEADERSHIP

In his Inaugural Speech, Falcam stressed responsible leadership as a means to bringing about social empowerment for his people. He also highlighted the importance of retaining a Micronesian identity while trying not to become isolationist in nature. His first goal in office was to establish an Administration that the citizens of FSM could trust; that could guide its people to prosperity. Development efforts were to be conducted through state planning and National Economic Summits in which both the public and private sectors could participate. His style has been open and active. During his first year in office, he criticized the UN for implementing the Barbados Program of Action too slowly, and for putting small island states into one generic category. He also wielded his veto power on a $6.75 million annual budget appropriations bill in October of 1999 because he desired that the money be used for "highest priority projects from each State's Public Sector Investment Program." FSM government officials had a history of corruption that President Falcam hoped to end, and the bill was more than $650,000 over budget. On 31 January of 2000, congress went ahead and passed the bill over Falcam's objections, putting his domestic influence into question.

## DOMESTIC POLICY

Because of FSM's special relationship with the US and the country's dependence on international aid, domestic and foreign issues are closely intertwined. If the nation is to continue to enjoy its present standard of living after the Compact of Free Association ends in 2001, internal sources of revenue must be greatly increased. Falcam has understood that this involves reducing the size of government and encouraging private enterprise wherever possible. However, this domestic policy has inevitably meant seeking foreign financial assistance.

There are an estimated 6,500 government workers at the national and state levels in FSM. In order to reduce the cost of governing the country, and increase revenues, Falcam planned to privatize postal services, and increase taxes. The rate to receive a valid passport was raised by 230%, from $15 to $50. However, these measures went only part of the way towards shoring up the FSM economy in the event that foreign aid from the US is cut. In a visit to China during March 2000, President Falcam obtained $150,000 in economic aid, and a 600-ton ship, in return for FSM's commitment to the One China Policy in the Taiwan conflict.

Falcam also recognizes the potential of the fishing industry to put the nation on a firmer economic footing. FSM obtained a $934,000 technical assistance grant from ADB to modernize its fisheries sector management. The grant will be used to coordinate the efforts of government, private sector, and other agencies concerned with fishing. Falcam's long-range goal is to create a business with good equipment, personnel, and accounting principles which can be turned over to the private sector—free of government involvement. He wants to encourage similar privatization in developing tourism and agriculture.

## FOREIGN POLICY

No foreign policy issue looms larger for FSM than the impending end of its Compact of Free Association with the US. Here Nena has been proactive, joining national and state governments to establish a Joint Economic Commission in anticipation of the new negotiations that will be required. In 1999, Chief US negotiator Allen Stayman said the FSM had done well in its political transition, developing into successful self-government, but the islands had not met economic expectations. The United States, with a new compact, was prepared to continue helping the FSM by promoting growth, reforms and good government. But, Stayman warned that US legislators and federal officials would ask tough questions before approving a new compact. First, several members of Congress wanted the FSM to account for all the money invested by the United States in the islands during the life of the compact. Those same officials wanted a strategy for advancing economic self-sufficiency before more funding would be approved. As FSM has grown further apart from the US, it has increased its relations with China, Australia, and other Asian countries. Falcam claims he will continue to ask for aid from the US, but the willingness of the US is in question.

In July 2000, FSM saw the worst cholera outbreak in decades, prompting the President to request over $41,000 in aid from the Australian government to put on preventative and educational programs about the disease. Several countries, including the Northern Mariana Islands and Guam, enacted quarantines on FSM; banning produce from the country for fear that the cholera would spread. The epidemic was worst in Pohnpei, Falcam's home-island.

## ADDRESS

Office of the President

PS53

Palikir Station, Pohnpei, FSM 96941

## REFERENCES

Bank of Hawaii. *Federated States of Micronesia Economic Report.* Autumn 1995.

*Pacific Magazine*, July–March 2000.

*Pacific Report*, December 1996–August 2000.

**Profile researched and written by Mary Sugar (8/2000); sections contributed by Eugene Ogan, Professor Emeritus, University of Minnesota (3/98).**

# MOLDOVA

## Petru Lucinschi
## President
*(pronounced "PET-ru loo-CHEEN-skee")*

*"I shall be a president who shall not divide people into good and bad. I shall be president for all."*

The Republic of Moldova (formerly named the Moldovan SSR), the second smallest of the former Soviet republics, straddles the River Dniestr (pronounced NYEH-stir) in the center of Europe. It borders Romania and Ukraine and lies adjacent to a small portion of the Black Sea. Its total land area is 33,657 sq km (13,000 sq mi). Moldova's total population has been estimated at nearly 4.5 million, of which 64.5% are Moldovan, 13.8% Ukrainian, 12.8% Russian, 3.5% Gagauzi, 2.0% Bulgarian, and the remainder other nationalities. The majority of Moldovans are Orthodox Christians. The 1994 Moldovan constitution identifies the state language as Moldovan although most linguists classify the language as a dialect of Romanian. (The name of the language is a significant political issue in Moldova: supporters of the "Moldovan" designation tend to favor Moldova's independence while some supporters of "Romanian" favor merger with Romania).

Moldova has a temperate continental climate and very fertile soil. Agriculture is the backbone of its economy, especially tobacco, fruit growing, and wine production. Moldova's per capita GDP has been estimated at US$2,200.

## POLITICAL BACKGROUND

The area which incorporates Moldova is known as Bessarabia, which is geographically delimited by the Prut River on the west, the Dniestr on the north and east, the Black Sea on the southeast, and the Chilian arm of the Danube delta on the south. This entire area, Bessarabia, became an integral part of the Romanian principality of Moldova in the fourteenth century. In 1812 it was ceded to Russia by the Ottoman Empire and was incorporated into the Russian empire. Russia retained control of the region until World War I, with the exception of a strip of southern Bessarabia. In December 1917 the Moldovan Democratic Republic was established, and in March 1918 the rest of Bessarabia declared its independence and united with Romania.

In June 1940, as a consequence of the Nazi-Soviet pact, Soviet troops occupied Bessarabia. The Soviet government then split Bessarabia into several parts. The Moldovan Soviet Socialist Republic was created (August 1940) out of the central districts of Bessarabia and a strip of Ukrainian territory on the eastern side of the Dniestr River. Under Stalin Moldova was subject to intense Russification. The Moldovan language could only be written with the Cyrillic alphabet. Moldova suffered organized famine, deportation of national leaders to Siberia, attempts to eradicate the national identity

of Moldovans, and forcible collectivization and industrialization of agricultural lands. Until 1988 the Communist Party of Moldova, part of the Communist Party of the Soviet Union, was the only political party allowed to function.

The dramatic events that dismantled the Soviet Union affected Moldova as well as other Soviet republics. In May 1990 the Republic's Supreme Soviet abolished clauses in article six of the Republic's constitution which had guaranteed the Communist Party a monopoly of power. The government also instituted important changes, including the reintroduction of the Latin alphabet, and on 23 May 1991, changed the state's official name from Moldovan SSR to the Republic of Moldova. On 27 August 1991, taking advantage of a failed coup in Moscow, the parliament in Kishinev unanimously adopted a resolution proclaiming the independence of the Republic of Moldova.

The road to independence has been marked by sharp inter-ethnic conflict in Moldova. The Turkic-speaking Gagauz minority declared independence and announced the creation of a separate republic, Gagauzia, in the southern part of Moldova in August 1990. A month later the majority Russian population in the eastern section of the Dniestr valley created the Dniestr Soviet Republic. Both secessions were declared void by the government.

The conflict between ethnic Russians and Moldovans flared up again in March 1992. Armed confrontation began after Moldovan nationalists intensified a campaign to unite with neighboring Romania. The Russian population feared that such a merger would make them second-class citizens in Romania. More than 150 deaths preceded the cease-fire of July 1992. The Dniestr Republic leadership is dominated by hard-line Communists and nationalists who look to other hard-liners in Moscow for support. They want Dniestr to be an independent state with control over foreign affairs, internal security, and defense. Moldovan authorities offer Dniestr an autonomous "special status" within Moldova that would give significant powers to the region yet not relinquish Moldova's sovereignty.

Negotiations between Gagauz and Moldovan leaders have been more successful. In 1993 Gagauz negotiators accepted a federalized framework similar to that offered to the Dniestr leadership. On 28 July 1994, the Moldovan parliament adopted a law and negotiated with Gagauz officials, establishing a "national-territorial autonomous unit" for the Gagauz. The region has its own elected legislative and executive authorities and will be entitled to secession from

Moldova in the case of Moldova's reunification with Romania.

Moldova held its first popular elections for president of an independent Moldova in December 1991. Mircea Snegur, who was unopposed, was elected. In February 1994 Moldova elected a new parliament to replace the old Supreme Soviet elected in 1990. The Agrarian Democratic Party (ADP), composed largely of former Communist Party officials and collective farm chairmen, won a majority of 56 out of 104 seats. Following the most recent elections, held in March 1998, 101 parliamentary seats were distributed as follows: the Party of Moldovan Communists, 40; the Democratic Convention of Moldova, 26; the Bloc for a Democratic and Prosperous Moldova, 24; and the Party of Democratic Forces, 11.

## PERSONAL BACKGROUND

Petru Lucinschi was born in 1940 in the village of Radulenii-Vechi. He received a philosophy degree from the State University of Chisinau and later studied at the High Party School in Moscow. He spent most of his career as a Communist Party functionary. Between 1971 and 1976 he was a Central Committee secretary; between 1976 and 1978 he was a member of the Central Committee's bureau, its key policy-making organ. After serving as a deputy head of the propaganda department, Lucinschi was sent to Tajikistan, where he was a second secretary of the Central Committee of the Communist Party of Tajikistan. This post was traditionally used by Moscow to monitor and control local Communist party leaderships. In November 1989 Lucinschi was elected first secretary of the Moldovan Communist Party's Central Committee. Soon afterward he took the high-ranking post of secretary of the Soviet Communist Party Central Committee in Moscow. After the failed August 1991 coup against Gorbachev and the outlawing of the Communist Party, Lucinschi returned to Moldova, where he was elected to the local legislature, the Supreme Soviet. In 1992–93 he served as Moldova's ambassador to Moscow. Lucinschi was elected chairman of parliament in January 1993, and began a second term on 31 March 1994, after winning the February 1994 parliamentary elections.

## RISE TO POWER

Lucinschi was able to build a base of support in parliament and in the ruling Agrarian Democratic Party. In August 1995 President Snegur broke with the ADP and formed his own party, which took on a nationalist orientation and accused the ADP of failures in economic reform. Some analysts believe Snegur made the move because the ADP would not support his reelection bid. This left Lucinschi and Prime Minister Andrei Sangheli free to contend for support within the ADP and among center-left voters. After Sangheli was nominated as the ADP candidate for the presidency, Lucinschi supporters collected enough signatures to put Lucinschi on the ballot as an independent candidate. In the first round of the Moldovan presidential election on 17 November 1996, President Mircea Snegur won 38.7% of the vote, while Lucinschi won 27.7%. Communist Vladimir Voronin won 10.2% of the vote, while Prime Minister Sangheli won only 9%. Since neither candidate won 50% of the vote, the Moldovan electoral law required that a runoff election be

held between Snegur and Lucinschi. On December 1 Lucinschi upset Snegur by 54% to 46% of the vote to become Moldova's new president.

## LEADERSHIP

Lucinschi's victory was in no small part due to his ability to project an image of a moderate, pragmatic, and independent figure. Lucinschi's status as an independent candidate (despite his long-standing ties with the ruling elite) cleverly distanced him from the perceived failures of Prime Minister Sangheli and the ruling Agrarian Democratic Party. Aside from those angered by the economic situation in Moldova, Lucinschi drew support from leftist voters, many of whom supported Voronin in the first round. Lucinschi's moderation won votes among those opposed to President Snegur's nationalist orientation, especially the Russian, Ukrainian, and Gagauz minorities in Moldova. Lucinschi's pragmatism, political skills, and wide range of contacts both within and outside Moldova were expected to help him tackle Moldova's daunting problems.

However, as of 1999 Moldova's problems had not improved significantly, and Lucinschi was advocating constitutional changes providing for a stronger presidency in order to overcome the parliamentary gridlock that he blamed for Moldova's lack of economic and political progress.

The question was presented to voters in a nonbinding referendum accompanying the May 1999 local elections. A majority of voters approved the measure, but a low overall turnout placed the results in doubt. They were upheld by the central electoral commission but declared void by parliament.

## DOMESTIC POLICY

Lucinschi's primary domestic policy goal has been to improve Moldova's economic situation. He has attempted to continue economic reforms while taking steps aimed at reducing their negative social impact. The collapse of the Soviet Union hurt Moldova's economy, which has shrunk by two-thirds in the intervening years. In 1993 Moldova began implementing an IMF-backed economic reform program. A voucher privatization program got under way in July 1994. By the end of 1995, two-thirds of state-owned property was privatized. However, the IMF has continued to demand further privatization as a condition for aid, and when parliament defeated a government privatization package in late 1999, the IMF suspended further loans. Living standards in Moldova remain low. External debt was expected to exceed US$1.1 billion in 1999, and the nation remained largely dependent on foreign aid.

Resolving the quest for autonomy in the breakaway Transdnietra region on Moldova's northern border has been another key concern for Lucinschi. In 1997, he signed an agreement with the region's unilaterally elected "president," but fundamental disagreements remained. Multilateral talks involving leaders from Ukraine and Russia took place in 1999. Although the impasse over the area's status continued, all sides agreed to work toward a gradual resolution of the dispute that would include demarcation of the area's boundaries.

## FOREIGN POLICY

According to the constitution, Moldovan foreign policy is based on neutrality. However, Moldova does favor cooperation with NATO and participates in NATO's Partnership for Peace program. Lucinschi is anxious to establish closer economic ties with the West. To that end, Moldova has pledged its cooperation with the European Union (EU) and, in 1997, declared its interest in pursuing negotiations toward associate membership, and possibly eventual full membership, in the organization. Moldova is working with Russia, Ukraine, the Organization for Security and Cooperation in Europe (OSCE), to work out autonomy arrangements for the Gagauz and Transdniestr regions. One of the most sensitive issues in the Republic's foreign relations is reunification with Romania. In a 1994 referendum, the overwhelming majority of Moldovans rejected reunification, although an outspoken minority continues to favor the union. Many Romanian officials have expressed strong support for reunification, which has caused tension with Moldovan leaders.

One of Lucinschi's key priorities has been improving relations with Russia. Most of Moldova's exports and nearly all of its energy imports come from Russia and other CIS states. Moldova is a member of the CIS economic union. Moreover, Moscow's cooperation will be necessary to secure the removal of Russian troops from Moldova. The 14th Army (renamed the Operational Group of Russian Forces in Moldova) remained in the country after the collapse of the Soviet Union in 1991. After years of negotiation, on 21 October 1994, Russian prime minister Viktor Chernomyrdin and former Moldovan prime minister Andrei Sangheli, signed an accord on withdrawing Russian troops from Moldova within three years.

## ADDRESS

President Petru Lucinschi
Kishinev
Moldova

## REFERENCES

Banks, Arthur and Thomas Muller, eds. *Political Handbook of the World*. Binghamton, NY: CSA Publications, 1999.

Congressional Research Service Report 95-403, 4 December 1996.

Dima, N. *Bessarabia, and Bukovina: The Soviet-Romanian Territorial Dispute*, 1982.

Foreign Broadcast Information Service. *Daily Report: Central Eurasia*. Infotag News Agency, 2 December 1996.

"A Happy Ending to a Sad Winter's Tale." *Business Week*, 27 March 2000, p. 18.

"Nowhereland." *The Economist*, 26 June 1999, p. 61.

Open Media Research Institute Analytical Briefs 478, 500. [Online] Available http://www.omri.cz. (Accessed November, December 1996).

*PlanEcon Review and Outlook for the Former Soviet Republics*. PlanEcon Inc., August 1996.

**Profile researched and written by Steven Woehrel, Congressional Research Service (12/96; updated 5/00).**

# MONACO

### Rainier III
### Chief of State
*(pronounced "ray-NEER")*

*"I would like to be remembered as the person who corrected
and got rid of the bad image and bad legend of Monaco."*

The Principality of Monaco is a celebrated European microstate. The enclave is 21 km (13 mi) from Italy on the Mediterranean coast, surrounded on three sides by France. Its total area is 1.81 sq km (0.70 sq mi). As the second-smallest independent city in the world after Vatican City, it has an estimated population of 32,150, 85% of whom are foreigners. Although French is the official language, Monegasques native to the principality speak their own language, a combination of French and Italian. English and Italian are also spoken. The official currency is the French *franc* although a limited supply of Monegasque currency circulates at par with the *franc*. In terms of ethnic composition, the population is 41% French, 17% Monegasque, 16% Italian, and 25% other. Roman Catholicism, the official religion, is practiced by 95% of the population although freedom of religion is guaranteed by the constitution. Monaco is extremely prosperous and provides full employment for its 32,000 residents plus another 25,000 jobs for French and Italian commuters. Gambling, conference facilities, banking, real estate, and tourism account for much of the principality's earnings.

## POLITICAL BACKGROUND

Founded in 1215 as a colony of Genoa, Monaco achieved independence in 1419 and has been ruled by the Grimaldi family ever since, with persistent influence by France in its domestic and foreign relations. Its first constitution was authored in 1911; it formally achieved the status of constitutional monarchy in 1962 with a constitution that abolished the principle that Grimaldi princes rule by divine rights. The current leader, Prince Rainier III, shares power with a unicameral 18-member National Council that has the right to veto any legislation the prince and his three-member Council of Government devise. The National Council is elected directly by true-born Monegasque citizens, ages 25 and over. The prince chooses a head of government from a list of French civil servants provided by Paris, but in effect, the prince is both the head of state and government, retaining dual powers assumed by a typical president and prime minister.

Although formal political parties do not exist, political organizations have influenced Monaco's politics. Formed in 1962, the National and Democratic Union (UND) has largely dominated Monaco's elections and has secured all 18 seats in the February 1998 election. Should the prince dissolve the National Council, new elections must be held within three

months. The chief justice of the Supreme Court and the head of the Monaco Police are designated by France. As stipulated in a 1918 protection treaty with France, if an heir is not available to take the throne, then the principality reverts to French control.

## PERSONAL BACKGROUND

Rainier Louis Henri Maxence Bertrand de Grimaldi was born in Monaco on 31 May 1923, the only son of the late Comte Pierre de Polignac and Princess Charlotte of Monaco. His education began in England at Summerfields, Hastings, and the Stowe School. From there he continued at Rosey, Switzerland, and the University of Montpelier in France, graduating from the *Ecole Libre des Sciences Politiques* (Paris) after a noted military career. During World War II he enlisted in the French army and served with the Seventh Regiment of Tirailleur Algeréins as Lieutenant Grimaldi. In combat during the Alsatian campaign, Prince Rainier was cited for bravery and offered a colonelship, which he declined. The French, Belgian, and Greek governments awarded him medals of honor. He founded the Monaco Red Cross and American Friends of Monaco.

In his youth, the prince devoted his leisure time to tennis and skiing, car racing, and cruises to Africa to obtain live animals for the Monaco National Zoo. From an early age he had no personal interest in gambling, an industry that has symbolized Monaco since its inception in Monte Carlo in 1860. His marriage in 1956 to American movie star Grace Kelly lent a magical aura to his personality and placed him and Monaco in the limelight. The couple had three children: Caroline, Albert, and Stephanie. Princess Grace's accidental death in 1982 plunged him into mourning for several years, but he is said to have recovered his zest for life and his job.

Some observers mistakenly speculated that he might step down and relinquish the throne to his son Prince Albert on his sixty-fifth birthday in 1988. In 1999, he reiterated his earlier promises to retain the helm until Prince Albert marries.

## RISE TO POWER

Prince Louis II, Prince Rainier's grandfather, became the sovereign leader of Monaco in 1922. In 1944 Princess Charlotte wrote to her father, Prince Louis II, renouncing her rights to the throne in favor of her son, Prince Rainier. In May of 1949, after several months of ill health, Louis II relinquished the throne to Prince Rainier, who on 5 May became

## MONACO

the thirty-first hereditary ruler of Monaco. Prince Louis II died a week later.

### LEADERSHIP

The young prince, acceding to the throne at age 26, was said to have taken his responsibilities very seriously and shepherded the principality through the uncertain 1950s when casino and tourist revenues were rapidly declining. Under his reign, the principality has experienced intensive economic and real estate development, especially in the tourist industry. The success of his leadership has depended upon the near homage Monegasque citizens voluntarily feel towards him and the supportive composition of the National Council. Several disputes and challenges in the 1960s and 1970s left his reputation virtually untarnished if not stronger.

In 1962, Prince Rainier initiated constitutional reforms that provided for the right of association, trade union freedom and the right to strike, the National Council's election by universal franchise (instead of via the delegate system), and the extension of the franchise to women. Monegasque citizens perceive that they are treated well by the Rainier government and appreciate living in a state which does not tax them yet provides all social and medical services. The only serious domestic political opposition Prince Rainier faced was from a Monegasque Communist, Charles Soccal, the head of the Federation of Trade Unions who served on the National Council during part of the 1960s and 1970s and spoke out forcefully against many of the Prince's projects and edicts. Since Soccal's defeat for re-election in 1978, the Prince has not faced any major political challenge in the National Council.

Prince Rainier has had to consider the French when formulating his policies. For example, in 1962 President De Gaulle became irritated because wealthy French citizens were living in Monaco and avoiding French taxes. This dispute was fueled in part by Prince Rainier's campaign to introduce international businesses to the fiscal advantages of establishing headquarters in Monaco. A compromise with the French government was reached in 1963 as Monaco agreed to collect a turnover tax of up to 40% of the value of exports of local firms that do at least 25% of their business outside of Monaco. The French customs service in turn collects the duties on cargoes delivered to Monaco and returns a share to Monaco.

### DOMESTIC POLICY

Under Prince Rainier, Monaco has evolved from a declining gambling enclave to an economically and culturally diverse principality. Land reclamation projects, such as the Fontvielle Quarter in 1985, have increased Monaco's territory by 20% and provided a location for new industrial plants. The arts and especially oceanography are given generous support by Prince Rainier's government.

Monaco's government has also been instrumental in ensuring that all residents share in the prosperity. Native-born citizens are guaranteed jobs in government services. A law also stipulates that companies must first offer jobs to native-born Monegasques, who represent nearly 5,000 of all inhabitants, then to local residents, and finally to the inhabitants of the four communities surrounding Monaco. Social unrest is rare, therefore, although in December 1999, government workers went on strike for the second time since World War II to demonstrate for a 35-hour work week, in line with the law debated in the French National Assembly.

Gambling now accounts for only 4.35% of total revenue while value-added taxes on hotels, banks, and industry generated 55% of public revenues in 1999. Monaco levies the same rate of VAT as the French rate of 21%. France, however, is under pressure by the Commssion to bring its rate closer in harmony with European-wide rates, and it is possible that French VAT will drop by 2% in the near future. Such adjustments would result in a drop of 10% in Monaco's overall revenues. A quarter of government revenue comes from tourism.

Prince Rainier has more or less realized his agenda for making Monaco thrive economically and culturally apart from its previous mainstay gambling. Yet its economic prosperity is constrained by its reliance on France. An economic downturn in France has a ripple effect on Monaco. The next phase in reducing dependence on France has been to promote business conventions and conferences. In July 2000, the Prince opened a new convention center.

### FOREIGN POLICY

Monaco has been closely linked to France since 1918 when a treaty made between the two countries formalized France's commitment to defend Monaco and respect its sovereignty "so long as it is exercised in conformity with the political, military, naval, and economic interests of France." During his reign, Prince Rainier has negotiated two additional treaties of significance (in 1954 and 1963) with France, updating but not fundamentally altering this relationship. France may station troops in Monaco and make use of Monaco's territorial waters because of the customs union arranged with France.

Monaco sends ambassadors to the Vatican, Paris, and a few European capitals. France finally allowed Monaco to join the United Nations in 1993. The principality is a member of the United Nations Educational, Scientific, and Cultural Organization (UNESCO) and other affiliated UN organizations. It also participates in the Conference for European Security and Cooperation. Several international organizations have their headquarters in Monaco, including the International Commission for the Scientific Exploration of the Mediterranean Sea, the International Hydrographic Bureau, and the International Commission for Legal-Medical Problems. It is also the seat for the International Academy of Tourism, founded in 1951 by Prince Rainier III.

## ADDRESS

Palais de Monaco
Monte Carlo
Principality of Monaco

## REFERENCES

Agence France Presse, 1 December 1999.

*Current Biography*, 1955.

*Janet Matthews Information Services*, 11 November 1999.

Monaco Web Site. [Online] Available http://www.monaco.mc/monaco/info/institutions.html (Accessed 5/2000).

*New Yorker*, 5 October 1987.

**Profile researched and written by Elizabeth Gittelman (7/90; updated 5/2000).**

# MONGOLIA

### Rinchinnyamiin Amarjargal
### Prime Minister
*(pronounced "rin-shin-YAH-myin ah-mar-YAR-gall")*

*"I firmly believe that liberalism throughout every segment of society is the engine of prosperity for Mongolia."*

Mongolia is a large landlocked country sandwiched between two larger neighbors, China and Russia. Located at the center of the Asian continent, it covers 1,566,500 sq km (694,100 sq mi). Most of the landscape consists of pasture or desert wasteland, including the famous Gobi desert, known for its extreme daily temperature changes. The Mongolian climate is arid, with surrounding mountains acting as barriers that prevent moist air flow and precipitation. About 10% of the country is forested, supporting an abundance of wildlife—including boar, elk, deer, and bear. Only 1% of the land is arable, and is used to produce wheat, barley, oats and vegetables.

The sixth largest country in Asia, Mongolia is sparsely populated, with a population estimated to be 2,617,379 or about four inhabitants per sq mi. Its population is growing at a rate of 2.5% annually. About 85% of the people are Mongols (mostly Khalkha), 7% are Turkic, 4.6% Tungusic, and 3.4% other. More than four million Mongolians reside outside their country. The primary religions are Tibetan Buddhist Lamaism (94%) and Muslim (6%), the latter confined to the Turkic population mainly in southeastern part of the country. Most people speak Khalka Mongolian, the official language. However, instead of using the traditional script, Mongolians have adopted the Russian Cyrillic alphabet since the Communist revolution. A move to revert back to the Mongolian script was begun recently, with Cyrillic to eventually become the second script. Many college-educated Mongolians were trained in the former Soviet Union and are fluent in Russian. The country's literacy rate exceeds 80%. Life expectancy is 59.1 years for males and 63.2 years for females.

Mongolia's GDP is approximately US$2,250 per capita. The national currency is the *tugrik*. One-third of the economy revolves around subsistence agriculture and livestock production. Primary exports are copper, minerals, hides, and skins; major imports include petroleum products, industrial equipment, and consumer goods. Significant trading partners are Russia, China, Japan, and Kazakstan.

## POLITICAL BACKGROUND
In the 13th century, Genghis Khan and his successors created the largest land empire in history. However, by the 17th century, Mongolia came under Chinese control, which lasted until the fall of the Manchu dynasty in 1911. From 1911 to 1919, Mongolia declared its independence from China with Russian protection. In 1919, the Chinese successfully reestab-

lished control over Mongolia, only to be defeated by Mongolian nationalists, Sukhe Bator and Khorloin Choibalsan. After a short-lived constitutional monarchy, the Mongolian People's Revolutionary Party (MPRP) founded the Mongolian People's Republic (MPR) under Choiblasan. He dominated government until his death in 1952 and resorted to Stalinistic practices to eliminate dissent. A series of authoritarian leaders ruled Mongolia after Choiblasan.

Mongolia remained a one-party state until 1989, when reforms in Eastern Europe and Russia affected Mongolia's domestic politics. In response to demonstrations calling for former leader Yumjaagiyn Tsedenbal's return to face trial for Stalinist crimes, the government agreed to embark on a political liberalization process. The National Democratic Party (NDP), which later contributed members to the Democratic Union (DU) coalition, formed an opposition group and pressured the government for a new constitution that would abandon the one-party system of government.

In 1990, a meeting of the Great Hural (National Assembly) reformed the constitution and set the framework for multi-party elections later that year for the lower house. Based on the newly adopted 1992 constitution, which created a unicameral legislature, elections for the Great Hural were held. The reformed MPRP (communists) won 70 of 76 seats. On 21 July 1992, the Great Hural selected Puntsagiyn Jasray, a free-market economist, as prime minister. In 1993, Punsalmaagiyn Ochirbat, formerly elected president as a member of the MPRP, was reelected as a candidate of the DU.

The latest election for the Great Hural was held on 30 June 1996, and resulted in the MPRP's stunning loss of its majority control by winning only 25 of 76 seats. The Democratic Union Coalition, consisting of four parties—headed primarily by the National Democratic Party and the Social Democratic Party—won 50 seats. It was a stunning electoral victory for the opposition DU resulting in a generational change, with the rise of ambitious, but young and inexperienced leaders taking over the helms of government. Over the next three years, Mongolia had four different prime ministers and experienced a four-month political crisis during which the country was ruled by an interim government, with the president and the DU-controlled legislature unable to agree on a new candidate for the position.

According to the 1992 constitution, 76 members of the Great Hural are popularly elected for four-year terms. The Great Hural, which meets at least 75 days every six months, appoints and dismisses the prime minister and other administrative officials. The president is chosen by popular vote for four-year terms and nominates the prime minister in consultation with the largest legislative party. He also serves as the commander-in-chief of Mongolia's armed forces. The president guides the nation in foreign policy and serves as head of state; the prime minister, as head of government, oversees and organizes the implementation of policies and the constitution. At local levels, Mongolia is presently a unitary state divided into 21 *aimags* (provinces) and 334 *soums* (counties). Most local policies and fiscal decisions are made at the national level.

## PERSONAL BACKGROUND

R. Amarjargal was born on 27 February 1961 in Ulaanbaatar, Mongolia, where he attended primary and secondary school, except for a four-year period spent in Moscow when his father worked at the Mongolian embassy in that city. Amarjargal returned to Moscow on scholarship for his university education, at the Plekhanov Economics Institute, where he earned a Bachelor's degree in finance and credit in 1982. After graduation, he worked for the Central Council of Mongolian Trade Unions for a year before entering the military for his term of national service, rising to the rank of captain and continuing to serve as a lecturer in finance and economics at the military academy until 1990.

After a year of teaching at the Mongolian Technical University, Amarjargal became the head of the Economics College in Ulaanbaatar, where he helped prepare a new generation of economists for the nation's shift to a market economy. As part of this task, he joined with his colleagues in writing the country's first textbooks covering such subjects as macroeconomics, privatization, and securities. Amarjargal served as director of the college from 1991 to 1996, during which time he also participated in management training programs both in Ulaanbataar and the Netherlands, in addition to earning a master's degree in macroeconomic policy and planning from the University of Bradford in the United Kingdom. Amarjargal is married and has a son. An avid soccer fan, he was named chairman of the Mongolian Football Federation in 1997.

## RISE TO POWER

Amarjargal was active in Mongolia's pro-democracy movement from its inception in the early 1990s, joining the forerunner of one of the parties that was merged to form the Mongolian National Democratic Party in 1992. During his years as head of the Economics College, he made a conscious effort to turn it into a "think tank" for the development of policy in such areas as economic restructuring and privatization. When the Democratic Union coalition came to power in 1996, many of the new government's economic policies reflected the ideas developed at the college during this period; in the same election, Amarjargal himself won a seat in the Mongolian parliament. From April to December 1998 he was Minister of External Relations; during this period he was one of the nominees for prime minister rejected by the parliament. He was once again nominated when the government of J. Narantsatsralt collapsed in July 1999, and the nomination was approved by parliament on July 30, making Amarjargal the nation's twentieth prime minister at the age of 38. In

November 1999, he was also elected chairman of the Mongolian National Democratic Party.

## LEADERSHIP

Amarjargal faces the challenge of bringing his coalition and nation together after a protracted period of political paralysis and dissension. He became prime minister in the wake of a five-month deadlock and constitutional crisis and the collapse of yet another government—the third in 15 months. The ruling coalition's handling of privatization and market reforms has come under increasing attack by members of the opposition MPRP for the social dislocation it has created and for the corruption that has accompanied the process. In addition, the nation has become increasingly polarized by the economic havoc wreaked by the Asian recession.

President Bagabandi, who opposes continued rapid economic reforms, has emerged as a major critic of the NDU, and in the spring of 2000, it was seen as likely that his MPRP party would increase their electoral representation in upcoming legislative elections scheduled for July.

As a professional economist and a national authority on economic reform and privatization, Amarjargal can be expected to continue steering his country toward a free-market economy. Soon after taking office, Amarjargal articulated his primary leadership goals as continuing and deepening economic reform, building a national consensus on development strategies, and achieving a sound and transparent government through discipline and accountability off public employees and reconciliation among opposing political parties and factions.

## DOMESTIC POLICY

Mongolia is a relative newcomer to a market economy. Prior to the NDU's ascension to power, an estimated 80% of the Mongolian economy was under state control and the government budget remained unbalanced. Amarjargal belongs to a new generation of young well-educated technocrats, dedicated to controlling government spending and to continuing privatization. Soon after being approved as prime minister, he expressed his commitment to continuing and extending Mongolia's free-market reforms.

As prime minister, Amarjargal also needs to address some of the significant social and economic dislocations caused by the previous decade's economic changes, particularly increased homelessness, hunger, and crime. His government must work to lessen the social and economic hardship on the average Mongolian, who has seen a decrease in economic opportunities and an increase in the price of imports. In the wake of severe blizzards that wreaked millions of dollars' worth of damage on the country in the winter of 1999/2000 Amarjargal reaffirmed his commitment to strengthening the country's social safety net. He also sought foreign disaster aid for immediate relief to herders affected by widespread loss of livestock.

Amarjargal has also declared his strong dedication to democracy. As a highly educated man and former academic, he has placed special emphasis on the importance of a well-informed public to maintain the democratic process. In the autumn of 1999 he initiated an "Open Government" program to give all citizens expanded access to printed and online information about government activities, as well as information about a variety of business and economic information.

## FOREIGN POLICY

Amarjargal, a proponent of economic globalization, has stressed the importance of international cooperation, both for regional political stability and for the economic opportunities it can offer to his land-locked country. During the Soviet era, the USSR was Mongolia's dominant ally. When the Soviet Union collapsed and Russia experienced grave economic dislocations, Mongolia suffered a loss of foreign aid. As a result, Mongolia's post-communist governments sought to rely less on Russia by reaching out to the West and to other Asian nations, including China and South Korea. These new relations produced increased trade and investment in Mongolia, further driving the domestic privatization effort. In turn, the newly developed commercial ties have improved diplomatic relations with these trading partners.

Amarjargal has continued a balanced approach to foreign policy, stating his belief that it is crucial for Mongolia to have good relations with both Russia and China, the two countries that are its sole neighbors, and to encourage foreign investment by both of these neighbors. He also recognizes the importance of reaching out to nations elsewhere in Asia and the world. Among other efforts, he has worked toward reviving Mongolia's formerly close ties with Vietnam, meeting with that country's prime minister in Ulaanbaatar in the fall of 1999.

Prime Minister Amarjargal has also expressed his belief that industrial growth will be a key factor in integrating Mongolia's economy into the world economy and has noted the importance of direct foreign investment in ongoing modernization efforts.

## ADDRESS

Office of the Prime Minister
Ulaanbaatar, Mongolia

## REFERENCES

Agnihotri, Newal K., ed. *Mongolia: International Relations* (Extended interview with then foreign minister Amaryargal)

Banks, Arthur and Thomas Muller, eds. *Political Handbook of the World*. Binghamton, NY: CSA Publications, 1999.

*BBC World Service*, interview, 3 March 2000.

Permanent Mission of Mongolia to the UN [Online] www.undp.org/missions/Mongolia/mngintro.htm

*Presidents and Prime Ministers*, Sept 1998 vol. 7 no. 5 p17(1).

Prime Minister of Mongolia. [Online] www.pmis.gov.mn/primeminister/

**Profile researched and written by Rosalie Wieder (5/2000); sections provided by Robert W. Compton, Jr., Western Kentucky University.**

# MOROCCO

## Mohamed VI
## King

*(pronounced "moh-HA-med")*

*"We all aim to achieve reconciliation and cooperation by overcoming the negative aspects
of the present and looking forward to the future, on the basis
of our rich common history, our civilization and culture, and our true religion."*

The Kingdom of Morocco is located on the westernmost part of North Africa. It occupies a strategic location that controls the lower half of the Strait of Gibraltar on the Mediterranean Sea while enjoying a long coastline on the Atlantic Ocean. Morocco is bordered on the east by Algeria and on the south by the Western Sahara territory. It has an area of 446,565 sq km (172,419 sq mi), a large part of which is desert.

Morocco is inhabited by 29.7 million people. The official language is Arabic, but French is widely spoken as well. Ethnically, Morocco is made up mostly of Arabs and a large minority of Berbers (40%). The religion of the majority of Moroccans is Islam.

Morocco is a lower-middle income country with a free-market economy based on the private sector, but with major governmental participation that is being curtailed by sweeping privatization. It has an important agricultural sector that remains mostly traditional and that provides 25% of export earnings and employs 40% of the labor force. Morocco has 75% of the world's phosphate reserves and is the largest exporter of that commodity. It also has the richest fishing waters in the world, a sophisticated tourist industry, and a small manufacturing sector. The Moroccan currency is the *dirham*.

## POLITICAL BACKGROUND

Most of Morocco became a French protectorate in 1912 while a smaller Spanish protectorate was instituted in the north and far south of the country. Spain also retained control of Spanish Sahara (now Western Sahara). A nationalist movement developed during the 1930s and 1940s, leading to eventual independence in 1956. The first head of state was Sultan Mohammed V, who had been a key supporter of the independence movement and took the title of king in 1957. After Mohammed's death in 1961, his son Hassan II was crowned and became head of government. On 23 July 1999, King Hassan died of illness and was replaced by Crown Prince Sidi Mohamed, who became known as Mohamed VI.

Morocco is a constitutional monarchy where power is theoretically shared by the king, the government, and a bicameral parliament. In reality, however, most power is concentrated in the hands of the monarch. The current constitution, which was adopted by referendum in 1992 and amended in 1996, gives executive powers to a government that emanates from parliament and is approved by the king. While the legislative body initiates legislation, the king must

agree before any law takes effect. He can dissolve parliament by decree and call for new elections, and propose his own legislation for popular approval by means of referendum. The monarch signs and ratifies international treaties, can declare a state of emergency, and can rule by decree. He appoints the prime minister and his cabinet, and presides over meetings of the Supreme Judicial Council.

Morocco has a multi-party system with 28 parties, the most important of which is the *Union Socialiste des Forces Populaires* (USFP). None of these parties challenges the supremacy of the king, and all have joined coalition governments formed under the control of pro-monarchy formations. The 1993 parliamentary elections caused a major political malaise in the country after the state was accused of having manipulated the results in order to deny the opposition a victory. To end the political crisis, the constitution was amended, and new elections took place in the fall of 1997. In these elections, three major party blocs, the *Koutla* (traditional left opposition), the *Wifaq* (monarchists), and the center received an almost equal number of seats each (102, 100, and 97, respectively). The USFP of the *Koutla* bloc won the largest number of seats (57) in the Lower House, and its leader, Abderrahman Youssoufi, was appointed prime minister at the head of a coalition government. This event constituted a major departure from past practices but did not fundamentally alter the political map and political process. However, for the first time, members of moderate Islamist movements were allowed to run for office. Nine members of the *al-Tawhid Wal Islah* (Unity and Reform of Abdelilah Benkirane) movement and the Popular Democratic and Constitutional Movement (MPDC) were elected.

## PERSONAL BACKGROUND

Sidi Mohamed Ben al-Hassan, who was born in 1963, is one of five children of Hassan II. He was educated in French and Arabic and also speaks some English and Spanish. Sidi Mohamed received a degree in international law from a French university and wrote a thesis on relations between the European Union and North African countries. He is known for being studious, quiet, and interested in technology and social issues. In his younger years, Sidi Mohamed gained a reputation as a playboy, showing a fondness for fast cars and nightclubs. He never married—causing some gossip in a country where a man of his age is widely expected to have begun a family.

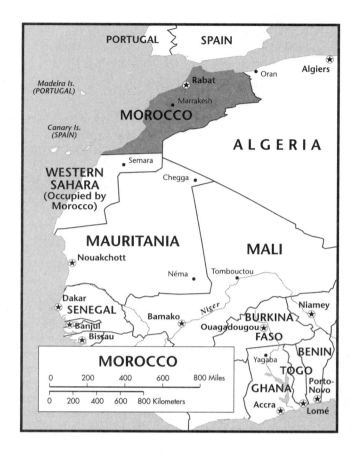

## RISE TO POWER

Sidi Mohamed was named crown prince by his father well before he was to become the new monarch. He had learned much about politics from his father and from the various duties he was assigned. In 1994, he was promoted from major colonel to a four-star general and served as coordinator of the 200,000-member Royal Armed Forces while his father remained commander-in-chief. In July 1999, Hassan II died of a heart attack after a long illness. Sidi Mohamed, who had spent his life in the shadow of his father, was thrust into the role he had been groomed to play for a lifetime.

## LEADERSHIP

When suddenly called upon to assume his father's office as King Mohamed VI, he did not seem to have enough experience to lead Morocco. At the start of his reign it was not clear whether he would acquire his father's ability to do so in the long run. Lacking the appeal and political skills of his father, who governed the country for 38 years with a mixture of authoritarianism and relative parliamentary politics, Mohamed sought to consolidate his power. At the same time he hoped to impose a new political style characterized by some political openness in the context of a constitutional monarchy. However, he is likely to maintain control of the instruments used by his father (e.g., the army, the security services, and patronage) to ensure the preeminence of the monarchy. Mohamed will gradually impose his authority in Morocco where his legitimacy is based on traditional and religious sources. As the twenty-second ruler from the Alaoui dynasty, he claims descent from the prophet Mohammed.

Because of this religious ancestry, he inherited the title of *amir al-muminnin* (the commander of the faithful). However, these qualities alone are not enough for the young king to rule a country that is facing a host of problems and a potentially dangerous elite.

Hassan II alternated between policies of repression and intimidation on one hand and relatively stable parliamentary politics on the other. As his political position gradually improved, he eased restrictions on political life, released hundreds of political prisoners, lifted press censorship, and allowed local and parliamentary elections to proceed. A very slow process of political opening finally led to municipal elections in 1992 and 1997, parliamentary elections in 1993 and 1997, and a constitutional amendment in 1996 related to the structure and election of parliament. These actions resulted from domestic pressures, but also—and perhaps primarily—from international pressure for political liberalization as a precondition for continued economic assistance and for a special relationship with the European Union (EU). With regard to the Islamist opposition, moderate groups became slowly tolerated, and the crackdown on radical ones increased, partly in response to the violent Islamist rebellion in neighboring Algeria.

Even though they did not alter Morocco's power structure, the parliamentary elections of 1997 allowed the emergence of an informal center bloc and the appointment of opposition leader, Abderrahman Youssoufi, as prime minister. In spite of the relative gains of the *Koutla* parties, most parliamentary seats have remained in the hands of pro-monarchy parties. The parliamentary reform and the control of government by the former opposition constitutes a major step in bringing about much needed political changes, such as allowing more participation from below and making office holders more accountable. After having been in power for close to two years, the Youssoufi government, known as the *gouvernement d'alternance,* must deal with major domestic pressures to solve many social and economic problems faced by the majority of Moroccans. Mohamed took over at a time when the challenges are immense, but he seems ready to face them head on. What may help him in this endeavor is the fact that, before his death, his father paved the way for a smooth succession by enacting major political reforms and by placing the "tolerated" opposition in power. However, it remains to be seen whether these reforms will translate into an effective overhaul of political practices in Morocco.

## DOMESTIC POLICY

Starting in the late 1970s, Morocco experienced a serious economic crisis due to the heavy cost of the campaign to annex the Western Sahara, a fall in phosphate prices, an alarming balance of trade deficit, and an escalating foreign debt. In 1983, the king agreed to an IMF-sponsored austerity program, which caused riots throughout the kingdom. After 15 years of intense economic restructuring, the aggregate outlook has improved as privatization gained momentum and as foreign investments increased. Between 1984 and 1995, the state's budget deficit declined from 12% to 3% of the GDP; exports increased by 9.7%; the debt-to-GDP ratio fell from 123% to 81%; and the debt-servicing ratio fell from a high 70% to 33% of export earning. However, in 1999 Morocco's total external debt stood at $22 billion as the country struggled with rising unemployment, a series of severe droughts that cut crops by 75% in 1995 alone, and a generally poor performance in most sectors. The economic growth rate fell to 0.6% from 6.3% in 1998, mostly as a result of a severe drought.

Because structural adjustment requires efficiency and tightening of state spending, unemployment is likely to rise from the already high 20%, and public expenditures on social services will continue diminishing as the state retreats from many activities. There is still widespread poverty, and the gap between rich and poor Moroccans keeps widening as gross income disparities across social classes and regions have increased in recent years. The population continues to grow at a burdensome rate of 2% a year, and the number of new job seekers continues to rise faster than job availability.

In the late 1990s, several strikes and demonstrations shook many professions and universities, calling attention to the urgency of dealing with the negative fallout from economic restructuring and inadequate public policies. The new king is well aware of the potential dangers that an ever-expanding poverty may bring about. In 1995, while he was crown prince, Mohamed began playing a very active role in public affairs, becoming particularly concerned with social issues. He initiated a yearly weeklong series of activities to combat poverty in the country. If the most pressing concerns (unemployment, housing, poverty) are not effectively addressed, they may turn into serious political liabilities. Economic conditions have not improved for most Moroccans, and either a militant Islamist tide or the military may, at an opportune time, forcefully challenge the throne.

## FOREIGN POLICY

Foreign policy decisions are made mostly by the king, helped by a very narrow circle of close advisors. Morocco never ceased to cultivate friendly ties with the West (mainly Europe and the US) in order to reap economic and political benefits while maintaining a fairly independent foreign policy. This has brought economic assistance and generous supplies of military hardware, especially from France and the US. Though Morocco was unable to obtain full membership in the European Union, it signed an agreement of Free Trade Association with the EU that will come into effect in 2010.

Close ties with the countries of the Middle East and contributions to the Palestinian cause have brought Morocco generous financial assistance from Saudi Arabia. Participation in the 1992 Gulf War on the side of the US-led international coalition brought more consideration and assistance from its Arabian Peninsula friends and the West, even though popular sentiment overwhelmingly supported Iraq. After the signing of the peace accord with the Palestine Liberation Organization (PLO) in 1993, the Israeli prime minister, Itzhak Rabin, visited Morocco. The following year, Morocco hosted the first Arab-Israeli conference on regional economic integration.

The dispute over the fate of the Western Sahara continues to affect Morocco's relations with Algeria and with other Maghrib territories. When the Sahrawi Republic was recognized by the Organisation of African Unity and admitted to membership in 1984, Morocco withdrew from the organization. It remains withdrawn from the organization. In 1999, Morocco tried to persuade the Organization of African Unity to cancel the membership status it awarded to the self-declared republic of Western Sahara. The final fate of that territory is to be decided by a UN-organized referendum scheduled to take place in July 2000. It will be no surprise if this event is postponed. Morocco wants to make sure that the vote confirms its control over the territory. A contrary result may usher in serious problems for the monarchy and the entire region.

## ADDRESS

Royal Palace
Rabat, Morocco

## REFERENCES

Brendan, Horton. *Morocco: Analysis and Reform of Economic Policy.* Washington, DC: Economic Development Institute, World Bank, 1990.

*The Economist*, 1 February 1997.

*Financial Times*, 15 December 1994.

*Guardian Weekly*, 22 February 1998.

Layachi, Azzedine. *Society, State and Democracy in Morocco: The Limits of Associative Life.* Washington, DC: Center for Contemporary Arab Studies, 1998.

Maroc Hebdo. [Online] Available http://www.maroc-hebdo.press.ma (Accessed 6/2000).

*MERIP*, March–April 1993.

Ministry of Communication. [Online] Available http://www.mincom.gov.ma (Accessed 6/2000).

Morocco Today. [Online] Available http://www.morocco-today.com (Accessed 6/2000).

Munson, Henry Jr. *Religion and Power in Morocco.* New Haven, CT: Yale University Press, 1993.

*New York Times*, 25 September 1993–29 July 1999.

Radio Station Medi1. [Online] Available http://www.medi1.com/medi1 (Accessed 6/2000).

*World Development Report.* Washington, DC: World Bank, 1994–98.

Vie Economique. [Online] Available http://www.marocnet.net.ma/vieeco (Accessed 6/2000).

**Profile researched and written by Azzedine Layachi, St. John's University (12/99; updated 6/2000).**

# MOZAMBIQUE

## Joaquím Alberto Chissano
## President

*(pronounced "wah-KEEM al-BAIR-toh shih-SAH-no")*

*"Each country must have a serious development program rooted in its own reality, and promote social justice through development."*

Officially known as the People's Republic of Mozambique and formerly known as Portuguese East Africa, Mozambique is situated in southern Africa. Mozambique is a long country that straddles the Indian ocean to the east; to the south are Swaziland and South Africa; to the west, Zimbabwe, Zambia, and Malawi; and to the north, Tanzania. Its total area is approximately 801,590 sq km (309,493 sq mi), and its population is estimated at 19,124,335. The Mozambique unit of currency is the *metical*. Portuguese is the national language with at least nine local languages spoken widely, and ethnically, Mozambique is comprised of nine large and 20 small ethnic groups. Mozambique's religion is about 50% traditional, 25% Christian (mainly Catholic), and 25% Muslim. Mozambique is a low income country with GNP per capita of US$900. Its primary exports are prawns, cashews, tea, cotton, sugar, and refined oil.

## POLITICAL BACKGROUND

Mozambique is a republic. Since independence, the president of the republic has also been the president of the Mozambique Liberation Front (Frente de Libertação de Moçambique—FRELIMO), the Marxist mass movement/party that led the county to independence from Portugal in 1975. In the same year, a constitution was formulated which created the People's Assembly as the supreme decision-making body of state and the highest legislative organ of the republic, with no more than 210 seats. Executive power was vested in a Council of Ministers, presided over by the president of the republic and charged with implementation of domestic and foreign policy decisions taken by the People's Assembly.

FRELIMO, which ruled the country as the sole political party of the state until the end of civil war in 1992, was formed as a national liberation movement in June 1962 and has had five party congresses in which delegates have decided the political direction of the republic. At the Fifth Party Congress held in July 1989 major discussions were begun on the creation of a new constitution, which could drastically change the established political and economic orientation of the republic. The new constitution was adopted in 1990. This constitution enshrined the principles of political pluralism and election by secret ballot of a government based on majority rule rather than proportional representation. These changes ultimately paved the way for multiparty politics and the end of the 16-year civil war. The first elections were held in 1994.

## PERSONAL BACKGROUND

Joaquím Alberto Chissano was born on 22 October 1939, in Malehice, in the Chibuto District of Gaza province in southern Mozambique. He was one of the few children from that area ever to attend school. After primary school in Gaza, he was sent by his parents to Lourenco Marques (now Maputo) where he completed high school. As a student, he was regarded as a leader. He joined the small Nucleus of Mozambican African Secondary Students (NESAM) and was its president from 1959 to 1960. He received a scholarship to study in Portugal in 1960, but fled secretly to Paris in 1961 to join the anti-colonial movement. In Paris, he helped found the Paris branch of the National Union of Mozambican Students (UNEMO), which cooperated with nationalist movements from all the Portuguese colonies and those of other African countries. Chissano became known as a young militant among African student nationalists.

In 1962, Chissano participated in the founding of the Mozambican Liberation Front (Frente de Libertação de Moçambique—FRELIMO) and in 1963 was elected to its Central Committee. Chissano served as secretary to the first president of FRELIMO, Dr. Eduardo Mondlane. FRELIMO was based on a policy of non-racialism and non-tribalism and was prepared to wage a military campaign if necessary to gain independence. Chissano joined the guerilla army that was launched from independent Tanzania in 1964.

## RISE TO POWER

Joaquím Chissano held a number of prominent posts in FRELIMO before his presidency in 1986. In addition to remaining on the Central Committee, Chissano was made secretary of the highly sensitive security department in 1965. He was appointed to both the Political Military Committee and the Executive Committee at the Second FRELIMO Congress held in a liberated zone in northern Mozambique in 1968. From there he was assigned as FRELIMO's Chief Representative to Tanzania, a post he held until the end of the war in 1974.

Chissano participated in the peace negotiations that culminated in the Lusaka Agreement of 7 September 1974 and led to full independence from Portugal. After the Lusaka negotiations, Chissano was appointed prime minister in the transitional government by the second FRELIMO president, Samora Machel. Chissano was named Foreign Minister in the first government of the Peoples Republic of Mozambique formed in June of 1975 and, as such, served in the People's

Assembly and in the Council of Ministers. He held the post of foreign minister until 1986.

On 19 October 1986, Samora Machel, president of FRELIMO and of the Republic of Mozambique, died along with other prominent Mozambican officials in a plane crash in South Africa. The South African government has been implicated in this accident. Subsequently, the Central Committee of FRELIMO named Joaquím Chissano president of FRELIMO and the People's Assembly confirmed him as president of the republic on 6 November 1986.

## LEADERSHIP

Chissano's political transition from foreign minister to president of the country was a smooth one. Because he was a trusted friend and comrade of the very popular Samora Machel and came out of the FRELIMO tradition of mass participatory politics, there have been few challenges to his assuming the presidency. However, Chissano maintains a very different public personality than Samora Machel. Machel was a fiery and flamboyant leader while Chissano is soft-spoken and unassuming.

Chissano had to address a growing divisiveness in the People's Assembly that began around the time of the 1994 elections. Some members of the People's Assembly believed that the country should maintain its socialist objectives, while others are pushing for a more capitalistic model. Chissano has tried to develop pragmatic compromises while moving the country towards a new economic agenda and constitution. The major challenge to Chissano and the FRELIMO government is to be found in the form of the Mozambican National Resistance Movement (RENAMO), which waged a 16-year war (1976–92) against Mozambique's army and its civilian population. Between 1989 and 1992, Chissano entered into negotiations with RENAMO and, with major constitutional reforms, was successful in convincing RENAMO to end the civil war and enter into a new political arrangement based on multi-party politics rather than the barrel of the gun. Implementation of the agreement was sluggish, as both sides jockeyed for power. Elections scheduled for 1993 weren't held until October 1994. Chissano won 53.3% of the vote, while Dhlakama of RENAMO won 33.7%. In the presidential and parliamentary elections held in December 1999, Chissano's margin of victory narrowed, when he won 52.3% to Dhlakama's 47.7% in the presidential vote. RENAMO also strengthened its position in parliament, taking 117 parliamentary seats against 133 for the ruling FRELIMO.

## DOMESTIC POLICY

Mozambique experienced growth in its economy between 1975 and 1980 but, largely due to the war waged by RENAMO and inadequate planning, it experienced a devastating decline between 1980 and 1993. The single most important domestic policy initiative undertaken by Chissano was to end the war through major political and constitutional reforms. RENAMO was founded in 1976 by the Rhodesian and Portuguese governments and, from 1980 until the end of the civil war in 1992, received most of its support from the white minority South African government. According to International Red Cross and Christian relief agencies and a 1988 US State Department Report, the goals of RENAMO

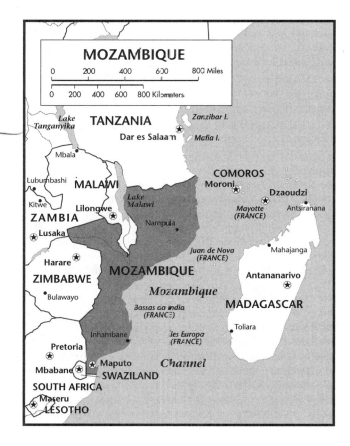

were to destabilize the country "without regard to a political program." In early 1988, it was conservatively estimated that 100,000 civilians may have been murdered by RENAMO. By the end of the civil war in 1992, over four million people were at risk of death due to food shortages and lack of health care because RENAMO primary targeted food crops, railroads, schools, and hospitals. Additionally, the Beira Pipeline, which transports oil from the port city of Beira, Mozambique to Zimbabwe and brings in much-needed foreign capital, was blown up many times by RENAMO in its campaign of terror.

In addition to negotiating peace with RENAMO, Chissano implemented land reform and privatization programs with the aim of creating economic stability. In order to do this, he established better diplomatic relations with Western countries, especially the US, and consolidated working agreements with the World Bank and the IMF. Because of such activities he has become known by members of his cabinet as the father of Mozambican diplomacy and a man who seeks a dignified peace.

The 1990 constitutional reforms were a direct result of years of war and were genuinely aimed at creating a climate in which new policy initiatives could be implemented. FRELIMO, which established an avowedly Marxist government, changed direction towards a market economy and a capitalist democracy. In the aftermath of these changes, Mozambique's economy began to recover after almost two decades of war and underdevelopment. The government's reconstruction and reform program won approval from the international financial institutions and from donors. Growth from the middle 1990s has been strong, and as of 2000 new confidence in the economy is attracting investment. However, it should be noted that this growth begins from a very low base: Mozambique is still the world's poorest country, and two-thirds of the population live in poverty as a result of drought, chronic underdevelopment which dates from Portuguese colonization, and most importantly from the 16 years of war. Unfortunately these advances were been set back by devastating floods that occurred in February and March 2000 affecting over a million people and destroying major economic infrastructure and thousands of hectares of crops and livestock.

Chissano continues to rule Mozambique as an elected president. The first multi-party elections were held in 1994. In December 1999, Mozambique had its second multi-party parliamentary and presidential election, which resulted in an extremely narrow victory for the incumbent FRELIMO government and president. The opposition party RENAMO claimed the election result to be falsified and attempted to get a Supreme Court ruling, demanding a recount of the votes. The Supreme Court rejected this.

## FOREIGN POLICY

Chissano has maintained relations with friendly neighboring African countries and the nonaligned and socialist countries. FRELIMO has always had close ties with the Zimbabwean government and is a key member of the Southern African Development Coordinating Conference (SADCC), a regional organization that promotes cooperative development initiatives. The Beira Pipeline, which transports oil from the Beira port in central Mozambique to landlocked Zimbabwe, is a project initiated through SADCC.

Upon his ascendancy to the presidency in 1986, Chissano continued the controversial policy of negotiating with the apartheid white minority government in South Africa to end South African support for RENAMO and to expand economic relations between the two countries. The first agreement, the Nkomati Accord, was negotiated between the two governments in 1983. Since the signing of the accord Chissano held two highly publicized meetings with South African officials. At both meetings South Africa gave its assurances that it would stop supporting RENAMO, but South African arms and personnel continue to be discovered by Mozambican officials and foreign observers. South Africa did offer to buy hydroelectric power from Mozambique's Caborra Basso Dam, which has been only sporadically operational since independence because of economic and technical problems as well as RENAMO attacks. A joint Security Commission was established by Mozambique and South Africa to protect the Dam from attacks and to sustain power transmissions.

One of Chissano's most important diplomatic goals was to end the hostile relationship between Mozambique and the US, a relationship attributed by the US to Mozambique's Marxist system. In this arena, Chissano has been successful. In 1988, full embassies were exchanged between the two countries and a warming of relations evolved. The United States now sees Mozambique as a country with a promising future and is now one of the principal bilateral aid donors to Mozambique. Under Chissano's leadership Mozambique has reached a lasting peace and a growing economy.

## ADDRESS
People's Republic of Mozambique
Office of the Presidency
Maputo, Mozambique

## REFERENCES

All Africa News Agency. "Facts About The Flooding/Mozambique Country Profile." 10 March 2000.

Cumbane, Evaristo. "Instability Threatens Mozambique After Disputed Poll." *Agence France-Presse*, 8 February 2000.

*Mozambique Press and Information Office Press Release*, 6 March 1990.

*Mozambiquefile*, November 1988.

*Mozambique Information Agency (AIM)*, 30 July 1990.

*Mozambique Support Network Newsletter*, various issues.

*Mozambique Update*, various issues.

*New York Times*, various issues.

Pan African News Agency, "Court Rejects RENAMO's Appeal Against Election Results." *Pan African News Agency*, 5 January 2000.

*Washington Post*, various issues.

**Profile researched and written by Lisa Brock (7/90; updated by Ezekiel Kalipeni, University of Illinois 3/2000).**

# MYANMAR

Than Shwe
Prime Minister
*(pronounced "THAN sh-WEE")*

*"National unity has been fostered"*

The Union of Myanmar (Burma) is the largest country on the Southeast Asian mainland, covering 678,500 sq km (261,970 sq mi). It shares borders with Bangladesh and India to the west, China to the north, and Laos and Thailand to the east. Its southern boundary is a coastline extending along the Andaman Sea and the Bay of Bengal. The capital is Yangon.

The population of 48,081,300 is ethnically diverse: 70% are ethnic Burmans, but other important groups include Indian, Pakistani, and Bangladeshi (2%); Chinese (3%); Karens (6%); Shans (7%); Arikanese (4%); and Chins, Kachins, and Mons (together 2%). Although the different groups speak a variety of languages and dialects, the official language is Burmese. English has been the most common second language. An estimated 80–90% of the population adheres to some form of Buddhism. There are also Christians, Muslims, Hindus and Animists among the population.

The economy, heavily dependent on agriculture and the export of raw materials, is in shambles, with no recovery in sight. Factories are estimated to be operating at 10% capacity. Inflation is 60% annually. The government has tried to stabilize the vaule of the *kyat,* the national currency, against the dollar, but this attempt has been largely unsuccessful due to the interference of the black market. The black market rate much more accurately reflects the *kyat's* real value than the rate that has been set by the government. Per capita GNP is US$1,200 annually. Primary exports include rice, teak, and other hardwoods, rubber, and cotton. Illicit narcotics, mainly heroin and methamphetamine, are produced and exported on a large scale. The foreign debt totals over US$4 billion.

## POLITICAL BACKGROUND
Myanmar (Burma), was annexed to British India in 1885 after a succession of wars. It did not gain full independence until January 1948. For ten years following independence the country, then known as the Union of Burma, maintained a parliamentary democracy headed by Prime Minister U Nu. In May 1958, in the face of a mounting political crisis, U Nu asked the military, headed by General Ne Win, to form a caretaker government until elections could be held. U Nu was returned to office in the elections of February–March 1960. Although the crisis had eased, the nation was confronted with serious problems of internal factionalism, insurgency, and lack of economic development. Taking advantage of these conditions, General Ne Win staged a coup d'etat in March 1962. The general abolished the national legislature and

organized a Revolutionary Council of senior army officers to run the government. The plan was to set the country on the "Burmese Road to Socialism," an eclectic mix of Marxism and spiritualism. In July, the Burmese Socialist Program Party (BSPP) was founded as the political arm of the military government, and Ne Win was designated chairman of the party.

In 1973, the name of the country was changed to the Socialist Republic of the Union of Burma. In 1974, after 12 years of military rule, the regime promulgated a new constitution, which codified Ne Win's BSPP ideals. At the same time, the national legislature was revived as the unicameral 489-member People's Assembly (*Pyithu Hluttaw*).

The 1974 constitution vested executive power in the 29-member Council of State (the chairman of which was also state president) and the 22-member Council of Ministers (which designated one of its members as the prime minister). The People's Assembly was the supreme organ of state authority, and members of both executive councils were chosen from within the Assembly. The voting age is 18. Since 1988, there has been no People's Assembly. In that year, following a coup d'état, the State Law and Order Restoration Council (SLORC) was created, made up primarily of ministers drawn from the military to run the country. As of early 2000, the May 1990 general elections, in which the opposition National League for Democracy won an overwhelming 87.7% majority, had still not been recognized by the SLORC, and those elected had not been seated.

Although Ne Win stepped down as president in 1981 and as chairman of the BSPP in 1988, many observers believe that he has continued to exert strong influence behind the scenes. The SLORC announced on 18 June 1989 that the name of the country would no longer be the Union of Burma, but *Myanmar Naing Ngan,* an ancient, formal term. The country is commonly referred to as "Myanmar," while democracy advocates such as the NLD use the old name, "Burma." City and other place names were changed by the SLORC as well.

## PERSONAL BACKGROUND
Than Shwe is originally from Kyaukse in central Myanmar. After graduating from high school, he went to work as a clerk in the post office. In 1953, at the age of 20, Than Shwe attended the Officer Training School's 6th course, after which he received his commission in the army. In 1963, one year after Ne Win crushed the Burmese democracy, Than Shwe was appointed an instructor at the Central Institute of

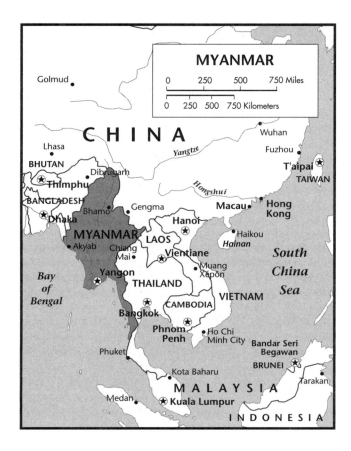

Political Science, the ideological training center of the BSPP. He rose gradually through the ranks of the army and in 1980 was promoted to the influential post of commander of the 88th light infantry division. He was considered an able field commander, though some analysts depict him as ruthless and more feared than respected by underlings. In 1983, he took over the Southwest Regional Command, and became chairman of the regional committee of the BSPP. Promoted to major general in 1985, he was then named deputy chief of staff of the army.

## RISE TO POWER

Myanmar in 1988 was rocked by a mass movement pressing for democratization. Initiated in March by students, the protest soon included ordinary citizens, Buddhist monks, government bureaucrats, and even some junior military officers. In the face of demonstrations, General Ne Win convened an extraordinary meeting of the BSPP, the nation's ruling (and sole legal) political party. On 23 July 1988 at the congress, Ne Win resigned as party chairman, and in his farewell speech, suggested far-reaching economic reforms and a referendum to decide the issue of multi-party elections. Although no one believed Ne Win would relinquish all power, the move nevertheless caught many observers by surprise.

On 18 September 1988, after mounting unrest, the army staged a coup d'etat and put in place the SLORC, composed of 19 members of the military and headed by General Saw Maung. Than Shwe was named vice chairman, deputy minister of defense, and army chief of staff. In 1990, he received promotion to full general. In March 1992, he assumed the defense portfolio, and on 23 April 1992, upon

the resignation of Saw Maung, who had been behaving erratically, Than Shwe was named chairman of SLORC. The following day he was designated prime minister.

## LEADERSHIP

Than Shwe's first move upon coming to power was to announce, and immediately follow through on, the release of significant numbers of political prisoners. It was widely believed that this was an attempt to placate the international community. Myanmar had been condemned by most Western states for massive human rights violations and most foreign economic aid, including that from multilateral lending institutions, had been cut off pending improvement in this area.

Than Shwe's main rival for attention, legitimacy, and power has certainly been Aung San Suu Kyi, leader of the National League for Democracy (NLD), landslide victor of the May 1990 elections, and winner of the 1991 Nobel Peace Prize. She was arrested in July 1989 and held in her home, incommunicado, until her July 1995 release. As his time at the head of the SLORC junta has gone on, Than Shwe has shown himself disinclined to open any kind of dialogue with Suu Kyi, and the NLD has been subjected to mass arrests, public attacks, restriction of movement, and vitriolic smear campaigns in the state-run press.

Some observers feel that Than Shwe has served as a balance between the junta's "pragmatists," exemplified by First Secretary Lt.-General Khin Nyunt, and the "hard-liners" typified by army chief Gen. Maung Aye. Both wings work against a hand-over of power to the NLD, but prefer different tactics in pacifying ethnic insurgencies. Than Shwe is thought to be planning to step down in favor of either Khin Nyunt or Maung Aye, but may be reluctant to do so as the succession could bring an intra-junta power struggle out in the open for the first time. The SLORC renamed itself the State Peace and Development Council in November 1997, and reshuffled the lineup of members, ousting and arresting some high-ranking officers for corruption.

## DOMESTIC POLICY

During Than Shwe's years in office, the ethnic insurgency in the frontier areas has been largely pacified, using a combination of Lt.-General Khin Nyunt's strategy of negotiating ceasefire deals and General Maung Aye's military offensives. In some regions, narcotics warlords such as Khun Sa have been allowed to legitimize their business activities as long as they lay down arms. A few rebel groups (most notably the Karen National Union) continue to battle the government, but their numbers and territory are much reduced. With the junta's army in control of most of Myanmar, large-scale forced labor has been reported on infrastructure projects such as roads, railways and dams, along with forced village relocation and other human rights violations, particularly in ethnic minority areas. These abuses have been repeatedly condemned by the UN General Assembly, the International Labor Organization, and independent human rights groups.

Under the SPDC, military spending accounts for as much as 50% of Myanmar's budget, at the expense of health, education, and welfare programs. The World Bank in early 2000 issued a scathing report on Myanmar's economic and political situation. Accusations have been leveled by observers that the economy relies on forced labor, and (with overt money-laundering) depends on the proceeds from trafficking in heroin and methamphetamine. Rampant deforestation and other environmental problems have gone unchecked under Than Shwe's government, along with a precipitous rise in HIV/AIDS and other infectious diseases.

## FOREIGN POLICY

Myanmar's relationship with China has been a high priority for Than Shwe, who visited Beijing in 1989 as a SLORC emissary and again, on as head of state in 1996. His efforts at arms procurement from China and improved border trade were quite successful, although they led to opposition charges that Myanmar was becoming a client state of the northern neighbor.

Association of South East Asian Nations (ASEAN) countries adopted a "constructive engagement" policy towards Myanmar, which was accepted for membership in the organization in July 1997. ASEAN investment in Myanmar declined with the Asian economic crisis of the late 1990s, however. Thailand, Myanmar's close neighbor, suffered from waves of refugees and an influx of Burmese methamphetamine, while engaged in a controversial gas pipeline venture with the junta, French and US companies. Japan similarly promoted business ties with Myanmar, but its investments were on the wane at the turn of the new century, due to corruption and other difficulties of ventures in Myanmar.

The United States imposed limited economic sanctions on Myanmar in 1996, followed by the European Community. The US and EC also observe an arms embargo against the SPDC. Pro-democracy exiles and overseas activists have organized boycotts of companies involved in Myanmar, and cities have passed "selective purchasing" laws aimed at pressuring those firms. One such law, challenged in Massachusetts, is being appealed at the US Supreme Court.

Than Shwe has proved impervious to outside pressure as well as economic inducements aimed at bringing him to the table for a tri-partite dialogue with Aung San Suu Kyi's NLD and ethnic leaders. In the process, Myanmar has grown poorer and more repressed. Perhaps Than Shwe's main accomplishment has been preserving the intact unity of the junta itself, under such besieged conditions.

## ADDRESS

Office of the Prime Minister
Yangon, Myanmar

## REFERENCES

*Beaters Library Report*, 24 April 1992.

Aung San Suu Kyi and Clements, Alan. *The Voice of Hope*. New York: Seven Stories Press, 1997.

Beyrer, Chris. *War in the Blood: Sex, Politics and AIDS in Southeast Asia*. London: Zed Books Ltd., 1998.

*The Economist*, 29 February 1992; 2 May 1992.

*Far Eastern Economic Review*, 13 February–7 May 1992.

*Far Eastern Economic Review Asia Yearbook*, 1991, 1992.

*Japan Economic Newswire*, 24 April 1992.

*New York Times*, 24–29 April 1992.

Open Society Institute. *Burma. Country in Crisis*. New York, 1998.

Rothberg, Robert, ed., *Burma: Prospects for a Democratic Future*. Washington DC: World Peace Foundation, 1998.

Smith, Martin. *Burma: Insurgency and the Politics of Ethnicity*. London: Zed Books Ltd., 1991, updated 1999.

**Profile researched and written by Alison Doherty Munro (10/92; updated by Edith Mirante 5/2000).**

# NAMIBIA

## Sam Nujoma
## President
### *(pronounced "nu-YO-ma")*

*"The years spent abroad have at times been characterized by loneliness.
We never lost sight of our principal objective—freedom and independence for Namibia."*

Namibia, formerly known as South-West Africa, became independent on 21 March 1990. Long considered Africa's lost colony it was colonized by Germany for 36 years before South African took control during World War I. Seven decades of South African rule saw the imposition of apartheid and patterns of uneven economic development between black and white segments of the populace. Whites, who make up about 70% of the population, have one of the highest standards of living in the world, while the majority of blacks live in dire poverty.

Covering an area of 823,290 sq km (317,873 sq mi) but with only 1.7 million people, Namibia is the most sparsely populated country on the planet. Over half the population lives in the northern third of the country, an area where higher rainfall makes subsistence agriculture possible. Despite its small size, the people of Namibia are ethnically diverse ranging from small groups of Khosian hunter-gatherers to the majority Ovambo cluster of ethnic groups. English is the official language; however, 13 indigenous languages are spoken in the country, as well as Arikaans and German.

Mining is the backbone of the economy, and uranium, diamonds, copper, and gold are major exports. Other rich mineral deposits such as coal, silver, and natural gas give the country the potential to become one of the wealthiest in Africa. Beef, mutton and karakul wool pelts are the principal products of the agricultural sector. Agricultural production in the heavily populated northern region has great potential. Prolific fishing grounds lie just off Namibia's coast in the South Atlantic Ocean. Namibia's per capita GNP is US$4,100, high compared to other sub-Saharan African nations but putting it in the lower medium income group overall. The currency of Namibia is the Namibian Dollar.

## POLITICAL BACKGROUND

Namibia is a constitutional democracy, and one of the newest members of the family of nations. Its independence marks the end of a century of sometimes-brutal colonial rule, as well as 23 years of guerilla war between the South-West Africa Peoples Organization (SWAPO) and the South Africa Defense Force. In a deal brokered by the two then-superpowers (the US and the USSR), Angola, Cuba, and South Africa agreed in late 1988 to give Namibia its independence in return for a Cuban troop pullout from Angola. This process began on 1 April 1989 when a UN-supervised cease-fire took effect. The UN effort, the largest of its kind, included over 6,000 civilian and military personnel to monitor both the cease-fire and the

subsequent election to determine Namibia's first government. In the early months of the peace plan, over 40,000 political exiles returned to the country. Again, this was the largest repatriation of political exiles ever in the history of the UN.

Elections for the Constituent Assembly, the body that was to write the country's constitution, were held in November 1989. The election was universally praised for being fair and free, a condition of the UN Peace Plan known as Resolution 435. Over 95% of eligible voters cast their ballots, a remarkable figure given the vast distance most had to cross to reach a polling station. Of the 72 seats in the Constituent Assembly that were contested, SWAPO took a clear majority of 41 seats. At the same time, the balloting also created a viable and strong opposition, consisting of six parties that range across the political spectrum.

The constitution was written by the Constituent Assembly, and formally adopted on 9 February 1990. Considered one of the most liberal in Africa, the constitution establishes a system of checks and balances between independent judiciary, executive, and legislative branches. Most forms of discrimination as well as the death penalty are abolished. Fundamental rights such as freedom of religion, speech, peaceful association, and the press are guaranteed. The right to legal representation, prevention of cruel and inhuman treatment, and a fair trial within a reasonable time also figure prominently throughout the document.

The president is limited to two five-year terms of office, and is directly elected by universal suffrage of all Namibians over the age of 18. A 72-member National Assembly also has the power to dissolve it and call new elections. Soon after independence legislation was passed with a new structure of regional and local governments. New constituency boundaries served to reduce the impact of ethnic voting blocks.

## PERSONAL BACKGROUND

Sam Nujoma was born on 12 May 1929 in Etunda Village in the remote northern region of Namibia known as Ovamboland. His origins are humble. He is said to have spent his early years herding goats at his family's homestead. Like many black Namibians, he received little formal education. Though he did not complete high school, he boasts that he enabled many in SWAPO to further their education over the years while he stayed behind to do necessary political work. Little is known of his early life because, like Nelson Mandela, he was a "banned person" under South Africa's restrictive security legislation. For many years it was illegal either to quote Nujoma or to print his picture inside Namibia. As early as 1957, he was fired from a job on the South African Railways for attempts to organize a trade union. In 1959 he joined the Ovamboland Peoples Organization (OPO) while in Cape Town, South Africa. The OPO consisted of a group of Ovambo workers who gathered to discuss their grievances with the contract labor system. The early meetings of this group took place in a barbershop in Cape Town that is now part of Namibia's folklore.

After his termination from the railways, he returned to Windhoek, the capital of Namibia, where he became a leading figure in the protest against the removal of the Old Location, or ghetto, to its present site. South African authorities wanted to move the entire African section of Windhoek to this new location in order to place as much distance as possible between whites and non-whites. For blacks dependent on jobs in the city, the move was considered a severe hardship because it would add many commuting hours to the workday. The Africans called the new ghetto *Katatura*, which means "a place where we do not stay" in a local language. Demonstrations against this removal led to a bloody confrontation in December 1959 between police and demonstrators during which 13 unarmed civilians were shot and killed. Shortly afterward, Nujoma was detained for his role in the demonstration.

On his release, he fled the country. While visiting the UN in April 1960, Nujoma joined with other Namibian exiles to help reform OPO into SWAPO. He was chosen president of the new group and returned to Dar es Salaam, Tanzania to build the organization of the party. His position was ratified by a party congress in 1963. Since that time he has traveled the world in order to obtain international support both for SWAPO and for Namibian independence. In this effort, he met with considerable success; SWAPO was granted Observer Status at the UN, admitted as a member of the Organization of African Unity, and allowed to establish diplomatic missions in many countries around the world.

In 1966 SWAPO began a guerilla war against the South African government. Often described as a low-intensity conflict, this war lasted 23 years. By the war's end the military wing of SWAPO had approximately 10,000 troops including armored units. On the other side, South Africa was forced to commit large numbers of troops, and spend millions of dollars in scarce foreign currency on the conflict. Much of the northern part of Namibia was turned into a war zone, with thousands of soldiers and civilians killed. SWAPO also maintained a system of refugee camps in Angola and Zambia for Namibians fleeing political persecution and apartheid. It is estimated that over 60,000 people were cared for in these camps.

## RISE TO POWER

In September 1989, after almost 30 years in exile, Nujoma returned to Namibia. Thousands of his countrymen gathered in Windhoek to greet him. He settled in *Katatura*, the ghetto in which he had refused to live three decades previously. A man noted for his headstrong views, Nujoma surprised his critics by holding a series of conciliatory meetings with political rivals. For this he received high acclaim even from

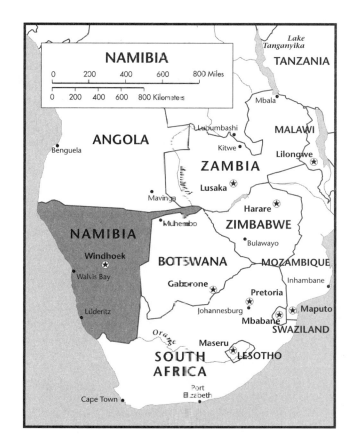

white politicians who had literally been his enemies only a few months previously.

In the November 1989 elections, his party failed to capture the two-thirds majority necessary to implement its own constitution. A key factor in this defeat was the issue of SWAPO detainees during the decades-long war and its commitment to human rights. This, too, Nujoma turned to an advantage by compromising with his opponents and incorporating specific human rights guarantees into the constitution. The result was a document that has been praised around the world. On 16 February 1990, he was unanimously elected by the Constituent Assembly as the first president of Namibia.

The issue of SWAPO detainees and alleged human rights abuses resurfaced with the publication in 1996 of a damning book by Siegfried Groth, a German pastor of the Lutheran Church, titled *Namibia: the Wall of Silence*. SWAPO defended itself in a book of its own published the same year as a rejoinder, titled *Their Blood Waters, Our Freedom*. To date (mid March 2000) the SWAPO Government has persistently refused to apologize, or to set up a South African-style "truth commission" to hold hearings on the alleged abuses, as church and human rights groups demand. SWAPO argues that this is unnecessary and will only open wounds that Nujoma's policy of "reconciliation" has helped to heal. The opposition DTA agrees with SWAPO on the issue

## LEADERSHIP

In choosing his cabinet, President-elect Nujoma continued his conciliatory theme by naming opposition members to cabinet positions. On 21 March 1990 Namibia became independent, and Sam Nujoma became its first president, sworn into office by UN Secretary Javier Pérez de Cuellar. Many observers view the process of reconciliation taking place in Namibia as a precursor to an ultimate end of apartheid in South Africa itself.

Nujoma and his SWAPO won a second term of office in the 7–8 December 1994 elections, taking 76% of the vote and 53 of the 72 seats in the National Assembly. Mushake Muyongo got 23% of the vote, and his Democratic Turnhall Alliance (DTA) was second with 15 parliamentary seats. Three other parties shared the remaining two seats.

The SWAPO government has been considered a shining role model of an emerging democracy. As the second term wore on, however, SWAPO consolidated its monopoly on power to the extent that the opposition became nonexistent in influencing decisions. Government priorities began to change. In a country with a poor black majority, members of parliament rushed through a bill prior to the 1999 elections giving themselves huge retirement packages whether they leave office or not. Allegations of corruption (still not as bad as in many African countries) and human rights abuses, especially in the Caprivi region, started surfacing.

Abuse of such a monopoly on power as SWAPO holds was demonstrated in November 1998, when Nujoma himself supported constitutional amendments proposed by his party allowing him to seek a third term. Seen by many as backtracking into dictatorial footsteps, and as "a torpedoing of democracy," but defended by SWAPO as a reflection of "the way that people perceived SWAPO," and "a result of democracy in action," the move sparked both local and international criticism. Resigning his position as Namibia's High Commissioner to Great Britain in protest over this eventuality, opposition candidate Ben Ulenga was quoted as saying, "I have...reached the firm conviction that the proposal to increase the presidential terms for the present incumbent would be to the total detriment of the country, the SWAPO party, and the cumulative process of political democratization and good governance in the country."

With its backbone support in the densely populated north, Nujoma's home area, as well as the majority of his fellow senior ministers, SWAPO went on to win three-quarters (55) of the 72 parliamentary seats and Nujoma got 77% of the vote in the elections held on 30 November and 1 December 1999. Ben Ulenga of the Congress of Democrats got the highest opposition vote (10.5%); but his party was tied with the DTA for number of parliamentary seats (seven each). The elections were declared substantially free and fair.

## DOMESTIC POLICY

Realizing Namibia's vast potential will not be an easy task. The new government inherits serious economic problems. Decades of apartheid rule have skewed the economy in favor of the tiny white minority. Unemployment in the black majority runs about 40%. Underemployment is also an issue; many black workers do not earn enough to support either themselves or their families. Apartheid policies, particularly in education, have prevented blacks from developing managerial and entrepreneurial skills. These are precisely the skills that are needed to lift Namibians out of poverty. Despite these disparities, the SWAPO government has

pursued a policy of reconciliation in a dynamic non-racial society.

As of early 2000, Nujoma and his government were faced with the delicate task of redressing major imbalances in the distribution of wealth while at the same time continuing to foster economic growth. Namibia relies on technical and financial assistance from donor countries in Europe, Scandinavia, and North America, and as of the late 1990s, China. President Nujoma has modified his socialist beliefs and embraced the private sector as a principal force for economic development. Learning from the mistakes of other newly independent countries, Nujoma has called for a mixed economy, with legislative codes for the regulation of foreign investment. In a move designed to bolster confidence in the business community, he appointed Otto Herrigel, a conservative white businessman, as finance minister. As of early 2000, this approach appeared to be working. Namibia has a robust economy, with inflation rates in single digits since 1995. In December 1999, Namibia was ranked (along with Mauritius) as one of the only consolidated democracies in the 14-member Southern African Development Community (SADC). According to Anthoni Nieuwkerk, research director of the Johannesburg-based Institute for Global Dialogue, the agency that compiled the ranking, this reflects Namibia's performance in fighting the enemies of democracy: unemployment, poverty, corruption, and social decay.

Namibia, along with South Africa, Botswana, Zimbabwe, and Swaziland, is at the epicenter of the AIDS pandemic. An estimated one in four adults is believed to be infected with the HIV virus. UNAIDS reports that in 1996, 46.7% of Namibian women at a prenatal clinic tested positive for HIV. Namibia is committed to addressing the growing AIDS pandemic, and in September 1999, was praised by the WHO as the only sub-Sahara African country that had made adequate health provisions (dedicated 15% of the budget, compared to less than 6% for other countries).

## FOREIGN POLICY

Namibia is the UN's 160th member, and is also a member of the Commonwealth of Nations, the association of former British Colonies. Namibia's most pressing foreign policy issue, at least for the first five years of independence when South Africa was still under apartheid rule, was managing relations with South Africa, its former colonial master. South Africa had regularly used its economic and political clout to destabilize its neighbors, particularly those who showed strong opposition to its apartheid system. With 85% of its imports coming from South Africa, and the remaining 15% coming through South Africa, Namibia could ill afford an adversary relationship with its close neighbor. Namibia handled the situation well, and on 1 March 1994, Walvis Bay (Namibia's main deep water port), over which South Africa had kept control, was fully handed back to Namibia. This significantly freed the country from South Africa's economic stranglehold, putting Namibia in an advantaged position over other land-locked southern African countries.

The SWAPO government has, since independence in 1990, pursued neutrality and a principal of contact and dialogue that is enshrined in its constitution. Namibia referred its 10 year-old territorial dispute with Botswana over Kasikili (a 3.5

sq km island, known in Botswana as Sedudu) located in the Chobe River, to the International Court of Justice (ICJ) in the Hague. In December 1999, the ICJ ruled in favor of Botswana, and Namibia accepted the ruling. However, during 1999, Namibia joined two civil wars: It sent an estimated 2,000 solders to help President Laurent Kabila of the Democratic Republic of the Congo (DROC) fight rebels; and in December 1999, Nujoma allowed Angolan troops to use its territory to pursue UNITA rebels. Namibian involvement in both conflicts, criticized by the opposition and some quarters of society, has the potential to increase insecurity in that country. As of early 2000, the negative effects of this are already apparent in the Caprivi border region with Angola, where Namibians have suffered scores of injuries and deaths from UNITA rebel attacks and harassment. Many men, struggling to escape from the poverty in this region, have been convinced by Angolan army recruitment efforts to fight in a foreign war. The Namibian government has also come under fire for human rights abuses in the area, on occasions in complicity with the Angolan government. As the country begins its second decade of independence in 2000, the handling of these conflicts, balancing domestic and international obligations, is a challenge the SWAPO government must handle with care.

## ADDRESS

Office of the President
Windhoek
Namibia

## REFERENCES

*Boston Globe,* 10 October 1999, 6 December 1999.

Bureau of Democracy, Human Rights, and Labor U.S. Department of State, 1999 Country Reports on Human Rights Practices. [Online] Available http://www.state.gov/www.global/human_rights/1999_hrp_report/namibia.html. (25 February 2000; accessed 10 April 2000).

*Namibia Report,* February 1990.

*New York Times,* 21 March 1990.

Putz, J. et al, *Political Who 's Who of Namibia,* 1987.

*Reuters,* 3 December 1999.

SAPPA News Agency, Johannesburg, BBC Monitoring International as provided by EBC World Monitoring Service, 12 May 1999, 7 August 1999.

*Washington Post,* 13 June 1996; 17 December 1999; 27 January 2000.

World Bank. [Online] Available http://www.worldbank.org/data/countrydata/countrydata.html (accessed Arpil 10, 2000).

**Profile researched and written by Bennet Fuller, Jr. (7/90; updated by Leo Zulu, University of Illinois at Urbana-Champaign 4/2000).**

# NAURU

## Bernard Dowiyogo
## President

*(pronounced "doh-ee-YO-go")*

*"Our priorities are, in essence, to cut our losses and to maximize our human resources potential."*

The Republic of Nauru (pronounced "NAH-roo") is distinctive in many ways. With an area of less than 22 sq km (little more than 8 sq mi), Nauru is the world's smallest independent nation. The single, tiny island lies 41 km (25 mi) south of the equator at a latitude of 0° south and a longitude of 167° east. On the inland side of the island, a coral cliff rises up to 300 m (less than 1000 ft) above sea level; this central plateau was the site of phosphate deposits. Because of its isolated location, birds nested on Nauru for thousands of years, leaving behind vast deposits of phosphate-rich guano. The island was once covered in dense tropical forest, but mining for phosphate during the past 90 years stripped this vegetation, leaving most of Nauru a strange, jagged landscape. A narrow fertile belt rimmed by sandy beaches still encircles the island. Temperatures range from 23° to 32° Celsius (73° to 90° Fahrenheit) year round. Rainfall is heavy from November through February and sporadic during the other months.

The population of Nauru is estimated at 10,605, about two-thirds of which are ethnic Nauruan. The remainder consists of migrant workers from Tuvalu and Kiribati, ethnic Chinese, and Europeans, almost all employed in some capacity in the phosphate industry. After years of population decline, ethnic Nauruans are now increasing rapidly in numbers. Half of the current population is estimated to be under the age of 15. The official language is Nauruan, classed within the Micronesian family of Austronesian languages. Most Nauruans also speak English, the language of commerce, government, and education. Representatives of the London Missionary Society brought Christianity to Nauru more than 100 years ago. Today 60% of Nauruans are members of the Nauruan Congregational Church; most of the remainder are Roman Catholics. Nauruans enjoy a high standard of living in terms of a Western lifestyle. However, this has resulted in both the loss of cultural traditions and increasing health problems. Changes in diet, including use of alcohol, have resulted in obesity and what some experts claim is the highest rate of diabetes in the Pacific, if not the world.

Throughout the 20th century, the economy of Nauru has been synonymous with phosphate mining. Phosphate is a key ingredient in agricultural fertilizers. This export has let Nauruans enjoy one of the highest per capita incomes, at approximately US$10,000, in the region. All modern infrastructure (the airport, national airline, railroad, paved roads, telephone system, and the single luxury hotel) was developed to support that industry. Apart from coconuts, there is no agricultural activity on the island. Almost everything is imported, including fresh water.

Phosphate reserves began to decline significantly in the 1990s. It is expected they will be completely exhausted shortly after the turn of the century although authorities disagree as to the actual date. When phosphate mining ceases, Nauru's economic prospects seem very limited. Every government since independence has invested a significant portion of phosphate revenues, much of it in overseas real estate, in an effort to cushion the effects of the loss of this income. However, the loss of millions of dollars to swindlers in 1993, a failed backing of a musical comedy in England, and unsuccessful investments in the Philippines and India have caused a financial decline in recent years. Ten years of deficit spending to make up for lost revenues has created substantial debt which, in early 1996, made Nauru incapable of meeting the salaries for its civil servants and placed the country in default on its external debt service.

Some attention has been given since 1995 to creating a tourist industry, but this would be dependent on developing public and private infrastructures that have been allowed to fall into disrepair. Nor does the recent Asian economic situation make tourism from that part of the world a likely prospect. Fishing has some economic potential. The national currency is the Australian dollar.

## POLITICAL BACKGROUND

Nauru became an independent republic on 29 January 1968, after 75 years of colonial rule. In 1999, it became a full member of the Commonwealth of Nations. When the UK and Germany reached an agreement over their interests in the Pacific, Nauru fell within the German jurisdiction. Though Germany controlled Nauru until the outbreak of the first World War, politics took second place to the interests of phosphate mining, which began in 1907. Agreements between Germany and a British firm to exploit deposits shaped the administration until the League of Nations mandate was given to Australia, New Zealand, and Britain after the war. Actual administration was in the hands of Australia through the British phosphate commissioners.

The island and its people suffered terribly during World War II. Even before Japan began its Pacific campaign, German raiders disguised as merchant ships shelled oil storage tanks in December 1940. The same week as the Pearl Harbor attack, Japan bombed Nauru and took control the following August. Japan occupied Nauru from 1942 until the end of the war. The Japanese tried to continue phosphate mining, using islanders as slave labor, but Allied bombing through most of 1943 and all of 1944 prevented this. The Japanese deported 1,200 Nauruans, or two-thirds of the indigenous population, to the Caroline Islands to work as laborers. Five hundred of them died of starvation, mistreatment, and disease. Of those who remained on Nauru, 50 died of the same suffering. Thus one-third of the Nauruan population perished in the war. The magnitude of this loss completely disrupted their society, and the shared experience united the survivors in a new resolve. Wartime suffering was the defining experience for those who would lead the way to nationhood 20 years later. When peace came, the old mandate was replaced in 1947 by a United Nations trusteeship, administered by Australia on behalf of the other two trust powers. In 1966, Nauruans were granted self-rule as a prelude to independence.

At independence, Nauru's constitution established the nation as a republic with a parliamentary system of government. The president might more properly be called prime minister; he is the *de facto* head of state as well as head of government. He is elected by parliament from among its elected members and appoints and removes the four or five ministers who make up the cabinet. The cabinet is collectively responsible to parliament, which can remove them along with the president by a no-confidence vote of at least half the members. If parliament fails to choose a new president within seven days, it is dissolved. The single-chamber parliament consists of 18 members, elected from eight constituencies for three-year terms. Parliament elects one of its members to preside as speaker; the speaker cannot at the same time be a member of cabinet.

A second tier of government, the Nauru Local Government Council, was created after the war to help build local government structures, address community issues, and link the local traditional level with the central government. However, after independence, the council took over ownership and control of many of the country's numerous enterprises and investments and thus gained considerable power. The council was dissolved in 1992 amidst allegations of mismanagement. Following an evaluation of investment performance, a new organization, the Nauru Island Council, was formed with a limited mandate to help revitalize the central government on local issues. Responsibility for managing investments was temporarily centralized in the cabinet until they could be brought in line with current financial management policy. These changes required new legislation to set out strategies for handling investments.

The economy and politics of Nauru have been thoroughly intertwined because it was common for individuals to hold seats in both parliament and the council. Hammer DeRoburt was Nauru's first president and held the office for all but 18 months until August 1989 when a vote of no-confidence forced him to step down. He also served as head chief of the council from 1955 until his death in 1990. Since there are no political parties, electoral politics has more to do with kin relations and personal factions than with issues. Furthermore, the performance of Nauruan business interests affects electoral outcomes, especially when business decisions have been criticized and accusations of corruption raised. The constitution created a form of government that, combined

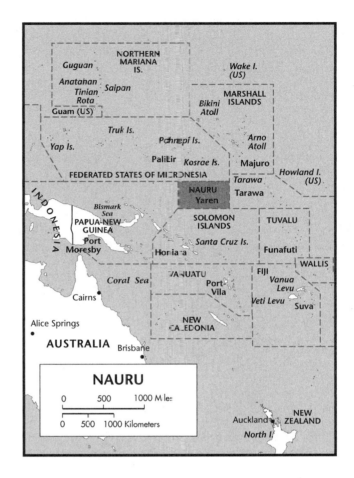

with the above factors, has since 1995 led to a "revolving door" kind of presidency. Bernard Dowiyogo, who had replaced DeRoburt, was defeated in 1995 by Lagumot Harris by one vote. Within a year, parliament ousted Harris, once again by a narrow margin. There followed a series of no-confidence motions that brought down another two presidents in less than four months. In February 1997, an island-wide election was held a year earlier than expected in an effort to return political stability to the country. Following the general election, parliament chose Kinza Clodumar as president, but within 18 months yet another no-confidence vote removed him from office

Government policies have only recently begun to adjust to the reduced income potential. Much of the political instability and shifts of leadership that have characterized the past few years stem from disagreements over the best ways to deal with this situation.

In 1999, Nauru finally joined the international community by joining the Commonwealth on Nations (May) and the United Nations (September). Parliament gave Dowiyogo a no-confidence vote in April. Rene Harris became the new president after defeating Dowiyogo by a 10–7 vote in Parliament. It was the seventh government in three years. Harris became a Member of Parliament in 1977, and held several government posts, including the chair of the Nauru Phosphate Corporation. A year later, in April 2000 elections were called again, and Dowiyogo defeated Harris and resumed his presidency after a year out of office.

## PERSONAL BACKGROUND

Bernard Dowiyogo was born in February 1946. Like a number of Nauruans who grew up in the postwar era, he received his post-primary education overseas. After completing secondary school at Ballarat College, Victoria, Australia, he went on to the Australian National University to obtain his law degree.

## RISE TO POWER

Dowiyogo is typical of his generation of Nauruan leaders, many of whom have been at times his political allies, but at other times his rivals for the presidency. He was first elected to parliament in 1973. He has served continuously ever since, making him the longest serving member in the nation's history. In 1976, he and other younger parliamentarians engineered a no-confidence vote, bringing down Hammer DeRoburt. He and his allies were perceived at the time as Nauru's first political party. Dowiyogo was then chosen to be president. However, he was unable to hold his group together. In 1978, former allies joined with other members in a no-confidence vote, removing him and returning DeRoburt to office.

When DeRoburt was deposed for good in August 1989, parliament chose Dowiyogo as president, and he was able to retain that office for six years, a record second in length only to that of his predecessor. The term ended when Lagumot Harris was chosen, and this pattern continued through the presidential turnovers from 1995 until the present. After Kinza Clodumar was deposed by a no-confidence vote, Dowiyogo was returned to the presidency by a larger margin, which might bring greater stability to a political scene that has in recent years been treated as farcical by outside observers. It is typical that Dowiyogo served as education minister in Clodumar's cabinet and in turn has promised a major role for Clodumar in his own new government.

## LEADERSHIP

In 1989, Dowiyogo drew on his training in law to formulate a challenge against Australia in the International Court of Justice over responsibility for rehabilitating mined-out phosphate lands. This issue was in keeping with Dowiyogo's concern for the environment. A settlement was reached in August 1993. As part of the settlement, Nauru received a one-time payment of A$57 million, followed by annual payments of A$2.5 million (adjusted for inflation) for 20 years. Nauru agreed to drop all claims against Britain and New Zealand, the other administering powers before independence.

## DOMESTIC POLICY

Every incoming president in the 1990s stressed the necessity for fiscal responsibility and careful management of available resources as phosphate revenues come to an end. Dowiyogo is no exception. In his previous position as education minister, he expressed concern for an economic development plan that would provide employment for educated Nauruans to avoid a "brain drain." During his earlier term as president, he spoke of developing a small but controlled tourism industry.

Although he has yet to put forth any specific proposals, critics of the country's economic policies have commented on Nauru's lack of any tariffs, income, or sales taxes. Imposition of such taxes would be a major move toward the kind of financial management Nauru needs. Dowiyogo may not have enough support in parliament to act on such politically volatile ideas.

## FOREIGN POLICY

Nauru's size, history of mining exploitation, and isolated location have led the country to take strong stands on environmental issues within the Pacific Island community. Dowiyogo's own sympathy toward environmental concerns strengthens this stance, and he is expected to continue Nauru's battle against pollution from industrialized nations, which is blamed for global warming. Global warming and the possibility of rising sea levels constitutes a particular threat to small island nations, and Dowiyogo is certain to use his country's membership in the South Pacific Forum to sound warnings on this issue. He must also work closely with Australia in establishing a Rehabilitation Authority to repair mining damage.

## ADDRESS

Office of the President
Government Offices
Yaren District, Nauru

## REFERENCES

"Air Nauru records first profit in 30 years," Pacific Islands Development Program/East-West Center, Center for Pacific Islands Studies/University of Hawaii at Manoa, 28 June 1999 [online archives]

"Big tasks for a small island," BBC Online Network, 30 April 1999 [online archives]

"Former Nauru president calls for rehabilitation of land," Pacific Islands Development Program/East-West Center, Center for Pacific Islands Studies/University of Hawaii at Manoa, 26 February 1999 [online archives]

Islands Business, 1990–1998.

"Nauru becomes member of the United Nations," Reuters, 15 September 1999.

"Nauru public service to be cut by half by 2001," Pacific Islands Development Program/East-West Center, Center for Pacific Islands Studies/University of Hawaii at Manoa, 26 February 1999 [online archives]

"Nauru to cut 400 government jobs," Pacific Islands Development Program/East-West Center, Center for Pacific Islands Studies/University of Hawaii at Manoa, 5 April 1999 [online archives]

Pacific Economic Bulletin, November 1996.

Pacific Islands Monthly, 1990–1998.

Pacific Magazine, 1990–1998.

"Shipping rates reduced between Australia and Nauru," Pacific Islands Development Program/East-West Center, Center for Pacific Islands Studies/University of Hawaii at Manoa, 11 June 1999 [online archives]

**Profile researched and written by Eugene Ogan, Professor Emeritus, University of Minnesota (12/98; updated 5/2000).**

# NEPAL

## Girija Prasad Koirala
### Prime Minister

*(pronounced "JEE-ree-jan prah-SAHD quoi-RAH-lah",*

*"As the new prime minister, my priorities will be to maintain law and order, eradicate corruption, and good governance."*

The Kingdom of Nepal is a small, land-locked country in South Asia which lies between the Tibetan region of China to the north and India to the east, south, and west. Occupying an area of 140,800 sq km (54,362 sq mi), Nepal is well known for its rugged, scenic beauty.

Nepal has an estimated population of 24 million people. Ethnically, 80% of the people belong to the Indo-Nepalese group that includes Paharis, Newars, Tharus, and recent Indian immigrants. Those of Tibetan origin make up the remainder of the population. Nepali is the official language, but there are also several local languages and dialects. Nearly 90% of Nepalese practice Hinduism, which is the country's official religion. Buddhists comprise the largest religious minority, followed by Muslims.

Nepal's economy is primarily agrarian, with almost 90% of the people employed in subsistence farming and related activities. The manufacturing and service sectors, though small, have grown in recent years. Tourism is a significant source of foreign exchange earnings and shows robust growth potential. With an estimated per capita GNP of US$1,100, Nepal ranks as one of the least developed countries. The currency unit is the Nepalese *rupee*.

## POLITICAL BACKGROUND

Nepal has historically been an absolute fiefdom of one family or another. From 1796 to 1846 Prithvi Narain Shah and his descendants ruled. They were followed by the Rana family of hereditary prime ministers. The Ranas were overthrown in 1950, and the royal line of King Tribhuvan came into power. In 1955, his son Mahendra succeeded Tribhuvan to the throne. Elections held in 1959 brought the Nepali Congress (NC) Party into power as the first parliamentary government. They remained in office for little more than a year before the king dismissed the government and banned all political parties.

Under a constitution promulgated in 1962, King Mahendra established a partyless *panchayat* (assembly) system. Members of this assembly served only at the king's behest. Even after Mahendra's son, Birendra Bir Bikram, assumed power in 1972, only minor reforms were made.

A coalition of the two major political forces in the country—the NC and the United Left Front (comprised of seven communist parties)—provided the vanguard for widespread political protests that began in 1990. With growing domestic and international pressure, King Birendra announced an end to the *panchayat* system and agreed to the restoration of multi-party parliamentary democracy. Officially promulgated on 9 November 1990, the new constitution transferred effective sovereignty to the people. A bicameral legislature was established, consisting of a 205-member *Pratinidhi Sabha* (House of Representatives), directly elected by universal suffrage every five years, and a 60-member upper house, the *Rashtriya Sabha* (National Council), most of whose members are indirectly elected by the lower house.

The first elections to the *Pratinidhi Sabha* resulted in a victory for the NC party. However, factionalism led to the government's collapse and new elections in November 1994. The Communist Party of Nepal-United Marxist Leninist (CPN-UML) won the largest number of seats in the new parliament, but not an outright majority. It formed a minority government that survived less than a year before being ousted in a no-confidence motion tabled by the NC. The NC then forged an alliance with the *Rashtriya Prajatantra Party* (RPP) and the *Nepal Sadbhavana Party* (NSP) to form Nepal's first coalition government. In March 1997, the NC-led coalition fell when several RPP parliamentarians joined the CPN-UML to defeat a confidence motion tabled by the government. Lokendra Bahadur Chand, leader of the RPP revolt, became prime minister of the new government formed by a coalition between the RPP and the CPN-UML. Shifting allegiances took their toll on political stability again in October 1997 when most of the RPP parliamentary delegation defected from the government to join the NC in voting to bring down Chand and the RPP-CPN-UML coalition. On October 7, Surya Bahadur Thapa of the RPP was sworn in as prime minister of a new NC-RPP-NSP coalition. Three months later, dissension within the RPP split the party, weakening Thapa. In March 1998, the opposition CPN-UML also fractured into majority UML and minority ML splinter groups.

These intra-party upheavals left the NC as the single largest parliamentary party. In early April, Thapa resigned under pressure and the NC's G. P. Koirala became the country's fifth prime minister in less than four years. Koirala formed a minority NC government with the parliamentary backing of the UML. Soon after winning a vote of confidence, he announced plans for holding elections by May 1999. In August 1998, the ML and NC joined forces, forming a majority coalition.

The arrangement did not last. In December, the ML withdrew from the government. Faced with an impending vote of no confidence, Koirala scrambled for new allies. The

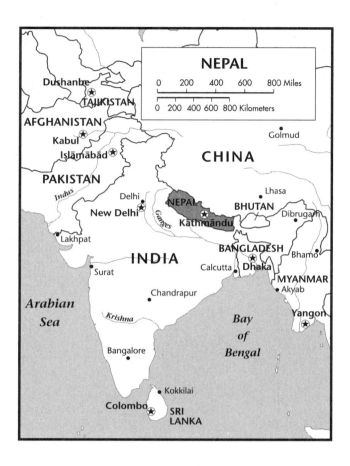

UML agreed to throw its support behind Koirala, provided he stuck to his promise of early elections. Subsequently, Koirala's minority government resigned. He then formed a majority coalition government with the UML and the NSP. In January 1999, the new government won a resounding vote of confidence. Soon after the vote, the king announced elections in May. In April 1999, the leftist movement in Nepal suffered a severe blow with the death of the CPN/UML president Man Mohan Adhikari, the only moderate Communist leader in Nepali politics. This may have contributed to the Communists relatively poor showing in the May elections—they won 68 parliamentary seats compared to 88 in the 1994 general elections. The Nepali Congress won a clear majority, with 110 seats in the 205-member *Pratinidhi Sabha*. The veteran K. B. Bhattarai ran unopposed for the NC parliamentary party leadership and was sworn in as prime minister on May 31. His tenure in office lasted less than ten months, however. Bhattarai was forced to resign as prime minister in March 2000 and was replaced by G. P. Koirala.

## PERSONAL BACKGROUND

Girija Prasad (G. P.) Koirala comes from a family with a long history of involvement in Nepalese politics. His father, Krishna Prasad Koirala, was a revolutionary during the Rana period who was forced to flee Nepal to avoid arrest by the government. As a consequence, G. P. Koirala was born in the northern part of the state of Bihar in India, near the Nepalese border, in 1925. Two elder brothers, M. P. Koirala and B. P. Koirala, were instrumental in the founding of the Nepali Congress (NC) in India in 1950, and both were later to become prime ministers of Nepal. Before completing his

higher education, G. P. Koirala became active in politics, getting involved in both the Indian independence movement and the Nepal revolution of 1950–51. He married (the late Sushma Koirala) and had one daughter.

## RISE TO POWER

G. P. Koirala began his active career in politics organizing the labor movement at the Biratnagar Jute Mills (BJM) in the town (Biratnagar) in Nepal that had formerly been the home of his father, K. P. Koirala. G. P. Koirala was also active in the Youth Nepali Congress for many years. He was arrested after the Royal Takeover in Nepal in 1960, and spent seven years in prison. Following his release, he continued to work for a multi-party democracy in Nepal. His political activities put him at risk, and he fled to India where he spent eight years (1971–79) in exile. In 1976, Koirala was elected general secretary of the NC in Patna, India. Returning to Nepal in 1979, G. P. Koirala played a key role in the country's struggle for democracy. He was a leader in the NC's civil disobedience movement of 1985, and in 1990 became the founding chairman of the Nepal Trade Union Congress. Koirala was elected to parliament in 1991 in the first general elections ever to be held in the country's history. He was prime minister of Nepal from 1991–94, and held the office again twice in 1998, first as leader of a minority NC government and then as head of a short-lived coalition with the UML and NSP. In 1996, Koirala was elected president of the NC, a position he still holds. Although he supported K. B. Bhattarai, a veteran of Nepal's democracy movement and a founding member of the Nepali Congress, in his candidacy for the prime ministership in May 1999, Koirala was extremely critical of Bhattarai's performance in office. Citing the need to maintain law and order, eradicate corruption, and restore good governance, Koirala forced Bhattarai to resign in March 2000. He subsequently defeated Sher Bahadur Deuba in elections for the leadership of the NC parliamentary party, and was sworn in as prime minister by King Birendra on 20 March 2000.

## LEADERSHIP

As a veteran of Nepal's faction-ridden politics, Koirala is well aware of the difficult task that faces him in running the country. In his first tenure as prime minister, Koirala proved a strong and capable leader, equal to the challenge of maintaining discipline in his party as well as in parliament. He was also responsible for breaking away from the concept of collective leadership that was prevalent in the Congress party in its early days, effectively establishing one-man leadership in the party. Nearly a decade later, however, the situation is different. The powers of the prime minister have been weakened by decisions handed down by the Supreme Court. And, at a time when Koirala has to deal with mounting national problems, he faces serious opposition within his own party. On the one hand, he has to satisfy his supporters, many of them younger MPs who voted for Koirala in the hope of electing a strong and dynamic leader who can deliver on his promises. On the other, he faces a sizeable block of Bhattarai supporters who supported Sher Bahadur Deuba, a younger generation politician, in the leadership elections. Many of these see Koirala's ouster of Bhattarai as a grab for power rooted in personal ambition rather than in any concern for the well-being of the country.

Bhattarai and Koirala have been feuding for years, and it is likely that Bhattarai's supporters are waiting for the appropriate time to strike back at Koirala. Koirala's cabinet choices have caused dissatisfaction among both friends and enemies within the party, and NC MPs have already begun boycotting events being addressed by the new prime minister. It will take all of Koirala's political skills to balance the feuding factions in the NC while, at the same time, deal with Nepal's pressing social and economic problems.

## DOMESTIC POLICY

Nepal is one of the world's most impoverished nations. Nearly half its population lives in absolute poverty; bureaucratic corruption is rampant; and a violent Maoist uprising in western Nepal threatens domestic security. Years of political instability have resulted in economic neglect, causing a decline in development spending, a drop in GDP growth, and erosion of living standards. Key economic statsitics for 1998 have been described as varying from "the dismal to the potentially disastrous," with growth rates projected to decrease to 1.9% in the 1998–99 fiscal year. Whether the new Koirala government has the ability or the longevity to achieve improvements in the economic situation remains to be seen. Past experience suggests that its policies will differ little from those of previous governments. Although one of its aims, like its predecessor's, will be to alleviate poverty, like its predecessor, Koirala's government has limited resources and is largely dependent on foreign aid. But, as a World Bank analysis states, Nepal is losing the trust of international aid organizations because of political interference, corruption and irresponsibility. Such problems contributed to the American multi-national ENRON withdrawing from a multi-billion dollar hydro-electric development projects in Nepal in early 1998.

## FOREIGN POLICY

Hemmed in by India and China, Nepal has historically followed a policy of non-alignment, regionally and globally. However, the country's dependence on India for trade and transit routes to the south, and both nations' reliance on common water resources, have made Nepal's relations with India especially sensitive. Since 1950, these relations have pivoted around a Treaty of Peace and Friendship which gives India significant leverage over the kingdom on economic and security matters. Historically, the NC has advocated closer ties with India, but the communist parties, particularly the ML faction, have resisted accommodating India's influence in the kingdom. Tapping into popular resentment against perceived Indian hegemony, "nationalists" have urged maintaining equal distance between India and China. Recently, there has been bitter debate over the provisions of the 1996 Mahakali River Treaty. This treaty, which provides for joint development and utilization of the river's irrigation and hydroelectric potential by the two countries, has drawn fire as a sell-out of Nepal's sovereignty and interests. The *Pratinidhi Sabha* has ratified this treaty, but agreement on its implementation remains elusive. Other outstanding issues include the border dispute over the strategic Kalapani territory in western Nepal and the fate of the over 100,000 ethnic Nepalese refugees from Bhutan housed in camps in Nepal.

## ADDRESS

Prime Minister's Office
Central Secretariat Singha Durbar
Kathmandu, Nepal

## REFERENCES

*EIU Country Reports: India and Nepal,* The Economist Intelligence Unit Ltd., 1997, 1998.
*Europa World Yearbook.* London: Europa Publications Ltd.,1999.
*Explore Nepal Weekly,* 22 June 1999.
*Kathmandu Post,* 4 December 1998–12 July 1999.
*The People's Review,* 23 March–29 March 2000.
Rose, Leo E. "Nepal and Bhutan on 1998: Two Himalayan Kingdoms." *Asian Survey,* 39, 1 (Jan–Feb 1999): 155.
*Spotlight,* 28 May–3 June 1999; 24 March–30 March 2000.

**Profile researched and written by Deryck Lodrick, University of California (5/2000).**

# THE NETHERLANDS

**Wim Kok**
**Prime Minister**
*(pronounced "VIM COOK")*

*"We know that it is sometimes difficult to compete, but it's better to be competitive
and to have a good performance than just be protected,
because protectionism leads to laziness and to a lack of modernization."*

The Kingdom of the Netherlands is the largest of the three Benelux countries, the other two being Belgium and Luxembourg. The country shares its borders with Belgium to the south and Germany to the east; the northern and western shores face the North Sea. Though the Netherlands is often called Holland, this is in fact the official name of two of its 12 provinces, Nord Holland and Zuid Holland. Also considered part of the Netherlands is the Netherlands Antilles, an island group in the Caribbean. The Netherlands' 33,939 sq km (13,104 sq mi) are home to 16 million people making it the most densely-populated nation in Europe. A quarter of the country's land has been reclaimed from the sea by the use of dikes and coastal dunes, and nearly two-thirds of the population lives below sea level. The capital and largest city is Amsterdam, while the seat of government is The Hague. Approximately 40% of the population are Roman Catholics while 31% are Protestants. The official language is Dutch.

The Netherlands has traditionally been a major maritime power and still boasts a large merchant fleet; Rotterdam is the world's busiest port. Foreign trade plays a large part in the economy and merchandise exports are equal to almost 50% of the country's GDP. Major exports include machinery, chemicals, and agricultural products. The Netherlands is a member of the EU and nearly 80% of its trade is with other EU-member nations, with the primary destinations being Germany, Belgium, and the UK. The Netherlands has, by and large, avoided the economic sluggishness that has plagued continental European economies over the last few years. Unlike some of its neighbors, the Dutch economy has continued to grow and is currently averaging about 3.5% per year. The per capita GDP stands at close to $22,200. The official currency of the Netherlands is the *guilder*.

## POLITICAL BACKGROUND

Having been under successive control of the Dukes of Burgundy, the Habsburg empire, and the Kingdom of Spain, the Netherlands effectively achieved independence in 1581. Dutch sovereignty was later codified in the Treaty of Münster, signed in 1648. Following a period of Napoleonic rule, beginning in 1795, the Dutch reasserted their independence in 1813. A constitutional monarchy was installed together with a strong States-General (parliament), effectively laying the foundations for the present political system. The constitution was revised in 1848 giving greater power to the States-General, and has existed almost unchanged since that time. Within the present system, the role of the monarch is largely ceremonial; power rests mainly with the bicameral States-General and through it the government. The 150-member Second Chamber of the States-General is directly elected and is the more powerful of the two houses, having the ability to propose and amend legislation. In comparison, the First Chamber, which consists of 75 members elected by the 12 provincial councils, can only approve or reject legislation. Elections for both the First and Second Chamber are held every four years, though never in the same year. The government is usually formed by the largest party in the parliament which, either on its own or through forming a coalition, controls a majority of votes in both chambers. In reality, no single party since World War II has been able to obtain an absolute majority; all post-war governments have been the products of various coalitions.

The electoral system is based on the principle of proportional representation, which ensures that each party in parliament receives an amount of seats roughly proportional to its share of the national vote. Thus, if a candidate in a given district is defeated, his votes are not lost but are added to a pool that will then determine the distribution of seats in a second round of allocation. This system, unlike the "first past the post" voting practiced in countries such as the US, makes it much easier for smaller parties to gain representation. Since the election of 6 May 1998, the Second Chamber has contained representatives of nine separate parties.

For more than half a century, starting in 1917, Dutch politics was dominated by political parties closely tied to the two major religious denominations, Catholic and Protestant. These religious-based parties, either alone or in coalition, participated in each government that was formed. In 1980, a number of these parties merged to create the Christian Democratic Appeal (CDA) Party which went on to form successive governments until being removed from power after the election of 4 May 1994. That election, which resulted in a coalition government under the leadership of Wim Kok and his Labor Party (PvdA), marked the first time since World War I that the traditional religious parties had been excluded from power. This situation was confirmed by the May 1998 election, from which the PvdA emerged as the largest party, with 45 seats. As was the case in 1994, Kok may again choose to form a so-called "purple" coalition with the Liberal Party (VVD) and a smaller center-left party named D-66, again excluding the CDA. The term "purple" in this case describes a melding of the three parties' colors—red for the

Labor party, blue and orange for the Liberals, and green for D-66.

## PERSONAL BACKGROUND

Willem (Wim) Kok was born at Bergambacht on 29 September 1938; his father was a carpenter. After finishing his secondary education, Kok attended the prestigious Nijenrode Business School. He then completed his military service and worked for a trading company for a short time. In 1961, Kok was appointed Assistant International Officer of the Netherlands Federation of Trade Unions. In the space of 12 years, he worked his way to the top of the Dutch trade union movement, becoming chairman of the Netherlands Federation of Trade Unions (NVV) in 1973. He held this post for the next 13 years. From 1979 to 1982 Kok also served as chairman of the European Trade Union Confederation.

Among his other achievements, Kok has served on the Socioeconomic Council, the Joint Industrial Labor Council, and the Nederlandsche Bank. He has also been a visiting lecturer at the Institute of Social Studies and advisor to the European Commission. He is well known for his simple tastes. Voters approve of his austere ways, which extended to the elimination of the traditional cocktail break during cabinet meetings. Kok is married and has three children.

## RISE TO POWER

Kok was elected to the Second Chamber of the States-General in 1986 and almost immediately succeeded Joop den Uyl as head of the Labor Party. In 1989, he was elected deputy chairman of the Socialist International. On 7 November 1989, Kok led the Labor Party into a coalition government with the CDA, taking his place as minister of finance and deputy prime minister. Kok became prime minister on 22 August 1994, after his party formed a governing coalition with the VDD and D-66, following the election. His position as prime minister was reaffirmed by the election of 6 May 1998.

## LEADERSHIP

One of the keys to the Labor Party's electoral successes has been its identification with the economic upsurge in the Netherlands. During the mid-1980s, in the face of a stagnating economy and rising unemployment, all of the major political parties began to coalesce around a set of policy measures intended to restore the flagging economy. These measures included lowering taxes, cutting government spending (particularly on social welfare programs), and increasing labor market flexibility. To a large extent these initiatives have succeeded and the Dutch economy, in comparison with its European neighbors, is performing strongly. The Labor Party is viewed as having played a major part in this success. Using traditionally strong ties to the unions, it has been able to persuade workers to support a reduction in benefits. Kok, who had led the nation's largest trade union before entering government service, is viewed as having played a central part in this process.

As a result of the relative success of the government's economic policies, the 1998 election lacked any major political issues and became, instead, a personality contest between the various party leaders. In this type of race, Kok had a clear advantage over his opponents as he has long been considered one of the most popular politicians in the Nether-

lands. Surveys before the election indicated that Kok himself was five times more popular than any of the other major party leaders.

Although the previous Kok government enjoyed considerable success, leadership of the coalition sometimes proved difficult. While Kok himself has a reputation for being a firm economizer, the Labor Party has traditionally worked to defend the provision of generous national welfare programs. On the other hand, Labor's main coalition partner (the free market, liberal VDD), has moved increasingly toward more conservative economic policies. The potential for discord between the two was evidenced a month after the 1994 election, when an initial attempt to build a coalition foundered on the Liberal's demands for deeper cuts in the social welfare system. Three months after the election a coalition was finally formed without VDD leader Frits Bolkstein, who chose to stay out of the cabinet. D-66 was the biggest loser in the 1998 election, dropping from 24 seats to 14. Nevertheless, another purple coalition was formed with D66, and the new government continued its path of modest privatization and liberalization. One source of friction in the cabinet is what to do about the budget surplus. The VVD wants to lower tax rates while the PvdA wishes to use the money for redistribution. In several interviews, Kok has indicated his intention to stand again for election in 2002, thereby increasing the likelihood that the PvdA will be in government until the middle of this decade.

## DOMESTIC POLICY

At the top of the Dutch domestic agenda is the continuing reform of the country's social security system. The first phase of this reform started in 1989 and was followed by a second phase beginning in 1992. These reforms have continued under the Kok government and a great deal of headway has been made. Non-wage costs, such as social welfare contributions, have been reduced considerably since the late 1980s. The government has also tightened the conditions under which Dutch workers can claim disability and employment benefits and has reduced the size of these payments. As a result of these and other changes, overall manufacturing wage costs in the Netherlands have risen far less than in neighboring Germany or France, making Dutch businesses more competitive.

Despite these successes, a number of domestic economic challenges remain. One of these is the question of unemployment. While the official unemployment rate is near 5%, one of the lowest levels in Europe, the accuracy of these figures has been challenged. Significantly, the Netherlands has the highest percentage of part-time workers of any country—more than one employed person in three works part-time. In addition, its has been speculated that the unemployment rate would almost double if it included jobless people who have been reclassified to get sickness benefits.

## FOREIGN POLICY

The defining feature of Dutch foreign policy is the country's membership in the EU. The Netherlands has been part of the EU since the organization's inception as the European Community (EC) in 1958. As a result of the EU's single market program completed in 1992, all trade between the Netherlands and the other members of the EU is tariff-free. In addition, a large part of the Netherlands' social, environmental, and financial policy follows guidelines that have been laid out by the EU's secretariat in Brussels. Similarly, relations between the Netherlands and countries outside the EU are strongly influenced by the mechanisms of both the European Political Cooperation and the Common Foreign and Security Policy by which EU members endeavor to coordinate their foreign policy positions. As part of its commitment to the EU,

the Netherlands has also pledged itself to the process of European monetary integration. In accordance with this process, beginning in 1999, a number of European currencies, including the Dutch *guilder* will gradually be replaced by a common European currency, the *euro*. In preparation for this step, the *guilder* has, for some time, been part of the European Monetary System and is currently closely pegged to the German *mark*. In early 1998, it was decided that the first head of the European Central Bank, a new body that will be responsible for monetary policy in the *euro* zone, is to be a Dutchman—Wim Duisenberg. It is expected that Dutch support for the European process will continue under the Kok government. Kok, himself, is a committed European and was one of the crucial figures behind the 1991 Maastricht Treaty.

Beyond its membership in the EU, the Netherlands is also a partner in NATO and the Western European Union. It is through NATO and the UN that the Netherlands has historically participated in numerous peacekeeping operations, including that in the former Yugoslavia.

The Netherlands is one of the most generous providers of foreign assistance in the world. In fact, only the Scandinavian countries regularly devote more of their GDP to foreign assistance.

## ADDRESS
Office of the Prime Minister
Binnenhof 20, POB 2001
2500 EA, The Hague, Netherlands

## REFERENCES
*The Economist*, 2–9 May 1998; 19 February 2000.
*Financial Times*, 23 October 1997.
*The Guardian*, 6 May 1998.
*New York Times*, 16 June 1997.
*Newsweek*, 2 June 1997.
*Washington Post*, 17 July 1997.

**Profile researched and written by Christopher Dall, College of William and Mary (9/98; updated by Paulette Kurzer, University of Arizona 3/2000).**

# NEW ZEALAND

## Helen Elizabeth Clark
### Prime Minister

*(pronounced "HEH-len ee-LIZ-ah-beth CLARK")*

*"My hopes for the future are simply expressed: a world where no child goes hungry or homeless,
where all communities experience peace and decent living standards
and show tolerance towards others, where the environment is clean and green
and where affirmation occurs through cultural and creative expression"*

The Dominion of New Zealand is an island nation situated in the South Pacific Ocean. Its closest neighbor is Australia, which lies approximately 2,400 km (1500 mi) to the northwest across the Tasman Sea. Only half that distance to the east lies the International Date Line. Consisting of two major islands and several smaller ones, New Zealand occupies 269,057 sq km (103,833 sq mi). The southern island, extending about 800 km (500 mi) from southwest to northeast, is largely mountainous. The northern island is smaller and less mountainous but spotted with several volcanoes.

The population of New Zealand is estimated at 3.6 million, with three-fourths living on the northern island. The vast majority of the people of New Zealand descend from European ancestry, with 88% claiming such a heritage. The indigenous peoples of the islands, the Maoris, make up 9% of the population while other Pacific islanders and Asians make up the remaining 3%. English is the principal language, but Maori is also considered an official language.

The economy of New Zealand is based principally upon the export of primary goods, such as wool, lamb, mutton, beef, fruit, fish, and timber. Imports include oil, motor vehicles, industrial equipment, and consumer goods. Its major trading partners are Australia, the European Union, the US, Japan, and China. Trade with a variety of Asian countries has been increasing in recent years. The GDP is US$61 billion with a per capita income of US$17,000. The unit of currency is the New Zealand dollar.

## POLITICAL BACKGROUND

New Zealand was originally settled by Maori voyagers from Polynesia in the 9th century. The first European to sight it was the Dutch explorer, Abel Tasman. In 1769, Captain James Cook claimed it for the British. New Zealand did not become a formal colony until 1841. It retained this colonial status until 1907 when it was made an independent member of the British Commonwealth.

New Zealand was one of the first countries to introduce universal adult suffrage and establish a welfare state. Beginning in 1898, the state passed laws guaranteeing old-age pensions and regulating labor practices. In the 1930s, a comprehensive social security system was introduced, which eventually guaranteed medical care to all New Zealanders. The success of the European settlers was not originally shared by the indigenous population. In 1840, a treaty guaranteed the Maoris possession of their land, but a series of wars forced them to make room for expanding British settlements. These military defeats, along with the proliferation of new diseases from Europe, reduced the Maori population to 40,000 by the turn of the century. It is only in the 20th century that they have recovered and become a strong political force, electing several members of parliament.

New Zealand continues to maintain its status as an independent democratic state within the British Commonwealth. Organized as a constitutional monarchy, the formal head of state is Queen Elizabeth II, who is represented by an appointed governor-general. Since 21 March 1996, Sir Michael Hardie Boys has been New Zealand's governor general. Real political power, however, rests with the Parliament, which consists of a single body—the House of Representatives. The House has 120 members who are elected for three-year terms. Every citizen over the age of 18 is eligible to vote. Executive authority is held by the prime minister; based on legislative elections, the leader of the majority party or the leader of the majority coalition is usually appointed prime minister for a three-year term. The deputy prime minister is appointed by the governor general.

In 1996, a new electoral system, called multi-member proportional (MP) representation, was introduced. Voters are asked to cast two ballots: one for a candidate to represent a particular constituency; the other for a political party. Any party receiving more than 5% of the vote is entitled to representation in Parliament even if none of its members won a single district. The effect is to ensure proportional representation. The party or coalition of parties that controls the House forms the government. From November 1996 until November 1999, the National Party led a majority coalition with a nationalist party called New Zealand First, led by Winston Peters. The major opposition party during that period was the Labor Party led by Helen Clark. Following the 1999 elections, the Labor Party formed the majority government, with Helen Clark as Prime Minister.

## PERSONAL BACKGROUND

Helen Elizabeth Clark was born 26 February 1950, in Hamilton on the North Island of New Zealand. She attended Epsom Girls Grammar School in Auckland, and studied Political Studies at the University of Auckland. In 1974 she graduated with an MA with Honors from the University of Auckland. Her research was on political behavior and representation. From 1973–75 she was a junior lecturer in Political Studies at the University of Auckland. In 1976 she studied

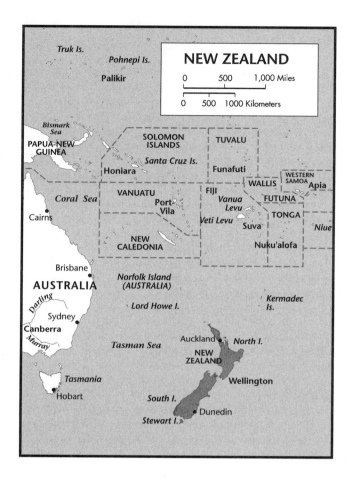

## LEADERSHIP

As a Labor MP since 1981, Helen Clark has held important positions in the NZLP and the New Zealand government. During her 19 years in Parliament, her unofficial title was "Mother of the House," reflecting her role as the longest-serving woman member among the then-current members of the New Zealand parliament.

In 1984 she was Chair of the ad hoc Disarmament and Arms Control Committee and Foreign Affairs and Defense Committee. She was also a member of the Government Administration Select Committee. She was the convener of the Government Caucus Committee on External Affairs and Security from 1984–87. In 1986 she was awarded the annual Peace Prize of the Danish Peace Foundation for her work in promoting international peace and disarmament.

From August 1987 until January 1989 Clark was Minister of Conservation, and was Minister of Housing from August 1987 until August 1989. In 1989–90 Clark was Minister of Labor and Minister of Health. While Minister of Health, she introduced tobacco-control legislation designed to provide protection against second-hand smoke in workplaces and public places, and to eliminate tobacco advertising and tobacco-company sponsorship of sporting events.

She was the first New Zealand woman to hold the cabinet-level position of Deputy Prime Minister (1989–90); while in this post, she chaired the Cabinet Social Equity Committee and was a member of the Cabinet Policy Committee, Cabinet Committee on Chief Executives, Cabinet Economic Development and Employment Committee, Cabinet Expenditure Review Committee, Cabinet Honors Appointments and Travel Committee, and Cabinet Domestic and External Security Committee.

Clark became the first New Zealand woman Privy Counselor upon her appointment to the Privy Counsil in 1990. Deputy Leader of the Opposition in 1990–93, she became Leader of the Opposition in December 1993. She led the Opposition until 1999 when she was elected Prime Minister on 27 November 1999. She is also Minister for Arts, Culture and Heritage and Minister in Charge of the New Zealand Security Intelligence Service and Ministerial services.

## DOMESTIC POLICY

Helen Clark's areas of interest include welfare state redistributive policies, international affairs, and equality for women. As a member of the New Zealand Labor Party since 1971 and as a Labor Member of Parliament since 1981, Clark's domestic policy interests are fully fashioned on Labor Party's principles and follow Labor's policies for the economy, employment, tourism, small business, employment rights and occupational safety, transport, fisheries, research science and technology, rural affairs, energy, e-commerce, employment relations, accident coverage and compensation, and industrial development.

The New Zealand Labor Party's objectives are full employment, higher real incomes, and a more equal distribution of income for all New Zealand citizens. The NZLP also believes that economic and social policies are cooperative ventures of public and private investment in people, infrastructure, and communities. Labor's public health policies emphasize prevention and primary health care, including such

abroad on a University Grants Committee post-graduate scholarship. From 1977 until her election to Parliament in 1981, she lectured in Political Studies at Auckland. She enjoys classical music, films, theater, opera, and racquet sports.

## RISE TO POWER

Clark joined the Labor Party in 1971. She has held office at every level of the New Zealand Labor Party (NZLP). In 1973–75 she was President of the Labor Youth Council and a member of the Auckland Labor Regional Council. In 1975 she ran unsuccessfully for a seat as a Member of Parliament (MP) in Piako. Clark was Secretary of the Labor Women's Council in 1977. She was a Labor Party Executive in 1978–88. Clark represented the Labor Party at congresses of the Socialist International and the Socialist International Women in 1976, 1978, 1983, and 1986 at an Asia-Pacific Socialist Organization Conference held in Sydney, Australia, in 1981, and at the Socialist International Party Leaders Meeting in Sydney in 1991. Clark was also a Government delegate to the World Conference to mark the end of the United Nations Decade for Women in Nairobi, Kenya in 1985. In 1981 Clark was elected as the Labor candidate for Member of Parliament (MP) for Mt. Albert. In 1996–99 Clark stood successfully as the Labor candidate for Member of Parliament (MP) for Owairaka. On 27 November 1999, the New Zealand Labor Party won the majority and Helen Clark was elected as Prime Minister of New Zealand.

issues as increasing immunization rates and reducing smoking rates.

In the 1999 election Clark's centrist New Zealand Labor Party patterned their strategy after that of the British Labor Party's successful 1997 election. In 1999 the Labor platform included turning back economic reforms, freezing tariffs, the repeal of the Employment Contracts Act with the objective of restoring a role for unions, and social spending on hospitals and schools.

The government formed under Clark in 1999 is a coalition government. Clark's government functions under a coalition agreement with Alliance, a party whose policies are more left-leaning than those of Labor. The Alliance is a coalition of five small parties—New Labor Party, Democratic Party, New Zealand Liberal Party, Green Party, and Mana Motihake. When the governor general, Sir Michael Hardie Boys, opened the 46th Parliament on 21 December 1999, his speech detailed the objectives set out in the coalition agreement signed on 6 December 1999, between Labour and Alliance.

Under Clark the coalition government is committed to a policy platform that reduces inequality, is environmentally sustainable, and that benefits the social and economic welfare of all New Zealanders. The government is also committed to a cooperative relationship with the Greens. The government is committed to continue efforts to right the wrongs done the Maori. (The Maori are a Polynesian people believed to have arrived in New Zealand in the 14th century.)

Clark's Government also recognizes the Treaty of Waitangi. The Treaty of Waitangi is New Zealand's founding document. The treaty was signed by 50 Maori chiefs and Captain Hobson, the Crown's representative, on 6 February 1840. This treaty with the Maori has been breached in the past. In 1999 the Maori comprised about 9–10% of New Zealand's population. Clark's government is committed to closing the economic and social gaps between the Maori and other New Zealanders.

Clark's first 100 days in office involved "feel-good" policies: a bill preventing Members of Parliament (MPs) from defecting to other parties; restructuring the student loan repayment scheme, and initiating an inquiry of genetically modified foods. The government also increased the subsidies for fees for dental education to be on a par with those granted to medical students. This decision combined the Labor-Alliance commitment to reducing cost of study to tertiary, for example, university students. Under Clark, the lifespan of the Mental Health Commission was extended. An inquiry into the efficiency of the electric industry and into its benefits to the ordinary consumer is also pursued.

PM Clark introduced a broad public policy debate over the responsibilities of public interest broadcasting. Her government did not approve of a joint venture proposal to Television New Zealand to inaugurate digital television service. Instead, Clark and Minister of Broadcasting and Minister in Charge of Television New Zealand, Marian Hobbs, wanted to establish a charter emphasizing more programming reflecting New Zealand perspectives, culture, and identity. The dominant commercial objective of digital television service and the thrust of the previous operation of Television New Zealand would act as barriers to this redirection.

## FOREIGN POLICY

New Zealand became independent from the United Kingdom on 26 September 1907. Although the 1931 Statute of Westminster granted equal status to all members of the Commonwealth, independent New Zealand's foreign policy dates from 1935, when the Labor government made treaties and exchanged diplomatic representatives. In 1943 the government established a career foreign service.

The Ministry of Foreign Affairs and Trade (MFAT) is responsible on behalf of the government for all major policy functions related to New Zealand's external relations, including bilateral relations with other countries, interests in international institutions, official development assistance, provision of consular services, and support services to government agencies overseas. Hon. Phil Goff is the Minister of Foreign Affairs and Trade under PM Clark.

As of 1999 New Zealand maintained 49 diplomatic and consular posts in 41 countries and territories. It was a founding member of the United Nations in 1945. New Zealand maintains interests in other international organizations: the World Trade Organization (WTO), the World Bank, the Asian Development Bank, as a member of the Commonwealth, and the Organization for Economic Co-operation and Development (OECD), among others.

New Zealand also administers Tokelau, made up of three small atolls in the South Pacific—Atafu, Fakaofo, and Nukunonu. Self-government and self-sufficiency are New Zealand's objectives for its relationship with the Tokelau population of around 1,500. New Zealand also takes on external affairs and defense functions for the Cook Islands and Niue.

Since 1923 New Zealand has exercised jurisdiction over the Ross Dependency, comprised of the land, permanent ice-shelf, and islands of Antarctica. Scott Base on Ross Island is preserved by New Zealand as a permanent scientific research base. Other than these researchers, Ross Dependency is an uninhabited ice-covered land.

Prime Minister Helen Clark's new government vigorously supports nuclear disarmament. New Zealand nuclear disarmament policy includes forging strong alliances with other non-nuclear states; building co-operation between nuclear weapon free zones, and strengthening New Zealand's Nuclear Free Zone in the South Pacific. In addition, the Clark government continues to express New Zealand's opposition to Japanese whaling. Clark questions whether Japanese whaling is conducted for the "scientific research" purposes upheld by the international Convention for the Regulation of Whaling. Clark continues to oppose Japan's whaling program at meetings of the International Whaling Commission.

As a Labor leader, Clark questioned excessive military defense spending. She also questioned the lease of 28 F-16s from the United States and the necessity of a bluewater frigate navy capable of anti-submarine warfare. Clark advocated that New Zealand's air force maintain its A-4 Skyhawk capability. She also advocated the position suggested in 1999 by the Foreign Affairs and Defense Select Committee that New Zealand should build its future defense capacity around the core role of the army.

Furthermore, Clark was severely critical of the previous government's relationship with Indonesia over Indonesia's actions in East Timor. Clark suggested that the resolution of the East Timor crisis receive top priority at the summit of the leaders of APEC (Asia Pacific Economic Cooperation).

## ADDRESS
Office of the Prime Minister
Parliament House
Wellington, New Zealand

## REFERENCES

*Christian Science Monitor*, 2 November 1999.
*Economist*, 4 December 1999.
New Zealand Information. [Online] http://www.odci.gov/cia/publications/factbook/nz.html

New Zealand Labor Party. [Online] http://www.labour.org.nz/InfoCentre1/Policies/
New Zealand News. [Online] http://www.scoop.co.nz/archive/scoop/stories/
New Zealand Parliament. [Online] http://www.ps.parliament.govt.nz/mp19.htm and http://www.labour.org.nv/MediaCentre1/Speeches/991221.html
New Zealand Statistics. [Online] http://www.stats.govt.nz/
NZLP Speeches. [Online] http://www.labour.org.nz/MediaCentre1/media.htm
*Time International*, 6 December 1999.

**Profile researched and written Jeanne Marie Stumpf (2/00).**

# NICARAGUA

**Arnoldo Alemán**
**President**
*(pronounced 'ar-NOHL-doe ah-le-MAHN')*

"*I think that for Nicaragua's sake we should begin the reconstruction process now.
I invite the Sandinistas to help us rebuild Nicaragua.*"

The Republic of Nicaragua is the largest and least densely populated country in Central America. Approximately the size of New York State, the 120,254 sq km region (74,738 sq mi) is home to 4,717,132 inhabitants. With the Pacific Ocean on the west coast and the Caribbean Sea on the east coast, Nicaragua lies between Honduras in the north and Costa Rica in the south. The capital city of Managua has a population of approximately 1,319,000. Comprised of a mainly mestizo (mixed Amerindian and Caucasian) population (69%), the population also includes a significant number of whites (17%), blacks (9%), and Amerindians (5%) in the country. While most whites live in Managua, blacks and Amerindians are concentrated on the east coast. Roman Catholics comprise 95% of the population and the remaining 5% are Protestant. Spanish is the official language, but English is widely spoken on the Caribbean coast and in Managua. Life expectancy at birth is 67 years. Infant mortality remains high 41 deaths per 1,000 live births. Literacy (defined as the population above the age of 15 that can read and write) is estimated to stand at 66%.

The unit of currency is the gold cordoba. The per capita GDP is approximately US$2,500. From 1996–2000, the GDP has steadily increased. Until 1998, Nicaraguan President Arnoldo Alemán's efforts to instill economic stability had paid off—reforms were reaping some success, even amidst the muddied waters the legacy of civil war and years of financial mismanagement had left behind. Then came Hurricane Mitch in 1998, devastating Nicaragua and neighboring Honduras and leaving Nicaragua, already the poorest country in Central America, with $1 billion worth of damage. Worst hit was the agricultural sector, which the country depends on for the majority of its exports. By 1999, President Alemán was forced to deal with a trade deficit approaching US$900 million. However, despite the destruction caused by Hurricane Mitch, Nicaragua's economy has continued to grow slightly. Aid and debt relief have contributed to this and helped to stabilize the economy, but the hand of President Alemán and his commitment to free market reforms and economic growth have played a key role as well.

However, Nicaragua is still one of the poorest nations in the hemisphere, and the poorest in Central America, with approximately 70% of the population living below the poverty line.

## POLITICAL BACKGROUND

For most of this century Nicaragua lived under the dictatorship of the Somoza family. After gaining power in a country torn by corruption and conflict between the Liberal and Conservative parties, Anastasio Somoza emerged as leader of the National Guard. Trained by US Marines, Somoza kept close links with the American military. After winning an uncontested election in 1936, Somoza controlled political power as president or through puppet presidents of his own choosing. After his assassination in 1956, Somoza was succeeded by his eldest son, Luis, who held office for six years. His brother, Anastasio Jr., became chief of the military. Supporters of the Somoza family held the presidency from 1963 to 1967. In 1967 Anastasio Jr. won the presidency in an election filled with fraud and repressive tactics. Despite opposition from his own Liberal Party, Anastasio Jr. was reelected in 1974. By the time of the 1979 revolution, his wealth was estimated to reach US$400 million. Somoza was gunned down years later while living in exile in Paraguay.

The July 1979 revolution, widely supported by the population, ended the 45-year Somoza family dictatorship. A critical moment came when Joaquín Chamorro, owner of the opposition newspaper *La Prensa* was gunned down on 10 January 1978. A year later the triumphant Sandinista Front (FSLN), (named for a martyred dissident to the Somoza dictatorship), gained power and formed a revolutionary junta. The junta governed for five years and the political process was restricted to workers' unions, peasants, students, women, and neighborhood organizations. Land reform, literacy campaigns, and health care access were central pieces of the new revolutionary government program. However, disappointed with the Marxist orientation of the Sandinistas, and opposed to their absolute control of the new Revolutionary Army, key leaders of the July 1979 uprising left the government and boycotted the 1984 elections. One of the most outspoken critics was Violeta Chamorro, editor of *La Prensa*. She led the democratic opposition to the Sandinistas. In 1984, despite the boycott, 75% of the electorate voted. FSLN's Daniel Ortega took 68% of the vote, and the Sandinistas gained 61 of the 96 available seats in the National Assembly. The validity of the elections, however, was called into questions as no opposition leader ran for the presidency.

Ortega and the Sandinistas had to fight a US-funded guerilla movement, the Contras (Spanish shortened word for "counterrevolutionaries") which they associated with the Somoza dictatorship. The role of the US in aiding the Contras

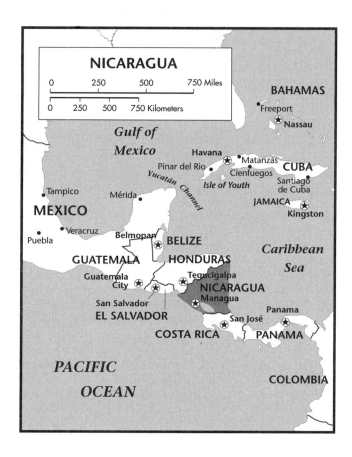

NICARAGUA

0        250        500        750 Miles

0      250      500     750 Kilometers

count votes and send official tallies to the national electoral office. Consequently accusations of fraud flourish from all political parties.

## PERSONAL BACKGROUND

Arnoldo Alemán was born in Managua on 23 January 1946. The son of a minister of education during the Somoza dictatorship, Alemán studied law at the Universidad Nacional Autónoma in León, Nicaragua. He graduated in 1967 and practiced law until 1979, representing banking and commercial institutions during the Somoza dictatorship. Alemán became politically active in opposition to the Sandinista revolution. During the Somoza dictatorship, he did not hold government posts but was seen as supportive of the regime. After the 1979 revolution, Alemán adopted a wait-and-see attitude, then opposed the Sandinista's attempt to make Nicaragua a second Cuba in the hemisphere. He became politically involved in the country and developed close links with the exiled Nicaraguan and Cuban-American communities in Miami. He was president of the Coffee Growers Association of Managua (1983–86), vice-president of the National Farmers Union (1986–90) and president of the Nicaragua Coffee Growers Union (1986–90).

A widower with four children, Alemán is the leader of the ultraconservative Liberal Party. In 1990 he supported the National Opposition Union (UNO) and its presidential candidate, Violeta Chamorro, and was the UNO candidate for mayor of Managua. He defeated the Sandinista candidate to become mayor of Managua in 1990. Alemán's close ties with the Cuban-American community in Miami and the former Contra leaders helped him gain access to the vast financial resources and efficient political network of the Nicaraguan exile community in the US.

## RISE TO POWER

His strong stand against the Sandinistas and his close links with local and American entrepreneurs gave Alemán a pivotal role in Nicaragua's transition to a market economy. His support for Chamorro waned when she was unable to control the UNO coalition and when her son-in-law and chief of staff, Antonio Lacayo, gathered strength. At that point Alemán turned to the century-old Liberal Party to launch his own presidential campaign in 1996.

The UNO coalition disbanded soon after Chamorro's election because its only purpose was to defeat Ortega. With no party of her own, Chamorro had to forge alliances with the Sandinistas in Congress to successfully govern. In turn she allowed the Revolutionary Army to remain in Sandinista hands. Daniel Ortega's brother remained head of the army, and the Sandinistas exercised veto power over Chamorro's weak government through their congressional delegation.

Many leaders of the conservative parties that supported the UNO coalition resented Minister of State Antonio Lacayo because his intentions to succeed Chamorro were well known. Alemán used his position as mayor of Nicaragua's capital and his links with the exiled Cuban community in Miami to prevent Lacayo from running for office. With Lacayo out of the race, Alemán became the most likely candidate to prevent the Sandinistas from regaining power.

In the 20 October 1996 elections, 23 presidential candidates ran for office but Ortega and Alemán emerged as the

came under heavy criticism and proved to be one of the enduring battles between President Reagan and the Democratic Party-controlled Congress. Aided by Soviets and Cubans, the Sandinistas stayed in power. The conflict produced more than 30,000 deaths and half a million displaced and exiled persons, most of whom sought political asylum in the US. A broad Central American peace accord was finally signed in 1988 under the leadership of Costa Rican president Oscar Arias. The Esquipulas Accord called for a cease-fire and democratic elections to be held in 1990.

In February 1990 Ortega's bid for reelection was challenged by Violeta Chamorro. She questioned the Sandinistas' close links with Cuba and the Soviet Union and reached out to center and conservative parties to help defeat Ortega and regain what she thought to be the true path of the 1979 revolution. The results of the election upset the Sandinistas and surprised local and foreign pollsters, who had expected Ortega to win. During her six-year presidency Chamorro attempted to control inflation, resume growth, and regain civilian control over the Sandinista National Army. Although prevented from seeking reelection and having no political party of her own, Chamorro succeeded in stabilizing the country's economy, dismantling the Contras, and regaining limited control of the army.

The electoral ballot in Nicaragua is probably one of the most complex in the Americas. Voters select candidates for the presidency, National Assembly, and local municipalities from a vast array of political parties. The tedious, complicated process goes forward without the help of technology to favorites. Filled with irregularities and disorganization, and after several days of vote counting, Alemán was declared winner with 51% of the vote; Ortega came in second with 38%. In the 93-seat Chamber of Deputies, the Liberal Party came short of a majority with 41 seats; the Sandinistas took 38; and the remaining 14 seats went to leftist and conservative groups. After several days of flip-flopping, Daniel Ortega conceded defeat but questioned the legitimacy of Alemán's government. The Sandinistas are still challenging the results for the mayorship of Managua, also won by the Liberal Party.

## LEADERSHIP

Alemán is the leader of the Liberal Alliance, a conservative group that supported the Somoza family dictatorship, vehemently opposed the Sandinistas, and supported Chamorro in 1990. He enlisted support from the Cuban-American community and the exiled Nicaraguan community, and thus forged a very conservative coalition of right-wing groups, entrepreneurs, and others opposed to the Sandinistas. The powerful archbishop of Managua, Miguel Obando, granted unofficial support of the Catholic Church to Alemán. Aleman has led a government of technocrats and former landowners of the Somoza government, and is expected to reach out to former Sandinistas who left the party. His first cabinet appointments favored technocrats over traditional politicians, and he is likely to appoint an economic team trained in American universities who will support free market policies. By 1999, Alemán was forced to deal with a trade deficit approaching $900 million. He has been commended for increasing talks with the Sandinistas during his term, and the two parties have indeed found common ground in one area: scandal allegations. In 1998, Daniel Ortega, the Sandinist former president, faced accusations from his stepdaughter of sexual abuse dating back to her childhood. Meanwhile, Alemán faced charges that the presidential plane he had been using was actually reported stolen in the United States and that it had been used throughout Central America and Colombia to carry cocaine. Both Ortega and Alemán denied all charges against them.

Alemán has had his share of troubles during his presidency. Student protests for increased educational funding and new deals that many say penalize the poor have caused large protests. A Sandinista-supported transportation strike in 1999 virtually paralyzed the country and forced Aleman to quell concerns that his government could be toppled at any moment—as suggested by Ortega and the Sandinistas. Alemán has been criticized for continually increasing the wealth of government officials, while his country still maintains its status as the 2nd poorest nation in the Western Hemisphere—second only to Haiti. Alemán has also faced border disputes during his term: in March 2000, his government coupled with Costa Rica to continue an ongoing battle over its border with Honduras, each claiming sovereignty over the Gulf of Fonseca. Other challenges during Alemán's presidency have been land reform and the land distribution process (favoring Sandinistas and their supporters), as well as growing poverty and migration issues. Alemán signed a new agreement with the International Monetary Fund (IMF) in 1999 and promised to implement an aggressive policy to cut the government fiscal deficit, to implement structural reforms, and to maintain overall monetary stability.

## DOMESTIC POLICY

Alemán has continued the effort to keep inflation low and carry on structural reforms in order to achieve economic growth. His entrepreneurial experience and commitment to the free market has helped take Nicaragua's economy away from policies of the Chamorro regime, depite the devastating economic damage done by Hurricane Mitch. A sharp decrease in capital gains taxation and other incentives to increase savings and investment have been part of his reform efforts. Alemán's faced his greatest challenge—to find common ground with the Sandinistas—by opening a dialogue, for which he has received much praise. As of 2000, unemployment in Nicaragua remained at close to 70% with more than 40% of the population living on less than US$1 per day.

The issue of land reform and the land distribution process accelerated by the Sandinistas has assumed a central role in Alemán's policies. Although Chamorro attempted to straighten out the distribution of land during her government, fierce opposition from the Sandinistas prevented her from addressing the issue. Alemán is strongly supported by former landowners, whose lands were nationalized by the Sandinistas and taken away from them, then distributed to Sandinista supporters. Support from the US, Latin American governments, and the international financial community have all helped Alemán gain control over military appointments and continue economic growth, however slight.

## FOREIGN POLICY

In light of the growing anti-immigrant sentiment in the US, Alemán will have to deal with the thousands of Nicaraguans currently living in the US who face deportation. He has continued to denounce the Castro government in Cuba and support free market talks for Central American nations and Mexico. Alemán's economic team has strived to develop more links with the international financial community, though its economy is predominantly agricultural with a small manufacturing base. He will encourage the US, (especially the exiled Nicaraguan community), the European Union, and other Latin American countries to invest in infrastructure development for Nicaragua. Indeed, Alemán has been responsible for liberalizing foreign trade, sharply reducing taxes, and eliminating most currency exchange controls.

The United States is Nicaragua's largest trading partner: two-way trade in 1998 totaled US$790 million. As of 2000, this continued to increase and US business presence in Nicaragua increased with the fast-food chain, McDonalds, opening a franchise in Managua.

## ADDRESS

Office of the President of the Republic of Nicaragua
Casa de Gobierno
Antiguo Banco Central
Managua, Nicaragua

## REFERENCES
CIA World Fact Book 1999. [Online] (Accessed 2000).

CNN. [Online] (Accessed 21 October 1996, 22 October 1996, 28 October 1996, 1 November 1996).

El País (Spain). [Online] Available http://www.elpais.es (Accessed 24 November 1996).

La Jornada (Mexico). [Online] http://www.serpiente.dgsca.mx/jornada/ (Accessed 11 October 1996, 20 October 1996, 21 October 1996, 9 November 1996, 11 November 1996).

Nicaraguan Central Bank. [Online] Available http://www.bcn.gov.ni/ (Accessed 5 May 2000).

US Library of Congress. *Country Studies: Nicaragua*. [Online] Available http://lcweb2.loc.gov/frd/cs/nutoc.html.

**Profile researched and written by Patricio Navia, New York University (12/96; updated 5/2000).**

# NIGER

## Mamadou Tandja
### Head of State
*(pronounced "MA-ma-dou TAN-ja")*

*"This victory is the victory of all the Nigerien people, of democracy, and of political, social, and institutional stability for a new beginning."*

The Republic of Niger, the largest nation in West Africa, occupies an area of 1,267,000 sq km (489,191 sq mi). It shares borders with seven other countries: Libya and Algeria to the north, Chad to the east, Nigeria and Benin to the south, and Burkina Faso and Mali to the west. Two-thirds of the country is desert, and most of the northeast is uninhabitable.

The population of Niger is estimated at ten million. That number is expected to double by 2015, adding even more strain to the already limited food and water resources. Approximately 53% of the people belong to the Hausa ethnic group, with Djerma Songhai peoples making up 22%, and Tuareg and Fulbe, 10% each. French is the official language. The people of Niger are predominantly Muslim (estimated at 85–90% of the population); some Christianity and traditional animism is also practiced.

The vast majority of the people make their living from agriculture. Peanuts, cowpeas, cotton, and livestock are the primary export products. In addition, hides and skins and uranium are important sources of foreign exchange. Niger is consistently ranked as one of the poorest countries of the world. The gross domestic product (GDP) is estimated at us$220 per head. The currency unit is the CFA *franc* with 640 *francs* = us$1.00.

## POLITICAL BACKGROUND

Niger was brought into the French African empire at the end of the 19th century as part of the French West African Federation. It achieved its independence, along with the other colonies of that federation, in 1960. The military played an active role in the independent Nigerien government from the beginning and definitively captured the government in 1974 in a military coup under General Seyni Kountché. Preparations for a transition to a multi-party state began in 1990. However, Ali Saibou, military and political successor to his cousin, Kountché, stayed as interim president until the elections held in 1992. The country experienced three very turbulent years of experimentation with Western-style democracy under a constitution for the Third Republic that had been approved by 90% of the voters in December 1992.

Under the co-habitation system, implemented under the 1992 constitution, the president was the head of state, but the prime minister (who could be from a competing political party) had powers that could conflict significantly with those of the president. In this system there was also a unicameral legislature with a Head of Assembly who could effect a compromise in the event of an impasse resulting from conflict between the president and prime minister. Until January 1996, the president was Mahamane Ousmane. He became embroiled in a political feud with the prime minister, which led to a January 1996 coup d'etat and the installation of Ibrahim Baré Mainassara as head of state and president of the Council of National Salvation (CSN).

Once in power, Mainassara attempted to gain legitimacy for his government by implementing presidential elections. He was declared to have won, despite widespread allegations of fraud. On 9 April 1999, Mainassara was assassinated by members of his personal security guard. Daouda Malam Wanké, head of the Presidential Guard unit responsible for the assassination, became the country's new leader. The junta called Mainassara's murder "an unfortunate accident" and reassured the international community that civilian rule would be restored within a year. It presided over yet another constitutional revision, which ushered in Niger's Fifth Republic.

The new constitution was passed in July 1999 and adopted the following month. It provided for a semi-presidential government. The president is head of state and appoints the prime minister (head of government) from a list of three candidates proposed by the parliamentary majority. Presidential actions must be counter-signed by the prime minister. The president can dissolve the national assembly, assume emergency powers, and convene the Council of the Republic in the event of a constitutional crisis. Amnesties for those involved in both the 1996 and 1999 coups were part of the constitutional draft.

In November 1999, elections were held for a new president and parliament. President Mamadou Tandja, elected with 60% of the vote, took office on 5 January 2000, an occasion that marked the country's return to civilian rule.

## PERSONAL BACKGROUND

Mamadou Tandja was born in 1938 in Maine-Soroa, in southeastern Niger near the country's border with Chad. He belongs to the ethnic minority Kanouri community. Attending military schools in Madagascar and Mali; he joined the army in the mid-1950s, rising to the rank of colonal. In 1974, Tandja participated in the military coup that ousted Niger's first post-independence president, Hamani Diori, and brought General Seyni Kountché to power. During the Kountché regime, Tandja served as prefect of the Tahoua and Maradi regions, ambassador to Nigeria, and two-term

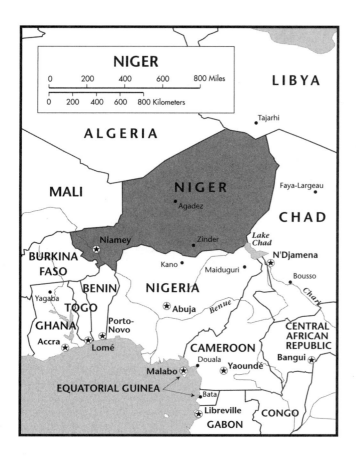

minister of the interior. In addition to carrying out the duties of his political posts, Tandja also served as commander of several army garrisons. He was known for hard work and efficiency, winning the nickname "the working chief." However, his reputation was marred by his role, as interior minister, in the violent repression of activities by Tuareg rebels in the north in 1990. During the massacre, Nigerien troops shot dead 63 Tuareg protestors and sparked five years of rebellion in the northern part of the country.

An asset declaration made upon Tandja's election to the presidency showed him to be a substantial property owner, with large livestock holdings. Tandja has ten children.

## RISE TO POWER

In 1991, Tandja retired from the army and assumed the leadership of the MNSD (Mouvement national pour la société), which had formerly been Niger's sole political party. He ran for president in 1993 and 1996, losing by a narrow margin in the 1993 election. He was beaten in the runoffs by Mahamane Ousmane, who had garnered the support of a nine-party coalition. Tandja lost again in 1996 to General Mainassara, whose reign was known for nepotism, imprisonment of opposition leaders, and military mutinies. Students, civil servants, and union members staged protest demonstrations. When Major Daouda Mallam Wanké agreed to hold elections (shortly after murdering Mainassara), Tandja had his chance to win the presidency.

In run-off elections held in November 1999, Tandja was elected president of Niger with 60% of the vote. His inauguration on December 22, 1999 marked his country's return to civilian government.

## LEADERSHIP

Tandja has named political and social stability and financial recovery as his top priorities. He has also pledged to improve living standards for workers and uphold the principles of democracy. In June 2000 Tandja issued a statement rejecting the possibility of adopting Islamic shari'a law in Niger, as has been done in the northern states of neighboring Nigeria. Citing provisions of the 1999 constitution, he pledged that Niger would remain a secular state.

At the end of December 1999, Tandja appointed seasoned politician Hama Amadou as prime minister. Upon taking office, he had declared his intention of cooperating with political opposition forces; however the opposition rejected the posts it was offered in the new government. Tandja had made it known that there was no money in state coffers to pay their salaries. Tandja's new cabinet, sworn in the following month, included members of both parties that had supported him in the November run-off elections: the MNSD (Mouvement national pour la société) and the CDS (Convention Démocratique et Sociale). He gained 55 votes out of the 83 seat National Assembly, ensuring cooperation from the Assembly and amnesty to the perpetrators of the 1996 and 1999 coups.

## DOMESTIC POLICY

Niger's greatest concerns are its economic situation and the need to achieve political stability. Tandja's government faces numerous domestic problems. The economy is close to complete bankruptcy. For months preceding Tandja's inauguration the nation had been beset by strikes by teachers, health-care workers, and other public employees, many of whom had gone for months without being paid. When the government was installed in January 2000, Prime Minister Hama Amadou announced that its coffers were empty. In March he announced that there was no money to pay the salaries of members of parliament.

With the restoration of civilian government, the resumption of foreign aid (which accounts for roughly half the country's revenue) is expected to help alleviate the financial crisis. However, in June President Tandja proposed an emergency action plan designed to effect a significant economic improvement within three months.

Political stability and peace are needed to convince foreign companies to invest exploration and extraction of uranium and other minerals. The Tuareg and eastern autonomy (FDR) rebellions have also caused grave concern among outside investors. Rebel groups have signed peace agreements with the government, but Niger is relying on foreign donors— primarily France—for the financial support needed for implementation of these agreements. In addition, unexplained deaths of repatriated rebels and civilian members of the minority populations also jeopardize the agreements.

Tandja faces other domestic problems as well. The Tuareg rebellion has led to a decline in tourism. Like most nations in West Africa, Niger faces a growing rate of HIV-infection, fueled by the large percentage of the population that seeks work outside the country. There is substantial unrecorded trade between Niger and Nigeria, with some reports suggesting that the products involved account for at least one-third of Niger's national consumption. The World Bank estimates that this "grey" economy represents about 70% of all economic activity in the country. This cross-border trade represents a significant loss in tax revenue for the government.

## FOREIGN POLICY

The seizure of power by Major Daouda Mallam Wanké in 1999 isolated Niger internationally. France, Japan, and the European Union suspended both foreign aid and trade to protest the imposition of military rule. (However, an accord for economic and technological cooperation with the People's Republic of China was signed in June 1999, when Wanké's minister of foreign affairs visited China.) Ties with Western donor nations were renewed with the return to civilian rule. In February 2000, France announced the resumption of development aid, including an aid package of $9 million to help pay the salaries of civil servants, some of whom were owed more than a year of back pay.

Tandja has built upon his success. Besides France, he has made visits to Burkina Faso, Liberia, Nigeria, and Libya. Libya, which has been remotely associated with supporting past coups, has offered to handle the delivery of oil and gas derivatives to the Nigerian market, and the two countries have agreed to form a joint oil exploration and production company. Nigeria ranks as a key business partner for Niger. It provides electricity to Niger and is Niger's largest market for livestock. Nigerian President Obasanjo, himself a military man now presiding over a return to democracy, may provide a mentor for Tandja. Niger may also look to African neighbors Ghana and South Africa for capital and mining experience.

## ADDRESS

Office of the President
Niamey, Republic of Niger

## REFERENCES

AfricaNews Online. [Online] Available http://www.africanews.org/west/niger/stories/19990622_feat2.html (Accessed 17 August 2000).

*Africa South of the Sahara*, 28th ed., London: Europa Publications Ltd., 1999.

BBC News [Online] Available http://news2.thdo.bbc.co.uk/hi/english/world/africa (Accessed 17 August 2000).

CNN Interactive [Online] Available http://cnn.com/WORLD/africa/ (Accessed 17 August 2000).

*The Independent* (Accra), 22 June 1999.

IRIN: Integrated Regional Information Network, United Nations Office for the Coordination of Humanitarian Affairs [Online] Available http://www.reliefweb.int/IRIN/wa/countrystories/niger/ (Accessed 17 August 2000).

*Niger News: Kakaki.* [Online] Available http://users.idworld.net/jmayer/kakaki (Accessed 17 August 2000).

Panafrican News Agency, 9 April–18 August1999.

**Profile researched and written by Kathryn L. Green, California State University, San Bernardino (9/99; updated 2/2000) and added to by Robert J. Groelsema (6/2000).**

# NIGERIA

## Olusegun Obasanjo
## President
*(pronounced "oh-LOOS-eh-gun oh-ba-SAN-jo")*

*"It is my determination to run an open, fair, and transparent government throughout the period of my mandate."*

The Federal Republic of Nigeria occupies 923,768 sq km (336,667 sq mi) with a population of 114 million, making it Africa's most populous country. The nation's capital city of Ajuba is centrally located in the nation's interior. Lagos, the former capital with over 10 million people, remains the country's financial and cultural center. Its southern boundary lies on the Gulf of Guinea while northern neighbors include Niger and Chad. Nigeria shares a border with Benin in the west and Cameroon to its east. Nigeria's widely varied topography consists of tropical swamp-like mangroves along coastal areas, with tropical rainforests extending 100–150 miles inward, becoming a savannah and wooded plateau and a semi-desert in the northern region of the country. The climate ranges from humid tropical weather in the south to arid and dry conditions in the north.

Nigeria's diverse ethnic, linguistic, and religious characteristics contribute to cultural and artistic enrichment and fractious political conditions. The major ethnic groups include the Hausa (21%), Yoruba (21%), Ibo (17%), and Fulani (9%). The Hausa have traditionally dominated the northern region of the country while the Yoruba have a pronounced influence in Nigeria's western region, and the Ibo's reside largely in the country's eastern region. While more than 250 languages and dialects are spoken throughout the country, two-thirds of Nigerians speak either Hausa, Yoruba, or Ibo. The official language, reflecting Nigeria's colonial experience, is English. Approximately 50% of Nigerians are Christians, 40% Muslim, and 10% practice traditional African religions. Life expectancy is 53.3 for males and 56 for females and the literacy rate is 57%.

The Nigerian economy is based on petroleum products, which account for 90% of all exports and 20% of its total economic activity. In the 1980s, Nigeria benefitted from high oil prices and the average per capita income exceeded us$1,500. However, as prices declined in the 1990s, the country's economy experienced contraction and acute crisis. Coupled with the decline of the second most important economic activity—agriculture—Nigeria's per capita income declined to the equivalent of us$960. Nigeria's major trading partners are the European Union (EU) and the United States. The national currency, the *naira*, has experienced continued devaluation.

## POLITICAL BACKGROUND
From 1100–1400 major African civilizations blossomed around the Niger River. Europeans appeared in the 15th and 16th centuries and established the slave trade. By the end of the 19th century, the British colonized the coastal areas, began to penetrate inland, and established a protectorate over Northern Nigeria by 1900. The British controlled Nigeria through a divide-and-rule method, pitting the various ethnic groups against each other. In the south, the British introduced Christianity, primarily to the Ibo.

After a half century of British rule, Nigeria became fully independent on 1 October 1960. It became a federal republic in 1963 with the country divided into three states based on ethnicity: the Northern Region, the Western Region, and the Eastern Region. During the 1960s leaders of the different states threatened secession from the federation. By 1966, the First Republic ended with a military coup. Subsequently, the Eastern Region declared its independence as the Republic of Biafra. In the ensuing civil war, the federal government blockaded Biafra and sent troops to reunite the country by force. During the three-year civil war, an estimated two million people died from mass starvation, mostly Christian Ibos.

When the civil war ended in 1970, Major-General Yakubu Gowan created a federal system consisting of 12 states and emphasized national reconciliation. Gowan was aided by new public works projects carried out by the central government's revenues from the oil boom. In July 1975, Gowan was overthrown by Brigadier Murtala Muhammad who, in turn, was assassinated on 13 February 1976. Muhammad's chief-of-staff, Lieutenant General Olusegun Obasanjo became the next head of state. As leader of the Supreme Military Council (SMC), Obasanjo oversaw the drafting of a new constitution by the National Constituent Assembly and the termination of a 12-year state of emergency. Obasanjo also legalized political parties and paved the way for democratic elections in 1979 and the inauguration of the Second Republic under Alhaji Shagari.

On 31 December 1983, a bloodless coup led by Obasanjo's followers displaced Shagari, who had been democratically reelected in 1983. The military officers seized power, citing increased corruption and economic mismanagement. Led by Major-General Ibrahim Babangida, Nigeria's military repeatedly postponed deadlines for return to civilian rule and repressed political opponents and curtailed civil liberties. In September 1987, Babangida announced a five-year plan for return to civilian rule. Elections for the Third Republic were finally held on 12 June 1993, amid rioting and inter-communal violence.

Mashood Abiola, a Yoruba businessman, was widely viewed as the winner of the 1993 elections, but the government never released the election results and instead annulled the results. Babangida refused to relinquish power but later resigned after naming Ernest Shonekan as interim head of state. In November 1993, General Sani Abacha assumed power and dissolved the National Assembly after a military coup. Despite pledges for civilian rule, Abacha increased his repression of political dissidents and inaugurated himself president in July 1994. Subsequently, Abiola was imprisoned. Abacha consolidated his control over a regime characterized as Nigeria's most corrupt and brutal government. The execution of Ken Saro Wiwa, an Ogoniland political activist, inflamed ethnic tensions and sealed the Abacha government's fate as a pariah state.

The death of Abacha from a massive heart attack on 8 June 1998, paved the way for a democratic transition. Major General Abdulsalan Abubakar was selected as head of state in a closed-door meeting of the Provisional Ruling Council the following day. Abubakar honored his promise to restore democracy by releasing political prisoners, including Abiola and Obasanjo, in preparation for presidential elections. Obasanjo was elected president on 27 February 1999, and Abubakar stated, "I have no doubt democracy has come to stay."

## PERSONAL BACKGROUND

Born on 6 March 1935, at Abeokuta in Ogun State (southwestern Nigeria), Olusegun Obasanjo belongs to the Yoruba ethnic group. He attended primary and secondary school at the Baptist Boys High School in Abeokuta and enlisted in the Nigerian Army in 1958. He trained at Mons Officers Cadet School in Aldershot, England, and at the Royal College of Military Engineering at Chatham, England. In 1959 he was commissioned second lieutenant, and then in 1960 Obasanjo was promoted to lieutenant.

After serving with the United Nations Peacekeeping Force in the Congo (formerly Zaire) in 1960, Obasanjo began a rapid rise in Nigeria's officer corp. By 1963, he became the commander of the Nigerian army's only engineering unit and received a promotion to captain. He received further education with the Indian Army Engineering School, and upon completion of the program in 1965, he was again promoted to major.

By the time the Biafran Civil War broke out in 1967, he had been placed in commanding positions and promoted to lieutenant colonel. In 1969, Obasanjo commanded the 3rd Infantry Division of the South-Eastern State and accepted the surrender of the Biafran forces, giving him national publicity. He was promoted to brigadier general shortly thereafter and became commissioner for works and housing in 1975. Later in 1975, he was appointed chief of staff of the Nigerian army. In 1976, Obasanjo became commander-in-chief of the armed forces and a lieutenant general. After General Muhammed was killed in a 1976 coup attempt, the Supreme Military Council appointed Obasanjo head of state. In 1979, he successfully organized Africa's first voluntary transition from military rule to democracy. After being promoted to general, Obasanjo retired to Ota, near Lagos, and became a poultry farmer. However, he remained active in African issues,

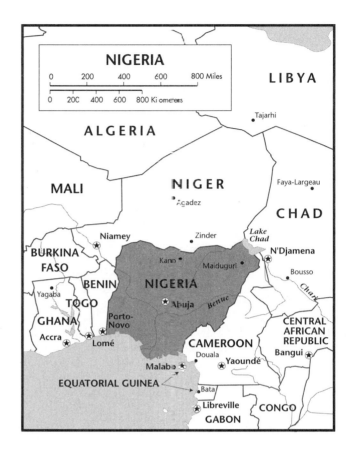

attending conferences and committee meetings and forming the African Leadership Forum.

Obasanjo is currently married to Stella Ajike Abede, whom he met in 1971. Prior to his marriage to Abede, he had a previous marriage to Oluyemi Akinlaja, with whom he had five children. Obasanjo's hobbies include table tennis and squash. He is also the author of several publications on African politics and the military. In 1991, his bid to become secretary general of the UN failed. General Abacha sentenced him to prison in 1995 for an attempted coup plot.

## RISE TO POWER

Obasanjo's transfer of power to an elected civilian leader in 1979, increased the nation's respect for him. However, his support of Shagari over Chief Awowolo, a fellow Yoruban, caused Obasanjo to lose the support of his ethnic group. He enjoys widespread support from many in the Hausa-speaking north.

After being imprisoned for allegedly plotting a coup attempt against General Sani Abacha in 1995, human rights groups began a public campaign for his release. Following the execution of Saro Wiwa, Nigeria was expelled from the Commonwealth of Nations. The death of Abacha and the ascendence of Abubakar opened the opportunity for a transition to democracy. Upon release from prison, Obasanjo decided to recommit himself to politics by running for the presidential nomination of the People's Democratic Party. His close relationship with the military and his commitment to democracy helped him capture his party's nomination in February 1999. Obasanjo defeated Chief Olu Falae by garnering 63% of the popular vote.

## LEADERSHIP

As Nigeria's newly elected leader, Obasanjo enjoys strong domestic and international support. Yet, his domestic critics are highly vocal and criticize him for his past ties to the military. Obasanjo's ethnic group, the Yoruba, continue to distrust him and a turnaround in relations are vital for healing ethnic relations. Human rights groups want him to establish a committee to investigate and punish former military leaders for corruption and human rights abuses. Obasanjo, however, while promising a truth commission, remains disinclined to punish the military. Furthermore, his own people, the Yoruba, continue to distrust and despise him because of his role in Shagari's presidential election in 1979.

Obasanjo is considered to be a wily politician with good oratory skills. Given the years of military rule, the neglect of the nation's infrastructure, and increased ethnic tensions, Obasanjo must be able to convince his opponents that he will govern in the nation's best interests. His experience as a military engineer is invaluable for restoring the nation's transportation network, and his close relations to the military could assist in keeping the soldiers in their barracks. However, some believe that he is merely a military front man who might be tempted to act undemocratically whenever he experiences criticism. In fact, General Babangida, a former president and a major power broker, strongly supports Obasanjo. Media criticism led Obasanjo to lash out at critics.

## DOMESTIC POLICY

Over the past years of military rule, Nigeria slowly descended into financial and political ruin. Once viewed as the pride of black Africa, Nigeria became synonymous with mismanagement and domestic chaos. In particular, the once vibrant agricultural sector has been weakened due to over-reliance on the petroleum industry. Meanwhile, petroleum prices have plummeted with decreased global demand and over-supply.

Obasanjo will have significant responsibility for restoring confidence in government. He will need to decrease corruption and work toward a more equitable distribution of the nation's resources. In particular, significant potential exists for ethnic flare-ups, especially among the Yoruba and Ibo. For years, the Ibo have not had the opportunity to share in the petroleum wealth while the Muslim-dominated government and military benefited financially. Furthermore, his opponent in the presidential race, Chief Olu Falae, who draws significant support from the Yoruba, has repeatedly charged electoral fraud. While most international observers agree that electoral fraud was fairly widespread, they acknowledge that it did not alter the results. Therefore, Obasanjo needs to appeal to those who are discontented by building an inclusive government.

In his victory speech, Obasanjo stated that his goals were to revitalize the economy, especially in agriculture, and to bring about more a transparent and accountable government. He has promised to revitalize agriculture, modeled on his modestly successful program—Operation Feed the Nation—from his previous administration. However, because of declining oil revenues, he must operate under austere financial conditions, making it difficult to spend money on projects. Already, the incoming government has indicated that it will be unable to pay the increased minimum wages negotiated last year. The tone that his administration will set for civilian rule will be important for future governments, possibly resulting in a renewed civil society as a foundation for democracy and defining a non-political role for the military.

The conviction of the former Speaker of the House of Representatives in July 1999 on two counts of perjury and forgery sent a message to elected officials that a new ethical standard would be enforced for public behavior. Salisu Buhari was caught falsifying his age, and among other things, forging a BA degree from the University of Toronto. The Buhari affair resulted in a decision by the independent electoral commission to re-screen all assembly members to ascertain their ages and educational qualifications. In late July, the speaker of the house of representatives of the southeastern state of Abia became the first victim of impeachment by colleagues under the Fourth Republic.

## FOREIGN POLICY

The return of democracy to Nigeria will improve the country's image abroad and will allow the country to take a more active and productive role regionally and on the global stage. During the Abacha regime, Nigeria became a pariah state. Even the Commonwealth of Nations expelled Nigeria and imposed economic sanctions. However, with Obasanjo's international stature, Nigeria will play a major role in regional economic and security affairs. It will be readmitted into the Commonwealth, with sanctions lifted, and will continue to play a greater military and diplomatic role in stabilizing weak governments in West Africa. Nigeria currently participates in ECOMOG (West African Peace Monitoring Force) of ECOWAS (Economic Community of West African States), which has military troops stationed in Liberia and Sierra Leone.

In March 1999, Obasanjo visited the United States and European nations in an attempt to increase foreign investment into Nigeria. He stressed his country's abundant natural resources and agricultural potential during his meetings with political and corporate leaders. Obasanjo promised to re-evaluate Nigeria's debt payments to international financial institutions, which were suspended by Abacha. He hopes to create an economic environment more conducive to foreign investment. Obasanjo maintains close personal ties to South Africa's Nelson Mandela, and trade relations with South Africa are likely to increase.

## ADDRESS

Office of the President
Abuja, Nigeria

## REFERENCES

*Detroit News*, 11 March 1999.
*Global Studies, Africa*, Nigeria: Country Report.
*Herald Tribune*, 9 March 1999.
*The New Republic*, 22 March 1999.
*The News*, (Nigeria), 22 February 1999.
*The Nigerian Drum Messenger*, 4 March 1999.
*Pan African News Agency*, various reports, March and April 1999.
*Post Express*, 11 March 1999.
*Tempo*, (Nigeria), 25 February 1999.
*Today Newspaper*, 7–13 March 1999.

**Profile researched and written by Robert Compton, Western Kentucky University (6/99; updated 2/00).**

# NORWAY

**Jens Stoltenberg**
**Prime Minister**

*(pronounced "JENS stol-TEN-berg")*

*"The Government exists to serve the people. We take up our duties with humility and optimism. Norway is truly a country of opportunity."*

The Kingdom of Norway occupies the western portion of the Scandinavian peninsula. The country's northern regions are in the Arctic Circle and share a 196 km (130 mi) border with Russia, an important factor influencing Norwegian foreign policy. Norway also shares a long border with Sweden to the east, and its territory fronts Finland in the northeast. At the same time, Norway's long coastline looks west across the North Sea to Great Britain, and south toward Denmark. These geographic characteristics play a political and economic role in linking Norway to Western Europe. The capital and largest city is Oslo.

The estimated population of Norway is 4,400,000. Nearly 89% of Norwegians describe themselves as members of the Evangelical Lutheran Church, which is the official state religious institution.

Norway covers 323,878 sq km (125,050 sq mi) of territory. Fishing and forestry once dominated commercial life, but the development of petroleum and natural gas fields since the 1970s has made hydrocarbons the driving force of the economy. Second globally only to Saudi Arabia, Norway pumped 3.327 million barrels/day of petroleum. Norway is also Europe's leading producer of natural gas and one of the world's wealthiest countries. Per capita income averages US$24,700. The Norwegian currency is the *krone*.

## POLITICAL BACKGROUND

In 1814, in the wake of the Napoleonic wars, Norway was forced to merge with Sweden, but managed to maintain elements of autonomy. Influenced by the French democratic revolution of 1848, Norway developed its own parliament, with limited powers, in the late nineteenth century. A strengthening sense of national identity led the Norwegians to negotiate their independence from Sweden in 1905. In that year, Prince Karl of Denmark was chosen as Norway's constitutional monarch, and took the name Haakon VII. His grandson, Harald V, became king in 1991 and reigns today. Norway followed a policy of strict neutrality from 1905 until 1940. In 1940, Germany invaded Norway and carried out an exacting occupation until 1945. The bitter experience of the German occupation shredded the long dominant political sentiment for neutrality, and led Norwegians to join NATO in 1949.

Norway is a constitutional monarchy, and the head of state enjoys only limited power. The monarch designates the prime minister, who is the chief of government, but only at the direction of the *Storting* (Parliament), the unicameral legislature where real power resides. The *Storting* has 165 seats, split among eight parties in the election of 1997. Elections are held every four years and the next one is scheduled for fall 2001. Unlike most parliamentary systems, an election is not called if a government loses a vote of confidence.

Due to the large number of parties and a system of proportional representation, coalition governments are the rule in Norwegian politics. Because most governments over the past decade have been minority governments, changes of government are a relatively frequent occurrence, even by the standards of European parliamentary systems. The ability to build consensus is thus an important political trait for politicians and for parties. Ideological parties tend, therefore, to be small because they are often exclusive. Women play a greater role in Norwegian politics than in any other European country. For many years, a woman, Gro Harlem Brundtland of the Labor Party, dominated Norwegian politics and served intermittently as prime minister. Kjell Bondevik, a Christian-democrat and prime minister from 1997 until early 2000, had nine women in various cabinet positions. The minority Labor government, under the leadership of Jens Stoltenberg, counted eight female ministers.

## PERSONAL BACKGROUND

Jens Stoltenberg was born in Oslo on 16 March 1959. He studied economics at the University of Oslo and worked part-time as a journalist on the national daily, *Arbeiderbladet* from 1979–1981.

Stoltenberg is Norway's youngest prime minister and turned 41 a few days after coming to power. He is known for his considerable charm and energy. He has been active in politics since his student days and has lived his whole life in Oslo. He is married to Ingrid Schulerud, a civil servant at the Ministry of Foreign Affair. The couple has two children.

## RISE TO POWER

Stoltenberg's political career started with a stint as vice-president of the International Union of Socialist Youth from 1985 to 1989. Subsequently, he became the local leader of the Oslo branch of Labor Party in 1990–1992. The party leadership recognizing his talents and energy, gave him a seat in parliament in 1993. At the relative tender age of 34, he held the portfolio of the Ministry of Trade and Energy in the Brundtland cabinet (1993–1996). After the resignation of Brundtland in 1996, Stoltenberg moved to the Ministry of

## NORWAY

Finance in Thorbjørn Jagland's government. During his time as Finance Minister, Stoltenberg supported the decision to invest half of Norway's state petroleum fund in international equities. The fund was set up in 1990 to save oil revenues for future generations once the oil stops flowing. Stoltenberg justified the controversial move by saying that long-term investments in equities promised better returns than bonds.

Norwegians judged Jagland an able steward of the government and the economy, which boomed under the country's wealth of petroleum and natural gas. However, polls indicated that family and personal values were suffering at the expense of the promotion of material values. Public opinions showed that the Labor party would easily be again Norway's largest party but prime minister Jagland pledged to step down if the Labor Party failed to improve on its 1993 total electoral vote of 39.6%. Unexpectedly, the Labor party did not make it and slipped to 35.2% of the vote. It lost two seats (67 to 65) in the *Storting*. As promised, Jagland stepped down as prime minister, although the Labor party was the largest party with 65 seats out of 165-seat parliament. Nevertheless, it went into opposition, a rare situation for a party which has been in office nearly continuously since 1935. Because of Jagland's pledged not to join the next government, the task of creating a workable coalition fell to Kjell Bondevik, a Christian-democrat.

Supporters and opponents alike viewed Bondevik as non-confrontational and a consensus-builder—necessary traits in forming yet another of the country's minority governments. He was duly chosen prime minister on 17 October 1997, and formed a coalition consisting of his Christian Democratic Party, the Conservatives, and the Liberals. Bondevik placed strong emphasis on such economic values as efficiency and productivity. But his three-party coalition government held only 54 of the *Storting's* 165 seats. In such circumstances, the coalition would have to tread carefully, with the acquiescence of the other party groupings that could easily outvote them. The media quickly dubbed the Bondevik government "the Slalom Coalition" due to its need to maneuver through the tricky slopes of the Norwegian political thicket.

In March 2000, the Bondevik government lost a vote of confidence. The immediate reason was an environmental dispute on the construction of natural gas power plant. Bondevik argued that Norway should wait with the construction of a new power plant until the introduction of new anti-pollution technology. Both Labor and Conservatives disagreed and argued that Norway should go ahead with new gas-fired power plants. When Bondevik refused to budge, he was forced to resign.

In February 2000, the Labor leadership appointed Stoltenberg to replace Jagland as the new party leader. Stoltenberg served on the standing committee on oil and energy affairs since 1997 and became prime minister on 11 March 2000 after the collapse of the Bondevik government. The minority Labor government has no promises of support from the six opposition parties. The Stoltenberg cabinet will have to negotiate with each of the political parties to obtain the necessary parliamentary support for its legislation. He faces a tough task because environmentalists are arrayed against him and support from other political parties is uncertain. Moreover, Stoltenberg can even expect opposition from within his own party on environmental issues. Brundtlandt, a hero for many Labor activists, gained an international reputation for championing the global environment.

## LEADERSHIP

The Labor government pledged to reform Norway's public sector, maintain strong bonds with Europe, and continue its efforts to broker international peace especially in the Middle East. Part of the reforms entails the partial privatization of the state-owned communication company, Telenor and Statoil. Especially Statoil, the state-owned energy company, holds important symbolic value as the guardian of the nation's oil and gas wealth. But Labor under Stoltenberg is determined to open up the state-owned company to private (foreign) capital and shake off the image abroad that Norway drives a nationalistic agenda to keep foreigners from buying its assets.

Stoltenberg, in his augural speech, also called upon the people and leadership to embrace the restructuring of the public sector to prepare for the new economy based on knowledge industries and to improve labor force participation rates of minorities. The public sector reforms contemplated by the Labor government include ways to attract skilled people in professions with looming labor shortage (nursing, for example), to involve private associations in the delivery of public services, and to bring about greater choice and freedom in health care, education, and other public services. At the same time, the government pledged to preserve the high level of services available to all Norwegian citzens.

## DOMESTIC POLICY

In the late 1980s, economic difficulties unsettled the Norwegian political landscape. A vigorous debate took place about the advantages and disadvantages of joining the European Union (EU). In 1990, a Labor government under Brundtland took power, and decided to press for Norwegian membership in the EU. To those worried about Norway's failure to sustain economic growth, EU membership held out the promise of greater access to the European market and a voice in EU decision-making. The country was already a member of the European Economic Area (EEA), which provided a restricted measure of access to the EU market, but did not subject independent-minded Norway to the EU's regulatory machinery. The other Nordics were already in the EU or seeking admission: Denmark was a member, and Finland and Sweden would soon join. Balanced against those advocating membership for Norway was a strong sense of localism.

As part of the price of membership, the EU was demanding that Norway open its waters to fishing by fleets from current member countries. In addition, cheaper agricultural products from the EU would compete with the more expensive products from Norway's rural population. Neither fishing (accounting for only 7.7% of Norway's exports in 1994) nor farming (less than 3% of the land is cultivated) plays a major role in the country's economy, but virtually every Norwegian has a strong cultural link to the sea and to the land. This link to the purportedly simple and pure values associated with the hard lives of fishermen and farmers appeared sentimental to some, but to many Norwegians coastal communities and rural villages express the ethos of Norway's sense of tradition and independence, and thereby play a strong role in forging the national identity. EU membership was defeated by a majority of 52.4% in a 1994 referendum.

Stoltenberg is on record to favor EU membership. But his hands are tied after two referendums in which the people have said no to membership.

The Norwegian economy is currently booming, but many economists are worried about the longer term. Norway's key domestic problem is to diversify its economy before hydrocarbon production declines. Its non-hydrocarbon industries are weak. Approximately 30% of the work force is in state industry (which includes petroleum and gas). Norway has used the generous petroleum revenues to modernize its infrastructure and has established a Petroleum Fund that invests in highly-rated equities and foreign government instruments. The government surplus, which reached US$7 billion in 1997, is placed in the Petroleum Fund. After 2000, when oil revenues may decline, the baby boomer generation will begin to retire, placing greater strain on the pension and state health care systems. The new government's challenge is to formulate politically acceptable steps to utilize the Fund to build a diversified economy for the long term.

## FOREIGN POLICY

Norway faces no immediate external threats, given the collapse of the Soviet Union in 1991. At the same time, Norwegian officials place paramount importance on maintaining friendly relations with Russia, a country that they believe in time could once again threaten Norway's future.

Norway has acquiesced to the US desire to expand NATO, but has had misgivings, since this could isolate and antagonize Russia. Expansion could also dilute the alliance's long-held central mission of collective defense should new, and presumably weaker, central European states join. Polls in 1996 and 1997 indicated that the Norwegian people place commitments abroad and expenditure for defense as low priorities. NATO enlargement could require extensive financial commitments to modernize new member states' militaries.

The government's new foreign minister, Jagland, has said that he will work to bring peace and stability to such countries as Bosnia. Norway, both under Labor and center-right coalition, took a leadership role in attempting to forge a lasting peace between Israel and Palestinians living in Israeli-occupied territory.

In addition, the new Labor government aims to reform and strengthen the UN. The Labor government is working to secure Norway a seat on the UN Security Council for the period 2001–2002 and will give priority to efforts to promote human rights and democracy and to mobilizing international efforts to combat corruption and crime. It also proposed to take a leading role in the global vaccine initiative (Global Alliance for Vaccination and Immunization) headed by the World Bank, UNICEF, the World Health Organization and private donors. In other words, the Labor government will continue Norway's established tradition of attempting to bridge the gap between the rich and the poor.

## ADDRESS

Office of the Prime Minister
Regjeringskvartalet
Akersgata 42
Oslo, Norway

## REFERENCES

The Associated Press, 11 March 2000.
*The Economist*, 1 November 1997.
*The Financial Times*, 25/26 March 2000.
*The Financial Times*, 10 March 2000.
*Financial Times*, 10 November 1997.
Janet Matthews Information Services. *Hilfe Country Report*, 7 December 1999.
*Official Site of Norwegian Government* http://odin.dep.no

**Profile researched and written by Paulette Kurzer, University of Arizona (4/2000); sections contributed by Paul E. Gallis, Congressional Research Service (3/98).**

# OMAN

## Qaboos Bin Al Sa'id
## Sultan

*(pronounced "kah-BUSS BIN AL sigh-EED")*

*"I have undertaken the action against my father in an effort to place the country along the path of reconstruction and development."*

Known as Muscat and Oman prior to August 1970, the Sultanate of Oman occupies the extreme east and southeast of the Arabian peninsula. It is surrounded on the northwest by the United Arab Emirate (UAE), on the west by Saudi Arabia, and on the extreme southwest by Yemen. On the tip of the Musandam peninsula lies a detached portion of Oman, separated from the rest of the country by the UAE, which extends into the Strait of Hormuz. Oman has a coastline of about 1,600 km (1,299 mi) on the Indian Ocean, and its total area is about 300,000 sq km (120,000 sq mi). Most of its borders with its neighbors are not clearly demarcated.

Because no census has ever been taken, population estimates vary greatly. Oman's population is approximated at 2.4 million, about 400,000 of whom are expatriate workers. Omanis constitute about 45% of the total labor force. The majority of the population are Ibadi Muslims, a small religious sect that is the only surviving offshoot of an early radical sect, the Khawarij. Around 25% are Sunni Muslims. Ethnically, the Omani population is predominately Arab. Small communities of Iranians, Baluchis, Indians, Pakistanis, and East Africans also inhabit the country. While Arabic is the official language, Persian, English, Urdu, and several other South Asian dialects are also spoken. The Oman *riyal* is the currency of the country. Although Oman's GDP is approximately US$18.6 billion, it declined in the 1990s because of decreasing oil revenues. Oman's economy is largely based on petroleum exports. However, Oman's oil reserves and production are not as extensive as UAE's or Kuwait's and, therefore, it has had to rely on grants from the Gulf Cooperation Council for its development projects.

Oman's economic growth has been concentrated on coastal urban areas while the interior has remained poor and undeveloped. Although 70% of the country's population is rural and engaged in traditional farming, herding (cattle breeding), or fishing, Oman has to import most foodstuff. It exports dates, nuts, limes, and fish. Oman's main trade partners are the Middle Eastern countries, Western Europe, Japan, and the US.

## POLITICAL BACKGROUND

Oman is an absolute monarchy with no constitution, elected legislature or legal political parties. After becoming the Sultan, Qaboos appointed his uncle, Tariq Bin Taymur, as prime minister. Tariq resigned in 1971, and since then the Sultan has presided over the cabinet meetings and acted as his own prime minister, minister of defense, and minister of foreign affairs. The cabinet, which consists of personal aides, assists the Sultan in running the government and is permitted to make decisions in the Sultan's absence. In 1981 the Sultan established a Consultative Assembly, which consists of appointed members and meets quarterly. In 1983, its membership was expanded to 55 members. The Assembly's role is purely advisory.

## PERSONAL BACKGROUND

Qaboos Bin Sa'id was born on 18 November 1940, in Salalah, Oman. He is the only son of Sultan Sa'id Bin Taymur who ruled over Oman from 1954 to 1970. Little is known about his early life as he was kept secluded within the palace wall by his father and grew up a shy and withdrawn child. He was educated by private tutors and later attended Britain's Royal Military Academy at Sandhurst. He obtained further military training in West Germany with a British regiment, after which he returned to London where he studied political science with private tutors. Upon returning to Oman in 1964, he lived under virtual house arrest until he became ruler.

## RISE TO POWER

Sultan Sa'id Bin Taymur was a reactionary and reclusive man. Instead of using oil revenues for development projects, he insisted on their exclusive use for defense. As a result, the country experienced minimal modernization even though it prospered from oil exports. For example, until 1970 there were three schools and 10 km (6 mi) of paved roads. In protest, several educated and talented Omanis, including the then-Sultan's own brother, went in voluntary exile.

Qaboos grew impatient with his father's antiquated administration. With British approval on 23 July 1970, Qaboos led a coup against his father forcing him to abdicate and sending him to London in exile. Qaboos then became the Sultan on Oman.

## LEADERSHIP

Sultan Qaboos' accession to power was welcomed by the vast majority of Omanis, who resented his father's reactionary attitude. Initially, Qaboos' main opposition was centered in Dhofar province, where rebels united against his father's rule. Qaboos requested cooperation from the rebels but only one of the factions surrendered. In 1971–72, two left-wing guerrilla groups merged to form the Popular Front for the Liberation of Oman and the Arabian Gulf; in 1974 they dropped "the Arabian Gulf" from their name. The Popular

Front continued their opposition activities, this time against the new Sultan. With the assistance of Iran, the UK, Pakistan, and Jordan, Sultan Qaboos was able to establish his control over the region. Though the Popular Front still opposes the Sultan, it is no longer a serious threat.

Qaboos has gained the support of the Omanis mainly by his use of oil income for economic development and increased social services, including education. Under Qaboos' rule, a large number of exiled Omanis have returned to their homeland. These repatriated citizens have offered skills and education that have been an asset to the country's development.

## DOMESTIC POLICY

Oman has seen tremendous changes since Qaboos came to power. Virtually the whole country has been transformed as a result of advances in housing, education, health, and communication. Internal migration from interior rural areas to urban centers has also contributed to social transformation. The government responded by taking steps to minimize the dislocating effects of its programs.

The economy of Oman, heavily dependent on its annual production of 900,000 barrels of crude oil, was adversely affected when the price of oil dropped below US$10 per barrel in 1998, a 25-year low. In the first three quarters of 1998, Oman's gross domestic product (GDP) had dropped by an annualized rate of 8.5%, and Omani oil production had similarly fallen by 32% in the same period. In January 1999, the Omani Finance Minister announced that the country's budget deficit was expected to double within the year. Seeking to offset the loss in oil revenue through other sources, the government raised customs duties from 5% to 15%, corporate income tax from 7.5% to 12%, and the cigarette tax from 75% to 100%, though it did not institute taxes on personal income or consumption. Oman is not a member of the Organization of Petroleum Exporting Countries (OPEC); however, in March 1999, Omanis agreed with OPEC to reduce global oil production by 2.1 million barrels of crude per day until April 2000 in the hope of raising oil prices to US$18 per barrel and stabilizing the oil market. In October 1999, the Omani Oil Minister recommended extending global oil production cuts beyond the date originally proposed for their expiration.

In an effort to ease its dependence on oil, Oman has sought to diversify its economy. A gas liquefaction plant at Sur is slated for completion sometime in 2000, though plans for a power station, an aluminum processing plant, a steel mill, and petrochemical and fertilizer plants at Salalah and Sohar and the gas pipelines to fuel them remain unrealized. While oil production constitutes less of Oman's GDP than was the case two decades ago, oil is still the major source of revenue for Oman's government, which is the mainspring of the country's economy. Manufacturing still accounts for only 5% of the GDP.

The Omani government has made a similar move toward greater privatization. At the successful new port at Salalah, a free zone is to be built solely by private investors. The private sector will also finance a new airline to service Salalah, a tourist destination as well as a trade center. Legislation barring expatriates from certain sectors of the economy has encouraged private employment of Omani nationals, most of

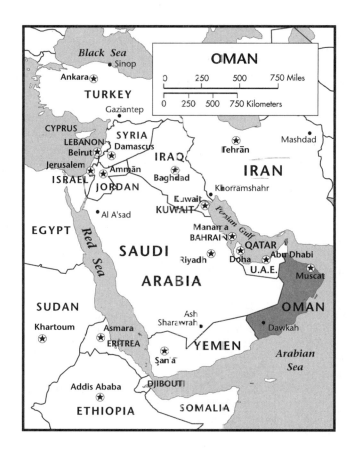

whom work for the government, and the industrial sector, comprised of 19% Omani nationals in 1995, was 28% Omani in 1997.

## FOREIGN POLICY

Once in office, Qaboos reversed the isolationist policy of his father and started establishing relations with most Arab and Western countries. By 1987, he had even developed ties to countries of the Eastern bloc, including the USSR and People's Republic of China. However, Oman has maintained a very pro-Western tilt in its foreign policy. Oman was one of the only two Arab states that endorsed the Egypt-Israel Peace Treaty of 1979. In June 1980 Oman concluded an agreement with the US granting access to Omani air and naval facilities, thus making Oman a base for US activities in the Persian Gulf. Oman has pursued its US policy despite concerns expressed by fellow members of the Gulf Cooperation Council. The outbreak of the Iran-Iraq war further underlined Oman's strategic importance, particularly with regard to the Strait of Hormuz, which is a narrow waterway at the mouth of the Persian/Arabian Gulf between Oman and Iran. About two thirds of the world's oil traffic passes through the Strait.

Most of Oman's foreign policy concerns are regional. When Qaboos took control, the rebellion in the Dhofar province of the country affected his relation with other states in the region. South Yemen (then the People's Democratic Republic of Yemen) and Iraq proved to be unfriendly neighbors at that time because they supported the rebels. Since a reconciliation summit in 1982, relations with Yemen have improved and have culminated in completion of a cooperation pact between the two neighbors in October 1988.

Despite its close relations with the West, Oman has tried to maintain a lanced regional policy. In early 1989, it restored diplomatic relations with Chad. In 1990, negotiations with the Palestinian Liberation Organization (PLO) indicated a desire to pursue a foreign policy that was in line with regional sentiment.

By 1999, Oman held to a middle-of-the-road stance of conciliation and compromise in Middle Eastern politics. In January 1999, Oman's foreign minister met with his counterparts from Egypt, Saudi Arabia, Syria, and Yemen at a closed meeting in Cairo to forge a position on the question of Iraq for the upcoming meeting of the 22-member Arab League later in the month. In February, Qaboos attended the funeral of King Hussein of Jordan, a gesture that expressed the close ties between Oman and Jordan. US Defense Secretary William Cohen included Oman in his tour of Persian Gulf allies, which was aimed at allaying concerns regarding extended US actions against Iraq. Newly enthroned King Abdullah of Jordan, accompanied by his Prime Minister and Foreign Minister, met with Qaboos in April 1999 to maintain the good relations between Jordan and Oman, which alone among the Gulf states refrained from criticizing Jordan for its non-oppositional stance toward neighboring Iraq during the Gulf War. Also in April, South African President Nelson Mandela spent three days in Oman, where he met with high-level government ministers and business leaders to encourage commercial ties between Oman and South Africa. Later in the month, Qaboos signed an agreement with the president of the United Arab Emirates defining the borders between Oman and the emirate of Abu Dhabi. Qaboos met with President Mubarak of Egypt in September. US Defense Secretary William Cohen once again visited Oman in October and met with Qaboos to discuss the Middle East peace process in light of Ehud Barak's election as Israeli prime minister and the future of Iran under Khatami's presidency. Qaboos was optimistic about the prospects of peace and saw Khatami as a tempering influence on Iran.

## ADDRESS
The Palace
Muscat
Sultanate of Oman

## REFERENCES
Khadduri, Majid. *Arab Personalities in Politics*. 1981.
*New York Times*, various issues.
Oman News Service. [Online] Available http://www.omannews.com/homee.htm (Accessed April 2000).
Peterson, J.E. *Oman in the Twentieth Century*. 1976.
Zahlan, Rosemarie Said. *The Making of the Modern Gulf States*. 1989.

**Profile researched and written by Bashir Ahmed (7/90; updated 5/2000).**

# PAKISTAN

## Pervez Musharraf
### Chief Executive
*(pronounced "PEAR-vezz moos-HAR-off")*

*"I would like to move away from the sham democracy we have had in Pakistan
I want a true democracy..."*

Pakistan, officially known as the Islamic Republic of Pakistan, is located in the northwest corner of the Indian subcontinent, and is surrounded by Afghanistan, Iran, China, India, and the Arabian Sea. It is comprised of four provinces: Sind, Baluchistan, the North West Frontier Province, and Punjab. Major urban centers include its capital Islamabad, Karachi, and Lahore. The currency unit is the *rupee*. Pakistan's total geographical area, excluding the disputed Jammu and Kashmir regions controlled by India, is 803,943 sq km (310,402 sq mi).

The population, estimated at 138,123,000, is composed of five ethnic groups: Punjabi, Sindhi, Pashtun (Pathan), Baloch, and Muhajir (immigrants from India and their descendants). Ethnic and linguistic groups generally coincide. Urdu, which is the official language, is mainly spoken by the Muhajirs. The dominant language is Punjabi (64%), followed by Sindhi (12%), Pashtu (8%) and Urdu (7%). English is widely used in business, higher education, government and the military. Less than 30% of the population is literate. The state religion is Islam. It is professed by 97% of the population (of which 77% is Sunni, and the remainer Shi'a). Other religious groups are Christians, Hindus, and Buddhists.

Pakistan's natural resources include extensive natural gas reserves, quality coal, iron ore, salt, and limestone. It's economy is primarily agricultural. 25% of the GNP comes from the agricultural sector. The principal crops are cotton, wheat, barley, sugarcane, millet, rice, and maize. The industrial sector occupies 20% of the formal work force. Textiles make up the largest manufacturing industry, followed by cement, sugar, and rubber industries. Pakistan's primary exports are textile and agricultural products. The average growth rate is estimated as 5% and the per capita GDP is approximately US$2,000.

## POLITICAL BACKGROUND

Since its independence in 1947, Pakistan has oscillated between military and civilian forms of government. The political system has been marked by instability and prolonged military influence. The army has run the country directly for almost half of its past 50 years. The first prime minister, Liaquat Ali Khan, was assassinated in 1951. A brief attempt at civilian government, marked by considerable upheaval, ended when Field Marshal Ayub Khan took power in 1958. He was then removed by General Agha Mohammed Yahya Khan in 1969. Yahya Khan's role as ruler ended when

Zulfikar Ali Bhutto was appointed as prime minister in 1973. The Pakistan People's Party (PPP) led by Bhutto won most of the seats in the March 1977 election, but General Zia ul Haq declared martial law and suspended all political activities, following allegations of electoral fraud and subsequent unrest. In October 1979, political restrictions were tightened, and Zia ordered the elections in February 1985 to be held on a non-party basis.

Although a civilian government resumed control after the February 1985 elections, the army's influence on politics continued. Complete civilian rule was not restored until Zulfikar Ali Bhutto's daughter, Benazir Bhutto, was elected as prime minister by the National Assembly in December 1988. Gulam Ishaq Khan, who had become president after Zia ul Haq, accused the government of corruption and dismissed Bhutto in August 1990. Subsequently, Nawaz Sharif, leader of the Islamic Democratic Alliance (IDA), was sworn in as prime minister on 6 November 1990. Sharif's service, however, was interrupted on 18 April 1993 when President Ishaq Khan dismissed his government after Sharif tried to curtail the president's constitutional power. Although Sharif was reinstated by the Supreme Court, both he and Ishaq Khan were forced to step down on 18 July 1993 under pressure from the army.

In the elections of October 1993 Benazir Bhutto's PPP gained a victory and she was inaugurated on October 19. Serdar Farooq Ahmad Khan Leghari became the new president on 14 November 1993. Leghari and Bhutto's elections, however, did not bring stability to Pakistani politics. Leghari dismissed Bhutto's highly unpopular government in November 1996 and established a new National Defense and Security Council (NDSC) which included the country's four most senior military men. Nawaz Sharif was returned to power on 3 February 1997, when his Pakistan Muslim League-Nawaz (PML-N) party won a landslide victory. The new prime minister greatly strengthened his hold on power when, in April 1997, the National Assembly and the Senate unanimously repealed key elements of the 1985 Eighth Constitutional Amendment. This divested the president of the power to appoint and dismiss the prime minister, cabinet, the legislature, provincial governors, and armed forces chiefs. In October 1999, Nawaz Sharif attempted to dismiss his own Army Chief and Chairman Joint Chiefs of Staff Committee, General Pervez Musharraf. This

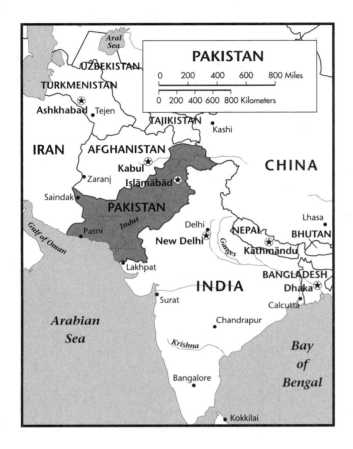

led to a military coup on 12 October 1999, with General Musharraf taking over the reins of government.

## PERSONAL BACKGROUND

Pervez Musharraf was born in Delhi, India, on 11 August 1943 to an educated Sayed family. When British India was partitioned into India and Pakistan in 1947, the family, like many other Muslims, migrated to Pakistan and settled in Karachi. Pervez's father, the late Syed Musharaff-ud-Din, was a career diplomat. The young Pervez attended some of Pakistan's elite schools before entering the Pakistan Military Academy in 1961. He married his wife, Sehba, on 29 December 1968, and has a son (Bilal) and a daughter (Ayla). A devoted family man, Musharraf is a keen sportsman, enjoying squash, badminton, golf, and sailing. He is also an avid reader, with an interest in military history.

Pervez Musharraf was commissioned 2nd Lieutenant in an artillery regiment in 1964. He saw active service in the 1965 war with India, during which he was awarded a medal for gallantry. Musharraf later volunteered for the commandos and was a company commander in a commando battalion during the 1971 Indo-Pakistan war. In 1980, Musharraf caught the eye of General Zia-al-Huq, who selected him for advancement. His subsequent military career included command at the brigade, division, and corps levels, as well as appointments to the Command and Staff College, Quetta, the National Defence College, and the Royal College of Defence Studies in the United Kingdom. Musharraf became Chief of Army Staff with the rank of General on 7 October 1998 and was appointed Chairman of the Joint Chiefs of Staff Committee on 9 April 1999.

## RISE TO POWER

General Pervez Musharraf was a most unlikely leader of a political coup d'état. Apparently without political ambitions, he was appointed as Pakistan's Chief of Army Staff by the then-prime minister, Nawaz Sharif, over the heads of two senior generals to replace General Jehangir Karamat, who had publicly criticized the government's political and economic policies. Musharraf was known for his integrity and highly regarded within the Pakistani army.

Nawaz Sharif, meanwhile, was busy consolidating his political position. Constitutional reforms placed many of the president's former powers in the hands of the prime minister. He used new "anti-terrorist" laws to stifle political opponents and limit free speech. His sudden conversion to "Islamic government" was seen by many as a prelude to the imposition of dictatorial rule in the name of Islam. Moreover, as the Pakistani economy worsened, with unemployment, inflation, and prices spiraling upwards, Nawaz Sharif and his political supporters were widely seen to be lining their pockets. Within the army, there were concerns over Nawaz Sharif's increasing reliance on the United States. There was resentment in military circles that Nawaz Sharif ordered the withdrawal from Kargil under U.S. pressure. There were also fears that Sharif had secretly negotiated a settlement over Kashmir with U.S. help, and was ready to unilaterally sign the Comprehensive Nuclear Test Ban Treaty in exchange for economic aid.

Distrustful of his Army Chief, Nawaz Sharif made plans to replace him with General Khwaja Ziauddin, head of the powerful Inter-Services Intelligence Agency and an officer loyal to Sharif. On 12 October 1999, while Musharraf was returning from a visit to Sri Lanka, Sharif announced his dismissal and ordered his arrest. When the general's plane, a commercial Pakistan International Airlines flight with civilians on board, arrived at Karachi airport, it was denied permission to land. Military intelligence, however, had warned Musharraf of Nawaz Sharif's intentions and he had made his own plans. Troops loyal to Musharraf seized the airport, and the general's plane landed with reportedly only seven minutes of fuel remaining. The army assumed power in a bloodless coup with General Musharraf becoming the Chief Executive of Pakistan.

## LEADERSHIP

As an military leader whose interests apparently were purely professional, General Pervez Musharraf's seizure of power in Pakistan was as much a response to circumstance as a planned venture into the political arena. However, his coup was supported by many Pakistanis, who saw the army as the only counterbalance to a prime minister completely out of control. Musharraf himself claimed, in a speech televised to the nation, that the country's institutions had been systematically destroyed and that the economy was in a state of collapse. His stated aim was to restore "pure democracy" to the country.

Musharraf's power base is ill-defined. The Army supported his ouster of Nawaz Sharif, but the extent of his support in the military is unclear. Many in the military are known to be more fundamentalist in their religious outlook than Musharraf, who believes religion should be a private affair. Similarly, though many Pakistanis supported the coup and many of Musharraf's initial moves, with political parties sidelined and a state of emergency in effect, the extent of Musharraf's popular support and backing among Pakistan's population remains undetermined. One positive is that Musharraf, as a muhajir or immigrant from India, avoids identification with either the Punjabi or Sindhi factions in Pakistan's politics.

After six months in office, it still remained to be seen whether Musharraf has the will, the popular support, and the leadership abilities to restore democracy to Pakistan.

## DOMESTIC POLICY

As of early 2000, Musharraf faced a daunting array of domestic problems. These included a corrupt and inefficient political system, an enormous foreign debt, an economy on the verge of collapse, and a society with serious social problems (such as heroin-addiction) and riddled by sectarian violence and feuding political factions.

Musharraf is seen as favoring moderate economic reform at home. In a key policy speech on 15 December 1999, he outlined an ambitious program to deal with the troubled economy. Most of his measures focused on improved revenue collection. He created the National Accountability Bureau to pursue tax evaders, and his administration has issued ultimatums to defaulters on loans issued by government banks. He also increased benefits for disadvantaged Pakistanis, such as increasing compensation given to relatives of dead government employees, making government land available to landless peasants, and deferring electricity payments for agricultural users. However, while all of these are positive steps, they fall far short of the rebuilding of institutions and the economic infrastructure that seem warranted by Pakistan's economic situation. Such reforms can probably only be instituted over the long term and with substantial foreign aid and international support.

Other domestic issues include corruption, reforming Pakistan's tax structure, defining the role of the judiciary in the country's affairs, sectarian violence, and dealing with both Islamic fundamentalists and the inter-provincial rivalries endemic in Pakistani politics. But perhaps the most important question of all is the timetable for Pakistan's return to a civilian government and the manner in which this will be effected.

## FOREIGN POLICY

As a professional military officer, Musharraf has limited experience of foreign affairs. Relations with India, and particularly the problem of Kashmir, dominates Pakistan's foreign agenda. Musharraf, who planned the invasion of Kargil in May 1999, is considered a hawk over Kashmir. He supported militant Islamic groups fighting in Kashmir and reportedly also has ties with fundamentalist elements in Afghanistan. Pakistan's stance on Kashmir, and particularly the potential for a nuclear conflict with India, is a cause of great concern among western nations. It is unlikely that Musharraf will soften his position on Kashmir, even though this may directly affect the international community's continued willingness to provide economic aid to Pakistan. U.S. president Bill Clinton made a brief six-hour stopover in Islamabad on 25 March 2000 during his South Asian tour to visit General Musharraf. Although the meeting's primary aim was to "open lines of communication," Musharraf can hardly have been pleased at Clinton's blunt message on Kashmir and the need for democracy in Pakistan.

## ADDRESS

Chief Executive Secretariat
Constitution Avenue
Islamabad 44000, Pakistan

## REFERENCES

Banks, Arthur S., Alan Day, and Thomas Muller. *Political Handbook of the World*. 1995–1996.
*Christian Science Monitor*, 5 February 1997.
*The Economist*, 19 February 2000.
*Foreign Affairs*, 79, 2 (March–April 2000).
*The New York Times*, 13 October 1999.
*Pakistan Link* [Online] Available http://www.pakistanlink.com/ (Accessed 29 April 2000).
*Time International*, 25 October 1999.

**Profile researched and written by Deryck Lodrick, University of California (4/00).**

# PALAU

## Kuniwo Nakamura
## President
### (pronounced "koo-NEE-wo na-ka-MOO-ra")

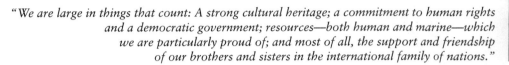

*"We are large in things that count: A strong cultural heritage; a commitment to human rights and a democratic government; resources—both human and marine—which we are particularly proud of; and most of all, the support and friendship of our brothers and sisters in the international family of nations."*

The Republic of Palau (pronounced "pull-OW"), the world's newest sovereign nation, is a collection of six island groups located in the western reaches of Oceania about 800 km (500 mi) east of the Philippines and 966 km (600 mi) north of Indonesia. Almost 350 islands form this Micronesian archipelago, but most are tiny and sparsely populated or uninhabited. The Rock Islands, a chain of about 300 small, low-lying coral islands, are known around the world for their great natural beauty. The main island of Babeldaob is the second-largest island in Micronesia after Guam. Distinguished by its high mountainous terrain, Babeldaob accounts for 396 sq km (153 sq mi) of Palau's total land area of 488 sq km (188 sq mi). The capital of Palau is Koror, a small but densely populated island and the political and economic hub of the country. It is connected to Babeldaob and some neighboring islands by a network of causeways. In an effort to relieve pressure on Koror and develop other regions of the country, a new capital is being built in eastern Babeldaob.

Palauans are a Micronesian people, a mixture of Polynesian, Melanesian, and Malayan races. The official language throughout the country is English. Sonsorolese is a second official language in the state of Sonsorol. Palauan is spoken in 13 of the country's 16 states, Anguar and Japanese are spoken in the southern most state of Anguar, while Tobi is the language of the state of Tobi. One-third of Palauans still practice the traditional religion, Modekngei. The other two-thirds of Palauans belong to a variety of Christian denominations. Public education is free and compulsory through the eighth grade. Literacy is high: 92% of the population 15 and older can read and write. The population of Palau is estimated at 18,467, but other sources give widely diverging estimates ranging from 13,000 to 20,000. It is not clear if any of these figures include the rapidly growing number of immigrant workers, mainly from the Philippines. There are 4,500 to 6,000 of these workers in Palau, many of whom are undocumented. Their numbers are growing so rapidly that government estimates predict that there may be 25,000 of them—more than the indigenous population—by the year 2000.

At present, Palauans enjoy one of the highest standards of living in the Pacific, but this is largely a result of US spending, rather than local economic productivity. Although Palauans are reputed to be sharp business people, the largest formal sector employer is the government, with a corps of about 2,000 people. In addition to the federal government, Palau's roughly 16,000 people are governed by 16 state administra-tions. The federal government is also the best-paying employer with average annual salaries of us$10,515. This contrasts sharply with the us$1.35 per hour earned by the Filipino immigrants working for the average private sector business. Such opportunities are limited, however, and many educated Palauans now must go abroad in search of jobs and decent salaries.

Although many Palauans still practice subsistence fishing and agriculture and produce handicrafts, the GDP has grown in recent years at about 10% per year. Palau's principal natural resource is its physical environment, and the fastest growing sector of the formal economy is tourism. Tourism grew from an average of 6,300 persons a year in 1983 to more than 40,000 in 1994. About half of the visitors come from Japan to enjoy scuba diving and snorkeling. Unfortunately for Palau, most of the profits are repatriated by foreign business owners. A second potential source of economic growth lies in exploiting the 322 km (200 mi) exclusive economic zone for its fisheries and undersea mineral deposits. At present, Palau earns some income from the sale of licenses to foreign fishing fleets, and it exports tuna and trochus (a shellfish). As with tourism, however, the vast majority of the wealth generated from fishing leaves the country. Palau also exports copra and handicrafts, but overall export earnings are dwarfed by import expenditures, which account for 80% of Palauan consumption.

## POLITICAL BACKGROUND

Palau became an independent nation on 1 October 1994, ending the *Taem era Marikel* or American era, that began with the US invasion of the islands in September 1944. One of the toughest battles of the Pacific war was fought between US and Japanese forces on the Palauan island of Peleliu. Palau was the last member of the UN Strategic Trust Territory of the Pacific Islands, a political trusteeship established by the United Nations after the end of World War II. The US assumed control of the islands in the aftermath of 30 years of Japanese colonial rule. Under the terms of the trusteeship, the US was given sole military base rights and was mandated to support the political, economic, and social development of Palauans in preparation for their return to self-rule or independence. During its five decades of administration, US policy makers failed to formulate a clear development policy for Palau, and the economy of the islands today reflects this ambivalence.

Palau has been ruled in this century by Germany, Japan, and the US. Before this, Spain ruled Palau as one of its vast holdings in Micronesia. Economic achievement during the US era was disappointing, but the Americans did leave a legacy of democracy, one that many Palauans seem to think blends well with their traditions. The US began building democratic institutions in Palau soon after the war. Universal suffrage and representative government were introduced, and the Palau District Legislature was convened in 1948. In the 1970s, the US began negotiating with Palau and the other Pacific Island trust territories about their political status after trusteeship. Palau began its journey to nationhood in 1978 when Palauans voted 55% to 45% against adopting the constitution of the Federated States of Micronesia. A national charter and development plan were drawn up the next year. In addition to outlining the political structure and process, the charter contained strict provisions for cultural and environmental protections, including a nuclear-free clause that ignited a controversy that continued until independence. The charter was passed in 1980, after three referenda. The first national elections were held in November of that year, and in January 1981, Haruo Remeliik took office as president of Palau's first constitutional government.

Remeliik served until 30 June 1985, when he was assassinated by a gunman hired by political rival John Ngiraked. His successor, former diplomat Lazarus Salii, shot and killed himself while in office in August 1988. Businessman Ngiratkel Etpison was elected Palau's third president in November 1988. He served one term and ran for a second in 1992 but lost. Kuniwo Nakamura won the November 1992 election for president.

Palauan politics since 1979 have been dominated by the question of approving a Compact of Free Association with the United States. The Compact provides for Palau's military defense and gives the US an option on one-third of the land for a period of 50 years. In addition, Palau will receive about us$500 million in economic aid over a 15-year period. The Compact was signed by the two governments on 10 January 1986, but failed to gain Palauan voters' approval in seven referenda on the subject. At issue was the fact that certain terms of the Compact conflict with the nuclear-free provision of the country's constitution and threaten to undermine environmental protections. A simple majority voted in favor of the Compact in each referendum, but Palau's constitution requires a two-thirds majority vote to override the nuclear-free provision, and this could never be obtained. In 1992, a citizen's initiative brought to the ballot a question asking voters whether or not they favored changing the majority needed to alter the nuclear-free provision from two-thirds to a simple majority. The initiative passed decisively but was followed by a series of challenges in court. These legal hurdles were eventually overcome, clearing the way for sovereignty and enacting the Compact on 1 October 1994.

Palau has a three-branch system of government. The executive branch is led by a president and vice-president. The 30-seat legislature, called *Otbiil Era Kelulau* (OEK), the House of Whisper Decisions, is made up of a 14-seat Senate and a 16-seat House of Delegates. A Supreme Court, National Court, and a Court of Common Pleas form an independent judiciary. Suffrage is universal at 18 years of age.

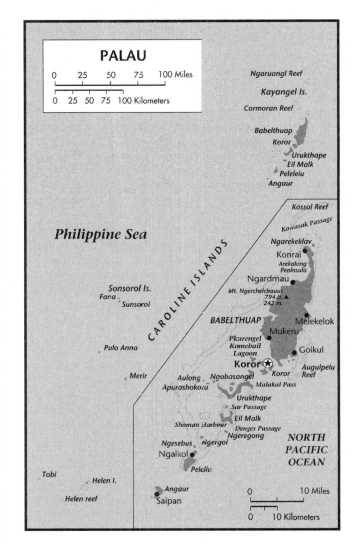

## PERSONAL BACKGROUND

Kuniwo Nakamura was born in Koror in 1941. He holds a degree in economics from the University of Hawaii. He was a teacher for some years until he became an economic advisor to the trust territory government.

## RISE TO POWER

Nakamura traveled a straight-line path to the presidency. He won his first election in the mid-1970s as representative from Koror to the District Legislature. He was elected to the Congress of Micronesia in 1975. During this period, Nakamura became active in the debate over post-territorial political status. He was floor leader during the 1979 constitutional convention and in 1980, was elected senator to the first national congress. He won a second term as senator in 1984, then ran for vice president in 1988. He won that election and served in the administration of Ngiratkel Etpison. Etpison also appointed him minister of justice.

The 1992 presidential race was the first in Palau. Nakamura ran against the incumbent Etpison and Johnson Toribiong, a 46-year old lawyer. Etpison was eliminated in the primary. With an 85% turnout, Nakamura squeaked by Toribiong in the general election, beating him by 134 votes

(4,841 to 4,707) and gaining the distinction of being the first president of Palau to rule with a majority.

## LEADERSHIP

Nakamura has assembled a cabinet of well-known business people and professionals. Vice President Tommy Remegesau Jr. is minister of administration. Minister of education is Billy G. Kuartei, a seasoned educational administrator. Minister of health Masao M. Ueda is the former administrator of federal programs for the Northern Marianas Commonwealth Health Center and special assistant to the director of the CNMI public health and environmental services. The minister of commerce and trade is George Ngirasaol, Nahamura's campaign manager and a successful businessman and political leader. The former director of the Palau public works department, Marcelino Melairei is minister of resources and development. He faces the challenge of making the most of the Compact funds, of setting a course for developing Palau's economic future, and of creating incentives for educated Palauans to stay there or return from abroad.

## DOMESTIC POLICY

Nakamura was elected on a platform of creating jobs and raising salaries for workers in Palau. Accomplishing this will be no mean feat in a country that is enormously dependent on government, faces a permanent withdrawal of budgetary support from the US, has purposely attracted cheap, temporary wage labor from abroad (Palauans refuse to do this kind of work), and is losing many of its educated citizens to opportunities overseas. In Nakamura's vision, Palau's economy will develop around tourism, agriculture, and foreign investment. He sees the Compact funds as a stabilizing force and has pledged to use them wisely. There is a keen need to expand the infrastructure to support economic development, and it is planned that Compact funds will finance the building of roads and infrastructure on Babeldaob. This is consistent with Palau's plans to attract people and economic activity to Babeldaob. Nakamura must ensure that this infrastructure serves Palau's long-term development needs and does not just support US military installations.

Paramount Chief Ibedul Yutaka Gibbons of Koror, the most powerful traditional leader in Palau and a key organizer of opposition to the Compact, has argued that the Compact will further erode Palau's autonomy and threaten traditional values. Koror has held a hegemony over Babeldaob for hundreds of years. Thus, Ibedul is sure to watch closely the spending of Compact funds, particularly as the scope of his authority is threatened by government plans to channel new resources away from Koror and to Babeldaob.

A controversial minimum-wage law went into effect on 1 January 1999. The new law set the minimum wage at US$2.50 per hour, but it exempted foreign workers. President Nakamura supported the new law and believed it would have a positive impact on labor practices. President Nakamura also signed into law an ethics-in-government bill which was intended to affirm the integrity of the electoral system and the fairness and honesty of government officials. In March 1999, President Nakamura directed the Minister of Justice to begin a crackdown on the unauthorized use of government vehicles, which had become a major issue with citizens. There was also a strong movement in the Palau Congress to change the present bicameral Congress (House of Representatives and Senate) to a unicameral form of government to reduce the cost of government. Such a proposal would eventually be put to the people in a vote, possibly in November 2000.

## FOREIGN POLICY

Nakamura has frankly and pragmatically characterized his country's recently won sovereignty as something less than full independence. Like the other former trust territories administered by the US, Nakamura has aligned his foreign policy with Washington's. Palau's regional orientation had traditionally been toward Micronesia, Guam, and Hawaii. Palau had not been an active player in South Pacific regional affairs, but this changed when a Palauan, Victorio Uherbelau, was chosen to head the Forum Fisheries Agency. Palau became the 185th member of the United Nations in December 1994. It became a member of South Pacific Forum, an organization of sixteen Pacific nations concerned with the economic and political stability and viability of the region, in 1995.

In October 1999, the Republic of Palau hosted the 30th South Pacific Forum with more than 300 foreign delegates, observers, and media members. President Kuniwo Nakamura, also the incoming Chairman of the South Pacific Forum, formally invited the United Nations Secretary General Kofi Annan to attend the meeting. The Forum considered issues on climate and sea level change, regional security and law enforcement, fisheries, and the United Nations Special Session on Small Island Developing States. Trade ministers of The South Pacific Forum endorsed the proposal for a Pacific Free Trade Area (FTA) that would create a regional market of six million people. The FTA allows goods produced in the fourteen island countries to be traded freely. In July 1999, Palau hosted the First Micronesian Traditional Leaders' Conference.

Also in 1999, there were several developments in the fishing industry. In January, President Nakamura threatened to cut off diplomatic ties with the Philippines because of continuing poaching by Filipino fishermen in Palau's exclusive economic zone. By September, the Philippines sent a delegation to Palau to address President Nakamura concerns. In April, Korean and Palauan trade officials signed an agreement to allow Korean fishing boats to catch tuna within Palau's territorial waters. In May, Micronesia, the Marshall Islands, and Palau signed a memorandum of understanding on fisheries management. The memorandum made the three island nations more efficient in managing marine assets and enforcing fisheries laws.

## ADDRESS

Office of the President
P.O. Box 100
Koror, Republic of Palau

## REFERENCES

*Islands Business Pacific*, Vol. 20, No. 10.
*Pacific Islands Monthly*, February 1993–January 1994.
*Pacific Magazine*, Vol. 20. No. 1, 4.

**Profile researched and written by N. Lynn Graybeal (updated 6/2000).**

# PANAMA

### Mireya Moscoso
### President

*(pronounced "meeh-REH-yu mos-KO-so")*

*"From now on we are in charge of our own destiny.
We don't want a divided country, we want a unified nation."*

The Republic of Panama is a central American country of 77,381 sq km (29,762 sq mi). It shares a western border with Costa Rica and an eastern border with Colombia. The Caribbean Sea lies north of Panama, and the Pacific Ocean is on the southern end of the country.

Panama has an estimated population of 2,778,526 and a population growth rate of 1.56%. With a birth rate of 22 births per 1,000 people and a death rate of 5.14 deaths per 1,000 people, Panama enjoys one of the highest standards of living in Central America. Life expectancy is 74.5 years and 90.8% of the population is literate. Approximately 70% of all Panamanians are mestizo (mixed Amerindian and white); 14% are West Indian; 10% are white; and 6% are Native American. A majority of the population (85%) is Catholic, but a significant number (15%) are Protestant. Spanish is the official language although English is also commonly used in urban areas.

A majority of the Panamanian workforce is employed by the service industry. The three main sources of employment are banking, commerce, and tourism. The purchasing power parity GDP is US$20 billion, (or US$7,300 per capita)—one of the highest in Central America and the Caribbean. In 1997, the economy expanded by 3.6% and early estimates for 1998 pointed toward a 5% expansion. Because more than 74% of Panama's economic activities are in the service industry, there has been little development in agriculture and industry in recent years. One of every three Panamanians is part of the country's labor force, but unemployment has remained high in recent years. Panama's exports totaled US$592 million in 1997 while the country imported almost five times as much. The main export products are bananas, rice, corn, coffee, and sugarcane. Panama's main trade partner is the United States. The unit of currency is the *balboa*, which has a fixed exchange rate of one *balboa* = US$1.00. Because of the large influence of the United States, the US dollars are commonly used as currency.

Panama is known around the world because of its 80 km long (50 mi) transoceanic canal built by the United States in 1914. The virtual monopoly held by the canal over trade between the Atlantic and Pacific Oceans has continued to fuel resources into the economy. Tolls for crossing the canal were raised by 8.2% in 1997 and 7.5% in 1998. The transit fee for small vessels now stands at US$1,500. These increases were justified by claims that the canal will need to be expanded by the year 2020 to meet the expected increase in demand.

## POLITICAL BACKGROUND

Rodrigo de Bastidas was the first Spanish conqueror to visit the Isthmus of Panama in 1502. A year later, Christopher Columbus established a temporary settlement in the region, and in 1513, Vasco Nunez de Balboa walked from the Caribbean Sea to the Pacific Ocean, proving that the Isthmus was the shortest passage to link the two oceans. Since then, Panama became a center of trade for the colonial power. Gold and other goods were shipped from South America and were hauled across the Isthmus to be loaded to other ships waiting on the Caribbean Sea. Because of its strategic importance and its convenient location for trade between Europe and South America, Panama became a key colony of the Spanish Empire from 1538 to 1821. After some unsuccessful attempts at independence, Panama was incorporated as a province of the newly formed Republic of Colombia, and it remained as such until 1903. In the late 19th century, French entrepreneurs eyed the Isthmus of Panama to build a new transoceanic canal. Ferdinand de Lesseps led the effort from 1890 to 1900, but the dense jungle, tropical diseases, and shortage of labor derailed his attempt.

In 1903, with encouragement from the US and financial support from the French, Panama declared its independence from Colombia. A treaty with the US set the legal and political basis for US involvement in building the canal. The Hay-Bunau-Varilla Treaty granted land rights to the US in perpetuity in a ten-mile wide corridor between the two oceans. In total, Panama ceded a 533-square mile strip of land that divided the west and east regions of the country. The US completed the 80 km (50 mi) long canal in 1914. From 1903 until the 1950s, a commercial elite controlled political power although Panama was nominally a constitutional democracy. The military began mounting pressure upon the government and demanded a greater role in the administration and in the profit sharing from the revenues of the canal. In addition, the large US military presence in the country caused discontent among the military elite.

In October of 1968, President Arnulfo Arias, who had been elected president twice before and had been ousted as many times, was removed from office a third time by the Panamanian military. Brigadier General Omar Torrijos, the head of the National Guard, emerged as the leader of the military junta and eventually seized total control. A charismatic leader, Torrijos continued the practices of corruption and repression that had characterized his predecessors.

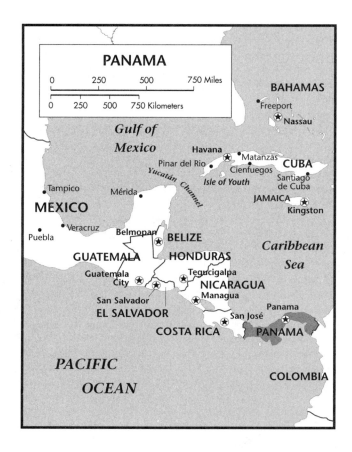

However, his leading cause was to repeal the 1903 Canal Treaty and recover control of the land where the canal had been built. Popular riots in 1964 led to the death of four US marines and more than 20 Panamanians. US and Panamanian negotiators proposed a new treaty in 1967, but neither country ratified the agreement. In 1973, new negotiations were initiated after the two countries signed a protocol known as the Kissinger-Tack declaration of principles. On 7 September 1977, President Jimmy Carter and General Torrijos signed the Panama Canal treaty in Washington D.C. After being approved by the Panamanians in a national plebiscite in October of the same year, the US Senate ratified the treaty in 1978. The new treaty granted the US primary responsibility for the operation and defense of the Canal until December of 1999. At that time, responsibility for the operation of the Canal would be transferred to Panama, but US military vessels would still have priority of passage. Panama would allow equal access to the Canal, and the US would have the right to ensure that the Canal remains open at all times. Together with the Canal treaty negotiations, Torrijos initiated a process of transition to democracy. He formed the Democratic Revolutionary Party and amended the 1972 constitution to allow for the reorganization of the unicameral legislative body. When Torrijos died in a plane accident in 1981, a political vacuum ensued.

Eventually, General Manuel Antonio Noriega emerged as the strongman of Panamanian politics. Although there were six different presidents during the 1980s, actual power remained in the hands of Noriega. In 1989, when an electoral defeat of his candidate was evident, Noriega suspended the presidential elections. Political and social turmoil, aggravated

by an ongoing economic crisis, threatened stability in Panama. Amid accusations of corruption and links to drug cartels, the US invaded Panama on 20 December 1989. Noriega was captured and brought to the US to face charges. He remains in a Florida prison to this day.

Guillermo Endara, a man of no political experience, was installed as president and governed until 1994. Inefficiency and corruption characterized his government, and the economic situation worsened. Ernesto Pérez Balladares of the Democratic Revolutionary Party (PRD) won the 1994 elections and assumed power. He restored political and social order and began a process of neo-liberal economic reforms aimed at restoring growth, reducing inflation, and creating employment. By the end of his administration, however, the economy was still in crisis. Pérez Balladares attempted to modify the Constitution to run for a second term in 1999, but he failed to muster a sufficient majority in the unicameral legislature. Elections held in May 1999 resulted in a victory for Mireya Moscoso, who became the first female president of Panama.

## PERSONAL BACKGROUND

Mireya Elisa Moscoso Rodríguez was born in Panama City on 1 July 1946. Moscoso's family came from the town of Pedasi, in the province of Los Santos. Her father was a teacher. She grew up and attended primary school in this small town. Her secondary education was completed at Maria Inmaculada Catholic School in Panama City. In 1964, she joined the presidential campaign of Arnulfo Arias, and two years later she became a sales manager for one of Arias's private companies. In 1968, at the age of 22, Moscoso worked as an assistant to President Arias and joined him in the US when he was forced into exile after being deposed by a military coup. In 1969, she and Arias were married in Miami. Moscoso attended Miami Dade Community College where she obtained a degree in interior design in 1974. She lived with Arias until his death in 1988 and returned to Panama after the 1989 US invasion.

## RISE TO POWER

Although she was not active in politics during her exile in the US and Spain, Moscoso accompanied her husband in his political career and vowed to defend his political goals after his death in 1988. Upon returning to Panama in 1990, she helped form the Arnulfista Party (named after Arnulfo Arias) in 1990. Moscoso made an attempt to win the presidency in 1994, but was defeated by Ernesto Pérez Balladares. Between 1994 and 1999, Moscoso worked to consolidate and strengthen the Arnulfista Party. Although she was the symbolic leader of the party, she faced opposition from other politicians who argued that a seasoned and experienced public official should contend for the presidency in 1999. In early 1999, she successfully defeated a primary challenge and was named presidential candidate of the Arnulfista Party. In part, her victory resulted from her strong and active opposition to Pérez Balladares' effort to amend the constitution to permit presidential re-election. Moscoso helped put together a coalition of opposition parties to block constitutional reform in the parliament. Elections were held on 2 May 1999, and Moscoso won 44.8% of the vote. She defeated Martín Torrijos, son of General Omar Torrijos—the man that had ousted Arnulfo Arias from power in 1968. Martín Torrijos was supported by the PRD, and he obtained 37.8% of the vote. She was inaugurated on 1 September 1999.

## LEADERSHIP

Moscoso will need to prove that she is more than just the widow of President Arias. Although she won the election, she will only have 14 seats in the 72-member parliament. In contrast, the PRD will have 34 seats—a sufficient force to constitute a formidable opposition. Moscoso campaigned against the re-election of Pérez Balladares and achieved national recognition for her efforts. However, her presidential program is generally regarded as lacking specificity, often relying on populist rhetoric. She will face a country left impoverished by the economic policies of Pérez Balladares. Approximately 36% of the population live in poverty, and unemployment stands at roughly 12%. Because she is perceived as more caring than Pérez Balladares, some of the reforms to control government spending and privatize government enterprises might be revised by the new administration as Moscoso tries to alleviate poverty and generate employment.

## DOMESTIC POLICY

Transfer of control over the operation of the Canal to Panama on 31 December 1999, was long an issue of sovereignty, as well as the driving force of Panamanian politics since the country was declared independent in 1903. Yet, this transfer is not the most urgent problem Moscoso will face. Dealing with the pressing economic problems that affect a large majority of the population (growing levels of unemployment, poverty, and worsening social services) will be monumental tasks for the inexperienced president. Moscoso will need to work hard to build a coalition in parliament in order to pass the legislation needed to stimulate growth, generate employment, and reduce poverty.

## FOREIGN POLICY

The main challenge for the Moscoso government will be to oversee a peaceful and trouble-free management of the Canal. Many experts predict that Panama will run into difficulties trying to operate the Canal and meet the 2020 deadline for the expansion, anticipating the expected increase in traffic. If Panama fails to successfully manage the operations of the canal, the US will be ready to step in, but national pride and the international reputation of the country will suffer tremendously. Moscoso needs to establish herself as a national leader, one who will unify opposing political interests in a country that is geographically positioned to play a key role in world economic growth of the 21st century. Many analysts have noted that Panama would probably not exist today as a country had it not been for the Canal. Moscoso will need to show that Panama is a country capable of operating one of the greatest engineering works of the 20th century and expanding its role to satisfy the demands of an ever more trade-interdependent world.

## ADDRESS

Presidente de la República de Panamá
Ciudad de Panamá, Panamá

## REFERENCES

BBC News. [Online] http://news2.thls.bbc.co.ok/hi/english/world/americas/newsid_334000/334161.stm (Accessed 2–3 May 1999).

*CIA World Fact Book. 1998 ed.* [Online] http://www.odci.gov/cia/publications/factbook/pm.html

CNN en Espanol. [Online] http://ccenespanol.com/latin/PAN/1999/05/06/moscoso.ap/index.html (Accessed 3–6 May 1999).

CNN interactive. [Online] http://cnncom/WORLD/americas/9905/03/panama.elex/ (Accessed 3 May 1999).

CNN interactive election watch. [Online] http://cnn.com/WORLD/election.watch/americas/panama2.html & http://cnn.com/WORLD/election.watch/americas/panama.html

*El Siglo Digital.* [Online] http://www.elsiglo.com/ediciones/3mayo99/principal.html (Accessed 3 May 1999).

*Encyclopaedia Britannica Year in Review 1998.* [Online] http://www.eb.com:180/bol/topic?eu=136632&sctn=1

Mireya Moscoso Home Page [Online] http://www.mireyaeselcambio.com/mireya.htm

Pastor, Robert. *Whirlpool. U.S. Foreign Policy Toward Latin America and the Caribbean.* Princeton University Press, 1992.

U.S. Department of State. *Background Notes: Panama,* March 1998. http://www.state.gov/background_notes/panama_0398_bgn.html (accessed 1/2000).

**Profile researched and written by Patricio Navia, New York University (12/99; updated 2/2000).**

# PAPUA NEW GUINEA

### Mekere Morauta
### Prime Minister

*(pronounced "may-KAY-ray moe-ROW-tah")*

*"We have chosen to give our children the chance of a decent life in their own country, in place of fearful descent into poverty, poor health and disorder."*

Papua New Guinea (PNG) is the Pacific Island nation that lies immediately north of Australia. It comprises the eastern half of the huge island of New Guinea, together with some 600 islands to the east, including the Bismarck Archipelago and Bougainville. Land area is about 463,000 sq km (almost 179,000 sq mi).

While most of the 4.7 million people are ethnically Melanesian, there are also small groups of Europeans, Chinese, and Polynesians. The official languages of government are English, Tok Pisin, and Hiri Motu. An estimated 800 distinct languages are still spoken, which is one of the obstacles to creating a sense of nationhood. The population is nominally Christian, but there are abundant traces of traditional forms of worship, often directed toward ancestral spirits.

Papua New Guinea has the potential to become the wealthiest Pacific Island nation, drawing on immense natural mineral and oil resources. It is estimated that if all known deposits were exploited, the country would replace South Africa as the world's leader in gold production. Copper mining and petroleum, as well as cocoa, coffee, and coconut products, are other significant export earners. Yet, the government budget regularly shows a deficit and remains heavily dependent on aid from Australia and international lending agencies. Though other Pacific Island nations are less well endowed with natural resources, PNG has the worst record in the Pacific in such social indicators as literacy, life expectancy, and maternal mortality rates. The unit of currency is the *kina,* which has fallen sharply in value since 1994.

## POLITICAL BACKGROUND

Initial colonization of what is now Papua New Guinea took place as part of contests between Great Britain and Imperial Germany over Pacific Island possessions.

After the First World War, in which Germany lost all its Pacific colonies, what had been German New Guinea became a Mandated Territory of the League of Nations, administered by Australia. The Mandated Territory consisted of the northeastern portion of the mainland, together with islands as far east as Bougainville. Australia retained control of the Territory of Papua, the southeastern portion of the mainland, and smaller adjacent islands. The Mandated Territory was distinctive for its greater prosperity, based on coconut plantations mostly operated by Australian firms and individuals. Papua had a small administrative budget and a paternalistic policy aimed at protecting the indigenous population from being exploited.

Japan's invasion of the Pacific in the second World War carried as far into PNG as the occupation of the north coast of the main island, and of New Britain and Bougainville. Allied counterattacks on Japanese positions brought destruction of property and considerable loss of life to the local people in these areas. During the war, both Papua and the Mandated Territory were administered as a single political unit, and this continued after military operations ended. Technically, the legal status of Papua remained distinct from that of New Guinea, which became officially a Trust Territory of the United Nations with Australia as trustee. However, the postwar Australian government treated the entire area as the single Territory of Papua and New Guinea.

Beginning in the 1960s, Australia came under considerable international pressure to grant independence to both Papua and New Guinea as a single nation. At that time there had been little development of political and social institutions, of the kind that would have made transition to independence an easy one. All real political authority was in the hands of Australians; Papua New Guineans (as they began to be called) occupied only the lowest echelons of the public service.

This would begin to change rapidly beginning in 1964 with the establishment of the first elected legislative body, the House of Assembly, empowered to enact legislation affecting the whole territory. Voting for the House of Assembly was the first experience of this kind for most of the indigenous population, and it launched the first steps toward the independence that was achieved in September 1975. At that time, the independent state of Papua New Guinea was established as a constitutional monarchy and a member of the British Commonwealth, with the British sovereign as head of state.

Papua New Guinea is governed by the so-called Westminister system. This means that an elected parliament is the national legislative authority. Parliament consists of 109 members chosen by universal adult suffrage for five-year terms; 89 of these are elected from local constituencies. The rest are elected from each of the nation's 19 provinces and the National Capital District (NCD) centered in Port Moresby. Executive authority resides in the prime minister and cabinet, all of whom are elected members of Parliament (MPs). The prime minister must demonstrate that he commands the support of a majority of MPs in order to form a cabinet. In Britain, where the Westminister system originated, this works smoothly enough because of long traditions, well-established and disciplined political parties, and an independent public service. However, these conditions do not exist in Papua New Guinea, leading to a degree of political instability that has attracted international concern.

Traditionally, indigenous politics operated on a very small scale in what became PNG. Few of the many language groups had what could be recognized as true chiefs with authority over large groups. Today many people still recognize first loyalties to a clan, an influential individual, or at most a language or geographic area. One consequence is large numbers of candidates, with no more than nominal party affiliation, running for Parliament in a single electorate. The successful candidate does not have to get a majority of votes cast. In 1992, the last election that has been completely analyzed, 87 of the winning candidates received less than 30% of the votes cast in their respective races. In such cases, MPs can hardly expect to enjoy the respect or long-term support of those they are supposed to represent. It is not surprising that each election sees a high turnover of MPs.

A Westminister system depends on the existence of a relatively small number of well-organized political parties, but in PNG even the most successful parties have difficulty commanding a majority in Parliament. Coalition governments have been the rule since independence. In 1997, 39 MPs were elected as Independents, without party affiliation or loyalty. The head of a party cannot even count on other MPs in his own group to back his attempt to form a government. Party switching is one of the most common features of PNG politics. This can lead to votes of no confidence in the governing prime minister, which makes formation of a whole new government necessary. No prime minister has ever served a full five-year term. All these factors have meant that there are few apparent links between party politics, voting, and actual governance of the country.

## PERSONAL BACKGROUND

Mekere Morauta was born in 1946 in Kukipi Village, in what is now Gulf Province. His father was a local government councillor and a church deacon with the London Missionary Society. Morauta received his primary education at local mission and government elementary schools. His secondary education began in the provincial high school at Kerema and was completed at the select Sogeri National High School in Port Moresby. He was among the first group of students to enter the University of Papua New Guinea when that institution was founded. He studied at Flinders University in South Australia on an exchange program and received his bachelor's degree in economics from the University of Papua New Guinea (UPNG) in 1970. Morauta is presently married to the former Roslyn McCullagh. He has one son by a former marriage.

## RISE TO POWER

Morauta's first employment after graduating from UPNG was as a researcher in the Department of Labour. He moved from there into the administration's Office of the Economic Adviser and eventually became the first native-born secretary of the Department of Finance on the eve of independence. During his tenure as finance secretary he was awarded an honorary doctorate by the University of Technology in Lae.

From 1983 until 1992, he served as managing director of the state-owned PNG Banking Corporation. In recognition of his service to finance and banking, Queen Elizabeth II knighted Morauta in 1990. Three years later, the government appointed him Central Bank governor. He left the Central Bank in 1994 and spent the next three years as head of his own private business, Morauta Investments Ltd., which combined fisheries, real estate, and publishing.

It was not until the 1997 national election that Morauta entered Parliament. Running as an Independent, he was elected Member for Moresby-Northwest. He initially joined a coalition government that elected Bill Skate as prime minister. Skate's own People's National Congress Party had won only six seats, and his government was soon in difficulty. His administration was accused of corruption and mismanagement. The kina's value fell below US30¢ for the first time in history. As the country's economic situation became worse, Skate attempted to obtain a large loan from Taiwan in exchange for recognizing that nation rather than the People's Republic of China. This proposal further eroded public confidence. By July 1999, Skate faced a vote of no confidence as 16 members of his own coalition abandoned him. On July 7, he resigned.

After being fired as minister for fisheries by Skate earlier that year, Morauta assumed leadership of the People's Democratic Movement (PDM), which had won 10 seats in the 1997 election. In the negotiations to form a new government, the speaker of Parliament, John Pundari, first allied himself with PDM, briefly shifted to Skate's group, then returned to the PDM fold. When Morauta was chosen prime minister on July 14, Pundari became deputy prime minister.

## LEADERSHIP

Morauta has the image of a technocrat, combining personal honesty with a concern for rational management, especially in financial matters. After becoming prime minister, he apologized publicly for not having taken a more effective role in the Skate coalition. He is popular with Australian academics and diplomats, who believe he is more likely to bring about the policies they would like to see instituted in PNG. This reputation is reflected in the slight rise in value of the *kina* after he took office.

## DOMESTIC POLICY

There is no question that Morauta's first goal is to restore economic well-being to his country. He declared after being sworn in that PNG was "bankrupt." Among his first appointments were a new secretary for finance and treasury and a new governor of the Central Bank. By instituting new monetary and fiscal policies, he hopes to stabilize the *kina* to a respectable position in the international currency markets. It is likely that he will be more aggressive than earlier prime ministers in privatizing government industries, like the national airline. A recent rise in world gold prices may assist him to reach his goals. He will also push for early development of a natural gas pipeline to Australia that has the potential of bringing US$200 million in annual revenue.

For more than a decade, armed conflict has wracked the island of Bougainville, where initial violence against a huge copper mine escalated into demands for the island's secession from PNG. Morauta seems committed to continue a policy of negotiation, rather than a military solution, following a cease-fire early in 1999. He first assumed the portfolio for Bougainville affairs himself, but in August 1999 he turned it over to Sir Michael Somare, PNG's first prime minister. Both Morauta and Somare are sympathetic to granting Bougainville the maximum degree of political autonomy, short of complete independence. Though there are many problems yet to be resolved among the different factions, peace seems more likely today than at any time since 1989.

## FOREIGN POLICY

Foreign policy issues come directly out of those which must be solved on the domestic front. Most pressing is restoring aid and loan support from other countries and international agencies that are vital to PNG's economic health. Australia, the World Bank, and the International Monetary Fund had withdrawn or suspended their assistance because the Skate government had failed to institute suggested fiscal reforms.

One of Morauta's first official acts was to attend the Asia Pacific Economic Cooperation forum's summit meeting in New Zealand. By presenting his administration's 1999 and proposed year 2000 budgets, he sought renewed international support. His efforts were rewarded in October 1999 when Australia's prime minister, John Howard, announced a new assistance package worth at least US$195 million. In addition, Australia is likely to continue its annual aid of US$200 million, tied to specific projects. Earlier the Asian Development Bank had pledged a US$25 million loan to support health services.

Morauta was quick to repudiate Skate's proposed deal with Taiwan in favor of continuing PNG's "two China" policy. While expressing regret for the tragic occurrences in East Timor, he has yet to make any firm commitment to international intervention in that island's affairs. He is more likely to actively pursue the free trade policy that has developed among the Melanesian Spearhead Group (MSG). Founded in 1988 by PNG, Vanuatu, and the Solomon Islands, MSG now includes Fiji and the New Caledonia independence coalition, the Kanak Socialist National Liberation Front. Beginning in 1994, the three founding nations agreed to eliminate any duties levied on tea from PNG, canned tuna from the Solomons, and beef from Vanuatu. Since then, the number of goods traded freely has grown to about 30, including fresh vegetables, coffee, animal feed, and bread.

In both domestic and foreign policies, Morauta is following paths that appeal to larger nations, like Australia. It remains to be seen if he can maintain the support of Parliament, which has yet to sustain a prime minister for a full five-year term of office.

## ADDRESS

Office of the Prime Minister
P.O. Box 6030
Boroko, Papua New Guinea

## REFERENCES

Economist Intelligence Unit. *EIU Country Profile: Papua New Guinea, 1999–2000.*
*Islands Business,* August–September 1999.
*Pacific Islands Monthly,* August 1999.
*Papua New Guinea Post-Courier,* June–September 1999.

**Profile researched and written by Eugene Ogan, Professor Emeritus, University of Minnesota (12/99; updated 2/2000).**

# PARAGUAY

## Luis González Macchi
### President
*(pronounced "loo-EES gohn-ZAH-lace MAH-kee")*

*"We must seize this great opportunity to change the destiny of this country."*

In the heart of South America lies the small Republic of Paraguay. This landlocked country is bordered by Bolivia on the north and northwest, by Brazil on the east, and by Argentina on the south and west. It has an area of 406,752 sc km (157,048 sq mi). The Paraguay River divides the country into two regions. The eastern region is the highlands area where 90% of the country's 5.4 million people live. It contains the densely forested Paraná Plateau, rolling foothills, marshes and grasslands. The western region, known as the *Chaco Boreal*, is a vast, flat plain with rough grasses, cacti, and thorny shrubs. Meteorological extremes of drought and flooding have discouraged settlement and agricultural development in the western region. The Paraná River defines the country's southeastern boundary and provides the only outlet to the sea. Asunción is Paraguay's capital and largest city, with a population of about 1,262,000.

Most Paraguayans are *mestizos* (people of mixed Spanish and Guaraní Indian ancestry). About 10% of the population is Guaraní, the first settlers in the region. Although Spanish is the official language, Guaraní is spoken with equal frequency. Government publications are produced in both languages. Almost all Paraguayans are Roman Catholic, although there are small pockets of Mennonites and other Protestant denominations. Life expectancy is high—70 years for males and 75 years for females. The literacy rate is about 92%.

Paraguay's market economy, once dominated by agriculture, forestry, and fishing, is now largely service oriented. Soybeans are the largest export crops, followed by cotton, meat, and timber. There is also a large informal sector of street vendors and those engaged in the re-export of imported consumer goods such as electronic equipment, office products, liquor, perfume, and tobacco products. Paraguay is a member of Mercosur, the Southern Cone Common Market. Brazil is Paraguay's most important trading partner, accounting for about one-third of all trade. Argentina is a distant second. In the late 1970s and early 1980s, construction of the world's largest hydroelectric dam, the Itaipu, on the Paraná River brought Paraguay the highest economic growth rate in Latin America. As of early 2000, however, Paraguay's economy was in recession following the devaluation of the Brazilian currency and a virtual halt in trading activity. Brazil is part owner of the Itaipu hydro complex, which not only employs 400,000 Brazilian peasants but also supplies 20% of Brazil's electricity. Paraguay's gross domestic product (GDP) contracted by 2.5% in 1999, continuing a seven-year trend. The country's banking sector collapsed in 1998 due to corruption and mismanagement, causing thousands of Paraguayans to lose their life savings. The unit of currency is the *guaraní*.

## POLITICAL BACKGROUND

Although both Portuguese and Spanish explorers came to Paraguay during the early part of the 16th century, by 1537 the territory was under Spanish rule. In 1609, the Jesuits arrived and over the next century they established more than 40 missions throughout the country. In 1767, however, King Charles III banished the Jesuits from the entire Spanish empire, that included Paraguay. On 14 May 1811, Paraguayans deposed the Spanish governor and declared their independence from Spain. Five years later, the educated, but authoritarian José Gaspar Rodríguez de Francia was declared ruler for life by the fledgling republic's legislature. Despite his isolationist policies, the country flourished and a tradition of dictatorial rule was established that prevailed for the next 150 years. In 1865, Paraguay's president, Francisco Solano Lopez, provoked a devastating five-year war with Brazil, Argentina, and Uruguay because they were refused access to the Paraná River basin. During the war three-quarters of Paraguay's male population was killed and the overall population decreased from one million to 221,000. In 1932, after the discovery of oil, Paraguay again went to war in a territorial dispute, this time with Bolivia. The three-year Chaco War gave the victorious Paraguay some additional land, but little else.

During the late 19th century, two political parties emerged, the Colorado Party and the Liberal Party. The Liberal Party held power during the first four decades of the 20th century. But for most of the last 120 years the Colorado Party has controlled Paraguayan political life. In 1954, after more than a decade of coups and revolts, General Alfredo Stroessner took the reigns of power and ruled with an iron fist for the next 45 years. The Stroessner administration, in a strong alliance with the Colorado Party, was characterized by corruption, persecution of political opponents, and human rights violations.

Stroessner was deposed in 1989 by Major General Andrés Rodríguez, who represented a rival faction within the Colorado Party. Rodríguez began a process of transition toward democracy in Paraguay. He ended censorship of the press and promoted a new constitution, adopted in June 1992. Under the new charter, the president is elected to a five-year term and may not succeed himself. Paraguay has a

## PARAGUAY

bicameral legislature, one chamber of 45 senators, another of 80 deputies. In 1993, Juan Carlos Wasmosy became the country's first civilian elected president in nearly 50 years. Wasmosy completed his five-year term and was succeeded by Raúl Cubas, the nominee of the Colorado Party, in May 1998.

The circumstances under which Cubas was elected sowed the seeds for his premature departure from office and the turmoil that engulfed his country. In 1996, Cubas served as finance minister in the Wasmosy government. He sided with his longtime friend, General Lino Oviedo, who led an unsuccessful coup attempt against Wasmosy. When Oviedo was stripped of his rank, Cubas campaigned to nominate him as the Colorado Party's presidential candidate. Oviedo selected Cubas as his vice-presidential running mate. When Oviedo won the primary election, Wasmosy had him arrested. After being convicted of insubordination, Oviedo was sentenced to 10 years in prison.

Cubas became the Colorado Party's presidential candidate and was elected with 52% of the vote. He was always seen as the stand-in for Oviedo. Even his campaign slogan was indicative: "Cubas in government, Oviedo in power." Cubas, who never had a strong political base, did not last long as the country's president. His decision to free Oviedo a few days after taking office proved to be his undoing. On March 28, 1999, under international and domestic pressure, he resigned and flew to Brazil. Luis González Macchi was installed as the country's new president.

## PERSONAL BACKGROUND

Luis Angel González Macchi was born on 13 December 1947, the son of Saul González, a former minister of justice and labor under Alfredo Stroessner. In his younger days he was a professional basketball player. He joined the Colorado party in 1966 and received his formal training in labor law at the National University of Asuncion. During the 1970s and 1980s González Macchi served in various posts in the Ministry of Justice and Labor. In 1993, he was elected to the Chamber of Deputies and served as its vice president in 1993–1994. In 1998, González Macchi was elected to the Senate and became its president. He is divorced from his first wife and is now married to a former Miss Paraguay, Susana Galli. They have a one-year-old child.

## RISE TO POWER

By the time Cubas was inaugurated on 15 August 1998, the Colorado Party was deeply divided between supporters of Oviedo (oviedistas) and his detractors. The split represented a division between those seeking a more democratic governance for Paraguay and those still wedded to the strong-man form of governance under former dictator Stroessner. Three days after his inauguration, Cubas commuted Oviedo's sentence, provoking a national uproar and infuriating many within the Colorado Party. Immediately, key leaders from all four political parties called for his impeachment. Although the Supreme Court annulled Cubas' decision, he defied the ruling and refused to return Oviedo to prison. The political crisis continued to brew over the next several months, with little evidence of resolution. In late March 1999, weeks before the legislature was set to launch impeachment proceedings, Vice President Luis Maria Argaña, who would have succeeded Cubas, was assassinated. Oviedo and Cubas were widely blamed for Argaña's death. Demonstrations and rioting broke out on the streets of the capital city of Asunción, and sniper fire killed five and injured hundreds.

Invoking the "democratic clause" in the Mercosur treaty, which requires member countries to be practicing democracies, representatives from Brazil, Argentina, and Uruguay, as well as Germany and the United States stepped in to resolve the crisis. The international delegation joined representatives of Paraguay's political parties and the Catholic Church to negotiate a peaceful settlement. On March 28, Cubas resigned and the Paraguayan legislature installed Luis González Macchi, president of the Senate and next in the line of succession, as the country's new president. Cubas was exiled to Brazil, joining former dictator Stroessner; Oviedo went to Argentina.

## LEADERSHIP

After an initial period of uncertainty about González Macchi's status as president, the Supreme Court ruled in May 1999 that he will serve out the unexpired term of Cubas (until 2003). A new vice president to replace the assassinated Argaña will be chosen in a November 1999 election.

The armed forces have pledged their support for the new government. González Macchi has already begun to purge the military and police of Oviedo loyalists. He is working with the legislature to extradite Oviedo and Cubas so that they can be tried for their roles in the deaths of Argaña and the demonstrators in Asuncion in late March.

González Macchi has signaled his intention to govern differently than his predecessors. He immediately established a government of "national unity" that included members of the two principal opposition parties: the *Partido Liberal Radical Auténtico* (PLRA), with its rural constituency, and the *Partido Encuentro Nacional* (PEN), an urban-based, left-of-center party. Of his first 11 cabinet appointments, González Macchi entrusted two key posts, the foreign ministry and the ministry of agriculture, to members of the PLRA. Likewise, PEN was given two posts: justice and labor, and industry and commerce. The Colorado Party retains control of the other seven ministries, including the key positions of finance and interior.

González Macchi faces many obstacles. Paraguay's democratic institutions are weak, political infighting is endemic, and the country's economic problems are far from solved. Moreover, the recent political crisis strengthened elements of Paraguayan civil society, including students, peasants, and unions. These groups have discovered new unity, purpose, and power as a result of their role in the ouster of Cubas. But they have turned down invitations to join González Macchi's "national unity" government and have begun pressing their own demands.

## DOMESTIC POLICY

González Macchi's cabinet appointments indicate that management of the economy will be a shared responsibility of all three parties. This is clearly the central priority of the new government, which faces severe funding problems. Nearly all of Paraguay's roadwork has been put on hold due to the lack of funds. Even the country's externally funded projects have been delayed because of the political crisis. Following the Colorado Party's traditional stance, González Macchi quickly distanced himself from a pure free-market philosophy toward economic development, indicating the need for government intervention in regulating the economy. Nonetheless, the new government has pledged to privatize the state-owned water, electricity, and telephone companies. He also announced plans to restart stalled projects and reinvigorate the economy through a series of investments and loans aimed at public works, agriculture, industry, and low-cost housing. But the government will need to move quickly to address high unemployment, the legacy of corruption from Wasmosy's presidency, and banking sector reform.

## FOREIGN POLICY

For more than a century Paraguay has been an isolationist country. In the past decade, however, it has slowly and cautiously emerged from its national cocoon and become part of the international community. The recent political turmoil, however, has threatened Paraguay's transformation. Brazil's president, Fernando Henrique Cardoso, warned that Paraguay must resolve its internal civil strife and restore its democratic credentials if it wants to remain part of the international community and, in particular, retain its trading relationships as a member of Mercosur. Moreover, Paraguay has had troubled relations with the United States and was decertified in February 1999 because of its participation in smuggling, money laundering, and international drug trafficking.

## ADDRESS

Oficina del Presidente
Palacio de Gobierno
Asuncion, Paraguay

## REFERENCES

Associated Press, 22 August 1998.
Economist Intelligence Unit, 2nd Quarter, 1999
Inter Press Service, 20 August 1998–29 March 1999.
*Latin American Weekly Report,* 9 March–25 May 1999.
*Michigan Daily,* 29 March 1999.
*New York Times,* 1 March–29 April 1999.
*Notisur,* 8 January 1999.

**Profile researched and written by James L. McDonald, Senior International Policy Analyst, Bread for the World, Silver Spring, MD (9/99; revised by Patricio Navia, New York University 4/2000).**

# PERÚ

## Alberto Fujimori
## President

*(pronounced "al-BARE-to foo-hee-MOH-ree")*

*"Power fascinates me."*

The Republic of Perú is located on the west coast of the South American continent, bordered to the north by Ecuador and Colombia, to the east by Brazil and Bolivia, and to the south by Chile. The third largest South American country, Peru's territory of 1.28 million sq km (496,222 sq mi) encompasses three distinct geographical areas: a narrow coastal plain along the country's 2800 km (1400 mi) Pacific Ocean coastline; the high sierra of the Andes; and the interior region of foothills, tropical rainforest and lowlands which includes the headwaters of the Amazon. The coastal area, home to one-third of the population of nearly 26.5 million, is the industrial and commercial center. Lima, the nation's capital, is located about midway down the coastline.

The official languages are Spanish and Quechua. Aymara is an important but not official language, which with Quechua, is spoken by Perú's Indians. Approximately 45% of the population is of Incan descent, and this sector remains largely unintegrated with the white (15%) and mestizo (37%) populations in Perú. Blacks, Asians and other groups make up the remaining 3% of the population. Roman Catholicism is the state religion, although there are some evangelical Protestant groups which have become increasingly powerful in the interior of the country.

The basis of Perú's economy traditionally has been the extraction of minerals such as copper, silver, zinc, and lead. Since the discovery in 1971 of petroleum in the northeastern jungle, oil has become the nation's leading export. Agriculture plays a significant role in the economy, with almost 40% of the labor force involved either in subsistence or commercial farming or fishing. The most important legal cash crops are coffee, cotton, and sugar. Coca, the plant from which cocaine is derived, brings in over US$1 billion annually in foreign exchange. The Peruvian unit of currency is the new *sol*. Per capita GDP is US$4,300, but nearly 70% of Peruvians live in extreme poverty.

## POLITICAL BACKGROUND

Perú's human history dates from at least 10,500 years ago. The seat of a series of indigenous ruling civilizations, Peru is perhaps most widely known for the last of these, the Inca Empire. The Spanish, led by Francisco Pizarro, landed in Peru in 1531, drawn by the search for the region's legendary mineral riches. The Incas, debilitated by a recent civil war, were easily conquered: the capital at Cusco fell in 1533, and by 1542, the Spanish had consolidated control. Pizarro founded Lima in 1535. Spear-headed by Simon Bolivar and José de San Martín, Perú's liberation from Spanish dominion was proclaimed on 28 July 1821, and achieved in December 1824. Although it took 55 years for Spain to recognize the new nation, Perú's independence marked the end of 250 years of Spanish rule in South America.

Since independence, Peruvian political life has been characterized by alternating periods of constitutional civilian government and extra-constitutional military regimes. Most of the military interventions were of brief duration, followed by a return to elected government. In October 1968, however, the military ousted Fernando Belaunde Terry of the Popular Action party in a bloodless coup, and maintained itself in power until May 1980. Military control of the government ended with the election of Belaunde once again to the presidency. In 1985, Alan Garcia Perez of the American Popular Revolutionary Alliance (APRA), Perú's oldest mass party, was elected to the presidency. Despite *Aprista* majorities in both houses of Congress, Garcia's administration was from the start mired in controversy and crisis. The economy was in a freefall, terrorists from both the *Sendero Luminoso* and *Tupac Amaru* movements were wreaking havoc, and Garcia and his ministers seemed unable to do anything to improve the situation.

The constitution provides for executive power to be held by the president, who is elected to a five-year term. Under a 1993 amendment, a president may serve consecutive terms. If no candidate for the presidency receives an absolute majority of votes, a second-round runoff between the two top vote-getters is necessary. There is a 20-member appointed cabinet, which may include a prime minister. Legislative power is vested in the bicameral Congress, composed of the Senate and the Chamber of Deputies. The Senate includes 60 members elected on a regional basis to five-year terms, plus former constitutionally-elected presidents as life members. The Chamber of Deputies is composed of 180 members elected to five-year terms on the basis of proportional representation. Voting is mandatory for all citizens over the age of 18, including illiterates.

## PERSONAL BACKGROUND

Alberto Fujimori was born in Lima on 28 July 1938, to parents who immigrated to Peru from Japan in 1934. Opponents have often claimed Fujimori was born in Japan, making him ineligible for the presidency, but the accusations have never been substantiated. His father owned a prosperous tire repair shop in Lima, which was confiscated

418

by the government in the wake of the Japanese attack on Pearl Harbor. Although Fujimori's parents remained Buddhists, and his mother never learned to speak Spanish, their five children were raised as Spanish-speaking Roman Catholics. Alberto attended a Catholic high school and earned an undergraduate degree from the National Agrarian University. He later earned a master's degree in math from the University of Wisconsin at Madison. His continued educational pursuits led to his eventually becoming an agronomist. He became rector of the National Agrarian University and president of the Association of University Rectors. Fujimori also hosted a widely viewed political talk show on the state television station. Prior to being elected to the presidency, Fujimori's political experience was limited to his participation in two government commissions.

Fujimori claims to be descended from a Japanese noble warrior, and during the 1990 campaign for the presidency, he appeared at photo sessions on several occasions wearing a kimono and brandishing a samurai sword. Fujimori is separated from his wife, Susana Higuchi. Her outspoken criticism of some of her husband's associates and her charges of corruption among some of Fujimori's advisors and his relatives led the president to relieve her of her role as first lady, and to ban her from the presidential residence. In 1995, Higuchi tried to run for the presidency, but the national electoral tribunal disqualified her. Congress also enacted a bill prohibiting presidential relatives from running for office. In 2000, Higuchi remained a popular former first lady, and was running for a congressional seat. While her criticisms against Fujimori had become milder, she remained a vocal critic of his administration. The couple has four children. Their daughter Keiko, who has been the most supportive of her father's political aspirations, has assumed many of the official duties vacated by her mother.

## RISE TO POWER

An agrarian engineer with no political experience or even party affiliation, Fujimori initiated his bid for the presidency late in 1989, well after the other candidates had begun campaigning. Dwarfed by the expensive, splashy campaign of front-runner Mario Vargas Llosa, Fujimori's low-key, low-budget, grass roots organization went virtually unnoticed by analysts. In the first round voting on 8 April 1990, Fujimori and his *Cambio '90* (Change '90) Party came within two percentage points of Vargas Llosa. The run-off, set for June 1990, was considered by most to be a dead heat. On 10 June 1990, with no support from Peru's traditionally influential sectors, Alberto Fujimori soundly defeated Vargas Llosa, with 57% of the votes, becoming the first ethnic Japanese head of state outside Japan.

The 1995 campaign again pitted Fujimori against a figure of international renown—former secretary general of the United Nations, Javier Perez de Cuellar. This time, however, Fujimori was the overwhelming favorite. Fujimori limited his campaign to personal appearances at groundbreakings and initiations of infrastructure improvements, and allowed his record to speak for itself. He did not address any of the issues being raised by other candidates. Despite frequent pessimistic polls showing erosion of his support, Fujimori again captured the presidency on 9 April 1995, with 64% of valid votes cast; Perez de Cuellar captured 22% of the vote. The president's

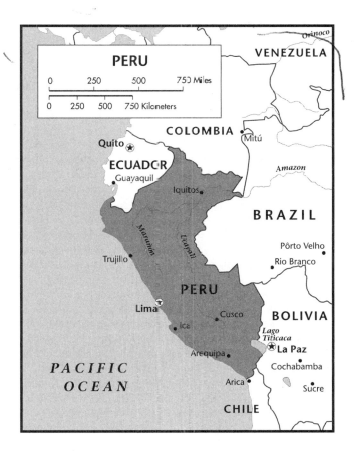

party also gained majorities in both houses of Congress, thus assuring Fujimori's control over Peru's direction in the next five years.

Although the Constitution prohibited the president from serving a third term, Fujimori argued that the Constitution was written after he was already in office and therefore would apply only to his bid for a fourth term. The Congress fired three Supreme Court justices who disagreed with this position. As the election year approached, Fujimori moved to neutralize important opponents, including former President Alan Garcia, who was considered a possible presidential candidate.

By 1999, Fujimori was falling out of favor in Perú and the international community. Despite a major shift in economic policy, unemployment and extreme poverty was widespread. The United States, a strong supporter of Fujimori, was now criticizing his government for clamping down on democracy. Fujimori controlled the press, which ridiculed and slandered all opposition candidates. But Fujimori was not untouchable. The respected *El Comercio* newspaper reported Fujimori's supporters had forged one million signatures to ensure his reelection. Fujimori raised the monthly minimum wage 18%, to US$118 and handed tiny pieces of land to more than 150,000 peasants. With pork-barrel politics, Fujimori seemed assured of a third term. By early 2000, a candidate with no political experience, much like Fujimori during his first campaign, began to gain a strong following. Alejandro Toledo, a 54-year-old business school professor, quickly established himself as Fujimori's main opponent. Educated in the US, Toledo came from a working-class family. His father was a bricklayer, and his mother sold fish at a street market.

His strong Indian features quickly gained him an important following from the nation's Amerindian population, traditionally strong supporters of Fujimori.

As Toledo's bid for the Presidency gained strength, it became clear he was in the midst of one of the dirtiest campaigns in Perú's history. Television and newspapers controlled by the Fujimori administration relentlessly attacked Toledo and the other candidates, and continually praised the president. The election held on 9 April 2000 was immediately criticized for serious and widespread accusations of fraud. United States officials warned Perú that a Fujimori victory would lead to economic sanctions. The Organization of American States said the election had been seriously compromised, and demanded a second round. Fujimori remained quiet during the counting of the votes, only saying that Peruvians needed to respect the outcome of the election. Tens of thousands of Peruvians demanded a second round. After long delays, the electoral board said Fujimori had received 49.84% of the 50% majority vote needed to prevent a runoff election. Toledo received 40.31%. A second election was called for June 2000. Fujimori, who had run a low-key campaign, became more active as he attempted to diffuse Toledo's growing popularity. By late April, national polls showed Fujimori with 46% and Toledo with 42%.

The Fujimori government set the second round of voting for May 28. Charging that Fujimori controlled the media by using threats to keep them from covering the Toledo campaign, Toledo declined to participate in the run-off election, a move that caused his support among some voters to erode. International observers, disappointed that the government would not postpone the elections until effective monitoring procedures could be established, left the country prior to the May 28 balloting. Fujimori won with 50.8% of the vote to Toledo's 16.7%. (Toledo, refusing to vote, also urged his supporters to stay away from the polls.)

## LEADERSHIP

Fujimori was an unusual candidate in Peruvian politics. Of Japanese descent, he had no support from the elite circles that had traditionally ruled the country. During his presidency, he emphasised his Japanese descent, in part to show that he was not part of the status quo. Unlike many past presidential candidates, he openly sought the backing of Perú's Amerindians, who came to see him as a defender of their rights. During his presidency, Fujimori ended hyperinflation, reducing it from a high of 7,500% per year to single digits by 1999. Yet, his most enduring claim was his crushing defeat of leftist groups, including the feared *Sendero Luminoso* (Shining Path guerrillas). The United States praised him for his actions, but in time, US officials became some of Fujimori's most vocal critics.

Fujimori's military and political victories are not simply of his own making. Early on, Fujimori established a strong relation with Vladimiro Montesinos, who became head of Fujimori's intelligence service, and was seldom seen in public. Montesinos has been credited with masterminding the offensive against the leftist guerrillas and Fujimori's hold on power. Throughout the 1990s and early 2000, the true value of Montesinos to Fujimori could never be fully established.

Inaugurated on 28 July 1990, Fujimori took the helm of a nation in crisis. *Sendero Luminoso* guerrillas controlled over half the national territory; GDP had declined 22%, and personal income had eroded 63% in the previous two years; over 70% of Peruvians lived in abject poverty; inflation was 7,650%; and the nation was in default on its foreign loans. Fujimori made it clear that he had two goals: to eradicate *Sendero Luminoso* (Shining Path) and to set the economy back on track. With no legislative base from which to accomplish these goals, but armed with sweeping emergency powers, Fujimori pushed through enormous amounts of legislation and economic reforms. Some of his anti-terrorist legislation alarmed Congress, which began to openly question Fujimori's commitment to due process.

On 5 April 1992, Fujimori dissolved the Congress and the judiciary, suspended the Constitution, and assumed dictatorial powers in what has come to be called an *auto golpe* (self-coup). The military backed this maneuver in return for a freer hand in combating terrorism and a blind eye towards their involvement in drug trafficking. The Peruvian people also supported the president, due to widespread contempt for allegedly corrupt politicians and judges. In response to a general outcry from the international community, Fujimori announced that a constituent assembly would be elected in November 1992, to rewrite the constitution. In the November elections, Fujimori's party won 45 of the 80 seats in the assembly; the best showing for any of the other 17 parties was six seats. The first act of the new assembly was to declare Fujimori a constitutional president.

Fujimori built his reputation on his unwillingness to negotiate with leftist terrorists and his tough stance against any perceived enemies. He scored a major victory with the arrest of Abimael Guzman, the intellectual leader of the Shining Path guerrillas, in 1992. In 1995, Perú went to war with neighboring Ecuador, stirring patriotic sentiments and leading to a victory at the polls for Fujimori. Four years later, the second-highest leader of Sendero, Elizabeth Cardenas Huayta, was arrested. In April 1997, military commandos stormed the Japanese Embassy, where Tupac Amaru rebels had been holding hostages since December 1996. All 14 of the guerillas were killed. As he had done before, a beaming Fujimori struck victory poses in front of cameras. While he appeared to be defending democracy, Fujimori was growing into a highly autocratic and authoritarian leader. By April 2000, Fujimori had lost a great deal of support among Peruvians and he was under great international pressure to open up the political process.

## DOMESTIC POLICY

Fujimori owes much of his success to improvements in the economy and his war against leftist guerrilla groups. Fujimori had vowed to correct the economic situation without hurting the poor. Nevertheless, he was forced to impose austerity measures under IMF guidelines for renegotiation of the nation's foreign debt. Despite brutal ramifications of the "Fujishock" for the poor, the reforms turned Peru's economy around in extremely short order. Inflation fell dramatically, the economy became productive, the state initiated an aggressive privatization plan, and foreign investment nearly doubled after Fujimori's agreement to abide by IMF economic guidelines. In 1994, inflation was 35%, and GDP growth was 12%, the highest in the world. The privatization that is occurring in Peru brought with it enormous costs; not the least of which was job losses in a nation already plagued by unsustainable levels of unemployment and underemployment. By 2000, Fujimori had slowed down the pace of economic liberalization and privatization of state-owned enterprises. He decided not to sell water companies, refineries, and hydroelectric plants. GDP growth for 2000 was predicted to reach 6.5%. Fujimori remained vague about any economic plans during a third term. In early 2000, he said Alejandro Toledo would bring disorder to the nation if he was elected.

Perhaps the single most important accomplishment of Fujimori's presidency was the capture on 12 September 1992, of the leader of *Sendero Luminoso*, Abimael Guzman Reynoso. Captured along with him were computer tapes outlining the structure of the terrorist organization and lists of other leaders. Within months, other leaders were captured, tried, and sentenced. Guzman pled guilty to being the leader of *Sendero* and was sentenced to life imprisonment.

In the 12 years between its inception and the capture of Guzman, the war with *Sendero Luminoso* claimed more than 20,000 lives, disrupted basic services, and necessitated the placement of nearly 50% of the national territory under emergency law. Army frustration with its inability to win the war led to widespread human rights violations, which were not discouraged by Fujimori in the period after the April 1992 coup. An increase in *Sendero* activity in spring 1995, led Fujimori to ask Congress to pass an amnesty law for those who commit human rights violations while combating terrorism.

## FOREIGN POLICY

Fujimori maintained an amicable relationship with neighboring countries and the United States early in his regime. The United States was especially pleased by Fujimori's vigorous fight against leftist guerrillas and his attempts to control coca production. But by 1999, members of the US House of Representatives had become concerned at the "erosion of democracy and the rule of law" in Perú. Also that year, the Inter-American Court of Human Rights had rejected Peru's bid to withdraw from its jurisdiction, saying it would continue to summon Peruvian officials to testify in reported abuses. Fujimori had come under increasing criticism for creating secret courts and tribunals that didn't respect a defendant's right to due process.

Fujimori was more successful with his neighbors. In January 1995, Ecuador challenged a disputed border with Perú, thus initiating a limited war between the two countries. In July 1995, the two countries established a demilitarized zone in the area of the disputed border. In 1999, both countries signed a historic agreement that ended the border dispute, which dated to 1941. That same year, Perú and Chile also signed an agreement to end a border dispute that dated to 1929.

Peru is a member of the Andean Community (ANCOM), created in March 1996 by leaders of Bolivia, Colombia, Ecuador, Peru, and Venezuela. In November 1997, Peru joined the Asia Pacific Economic Cooperation (APEC) forum. Peru is a full member in good standing of a variety of international organizations, including the Organization of American States, the United Nations, and the Andean Pact common market.

## ADDRESS

Oficino de Presidente
Lima, Peru

## REFERENCES

*Brookings Review,* Winter 1995.
*Christian Science Monitor,* 1995.
*Current History,* January 1987–March 2000.
Krauss, Clifford. "Runoff in Peru." *The New York Times,* 16 April 2000, p. WK2.
———. "Fujimori is Victor in Peru's Runoff Despite Protests." 29 May 2000, p. A1.
LaFranchi, Howard. "Peru's Fraud Factor—and the Politics of Tallying Votes." *The Christian Science Monitor,* 14 April 2000, p. 7.
*New York Times,* June–July 1990; April–June 1995, January–April 2000.
"Peru: Fujimori's Ploy May Blow Up in His Face." *Business Week,* 24 April 2000, p. 140.
"A Second Chance for Toledo, and Peru." *The Economist,* 15 April 2000, p. 31.
*Wall Street Journal,* June–July 1990; April–June 1995.
*The Washington Post,* 1999–2000.

**Profile researched and written by Alison Doherty Munro (8/95; revised by Ignacio Lobos 5/2000).**

# PHILIPPINES

### Joseph Estrada
### President
*(pronounced "JOE-seph e-STRAH-dah")*

*"What I am now, I owe to the masses. So when I step down, I would like to be known
as the president who championed the cause of the masses.
That's how I want to be remembered. Everything I have, I owe to the masses."*

The Republic of the Philippines is located on the southeast rim of Asia. Its total area of 300,000 sq km (115,831 sq mi) is composed of over 7,100 islands which stretch from north to south for almost 1,850 km (1,150 mi). The largest islands are Luzon and Mindanao. Quezon City is the official capital of the nation, Metropolitan Manila (which includes Quezon City) is the de facto capital.

The population, estimated at 79,345,812, is mainly of Malayan descent, and is predominantly Roman Catholic (85%). However, the Muslim minority in the south are a politically significant group. Linguistically, the Philippines is a diverse country: English, Spanish and over 70 local languages are spoken. Filipino, which is a derivative language of Malayan dialect, is the national language.

The per capita GNP is approximately US$3,500. The unit of currency is the *peso*. The country's traditional agricultural exports are wood, sugar, and coconut products. Products such as electronic equipment and parts, textiles, processed foods, and mining now dominate Philippine exports.

## POLITICAL BACKGROUND
Claimed for Spain by Ferdinand Magellan in 1521, the Philippines has had a long colonial experience. On 12 June 1898, the Philippines declared independence from Spain. That same year, it came under US rule as a result of American victory in the Spanish-American War. After several years of fighting, US military forces quelled the armed Philippine resistance to American colonial rule. Japan occupied and ruled the Philippines for much of World War II (1939–45). On 4 July 1946, the Philippines was accorded formal independence by the US government.

The political system of the Philippines is divided into three branches: the executive, the legislative, and the judiciary. Under the 1987 Constitution, the chief executive of the nation, the president, is directly elected to a single six-year term. The legislative branch is composed of a bicameral Congress consisting of 24 senators and 250 representatives. The judicial branch is led by 15 members of the Supreme Court.

## PERSONAL BACKGROUND
Joseph Marcelo Ejercito Estrada was born 19 April 1937. He grew up in the town of San Juan, now part of Metropolitan Manila. Estrada is the son of the late Emilio Ejercito, a government engineer, and Maria Ejercito, who were prosperous landowners. After three years of engineering

study, Estrada defied his parents and opted for a career in the movie industry. Barred by his parents from using the family name, he adopted the screen name "Estrada" (Spanish for street) and the nickname "Erap" (*pare,* Spanish for friend, spelled backwards). Estrada played the lead in over 80 Philippine movies and produced more than 70 films. A Robin Hood screen persona, he regularly was cast as an anti-crime figure in action films—combating drug lords, gangsters, and corrupt politicians—or as the romantic lead in sex comedies.

In 1968, Estrada entered politics as a mayoral candidate in San Juan. He served 16 years (1969–86) as mayor. Estrada was responsible for introducing a series of major infrastructure improvements to San Juan, including the establishment of the first municipal high school, the central post office, and the police and fire department headquarters, and paving the streets. Estrada is married to Luisa Loi Pimentel-Ejercito, a doctor of psychiatry. They have three children.

## RISE TO POWER
Estrada entered national politics as a candidate for the Philippine Senate in 1987, following the authoritarian rule of Ferdinand Marcos. He served in the Senate from 1987 to 1992, where he chaired the Committee on Rural Development and the Committee on Cultural Communities (responsible for policy affecting the indigenous peoples of the Philippines). He also served as vice-chair of the Committee on Health and the Committee on Natural Resources and Ecology. Estrada sponsored only three bills as a senator. An ardent nationalist, he was one of the most outspoken critics of the Philippines-US military bases agreement.

Philippine presidential elections prior to the imposition of martial law in 1972 were two-party contests, usually featuring a competition between the incumbent president and a single challenger. This pattern changed with the 1992 election: the 1987 Constitution barred then-President Corazon Aquino from reelection and seven candidates vied for the presidency. Estrada entered the (separate) vice presidential election as running mate to presidential aspirant Eduardo "Danding" Cojuangco, Jr., uniting the Nationalist People's Coalition and Estrada's *Partido ng Masang Pilipino.* Cojuangco, a close associate of former-president Marcos, finished third in the presidential contest, with 18% of the vote. Estrada won the vice presidency with 33%. Both candidates drew their electoral strength from Northern Luzon. Estrada, however, also enjoyed strong support in other regions of the country, demonstrating his appeal to voters other than former Marcos loyalists.

As vice president (1992–98), Estrada headed the Presidential Anti-Crime Commission and was directly involved in several high profile arrests of alleged kidnappers and other criminals. In other matters, he was marginalized by the Fidel Ramos administration and its coterie of former military officers.

## LEADERSHIP

Estrada's movie screen image as an anti-crime figure and his pledge to help the poor and revitalize agriculture have endeared him to the Philippine masses. His 1998 presidential campaign built upon this charismatic and populist image. Opponents and critics focused instead on Estrada's reputation for limited intellectual depth, drinking, womanizing, and late evenings at Manila nightclubs. Estrada dismissed these allegations and cut his consumption of alcohol, food, and tobacco to counter these charges and related concerns about his health. He also surrounded himself with a team of well-regarded advisers, allaying fears about his nationalist and populist instincts among some segments of the middle and upper classes. Estrada's advisers reflected the diversity of his appeal and his campaign message: they ranged from established bankers, lawyers, and wealthy businessmen who stressed a continuation of the free-market economic reforms introduced under Ramos to leftist social activists committed to social reforms intended to benefit the poor.

Estrada campaigned on a platform of law and order, promising a "true war" on drugs and a punishment of law enforcement personnel engaged in criminal activities. The second pillar of Estrada's campaign was his commitment to improving the welfare of the Philippine poor, providing them with access to health care, education, nutritional programs, and housing. He prioritized employment generation and rural development. Estrada further pledged to introduce effective governance, eliminate corruption, promote transparency in government operations, and increase local autonomy.

Estrada was the clear victor in the 11 May 1998 elections, notwithstanding allegations of electoral fraud. He ran under the LaMMP (*Laban ng Makabayang Masang Pilipino* or Fight of Nationalist Filipino Masses) banner, capturing 46.4% of the vote in a ten-candidate contest. His nearest challenger was former speaker of the house, Jose de Venecia, who garnered only 17.1% of the vote. De Venecia's running mate, Gloria Macapagal Arroyo, daughter of a former president of the Philippines, won the vice presidency with 50.2% of the vote. Estrada's running mate, Edgardo J. Angara, finished a distant second with 24.5% of the vote.

## DOMESTIC POLICY

During the first 20 months of Estrada's presidency, he faced challenges in keeping his diverse group of advisers and supporters united and satisfied. He confronted numerous social and economic problems: acute poverty, disparities in wealth, substantial foreign debt, and ongoing communist and Muslim insurgencies. Despite the "people power revolution" that began in the late 1980s, regional and provincial "strongmen" retain considerable power and influence. Among the poor, dependency relations, cultural norms, differentiated interests, repression, and electoral institutions stand

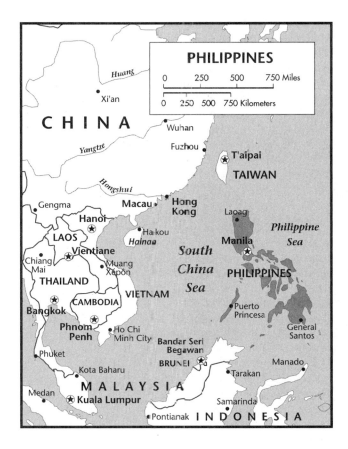

as obstacles to effective mobilization and political participation. Patron-client relations and personal and group identifications along regional and ethno-linguistic lines continue to shape Philippine politics.

Despite considerable economic growth in the 1990s, over 35% of the population still lives in poverty. Unemployment has declined but remains over 8%. Inflation declined to single digits in the mid 1990s, but the economic crises in East and Southeast Asia threaten the Philippine economy. High population growth rates also challenge its capacity for employment generation. Currency crises and economic downturns experienced elsewhere in Asia were less pronounced in the Philippines. Nonetheless, the *peso* depreciated significantly relative to the US dollar, and the Philippines has been much slower to recover than neighboring Thailand, Malaysia, and Korea. As of 2000, foreign debt remained substantial—over US$45 billion—and debt servicing obligations are a continuing source of political controversy. Annual payments of interest and principal amount to US$6 billion—roughly double the combined government expenditures on agriculture, education, and health. Exacerbating the pressures on the budget, agricultural output has been severely reduced by El Niño- and La Niña-related weather patterns.

Philippine government revenues are low by developing country standards, reflecting low tax rates and poor collection. Estrada must increase these revenues or attract substantial new private investment in order to address the daunting infrastructure and investment requirements of his country, notably in agriculture, education, health, and water resource management. The budget deficit was projected at 70 billion pesos for 1998. Estrada promised to increase revenues by simplifying the tax collection system and cracking down on tax evasion (after a brief tax amnesty).

At the outset of his presidency, Estrada angered many Filipinos by agreeing to permit the burial of former president and dictator Ferdinand Marcos in the national Heroes' Cemetery in Manila. In the face of strong opposition, Mrs. Marcos agreed to postpone the burial, temporarily defusing the controversy. To the dismay of his critics, Estrada has not definitively renounced his position.

Estrada has moved to consolidate his influence in the new Philippine Congress under the banner of his new party, *Lapian ng Masang Pilipino* (Party of the Philippine Masses). He wants Eduardo Cojuangco, Jr., his 1992 presidential running mate and a former Marcos crony, to chair the new party. Cojuangco disbanded his Nationalist Peoples' Coalition, advising party members to join Estrada's new party. Party-switching is common in the Philippines as national, provincial, and local leaders (and their coteries) seek advantage in access to government resources. Judging from events following the 1992 elections, Estrada can expect a significant number of congressmen to shift allegiance to his party.

In advance of the opening of the new Congress, Estrada has proposed over 20 bills aimed at improving the tax and customs systems and the performance of the related government agencies, continuing reforms in the banking sector, beginning a major program of school construction, strengthening the national nutritional program, providing guarantees for low-income housing, and reforming the energy sector. Estrada's proposed economic legislation includes a Fair Trade Act, an Anti-Dumping Act, and a Securities Regulation and Enforcement Act. In the political arena, he is proposing a ban on political dynasties (multi-generational office holding by leading families), the introduction of absentee voting for overseas Filipinos, and an end to the ban on political advertising prior to the official campaign period. To combat pork-barrel allocations by Congress, Estrada pledges to eliminate the sizable discretionary accounts awarded legislators by prior administrations. On the environmental front, he proposed a National Land Use and Water Code and a Clean Air Act which won approval by Congress in May 1999.

## FOREIGN POLICY

For more than a century, the Philippines maintained a close relationship with the US. In the latter part of the 1980s and early 1990s, this relationship came under heavy criticism as nationalists condemned the presence of US military bases in the Philippines. The Aquino government refused to renew the bases agreement beyond its September 1991 expiration date. The eruption of Mount Pinatubo in June 1991 caused extensive damage to the Clark Air Base, prompting its closure. A new treaty to permit continued US operation of Subic Naval Station was rejected by the Philippine Senate in late 1991.

Strong Philippine-US ties persist: the US is still the Philippines' leading trading partner. However, Japan is the second-largest trading partner and has become the nation's largest aid donor. Japanese investments, as well as investments from South Korea and Taiwan, helped fuel Philippine economic growth in the mid 1990s. If the economic crises facing Japan, South Korea, and several Southeast Asian countries continue, Philippine economic growth will be at risk. To stimulate foreign investment, Estrada supported an amendment to the 1987 Constitution to permit foreign ownership of land in the Philippines. He also is considering opening the retail sector to foreign competition.

Following the withdrawal of American military forces in 1992, the Philippine military has assumed increasing responsibility for external defense of the country. The dispute with China and several Southeast Asian nations regarding claims to the oil-rich Spratly Islands has heightened consciousness of this external role. Estrada's predecessor, Fidel Ramos, a former Secretary of Defense and career military officer, initiated a major modernization of the Philippine armed forces. During the 1998 presidential campaign, Estrada gave little public attention to the military, promising only to demilitarize the government bureaucracy. Estrada's ability to control the politicized Philippine military in the face of economic and social challenges to the nation will be a crucial test of his presidency and the consolidation of Philippine democracy. Worry about the lack of economic development grew stronger by December 1999 when Estrada's commitment to economic reforms came under question. The Philippine Congress ignored long-standing reform bills that include opening the retail trade to foreign investors, further liberalizing the banking sector, and privatizating the national power company. Also during the first 20 months of Estrada's presidency there were numerous complaints of a "midnight cabinet" of cronies making deals and influencing policy. This coincided with a lack of a strong legislative and policy agenda. However, beginning in January 2000, Estrada appeared to change his governing habits. He allowed the Economic Coordinating Council, a group of well-respected technocrats, to take over much of the economic planning and development for the government. The council combines veteran businessmen like Finance Secretary Jose Pardo, Bangko Sentral Governor Rafael Buenaventura and Trade and Industry Secretary Manuel Araneta Roxas, with academics, including new chief of staff Aprodicio Laquian, Socio-economic Planning Secretary Felipe Medalla, and Budget Secretary Benjamin Diokno.

## ADDRESS

Office of the President
152 Dr. J.P. Laurel St.
Metro Manila, Philippines

## REFERENCES

*Asiaweek*, 20 February 1998; 18 February 2000.

*Business World*, (Manila), 15–17 July 1998.

*Far Eastern Economic Review*, 14 May 1998; 2 July 1998; 23 December 1999.

*Los Angeles Times*, 27 June 1998.

Philippines Department of Environment and Natural Resources. [Online] Available http://www.hangin.org (Accessed March 20, 2000).

**Profile researched and written by Jeffrey M. Riedinger, Michigan State University (9/98; updated by John P. Ranahan 3/2000).**

# POLAND

### Aleksander Kwasniewski
### President

*(pronounced "ah-leck-SAHN-der kvash-nee-EFF-ski")*

*"Let us not allow the divisions that were so sharp in the generations of our grandfathers and fathers to burden endlessly our common future...I believe that we can overcome divisions, that we can look for whatever it is that unites the Poles and organize the Poles for the great and necessary deeds."*

The Republic of Poland encompasses an area of 312,680 sq km (120,725 sq mi) that is largely flat plains, with the exception of mountains along the southern border. To the north lies the Baltic Sea. To the east, Poland is bordered by Russia (Kaliningrad), Lithuania, Belarus, and Ukraine. To the south are Slovakia and the Czech Republic. Germany borders Poland to the west. Poland's population of about 38.6 million is predominantly ethnic Polish (97%) and Roman Catholic (95%). A small number of ethnic Germans, Ukrainians, Lithuanians, and Belorussians live in Poland. Poland introduced a new *zloty* currency to replace the old *zloty* on 1 January 1995. The per capita GDP is approximately US$6,800. Poland's natural resources included coal, natural gas, and minerals.

## POLITICAL BACKGROUND

Situated in the heart of Europe with few natural boundaries, Poland has had a long and troubled history marked by the ambitions of its great power neighbors. A Slavic tribe, the *Polanie*, became established in the 10th century in the area that became Poland. In the 14th century, the Polish kingdom was reestablished and united with Lithuania. Poland fought long wars over the centuries against powerful neighbors. Poles lost their country in 1795 with the partition of Poland by Prussia, Austria, and Russia. Poland achieved independence after World War I. In 1939, Nazi Germany invaded Poland from the west, and from the east, the Soviet Union invaded and occupied eastern Poland, as agreed to secretly with Germany. Poland lost about six million people during the course of World War II. After the war, the Polish Communists, the United Workers' Party (PUWP), seized power in 1947 and exercised monopoly rule, with allegiance to the Soviet Union for 40 years. In 1980, an independent trade union, Solidarity, was formed in the northern port city of Gdansk, and was the first independent workers' organization established in the eastern bloc. Led by shipyard worker, Lech Walesa, Solidarity swiftly broadened its membership to the millions. In an attempt to forestall a possible Soviet invasion, Communist leader General Wojciech Jaruzelski imposed martial law in December 1981 for one year, and Solidarity was banned.

Changes in the Soviet Union under the leadership of Mikhail Gorbachev in the mid- to late 1980s radically altered the international climate in eastern Europe. Poland established the first non-Communist-led government in the Warsaw Pact on the basis of a historic round table agreement made in April 1989, that split power between the Communist government and the opposition. Elections in June 1989 brought a resounding victory for Solidarity, which won almost all of the freely-contested parliamentary seats, and a sound defeat for the Communists. Solidarity leader Lech Walesa nominated Tadeusz Mazowiecki to be prime minister. Poland swiftly launched a radical "shock therapy" economic reform program designed by then-Finance Minister Leszek Balcerowicz. Lech Walesa won the presidential elections in December 1990.

In Poland's first free parliamentary elections in October 1991, the Democratic Union (a post-Solidarity party) "won" the extremely fragmented vote with about 13% of the vote. In total 29 parties entered the *Sejm*, the lower but more powerful house of parliament, ushering in an extended period of party and parliamentary impasse, political scandal, and an increasingly divisive political environment. Continued impasse on many issues led President Walesa to dissolve parliament on 29 May 1993, and call for early elections. Elections held on 19 September 1993, brought former Communists and Communist-allied parties into power. With 52.1% voter turnout, the Democratic Left Alliance (SLD), a coalition of leftist parties, won 20.4% of the vote; the Polish Peasant Party (PSL), another post-Communist party, won 15.4%; and the Democratic Union won 10.6%. The SLD and PSL signed a coalition agreement on 13 October 1993; combined they held majorities in both the *Sejm* and Senate. A government under Waldemar Pawlak of the Peasant Party was sworn in on 16 October 1993.

The Pawlak government found itself increasingly at odds with President Walesa over many issues. In January 1995, Walesa utilized brinkmanship tactics to remove Pawlak by refusing to sign the budget and threatening to invoke a constitutional clause and dissolve parliament, a move which would have led to early elections. The strategy ultimately succeeded. The ruling coalition agreed on February 7 to replace Pawlak of the Peasant Party with *Sejm* Speaker Jozef Oleksy of the Democratic Left Alliance. The Democratic Left Alliance and Peasant Part signed a new coalition agreement on February 15, assigning the SLD with nine cabinet posts, and the PSL with eight. The *Sejm* approved Oleksy' government on March 4.

Presidential elections were held in November 1995. After two rounds, incumbent President and former Solidarity leader Lech Walesa was defeated by SLD leader Aleksander Kwasniewski. Shortly after the presidential vote, Prime

Minister Oleksy was forced to resign amidst charges of espionage activities with the former Soviet secret service. Oleksy denied the charges, but resigned after the Polish military prosecutor opened a formal investigation in December 1995. A government headed by Wlodzimierz Cimoszewicz of the SLD was selected to be the next prime minister on 1 February 1996; his cabinet was approved by parliament on February 15.

## PERSONAL BACKGROUND

Aleksander Kwasniewski was born on 15 November 1954, in Bialogard. He studied transport economics at the University of Gdansk, but did not complete his degree. Kwasniewski remained a member of the Communist party during the period of martial law in the early 1980s, and worked as editor-in-chief of a weekly Communist youth magazine. In addition to Polish, Kwasniewski speaks Russian, English, German, and French. He married in 1979 and has a daughter.

## RISE TO POWER

Kwasniewski joined the Polish United Workers' Party (PZPR, the Communist Party of Poland) in 1977. He worked with, and later headed, socialist student organizations (the Socialist Union of Polish Students) in Gdansk in the late 1970s. He held government posts from 1985 to 1990. Kwasniewski also served as the chairman of the Polish Olympic Committee in the late 1980s. In 1989, he was selected by Communist Prime Minister Mieczyslaw Rakowski to participate in the Communist party's round table negotiations with Solidarity. After the PZPR dissolved in January 1990, Kwasniewski co-founded the Social Democratic Party of the Republic of Poland, the direct successor to the PZPR.

Kwasniewski entered parliament after the October 1991 elections. He served on the foreign affairs, economic policy, and budget and finance committees in the *Sejm*. After the 1993 elections, he chaired the parliamentary club of the Democratic Left Alliance (SLD) coalition. In November 1993, he became chairman of the Constitutional Committee of the National Assembly (comprising both the *Sejm* and Senate) which was charged with drafting a new constitution.

Going into the presidential elections in November 1995, Kwasniewski was a strong favorite to win by public opinion indicators, although incumbent President Walesa experienced a last-minute surge in public support. Kwasniewski's campaign slogan, "let's choose the future," contrasted with Walesa's attempts to rally against Poland's Communist past. In a televised debate, Kwasniewski charged that Walesa was "a man of the past." In the first round, Kwasniewski won 35.1% of the vote to Walesa's 33.1%. In the second round, Kwasniewski won 51.7% of the vote against Walesa's 48.3%. Kwasniewski was inaugurated as President of Poland on 23 December 1995.

## LEADERSHIP

Kwasniewski rose to political prominence early in his career. After the 1993 elections, Kwasniewski's Democratic Left Alliance (SLD) won the largest share of the votes, and formed a coalition with the Polish Peasant Party. Although the SLD was the more powerful partner, Kwasniewski chose not to enter into government, but rather prepared to challenge incumbent President Walesa in the 1995 presidential elections.

In the presidential campaign, Kwasniewski and his party emphasized social-democratic values, professionalism, and cooperative rather than confrontational tactics. The base of support is mixed, and includes the old Communist guard, the unemployed, peasants, and some of the youth vote. Kwasniewski won the largest share, but there was no win over 50% of the vote among 13 candidates in the first round of the presidential elections. Kwasniewski's victory over Walesa in the second round surprised some observers who had expected Walesa to be able to consolidate the fragmented support of center and center-right voters. After defeating Walesa, Kwasniewski renounced his membership in the Social Democratic Party (part of the SLD). Immediately after being sworn in as President, Kwasniewski was faced with the Oleksy affair that brought down the government. Kwasniewski negotiated with both coalition parties, and swiftly named a new premier and cabinet, which was approved in February 1996, forestalling the need to call for early elections. As of May 2000, Jaroslaw Kalinowski, leader of the Peasant Party (PSL), had announced his intention to challenge Kwasniewski for the presidency in elections scheduled for late that year. Observers predicted, that with Kwasniewski continuing to enjoy support of approximately 60% of voters, he would likely win reelection.

## DOMESTIC POLICY

In his inauguration speech, Kwasniewski emphasized unity and commonness over factionalism. He discounted any speculation that Poland would turn back or away from its course to a prosperous democratic system. Kwasniewski has also stated that he wished to improve relations with the

Catholic Church, which had backed Walesa. Kwasniewski came under some fire by the opposition over his silence over the Oleksy affair. While he accepted Oleksy's resignation, he did not call for it. Continuing official investigations into the Oleksy affair may continue to present challenges to the governing coalition and to the president.

Both the Oleksy and Cimoszewicz governments have pledged to continue economic reforms, and President Kwasniewski has also pledged to stay the course. They have prioritized continuing economic growth, instituting budgetary reform, curbing social spending, reducing unemployment, and progressing on mass privatization. As of 2000, Poland's economy was the strongest among the countries being considered for admission into the European union. Over 60% of the Polish population is working in the private sector. Exports, investments, and consumption have been driving economic growth.

## FOREIGN POLICY

Since 1989, Poland has sought to integrate with the West, forge new relations with the Soviet successor states to the east, and promote cooperation with neighboring states. A primary foreign policy priority has been to gain closer association with and eventually full membership in EU and NATO. Of the former Communist countries, Poland has been the most outspoken in demanding security assurances from NATO. While former President Walesa at first criticized the alliance's partnership proposal as inadequate, Poland has since participated actively in NATO's Partnership for Peace program (PFP). As in some other Central European countries, foreign policy issues did not appear to play an influential role in either the general or presidential elections, and the return of former Communists to power is not expected to diminish core foreign policy priorities. After the November 1995 presi-

dential elections, President Kwasniewski emphasized continuity in Polish foreign policy. European Union countries, and Germany in particular, dominate Poland's foreign trade. In 1998, Poland was one of six countries that began membership talks with the European Union. As of 2000, President Kwasniewski continued to press Poland to join the EU in 2003. Kwasniewski's May 2000 visit to France, the country that will assume the six-month rotating presidency of the EU in July 2000, would focus in part on winning French support for enlarging the EU membership.

## ADDRESS

Office of the President
YU. Wiejska 4/8
00–902 Warszawa
Poland

## REFERENCES

*Country Reports on Human Rights Practices for 1995, Poland*, March 1996.

*The Financial Times, Polish Foreign Trade and Finance Survey*, September 29, 1995.

Foreign Broadcast Information Service, *East Europe Daily Report*, various issues.

*The New York Times*, various issues.

"Polish Peasant Party Head in Presidential Bid." [Online] Available http://www.centraleurope.com/news/ (Accessed 15 May 2000).

US Department of State. *Background Notes: Republic of Poland*. August 1994.

US Library of Congress. *Poland, a Country Study*. Federal Research Division. October 1992.

*US News and World Report*, 6 November 1995.

**Profile written and researched by Julie Kim, Library of Congress (5/96; updated 5/2000).**

# PORTUGAL

### Antonio Manuel de Oliveira Guterres
### Prime Minister

*(pronounced "o-liv-YAIR-a goo-TEAR-rez")*

*"Increased (economic) competitiveness must be compatible with respect for human dignity."*

The Portuguese Republic is located on the western portion of the Iberian Peninsula in Western Europe. To the west lies the Atlantic Ocean and to the north and east lies its only bordering neighbor, Spain. The climate is mild and temperate, with an average annual temperature of 61°F (16°C). The total area of Portugal is 92,082 sq km (35,553 sq mi), with an estimated population of 9.92 million. Approximately 30% of the population live in urban areas. The capital and largest city is Lisbon (835,000), situated at the mouth of the Tagus River along the western coast. The Portuguese Republic also includes two archipelagos located in the Atlantic: the Azores and the Madeiras Islands.

Portugal is a culturally homogenous country, characterized by a Mediterranean identity comprised of Iberian, Latin, Teutonic, and Moorish elements. A widely shared sense of national identity developed as early as the 14th century. Black African immigrants constitute about 1% of the population. Over 94% of the population is affiliated with the Roman Catholic Church, with Muslim, Jewish, and Protestant minorities comprising most of the remaining 6%. Portuguese, the official language, is spoken by virtually the entire population.

Portugal has made great strides in catching up with its richer neighbors. Per capita GDP has been estimated at US$14,600, up from US$6,984 in 1990. Average annual growth between 1996 and 2000 was 3.2% and above the average for the euro-zone. Unemployment fell to 4.5%. There are still some weak spots. Portugal runs a trade deficit and economic growth is driven by domestic consumption. Its main exports are not very competitive, consisting of textiles and clothing (20%), footwear (7%), electrical machinery (19%), and agricultural commodities, such as fish, cork and cork products, wine, and timber. More than 80% of its exports go to the European Union. The Portuguese unit of currency is the *escudo*. Portugal joined EMU in 1999 after it brought down its budget deficit to 1.2% of GDP.

## POLITICAL BACKGROUND
The Portuguese Republic was proclaimed in 1910, following the bloodless revolution which deposed King Manuel II and ended one of the oldest European monarchies. The establishment of the Republic initiated a period of governmental instability and political violence. A military coup in 1926 paved the way for a former economics professor, Antonio de Oliveira Salazar, to become finance minister (1928) and then prime minister (1932). Influenced by Italian fascism, Salazar consolidated governmental authority and established a right-

wing dictatorial regime, known as the *Estado Novo* (New State). Under Salazar, political opposition was outlawed and at times brutally repressed by his secret police. With the support of the Church, the military, and his National Union Party, Salazar remained in power until illness forced him to resign in 1968. The political legacy of Salazar continued until 1974 when a bloodless coup led by left-wing military officers toppled the regime. A new constitution establishing a parliamentary democracy was promulgated in 1976.

The 1976 Constitution establishes the president as head of state. The president is elected by universal suffrage for a five-year term through an electoral system that ensures majority support; the top two candidates go to a second round of elections if no candidate receives a majority of first-round votes. The latest presidential election of January 1996 resulted in the victory of Jorge Sampaio, the former leader of the Socialist Party. Political power in Portugal, however, rests with the prime minister, who is the head of government. Members of the Assembly of the Republic, the unicameral 230-member legislative body, are elected to four-year terms through a system of proportional representation. The leader of the party with the most seats in the Assembly is officially appointed by the president to form a government. Reforms to the 1976 Constitution were implemented in 1982, establishing strict civilian control of the military, a reduction of the powers of the president, and the creation of an independent 13-member Constitutional Tribunal responsible for adjudicating the constitutionality of legislation. The 1989 constitutional reform allowed the privatization of previously nationalized industries. The two main political parties in Portugal are the center-right Social Democratic Party (PSD) and the center-left Portuguese Socialist Party (PSP). Other significant parties include the right-wing Social Democratic Center Party/Popular Party (CDS/PP) and the left-wing Portuguese Communist Party (PCP).

The legislative elections of 1 October 1995 marked a dramatic shift in the two major parties. The Socialists returned to power after a decade in opposition. Social Democrats, who had governed with a majority of seats, were hampered by financial scandals, declining economic growth, and the loss of their popular leader Anibal Cavaco Silva, who stepped down to run for the presidency. It was thought that many voters wanted a "breath of fresh air" after a decade of continuous center-right rule. The socialist government presided over an economic recovery, improved labor market, and Portugal's entry into the euro zone. The Socialist party stayed in power after the 10 October 1999 election.

## PERSONAL BACKGROUND

Antonio Manuel de Oliveira Guterres was born in Santos-o-Velho, Lisbon, on 30 April 1949, the son of middle-class parents. Socialism and Roman Catholicism are considered to be two early influences on his political views. Guterres became a member of the Catholic University Youth during his college years. It is said that Guterres developed an affinity toward socialist ideas and principles through his work with Catholic organizations in the shanty towns of Lisbon. He studied electrical engineering at Lisbon University and received his degree from the *Instituto Superior Tecnico* in Lisbon. Guterres was subsequently appointed assistant lecturer there (1973–75). He is considered to be both a devout Roman Catholic and a socialist, a rarity among the Portuguese left. He and his wife, Luisa, have one son and one daughter, and currently reside in Lisbon.

## RISE TO POWER

Guterres' rise to power began with the the 1974 revolution. During the long reign of Salazar, political opposition was outlawed and repressed. At times, Salazar's party, the National Union, held every seat in the legislature. Guterres joined the reconstituted Socialist Party in 1974, founded by the previously exiled socialist Mario Soares. In that same year, Guterres became the ministerial assistant for Soares. He remained in that role under various Soares governments that followed. Guterres was elected deputy to the Assembly in 1976 as a member of the Socialist Party and continued his parliamentary service until 1983. He lost his seat that year but returned after a two-year hiatus to again become deputy in 1985 and has served continuously to the present. He has held several parliamentary positions, including chairman of the Parliamentary Committee on Economy and Finance (1977–79); chairman of the Parliamentary Committee of Demography, Migrations, and Refugees of the Parliamentary Assembly of the Council of Europe (1983); and chairman of the Parliamentary Committee on Regional Planning, Local Authorities, and Environment (1985–88). He rose within the ranks of the Socialist Party by being appointed a member of the socialist shadow government responsible for Industry (1985–86), then becoming a member of the National Bureau of the Socialist Party (1986–88). Guterres' rapid rise within the ranks of the Socialist Party can be attributed in part to his ability to appeal to both the traditional left and the more rightist sections of his party. He became president of the Parliamentary Group of the Socialist Party in 1988. In 1992, Guterres became leader of the Socialist Party, replacing Jorge Sampaio after a poor electoral performance by the Socialists in 1991. Later, in 1992, Guterres became one of the many vice-presidents of the Socialist International. Assuming office on 28 October 1995, Guterres succeeded Cavaco Silva. He was reappointed prime minister after the 10 October 1999 elections.

## LEADERSHIP

Guterres led his Socialist Party along a more centrist political path and presided over strong economic recovery in the second half of the 1990s. After Spain had announced its intention to be part of the first group of countries to join to

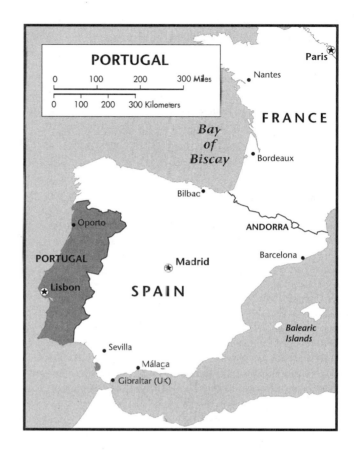

euro-zone, Guterres was able to coopt the opposition in order to follow Spain's decision. Although his government passed difficult legislation to bring down the public deficit, the opposition parties abstained from voting on the budget. Guterres suffered two legislative setbacks, both in 1998. First, the PS lost a referendum on abortion in June 1998 and then a referendum on regional decentralization in November 1998.

His second term as leader of Portugal will probably be more turbulent. Guterres cannot expect the same kind of accommodation from the opposition or from his own backbenchers. The program of the second Guterres minority government involves the promotion of economic growth through investments and exports and increased spending on education and health. Since public deficits are set to remain at 1.2% of GDP, increased social spending can only come from decreased spending in other areas. The government plans to save public monies by streamlining the cumbersome bureaucracy and reforming the judicial system. But the rationalization of the public administration will probably cost money and may leave little room for increased social spending. Many members of the parliamentary faction of the PS insist, however, on increased social spending after years of budgetary austerity to meet the tough EMU criteria. In addition, economic modernization will depend on the accelerated privatization of state-owned enterprises. Here, too, Guterres can expect opposition from leftwing PS parliamentarians. In May 2000, civil service and transport unions affiliated with the Communist and Socialist parties went on strike to press for higher wages. Guterres told the public sector to keep pay increases low to avert a spiral of inflation at the same time that the government raised fuel taxes by 11%.

Public sector workers fear an erosion of purchase power with a higher fuel tax.

The main opposition party, the center-right Social Democratic party, is debilitated by intense internal struggles and is not able to offer a real governing alternative. At the same time, now that the pressure to join EMU is gone, it has no reason to abstain from voting against the government. The PS cannot rely on consistent support from the left either. The Communist party is willing to cooperate with the PS on an issue-by-issue basis. It has not pledged to support the government during its entire four-year term.

## DOMESTIC POLICY

Prior to Guterres' election, Portugal moved along a path of free-market policies with austere economic measures instituted by Cavaco Silva. Many consider these policies, coupled with the billions of dollars in aid provided by the EU and other foreign sources, to have precipitated economic prosperity and, consequently, political stability in the 1980s and early 1990s. Guterres kept to his promises not to dismantle the privatization efforts and free-market reforms of the previous government and pursued a conservative, neoliberal economic program after 1995. After his 1999 election, Guterres announced that the Socialists were still committed to privatization and economic modernization with the result that programmatic differences between the center-left and right had more or less disappeared. The 1999 election was therefore more a contest of personalities than of policy options.

With pressure to modernize the country, Guterres has promised that the "priority of priorities" is bureaucratic reform. The Portugese judicial system is inefficient and incapable of dealing with corruption and sleaze. To attract foreign investment, however, corruption must be brought under control. Portugal also possesses a cumbersome administrative bureaucracy. Here, too, Guterres envisions reforms and rationalizations.

## FOREIGN POLICY

Portugal continues to express interest in fostering closer ties to its former colonies, especially Brazil. Guterrez celebrated Brazil's 500 years of discovery. He has also been involved in trying to settle the East Timor conflict, and the PS has also taken an interest in the difficult situation in Angola, another former colony. The Socialists under Guterrez are intent on expanding Portugal's export markets outside the European Union. Portugese-speaking countries are obvious targets.

Over the years, Portugal has been a major recipient of EU regional aid. This flow of money will most likely diminish with the proposed enlargement of the EU to eastern Europe. The PS played hardball during the five-year budget negotiations in Berlin in March 1999 to ensure that the EU would not cut off the flow of structural funds to Lisbon. The PS threatened to veto plans to reform the EU budget unless the richer states made concessions. With the PS facing an election six months later, a subtantial reduction in funds would have resulted in an electoral backlash. Portugal succeeded in retaining the same proportion of funds from the previous package and secured a 10.4% share of the structural aid funds over the 2000–06 period, the equivalent of EUR\$27.18 billion. Portugal also extracted the compromise of another EUR\$18 billion in cohesion funds set aside for countries with a GDP below 90% of the EU average. Nevertheless, once the applicant countries join, transfers from the EU will diminish.

Guterres has garnered the reputation of an international stateman thanks to his robust response to the East Timor crisis and his country's Council presidency during the first part of 2000. Guterrez delivered a virtuosity performance during the March 2000 EU summit meeting in Lisbon. Other European leaders, not knowing him too well, did not have high hopes for the summit but were able to conclude a memorable "dotcom summit" in which the member states pledged to create 20 million jobs by embracing the internet age.

## ADDRESS

Office of the Prime Minister
Presidencia do Conselho de Ministros
Rua du Imprensa 8
1300 Lisboa, Portugal

## REFERENCES

*Barclays Bank Country Report,* 28 April 2000.
*Financial Times,* various issues.
*Hilfe Country Report,* 27 January 2000.

**Profile researched and written by S. Martin Hwang, Binghamton University (SUNY) (2/96; updated 5/2000).**

# QATAR

### Hamad bin Khalifa al-Thani
### Emir

*(pronounced "HAH-mahd bin kah-LEE-fah al THAH-nee")*

*"[Arab unification] will not be achieved unless an all-out Arab summit is held
to discuss the best ways to overcome the state of fragmentation we suffer,
and bridge the gaps between Arab countries. In such a case we can achieve
Arab solidarity and consolidate joint constructive cooperation that enables us
to adopt a unified stand to confront any challenges or dangers threatening our nation."*

The country of Qatar is located on a peninsula extending into the Persian Gulf from the Arabian mainland. Qatar is bordered by Oman, United Arab Emirates, Saudi Arabia, and across the Gulf of Bahrain and Iran. Qatar's total area is 11,437 sq km (4,416 sq mi) with a total population of 724,000 of which only 30% are Qatari citizens. Most Qataris follow the Wahabi tradition of Sunni Islam, although a large number of Shi'as can be found among the Iranian population. The official language is Arabic with English widely spoken among the educated groups. As in other oil-producing Persian Gulf states, economic development in Qatar has resulted in the influx of large numbers of foreign workers. The non-Qatari population includes large numbers of Indians, Iranians, Pakistanis, and Palestinians. Qatar's arid climate and the absence of suitable sources of underground water has resulted in the concentration of the population in a few large ports. The capital Doha accounts for 60% of the total population. De-salination plants provide more than half of the country's water needs.

Prior to the discovery of oil in 1939, Qatar's economy was based on fishing and pearling. Since the 1950s, however, rising oil prices have turned Qatar into one of the wealthier nations in the world by transforming the economic and social structure of the country. Qatar's total hydrocarbon reserves include 3.7 billion barrels of oil and 380 trillion cubic feet of natural gas. The North Field in the Gulf is believed to contain the world's largest single deposit of natural gas. Petroleum products account for more than 80% of total exports and have allowed the country to enjoy unprecedented prosperity. The per capita GNP is US$17,110, making it one of the wealthiest countries in the world. The local currency is the Qatar *Riyal*.

## POLITICAL BACKGROUND

Until 1872, when it became part of the Ottoman Empire, Qatar was under the influence of the Khalifa family of Bahrain. Upon the withdrawal of Turkish forces in the early days of the First World War, Qatar came under the stewardship of Britain with whom it signed a treaty in 1916. The recognition of Sheikh Abdullah al-Thani by the British as the emir of Qatar established the al-Thani family as the ruling dynasty in Qatar, a position that they continue to hold to this time.

The 19th and early 20th century witnessed the domination of the Persian Gulf by Britain. Through a series of agreements, Britain was able to extend protectorate status to most Gulf countries including Qatar. The 1916 Anglo-Qatari agreement and a later agreement signed in 1923 committed Britain to the defense of Qatar while Qatar undertook not to enter into any agreements with foreign governments without British consent.

Britain's decision to withdraw from all areas east of the Suez by 1971 brought independence to Qatar and other Persian Gulf nations. After the failure of talks on a proposed federation with Bahrain, Qatar became fully independent on 1 September 1971. Anticipating independence, Qatar adopted a written constitution in April 1970. The emir is both the head of state and the head of government. He appoints the Council of Ministers and acts as the prime minister. The appointed Advisory Council has limited powers and assists the emir in ruling the country, but it has no independent legislative powers. The ruling al-Thani family dominates both the Advisory Council and the Council of Ministers in addition to other important economic and political institutions.

## PERSONAL BACKGROUND

Sheikh Hamad bin Khalifa al-Thani was born in Doha in 1950 as the eldest son of Sheikh Khalifa, who at the time was the heir apparent. Like his father, Sheikh Hamad received his early education in Qatar and later attended the Royal Military Academy at Sandhurst, United Kingdom. Upon graduation with the rank of lieutenant-colonel in 1971, he returned to Qatar and assumed the command of a mobile brigade. In February 1972, shortly after Hamad's return, Sheikh Khalifa deposed the ruling emir who was at the time on a hunting vacation in Iran and proclaimed himself the new ruler of Qatar. Sheikh Hamad became the Sheikdom's new army chief-of-staff with the rank of general. He was later appointed as the commander-in-chief of the military. Sheikh Hamad was also responsible for the formation of the engineer's corp. and the military police. In 1977, Sheikh Hamad was appointed as the crown prince and defense minister.

## RISE TO POWER

Sheikh Hamad's rise to power began with his appointment as the commander of a military brigade upon his return from England. Under Sheikh Hamad's command, the brigade became one of the best-trained and most effective military forces in the Gulf region. During the Gulf War, the members

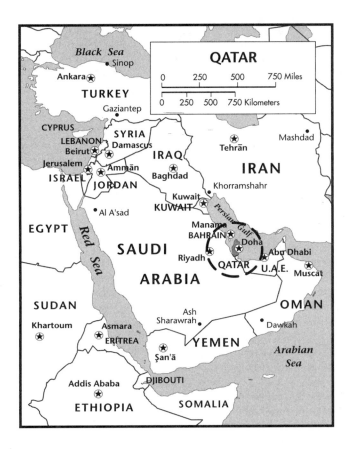

of the brigade distinguished themselves in recapturing the town of Khafji from Iraqi forces.

Hamad's rise to power was made possible by his ability to establish close ties with other influential families in Qatari politics and by his successful use of these alliances to defeat potential rivals within the royal family, including his younger brother Abdel Aziz. By late 1989, when he was given more responsibilities in running the country, Sheikh Hamad had already established himself as the second most influential person in Qatari politics, the first being the emir himself. Hamad's court had emerged to rival the emir's court in influence and prestige. In July 1989, using his influence he was able to replace potential rivals in the Council of Ministers by younger men close to himself. He was also successful in curbing some of the more extravagant privileges of the members of the royal family and other high officials in the government.

Sheikh Hamad's political ascent continued. In June 1993, he was appointed deputy emir. On 27 June 1995, Sheikh Hamad in a bloodless coup deposed his father Sheikh Khalifa, who was vacationing in Switzerland, and proclaimed himself as the new emir and prime minister of Qatar. His ascent to power was met with the approval of Qatar's foreign allies including the US and neighboring Gulf States. It was also supported by significant portions of the al-Thani family and the business community, both Qatari and foreign, who found the former emir too conservative in carrying out economic reforms.

## LEADERSHIP

Under Sheikh Khalifa, Qatar experienced rapid social and economic change. His style of leadership was generally seen as conservative and cautious. As crown prince and deputy emir, Sheikh Hamad, on the other hand, was seen as more decisive and assertive, particularly on issues related to economic development and foreign policy. As Sheikh Hamad was already responsible for day-to-day affairs prior to this formal rise to power, his rise to emir has not created any major discontinuities in Qatari politics. A cabinet reshuffle in July 1995 did not result in any major changes. While most ministers were able to retain their position, Sheikh Hamad kept the defense portfolio for himself. He is expected to continue the push for economic development and for an independent foreign policy while also balancing the interest of domestic and foreign allies. Sheikh Hamad's leadership style is more open compared to other rulers in the region. Since assuming power he has decreased press censorship and has even signaled that he might be willing to accept an elected assembly.

## DOMESTIC POLICY

Although Qatar is among the wealthier countries in the world, in recent years it has faced some economic problems. The economy's heavy reliance on hydrocarbons, particularly oil, has meant that the drop in the price of oil since the early 1980s has had adverse economic consequences for the country's economy, producing a negative growth rate in recent years and budget deficits since 1989. The economic problems were further compounded after it became known that the deposed emir had managed to maintain control of considerable sums of money following the 1995 coup. While the exact amount of the funds appropriated by the deposed emir is not known, it is clear that it is considerable with estimates as high as US$17 billion, while more conservative estimates put it at US$3–5 billion. The Qatari government is trying to regain control over some of this money.

Sheikh Hamad's ability to deal with economic problems depends on his ability to reform the economic system. Sheikh Hamad has always taken a keen interest in the economic development of Qatar. In 1989, he was responsible for organizing the Supreme Council for Planning to coordinate and encourage industrial and agricultural development. Qatar's industrialization program increased its debt service obligations. In 1998 hydrocarbon revenues dropped by 25%; however, by 1999 revenues returned economic growth to 1997 levels. Qatar is practicing fiscal discipline and creating low-cost efficiencies.

Sheikh Hamad has also been an advocate of the rapid development of Qatar's vast offshore natural gas reserves and other industrial projects as an alternative to oil. The development of the North Field natural gas reserves, however, depends on Qatar's success on securing foreign financing. Under Sheikh Hamad, the Qatari government has continued to work closely with foreign and domestic investors in developing the country's economic resources, and it is expected that these ties will continue to grow in the future. In 1999, proven oil reserves ensured continued output at current levels for 23 years; Qatar has the third largest natural gas reserves in the world. Liquefied Natural Gas (LNG) earnings will increase as Qatar supplies the Asian market. Qatar supported the Organization of Oil Exporting Countries (OPEC) efforts to increase oil prices by cutting back crude oil production by 4.3 million barrels per day from March 1999 to March 2000.

As of 1999, plans were in the works to implement a foreign investment code in agriculture, industry, tourism, and education ventures. Qataris have received water and electricity free of charge, but the government is developing a tariff structure with a monthly ceiling.

The former emir, who still claims to be the legitimate ruler of Qatar, and his allies within the ruling elite are still a source of problems for Sheikh Hamad. The deposed emir has not given up on the possibility of resuming his former position. His presence in the region, (he resides in the United Arab Emirates), and the royal treatment that he has received while visiting Saudi Arabia, Bahrain, Egypt, and other countries in the region has been a source of concern for the Qatari government. It was widely believed that Sheikh Khalifa was behind a plot discovered in February 1996 to return him to power.

## FOREIGN POLICY

As a member of the Gulf Cooperation Council (GCC) which also includes Bahrain, Kuwait, United Arab Emirates, Oman, and Saudi Arabia, Qatar maintains close ties with its neighbors. Through the GCC, Qatar also has defense ties to Egypt and Syria. Shortly after taking power, Sheikh Hamad dispatched personal envoys to the GCC countries to assure them of continued cooperation and friendly relations. Membership in GCC, however, has not prevented Qatar from following a more or less independent course. Unlike other GCC members, Qatar has cordial relations with both Iran and Iraq and continued to maintain contacts with both governments at very high levels. Nor has membership in GCC prevented Qatar from asserting its position within the GCC. In December 1995, the Qatari emir boycotted the last session of the GCC summit to protest the choice of a Saudi Arabian citizen as the new secretary-general of the organization. Additionally straining relations with Saudi Arabia is a border dispute that resulted in violent clashes between the two countries in October 1992. Both countries have chosen to resolve their differences through negotiations.

A second border dispute with Bahrain exists over a number of islands, including the potentially oil-rich Hawar chain in the Persian Gulf. In April 1986, after Bahrain tried to build a coast guard station on the artificially constructed Fasht al-Dibal island in the Persian Gulf, Qatari forces raided the island taking the Bahrain workers as prisoners. Although the workers were freed shortly afterwards, sovereignty of the island and nearby Hawar islands continued to cloud relations between the two countries. In November 1994, Sheikh Hamad submitted the dispute to the International Court of Justice in The Hague, Netherlands, although he also indicated that the case will be withdrawn if Saudi Arabian mediation results in satisfactory arrangements. As deputy emir and heir apparent, Sheikh Hamad was known to have advocated a tough stand against both Saudi Arabia and Bahrain.

Sheikh Hamad is generally viewed as an advocate of close relations with the United States and the West in general. Qatar supported the allied effort in the Gulf war, where Qatari troops distinguished themselves in the defense of the town of Khafji against the Iraqi forces. In 1992, Qatar signed a defense pact with the US. Qatar also has signed various forms of defense understandings with the UK and France. Sheikh Hamad's close ties to the US won him quick recognition after the 1995 coup and helped overcome any reservations that neighboring countries such as Saudi Arabia might have had.

Since the conclusion of the peace accords between Israel and the Palestinian Authority, Qatar has taken the lead in developing ties to Israel. In addition to diplomatic exchanges between the two countries, Qatar has also agreed to sell liquefied natural gas to Israel. Qatar's ties to Israel can become another point of dispute within the GCC. Some of the members, notably Saudi Arabia have advocated a more cautious approach. The warm reception afforded to the former emir during his tour of the Gulf states in early 1996 is regarded to have been a signal to the Qatari government to modify its foreign policy behavior.

## ADDRESS

Office of the Emir
Doha, Qatar

## REFERENCES

Arabic News. [Online] Available http://www.arabicnews.com (Accessed 6/2000)

Crystal, Jill. *Oil and Politics in the Gulf: Rulers and Merchants in Kuwait and Qatar.* New York: Cambridge University Press, 1990.

Gause, F. Gregory III. *Oil Monarchies: Domestic and Security Challenges in the Arab Gulf States.* New York: Council on Foreign Relations Press, 1994.

**Profile written and researched by Hootan Shambayati, Middle East Center, University of Utah (6/96; updated 6/2000).**

# ROMANIA

## Emil Constantinescu
## President

*(pronounced "ay-MEEL cahn-stan-tin-ESS-kew")*

*"A majority of Romanian people has proved that it can engineer democratic change quietly and calmly, and that it can achieve in a world tormented by open and even bloody conflicts a zone of understanding and stability."*

Romania lies in southeastern Europe. Its geography is influenced by the Carpathian Mountains and the Danube River. It comprises an area of 237,500 sq km (91,699 sq mi) and is bounded by Ukraine to the north, Moldova to the northeast, the Black Sea to the east, Bulgaria to the south, Serbia to the southwest, and Hungary to the northwest. Its population has been estimated at 22.3 million: 87% being Orthodox, 5% Roman Catholic, and 3.5% Reformed Protestant. About 90% of the people speak Romanian (a Latin-based language); 7.1% speak Hungarian; and 3.4% speak other languages.

Romania's per capita GDP has been estimated at US$4,050. The country's currency is the *lei*. The agricultural sector includes wine production, forestry, and farming. The industrial sector includes mining, manufacturing, power, and construction. Among Romania's natural resources are crude petroleum, brown coal, salt, iron ore, bauxite, copper, and other minerals.

## POLITICAL BACKGROUND

The Ottoman Empire ruled the territory of modern Romania from the early 16th century until the late 19th century. Romania became an independent kingdom in 1881. During the 1930s, a fascist dictatorship allied the country with Nazi Germany, but in late 1944 Romania sided with the Allies against Germany. Soviet forces installed a communist government in 1945. The Paris peace treaty of 1947 forced Romania to cede territory to the Soviet Union and Bulgaria. It also granted Romania northern Transylvania. Romania's King Michael was forced to abdicate in 1947, and Romania became a Socialist Republic. Nicolae Ceausescu became Communist Party General Secretary in 1965. During the Ceausescu era Romania was known for its repressive leadership, highly centralized government, maverick foreign policy, and unpredictable behavior within the Soviet East Bloc. Among the "old guard" of Communist Party leaders, Ceausescu was seen as one of the most resistant to change. Romania's overthrow of communism in late 1989 was the only bloody revolution to occur in Eastern Europe. Demonstrations in December 1989, sparked by ethnic Hungarians, turned violent and quickly spread to other cities. A group calling itself the National Salvation Front (FSN) formed a provisional government. The Romanian armed forces joined the demonstrators and fought against Ceausescu's secret police, the Securitate. Ceausescu and his wife Elena were captured as they tried to escape the capital. They were executed on 25 December 1989.

FSN leader Ion Iliescu became provisional president, and Petre Roman became prime minister. Elections held in May 1990 resulted in an overwhelming victory for Iliescu and the FSN, but opposition continued to grow. Iliescu called in miners from the countryside to forcibly quell student demonstrators in Bucharest who were demanding his resignation. The miners returned to Bucharest in 1991 to join protesters in opposition to Iliescu. More violence ensued, and Roman was forced to resign. Iliescu broke away from FSN and formed the Democratic National Salvation Front (FDSN), which later became the Social Democracy Party of Romania (PDSR).

In the 1992 elections, the Democratic National Salvation Front-Social Democracy Party won a plurality of the vote but lacked a parliamentary majority. Independent Nicolae Vacaroiu became prime minister, but his government was supported by less than a majority in parliament. Vacaroiu had to rely on the support of three small extremist parties, two right-wing nationalist parties, and the leftist Socialist Labor Party. The opposition Democratic Convention (CDR), which included over a dozen parties and organizations, came in second with about 20% of the vote.

In 1996 the CDR won a plurality of the vote (30%) in both the Senate and House of Representatives, beating the PDSR. Victor Ciorbea of the Democratic Convention became Prime Minister of a coalition government that included the Social Democratic Union (USD) and the ethnic Hungarian party, the UDMR. Together the coalition had the support of a majority in parliament. In presidential elections, Emil Constantinescu of the CDR defeated Iliescu in the second round.

## PERSONAL BACKGROUND

Emil Constantinescu was born on 19 November 1939 in the town of Tighina (currently located in Moldova). He studied law and geology at the University of Bucharest. He worked briefly as an assistant judge but left the field of law, which was under the strict control of the Communist Party, and returned to the study of geology. In 1979 he received a Doctorate in Science from the University of Bucharest. Constantinescu has written numerous books on mineralogy. In 1992 he became rector at the University of Bucharest and continued an academic career until his electoral victory in 1996. He is married to Nadia Ileana, a jurist, and has two children, Dragos and Norina.

## RISE TO POWER

Constantinescu entered the political foray after the 1990 miners' attack on student protesters in Bucharest. He was one of the leaders of University Solidarity, an organization that was created in response to the 1990 street riots. He became a founding member of the Civic Alliance party and the umbrella anti-communist forum, the Democratic Convention of Romania (CDR). Constantinescu became CDR president in 1992 and the CDR candidate to run in the first popularly contested presidential elections. Ion Iliescu defeated Constantinescu with 61% of the popular vote. Despite the loss, Constantinescu remained president of the CDR.

Four years later, the CDR again nominated Constantinescu as its candidate for the 1996 presidential elections. In the campaign, Constantinescu outlined a future program for a CDR government known as the "contract with Romania." He pledged speedier economic reforms and closer ties with NATO and the European Union. On 3 November, Romania held parliamentary and presidential elections. In the first round, incumbent President Iliescu won a plurality of the vote but not enough to win the presidency. Two other candidates, Petre Roman of the Social Democratic Party and Gyorgy Frunda of one of the Hungarian parties, endorsed Constantinescu in the second round. On 17 November, Constantinescu received 55.15% of the vote to President Iliescu's 44.85%. Iliescu conceded defeat and expressed respect for the results chosen by the Romanian electorate. Constantinescu was inaugurated as President before both houses of parliament on 28 November 1996.

## LEADERSHIP

After losing his first bid for the presidency in 1992, Constantinescu remained leader of the most significant opposition group and constantly presented himself as the alternative to the Iliescu regime. He remained president of the Democratic Convention of Romania, which itself was wrought with internal differences among its many component groupings. Some constituent member organizations of the Democratic Convention left the coalition in 1995. However, in 1996 the opposition coalesced around Constantinescu and joined ranks against Iliescu.

Constantinescu emphasized the future tasks facing the country rather than dwelling on past problems. He pledged not to seek retribution against those formerly in power, nor to tolerate any form of political punishment. However, the reforms he envisioned have been hobbled by differences among coalition members—the CDR, Social Democratic Party, and Hungarian party—that Constantinescu has not been able to smooth over. In the space of three years, he has had to appoint three different prime ministers. By 2000, Constantinescu's popularity had declined significantly, thanks to Romania's continuing economic woes and also to his support for NATO during the Kosovo crises of early 1999. His prospects for the 2000 elections were also threatened by the resurgence in popularity of PSDR leader and former prime minister Ion Iliescu.

## DOMESTIC POLICY

Romania has made progress toward the development of democratic institutions and a market economy since the 1989 revolution, but lacking the reformist traditions in other developing countries, Romania's transition has lagged somewhat.

After bottoming out in 1993, its economy rebounded, and annual growth improved. Constantinescu and the coalition government pledged to accelerate privatization of the enormous industrial state sector, reduce the budget deficit, and lower inflation. Constantinescu also pledged to open the economy to foreign investment. Both Constantinescu and Prime Minister Victor Ciorbea emphasized that further economic pain and sacrifice were unavoidable. In cooperation with the international financial institutions, the government drafted a tough "shock therapy" economic program. Over the following years, however, Constantinescu's promises of economic improvement went largely unfulfilled. In the first half of 2000, inflation was running at over 40%; unemployment had doubled since 1996, rising to 12%; both foreign and internal debt had risen; and privatization efforts had stalled.

Romania's 1.7 million ethnic Hungarians account for the country's largest ethnic minority. Most of the Hungarians live in Transylvania, in the western part of the country. Many Hungarians seek greater minority rights and even autonomy. In turn, these demands have sparked anti-Hungarian responses from nationalist leaders. However, the presence of the Hungarian Democratic Union of Romania party in the coalition, which came to power after the 1996 elections, promised a shift toward more pro-Hungarian policies.

## FOREIGN POLICY

Since the end of the Cold War, Romania has sought to integrate with Western institutions, in particular the European Union (EU). Its efforts, however, were hindered by Romania's slow pace of reform and lingering communist legacy. In 1993 Romania signed an agreement with the EU, which called for greater economic cooperation, expanded trade relations, and political integration. In 1995 Romania formally applied to become an EU member. However, it was not among the "first wave" of prospective Eastern and Central European candidates for membership. As of 2000 the EU formally accepted Romania as a candidate for membership, but extensive negotiations (and probably several more years) remained before membership could become a reality.

Romania was the first country to sign up for NATO's Partnership for Peace program, which is designed to enhance cooperation with partner states via consultations, joint exercises, and information sharing. Romania also joined the growing ranks of former Warsaw Pact countries that sought full NATO membership. After the 1996 elections that brought the Democratic Convention to power, Romania's prospects for future membership in NATO appeared to have improved significantly. Romania's new leaders have especially pressed NATO to be among the first group of countries to be invited to join the military alliance; however, ultimately it was not included among the countries admitted in 1999 and was still waiting for membership consideration as of 2000.

With its neighboring countries, Romania has sought to normalize relations in the post-communist era. After the collapse of the Soviet Union in 1991, the leaders of Romania actively sought unification with the former Soviet republic of Moldova (with which Romania has longstanding historical ties). Romanian officials likened unification with Moldova with the 1990 unification of Germany. However, in early 1994 forces that rejected joining Romania came to power in Moldova, and the drive for unification has since receded.

Efforts to normalize relations with Hungary were held up over concerns about the rights of ethnic Hungarians living in Romania and Romanian concerns about potential Hungarian irredentism. After years of stalemate, Romanian and Hungarian leaders accelerated efforts in 1996, with both countries aware that lack of progress on this issue was hampering their efforts to integrate with the European Union and NATO. In September 1996, the Romanian and Hungarian prime ministers signed a Treaty of Understanding, Cooperation, and Good-Neighborliness. Among other things, the pact declared that the two countries harbor no territorial claims, and outlined the rights of national minorities according to European standards.

During the brutal wars in Bosnia and Croatia in 1991–95, Romania supported international efforts to isolate and punish Serbia-Montenegro with comprehensive UN economic sanctions. Observance of the embargo and the disruption of trading routes entailed significant financial costs to Romania. In addition, President Constantinescu paid a political price at home when he supported the NATO compaign against Serbia during the Kosovo crisis of 1999.

Romania is an active participant in the Black Sea Economic Cooperation group, a forum of Balkan countries which seeks to encourage regional trade and economic ties. Romania is also a member of the Central European Free Trade Association (CEFTA).

## ADDRESS
Office of the President
Bucharest, Romania

## REFERENCES

Bachman, Ronald D. *Romania, a Country Study.* Washington, DC: US Library of Congress. Federal Research Division, 1991.

Banks, Arthur and Thomas Muller, eds. *Political Handbook of the World.* Binghamton, NY: CSA Publications, 1999.

*The Economist,* 6 February 1999, p. 55.

*The Economist,* 25 December 1999, p. 16.

*The Economist,* 10 June 2000, p. 57.

*Europa World Year Book 1996.* London: Europa Publications Ltd., 1996.

*Financial Times,* December 1996.

*Financial Times Survey,* 9 July 1996.

*New York Times,* 19 November 1996.

Sanborne, Mark. *Romania.* New York: Facts on File, 1996.

US Department of State. *Country Reports on Human Rights Practices for 1995: Romania.* 1997.

**Profile researched and written by Julie Kim, Library of Congress (4/97; updated 6/2000).**

# RUSSIA

## Vladimir Putin
## President
*(pronounced "vlad-EE-mir POO-teen")*

*"We must safeguard what has been achieved, maintain and develop democracy, ensure that the authorities elected by the people work in their interests, defend Russian citizens everywhere, including both inside and outside our country, and serve the society."*

Russia, also officially called the Russian Federation, was by far the largest republic of the USSR. Its population of about 150 million accounted for slightly more than half the Soviet total. Its 6.6 million square miles comprised 76% of the territory of the USSR, stretching across Eurasia to the Pacific across 11 time zones. Russia also inherited the lion's share of the natural resources, industrial base, and military assets of the former Soviet Union. Much of its territory in the north and Far East, however, is sparsely populated. Although Russia is nearly twice the size of the United States, its population is only a bit more than half the US total.

Russia is a multinational, multi-ethnic state with over 65 nationalities and a complex federal structure inherited from the Soviet period. Within the Russian Federation there are 21 ethnic republics (including Chechnya) and 18 other administratively distinct ethnic enclaves. The principal political subdivision of the ethnically Russian parts of the federation is the oblast, of which there are 49. In some respects Russia's multinational federal structure resembles that of the former Soviet Union, on which it was patterned. The demography, however, is different. Ethnic Russians, comprising 81.5% of the population, are dominant. The next largest nationality groups are Tartars (3.8%), Ukrainians (3%), and Chuvash (1.2%). Traditionally, Russians belong to the Russian Orthodox Church. Other major religious groupings in Russia include Islam, Buddhism, Catholicism, various Protestant faiths, Judaism, and animism.

## POLITICAL BACKGROUND

Russian history dates from the late 9th century AD. The earliest Russian state, known as Kievan Rus, had its capital for the most part in Kiev (in present day Ukraine). The ruling dynasty came from Scandinavia and had cultural and commercial ties to northern Europe. Christianity came to Russia in the late 10th century via Constantinople, bringing Russia spiritually into the orbit of Byzantium. Kievan Rus was overrun and destroyed by the Mongols in the mid-13th century. The modern Russian state emerged from the territory around Moscow during the later part of the Mongol domination (late 14th through 15th century). As Mongol power declined, Muscovy grew, absorbing large parts of the Mongol Empire and most of the lands of old Kievan Rus. But $2^1/_2$ centuries of Mongol domination had cut Russia off from Europe at a critical time, leaving a legacy of oriental despotism in Russia while northern, central, and western Europe experienced the renaissance and reformation instead.

Thus, when Russia "rejoined" Europe in the 16th century, there was a big developmental gap between them. With no natural boundaries in the east or west, Russia continued to expand through the Eurasian corridor, absorbing lands populated by non-Russian peoples. During this empire-building, Russia often felt itself under pressure from surrounding states that were more highly developed, as well as from the harsh northern climate. The Russian Empire became a highly militarized state whose activities were often dominated by the requirements of national defense and human subsistence.

The Tsarist Russian Empire, fatally weakened by defeats during the First World War, was overthrown in 1917. A provisional government was set up, which aimed to create a modern republic, but it was swept away by Communists led by Vladimir Lenin, leading to several years of civil war. The victorious Communists proclaimed the Soviet Union in 1922, comprising most, but not all, of the previous Russian Empire. It was organized into ethnically based Soviet Socialist Republics, of which there were eventually 15. The Russian Republic was bigger and more populous than all the others combined, and Russians dominated the republics on the periphery even while they were all subject to the authoritarian control of a government that was federal in form but became highly centralized in function under Stalin, who ruled from 1924–1953.

After the Soviet victory in World War II, the Russians and other Soviet peoples hoped for a relaxation of authoritarianism, but Stalin launched new repressions against soldiers and others who had contacts with the West during the war and established an "iron curtain" against further Western contacts. At the time of his death, he appeared to be launching new wide-scale repressions against Soviet Jews and others. Khrushchev's partial reforms (1954–1964) were mostly reversed by Brezhnev (1964–1982) and his two short-term successors. Major change came when Mikhail Gorbachev became the Soviet leader in 1985. By that time, the Soviet economy had run out of steam, hampered by a highly centralized command system that proved increasingly inefficient and unable to cope with the requirements of post-industrial development. Economic growth stagnated and began to decline, belying Khrushchev's famous goal of soon "overtaking" and "burying" (outlasting) the capitalist West.

Gorbachev launched a series of reforms intended to reverse this downward trend and revive the Soviet system. His political reforms unleashed a process of democratization that

went beyond what he intended. His economic reforms, however, were ill-conceived and half-hearted. The power of the Soviet government and the Communist Party, economic output, the standard of living, and Gorbachev's prestige and popularity, all declined dramatically. More and more power devolved to the Soviet republics, and some sought autonomy or full independence. In June 1991, Boris Yeltsin was elected president of the Russian Republic, despite Gorbachev's opposition. In December 1991, Yeltsin, together with the leaders of Ukraine and Belarus, declared the dissolution of the USSR, making Russia a fully independent state—but considerably smaller than the Soviet Union or the old Russian Empire. Yeltsin's popularity declined during his first presidential term because he was unable to reverse economic distress and growing crime. Nonetheless, he was re-elected president in 1996 following a vigorous campaign that emphasized the threat to democratization if his main opponent, Communist Party leader Gennadiy Zyuganov, was elected. The strain of the campaign caused Yeltsin to suffer a heart attack in the last days of the race. Yeltsin's second term was characterized by his precarious health and frequent and prolonged absences from public life, causing policy drift punctuated only by his arbitrary purges of prime ministers.

The structure of the Russian Government has been radically transformed four times since 1990, most recently by the Constitution of December 1993, personally tailored for Yeltsin after he forcibly disbanded the old legislature in October 1993. The new government is a strong presidential republic. The president is directly elected for a four-year term and can be re-elected only once. The Federal Assembly is a bicameral legislature, in which the more powerful lower chamber, the *Duma*, is popularly elected. The upper chamber, the Federation Council, is comprised of leaders of the executive and legislative branches of the 89 republics and regions of the Russian Federation. Legislative deputies also serve four-year terms and can be re-elected once. The judicial branch, which is nominally independent, is the least well developed of the three. Federal judges are appointed by the president and confirmed by the legislature. There is a Constitutional Court that rules on legality and constitutionality of governmental acts and on disputes between branches of government or federative entities. The Supreme Court is the highest appellate body.

## PERSONAL BACKGROUND

Vladimir Putin was born in Leningrad (now St. Petersburg) on 7 October 1952. In a 1999 memoir, he stated that his paternal grandfather had been a cook for Lenin and Stalin, and that his father had worked for the security apparatus. He graduated from the Law Department of Leningrad State University in 1975, with a Masters of Economics, and immediately joined the Committee for State Security (KGB). He then attended the Red Banner Intelligence School, learning spycraft and fluency in German, and attaining his black belt in judo. In the 1999 memoir, he stated that he had tried to join the KGB as a teenager, but was told to pursue a law degree. He is fluent in German. His wife's name is Lyudmila, and they have two daughters, Maria and Katerina. Putin plays several sports, including skiing and judo.

## RISE TO POWER

In 1975, he joined the staff of the First Chief Directorate for Foreign Intelligence of the Committee on State Security (KGB), and was assigned to the Leningrad branch, where until 1978 he helped to shadow foreign visitors. In 1985, he was assigned to counterintelligence duties in Dresden in then-East Germany, where he served for five years. Reportedly, he checked the loyalty of Soviet diplomats and other personnel and recruited secret informants who could report on NATO affairs. In 1990, he returned to Leningrad after the collapse of East Germany and assumed the post of Assistant Rector (Dean) for International Affairs at Leningrad State University, working for his former teacher, Rector Anatoliy Sobchak. Reportedly, there he also checked on the loyalty of students and monitored foreigners. In 1991, upon Sobchak's election as Chairman of the Leningrad City Council, Putin became his advisor, and retired from the KGB with the rank of Lt. Col. From 1991–1994, Putin was Chairman of the Foreign Relations Committee of the City Council, and in 1992–1994 was also the Deputy Mayor of St. Petersburg. From 1994–1996, Putin was appointed First Deputy Chairman of the City Council (renamed First Deputy Mayor of St. Petersburg).

When Sobchak lost a re-election bid in 1996, Putin asked his Moscow friends for help in finding a job, and Pavel Borodin, Head of the State Property Administration under the Russia Presidency, brought Putin to Moscow to work as his Deputy Business-Manager. In this post, Putin gained major recognition as an efficient and discrete manager of presidential assets and properties, such as dachas, limosines, hospitals, and spas. Success led to his being appointed Head of the Presidential Administration and Chief of the Control (disbursing) Department of the Presidency from 1997–1998. In 1998, he was named Director of the Federal Security Service (counterintelligence agency), and from March 1999 until August 1999, was also the Secretary of the Russia Security Council, the top national security decision-making body, headed by the President. On 9 August 1999, Yeltsin appointed him acting Prime Minister, and on 16 August 1999, he was confirmed by the legislature.

In 1999, President Yeltsin faced increasing scandal as international investigations seemingly pointed to his family's involvement in financial crimes. He resigned on 31 December 1999, a few months before his term would normally end. He had appointed a member of his presidential apparatus, Vladimir Putin, as prime minister in August 1999, and hailed him as his choice for the presidency. Early presidential elections were scheduled for 26 March 2000. Some observers speculate that Yeltsin and his supporters viewed Putin as a capable leader who would be able to shield Yeltsin from prosecution for corruption. They note that Putin's first move after being appointed acting President was to sign a decree granting Yeltsin immunity from prosecution.

During the March 2000 presidential election, Putin refused to outline his policy program in any detail or debate other candidates, but took positions on some issues. He called for a strong and stable Russia, fighting crime, and law and order (exemplified by fighting Chechen terrorists as convenient scapegoats). He stressed that "the stronger the state, the freer the individual," trying to equate safety and freedom. He also argued that a strong state is "part of Russia's genetic code." His other major campaign themes and promises included creating a level playing field in economy with no favors for oligarchs; raising pensions to seniors from $25 to $35 as a moral necessity; making an inventory of Russia's resources and assets; retaining some nationalized defense industries; and increasing support for the armed forces and defense industries. He also stressed the need for low taxes that are widely collected, rather than high taxes that are rarely collected, and land reform (though he was vague on private property rights). Putin's vague promises and themes aimed at a middle-of-the-road, inclusive campaign that did not alienate possible constituencies. A slight decline in Putin's lead near election day led pro-Putin media to launch an ominous anti-Semitic attack against liberal Yabloko Party candidate Grigoriy Yavlinskiy, and Putin put added pressure on regional leaders to deliver votes for him. According to officially reported results, Putin squeaked to a victory in the first round, something Yeltsin was not able to do in 1996. The Central Electoral Commission reported that Putin gained about 53% of 75.2 million votes cast.

## LEADERSHIP

Most observers have credited Putin with being a cautious but decisive leader who likes to work outside the glare of media or public scrutiny. His early popularity was derived from his resolve in fighting in Chechnya rather than decisive economic measures or moves against corruption. He also appeared to benefit greatly from the coincidences that Chechen guerrillas invaded Dagestan and apartment bombings in Russia occurred at the time he was being positioned by Yeltsin as his successor. Putin's leadership of the Chechnya conflict provided a major boost to the government-created Unity Party and other pro-Yeltsin parties during the December 1999 Russian legislative elections, and a major blow to the Yeltsin opposition Fatherland-All Russia bloc, headed by former Prime Minister Yevgeniy Primakov and Moscow Mayor Yuriy Luzhkov.

Kremlin politics at time when Putin was named prime minister was focused more on the corruption scandal of the Yeltsin family than on Chechnya. Ousted Prime Minister Sergey Stepashin was advocating a more cautious, step-by-step action against Chechen terrorists, but Putin quickly endorsed giving the military a basically free hand. Putin's vigorous prosecution of the Chechnya conflict was viewed in a positive light be most Russians, providing him a major boost in his run for the presidency. In his 1999 memoir, Putin

presented himself as the savior of Russia, stating that he decided, at the possible cost of his career, that he would combat the mortal threat to Russia posed by Chechen terrorists who aimed to "break up" and "Islamize" it.

From his KGB experience and role in St. Petersburg, he was a master in media manipulation and "spin," understanding that the media should not be permitted to freely cover the Chechnya conflict. Instead, the media were shown Putin's decisiveness and energy in co-piloting a jet fighter to visit the troops in Chechnya. The Putin government stressed that it was combating anti-terrorism in Chechnya, and highlighted Chechen guerrilla atrocities and the freeing of kidnap victims and "slaves" held by the guerrillas. Many Russians also liked Putin's use of common language or even prison slang, such as his talk of flushing the Chechens and annihilating them.

## DOMESTIC POLICY

President Putin enjoys a much stronger domestic political position than did Yeltsin during most of his presidency, who had to contend with a legislature dominated by Communists and nationalists. A majority of deputies in the newly elected State Duma broadly back Putin, so a "honeymoon" period appears likely where Putin's legislative proposals may be supported. On April 2, Putin stated that his government would be dedicated to "strengthening the state and a continuation of market transformation." His campaign, vaguely endorsed land reform legislation, customs and tax reforms, consistent tax policies in regions, and attractive legal conditions for international investment. He has appeared to support religious freedom, but his new national security concept warns against "the negative influence of foreign missionaries." The rescheduling of Russia's international debt is necessary, since servicing of external and internal debt would consume most of the 2000 budget. If rescheduling fails, then monetary emissions and inflation may ensue.

There is a debate whether Putin will continue market reforms. Some observers believe Putin could implement the "China model": improving economic ties with the West but also rolling back democratization.

There are major humanitarian and economic costs and unintended consequences of the Chechnya conflict. Civilian and military casualties may well be higher than in the 1994–1996 Chechnya campaign, when 80,000–100,000 died, and military costs appear to rival the us$12–15 billion estimated for the earlier conflict. Infrastructure damage too may match or exceed that of the earlier conflict. Most Chechens are displaced and their homes damaged or destroyed. The military's indiscriminate bombing, tacit support for looting, and inadequate investigation of alleged atrocities undermine democratization, human rights, and the rule of law, according to many observers. Putin's statements about the conflict also have raised concerns about his commitment to human rights and law, including the presumption of innocence. Putin long rejected allowing the Organization for Security and Cooperation In Europe (OSCE) into Chechnya, except "where and when we say, where we permit it and deem it expedient," despite Russia's assurances at the November 1999 OSCE Summit to cooperate in resolving the conflict.

Personnel changes made by Putin have mainly included bringing in people he worked with in St. Petersburg or in the security apparatus. Putin has stated that he is seeking a professional government that could include members of various political factions, but this may risk policy gridlock. Some observers raise civil rights concerns about a government that is heavily staffed by personnel with long careers in the Soviet-era security apparatus. Putin has formed a special group of reputed reformers, including his new Prime Minister Mikhail Kasyanov, Presidential Administration head Aleksandr Voloshin, First Deputy Finance Minister Alexey Kudrin, and economic advisor German Gref, to come up with draft economic legislation to implement "radical" economic reforms. Putin has indicated that he will retain Igor Sergeyev, Defense Minister during the Chechnya conflict. Current or former security officials Putin has promoted include Sergey Ivanov, Secretary of the Security Council, who is an ex-KGB officer and close friend and Nikolay Patrushev, Director of the Federal Security Service, who knew Putin in the Leningrad KGB. Putin also quietly replaced 14 presidential representatives in the regions with former security officers.

## FOREIGN POLICY

After Putin became acting president, he gave assurances that Russian foreign policy would not change. A debate on Russia's foreign policy course, however, soon began, encompassing such traditional themes as whether Russia should be oriented toward the West or the East, should embrace "globalism" that includes ties with the West or "multipolarity" that emphasizes forming an anti-Western bloc. Putin in his election campaign stressed domestic issues, but did appear to reject an anti-Western foreign policy. In his letter to the Russian People, Putin stated that "Russian foreign policy should promote national interests. The real, especially economic, interests of the country alone should determine what Russian diplomats do." Harking back to traditional themes, however, he also stated that "it would be unreasonable to be afraid of a strong Russia, but one should reckon with it," and that "one can insult us only at one's own peril." Putin stressed that the Foreign Ministry would coordinate foreign policy, including foreign economic relations, indicating that Putin might be trying to reconcile clashing interests between some pro-Western elements in the ministry and hard-line military elements with anti-Western sentiments who now appear dominant in the Defense Ministry.

Some observers believe that Putin will be able to receive majority support in the Duma for whatever foreign policies he pursues, whether pro- or anti-Western. On the one hand, anti-Western proposals might receive backing from nationalists, and from his Unity Party's alliance with communists in the Duma. On the other hand, if he follows pro-Western policies, his Unity Party, other pro-government factions, and liberals in the Duma may well provide ample backing. Contradictions emerge, however, if Putin plans a mix of pro-Western and anti-Western policies. The Russian military pressing the need to confront NATO would be incompatible with cooperation with the European Union and international financial institutions. Contradictory policies pursued by Putin that have already resulted in more contentious US-Russian relations include seeking friendly US relations while constraining a free press in Russia and violating human rights in Chechnya. Others have argued that Putin may seek to consolidate power by using the bugaboo of a hostile West, perhaps by pointing to US national missile defense plans.

Security Council secretary Sergey Ivanov, Putin's appointee, stated on 31 March 2000 that internal economic threats to Russia's security were more worrisome than external threats, and would be of most concern to Putin. Russia's need for foreign investment suggests continued ties with the West, according to many observers. Putin in BBC interview on March 5 indicated his desire for close ties with the West and more influence in NATO affairs, reflecting his decision to renew some Russian ties with NATO broken during the Kosovo conflict. He stated that "we believe we can talk about more profound integration with NATO, but only if Russia is regarded as an equal partner." Russia had opposed eastern expansion of NATO, Putin suggested, only because Moscow had been excluded from discussion of the issue, "but this does not mean we are going to shut ourselves off from the world. Isolationism is not an option." Following criticism of these comments by Zyuganov, Russian Foreign Minister Igor Ivanov stressed that Putin's main point was not that Russia wanted to join NATO but that "Russia wants to play a role in Western European institutions."

Putin's early arms control announcements sent mixed messages to the West, but he clearly demonstrated his support for some strategic arms control by convincing the Duma on 14 April 2000, finally to ratify START II. However, he has continued to question amending the Anti-Ballistic Missile Treaty. In his first major foreign policy statement as president-elect, Putin on March 31 told nuclear weapons industry officials that he wanted "to make our nuclear weapons complex more safe and effective," as well as "preserve and strengthen" it. He rejected the use of "phony values" to keep Russia out of international nuclear markets, possibly referring to the US opposition to Russia's nuclear reactor sales to Iran.

Just before Putin's election, he and his Security Council approved a draft foreign policy concept, a traditional Soviet-type set of guidelines that are supplemented by a military doctrine and ostensibly flow from an overarching national security concept. (Putin approved the national security concept in January 2000 and a draft military doctrine in February 2000.) The national security concept highlights Russia's economic crisis and social and political instability as its main national security problems. It also threatens the use of nuclear weapons to deter conventional attacks. The draft military doctrine places some emphasis on the possibility of counterbalancing NATO expansion and operations. During Putin's premiership, the defense budget has been increased and he has called for more support for the defense and security agencies, indicating his possible future actions. The foreign policy concept highlighted Russia's foreign economic interests and concerns about the treatment of the 20 million Russians residing in the "near abroad" former Soviet republics. Also in line with the foreign policy concept, Putin has supported ties with China to counter what Russia and China have termed US "hegemony." Putin's government in March 2000 conducted talks with China on arms and oil sales. Russia has supported China on the Taiwan issue, and China has supported Russia on Chechnya.

## ADDRESS
The Kremlin
Moscow
Russian Federation

## REFERENCES
Billington, James H., *The Icon and the Axe: An Interpretive History of Russian Culture*. New York: Vintage Books, 1970.

Florinsky, Michael T., *Russia: A Short History*. New York: Macmillan, 1969.

Franchetti, Mark. "Agent Reveals Young Putin's Spy Disaster." *London Sunday Times*, 19 March 2000.

Golts, Aleksandr, and Dmitry Pinsker. "Putin: A Man Without Guarantees." *MSNBC*, 8 March 2000.

Karasik, Theodore. "Putin's Chechen War and the Rebirth of Yuriy Andropov." *Analyst*, 5 January 2000.

Kramer, Mark. "If It Looks Like the KGB, and Acts Like the KGB." *Washington Post*, 19 March 2000.

Lloyd, John. "The Logic of Vladimir Putin." *New York Times*, 19 March 2000, Sect. 6, p. 62.

Nesirky, Martin. "Putin Aims to Restore Pride of Armed Forces." Reuters, 20 March 2000.

Paddock, Richard C. "Putin's Obscure Path." *Los Angeles Times*, 19 March 2000, p. A1.

"Paper Carries Putin Biography." Foreign Broadcast Information Service, *USSR Daily Report/Central EurasiaDaily Report (hereafter FBIS)*, 23 March 2000.

"Putin Inaugural Address 7 May." *FBIS*, 7 May 2000.

"Putin Remarks in Book Criticized." *FBIS*, 21 March 2000.

"Putin Sets out Campaign Principles." *FBIS*, 29 Febraury 2000.

"Putin's Foreign Policy: Four Viewpoints." *Russia Brief*, Center for Strategic and International Studies, April 2000.

Radio Liberty. *Report on the USSR*, various dates.

"Russia: TASS Carries Updated Biography of President Putin." *FBIS*, 27 March 2000.

Treadgold, Donald W. *Twentieth Century Russia*. 8th ed. Boulder, Colo.: Westview Press, 1995.

Yeltsin, Boris N. *Against the Grain: An Autobiography*. New York: Summit Books, 1990.

Yeltsin, Boris N. *The Struggle for Russia*. New York: Times Books, 1995.

**Profile researched and written by Jim Nichol, Library of Congress (5/2000).**

# R W A N D A

## Paul Kagame
## President
*(pronounced "PAUL ka-ga-ME")*

*"The rehabilitation of Rwanda will be first and foremost a rehabilitation of individuals,
a moral rehabilitation, before being a material rehabilitation."*

The Republic of Rwanda is a small land-locked country in East Africa, occupying 26,338 sq km (10,288 sq mi). It is bordered by Burundi to the south, Tanzania to the east, Uganda to the north, and the Democratic Republic of Congo to the east. The capital is Kigali, located in the central region.

Rwanda's population has been estimated at nearly 8.12 million. A population density of 290 people per sq km in such a small territory made it second in the world in population density in 2000. The population consists of three ethnic groups: the Hutu, the Tutsi, and the Twa. The Hutu are an overwhelming majority, followed by the Tutsi and the Twa. Exact populations are unclear, due to recent ethnic violence. The groups have in common the national language, Kinyarwanda, as well as religious practices. French is also recognized as a national language and is becoming more widely used, especially among the educated classes. Slightly more than half of Rwandans belong to the Roman Catholic Church, and an additional 20% are members of Protestant sects. Indigenous animist religions are still prevalent, even among Christians. Only 1% of the population is Muslim.

Rwanda has few natural resources and little industrialization. The economy thus depends heavily on agriculture, with coffee and tea providing over 80% of the country's export earnings. Other exports include pyrethrum (an organic insecticide), tin, and gold. As many as 95% of Rwandans are peasants in the mountainous countryside. Population pressures have led to serious soil degradation and declining agricultural production. The economy collapsed during the civil war in 1994 and has still not recovered to levels seen before the war. As a result of these conditions, Rwanda ranks among the poorest countries in the world, with per capita GDP estimated at $690, and this poverty has been at the root of serious social and political turmoil in the country. The currency is the Rwandan *franc*; recent political events have eroded its value.

## POLITICAL BACKGROUND

Rwanda was a German colony from 1895 to 1916, after which it became a Belgian protectorate. Belgian colonial policies, including indirect rule, served to solidify ethnic divisions and identities and allowed the minority Tutsi rulers to become increasingly enriched at the expense of the Hutu majority. This resulted in a peasant uprising in 1959 that drove Tutsi officials from office. By 1962, when Gregoire Kayibanda became president of the independent Republic of Rwanda, thousands of Tutsi had fled the country, and only a

handful remained in government posts. Ethnic conflict continued throughout the 1960s, driving thousands more Tutsi from the country and creating insecurity that discouraged international investment and kept the economy stagnant. After a fresh outbreak of ethnic violence in 1973, the minister of defense and head of the military, Major General Juvenal Habyarimana, a Hutu, led a military coup and became president.

Under the slogan "peace, unity, and development," President Habyarimana quickly moved to end ethnic violence in the country and to initiate economic development. For more than a decade, Rwanda experienced stability and economic growth, but by the late 1980s, discontent with Habyarimana had become widespread. Corruption and nepotism was rampant, and the beneficiaries were primarily Habyarimana's relatives or cronies from his home region in the north. A collapse in the price of coffee in 1987 increased the poverty of the masses and inspired open criticism of the regime. In response, Habyarimana moved to consolidate power more fully in the hands of trusted friends and relatives. In 1990, a democracy movement emerged, primarily among Tutsi and southern Hutu who felt excluded from power. To regain popular support, Habyarimana promised political reforms, but behind the scenes, he continued to harass political opponents.

On 1 October 1990, the Rwandan Patriotic Front (RPF) invaded northern Rwanda. The RPF, a movement comprised primarily of Tutsi refugees, many of whom had been living in Uganda and neighboring countries for more than 30 years, demanded the installation of a democratic government in Kigali and the right of refugees to return to Rwanda. The combined pressures of the war and the democracy movement forced Habyarimana to accept political reforms. In June 1991, the national legislature approved a new constitution and allowed the formation of opposition parties. A variety of parties soon emerged and demanded inclusion in the government. In March 1992, Habyarimana named a new government with a prime minister from the *Mouvement Democratique Republicain* (MDR), an opposition party. Meanwhile, political harassment and violence continued unabated. When government representatives signed a peace accord with the RPF in August 1993, the level of violence in the country increased as supporters of the regime struggled to maintain control. After Habyarimana died in a plane crash on 6 April 1994, members of the Presidential Guard and other supporters of the regime (primarily Hutu) systematically killed those they considered political opponents, primarily Tutsi but also many Hutu.

Under the 1991 Constitution, the national government consists of two parts: the executive and the legislative. Executive power is held by the president, who relies on the assistance of his appointed council of ministers, which includes a prime minister. Legislative power is held by the president in conjunction with the *Conseil National de Developpment* (CND), which has 70 members. Elections for the president and the CND are by universal adult suffrage for five-year terms. In practice, the military continues to take an active role in governing the country, thus limiting the activities of the ministries and giving greater power to the president.

## PERSONAL BACKGROUND

Paul Kagame was born in 1956 in Rwanda of Tutsi parents. In 1959, barely three years old, he was forced into exile with his parents. He fled Rwanda to Uganda in the first great mass exodus of the Tutsi after the overthrow of the Tutsi monarchy by the majority Hutu. He remained a refugee for 30 years in Nshungerezi refugee camp, near Mbarara in western Uganda. Life as a refugee and the persecution of his people experienced in Uganda under Milton Obote's second rule (1980–85) were formative in his determination to return to Rwanda in the future. In 1983 Obote expelled 40,000 Rwandan refugees from Uganda because of their support for rebels under Museveni's leadership that were intent on overthrowing Obote's regime in Uganda. Some estimates put the number of Rwandans killed in the fighting with Obote at 10,000. Outraged by the injustice of the Obote government, he left Makerere University to join Museveni's rebels in the bush.

Once Obote's government was defeated by Museveni's National Resistance Army, Kagame was rewarded with an influential position as chief of military intelligence in Museveni's government in Uganda. As director of military intelligence he helped to restore peace and order in Uganda. His subordinates knew him as a stern leader with self discipline. However, a good influential position as chief of military intelligence in Museveni's National Resistance Army in Uganda did not make him forget his goal of returning to Rwanda. Instead, he abandoned the job and, in the early 1990s, went to reorganize his fellow Rwandese in exile and returned to the bush again before marching to a military victory into Kigali. He found the city littered with corpses of hundreds of those who fell victim to the 1994 three-month-long barbaric Rwandan genocide.

## RISE TO POWER

When the RPF first invaded Rwanda in 1990, Paul Kagame was taking further military training in the United States. His fellow officers who initially led the invasion—namely Major-General Fred Rwigyema, Major Dr. Peter Baingana, and Major Chris Bunyenyezi—were killed in the first week. Kagame returned from the US to take over the reigns of RPF, which he found demoralized and in disarray. Kagame quickly reorganized the RPF and introduced some ethnic balance by including as many Hutus as possible. In response to the massacres that spread across Rwanda after the death of Habyarimana in April 1994, the RPF launched a major

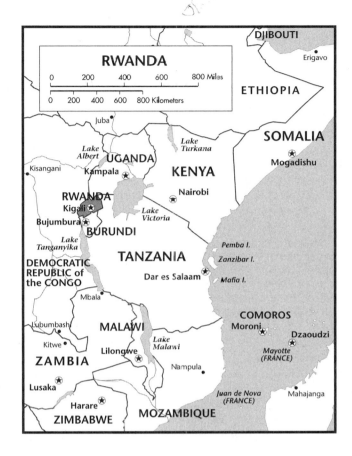

offensive and quickly captured much of northern and eastern Rwanda and, over a period of three months, gradually gained control of most of the rest of Rwanda. By July 1994, the remnants of the Habyarimana regime, along with hundreds of thousands of Hutu civilians, fearing retribution for the massacres, fled before the advance of the RPF troops, creating one of the largest movements of refugees in modern world history. Approximately two million people fled Rwanda, half to Tanzania and half to the Democratic Republic of Congo; another two million became internal refugees. With the capture of the city of Gisenyi on 17 July 1994, the RPF controlled all of Rwanda except for a small area in the southwest that was controlled by French troops. The victorious RPF then set about establishing a new government.

Military victory, however, did not guarantee the RPF's ability to rule the country. The Rwandan population perceived the RPF to be a Tutsi movement because the top military commanders and the majority of soldiers were Tutsi. To gain legitimacy and attract the predominantly Hutu refugees back into the country, the RPF needed to present itself as a multi-ethnic coalition. Thus, the RPF struck an accord with the opposition parties that had served in the 1992 multi-party government. As one of the senior Hutu in the RPF, Pasteur Bizimungu was named president for a five-year term on 17 July 1994. Faustin Twagiramungu, another Hutu from the MDR and the man designated to become head of government in the peace accords of August 1993, was named prime minister. Despite formally holding the highest state office in Rwanda, Bizimungu's power is thought to have been relatively limited. Because he left the country before the outbreak of the war and joined the Tutsi-dominated RPF, many Hutu did not trust Bizimungu, particularly in his home region of the north, where Habyarimana was popular and the RPF hated. In the new government named on 19 July 1994, Major-General Paul Kagame, the head of the RPF, became vice president and minister of defense. Because of his control of the military, Kagame was widely perceived to be the "power behind the throne." Together, Bizimungu and Major-General Kagame ruled the country, with the latter seen as the real wielder of power.

On 23 March 2000, President Pasteur Bizimungu resigned as president after accusing the Tutsi-controlled parliament and cabinet ministers of unfairly investigating his allies on corruption charges. Kagame, Bizimungu's vice president and the rebel leader who propelled the mostly Tutsi Rwandan Patriotic Front (RPF) to victory in 1994 and ended the country's genocide, was inaugurated the new president of Rwanda on 22 April 2000. He was overwhelmingly elected president on 17 April 2000 during a special joint session of parliament and the cabinet. Kagame became the country's first Tutsi president since independence from Belgium in 1962.

## LEADERSHIP

During his tenure, President Pasteur Bizimungu and the Tutsi-led RPF were locked in a dispute that illustrates the political and ethnic difficulties of the country's post-genocide power-sharing agreement. Senior RPF members and some legislators charged that Bizimungu was invoking ethnic problems as a smokescreen and that he opposed the campaign against corruption for fear of being accused himself. On the other hand, Bizimungu's supporters accused Kagame of usurping power and being the real force behind the scenes. The ruling pair of Kagame, English-speaking and Tutsi, and Bizimungu, French-speaking and Hutu, meant to be a symbol to the world of Rwanda's post-genocide reconciliation, proved to be a cosmetic and tense pairing. Thus, the long-awaited ascendancy to power of Kagame as president of Rwanda has the benefit of clarifying the situation with power at last corresponding with office. Over the years Kagame has displayed strong leadership qualities. He and his personal staff are known to be well disciplined, shunning alcohol and smoking. His ambition is to restore hope in a country torn asunder by ethnic animosities and to introduce "social justice for all based on the rule of law." He himself a victim of Rwanda's decades of ethnic tensions, Kagame's ambition is to reconcile the Hutus and the Tutsis, but he is faced by the tough task of reconciling a nation ruptured by massive killings. Critics say his elevation to the presidency shows he is trying to consolidate power at the expense of reconciliation between the Hutus and the minority Tutsi population.

## DOMESTIC POLICY

Kagame assumes office in a country devastated by a brutal war. The battles between the Rwandan army and the RPF destroyed much of the country's infrastructure. Many hospitals, churches, and schools were leveled; roads and bridges destroyed; and water and electric lines cut. The massacres killed more than one-half million people, many from the educated elite. Thus, one of the primary goals of the Kagame administration has been to encourage refugees to return to Rwanda to help rebuild the country, sometimes through the use of force or closing camps in neighboring Democratic Republic of Congo.

Many Hutu refugees were initially reluctant to return for fear they would face reprisals from the mostly Tutsi military for the massacres in 1994. A number of instances of revenge killings by RPF soldiers convinced Hutu refugees that their return would be dangerous. The Kagame regime, however, has attempted to allay those fears. In contrast to the massacres that began in April 1994, killings by RPF soldiers have not had official sanction: they have been condemned by Kagame. Kagame has vigorously investigated reports of violence by his soldiers, and perpetrators have been arrested. To discourage vigilante justice by RPF troops and others, the government has promised that those who organized and carried out the massacres will be brought to trial. They have arrested as many as 130,000 people believed to have taken a leading role in the massacres. With this many genocide suspects being held in prison, the government faces a dilemma over what to do with those accused of committing genocide. Kagame has to maintain a careful balance between pursuing justice and guaranteeing the safety and freedom of Hutu who wish to return to Rwanda. Despite reservations about safety, most of the refugees from the camps in the Democratic Republic of Congo and Tanzania had returned to Rwanda by early 1995.

In late April 1995, the government ordered the last of the internal refugee camps closed in an attempt to force the people to return to their homes and to rout Hutu militants believed to be hiding in the camps. Supply lines were shut off, and no relief workers were allowed into the camps. Violence ensued, and government troops were accused of killing thousands of refugees. The government accepts responsibility for the violence but maintains that just 338 refugees were killed. International agencies maintain that deaths were indeed in the thousands. By mid-May, the last of the refugees had left the squalid camps, electing to attempt to return to their homes rather than face certain death in the disease-ravaged camps.

While Hutu refugees who fled the country in 1994 have been reluctant to return, thousands of Tutsi refugees from earlier conflicts have been returning to Rwanda. Many of these refugees were born in exile and had never previously visited Rwanda. The integration of these refugees into Rwanda is a major domestic policy problem for Rwanda since since 1994. Many of the refugees do not speak Kinyarwanda or French, the two major languages of the country. They have settled primarily in the urban centers and occupy houses and businesses emptied either by the massacres or by the flight of refugees. The government faced the difficult task of determining which properties were actually available and how they would be distributed.

In addition to dealing with issues of justice and resettlement, Kagame will need to focus on revitalizing an economy devastated by war. The government has sought international assistance to rebuild the infrastructure. It has encouraged farmers to return to their fields and has attempted to renew the trade in coffee and tea, Rwanda's main exports. Given the severe social disruptions caused by the war, it may take years before the economy begins to function effectively.

## FOREIGN POLICY

While it is too early to write about Kagame's foreign policy, his involvement in the previous government of Bizimungu is a useful guidepost. During the Bizimungu era, Kagame, who was then vice president, traveled widely throughout the world to drum up support for the rebuilding of Rwanda. It can be expected that two major issues will occupy his new regime in terms of foreign policy: (1) seeking international support for the rebuilding of Rwanda and (2) continued involvement in the geopolitics of Great Lakes region. Under Bizimungu's regime, Kagame travelled widely to European and African capitals, seeking material and financial support for repairing Rwanda's infrastructure. He also worked closely with the United Nations in the efforts to resettle refugees and to maintain peace in the country. In collaboration with the international community, war crimes tribunals were created to find and prosecute the perpetrators of the 1994 massacres. He has been critical of the inadequate international response to the Rwanda crisis and the limited financial resources made available to his government. He even has accused certain organizations of complicity in the Rwanda tragedy. As an English-speaking Tutsi with some US training, his administration can be expected to continue the maintenance of close ties with the governments of Belgium and the US. Relations with France, which actively supported Habyarimana, are quite chilly. Over the past five years or so, Rwanda has received military support from the United States in the form of military training of the Rwandan army within Rwanda itself, including combat, military management, disaster relief, soldier team development, land-mine removal, and military and civilian justice.

The other foreign policy issue facing Kagame concerns the regional geopolitics within the Great Lakes region, which threaten to widen the civil strife in Rwanda and Burundi to the larger central African region. In 1994, with French support, the former Rwandan army was able to flee into the Democratic Republic of Congo (DRC) with much of its equipment and artillery and was able to regroup. The presence of this military force posed a continuing threat of invasion for the new Rwandan government. Supporters of the former Hutu regime, including many military personnel, operated actively in the refugee camps, using threats to dissuade people from returning to their homes in Rwanda. Furthermore, this force terrorized the Tutsi living inside the borders of the DRC. Fearing another genocide of the minority Tutsi inside the DRC and to flush out the remnants of the former Rwandan army, Kagame's army and the Ugandan army invaded the northeastern part of the DRC in 1997. They also helped sweep dictator Mobutu Sese Seko from the country he called Zaire (now the DRC) and installed Laurent Kabila as the new ruler. Dissatisfied with Kabila's independence and lack of allegiance to his benefactors, Rwanda and Uganda, the two armies re-invaded the DRC to support a rebellion aimed at ousting Kabila. Kabila called upon other African governments, including Zimbabwe, Namibia, Botswana and Zambia, to come to his rescue and repel the second Ugandan-Rwandan invasion. Zimbabwe and other African countries joined the war on the side of Kabila, which threatened to widen the conflict from a local to a regional one.

But differences over how to conduct the current war led to divisions in the principal rebel group, the Rally for Congolese Democracy, which splintered into two factions—one backed by Rwanda, the other by Uganda. In August 1999, fighting between the Ugandan and the Rwandan armies erupted at the Kisangani airport and spread to the rest of Kisangani, a town that had been held jointly by the Ugandan and Rwandan forces. By May 2000 the two sides had not resolved their differences and were continuing to exchange fire sporadically. Museveni and Kagame, two of Africa's oldest and closest allies, turned their guns on each other in the eastern Congolese town of Kisangani, wrecking what little chance remained that they would resolve their differences and dealing a further blow to efforts to bring peace to the Democratic Republic of Congo. The unraveling of the Uganda-Rwanda alliance leaves little chance that the 22-month war in Congo, which has displaced one million people and put another 10 million at risk of starvation, will end any time soon, despite an international pledge to install a UN force. In short, these events are a testament to Kagame's desire to play a crucial role, for better or for worse, in the geopolitics of the Great Lakes region.

## ADDRESS

Presidence de la Republique

Kigali, Rwanda

## REFERENCES

*Africa Confidential,* various issues.

*Africa South of the Sahara 1993.* London: Europa Publications, 1993.

Amnesty International. *Rwanda: Reports of killings and abductions by the Rwandese Patriotic Army.* April–August 1994; 20 October 1994.

Bezy, Fernand. *Rwanda 1962–1989: Bilan Socio-Economique d'un Regime.* Paris: Institut d'Etudes du Developpement, 1990.

*Dialogue,* various issues.

Duke, Lynne. "US Military Role in Rwanda Greater than Disclosed." *The Washington Post,* 16 August 1997, p. A1.

*Jeune Afrique,* various issues.

Kanhema, Newton. "Kagame, A Hardened Rwandan Guerilla Leader Turned Statesman." *PanAfrican News Agency,* 27 October 1997.

*New York Review,* 20 October 1994.

Pitman, Todd. "Rwanda's Elite Tightens Grip on Power." *Reuters,* 21 April 2000.

"Rwanda: Paul Kagame Stern Commander." *New African,* September 1994, no. 322, p. 35.

Santoro, Lara. "Congo Battle Ends Alliance of Uganda, Rwanda Against Kabila." *The Boston Globe,* 6 May 2000, p. A6.

Watson, Catharine. *Exile from Rwanda: Background to an Invasion.* Washington, DC: US Committee for Refugees, 1991.

"Who is Paul Kagame?" *West Africa,* 25 July 1994, no. 4008, p. 1300.

**Profile researched and written by Ezekiel Kalipeni (5/2000).**

# ST. KITTS AND NEVIS

### Denzil Douglas
### Prime Minister
*(pronounced "DEN-zihl DOUG-lass")*

*"We have all been motivated and sensitized as to the future role that we have to play as Caribbean leaders."*

The Federation of St. Kitts and Nevis (St. Kitts is an abbreviation for St. Christopher) is located in the eastern Caribbean at the northern end of the Leeward Islands group, part of a chain of islands known as the Lesser Antilles. The country's total area is 261 sq km (101 sq mi), encompassing two islands. The larger, St. Kitts, at 168 sq km (65 sq mi), is an oval-shaped island only about eight km (five mi) wide. Its highest elevation is 1,156 m (3,792 ft) on Mount Misery, an extinct volcano with a lake in its crater, forested mountain slopes, and streams. The smaller island, Nevis, lying 3.2 km (two mi) to the southeast of St. Kitts, covers 93 sq km (36 sq mi) and is a volcanic cone nearly circular in shape. More rocky and less fertile than St. Kitts, its highest elevation is 985 m (3,232 ft) at the summit of Nevis Peak. The two islands boast many beaches, a pleasant tropical climate, and a mean temperature of 80°F, all of which are valuable assets to the tourism industry.

English is the official and principal language of the country. Most of the population is of African descent—from ancestors who were brought to the Caribbean region to work as slaves on the sugar plantations. The estimated population stands at nearly 43,000, and approximately 19,000 of those live in the capital city of Basseterre, a coastal city on the island of St. Kitts and chief port of the country. The largest city on Nevis is Charlestown, with a population of about 1,800. The primary religion is Anglican, a Protestant religion originating in England and brought by the English who first settled the islands. The economy is primarily based on tourism and sugar cane. Other products include cotton, coconuts, tropical fruits, lobster, clothing, electronic equipment, and postage stamps while imports include foodstuffs, manufactured goods, machinery, and fuel. Major trading partners include the United States, Great Britain, Japan, Trinidad and Tobago, and Canada. The unit of currency is the East Caribbean (EC) dollar, adopted in the 1970s by a number of countries.

## POLITICAL BACKGROUND
St. Kitts-Nevis is an independent democratic state within the British Commonwealth of Nations. The formal head of state is Queen Elizabeth II, who is represented by an appointed governor-general. Since 1985 this largely ceremonial position has been occupied by Sir Clement Athelston Arrindell. Real political power rests with the cabinet and the National Assembly, which consists of 11 elected members (eight for St. Kitts and three for Nevis) and three appointed members. The

prime minister is head of the cabinet as well as the leader of the majority party in the Assembly. The cabinet and prime minister are responsible to the National Assembly, which can remove them through a vote of no confidence. There are four main political parties in the country. The party currently in power is the St. Kitts-Nevis Labour Party (SKNLP), which holds a majority of eight seats in the Assembly. The Nevis-based Concerned Citizens Movement (CCM) holds two while the Nevis Reformation Party (NRP) holds one. The conservative People's Action Movement (PAM) currently holds no seats. Should no one party command an outright majority, a coalition between two or more parties may be formed.

The island of Nevis also maintains its own Assembly and premier. It has the constitutional right of secession from St. Kitts if a majority of the legislators approve it. In 1990, the premier of Nevis announced that he intended to seek an end to the federation with St. Kitts by the end of 1992, but an election in that same year removed the threat of secession for the time being.

Originally inhabited by the Carib Indians, for whom the Caribbean is named, St. Kitts and Nevis were named by Columbus in 1493. He named the larger island St. Christopher, for the patron saint of travelers, but when English settlers arrived in 1623, they nicknamed it St. Kitts. The French also founded settlements, and for more than a century the two countries disputed the ownership of the islands until Britain was awarded them in a treaty in 1783. In 1967, St. Kitts and Nevis became a state as part of the West Indies Associated States, a free association between several Caribbean islands and Great Britain, in which each member enjoyed internal autonomy while Britain retained responsibility for defense and foreign affairs. On 19 September 1983, St. Kitts-Nevis became fully independent, joining the United Nations but also maintaining its membership in the British Commonwealth.

## PERSONAL BACKGROUND
Denzil Douglas was born in St. Kitts-Nevis on 14 January 1953. After attending primary and secondary schools on his home island, he entered the University of the West Indies, where his interests were less in politics and more in science and medicine. He first received his Bachelor of Science degree and then turned to the study of medicine, earning degrees as a Bachelor of Medicine and a Bachelor of Surgery. He returned home to St. Kitts-Nevis to practice medicine and became the president of the St. Kitts and Nevis Medical Association.

While practicing medicine he became active in politics as a member of the St. Kitts-Nevis Labour Party, rising through its ranks to become deputy chairman. In 1989, after the Labour Party lost its third-straight election to Prime Minister Kennedy Alphonse Simmonds' party (PAM), the party leader resigned, and Douglas was chosen as his successor. With this promotion he became not only the head of his party, but also the official leader of the opposition in the National Assembly.

## RISE TO POWER

Denzil Douglas is only the second prime minister of St. Kitts-Nevis. His predecessor was elected in 1983 when the country became independent and had been prime minister until the July 1995 elections, which took place almost three years before they were required by the constitution. The elections were held early, as many believed they would be, due to the political fallout from the previous elections in November 1993. At that time, PAM won only four seats, with 41% of the popular vote. The SKNLP also won four seats, yet it had won a greater percentage of the popular vote, 54%.

However, Simmonds joined forces with the NRP, which controlled one seat, and formed a majority in the National Assembly. The SKNLP's supporters responded with violent street demonstrations, arguing that the government had no legitimacy. The authorities promptly imposed a curfew and state of emergency, something which has left a continual state of tension in the political landscape.

In September 1994, cocaine worth millions of dollars was found buried in the sand by a fisherman searching for turtle eggs. Shortly thereafter, two sons of the deputy prime minister, Sydney Morris, were accused of conspiring to sell cocaine and possessing weapons. A third son disappeared. Such serious charges would normally be enough to keep the suspects behind bars, but the two were released on bail. Their release prompted not only charges of corruption to be hurled at the government, but a riot at the prison by 150 inmates. The rioters set fire to the prison and many escaped, forcing the government to call for help from the regional security and police forces to restore order and capture the escapees. In the wake of this, the deputy prime minister resigned.

This incident, which occurred after a number of unsolved crimes, reflected the sense among many in the country that St Kitts-Nevis was coming to play an increasing role in the international drug trade. The crisis that it prompted led to the formation in November 1994 of a "forum for national unity," attended by the four political parties, the Chamber of Industry and Commerce, church organizations, the Hotel and Tourism Association, the St. Kitts-Nevis Trades and Labour Union, and the Bar Association. All parties agreed that the increase in drug-related crime was creating adverse publicity and eroding the confidence of local and foreign investors. The forum called for immediate action to strengthen security and agreed to hold elections within one year.

Prime Minister Simmonds further embarrassed the government when he appointed Sydney Morris as an advisor to the ministry of education only one month after Morris had resigned in the wake of scandal. Douglas, leader of the opposition at the time, called for the prime minister to resign, claiming that Simmonds made a "callous and insensitive" decision in appointing Morris to a post that was tantamount to making him junior education minister.

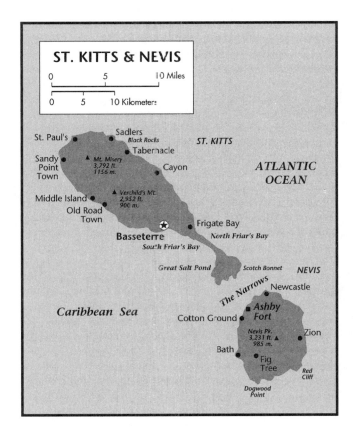

The cumulative effect of political scandal, rising drug crime, and the 12-year hold on power left the Simmonds government open to attack and criticism. When the elections were held on 3 July 1995, Dr. Douglas, who had spent six years in the opposition as leader of the SKNLP, swept into office in a landslide victory. His party captured seven of 11 seats, ousting Prime Minister Simmonds not only from his position as head of government, but also from his seat in the Federal Parliament. Douglas became prime minister on 4 July, the following day.

## LEADERSHIP

Upon entering office, Douglas faced several formidable challenges to his leadership. The most important was to address the breakdown of law and order which had increasingly plagued St. Kitts-Nevis. During the campaign he had pledged to clean up the federation's image as a haven for drug traffickers and money launderers. In his first speech as prime minister, he outlined an ambitious program to reorganize the police forces and to remove them from the country's political battles. All too often the police had not remained an impartial organization dedicated solely to its stated mission. Thus, Douglas announced that his government would work in cooperation with the British in a major effort to improve the police. During the campaign, Dr. Douglas committed himself on several major fronts. He criticized the government for its performance on keeping the economy strong. After assuming power, the Labour Party government proceeded to develop effective programs in the fields of tourism, housing, education, infrastructure development, health care, sports administration, and foreign relations, particularly as they relate to the enhanced image of St. Kitts and Nevis abroad.

As a result of the successes of the SKNLP's initial term, in March 2000, the voters of St. Kitts-Nevis returned Douglas and his party to office with an even greater mandate by voting all eight of the St. Kitts' seats to the SKNLP, completely rejecting PAM Party of former prime minister, Dr. Kennedy Simmonds. The CCM retained its two seats in the parliament, and the NRP held its one seat.

## DOMESTIC POLICY

In 1994, the growth of the Gross Domestic Product declined, falling to 3% from 4.5% the previous year. To convince voters that economic conditions would improve under new leadership, they promised to provide a boost to the tourism industry, outlining a strategy involving the construction of new hotels, a program that would create 1,700 new jobs, according to their estimates. In the past two years, the construction industry had declined, as several large projects had been completed and few new ones were started. Among the new prime minister's favored projects is an "energy and environment friendly" international yachting harbor. The party also campaigned on a plank to abolish or reduce many of the country's different taxes. The government worked throughout its first term to reduce the tax on companies' net profits.

The Douglas government also targeted sugar cane production. As the major crop grown in the country, the health of the sugar industry is vital to the country's economic well being. Dr. Douglas has promised to revitalize the industry in the face of a 6.1% drop in production. The decrease was due partly to the effects of drought but also to difficulties with transport and labor unrest. Production was further curtailed when two devastating hurricanes hit the island in the fall 1995, causing US$100 million in damage, including 75% of all the houses in St. Kitts-Nevis. However, despite the damage caused by the storms, the economy experienced a remarkable upswing, growing by 5.1% and achieving almost full employment.

Douglas also attempted to fulfill promises made to small farmers during the 1995 campaign, many of whom occupy and farm small parcels of land owned by their village. The SKNLP said that these lands would be transferred to the people who live and labor on them and that the purchase price would be the cost of the legal services necessary to make the transfers. This program aimed to increase agricultural production and reduce the country's need to import so much of its food.

## FOREIGN POLICY

Another top priority for Douglas' government was to continue to boost the island's exports. To this end, he supported the country's membership in the Caribbean Community and Common Market (CARICOM), a regional trade organization that regulates trade within the Caribbean and negotiates with other countries and trading blocs. Douglas, along with the other heads of government of the CARICOM countries, met in Guyana in July 1995 to discuss prospects for further integration of the economies of the region. The prospect of being left to languish by the consolidation of other regional trading blocs, like NAFTA (US, Canada, and Mexico), Mercosur (Argentina, Bolivia, and Paraguay), and the Central American Common Market, prompted the leaders to agree upon the creation of a single market in which all countries could trade freely with one another without any tariff barriers. As a part of this effort to promote economic unity, the next step would be to adopt a single currency for all member nations. The Douglas government continues to play an active role in furthering the CARICOM goals. St. Kitts-Nevis deputy prime minister and minister of foreign and CARICOM affairs, the Hon. Sam Condor, became the chairman of the Community Council in June 2000.

Until these long range goals can be adopted, Douglas and his counterparts agreed on short-term measures, such as eliminating the mass of red tape that restricts trade between CARICOM members, reducing the common external tariff from 35% to 30%, and allowing the free movement of the population among countries. Plans call for the latter provision to apply initially only to graduates of regional universities, as Douglas and others have expressed their hesitation to open their borders completely to those without jobs or skills. However, local businesses, represented by the Caribbean Association of Industry and Commerce, have pressed the heads of government to go further, providing work permits when there is a bona fide offer of employment by a regional employer to fill an identified professional or technical vacancy.

## ADDRESS

Office of the Prime Minister
Government Headquarters
PO Box 186
Church Street
Basseterre, St. Kitts

## REFERENCES

*Caribbean and Central America Report,* various issues (1995–96).

*Caribbean Update,* various issues (1995–96).

*Latin American Weekly Report,* various issues (1995–96).

Marcus, Frances Frank. "Doing What the Islands Do Best." *New York Times,* 24 October 1999, p. TR10.

Myers, Gay Nagle. "Resilient People, Island Shake off Georges' September Visit." *Travel Weekly,* 19 November 1998, p. C8.

"The 1999 New Year's Message" (Prime Minister Denzil Douglas); "St. Kitts and Nevis Prime Minister Douglas Presents Caribbean Concerns to United States Secretary of State." [Online] Available http://www. stkittsnevis.net (Accessed January 2000).

*The World Almanac.* 1996.

**Profile researched and written by David Bernell, Johns Hopkins University (2/96; revised 6/2000).**

# ST. LUCIA

**Kenny Anthony**
**Prime Minister**
*(pronounced "KEN-ee AN-thon-ee")*

*"I solemnly pledge that we will effectively and fearlessly attack all those problems which today remain unsolved...we promise you a better, richer and more satisfied St. Lucia."*

Located in the southern end of the crescent formed by the Windward Islands group in the Caribbean Sea, St. Lucia is an irregularly shaped oval, 44 km (27 mi) long and 23 km (14 mi) wide. This island country is characterized by rolling hills and two prominent volcanic mountains (The Pitons). It occupies an area of 616 sq km (238 sq mi).

St. Lucia's population has been estimated at 154,020. More than 85% are of African descent while the remainder consists of 9% mixed races, 3% East Indian descendants, 1% European descendants, and 1% Caribs. While English is the official language, French Creole is also widely spoken. St. Lucia is almost entirely Christian (95%), with Catholicism the largest denomination (85%). Although most St. Lucian women fill the traditional household role, they are also well represented in government and the leading professions. The participation of women in other sectors of society is expected to increase as more women take advantage of public schooling and other government programs.

The economy has traditionally been tied to agriculture, principally the production of bananas. Other major crops include coconuts and cocoa. In recent years tourism and related services have assumed greater importance. Besides agricultural products, St. Lucia exports excavating machinery, iron sheets, electrical switches, beverages, clothing, and cardboard boxes. The US, the UK, the US Virgin Islands, Jamaica, and Trinidad and Tobago are St. Lucia's major markets. The unit of currency is the Eastern Caribbean (EC) dollar.

## POLITICAL BACKGROUND

By the time the islands were discovered by Europeans around 1502, they were already inhabited by Arawak and Carib peoples. The first known European settlement was by 67 Englishmen in 1624. The French established a colony in 1651. For more than a century, the French and British fought for possession of the island, with the British finally winning in 1803. St. Lucia remained under British rule for the next 165 years. Representative government was introduced in 1924. In 1967, St. Lucia became one of the West Indies Associated States, gaining full autonomy in internal affairs, with the British retaining responsibility for defense and foreign relations only.

Today St. Lucia is a constitutional monarchy. Executive power is vested in the British sovereign, the titular head of state, represented by the governor-general. The governor-general is appointed on the advice of the prime minister, who is the head of government and leader of the cabinet. The prime minister must have the majority support of the House, to which he and his cabinet are responsible.

The bicameral legislature consists of an 11-member Senate composed of six members appointed on the advice of the prime minister, three appointed on the advice of the leader of the opposition, and two on the advice of the governor-general. The House of Assembly, by contrast, is a 17-member body composed of representatives elected by universal adult suffrage for up to a five-year term. The highest judicial body is the Privy Council of the United Kingdom, with a legal system based on English common law and the "Code of Napoleon".

Historically, St. Lucian political life has been dominated by two parties: the United Workers' Party (UWP), which was founded in 1964, and the incumbent St Lucia Labour Party (SLP), founded in 1946. St. Lucia became an independent country in 1979 under the leadership of the UWP. Nevertheless, the historic links with Britain continue to be maintained at pre-independence levels.

## PERSONAL BACKGROUND

Kenny Anthony was born on 8 January 1951 in St. Lucia. He began his academic career at the Vieux Fort Senior Secondary School and then attended the St. Lucia Teachers' College. He obtained first class honors from the University of the West Indies (UWI), where he read for a bachelor's degree in government and history. Following this, he received his LLB and master's degree in law, both from UWI. He then attended the University of Birmingham, where he obtained a doctorate in law.

Complementing his academic achievements is an equally impressive professional career. He taught at both the Castries Anglican Primary School and at his alma mater, the Vieux Fort Secondary School. He became a part-time tutor in the Faculty of Social Sciences at the St. Augustine Campus (UWI) in 1978. In 1981 he began teaching at the Cave Hill Campus (UWI), eventually becoming a department head. Anthony was appointed director of the Caribbean Justice Improvement Project in October 1993. He has served as an advisor to the Regional Constituent Assembly of the Windward Islands and as a consultant for the Organization of Eastern Caribbean States (OECS) and the United Nations Development Program (UNDP).

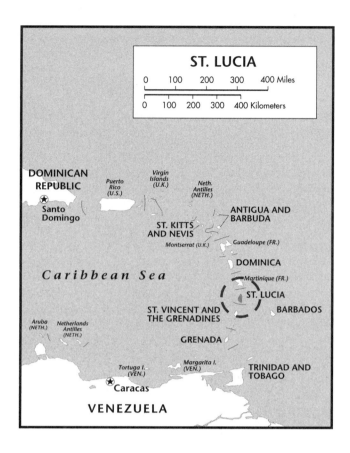

## ST. LUCIA

0    100    200    300    400 Miles

0    100    200    300    400 Kilometers

## RISE TO POWER

In August 1979, Anthony was appointed special advisor in the St. Lucia Ministry of Education and Culture, and in 1980 he became minister of education. He served as general counsel to the Caribbean Community Secretariat in March 1995 until his resignation in 1996. At that time Anthony was elected political leader of the St. Lucia Labour Party. He led the SLP to victory in the May 1997 general elections when they defeated the UWP by obtaining 60% of the votes cast. The former opposition party was returned to power after 18 years with the largest mandate ever given to any political party in the country's history.

## LEADERSHIP

The dramatic success of the SLP in the 1997 elections demonstrated St. Lucians' confidence in Anthony. One political observer described the victory of the Anthony-led SLP as "deliverance." The mistakes of his predecessors also contributed to his success. The government of St. Lucia's first prime minister, John Compton, was associated with numerous scandals. Anthony's immediate predecessor, Vaughan Lewis, offered an approach to politics that was more textbook in nature than it was creative or populist. He was seen more as a stiff technocrat holding the reins of power than as a flexible politician who would be prepared to bend where necessary. These past failures of leadership left Anthony with the image of a "savior." His election campaign made no extravagant promises to the people. However, it did promise change.

Soon after taking office, Anthony followed through on his campaign pledges by introducing several significant changes. He appointed new people to positions of leadership at state corporations. He also announced that the governor general would be replaced and that an audit team would be assembled to review state finances in order to let the people know where the country stood. The number of ministerial portfolios was reduced to ensure that the government was not overstaffed during this difficult economic period. Anthony has taken a very populist approach to his new position, promising to hold meetings with each representative national body in the country.

## DOMESTIC POLICY

Prime Minister Anthony and the SLP have formulated policies aimed at increasing tourism through more intense marketing and the transformation of St. Lucia's image by measures such as the development of more eco-tourism and heritage sites. Anthony has set a goal of raising St. Lucia's share of Caribbean tourism from its 1997 level of 1.3% to 5% by 2003.

The Anthony government has interwoven the expansion of the tourism industry with its goal of increasing employment. Anthony also aims to create more public-sector jobs while implementing skills training, apprenticeship, and skills registration programs. In 1996 the unemployment rate stood at 29%. The major factors that contributed to this situation include lack of appropriate education, training, and capital. By 1999, unemployment had been reduced to 18%. In his 2000–01 budget statement, Anthony outlined the additional employment strategies of stimulating the tourism and construction sectors, creation of more opportunities for self-employment, and diversifying the agricultural sector. His government has recognized the importance of absorbing the debt of the St. Lucia Banana Growers Association and restoring the banana industry to its former status. Tax incentives have been introduced to encourage the development of non-traditional crops. The existing tax structure has been reviewed with the aim of reducing the consumption tax on manufactured exports and eliminating duties on imports. The SLP also hopes to encourage economic democracy through the promotion of cooperatives.

## FOREIGN POLICY

St. Lucian diplomacy focuses primarily on relations with the US and Caribbean countries although historic links with the UK continue. All of these areas have been involved in the ongoing dispute over the US's challenge to the preferential treatment traditionally accorded to Caribbean banana exporters by EU countries. Prime Minister Anthony has been actively involved in protesting the 1999 WTO ruling that imperils that arrangement. However, Anthony has also declared the importance of protecting St. Lucia's farmers through agricultural diversification.

Anthony intends to boost the economic and political status of St. Lucia by entering into trade and diplomatic partnerships based upon mutual respect and reciprocal benefits. To this end, he has established diplomatic relations with China. In February 1999, he made a week-long visit to China, winning pledges of financial support for a number of projects, including a US$4-million sports complex. Among the other countries visited by Anthony are Japan and Cuba. On a regional level, the government intends to deepen its relations with Guadeloupe and Martinique because of St Lucia's shared cultural and historic ties with these French islands.

Another form of investment which Anthony hopes to encourage is from St. Lucian citizens residing abroad, who are being encouraged to return home through programs easing their re-integration into society, amending the customs regulations to provide concessions on household and personal effects, and increasing investment opportunities. Returned nationals who invest in St. Lucia should help to develop the retirement industry and assist in the expansion of local economic opportunities.

Anthony wants his foreign policy to focus on economic and social development and hopes to create a St.-Lucian niche in the global economy. The focus of the Ministry of Foreign Affairs and its overseas offices will be directed at creating trade and investment opportunities.

## ADDRESS

Office of the Prime Minister
Government Buildings
John Compton Highway
Castries, St. Lucia

## REFERENCES

Anthony, Kenny. "Strengthening, Modernizing, and Repositioning the Economy: The 2000/01 Budget Statement." 28 March 2000.

*Caribbean Development Bank Annual Report, 1996.* St. Michael, Barbados.

*Caribbean Week,* 20 June 1997.

*Elections '97 Manifesto Castries.* St. Lucia: St. Lucia Labour Party, 1997.

*Political Handbook of the World.* Ed. Arthur Banks and Thomas Muller. Binghamton, NY: CSA Publications, 1999.

St. Lucia Government Web Site. [Online] Available http://www.stlucia.gov.lc/primeminister/pmonwtoruling.htm (Accessed June 2000).

St. Lucia One Stop News Web Site. [Online] Available http://www.sluonestop.com (Accessed June 2000).

**Profile researched and written by Rachel and Ian Boxill, University of the West Indies (8/97; updated 6/2000).**

# ST. VINCENT AND THE GRENADINES

**James Mitchell**
**Prime Minister**

*(pronounced "JAIMZ MITCH-ul")*

*"We must prepare to make an act of faith and take a great leap toward regional unity."*

St. Vincent and the Grenadines is located in the Windward Islands group of the eastern Caribbean, south of St. Lucia and west of Barbados. Its jurisdiction covers the northern Grenadine islets of Bequia, Canouan, Mayreau, Mustique, Prune Island, Petit St. Vincent, and Union Island. The national capital is in Kingstown, located on the island of St. Vincent. All of the 32 islands that make up this country are volcanic in origin, and some are privately owned. The country's total area is 389 sq km (150 sq mi).

The population is estimated to be 120,512, with growth at 0.57%. Ethnic composition is 66% African and 19% mixed origin, with some Carib Indians, East Indians, and Europeans. About 65% of the islanders are descendants of slaves who were brought from Africa to work the plantations. While English is the official language, a French patois is also spoken as a result of French 18th century colonization. Almost half of Vincentians belong to the Anglican Church while 28% are Methodists. Roman Catholics and Seventh-Day Adventists make up the remainder of the population. Life expectancy is 74.8 years for women and 71.7 years for men.

The economy is based almost entirely on tourism and agriculture, with bananas, arrowroot, and coconuts being the primary exports. The unit of currency is the East Caribbean dollar. The per capita GDP is US$2,400, with a growth rate of 4%.

## POLITICAL BACKGROUND

The Arawak Amerindians, who migrated from South America, are the earliest known inhabitants of St. Vincent and the Grenadines. Subsequently, the Caribs took control of the islands, and were there when Christopher Columbus reached St. Vincent in 1498.

St. Vincent was one of the last of the West Indies to be settled by Europeans. Left to the Carib Amerindians by British and French agreement in 1660, the islands continued to have a sizable Amerindian population until the first quarter of the 18th century. This isolation from European influence resulted in the evolution of the Black Caribs, who descended from the intermarriage of runaway or shipwrecked African slaves with the Amerindians. The islands were taken formally by the British in 1763, who ruled thereafter, except from 1779 to 1783 when they were in the hands of the French.

The islands changed their ethnic character during the next century. When the Black Caribs and the remaining Amerin-

dians rebelled against the British in 1795 at French instigation, most of the defeated insurgents were removed to the Bay of Honduras. Those who remained were decimated by a volcanic eruption in 1812. They were supplanted by African slaves, who were freed in 1834, Madeiran Portuguese, who immigrated in 1848 because of a labor shortage, and Asian indentured laborers, who arrived in the latter half of the 19th century.

St. Vincent was administered as a crown colony within the Windward Islands group from 1833 until 1960 when it became a separate administrative unit with the Federation of the West Indies. The federation fell apart in 1962, and after lengthy discussion, St. Vincent became a self-governing state in association with the UK seven years later.

St. Vincent gained complete independence on 27 October 1979, and is now a member of the British Commonwealth, with Queen Elizabeth II as its formal head of state. Representation is through a governor general who appoints as prime minister the leader best able to command a majority within the legislature. In turn, the prime minister appoints the cabinet ministers. The governor general normally acts on the cabinet's advice, and real executive power is exercised by the prime minister and his cabinet. The legislature is the unicameral House of Assembly, comprised of 15 representatives elected by universal adult suffrage and six senators (four nominated by the ruling party and two by the opposition party). Elections are held every five years although the prime minister may call elections at any time.

The People's Political Party (PPP) was the first major political party and was dissolved in 1994. The principal political parties are the centrist New Democratic Party (NDP) and the Unity Labor Party (ULP), which was formed by a coalition of the moderate leftist Movement for National Unity and the moderate socialist St. Vincent Labour Party (SVLP).

## PERSONAL BACKGROUND

James Fitz Allen Mitchell, nicknamed "Son," was born on the island of Bequia on 15 March 1931. His father was a mariner by trade. After attending the St. Vincent Grammar School, he studied agriculture at the Imperial College of Tropical Agriculture in Trinidad and the University of British Columbia. Mitchell then studied history at the University of Toronto. From 1958 to 1960, he was employed as an agricultural research officer and then spent two years as a teacher. Mitchell then edited reports for the British Ministry of

Overseas Development in London for 18 months. He has authored several books on Caribbean agriculture and, in addition to English, can speak French and Spanish. Mitchell is divorced and has three daughters.

## RISE TO POWER

Mitchell's political career began in 1966 after winning a seat in the legislature as a member of the SVLP representing the Grenadines. In 1967, he was appointed minister of trade, production, labour, and tourism in the SVLP government headed by party founder Robert Milton Cato. As leader of the SVLP, Cato was elected premier in 1967 and governed St. Vincent for 15 of the next 17 years. As part of a generation of Caribbean leaders who rose through the ranks of the labor movement in the 1960s, Cato ruled with repressive policies designed to intimidate any opposition to his party.

In 1972, Mitchell left the SVLP but retained his seat in parliament as an independent. In the election of that year, the SVLP was deadlocked with the PPP for legislative support, thus making the independent Mitchell the compromise choice for premier. Two-and-a-half years later he lost the position in a vote of no confidence. In 1979, Mitchell formed the New Democratic Party (NDP), which immediately became the second ranked party with official status as loyal opposition. Just as his new party was coalescing, he lost his seat in parliament to the leader of the PPP, Ebenezer Joshua.

In a surprising upset, the Labour Party, which had dominated the island's politics for so many years, was thrown out of power in 1984. A resurgent economy, as well as suspicions of corruption, scandals, and political repression, brought nearly 89% of the electorate to the polls. Mitchell's NDP swept all nine seats in the house of assembly, thus making majority leader Mitchell the prime minister once again.

In 1994, the opposition submitted a motion of no confidence in an attempt to have Mitchell removed from office. The ULP charged that the government failed to address the marked decline in banana production, the crisis in health and education sectors, and allegations of drug-related activities on the islands. The motion was defeated by a vote of 10–3, and Mitchell remained in power.

In the elections of 15 June 1998, the opposition ULP narrowly lost to Mitchell's NDP. Elections to the 15-seat parliament were called a year earlier than constitutionally required. Vincent Beache, a banana grower and former cabinet minister, led the opposition. Although Mitchell succeeded in retaining leadership, his party (which once held 12 of 15 seats in parliament) received only a one-seat majority. Voters reflected their disillusionment with a troubled banana industry and the 35% to 40% unemployment rate. The opposition ULP out-polled Mitchell's NDP in the popular vote, 27,506 votes to 23,219. However, under a system of proportional representation, Mitchell's party won eight seats to the opposition's seven.

## LEADERSHIP

Mitchell has been a dominant figure in St. Vincent for nearly three decades. He is a liberal reformer who believes in working within the existing system to improve economic and social conditions. He has emphasized land reform and backs tighter restrictions on the foreign ownership of land, an issue

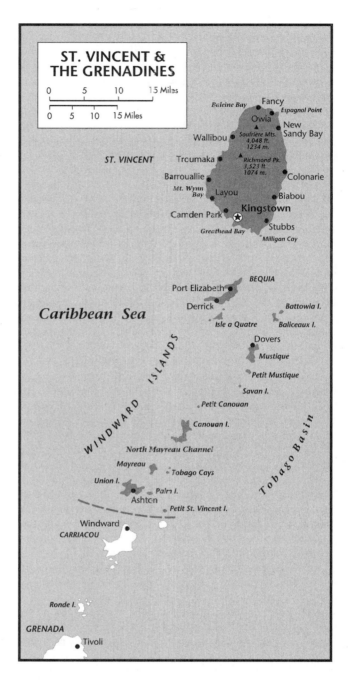

widely perceived as a problem under the Cato government. At the same time, the pro-business Mitchell does not favor heavy state investment in productive enterprise but advocates government investment in infrastructure to help the private sector. The people have generally accepted these changes in the government's political direction and development strategy.

However, Mitchell's popularity is at an all-time low. With 14 consecutive years in power, he is the longest-serving leader in the English-speaking Caribbean. As is the case with many entrenched governments, allegations of corruption and conflict of interest have been raised while the opposition pledges to create new jobs and reduce crime and drugs. The 1998 election results were hotly contested. Opposition leaders considered protests and strikes to force a new election within six months. Now in his fourth term, Mitchell has stated that he wants to finish projects his government has started, such as an upgraded international airport. Other accomplishments include his work on regional cooperation and stability. He believes that he can strengthen political and economic conditions in his country by improving the stability of the entire region. Mitchell's attempts to ease conflicts and tensions while promoting economic development in the region have placed him in a leadership role that extends beyond St. Vincent.

## DOMESTIC POLICY

St. Vincent has always been considered one of the poorest countries in the hemisphere, second only to Haiti. It was severely damaged by a volcanic eruption in 1979 and a major hurricane in 1980, both of which damaged the banana crop. This vital economic sector accounts for 60% of the workforce and 50% of merchandise exports. As a result of drought conditions in 1994, a Banana Rehabilitation and Replanting Programme (BRRP) was established with financial support from the EU. Tropical storms again threatened agricultural production in 1994 and 1995. Bananas were severely damaged.

The exporting of bananas has been under attack by a force that could prove deadlier than any hurricane. Four rival banana-producing countries, including the US, are challenging the legality of the trade preference given to Caribbean bananas in European markets under the Lome Convention. Vincentian banana growers fear they will be unable to compete against the larger South and Central American producers if they lose trade preference. The overall result could further weaken St. Vincent's fragile economy. The government has been unsuccessful in its efforts to introduce new industries, and unemployment rates remain high. The continuing dependence on a single crop (bananas), despite attempts to diversify the economy, represents the biggest obstacle to the country's development.

Mitchell has attempted to develop links between the agricultural and tourist sectors to maximize the benefits of both. Tourism has grown to become a very important part of the economy. In 1993, it supplanted banana exports as the chief source of foreign exchange. The Grenadines have become a favorite destination for the upscale yachting crowd.

St. Vincent and the Grenadines are a popular transshipment point for South American drugs destined for US and European markets. This clandestine activity, which reportedly has already infiltrated the mainstream economy, is abetted by the fact that some islands are privately owned and difficult to reach without private airplanes. St. Vincent has worked closely with the US to eradicate the drug manufacturing and trafficking problems, having signed a maritime law enforcement agreement in 1995 and an extradition treaty the following year.

## FOREIGN POLICY

Mitchell has pressed hard for formal regional unity. He believes that a unitary state made up of St. Vincent, St. Lucia, Dominica, and Grenada, could gain political influence and increase their chances for economic growth. In the late 1990s the leaders of the four countries created the Regional Constituent Assembly, stating that they were committed to the establishment of economic and political union under a federal system. St. Vincent is also a member of the Organization of Eastern Caribbean States, the Association of Caribbean States, and the Caribbean Community and Common Market (CARICOM). As a member of CARICOM, St. Vincent and the Grenadines strongly backed efforts by the US to facilitate the departure of Haiti's de facto authorities from power. Personnel were contributed to the multinational force, which restored the democratically elected government of Haiti in October 1994.

At the same time, the foreign policy of the Mitchell government has demonstrated an independence vis-a-vis the US. Although his predecessor assisted in establishing the US-backed Regional Security System (RSS), Mitchell has strongly opposed militarization of the region. He canceled St. Vincent's participation in US-Eastern Caribbean joint military exercises in 1986. Essentially, he believes that the greatest threat to stability is poverty, not leftists. Money should therefore be spent on solutions to the region's economic crises rather than the military.

## ADDRESS

Office of the Prime Minister
Kingstown, St. Vincent

## REFERENCES

CIA World Factbook. [Online] Available http://www.odci.gov/cia/publications/factbook/vc.html
The Economist, 13 June 1998.
Europa World Yearbook 1997. London: Europa Publications Ltd., 1997.
U.S. Department of State. Background Notes: St. Vincent and the Grenadines, April, 1997.

**Profile researched and written by Christina Siracusa (12/98; updated 2/2000).**

# SAMOA

## Tuilaepa Sailele Malielegoai
### Prime Minister
*(pronounced "too-ee-lah-EH-pah sye-LAY-lay mah-lee-eh-lane-GO-eye")*

*"We put in place our fiscal and monetary policies which focused on ensuring that we have discipline in our own budgetary management. We are very confident that this will bring additional impetus to the economy."*

In July 1997, the Independent State of Western Samoa officially dropped "Western" from the country's name, sharpening the contrast between its status as an independent nation and that of the US Territory of American Samoa. Samoa lies in the center of the South Pacific, between longitudes 171 and 176 degrees west, and latitudes 13 and 15 degrees south. Its closest neighbors are Tuvalu and Kiribati to the north, American Samoa to the east, Tonga to the south, and Fiji to the southwest. New Zealand, further to the southwest, is the largest nation with which Samoa has historically maintained close economic, political, and social ties. Samoa comprises a chain of islands formed by volcanic action millions of years ago. The total land area is 2,831 sq km (1,093 sq mi). Only four of the islands are inhabited, but the nation also claims 120,000 sq km (46,332 sq mi) of ocean territory. The capital city of Apia is located on the island of Upolu, the second largest island and burial site of the writer Robert Louis Stevenson. Stevenson's former home, Vailima, has been renovated to serve as the official residence of the head of state.

Samoa's population is estimated at 230,000. Many Samoans have moved to New Zealand, where they are estimated at more than 60,000. Others live in American Samoa and the United States, especially in Hawaii and California. The Samoan language is one of a large family of Polynesian languages and is one of the country's official tongues. The second official language is English. The ancestors of the present population arrived in the islands by voyaging from the west almost 3,000 years ago, before the original settlements of Tahiti, New Zealand, or Hawaii. Almost 90% of the people living in Samoa today are of pure Polynesian ancestry; the remainder is of European or combined descent. Samoa is a profoundly religious nation, as demonstrated by its motto *Fa'avae I le Atua Samoa* (Samoa is founded on God). Missionaries were active in the 19th century, and even today church schools are an important part of the educational system. Approximately half the population is affiliated with the Congregational Church; about one quarter is Catholic; and the rest are divided among Methodist, Mormon, and other faiths.

Samoa's economy is primarily agricultural and has suffered in the 1990s from a series of natural disasters. Three successive cyclones in 1989, 1990, and 1991 not only destroyed coconut plantations but also devastated roads and communications. These storms were followed in 1993 by a leaf blight that severely damaged a basic food crop, taro.

Since then, agricultural production (but not taro) has begun to recover. Tourism was also disrupted by the storms but has great potential for economic development. GDP grew 9.6% in 1995, and 6% in 1996, but only an estimated 3% in 1997. Though the country showed a fiscal surplus amounting to 1.9% of GDP in 1995–96, it is still burdened by high levels of external debt. Most of this is owed to the Asian Development Bank and amounted to almost 95% of GNP in 1996. The budget is heavily dependent on foreign aid; the largest donor in 1996 was Japan. The GDP of Samoa is US$470 million, with an estimated per capita GDP of US$2,100. An important source of income is the money that is sent home by Samoans living abroad. The Samoan unit of currency is the *tala*.

## POLITICAL BACKGROUND

When Europeans contacted the Samoan islands in the late 1700s, there was no single political structure that governed all the people. Warfare among the islanders was made more violent when whalers and other outsiders introduced muskets and gunpowder. European rivalry for Pacific Island possessions led Germany to annex the western portion of the archipelago in 1900. In 1914, New Zealand took over what came to be called Western Samoa under a mandate from the League of Nations. That mandate evolved into a United Nations trusteeship after World War II. In 1962, Western Samoa became the first independent Pacific Island nation, joining the British Commonwealth in 1970 and the United Nations in 1976. Changing the country's name in 1997 reflects the pride in these early political achievements, particularly in contrast to the dependent status of American Samoa.

Samoa's constitution combines European concepts and practices with those of *fa'a Samoa* (Samoan custom). Basic to the latter is an elaborate system of chiefly titles, the *matai* system. Holders of the two highest titles (*tama-a-'aiga*) became joint heads of state at the time of independence. The surviving title-holder, Susuga Malietoa Tanumafili II, is currently sole head of state; it is not clear what will happen when the time comes for him to be succeeded.

The laws that govern the nation are enacted by the legislative assembly, or *Fono a Faipule*. An important constitutional change was made in November 1991. Until that time, only holders of *matai* titles were allowed to elect members of the *Fono*. This meant that most women and many young men could not vote since few of them were *matai*. Under the 1991 constitutional reforms, the vote was granted to all Samoans 21 years or older although only *matai* are eligible to run for

Fono office. The term of the *Fono* was increased from three to five years and the number of cabinet members from eight to twelve. Two *Fono* members are elected by non-Samoans of European or mixed descent on a separate electoral roll.

The legitimacy of the *matai* electoral system had been a matter of controversy for more than a decade and led to the formation of political parties. It is not clear how the new system of universal suffrage will affect the composition of these parties, and there is still sentiment that all Samoans, not only *matai*, should be eligible to run for election to the *Fono*. Some object that the 1991 reforms were never voted on by all the people. So far the Human Rights Protection Party (HRPP) has been able to hold power for an unprecedented five terms against the opposition of the Samoa National Democratic Party, the Samoa Labour Party, and smaller groups. However, HRPP's dominance has not been maintained without trouble.

In July 1999, Samoa's Minister of Public Works, Luagalau Levaula Samuelu Kamu, was shot and killed at a political function hosted by the ruling Human Rights Protection Party, as it celebrated its 20th anniversary. A Samoan legislator, a Cabinet minister's son, and a third man were charged with murder in the assassination.

## PERSONAL BACKGROUND

Tuilaepa Sailele Malielegoai was born in Lepa Village in 1946. "Tuilaepa" is a *matai* title he assumed as an adult. When he became prime minister, media attention focused on the sacrifices his family made for his education. These made it possible for him to obtain secondary education at the Marist Brothers' St. Joseph's College at Latopa, Samoa. He then received a scholarship to attend St. Paul's College in Auckland, New Zealand. He was awarded bachelor and master of commerce degrees from the University of Auckland, with specialization in accounting and economics. He is married and has several children.

## RISE TO POWER

The political career of Tuilaepa Sailele (as he is referred to by the media) has long been overshadowed by the towering presence of the former prime minister, Tofilau Eti Alesana. Three decades of Tofilau's leadership began with his election to the first post-independence *Fono* in 1967. At that time, he was allied with the first prime minister, Tupua Tamasese Lealofi IV. However, this group was defeated in 1976 when Tupuola Taisi Efi became prime minister. Amidst the controversy over the *matai* electoral system, Tofilau was among the politicians who formed the HRPP, in opposition to Tupuola. The general election of 1982 was followed by a series of legal challenges and changes in leadership. In December of that year, HRPP's by-election victory made Tofilau prime minister, beginning an unprecedented 16-year reign.

For his part, Tuilaepa Sailele returned from his education in New Zealand to take up public service positions in the economic and finance ministries. In this capacity, he participated in international conferences on economic matters. In 1981, he was elected to the *Fono* as an HRPP supporter. His educational qualifications and public service experience made him a natural choice for finance minister in 1988, a position he held continuously until 1998. In 1991, he was named deputy prime minister.

During the 1990s, Tofilau's leadership was shaken by the nation's poor economic performance and some questionable policies, such as the proposed sale of Samoan passports to Asians. Most recently, poor health frequently sent him to New Zealand for medical treatment. During these periods of absence or incapacity, Tuilaepa Sailele was in effect the prime minister, speaking for the country and its government. Finally, when death became imminent, Tofilau resigned his office. In November 1998, the *Fono* elected Tuilaepa to become the next prime minister by a margin that surprised many observers.

## LEADERSHIP

Tuilaepa Sailele has based his leadership on a "no-nonsense" approach to Samoa's economic problems. In carrying out his program, he has been willing to face up to more senior politicians. This has not always been favorably regarded in a society that emphasizes hierarchy and deference. He is viewed by some as being arrogant and high-handed. Because he is more than two decades younger than his predecessor, others questioned his readiness to assume the highest office. However, when the vote was taken, his margin of victory apparently assured his position until the next general election, scheduled for 2001.

## DOMESTIC POLICY

Tuilaepa Sailele's long service as finance minister and deputy prime minister meant that he was largely responsible for many of his predecessor's domestic policies. There is little doubt that he will actively continue those policies now that he occupies the highest office. He supported the controversial implementation of a 10% Value Added Goods and Services Tax in January 1994. The tax, imposed to help curb imports and correct Samoa's severe trade imbalance, led to noisy protest marches and speculation that this strong opposition might spell disaster in the coming election. A 10% reduction in public service pay was almost as unpopular. However, in

1996 the HRPP won 28 of 49 seats in the *Fono*, a very healthy margin of victory.

Another policy initiated while Tofilau was prime minister, certainly based on his successor's views, was that of privatizing what had been government activities and industries. This policy was apparently triggered by the financial troubles of the government-owned national airline, which amassed losses amounting to US$40 million. Beginning in 1995, the government issued a strategic plan of partnership with the private sector. The success of a Japanese auto parts plant, Yazaki Samoa, established in 1991 and employing about 3,000 Samoans, is often pointed out as an example of what can be accomplished by utilizing market forces rather than government management. This firm accounts for 20% of the nation's manufacturing output.

Diversification is regarded as essential to cushion Samoa's economy against natural disasters affecting agriculture. Although recent growth in the fishing industry is encouraging, Tuilaepa Sailele's plan clearly looks in another direction. He intends to develop tourism as a leading industry and argues for creating the infrastructure necessary to support this expansion, including the construction of larger resort hotels. All such steps are to be taken in cooperation with private investment. The new prime minister is alert to the record of shady outsiders who have taken advantage of Pacific Island nations to operate confidence schemes, sometimes fleecing governments of huge sums. He has established a system of character and credit checks to foil anyone who would try to operate such schemes in Samoa.

## FOREIGN POLICY

Ties with New Zealand have remained close since independence, but New Zealand has taken steps in recent years to reduce immigration by lowering quotas.

Because of his active role in managing Samoa's economy, the new prime minister has yet to establish a specific foreign policy distinct from that of his predecessor. He is expected to continue efforts to attract funds from overseas donor countries for needed projects. Japan has been the most generous donor in the past. In 1998, the national university opened a new physical plant built with Japanese funds. Whether such generosity will survive the Asian economic crisis is not clear, and it may be necessary to seek new international ties to ensure assistance for continued development.

The career of Tofilau, which developed over 30 years as a senior Pacific Island leader, gave him a prominence on the international scene which Tuilaepa Sailele has yet to achieve. Samoa is certain to continue its active role in the preeminent Pacific Islands regional organization, the South Pacific Forum. Together with Tonga, the nation represents a counterweight to the Melanesian nation-states like Papua New Guinea and the smaller island countries like Tuvalu. Like other forum members, Samoa is concerned with environmental and security issues, such as nuclear testing and forestry and fishery management. What Tuilaepa Sailele is likely to add to international relations is a concern for mutually profitable economic relations with Pacific Island neighbors. One such example is the import of coconuts from Tonga for processing in Samoa's mill for manufacturing dried coconut products.

## ADDRESS
Government House
Apia, Samoa

## REFERENCES
Douglas, Norman and Ngaire Douglas, eds. *Pacific Islands Yearbook*, 17th ed. Fiji Times Ltd., 1994.
Economist Intelligence Unit Ltd. *Country Profile: Samoa*. 1998–99.
*Islands Business*, selected issues, 1997–1999.
Meleisea, Malama. *Lagaga: A Short History of Western Samoa*. University of the South Pacific, 1997.
Stanley, David. *South Pacific Handbook*. 5th ed. Moon Publications, 1993.
*Talamua: The Samoa Monthly Magazine*, selected issues, 1996–1998.

Profile researched and written by Eugene Ogan, Professor Emeritus, University of Minnesota (6/99; updated 2/00).

# SAN MARINO

## Gabriele Gatti
### Secretary of State for Foreign Affairs

*(pronounced "gah-bree-ELL GAH-tee")*

*"There emerges the conviction that the micro-states can offer significant contributions to the solution of those problems that above all are concerned with the basic principles of international society."*

The Republic of San Marino is a landlocked state on the Italian peninsula about 225 km (140 mi) north of Rome and between the Italian regions of Emilia-Romagna and Marchesa. Situated on the slopes of Mount Titano, San Marino claims to be the oldest republic in Europe. Its total area comprises 60 sq km (20 sq mi). Approximately 25,000 citizens made up the Sanmarinese population in 1999. San Marino principally uses the Italian *lira* as its currency, but since 1971 the government has issued its own coins (in denominations of one *scudi* and two *scudi*). Vatican currency is also legal tender. Italian is the official language, but English and French are also spoken. The ethnicity of the Sanmarinese derives from a mixture of Mediterranean, Alpine, Adriatic, and Nordic ethnic types. Most of the citizens are Roman Catholic. The country's ethnic composition is 80% Sanmarinese and 20% Italian. San Marino exports wine, woolen goods, furniture, and ceramics. The international sale of San Marino postage stamps and tourism (with 3.3 million visitors annually) constitute the largest shares of government revenue.

## POLITICAL BACKGROUND
San Marino is a republic, dating its sovereignty back to its founding in the 4th century by a Christian stone cutter named Marinas who fled persecution in Dalmatia. With the establishment of a monastery in the 9th century, the community grew and acquired statutes of government by the 12th century. The present constitution is based on the statutes of 1660. Papal recognition in 1631 officially gave San Marino independent status.

The Grand and General Council (*Consiglio Grande e Generale*) of 60 members exercises legislative power and is elected every five years by direct vote of all citizens over the age of 21. Every six months two members of the council are nominated to act as captains-regent; they preside over meetings of the Grand and General Council, as well as the Congress of State (the 12-member cabinet), but their functions are largely honorary. The office of secretary of state for foreign affairs has come to represent many of the functions of a prime minister. The secretary of state for foreign affairs has responsibilities that supersede the authority of the captains-regent, but the captains-regent are personally answerable for the mandate given them by the Grand and General Council. The captains-regent must also respond to citizen proposals and requests presented to them (traditionally on the Sunday after 1 April and 1 October in any given year). Full executive power rests in and is shared by members of the Congress of State (cabinet) nominated by the Grand and General Council: the three secretaries (foreign affairs, internal affairs, and finance), the two captains-regent, and the seven ministers heading various administrative departments.

Although San Marino has no written constitution per se, a 1926 electoral law serves some of the functions of a constitution. Women voted for the first time in the 1964 elections.

Although legally sovereign, San Marino's government and political parties are influenced by Italian politics and political parties that are counterparts to those in San Marino. The largest party in the Grand and General Council is the San Marino Christian Democratic Party (*Partito Democratico Cristiano Sammarinese*—PDCS). Other influential parties include the San Marino Socialist Party (*Partito Socialista Sammarinese*—PSS); the San Marino Democratic Progressive Party (*Partito Progressista Democratico Sammarinese*—PPDS, formerly the Communist Party—PCS); the Popular Alliance of Sanmarinese Democrats (*Alleanza Popolare dei Democratici Sammarinese*—APDS); Socialists for Reform (*Socialisti per le Riforme*—SR); and Sanmarinese Communist Refoundation (*Refondazione Comunista Sammarinese*—RCS). The San Marino government will pay for part of the expenses for Sanmarinese living abroad to fly home to vote, and 80% of the population turns out on election day.

## PERSONAL BACKGROUND
Gabriele Gatti was born on 27 March 1953 in San Marino. He earned a degree in literature and philosophy. A member of the Sovereign General Council since May 1978, he has also been active in the San Marino Christian Democratic Party and has served as its secretary-general since July 1985. He became secretary of state for foreign affairs of the republic, the de facto leader of the country, on 26 July 1986.

## RISE TO POWER
Gabriele Gatti had been secretary-general of the Sanmarinese Christian Democratic Party (*Partito Democratico Cristiano Sammarinese*—PDCS) for one year when the existing leftist government collapsed in June 1986 owing to Communist and Socialist party withdrawal over foreign policy disputes. In July, the Grand and General Council approved a new mandate put together by the San Marino Christian Democratic and San Marino Socialist (*Partito Socialista Sammarinese*—PSS) parties. This unprecedented coalition was renewed with elections on 28 May 1988, whereby the

Socialist opposition lost four seats in the Grand and General Council. Gabriele Gatti's San Marino Christian Democratic Party won 27 seats, and the Socialist Party won 18. These two parties continued their coalition despite their obvious differences: the Christian Democratic Party is Catholic and conservative in outlook while the Communist Party follows the leftist line of its parent party in Italy. The elections held 31 May 1998 saw a new party, the Sanmarinese Progressive Democratic Party (*Partito Progressista Democratico Sammarinese*—PPDS) gain in representation, with the Christian Democrats winning 25 seats; the Socialists 14; and PPDS winning 11. The next month (June 1998), Gatti was re-elected for another five-year term as secretary of state for foreign and political affairs by the Grand and General Council. The next election has been scheduled for June 2003.

## LEADERSHIP

Under Gatti's leadership, the government has encouraged the establishment of small-scale industries and service-oriented enterprises by offering tax exemptions for five to ten years. In early 1999, when Italy ceded its monetary operations to the European Central Bank, San Marino joined the European Monetary Union.

## DOMESTIC POLICY

In addition to the sale of postage stamps and revenues from tourism, San Marino receives an annual budget subsidy from the Italian government stemming from the 1862 customs union agreement formed between the two countries. In exchange for this subsidy, San Marino relinquishes the rights to free transit of imports through Italian ports; the printing of paper currency and notes; the operation of commercial radio and television stations; and tobacco cultivation and production of other goods protected by Italian state monopoly. San Marino's trade policy is essentially governed by its customs union with Italy. A 1987 amendment to the relationship allows San Marino banks the right to conduct financial operations directly with foreign banks rather than via the Bank of Italy as was previously required. It also reinstates San Marino's right to operate a casino. This is a venture over which public opinion is divided. Some prefer to keep San Marino traditional, and others are eager to expand its tourist potential. In the late 1990s, San Marino came under pressure from Italian, UK, and US governments to enforce a law enacted in 1997 against music piracy.

## FOREIGN POLICY

San Marino is proud of its neutral status. While San Marino's foreign activities are limited, it maintains 50 consulates worldwide, including offices in China, the United States, and most of the nations of Western and Eastern Europe. San Marino has observer status at the United Nations and belongs to several UN agencies. San Marino was a signatory of the 1975 Final Act of the Conference on Security and Cooper-

ation in Europe and continues to participate in their review sessions. By virtue of its customs union with Italy, San Marino is able to have free access to EC markets. Approximately 7,000 Americans of Sanmarinese descent live in New York, Michigan, and Ohio.

## ADDRESS

San Marino Christian Democrat Party
Piazza Bramanti Lazzari
San Marino

## REFERENCES

Dezzani, Mark. "San Marina Acts Against Piracy—At Last." *Billboard,* 27 March 1999, vol. 111, no. 13, p. 68.

Duursma, Jorri. *Self-Determination, Statehood, and International Relations of Micro-states: the Cases of Liechtenstein, San Marino, Monaco, Andorra, and the Vatican City.* New York: Cambridge University Press, 1996.

*The Economist,* 27 August 1988.

*Washington Post,* 19 June 1938.

*World Press Review,* December 1988.

**Profile researched and written by Elizabeth Gittelman (7/90; updated 6/2000).**

# SAO TOMÉ AND PRÍNCIPE

**Miguel Trovoada**
**President**
*(pronounced "MEE-gwell TRO-voh-AH-da")*

*"We hope that this appointment [a new prime minister] will put an end to the atmosphere of poor relations between the President and the government."*

The Democratic Republic of Sao Tomé and Príncipe consists of two islands, Sao Tomé and Príncipe, located off Africa's west coast. Combined, the two islands comprise 964 sq km (372 sq mi), making it second only to the Seychelles Islands as Africa's smallest nation. Its nearest neighbors to the east are Cameroon, Gabon, and Equatorial Guinea. The islands form part of a chain of extinct volcanoes and are both quite mountainous. The climate is tropical, but temperatures vary a good deal with altitude. Coastal temperatures average around 81°F, but the mountain regions average only 68°F. Seasons are distinguished more by a change in precipitation than by a change in temperature. The rainy season extends from October to May, and average annual rainfall varies from 20 to 39 inches, most of it falling on the southern portions. The capital is the town of Sao Tomé, located on the northeast coast of the island of Sao Tomé.

Reflecting its colonial history and economic links to Portugal, over 90% of its population is Roman Catholic and the primary language is Portuguese. Many of its native-born people, called the *forros*, speak a Portuguese-based creole language while recent migrants from Mozambique and Angola, the *angolares*, speak Portuguese. In recent years, laborers from Mozambique and Angola have arrived in large numbers and have increased the country's population to over 154,000. Approximately 80% of the population resides on Sao Tomé with the remainder on Príncipe. A pattern of migration and colonialism forms the background to the modern politics and economy of this archipelago nation.

Sao Tomé and Príncipe's economy is based on the export of agricultural crops, such as cocoa, coconut, palm kernels, and bananas to Western Europe, especially Portugal. Together with fishing, agriculture accounted for 23% of GDP and more than 95% of exports in 1997. The currency unit is the *dobra*. The GDP is US$164 million, growing at an annual average rate of 2.5%. Per capita GDP is estimated at US$1,100. The inflation rate was reigned in from a 1997 high of 68.2% to 10.5% in 1999 and the local currency has stabilized. The national economy is nevertheless dependent on loans and development aid from programs of the World Bank and bilateral donors, which have agreed to new programs to aid the liberalization of the economy.

## POLITICAL BACKGROUND

The islands of Sao Tomé and Príncipe were colonized by Portugal in the late 1400s as a site for sugar plantations worked by West African slaves and Portuguese overseers. The mixing of these elements over several centuries produced a creole national culture, which blended African and European traditions, languages, and economic culture. Sao Tomé and Príncipe achieved status as an overseas province of Portugal in 1951 and local autonomy in 1973. A nationalist group called the *Comissao de Liberacao de Sao Tomé and Príncipe* formed in 1960, and in 1972 it reorganized itself as the *Movimento de Liberacao de Sao Tomé and Príncipe* (MLSTP) under the leadership of Dr. Manuel Pinto da Costa. Following a 1974 military coup in Lisbon, Portugal gave independence to all of its overseas colonies. In Sao Tomé and Príncipe, elections to a constituent assembly were held in July of 1975 and the MLSTP won all 16 seats. Pinto da Costa was elected as president. During the years 1976–85 he opened trade and diplomatic ties with Eastern Europe and accepted military advisors from the Soviet Union and Cuba. In spite of growing internal opposition, Pinto da Costa served three five-year terms as president.

In 1989 the MLSTP endorsed a plan for a new constitution, which guaranteed multi-party elections, universal suffrage, and freedom of the press. Pinto da Costa agreed to step down from office and was replaced as MLSTP head by Dr. Carlos da Graca, who had returned from exile in Gabon. The party also merged with an opposition group, the *Partido Social Democratica* (PSD), to form the MLSTP-PSD. In the 1990 elections 72% of the population voted to accept a new constitution. In the new system legislative power is vested in a national assembly, which comprises 55 members elected for four years. While executive powers are invested in the government, the president, who is elected to a term of five years, is nominally head of the armed forces and in charge of foreign affairs. The constitution also limits the president to two successive terms. The government is headed by the prime minister, who has both executive and administrative duties.

The 1990 constitution, however, contains two conflicting methods for the appointment of the prime minister. Under one clause, the president retains the right to appoint the prime minister. Another clause states that the prime minister should be selected by the party that wins a majority in the elections to the National Assembly, held every four years. This structural contradiction has resulted in considerable political instability since 1991. This contradiction has been partly blamed for frequent government changes (six since the introduction of a multi-party system), delays and/or blockage of many of the major political and economic decisions, including the privatization of public companies. The 1996–98

460

coalition government proposed a revision of the 1990 constitution to clarify and curb the president's powers, which has yielded no results, and no constitutional changes have been included in the current government's plans. A supreme court holds judicial authority and is responsible only to the National Assembly.

## PERSONAL BACKGROUND

Miguel Trovoada was born on Sao Tomé Island on 27 December 1936. He completed his primary education on Sao Tomé and his secondary education in Angola. From 1957 to 1960 he studied law in Lisbon. His political career began under the tutelage of Sao Tomé and Príncipe's founding president Manuel Pinto da Costa. In 1975 after the country's first elections, President Pinto da Costa named Trovoada as his prime minister. In 1979 after disagreements over national policies, Trovoada was dismissed and fled to Paris. Trovoada returned from exile in 1991 to stand for election under the new constitution as an independent candidate but with the support of the opposition party, the *Partido de Convergencia Democratica* (PCD). For the 1992 elections Trovoada founded his own party, the *Ação Democrática Independente* (ADI), to which he has remained closely allied.

## RISE TO POWER

The results of the 30 June 1996 elections took most observers by surprise. In that election President Trovoada narrowly outpolled the expected winner, former President Pinto da Costa, but failed to achieve a majority, forcing a second election. In the run-off election President Trovoada won 52% of the vote, while Pinto da Costa got 48%. The election was declared generally free and fair by international observers, although there were allegations of an unconstitutional modification of the voter lists between the first and second rounds. The victory marked a defeat for the MLSTP-PSD, which held a formal majority in the National Assembly until the 1998 legislative elections. The MLSTP-PSB was to increase its majority from 27 seats in the 1994 elections to 31 in the legislative elections of 8 November 1998, holding all 10 seats in the cabinet. The ADI and the PCD-GR got 16 and 8 seats, respectively.

The politics of the appointment of a prime minister has continued to be a thorny issue. Trovoada has often been criticized for acting without due consultation of the government or National Assembly, and for repeated dismissals of prime ministers and dissolution of parliament at his whim. During his first five-year term, President Trovoada appointed three different prime ministers. In 1994 the PCD lost the legislative elections to the MLSTP-PSD, the former ruling party. On 15 August 1995 Trovoada and Carlos da Graca, MLSTP-PSD leader and newly appointed prime minister, were deposed in a bloodless military coup, but re-instated a week later following wide international condemnation and Angolan intervention. Soon after the failed military coup and following a legislative stalemate, Trovoada dismissed Carlos da Graca.

In order to resolve the political crisis that the country was facing, a government of national unity headed by new Prime Minister Armindo Vaz d'Almeida, former secretary general of the MLSTP-PSD, was inaugurated in 1996. This government was short-lived and Trovoada named Raul Braganca,

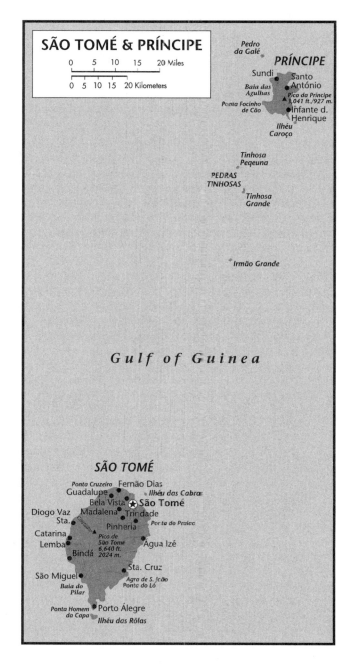

SÃO TOMÉ & PRÍNCIPE

MLSTP-PSD's assistant secretary general, to form the country's sixth government. In May 1997, Trovoada's unilateral decision to establish diplomatic relations with Taiwan without consulting cabinet or parliament led to six months of political stalemate. As political tension rose, a forum of national unity which all political parties attended, was convened in an attempt to solve Sao Tome's political stalemate, but failed to meet its objectives. In December 1998, Trovoada accepted the appointment of Guilherme Pósser da Costa, a lawyer and former foreign minister characterized as a reformist, as prime minister for the new MLSTP-PSD government. After Trovoada's veto of the first cabinet, new Prime Minister Guilherme Pósser da Costa formed a Government in January 1999, announcing an austerity program, and promising to revitalize the economy and fight corruption. Political life has since stabilized, although relations between the prime minister and the president remain touchy.

## DOMESTIC POLICY

At the time of independence from Portuguese rule in 1975, Sao Tomé and Príncipe inherited a national economy ill-equipped to provide for the welfare of its citizens. The country was dependent on protected markets in Portugal for its agricultural products. President Pinto da Costa took virtually all enterprises into state control, a reflection of his training as an economist in East Germany. The government exercised a monopoly over foreign trade and controlled prices and retail commerce through a network of "people's shops."

Implementation of socialist economic policies coincided with difficult economic conditions internationally. After 1979 world prices for cocoa, Sao Tomé and Príncipe's chief export, declined dramatically. Between 1980 and 1986 the economy grew at slightly more than 1%; between 1987 and 1991 it declined 1.2% per year. In the 1987–91 period, GNP per capita declined at a rate of 3.5% per year.

In 1985 Sao Tomé and Príncipe was faced with economic collapse and President Pinto da Costa initiated a process of economic liberalization prescribed by the World Bank and other international donors. The country invited foreign managers to bid for contracts to run state farms and sought foreign capital investment. "People's shops" were leased to private traders. In 1987 the World Bank and the African Development Bank agreed to support a three-year recovery program to increase agricultural production, reduce the trade deficit, and reduce public spending. The World Bank and the African Development Bank provided US$7 million and US$8.5 million respectively. As a part of this program the national currency, the *dobra*, was devalued twice.

Through the 1980s Sao Tomé and Príncipe's economic fortunes continued to decline despite international aid. In March of 1989 the International Monetary Fund (IMF) and the World Bank announced a structural adjustment program to accompany a new set of loans. These loans required that Sao Tomé and Príncipe reduce the size of its government payrolls and continue to privatize its economy, especially banking. The nation was slow to respond. In 1990 the IMF suspended loan payments and the World Bank threatened to follow suit. By the end of 1990 the budget deficit had reached US$4.5 million and inflation was 47%.

These economic woes set the background for the political reforms and elections of 1991. The government devalued the currency several times and reformed the banking system. By mid-1992 the IMF agreed to resume loan payments. The government announced the privatization of a series of government enterprises. In March of 1994 the government laid off 234 state employees in the first stage of its policy to reduce the budget deficit. By 1995 a total of 4,000 state workers were laid off. The 1995 bloodless and short-lived coup was fueled by massive popular unrest due to wage stagnation as the economy failed to improve. The military leaders held power only briefly before returning the civilian government to power.

Macro-economic instability, lack of economic diversification, government mismanagement, widespread corruption, political instability, forestalled economic expansion, and economic stagnation set in. The World Bank placed real GDP growth between 1985 and 1995 at an annual average rate of 1%. The World Bank structural adjustment policy which had squeezed the quality of life in the country gave way to World Bank negotiations for a new aid policy which emphasized improving the use of public sector funds and financial systems. In 1995 Sao Tome qualified for another IMF structural adjustment program. The Government faltered in its efforts at structural adjustment, and the economy continued to face serious difficulties. In 1997, the IMF suspended further disbursement for lack of compliance. Real GDP growth has remained at low levels since 1995, but it slightly improved to reach a growth of 2.5% (still slightly below the estimated population growth rate) in 1998 and 1999. Real wages for the public service had been declining since 1987. Increased militancy among the country's 3,500 civil servants (in mid-March 1998 they went on strike for the first time since independence) forced the country to effect hefty wage increases in 1997 and 1998, against IMF advice.

Signs of economic recovery are now beginning to show, bringing a ray of hope for the future. Improved budget management has brought down the inflation rate from 68.2% in 1997 to 10.5% in 1999, and the currency and interest rates are stabilizing. Despite initial resistance during the early 1990s, the privatization program has continued, and by April 1998 all companies, except four strategically placed public enterprises, had been privatized. In June 1999 the Government unveiled a major policy document: Strategic Options for the Medium Term and Action Plans 2000–2002. The document emphasizes social sector investment, macro-economic stabilization, and economic growth, and includes ambitious economic performance targets recently agreed with the IMF. The reform-minded Guilherme Pósser da Costa has promised to fight pervasive corruption, the worst corruption scandal being the issuing of fraudulent Treasury bonds worth US$500 million by the central bank. The Governor of the central Bank, Carlos Quaresma, was dismissed in relation to the fraud in December 1999, and later detained after an international warrant for his arrest was issued by Belgium. In December 1999 the IMF and World Bank endorsed the government's economic management and promised to approve a program of assistance in 2000, that may also help Sao Tome to qualify for debt relief under the IMF/World Bank heavily indebted poor countries (HIPC) initiative. In 1997 Sao Tome's external debt was equivalent to US$267 million. The potential exploitation of offshore oil and gas reserves holds promise for the improvement of the islands' economy.

## FOREIGN POLICY

Sao Tomé and Príncipe's foreign policy since 1975 has been a product of its small size and fairly unstrategic geopolitical location. Unlike the Seychelles, which are located near the Persian Gulf, Horn of Africa, and Indian Ocean shipping lanes, Sao Tomé and Príncipe have few strategic assets to offer to global powers. It has therefore adhered to a nonaligned, anti-imperialist stance which initially drew it close to the Socialist bloc. It also joined a number of international organizations. In 1975 Sao Tomé and Príncipe joined the Organization of African Unity and in 1977 became a member of the International Monetary Fund. With the collapse of its Soviet and Eastern European allies in the late

1980s, the country has enjoyed closer links with the United States and the European Union. The country was a founding member of the *Communauté Économique des Etats de l'Afrique Centrale* (CEEAC) in 1983, and the seven-member Lusophone community, the *Communidade dos Países de Língua Portuguesa* (CPLP) in 1996. In 1997 it also joined the 52-member community of Francophone countries, *La Francophonie*.

Sao Tomé and Príncipe is involved in disputes with neighboring countries over the country's maritime boundaries. Negotiations with Equatorial Guinea resulted in an accord on maritime boundaries in June 1999. Similar negotiations are continuing with Nigeria and Gabon, the outcomes of which may complicate Sao Tomé and Príncipe's oil development.

Sao Tomé and Príncipe's major trading partners are Portugal, Germany, Belgium, and Angola. France also has a number of business interests. Relations with the United States have been improving in recent years. The United States has provided economic assistance and has recently opened a branch of the Peace Corps. Trovoada's decision in 1997 to recognize Taiwan has angered China, but resulted in significant aid from Taiwan. The primary issue in Sao Tomé and Príncipe's foreign relations in the next few years will be the effect of domestic political policy on economic performance and the response of international donors to these measures.

## REFERENCES

Africa No 1 radio, Libreville, BBC Monitoring International Reports, as provided by BBC Worldwide Monitoring, 25 December 1998, 16 March 1998.

*African Research Bulletin* (1–3) June 1996).

Diario de Noticias. [Online] Lisbon, BBC Monitoring International Reports, as provided by BBC Worldwide Monitoring, 6 November 1998, 6 January 1999.

Economist Intelligence Unit. *Country Profile: Congo, Sao Tomé and Príncipe, Guinea-Bissau, Cape Verde 1997.*

Economist Intelligence Unit. *Country Profile: Congo, Sao Tomé and Príncipe, Guinea-Bissau, Cape Verde, 2000.*

Hodges, T. and M. Newitt. *Sao Tomé and Príncipe: From Plantation Colony to Microstate.* Boulder: Westview Press, 1988.

Radio National de Angola, Luanda, Summary of the World Broadcasts, as provided by BBC Worldwide Monitoring, 21 October 1996.

Radio Renascenca, Lisbon. Summary of the World Broadcasts, as provided by BBC Worldwide Monitoring, 13 November 1996.

RDP Antena 1 Radio, Lisbon, BBC Monitoring International Reports, as provided by BBC Worldwide Monitoring, 1 July 1998.

U.S. Department of State. Human Rights Reports. [Online] Available http://www.state.gov/www/global/human_rights/1999_hrp_report/saotomep.html (Accessed 10 May 2000).

Central Intelligence Agency. World Factbook 1999. [Online] Availabe http://www.cia.gov/cia/publications/factbook/tp.html (Accessed 10 May 2000).

**Profile researched and written by James C. McCann, Ph.D., Boston University, (9/96; updated by Leo Zulu, University of Illinois at Urbana-Champaign, 5/2000).**

# SAUDI ARABIA

### Fahd Bin Abdul Aziz Al-Saud
### King and Prime Minister

*(pronounced "FAHD bin AHB-dool ah-ZEEZ al-sah-OOD")*

*"The Kingdom of Saudi Arabia has always believed that no real peace can prevail in the Middle East unless a just and permanent solution to the Palestinian problem, which is the core of the struggle taking place in the region, is found."*

The Kingdom of Saudi Arabia was founded in 1932 when King Abdul Aziz Al-Saud, commonly known in the West as Al-Saud, consolidated his conquests. Saudi Arabia occupies about 80% of the Arabian peninsula and has an area of 2,149,690 sq km (829,995 sq mi). It is largely a desert country with no rivers or permanent bodies of water and has poorly defined borders. To the west lies the Red Sea; to the south, Yemen and Oman; to the southeast, the United Arab Emirates; to the east, the Persian/Arabian Gulf, Qatar, and Bahrain; and to the north, Jordan, Iraq, and Kuwait. Population figures are not reliable; however, estimates suggest Saudi Arabia has a population of 21.5 million, half of which live in urban areas. About three million of the total population are expatriates, who make up about 60% of the labor force. Virtually all indigenous Saudis are Muslims, as are more than half of the expatriate population. About 85% of the Saudis are Sunni Muslims, the majority of whom are followers of the Wahabbi movement; the remainder are Shias and are located mainly in the eastern province. Arabic is the official language, but English is understood and used in the private sector. Saudi Arabia is the site of two of the three holiest places of Islam: Mecca, the birthplace of the Prophet of Islam, with the Kaaba (the Grand Mosque) located there; and Medina, the burial place of the Prophet. Millions of Muslims from all over the world make pilgrimages to these two cities every year.

Saudi Arabia has the world's largest proven oil reserves. It is the third-largest producer and the largest exporter of crude oil. Massive agricultural development projects have helped the country achieve near self-sufficiency in wheat, eggs, milk, and vegetables. Its major trade partners are the US, the UK, Japan, and West Germany. Its main imports are machinery and equipment, foodstuff, textiles, minerals, and chemicals. The per capita GDP has been estimated at US$9,000. The *riyal* is the Saudi Arabian currency.

## POLITICAL BACKGROUND

Saudi Arabia is an absolute monarchy with the king heading the state as well as the government. There are no political parties nor any formal parliament. Neither does the country have a formal written constitution. Legislation is promulgated through royal decrees, which must be in accordance with the *Shariah*, the sacred law of Islam. The country has no formal administrative hierarchy. The Council of Ministers, appointed and headed by the king, serves both legislative and executive functions. Advisory councils and cabinet commis-

sions nominated by the king also assist mainly in the implementation of development projects.

Important and sensitive decisions are reached by consensus of the senior princes of the royal family. Additionally, members of the royal family head important ministries and hold sensitive positions in the armed forces. Since 1980, Saudi monarchs have announced several times that a committee is working to draft a basic system of rule and that a Consultative Assembly (*Majlis ash Shura*) would be established. However, no concrete steps have been taken as yet. Local government is administered through general municipal councils, district councils, and tribal and village councils.

## PERSONAL BACKGROUND

King Fahd Bin Abdul Aziz Al-Saud was born in 1920. His mother Hassa, the fifth wife of Abdul Aziz, belonged to the Sudayri clan. He obtained his early education at the palace school and later received practical training at his father's court. He was exposed to domestic and international political events at an early age. He accompanied his elder brother, Faisal, to the founding of the UN in San Francisco in 1945 and represented his country at the coronation of Queen Elizabeth II of the UK. In 1953, he became the first minister of education in the country's history. Since then, he has played a significant role in the modernization of the country. Under his supervision elaborate programs were launched to establish schools in all parts of Saudi Arabia and to encourage girls to enter public schools. In 1961, he became minister of interior when a new cabinet was formed under Faisal.

## RISE TO POWER

The line of succession to the Saudi throne passes one by one through the sons of the late King Abdul Aziz in order of seniority unless someone gives up this right voluntarily. When a king takes over, he appoints the new crown prince and heir-apparent with the consultation of the senior princes of the royal family. Even the ascension of the crown prince to the throne is not automatic as the senior princes of the royal family must confirm this step. The Saud royal family is highly secretive, and the whole process is shrouded in mystery.

Prior to becoming king, Fahd was an active member of the royal family. He supported Faisal in his dispute with his eldest brother, King Saud, in the 1950s. In the ensuing power struggle, Faisal was successful, and he was crowned king in 1964. Fahd's position was enhanced in the royal hierarchy, and he was appointed the as the interior minister by Faisal. When Faisal was assassinated in 1975, Khalid Bin Abdul Aziz became the king, and Fahd was appointed crown prince and first deputy prime minister. Because Khalid's poor health did not allow him to actively pursue the state business, he delegated the actual conduct of government to Fahd. On Khalid's death in 1982, Fahd became the king and prime minister of the Kingdom of Saudi Arabia.

## LEADERSHIP

The cohesion of the royal family and the consensus-building process have enabled the family to survive. So far, disagreements have not been highly divisive, and the royal family has been able to present a united front. Although Crown Prince Abdullah and King Fahd have not agreed on all major policy issues, the ailing Fahd has gradually turned his powers over to Abdullah since 1997. By 1999, Abdullah was widely considered to be king in all but name. Whereas Fahd was regarded as a modernist, Abdullah, only two years younger than his brother, is regarded as conservative, with a strong sense of Arab and Islamic identity. Since 1962, he has been the commander of the national guard.

Because he advocates modernization, Fahd historically has had the support of the middle class. However, the middle class lacks political leadership and does not possess the ability to organize an opposition movement. Religious and radical elements have been the most vocal opponents of the royal family. While radical Arab nationalists who were active in the 1950s and 1960s more or less lost their appeal, Islamic fundamentalists emerged in the 1970s, 1980s, and 1990s to challenge the regime. Islamic fundamentalists have criticized the royal family for its conspicuous consumption and privileges. Fahd has been a particular target due to his liberal and modern attitudes. Religious opponents demand strict observation of Islamic principles and rituals and see the process of development as leading the nation away from the pristine principles of Islam. The capture of the Grand Mosque (Kaaba) in Mecca by the Sunni Muslim extremists on the first day of the new Islamic century 1400 (November 1979) came as a surprise to the ruling family. In the past it regarded the Islamic opposition merely as an irritant devoid of serious political aspirations. The religious opposition poses a dangerous threat to the regime because it challenges the legitimacy of the royal family.

To neutralize Islamic activists and strengthen the religious basis of the ruling family, Fahd has taken various steps. He has adopted the title of the Custodian of the Two Holy Places. Islamic principles, such as the ban on liquor and segregation of sexes, are strictly enforced, and violations are severely punished. Increased funding has been allocated to religious educational institutions, and the proportion of religious studies in secular educational institutions has been increased. In the 1990s, increased activity by radical Islamists prompted a government crackdown that included widespread temporary detention of Muslim fundamentalists and long-term detention of their most prominent leaders, including radical clerics Salman al-Audah and Safar al-Hawali.

## DOMESTIC POLICY

Fahd took over as King at a time when the prices and the worldwide demand of oil were declining, which resulted in a

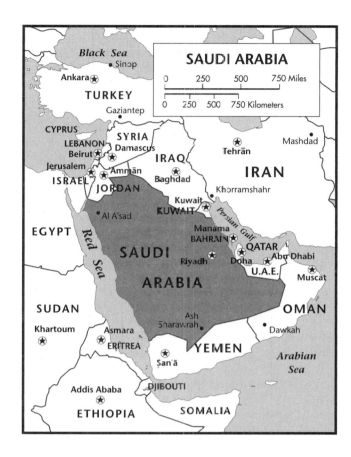

decrease in Saudi government revenues. Because defense spending was considered essential, domestic social programs were trimmed, and the cuts threatened the country's political stability. To deal with this situation, Fahd basically adopted a carrot-and-stick policy that proved rather successful. Despite continuing recession, the government undertook development programs in the poorer regions of the country to appease minorities like the Shiites, who are considered to be vulnerable to Iranian propaganda. At the same time, Fahd retained a tight grip on the government. Meanwhile, the modernization program started under Faisal to rebuild the country's infrastructure was completed.

At the end of the 1990s, Saudi Arabia's major domestic concern was the sharp decline in oil prices that took place in 1998, causing the nation's budget deficit to skyrocket. Although OPEC members agreed to cut production in March 1999, Crown Prince Abdullah warned that a boom period in the nation's economy was ending and that the Saudis would have to become accustomed to more modest oil revenues and work toward a more diversified economy.

## FOREIGN POLICY

While Saudi Arabia has always maintained close relations with the West and particularly the US, Fahd is considered to be more pro-West than other royal family members. Fahd took over as crown prince at a very crucial time. Since the October 1973 Arab-Israeli War, the oil embargo, and subsequent oil price hike, Saudi Arabia has emerged as a major actor in the international arena and is a leading power in the Arab world.

In August 1981, Fahd proposed a solution to resolve the Arab-Israeli dispute. The plan provided a compromise solution indirectly recognizing the legitimacy of Israel while providing for the creation of a Palestinian state. The Iranian revolution, the war between Iran and Iraq, and the Soviet invasion of Afghanistan in December 1979 were all alarming developments for the Saudis. In response to these events, defense spending, a major feature of Saudi expenditure, increased several-fold mainly because of the purchase or loan of armaments and military equipment from the US and other Western powers.

Although Saudi Arabia actively supported Iraq during the war with Iran, it sided with the US when Iraq invaded Kuwait in 1990, making a substantial contribution of arms, oil, and funds to the international coalition allied against Iraq. It also permitted foreign troops to be stationed on its soil, a decision at odds with its traditional policies.

In response to regional threats, Fahd has been actively involved in the formation of the Gulf Cooperation Council (GCC), which consists of Arab Gulf states in the Arabian peninsula. Saudi Arabia has had very close relations with the US since President Franklin D. Roosevelt met with King Abdul Aziz. The US has historically been a major supplier of arms to Saudi Arabia. However, the continued Arab-Israeli conflict and growing domestic opposition in the US to providing arms to Saudi Arabia have led the Saudis to find other arms suppliers, such as the UK and France. Still, Fahd is considered an advocate of close ties with the US, and during his reign, the two nations have maintained very friendly relations. US support increased following the Gulf War and Iraq's failure to comply with international pressure to disarm.

## ADDRESS
Royal Palace
Riyadh, Saudi Arabia

## REFERENCES

"Abdullah and the Ebbing Tide." *The Economist,* 23 January 1999, p. 41.

*Christian Science Monitor,* various issues.

Khuddri, Majid. *Arab Personalities in Politics.* 1981.

*New York Times,* various issues.

*Political Handbook of the World.* Ed. Arthur Banks and Thomas Muller. Binghamton, NY: CSA Publications, 1999.

"Royal Rivalry." *World Press Review,* September 1999, p. 24.

**Profile researched and written by Bashir Ahmed (7/90; revised by Rosalie Wieder 6/2000).**

# SENEGAL

## Abdoulaye Wade
### President
*(pronounced "AHB-doo-li WAD")*

*"You can rely on me. I am a candidate of the poor, farmers, youths, women and executives who all long for change at the highest office."*

Located in West Africa, midway between Arab-Mediterranean North Africa and the tropical rain forest countries along the Gulf of Guinea, the Republic of Senegal covers an area of 197,161 sq km (75,750 sq mi). Senegal was originally colonized by the Portuguese, who were followed later by the French. The country gained its independence from France on 4 April 1960 and was declared a republic on 20 August of the same year.

The capital of Senegal is Dakar, which with one million inhabitants is one of the great seaports and industrial complexes of West Africa. Senegal's total population exceeds 10 million. When the Federation of French West Africa was formed, Dakar became the federal seat of government. The country is bounded by the Atlantic Ocean on the west, and separated from Mauritania to the north by the Senegal River. On the east it is bordered by the Republic of Mali, and on the south by Guinea and Guinea-Bissau. The independent, English-speaking state of The Gambia, straddling the Gambia River, penetrates fingerlike into Senegal for over 320 km (220 mi).

The dominant ethnic group is the Wolof, who constitute about 40% of the population and whose language, Wolof, is the official language of Senegal. About 19% of the Senegalese are Serer, with the remainder belonging to other ethnic groups, including the Tukulor, the Mandinka, and the Peul. Ninety-two percent of the Senegalese are Muslim, with 6% practicing indigenous beliefs and the remaining 2% practicing Christianity. The national currency is the CFA *franc*. Per capita GDP has been estimates at US$1,600. Agricultural production includes peanuts, cotton, millet, sorghum, and rice. Fish are caught along the Atlantic coast.

## POLITICAL BACKGROUND

One of Africa's functional democracies, Senegal has a strong presidency, a national assembly of 140 members, and a 60-member Senate, a recent creation dating back only to 1998. The 7 March 1963 constitution was revised six times between 20 June 1967 and 24 April 1981. Rather than a sign of political instability, the changes reflected cautious movement away from a single dominant party to a liberal multi-party system. Presently, the president of the republic is elected by direct universal suffrage for a seven-year mandate.

Senegal was part of the Confederation of Senegambia, lasting from 1982 to 1989. The treaty called for the integration of security systems, the military, and the economic and monetary systems of Senegal and The Gambia. For a variety of reasons the union failed, and Senegambia never existed beyond the treaty. Since December 1983, Senegal has been unsuccessful in resolving a separatist insurgency in the southern Casamance region. The conflict has at times involved neighbors Guinea-Bissau and The Gambia. In 1989, Senegal found itself briefly at war with Mauritania over border and resource issues, and in 1998 Senegal sent troops in support of Guinea-Bissau's now-exiled President Vieira.

Free and fair elections in February–March 2000 ended 40 years of Socialist Party rule, producing the first change of government in Senegal's history since independence.

## PERSONAL BACKGROUND

Abdoulaye Wade was born on 29 May 1926 in the town of Kebemer. He did his primary schooling in Kebemer and Saint Louis, followed by middle school in Sebikotane at William Ponty, and high school at Van Vollenhoven in Dakar. He received a scholarship to study elementary and advanced math at Lycée Condorcet (High School) in Paris. After his college studies at Besançon, he earned his doctorate in law and economics. It was in Besançon that Wade met Viviane Vert, a student of philosophy. Both were involved in student union organization in 1952. They married several years later and have a son and daughter, Karim and Sindjeli.

Wade worked as a barrister for a few years in Besançon before returning to Senegal where he opened his own law firm and began teaching courses at the University of Dakar. He became a permanent faculty member in the law school and department of economics, and later served as dean of the law school. His many professional activities include his econometrics research at Boston University, lecturing in the faculties of law and economics at Paris II, and consulting for the OAU and the African Development Bank. He is a member of the Stockholm-based International Academy of Comparative Law. Wade has been awarded the French Legion of Honor.

Although Wade is not a soccer fanatic, he does enjoy the game, and in his younger years he enjoyed riding horseback. In his student days, he was a jazz enthusiast and collected classical, jazz, and blues. He played the violin and guitar at William Ponty and Sebikotane. His favorite poet is Clement Marot, a French author from the middle ages, and among his favorite books is Benoist-Mechin's biography of the Emperor Julian. Wade is fluent in French, English, and Wolof.

## RISE TO POWER

Abdoulaye Wade first dreamed of becoming president of Senegal so long ago he does not remember, but until joining the pan-africanist movement of Joseph Ki-Zerbo, and then working for the predecessor of the PS, his intentions were to stay in the background while inspiring others to that role. However, his teaching and law practice and his work with student unions and parties convinced him to create his own party, the *Parti Démocratique Sénégalais* (PDS), in 1974.

In 1978, Wade was elected parliamentarian on the PDS ticket and re-elected in 1983. Four-time defeated presidential candidate in 1978, 1983, 1988, and 1993, he considered the 1988 and 1993 elections "stolen" by Diouf. Nevertheless, he twice held the post of minister of state in Diouf's government, from April 1991 to October 1992 and from March 1994 to 1998. In October 1999, Wade returned to Dakar after being away for 373 days. He was met in Dakar by an estimated one million supporters and given a similar reception in St. Louis. In March 2000, he became Senegal's third president, winning 58% in the second round to defeat Abdou Diouf.

## LEADERSHIP

Wade's trademark is his shaved head, but he truly is the ionoclast of Senegalese politics. In the 1980s, he coined the word *sopi*, wolof for "change." He was charged with complicity in the murder of constitutional court Vice President Boubacar Seye and was arrested for his alleged involvement in the 1994 Dakar riots. In both cases he was acquitted of the charges. He takes great interest in events around the continent, having served as Diouf's emissary to

Zaire and personally intervening with General Sani Abacha for the release of General Obasanjo when he was imprisoned. He has written President Lansana Conté of Guinea for Alpha Conde's unconditional release from prison. A lesser man would have become discouraged over the past 26 years during his quest for the presidency.

Wade has urged youth to be active in developing the country and building a democratic society. Although he has backed off some of his campaign promises, he would like to dissolve the parliament, schedule new elections before the end of 2000, and draft legislation limiting presidential terms from seven to five years with a limit of two terms. He is a committed liberal and pan-Africanist, who advocates a federation of West Africa, excluding hegemon Nigeria. Wade is the vice president of the Liberal International and sees himself rebuilding Senegal with its youthful human resources.

## DOMESTIC POLICY

Abdoulaye Wade inherits a treasury, not empty, but hardly overflowing, and a government apparatus beset by corruption. In 1999, Senegal placed 58 out of 99 countries on Transparency International's list of most corrupt countries. In his campaign, he promised to fight corruption and to offer a brighter future for youth. To this end, he envisions giving future youth a head start by establishing nursery and pre-schools throughout the country. For the present generation, he plans to build upon existing programs to diversify employment in agriculture and in agricultural-related industries.

Approximately 80% of the population are employed in agriculture, and the groundnut (peanut) is the most important cash and export crop. Because of adverse weather conditions, including drought, output has been uneven in recent years, falling to disastrously low levels in the early and mid-1980s. The government has attempted to reduce dependence on groundnuts by encouraging diversification, in particular by expanding production of cotton, rice, and sugar. Wade has promised to initiate reforestation programs throughout the country.

Between 1988 and 1992, Senegal lost some 9,000 jobs due to structural adjustment programs. Urban unemployment rose to levels of 20% to 30%. Aside from these challenges, Wade had to configure a government able to address severe economic and social constraints and to deal with the fall-out sure to arise from the Socialist Party's survival instincts. Further, Wade had to find the means to resolve the 17-year Casamance conflict, which was still smoldering in June 2000.

## FOREIGN POLICY

Abdoulaye Wade is likely to lead a more pro-active, visible foreign policy than his predecessor. Besides his extensive European and American connections, he has contacts and acquaintances across the continent, ranging from Colonel Khaddafi to Denis Sassou-Nguesso. He will continue Abdou Diouf's good relations with Presidents Yahya Jammeh of The Gambia and Kumba Yala of Guinea-Bissau.

His previous experience gained as Diouf's minister of state will stand him well. In Zaire, for example, he attempted to mediate the impasse between Mobutu and the opposition. When Obasanjo had been imprisoned, he tried to negotiate with Nigerian General Sani Abacha for his release. He pleaded Sassou-Nguesso's cause and that of Eyadema to European donors. Wade's plan to meet President Lansana Conté for the release of Alpha Conde is straightforward: "As an African, I take on the right to implicate myself in everything happening on the continent."

Wade has said he will argue for the creation of a confederation of West African states based on the American federalist model. However, the 15-member federation would not include Nigeria, a behemoth he considers unstable. The confederation would take on construction of transportation networks, telecommunications, environment, and health. Wade would be ready to accept the post of governor of Senegal.

## ADDRESS

Office of the President
Avenue Roume
BP 1 68
Dakar, Senegal

## REFERENCES

*Africa News*, September 1989.
Africa News Online. [Online] Available http://www.africanews.org/west/stories/1999_feat1.html (Accessed June 2000).
*Africa Report*, November-December 1982.
*Africa Research Bulletin*, various issues.
Africaonline. [Online] Available http://www.africa-online.com (Accessed June 2000).
Economist Intelligence Unit Ltd. *EIU Country Reports*. February 2000.
Integrated Regional Information Network (IRIN). [Online] Available http://www.reliefweb.int/IRIN (Accessed June 2000).
*Jeune Afrique*, various issues.
*Le Monde Diplomatique*, April 1988.
USAID. *Democracy Assessment of Senegal*, 2 June 1997.
Villalon, Leonardo A. *African Affairs*. April 1994, vol. 93, no. 371, p. 163.

**Profile researched and written by Robert J. Groelsema (6/2000).**

# SIERRA LEONE

## Ahmad Tejan Kabbah
### President
*(pronounced "ah-MAD TAY-jun KA-ba")*

*"My duty is to serve the entire population of Sierra Leone, which means that no one religious or tribal group, and no one section of our population can lay claim to preferential treatment from my administration."*

The Republic of Sierra Leone is located on the coast of West Africa, bisected by the 8th degree of latitude. It is bordered by Guinea on the northwest and northeast, and by Liberia on the southeast. The country's total area of 71,740 sq km (27,699 sq mi) is characterized by dense rain-forests in the south, coastal lowlands in the west, and a steep escarpment rising to a rugged and hilly interior in the east. The largest city is the capital and principal port of Freetown.

The total population is estimated at 5.3 million. The official language is English, though Krio (a combination of English, Yoruba, and other West African languages) is widely spoken. Of the 16 ethno-linguistic groups found in Sierra Leone, the northern Mende and southern Temne are the largest, with about one million members each. Descendants of repatriated and "recaptured" ex-slaves, known as the "Krio" (Creole) dominate the area around the capital. Most Creole descendants are Christians, and many northerners are Muslims, with a large number of the remaining population practicing traditional religions.

The official currency is the *leone*. Sierra Leone is the world's second-largest producer of rutile (an important component in paints and non-stick cookware). Rutile has replaced diamonds as the country's main source of hard currency, largely because the diamond-rich eastern region has been outside of government control for several years. Other mineral exports include iron ore and bauxite. Coffee, cocoa, palm kernels, and rice represent the primary agricultural exports. With a GNP of US$2.7 billion, the average annual per capita income is only US$530—making Sierra Leone one of the world's poorest nations.

## POLITICAL BACKGROUND
The modern state of Sierra Leone has its origin in the settlement at Freetown of some 400 free blacks from England in 1787. This group was joined in the 1790s by free blacks from Nova Scotia and Jamaica. With backing from prominent British Abolitionists, the settlement grew and became a British colony in 1808. Over the next four decades, the original settlers were joined by some 40,000 "recaptives"—the cargo of slave ships intercepted by the British Anti-Slaving Squadron in operation along the West African coast. Thus, from its earliest years, Sierra Leone was one of the world's great cultural melting pots. The "Creoles," as the settlers came to be known, drew upon their knowledge of West Africa, Europe, and the New World to become influential merchants in the "legitimate" trade that developed in the period after the slave trade. Creole missionaries were instrumental in the spread of Christianity throughout West Africa. During the 19th century, Sierra Leone developed into one of the region's intellectual centers. Newspapers printed in Freetown were read throughout West Africa. The Foura Bay Teacher Training College was established in 1827, and in 1876 achieved University College status.

In 1896, the British declared the interior to the north and east of Freetown to be a British protectorate. The Creole population continued to play an influential role in the affairs and civil service of the colony up to the end of World War II. In 1951 a new unitary constitution, which granted universal adult suffrage, politically empowered the region's indigenous ethnic groups. Elections in 1953 and 1958 saw victory for the largely Mende-backed Sierra Leone Peoples Party (SLPP), with the party's leader, Milton Margai holding the positions of chief minister and prime minister, respectively. On 27 April 1961, Sierra Leone was granted independence within the British Commonwealth, with the SLPP still in power. In 1967, the All-Peoples Congress (APC), under the leadership of Siaka Stevens, succeeded in defeating the SLPP at the polls. A military coup prevented the APC from taking immediate control of the government. Within a year, however, a counter-coup displaced the military government and placed Stevens and the APC in power.

The 1970s were a decade of declining national revenues and growing corruption within the government. Stevens' regime survived a coup attempt in 1971 and in June of 1978 re-wrote the constitution to accommodate a new system of one-party rule under the APC. The early 1980's saw continuing economic decline and growing political strife, with violent clashes with workers and students becoming commonplace. In 1985, Stevens retired and Joseph Saidu Momoh (who was then a cabinet minister and head of the armed forces) was nominated as the sole candidate for president. Running uncontested, he received 99% of the vote. Momoh's acceptance of IMF austerity programs did little to improve the country's economic situation and caused considerable hardship among the poor. Momoh launched several highly-publicized anti-corruption campaigns, but these were frequently derided as no more than opportunities to purge his political opponents from the civil service.

In 1992, the Momoh government was overthrown by a group of junior officers. These men had been serving in combat against the Revolutionary United Front (RUF) in the country's southeast, near the Liberian border. They established the National Provisional Ruling Council and chose the 25-year-old Valentine Strasser as head of state. The NPRC vowed that they would bring a quick end to the civil war that had begun the year before and would return the country to civilian rule as soon as possible. Over the next four years, Strasser survived numerous coup attempts. Though the NPRC was unsuccessful in bringing an end to the insurgency of the RUF, the Strasser government did take concrete steps towards elections that would hand over power to a civilian government. In 1996, Strasser was overthrown in a bloodless coup. He was succeeded by his second-in-command, Julius Maada Bio.

Many observers feared that Bio's coup would mean an end to the transition to civilian rule. Nonetheless, during his short period as head of state of just under three months, Bio oversaw parliamentary and presidential elections—no small feat in the war-ravaged country. The presidential contest included a run-off election between the presidential front-runners: Tejan Kabbah of the Sierra Leone People's Party (SLPP) and Karefa-Smart of the United National People's Party (UNPP). The final results saw Kabbah and the SLPP win by a commanding three to two margin. Kabbah took power on 29 March 1996.

## PERSONAL BACKGROUND

Alhaji Ahmad Tejan Kabbah was born on 16 February 1932, in Pendemba, Kailahun District—part of the country's eastern province. His family moved to the capital of Freetown when he was one year old. Though a Muslim, he attended Catholic schools, including the elite Saint Edwards Academy. A distinguished student, Kabbah went on to study economics at University College, Wales, and later received a law degree. He is married to Patricia Tucker Kabbah, herself described as a "devout Catholic." She holds an MA in French from the University of Chicago as well as a law degree.

## RISE TO POWER

Kabbah's background is more that of technocrat than professional politician. He joined the SLPP in 1954. Upon completing his education abroad, he returned to Sierra Leone to serve as a district commissioner in the Moyamba, Kono, Bombali, and Kambia districts (thus having served in each of the country's major regions). He later served as a deputy secretary in the Ministry of Social Welfare and as the permanent secretary in charge of both the Ministry of Education and the Ministry of Trade and Industry. As the Stevens government became increasingly insular during the early 1970s, Kabbah sought administrative work outside of Sierra Leone with the United Nations. He first worked as a deputy chief for the UN's West African division, and then served as a United Nations Development Program (UNDP) representative to Lesotho (1973), Tanzania and Uganda (1976), and Zimbabwe (1979). In 1979, he became the chief of the UNDP eastern and southern African divisions, where he was directly responsible for assistance to liberation movements. Two years later, he became a UN director for administration and management.

Kabbah's work in Sierra Leone resumed when he was selected to chair an advisory council formed to review the 1991 constitution. Such an intimate knowledge of the constitution, combined with his extensive experience in national

and international administration, was a major factor in his selection as the presidential candidate for the SLPP in the 1996 elections.

## LEADERSHIP

Though the presidency is the first elected office held by Kabbah, he proved to be a savvy and resilient politician. Upon assuming office, he moved to secure a broad power base by establishing an unusually large cabinet which sought to accommodate as large a number of interest groups as possible. In the first few months of his presidency, Kabbah took several steps to end the civil war, which had raged since 1991. He continued peace talks with the Revolutionary United Front (RUF) that had been initiated by his predecessor. Kabbah ended the government's reliance upon South African mercenaries—instead counting on Nigerian military aid, his own army, and Kamajor militias to turn the tide against the RUF.

Despite this promising start, Kabbah was unable to accomplish all of his goals. On 25 May 1997, his government was unseated in a coup led by Johnny Paul Koroma, who was backed by both the Sierra Leonian military and the RUF—confirming suspicions that there had been extensive cooperation between the army and the rebels. Kabbah fled the country and called on the international community to aid in the removal of Koroma and the return of Sierra Leone to democratic rule. Koroma's government, the Armed Forces Revolutionary Council (AFRC), soon became an international pariah, failing to earn recognition from a single nation or international body. Further, Koroma's government soon found itself in conflict with a West African ECOMOG

(Economic Community Monitoring Group) force charged with returning Kabbah to power. On 15 February 1998, after months of unsuccessful negotiations, the ECOMOG forces, joined by Kamajor militias still loyal to Kabbah, launched a concerted attack. Within two weeks, ECOMOG had seized the capital and was making arrangements for the return of Kabbah. On 10 March 1998, Kabbah was reinstated as president.

## DOMESTIC POLICY

The most pressing domestic issue for Kabbah's government is to bring an end to the unfinished rebellion of the military and the RUF. Despite ECOMOG's defeat of the forces loyal to Koroma in urban centers, numerous pockets of former soldiers and rebels continue to fight a guerrilla war against Kabbah supporters. This creates a dilemma for Kabbah, who is clearly eager to reduce the size and influence of the military. He has called for the disarming of all combatants who supported Koroma and has asked the Commonwealth for aid in training the country's police force. Kabbah has also moved to consolidate his power by reducing the size of his cabinet to 15 members, though he has also established an additional advisory committee to demonstrate that he still represents the interests of the entire population.

Kabbah is aware that, for the country to move forward, the antagonisms spawned by years of civil war and corruption must be overcome. Since being returned to the presidency he has made repeated calls for tolerance and reconciliation, asking citizens to allow the country's judicial system to bring to justice those who committed atrocities and abused their power. Johnny Paul Koroma's AFRC, now allied with the Sierra Leone Army (SLA), could provide Kabbah with a useful ally in moving the provisions of the Lome Accord ahead.

Kabbah has stressed the importance of economic reforms. In this effort he has the support of the IMF, which issued a us$21 million post-war loan for emergency assistance to help speed disarmament, demobilization, rehabilitation, and reconstruction. The IMF and the World Bank have issued an additional us$155 million in credits and loans to boost a return to peace.

The revitalization of the Sierra Leone Produce Marketing Board, improved government cooperation with the private sector, the reinvigoration of the mining sector, improved national control over the maritime fishing sector, and the return of Sierra Leonians in the diaspora have all been highlighted as key components in the rebuilding of the country's devastated economy. Reasserting government control over the diamond fields—by military force if necessary—is seen as essential to end the war. Such demands will sorely test Kabbah's considerable leadership skills.

## FOREIGN POLICY

The key objective for Kabbah must be to build upon the international support which he assembled for his return to Sierra Leone. It is likely that Kabbah will rely on the continued presence of UNAMSIL (UN peacekeepers) in lieu of ECOMOG troops as a means of ensuring the stability of his government. If he is to be successful in cutting off the RUF's diamond smuggling, he will also need international cooperation to control the country's diamond trade. This will require concerted diplomacy with neighbors Liberia and Guinea, as well as Ghana and Nigeria. His dependence on the Commonwealth also demands continued efforts to clear up allegations of human rights abuses.

Tensions are likely to continue between Kabbah and Charles Taylor, president of Liberia. Taylor has had a very uneasy relationship with both ECOMOG and Nigeria. He also covertly supported Koroma's government and the RUF.

Beyond the West African region, both the Commonwealth and US have shown strong support for Kabbah, hailing his return as a victory for African democracy. Such praise has translated to much-needed foreign aid, at least to the present. Nine years of civil war and political turmoil have weakened international confidence in Sierra Leone, and Kabbah is aware that his country must show progress towards long-term stability quickly in order to avoid donor fatigue and the discouragement of international investors. Such foreign investment is crucial to any sort of long-term economic recovery.

## ADDRESS

The State House
Siaka Stevens Street
Freetown, Sierra Leone

## REFERENCES

Africa News Online. [Online] Available http://www.africanews.org/west/stories/1999_feat1.html (Accessed 6/00).

Africaonline. [Online] Available http://www.africa-online.com (Accessed 6/00).

Agence France Presse, 17 January–3 March 1996.

BBC Summary of World Broadcasts, 21 January–4 March 1996.

CIA World Factbook, 1999.

Deutsche Presse-Agentur, 3 March 1996.

The Economist, 20 January 1996.

Economist Intelligence Unit Ltd. EIU Country Reports. 15 February 2000.

Government of Sierra Leone. Press Release, 13–14 January 1998.

Integrated Regional Information Network (IRIN). [Online] Available http://www.reliefweb.int/IRIN (Accessed 6/00).

Inter Press Service, 22 January 1996.

Jane's Defense Weekly, 24 January 1996.

Jerusalem Post, 6 February 1996.

Kabbah, Ahmad Tejan. "Address to the Nation," 10 March 1998.

Panafrican News Agency, 3–17 March 1998.

Periscope Daily Defense News Capsules, 22–25 January 1996.

Reuters Ltd., 17 January–3 March 1996.

Sierra Leone News Archives, 1997–1998. Available http://www.sierra-leone.org/slnews0398.html (Accessed 6/00).

USAID. Sierra Leone Options Paper for Development Assistance. 28 February 2000.

US Department of State. Sierra Leone Country Report on Human Rights Practices for 1999.

Xinhua News Agency, 25 January–3 March 1996.

**Profile researched and written by Jonathan T. Reynolds, Livingstone College (6/98; updated by Robert J. Groelsema 6/00)**

# SINGAPORE

## Goh Chok Tong
### Prime Minister
*(pronounced "GO CHUCK TUNG")*

*"We must seek common ground and forge consensus on major issues. Then we will continue to have political stability, the bedrock of our social harmony and economic prosperity."*

The Republic of Singapore is a city-state located on the southern tip of the Malay Peninsula. Singapore's total area of 622 sq km (240 sq mi) is comprised of a single large island and 50 other islets. The population is estimated at 3.5 million, growing at a rate of 1.15% per year. Because of its limited area, Singapore is among the most densely populated countries in the world. The population is ethnically diverse, consisting of: 77% Chinese, 15% Malays, 7% Indians and Pakistanis, and a small percentage of other groups. Major religions include Buddhism, Taoism, Confucianism, Hinduism and Islam. Christianity is also a major religion in Singapore due to the controversial activity of evangelical groups. English is the major language on the island, but Malay, Tamil and Mandarin Chinese are also common. The diverse nature of Singapore's population is seen as a source of potential conflict by the government, which sometimes takes steps to counter movements which might spark conflict. For example, English is promoted as a common language since it is the first language of none of the major ethnic groups.

Singapore originally served as an intermediary center of trade, acting as a site for transshipment of rubber, timber, petroleum and other regional products. Since the 1960s its economy has grown at an average rate of 8.5% per year. Because of this rapid industrial development, Singapore is known as one of the four "little dragons" or "little tigers" of Asia, along with South Korea, Taiwan and Hong Kong. Major exports include office and data machines, machinery, petroleum products, telecommunications equipment, chemicals, textiles, and garments. GDP is US$91.7 billion, and Singaporeans enjoy an average per capita income of over US$26,300. The currency is the Singapore dollar.

## POLITICAL BACKGROUND
Colonized by the British in 1861, Singapore achieved self rule in 1959. It joined the Federation of Malaysia in 1963, but seceded and declared itself an independent republic on 9 August 1965. Under the constitution of 1959, Singapore has a parliamentary system of government. The unicameral parliament is composed of 83 members. Voting is compulsory and suffrage is universal for all citizens who are at least 21 years old. The ruling party in parliament must call a national election after no more than five years in power. The prime minister heads the cabinet and plays a leading role in the government. Previously ceremonial, the office of the president was recently expanded to included veto power over official appointments and some government spending. The president

may also appoint a small number of "non-constituency members of parliament" (NCMPs), who are not allowed to vote on some major matters, such as constitutional amendments and government expenditures.

The People's Action Party (PAP), founded in 1954, has always dominated the parliament. Since a major opposition party withdrew in 1966, the highest number of seats held at one time by opposition parties has been four. The PAP received 65% of the vote in the most recent general elections on 2 January 1997, winning 81 of the 83 seats. It is expected that the president will appoint a NCMP from the losing opposition party candidates with the best showing at the polls.

## PERSONAL BACKGROUND
Goh Chok Tong was born in Singapore on 20 May 1941. Because his father died when he was nine and his mother worked as a teacher during the day, Goh and his four younger brothers and sisters were raised mainly by relatives. He earned first class honors at the University of Singapore, receiving a Bachelor of Arts degree in economics in 1964. Two years later he was awarded a Master of Arts degree in development economics from Williams College in the US. He is married to Tan Choo Leng, a lawyer. They have two children.

## RISE TO POWER
Two main factors propelled Goh through the ranks of the People's Action Party (PAP) in the 1970s and 1980s: his effectiveness as a technocrat and the belief that Singapore needed to develop a younger generation of leaders. After serving as an administrative officer in the economics planning unit of the government, he became managing director of the Neptune Orient Lines. The success of this shipping company attracted the attention of finance minister, Hon Sui Sen. Hon convinced the 35-year-old Goh to run for parliament in the 1976 general election as a member of PAP. Despite his lack of political experience, by 1979 Goh was already the trade and industry minister and the PAP's second assistant secretary-general, with important election responsibilities.

In the early 1980s Goh held various cabinet posts in the health and defense ministries. He also chaired PAP campaigns in the 1981 by-election and the 1984 general election—in which opposition party candidates won seats in parliament for the first time in over a decade. Despite this setback, the PAP leadership continued to groom him for higher positions,

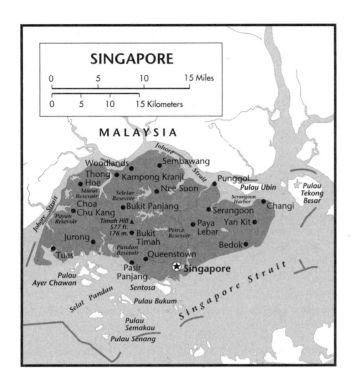

## SINGAPORE

and Goh was made first deputy prime minister and minister for defense after the 1984 election. Goh was now formally in line to succeed Prime Minister Lee Kuan Yew, and took over many of the day-to-day responsibilities of running the government. When Lee relinquished the premiership in November 1990, he chose Goh to replace him. Goh thus became the second prime minister in Singapore's history. He works with President Ong Teng Cheung, president since 1 September 1993 and reelected in 1999.

## LEADERSHIP
When Goh was chosen prime minister, it was widely believed that he would bring a new leadership style. The former prime minister, Lee Kuan Yew, was authoritarian in his vengeful pursuit of prominent political opponents. He tolerated little dissent as he practiced a strict form of social engineering. In contrast, Goh had a reputation for seeking consensus and hearing other opinions. But his leadership style has not marked a major transition from that of Lee.

In August 1991 Goh called a general election two years before it was required, as a way of consolidating his position. And although PAP won handily, with 61% of the total, the result was considered a boost to opposition parties. The PAP's percentage of the total vote had fallen for the third straight election, and the opposition had increased its number of seats to a 25-year high.

Goh was determined to reverse that pattern when he called the 1997 election. His reelection was certain; opposition parties repeated their 1991 strategy of contesting fewer than half the seats in parliament. This encouraged people to cast a "protest" vote for the opposition by removing any concern that the PAP might actually be defeated. Goh countered that through reforms and redistricting, which tied PAP members more closely to local politics and made it easier to see which neighborhoods had voted for opposition parties. He then

made it clear that neighborhoods with high vote totals for opposition parties would be the last to receive government upgrades for housing projects. Goh was an energetic force during the campaign, focusing attention on two electoral districts with high opposition support. The results—an increase in the PAP's percentage of the vote total and the recapturing of seats lost in previous elections—marked a major victory for Goh.

The PAP under Goh is decidedly intolerant of opposition politicians or foreign publications whom it feels have overstepped the bounds of reasonable dissent. A favorite tool for striking back is the lawsuit; several opposition leaders and international newspapers have been successfully sued for libel. After the 1997 election, PAP leaders filed 21 lawsuits against two members of the Workers' Party, mainly based on comments made during the campaign. One of the two fled to Malaysia and the court ordered him to put US$11 million in escrow.

Goh is a champion of "Asian values" and criticizes the West for its abandonment of family values. He complains about the treatment of Singapore by the Western media, arguing that they attempt to influence domestic politics and are culturally insensitive. He claims that the 1997 PAP victory proved that Singapore had "rejected Western-style liberal democracy and freedoms, putting individual rights over that of society." He defends Singapore's style of governance and argues that the Western media focuses too much attention on restrictions to information rather than emphasizing those information sources which remain available.

One reason that leadership styles have not changed may be that Lee Kuan Yew is still an active and influential voice. He has remained a senior minister without portfolio ever since stepping down from the top post, and his public statements carry great weight. Since Goh had been involved in the Lee government for several years, it is not surprising that few major policy or stylistic changes would occur when he took over as prime minister. Another factor is the PAP's fear that younger generations will forget how they achieved their current level of prosperity, and thus will undermine the foundations of that success. Aware of this, Goh seems determined not to make any major break with past approaches to governance.

## DOMESTIC POLICY
For years Singapore has been known for its phenomenal economic growth. The Organization for Economic Cooperation and Development (OECD) considers Singapore to be a "developed" country and World Bank statistics rank it as one of the richest countries in the world in terms of per capita GNP. Singapore's *surplus* totaled nearly 13% of the total 1996 GDP—providing the government with a powerful tool to direct future economic development. Despite major disruption from the Asian Crisis in 1997 and 1998, the economy survived intact. By 2000, the government was again projecting a budgetary surplus amidst modest tax cuts.

This rapid growth creates concern that the high cost of property and wages will cause the manufacturing sector to decline in the face of competition from other countries in the region. In finance, services, and transport Singapore is a regional economic leader and has become a major investor in Southeast Asia and China.

Common social problems such as crime, homelessness, poverty, and pollution are almost nonexistent. Some attribute this success to unique government policies. Many key aspects of life have been closely regulated. For example, the ownership and use of automobiles are discouraged, but an effective mass transit system provides an attractive alternative. The Housing Development Board spearheaded residential development which allows most citizens to own their own apartments in government-owned buildings. The upgrading policy which Goh used to spark his victory in the 1997 elections is a multi-billion dollar program to improve these buildings. In addition, Singapore has harsh criminal laws. Convicted drug dealers are executed, and even minor offenses such as chewing gum or feeding pigeons can lead to fines of hundreds of dollars.

One problem which concerns Goh's government is the aging of the population. Within the next 25 years more than a quarter of the population is expected to be over 60. In 1996 a Tribunal for the Maintenance of Parents was established to intervene when adult children are accused of neglecting their aging parents. This policy enforces the traditional value of respect for elders and seeks to ensure that a large part of the population does not become reliant on the government in their old age.

## FOREIGN POLICY

With a small population and no territorial ambitions or major strategic rivals, Singapore's global concerns are primarily economic in nature. It is a regional center for business and an increasingly important source of foreign investment in Asia. Despite a population of only three million people, Singapore's total volume of trade is the 13th highest in the world. In 1996 Singapore's importance in the economic growth of Asia was acknowledged as it hosted the World Trade Organization's first-ever meeting of trade ministers, with representatives from 160 countries.

Singapore's economic might gives Goh's government significant clout in the region, as in its 1994 decision to invest US$15 billion in development projects in Asia. But economic concerns can also create rivalries. Singapore has had a longstanding rivalry with Hong Kong in areas like financial services, communications, and regional headquarters of major corporations. Singapore's government, which fears becoming too economically reliant on service sectors, wants very much to maintain a manufacturing base for its economy. This forces it into competition with neighboring Thailand, Indonesia, and Malaysia, which can offer improving infrastructures, larger markets, cheaper wages, and lower property

costs to investors. Responding to some of these pressures, Goh announced that his government would review the major factors affecting Singapore's economic competitiveness.

Singapore's domestic policies have sometimes been a source of international conflict. Relations with the Philippines were strained in 1995 when a Filipino maid convicted of murder was executed. In 1994 the caning of an American teenager convicted of vandalism created tensions with the US. During the most recent campaign, Goh reacted angrily when the US government criticized the PAP for promising to consider electoral results when implementing its program of housing improvements. Goh and Lee sparked diplomatic incidents with Malaysia in 1996 and 1997 with remarks which were taken as insults. However, in April 1999, Singapore conducted joint military exercises with Malaysia, reflecting a turnaround from 1998 when Malaysia withdrew from military exercises stipulated in the Five-Power Defense Agreement involving Australia, New Zealand, UK, Singapore, and Malaysia.

Aside from these diplomatic incidents, Singapore's foreign relations are generally smooth. Although China and the US are political rivals in Asia, good relations with both are maintained. The Goh government feels a significant cultural bond with China and enjoys growing economic ties to the country. The US is already a major trading partner and has been granted access to its air and naval facilities.

## ADDRESS

Prime Minister's Office

Istana Annexe

Orchard Rd.

Singapore 238823

## REFERENCES

*Current World Leaders,* February 1997.

*The Economist,* 21 August 1993–8 February 1997.

*Far Eastern Economic Review,* 12 December 1996–6 February 1997

*Forbes,* 29 March 1993.

*New York Times,* 23 December 1996–27 March 1997.

"Singapore." US Department of State Publication #8240. Washington DC: US Department of State, Bureau of Public Affairs, December 1995.

*Straits Times* (Singapore), 4 January–8 February 1997.

Westlake, Michael, ed. *Far Eastern Economic Review Asia 1996 Yearbook.* Hong Kong: Review Publishing, 1995.

**Profile researched and written by Scott Hvizdos (4/97; updated 5/00).**

# SLOVAKIA

## Mikulas Dzurinda
## Prime Minister

*(pronounced "MI-ku-lash dzuh-RIN-dah")*

*"The basic precondition for a successful fulfillment of tasks that stand ahead of us is political stability. There is no time for artificial ideological conflicts."*

The Slovak Republic is located in Central Europe and shares its borders with five states: Austria, the Czech Republic, Hungary, Poland, and Ukraine. Its total area is 49,034 sq km (18,932 sq mi).

Slovakia's population is 5.4 million. Approximately 86% of the people are Slovaks. Other nationalities include Hungarians (10.76%), the Roma (2.30%), Czechs (0.80%), Ruthenians, Ukrainians, Germans, Jews, Poles, and Croats. The official language is Slovak, a Slavic language. Religious affiliation is 60% Roman Catholic, 10% atheist, 8% Protestant, 4% Orthodox, and 18% unidentified.

Slovakia's currency is the Slovak *Koruna* (Sk). More than 83% of the country's industry is privately owned. The GDP has grown steadily since 1993 at the rate of 4.2–7% yearly—reaching a per capita GDP of US$8,300. The unemployment rate stands at 14% of the workforce.

## POLITICAL BACKGROUND

During the past several centuries the lands of the Czech Crown were ruled from Vienna, while Slovakia fell under the Hungarian domain. The Czechs enjoyed a relatively high degree of cultural autonomy from Vienna. The Slovaks, however, were subjected to the policies of Magyarization—becoming Hungarian through forced linguistic assimilation. Consequently, the Czechs were better prepared for independent statehood when the Czech lands and Slovakia were joined in the common state of Czechoslovakia in 1918. As a result, the republic was ruled and administered, to a great extent, from Prague. More that one million Czech professionals moved to Slovakia and played a key role in the urbanization and industrialization of the republic, and in the development of its educational system.

The governance of the inter-war Czechoslovak Republic was derived from the doctrine of "Czechoslovakism," meaning that the Czech and Slovaks comprise one nation that speaks two similar languages. The main purpose of the doctrine was to minimize the influence of large German and Hungarian minorities that remained in Czechoslovakia after the partition of the Austro-Hungarian monarchy. Although the Czechoslovak state became one of the most stable and prosperous democracies in Central Europe, it was dismembered by Nazi Germany in 1938. The Czech lands and Moravia fell under German control and formed a so-called *Protektorat,* while Slovakia was turned into Hitler's puppet state under the leadership of Jozef Tiso. Both, the Slovak State and the *Protektorat* lasted until the end of the Second World War. In 1945 Czechoslovakia was reunified.

The Czechoslovak Communist Party staged a coup in 1948, and Czechoslovakia became one of the satellites of the Soviet Empire. The 1949 Constitution proclaimed that Czechoslovakia is a unitary state comprised of two equal nations, Czechs and Slovaks. In 1968, Alexander Dubcek, a Communist Party leader, initiated the democratic reform movement known as "Prague Spring." His attempt to build "socialism with a human face" was crushed, however, by an invasion of the Soviet-led armies of the Warsaw Pact in August 1968. An amendment to the Constitution gave Slovakia a nominal degree of autonomy, including its own government and legislature, making Czechoslovakia a federation of two republics. In practice, however, the federation was ruled from Prague, and the federal arrangements were unnoticed in the repressive aftermath of the "Prague Spring," the so-called "period of normalization."

After 20 years of "normalization," the hard-line Communist regime of Czechoslovakia crumbled in only 10 days, as the 1989 "Velvet Revolution" led to a peaceful transfer of power. In December 1989, a former dissident playwright, Vaclav Havel, became the president of Czechoslovakia. Free elections were held in Czechoslovakia on 8 June 1990, and new political parties, the Civic Forum (CF) and its Slovak counterpart, the Public Against Violence (PAV), won. Yet, in Slovakia the PAV faced a strong challenge from Jan Carnogursky's Christian Democratic Movement (ChDM). The transitional process soon ran into inter-republic disagreements over the structure of the federation, competencies of republican governments, and the pace and strategy of economic reforms. By 1991, strong political parties emerged in both republics, each with its own national agenda. Vaclav Klaus and his Civic Democratic Party (CDP) represented the interests of the Czech Republic. In Slovakia, the Movement for a Democratic Slovakia (MDS) was led by Vladimir Meciar. Both parties won electoral victories in their respective republics in the June 1992 elections. Despite public opinion polls that favored the continuation of a unified Czechoslovakia, the party leaders swiftly agreed on the dissolution of the federation. The peaceful dissolution, or the "Velvet Divorce," was preceded by more than 60 agreements, signed by political representatives of the Czechs and Slovaks. In December 1992, the Federal Assembly voted to dissolve the union and itself. Slovakia became a sovereign, independent state on 1 January 1993.

In Slovakia, Meciar and the MDS were plagued by internal fragmentation and by the absence of a stable parliamentary majority. Meciar's authoritarian and confrontational style quickly alienated many of his former supporters. Several party leaders deserted the governing MDS and formed smaller splinter-parties. These splinter-groups, the opposition (comprised mainly of the ChDM and the Party of the Democratic Left-PDL), and ethnic Hungarian parties gained strength as more deputies left the MDS. Finally, in March 1994, the opposition managed to pass a no-confidence vote with the help of President Michal Kovac. Following Meciar's resignation, the government of Jozef Moravcik retained power for only six months.

Meciar's MDS bounced back in the September–October 1994 elections, winning 35% of the vote. The MDS formed a coalition government that remained in power until the September 1998 elections. During his four-year term, Meciar attempted to consolidate the political power of the MDS. His new governing coalition excluded all opposition forces from the political process and reversed some policies of the Moravcik government. Privatization of state-owned property became an instrument for rewarding political loyalty. Election laws were changed in a way that favored the MDS, and Meciar was accused of manipulation and gerrymandering. Much legislation introduced by his government was found to be unconstitutional.

In reaction to the new election laws, five opposition parties combined to form the Slovak Democratic Coalition (SDC) in 1997. Mikulas Dzurinda emerged as the spokesman and leader of the group. In the September 1998 elections, the SDC gained 26.33% of the vote and was able to form a coalition government. Dzurinda was sworn in as the new prime minister on 30 October 1998.

## PERSONAL BACKGROUND

Mikulas Dzurinda was born on 4 February 1955, in Spissky Sturtok. He attended a technical high school in Spisska Nova Ves and studied economics at the University of Transportation and Telecommunications in Zilina. After finishing his university studies, Dzurinda worked at an economic research institute in Zilina. In the mid 1980s, he accepted employment at Bratislava's district directorate for the national railways and helped to automate Czech rail transport. Dzurinda is married and has two daughters. His hobbies include sports, particularly long distance running.

## RISE TO POWER

Dzurinda served as a deputy to the Slovak minister of transportation and communications from 1991 until 1992. He was elected to parliament in 1992 and became the minister of transportation, telecommunications, and public works in the government of Joszef Moravcik. He was reelected in 1994 but remained in the parliamentary opposition, often criticizing the economic policies of the ruling coalition.

As a founding member of the ChDM, Dzurinda served as spokesman for the party's Transportation Club. An expert on economics, he soon became chairman of the ChDM's Economics Club. Dzurinda represented the views of the younger, more pragmatic and more moderate wing of the party on issues such as the relations between church and state, Slovakia's foreign policy towards the Vatican, and

abortion. Dzurinda's moderation and popularity with young voters were the main reasons why the ChDM nominated him to represent his party in the SDC after its formation in October 1997. He began as spokesman for the five-party coalition and rose to its chairmanship in June 1998. Following the September elections, the SDC emerged as the strongest member of the four-party coalition government.

## LEADERSHIP

The problems of the coalition are numerous. The new prime minister has no previous experience in governing a country. After six years of Meciar's rule, the economy, health care services, and educational system are on the verge of collapse. The industrial giant, VSZ Kosice, came close to bankruptcy in November 1998, when it was unable to repay a foreign loan of US$35 million. The Slovak Electric Energy Industry managed to go from a 6.33 billion Sk profit in 1994, to a 2.55 billion deficit in 1998. Slovak universities accumulated more than 6 billion Sk in debt, to which 0.6 billion was added in 1998. Many schools were forced to operate without heating in the winter. The health care department started 1998 with a 5 billion Sk deficit which increased to 12 billion by the end of the year. As a result, pharmaceutical companies refused to supply hospitals and pharmacies with essential medication.

The broad governing coalition was formed by four political parties, two of which are coalitions themselves. These parties represent views, agencas, and ideologies from across the political spectrum, and their policy preferences are often incompatible. Moreover, Meciar's MDS—despite the fact that it is in parliamentary opposition—actually won the election by a few tenths of a percentage point. Meciar has proven that he can orchestrate a political comeback and should not be underestimated. Adding to the already unstable political situation was the fact that the Slovak parliament was unable to elect a president after Michal Kovac's term expired in March 1998. The new president, according to the coalition agreement, was to be chosen directly by the electorate in the first half of 1998. In May 1999, Rudolf Schuster, the mayor of Kosice, became the first directly elected president of Slovakia.

The greatest challenge to Dzurinda's leadership comes from the ranks of his very own party. In 1999, Jan Carnogursky, leader of the ChDM, succeeded in splintering the SDC into the five parties from which it was originally created. The coalition partners in the government, and most of the SDC leaders themselves, strongly oppose this fragmentation. They fear it could lead to instability and eventually force early elections.

It seems reasonable to anticipate that Mikulas Dzurinda will have numerous opportunities to prove his leadership abilities should his governing coalition hold on for the full four-year term.

## DOMESTIC POLICY

The new government has emphasized the need to improve the legal system, revive the crumbling economy, normalize relations between the governing coalition and the parliamentary opposition, and end Slovakia's international isolation. This program was approved by the parliament in December 1998 when the legislators passed a vote of confidence in the Dzurinda-led governing coalition.

Having learned from the mistakes of the Moravcik government, which was undermined from within by the remaining MDS members, a full-scale replacement of state and local administrators was one of the first steps taken by Dzurinda. The election law was found to be unconstitutional by the courts and changed. In a controversial decision, Dzurinda revoked the amnesty given by Meciar to the people implicated in the kidnapping of President Kovas' son in 1995. The National Assembly also repealed a language law, initiated by the SNP under Meciar, because it discriminated against minority languages. For the first time in a Slovak government, political parties representing Hungarian minorities are being given a voice.

The Dzurinda government introduced an austerity package as its first step in developing a new economic policy. Other anticipated changes include new tax policies, a rollback of subsidies on energy and water, and an end to price regulations on some basic food items. One of the primary tasks of the new administration will have to be the reduction of a massive foreign debt, which increased from 3.7 billion Sk in 1993 to 12.5 Sk in 1998. These measures are not popular, but their proponents argue that they are needed in order to improve an economy that has been devastated by the reckless policies of the Meciar government.

After one year in power, the new legislature was able to pass 71 bills. By the end of 2002, they need to pass more than 250 bills in regard to requirements for European Union (EU) integration alone.

## FOREIGN POLICY

The primary goals of Slovakia's foreign policy are to end its international isolation and to integrate the country into European and North Atlantic economic, political, and security structures. Membership in the EU was delayed because Slovakia was found to be the only country in Central Europe that lacked those democratic institutions needed to protect its ethnic minorities. At the 1998 summit in Vienna, the EU representatives agreed to re-evaluate Slovakia's accession status by the end of 1999. To improve its image, Foreign Minister Eduard Kukan introduced legislation intended to foster the languages of minority groups, return multilingual report cards to schools, and initiate measures to improve relations with Hungary and the Czech Republic. In April 1999, the government opened Slovakia's air space for NATO planes. Upon re-evaluation in October 1999, the European Commission recommended to begin negotiations with Slovakia.

Also in 1999 the Dzurinda government intended to reapply for membership in the Organization for Security and Cooperation in Europe. The defense minister, Pavol Kanis, proposed that new security treaties be made with Poland, Hungary, and the Czech Republic, three Central European countries being considered for admission to NATO. In February 1999, the premiers of Hungary and Slovakia signed a protocol on implementation of the Slovak Hungarian Agreement. By October 1999, the prime ministers from all four countries met in the Slovak resort Tatranska Javorina, coordinating efforts to combat organized crime and international money laundering.

## ADDRESS
Urad Vlady SR
Namestie Slobody 1
Bratislava, Slovakia

## REFERENCES
Butora, Martin and Michal Ivantysin, eds. *Slovensko 1997: Suhrnna sprava o stave spolocnosti.* Bratislava: Institut pre Verejne Otazky, 1998.
*Domino Forum,* 10 January–10 July 1998.
Karatnycky, Adrian and Alexander Motyl, eds. *Nations in Transit, 1997.* New Brunswick, NJ: Transaction Publishers, 1998.
"A New Day in Slovakia." *The Economist,* 6 March 1999, vol. 350, p.100.
"Slovakia." *Newsweek International,* 26 April 1999, p.31.
*Ustava Slovenskej repubky.* Bratislava: Remedium, 1992.
*Verejna Sprava: Revue pre miestnu statnu spravu a samospravu,* 1998.

**Profile researched and written by Tibor Papp, Columbia University (3/99; updated 6/2000).**

# SLOVENIA

Milan Kucan
President

*(pronounced "MEE-lahn KOO-chahn")*

*"Full membership in the European Union is a vital issue for Slovenia."*

The Republic of Slovenia, o.ne of the five successor states to the Socialist Federal Republic of Yugoslavia, is bordered by Austria to the north, Italy to the west, Croatia to the south, and Hungary to the east. It has 40 km (25 mi) of shoreline on the Adriatic Sea. Slovenia covers an area of 20,041 sq km (7,738 sq mi). The capital city is Ljubljana.

Slovenia has an estimated population of nearly two million, 91% of whom are Slovenes. The remaining 9% are Serbs, Croats, Italians, and Hungarians. The official language is Slovene, written with the Latin alphabet. The population is 96% Roman Catholic.

The official currency is the *tolar.* Slovenia's per capita GDF is approximately US$10,300. Some 70% of total exports gc to EU members. Consumer goods, manufactured goods, and machine and transport equipment each account for about 26% of Slovenia's exports.

## POLITICAL BACKGROUND

With the collapse of the Hapsburg monarchy in 1918, the Slovenes, with Croats and Serbs from the Austro-Hungariar empire, joined with the Serbian kingdom to form the Kingdom of Serbs, Croats, and Slovenes, later renamec Yugoslavia. During the World War II (1939–45), much of Slovenia was incorporated into the Third Reich, with the remainder split between German allies Hungary, Italy, and the Nazi puppet state in Croatia. Following the war, Slovenia became one of the six constituent republics of the Socialis: Federal Republic of Yugoslavia.

From 1945 to 1980, Yugoslavia was ruled by Josip Broz, popularly known as Marshal Tito. Though a communist, one-party state, Tito steered the country on an independent course from the Soviet Union. After 1980, Yugoslavia was ruled by a collective presidency. In this Yugoslav state, Slovenia was consistently the most progressive region. The Slovene members of the federal communist party were usually in the forefront of economic and political reform. Slovenia was by far the most developed of the Yugoslav republics, with only 8% of Yugoslavia's population contributing up to 20% of its GNP and 30% of its foreign trade. By the early 1980s, as the Yugoslav national economy faced growing crises, the Slovenes pushed for a greater reliance on market forces and greater acceptance of political pluralism.

By the mid-1980s, Slovenia's communist party had been rebuffed on economic issues by conservatives in the Serbian party who sought to recentralize the economy and party. The Slovenes also saw Serbian repression in the Albaniar-populated province of Kosovo as a major obstacle to Yugoslav membership in the European Community, which was a priority for the Slovene leadership.

Although many independent political movements arose in Slovenia in the mid-1980s, the major turning point in Slovene politics came in May 1988 when two Slovene journalists uncovered an alleged plot by the Yugoslav army to arrest 200 Slovene officials, intellectuals, and journalists and to use armed intervention to put down any protests. This event destroyed any hope in the Slovene party and society for reforming Yugoslavia through the federal government in Belgrade. From this point on, despite continued political, economic, and even military pressure from the Serbian communists, the Slovenes moved on their own. Independent political parties were formed, and in January 1989 the Slovene Communist Party admitted the need to accept a multi-party system. Slovene party chief Milan Kucan continued to defend the human rights of Albanians in Kosovo. At the federal party congress in January 1990, the Slovene delegation rejected Serbian demands for a recentralized party and called instead for the independence of republic parties, free multi-party elections, and respect for human rights. The Serbs rejected Slovenia's proposals, and the Slovenes walked out of the congress, marking the end of the Federal League of Communists of Yugoslavia.

The Slovene Communist Party renamed itself the Party of Democratic Renewal (PDR) and adopted a platform similar to the social democratic parties of Western Europe. It established a multi-party system in Slovenia, with the hope that by championing Slovenia's rights in the face of Serbian pressure, it had gained the legitimacy needed to win the upcoming elections. In the April 1990 elections, however, a coalition of six center and rightist parties, founded in 1989 under the name of the United Democratic Opposition of Slovenia (DEMOS), won 123 of 202 seats in parliament. But the head of the PDR, Milan Kucan, won the presidency with 58% of the vote.

In December 1990, the Slovenes overwhelmingly voted in a referendum for independence, giving the leadership six months to negotiate a new form of association with the other Yugoslav republics. In subsequent negotiations between the presidents of the Yugoslav republics, Kucan and Croatia's president, Franjo Tudjman, insisted on a new, confederal form of Yugoslavia while the Serbian and Montenegrin leaders insisted on a more centralized federation. By June 1991, the Slovene Parliament declared that Slovenia would

begin the process of dissociating from Yugoslavia. Although it allowed that the Yugoslav army would remain in Slovenia for three years and explicitly recognized the legitimacy of existing Yugoslav institutions, this was taken as an illegal declaration of independence by the Slovene army. On 25 June 1991, units of the Slovene territorial defense force took control over border crossing posts on Slovenia's international borders from the Yugoslav customs service.

The federal Yugoslav army, which was allied with the Serbian Communist Party and had all along opposed Slovenia's reformist moves, took this as the excuse to move into Slovenia to crush the new Slovene government and bring it back under Belgrade's control. But the army was met with surprisingly strong Slovene resistance. After diplomatic intervention by the EC, both sides agreed to a ceasefire. Slovenia froze its moves toward independence for three months while negotiations on the future of Yugoslavia continued. Stunned by their de facto defeat, the federal army agreed to pull out of Slovenia. The attack solidified full and unconditional support for independence within Slovenia. This support was reinforced by the full-scale attacks by the Yugoslav army on civilian targets in neighboring Croatia in the summer and fall of 1991. By December, the Slovenes had officially requested diplomatic recognition from the EC, which was granted on 15 January 1992. The United States recognized Slovenia in June 1992.

## PERSONAL BACKGROUND

Milan Kucan was born in Krizevci in northeastern Slovenia on 14 January 1941. He attended school in the northeast Slovene town of Murska Sobota and in 1963 graduated with

a degree in law from the University of Ljubljana. He joined the League of Communists of Slovenia in 1958 as a student and was a member of the University Committee of the Slovene party and a member of the central committee of the Youth Association of Slovenia.

President Kucan has received a number of awards, including a medal of the Order of Pope Pius from Pope John Paul II in 1993 and the Crans Montana Prix de la Fondation for his contributions to peace and cooperation in Europe in 1999.

## RISE TO POWER

After receiving his law degree, Kucan joined the staff of the central committee of the Slovene party's Youth Association, taking the post of president of its educational and ideological commission. After fulfilling his military service, he was elected president of the Youth Association for 1968–69. He was a member of the Central Committee of the Slovene party in 1969–73, a period of great reformist fervor, and was a secretary of the Slovene conference of the Socialist Alliance of Working People, the official mass mobilization group, in 1973–78. Kucan was elected president of the Slovene Parliament in 1978 for a four-year term. He had managed to survive both the purges of liberals and reformers that swept the Yugoslav Party (1971–72) and the period of hard-line dominance of the Slovene Party (1972–82), apparently by remaining on the very fringe of acceptable official party policy.

In 1982, Kucan was chosen to be one of the two Slovene representatives in the Presidency of the League of Communists of Yugoslavia, the top party decision-making organ. In 1986, he assumed the leadership of the Slovene Communist Party and was instrumental in resisting the Serbian Party's pressures to recentralize the Yugoslav federal party and state. It was this position as champion of Slovene rights and his role in getting the Slovene Party to accept the need for a multi-party system that enabled him to win the April 1990 election when Slovenia was still part of the Yugoslav federation. In the first post-independence election in 1992, Kucan won 64% of the vote. He was reelected to a second five-year term in 1997 when he ran as an independent candidate against seven opponents. His second term began on 23 December 1997.

## LEADERSHIP

Throughout the Yugoslav crisis, Kucan has been a visible and active proponent of Slovenia's rights, first by championing a new confederal form of Yugoslavia, then, after the July 1991 invasion by the Yugoslav army, by pushing for international recognition of Slovenia. After independence he forcefully argued Slovenia's case before international bodies, including the EU. His goal since independence has been to solidify the democratic institutions introduced in those early years; to help create a democratic political culture and overcome the divisions of the communist past; and to argue forcefully that Slovenia's future lies in joining regional political, economic, and military groupings—in particular the EU and NATO. He was rewarded for these efforts and for his integrity with 56% of the vote (in a field of eight candidates) in the November 1997 presidential elections.

## DOMESTIC POLICY

Slovenia was governed from independence until April 2000 by centrist coalitions headed by Prime Minister Janez Drnovsek. In April 2000, the coalition collapsed and a right-wing coalition, growing in influence, was taking control of the government although no one had been named to replace Drnovsek as prime minister.

The main domestic issue since independence has been the attempt to shift the Slovene economy to private ownership and market principles, and to bring the country's laws and regulations into line with the EU. Given the almost unanimous support for EU membership among Slovenia's political parties, and the fact that Slovenia was invited in July 1997 to begin talks on EU membership, this issue is most pressing. Slovenia is the only potential member that already meets all of the Maastricht Treaty criteria. However, the main stumbling block was the issue of foreign ownership of property, which EU rules require, but which had been forbidden under Slovene law. In 1997 this issue was finally resolved when the legislature enacted regulations to allow foreign nationals to buy land as of 2001; two years later, in 1999, regulations were enacted to allow foreign banks to open branches in Slovenia.

Another controversial issue is whether those people who had worked for the Communist Party when Slovenia had been part of Yugoslavia should be allowed to take part in current politics. President Kucan has called for this issue to be removed from political debate, noting that it detracts from Slovenia's attempts to move forward.

Slovenia's economy has been quite strong since 1994, despite the loss of its major markets in the former Yugoslavia. Its per capita GDP is $10,300, higher than most other Eastern European countries. Its economy grew at an annual rate of about 4% during the late 1990s, and foreign investment in the country has been steadily increasing.

## FOREIGN POLICY

Slovenia has been successful in achieving its foreign policy goals. It obtained international recognition in 1992 and immediately began seeking membership in the EU and NATO. Slovenia is a member of the Partnership for Peace program of NATO and continues to seek full membership. Although it was not included in the NATO expansion announced in July 1997, Slovenia has been identified as one of the strongest candidates for future expansion.

The goal of EU membership is at the top of Slovenia's foreign policy agenda. Seventy percent of Slovenia's exports go to the EU, and Slovenia was seeking membership in the organization even before the breakup of Yugoslavia. Slovenia has signed an association agreement with the EU and in July 1997 (along with four other central European countries) was invited to talks on EU membership. Given the economic successes of the country and the efforts of Kucan and

Drnovsek, it is likely that Slovenia will be included in the next expansion. With the coming to power of the center-left coalition of Romano Prodi, Italy has shifted from being the main obstacle to Slovene membership to being an ardent proponent.

The Kucan government has attempted to improve relations with Croatia in recent years. The failure of Croatia to come to the aid of Slovenia during the 1991 invasion by the Yugoslav army had caused considerable strain between the two countries. Other unresolved issues include the fate of the jointly owned Krsko nuclear power plant, the fate of Croatian hard currency deposits in Slovene banks, and a dispute over Slovenia's access to the Adriatic Sea. Yet despite these differences, the two countries were able to sign a free trade agreement in October 1997, and trade relations have indeed improved. Slovenia has also been working to normalize its relations with the Serbian-dominated Yugoslav state. In 1999, Slovenia, along with Croatia, Macedonia, and Bosnia and Herzegovina, asked the United Nations to force Yugoslavia to reapply fo UN membership. Yugoslavia, consisting of Serbia and Montenegro after the break-up, holds the UN membership that was granted to the former Socialist Republic of Yugoslavia in 1945 when the United Nations was founded.

In 1999, Slovenia received visits from US President Bill Clinton and Irish Prime Minister Bertie Ahern, both signs of Slovenia's increasing interest and participation in world affairs and international trade.

## ADDRESS

President Erjavceva
17 1000 Ljubljana
Slovenia

## REFERENCES

Bennett, Chris. "Yugoslavia's Bloody Collapse. New York: 1995." *The Economist*, 11 January 1997.

CIA World Factbook. [Online] Available http://www.odci.gov/cia/publications/factbook/si.html (Accessed June 2000).

Goodman, Anthony. "Four States Seek to End Belgrade's UN Status." Reuters Limited, 2 November 1999.

President of Slovenia. [Online] Availabe http://www.sigov.si/upr/ang/index.html (Accessed November 1999).

Radio Free Europe/Radio Liberty Newsline. [Online] Available http://www.rferl.org/newsline (Accessed June 2000).

Silber, Laura, and Allan Little. *Yugoslavia: Death of a Nation.* New York: 1997.

"Slovenia: The View from the Outside Looking In." *Time International*, 22 March 1999, vol. 153, no. 11, p. 31.

**Profile researched and written by V.P. Gagnon, Jr., Ithaca College (3/98; revised 6/2000).**

# SOLOMON ISLANDS

**Bart Ulufa'alu**
**Prime Minister**
*(pronounced "oo-loo-fah-AH-loo")*

*"The move to achieve change is not easy and so it could mean sacrificing with pain."*

Lying to the east of Papua New Guinea, the Solomon Islands are a scattered double chain of islands, forming the third largest archipelago in the South Pacific. The land area totals more than 27,500 sq km (10,640 sq mi) spread over 1.35 million sq km (521,235 sq mi) of ocean. Volcanic action produced many of the islands, including the largest—Guadalcanal, Malaita, New Georgia, Santa Isabel, Makira, and Choiseul. Such seismic disturbance, including two submarine volcanoes in the Western Province, continues to the present day. There are also coral atolls of varied size. Altogether, the country consists of more than 900 islands, 347 of which are populated.

Population is estimated at 455,429. Until the mid-1980s, Malaita was the most populated island. Since then, there has been considerable immigration to the capital, Honiara; Guadalcanal now boasts the largest number of residents. Though overall population density (16.6 per sq km) is one of the lowest in the Pacific, it is unevenly distributed, and the smaller eastern atolls are crowded. The annual growth rate of 3.2%, could aggravate the problem for the entire nation. More than 94% of Solomon Islanders are ethnically Melanesian. Slightly less than 4% are Polynesian. From 1955 to 1971, the ruling British government moved people from what were then the Gilbert Islands (now Kiribati) to ease overcrowding; there are some 4,000 Gilbertese presently living in the Solomons. The remainder of the population is of European or Chinese ancestry.

More than 90% of Islanders are Christian, but speakers of the Kwaio language on Malaita still proudly identify themselves as "pagan." The Anglican Church of Melanesia claims the most members, and there is a substantial number of Catholics, Seventh-Day Adventists, Methodists (United Church), and followers of the South Seas Evangelical Church. More than 80 indigenous languages and dialects are spoken, most of them of the widespread Austronesian language stock. Although English is the official language, the Solomon Islands Pijin is the most widely understood.

Like many Pacific Island nations, the Solomon Islands are heavily dependent on foreign aid, with Japan being the largest donor. Government expenditures are regarded as excessive, and estimates of national debt range between US$170–200 million. Serious efforts have been made in the past two years to bring financial well-being to the country. One encouraging sign is the Gold Ridge mine which completed its first year of full operations in 1999. Logging continues to be a problem. Carried out by foreign firms, levels of deforestation are not

sustainable. The country continues to have a very poor record of providing services to the people; literacy and health statistics are among the worst in the Pacific. The official currency is the Solomon Islands dollar.

## POLITICAL BACKGROUND

Alvaro de Mendana, a Spanish explorer, was the first European to see the Solomon Islands in 1568. The Spanish named the archipelago, which they mistakenly believed to be a continent, after King Solomon, hoping that riches like that credited to him in the Bible would be found there. At that time, Westerners had yet to discover a method of reckoning longitude so the Solomons were "lost" on European maps for almost 200 years. The English and French explorers of the late 1700s were finally able to chart the islands for other seafarers. Early contacts between European sailors and Islanders were often marked by violence and mistrust, but the former's need for fresh water and other supplies and the latter's desire for iron tools and weapons promoted trade that increased through the 1800s. Early in that century, exchanges with whaling ships were important, followed later by trade for tortoise shell and other tropical products. Beginning in 1870, Islanders were recruited to work on plantations in Australia, Samoa, and Fiji. Some of their descendants are found in those nations today. Trade also put firearms in the hands of the Islanders, adding a new element to conflict among different local groups. Diseases introduced by Europeans took their toll, and were further spread as Islanders began to travel more widely within the archipelago.

In the late 1800s Great Britain began to be concerned about the unregulated activities of outsiders in the South Pacific. These included labor recruiting that more closely resembled kidnaping and trading by beachcombers who were little more than criminals on the run from their home countries. The Western Pacific High Commission was established in Fiji in 1877 to protect British interests and those of British subjects living in the Solomons. France and especially Germany began colonial expansion into the Pacific during this period. Rivalry between Britain and Germany created a series of confrontations and ultimately treaty negotiations. The Solomons constituted one of the disputed areas in this process. Finally, the islands were divided between the two nations. Bougainville, the northernmost of the chain, became part of German New Guinea, ultimately to become a reluctant province of independent Papua New Guinea. The rest of the Solomons became a British Protectorate (BSIP) in 1893.

The Protectorate was a tiny part of the vast British Empire, regarded as having little economic potential. Administration concentrated on pacifying the more violent local groups and, to a lesser extent, easing the way for foreign commercial interests to develop a plantation economy with copra (dried coconut meat) as the major export. Christian missions provided most of the health and education services for Islanders, while administrators tried to prevent mission rivalry by keeping the different sects in separate parts of the Protectorate. One result was differing rates of social development among the various islands; for example, the aggressive Methodist mission created a noteworthy level of practical education in what is now the Western Province. Generally, however, the pace of change was slow until the Second World War.

The Japanese invasion of the Solomons in 1942 and Allied counterattacks brought great devastation. Military action on Guadalcanal was particularly fierce. Allied troops with vast amounts of European goods were a new stimulus to change among the local population. According to postwar British administrators, one consequence was the appearance of various social movements seeking to overturn the colonial status quo. The most famous of these was "Marching Rule" on Malaita, described on one hand as a "cargo cult" and on the other as the beginnings of Solomon Island nationalism.

Decolonization of the Pacific Islands began in the 1960s, but the Protectorate remained in place until independence was granted in July 1978. The new constitution established a modified Westminister system of government with the British monarch as head of state. A Solomon Islands citizen is appointed, on the recommendation of the National Parliament, as governor general to represent the monarch, but has limited powers. Effective executive power is exercised by the prime minister and his cabinet. The prime minister is elected by and from the members of Parliament, and appoints ministers for parliamentary membership. Parliamentary elections occur every four years but without the support of a majority of members, the prime minister can be forced to step down between elections. Parliament can also dissolve itself before its four-year term is over by an absolute majority vote. In that case, a general election must be held within four months.

The geographic and linguistic fragmentation of the islands creates particular strains within the political system, including pressures to decentralize government functions. Parliamentary constituencies have increased in number since independence. There are presently 50 members—47 from electorates in the 10 provinces, and three from the Honiara Town Council area. Provincial governments have been established, each with an assembly, a premier, and a staff. This adds to the cost of government.

Although political parties are basic to a Westminister system, those in the Solomon Islands have been loose factions. There are frequent defections from one party to another. No single party has been able to command a parliamentary majority so coalition governments have ruled since independence. Furthermore, there is considerable turnover at each general election. In 1997, 22 parliamentary incumbents failed in their bid for reelection. Outside observers have

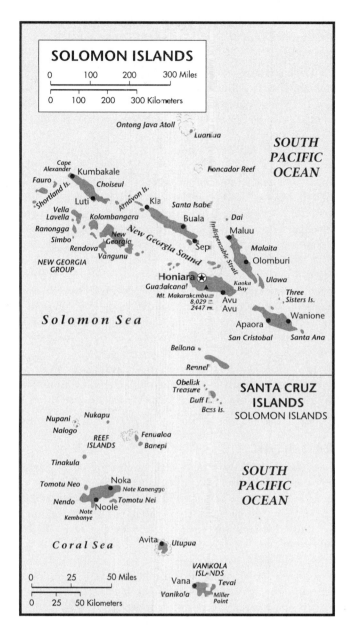

blamed the instability of political leadership, together with the constant manipulation of offices and perquisites in exchange for coalition support, for recent economic problems in the Solomons.Personal Background

Bartholomew Ulufa'alu was born in Alite'e Village in the Laulasi area of Malaita in 1950. After attending village primary schools, he received his secondary education at St. Joseph's Tenaru School and Aruligo Secondary School. In 1970–74, he attended the University of Papua New Guinea in Port Moresby, where he was active in student politics. He graduated with a degree in economics. Ulufa'alu is a Roman Catholic and married with two children.

## RISE TO POWER

Upon completion of his university education, Ulufa'alu returned to the Solomons and became associated with a small group regarded by the British as "radical" or "socialist." He began his career by setting up a cooperative society, and is credited with helping to organize the first labor unions in the Protectorate. Ulufa'alu was also a prominent agitator for independence.

For almost two decades, the most prominent figure in Solomon Islands politics had been Solomon Mamaloni, who served as prime minister in 1981–84, 1984–93, and 1994–97. Ulufa'alu's career has inevitably intersected with Mamaloni's. Ulufa'alu entered electoral politics in 1976 and served as Member for East Honiara until 1983. He served as finance minister in the first Mamaloni government of 1981–83, but resigned his seat at Mamaloni's request in order to set up a pool of business and development consultants. Mamaloni found their recommendations to be too costly and Ulufa'alu moved into opposition. He was an unsuccessful candidate for Parliament from the Aoke/Langalanga electorate (Malaita) in 1993. By 1997 widespread dissatisfaction with Mamaloni's regime—including accusations of financial mismanagement and even corruption—created the opportunity for a new coalition to assume power. In the July 1997 election, Ulufa'alu's bid to represent Aoke/Langalanga was successful. On the second ballot for prime minister, Ulufa'alu won by a two-vote margin. The members who supported him, many of whom had been in opposition to Mamaloni's previous government, formed a coalition taking the name Alliance for Change, with Ulufa'alu as leader. Mamaloni died on 11 January 2000, ending a remarkable political career.

## LEADERSHIP

From the time he was organizing student protests at the University of Papua New Guinea, Ulufa'alu has had a reputation for outspokenness and willingness to take radical action. However, his career has been marked by shifting directions. Media have described him as the best finance minister the country has had. He is credited with achieving the only positive balance of payments account since independence. After he left political office in the 1980s, he kept a relatively low profile as an entrepreneur and a private business consultant. His education, intellect, and past accomplishments lead some to expect genuine change if his coalition can survive the historical instability of Solomon Island politics. Ulufa'alu's Malaitan origins are a double-edged sword. This populous province sends 11 members to Parliament, but fears of Malaitan dominance loom large in the country's politics.

## DOMESTIC POLICY

Ethnic conflict has dominated all other domestic political issues since late in 1998. Animosity had long existed between Guadalcanal Islanders and Malaitans, but escalated in the 1970s with new migration into the capital, Honiara. Issues include disputes over land; Guadalcanal landowners fiercely resist any claims by Malaitans to any rights on their island. Ulufa'alu's position as a Malaitan fuels suspicion, while the premier of Guadalcanal province was accused of backing a Guadalcanal militant group. By July 1999, Ulufa'alu had declared a state of emergency. The British Commonwealth appointed a former Fijian prime minister to broker a peace agreement, and police contingents from Fiji and Vanuatu were assembled to serve in the Solomon Islands. Guadalcanal militants adopted the name Isatambu Freedom Fighters, while Malaitans formed a group called the Malaita Eagle Forces. The latter are demanding compensation for property lost on Guadalcanal. As of April 2000, there is little hope of settlement.

## FOREIGN POLICY

The issue of ethnic violence has so completely dominated Solomon Island politics for almost two years that foreign policy has faded into the background. Observers continue to watch with particular care how relations develop between the Solomons and Papua New Guinea. The long-standing dispute over the attempt by PNG's Bougainvile Province to secede seems to be approaching resolution. However, the kind of conflict that now faces the Solomon Islands has uncomfortable echoes for all small island nations separated by linguistic and cultural differences.

## ADDRESS

Office of the Prime Minister
Honiara
Solomon Islands

## REFERENCES

Bennett, Judith. *Wealth of the Solomons*. University of Hawaii Press, 1987.
Economist Intelligence Unit Ltd. *Country Profile: Solomon Islands*. 1999–2000.
Harcombe, David. *Solomon Islands: A Travel Survival Kit*. Lonely Planet Publications, 1993.
*Islands Business*, January 1999–March 2000.
*Papua New Guinea Post-Courier*, June–December 1999.

**Profile researched and written by Eugene Ogan, Professor Emeritus, University of Minnesota (3/98 updated 6/2000).**

# SOMALIA

## Interim Profile

Somalia occupies the area known as the "horn" of Africa, with coastline fronting the Gulf of Aden on the north and the Indian Ocean to the east. It is bordered on the northwest by Djibouti, on the west by Ethiopia, and by Kenya to the southwest. The country's borders contain some 638,000 sq km (246,300 sq mi). Political disturbances over the course of the 1990s have rendered population estimates unreliable. Recent UN estimates place the national population at around 10 million, with as much as 25% living in urban areas.

Somalia is unique in Africa, being ethnically homogeneous. Over 95% of the population characterize themselves as "Somali." Nonetheless, divisions between family lineages ("clans"), have tended to weaken the unity of the national government and led to chaos in the 1990s. Somali is the official language and is spoken by almost all inhabitants. Arabic, English, Italian, and Swahili are also commonly spoken.

The great majority of rural Somalis earn a living from the herding of goats, sheep, camels and cattle. Indeed, livestock exports to the Arabian peninsula and Middle East are a major source of foreign exchange for the country. A small proportion of Somalis earn a living from fishing. In the southern region irrigated farmlands produce citrus fruits and bananas for export. Grain is grown to a limited extent in the southern and northern regions of Somalia, but not in great enough quantities to guarantee a regular supply of staples for the country. As a result, Somalia has been a net food importer for the past several decades.

## POLITICAL BACKGROUND

The coast of Africa's eastern horn has long been a region of strategic significance and of cultural ferment. During the "scramble for Africa" in the late 1800s, the British were able to secure several treaties from local Somali leaders in the northern plateau area and declared the region a protectorate (called "Somaliland") in 1886.

In the southern portion of the horn and elsewhere along the East African coast, the Italians were pursuing treaties with the Arab or Swahili sultans who controlled most of the area's significant trading cities. In 1905 the Italians had declared the colony of "Italian Somaliland"—which included the modern capital of Mogadishu. From 1936 the region of southern Somalia served as a base for Italian operations in Ethiopia, as the Italians sought to expand their colonial holdings. During World War II there were clashes between the forces of British and Italian Somaliland, with the British eventually seizing control of all Italian holdings. In 1950 the area of Italian Somaliland was returned to Italian administration, but under the aegis of a UN trusteeship.

The combination of nationalist agitation in both Somalilands and UN pressure for decolonization led to the two regions being unified as an independent Somalia on 1 July 1960. Elections in 1959 gave a strong majority to the Somali Youth League (SYL) party, but the first independent government was a coalition formed between the SYL and two smaller parties from the northern region. The first prime minister was Abdirashid Ali Shirmake, with Aden Abdullah Osman Darr as president.

From the first years of independence, Somalia's government pursued a policy of "Somali self-determination" which led to tensions and conflict with neighboring states. Tens of thousands of ethnic Somali lived in the Ogaden region of Ethiopia, northeastern Kenya, and French Somalia (now Djibouti). The Somali government stated that these regions rightfully belonged to Somalia. Border skirmishes between Somali forces and those of Ethiopia and Kenya were common in the 1960s. These tensions were further fueled in 1962 when Somalia signed an agreement with the Soviet Union for the provision of military aid.

During the course of the 1960s Somalia saw not only regional, but growing internal conflict. Rivalries between clans saw the fragmentation of political parties into smaller and smaller units. By the late 1960s there were over 60 political parties in the country. When President Abdirashid Ali Shermake was assassinated in October of 1969, the military seized power under the leadership of Siad Barre. Barre's government disbanded the parliament, suspended the constitution, and formed the Supreme Revolutionary Council. Declaring a policy of "scientific socialism" the government nationalized many foreign-owned firms, drawing the ire of already-suspicious Western powers. The new government launched ambitious development and infrastructural programs, created an alphabet for the Somali language, and launched a major literacy campaign.

By the middle of the 1970s, Somalia was embroiled in regional and international conflicts. In 1975 the US alleged that Somalia was allowing the Soviet Union to establish military bases along the strategic Gulf of Aden. In 1977 Barre officially recognized the Western Somali Liberation Front, which had been fighting for Somali self-determination in the Ogaden region of Ethiopia, and then sent in Somali troops. Substantial gains were made until the Ethiopians signed a

mutual defense treaty with the Soviet Union, leading to massive military aid and an airlift of some 17,000 Cuban troops. Unable to face such overwhelming odds, the Somali troops were soon pushed out of the Ogaden. Soviet advisers were expelled from Somalia in retaliation, and the Barre government turned to the West for support. The Reagan years of the 1980s saw increasing American military and economic aid to the Barre government. Such aid was essential to the Somali repulsion of an Ethiopian-backed invasion in 1982.

## THE FALL OF BARRE AND DESCENT INTO CIVIL WAR

By the mid-1980s, both the Somali and Ethiopian governments were faced with growing internal conflicts, and in 1988 they signed an agreement to respect one another's borders. By the late 1980s Barre's hold on power was becoming increasingly tenuous. The Somali National Movement (SNM) began operating in the northern region in 1988. The Barre government reacted with brutal force, but was not able to destroy the SNM. Beginning in 1989 the central government was also faced with insurrection in the south, particularly by the Somali Patriot Movement (SPM). By the early 1990s additional insurgent groups, organized along regional and clan lines, were formed. These included United Somalia Congress (USC), the Somali Democratic Front (SDF), and the Somali Salvation Democratic Front (SSDF). Widespread conflict disrupted food production and distribution. By the late 1980s hundreds of thousands were at risk for malnutrition and starvation. By late 1990, Barre's government found itself in control of little other than Mogadishu and the

surrounding environs. He was forced to flee the capital in January of 1991.

Following Barre's exodus, the USC seized Mogadishu. Though its leadership stated that they had no plans to form a permanent government, the other factions showed little trust. Factions which had previously focused their efforts on unseating Barre now threatened to turn upon one another—despite the efforts of "reconciliation" conferences sponsored by Djibouti and numerous calls for dialogue. The USC itself split into two antagonistic factions led by Muhammad Fara Aidid and Ali Mahdi. Mahdi later formed the Somali Salvation Alliance (SSA) and declared himself "president of Somalia." In the north, the SNM declared the independence of their sphere of influence as "Somaliland"—roughly re-creating the borders of the old British protectorate. Leaders of the Isaaq clan then "elected" Mohammad Ibrahim Egal, who had been prime minister of Somalia in the 1960s, as "president of Somaliland." Barre and his supporters regrouped at Guerbaharre and reorganized under the name as the Somali National Front (SNF). In September of 1991 open combat broke out among the various groups and continued for nearly six months.

## INTERNATIONAL INTERVENTION

In March of 1992 the UN organized a tenuous a cease-fire in the capital. The Security Council called for an arms embargo and moved to create the United Nations Operation in Somalia (UNOSOM),a group assigned to encourage peace talks and observe the distribution of food aid. UNOSOM had no military capacity. Certain factions, particularly the Aidid-led USC group, alleged that the UN was supplying their enemies with arms, and interrupted or seized relief supplies. During this time Barre's SNF attempted to retake Mogadishu, but was driven back. This defeat effectively cost Barre what little support and legitimacy he retained. After 21 years of rule, he fled the country.

Adding to Somalia's woes was a severe drought. Pastoralists and farmers, whose livelihoods had already been disrupted by the civil war, found themselves both unable to produce food and unable to find safe haven. Nearly half a million are estimated to have fled the country for camps in Kenya, Ethiopia and Djibouti. Hundreds of thousands were threatened with starvation, and the political turmoil prevented effective distribution of relief supplies. In response to this deteriorating situation, the UN and US government organized the United Nations International Task Force (UNITAF). Composed of over 30,000 troops from over 20 countries, the UNITAF forces staged a dramatic landing in Mogadishu in December of 1992. Given the moniker "Operation Restore Hope" the troops occupied urban centers throughout Somalia over the next several weeks, opening roads and establishing food-distribution networks. UNITAF forces also undertook efforts to establish a more stable peace—arranging talks between two of the most powerful Mogadishu-based warlords, Mohammad Fara Aidid and Ali Mahdi. Divisions within the UNITAF administration became evident when the UN contingent pressed for active disarmament of the various armed factions. Despite US reluctance, limited disarmament operations were undertaken.

In the early months of 1993, UNITAF forces were being substantially reduced, though conflicts between factions continued in many parts of the country. Ethiopia hosted representatives of 15 factions for a "national reconciliation" conference in March of 1993. After extended debate, the conference established a transitional committee which was to serve as the supreme administrative body for Somalia, and which had a mandate to hold elections within two years. This outcome also prompted the UN to make arrangements for UNITAF to be disbanded and replaced by UNISOM II—which was to have a more rigid command structure and a clearer mandate to disarm the Somali factions.

The situation in Somalia had become increasingly tense by June of 1993. Tensions between UNISOM II and Mohammad Fara Aidid's Mogadishu-based group (now called the Somali National Alliance) increased over issues of disarmament and UN accusations that Aidid was hindering peace talks. On 5 June a conflict between UNISOM II and Aidid's forces resulted in the deaths of 23 Pakistani peacekeepers. A warrant was later issued for Aidid's arrest. Attempts to capture Aidid over the next several months led to hundreds of Somali's being killed or wounded. Such incidents led to an erosion of Somali goodwill towards the peacekeeping forces. On October 3 US Rangers entered an area of Mogadishu under Aidid's control. In the ensuing battle, 18 American combatants were killed and dozens injured. The incident also resulted in hundreds of Somali casualties. Negative public opinion issuing from the clash led to plans being laid for an accelerated US withdrawal.

In late 1993 and early 1994, several conferences between faction leaders were held in Ethiopia and in different regions of Somalia. Various factors, including conflicting strategies from within UNISOM and strife between Somali factions, prevented the reaching of any substantive agreements. In February of 1994 the UN voted to gradually reduce its troop strength. This process continued until March of 1995, when the last of the UN and US troops left Somalia.

With the withdrawal of international forces, conflict between regional and clan-based factions continued. Further, unarmed UNOSOM personnel and relief workers who remained in Somalia became increasingly vulnerable to banditry. Some aid organizations simply declared the situation unworkable and pulled out of Somalia altogether. Others have taken to hiring bodyguards and paying "protection" to local leaders for the right to continue humanitarian operations in the area.

As Somalia entered the 21st century, it did so without a national government. However, the situation had somewhat stabilized with the establishment several regional governments. Under the leadership of the SNM, the "Republic of Somaliland" in the north has maintained a modicum of stability. Courts have been established and currency has been printed. Still, ongoing conflict with smaller factions in the region has led to calls for recognition to be rebuffed. In the south, Aidid's SNA and Mahdi's "Group of Twelve" have emerged as the most powerful factions. Aidid's group is based in South Mogadishu and Mahdi in North Mogadishu. On August 1 Mohammad Fara Aidid was killed in an ambush, and leadership of the SNA was taken over by his son Hussayn Muhammad Aidid—himself a former corporal in the US Marines. Despite numerous assassinations within both camps, large-scale confrontations have been few. Hussayn Aidid has not, though, attended recent peace talks sponsored by the Arab League in Djibouti and Yemen. Rather, he has repeatedly alleged that the UN and other groups are supplying his enemies. Mahdi, in turn, has stated that Aidid is receiving military aid from Libya and Sudan.

Northeastern Somalia under the leadership of Col. Abdullahi Yusuf, formed its own government called the Puntland regional government. Elsewehre in Somalia, Islamic courts have been created to deal with lawlessness. Due to the efforts of these courts, security has improved significantly and law and order in some parts of the country, particularly Mogadishu has been restored. During the 1990s decade efforts at mediation of the Somali internal dispute have been undertaken by many regional states. Ethiopia has played host to several Somali peace conferences and initiated talks at the Ethiopian city of Sodere, which led to some degree of agreement between competing factions. The Governments of Egypt, Yemen, Kenya, and Italy also have attempted to bring the Somali factions together. In 1997, the Organization of African Unity and the Inter-Governmental Agency on Development gave Ethiopia the mandate to pursue Somali reconciliation but with little success.

During the early months of 2000 the Djibouti government attempted to bring together 50 Somali scholars and elders to work out modalities and procedures for the establishment of a national Somali government. However, at the same time Libya was engaged in drawing up a plan for setting up a Somali government composed of the Sodere (Ethiopian town where pro-Ethiopian Somali factions held a conference several years ago) and Salballar (factions allied to principal Mogadishu faction leader Husayn Muhammad Aydid) groups. Libya informed the Djibouti government of its intention to revive the resolutions of the Cairo peace conference which called for the formation of a national government. Subsequently, Libya told Djibouti to stop organizing a Somali national conference. The political future of Somalia remains in limbo.

## REFERENCES

*Africa South of the Sahara*. London: Europa Publications Ltd., 1995.

*Agence France Presse*, 2, 5, 14, 15, 16, 19, 22 September 1996.

*BBC Summary of World Broadcasts*, 2, 4, 5, 9, 20 September 1996.

"Djibouti President Invites Somali Scholars, Elders for Talks on New Government." *'Ayaamaha'*, Mogadishu, BBC Worldwide Monitoring, 6 March 2000.

*The Economist*, 31 August 1996.

*Global Studies: Africa*, 1995.

*Indian Ocean Newsletter*, 28 September 1996.

"Islamic Clerics Combat Lawlessness in Somalia." *Christian Science Monitor* (Boston, MA), July 13, 1999, p.1.

"Libya Reportedly Urging Djibouti not to Host Somali Conference." *'Ayaamaha'*, Mogadishu, BBC Worldwide Monitoring, March18, 2000.

*Reuters Financial Service*, 18 September 1996.

*Xinhua News Agency*, 9 September 1996.

**Profile researched and written by Dr. Jonathan T. Reynolds, Livingstone College (12/96; updated by Ezekiel Kalipeni, University of Illinois, Champaign-Urbana 5/2000).**

# SOUTH AFRICA

## Thabo Mbeki
## President
*(pronounced "TAH-bow em-BEEK-ee")*

*"Affirmative action isn't a philosophy. It's not an end in itself. It's an instrument to get a more equal society, broadly representative of South African demography."*

The Republic of South Africa, located at the southern tip of the Africa continent, is bordered to its northeast by Swaziland, Mozambique, and Zimbabwe, to the north by Botswana, and to the northwest by Namibia. Lesotho, an independent kingdom, is an enclave within South Africa. The country has a total land area of 1,219,584 sq km (470,882 sq mi).

South Africa's population of 43,426,386 is composed of four distinct groups: 80% black, consisting mainly of Xhosa, Zulu, and Sotho, (collectively known as Bantu); 8% white, comprising Dutch-descended Afrikaners and whites of British descent; 9% of mixed heritage ("colored"); and 3% Asian, primarily from the Indian subcontinent. Reflective of this multicultural society, there are 11 official languages with Ndeble, Sotho, Pedi, English, and Afrikaans most widely spoken.

South Africa has an advanced industrial economy with manufacturing and services accounting for 63% of total employment. The country possesses abundant natural resources, particularly minerals. It accounts for one-third of the world's gold output. Agriculture is South Africa's second major employer, accounting for 30% of the labor force. While the per capita income is US$6,800, the average income of whites is about tenfold greater than that of blacks. White unemployment is about 4%, but black joblessness exceeds 40%. The national currency is the *rand*.

## POLITICAL BACKGROUND
From 1948 to 1994, the National Party maintained dominance over South Africa's political system. The policy of apartheid, based on the separation of races, structured the political and economic life of the nation. After years of racial oppression and international condemnation, the opposition African National Congress (ANC) was legalized. Negotiations began with Nelson Mandela and other ANC leaders for a transition to multiracial democracy in 1990.

Three thousand international observers monitored the first all-race election (in which the franchise was extended to South Africa's non-white majority) in May 1994. This historic election effectively ended apartheid and the National Party's dominance. Mandela's ANC obtained 63.1% of the popular vote and 252 seats in the National Assembly.

The current government is again led by the ANC, which solidified its hold over the National Assembly based on results of the June 1999 elections. Mandela's successor, Thabo Mbeki and the ANC increased their majority to 266 seats, just shy of the two-thirds majority needed to unilaterally amend the Constitution. The Democratic Party, a multiracial party, emerged as the opposition leader with 38 seats while the Inkatha Freedom Party (IFP), representing primarily Zulus in Kwazulu-Natal, slipped to 34 seats. The former National Party (NP), reconstituted as the New National Party (NNP), saw its electoral fortune decline to 28 seats from 82 in 1994.

The current constitution went into effect in 1997 and maintains a federal system with significant powers reserved for the nine provincial governments. The president is elected by the National Assembly for a five-year term, not to exceed two terms. He is responsible for appointing the deputy president and cabinet, as well as leading his party in the passage of legislation. The president oversees the day-to-day operation of the government and distributes power and functions among the deputy president, ministers, and the deputy ministers. The president can call for new elections by dissolving Parliament if a majority of representatives seek its dissolution and at least three years have lapsed since the last election. However, the National Assembly may pass a no-confidence resolution that excludes or includes the president. If the majority of the National Assembly votes "no confidence" in the government, the president must reconstitute his cabinet. In the event that the National Assembly passes a no-confidence resolution that includes the president, both the president and his government must resign. The National Assembly must select a replacement from within its ranks.

Parliament consists of the National Council of Provinces (NCOP) and the National Assembly. The 400 members of the National Assembly are chosen by a proportional representation system through party lists for five-year terms. NCOP members consist of provincial officials chosen to reflect provincial parties' relative strengths. The National Assembly passes legislation, amends the Constitution, and oversees activities of the provinces in accordance with the Constitution. The NCOP passes legislation that pertains specifically to the provinces.

## PERSONAL BACKGROUND
Thabo Mbeki was born on 18 June 1942, in Mbewuleni, a village in Transkei province. He was the eldest son of Govan and Epainette Mbeki. Both of his parents were part of a rural aristocracy dating back to British colonial times. They operated a small general store. During his early years, political discussions engulfed Mbeki's life. His mother, a

teacher by training, became one of the first women members of the South African Communist Party (SACP). His father, also a teacher and SACP member, earned two university degrees and became a party activist among peasants. Highly literate by the age of 10, Mbeki read all the books in his home. From an early age, his parents instilled the values of self-reliance, empathy, and service.

As a result of his parents' activism, Mbeki was faced with the threat of disruptions in his life. He therefore spent most of his adolescent years away from home in boarding schools. At the age of 14, Mbeki joined the Youth League of the ANC. When his secondary education at Lovedale Institution was disrupted by a strike led by Mbeki himself in 1959, he was expelled from the school and continued his education at home. Early in the 1960s, Mbeki joined the SACP and studied under its brightest theoreticians. In 1962, one year before his father's arrest and subsequent life prison term, Mbeki left South Africa on ANC orders. He was elected secretary of the African Students' Association in London while completing a degree in economics at London University. In 1966, he completed a master's degree in economics from Sussex University and became an important fixture in the ANC's diplomatic efforts abroad. After receiving guerilla training and lessons in Marxist ideology in 1970 at the Lenin International School (in the Soviet Union), he worked for the ANC in Nigeria, Botswana, Mozambique, Zambia, and Swaziland.

Mbeki met Zanele Dlamini, the director of the Women's Development Bank, during a stay in Swaziland to organize that country's ANC headquarters. They were married in 1974. Kwanda Mpahlwa, Mbeki's son from a previous relationship, remains missing after going into exile in 1980. Mbeki's home is in Ecingwana, Eastern Cape province. His hobbies include chess, reading, and spending time with his family. Unlike most political leaders, Mbeki writes his own speeches. He recently published a book titled *Africa: Your Time Has Come*, outlining his belief in a coming African Renaissance.

## RISE TO POWER

Throughout his youth, Thabo Mbeki was groomed for leadership within the ANC under the tutelage of Oliver Tambo. Regarded as a brilliant political strategist and a man dedicated to hard work, Mbeki rose through the party ranks rapidly, serving in Swaziland and Nigeria to establish ANC branch offices and to build support abroad. In 1978, when he returned to the ANC headquarters in Lusaka, Zambia, Mbeki became the political secretary in the office of its president, Oliver Tambo. He was later promoted to director of information. Through repeated trips abroad, Mbeki polished his diplomatic skills by meeting with foreign dignitaries and business leaders. In 1985, Mbeki became a member of the National Executive Committee (NEC) of the ANC.

During the 1980s, he spearheaded a campaign to involve more white South Africans in anti-apartheid activities, including a meeting between the ANC and influential Afrikaners from the Institute for a Democratic Alternative for South Africa in 1987 at Dakar, Senegal. He emerged as the primary public relations spokesperson and diplomat of the ANC. In 1989, he headed the ANC's international affairs department and participated in secret talks with the South

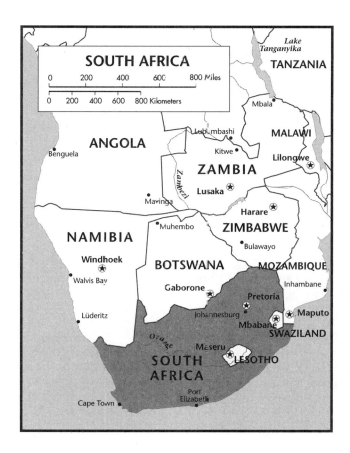

African government for legalization of the ANC and release of political prisoners, including Nelson Mandela.

Mbeki returned to South Africa in 1990 when the ANC was unbanned. He emerged as a key figure in negotiating the rules for South Africa's first all-race elections, the content of an interim constitution, and the transition to majority rule. Upon Mandela's election to the South African presidency in 1994, Mbeki was appointed deputy president of the Government of National Unity. As Mandela aged and decided not to run for another presidential term, Mbeki began to perform presidential duties with Mandela's blessing. On 18 December 1997, he was elected president of the ANC and received Mandela's support during the 2 June 1999, elections. The ANC won, virtually assuring Mbeki's election as president. He was inaugurated on June 16 in an elaborate ceremony with 60,000 spectators and dignitaries from 30 countries.

## LEADERSHIP

Mbeki brings important leadership skills and experiences to the office of the presidency. His negotiating experiences involving many diverse ethnic and economic interests over the years make him an ideal person to lead South Africa during the second stage of post-apartheid governance. Mbeki is a pragmatist, one who studies the issues and positions meticulously and seeks to resolve conflict through compromise. He is well respected within the South African business community and internationally, as a statesman and an intellectual. Furthermore, Mbeki enjoys the full support of Nelson Mandela, who remains almost universally popular.

Despite these strengths, Mbeki remains somewhat of an enigma to many who did not observe his international activities. His support within some quarters of the ANC, especially among the poor and militants, remains weak. He is sometimes viewed as detached and too cerebral by radicals because he did not participate in the armed struggle from within South Africa.

Mbeki maintains good relations with most leaders of the ANC and a working relationship with Chief Mangosuthu Buthelezi of the Inkatha Freedom Party—who is viewed as an important player in maintaining ethnic harmony in Kwa-Zulu Natal Province. His cabinet, which was announced on 17 June 1999, consisted mostly of ANC members. Buthelezi turned down the offer of deputy president and became instead minister of home affairs. During his administration, Mbeki needs to convince the skeptics in his party and the rank-and-file ANC members that he can move the transition several steps forward by transforming the condition of most blacks. To do this, he needs to maintain a delicate balance between all the contending interests.

## DOMESTIC POLICY

The first post-apartheid government brought significant changes to the nation, including the incorporation of ANC's armed guerillas, known as the *Umkonto we Sizwe* (Spear of the Nation), into the South African Defense Force; the creation of a multiracial civil service and national police; and increased public spending for social programs for the disadvantaged through the National Reconstruction and Development Program. The most significant achievement was the creation of 500 rural clinics and the establishment of free medical care for children under age six and pregnant women. All of these changes were accomplished with sustained economic growth. However, the disparities between racial groups remain potentially explosive.

Mbeki's major challenge, to uplift the economic condition of the black majority, constitutes an extremely difficult task. The government will remain committed to major public works projects, including rural electrification, education funding, the building of affordable homes, and the creation of sanitation systems. However, it needs to maintain the support of the predominantly white business community, which looks at Mbeki and the ANC with concern and suspicion. At the same time, more militant members of the ANC believe that the Mandela administration did not go far enough in redressing the inequity of resources and opportunities persisting from the apartheid era. Mbeki's experience in conflict resolution and negotiating skills can help create policies and programs acceptable to multiple constituencies.

While a modest level of white out-migration to Australia, Great Britain, and Canada has taken place since the fall of the apartheid government, the major problem for South African immigration policy remains the migration to South Africa from nearby nations by those seeking economic improvement. The new government must come up with a policy to manage this issue, especially because of its relation to increased crime. In the past five years, the judicial system failed to deal adequately with increasing crime. Mbeki will likely take measures to reform the system based on crime prevention and community policing.

## FOREIGN POLICY

During the apartheid era South Africa was a pariah state. It now enjoys full membership in the international community. Over the past five years, South Africa has gradually assumed an important role as an economic and moral leader for sub-Saharan Africa. Relations with neighboring nations have become strong, and South Africa has begun to provide economic and technical assistance to neighboring states through the Southern African Development Community (SADC). Mbeki's message of an "African Renaissance" resonates well in a region that has been largely ignored, both economically and culturally, since the end of the Cold War. He is well respected among African leaders.

Because the ANC government remains deeply committed to domestic resource redistribution and maintains close ties with Cuba and Libya, the West remains cautious toward Mbeki's government. During the apartheid era, Cuba and Libya provided financial assistance and training to ANC guerrillas, and the new government remains appreciative of that support. As a result, South Africa may not always pursue interests that are aligned with those of the West. However, because South Africa seeks a major infusion of foreign investment, Mbeki's government cannot antagonize Western investors and governments. In the end, Mbeki's pragmatism and diplomatic skill should allow the government to craft an independent foreign policy while winning acceptance and respect from the West.

## ADDRESS

State President's Office
Union Buildings, Western Wing
Private Bag X1000
0001 Pretoria, South Africa

## REFERENCES

ANC Official Website. [Online] Available http://www.anc.org.za/ (Accessed 10 February 2000).
*Business Day* (Johannesburg, South Africa), 31 May 1999.
*Panafrican News Agency,* 9 June 1999.
*The Sowetan* (Johannesburg, South Africa), 9 June 1999.
*Sunday Times* (South Africa), May–June, 1999.
*Washington Post,* 31 May–4 June 1999.

**Profile researched and written by Robert W. Compton, Jr., Western Kentucky University (9/99; updated 2/2000).**

# SPAIN

## José María Aznar
### Prime Minister
*(pronounced "ho-ZEY mah-REE-ah AZ-nar")*

*"Spaniards have been very generous to us and we know how to thank them: with hard work and collaboration."*

The Kingdom of Spain occupies four-fifths of the Iberian peninsula in Southwestern Europe. The national territory also includes the Balearic Islands in the Mediterranean Sea, the Canary Islands in the Atlantic Ocean, and a few small enclaves in Morocco. Together, these parts cover 504,750 sq km (194,884 sq mi). Mainland Spain shares its northern border with France and its western border with Portugal. The Mediterranean Sea lies to the east. Morocco is 30 km to the south. The capital and largest city is Madrid; metropolitan Madrid is home to 4 million Spaniards. The nation's population of 40 million is largely Roman Catholic, although there has been no state religion since 1979. Castilian Spanish is the official language, but the distinct ethnic groups within Spain—Catalans, Valencians, Gallegos, and Basques—have preserved their languages. Regional divisions within Spain have led to the formation of 17 autonomous regions within the country, each with its own political parties and government.

Spain's economy is one of the largest of the OECD nations. Its GDP was expected to account for 8% of the combined GDP of the "euro-zone" countries that adopted the new "euro" currency in January 1999. The country's GDP is estimated at US$646 billion. Per capita GDP is approximately US$16,500. As a member of the European Union, Spain has tied its economy closely to the regulations that govern that alliance. Almost 75% of trade—both imports and exports—is carried on with other EU nations. Principal exports include automobiles, fruit, minerals, metals, clothing and textiles. Imports include petroleum, aircraft, grains, chemicals, machinery, and transportation equipment. The currency is the *peseta*. Devaluations have occurred in order to participate in the EU's anticipated monetary union. Unemployment has decreased from over 24% (1996) to 15% (fourth quarter of 1999). The country's economy was expected to grow by 3.3%, with inflation at about 1.9% and unemployment at 15% in 2000.

## POLITICAL BACKGROUND

Present-day Spanish language, law, and religion date from the Roman conquest, which began in the second century BC, and lasted until the fifth century AD, with the invasion of the Visigoths. The arrival of the Moors in 711 AD spelled the end of Visigoth power, and it was not until 1492 that the Moors were driven out. By 1512, the unification of present-day Spain was complete.

During the 16th century, Spain was the most powerful of the European nations, due largely to the immense wealth derived from its colonial expansion into the Americas. The defeat of the Spanish Armada by the British in 1588 was the beginning of a steady decline of Spanish influence in Europe. The 19th century brought with it the revolt and subsequent independence of most of Spain's colonies.

The 20th century saw no great improvement in Spain's fortunes. In 1931 a democratic republic was established. In 1936 the Army, led by General Fransisco Franco y Bahamonde revolted against the republic. A bloody civil war lasted until 1939 when Franco's Nationalist forces defeated the Loyalist forces. The Nationalist victory in 1939 swept into power General Franco, who established an authoritarian government which severely restricted individual liberties and repressed any challenge to its power. General Franco died in November 1975 and was succeeded by King Juan Carlos. A new and more liberal council of ministers was formed and restrictions on political activity were lifted, but long pent-up pressures and frustration at the pace of reforms led to widespread demonstrations. In July 1976 Prime Minister Carlos Arias Navarro, who had been appointed by General Franco, resigned at the king's request, and was replaced by Adolfo Suárez González. Political reforms then proceeded rapidly, including the establishment of a bicameral legislature.

General elections in October 1982 brought decisive victory to the *Partido Socialista Obrero Español* (PSOE—the Socialist Workers' Party) and to the party's leader Felipe González Márquez. Despite gradual but continual erosion of support over the years, González and the PSOE remained in power throughout the 1980s and early 1990s. It was during González's tenure that Spain faced a range of controversial issues, and it is due in part to these factors that the popularity of the government suffered. Economic rationalization met with bitter opposition from trade unions, education reform met with resistance from the public, and Spain's continued membership in NATO was the source of large-scale public demonstrations. Despite these obstacles, economic rationalization did take place, paving the way for Spain's full membership in the European Union; education reform went forward; and Spain remained a full member of NATO after a general referendum on the question in March 1986. In the early 1990s, the government was rocked by a series of financial scandals involving family members of some government officials. Following an eruption of even more scandalous allegations concerning the PSOE's financing, early

**SPAIN**

0      100      200      300 Miles

0    100   200   300 Kilometers

*Bay of Biscay*

Paris

Nantes

FRANCE

Bordeaux

Bilbao

Oporto

ANDORRA

Barcelona

PORTUGAL

Madrid

SPAIN

Lisbon

*Balearic Islands*

Sevilla

Málaga

Gibraltar (UK)

elections were called for 6 June 1993. The PSOE was once again returned to office, but for the first time lost its majority in the *Cortes*. By 1996, Spanish voters had put the conservative Popular Party (PP) in power, with José María Aznar as head of government. Unknown outside conservative circles, Aznar ruled the country during a prosperous time. While his party lacked a majority, and had to broker agreements with minority parties to rule, the country was taking a decisive turn to conservatism. In March 2000, the PP obtained a resounding victory, capturing a majority of seats in the Congress of Deputies. With an absolute majority, the PP didn't need help from any party to govern.

Under the 1978 constitution, Spain is a hereditary monarchy, and the king is head of state. The king appoints the president of the government (prime minister) and the council of ministers on the prime minister's recommendation. Legislative authority is vested in the *Cortes Generales*, which consists of the 350-seat Congress of Deputies, elected by proportional representation; and the Senate, comprised of 208 directly elected members and 47 regional representatives. Both houses are elected by universal adult suffrage to four-year terms, subject to dissolution.

## PERSONAL BACKGROUND

José María Aznar was born 25 February 1953 in Madrid, to a family that included several well-known conservative journalists, one of whom chronicled the Spanish Civil War from General Francisco Franco's perspective. Aznar's father and one of his grandfathers held political posts in Franco's authoritarian government. Aznar was educated at the University of Madrid, where he trained as an attorney.

During the 1970s and 1980s, Aznar was employed as a tax inspector in Madrid. It was during this time that he became active in the right-wing Popular Alliance.

Aznar is married to Ana Botella, who is also a lawyer. In 1996, Botella played a minor role in her husband's campaign. During the 2000 campaign, however, she made visits to every region of the country, speaking with voters and pushing her husband's agenda. The couple has three children. For recreation, Aznar enjoys playing paddle tennis.

## RISE TO POWER

José María Aznar was first elected to the Spanish parliament in 1982, after which his rise to prominence within the Popular Alliance was rapid. In the mid-1980s, he served as chief minister of the Castile-Léon region. He also led a faction within the party which advocated a shift toward the political center and a break with Franco's remaining adherents. In 1989 Aznar was elected leader of the Popular Alliance, which was then renamed the Popular Party (PP). Throughout the early 1990s Aznar continued to steer the party toward the center, avoided ties to groups on the extreme right, advocated conservative fiscal and economic policies, and made a concerted effort to recruit women and young people into the party.

In the first elections contested under Aznar's leadership in 1989, the PP lost by a wide margin to the PSOE. Nevertheless, Aznar was credited with having refashioned the PP into a "clean" party of the right—devoid of fascist and extreme elements devoted to Franco. The 1993 general election, although still won by the PSOE, brought the PP within a narrow margin of capturing a majority of seats in the *Cortes*. The continuing scandals within the PSOE allowed Aznar to capitalize on the PP's recent electoral strength by making ethics an issue.

Continued erosion of support for the PSOE, coupled with the widening inquiry into corruption at the top levels of the party forced Prime Minister Felipe González Márquez to call early elections for 3 March 1996. As the principal opposition party, the PP was expected to gain an outright majority in the March elections, with no need for coalitions with regional parties. However, despite commanding leads in all the polls, when the vote was counted Aznar and the Popular Party had won only 156 seats in the Congress of Deputies—20 seats short of the majority needed to form a government. In fact, with only 38.8% of the 25 million votes cast, the PP garnered only 1.4% more than González and the PSOE.

To rule, Aznar was forced to forge a coalition with the Catalan Convergence and Union (CiU) party, which was led by Jordi Pujol, a powerful political figure. Aznar had counted on an outright victory and had attacked the Catalan party during the campaign. Yet Pujol was willing to forget in exchange for concessions and political power. For the next four years, Aznar's party ruled with CiU on its side.

In March 2000, Aznar and the PP were expected to barely win against a leftist coalition intent on gaining power back. The PSOE aligned itself with the United Left, but couldn't muster much support from Spaniards, who are overwhelmingly left of center. Yet, voters were disillusioned with continued political scandals and accusations of corruption that had shocked the left. In 1999, the PSOE's presidential candidate, the popular Jose Borrell, was forced to resign when two of his underlings were charged with allegations of wrongdoing. The PSOE then settled on Joaquín Almunia to lead the party. By all accounts, the campaign for the March 2000 elections lacked drama or major ideological differences. Aznar, Almunia, and other candidates were left to exchange personal insults. Aznar was especially hard on Basque separatist nationalists, an easy position to take since most Spaniards were tired of E.T.A. terrorist attacks. What really worked in favor of Aznar was the thriving Spanish economy. Under Aznar, the economy was one of the fastest growing in Europe. The liberalization of the economy had been one of Aznar's major goals in 1996, and many of his policy decisions had worked. By 1999, the economy was growing at more than 3% per year, and unemployment had decreased from about 24% when he took power, to about 15% by late 1999. Faced with those numbers, the left didn't have much to offer, except to accuse Aznar of being too far to the right. But Aznar would not concede much in ideology. During the latter part of his presidency, he continued to claim a more centrist position, talking both about family values and creating more jobs.

Since 1996, Aznar had grown in confidence if not in style. Still considered a bland orator with a serious lack of charisma, Aznar had become an able politician who had managed to maintain the fragile alliance with Pujol and the CiU. As more European countries leaned to the left in the late 1990s, the successful economic policies of Aznar became powerful symbols for conservative leadership. By 2000 elections, Aznar was seeking a majority so he would not have to negotiate with Pujol or any other party, as he sought further economic reforms. What happened at the polls caught even Aznar by surprise. The PP captured 44.5% of the vote and increased its seats in the Congress of Deputies from 156 to 183, a majority. The PSOE lost 16 seats (from 141) and the United Left lost 13 (from 21). The CiU held on to 15 seats, but lost its political leverage since the PP no longer needed anyone to form a government.

## LEADERSHIP

In 1996, Aznar spent six difficult weeks negotiating with regional party leaders before he inauguration as Prime Minister. He came to terms Jordi Pujol and leaders of parties representing the Canary Islands and Valencia. Without the alliance, he would not have been able to govern. Even the Basque Nationalist Party signed a formal agreement with the PP, giving Aznar's government a great deal of stability.

The PSOE, which won 140 seats in that election, was the principal opposition to the PP. Together with the United Left, they were expected to make Aznar's four years in office difficult at best. But plagued by internal difficulties and political scandals, the left never managed to cause problems for his government. Pujol, who relished his role as kingmaker, was more concerned with winning political and economic concessions for the Catalan region than creating problems for Aznar.

Political terms were quite different after the 2000 elections. With majority rule, Aznar won't have to seek any alliances with other parties to pursue his policies. Yet, Aznar was conciliatory during his victory speeches, saying he would seek the cooperation of other parties to push further reforms to Spain's economy. Aznar, who has been criticized for his conservative politics, stressed democratic themes in graciously accepting his victory. But that may not be enough with some sensitive issues that face the nation, including separatists in Basque country.

## DOMESTIC POLICY

In 1996, Aznar inherited an economy with several notable strengths—annual growth of nearly 3% and inflation under 4%—and one overwhelming weakness—unemployment that hovered near the 25% mark, despite two years of sustained economic recovery. He also inherited an entrenched welfare state, established during 14 years of Socialist governments. Fears of a weak or unstable government were laid to rest with the emergence of a strong coalition that supported Aznar's pro-business, pro-European Union position. From 1996 until early 2000, Aznar guided Spain into the European monetary unit, privatized many state assets, and lowered taxes. Yet, Spain's standard of living remained below that of other members of the EU. Economists have pointed out that Spain's economy must continue to grow at 4% annually to catch up, a difficult goal.

In his second term, Aznar has promised to continue to liberalize the economy. He wants to trim what he sees as a bloated bureaucracy; cut more taxes for citizens in the upper-income brackets; introduce competition in the energy and telecommunications industries to reduce prices and increase quality of service. He has proposed to increase the hours of operations for commerce, potentially disturbing a Spanish lifestyle that has endured for centuries. A higher GDP has meant greater energy consumption, which could lead to inflation. And while unemployment has decreased significantly, it remained at 15% in early 2000. To accomplish his goals, Aznar has said he will make "democratic use" of his majority in Congress. That means he doesn't want to upset the many leftists who crossed party lines to vote for him. And it means he would not be likely to simply ignore those who do not agree with his policies.

Aznar also faced the difficult task of dealing with Basque separatist violence. In late November 1999, the ETA (Euzkadi ta Askatasuna or Basque Nation and Liberty) ended a self-declared cease-fire. Three people were killed in terrorist attacks in the first quarter of 2000. The Nationalist Basque Party (PNV), which believes that only through negotiation peace can be achieved, was concerned that Aznar's resounding victory in March would hurt the peace process. Aznar has attacked the PNV for not isolating Euskal Herritarrok (EH), the party that is considered the political arm of ETA. Moderate nationalists fear Aznar will not negotiate with ETA, or even hold a dialogue with Basque separatists, perhaps leading to more violence. "I don't know what (Aznar) is thinking," PNV president Xabier Arzalluz told the press in early 2000. "Now he talks about dialogue. Before, he didn't want to talk. I can't have too much trust in Mr. Aznar." Aznar has simply responded "Spain is one nation."

## FOREIGN POLICY

Upon the death of General Franco and the subsequent return to democratic government, Spain's first foreign policy priority was to re-enter the international community from which it had been isolated during the Franco regime. To this end the nation actively pursued diplomatic relations with other nations. Spain became a member of NATO in 1982, and has become a major participant in multinational security activities. Spain became a full member of the European Community (now the European Union) in January 1986, further strengthening its ties to its neighbors. The country often coordinates its response to international policy issues through the EU political cooperation mechanism, even on issues outside Western Europe. Spain retains a special identification with Latin America, and advocates the concept of *Hispanidad*, which emphasizes historical and cultural ties between Spain and Spanish-speaking American nations. Spain also maintains economic and technical cooperation programs with the region. Many of its corporations have major holdings in Latin America. In some of those nations, Spain is the top foreign investor.

Spain has been positioning itself as the gateway between Latin America and Europe, but its relations with some Latin American countries were strained starting in October 1998, when Spanish judge Baltazar Garzon asked British authorities to arrest former Chilean dictator Augusto Pinochet, who was recovering from surgery in London. Garzon was trying to prosecute Pinochet, one of the most notorious dictators of the 20th century, for human rights violations. Garzon's efforts were applauded nationally and internationally, but it strained relations between Spain and Chile, Spain and Britain (both countries also had issues over Gibraltar in 1999), and other Latin American countries that came to the defense of Chile's sovereignty. Aznar was criticized for twice trying to intervene to prevent Pinochet's extradition to Spain. Chile threatened to end relations with Spain, which is the largest foreign investor in that country. Many Spanish citizens left Chile after being threatened by right-wing supporters of Pinochet. In August 1999, Aznar said he would respect the independence of his country's judicial system and allow Garzon to continue to petition Pinochet's extradition from Britain. While a British judge finally agreed that Garzon could extradite Pinochet to Spain, the dictator was released for humanitarian reasons in March 2000. Aznar may be forced to appease other nations during his second term. Spanish judges agreed in early 2000 to investigate human rights cases in Guatemala, and they continued to investigate human rights abuses committed during the Argentinean "dirty war" of 1976–83.

Spain and the United States have long maintained official and cordial relations. Recent years have seen the strengthening of these ties with the exchange of high-level visitors. The two countries cooperate in NATO and bilaterally in defense and security areas, whereby Spain permits US use of some Spanish military facilities. There is also long-term cooperation in support of aerospace research and exploration. Cultural and educational relations are maintained through both the Fulbright Scholarship program and a US Embassy exchange program.

## ADDRESS
Office of the Prime Minister
Complejo de la Moncloa
Edif. INIA
28071 Madrid, Spain

## REFERENCES
"The Pinochet Case: The Law's Web." *The Economist,* 2 October 1999, p. 65.

"Long Shadows: Conflict Over What to Do with Augusto Pinochet Continues." *The Economist,* 7 August 1999, p. 38.

"Spain and Race: Trouble." *The Economist,* 24 July 1999, p. 47.

"Spain's Socialists: Who Next?" *The Economist,* 22 May 1999, p. 57.

"Spain: Slinging Mud." *The Economist,* 1 May 1999, p. 50.

**Profile researched and written by Ignacio Lobos (6/2000).**

# SRI LANKA

## Chandrika Bandaranaike Kumaratunga
### President

*(pronounced "chan-DREE-ka bon-dar-a-NAH-e-kee koo-mar-ah-TUNG-ah")*

*"The fundamental obstacle to increased foreign investment is Sri Lanka's costly and prolonged ethnic conflict."*

The Democratic Socialist Republic of Sri Lanka (formerly called Ceylon), is a teardrop-shaped island country in the Indian Ocean, situated off the southeastern coast of India. The Maldive Islands lie to its west. It has an area of about 65,610 sq km (25,332 sq mi). Major cities include Colombo, the capital, Dehiwala-Mount Lavinia, Jaffna, and Kandy.

The island has a population of 19.1 million. Official languages are Sinhala and Tamil, but English is also recognized as a national language. Since independence, one of the constant issues bedeviling Sri Lankan life has been ethnic conflict. Almost 75% of the population is Sinhalese. Tamils form about 18%, Muslims about 7%, and smaller groups such as the Burghers (people of Eurasian descent), Malays, and Veddah aborigines are also to be found in the country. About 70% of the population is Buddhist, but Hinduism, Islam and Christianity are also followed by smaller groups of the population. The Tamils themselves are divided into two groups: Sri Lankan Tamils, who have lived in the country for centuries, and Indian Tamils who were brought by the British colonizers as plantation laborers in the 19th century. Most of the ethnic conflict has been between the Sinhalese and the Tamils, particularly the Sri Lankan Tamils.

The per capita GNP is estimated at US$2,500. The unit of currency used in Sri Lanka, as in several other South Asian states, is the *rupee,* which is divided into 100 cents. The Sri Lankan economy is heavily dependent upon agriculture, which contributes about a quarter of the country's GDP and employs about 44% of the labor force. In recent years, the economy has diversified. Attempts have been made to boost the tourism and banking sectors. Textiles and clothing are the most important sources of foreign exchange, but traditional exports such as tea, rubber, and coconuts form over 20% of export earnings.

## POLITICAL BACKGROUND
On 4 February 1948, Sri Lanka obtained independence from the United Kingdom, which had colonized it in 1815. Established as a parliamentary system within the Commonwealth, the country became a republic in May 1972 and, in the fall of 1978, switched to a presidential-parliamentary system. This largely unitary system is akin to the French presidential system and concentrates power in the president, who is limited to two six-year terms. The president appoints and dismisses the prime minister and other ministers and can also dissolve parliament. The unicameral legislature is composed of 225 members who are elected by proportional representation for six-year terms. The Supreme Court judges are appointed by the president, and the Court has sole jurisdiction over constitutional issues.

Several parties are active in Sri Lankan politics, but the two most important ones are the United National Party (UNP) and the Sri Lankan Freedom Party (SLFP). The UNP is a moderate, liberal, and generally pro-Western party, while the SLFP, which is currently in power, is a more leftist-oriented party. Two of the more prominent groups implicated in guerrilla attacks against the government are the *Janatha Vimukhti Peramuna* (People's Liberation Front), with a militant Sinhalese ideology, and the Liberation Tigers of Tamil Eelam (LTTE), which is the leading force in the fight for a Tamil homeland in Sri Lanka. Large-scale repression and the death of top JVP figures, allegedly at the hand of security forces in late 1990, reduced the organization's effectiveness, but by early 2000 the JVP had re-emerged as a third political force on the island.

The ethnic conflict in Sri Lanka has been simmering for decades. Government policy in the 1950s aimed at enhancing the political and social status of Sinhalese and embittered the Tamils. While there was some violence during the 1970s, the conflict escalated into a civil war in the 1980s, sending many Tamil refugees to Tamil Nadu in India. Indian attempts at mediation between the LTTE and the Sri Lankan government in the mid-1980s were ineffectual. Fighting between the Tigers and Sri Lankan forces have continued, although the former have suffered severe losses with the withdrawal of Indian support, weakening of support from the Tamil population and increasing success of the Sri Lankan Army attacks. But the Tigers continued to demonstrate their power. In May 1991 they were implicated in the assassination of India's Rajiv Gandhi, and, according to the Sri Lankan government, the Tigers are the likely suspects in the 1 May 1993, assassination of President Ranasinghe Premadasa and the October 1994 assassination of Gamini Dissanayake, the UNP's candidate for the Sri Lankan presidency. The latter was perceived as being a hard-line anti-Tamil politician. In January 1995, the Tamils agreed to a "cessation of hostilities" with Chandrika Kumaratunga, the newly-elected SLFP president who was perceived as being more moderate. Within three months, this truce collapsed and the LTTE resumed its attacks on government forces. The Sri Lankan army went on the offensive, and by early 1996 appeared to have control of the northern peninsula. Tamil resistance continued, however, with attacks on the military in the north and bombings elsewhere on the island. After a suicide bombing at Sri Lanka's most sacred Buddhist shrine, the 'Temple of the

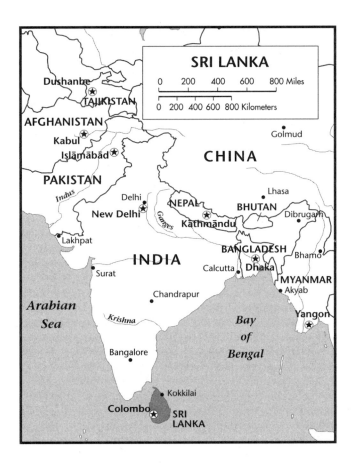

Tooth' in Kandy in 1998, the government formally outlawed the LTTE. President Kumaratunga continued to offer the Tamils limited regional autonomy, a position that was opposed by the UNP opposition and rejected outright by the Tamils. By late 1999, the LTTE had regained much of its lost territory in the north, inflicting a series of major defeats on government forces. Despite this, Kumaratunga was elected to a second term as president in December 1999. By May 2000, the government's position in the Jaffna peninsula had deteriorated alarmingly, with some 40,000 soldiers isolated in the north by Tamil rebels. Not surprisingly, the Tamils rejected a renewed effort by Kumaratunga to begin peace talks.

## PERSONAL BACKGROUND
Chandrika Kumaratunga was born on 29 June 1945, in Colombo, the capital of Sri Lanka. She received training in political journalism with *Le Monde* in Paris and a degree in political science from the University of Paris, where she also studied for a PhD. in development economics. Kumaratunga studied law and group leadership as well. Between 1976 and 1979, she served as an expert consultant with the Food and Agricultural Organization of the UN. Kumaratunga was a guest lecturer at *Jawahar Lal Nehru University* in India and Bradford University in the United Kingdom, and a Research Fellow at the Institute of Commonwealth Studies, University of London. She has authored several research papers on land reform, political violence, and agriculture. Between 1977 and 1985, she served as the chairperson and managing editor of the *Dinakara Sinhala*, a daily newspaper. Kumaratunga married Vijaya on 20 February 1978. She has a son and daughter.

## RISE TO POWER
The ascension of Chandrika Bandaranaike Kumaratunga to the presidency of Sri Lanka continues the South Asian pattern of family ties leading to democratically elected political power. The Bandaranaikes have been major political figures throughout the country's political history. Kumaratunga's mother, Sirimavo Bandaranaike, was the first female prime minister anywhere in the world. She has held the office of prime minister three times: from 1960–65, 1970–77, and again in 1994. Kumaratunga's brother, Anura Bandaranaike, was a cabinet minister in the UNP cabinet that lost power in the elections. He defected from the SLFP in April 1994, as a result of their rivalry.

Part of her popularity is due to the perception among the electorate that the family has paid a bloody price for public service. Kumaratunga's husband, Vijaya, a popular actor and politician, was assassinated by Sinhalese extremists on 16 February 1988; her father, Solomon W.R.D. Bandaranaike, prime minister between 1956–59 was assassinated in September 1959.

As a member of this illustrious Sri Lankan family, it was only a matter of time before Kumaratunga joined the political fray. She was first appointed to the position of additional principal director of the Land Reforms Commission during her mother's second term in office. She has also served as chairperson of the Janawasa Commission, Executive Committee member of the Women's League of the SLFP, member of the Executive Committee and the Working Committee of the SLFP, and as the vice president and president of the Sri Lanka Mahajana Party (SLMP), a party formed with her late husband, Vijaya.

Kumaratunga left the country after her husband's assassination in 1988 but returned in 1990 to help her mother, Sirimavo Bandaranaike, in leading the SLFP. The party was at the head of the People's Alliance that had been formed in the prelude to the 1993 provincial elections. Kumaratunga was instrumental in the victory of the coalition in the Western Province, where she became the chief minister. On 24 June 1994 President D.B. Wijetunga dissolved parliament and ordered elections for 16 August 1994. By then, Kumaratunga had supplanted Anura Bandaranaike as her powerful mother's heir apparent.

Although Kumaratunga was unable to win a clear victory, she was able to form a government and became the prime minister. In the presidential elections in November 1994, after the assassination of UNP candidate Gamini Dissanayake, she faced the latter's widow, Srima. Although Srima was expected to get a lift from the "sympathy" vote, Kumaratunga was able to carve out an impressive victory, with 62% of the vote, becoming the first female president of Sri Lanka. Escaping an assassination attempt three days before polling, Kumaratunga narrowly won a second six-year term as president on 21 December 1999.

## LEADERSHIP
Kumaratunga is an experienced politician who comes from a family with a prominent place in Sri Lankan politics. She can call on the expertise of her mother, a political veteran and Sri Lanka's current prime minister. In her own political career, Kumaratunga has demonstrated many of the qualities necessary for someone in her position. She is renowned

among her supporters for her energy and intellect. However, the task she has faced as Sri Lanka's president would test anyone's abilities to the utmost. Kumaratunga was elected to office by a populace that expected her to restore peace and prosperity to a violence-torn country. Despite being able to negotiate a short-lived "cessation of hostilities" with the Tamil rebels in January 1995, she has been unable to fulfill her electoral promises. Her offers of a negotiated peace have repeatedly been turned down by the Tamils extremists who want nothing short of a separate state. On the other hand, she has had to control the militant sections of Sinhalese society and the army in the face of Tamil provocations. Though re-elected as president, the euphoria of Kumaratunga's 1994 victory is gone. The war drags on with the government apparently losing; the army is demoralized and experiencing high rates of desertion; the UNP, which is gaining in strength, opposes Kumaratunga's plans for peace; and the country suffers from the economic burden of the war. Kumaratunga's second term in office will be an even greater test of her political skills and leadership than her first.

## DOMESTIC POLICY

The most important domestic problem in Sri Lanka remains the ethnic conflict between the Tamils and the Sinhalese. Since 1984 the conflict has defied solutions, its annual cost now runs about US$850 million, and it has taken over 61,000 lives. After the collapse of her peace overtures to the Tamils when she first took office, Kumaratunga has followed a dual strategy in relation to the war: military defeat of the Tamil Tigers coupled with a constitutional settlement that would grant regional autonomy to Tamil majority areas. By 1996, the government's military strategy appeared to be on the verge of success. Tamil resistance continued, however, and in late 1999 and early 2000 the LTTE inflicted a series of major defeats on Sri Lankan government troops in the north. In May 2000, following these setbacks, Kumaratunga's government placed the country on an emergency war footing.

The second element in the president's strategy, constitutional reform, has also run into problems. Kumaratunga proposes establishing a British-style government, with power concentration in the hands of a prime minister. Tamil areas in the north and east would be given control of health and education, and considerable influence over the areas of finance and policing. This is not enough for Tamil separatists, who want an independent Tamil state in Sri Lanka. On the other hand, it is too much for the UNP which sees it as breaking up Sri Lanka as a unitary state. Constitutional reforms require a two-thirds majority in parliament, and so far the UNP has succeeded in blocking the changes proposed by Kumaratunga. In March 2000, the president met with Ranil Wickremesinghe, the opposition leader, to discuss common ground for a peace plan. The Norwegian government has also become involved in an initiative to bring peace to Sri Lanka.

On the economic front, Kumaratunga has abandoned most of her socialist beliefs and is a firm supporter of Sri Lanka being a free-market economy. Although she has made some progress in promoting privatization, reforming finances, and restructuring the tax system, other economic problems remain. These include unemployment, a fiscal deficit, inflation, and the burden of the Tamil conflict. The Institute of Policy Studies in Colombo has calculated the cumulative cost of the civil war to be 170% of Sri Lanka's 1996 GDP. In addition to losses in men and material, indirect costs include disruption of trade, loss of tourist income, and declining foreign investment. The government imposes a National Defence Levy (a tax to pay for the war) on most consumer spending and imports. In May 2000, it announced price increases in essential goods and services (e.g. domestic cooking gas, telephone charges, and water) for the same purpose. In the mean time, government spending on social services averaged only 1.3% of the GDP between 1990 and 1997. Clearly, the future growth of Sri Lanka's economy and the well-being of its people depend on a peaceful and lasting resolution of the country's on-going ethnic conflict.

## FOREIGN POLICY

Although there have been problems with India in the past, particularly because of the latter's support of the Tamils in the 1980s, Sri Lanka maintains cordial relations with its neighbors in South Asia. Kumaratunga's peace efforts are welcomed by India, which is facing its own secessionist struggles in Kashmir and some of its northeastern states. After being burned by its abortive peacekeeping efforts in Sri Lanka, the Indian government is reluctant to get involved with the Sri Lankan conflict. India did, however, after an initial refusal, agree to a Sri Lankan request to provide assistance in evacuating some 35,000–40,000 government troops trapped in the northern part of Sri Lanka during the Tamil offensive of May 2000. This help was not necessary, as government forces withstood the Tamil threat. There are some analysts, however, who see a possible role for India in negotiating a peace between the warring parties in Sri Lanka. Kumaratunga is actively seeking diplomatic support abroad for her efforts to bring the conflict in Sri Lanka to an end.

Kumaratunga adheres to the traditional Sri Lankan foreign policy of nonalignment. The country enjoys good relations with major countries like the US and the UK. Kumaratunga's efforts to democratize the political and social structure, investigate human rights violations, and bring peace to the island are supported by the global community.

## ADDRESS

Office of the President
Republic Square
Colombo 1, Sri Lanka

## REFERENCES

*Asiaweek*, 1999–2000.

*The Economist*, 1999–2000.

*Europa World Yearbook*. London: Europa Publications, 1999.

*Far Eastern Economic Review*, 1994–95.

Nilan, Fernando. "Sri Lanka in 1998: Political Stalemate and Economic Drift." *Asian Survey*, January–February 1999, v. 39, no. 1 p. 185.

*Sri Lanka Country Profile*, Economist Intelligence Unit, 1994–95.

*Times of India*, 1994–2000.

**Profile researched and written by Thomas Uthup, Binghamton University (SUNY) (3/95; updated by Deryck Lodrick, University of California 6/00).**

# SUDAN

## Omar Hassan Ahmed al-Bashir
## Prime Minister

*(pronounced "oh-MAR hah-SAHN ah-MED al bah-SHEER")*

*"As soon as we feel that the Sudanese people are capable of making good decisions free
from sectarian considerations and party politics, we will relinquish power."*

The Republic of the Sudan, historically known as the land of Kush, borders on eight neighboring states and is the largest country in Africa. To the north of Sudan are Egypt and Libya; to the west are Chad and the Central African Republic; to the south are Zaire, Uganda and Kenya; and to Sudan's east are Ethiopia and the Red Sea. Its total area is 2,505,813 sq km (967,494 sq mi). The population is estimated to be 34.5 million. The unit of currency is the Sudanese pound. Arabic, the official language, is spoken by about half of the population. Nubian and Ta Bedawie are also spoken. Over 100 dialects of Nilo-Hamitic, Sudanic, Bantu and Darfurin languages are also used, while English is spoken in major urban areas. Ethnically, Sudan is complex, with over 500 different tribes composing 19 major ethnic groups: in the north are mostly Arab peoples; in the south are the Nuba, Beja, Fur, Sudanic, Nilotic and Para-Nilotic groups, among them the Dinka, Nuer and Shilluk. Sudan's religion is predominantly Sunni Muslim (70%, mostly in the north), but traditional belief systems (20%) and Christianity (10%, mostly in the south) also exist. The per capita GNP for the country is US$930. The country's primary exports are cotton, gum arabic, livestock, peanuts and sesame.

## POLITICAL BACKGROUND

After gaining its independence from Egypt and the UK in 1956, Sudan initially was established as a civilian parliamentary republic. However, democratic mechanisms have faltered over the years as a series of military and civilian coups brought non-elected leaders to power. In the coup of 6 April 1985 President Gaafar al-Nimeri was overthrown by General Abdul Rahman Suwar al Dahab, who had been promoted to minister of defense only three days earlier. Suwar al Dahab suspended the constitution, declared martial law and formed the Transitional Military Council of 15 senior military leaders to act collectively as the heads of state. Civilian government was restored in 1986 and, in elections held between 1–12 April 1986, Sadiq al Mahdi was chosen prime minister. Mahdi's Umma Party formed a coalition with the Democratic Unionist Party to oppose the militant fundamentalist National Islamic Front (NIF). A Constituent Assembly was established to govern the country as its legislative body, while a Council of Ministers, headed by Mahdi, implemented government policy. The executive branch consisted of a five-man Supreme Council which acted collectively as president.

After the 30 June 1989 coup led by Omar Hassan Ahmed al-Bashir, Bashir declared a state of emergency, suspended all political activity, and established a 15-member Revolutionary Council. Although initially Bashir's junta ruled Sudan in an autocratic manner with no apparent links to political parties, his group eventually allied itself with the NIF, which sought to reinstate Islamic law (*shariah*). Civilian government was nominally restored in 1993, but Bashir and the NIF remained in control through the 1990s as warfare continued between government forces based in the north and non-Muslim rebels in the southern part of the country.

## PERSONAL BACKGROUND

Relatively little has been published on Bashir's personal background, but it is known that he was born in 1944. He received some of his military training in the USSR, although he later held distinctly anti-Communist views. Bashir served in the Sudanese army, rising to the rank of brigadier, and he was the third-ranking paratroop and airborne commander in the civil war between the central government and the southern rebels of the Sudanese Peoples Liberation Army (SPLA), led by John Gurang.

It is believed that he is a member of a northern Muslim sect which opposed Sadiq al Mahdi's efforts to suspend the imposition of Islamic law.

## RISE TO POWER

Bashir, who has said that he had considered taking power ever since Suwar al Dahab returned Sudan to democracy in 1986, reportedly arrived in Khartoum only three weeks before the 1989 coup. Prime Minister Sadiq al Mahdi's inability to end the civil war or to rehabilitate Sudan's crippled economy led to months of growing confrontation and animosity between the military and the government. In February a group of military officers presented Prime Minister Mahdi with an ultimatum, demanding that he either settle the civil war through negotiation or give the military the means to gain victory on the battlefield. Bashir is said to have been involved in the planning of a coup attempt set for 22 June 1989, though he was not among those arrested in a June 18 preemptive roundup of conspirators.

On June 30, a group of military officers, dissatisfied with Sadiq al Mahdi's progress in ending the war and solving Sudan's endemic food crisis, moved to arrest the prime minister and dismissed 28 generals loyal to his government. The coup was for the most part bloodless, as it was reported that only two officers were killed in the take-over. The little-known Bashir soon announced on the official Omdurman radio that he was the leader of this coup and that henceforth Sudan would be ruled by a new Revolutionary Command Council of National Salvation. He further announced that the junta's primary goals would be achieving peace and putting the *shariah* issue to the people in the form of a referendum.

## LEADERSHIP

After the 1989 coup, Bashir moved to monopolize power within his 15-member Revolutionary Council. He dissolved parliament, established a state of emergency and a curfew in Khartoum, suspended all political activities, and freed 14 army officers who had been arrested earlier for plotting Mahdi's overthrow. He promoted himself to Brigadier General and declared himself prime minister, defense minister, and commander in chief of the armed forces. He also purged the military of dozens of officers who were thought to have loyalties to the old regime, thereby cementing his own position of dominance vis-a-vis the military. Bashir appointed officers loyal to him to head the air force, the infantry institute, and military intelligence. He then traveled throughout the country to solidify his position by reappointing regional governors that would support him.

By 1990, Bashir had formed an alliance with the National Islamic Front (NIF), an Islamic fundamentalist party led by Hassan al-Turabi, and the two men remained the country's most powerful political figures throughout the decade, even after the nominal restoration of civilian government in 1993. Al-Turabi served as the political and ideological leader of the country's program of Islamization, while Bashir maintained the military power behind the government. In December 1999 a growing power struggle between the two men led to the removal of al-Turabi and the appointment of new political leadership by President Bashir.

## DOMESTIC POLICY

The cornerstone of Bashir's domestic policy has been the imposition of Islamic law and institutions through severe political repression involving widespread human rights abuses. All real political opposition has been driven underground or into exile. *Shari'ah* was reinstated in 1991, although it is not observed in the non-Muslim southern provinces. Despite the 1998 adoption of a new constitution providing for a multi-party political system, civil liberties in Sudan remain heavily restricted.

Periodic ceasefires and negotiations have failed to end the civil war that has ravaged the country since the early 1980s, killing two million people, internally displacing over four million, and exacerbating famine conditions in the south. As the 1990s came to an end, it appeared that neither the government nor the rebel forces were capable of winning the war militarily. Government and rebel negotiators continued to meet in 1999, reaching agreement on transit routes for humanitarian relief.

Although the war has occupied most of Bashir's energies, his country's pressing economic problems have forced him to implement harsh programs aimed at cutting government expenses and boosting Western lenders' confidence in his regime. In spite of the government's privatization program

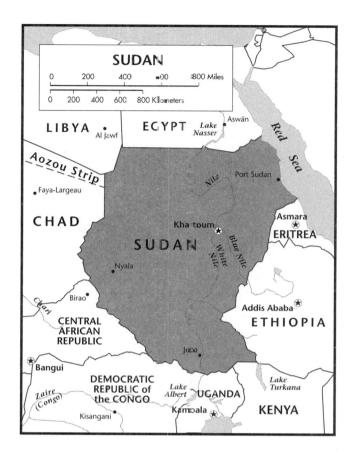

and efforts at stimulating foreign investment, Sudan's economy at the end of the decade was still weakened by massive foreign debt and heavy military expenditures.

## FOREIGN POLICY

Bashir has made clear his intent to take a strongly pan-Arabist approach to foreign relations, voicing his desire to make Sudan a model Islamic state in the region. Shortly after coming to power, Bashir approached many Arab countries such as Saudi Arabia, Kuwait, the United Arab Emirates and Iraq, seeking assistance in the form of money, medical supplies, oil and weapons. Capitalizing on his self-proclaimed solidarity with the Arab world, Bashir personally visited Iraq, announcing soon afterwards that President Saddam Hussein had promised to meet Sudan's requirements for aid and weapons.

During Bashir's period in power, Sudan has acquired an international reputation for political repression, human rights abuses, and support of terrorism. The US added Sudan to its list of countries spawning international terrorism in August 1993 and implemented economic sanctions in 1996. Sudan has also been censured by the UN for human rights abuses.

## ADDRESS

Office of the Prime Minister
Khartoum, Sudan

## REFERENCES

*Africa Confidential*, 28 July 1965.
*African Report*, September–October 1989.

Banks, Arthur S. and Thomas Muller, eds. *Political Handbook of the World*. Binghamton, NY: CSA Publications, 1999.

*The Economist*, various issues.

*New African*, October 1989.

*New York Times*, various issues.

"Sudan: Palace Coup." *The Economist*, 18 December 1999, p.41.

"Sudan: The Human Price of Oil." Report summary. Amnesty International, 3 May 2000.

*Sudanews*, 1990.

"Sudan's Chance for Peace." *The Economist*, 22 January 2000, p.45

US Department of State, *Human Rights Report for 1999— Sudan*.

**Profile researched and written by Craig Schultz (7/90; updated 5/00).**

# SURINAME

## Jules Albert Wijdenbosch
## President
*(pronounced "WY-den-bush")*

*"I shall endeavor to forge the Surinamese people into a truly democratic nation in which the quality of life of every citizen is equal and guaranteed."*

The Republic of Suriname (pronounced "suh-ri-NAM-uh," but also pronounced in English without the last syllable) is situated on the north central coast of South America and covers an area of 163,266 sq km (63,037 sq mi), excluding 17,635 sq km (6,809 sq mi) disputed with Guyana. More than 95% of the country's area is covered by tropical forest. To the north lies the Atlantic Ocean, to the east French Guiana, to the south Brazil, and to the west Guyana. The population is estimated at 431,156. More than 90% of the population is settled in the northern coastal region, the site of extensive plantation agriculture in the 17th through 19th centuries. Movement out of agriculture has produced an urban sprawl around the capital city of Paramaribo with an estimated population of 180,000.

Dutch is the official language, but the majority speak Sranang Tongo, a local pidgin. Also widely spoken are Sarnami Hindostaans (a derivative from Hindu and Urdu) and Maleis (a forerunner of Indonesian). There are also a number of tribal African and Amerindian tongues spoken by the Maroons (descendants of runaway slaves) and the Carib and Arawak groups living along the rivers of the interior and in other scattered locations. English, Chinese, French, and Spanish are also spoken. Ethnically the population is a rich composite of peoples, most of them brought to the country by the Dutch to work on sugar and other plantations: Creoles (or blacks) now make up about 31% of the population, Hindustanis (from India) about 37%, Javanese 14%, Bush Negroes (or Maroons) 9%, Amerindians 3%, Chinese 3%, and others (including Dutch and Lebanese) 3%. The population also exhibits a rich variety of religious faiths: Protestants and Catholics each comprise about half of the total Christian community, making up 42% of the population. Hindus add another 27%, Moslems 20%, and smaller numbers of Jews, Buddhists, and animists (among the forest peoples) round out the figures.

The currency unit is the guilder, or Surinamese florin (Sf). Suriname's primary export products are alumina, rice, bauxite, aluminum, shrimp, and bananas.

## POLITICAL BACKGROUND
Suriname was a prosperous British settlement on the banks of the Suriname River of northeast South America. The settlement was transferred to the Dutch in 1667 by the Treaty of Breda with the British receiving New York, New Jersey, and Delaware in return. Slaves imported from Africa furnished labor for the vast plantations, and after slavery was abolished in 1863, indentured laborers were brought in from British India and the Dutch East Indies for this purpose. Suriname has been a fully self-governing member of the Dutch Kingdom since the end of World War II. In 1975, upon being granted independence, the country dropped its former name of Dutch Guiana. Although originally governed as a parliamentary state, the constitution was suspended in early 1980 following a military coup. Civilian rule was restored in 1988 under a new constitution that had been approved in September 1987. This constitution gave Suriname a mixed presidential and parliamentary form. In 1990 Suriname again suffered a military coup, but constitutional government was maintained, and elections were held in May 1991.

Under the terms of the 1987 constitution, Suriname is a parliamentary republic with one legislative house, the National Assembly. Ultimate authority rests with this 51-member body which is elected for a five-year term. The National Assembly reflects the diverse population through ethnically-based political parties. Elections are not prescheduled and can take place at any time during the five-year period. Executive authority rests with the president, who is elected by the National Assembly. The president serves as head of state, head of government, head of the armed forces, and chair of the Council of State, which is an advisory body. The president shares some of his powers with his vice president, who heads the Cabinet and oversees day-to-day policy-making and administration.

## PERSONAL BACKGROUND
A native of Paramaribo, Jules Wijdenbosch was born 2 May 1941. He became involved in government as a bureaucrat in the harbor office of Paramaribo, rising to the rank of customs house officer by age 21. He was a public servant for the city of Amsterdam, where he studied political science, specializing in issues of public administration. In September 1996 Wijdenbosch was elected president of Suriname at age 55.

## RISE TO POWER
Wijdenbosch's political career was advanced by a close association with army commander Desi Bouterse, who was in effect the military dictator of Suriname from 1980 to 1987. The arrest and execution of 15 prominent civilians by Bouterse's government resulted in internal and external pressures for the drafting of a new constitution and subsequent free elections in 1987. In preparation for the elections, Lt. Colonel Bouterse created the National Democratic Party

**SURINAME**

0      250      500      750 Miles

0    250    500    750 Kilometers

(NDP), a political vehicle for him and his supporters. Bouterse's NDP won only three seats in the National Assembly. Nevertheless, after Bouterse staged a 1990 Christmas Eve coup, the National Assembly rapidly approved a new government dominated by the NDP that had the strong backing of the army. Wijdenbosch has proved himself a key civilian supporter of Bouterse, periodically having held the chairmanship and vice chairmanship of the NDP through 1996. After the 1990 coup Johan Kraag was installed as president, although the government was dominated by the vice-president and premier Jules Wijdenbosch.

This short-lived government was replaced by the democratically elected government of Renaldo Ronald Venetiaan who vowed to eradicate military influence in politics. Relations with the armed forces remained tense during the Venetiaan administration. Desi Bouterse resigned as army commander in December 1992 but has continued to play a role in politics as leader of the opposition National Democratic Party. He continues to have close ties with the military.

In the general election on 23 May 1996, President Venetiaan's New Front coalition of five parties narrowly won the National Assembly. The NDP won only 16 of the 51 National Assembly seats. It subsequently increased its strength to 28 when the New Front coalition, headed by Venetiaan, disintegrated. Members of the Hindu (VHP) and Indonesian (KTPI) parties joined a new coalition with the NDP, giving the election to Wijdenbosch and the NDP. Wijdenbosch won 437 votes of the United Peoples' Assembly against 407 for the former president Ronald Venetiaan, an outspoken defender of democracy over military government.

The new recruits to the NDP-led coalition, however, stipulated that Bouterse should not hold office in the new government. Wijdenbosch's close association with former dictator, Desi Bouterse, and his September 1996 election to the presidency has reawakened fears of a resurgence of the bloody civil war of the 1980s.

## LEADERSHIP

Upon taking office Wijdenbosch promised two things: economic development of human and natural resources, and more democratic practices and institutions. His inaugural speech reflects a populist policy of state control over natural resources and the economy to provide for social needs. Wijdenbosch's call for an export-oriented and import-restrictive economy is nationalistic in its overtones, yet the privatization of many government industries will make such policies difficult to realize. The NDP has run into trouble in trying to piece together a cabinet acceptable to its supporters. Wijdenbosch's vice-president, Pretaap Radhakishun, objected to the nomination of the former head of the state-owned Surinam Airways for the position of finance minister on the grounds that the nominee, Modilal Mungra, had been implicated in a financial scandal with the airline in the 1980s. Many of the problems confronting Wijdenbosch's new government will undoubtedly stem from a long-standing rivalry between Creole and Hindustani political groups.

## DOMESTIC POLICY

By June 1999, Suriname's currency had lost a third of its value, and inflation was running at about 10% a month. The government was quick to blame forces beyond its control. Any disturbances in the economy has profound effects on this small, impoverished nation, where 63% of the people live below the poverty line, and frustrated citizens didn't wait to stage protests against the government, asking for the president's resignation. Suriname's finance minister blamed the currency's slide on a major cocaine bust in the Netherlands, but opposition leaders didn't accept the excuse. In the meantime, the government came up with another idea to save the economy. President Jules Wijdenbosch told the nation he had sent a delegation to Phoenix, Arizona, to negotiate for US$26 million in aid, but didn't provide any other information. Surinamese were tired of excuses and promises.

National strikes, a sinking economy and protests throughout the country finally convinced Wijdenbosch to call for early elections in June 1999. The president was trying to win time, but his decision didn't earn any praise from opposition parties, which demanded his immediate resignation. Wijdenbosch has not been a popular president. He assumed his post with crucial help from the former military leader and dictator Desi Bouterse. His links to the former dictator, who acts as government counselor, have hurt him. Bouterse staged coups in 1980 and 1990 and is being pursued by human rights groups over political killings. To make matters worse for the government, Bourterse was convicted of cocaine trafficking by a court in The Hague in July 1999. A judge sentenced him in absentia to 16 years in prison, and fined him US$2.18 million. Suriname has protected and defended Bouterse, hurting diplomatic relationships with the Dutch, who keep the tiny nation's economy going.

Yet, it was the economy that turned Suriname against Wijdenbosch. He has been blamed for a major budget deficit that fueled price increases and devalued the national currency. And despite calling for early elections, Surinamese were not expected to go to the polls for six to nine months, the time it takes to prepare an election for a country of 400,000 people. In the meantime, President Wijdenbosch announced he was firing his entire cabinet, promised emergency measures to improve the economy, and said he would form a new government. Elections are scheduled to take place in May 2000, and one of the unlikely candidates is Bouterse, whose popularity seems unaffected by the Dutch sentence. A strong opponent may be Stanley Rensch, leader of a human rights group that wants to try Bouterse and his colleagues for political killings and other crimes.

## FOREIGN POLICY

Suriname is a member of the UN, the Organization of American States (OAS), and the nonaligned movement, and is associated with the European Union under the Lomé Convention. In 1995 Suriname became a member of Caricom, the Caribbean common market. Suriname is making efforts to boost its political and economic ties with India and Indonesia. Relations with France have become strained because of the influx into French Guiana of 8,000 to 12,000 refugees from eastern Suriname and fears of Haitian refugees entering French Guiana via Suriname. Surinamese refugees have been fleeing in order to avoid human rights abuses by the army.

The Ministry of Foreign Affairs in the Netherlands reacted cautiously to President Wijdenbosch's election, saying that it would decide its position on future cooperation with Suriname once the new government's composition and program were known. However, by 1999 diplomatic relations with the Dutch were damaged as the Surimanese protected and defended former dictator Desi Bourterse, who was convicted of cocaine trafficking by a court in The Hague in July. Suriname has a lot at stake in its foreign relations with the Dutch since it needs US$1 billion in Dutch development aid.

Suriname has also gained international attention with the commercial exploitation of 40% of its rainforest, under contract to three Asian companies. This has prompted international organizations, including the Inter-American Development Bank (IDB), UN Food and Agricultural Organization (FAO), and European Union (EU), to offer financial assistance to maintain a healthy level of resources through replanting and managed harvesting.

## ADDRESS

Z.E. De President van de Republiek Suriname
Paramaribo
Suriname

## REFERENCES

Banks, Arthur S., Alan J. Day, and Thomas C. Muller. *Political Handbook of the World, 1995–1996.* CSA Publications, 1996.

*Caribbean Insight 19,* no. 10 (October 1996).

*EIU Country Profile: Suriname, 1995–96.* London: Economist Intelligence Unit Ltd., 1995.

*Latin America Monitor: Caribbean 13,* October 1996, no. 10 p. 7.

Lawson, Edward. *Encyclopedia of Human Rights.* New York: Taylor & Francis Inc., 1987.

**Profile researched and written by David Kyle, Ph.D., Texas A&M University (12/96 updated 5/2000).**

# SWAZILAND

## Mswati III
## King
*(pronounced "em-SWAH-tee")*

*"I call on the whole Swazi nation to remain united in our commitment to overcome the difficulties we face, with honesty and openness in our dealings with one another. And may Almighty God continue to watch over us as we make every effort to create the right conditions to allow all Swazis the opportunity to live in peace and prosperity."*

The Kingdom of Swaziland, surrounded by South African territory but for a short border with Mozambique, lies in Africa's southeastern corner. Topographically diverse, Swaziland's 17,363 sq km (6,704 sq mi) area changes from rugged, mountainous terrain in the west to low plains in the east. The population is estimated to be 985,335, of whom 90% are Swazi, with 10% of the population split between Zulu, Tonga, Shangaan and European peoples. Nearly 60% of the Swazis are Christian, and 43% practice indigenous beliefs. The currency is the *lilangeni*. Swaziland's economy is heavily biased toward agriculture. Swaziland's principle cash crop is sugar, followed by forest products. Asbestos and coal are also exported.

## POLITICAL BACKGROUND

Swaziland, theoretically a constitutional monarchy, is ruled strictly by King Mswati III. The Swazi nation originated with the Ngwane people of the Nguni language group. The Ngwane moved into what is today Swaziland in the latter half of the 18th century. King Sobhuza I was responsible for conquering and incorporating other groups of Africans into the burgeoning Swazi Kingdom. Swaziland was administered for a short period by Afrikaners until the British declared the Swazi state a protectorate. Swaziland maintained this status from 1902 until 6 September 1968, when it received its formal independence.

At that time a parliamentary style of government was put in place with a House of Assembly and Senate. After the Ngwane National Liberation Congress (NNLC) won the right to represent one of Swaziland's eight constituencies in 1972, King Sobhuza II banned all political parties, including his own Imbokodvo National Movement. King Sobhuza enacted a new electoral system in 1978, utilizing the *tinkhundla,* or local councils composed of two or three chieftaincies. Each *tinkhunda* sends two representatives to an electoral college, which selects 40 members of Parliament from a list provided by the king. The king also appoints 10 House members and 10 of the 20 senators. The traditional *Liqoqo,* or King's Council, remains an alternate power base for the Swazi monarch.

The *tinkhundla* system has been a source of antagonism and uncertainty for many chiefs, who fear that the new system of representation has detracted from their traditional authority. The king appoints *tindyuna,* or governors, to head each *tinkhundla,* and the chiefs have voiced concern that their powers are being usurped by the *tindyuna.* A meeting of chiefs was held at Ludzidzini, the royal *kraal* (cattle enclosure) in 1986. The chiefs wanted clarification from the king as to the duties and rights that the chiefs would keep in relation to the king's *tindyuna.*

In fact, the trend in Swazi politics and government has been toward the centralization of power in the hands of the king and the expanding bureaucracy surrounding him. This tendency has decreased the power of chiefs and the Swazi people, which has in turn been reflected in elections to the *tinkhundla.* The 1988 turn out for the *tinkhunda* elections was lower than the 1983 poll, and of all eligible voters, only 135,000 voted. In the towns of Mbabane, Manzini and Lobamba, with a potential of 60,000 adult voters, fewer than 20,000 voted.

## PERSONAL BACKGROUND

The present monarch, King Mswati III, known as Crown Prince Makhosetive prior to ascending the throne, was born in Swaziland on 19 April 1968 to Queen Ntombi. Prince Makhosetive was one of possibly as many of 200 children born to King Sobhuza II, who ruled Swaziland from 1921 for 60 years. With Sobhuza's death in August, 1982, Prince Makhosetive was chosen heir apparent. Prince Makhosetive was 16 at the time, and was attending a private school in Dorset, England.

## RISE TO POWER

Prince Makhosetive faced a number of challenges between the time of his selection in 1982 and his installation as King Mswati III in 1986. In the four years prior to his installation, the country was ruled by a number of regents. Queen Dzeliwe, one of Sobhuza's 50 wives, was the first to rule Swaziland after the King's death. After refusing the *Liqoqo's* request to remove Prince Mabandla Dlamini as prime minister, Queen Dzeliwe was removed as regent in August, 1983. A new regent, Ntombi, mother of the soon-to-be King, was chosen, and Prince Makhosetive was then presented to the nation. In 1984, the *Liqoqo* attempted to purge itself of a number of opponents, including the head of Makhosetive's lineage, Prince Mfanasibili. Queen Ntombi and a number of cabinet ministers repudiated these purges, and the heads of the army and police were dismissed. However, Mfanasibili was at the center of the struggle for power in the *Liqoqo* and only when he was arrested was the attempt to maintain the *Liqoqo's* supremacy thwarted. This move restored governmental power to the prime minister and cabinet, and permitted Prince Makhosetive's coronation on 25 April 1986 at the age of 18.

## LEADERSHIP

King Mswati's first two years of rule were characterized by a continuing struggle to gain control of the government and consolidate his rule. Immediately following his coronation, Mswati disbanded the *Liqoqo* and revised his cabinet appointments. In October of 1986 Prime Minister Bhekimpi Dlamini was dismissed and for the first time a non-royal, Sotsha Dlamini, was chosen for the post. Prince Bhekimpi and 11 other important Swazi figures were arrested in June 1987. Mfanasibili, Bhekimpi, and eight others were convicted of high treason. However, eight of those convicted were eventually pardoned. In early 1989, rumors circulated to the effect that Prince Mfanasibili had attempted to orchestrate a coup while in prison. Other rumors suggested that Mfanasibili was planning an escape from prison to be followed immediately by a coup. Three years after Mswati's coronation, royal infighting and intrigue remained very much an aspect of Swazi governance.

Mswati also faced non-royal challenges to rule in 1989. Dr. Ambrose Zwane, a Swazi nationalist from the pre-independence period was caught with pamphlets promoting a People's United Democratic Movement, which reflected popular displeasure with the endemic royal infighting. In 1989 Mswati replaced his prime minister, Sotsha Dlamini, with Obed Dlamini, a former unionist and activist. Mswati hoped that his new prime minister would be able to quell labor unrest that had surfaced in the country in 1989, particularly at the Havelock asbestos mine.

King Mswati has earmarked corruption as one of the major challenges to stability and prosperity in Swaziland, although corruption appears to be ubiquitous. Opening the 1988 Parliamentary session, King Mswati suggested that corruption was undermining the nation's stability. Examples of corruption are numerous. In 1984, Minister Mhambi Mnisi allegedly embezzled aid monies sent to Swaziland in the aftermath of Cyclone Domoina. In 1987, Minister of Justice David Morse appeared in court as co-director of a company that was charged with evading payment of customs duties. In 1988 ranking members of the Swazi police and the attorney general were charged with illegally selling stolen autos and pocketing the proceeds. During the 1990s corruption in high circles continued fomenting discontent among the general populace, particularly those vying for a more democratic system. In January 2000 King Mswati identified poverty alleviation and fighting corruption as key priorities for his government.

As a concession to the pro-democracy movement in Swaziland, Mswati appointed in 1996 a constitutional review commission to review the constitution that was banned by his father in 1973 and design a new one. However, controversy and allegations of irregularity have plagued the Constitutional Review Commission since its inception and threaten the credibility of the resulting document. The opposition has voiced its concerns over the make-up of the Constitutional Review Commission, which is full of royals, traditionalists, and those with the most to lose from the reform.

The media have found it increasingly difficult to function with independence in a country where the monarch's reign is

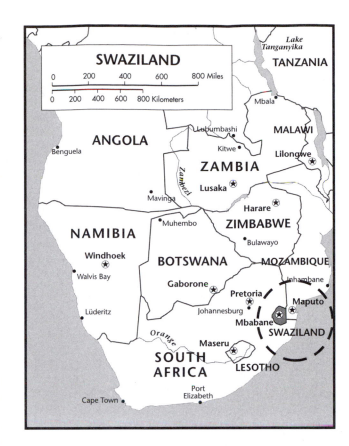

supreme. In September 1999, authorities charged the editor-in-chief of the *Times of Swaziland*, Bheki Makhubu, with criminal defamation for publishing the profile of a fiance of King Mswati, the eighth wife-to-be. But popular discontent is starting to increase, and people are overtly asking for major reforms. By 2000, Mswati was forced to allow a few reforms and released political prisoners.

## DOMESTIC POLICY

The Swazi economy, intimately tied to the South African economy, has remained strong despite South Africa's economic difficulties and currency crisis. Swaziland receives over 80% of its imports from South Africa and sends nearly 40% of its exports there. The Swazi economy remains highly dependent upon sugar exports for foreign exchange. Swaziland's reliance on sugar and timber sales makes for many economic fluctuations, with prosperity dependent on world commodity prices and good weather. The manufacturing sector has enjoyed some expansion, which helps to offset Swaziland's reliance on primary product exports. Coca-Cola's 1986 decision to move its concentrate plant from South Africa to Swaziland was a boon to the latter country, adding nearly 5% to Swaziland's manufacturing value in 1988. As Swaziland entered the 21st century, it was one of the wealthier countries in the region, with GDP of US$4 billion and GDP per capita of US$4,200. Real GDP growth is estimated at 2.6%.

## FOREIGN POLICY

Swaziland's foreign policy is largely dictated by geographical and economic realities and the inherent conservatism of the monarchy. Nearly surrounded by South Africa, Swaziland has little choice but to maintain cordial relations with its powerful neighbor. This relationship has involved the coordination of security and intelligence operations. During the apartheid era, members of the African National Congress, banned in South Africa, were not welcome in Swaziland. In February 1982 King Sobhuza II signed a secret security pact with South Africa, for which he came under criticism from a number of other southern African countries for establishing close ties to South Africa. The experiences of the direct raids by South African military forces against members of the African National Congress in Swaziland during the 1980s repeatedly demonstrated the country's vulnerability to South African might.

Outside of Africa, Swaziland's international relations during the Cold War were decidedly pro-Western. Swaziland, during this period, did not maintain diplomatic relations with any nations of the Eastern bloc. As of 2000, Swaziland continues to receive security assistance from the US and enjoys strong diplomatic relationships with Israel and Taiwan.

## ADDRESS

Ministry of Foreign Affairs
PO Box 518
Mbabane, Swaziland

## REFERENCES

Makhubu, Bheki. "Young Swazi Activists Rock the Boat." *Mail and Guardian (Johannesburg)*, 24 August 1999.

"Nigeria: Swazi King Mswati Arrives, Meets Abubakar." Radio Nigeria-Lagos, BBC Monitoring International Reports, 23 May 1999.

"Swazi King Begins Visit In Belgium." Panafrican News Agency, 4 October 1999.

"Swazi Prosecutor Considers More Press Charges." *Mail and Guardian*, 1 October 1999.

"Swaziland Mediates Between Angola, Zambia for Peace." Radio Swaziland, Mbabane, BBC Monitoring International Reports, 11 May 1999.

"Swaziland: US Officials Arrive to Discuss Defence, Security Cooperation." Radio Swaziland, Mbabane, BBC Monitoring International Reports, 28 April 1999.

**Profile researched and written by Joshua Lazerson (7/90; updated by Ezekiel Kalipeni 3/2000).**

# SWEDEN

**Göran Persson**
**Prime Minister**

*(pronounced "YUR-an PERSH-on")*

*"The mandate our citizens expressed in the [1998] election is clear. Sweden will enter the next decade with more jobs, increased justice and broader cooperation."*

The Kingdom of Sweden, situated in northern Europe between Norway and Finland, is part of the Scandinavian peninsula. The total area is 449,964 sq km (173,731 sq mi) with an estimated population of 8.9 million. Approximately 80% of the people live in urban areas. Stockholm, located on the eastern Baltic coast, is the capital and largest city.

Sweden is ethnically and culturally homogeneous, but much less so than a generation ago. Although virtually everyone speaks Swedish, post-1945 immigration has introduced significant multicultural elements. Two traditional minority groups are the Sami (formerly known as Lapps) and Finnish-speaking Swedes in the northern provinces. In addition, another 10% of the population is foreign born and 5% are foreign nationals. While many come from neighboring countries (including 103,000 immigrant Finns), almost 100,000 are from former Yugoslavia, with significant numbers from the Middle East, Asia, Africa, and even Latin America. The Swedish Lutheran church is nominally the faith of 90% of the population.

Famous for adopting a "middle way" between state socialism and competitive capitalism, Sweden enjoys a high living standard coupled with one of the most extensive social security systems among developed "welfare states." Nevertheless, slow economic growth, coupled with economic turmoil in the early 1990s, has reduced Sweden's relative economic prosperity. Per capita GDP is approximately US$19,700. Unemployment, long among the lowest in Europe, soared to nearly 13% in the early 1990s but has since declined to less than 7%. Sweden's wealth was built first on its rich natural resources, including minerals, timber, and fish. Its economic prosperity rests on exports, which amount to more than 30% of GDP. In addition to raw materials, Sweden has a sophisticated industrial sector, known for its automobiles, specialized machinery, and biotechnology products. The Swedish currency unit is the *krona*.

## POLITICAL BACKGROUND

Sweden is a constitutional monarchy with a parliamentary form of government. The gradual development of parliamentary democracy was realized in the early 20th century with the expansion of suffrage and with elected leaders being accountable to the parliament, simultaneously reducing the role of the monarchy. Since 1975, King Carl XVI Gustav has served as a unifying force and a symbol of national identity, performing largely ceremonial roles.

Whereas the Swedish parliament or *Riksdag* consisted of two houses between 1866 and 1970, the constitutional amendments of 1968–69 established a single chamber, popularly elected through universal suffrage. Members of the 349-member *Riksdag* are elected to three-year terms through an electoral system of proportional representation. The speaker of the *Riksdag* nominates the prime minister, usually the leader of the largest party in parliament. This selection must be confirmed by the *Riksdag* with a simple majority of votes.

The Social Democratic Party (*Socialdemokratiska Arbetarpartiet* or SAP) is both the oldest and largest among the major parties in Sweden, having controlled government or participated in governing coalitions almost continuously since 1932. The SAP was forced into opposition from 1976 until 1982 and again from 1991 until 1994. This long period of governance has allowed them to pursue goals of economic prosperity, social security, full employment, and equality. The SAP is closely tied to the Swedish labor movement, which organizes more than 80% of employees. Between 1994 and 1998, it governed as a minority government with support from centrist parties. In the September 1998 election, the SAP won 131 seats (a loss of 30 from 1994). It must now rely on two untried coalition partners: the Left Party (*Vänsterpartiet* or VP) and the Green Ecology Party (*Miljöpartiet de Gröna* or MP). This bloc will have a solid majority of 190 seats, but there may be problems between the moderate leftist Social Democrats, the radical socialist Left Party, and the countercultural Greens.

The main opposition party is the Moderate Conservative Party (*Moderata Samlingspartiet* or M), the second largest party, with 82 seats in the new parliament. The center-right Christian Democrats (*Kristdemokratiska Samhällspartiet* or KDS) gained 27 seats and now hold 42. The other parties include the Center Party (*Centerpartiet* or C) and the Liberals (*Folkpartiet Liberalerna* or FP). Each lost nine seats and hold 18 and 17 mandates respectively.

Göran Persson took over leadership of the SAP and the government in August 1995 and faced his first election as prime minister in September 1998.

## PERSONAL BACKGROUND

Göran Persson was born on 20 January 1949, in Vingåker, Sörmland, the fourth of five children. Upon completing his secondary education, specializing in chemistry, he went on to study sociology and later political science at the University

SWEDEN

0      100      200      300 Miles

0   100   200   300 Kilometers

*Norwegian*

*Sea*

Narvik

Kiruna

Umeå

SWEDEN

Trondheim

Gulf of Bothnia

NORWAY

Bergen

Gävle

Åland
Islands

Oslo

Stockholm

Gotland

*North*

*Sea*

Göteborg

Baltic Sea

Öland

DENMARK

København
(Copenhagen)

College of Öbrero. In 1971, he left his studies to work in the district organization of the Swedish Social Democratic Youth League in Sörmland. After completing his military service (1973–74), Persson became an official of the Workers Educational Association in Sörmland and taught economics, mathematics, and social studies at various high schools. He became chairman of the Katrineholm Local Educational Committee (1977–79) prior to his entry into Swedish national politics in 1979. Persson married in 1995 and lives in central Malmö with his wife, Annika, and her two sons. Persson has two daughters from his first marriage. His personal interests include reading, art, architecture, and cooking.

## RISE TO POWER

Persson first entered national politics in 1979, becoming a member of parliament. During his legislative tenure, he has gained considerable and varied political experience. Persson was appointed to the Ministry of Education and Cultural Affairs with special responsibility for schools and adult education in 1989 during the Ingvar Carlsson administration. While the Social Democrats were in opposition between 1991 and 1994, Persson was chairman of the Standing Committee on Agriculture (1991–92), a member of the Standing Committee on Industry and Trade (1992–93), and vice-chairman of the Standing Committee on Finance (1993–94). After the return of the Social Democrats to power in 1994,

Persson was appointed minister of finance, achieving considerable success by reducing welfare benefits and cutting government expenditures. The economic difficulties of the 1990s precipitated in the minds of many the need for fiscal conservatism, for which Persson was selected. Although it is widely perceived that Carlsson was grooming Mona Sahlin, then deputy prime minister, to succeed him upon retirement, a minor scandal involving the misuse of a government credit card compelled party leaders to seek an alternative candidate to lead the Social Democratic Party. In March 1996, Persson was selected to become chairman of his party. He was confirmed as prime minister one week later.

## LEADERSHIP

Persson is considered to be a decisive and determined politician; a tough-minded technocrat, with "strong views and strong methods." The disappointing results of the 1998 election must be kept in perspective. In 1994 his party was the main opposition to a non-socialist coalition and garnered only 36.5% of the vote. It was the worst Social Democratic showing since 1921. His ability to form a working, informal coalition with two radical parties demonstrates his political skill, as well as the pragmatic Swedish political culture.

Persson has continued the program of economic reform and recovery from the 1990–93 recession begun under Carlsson. The Social Democrats were in opposition during the worst years of the recession. Although they criticized details of the non-socialist coalition's austerity policies, they accepted the need for significant cuts in government expenditure and support for economic change. By 1994, recovery was underway, and the staggering government budget deficits were falling. Persson's government believed that exports and private consumption would restore economic balance. His government relied upon the Center Party (and to a lesser extent the Liberals) for political support in parliament. For decades prior to 1990, Sweden had enjoyed remarkably low unemployment rates, often less than 2% of the labor force. In the 1990s, unemployment soared to over 8%. The public sector employed nearly 32% of the total labor force. Efforts to further expand that sector were opposed by the Persson government. Swedish tax rates were quite high in 1997, exceeding 53% of GDP, but have since been reduced significantly.

Persson has not abandoned Sweden's famous welfare state, which is especially generous in health, education, and social security programs. Support for these programs remains strong across the political spectrum despite serious critiques from foreign media commentators and academics. The Social Democrats restored some of the cuts in unemployment and sickness insurance. Persson continued efforts to reduce bureaucratic inefficiencies and encouraged cautious measures aimed at stimulating competition and even outsourcing in the public sector. Public sector labor unions and the left-wing of the Social Democratic Party object to many of these measures. Traditional voters showed their displeasure by abandoning the SAP for the more collectivist Left Party. Dissatisfaction also hurt Persson's two centrist parliamentary allies. Social Democrats who work in the private sector, especially Sweden's large engineering and high technology sectors, have been more supportive and have enjoyed growing employment fueled by dynamic exports. Overall economic recovery helped stabilize and stimulate property values.

Some significant changes were introduced at the opening of parliament, three weeks after the 1998 election. Eight ministers in the former Persson government were dismissed. Among their replacements was Mona Sahlin, the former Social Democratic deputy prime minister and heir to the leadership until a minor scandal forced her out of the government. She has been made a "junior minister" in a new super ministry responsible for industry, commerce, communications, and home affairs. The outgoing foreign minister, Lena Hjelm-Wallen, has been named deputy prime minister, with special responsibility for relations with the European Union. Her replacement in the foreign ministry is Anna Lindh, formerly environmental minister.

## DOMESTIC POLICY

Persson demonstrated his ability to gain support from across the political spectrum by adopting a major old-age national pension reform in June 1998 after years of planning and discussion. The new program is one of the first national pension schemes to move in the direction of "defined contributions" rather than rely on other public revenues to guarantee benefits. Although it will be phased over many years, the new system ties benefits to economic performance and demographic changes. Moreover, it invites citizens to make individual investment decisions with a modest portion of their obligatory pension contributions. While voluntary pension plans have long allowed such personal discretion, extending it to the entire public system is a radical reform.

Persson is committed to reducing unemployment. A tentative budget agreement has been reached with the supporting Left and Green parties, calling for increased child benefits and pension provisions but still keeping within the government's spending limits. Those include a 2% budget surplus and gradual reduction of public sector debt. The Persson government intends to resist the Left Party's demands for 100,000 new public sector jobs and increased subsidies to local authorities. Sweden's economy has been growing rapidly since 1993, depending upon a rapid expansion of exports. Global economic difficulties apparent in late 1998 threatened that growth.

Several non-economic issues remain prominent as well. The presence of 12 nuclear power plants has been a contentious issue for more than 20 years. Promises to phase out nuclear power by the year 2010 have been postponed repeatedly as economic and other environmental issues have intruded. Both the Left and the Green parties want to accelerate the nuclear phase-out.

To be successful, Persson must find ways to improve the nation's healthcare and education systems while integrating a substantial immigrant population into the mainstream.

## FOREIGN POLICY

Sweden has maintained a policy of neutrality throughout the 20th century, avoiding both world wars and remaining nonaligned during the postwar period. Unlike Denmark and Norway, Sweden declined membership in the North Atlantic Treaty Organization (NATO) in 1949, wanting to remain outside of all military alliances. Moreover, Sweden's decision not to join the European economic alliance was based on a concern that membership would undermine its traditional policy of neutrality. Sweden has, however, participated actively in many international organizations, including the UN, the International Monetary Fund (IMF), the Organization for Economic Cooperation and Development (OECD), and the General Agreement on Tariffs and Trade (GATT). With the end of the Cold War and the necessity to strengthen its economy, Sweden applied for EU membership in 1991. A referendum concerning EU membership passed in November 1994. Sweden officially joined on 1 January 1995.

Persson's new government will depend on parties skeptical of membership in the EU, opposed to Swedish participation in the European Monetary Union (EMU), and opposed to closer ties with NATO. Along with Denmark and Britain, Sweden has chosen to remain outside of the EMU but reserves the right to join later. Sweden is committed to keeping its economy and currency closely tied to the EMU. With the economic improvements of recent years, it is now in substantial compliance with the criteria for EMU participation. Sweden has historically allowed its currency to depreciate significantly in order to maintain international competitiveness. EMU membership would close that option. Public opinion polls indicate that 44% of Swedes are opposed to EMU membership while 39% are in favor. This is a substantial strengthening of the pro-EMU camp and may complicate the government's EU policies.

Sweden has modified its non-alignment policy to include participation in the NATO-sponsored "Partnership-for-Peace." As NATO expands into central Europe, Swedes have discussed closer ties to the alliance. While a majority of Swedes support NATO membership, the Left and Green parties, as well as more traditional Social Democratic circles, are opposed. Persson will continue to maintain an activist role in peacekeeping operations, assertive diplomacy, and generous foreign aid programs.

In February 1999 Sweden became the fourth country to sign the UN treaty to imprison war criminals convicted by The Hague's Yugoslavia war crimes tribunal. In April of the same year, the government refused NATO's request for troops to handle the Kosovo refugee crisis in Albania, claiming that it could only send troops for campaigns authorized by the United Nations and the Organization for Security and Cooperation in Europe. However, the government did offer to send logistics staff to resolve issues and agreed to offer asylum to as many as five thousand Kosovar refugees from Macedonia.

## ADDRESS

Office of the Prime Minister
Riksdagshuset
Stockholm, Sweden

## REFERENCES

*The Economist,* 15 August 1998.
*Financial Times,* September–October 1998.
*The Guardian* (London), September–October 1998.
Nordic Council of Ministers. *Newsletter,* October 1998.
OECD. *Economic Outlook,* June 1998.

**Profile researched and written by Eric S. Einhorn, University of Massachusetts, Amherst (3/99; updated 2/00).**

# SWITZERLAND

## Adolph Ogi
### President
*(pronounced "A-dolf OH-ghee")*

*"There is no longer the possibility for economists to escape social responsibility…
Global economic progress must find its social corollary."*

The Swiss Confederation is located in the heart of Western Europe and is bordered by Germany, France, Italy, Austria, and Liechtenstein. Of the country's 41,292 sq km (15,943 sq mi), 60% are covered by the Alps and contain some of the highest mountain peaks in Europe. The remaining 30% is referred to as the *Mittleland* or central plateau. This area supports the majority of the nation's urban, economic, and agricultural activity.

Switzerland's population numbers approximately 7.3 million. The native Swiss are an amalgam of different ethnic traditions—74% German, 20% French, 4% Italian, and 1% Romansch. The majority of Swiss speak German, with smaller percentages speaking French, Italian, and Romansch. All four are official languages of the country's federal administration. Nearly 48% percent of Swiss are Roman Catholic while 44% are Protestant. The largest city in Switzerland is Zurich, although Berne is its capital. Both cities are located in the German-speaking section of the country.

Switzerland is one of the wealthiest countries in the world and boasts a higher per capita GDP than any other country in Europe. It is home to some of the largest banks and multinational corporations in the world. Major exports include machinery, chemicals, watches, chocolate, and cheese. The primary destination for these goods is the European Union (EU), which takes about 60% of all Swiss exports. The unit of currency is the Swiss franc. After undergoing a period of economic stagnation during most of the 1990s, the Swiss economy is now beginning to revive. Unemployment, which had peaked at a historically high level of 5.4% in 1997, has now fallen to 3.6%.

## POLITICAL BACKGROUND

The origins of Switzerland can be traced back to 1291 when the cantons of Schwyz, Unterwalden, and Uri signed a defensive alliance to oppose Austrian domination. Other cantons joined the alliance and, by the late 15th century, the coalition was able to achieve virtual independence within the Austro-Hungarian Empire. Following a period of occupation by France, the place of the Swiss federation in post-Napoleonic Europe was affirmed at the Congress of Vienna in 1815. In that same year, the federation was joined by the cantons of Geneva and Valais, and was declared to be perpetually neutral. After a brief civil war in 1847, the federation was replaced by a more unified confederation that became a federal state in 1874.

Reflecting the country's variegated geography as well as its diverse cultural and historical roots, Swiss politics is firmly anchored at the local level. The 26 cantons and 3,000 smaller communes exercise a large degree of autonomy over many areas including policing, school administration, health systems, and tax collection. The confederation, on the other hand, is responsible for issues such as the military, social insurance, and foreign affairs.

The Federal Assembly is comprised of the 46-member Council of States and a 200-member National Council. Two members are drawn from every canton for the Council of States. Membership in the National Council is based on a system of proportional representation, the number of seats gained by a political party being directly proportional to the number of votes it receives. Elections for all legislative seats take place every four years.

The Federal Council is a seven-member executive body, elected by the Federal Assembly. Each member of the Council is of equal rank and holds a cabinet portfolio assigned by common agreement with his or her colleagues. This emphasis on collegiality is carried over into the Council's decisions, which are presented as unanimous. Each December the Federal Assembly elects a president and vice president from among the councilors, though in practice the previous year's vice president is usually moved to the higher position. Swiss presidents serve for one year at a time and are also cabinet ministers in their own right. The role of a Swiss president is akin to that of a prime minister—a first among equals, whose job is to lead and channel debate among his or her colleagues. Throughout the 20th century the power of the Federal Council relative to that of the Assembly has steadily increased. Today, the great majority of legislation is initiated by the Council, after which it is submitted to the Assembly for review and alteration. The final decision on a policy rests with the general public, in the form of a referendum.

The third component of the confederation is the Federal Supreme Court, which is empowered to decide constitutional law issues, primarily cantonal and communal law. Federal statutes passed by the Assembly are not subject to judicial review. The rational behind this limitation lies with the right of referendum, which allows the public to submit any federal statute to a popular vote. Thus, it is the general public, and not the judiciary, that decides on the constitutionality of a federal statue.

The right of referendum is an important element in Swiss politics. Since the practice was begun in 1848, Switzerland has held over 450 nationwide referendums, more than all other countries combined. Any bill approved by the Federal Assembly can be challenged in a national referendum. For this to occur, a petition signed by 50,000 citizens or eight cantons must be presented within eight days of the bill's passage. The outcome of the referendum is then decided by popular majority vote. Swiss voters can also exercise direct democracy by means of the constitutional initiative. Any seven Swiss voters can begin this process by submitting a request for an initiative and a description of the desired changes in the constitution. They then have 18 months to collect the 100,000 signatures necessary to force the initiative to a referendum. Such proposed changes to the constitution must be accepted by both a majority of the voters and by more than half the cantons. This so called "double majority" applies also to any constitutional changes proposed by the Council or Assembly, as well as to Swiss membership in supranational bodies such as the EU or UN.

## PERSONAL BACKGROUND

Adolf Ogi was born 18 July 1942 in Kandersteg, a town in canton Berne, the son of Anna and Adolf, Sr. Both he and his brother, Rudolph, attended the local schools in Kandersteg. Ogi obtained his commercial diploma from the Ecole Supérieur de Commerce in La Neuveville (canton Berne) and then studied at the Swiss Mercantile School in London.

From 1963 to 1964, Ogi managed the Meiringen-Haslital Tourist Information Office. He then led the Swiss Ski Association as technical director from 1969–74 and as director from 1975–81. From 1971–83, Ogi was the vice-president of the World and European Committee of the International Ski Federation. He was appointed Director General and a member of the management council of Intersport Schweiz Holding AG in 1981.

Ogi also served in the national defense. He commanded a mountain rifle battalion (1981–83) as a major in the Swiss Army. He then served as a liason officer for a redoubt (fortress artillery) brigade until 1987, and acted finally as an officer in a special strategy group at army headquarters.

Ogi is married with two children.

## RISE TO POWER

Ogi became a member of the Swiss People's Party (SVP-Schweiz) in 1978 and was elected to Parliament in 1979. He worked in the Military Commission of Parliament from 1982–87 and was chairman of the commission beginning in 1986. He then served as president of the SVP until he was elected to the Federal Council on 9 December 1987. On 1 January 1988, Ogi became head of the Federal Department for Transport, Communications, and Energy (EVED), where he served until 1995. At this time he became head of the Federal Military Department, later to be called the Federal Department of Defence, Civil Protection, and Sports (DDPS). In 1999 Ogi served as Vice President of the Federal Council and from August 1998 to June 1999 he chaired the Candidature Committee for the Winter Olympic Games in 2006.

Ogi first became president of the Swiss Confederation in 1993. In 2000, he holds this one-year rotating position for the second time.

## LEADERSHIP

Talk of an organized "leadership" or "opposition" is not really applicable to Switzerland. Since 1959, a power-sharing coalition has existed between the four largest political parties. The seven seats on the Federal Council are divided between the Christian Democratic Party (CVP), the Radical Democratic Party (FDP), and the Social Democratic Party (SPS), with one seat going to the smaller Swiss People's Party (SVP). Four or five councilors are usually selected from German-speaking sections of the country, while two are from French-speaking regions. As a rule, there should be no more than one councilor per canton. Traditionally, Council seats have been divided equally between Protestants and Catholics. Popular support for the four major parties has remained strikingly consistent over the past 40 years. They collect about 75% of the vote in each parliamentary election.

## DOMESTIC POLICY

Stability, continuity, and collegiality are the hallmarks of the Swiss political system. As a rule, changes happen very slowly and only after much consensus building. This tradition has been strained by a number of contentious issues in the 1990s. In a 1992 referendum, voters opposed Switzerland's entry into the European Economic Area (EEA), thereby turning their backs on closer ties with the EU. The EEA referendum was accompanied by considerable domestic political fallout. The final vote split almost completely along partisan German and French-speaking lines, with all 19 German-speaking cantons and the Italian canton of Ticino coming out against the treaty. Though the popular vote was a tight 1.79 million to 1.76 million, only the remaining seven French cantons voted for the agreement.

That a cultural divide between French and German speakers existed has always been tacitly, and sometimes explicitly, accepted. For instance, in 1979 the first new canton since 1815 was established when the French-speaking region of Jura seceded from the German-speaking canton of Berne. The EEA vote demonstrated how much this divide has now become a political issue, with French speakers favoring closer ties with the EU as a way of mitigating the power of the German-speaking majority.

## FOREIGN POLICY

Historically, Switzerland has maintained a stance of neutrality and limited engagement in its foreign policy. Increasingly, however, this position has been brought into question by the demands of a much more integrated world. In an attempt to mitigate some of the damage done by the electorate's rejection of the EEA agreement, the Swiss government has entered into a number of bilateral agreements with the European Union. The agreements, which focus on issues such as the removal of trade barriers, the development of road and air links, and the movement of job-seekers, are designed to ensure that Switzerland does not remain totally isolated as the surrounding countries move to ever closer integration. In the long-term, it is the Federal Council's goal to seek full EU membership for Switzerland.

The government has also been forced to relax the country's tradition of limited international engagement. In 1992, Switzerland became a member of both the IMF and World Bank. In addition, it has recently joined the World Trade Organization as well as the Organization for Security and Cooperation in Europe. Switzerland has also moved to strengthen its relations with the United Nations and is now a participant in a number of UN peacekeeping and humanitarian missions. The Federal Council has announced that it is planning to seek full UN membership for Switzerland.

The most recent challenge to Switzerland's tradition of neutrality has come from revelations concerning the country's role during the Second World War. In 1996, allegations were made that Switzerland profited from wartime ties to Germany by purchasing over US$500 million of Nazi gold. This was followed by evidence indicating that a number of Swiss banks still held millions of dollars that had belonged to Jewish holocaust victims. Responding to these disclosures, the Swiss government set up two commissions to locate assets of Nazi victims in dormant bank accounts, and to examine the historical relationship of Switzerland to Nazi Germany. In August 1998 it was agreed that Swiss banks would pay out US$1.25 billion to settle claims made against them by Jewish groups and individuals. In addition, the Federal Council has proposed the creation of a US$4.7 billion Swiss Foundation for Solidarity to benefit all human rights victims. Overall, these issues have led to a considerable amount of soul searching among the Swiss and a questioning of the country's continued policy of neutrality.

## ADDRESS

Office of the President
Federal Chancellery
Bundeshaus-West, Bundesgasse
3003 Berne, Switzerland

## REFERENCES

*The Economist*, 14 February 1998; 26 September 1998.
*Financial Times*, 6 May 1993; 8 April 1994; 17 May 1997.
*International Herald Tribune*, 28 December 1998.
Kobach, Kris W. *The Referendum: Direct Democracy in Switzerland*. Aldershot, England: 1993.
*New York Times*, 27 December 1998.
*Swiss Review of World Affairs*, Zurich: Neue Züricher Zeitung, July–December 1998.

**Profile researched and written by Jennifer Wallace (6/2000).**

# SYRIA

## Hafiz al-Assad
### President
*(pronounced "HAH-fez all ah-SAHD")*

*"No one in Syria can relinquish an inch of the land; he who relinquishes a part of his land or sells out any part of his homeland is a betrayer of the people. This is an axiom believed by each Syrian citizen."*

The Syrian Arab Republic covers an area of 184,050 sq km (71,043 sq mi) and is bordered on the north by Turkey, on the east and southeast by Iraq, on the south by Jordan, on the southwest by Israel, and on the west by Lebanon and the Mediterranean Sea. The capital of Syria and its major city is Damascus.

Syria's population is estimated at 17.2 million inhabitants, with an annual growth rate of 3%—one of the highest in the world. Approximately 80% of the people are Sunni Muslims. Other religious groups include various branches of Shi'ism, Druze, and Christianity. Racially, the Syrians are varied, and except where ethnic distinctions have found religious expression, racial types are generally intermixed. It is estimated that Arabs make up about 90% of the population. Other ethnic groups include Kurds, Armenians, Turkomans, Circassians, Assyrians, and Jews. The official language is Arabic, although Kurdish is also widely spoken. Syria has three remote villages where ancient Aramaic, the language of Christ, is still spoken.

The country's GNP is estimated at US$41.7 billion, and per capita income is US$2,500. The national currency is the Syrian pound. Despite recent reforms, Syria's economy continues to be dominated by the government. The country's four banks are all state owned, and interest rates are fixed by law. Syria's large public sector industrial firms are unproductive and unprofitable. Agriculture provides a livelihood for 32% of the workforce. Wheat, barley, and cotton are the main cash crops. Although its oil production is small by Middle Eastern standards, oil accounted for 66% of Syrian exports in 1996.

## POLITICAL BACKGROUND

Archaeological evidence suggests that Syria was the center of a great Semitic empire extending from the Red Sea to Turkey and Mesopotamia around 2500 BC. In the 4th century BC, Syria fell to Alexander the Great, first in a long line of European conquerors. In 637, Damascus was conquered by the Arabs. Most Syrians were converted to Islam, and Arabic gradually became the language of the area. Ottoman forces gained control of the territory in 1516 and Syria remained a province of the Ottoman Empire for the next four centuries. Following World War I, Syria was divided into British and French mandates until gaining its independence in 1944.

Two parties that had led the struggle for independence dominated Syrian political life immediately after World War II. They were eventually discredited and replaced by pan-Arab and left-of-center political forces. For three years, Syria joined with Egypt to form the United Arab Republic (LIAR). Syrians chafed under Egyptian rule and, in 1961, seceded from the LIAR. A period of political instability followed until power was seized by a group of leftist army officers and a radical socialist government was formed. On 16 November 1970, a former chief of the air force and defense minister named Hafiz al-Assad took control of the government.

Today, Syria is a republic under a military regime. The constitution of 1973 defines Syria as a "socialist popular democracy," and provides for a 195-member People's Assembly, elected by universal adult suffrage. In 1990, the seats in the Assembly were increased to 250. The president is vested with the power to appoint and dismiss vice presidents, the prime minister, ministers, and other high officials. He is also the commander in chief of the armed forces. Elections for the presidency are held every seven years, while members of the People's Assembly are elected every five years.

Although a number of parties operate in Syria, for the past 27 years politics have been dominated by the Baath Party, which advocates socialism and Arab unity. Three of the smaller parties (Arab Socialist Union, Unionist Socialist, and Arab Socialist) have combined forces with the Baath, forming a coalition known as the National Progressive Front. In August 1994, the Baath won 167 of the 250 Assembly seats. The president of the republic is also the secretary general of the Baath Socialist Party.

## PERSONAL BACKGROUND

Hafiz al-Assad was born on 6 October 1928 (some sources claim 1930) in the Syrian village of Oardaha. In 1952, he joined the Syrian Military Academy at Horns, and subsequently the Air Force Academy in Aleppo. Graduating as a combat pilot at the top of his class, he rose through the ranks rapidly and, by 1957, became a squadron commander. Shortly thereafter he went to the USSR for training with the Soviet air force. Assad also spent time in Cairo during the short-lived political union between Syria and Egypt.

Assad is married with four sons and one daughter. In recent years questions about his health have been raised periodically and it is believed that he suffers from a heart ailment. Although denied by the Syrian government, it was reported that Assad had suffered a heart attack in 1983.

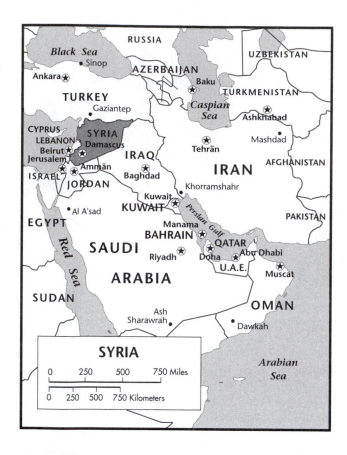

## RISE TO POWER

Assad joined the Baath Party in 1946. Later, while in Cairo, he founded the Baath Military Committee. After Syria withdrew from the United Arab Republic in 1961, Assad and other members of the committee were imprisoned a short while by Egyptian authorities. Upon his return to Syria, Assad was dismissed from the military by the new government and given a low level job in the ministry of transportation.

In March 1963, a military junta dominated by the Baath came to power. Assad rejoined the air force and was given command of an airfield. At the end of 1964, he was promoted to the rank of major general and became commander of the air force. In February 1966, Assad headed the Ministry of Defense, a position that he held until November 1970 when he seized control of the government through a military coup. He remained prime minister until March 1971, when he was elected president for his first seven-year term. Assad has since been reelected three times. Since November 1970, Assad has also been the secretary general of the Baath Socialist Party.

## LEADERSHIP

Although a number of political parties and a parliament operate in Syria, Assad has tried to silence political dissent, at times through violence. Some observers have labeled the country a military dictatorship, and a number of international organizations have criticized its poor human rights record.

Opposition activities reached their peak in the early to mid-1970s. One group that has been especially active in opposing Assad is the Syrian branch of the Muslim Brotherhood. A fundamentalist Islamic group, the Brotherhood draws its main support from Syria's Sunni majority. One

source of friction between the government and the Muslim Brotherhood is the prominent role of Alawites in the Syrian politics. The Shi'i Alawites (of which Assad is a member), represent only about 12% of the total population, but play a disproportionately influential role in the government, particularly in the military and security apparatus. Consequently, resentment towards the Alawites has been growing among the general population. In June 1979, the government accused the Muslim Brotherhood of attacking the military academy and killing 60 army cadets, most of whom are believed to have been Alawites. Further disturbances occurred in 1982, resulting in a showdown between the government and the opposition. In February of that year an uprising in the city of Homo was suppressed by the Syrian military. In March and April of 1986, a number of bombs exploded in Damascus and other major Syrian cities. Government officials have blamed most of these attacks on the Muslim Brotherhood, although it is thought that other groups and foreign countries (including the US, Jordan, and Iraq) are also involved.

In 1991, Assad proposed a reformation of Syrian politics and released more than 2800 political prisoners. Then, in 1992, he suggested that new parties might be established within Syria's political framework, while rejecting any foreign systems as models. In an effort to improve his human rights record, Assad pardoned approximately 1200 political prisoners in 1995 and lifted a ban on the Muslim Brotherhood. During the 1990s, increasing concern was focused on the state of Assad's health and its effect on his ability to govern, particularly since his mental alertness had declined and it was suspected that he was suffering from some form of dementia. Nevertheless, he was reelected once again in 1999, amid fears that he might not live to complete another seven-year term. Meanwhile, Assad's son Bashir was being groomed to succeed him, although he was relatively inexperienced and would confront numerous political rivals upon his father's demise or incapacitation.

**Note:** Assad died on 10 June 2000 of a heart attack, according to medical officials quoted by Agence France-Presse. A week later, Bashir Assad was unanimously elected by the Baath Party as its secretary-general on the second day of its party congress—its first in 15 years. The younger Assad is expected to be formally nominated as president later in the convention. The country's parliament has already amended the constitution to lower the minimum age for a president from 40 to 34, making Bashir Assad eligible for the position. While Syrians used Hafiz Assads' funeral to show their support for his son, Assad's exiled brother, Rifaat Assad, contended that he, not his nephew, should rule Syria. In response, the prime minister of Syria ordered Rifaat Assad arrested if he tried to enter the country. If Bashir Assad completes the succession process, it would be the first father-to-son transfer of leadership in a nominally republican Arab state.

## DOMESTIC POLICY

A deteriorating economy has been fueling dissatisfaction with the regime. The Syrian economy has been in decline since the early 1980s, and despite short term successes, Assad has been unable to reverse the general trend. The economy is heavily dependent on foreign aid and loans from its Arab neighbors and other countries. The decline in oil prices has meant that some of the Arab countries, Kuwait in particular, have reduced aid. At the same time Russia and international banks have been pressuring Syria to repay loans. The result has been economic stagnation and periodic shortages of goods. In the late 1990s, Assad's ability to deal with the economy was compromised by failing health and preoccupation with foreign policy, especially efforts at achieving peace with Israel. As of 1999, a record drought and falling oil prices suggested that Syria's economic problems would be among the most serious challenges inherited by Assad's successor.

## FOREIGN POLICY

Under Assad, Syria's foreign policy has been guided by two principles: refusal to compromise with Israel, and the desire to transform Syria into a major regional player.

As one of the Arab countries that shares a border with Israel, Syrian forces were involved in both the 1967 and the 1973 Arab-Israeli wars. In 1973, Syria lost control of the Golan Heights, which were officially annexed by Israel in December 1981. Ten years later, Assad agreed to engage in a regional peace conference with Israel, in an attempt to recover the Golan Heights. These peace talks have continued on and off over the years, but no agreement has yet been attained. The election of Binyamin Netanyahu as prime minister of Israel in 1996 jeopardized the viability of these talks since he rejected the land-for-peace policy and insisted that Israeli sovereignty over the Golan Heights would not be compromised. The collapse of Netanyahu's government at the end of 1998 and the election of Ehud Barak as prime minister in 1999 revived the prospects for a Syrian-Israeli peace agreement, and talks resumed at the beginning of 2000.

Despite repeated calls for Arab unity, Syria's relations with its neighbors have often been characterized by conflict. Although both the Syrian and the Iraqi regimes subscribe to the Baath ideology, relations between the two countries have been antagonistic for most of the past 20 years. Syrian support for Iran during its war with Iraq caused considerable strain. Despite a reported meeting between Assad and Saddam Hussein of Iraq in April of 1987, relations between the two countries have not improved. Further tension occurred when Syria joined the multinational effort to expel Iraq from Kuwait in 1990.

Syria has also had problems with its other Arab neighbor, Jordan. Assad has accused Jordan of supporting the Muslim Brotherhood and other groups that opposed his regime. Since 1985, however, the two countries have been able to resolve some of their differences and relations between them have improved.

Syria made repeated attempts to establish a cease-fire among warring factions in the Lebanese civil war. Despite the presence of Syrian troops, the situation has continued to deteriorate. In 1989, Michel Aoun, commander-in-chief of the Lebanese army, attempted to drive the Syrian military out of Lebanon. Aoun was defeated by the Syrian army and, in 1990, the Lebanese government implemented the Taif Agreement, which solidified Syria's presence in Lebanon. In 1991, Syria and Lebanon signed a treaty of fraternity and cooperation. At times the Syrian government has been able to use its influence in Lebanon to obtain the release of Western hostages. Under the terms of the Taif agreement, Syrian troops were to have been withdrawn from Beirut by 1992, but the withdrawal was still pending as of 1999.

During the Cold War era, Assad maintained friendly relations with the USSR and the Soviets were the major supplier of armaments for Syrian troops. Since the breakup of the Soviet Union, however, financial and military support has sharply declined.

Relations with the US and Britain have improved in recent years. Though the Assad regime has been condemned for assisting terrorist groups, this charge has been played down since Syria joined the US-led multinational effort to expel Iraq from Kuwait in 1990 and agreed to participate in direct peace talks with Israel in 1991.

## ADDRESS

Office of the President
Damascus, Syria

## REFERENCES

Banks, Arthur and Thomas Muller, eds. *Political Handbook of the World*. Binghamton, NY: CSA Publications, 1999.

*The Economist,* various issues.

*Europa World Year Book, 1997*. London: Europa Publications Ltd., 1997.

Fisher, W.B. *The Middle* East *and North Africa*. 1990.

*Middle East Review,* 1989.

New York Times. [Online] Available http://www.nytimes.com (Accessed 21 June 2000).

"Peace Talks Move Ahead on Both Tracks." *Middle East Economic Digest,* 14 January 2000, p.13.

Plain Dealer. [Online] Available http://www.cleveland.com/news (Accessed 21 June 2000).

"The Riddle of the Sphinx." *U.S. News & World Report,* 20 March 2000, p.14.

Syria Online: Website of Golan. [Online] Available http://www.golan-syria.org/wordr.htm (Accessed 21 June 2000).

"Taking Assad's Pulse." *Newsweek International,* 8 March 1999, p.38.

*Worldmark Encyclopedia of the Nations*. 9th ed. Detroit: Gale Research, 1998.

**Profile researched and written by Hootan Shambayati (7/90; revised 6/2000).**

# TAIWAN

## Chen Shui-bian
## President
*(pronounced "SHEN shoo-EE BEE-on")*

*"We should insist on Taiwan's independent sovereignty. This is not our job; it is our mission."*

Taiwan, known officially as the Republic of China on Taiwan since 1949, is a semitropical island about 145 km (90 mi) off the southeastern coast of mainland China. With a total land area of 35,203 sq km (13,592 sq mi), Taiwan has an estimated 22,113,250 inhabitants. The P'eng-hu (Pescadores) Islands and 13 scattered offshore islands, including Quemoy and Matsu, are also part of Taiwan. Approximately 98% of the population is ethnically Chinese and the remainder consists of nine aboriginal tribes of Mayalo-Polynesian ancestry. The Chinese are divided into three groups: the majority Amoy Fukienese; the minority Hakkas; and the "mainlanders" who fled the mainland when the Communists seized power in 1949. Mandarin Chinese is the official language and Taiwan's main religions are a mix of Buddhism, Taoism, and Confucianism (93%) and Christianity (4.5%). The literacy rate is 94%.

Taiwan is a rich and recently industrialized nation, with a per capita income of US$16,500. Primary exports consist of textiles, clothing, chemicals, machinery, and consumer electronics. Its major trading partners include the United States, Japan, Hong Kong, Germany, and the United Kingdom. The national currency is the New Taiwan dollar. The capital and largest city is Taipei, with an estimated population of 2,880,000.

## POLITICAL BACKGROUND

Taiwan was a part of China before the Japanese Occupation in 1895–1945. In 1949, the Kuomingtang (KMT) regime, also called the Nationalists, was driven from the mainland by the Communists who were led by Mao Zedong. The Nationalists retreated to Taiwan, taking along with them approximately two million soldiers, officials, merchants, and dependents. Both the People's Republic of China (PR China) and Taiwan claim to be the legitimate government of China, resulting in frequent political hostilities and occasional military skirmishes. PR China considers Taiwan as a renegade province.

According to the constitution promulgated 1 January 1947, the popularly elected National Assembly is the highest organ of state power for all of China. Its responsibilities include recalling the president and vice-president, amending the constitution and the power of consent for presidential appointees. The Legislative Yuan, which is the *de facto* legislature for Taiwan, however, performs primary parliamentary functions. The first National Assembly was elected in 1947, with 2,961 delegates serving six-year terms. Since Commu-

nists took over the mainland in 1949 and the Nationalist government moved to Taiwan, subsequent elections were impossible. Thus the terms of National Assembly members, along with those of the legislative and control branches, were extended indefinitely until constitutional reforms in 1991 paved the way for Taiwanese control of the legislature. The original members either retired or contested local Taiwanese seats.

The Legislative Yuan functions as the legislative organ for the Republic of China. Its representatives are elected by universal suffrage of adults older than 20 years old for three-year terms through a system of proportional representation. It exercises legislative power over statutory and budgetary bills and other important affairs.

The president, directly elected for the first time in 1996, is head of state and acts as mediator and arbiter among the government's five branches or yuans: executive, legislative, judicial, examination, and control. The president is also responsible for choosing the premier with the consent of the legislative branch. Furthermore, the president, with the recommendation of the premier, appoints the vice-premier and ministers of the cabinet.

Despite recent political liberalization, the Kuomingtang (KMT) remains in control of the legislative yuan. Until recently, it was the only legal political party; but presently the other major parties include the Democratic Progressive Party (DPP), formed in September 1986, and the New Party (NP). The ideology of the KMT espouses a foundation of traditional Chinese culture and adds Western political, economic, and social theories as the building blocks of a successful Taiwan. The DPP's party platform is pro-independence and anti-corruption. The Legislative Yuan's election, last held in December 1998, resulted in a slim majority for the KMT with 123 seats. The recent election of Chen Shui-bian as president signaled an end to KMT's dominance in Taiwanese politics.

## PERSONAL BACKGROUND

Chen Shui-bian was born in Tainan province (southern Taiwan) to a poor farming family on 18 February 1951. Throughout his elementary and secondary education years, Chen was normally at the top of his class despite gripping poverty reflected by life in a mud hut. He attended the prestigious National Taiwan University, graduated with a bachelor's degree in law in 1974 and won the Outstanding Performance Award for Academic Achievement. In 1973, he passed the Examination Yuan's legal qualification test as a top performer. In 1976, he began a successful legal career practicing maritime law with the Formosa International Marine and Commercial Law Office. Shortly thereafter, he married Wu Shu-jen, the daughter of a wealthy doctor.

In 1980, Chen became the defense attorney for two dissident leaders and publishers of the "Formosa Magazine" who were charged with sedition in what came to be known as the Formosa Incident. That violent protest in Kaohsiung left 140 police injured and 50 people jailed for inciting civil disorder. He lost the case, but became convinced that political activism was necessary to reform the authoritarian political system. One defendant, Annette Lu, served five years in prison for sedition. Lu became Chen's vice-presidential running mate and upon Chen's victory, the first female Taiwanese vice-president.

Chen remained active in legal circles throughout the 1980s but also became active in politics. In 1981, he was elected member of the Taipei City council. His anti-government stance gained him a reputation as a populist and anti-KMT politician. The KMT government sought to contain his growing influence. In 1985, he was sentenced to a one-year prison term for libel resulting from his article in "Formosa Magazine" which accused a pro-government university professor of perjury. He served eight months in prison. During his incarceration, his wife was elected to the National Assembly at a heavy cost. A truck struck his wife in what Chen claimed was an assassination attempt by KMT thugs. Wu's spine was shattered in 30 places and resulted in paralysis below the waist and confinement to a wheelchair. In 1998, he wrote an autobiography, *Son of Taiwan*. Chen's hobbies include membership in the Rotary Club and Western movies.

## RISE TO POWER

The legalization of DPP and the introduction of multi-party politics coincided with Chen's release from prison. His political conviction was cemented after the Formosa incident as he stated, "what I discovered was that the best way to help was not to appeal their sentences or seek a retrial, but to join them in their democratic cause, to help them complete their task." Upon his release from prison in 1985, Chen joined the DPP and became an assistant for a national legislator. From 1987–1989, he was a member of the DPP Central Standing Committee where he developed a strong network with the party in preparation for seeking a seat in the National Assembly.

In 1989, Chen was elected to the Legislative Yuan and became a major spokesperson for the DPP. As a leader of the party, he championed political democracy and governmental reform. His calls for political and economic reform created enemies in the government, but increased his popularity among the people. From 1990–1994, Chen's political stature increased as he assumed greater political responsibility and prominence. He became the co-chairman of the National Defense committee in the Legislative Yuan, a member of the DPP Central Executive Committee, and Director of the DPP Caucus in the Legislative Yuan. In recognition of Chen's rising star, *Time* declared him one of the "Global 100" roster of "Young Leaders for the New Millenium."

Chen took advantage of Taipei's environmental and political problems and was elected mayor in 1994. As Taipei's

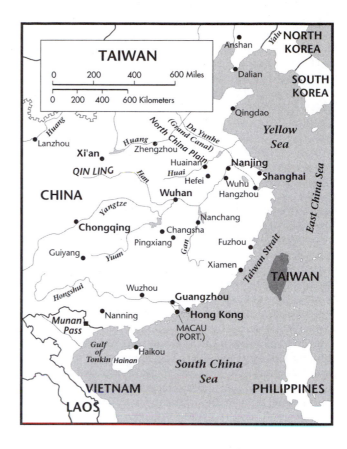

first popularly elected mayor, he obtained a significant electoral following during his administration. Many came to appreciate his proactive administrative style and increased attention to administrative efficiency. Others saw him as an abrasive and confrontational leader who could bring about harmony and consensus. However, supporters point to improved traffic conditions, decreased crime, prostitution and corruption, and the creation of large city parks. He hired additional police officers and used the zoning system to move the vice industry from residential to industrial zones. Periodically, he appealed to younger voters by holding massive downtown dance parties and appeared wearing Superman and other costumes. Despite polls indicating an approval rating of over 70% at the height of his popularity, in 1998, Chen suffered an electoral defeat by losing his reelection bid for mayor to a KMT candidate.

In 1999, Chen was chosen by the DPP as the party's candidate for president. He chose Annette Lu as his vice-presidential mate. Like Chen, Lu rose to political prominence from a low-income family. In his policy statement made in Europe, he stated, "Taiwan is a country and I am running for its presidency" provoking the anger of PR China's leaders. Chen and Lu's campaign centered on the themes of Taiwanese independence, an end to KMT dominance, and political and economic reform. As a maverick candidate, he appeared at campaign functions dressed as James Bond and Superman. His campaign web site painted him as an underdog candidate by showing him in a black jumpsuit, suspended above a computer alluding to the theme "Mission Impossible." In the three-way race that divided the establishment vote in two, Chen captured 39% of the vote. The KMT candidate, Lien

Chan, garnered 23%, and James Soong an independent candidate and KMT defector embarrassed the KMT by obtaining 37% of the votes. The poor performance of the KMT and President Lee's support of Chan led to a crisis within the KMT and his eventual resignation as party leader.

## LEADERSHIP

In his victory speech, Chen rejected China's "one country, two systems" formula for reunification by stating that Taiwan's sovereignty must be protected. He also invited the People's Republic of China's leadership to engage in a dialog with him to resolve the future of Taiwan-China relations.

Chen faces major leadership challenges which will require him to use his leadership and communication skills to bring about effective government. For the past half-century, the KMT controlled national politics and the stability that it brought can no longer be taken for granted. Significant uneasiness exists among the population regarding policies the government will pursue. The DPP and Chen remain unproven in national politics. Further complicating the political environment is the KMT control over Taipei and the Legislative Yuan.

Chen's popularity and image as an anti-corruption crusader will be invaluable in maintaining the unity of the DPP. A minority of DPP members distrust the youthful Chen. What unites the party is a desire to change the political system and redress the concentration of economic and political power and favoritism that occurred over decades of KMT rule. If Chen can maintain his popularity with younger and urban voters, the chances for maintaining the unity of the DPP will increase. DPP unity and Chen's ability to work with a KMY dominated Legislative Yuan will determine the effectiveness of Chen's regime.

## DOMESTIC POLICY

The major focus of the Chen's administration in domestic policy is governmental reform. In particular, the government will work on improving the delivery of governmental services and reforming the economy. Over the past decades, the KMT became a major economic player by owning manufacturing and service sector firms. Over the past six months, the KMT began to divest from its economic holdings by selling banks, factories, and services it owned. It is likely that as these changes continue to take place, instances of KMT misappropriation and governmental ethics will become important issues.

The KMT's economic growth mantra failed to energize voters who are becoming increasingly interested in quality-of-life issues. DPP's record in Taipei, of improving the quality-of-life could serve as a guideline for national policy. Taiwan continues to face major environmental problems including traffic congestion, water and air pollution, and the scarcity of recreational opportunities. At the same time, however, the government must continue to nurture the economic recovery from the 1997 Asian economic crisis by diversifying the country's economy. Thus far, there is discussion of increasing economic cooperation with the mainland by ending the long-term official ban on direct economic linkages. Taiwan continues to seek to become a major center, which integrates manufacturing, transport, finance, and communications for international corporations.

## FOREIGN POLICY

Relations with mainland China are a serious challenge to the Chen government. Mainland China is particularly bellicose to any movement by Taiwan to become independent or seek a greater role in international affairs. For example, during the recent presidential elections, PR China made intense efforts to prevent the Taiwanese from electing Chen. Chinese pressure on the Taiwanese increased because the DPP's party program calls for the independence of Taiwan. As the election neared, the country's stock market experienced significant volatility in response to Chinese statements about impeding military action.

Now that the elections are over, it will be necessary for Taiwan to bring some normalcy to its relations with the People's Republic of China. So far, Chen has decreased his rhetoric regarding independence and is calling for a more constructive relationship with China. Support from the United States is essential in controlling Chinese influence and for providing Taiwan a sense of national security. The new government's foreign policy will be based on supporting democracy in the region and providing economic aid to the developing world. Because of Taiwan's successful economy, it now provides a significant amount of foreign aid and technical assistance to the developing world. In return, some emerging countries have recognized Taiwan by establishing formal diplomatic relations. In addition, Taiwan has established significant relations with over 120 nations. Now that democracy is consolidated in the country, international prestige will likely increase.

## ADDRESS

Office of the President
Chiehshou Hall, Chungking S. Road
Taipei, 100, Taiwan

## REFERENCES

BBC News. [Online] Available http://news.bbc.co.uk/ (Accessed 18, 19, 20, 24 March 2000).

Central Election Commission, R.O.C. [Online] Available http://www.elect2000.gov.tw/english/

Democratic Progressive Party. [Online] Available http://www.dpp.org.tw/English/

*Far Eastern Economic Review,* 22 July 1999 and 16 March and 30 March 2000 issues.

Pun, Allen. "Chen Campaigns in Middle Ground." *Free China Journal,* 10 December 1999.

*The Straits Times,* 20 March 2000.

**Profile researched and written by Robert W. Compton, Jr., Ph.D., Department of Government, Western Kentucky University (5/00).**

# TAJIKISTAN

### Imomali Rakhmonov
### President

*(pronounced "ee-MOM-all-i rah-MON-off")*

*"The people of Tajikistan are not indifferent toward the homeland's destiny,*
*and all are disposed toward peaceful and creative endeavors."*

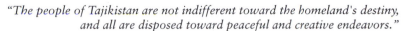

The Republic of Tajikistan borders Uzbekistan to the west; Kyrgyzstan to the north; China to the east; and Afghanistan to the south. Tajikistan is only 20 miles away from Pakistan on one section of its southern border, separated by a narrow Afghan corridor. Tajikistan has a total land area of 139,909 sq km (54,019 sq mi) and is largely mountainous. The Pamir Mountain range, known as the "roof of the world," runs through Tajikistan, China, and Afghanistan. Major administrative subdivisions include the Gorno Badakhshan Autonomous Region (an ethnic enclave enjoying theoretical rights) and other regions. The population of Tajikistan is estimated at 6.1 million.

Tajikistan has been subject to myriad historical influences. While Tajikistan's language and ethnic background are heavily Persian, its religion and culture were influenced by Turkey. Though it only became an independent nation in 1991, its culture has produced impressive architecture in Bukhara and Samarkand, cities now in Uzbekistan, and contributions to Persian literature. A Soviet-era census reported that 62% of the population is ethnic Tajik, 23% Uzbek, and 8% Russian. Since the 1989 census, up to three-quarters of these Russians have emigrated because of Tajik economic distress and fears of civil conflict. Clan and regional identities are also significant among most Tajiks and can transcend national identity. These include the Khjoent, Kulyab, Garm, and Pamiri regional focuses. More than a million Tajiks also reside within Uzbekistan and four million in Afghanistan. The official language is Tajik, closely related to Farsi, the chief language in Iran; but 36% of the population is fluent in Russian. Most Tajiks belong to the Sunni branch of Islam, common to the other Turkic peoples of Central Asia, rather than the Shi'a branch, dominant in Iran. Tajikistan has the highest percentage of rural population, the lowest educational level, and the highest infant mortality rate of the former Soviet republics. Most of the people live in tiny rural *qishlags* or hamlets with as few as 15 to 20 cottages in the most mountainous areas.

Following independence, Tajikistan, unlike other former Soviet republics, agreed to subordinate its economy to Russia, but was forced by 1995 to introduce its own currency, the Tajik ruble. The breakup of the Soviet Union and civil conflict in Tajikistan severely harmed its economy. By some estimates, gross domestic product had declined by more than 75% by 1993, 80% of Tajik industries were damaged or idle, and total war damage was estimated at over US$12 billion. In late 1997, Tajikistan's economic decline appeared to reverse as the peace accord began to take hold, allowing economic activities to recover. The GDP of Tajikistan is estimated at US$6 billion and per capita GDP is about US$990. Declines in world commodity prices harmed exports in 1998. Inflation in consumer prices slowed from over 500% in 1996 to 46.3% by the end of 1998. By mid-1999, most small enterprises had been privatized, but most major firms remain in state hands. Tajikistan's major industry is the aluminum smelter in Tursunzade, one of the world's largest, although it is currently producing well below capacity. Tajikistan's other exports include hydroelectric power and cotton. Tajikistan and Kyrgyzstan are the main suppliers of water to the rest of Central Asia. Tajikistan's cotton production was about the same in 1999 as in 1998 despite ambitious plan targets because of bad weather and inadequate investment. Cotton and silk production and sheep herding are the main livelihoods. Crime and corruption, mainly drug-related, threaten the emergence of a market economy.

## POLITICAL BACKGROUND

From ancient times, what is now Tajikistan has been subject to Persian, Greek, Arabic, Turkic, Mongol, Uzbek, Afghan, and then Russian control. Northern Tajikistan was annexed by the Russian Empire in 1868, while the southern parts remained under the sovereignty of the Uzbek Bukharan Khanate. After the Bolshevik revolution in Russia in 1917, the northern parts of Tajikistan were included in the Turkestan Autonomous Soviet Socialist Republic, while a Communist-run and nominally independent People's Republic of Bukhara was proclaimed in the south, which was eliminated in 1921. In the early 1920s, many Tajiks revolted against Communist rule. These rebels, termed *Basmachi* (bandits) by the Russians, were finally suppressed in the early 1930s, though with large Tajik casualties. Many Tajiks fled to Afghanistan at that time and after the beginning of collectivization and during the purges in the early 1930s. In October 1924, the Tajik ASSR was created as part of the Uzbek Soviet Socialist Republic, recognizing the historical dominance of Uzbeks over Tajiks. In 1929, however, a Tajik Soviet Socialist Republic was created as a nominally sovereign subunit of the Soviet federation.

Tajikistan declared its sovereignty over its land and resources on 24 August 1990, and its independence on 9 September 1991. It was among the Central Asian republics least prepared and inclined toward independence, and its Communist-dominated elite, largely composed of members of

## TAJIKISTAN

established a UN Mission of Observers in Tajikistan (UNMOT) in December 1994, consisting of several dozen observers, to monitor the cease-fire. This committee was later expanded to investigate cease-fire violations, monitor the demobilization of United Tajik Opposition (UTO) fighters, assist ex-combatants to integrate into society, and offer advice for holding elections. A small Organization for Security and Cooperation in Europe (OSCE) mission also promoted peace. In 1993, the Commonwealth of Independent States (CIS) authorized joint Russian and Central Asian "peacekeeping" in Tajikistan under the auspices of its Collective Peacekeeping Forces (CPF) treaty to protect what Yeltsin termed "CIS borders." CPF consisted of Russia's 201st Rifle Division, based in Tajikistan, and token Kazak, Kyrgyz, and Uzbek troops. In late 1998, Karimov pulled Uzbek "peacekeepers" out of Tajikistan to protest charges made by Rakhmonov that Uzbekistan had fostered an insurrection there, and Kyrgyzstan pulled out as well, citing costs. Russian media reported in late 1999 that there were about 20,000 CPF, border, and other Russian troops in Tajikistan. In August 1999 the commander of the CPF troops stated that the role of his forces had largely shifted to the delivery of humanitarian cargos, clearing mines, and giving medical assistance. Nonetheless, plans to withdraw the CPF have not been announced, perhaps because in April 1999, Russia and Tajikistan signed a basing agreement for the 25-year presence of Russian troops.

In December 1996, the two sides agreed to set up the National Reconciliation Commission (NRC), an executive body composed equally of government and opposition emissaries. In June 1997, Rakhmanov and UTO leader Seyed Abdullo Nuri signed the Comprehensive Peace Agreement. Under this accord, Rakhmanov remained president but 30% of ministerial posts were allocated to the opposition with Nuri heading the NRC. Benchmarks of the peace process have largely been met, including the return of refugees, demilitarization of rebel forces, legalization of rebel parties, and the holding of presidential and legislative elections. Stability in Tajikistan remains fragile, however. An unsuccessful insurrection in the Leninabad region of northern Tajikistan launched by notorious warlord Mahmud Khudoyberdiyev in November 1998 highlights concerns by some observers about secessionist tendencies in the region and about ethnic tensions between ethnic Tajiks and Uzbeks in Tajikistan.

## PERSONAL BACKGROUND

Imomali Rakhmonov, a Tajik belonging to the Kulyabi clan, was born in October 1952 in the town of Dangar in the Kulyab region. He studied economics at Dushanbe's Lenin State University. After serving in the Soviet armed forces, he held several low-level jobs, including: electrician salesman, head of a trade union committee, and secretary of a Communist Party organization at an agricultural enterprise. In 1988, he became the director of a state farm in his native Dangar *raion* (county). He was elected chairman of the Culvert region government (oblast executive committee) on 2 November 1992.

## RISE TO POWER

Rakhmonov's rise to power was meteoric, boosted by his clan and political links to the Kulyabi paramilitary leader and ex-

the Khjoent and Kulyab clans, has endeavored to rebuild traditional ties with Russia. In August 1991, the Communist Party chief fully supported the coup attempt against Gorbachev; he was later forced to resign. The Communists continued to rule, however, and supported former Tajik Communist Party chief Rakhmon Nabiyev's popular election as president in November 1991. This election was condemned as fraudulent by groups opposed to continued Communist Party rule, leading to massive demonstrations and an agreement by Nabiyev in May 1992 to form a coalition government. In September 1992, however, opposition forces, largely composed of members of the Pamiri and Garm clans, who had long been excluded from political power and many of whom were supporters of the Islamic Renaissance Party (IRP) or the liberal Democratic Party, forced Nabiyev from office and tried to consolidate power. Hard-line Communists resisted these efforts. By December 1992, these forces had succeeded in routing the oppositionists from the capital, and launched a concerted countrywide offensive, resulting in 20,000–40,000 or more casualties and over 350,000 displaced persons, many of whom fled to Afghanistan. Uzbekistan and Russia contributed arms and troops to assist Tajik pro-Communists in routing the opposition.

The armed conflict between the two sides continued throughout 1993 and early 1994 with border attacks launched by Tajik rebels based in Afghanistan. At a UN-sponsored meeting in Tehran, the Tajik government and opposition emissaries agreed on 17 September 1994 to a cease-fire, to begin when UN observers were in place along the Tajik-Afghan border. The UN Security Council formally convict Sangak Safarov, his relationship with ex-president Nabiyev, and the opportunity for upward mobility presented by civil war. After Safarov shot the previous chairman of the Kulyab regional government, Rakhmonov was installed in the post. Three weeks later, he was selected by the Communist-dominated Supreme Soviet as its chairman when they met in exile in Khojent. Rakhmonov was further considered an attractive candidate for the chairmanship because of his Communist Party ties and his hard-line position against reconciliation with the opposition. After the Communist forces retook Dushanbe at the end of 1992, the Rakhmonov-led Supreme Soviet was able to return to the capital.

## LEADERSHIP

Rakhmonov is described by the Russian independent media and others as a tough and skillful politician who has managed to retain power despite years of political opposition, a difficult peace process, internal separatism and ethnic dissidence, economic collapse, and fragile political relations between his Kulyabi regional supporters and other regional interests, particularly the previously dominant Khojent clan.

Moving to consolidate his hold on political power, Rakhmonov decided to hold presidential elections and a referendum on a new constitution in November 1994. Tajikistan was the last of the Central Asian states to replace its Communist-era constitution. The main Tajik democratic and pro-Islamic opposition groups announced that they would boycott the election and referendum because they had no say in drawing up the draft constitution and would not be allowed to field their own candidates. The election and referendum restored the presidential system of rule and witnessed the further consolidation of Rakhmonov's power when he was elected by a wide margin and his constitution was overwhelmingly approved. Only one candidate besides Rakhmonov was permitted to run, Abdumalik Abdullojanov, a prominent politician in the northern Leninabad region and a former Tajik prime minister. Abdullojanov alleged widespread election fraud. The OSCE declined to send monitors because it viewed the electoral process as not meeting its standards. Elections to a new 181-member legislature took place in February 1995. Four parties were allowed to compete, but restrictive nomination procedures ensured that about 40% of candidates ran unopposed. The election excluded virtually all opposition parties, and Western groups refused to monitor the "seriously flawed" vote.

## DOMESTIC POLICY

After defeating the oppositionists in 1992, Rakhmonov followed the path of other authoritarian leaders in Turkmenistan and Uzbekistan by putting into place one of the most authoritarian political systems in Central Asia. Opposition political parties were banned or suppressed, press freedoms were circumscribed, and human and civil rights were frequently violated.

According to the Rakhmonov-drafted constitution approved by referendum in November 1994, the Oliy Majlis (legislature) enacts laws, interprets the constitution, determines basic directions of domestic and foreign policy, sets dates for referenda and elections, and approves key ministerial and other appointments. The legislature also approves the state budget, determines tax policy, ratifies treaties, and approves a state of war or emergency as decreed by the president. The constitution also calls for creation of a presidium to "organize work," to be elected by the legislators and to be headed by the speaker. Laws are required to be passed by a two-thirds majority of the total number of deputies, and a presidential veto may be overridden by the same margin. The main Tajik opposition groups boycotted the November 1994 presidential election and constitutional referendum because they had no say in drawing up the draft constitution and would not be allowed to field their own candidates.

The Tajik legislature in June 1999 rubber-stamped constitutional changes proposed by Rakhmonov calling for a seven year presidential term, a two-house Supreme Assembly (legislature), and the legalization of religious parties. A popular referendum approved the changes on 26 September 1999, and the legislature scheduled a presidential election for November 6. Tajik opposition candidates, given just a few days to gather 150,000 signatures countrywide, alleged that governmental harassment prevented them from gathering the signatures. The Central Electoral Commission (CEC), controlled by Rakhmonov, pronounced him the only candidate. This prompted the resignation of opposition members of the NRC and calls for an electoral boycott. To provide the gloss of a multi-candidate race, the CEC "registered" Islamic Renaissance Party nominee Davlat Usmon, though he refused to run. The CEC announced that 98% of the population had turned out and 96.9% had voted for Rakhmonov, and only 2% for Usmon. The OSCE refused to monitor the election. Seeking to avert renewed civil war, Nuri agreed on November 5 to respect the outcome of the election and rejoin the NRC in return for pledges by Rakhmonov to allow fair legislative elections scheduled for February 2000. An electoral law was approved with input from the UTO on 10 December 1999. The law called for the upper legislative chamber, the National Assembly (representing regional interests), to consist of 33 members, and the lower chamber, the Assembly of Representatives, 63 members.

Elections to the Assembly of Representatives were set for 27 February 2000 with a runoff election on March 12. Nearly 300 candidates competed for the 63 seats. Turnout was reported by the CEC at 93.23%. In the party list voting, Rakhmanov's People's Democratic Party (PDP) won fifteen seats, the Communist Party won five seats, and the Islamic Renaissance Party won two seats. Over 107 UN and OSCE observers monitored the race. They praised the "political pluralism" of the vote, since voters "were presented with a genuine and broad range of alternatives," but concluded that the electoral process must be improved "to meet the minimum democratic standards for equal, fair, free, secret, transparent, and accountable elections." They raised questions about freedom of the media, the independence of electoral commissions, the questionable de-registration of some candidates, apparently inflated turnout figures, and the transparency of vote tabulation.

In the National Assembly, 33 upper legislative chamber seats were filled on March 23 by indirect voting by local council assemblies and the appointment of eight members by Rakhmonov. Addressing the first session of the newly elected National Assembly on 17 April 2000, President Rakhmonov hailed the meeting as marking a new era of peace in

Tajikistan's history. He stated that the top policy priorities were to preserve Tajikistan's stability and independence and to raise the living standards of the population.

In line with the peace accords which set presidential and legislative elections as the culmination of the peace process, on 26 March 2000, Tajikistan disbanded its NRC. Nuri, chairman of the NRC, called for quick settlement of remaining peace issues. The UN Security Council on 21 March 2000, praised the legislative elections and work of the NRC, and supported withdrawing UN observers in May 2000.

## FOREIGN POLICY

President Rakhmonov has proclaimed Tajikistan's willingness to establish amicable relations with all countries, and has supported stronger ties with the neighboring states of Iran, Afghanistan, Pakistan, and other countries sharing Tajikistan's language, history, or culture. He has emphasized cooperation with China and India, and has called for increased economic ties with the United States, Europe, and Japan. Some elements of the Tajik opposition advocate closer ties with Iran or Afghanistan's Taliban group. Iran has helped mediate the civil war and is a guarantor of the peace settlement. Tajikistan's civil conflict and economic straits have restrained its ability to open legations abroad, but it is active in the UN and the CIS.

The top priorities of Tajik foreign policy, Rakhmonov stated in October 1999, are close ties with Russia and other former Soviet republics. Critics of Russia's large role in security in Tajikistan argue that it jeopardizes Tajikistan's independence, while still failing to safeguard it from drug trafficking, arms smuggling, terrorism, and other transborder criminal activity. Uzbekistan, Kazakhstan, and Kyrgyzstan assisted Russian "peacekeepers" in guarding Tajik borders. In February 1999, Tajikistan gained membership in the CIS customs union (composed of Belarus, Russia, Kazakhstan, and Kyrgyzstan) and in March 1998 gained membership in a customs unit formed by Kazakhstan, Kyrgyzstan, and Uzbekistan, though these remain largely moribund. Tajikistan's relations with Uzbekistan have been mercurial. Tajikistan has accused Uzbekistan of harboring separatists, and Uzbekistan has accused Tajikistan of harboring Uzbek and Tajik terrorists intent on overthrowing the government. Appearing to brush aside Tajikistan's sovereignty, Uzbek President Islam Karimov ominously stated in October 1999 that "we have the right to carry out the same kind of operations against terrorist bases in Tajikistan as Russia has carried out on the Chechen-Dagestani border." A Taliban victory in Afghanistan might present the current Tajik government with regimes to both the north (Uzbekistan) and south (Afghanistan) that seek to gain undue influence, according to some observers. Iran and Uzbekistan have backed different sides in the Tajik civil war, but both oppose Afghanistan's Taliban group. Some Tajik opposition ties with Iran provide friction with Afghanistan's Taliban. Tajikistan's instability and regional concerns tend to lead the Rakhmonov government to rely more on Russia which, by granting Russia basing rights, antagonizes Uzbekistan and the Taliban.

## ADDRESS
Prospekt Lenina 42
Dushanbe, Tajikistan

## REFERENCES

*The Economist,* 12 November 1994.
*FBIS Daily Report, Central Eurasia.*
*Los Angeles Times,* 25 October 1994.
*New Times,* January 1993.
*RFE/RL Research Report,* 7 January 1994.
*Survival,* Winter, 1993–1994.
"Tajikistan: Edging Towards Democracy." *The Economist,* 4 March 2000, p. 43.

**Profile researched and written by Jim Nichol, Library of Congress (5/2000).**

# TANZANIA

## Benjamin William Mkapa
## President
*(pronounced "em-KA-pa")*

*"We do not want to be a scapegoat for procrastination in the negotiations, and we abhor even the perception that Tanzania is an obstacle to the speedy resolution of the Burundi conflict."*

The United Republic of Tanzania was created by the formal union of Tanganyika, on the East African mainland, and the island nation of Zanzibar (comprised of the islands of Zanzibar and Pemba). Tanzania is bordered to the east by the Indian Ocean; to the north by Uganda and Kenya; to the west by Rwanda, Burundi, and Zaire; and to the south by Zambia, Malawi, and Mozambique. The national territory occupies a total area of 945,090 sq km (364,898 sq mi); over 99% of which is mainland Tanzania. The population of 31.3 million is largely rural, with only about 31% of the people living in or near metropolitan areas. The official capital is Dar es Salaam, which is home to two million Tanzanians. Official languages are Kiswahili and English, although numerous indigenous languages are spoken among the nation's more than 120 ethnic groups. The majority of Tanzanians are African; non-Africans make up less than 1% of the population. There is no official religion in Tanzania and Christian, Muslim, and indigenous beliefs are each professed by roughly one-third of the people. Zanzibar, however, is overwhelmingly Muslim. Agriculture dominates the economy, accounting for 56% of GDP and 85% of employment. Cash crops such as coffee, tea, cotton, cashews, sisal, cloves (from Zanzibar), and pyrethrum are important for export earnings. Industry in Tanzania accounts for 15% of GDP. The currency is the Tanzanian shilling. Per capita income is estimated at US$730. The country relies heavily on foreign economic assistance.

## POLITICAL BACKGROUND

Arab traders were active in Tanganyika's coastal region by the 8th century. By the 12th century traders from India had arrived. In 1506, the Portuguese claimed control of the coastal region, although they neither colonized nor explored it. By the early 18th century indigenous coastal dwellers, with the assistance of Omani Arabs, had driven the Portuguese from the area. The Omani Sultan, Seyyid Said, claimed the coastal region for himself and eventually moved his capital to Zanzibar in 1841. The mid-19th century saw the arrival of European explorers. Germans reached Mt. Kilimanjaro in the 1840s, and the British reached Lake Tanganyika by 1857. Colonial rule soon followed. The Germans contrived to bring African societies under their "protection" by negotiating fraudulent treaties with illegitimate African leaders. In 1886 and 1890, Anglo-German agreements were reached stipulating specific spheres of influence for each nation. The United Kingdom took control over Zanzibar and Germany over Tanganyika. Germany's defeat in World War I spelled the end of its African colonial empire and Tanganyika was passed to the United Kingdom under a League of Nations mandate. After World War II, Tanganyika became a United Nations trust territory under British control. The first Tanganyikan political party was formed in 1954 by Julius K. Nyerere. The Tanganyika African National Union (TANU) and Nyerere were instrumental in guiding Tanganyika to independence. In May 1961, the country became autonomous with Nyerere as prime minister under a new constitution. Full independence came in December 1961, and Nyerere was elected president of Tanganyika when the country became a republic within the Commonwealth in 1962.

Zanzibar, the other part of the United Republic of Tanzania, had a stormier path to independence than the mainland. British interests became established in Zanzibar for both commercial purposes and in an attempt to end the slave trade. The British reached an agreement with the Sultan in 1822 to end the slave trade, but it was more than 50 years until it finally came to an end. The Anglo-German agreement in 1890 made Zanzibar a British protectorate and the British incorporated the sultan into their colonial administration. The British created a strict racial hierarchy on the islands with Europeans on top and Arabs favored over Africans. According to the British, Zanzibar was an Arab state. In December 1963, Zanzibar became an independent sultanate; in January 1964, the sultan was deposed by an armed uprising of members of the African nationalist Afro Shirazi Party and a republic was proclaimed. In April 1964, the Zanzibari government signed an Act of Union with Tanganyika and the United Republic was formed.

The political history of the Tanzania has been largely shaped by the political stature of Tanganyika's first president, Julius Nyerere. Considered the father of the country, Nyerere was president of Tanzania from 1962 to 1985. Under his leadership the country embarked on a course of democracy within a one-party state. TANU was the only recognized political party and all candidates for any office were TANU members. This, however, did not preclude sometimes hotly contested races among several candidates from within the party. In 1977, TANU, under Nyerere's leadership, merged with the Afro Shirazi Party, the sole political party on Zanzibar, to form CCM (*Chama cha Mapinduzi* or the Revolutionary Party). Nyerere implemented a sweeping economic reorganization known as *ujaama*, a system intended to produce a uniquely African form of socialism.

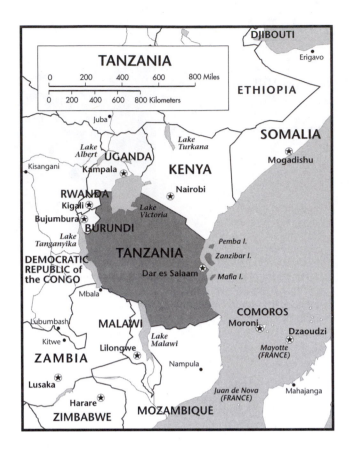

State control of everything from agricultural collectivization to transportation and utility services was initiated. Widely viewed as a failure, the system nevertheless remained in place until the 1980s when Nyerere's hand-picked successor, Ali Hasan Mwinyi, began the slow process of dismantling *ujamaa*.

The Constitution of Tanzania, as adopted in 1977 and subsequently amended, articulates the structure of government. The president is head of state and head of government, and is elected to no more than two five-year terms. Universal suffrage is granted at age 18. The National Assembly is made of 274 legislators. There are 232 who are elected to five-year terms by popular vote. The president then nominates the remaining 42 members of parliament. The Union of Tanzania is a carefully structured balance of interests, with guarantees of Zanzibari representation in the National Assembly and at the executive level. Zanzibar continues to elect its own President and House of Representatives, which have authority over the two islands' internal affairs. In 1992, the move toward a multi-party state was initiated, and the 1995 elections were the first multi-party elections held in Tanzania since the early 1960s and they marked the rise of Benjamin Mkapa to the Presidency of the Republic.

## PERSONAL BACKGROUND

Benjamin William Mkapa was born on 12 November 1938, in Ndanda, Tanganyika. Educated at Makerere University College, Mkapa held positions in the civil and foreign service in the early 1960s. Later he was appointed the managing editor of two national newspapers, served as press secretary for President Nyerere in 1974, and was a founding director of the Tanzania News Agency in 1976. Beginning in the late 1970s, and continuing until his election as president, Mkapa was appointed to a series of high level ministerial and ambassadorial positions. Mkapa served abroad as High Commissioner to Canada and Ambassador to the United States, during which time he also continued his education at Columbia University. Mkapa has been married to Anna Joseph Maro since 1966. The couple has two sons, Nico and Steve.

## RISE TO POWER

Benjamin Mkapa has been active in CCM for much of his adult life, and has worked closely with both President Nyerere and President Mwinyi. He has been a protégé of Nyerere, and it was with the first President's backing that Mkapa emerged as the CCM candidate for the nation's first multi-party election in decades. Mwinyi was himself ineligible, having already been twice elected to the presidency. In the 1995 elections, the newly organized political parties that emerged after the opening of the system in 1992 were no match for the decades-old political power of the CCM. Mkapa further benefited from the active role Nyerere took in campaigning on his behalf.

The vote on 29 October 1995 was marred by procedural errors and delays, which led to the returns from Dar es Salaam being nullified. A revote for Dar es Salaam was held on November 19. Many of the opposition parties boycotted the re-run, charging that insufficient procedural guarantees were in place. Since the October 22 Zanzibari presidential election had been tainted with fraud, leading to a disputed victory for the CCM candidate, tensions were high for the Tanzania election. There were no allegations of fraud in the elections and Benjamin Mkapa won the presidential balloting with 61.8% of the 6.1 million votes cast. CCM candidates also won 75% of the seats in the National Assembly, thus handing Mkapa a stable legislative base for his first five-year term.

## LEADERSHIP

Benjamin Mkapa was sworn in as Tanzania's third president on 23 November 1995. Omar Ali Juma (the former First Minister of Zanzibar), who was Mkapa's running mate, became vice president. Mkapa inherited the leadership of an economically disadvantaged, agriculturally unproductive, donor-dependent nation of millions of desperately poor people. His immediate predecessor initiated the process of freeing the market for competition, repairing infrastructure, and meeting IMF (International Monetary Fund) guidelines for continued economic assistance. Marking a departure with the Mwinyi regime, Mkapa shunned many long-standing politicians when he named a new council of Ministers with Fredrick Sumaye as prime minister. Mkapa has succeeded in deepening market reforms and winning the confidence of donor countries that had been shaken by the widespread corruption under the Mwinyi government.

During his election campaign, Mkapa pledged a war against corruption. In January 1996 he appointed a special presidential commission chaired by a former Prime Minister Joseph Warioba to undertake a full investigation of corruption in Tanzania. In its final report issued on December 1996, the commission established a number of causes and remedies for corruption. It also pointed out some individuals who seemed to be involved with corruption. Despite the report, many of the named individuals escaped prosecution although two high ranking government officials eventually were forced to resign and another was brought to trial in 1999. While some Tanzanians questioned the sincerity of his government to curbing corruption, the Mkapa administration has generally received high marks from donors for its efforts to reduce this problem.

## DOMESTIC POLICY

Mkapa is from a new generation of African leadership. His government represents a passing of responsibility from the generation of leaders who won independence to a new generation that must figure out how to bring economic development to a continent that has played a marginal role in the global economy. Symbolic of this change was the death of the first President Julius Nyerere on 14 October 1999. While there was some speculation that instability might follow in the wake of the passing away of the father of the country, Tanzania has continued with its tradition of peace and stability.

Mkapa's skills as a conciliator and negotiator have been put to the test over the issue of the Union. Zanzibari resentment toward the mainland has been on the increase and the activities of CCM operatives in the 1995 Zanzibari presidential elections fueled resentment. Mkapa was accused of refraining from taking a firm line in the CCM-CUF (Civic United Front) dispute over the 1995 election results. However, Mkapa tried to strike a difficult balance between guiding the whole country, including Zanzibar, to a more open political system while appeasing those who held power on the islands. In an attempt to reduce political tensions on the islands, Mkapa allowed external mediation into the Zanzibar political stalemate from the Commonwealth. During the June 2000 CCM extra ordinary party conference, Amani Abied Karume, a moderate, was selected as the party's Zanzibari Presidential Candidate, opening the possibility that a political solution can be reached in the islands. President Mkapa was endorsed as the party's candidate to seek re-election for a second (and last) five-year term as Tanzania's president.

## FOREIGN POLICY

Tanzania has long been at the forefront of African affairs and has taken a leadership role in East Africa. Tanzania's influence has been greatest in the regional arena, and the country adopted an active role in the Organization for African Unity and the Southern Africa Development Community. From the time of Tanzania's own independence, the government has openly supported liberation movements throughout southern Africa. Tanzania maintains close ties with Uganda, Mozambique and Zambia. The East African Community's collapse in 1977 resulted in a complete breakdown in relations between Tanzania and Kenya. However, under the leadership of Mkapa and his colleagues, President Yoweri Museveni of Uganda, and President Daniel arap Moi of Kenya, a close relationship between the three countries was re-established with the signing of an East African Cooperation treaty in Arusha, Tanzania on 31 November 1999.

During Mkapa's first term, relations with Burundi were problematic. In July 1996 the Mkapa administration, in cooperation with other regional governments, imposed sanctions on the Burundi military regime following the overthrow of a democratically elected Hutu led government by Tutsi extremists. Relations remained uneasy as a civil war erupted in Burundi and Tanzania was accused with complicity in rebel attacks. This issue was exacerbated by an increasing number of Burundians seeking refuge in Tanzania throughout 1996 and 1997. Despite the tension between the two states, peace talks aimed at bringing an end to Burundi's civil war were hosted in Tanzania's northern city of Arusha. The slow moving talks were facilitated by Julius Nyerere, and after his death, Nelson Mandela, the former South African President.

Another major foreign policy concern for the Mkapa government was the hundreds of thousands of refugees from Rwanda, Burundi, and Congo who fled to Tanzania to escape the widespread violence unleashed by the Rwandan genocide in the Great Lakes region. In addition to facilitating regional peace talks, the Tanzanian government attempted to mobilize international humanitarian support and to repatriate refugees.

On 7 August 1998 the terrorist bombing of the US embassy in Dar es Salaam shocked the Mkapa administration. The explosion claimed 12 lives and was attributed to an international terrorist group with links to Osama bin Laden. The Mkapa government worked closely with the United States in conducting investigations into the attack.

A cornerstone of the Mkapa government's foreign policy has been to mobilize foreign resources for economic development. Since coming to power, Mkapa has been travelling to meet heads of state and encourage foreign investment. In 1996 his government established the multilateral debt fund to help the country service its external debt. Tanzania was offered debt relief of US$1.1 billion in January 1997 and pledges were made by foreign donors for US$2 billion more in early 2000.

US-Tanzania relations date to the early 1950s, when the United States began a program of assistance through the US Agency for International Development. Although relations were strained shortly after independence until the 1990s, ties between the two countries, especially after the embassy bombing, have become strong. USAID programs have provided training for thousands of Tanzanians in a range of areas. In the 1990s, the emphasis of the assistance has shifted to infrastructure improvement in the rural parts of the country, AIDS control, and enhancing private sector economic development. US companies have become interested in business opportunities while tourists are traveling in increasing numbers to Tanzania's spectacular game parks.

## ADDRESS

Office of the President
Dar es Salaam
United Republic of Tanzania

## REFERENCES

*Business Times* (Dar es Salaam), 19–25 May 2000.

Due, Jean M. "Liberalization and Privatization in Tanzania and Zambia." *21:12 World Development,* 1981–88 *The Economist,* 1995–96.

Gonza, Sam. "Were Elections Free and Fair in Zanzibar?" *The Africa Church Information Service* (Nairobi, Kenya), 16 November 1995.

Integrated Regional Information Network. [Online] Available http://www.reliefweb.int/IRIN/cea/countrystories/tanzania/19991202.htm (Accessed 6/00).

Kilimwiko, Lawrence. "Tanzania: Elections in October." *Africa Information Afrique,* 19 September 1995.

"Mkapa Is Sworn in As President." *The Africa Church Information Service* (Nairobi, Kenya), 27 November 1995.

**Profile written and researched by Alison Doherty Munro (7/96; updated by Bruce Heilman and Miraji Kitigwa, University of Dar es Salaam 6/00).**

# THAILAND

**Chuan Leekpai
Prime Minister**
*(pronounced "CHEW-on LEEK-pie")*

*"We must enhance our ability to maximize benefits and minimize the negative effects of globalization...While we address the economic dimension of development, we must not overlook its social or human aspect."*

The Kingdom of Thailand is located in the heart of Southeast Asia's mainland. To its northwest is Myanmar (formerly Burma); to the northeast, Laos; to the southeast, Cambodia; and to the south, Malaysia. The total area is 514,000 sq km (198,456 sq mi) and its total population is 60.6 million, of whom 75% are Thai, 14% are Chinese, and 11% are from various other ethnic groups. It is a nation abundant in natural resources, including fertile farmlands in the central part of the country surrounding the Chao Phraya River, lush tropical rainforests in the south, and forested mountains in the north. The capital and largest city, Bangkok is the country's major commercial, financial, and administrative center.

Thailand is rapidly becoming a more urban nation. While farming employs the majority of Thais, the level of urbanization doubled from approximately 15% to 30% from the 1970s to the 1990s. The official language is Thai and many of the ethnic Chinese have adopted Thai surnames. The literacy rate is 93%. More than 95% of the people are Buddhists, Thailand's official religion. Buddhism and its temples play an important role in daily life.

During the early 1990s, the Thai economy grew by 7–9% annually. In 1997, that trend came to a halt, when the economy contracted by 0.4%. In 1998, the economic downturn worsened, with the economy shrinking another 8.5%. Thailand's primary exports are textiles, computer parts, electrical appliances, precious stones and jewelry, rubber, shrimp, rice, and auto parts. In the future, Thai leaders envision the development of a regional communication hub in Thailand, and further growth in the auto parts segment. The unit of currency is the *baht*.

## POLITICAL BACKGROUND

Thailand, known as Siam until 1939, was the only nation in Southeast Asia to avoid direct colonization. During World War II, Thailand was sympathetic to the Axis Powers and supported Japan to avoid colonization. Initially governed as an absolute monarchy, a subsequent series of military coups limited the power of the king in 1932. Siam became a constitutional monarchy and was renamed Thailand in 1939 to reflect a movement toward modernization. King Bhumipol Adulyadej, monarch since 9 June 1946, plays a largely ceremonial role, but his opinions are highly regarded and his influence on politics is significant. His major influence and power stems from his role in dealing with political crises by granting or withholding legitimacy. In 1996, King Bhumipol celebrated his 50-year golden jubilee, making him the longest

reigning monarch in the world. December 5, his birthday, is a national holiday.

Thailand has a long history of military regimes and military intervention in politics. There have been at least 18 coups and attempted coups since 1932. The three decades following World War II (1950s, 1960s, and 1970s) were characterized by authoritarian rule. Gradually, however, Thailand evolved toward a semi-democratic government that showed high levels of instability until a coalition of civilian parties led by Chuan Leepai won power in 1992.

The Thai Parliament approved a new constitution on 11 October 1997. Drafted by a 99-member charter committee, the document is, by far, Thailand's most democratic constitution. It requires that the prime minister be an elected member of Parliament. It continues the tradition of a bicameral Parliament with a 500-member House of Representatives (400 elected form geographic districts and 100 from a national list). Contrary to earlier constitutions that provided for an appointed Senate, the new Senate of 200 members is elected nationally from throughout the country. As before, elections for prime minister are held every four years or whenever Parliament is dissolved. The leader of the party that gains the most seats in an election is charged with forming a government and presenting the list of cabinet members to the king for formal approval. The basic goal of the 1997 constitution is to reduce the influence of money in politics and to make Thailand a more genuinely democratic society with greater local involvement.

## PERSONAL BACKGROUND

Chuan Leekpai was born on 28 July 1938 in the Muang District of the small southern province of Trang. He is one of Thailand's few modern political leaders who has neither an aristocratic nor a military background. His father was a Chinese immigrant school teacher and his mother a market merchant. Chuan is the third son in a family of nine children. He received his primary education at Wat Kuang Viset school and his high school certificate from Trang Wittaya school, both in Trang province. He was an artist as a student, and earned a certificate in painting and sculpture at Silpakorn Pre-University. Like many other ambitious rural students, Chuan left his home province to pursue further education in Bangkok. In 1958, Chuan enrolled an Thammasat University, one of Thailand's most prestigious universities. He earned room and board by working in a Buddhist temple for eight years. Chuan earned a bachelor's degree in 1962, and

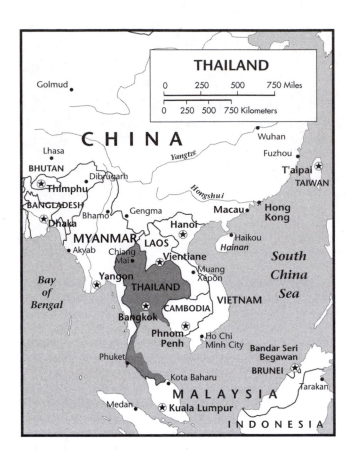

the house (1986–88), and deputy prime minister under Chatichai Choonhaven in 1990.

Chuan enjoyed equal success within his own party. After a 25-year membership in the Democrat Party, one of Thailand's oldest political institutions, he rose to the post of party leader in 1990. This was a time of great turmoil within the country. In 1991, a military junta staged a bloodless coup, ousting Prime Minister Chatichai. Popular pro-democracy and anti-military movements gained momentum. A 1992 general election resulted in a major victory for the pro-democracy parties, who captured 185 out of 360 seats in the House of Representatives. As leader of the party with the most seats, Chuan was able to forge a coalition government, providing a 202-seat majority. With the formal approval of the king, Chuan became the new prime minister and assembled his cabinet on 23 September 1992. The Chuan government managed to retain power for nearly three years, despite repeated challenges. Finally, a land reform scandal forced Chuan to dissolve the House of Representatives and schedule new elections. His party was voted out of power in July 1995. Chuan remained in Parliament as an opposition leader until he was able to gather enough support to form a new government in November 1997.

## LEADERSHIP

Chuan has maintained leadership of his party since August 1990, demonstrating remarkable political strength. Every prior Democrat Party leader had been overthrown by a military coup within a year. He maintains a reputation for moderation and integrity. During his 28 years in Parliament, Chuan has been untainted by corruption—a rare accomplishment for a Thai politician. One of Chuan's strongest leadership traits is his ability to surround himself with highly able and respected talent. In Chuan's first cabinet, 15 members had advanced degrees. His economic team, including Supachai Panitchpakdi (deputy prime minister and minister of commerce) and Tarrin Nimmanhaeminda (minister of finance), is well-respected, forming the foundation of a cabinet that has been described as the most professional cabinet in Thailand's history. Chuan was also able to persuade former prime minister Anand Panyarachun and his colleagues to assist the government with economic issues.

Major criticisms of Chuan as a leader have focused on his lack of skill as an administrator, charging that he is weak and indecisive, and is not a dynamic leader. Others argue that Chuan has undergone change and growth during his years as a politician, and is no longer the soft-spoken individual that started out in Thai politics, committed to avoiding confrontation at all costs. Some critics suggest that the Democrat Party needs to broaden its base of support beyond the south and Bangkok. The new constitution, which attempts to reduce the influence of money in future elections and provide a system of proportional representation, may help Chuan and his party significantly in this regard. Finally, Chuan's cabinet includes a number of ministers, appointed to satisfy the coalition partners, with poor public images. His management skills are being tested with the challenge of managing these diverse personalities.

graduated with a law degree in 1962. After passing the Thai bar examination in 1964, he practiced law. He has been awarded honorary degrees from a number of universities, including Srinakharinwirot University (political science, 1985); Ramkhamhaeng University (political science, 1987); University of Philippines (law, 1993); University of Silpakorn, where as a young man he had earned a painting and sculpture certificate (painting, 1994); Vongchavalitkul University (law, 1998); and National University of San Marcos, Lima, Peru (1999).

## RISE TO POWER

In 1969, Chuan decided to give up his legal career to run for a seat in the House of Representatives in his home province of Trang, under the banner of the Democrat Party *(Pak Prachatipat)*. Despite a poorly funded campaign, Chuan won his first bid for political office and, at the age of 33, became one of the youngest members of Parliament. He continued to hold his seat through 11 national elections. Observers credit this remarkable electoral success to his honesty and integrity and his close contact with voters in his province. Chuan also has the reputation of being a politician who fights for the poor and the common man. In giving speeches in the south, he will often shift to speaking in the southern Thai dialect.

Chuan gained extensive and diverse political experience at the highest levels of government. Between 1975 and 1990 he held nine different ministerial positions including deputy minister of justice (1975), justice (1980), commerce (1981), agriculture and cooperatives (1982–83, 1990), education (1983–86), and public health (1988). He served as speaker of

## DOMESTIC POLICY

The most serious challenge that faced Chuan when he took office in 1997 was Thailand's economic crisis, the worst since World War II. The crisis was triggered by excessive private sector borrowing abroad (this debt reached approximately US$80 billion) and related non-productive investments, runaway inflation of real estate prices, and problems with the exchange rate. The previous two governments had stubbornly maintained a fixed exchange rate for the baht and the US dollar, even though the value of the dollar was soaring globally. The result was dangerously low international exchange reserves, leading the International Monetary Fund to structure a rigorous set of conditions tied to a US$17 billion bailout of the Thai economy. In late 1997, the Chuan government closed 56 of 58 ailing financial institutions, an act described by the *Bangkok Post* as "decisive, painful, and necessary." The conditions imposed by the IMF in exchange for financial assistance represented Thailand's first loss of economic sovereignty since World War II.

By 1999, the Thai economy was on its way to recovery. The economic stimulus package enacted by the government had positive results during the summer of 1999. The plan focused on business loans, property tax cuts, tariff reductions, and corporate tax relief. By fall, the economy had recovered sufficiently so that the Thailand was able to decline US$3 billion in available loans from the IMF. In December 1999, the government projected that economic statistics for the year would show economic growth at 3–4%.

## FOREIGN POLICY

In presenting his foreign policy statement to Parliament in November 1996, Chuan gave highest priority to Thailand's relations with the nine-member Association of Southeast Asian Nations (ASEAN). In fact, Chuan has had more interactions with ASEAN leaders than any other Thai prime minister. In November 1999, at a meeting in Manila, Philippines, six ASEAN members—Brunei, Indonesia, Malaysia, Philippines, Singapore, and Thailand—agree to establish a free-trade zone in the region by 2010. The remaining four nation members—Cambodia, Laos, Myanmar (Burma), and Vietnam—are expected to join the free-trade zone by 2015.

Chuan also has demonstrated an impressive commitment to human rights. He pushed the other members of ASEAN to agree to include the concept of an open society in the ASEAN Vision 2020 statement. In 1993, despite opposition from his own military leaders, he allowed eight Nobel peace laureates to visit Thailand as part of a campaign aimed at winning the release of Myanmar's opposition leader, Aung San Suu Kyi. Chuan is also committed to working with neighboring nations on joint projects, such as the Mekong Basin Development Project involving Laos, Myanmar (Burma), Yunnan (southern China), and Vietnam. In January 2000, the Thai government agreed to stop sheltering members of the Khmer Rouge (the faction responsible for crimes against humanity in the 1960s, 70s, and 80s that led to as many as 1.7 million deaths). When Khmer Rouge leader Ta Mok was captured in a Thai-Cambodian border region, he asked Thailand for asylum but Thai officials declined to interfere with the Cambodian legal proceeding and refused his request.

Wielding considerable influence in the foreign policy of the Chuan government is Harvard-educated foreign minister, Surin Pitsawan. Surin's Muslim background is expected to enhance Thailand's relations with the Islamic world. He is ably assisted by M.R. Sukumbhand Paribatra, a Chulalongkorn University political science professor.

## ADDRESS

Office of the Prime Minister
Government House
Bangkok, Thailand

## REFERENCES

*Asiaweek*, 21 November 1997.

*Bangkok Post*, 8 November–28 December 1997.

*Far Eastern Economic Review*, 20 November 1997.

Leifer, Michael. *Dictionary of the Modern Politics of Southeast Asia*. London: Routledge, 1995.

*The Nation*, 8 November–15 December 1997.

Office of the Prime Minister, Thailand. [Online] Available http://www.thaigov.go.th/em-prime.htm (Accessed 15 June 2000).

Raengsak Kumthorn. *From Commoner to Prime Minister: A Biography of Chuan Leekpai*. 1992.

Sutichai Yoon. *Political Offensive, Chuan Leekpai Style, Thai Talk*. Bangkok: Nation Publishing Group, 1995.

"Thai PM Signs Agreement in Cambodia." BBC News, 14 June 2000. [Online] Available http://news6.thdo.bbc.co.uk/hi/english/world/asia%2Dpacific/newsid%5F790000/790388.stm (Accessed 14 June 2000).

"Thailand: the Next Test." *The Economist*, 3 July 1999, p. 32.

Win, May Kyi, and Harold E. Smith. *Historical Dictionary of Thailand*. Lanham, MD: Scarecrow Press, 1995.

**Profile researched and written by Gerald W. Fry, University of Oregon (3/98; revised 6/2000).**

# TOGO

### Gnassingbe Eyadema
### President

*(pronounced "nyah-SING-bay ey-YAH-deh-mah")*

*"The tenets of my new five-year term will be maturity, peace, security, reconciliation, and forgiveness."*

The Togolese Republic is a West African country whose political culture reflects its colonial history and the economic roller coaster of post-independence Africa. Situated along a narrow north-south axis, Togo stretches across several ecological zones. It includes 50 km (31 mi) of Atlantic coastline on the Gulf of Benin, a zone of tropical rain forest, and a northern region comprised of semi-arid savannah. Ghana borders Togo to the west, Burkina Faso to the north, and Benin to the east. Its total area is 56,786 sq km (21,925 sq mi)—roughly the size of West Virginia.

The population is estimated at 5 million—though census figures are complicated by the large number of Togolese living in neighboring countries. The capital city of Lome has a population of approximately 800,000.

Togo's population parallels the diversity of its landscape, with some 40 ethno-linguistic groups. The largest group, the Ewe, make up some 40% of the population and reside primarily in the south. The next largest group, the Kabye, represent some 25% of the population and live primarily in the north, though many have migrated south in search of work. Other ethnic groups include the Mina, Cotocoli, and Moba. There are significant numbers of Christians (mostly in the south) and Muslims (in the north) though a majority of the population practice indigenous religions, often blended with elements of Christianity and Islam. The official language is French, used for government, business, and in the schools. Many other languages, such as Ewe and Kabye, are used in daily life.

Togo's economy is largely agricultural, with over 60% of the labor force involved in growing food and export crops (of which cotton and cocoa are the most important). Calcium phosphate and marble are the principal non-agricultural exports. The per capita GDP is estimated at us$1,670. The currency is the CFA *franc*, which is shared with most other former French colonies in Africa.

## POLITICAL BACKGROUND

The Ewes, a tribe of hunters and farmers, moved into the area which is now Togo from the Niger River Valley between 1100 and 1300. During the 15th and 16th centuries Portuguese explorers and traders visited the coastal region, which became a major slave-trading center. As European powers struggled to gain control of overseas territories in the late 19th century, a German diplomat named Gustav Nachtigal signed a treaty with Chief Mlapa III in 1884 that led to the creation of the German protectorate of Togoland. Following the German defeat in World War I, Britain and France divided the colony, which they held under a League of Nations mandate. The British administered the western portion of Togo as part of its Gold Coast colony, while the French retained the east. The division left the Ewe people divided between two different colonies ruled by different European powers, a legacy which has been a source of political tension ever since. In 1956, the UN supervised a plebiscite in British Togoland. Despite vocal Ewe opposition, a majority in that district supported formal union with the Gold Coast colony, which in 1957 became the independent nation of Ghana. French Togoland achieved its own independence on 27 April 1960.

During the campaign for independence, Sylvanus Olympio, a Ewe nationalist, emerged as Togo's most powerful political leader. On 27 April 1960, in a smooth transition, Togo severed its ties with France, shed its UN trusteeship status, and became a fully independent nation with Olympio as its first elected president. On 13 January 1963, Olympio was killed in a military coup led by a young army officer named Gnassingbe Eyadema. The military installed a new civilian government with Nicholas Grunitzky as president. In 1967, the military overthrew Grunitzky and installed Colonel Kleber Dadjo as head of state. Within a few months Eyadema seized power and named himself to the top leadership position. In 1969, Eyadema's government established a party called the *Rassemblement du Peuple Togolaise* (RPT), which integrated the military rulers into civilian roles. In 1972, 1980, and 1993, Eyadema ran for office unopposed.

## PERSONAL BACKGROUND

Gnassingbe Eyadema was born on 26 December 1937, at Pya, in the northern region of Togo. His father was a peasant who died at an early age. Eyadema was raised by his mother and other relatives. Though he enrolled at a mission elementary school, he dropped out to join the French colonial army in neighboring Dahomey (now Benin) in 1953. His military career took him overseas to fight in French colonial wars in Indochina and Algeria. During the course of these campaigns, he rose to the rank of sergeant. He later served in Niger before the French colonial army was demobilized in 1963.

## RISE TO POWER

Eyadema was a central player in the demise of Togo's post-colonial democratic government. In 1963, the demobilized colonial soldiers demanded integration into the Togolese army. When President Olympio refused, his government was overthrown in a military coup. Eyadema was instrumental in planning that coup and is rumored to have personally executed Togo's first head of state. He was immediately promoted and, within two years, attained the rank of lieutenant colonel and chief-of-staff of the armed forces.

As chief-of-staff, Eyadema held considerable power over the civilian government he and his colleagues installed. By 1967, Eyadema had grown dissatisfied with the authoritarian leadership of Grunitzky and overthrew him in a bloodless coup. A new government under Colonel Kleber Dadjo lasted only a few months before Eyadema seized power again—this time for himself.

## LEADERSHIP

As Africa's longest-ruling head of state, Eyadema has proven himself time and again to be a shrewd and often brutal political pragmatist. He rose to power as a populist leader whose main base of support lay with the army and Togo's more northern ethnic groups. Eyadema's popular image has been enhanced by his survival of several assassination attempts and one plane crash. He has also promoted a cult of personality in which his image is found in all public places and on lapel badges worn by all civil servants. From the mid-1970s, Eyadema initiated a national program of cultural "authenticity" in which foreign toponyms were abandoned in favor of African names, and the languages of Ewe and Kabiye were encouraged to replace French as the language of education and cultural life.

Shortly after seizing power, Eyadema suspended the constitution, abolished all opposition parties, and dissolved the National Assembly. From 1969 to 1992, opposition voices were suppressed. The central government maintains tight control of all media, including the only television station. Opposition to Eyadema's government has been fierce and is increasingly well organized. In 1985, for example, a wave of bombings rocked the capital of Lome. In 1986, armed dissidents invaded from Ghana and attempted to overthrow the Eyadema government. French paratroopers and troops from Zaire helped Eyadema maintain his hold on power. The RPT government responded to these attacks with a wave of arrests. Many defendants were tried and sentenced to death. In addition, Eyadema took steps to improve his own personal security. Outside observers, particularly Amnesty International, accused the Eyadema government of using torture and murder as a means of suppressing political discontent. Such condemnation, in addition to continued internal dissent, helped pressure Eyadema to undertake a series of reforms that hinted at eventual democratization. In particular, Eyadema appointed a commission on human rights and extended amnesty to many members of the opposition—including those jailed in the 1986 coup attempt.

In 1990, the RPT met to consider party reforms. A multi-party system was rejected, but calls for greater freedom of expression were voiced. In 1991, following a wave of protest that included demonstrations and a general strike, Eyadema agreed to a national conference that would include members of the opposition. Opening in July of 1991, the conference immediately took an aggressive stand against Eyadema's government—declaring itself sovereign and drafting an

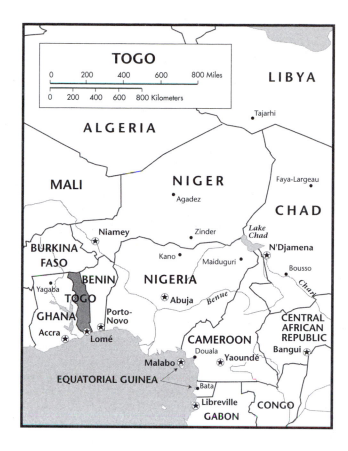

interim constitution. The conference also named a "transitional government" and elected Kokou Joseph Koffigoh as "transitional prime minister." Eyadema responded by using troops and security forces to harass the opposition. Following an attempt by the transitional legislature to ban the RPT, Eyadema ordered troops to seize Koffigoh and force him to form a transitional government more friendly to the RPT. Other opposition leaders were treated more harshly. Gilchrist Olympio (son of the slain president) was ambushed and wounded by armed assailants in May of 1992, and Tavio Amorin was assassinated in July. In October, the military seized and shut down the interim legislature, and Eyadema soon declared the transition process to be finished. Another wave of strikes and protests ensued, and on 25 January 1993, French and German diplomats witnessed security forces fire on peaceful demonstrators in Lome, killing at least 19. Eventually, Eyadema agreed to hold multi-party legislative and presidential elections. Disputes led to a boycott by opposition candidates, and Eyadema ran once again unopposed. On 25 August 1993, he was elected with 96% of the vote. Eyadema survived another coup attempt by Ghana-based dissidents in January of 1994.

Legislative elections were held the following month and were generally considered to be free and fair. Eyadema threw the opposition into turmoil by selecting Edem Kodjo as prime minister, despite the fact that Kodjo was a member of one of the least powerful opposition parties. Over the next several years, Eyadema slowly increased the representation of his RPT party in the government.

Presidential elections in 1998 introduced a semblance of multi-party democracy. Six candidates contested the presidency, and opposition members were even allowed to make brief statements on RPT-controlled state TV. The sudden resignation by chief members of the National Electoral Commission, particularly chairwoman Awa Nana, during the counting of returns shook both national and international confidence in the vote. The NEC members alleged that they had received death threats. Eyadema's own internal security minister took over the count and declared Eyadema to be the victor with 52% of the vote—just enough to avoid a run-off with Gilchrist Olympio, who was said to have garnered some 30% of the vote. Riots ensued, and the headquarters of Olympio's *Comite d'Action pour le Renouveau* party was burned when police broke in to "restore order." Despite condemnation by international observers, Eyadema hailed the elections as "free and fair" and a popular mandate for his continued rule. However, his dominance would not go unchallenged.

Eyadema tightened his grip on power in March 1999 when his party, the RPT, captured 77 of 81 seats in the National Assembly. The government claimed that 66% of eligible voters participated in the elections, but opposition parties, which called for a boycott, said only 10% voted. The main opposition party, the Union des forces de changement (Union of the Forces of Change or UFC), led by Gilchrist Olympio, called for a boycott to pressure the government to hold new presidential elections.

In May, the opposition called for a one-day stay-at-home campaign that was moderately successful. In the same month, European mediators arrived in Togo to discuss ways to lift the political impasse. French President Jacques Chirac visited Togo during the negotiations in July and pressured Eyadema to find a solution. The government agreed to hold new parliamentary elections sometime in 2000, which will be overseen by a newly independent electoral commission.

During negotiations, the government was embarrassed by a new report published by a Benin-based human rights group, which said Togo's troops executed hundreds of opponents during the 1998 presidential elections. That report confirmed findings by Amnesty International that leveled similar accusations earlier in the year. In its 45-page report, Amnesty International said political opponents were detained without trial, tortured, and hundreds were executed by security forces both before and after the elections. The group said bodies of victims, some handcuffed, washed ashore on the beaches of Togo and Benin. Eyadema's government reacted angrily to the report and threatened to sue Amnesty International, claiming the group fabricated a "pack of lies." The government arrested and later released Togo human rights workers who allegedly had provided the information to Amnesty.

Ultimately, after 10 days of negotiations with opposition parties in July, Eyadema agreed he would not run for re-election in 2003, ending one of the longest periods of rule by an African leader.

## DOMESTIC POLICY

Eyadema maintains a strong grip on the military (most members of which hail from his own northern region), and

continues to show a willingness to use force to maintain his hold on power.

Economically, Eyadema has attempted to expand the export economy. Restrictions on foreign investment have been eased, and an Export Processing Zone has been established in the south. Attempts have also been made to improve returns from tourism. Any true economic progress, though, will be endangered if political stability is not somehow achieved—particularly with Western donor nations threatening to withhold much-needed economic aid. The devaluation of the CFA in 1994 has continued to place hardships on Togo's middle class.

## FOREIGN POLICY

Despite Eyadema's authoritarian rule, Togo maintained good relations with most Western powers until the early 1990s—frequently advertising its "pro-Western market economy." With the end of the Cold War, former supporters have grown increasingly displeased with Eyadema's unwillingness to step down or even share power. Indeed, the widespread use of force against his opposition from 1991 to the present has led the US, the EU, and even France (traditionally Eyadema's closest ally) to suspend foreign aid. The controversy over the 1998 elections, for example, has led the EU to withhold a much needed US$50 million loan. Further sanctions have been threatened.

Togo has generally enjoyed positive relations with other African states—with the exception of Ghana, which Eyadema has frequently accused of sponsoring coups. Indeed, opposition leader Gilchrist Olympio has lived in exile in Ghana since 1982. When Mobutu Sese Seko, the former ruler of Zaire, was driven from power in 1997, Eyadema lost a valuable ally. Mobutu fled to Togo from Zaire (since renamed the Democratic Republic of Congo), but Eyadema allowed him to remain in his country for less than a week.

Togo maintains membership in the UN, the Economic Community of West African States (ECOWAS), and the Organization of African Unity (OAU).

## ADDRESS

President de la Republique
Lome, Togo

## REFERENCES
Africa News. [Online] Available http://www.africanews.org
*Africa South of the Sahara,* 1994
CIA World Factbook. [Online] Available http://www/pdco/gpv/cia/publications/factbook/to.html
*Deutsche Presse-Agentur,* 4 July 1998.
*The Economist,* 4 July 1998.
*Economist Intelligence Unit: Togo and Benin,* 1994.
Piraux, M. *Le Togo aujourd'hui.* Paris: 1977.
Togo Home Page. [Online] Available http://www.africa.com/togo
US Department of State. *Background Notes: Togo.* June 1996
*Washington Post,* 25 June 1998.
*Washington Times,* 5 July 1998

**Profile researched and written by Jonathan T. Reynolds, Livingstone College (12/98; updated 2/00).**

# TONGA

## Taufa'ahau Tupou IV
## King

*(pronounced "TOW-fa-ah-how TOO-po")*

*"It is difficult for anybody to know what will happen in the future, but there are problems because it is difficult to control a democratic government."*

The Kingdom of Tonga is a small Polynesian kingdom located in the central South Pacific consisting of 160 islands with a total land area of 748 sq km (289 sq mi). Tonga's neighbors include Western Samoa to the north, Fiji to the northwest, and New Zealand to the south. Recent archaeological evidence indicates that the Tongans were associated with a *lapita* (a type of pottery) culture group originating out of Southeast Asia. Slowly migrating eastward through Melanesia, these peoples settled in Tonga around 1000 BC. Contemporary Tongan society, often characterized as deeply religious and traditionally conservative, is largely composed of semi-subsistent farmers and noble elite. Tonga's population is estimated at 109,000. Approximately 95% of the population are practicing Christians. The per capita GNP averages about US$2,100. The unit of currency is the *pa'anga*.

As in all Polynesian cultures, kinship and collectivism predominate. Even today, groups based on kinship are often formed to carry out activities. Similarly, many valued possessions are corporately owned. Women command a strong position in Tongan society, and many tasks are shared between the sexes.

Agriculture is the mainstay of the Tongan economy. Nearly 50% of the GNP and more than 60% of the active wage labor force originate in this sector. Although manufacturing and tourism are on the increase, partly due to government efforts to diversify the economic base, the bulk of Tongan exports are agricultural. These include copra, coconut oil, bananas, melons, vanilla beans, and vegetables.

## POLITICAL BACKGROUND

Renowned for its highly stratified, ascribed status society, consisting of king, chief, and commoner classes, Tonga established an elaborate political structure long before European contact in the 18th century. By 1835, after a period of political unrest and civil wars between the various clans, a chief named Taufa'ahau emerged as the dominant leader. He eventually became King Tupou I, Tonga's first modern ruler, and in 1875, established Tonga as a constitutional monarchy.

Although Tonga distinguishes itself as the only Pacific island nation never to have been colonized, in 1899, at the invitation of King Tupou II, Tonga became a British protectorate, and all foreign affairs were transacted through the UK. Full independence was restored in 1970.

Tonga's political structure today has changed little since its inception in 1875. It still consists of three bodies: the Executive Council, the Legislative Assembly (parliament),

and the Judiciary, with the king exercising wide influence over all three. The Executive Council is comprised of the king, the Privy Council, and the Cabinet. When the king presides, the Cabinet becomes the Privy Council. The Monarch, His Royal Highness Taufa'ahau Tupou IV, personally appoints the members of Cabinet without election or public involvement. This includes Tonga's two governors and 10 Ministers of the Crown. All Cabinet members also act as heads of government ministries, and ministers maintain their positions until retirement. The prime minister of Tonga is the king's younger brother, Prince Tu'ipelehake.

The Legislative Assembly, traditionally the government's debating chamber, consists of only one house that meets annually. Sessions last three to five months and are opened and closed by the king. Parliament is comprised of the speaker, who is selected by the king, the 11 appointed Cabinet members, nine noble's representatives (elected by the 33 nobles of the realm), and nine people's representatives (elected by the commoners.) There are no political parties. Unlike other constitutional monarchies, Tonga's king is not a figurehead. He has absolute veto power over any laws put forth by parliament.

## PERSONAL BACKGROUND

Taufa'ahau Tupou IV is the direct descendant of King George Tupou I. He was born on 4 July 1918, and was christened Crown Prince Siaosi Taufa'ahau Tupoulahi. Tupou received his early education in Tonga where he was both an outstanding student and sportsman. He then attended secondary school at Newington College in Australia and received his bachelor of arts and bachelor of laws degrees from the University of Sydney. He was the first Tongan citizen to receive a university degree. In 1947, he married Halaevalu Mata'aho, the daughter of the noble 'Ahome'e. They have three sons and a daughter.

## RISE TO POWER

Shortly after his return from studies in Australia, Taufa'ahau was appointed to the Cabinet as the Minister of Education. A year and a half later, the portfolio of Minister of Health was added to his duties. He held these two portfolios until December, 1949, when he became Premier of the Kingdom, combined with the portfolios of Education, Agriculture, and Foreign Affairs. In 1962, the portfolio of Works was added to his many duties.

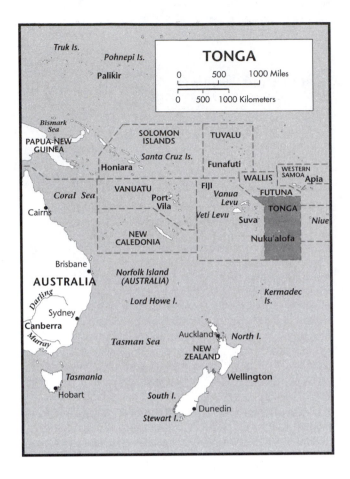

During the 16 years that the Crown Prince was appointed premier, Tonga underwent a number of important economic and social changes. One of his earliest aims was to improve the standard of education in the kingdom, and he was the moving force behind the establishment of Tonga's Teacher Training College and Tonga High School. Today, Tonga has one of the highest literacy rates in the Pacific Basin region.

Taufa'ahau was also instrumental in developing Tonga's agricultural sector via the establishment of a number of boards and councils whose duties were to facilitate the handling and marketing of Tongan produce locally and regionally. The Tongan Broadcasting Commission, the International Dateline Hotel, Queen Salote Wharf and the government newspaper, the *Tongan Chronicle*, were all established under the Crown Prince's leadership. Because of these many achievements, the British accorded him a Commander of the Order of the British Empire and a Knight of the British Empire in 1951 and 1958 respectively.

## LEADERSHIP

In 1965, Her Highness Queen Salote Tupou III died. Two years later, on 4 July 1967, after a year of mourning and another year of preparation, Crown Prince Taufa'ahau Tupou IV was crowned King of Tonga in the Royal Chapel in Nuku'alofa, the capital of Tonga.

As Tonga entered the 21st century, its political stability was threatened by a number of growing problems. These include an increasing national debt; overpopulation; limited land resources; high under- and unemployment; decreasing productivity in the primary sector; and an heightened awareness by the majority of citizens of Tonga's socio-political and economic imbalances.

Cognizant that Tonga must come to grips with its socio-economic problems in order to maintain an independent state, Tupou IV's reign has been marked by concerted efforts to meet these challenges and bring Tonga up-to-date with the 21st century. Tupou IV has encouraged the diversification of the economic base, the development of basic infrastructures, and the strengthening of Tonga's position regionally. Over the last 20 years, a Development Bank has been established, and several loan schemes for new entrepreneurs have been initiated. Foreigners, with their capital and business acumen, are now encouraged to settle in Tonga as never before in its history.

Although the King is also aware that additional political reforms must be introduced for the monarchy to survive, Tongan monarchs historically have been reluctant to tamper with the foundations of the political structure. This is because they fear that once such reforms are underway, there may be no end to them until they eventually overwhelm and terminate the monarchical structure. The political changes most recently introduced have only been piecemeal, delaying actions that effectively keep ultimate power (especially on matters concerning land allocation) in the hands of the traditional elite.

Fortunately, the demand for far-reaching structural changes in the political system has not yet arisen. This is in large part due to a combination of factors including emigration, remittances, and a genuine affection for and strong national pride in Tonga's monarchy. But Tupou IV, perhaps more than any of his ancestors, may find himself forced to initiate reform precisely because of his own liberalism in allowing other influential changes to filter into the Kingdom. Such reforms could include the creation of political parties, an increase in political influence in parliament, the readjustment of parliamentary participation, or more radically, the abolition of the formal legal elements of the noble system. Commoners are already demanding increased opportunities for political participation.

Although Tonga is going through a period of upheaval and change, Tongans are very protective of their political independence and their Monarch, and with good reason, having witnessed the plight of other Pacific Islanders in the wake of foreign encroachment. The majority of Tongan citizens still appear to have an abiding affection for their Monarch, although a growing ambivalence surrounds Tonga's nobles, who often serve as convenient scapegoats for Tupou IV. Like his great-grandfather, this King appears to be a master at playing both sides of the fence: appeasing the nobles while simultaneously attending to the needs of the commoners. He is a religious man who does not, for instance, have an opulent lifestyle. He does not rule by force but by reason and suggestion, apparently willing to change his position on specific matters if public support is not forthcoming. This occurred recently when the public strongly contested the construction of a waste treatment plant Tupou IV supported. Eventually, plans for the plant were withdrawn.

## DOMESTIC POLICY

Tonga is at a crossroads in its history as never before. Land reform issues, for instance, are a recurrent theme; because of a growing population and finite land mass, many persons legally entitled to land can no longer obtain it. This situation is further aggravated by the tendency of some nobles to take advantage of their status by leasing out estate land to those who would be undeserving according to Tongan law. To date, little progress has been made on land reform, though Tupou IV has set an example by dividing his 'api (land) allotments in half, thus allowing the redistribution of more land to the commoners. Unfortunately, few other members of the traditional elite have followed suit.

The King has been criticized, however, as one who is ready to jump on the bandwagon of any scheme that might prove profitable for the Kingdom. He promoted tourism with great enthusiasm, touting it as Tonga's salvation from economic impoverishment and underemployment, though little came of it. Through the years, a variety of other, perhaps less realistic schemes have been considered and sometimes pursued: Tonga as a duty-free port, a tax shelter, a Pacific Monte Carlo. More recently, administrative emphasis has been placed on manufacturing and export industries. Meanwhile, until the government strikes it rich, projects in the agricultural sector are kept afloat to buoy the balance of trade and keep the Tongan people fed and occupied. Subsistence activities, kingship networks and overseas remittances (which are steadily increasing) are not discouraged since they ensure that the social welfare of the Tongan people will be provided for while the government continues to look for Tonga's lucky break.

In January 1999, Tonga's cabinet approved budget guidelines to help the economy recover from the 1998 depression. With gross domestic product and foreign reserve figures continuing to drop, the government said Tonga was facing an alarming situation as the budget deficit continued to grow. According to government figures, the GDP fell by 4.4% in the 1996–97 financial year and another 1.5% in the 1997–98 fiscal year. Pro-democracy supporters said the government needed to cut spending to help revive the economy. Some other measures that were proposed included privatizing some government services, including the post office, government stores, and the government newspaper, and offering early retirement to government employees. Despite the growing deficit, the kingdom kept inflation under control. The average inflation rate for 12 months ending in April 1999 stood at 4.1%.

The Tonga Visitors Bureau reported that tourism earnings decreased in 1998, even though there was a slight increase in visitors. In 1998, 27,000 people visited Tonga, an increase of 970 visitors from 1997. But earnings dropped significantly, from $7.65 million in 1997 to only $2.17 million in 1998. The government hoped Millenium celebrations would boost tourism in the island.

## FOREIGN POLICY

Though staunchly anti-Communist, the King encourages the practice of tolerance and political nonalignment with all nations regionally and internationally. This is an astute stance on Tupou IV's part. Because the Kingdom was never colonized like its Pacific neighbors, and thus does not benefit (or suffer) from financial assistance from one donor nation, Tonga must rely on piecemeal assistance from whatever source is available. Over the years, the King has negotiated with government and private parties from the US, New Zealand, Japan, Australia, India, Germany, Saudi Arabia, Russia, France, Sweden, Libya, the UK, and China. Several negotiations, particularly with Japanese and German businessmen, have led to long term friendships, business, investments, gifts of aid, or equipment. Where some negotiations have resulted in suspect deals and losses for the Kingdom, others have given the King additional leverage in aid requests. The courting of the Soviets, whether intended or not, attracted concern and notice from New Zealand, Australia, the UK, and the US. Although this can be a dangerous game politically, the King has been fairly successful to the extent that he has secured funds for many projects without politically alienating any one country.

In 1998, Tonga established diplomatic relations with China, ending a 26-year relation with Taiwan and securing the unopposed endorsement of the United Nations (UN) Security Council, where China has a veto. A UN Security Council committee recommended Tonga's admittance to the UN in July 1999.

In November 1999, Tonga joined seven other Pacific island nations to criticize worldwide lack of action to reduce greenhouse gas emissions and help vulnerable nations adapt to climate changes. The eight nations held a press conference in Bonn, Germany, described damages already being felt in their nations, and said it was time to stop global warming before problems grew worse.

## ADDRESS

The Palace
PO Box 6
Nuku'alofa, Tonga

## REFERENCES
Development in the Kingdom of Tonga. May 1986.

Honolulu Star Bulletin, 12 February 1990.

Marcus, George, E. Power on the Extreme Periphery: The Perspective of Tongan Elites on the Modern World System. 1980.

Pacific Islands Monthly, various issues.

Ritterbush, S. Deacon. Entrepreneurship and Business Venture.

Taulahi, Amanaki. His Majesty King Taufa'ahau Tupou IV of the Kingdom of Tonga. Fiji: Institute of Pacific Studies, 1979.

**Profile researched and written by Deacon Ritterbush (7/90; revised 5/2000).**

# TRINIDAD AND TOBAGO

**Basdeo Panday**
**Prime Minister**

*(pronounced "BAHZ-day-o PAN-day")*

*"I assure you there is nothing we cannot do, if we do it together. If only we could unite as one people, the difficult we shall do immediately, the impossible will take a little while longer."*

The Republic of Trinidad and Tobago lies in the southern Caribbean just off the coast of Venezuela. The total area of Trinidad and Tobago is 5,128 sq km (1,980 sq mi). The population is estimated at 1.1 million, divided between the African descendants of slaves (40%) and East Indian descendants of indentured laborers (40.3%). European, Chinese, Syrian, Lebanese and mixed races comprise the rest of the population. The population is predominantly Roman Catholic (32%), Hindu (24.3%), and Anglican (14%), with smaller groups of various Protestant sects and Muslims. English is the official language of the country. Trinidad and Tobago, which has a per capita GDP of US$8,000, is one of the most industrialized Caribbean countries. Its economy is based primarily on petroleum and petroleum products. Industries include petrochemicals, methanol, and iron and steel. Sugar is the main agricultural export. The unit of currency is the Trinidad and Tobago dollar.

## POLITICAL BACKGROUND

The larger of the two islands, Trinidad, was captured by the British from Spain in 1797. The smaller island, Tobago, was disputed by the Dutch, French, and English until it was ceded to the British in 1814. The islands were administratively joined in 1888. Trinidad and Tobago became self-governing in 1956 and gained its independence from Britain in 1962. In 1976, they became a Republic within the British Commonwealth. Trinidad and Tobago has a parliamentary system patterned along the lines of the British Westminster system. General elections are held every five years. The prime minister is the leader of the party that has the majority of parliamentary seats. The president is the head of state and performs mainly ceremonial and procedural duties. Trinidad and Tobago is a multi-party state, but from independence to 1986 the Afrocentric People's National Movement (PNM) dominated. In 1986, an ethnically heterogeneous alliance, the National Alliance for Reconstruction (NAR), was voted into power by a populace seeking change. The NAR Alliance collapsed, however, and a segment formed the East Indian-based United National Congress (UNC). A revitalized PNM returned to power in 1991. In 1995, an early election vote produced a 17–17 stalemate in parliamentary seats between the two main parties, the PNM and the UNC. The NAR itself won its two traditional seats in Tobago and joined with the UNC in the country's first coalition government. This is also the country's first East Indian-led government.

## PERSONAL BACKGROUND

Basdeo Panday was born in the small southern town of Princes Town, Trinidad, on 25 May 1933. He graduated from Presentation College (high school) in San Fernando in 1951 and worked as a cane weigher, primary school teacher, and a civil servant before going to the United Kingdom to further his studies. He obtained a diploma in drama from the London School of Dramatic Arts in 1960, a law degree from Lincoln's Inn in 1962, and a B.S. in economics from London University in 1965. His legal career has mainly been in the field of labor law. In the 1970s, he served as legal adviser to the powerful Oilfield Workers Trade Union and to the sugar union-linked Association of Technical, Administrative, and Supervisory Staff. He also practiced law privately. He is married to Oma (former Ramkissoon) and has four daughters.

## RISE TO POWER

Panday's political career has been a story of dogged perseverance in a country marked since independence by political polarization along ethnic lines. Although Panday's early militant union activism crossed racial lines, his political base of support has been concentrated in the rural East Indian communities of south and central Trinidad. In the West Indies, unionist and political activism have often been intertwined, and Panday's career reflects both these influences. In the 1960s and 1970s, he was active on behalf of sugar and oil workers and was jailed a few times for organizing protests. Politically, he first joined the small short-lived Workers and Farmers Party in 1966, a vehicle for common labor-oriented action. His political involvement continued in 1971, when he participated in an opposition boycott of the general elections. At the time, a breakaway faction of the dominant but stagnating PNM had joined with a faction of the traditional East Indian opposition Democratic Labor Party (DLP) to pressure the government to change the system of voting by machine (perceived as rigged), and denial of the vote to 18-year olds. The opposition boycott facilitated total PNM parliamentary dominance and led to the marginalization of the DLP. The resulting vacuum in East Indian political participation was eventually filled by Panday in 1976, when he formed the United Labor Front (ULF). Despite a leadership struggle, the ULF emerged as a political force by winning 10 seats in the 1976 elections. Panday became the leader of the opposition in parliament, a position he held for the next 10 years. Meanwhile he continued his unionism, becoming head of the sugar union and retaining that position until 1995. In the 1980s, the popularity of the PNM waned as it lost its charismatic post-independence leader, Dr. Eric Williams, and became mired in successive corruption scandals. Moreover, the oil boom of the mid-1970s had given way to economic austerity. Conscious of his limited ethnic and geographical base of support, Panday merged his party in 1986 with a new urban middle-class party, the Organization for National Reconstruction (ONR). He had previously merged as well with two small parties, the socialistic Tapia House Movement and the Democratic Action Congress (DAC) based in disaffected Tobago. The merged grouping, the NAR, came to power in 1986, riding a wave of popular dissatisfaction with government and desire for change. Panday became minister of external affairs and international trade. Within two years, however, the ULF segment of the NAR found itself in disagreement with NAR's micromanagerial policies and unhappy with its relative lack of influence within the merged group. Panday was removed as external affairs minister in 1988 and was eventually expelled from the NAR. In the same year, he formed the Club 88, which became a full-fledged party, the United National Congress (UNC), in October. By 1990, defections from the NAR to the UNC allowed Panday to reclaim the role of official leader of the opposition from the PNM, which then held only three parliamentary seats. In 1991, the PNM was returned to power by a populace tired of the NAR's harsh austerity measures. However, once in power the new-look PNM continued the structural adjustment program, and also alienated the grassroots segments that were its traditional support base. At the same time, the UNC had tried to broaden its base by incorporating a few African elements into its primarily East Indian leadership. Demographically, the East Indian population was by then in the majority in Trinidad and Tobago, and was also somewhat less geographically concentrated than before. A highly mobilized UNC was therefore ready for the polls when a snap election was called by a too-confident PNM in November 1995. The result was a political stalemate that was brokered by the UNC's former ally, the NAR, which won its two traditional (former DAC) seats in Tobago. After two decades in opposition politics, Panday finally assumed the reins of leadership. Shortly after assuming power, Panday's government succeeded in bringing two opposition members of parliament into the UNC, so that Panday no longer needed to rely on the NAR to govern. This in turn led to increased tension between the Prime Minister and the President, NAR leader, Arthur Robinson.

## LEADERSHIP

As the country's first prime minister of East Indian descent, Panday has the exceptionally strong support of the East Indian community, as well as the Hindu, Muslim and Presbyterian communities. However, despite his alliance with the NAR, his support among the African segment is extremely weak. In particular, given his rural base, a major challenge is how to appease the urban, modernized sectors while rewarding his neglected rural base. Urban and non-Indian fears of loss of influence have to be allayed. To this end, Panday has stressed the theme of national unity, taking pains to note that his government is a government of all the people. However, early grumblings were heard with respect to the distribution of ministerial and cabinet posts, and the attempt by the government to place UNC loyalists on key state boards. Another source of dissatisfaction centered on the government's per-

ceived accommodation with the Jamaat-al-Muslimeen, Islamic adherents who laid siege to the parliament in 1990. The Muslimeen have openly supported the new government but the extent of the alliance remains unclear. In another area, Panday's links with and electoral financing from key business people have raised concerns about pork barrel politics and generated skepticism among the labor unions whose expectations were initially raised by Panday's victory. Again, the new government's honeymoon period ended rather quickly when Panday attempted to rein in criticism from the press. The ensuing uproar in a country that prides itself on its free press led the prime minister to back down temporarily, but the issue of ensuring responsible journalism apparently remains high on the government's agenda. Another leadership issue is Panday's closeness to his attorney-general, a human rights activist and lawyer seen as too sympathetic to criminals and drug offenders. The situation has generated uneasiness in significant sectors of the populace. Finally, Panday's electoral campaign and early days in office have been dominated by ethnic considerations rather than issues. As the ethnic issue becomes less remarkable, social and economic concerns are bound to reemerge. Skepticism is being expressed as to the ability of the government to carry out popularly desired social reform in view of international constraints, limited resources, and the need to redistribute revenue in favor of the rural sectors. Panday has attempted to reach out, however, to traditional PNM voters since assuming power in 1996. The success of this attempt is reflected in an estimated 15% increase in support from this segment of the electorate in April 2000.

## DOMESTIC POLICY

The new government has inherited an improved economy. Real GDP grew by 3.5% in 1995. It also grew an estimated

4.3% in 1998 est. Plans are to continue the basic development thrust but with a more people-centered approach and a consensual decision-making strategy that would involve a partnership between government, business and labor. Energy remains the centerpiece of the economy. The sector contributes 27.9% to total GDP and 68% of foreign exchange earnings. The government plans to concentrate on increasing oil production while monetizing gas reserves and will continue a variety of major industrial projects. In the other major sector of the economy, agriculture, the stated aim is domestic food and nutrition security. Agricultural diversification and sustainable management of natural resources are priorities. The government hopes to continue to attract foreign investment and has announced plans to streamline investment procedures. Encouraging business investment and improving the efficiency of the business sector are stated goals. To this end, corporate taxes have been lowered and small business financing is expected to be increased. Lastly, tourism development is envisaged, mainly through information enhancements, some resort development, and encouragement of convention and events-type tourism. Socially, two areas are being given attention. Poverty alleviation is important in a country where the poor are now estimated at 21% of the population. Some fiscal measures were introduced in the first budget presentation of the new government, including income tax relief and removal of value-added taxes and import duties on basic food items. In the other key social area, crime prevention, an area which has posed intractable problems for successive governments, the new government is focusing on community involvement and legislative and judicial reform. A university-level task force on the subject, supported by the government, has recommended various community-oriented measures as well as training and administrative initiatives. A central aspect of crime policy is drug interdiction. Trinidad and Tobago has become a regionally significant drug transshipment center and attempts to bring drug lords to justice have often been thwarted by the disappearance or murder of witnesses. The government is working with the US to hone investigation techniques and develop a more substantial witness-protection program. Despite its labor-oriented base, the new government is likely to continue adjustment policies. Because of the high level of subsidy to the public sector, reductions are likely in that segment of the labor force. Some diversion of capital expenditure from urban to rural areas is expected. In this respect, early casualties were plans for certain urban-based cultural projects, including construction of a much-heralded National Library Complex.

## FOREIGN POLICY

In terms of foreign policy, the new government has articulated support for regionalism including commitment to tariff reductions mandated by the Caribbean Community (CARICOM) and support for the Association of Caribbean States (ACS) headquartered in Trinidad. The ACS was formed in 1994 to bring together the states of the Caribbean Basin, both island and mainland. The government applied in 1997 for entrance into the North American Free Trade Area (NAFTA). Also on the agenda are initiatives to enhance cooperation with Mercosur (Latin American countries in the southern cone) and other Latin American countries. Bilateral negotiation of outstanding marine disputes with Venezuela is continuing. Finally, anti-narcotic cooperation with the US has been affirmed.

## OFFICE OF THE PRIME MINISTER
Central Bank Building
Eric Williams Plaza
Independence Square
Port-of-Spain

## REFERENCES
Caribbean Development Bank. *Annual Report 1994*. St. Michael, Barbados: CDB, 1995.

Trinidad and Tobago Central Statistical Office. *Statistics at a Glance 1994*. Port-of-Spain: Central Statistical Printing Unit, August 1995.

Trinidad and Tobago House of Representatives. *Budget Statement 1996*.

Trinidad and Tobago Ministry of Information. *Profile of Prime Minister Basdeo Panday*.

**Profile researched and written by Jacqueline Anne Braveboy-Wagner, The Graduate School of the City University of New York (2/96; revised by John Ranahan 4/2000)**

# TUNISIA

## Zine El Abidine Ben Ali
## President

(pronounced "ZIN-ah el ah-bih-DIN-ah ben AH-lee")

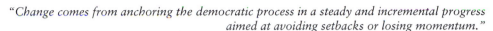

*"Change comes from anchoring the democratic process in a steady and incremental progress aimed at avoiding setbacks or losing momentum."*

The Republic of Tunisia is located on the Mediterranean shores of North Africa between Algeria on the west and Libya on the east. It has an area of 163,610 sq km (63,170 sq mi) and a population of 9.5 million, most of whom are Arabs. The population growth rate is 1.39%, one of the lowest in the Arab world. The religion of 98% of the population is Islam. Tunisia's national language is Arabic, but French is widely used and is the language in which business is transacted. The country is predominantly urban with two-thirds of its land area consisting of desert or high, arid plains. Tunisia's per capita income is US$5,200 with a GDP of US$49 billion. The currency unit is the *dinar*. Tunisia exports crude oil, textiles, phosphates and olive oil. Other important sources of foreign exchange are a very developed tourist infrastructure and emigrant workers' remittances.

## POLITICAL BACKGROUND
According to the 1959 and revised 1991 constitutions, Tunisia is a republic in which power is shared by a strong president who is elected for five years (except for Habib Bourguiba who nominated himself for life), and a unicameral legislative body, the National Assembly, whose members are directly elected for a five-year term. The president nominates a prime minister who is responsible to him; he can dissolve the National Assembly and call for new elections. He is both head of government and head of state and is an important initiator of legislation.

Since Tunisia's independence in 1956 from France, until 1987, the Tunisian political system was dominated by former President Habib Bourguiba, a heroic nationalist leader, and his Neo-Destour Party (changed to Destourian Socialist Party, PSD, in 1964). Under 31 years of Bourguiba's presidency, Tunisian politics alternated between one-man authoritarianism and relative liberalism with only one party in power. In December 1974 the National Assembly, controlled by the PSD, made Bourguiba president-for-life. Multi-partyism was then a remote possibility and the system moved toward stagnation and intolerance of opposition.

By the mid-1970s, opposition movements started to form at home and abroad to oppose the rule of the aging president and his prime minister, Hedi Nouira. The *Movement for Popular Unity* (MUP), led by Ahmed Ben Salah (former Minister of Agriculture) was formed in Europe, and former Minister of Interior Ahmed Mestiri created the *Movement of Social Democrats* (MSD). Both were banned in Tunisia and many of their sympathizers were arrested. More important

challenges came from the General Union of Tunisian Workers (UGTT) and Islamic fundamentalist groups. The labor confederation organized a major strike in January 1978 which was followed by street rioting across Tunisia. In retaliation, the army killed around one hundred people, arrested hundreds more, including the Labor leader Habib Achour. The Islamists, led by *Le Movement de la Tendance Islamic* (MTI) expressed its first challenges, both verbally and with violence, by the late 1970s, which resulted in the arrest of its leaders.

As the political and economic situation continued to erode, the Tunisian regime moved by the early 1980s toward the liberalization of the system by accepting independent candidates in elections and by releasing political prisoners. Opposition parties such as the MSD, the MUP and the Communist Party, PCT, were recognized. Only the Islamist group, MTI, was not given legal recognition. However, all these parties were too weak to compete with, or unseat, the PSD, which maintained its dominant position. New nationwide rioting took place in 1983 and 1984 after the announcement of an increase in the price of semolina and bread and other economic austerity measures. Many people were killed and many more arrested by the governmental forces. Bourguiba, who was then 81 years old, finally reversed the price increase decision and calm temporarily returned. It was in this context that the current president of Tunisia rose to power and overthrew Bourguiba with a bloodless coup on 1 November 1987.

## PERSONAL BACKGROUND
President Zine El Abidine Ben Ali was born on 3 September 1936 in Hammam Sousse. In Tunis, he pursued studies in electrical engineering. Before becoming president he held several state offices, notably that of director of Military Security (for 16 years), Secretary of State for National Security, and Minister of National Security. He received degrees from the French military academy of Saint Cyr and the French artillery school of Chalons sur Marne. He also trained in the US Army's School of Field and Anti-Aircraft Artillery in Texas and, at Ft. Holabird, Maryland, where he completed a course on intelligence and military security.

He started his career in 1958 as director of Military Security. After an alleged disagreement with Bourguiba, he was sent in 1974 to Morocco as military attaché, and to Poland in 1980 as ambassador. However, in the wake of the 1983–84 bread riots in Tunisia, he was recalled and made

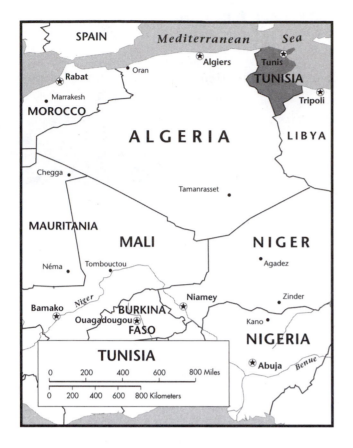

head of National Security. That was the beginning of his very rapid rise to power.

## RISE TO POWER

A few months after his return, he became Secretary of State for National Security; he was then named Minister of National Security in October 1985, and Minister of Interior in April 1986. In that same year he was made under-secretary general of the DSP party. The final appointment under Bourguiba came on 2 October 1987 when he was appointed prime minister and secretary general of the party.

According to Article 57 of the 1959 Tunisian constitution then in effect, the prime minister was to assume the presidency in case of death, resignation or permanent inability of the president. Using this provision, Ben Ali deposed Bourguiba on 7 November 1987. The former president, who was 84, was judged by most people as having become mentally unstable, senile, erratic and more dictatorial than ever. His ouster was, therefore, almost unanimously welcomed by the Tunisians.

Since taking power in 1987, Ben Ali has run for president three times. After his first election he pushed through amendments to the constitution that made the president of the National Assembly, rather than the prime minister, the successor to a president unable to continue in office. Furthermore, that individual would then be precluded from running for the office in new elections, thus precluding the route to power that he had used. In the first two elections, in 1989 and 1994, he ran unopposed. In the 1999 elections he faced two opponents, Mohamed Belhaj Amor of the (socialist) Party of People's Unity, who garnered 0.3% of the

votes and Abderrahmane Tlili of the (Arab nationalist) Unionist Democratic Union, who received 0.2% of the votes. Two other potential candidates were arrested after announcing their intention to run: Abderrahmane el-Hani, a lawyer and leader of a political party that the government would not recognize, and Moncef Marzouki, a vocal critic of the regime's human rights record.

## LEADERSHIP

From the start, the tasks facing the new president were numerous and challenging, particularly the struggling economy and the Islamic fundamentalist movement. Promising a democratization of Tunisia, Ben Ali moved quickly to reconcile the government with the various opposition groups, notably by freeing hundreds of political prisoners, establishing contacts with exiled opposition, abolishing the state security court, and paving the way for a multi-party system. He changed the name of the DSP to the Democratic Constitutional Rally (RCD), and recognized new political parties. However, he would not tolerate any party based on religion. Ben Ali has refused to recognize the MTI, which has since been renamed an-Nahda (the renaissance). His strong and unchanging opposition to the Islamist factions in Tunisia have won him praise from the West, though increasingly the means he uses to shut down opposition are causing concern both within the country and outside.

Ben Ali is facing an increasingly cynical public and alienated youth due to the tight control he has maintained over the political process, the suppression of effective opposition and his poor human rights record. Despite cosmetic changes to the constitution and electoral process, he and his RCD party refuse to allow any effective opposition to emerge.

## DOMESTIC POLICY

Contrary to the problems related to political pluralism and a disenchanted electorate, the economy of Tunisia has greatly improved in the final years of the 1990s. It has averaged a 5% annual growth rate since 1997, helped in part by its associate-membership in the European Union and the IMF-required economic stabilization program. Its associate status has led to a doubling of foreign investment in 1998–1999 over that of previous years. An estimated 600,000 Tunisian emigrants live overseas providing a substantial source of foreign exchange to the Tunisian economy with their remittances, as well as relieving the unemployment stress in Tunisia itself, where the unemployment rate is over 15%. Due to complaints from Europe, particularly Italy, regarding illegal immigration from Tunisia, the government encourages its citizens to find work in the Persian Gulf countries. Tunisia has also received more World Bank loans than any other Arab or African country in the past decade.

Ben Ali's government has engaged in economic policies, with varying success, to promote private investment in industry and agriculture; increase irrigation agriculture through a number of dam constructions; consolidate landholdings in order to achieve cereal self-sufficiency; search out new markets for its olive oil, date and citrus exports; encourage a broadening of manufacturing industries and modernization and improved marketing plans of the traditional industries of textiles (which accounts for 45% of

Tunisia's export earnings) and fish processing; promote petroleum exploration and export through liberal terms offered to the more than two dozen foreign companies currently involved in that industry in the country; renovate plants and promote its internal market for calcium phosphate, of which Tunisia is the world's fourth-largest producer; and promote industrial zones and its offshore banking sector to achieve an economic goal to make Tunisia a "Mediterranean Singapore."

The Islamic fundamentalist pressure in Algeria has provoked severe repression on the part of Ben Ali against Islamic groups in Tunisia and also against anyone seen to be in real opposition to the president and his party. It is estimated that there are currently over two thousand political prisoners in Tunisia.

## FOREIGN POLICY

Tunisia's foreign policy in the 1990s has been greatly affected by the troubles of its neighbors, Libya and Algeria; by its stance in the Gulf War in which it refused to condemn Iraq; and by the headquartering of the Palestine Liberation Organization in Tunis for over a decade. Western pressure to uphold the 1992 UN Security Council sanctions against Libya despite the close economic ties of the two countries has only recently eased due to the Libyan decision to turn over the bombing suspects for trial in the Pam Am explosion over Lockerbie, Scotland. Ben Ali's strong offensive against internal Islamic groups has brought support and praise from the West, though, increasingly, condemnation regarding the methods he uses to control these groups and other political opponents. The president's support of Iraq in the Gulf War brought a withdrawal of investment dollars from Saudi Arabia and Kuwait that have only begun to return in the late 1990s due to a significant lobbying effort by the president. Tunisia has consistently called for an end to the UN sanctions against Iraq, as it did regarding the sanctions against Libya.

Ben Ali's foreign policy has consisted of maintaining a careful balance between close relations with Western Europe and the US along with increasing inter-Arab cooperation (including a restoration of good relations with Egypt after a long hiatus following its signing of the Camp David accords) as well as seeking support and trade partnerships with Asian countries. France, its former colonial ruler, remains Tunisia's number one trade partner, with Italy following close behind. Ben Ali has played an important role in the Arab Maghrebi Union (AMU). The AMU became moribund in the mid-1990s due to strains between various members but in 1999 it appeared to be reviving under calls from Morocco and Tunisia. In 1993 Ali served as president of the AMU and in April 1994 was at the helm of the Organization of African Unity for one year. He used that platform to encourage greater cooperation between Europe and Africa, seek improvements in terms of trade for African economies, and to accomplish much-needed debt restructuring for African countries. Tunisia has also consistently supported demands of the Organization of African Unity to add two permanent African seats to the UN Security Council.

The Palestine Liberation Organization's (PLO) maintenance of its headquarters in Tunis continued until the movement of the organization to assume its leadership of the Palestinian Authority in Gaza in 1994. One year before Ben Ali became president, the Israeli air force bombarded the PLO headquarters, and shortly after he took over, the Israelis again violated Tunisian sovereignty by sending a team that assassinated the PLO chairman's principal deputy, Abu Jihad (Khalil al-Wazir). These events temporarily strained US-Tunisian relations because the American condemnation of the Israeli act was judged unsatisfactory by the Tunisians. US-Tunisian relations continued, however, to develop at economic and military levels. When the peace process began between the PLO and Israel, Tunisia moved toward normalization of relations with Israel, which continued until the election of the Netanyahu government in Israel in 1996. Despite the election of Ehud Barak in Israel in 1999, the normalization process is still on hold while the PLO and Israel continue to work towards peace.

## ADDRESS

Présidence de la République

Tunis, Tunisia

## REFERENCES

Fandy, Mamoun. *The Christian Science Monitor,* 25 October 1999.

*Jeune Afrique,* various issues.

Ling, Dwight L. *Morocco and Tunisia: A Comparative History.* 1979.

Long, David E. and Bernard Reich, eds. *The Government and Politics of the Middle East and North Africa.* 1986.

*Middle East and North Africa,* 46th ed. London: Europa Publications, 1999.

*New York Times,* various issues.

Spencer, William. *The Middle East.* 8th edition. Dushkin/McGraw-Hill, 2000.

Tunisia-Constitution. [Online] Available http://www.uni-wuerzburg.de/law/ts00000_.html (Accessed 6/00).

*Washington Post,* various issues.

*Washington Report on Middle East Affairs,* March 1990.

**Profile researched and written by Kathryn Green (6/00).**

# TURKEY

Bülent Ecevit
Prime Minister
*(pronounced "BEE-yoo-lent es-SEV-it")*

*"It is out of the question for us to make any compromises with the country's basic principle of a secular republic."*

The Republic of Turkey covers an area of 2,018,780 sq km (779,452 sq mi) in Europe and Asia. Turkey's neighbors include Greece and Bulgaria on the west, Syria and Iraq on the south, Iran on the east, and the former Soviet republics of Armenia and Georgia on the northeast. It borders the Black Sea to the north and the Mediterranean to the south. The Turkish straits, the Dardanelles and the Bosphorous, separate Turkey's Asian side from Europe.

The population is estimated at 65.6 million. Ethnically rather homogenous, 80% of the people are Turkish, with a substantial Kurdish minority, and small groups of Arabs, Circassians, Greeks, Armenians, Georgians, Lazes, and Jews. The official language is Turkish. A 1982 law banning the use of the Kurdish language was rescinded in early 1991. Turkey is an overwhelmingly Moslem country with 98% of the people adhering to one of the two main branches of Islam (Sunni or Shi'a).

The Turkish economy is primarily agrarian, with about 50% of the population engaged in agricultural pursuits. Grain, tobacco, cotton, nuts, and olive oil are the chief agricultural products. Natural resources include chrome, copper, iron ore, manganese, bauxite, borax, and petroleum. The most important industries are textiles, iron, steel, sugar, food processing, cement, and fertilizers. The currency is the Turkish *lira*.

## POLITICAL BACKGROUND

The Republic of Turkey is the political successor to the Ottoman Empire, whose domination extended over most of North Africa, the Middle East (with the exception of Iran), the Balkans, and much of Central Europe during the 15th and 16th centuries. The 19th century witnessed the disintegration of that empire, as different provinces gained their autonomy or independence. The final collapse came when the Ottomans entered World War I on the German side. The end of that war was followed by the War of Independence led by General Mustafa Kemal Ataturk, who defeated the occupying Allied forces and eventually dissolved the Ottoman dynasty.

A secular nationalist republic was declared on 29 October 1923, with Ataturk as its first president. He initiated a reform program under which Turkey abandoned much of its Ottoman and Islamic heritage. The new principles adopted by the republic were secularization, establishment of state control of the economy, and creation of a new national consciousness.

Multi-party democracy was introduced into Turkey in 1946 and the first peaceful change of government took place in 1950. Since the transition to a multi-party regime, Turkey has experienced three brief periods of military intervention (1960, 1971, and 1980), during which democratic principles were suspended. For the most part, however, Turkey remained a democratic country with free elections held at regular intervals.

The Turkish constitution has been rewritten three times (1924, 1961, and 1982). Under the present structure, legislative power is vested in a unicameral National Assembly. This 550-seat body is elected by universal suffrage for a five-year-term. The National Assembly in turn elects the president for a seven-year term. The prime minister, who heads the government, is appointed by the president and usually leads the majority party in the National Assembly. The president is also vested with some executive powers. At present, the presidency is held by Süleyman Demirel, while Bülent Ecevit, leader of the Democratic Left Party (DSP), is the prime minister.

## PERSONAL BACKGROUND

Bülent Ecevit was born into a well educated family in Istanbul, Turkey, in 1925. His father, Fahri Ecevit, taught forensic medicine at Ankara University and was later elected to the parliament. His mother, Nazli Ecevit, was a professional painter. Ecevit received his bachelor's degree in 1944 from Robert College, in Istanbul. He then studied English literature at Ankara University, and Sanskrit, Bengali, and art history at London University. In 1957, he spent eight months at Harvard University. Before starting his political career, Ecevit worked for the government press and publicity department in Ankara from 1944–46 and at the Turkish press attache's office in London between 1946–50.

Ecevit returned to Turkey in 1950 to work for *Ulus*, an Ankara daily newspaper and official organ of the Republican People's Party. He wrote art reviews and commentaries on international affairs, eventually becoming its editor. He also wrote a daily column for the Istanbul daily newspaper, *Milliyet*. For three months, Ecevit was a guest writer for the *Winston-Salem Journal*, in North Carolina. He also co-edited a fortnightly review, *Forum*, which provided a common democratic platform for writers with different ideological views. In the 1970s and 1980s, Ecevit edited two publications aimed at promoting democracy—the monthly review, *Ozgur Insan* and weekly *Arayis*.

## RISE TO POWER

Between 1957 and 1980 Ecevit served as a member of Parliament, with a brief interval in 1960–1961 due to a military take-over of the government. He was elected to the Constituent Assembly that prepared the Constitution of 1961. Between 1961 and 1965 Ecevit served as the minister of labor. In 1966, he was elected secretary general of the Republican People's Party (RPP). In protest against a new military intervention and as a result of internal party disputes, Ecevit resigned from this post in 1971. The following year, he regained the party leadership and withdrew his party's support from the government. He helped to block the election of a military candidate to the presidency. In 1973 elections, the RPP emerged with the largest number of seats in parliament. Between 1974 and 1979, Ecevit led three coalition governments.

## LEADERSHIP

During his first nine-month long premiership in 1974, Ecevit ordered troops to Cyprus in support of the Turkish minority, which led to the eventual partition of the island.

After the military intervention of 12 September 1980, his party, along with others, was banned. He faced numerous trials in military courts and was imprisoned three times. A 10-year ban was imposed on the political rights of all party leaders including Ecevit. He regained his political rights, as a result of a referendum held in September 1987, and was elected chairman of the Democratic Left Party (DSP). He was reelected to the Parliament in 1991. In July 1997, Ecevit was appointed deputy prime minister in a three-party minority government.

Between the elections of December 1995 and April 1999, political instability due to short-lived coalition governments marked the Turkish political scene. The coalition government formed by Ecevit after April 1999 elections is the sixth government since December 1995. Following the December 1995 election, Tansu Ciller of the True Path Party (DYP) and Mesut Yilmaz of the Motherland Party (ANAP) formed two succeeding coalition governments. Necmettin Erbakan of the pro-Islamic Welfare Party (RP) formed the third coalition government in June 1996. He was forced to resign from the premiership due to pressure from the military, which perceived Erbakan's coalition government as a threat to Turkey's secular politics. In June 1997, a coalition of Yilmaz and Ecevit came to power under the premiership of Yilmaz. This government too was short-lived; it fell as the result of a corruption scandal in November 1998. Ecevit was named interim prime minister. His minority government, backed by Yilmaz and Ciller, served until the early elections of April 1999.

In the April 1999 elections, Ecevit's DSP received the highest number of votes, with 22.2% of the total. The biggest factor in the success of his party appears to be the capture of Kurdish guerrilla leader, Abdullah Ocalan. Soon after taking office, in February 1999, Turkish commandos captured this most wanted fugitive. Ecevit emerged as a triumphant figure who might stabilize the country's turbulent political scene. Short of establishing a required majority in the Parliament, Ecevit formed a three-party coalition government with the extreme right Nationalist Action Party (MHP) and the Motherland Party on 28 May 1999. The 550-member

parliament voted 354–182 to approve the government and its program.

One of the most serious difficulties the coalition government is likely to face is to establish harmonious cooperation between DSP and MHP, senior partners of the coalition government. The embittered rivalry between these two parties was fueled in the 1970s by street battles between the supporters of extreme right and left ideologies, which cost more than 5,000 lives and led to deep political chaos. This resulted in the military take-over of 12 September 1980. Despite their differences, however, the leaders of the two parties are strong Turkish nationalists. Both take a hard line against the Kurdish movement and oppose any compromise with Greece over issues relating to Cyprus and the Aegean. They refuse an independent Kurdish identity and perceive the civil strife in Southeast Anatolia as a problem of terrorism.

Business leaders, secularists, and the military support Ecevit's coalition government. His disengagement from the traditional state socialism of the Turkish left and his advocacy for the market economy appear to be the biggest reasons for his increased support from business leaders. Many secularists are impressed by his ardent belief in the secular principles of government, in the wake of Islamic revivalism and the rise of the pro-Islamic Virtue Party (FP). Ecevit's solidified position as one of the country's most steadfast secularists, as well as his opposition to any compromise with Kurdish rebels, constitute the most important reason for his support by the military.

## DOMESTIC POLICY

Ocalan's fate is expected to be one of the coalition's first flash points. In late June 1999, Ocalan was sentenced to death on charges of treason and causing the death of 30,000 people in the *Partiya Karkere Kurdistan* (PKK)'s 15-year war for autonomy in southeast Turkey. According to the Turkish legal system, the death sentence must be ratified by the parliament and then by the president before it can be implemented. No death sentence has been carried out in Turkey since 1984. While the nationalists in the parliament support the execution of Ocalan, Ecevit opposes capital punishment. It is also unclear whether the nationalists will back Ecevit's proposal to introduce a bill that would allow lenient punishment for the Kurdish rebels who surrender.

The new government is embarked on a program of key reforms. Changes in the state security law have been introduced, and subsequently the Parliament voted in June 1999, with an overwhelming majority, for the removal of military judges in State Security Courts. The government is also reviewing measures to promote human rights reforms.

The coalition protocol indicated that the government would stand by the anti-inflationary policies and privatization plans of previous governments and would work to combat rising unemployment. Turkey seeks International Monetary Fund (IMF) backing for a "disinflation program" to cut hyper-inflation to single digits by the end of 2001. Social security reform, which is crucial for IMF support, is a priority issue for the Ecevit government. Reform is also promised in agricultural subsidies, which are a big drain on state finances. The IMF has urged Turkey to reform its pension system, which produces losses of around 3% of the GDP each year. Any such move will probably require an increased retirement age, which now stands at 43 years for men and 38 years for women. The government also passed a new banking law aimed at making Turkey more attractive to investors.

## FOREIGN POLICY

Turkey has been eager for membership in the European Union (EU). However, the EU is citing Turkey's underdeveloped economy and human rights violations as impediments to its entry. Relations with the EU had been in decline since Turkey was excluded from consideration for membership in the year 2000. The crisis over Ocalan's trial has worsened the situation. The Council of Europe had voiced strong objections to the presence of a military judge in the proceedings, and it warned Turkey against carrying out a death sentence. The coalition government's new reform package does not currently include a provision to remove the death penalty. Ties with the EU improved markedly, however, following the decision of the December 1999 EU summit in Helsinki, Turkey once again joined the list of candidate members although few political observers believe that Turkey has a realistic chance at entry for 10–15 years.

Although the Ecevit government has claimed that the Turkish public had lost interest in joining the EU, it is unlikely that the government will radically change its policies toward Europe. On the other hand, observers believe that the Pan-Turkist view of the senior coalition partner (MHP), may pressure the government to seek stronger ties with the Turkic republics of the former Soviet Union.

Relations with Greece will continue to dominate Turkey's foreign policy agenda. Ever since it joined the EU in 1981, Greece traditionally opposed the entry of Turkey into the union. The capture of Ocalan increased the strain in Greek-Turkish relations. Apprehended in Kenya after a secret stay in the Greek embassy, Ocalan stated at his trial that Greece was a major supporter of his organization. The Ecevit government was also expected to maintain a hard line on the issue of Cyprus. Nevertheless, beginning in the summer of 1999, Greek-Turkish relations have undergone significant improvement. The tragedy surrounding the major Turkish earthquake in August 1999 formed the catalyst for this thaw. Greece was among the first countries to offer aid to its traditional foe. When a smaller earthquake struck Greece the following month, Turkey reciprocated the Greek gesture. In the aftermath of the tragedies, Greece and Turkey continued a dialogue that resulted in the signing of cooperation accords in the areas of tourism and the fight against terrorism. In addition, Greece's support of the decision of the December 1999 EU summit in Helsinki to place Turkey as a candidate for EU membership also helped to continue the thaw in Greece's relations with its eastern neighbor.

## ADDRESS

Prime Minister's Office
Basbakanlik
Bakanliklar
Ankara, Turkey

## REFERENCES

Banks, Arthur S., Alan Day, and Thomas Muller, eds. *Political Handbook of the World*. 1997.

*Boston Globe*, 4 May 1996.

British Broadcasting Corporation. [Online] Available http://news.bbc.co.uk (Accessed 5/00).

Ministry of Foreign Affairs. [Online] Available http://www.mfa.gov.tr (Accessed 5/00).

*New York Times*, April–May 2000.

*Sabah*, June 1999.

*TurkC-L Turkish Press Review*.

**Profile researched and written by Ayse Betül Çelik and Cengiz Kirli, Binghamton University (9/99; updated 5/00).**

# TURKMENISTAN

## Saparmurad Niyazov
## President

*(pronounced "saa-par-MUR-ad nih-YAH-zoff")*

*"Right from the start of perestroika, we embarked on economic reforms, and we did this gradually, adapting to national features and the people's mentality and traditions."*

The Republic of Turkmenistan borders on Kazakhstan and Uzbekistan to the north and west, Iran and Afghanistan to the south, and the Caspian Sea to the east. It covers a total land area of 488,100 sq km (188,455 sq mi). The capital is Ashkhabad, near the border with Iran. The Caspian seaport of Krasnovodsk is called the "gateway to Central Asia." The least populous of the Central Asian states of the former Soviet Union, about 90% of the land area is covered by the Kara Kum desert.

The population is 4.37 million, of whom 72.0% are Turkmen, 9.5% are Russian, 9.0% are Uzbek, and 9.5% represent other ethnic backgrounds. The official language is Turkmen, a Turkic language; 74.6% of the population speak Turkmen fluently, and 38.6% speak Russian fluently. In a move to emulate the Turkish model of modernization and Westernization, the Latin alphabet has been chosen to replace the Cyrillic (Slavic) alphabet. The majority of the population is Muslim; most Russians are Russian Orthodox.

Turkmenistan's GDP increased by 5% in 1998, boosted by harvests of wheat and cotton, as well as increased oil production. A severe 32.8% drop in agricultural production in 1996 was reversed in 1997–1998, and Turkmen officials reported record grain harvests in 1999. Turkmen officials also have reported gains in oil and gas production during the first half of 1999. Turkmenistan is among the world's top ten in cotton production, and agriculture accounts for about one-half of employment. According to the World Bank, Turkmenistan's underlying fiscal position has weakened markedly over the years as public sector deficits have ballooned, amounting to 12% of GDP for 1998. Nonetheless, high consumer inflation rates eased from nearly 1,000% in 1995–1996 to 20% in 1998. The per capita GDP is estimated at US$1,630. Poverty is widespread and infant mortality and drug use are high. State subsidies for some food and other necessities provide some relief. Environmental problems center around the shrinkage of the Aral Sea and widespread water pollution.

## POLITICAL BACKGROUND

Beginning in the sixth century, the Urguz group of Turkish peoples migrated into western Asia and the Middle East, settling in areas in modern Turkmenistan in the 10th century and establishing the Seljukid Empire in southern Turkmenistan. In the 11th and 12th centuries, the Urguz Turkmen also established the Khorasan and Khorezm khanates, the root of the future Turkmen nation. In the 13th century, Mongols overran Central Asia including the area of modern Turkmenistan. In the 15th century, what is now southern Turkmenistan was divided between the Khivan and Bukharan khanates and Persia (now Iran). The Turkmen provided determined opposition to Russian Czarist forces in the 18th and 19th centuries, finally being annexed by the Czar in 1886 as part of what was called the Transcaspian Region.

After the Russian Bolshevik Revolution of 1917, a period of political disorder occurred, but in 1920 the Red Army occupied what is now Turkmenistan. Turkmen in the Basmachi resistance movement fought on for several years against the Bolsheviks. In 1924, Stalin established the Turkmen Soviet Socialist Republic. Forced collectivization in Turkmenistan in the late 1920s and early 1930s encountered massive resistance among the largely nomadic population and resulted in great loss of life.

Turkmenistan was long a relatively neglected republic of the Soviet Union; few investments in industry or other infrastructure development were made. Turkmen were also underrepresented as members of the Soviet Communist Party and in the leading ranks of the party. In the late 1950s, some Turkmen leaders called for preference to be given to Turkmen in filling top posts in the republic; Moscow responded by purging the Turkmen Party. In 1969, conservative Muhamednazar Gapurov became Turkmen Party leader, remaining in power until late 1985, when he was ousted from his position as part of Gorbachev's purge of Central Asian leaders. Gapurov was replaced as Turkmen Party leader by Saparmurad Niyazov.

During the abortive Soviet coup attempt in August 1991, Niyazov did not issue a statement condemning the coup until it had unravelled. Upon Gorbachev's return to Moscow, Yeltsin and public opinion forced Gorbachev to resign as party leader. A staunch proponent of authoritarian political power, Niyazov did not follow Gorbachev's example, but did announce his resignation from the Soviet Communist Party Politburo; later he nationalized some Communist Party assets in Turkmenistan. Instead of abolishing the Turkmen Communist Party, he attempted to preserve it by orchestrating its "transformation," renaming it the Democratic Party in December 1991. He serves as the chairman of this "new" party. While this party proclaims that it stands for the rule of law, a mixed economy, and a multi-party system, it also operates much like the old Communist Party through its cells in the workplace and elsewhere.

## PERSONAL BACKGROUND

Saparmurad Niyazov was born in May 1940. Despite his Russian sounding last name, he is an ethnic Turkmen. He began his career in 1969 as an instructor at a geological prospecting worker's union in Turkmenistan. He went to St. Petersburg (formerly called Leningrad) where he graduated from the Leningrad Polytechnical Institute with a degree in engineering physics. He joined the Communist Party in 1962. Returning to Turkmenistan, Niyazov became a foreman of a shop at the Bizmeyn district heat and power plant from 1967 until 1970, when he began full-time political work. As a promising young party official, he was invited to take part in the correspondence program of the Communist Party's Higher Party School in Moscow. Niyazov and his wife have two children.

## RISE TO POWER

Niyazov headed the Industrial Transport Department of the Turkmen Communist Party until December 1980, and then was appointed first secretary of the Ashkhabad City Party Committee. Although Askhabad's industries did not perform well during his tenure, Niyazov was viewed as a competent party boss. In 1984, he became an instructor in the Organizational Party Work Department of the Communist Party, then six months later he became chairman of the Turkmen Council of Ministers. At the end of the year, the relatively young Niyazov was appointed first secretary of the Communist Party of Turkmenistan as part of Gorbachev's efforts to reinvigorate the party elite, fight corruption, and find a scapegoat for economic decline in Turkmenistan. Because of his new post, Niyazov was elected a full member of the Central Committee at the Soviet Communist Party Congress in March 1986.

In addition to his party posts, he became chairman of the Turkmen Supreme Soviet in 1990, following Gorbachev's call for party leaders to head up legislatures. He played a prominent role in the July 1990 Soviet Communist Party Congress, being named to the presidium and presiding at a session. He defended Turkmenistan's caution in implementing Gorbachev's reforms in order to avoid the ethnic and political storms that had occurred in other republics, called for a renewed federation of republics, and for an independent and powerful Turkmen Communist Party. He and all other republic first secretaries were elected ex-officio full members of the Politburo of the Soviet Communist Party, at that time the leading decision-making body of the party.

In early October 1990, the Supreme Soviet changed the Turkmen Constitution to allow a quick popular presidential election, the first such election among the former Soviet republics. Niyazov was overwhelmingly elected, receiving 98.3% of the popular vote, to the newly created post of president of Turkmenistan (relinquishing formal leadership over the Supreme Soviet). He ran unopposed, being unanimously nominated for the post by the Turkmen Supreme Soviet. He remained Communist Party first secretary after winning the election.

Democratization in Turkmenistan has proceeded more slowly than in most other ex-Soviet republics. In May 1992, Turkmenistan became the first Central Asian republic to enact a post-independence constitution. It sets up a "secular democracy" embracing a presidential system of rule, granting Niyazov wide powers as head of state and government, though it formally upholds the balance of powers between executive, legislative, and judicial branches. Niyazov issues edicts that have the force of law and appoints and removes judges and local officials. The constitution includes an impressive list of individual rights and safeguards (though not freedom of the press), but cautions that the exercise of rights must not violate national morality and public order, or damage national security. A democratically-oriented provision calls for the direct popular election of the president, who by law must be an ethnic Turkmen. In line with this provision, a new presidential election was held on 21 June 1992, and Niyazov was elected unopposed, winning 99.95% of the votes cast. In a referendum in January 1994, he received the support of 99.99% of the vote for extending his term until 2002. A change to the Constitution was enacted in late December 1999 naming Niyazov president for life. Most observers viewed the referendum and the life term as serious setbacks to democratization in Turkmenistan.

## LEADERSHIP

Niyazov is president, supreme commander of the armed forces, first secretary of the Democratic Party of Turkmenistan (DPT, formerly the Turkmen Communist Party), head of the People's Council (Khalk Maslakhaty), and chairman of the Cabinet of Ministers and the National Security Council. He has created a "cult of personality" by awarding himself medals and titles, including the title of "Turkmenbashi," leader of all Turkmen. The national oath recited by office-holders and school children includes the phrase "[if] I betray...Turkmenbashi, may my breath stop." Niyazov has also formulated a *Rukhname* (spiritual book), which he envisages as dictating Turkmen national cultural and ethical standards.

President Niyazov rejects what he calls the "chaos and permissiveness" of multi-party democracy, favoring the collective "togetherness" of one-party rule. The DPT, like the TCP before it, is the only party allowed to operate. It is closely controlled by Niyazov. The DPT proclaims that it stands for the rule of law, a mixed economy, and a multi-party system, but it operates like the old Communist Party through cells in the workplace and elsewhere. The DPT reports that it has 60,000 members. Seeking to bring together most major cultural, religious, and public groups as a wider political bloc, in early 1994, Niyazov created a National Revival Movement, which he heads. Unregistered parties are tiny and have been severely repressed. Physician Pirkuli Tangrikuliyev announced that he wanted to create an opposition party and would run in the 1999 Mejlis election, but he was arrested and convicted of corruption.

## DOMESTIC POLICY

The 1992 constitution created a People's Council (Khalk Maslakhaty) with mixed executive and legislative powers, consisting of the president, ministers, the 50 legislators of the Supreme Council (Mejlis), 60 "people's representatives," and others. The people's representatives were elected by district in a virtually uncontested vote in December 1992. The Khalk Maslakhaty serves as a forum and rubber stamp for the president's policy initiatives. Resurrecting pre-Soviet customs, a Council of Elders, hand-picked by Niyazov, was also created to advise the president and choose presidential candidates. Oppositionists complained that both these bodies were designed to stifle dissent. A new Mejlis of 50 members was elected in December 1994. The candidates were all nominated by Niyazov, ran unopposed, and most were members of his DPT. The Mejlis routinely supports presidential decrees and has little legislative initiative. The court system retains its basic Soviet-era structure and functions. The President appoints all judges for five-year terms without legislative consent, except for the Chairman of the Supreme Court, and removes them by decree.

The lack of democratization in Turkmenistan was accentuated during the 11 April 1998 election of 60 unpaid "people's representatives" to the Khalk Maslakhaty. Turnout was reported at 99.5%, though some of the candidates ran unchallenged and no real campaigning or political party contestation occurred. Elections to the Turkmen 50-seat legislature (Mejlis) were held on 12 December 1999. Niyazov rejected a role for parties, stating that partisanship could lead to clan rivalries. Instead, he directed that nominating groups choose "professional" candidates, and they dutifully selected two candidates per constituency to run. There was no discussion of political issues or problems during the campaign. Prior to the race, Niyazov stepped up his repression of political and religious dissidents. The OSCE refused to send monitors, citing the government's control over the electoral process.

Niyazov has vowed to move slowly on reforms, and has tried to maintain some subsidies for food, water, and other necessities to placate the population. In December 1999, he stated that the economic and political transformation of Turkmenistan would not be completed until 2011. In April 2000, he rejected proposals to step up market reforms and allow political pluralism, averring that "the Turkmen people, given their mentality inherited from their forefathers, will not accept such things....we have honesty purity, and accord in our blood." But he has directed some legal reforms he claims increase human rights, such as abolishing the death penalty and holding yearly amnesties. He has also hailed a law he initiated to permit exile instead of a jail term. In May 2000 he called for representatives of elders' councils, members of the People's Council, and local administration heads to become responsible for endorsing arrest documents and monitoring the actions of prosecutors. Critics have objected that such a change would place criminal justice even more tightly under Niyazov's control.

Niyazov has stated that his country's neutrality in world affairs prevents it from heavily participating in multinational defense organizations, but permits bilateral military assistance. During Niyazov's May 1995 visit to Moscow, he and President Yeltsin signed agreements on air defense, military transport, Russian use of Turkmen military facilities, and others they typified as creating a "strategic partnership." However, actual cooperation has been minimal. In early 1995, Turkmenistan became the first Central Asian state to join NATO's Partnership for Peace (PFP), calling for aid in officer training. In keeping with the neutrality policy, however, Turkmen troops have merely "observed" PFP military exercises. Turkmen armed forces have numbered 17,000–19,000, including ground, air, and air defense forces. Niyazov has emphasized replacing the higher officer corps with ethnic Turkmen and has replaced almost all lower echelon officers from Russia. Turkmen are receiving officer's training in Russia, Ukraine, and Turkey. In 1993, Russia and Turkmenistan agreed that Russian border guards would work with Turkmen border guards under Turkmen command at borders with Iran and Afghanistan. In 1999, Niyazov canceled this agreement, and the last of Russia's 1,000 border troops in Turkmenistan left in late 1999.

## FOREIGN POLICY

Niyazov supports some of Russia's policies in the region while endeavoring, where possible, to resist, contravene, or reduce Russian influence. Russian military and border troops assisted Turkmenistan until it built up its own forces, and Russia's presence has been used to counter Uzbek policies in the region. In 1992, Turkmenistan and Russia signed a Friendship and Cooperation Treaty that contained security provisions. In 1993, Turkmenistan was the only former Soviet republic to agree to Russian demands for dual citizenship for the relatively small number of ethnic Russians residing in Turkmenistan, to assuage Russian criticism of Turkmen nationality policy and to encourage skilled ethnic Russians to remain. Russia objects to Turkmen efforts to reduce dependence on existing natural gas export routes that transit Russia. Turkmenistan at first supported Russia's and Iran's demands that Caspian Sea resources be exploited in line with Soviet-era treaties, but Niyazov in September 1999 decreed control over navigation, fishing, and resources within a national sector.

President Niyazov has resisted proposals by Kazakhstan and Russia to strengthen the Commonwealth of Independent

States (CIS) and has refused to sign several CIS agreements viewed as violating Turkmen sovereignty. In 1992, Niyazov "initialed" a CIS collective security arrangement, but then refused to participate in CIS "peacekeeping" in Tajikistan. After Kyrgyzstan joined Kazakhstan, Belarus, and Russia in a "deeper integration" customs union in 1996, Turkmenistan's Foreign Ministry noted that it rejected "entry into rigid supranational structures." Instead, Niyazov has stressed the establishment of bilateral ties with CIS states. Relations with Uzbekistan have been tense, with both states vying for regional influence and arguing over borders and water sharing. Uzbekistan has criticized Turkmenistan's ties with Iran as threatening the region's independence.

Turkmenistan's "neutral" foreign policy is enshrined in its constitution. Niyazov has declared that Turkmenistan's "open door" or "permanent neutrality" policy precludes joining political or military alliances and entails good relations with the East and the West, though priority will be placed on relations with Central Asian and other Islamic states. Turkmenistan joined the Non-Aligned Movement in 1995, and the United Nations General Assembly in 1995 recognized Turkmenistan's status as a neutral state. Turkmenistan has pursued close ties with both Iran and Turkey. In addition to growing trade ties with Iran, Turkmenistan is also interested in cultural ties with the approximately one million Turkmen residing in Iran. Turkey is the largest foreign investor in Turkmenistan and has far surpassed Russia in trade turnover with Turkmenistan.

## ADDRESS

Zdaniye Pravitel'stva
Ashkhbad, Turkmenistan

## REFERENCES

"Turkmen Head: Another Eleven Years Needed to Complete Reforms." *Foreign Broadcast Information Service (FBIS), Daily Report: Central Eurasia*, 27 April 2000.

"Niyazov on Plans for 'Humanization' of Turkmen Law System." *FBIS*, 5 May 2000.

*Handbook of Major Soviet Nationalities*, 1975.

"Central Asia." *Harvard International Review*, v. 22, Winter-Spring 2000: 44-54, 56-74, 76-79.

Anna Matveeva, "Democratization, Legitimacy and Political Change in Central Asia." *International Affairs*, v. 75, Jan. 1999: 23-44.

Richard Foltz, "Islam and Identity in Post-Soviet Central Asia: Some Historical Considerations." *Harriman Review*, v. 11, April 1999: 39-43.

Rajan Menon and Hendrik Spruyt, "The Limits of Neorealism: Understanding Security in Central Asia," *Review of International Studies*, v. 25, January 1999: 87-105.

**Profile researched and written by Jim Nichol, Library of Congress (5/2000).**

# TUVALU

### Ionatana Ionatana
### Prime Minister

*(pronounced "eye-oh-nuh-TAH-nuh eye-oh-nuh-TAH-nuh")*

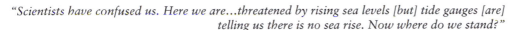

*"Scientists have confused us. Here we are...threatened by rising sea levels [but] tide gauges [are] telling us there is no sea rise. Now where do we stand?"*

The remote Pacific island nation of Tuvalu consists of a chain of nine atolls situated a few degrees south of the equator and just west of the international date line. Its nearest neighbors are Kiribati (formerly the Gilbert Islands) to the north, Rotuma and Wallis Island to the south, the Solomon Islands to the west, and Tokelau to the east. The Tuvaluan islands stretch over a distance of 560 km (350 mi). From north to south, they are Nanumea, Niutau, Nanumanga, Nui, Vaitupu, Nukufetau, Funafuti, Nukulaelae, and Niutaka. The last of these has not had a permanent population, so "Tuvalu" means "group of eight". The islands rise no higher than six meters (less than 20ft) above sea level. The total land mass is less than 26 sq km (approximately 10 sq mi), making Tuvalu second only to Nauru as the smallest Pacific Island state. However, Tuvalu's Exclusive Economic Zone, including fishing rights, extends over 898,700 sq km (347,000 sq mi), creating one of the country's major economic resources and giving Tuvalu the world's largest sea-to-land ratio. From March to November the weather is warm; the rainy season extends from November to March.

The population of Tuvalu was estimated at 10,588 in 1998. Ninety-five percent of the people are Polynesian, with the remainder being mostly Micronesian. Most Tuvaluans are members of the Tuvalu Christian Church—the local version of Protestantism originally brought to the islands in the 1860s by the London Missionary Society. Other religious affiliations include Seventh-Day Adventist and Baha'i. Except on Nui, where a dialect of I-Kiribati is spoken, the national language is Tuvaluan. English is the official language of government.

The Tuvaluan dollar is the unit of currency, convertible at par with the Australian dollar. The capital and administrative center is Fongatale on the island of Funafuti. Since 1980, migration to Funafuti has shifted the population so that the island is now home to some 45% of Tuvaluans. This rural-to-urban shift has been accompanied by a rapid shrinkage of the traditional activities of agriculture and fishing, although copra production remains one of the few sources of cash income for outer islanders. In 1998, the per capita GDP was reported to be $800. In February 2000, proceeds from a deal with a Toronto, Canada, company (Information.ca.Corp.) to license the Tuvalu ".tv" domain names for US$1,000 each reportedly doubled Tuvalu's GDP. Tuvalu received US$20 million for ".tv" domain name sales in 1999.

There are more skilled laborers than jobs on Tuvalu. The Tuvalu Maritime School trains seaman to work on large container ships. In early 2000, a German shipping company announced that it would award the contract of supplying 20 seaman to the Alpha Pacific Navigation Limited, a Tuvaluan firm. Tuvaluans historically worked in Nauru's phosphate industry but phosphate deposits will soon be exhausted and in the late 1990s and 2000, Nauru was repatriating Tuvaluans as jobs were becoming scarce.

Foreign aid provided much of Tuvalu's income. The Tuvalu Trust Fund was established in 1987 with initial grants from the United Kingdom, Australia, and New Zealand. These grants were subsequently increased with contributions from Japan and Tuvalu itself. The fund was originally designed to help balance the total government budget, though balance-of-payment deficits continue to be financed by aid funds. Careful management of the Fund's investments has produced an annual average return of 6.5%. This has permitted an expansion of social services, such as free public education through eighth grade. A 1997 UNICEF report found the status of Tuvalu's women and children to be higher than that in some larger Pacific countries.

## POLITICAL BACKGROUND

When a British sea captain discovered Funafuti in 1819, he named the island "Ellice" after a member of Parliament who owned the ship's cargo. In 1841, Charles Wilkes of the US Exploring Expedition gave that name to the entire group. Great Britain declared a protectorate over the then Gilbert and Ellice Islands in 1892; the islands were elevated to the status of colony in 1916. When preparations for the colony's independence began in the 1970s, the Polynesian Tuvaluans feared being overwhelmed by the larger Micronesian Gilbertese population. They voted overwhelmingly in a 1974 referendum, monitored by UN observers, to be treated separately, and the colony of Ellice Islands was established in 1975. Great Britain granted independence to Tuvalu in October 1978.

The original constitution was revised in 1986. Tuvalu remains a member of the Commonwealth on Nations and the British monarch is the head of state and is represented by a Tuvaluan governor general, whose functions are mostly ceremonial. The monarch, with advice from the prime minister and Parliament, appoint the governor general. The cabinet, made up of the prime minister and not more than four ministers, holds real executive authority. The prime minister is elected by Parliament.

Parliament consists of a single chamber of twelve members elected by all citizens over 18 years of age. Candidates must

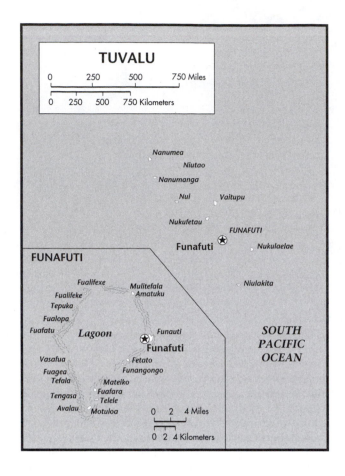

be at least 21. Elections are held every four years, more often if Parliament is dissolved by the governor general under provisions set out in the constitution. Four islands elect two members each, three islands elect one member each, and two islands elect one member to represent them jointly. Parliament can remove the prime minister by passing a no-confidence vote.

Funafuti, the main island, has a town council; the other inhabited islands have island councils. Each council consists of six members and is elected to four-year terms. Councils are responsible for the provision of local services and upholding law and order.

Like a number of other Pacific Island nations, Tuvalu inherited a British type of political system that does not always fit easily with traditional culture and values. There are no major political parties and personal alliances are much more important than ideology, and economic issues inevitably affect government. Accusations of financial mismanagement led to the ouster of the first prime minister, Toaripi Lauti, in 1981. In the late 1990s, substantial revenue has been generated for the country through licensing of both the country's area code and internet domain.

## RISE TO POWER

Most ministers in Tuvalu are responsible for more than one department. Prior to becoming prime minister, Ionatana Ionatana was both minister of education and culture and minister of health, women and cultural affairs.

In April 1999, the incumbent prime minister Bikenibeu Paeniu, received a vote of no-confidence and was ousted from

office by the Tuvalu Parliament. A few days later, Ionatana Ionatana was elected prime minister, and an inauguration was held on April 27, 1999 for Ionatana and his new cabinet. The new cabinet ministers included Lagitupu Tiulimu, Deputy Prime Minister and Minister of Finance and Economic Planning; Faimalaga Luka, Minister of Natural Resources and Environment and Minister of Internal Affairs, Rural, and Urban Development; Samuelu Penitala Teo, Minister of Works, Energy, and Communications; Teagai Esekia, Minister of Education, Sports, and Culture and Minister of Health, Women, and Community Affairs. The first parliamentary session of the new government was opened by Governor General Sir Dr. Tomasi Puapua on May 26, 1999.

## LEADERSHIP

Prime Minister Ionatana Ionatana may be the leader who brings Tuvalu into full republic status. In February 2000, Ionatana announced that he might consider leading a campaign for the island nation to leave the Commonwealth and become an independent republic. Ionatana and others in the government perceive that the British government has consistently mistreated Tuvalu in retaliation for Tuvalu's drive for independence in 1978. The terms of the separation from the Gilbert Islands were unfavorable to Tuvalu. A previous prime minister, Kumuta Latasi, had the British Union Jack removed from the Tuvalu flag.

## DOMESTIC POLICY

Governing a tiny island nation with limited economic resources presents particular challenges. A key issue is the attempt to reduce dependence on foreign aid. Shortly after taking office, Ionatana worked to prevent the deal to license Internet ".tv" domain names from collapsing. He was successful in negotiating with a Toronto-based firm, Information.ca.Corp, to allow the licensing arrangement to go forward. As a result, Tuvalu received us$20 million in early 2000 representing licensing fees earned during 1999.

The success of the Tuvalu Trust Fund is critical to the country's survival in the future. The government has explored other ways to increase revenue, such as offering passports for sale (mainly to affluent Chinese), a practice engaged in by several other Pacific Island nations. Selling special issues of stamps has been a source of income for the country for some time.

## FOREIGN POLICY

Conflicting reports about the possibility of a drastic rise in sea levels from the process known as "global warming" have caused Ionatana to be confused about what action to take. However, less than a year after becoming prime minister, Ionatana negotiated with New Zealand to allow Tuvaluans to move to New Zealand should the sea levels rise to a dangerous level. New Zealand agreed in June 2000 to help if necessary.

Under Ionatana's leadership, Japan agreed to provide a substantial grant in the amount of us$83,000 toward the purchase of a road roller for the Public Works Department to be used for road and runway maintenance.

Less dramatic, but regionally significant, is the signing of a treaty of friendship between Tuvalu and Kiribati in September 1997. This agreement covers a range of issues for cooperation, including trade and transportation. It remains to be seen what practical action will result, but the treaty serves as a symbol of the country's commitment to regional cooperation.

## ADDRESS
Office of the Prime Minister
Private Mail Bag
Vaiaku
Funafuti, Tuvalu
Telephone: (+688) 20100

## REFERENCES

*EIU Country Profile: Tuvalu, 1995–96.* London: The Economist Intelligence Unit Ltd., 1996.

*Islands Business,* January1997–November 1999.

"Tuvalu PM Admits Confusion Over Conflicting Reports on Sea Levels." *Pacific Islands Report.* [Online] Available http://pidp.ewc.hawaii.edu/PIReport/2000/February/02-25-09.htm (accessed June 29, 2000).

"New Zealand to Assist Tuvalu in Sea Level Battle." *Pacific Islands Report.* [Online] Available http://pidp.ewc.hawaii.edu/PIReport/2000/June/06-27-15.htm (accessed June 29, 2000).

*Pacific Magazine,* January1997–December 1999.

Stanley, David. *South Pacific Handbook,* 6th ed. Moon Publications, Inc., 1996.

**Profile researched and written by Susan Gall (8/2000); sections contributed by Eugene Ogan, Professor Emeritus, University of Minnesota (3/98).**

# UGANDA

## Yoweri Kaguta Museveni
### President
*(pronounced "YOU-ree muh-SEH-veh-nee")*

*"My mission is now almost accomplished, which is to orient my people toward modernization. We shall complete this process of democratization."*

The Republic of Uganda, a landlocked equatorial East African country, is bordered by Zaire to the west, the Sudan to the north, Kenya to the east, and Rwanda, Tanzania and Lake Victoria to the south. The capital is Kampala, located on the northern shore of Lake Victoria. Uganda occupies 235,885 sq km (94,354 sq mi), an area which is home to nearly 23 million people, 99% of whom are African, and 1% of whom are of European, Asian, and Arab ancestry. The indigenous African population is quite diverse, with different groups dominating particular geographic regions of the country: Bantu groups, 65% of the African population, are located largely in the south; Nilotic groups comprise roughly 10% of the population and are found in the north; the Turkana and Karamojong are among the Nilo-Hamitic groups in the northeast. The official language is English, although Luganda and Kiswahili are widely used. The majority of Ugandans are Christian, but there are those who profess Islam or practice traditional religions as well.

Although Uganda has attained a record of solid economic reform and sustained growth economic growth over the last decade, in the process winning the accolade of an African role model for economic development, the economy is still among the least productive in the world: per capita GNP is us$1,020. The economy is primarily agricultural, and Uganda's principal exports are cash crops, including coffee (70% of all exports) cotton, tea, and maize. The currency is the Uganda shilling.

## POLITICAL BACKGROUND

Several African kingdoms had been in place for centuries when the first Arab traders moved inland in the 1830s into what is now Uganda. British explorers, searching for the source of the Nile, arrived in the 1860s. Protestant and Catholic missionaries first entered the country in the late 1870s. In 1888, Britain assigned control of its emerging central African "sphere of interest" to the Imperial British East Africa Company. In 1890 an Anglo-German agreement confirmed British dominion over Uganda and neighboring Kenya. By 1893 the Company abandoned the territory, which became a formal British protectorate in 1894. It was not until 1955 that the terms of the protectorate were expanded to include constitutional changes that would eventually lead to Uganda's independence.

Uganda's first general elections were held in 1961, and internal self-government was granted on 1 March 1962, with Benedicto Kiwanuka as prime minister. On attaining independence on 9 October 1962, Kiwanuka had been succeeded by Dr. Milton Obote, leader of the Uganda People's Congress (UPC). At the time of independence, the country comprised four regions, including the Kingdom of Buganda, traditionally among the most powerful political entities in the area. In 1963 Uganda became a republic and Mutesa II, the king of Buganda, was named president. Executive power, however, remained with the cabinet and Prime Minister Obote. After several years of conflict between those who favored a centralized state and those who preferred a loose federation with strong roles for tribally based kingdoms, Obote led a coup against the King in February 1966. He suspended the constitution and assumed all government powers as executive president in April 1966.

In 1967 Obote promulgated a new constitution, which granted the president greater power, proclaimed Uganda a republic, and abolished the traditional kingdoms. All opposition parties were banned in 1969. In January 1971, Obote was overthrown by the army, led by Major General Idi Amin Dada, who assumed full executive power. In February, Amin dissolved the National Assembly, assumed legislative power, suspended the constitution, and declared himself head of state. In an "economic war" intended to free Uganda from foreign domination, Amin expelled all Asians, many of whom were engaged in trade and small industry. The next seven years were characterized by brutality virtually unmatched in history, with the ruthless extermination of any suspected opposition and an army which was allowed to trample on civil and human rights with impunity. Relations with nations around the world, and especially with the East African community, deteriorated steadily throughout the 1970s, leading to its collapse in 1977. In November 1978, Amin annexed the Kagera salient from Tanzania, which provoked the 1979 joint invasion of Uganda by Tanzanian troops and the Uganda National Liberation Army (UNLA), an umbrella organization of rebel forces. The invasion force quickly gained control of much of the southern region of Uganda, and Amin's troops capitulated. In April 1979 a Tanzanian assault force entered Kampala. Idi Amin fled to Libya and later to Saudi Arabia.

Elections held in 1980 were won by the UPC and Milton Obote became president for the second time. Obote's second term was marked by increasing guerrilla activity, to which he responded with repression and violence. Obote was overthrown in a military coup in July 1985. Over the next several months, agreement was reached between exiled opposition groups and the interim government. These talks were opposed by the National Resistance Movement (NRM) and its military wing, the National Resistance Army (NRA), led by Yoweri Museveni. Musveni assumed the presidency when the NRA took over the capital in January 1986.

## PERSONAL BACKGROUND

Yoweri Kaguta Museveni was born in 1945 in Ntungamo, in the Ankole district of southwestern Uganda. Museveni was provided with an excellent education by Ugandan standards, attending Kyamate Boys School (1953–1959); Mbarara High School (1959–1960); and Ntare School (1961–1966). He attended University College in Dar Es Salaam, Tanzania, where he graduated in 1970 with a Bachelor of Arts in economics and political science. He returned to Uganda in 1970 and joined the government of Prime Minister Milton Obote as a research assistant. When Obote's government was overthrown by Idi Amin Dada in 1971, Museveni fled to Tanzania.

Yoweri Museveni is married to Janet Kataaha. The couple have one son and three daughters

## RISE TO POWER

While in exile in Tanzania, Museveni formed the Front for National Salvation (FRONASA), a rebel army whose stated purpose was the overthrow of Amin. When this occurred in April 1979, Museveni assumed a prominent place on the Military Commission which was established as the new national leadership of the country. He served as minister of defense to the three presidents who served prior to the 1980 elections. Museveni was enormously popular, within the Military Commission and among the Ugandan general population. In November 1980, Museveni was promoted to vice-chairman. The December 1980 election of Milton Obote to the presidency again precipitated an exodus of resistance fighters from the country. As head of the National Resistance Army, Museveni was once more in the forefront of the effort to overthrow Uganda's government. After a bloody civil war Obote was overthrown in a 1985 coup, which brought Brigadier Basilio Okello to power. Most rebel groups soon reached agreement with the Okello government and were given positions on the Military Council; the NRA was not among those groups. The UNLA, now the official national army, continued its reign of terror.

The NRA continued its campaign to overthrow the government and succeeded in gaining control of large areas of the country. On 26 January 1986 they entered Kampala and dissolved the Military Council. Museveni was sworn in as president three days later. By this time, Uganda's 24-year turbulent history since independence had been through seven military coups, eight presidencies, two suspensions of the constitution, and loss of an estimated 400,000 lives.

## LEADERSHIP

In February 1986, Museveni named a new cabinet, which was comprised primarily of NRM and NRA members, but which also included representatives of other political parties and three members of the previous administration. A National Resistance Council was created to take over legislative duties until a new constitution was written. At the local and district levels, Museveni established a system of "resistance committees," whose duties included local security and the

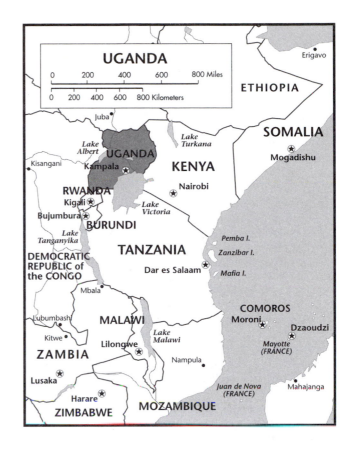

elimination of corruption. Throughout his career, Museveni witnessed the civil disruption which was occurring throughout Africa. He concluded that much of the unrest was the result of political party divisions based on regional, religious, and ethnic distinctions. This conclusion led Museveni to limit the role of political parties in Uganda. One reason for Museveni's widespread support is his steadfast adherence to a (professional) code of conduct for his troops, which prohibits rape, pillage, and the murder of civilians. While not without unsavory elements, and clearly responsible for violations of human rights, the NRA has historically identified and punished those within its ranks accused of these crimes. This earned him a lot of trust from the Ugandan people.

During the first three years of Museveni's government, guerrilla activity continued. By 1989 the war had ended. Museveni was determined to root out corruption among the security forces, and established commissions to investigate charges of corruption and human rights violations. As a result, more than 80% of the police force was dismissed from service. In June 1987, the NRC offered amnesty to all rebel troops except those accused of murder or rape; by mid-April 1988, more than 30,000 rebel forces had surrendered to the government.

In February 1989 national elections were held, the first since 1980. The NRC was expanded from 98 members to 278 members, 210 of whom were elected. Ministerial posts were no longer reserved exclusively for appointed members, and 14 ministers and deputy ministers lost their positions. A new constitution was promulgated in October 1995. It established a "no-party" state, at least through the year 2000.

New elections were scheduled for May and June 1996. The elections were open to all, provided they did not organize as candidates of particular parties.

Presidential elections held on May 9 and parliamentary elections in June 1996 were deemed to be generally free and fair, within the limits imposed by the "no party" or "movement" based system established by the constitution. Most observers and analysts acknowledged the advantage the system ceded to Museveni. Unable to organize under the auspices of political parties, Museveni's challengers were limited in their ability to raise funds and to campaign effectively during the short three-month electoral season. For many the election was essentially a referendum on the validity of Museveni's system.

The results of the presidential election were unsurprising. Museveni took 74.2% of the vote. His runner up, Paul Ssemogerere, got 24%. His challengers claimed massive vote rigging, but international observers were unable to find evidence of electoral fraud. Inaugurated on 12 May 1996, Yoweri Museveni pledged to continue the process of democratization and economic recovery, which was begun during his previous 10 years as Uganda's national leader. His critics accuse him of lacking democratic credentials; of being a despot, be it a benevolent one, for suppressing political parties. This matter will be settled through a national referendum on the choice of a political system scheduled for June 2000. Next general elections are scheduled for May 2001.

## DOMESTIC POLICY

Ravaged by decades of war and civil strife, Uganda's economy has made a remarkable recovery since the cessation of most rebel activity in 1989. Economic growth has since averaged 6–7% annually. This performance is largely based on continued investment in the rehabilitation of infrastructure, improved incentives for production and exports, reduced inflation (from 240% in 1987 to 42% in 1992, and to 5% by 1996, remaining in single digits until May 1999), gradual improvement in national security, and the return of Indian-Ugandan entrepreneurs. There is growing concern, however, that with the involvement of Uganda in the war in the Democratic republic of the Congo (DRC), growing corruption in government, and slippage in the government's determination to continue with reforms, this performance may decline.

Museveni has aggressively adopted free market economic policies and embraced sustained economic structural adjustment programs as prescribed by the IMF. This has won him praise as a role model for African Development, and much needed economic assistance, from the IMF, World Bank, and western countries. This level of performance also helped Uganda in 1999 to be the first among least developed countries to qualify for debt relief. With foreign debts totaling about US$3.631 billion, up to US$650 million may be forgiven under the scheme.

Museveni has tried to reduce the size of the military and security forces and to reform the civil service. A plan was implemented to guarantee a smooth transition for ex-soldiers upon their return to civilian life, including programs to retrain them for civilian employment, to assist in relocation for the soldiers, and to provide monetary assistance until they become self-sufficient. The plan is viewed as an effective way to reduce military expenditure while providing the skilled labor needed for an expanding economy.

In education, Uganda is making big strides, especially with the introduction of universal primary education in 1997. Before then, education was not compulsory in Uganda and all schools charged tuition, making attendance impossible for many Ugandans. Uganda, where 46% of the population subsists below the poverty line, has raised enrollment of school-age children dramatically from 54% (2.1 million) in 1997 to 90% (5.3 million) in 1999. "Progress on universal primary education is the most important legacy for any government in the developing world," Museveni's wife, Janet, was quoted as saying on receiving the Pencil Award from Oxfam's Education Now program in April 1999, for the country's success in using money saved from debt relief for universal education.

Uganda, hard hit by the AIDS pandemic which threatens to reverse the economic gains so far made, and once at the disease's epicenter, is acclaimed as a success for its all out commitment in controlling HIV/AIDS. The WHO reported that rates of infection are dropping, and in one area they decreased from 27–30% of the population in 1993 to 11–12% in 1997.

Several sources of civil unrest remain: the Lord's Resistance Army (LRA), a cult-like Christian rebel group that is continuing guerilla attacks in northern Uganda from bases in southern Sudan; the Allied Democratic Forces (ADF) which has stepped up rebel attacks in western Uganda from the DRC since 1997; and other groups, including Rwanda Hutu rebels, Uganda National Rescue Front-II, and the Uganda National Front/Army that mount sporadic attacks from time to time. These groups have been accused of rape, kidnapping, torture, child abuse (they use abducted children as combatants, or sex and labor slaves), and murder of several hundred non-combatants, and other human rights abuses. UNICEF estimates that LRA and ADF have abducted over 4,900 men, women and children since 1987, most of whom remain missing.

Museveni vowed to end the uprising and Ugandan troops have won significant victories over rebels. He agreed, though reluctantly, to an Amnesty Bill in January 2000, which provides for pardon to any rebels who surrender their arms within 6 months. Three months later, no rebels have surrendered their arms. This civil unrest is beginning to affect the country's efforts to attract foreign investment. Tourism is said to have dropped by 50% since the massacre of eight tourists by Hutu rebels in 1999 in a forest reserve in Bwindi.

In a March 2000 interview with the *Los Angeles Times*, Museveni reported that when he leaves office, he would like to be remembered as "a freedom fighter, who helped to give the people of Uganda a key to their future, to give them democracy, get rid of dictatorship."

## FOREIGN POLICY

Uganda is a member of the UN, the Commonwealth of States, and several related agencies, and is a founding member of the Organization of African Unity (OAU). It also belongs to the Non-aligned Movement, the Group of 77, and the Organization of the Islamic Conference. Uganda welcomes diplomatic relations with all nations, regardless of ideology.

Relations with African neighbors are strong, although there have been strains with Kenya over trade and dissident political activity by Ugandan exiles. Some African countries have voiced concern over Libya's provision of fuel and military supplies to Uganda. Relations with Sudan, which had led to the severing of diplomatic relations between the two countries in 1995, continued to be strained. Each country accuses the other of supporting insurgency movements against it: the LRA fighting against the Ugandan government and the Sudanese People's Liberation Army (SPLA) fighting against the Sudanese Islamic government. A peace accord signed between the two countries in December 1998 has resulted in the exchange of political prisoners and kidnapped civilians (by the LRA), but tensions remain.

Ugandan troops have been involved in a complicated war in the DRC since August 1998 involving six foreign armies and nine rebel groups fighting on multiple fronts. Uganda is fighting alongside Rwanda in support of rebel forces against the government of Laurent Kabila, whom Museveni and Rwanda had helped to bring to power in another rebellion against Mobutu Sese Seko only a year before. Kabila is said to be arming the rebel ADF against Uganda and harboring Hutu extremists engaged in cross-border killings of Tutsis in Rwanda.

Uganda's involvement in the DRC has been criticized internally as unconstitutional. In June 1999 the DRC took Uganda, Rwanda, and Burundi to the International Court of Justice for committing acts of armed aggression against it and violating DRC's territorial integrity. Analysts argue that Museveni is ill-equipped to provide policing in the region, and that the country, fighting several rebel groups with a poorly equipped army, cannot afford the intervention of Angola, Namibia, and Zimbabwe (in support of Kabila) in the war. In 2000, the UN was sending into the DRC some 5000 troops to oversee a shaky peace accord signed in Lusaka in July 1999 by the countries involved. A continuation of the war can only hurt Uganda's efforts at economic growth and development

Relations with the US have steadily improved since Museveni came to power. There has been continued diplomatic warming and a concomitant increase in the flow of economic, humanitarian and technical assistance from the US to Uganda. This was capped by President Bill Clinton's visit to the country in April 1998. Like other Western countries, the US is closely watching Uganda to ensure a free and fair electoral process in the lead up to and during Uganda's referendum on political party system in June 2000.

## ADDRESS

Office of the President
Parliamentary Buildings
PO Box 7168
Kampala, Uganda

## REFERENCES

*Africa Report,* July–August 1993; May–June 1994.

Agence France-Presse, 27 April 1999.

Aliro, Ogen Kevin. "Key Test for the Non-Party State." *Gemini News Service,* 26 April 1996.

Apter, David. "Democracy for Uganda: A Case for Comparison." *Daedalus,* Summer 1995.

*Atlantic Monthly,* September 1994, 22–30.

*Boston Globe,* 10–13 May 1996.

*CIA World Factbook.* [Online] Available http://www.cia.gov/cia/publications/factbook/ug.html

*Daily Telegraph,* (London, England) 1 March 2000, p.19.

Department of State. [Online] Available http://www.state.gov/www/background_notes/uganda_0298_bgn.html

*Economist,* 29 May 1993, 10 December 1994, 22 July 1995, 23 March 1996, 13 April 1996.

*Finance and Development,* June 1993.

Inter Press Service, 31 August 1998.

*Los Angeles Times (CA),* Opinion Desk, 12 March 2000, p.M-3.

*Los Angeles Times (CA),* Foreign Desk, 27 January 2000, p.A-1.

*New York Times,* 31 March 1996; 1 April 1996; 10, 11, 12 May 1996.

*New Vision,* Kampala, BBC Monitoring International Reports, as provided by BBC Worldwide Monitoring, 22 October 1999.

PanAfrican News Agency, as provided by PanAfrican News Agency; 7 September 1997; 3 October 1997; 24 August 1999; and 16 February 2000.

PANA News Agency. [Online] Dakar, BBC Monitoring International Reports, as provided by BBC Worldwide Monitoring, 3, 9 March 2000.

Reuters News Service, 1, 5–7, 9–10, 12–14 May 1996.

*Sunday Vision,* Kampala, BBC Monitoring International Reports, as provided by BBC Worldwide Monitoring, 23 January 2000.

World Bank. [Online] Available http://www.worldbank.org/data/countrydata/countrydata.html

**Profile researched and written by Alison Doherty Munro, independent researcher (12/96; updated by Leo Zulu, University of Illinois at Urbana-Champaign 4/2000).**

# UKRAINE

## Leonid Danylovich Kuchma
### President
*(pronounced "lee-a-NEED da-NEEL-o-vitch KOOCH-ma")*

*"The people of Ukraine have decided to put the economy right and we are prepared to bear the costs of adjustment."*

Bounded by Poland, Romania, and Moldova to the west, the Black Sea to the south, Russia to the east, and Belarus to the north, Ukraine covers 603,700 sq km (233,100 sq mi) and has nearly 50 million people. The capital is the city of Kiev, which has 2.9 million inhabitants.

Its population is divided among several ethnic groups, with 73% Ukrainian, 22% Russian, and numerous other minorities. Ukrainian is the official language, similar to Russian in its use of the Cyrillic alphabet, although other languages can be used in official proceedings. Ukrainians profess a variety of religions, including Unitate Catholicism, Russian Orthodoxy, Ukrainian Autocephalous Orthodoxy, and various Protestant sects.

Long the bread-basket of the Soviet Union, Ukraine consumes only half of the food it produces, exporting the rest to Russia and other states. It has a large industrial sector based on heavy industries, automobile production, and other consumer durables. In addition, it has sizable deposits of coal, petroleum, oil and gas, manganese, uranium, gypsum, and other minerals. The Ukrainian authorities are seeking to find export markets for all these products; to date, they have had most success in selling electric power to Eastern Europe. This power is produced by the more than 20 nuclear power stations in the republic. Chernobyl, scene of the world's worst nuclear plant accident, is located in the Ukraine.

Like Russia and the other post-Soviet successor states, Ukraine's economy has been in steep decline since independence. Its national currency, the *karbonovtsy*, has declined rapidly in value relative to the *ruble* and other currencies since its introduction in the summer of 1992. In 1993, Ukraine suffered hyperinflation, with prices increasing over 10,000%. These changes, and the partial privatization in some areas, makes any estimate of GDP highly problematic. Current estimates, however, place the inflation rate at 20% and the per capita GDP at us$2,200.

## POLITICAL BACKGROUND

Ukraine, the current name for this country, was not widely used until the 19th century. Meaning "at the border" or "at border region," its use was often seen as a pejorative or derogatory term. But important political units have existed on what is now Ukrainian territory for more than a millennium. From the 9th to the 13th centuries, Kievan Rus dominated most of what is now Ukraine, controlling much of the north-south trade between Scandinavia and Byzantium. Following the capture of Kiev by the Mongols, Ukrainian lands fell under a variety of outside rulers, more importantly Lithuania in the 14th century and then Muscovy. In 1569, Ukrainian territories were transferred from Lithuanian to Polish control, and Ukrainians were divided between Catholic and Orthodox subordination.

In 1654, the nominally independent Ukrainians under the leadership of Bohdan Khmelnitskiy sought Russian help against the Poles. The Russian state used this alliance to absorb and incorporate Ukrainian lands into the growing Russian state and gradually displaced many Polish nobles with Russian ones. By the end of the 18th century, all elements of local autonomy were suppressed. Russianization expanded rapidly, particularly after the annexation of Crimea in 1783, which opened the Black Sea coast for export of grain to Europe and beyond.

In response to Russian heavy-handedness, particularly Russian moves to restrict the use of the Ukrainian language in 1863 and 1876, a Ukrainian national movement emerged in the 19th century. Much of it was headquartered in those portions of Ukraine that remained under more liberal Austro-Hungarian control. By World War I, these groups had a broad network of activists throughout the Ukrainian lands. After the February 1917 overthrow of the czar, a Ukrainian Central Rada emerged under German protection. That government was replaced several times during a complicated civil war in which White Russians, Bolsheviks, Germans, anarchists, and Ukrainian nationalists alternated in power or, to be more accurate, in claims to power.

By the end of 1920, Soviet power was successfully imposed and a Ukrainian Soviet Social Republic proclaimed. It became a founding member of the USSR in 1922. Initially, Soviet policy was quite supportive of Ukrainian rights; Moscow pushed a policy of Ukrainianization of Russian and Jewish cadres who dominated the cities and the Communist Party organization. But by the end of the 1920s, Soviet policy shifted, with the imposition of brutal collectivization policies in which at least six million Ukrainians died and the equally brutal industrialization strategies which uprooted citizens and transformed Ukrainian life. By the end of the 1930s, virtually all the gains of the 1920s had been wiped out, but the existence of a Ukrainian state with its panoply of institutions encouraged Ukrainians to think that they might someday have greater autonomy or even independence.

Moscow added Galicia and Western Volhynia to Ukraine as a result of the 1939 Hitler-Stalin Pact. However, the German invasion of 1941, in which Ukraine was occupied, appeared to nullify these actions. After the Soviet victory, Ukraine was reconstituted in its current borders which include these west Ukrainian lands. In 1954, Moscow transferred Crimea from the Russian republic to Ukraine to mark the 300th anniversary of the incorporation of Ukraine into the Russian state, and, more importantly, to preclude the return of the Crimean Tatars whom Stalin had forcibly deported to Central Asia in 1944. Moscow helped to rebuild Ukraine but faced armed resistance from the population until the time of Stalin's death.

Ukrainian nationalism ebbed and flowed with the course of Soviet reforms after 1953. Finally, under Gorbachev, as a result of both his more open policies and the shock of the Chernobyl nuclear accident, Ukrainian nationalism exploded. A national movement, the *Rukh,* was founded, and the republic's leaders were forced by several rounds of elections to attend to its demands for autonomy and ultimate independence. Like other Soviet republics, Ukraine declared itself sovereign in July 1990. Following the August 1991 coup and the subsequent resignation of Mikhail Gorbachev in December 1991, Ukraine sought to achieve independence but agreed to work within the Commonwealth of Independent States as a transitional measure. It achieved international recognition, made easier by the fact that Ukraine has been in the UN since 1945. In 1996, the country adopted a new constitution that significantly broadened the powers of the president.

## PERSONAL BACKGROUND

Born in Chaikine in Ukraine's Chernihiv oblast on 8 August 1938, Leonid Kuchma graduated from Dniepropetrivsk University in 1960. He worked as an engineer and later manager first in a highly classified Soviet design bureau in Dniepropetrivsk and then at Baikonur, the Soviet space facility in Kazakhstan. Between 1986 and 1992, he was general director of the world's largest missile factory in Dniepropetrivsk. An avid tennis player and soccer fan, he is married and has a daughter and grandson.

## RISE TO POWER

Kuchma's entrance into public politics took place in February 1990 when he shocked a plenum of the Ukrainian Communist Party Central Committee by comparing the Soviet Communist Party to a captain who had steered his ship onto the rocks. After independence, he served as prime minister from October 1992 to September 1993 when he resigned over differences with then President Leonid Kravchuk. After leaving office, he served as president of the Ukrainian Union of Industrialists and Entrepreneurs, a body that became the power base for his successful bid for the Ukrainian presidency against Kravchuk in July 1994.

## LEADERSHIP

A pragmatist who believes that Ukraine must cooperate closely with both Russia and the West, Kuchma appeals to the intellect rather than the heart, quite the opposite of Kravchuk, his predecessor. This pragmatism also reflects his own power base: the industrial leaders of the country who want stability and more production. But it also means that he does not have much emotional resonance with the population.

Like Boris Yeltsin and the presidents of many of the other former Soviet republics, Kuchma has sought to reduce the power of the parliament in various spheres of life, particularly the economy, as a means of breaking the deadlock that has prevented Ukraine from initiating economic reforms. However, in spite of his insistence on the unilateral right to define the powers of the presidency, this deadlock persisted throughout his first term. In his second term, beginning in 1999, he still faces the challenge of bringing to fruition his stated commitment to economic reform.

## DOMESTIC POLICY

Early in his first term, Kuchma surprised everyone by pushing through a radical economic reform package. Kuchma's plan called for fiscal and monetary stabilization through the introduction of a new national currency, the *hryvna,* the reduction of budget deficits and subsidies, the reduction of taxes on enterprises, an independent state bank, privatization and capital accumulation in private hands, the development of Ukraine's first mortgage system, privatization of agriculture, the liberalization of the export-import regime, the delinking of social welfare from individual enterprise, and the creation of a stronger executive system to push through these reforms.

However, many in the Ukrainian parliament and population opposed these moves, which were certain to bring at least short-term suffering to some. Little of Kuchma's ambitious program had been implemented by the time of the 1999 presidential elections. Privatization lagged well behind his goals, foreign investment levels were low, and only a major effort by newly appointed prime minister Viktor

Yushchenko saved the country from defaulting on its debt to Western bond holders.

## FOREIGN POLICY

Kuchma surprised many observers in the foreign policy area, taking positions favoring both Russia and the West. This course has increased Ukraine's freedom of action, allowing it to act more like an independent country and Kuchma more like a president. With regard to Russia, he has shown himself willing to cooperate and even to defer to Moscow on important issues. Ironically, this has not increased Russian influence in Kiev but rather the reverse because it has led Moscow to back off from some of its more threatening interventions, as Russia has no interest in destabilizing a regime that wishes to cooperate. Since Kuchma's election, Moscow has withdrawn much of its support for the Russian community in Crimea, has been more forthcoming about the Black Sea fleet, and has toned down its rhetoric about Ukrainian energy purchases. In 1997, the leaders of the two countries signed a 10-year friendship treaty and reached a settlement regarding the Black Sea fleet. The Russian Duma ratified the treaty in 1999.

Kuchma's approach to the West has been equally liberating. During his first presidential campaign, Kuchma said he would not press for ratification of the Non-Proliferation Treaty (NPT). This angered the West by calling into question the January 1994 tripartite agreement on the withdrawal of nuclear weapons from Ukraine, and raised doubts about new aid from Western-dominated international agencies. But after the election, Kuchma reversed himself, pushed through the ratification and has been rewarded with sizable international assistance. Moreover, his removal of the nuclear question that had hung over Ukraine's relationship with the West has led many countries, including the US, to be more supportive of Ukrainian interests. During Kuchma's first term in office, Ukraine was admitted to the Council of Europe, the Central European Initiative, and the Central European Free Trade Agreement (CEFTA). It also signed a economic cooperation agreement with the EU, although it was not among the countries invited to begin negotiations for admission in 1998.

## ADDRESS

Office of the President
Government of the Republic of Ukraine
Kiev, Ukraine

## REFERENCES

Banks, Arthur and Thomas Muller, eds. *Political Handbook of the World.* Binghamton, NY: CSA Publications, 1999.

Embassy of Ukraine in the United States. *Leonid Kuchma,* 1994.

*Financial Times,* 30 September 1994.

"Leonid Kuchma, Ukraine's Dismal Choice." *The Economist,* 20 November 1999, p.64.

Nahaylo, Bohdan. *Soviet Disunion,* 1992.

RFE/RL Research Report.

"Right, Left, and Center." *Time International,* 29 November 1999, p.24.

"We Need Massive Assistance." *Newsweek,* 20 December 1999, p.26.

**Profile researched and written by Paul A. Goble, Carnegie Endowment for International Peace (11/94; updated 6/2000).**

# UNITED ARAB EMIRATES

## Zayid Bin Sultan Al Nuhayyan
### President

*(pronounced "ZAH-yid bin SUHL-tahn al NUH-hah-yahn")*

*"Money is of no value unless it is used for the benefits of the people."*

The United Arab Emirates (UAE) is a federation of seven former Trucial States (emirates): Abu Dhabi, Dubai, Sharjah, Ras at Khaimah, Ajman, Umm al-Qaiwain, and Fujairah. These states were known as the Trucial States because of truces concluded with the UK in the 19th century. The UAE was formed in December 1971, when the UK terminated its treaty relations and ended its security role in the Persian/Arabian Gulf. Its total area is estimated to be 77,700 sq km (30,000 sq mi) and it has a coastline of 650 km (400 mi.). Largely desert, the country's climate is characterized by extreme temperatures and sparse rainfall. The UAE has a population of 2.3 million, most of which is concentrated in the emirates of Abu Dhabi and Dubai. The majority of the native population is Sunni, though about 20% of the population is Shia. Native Arab inhabitants are outnumbered by non-Arab immigrant workers. These expatriate workers, who account for 70% of the population, are mostly from Pakistan, India, Iran and other Arab countries. Arabic is the official language but English, Persian and Urdu are also spoken.

The currency of the UAE is the *dirham*. In the past, the economy relied on trading, fishing and pearling. Since 1958 it has been largely dependent on oil and gas extraction, which together make up about 48% of its GDP. Oil revenues supply over 90% of public sector revenues and account for over 80% of export earnings. Abu Dhabi has the largest reserves within the UAE and the greatest petroleum production. Dubai has a large re-export trade and boasts one of the world's largest and most modern dry docks. Oil has led to rapid building of infrastructure and to development of health and education services.

UAE's major trade partners are Japan, the US, and Western European countries. Its major imports are consumer goods, machinery and transport equipment. Per capita GDP is US$17,400, one of the highest in the world.

## POLITICAL BACKGROUND

Prior to the 1960s, individual emirates lacked formal institutions of government. The British resident agent took care of foreign and defense affairs and intervened in internal tribal matters only to mediate. It was only in the 1970s that a formal governmental structure was established. When the federation was created in 1971, a provisional constitution was approved, which was meant to be replaced by a formal constitution five years later. However, the provisional constitution was repeatedly renewed and has remained in force throughout the period of independence. In 1996, the term "interim" was removed, officially changing the document's status from de facto to permanent.

According to the constitution, the highest government authority is vested in the Supreme Council, which consists of the rulers of the seven emirates. The president and the vice president are elected by the Supreme Council. The president in turn appoints the Council of Ministers, which exercises executive authority. A Federal National Council, consisting of 40 members appointed by the rulers of the seven emirates, acts as the legislature. This body reviews laws proposed by the Council of Ministers and can reject them or suggest amendments.

Under the present system, individual emirates retain a great degree of autonomy, and all powers not specifically reserved for the federal government belong to them. Each of these emirates has retained control over mineral rights, taxation and police protection. In November 1976, the Supreme Council amended Article 143 of the provisional constitution so that the right to control armed forces was placed exclusively in the hands of the federal government. This action represents an important step toward integration. Although there are no political parties in the UAE, secret political groups are known to exist.

## PERSONAL BACKGROUND

Sheikh Zayid belongs to the Al bu Falah (or Nuhayyan, after the name of the founder of the dynasty) section of the Bani Yas tribe, which traces its origins to the Liwa Oasis. Zayid was born near the end of World War I, probably around 1917. Zayid never acquired a formal education; he is largely self-taught and able to converse in several languages. He observed the conduct of public affairs in his oldest brother's palace; additionally, he spent considerable time in the desert, learning the style and traditions of tribal politics. As governor of Alain, he acquired the loyalty of the local tribes with his generosity, shrewdness, and effective methods of mediation. Zayid encouraged the economic development of the Alain region, particularly its agriculture. As governor, Zayid traveled to both Europe and the US, where his ideas about development of his country were stimulated.

## RISE TO POWER

After oil was discovered in Abu Dhabi in 1962, revenues from petroleum exports began to grow. However, the ruler, Sheikh Shakhbut, Zayid's elder brother, took a conservative

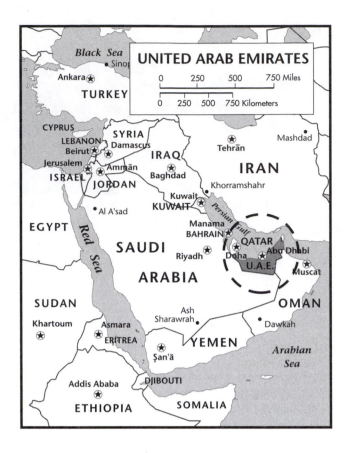

approach because he feared that development could lead to disintegration of the social fabric and an end of the traditional way of life. Zayid tried unsuccessfully to persuade his brother to change his views and to use the oil money for constructing infrastructure and for providing needed social services. With the approval of his family and the British, Zayid deposed his brother and acquired power in a coup in 1966. In 1971, when the federation was formed, Abu Dhabi was the largest and richest emirate. Not surprisingly, Zayid was elected president of the federation. Zayid has consistently supported the concept of the federation and has contributed significant funds to the federation budget as well as to the smaller emirates.

## LEADERSHIP

Zayid's main support comes from the bedouins of Abu Dhabi, particularly those of the Alain region. Zayid travels throughout the country and maintains close personal contacts with his constituents. Although previous successions in Abu Dhabi have been violent, the emergence of the federation and the elevation of Abu Dhabi's ruler to the presidency has brought about stability. Moreover, the steady flow of oil income has eliminated the need for taxes and has provided sufficient resources to placate opposing groups. Zayid has used oil revenues to expand education, health and other social services and to solidify his support throughout the UAE. He has been a strong proponent of economic development, including numerous joint ventures with foreign-owned companies.

In 1996 Zayid was elected to his sixth five-year term as president. In the same year, the nation staged gala festivities celebrating both the 30th anniversary of Zayid's accession to

the presidency and the 25th anniversary of the UAE's foundation as a federation. The occasion had added personal significance for Zayid, who was recuperating from recent, successful surgery in the US. In the weeks following his return, a succession of visits by both Arab and other foreign leaders had given evidence of the high regard in which the 79-year-old president was held in the international community.

## DOMESTIC POLICY

Zayid's domestic policies have been designed to enhance the integration and centralization of the federation. Despite his efforts, the process of integration has been slow. In December 1973, the separate cabinet of Abu Dhabi was disbanded and several ministries were upgraded to federation level. By 1976 the defense forces of emirates had emerged. Zayid used Abu Dhabi's financial leverage to accelerate the integration process. In 1976, impatient with the lack of progress in modernizing the government, Zayid threatened not to stand for a second term as president, a move which yielded positive results. The Supreme Council granted the federal government control over defense, intelligence services, Immigration, public safety and border control. In 1977 the National Council was inaugurated.

The main obstacles to integration are the differing interests of the two larger components of the federation, Abu Dhabi and Dubai. While Abu Dhabi's main source of income is oil, Dubai relies on trade and re-export to Iran and other countries of the region. The two sources of economic activity have led to differing political outlooks. Additionally, there has been a long-standing rivalry between the dynasties of Abu Dhabi and Dubai. However slow it may be, considerable progress towards integration has taken place; because of Zayid's efforts, it is unlikely that this process can be reversed.

In reaction to declining export revenues in the 1980s, the UAE moved to diversify and streamline its petroleum sector, building up its "downstream" refining and marketing business with positive results. The nation also took steps to exploit the potential of its vast natural gas reserves. In the 1990s Dubai was promoted as a hub for trade and finance.

## FOREIGN POLICY

Zayid's foreign policy has been motivated chiefly by his support for Arab unity. He was one of the leading figures in the establishment of the Arab Gulf Cooperation Council in 1981. The UAE has given considerable aid to various Arab causes and is particularly active with regard to the Palestinian issue. It was the first Arab state to totally ban all petroleum exports to the US after the October 1973 Arab-Israeli War. In November 1978, it supported the Baghdad Arab summit decision to ostracize Egypt. In 1983, it took part in GCC joint military exercises in Oman and has since then increased its defense budget substantially.

However, domestic divisions within the federation are reflected in its foreign policy. While Zayid provided financial support to Iraq in its war effort, Dubai maintained friendly relations with Iran, as it profited from the re-export trade. Dubai was the only emirate not to participate in the GCC defense exercises.

Several of the emirates of the federation have poorly demarcated borders, which have led in the past to tensions between UAE and its neighbors, Saudi Arabia, Qatar and

Iran. Abu Dhabi resolved its dispute over the Buraimi oasis with Saudi Arabia in 1974, and Sharjah reached an agreement with Iran in 1971 over the Island of Abu Musa. However, the dispute over the two Tumbs islands still remains unresolved between Rais al Khaimah and Iran. A dispute over the nearby island of Abu Musa reignited territorial tensions between the UAE and Iran in 1992 and led the UAE to seek international mediation. The status of these islands was still unresolved as of 1999, and tensions in the region continued.

During the Persian Gulf War in 1991, the UAE cooperated with the military coalition arrayed against Iraq and allowed deployment of foreign forces on its soil, as well as contributing a large sum toward the cost of the war. Having purchased weapons from the United States since 1987, the UAE signed a military cooperation pact with the US in 1994.

Zayid has taken a strong interest in the fate of the Muslim population in war-torn Bosnia, criticizing the international community for not intervening in the conflict sooner and raising money for the Bosnian Muslim community.

## ADDRESS

Royal Diwan

Abu Dhabi, UAE

## REFERENCES

Banks, Arthur and Thomas Muller, eds. *Political Handbook of the World.* Binghamton, NY: CSA Publications, 1999.

*Financial Times.*

Kadduri, Majid. *Arab Personalities in Politics,* 1981.

*New York Times,* various issues.

Office of the President. "Zayed: The Man and the President." [Online] Available http://www.ecssr.ac.ae/00uae.zayedin-justice.htm (Accessed 9 May 2000).

Zahlan, Rosemarie Said. *The Making of the Modern Gulf States.* 1989.

**Profile researched and written by Bashir Ahmed (7/90; updated 5/2000).**

# UNITED KINGDOM

**Tony Blair**
**Prime Minister**
*(pronounced "TOE-nee BLARE")*

*"The progressive parties of today are the parties of fiscal responsibility and prudence."*

The United Kingdom of Great Britain and Northern Ireland (UK), as it is officially called, is situated across the English Channel in northwest Europe and is comprised of England, Scotland, Wales, and Northern Ireland. The United Kingdom has a total area of 244,104 sq km (94,249 sq mi) and a population of 60 million inhabitants. England, accounting for half the total area, is the political and economic center of the United Kingdom. With 83% of the total British population, England is one of the most urbanized and densely populated regions in Europe. Scotland accounts for 9% of the population while Wales and Northern Ireland together only account for 8%. London, located on the Thames River in Southeast England, is the capital of the United Kingdom and its largest city, with 7.5 million inhabitants. Regional capitals are Edinburgh, Scotland; Cardiff, Wales; and Belfast, Northern Ireland.

The four regions of the United Kingdom have distinct ethnic and cultural identities. While English is the official and predominant language, Gaelic is spoken in parts of Scotland and Northern Ireland, and Welsh is spoken in parts of Wales. There are two established churches, the larger Church of England (Anglican) and the Church of Scotland (Presbyterian). Other practiced religions include Roman Catholicism, Methodist and Islam. Since the 1950s and 1960s, a greater influx of immigrants from former British colonies—primarily from India, Pakistan and the Caribbean/West Indies—have expanded the cultural and ethnic diversity of the British Isles. The inflow and concentration of nonwhite immigrants in urban centers have occasionally resulted in the swelling of racial tensions. About 5% of the current population is nonwhite.

The United Kingdom has one of the larger economies in Europe and has had average annual growth rates of over 2% from 1998 to 2000. Unemployment has dropped to 4%, which is the lowest rate in 20 years. A majority of the labor force is engaged in the service sector of the economy (60.6%) while a smaller proportion of workers are engaged in manufacturing and construction (27.2%). Women comprise 49% of the labor force and are concentrated in retail, clerical, and human services. Major exports include machinery and transport equipment, chemicals, petroleum, and manufactured goods. Major imports include foodstuffs, machinery, manufactured goods, and consumer goods. The United Kingdom's major trading partners are other West European countries as well as the United States. The British unit of currency is the Pound Sterling.

## POLITICAL BACKGROUND

The United Kingdom is a constitutional monarchy with a parliamentary form of government. The gradual development of parliamentary democracy has resulted in the diminished power and role of the monarch in political affairs. Today, the monarch acts as a unifying institution and a symbol of national identity. The monarch is the head of state, discharging primarily ceremonial functions. These ceremonial duties, however, are part of the unwritten British constitution and represent the continuity of the British political tradition. The current monarch is Queen Elizabeth II (1952). Her eldest son Charles, the Prince of Wales, is next in line to the throne.

Parliament, composed of the House of Lords and the House of Commons, is invested with supreme legislative authority. The House of Lords, comprised of nonelected peers, has a limited role in the legislative process. Precluded from vetoing any "money bills," it can only delay other bills for up to one year. However, the House of Lords is in a unique position to scrutinize, debate, amend, and legitimize governmental legislation without answering to any specific constituency. While both chambers are required for bills to become enacted into law, the real legislative power rests in the House of Commons. The 651 members of the House of Commons are directly elected from single member districts to five year terms, subject to dissolution. Normally, the leader of the largest party in the House of Commons is designated prime minister. The prime minister, who is the head of government, appoints ministers to head the various departments. While cabinet ministers are responsible for the functioning of their departments, the prime minister determines the direction and goals of government policies.

The two major parties in the United Kingdom are the Labour Party, led by the present prime minister, Tony Blair, and the Conservative Party, led by William Hague. Until Blair's administration, the Conservative Party had been in government since 1979, under Margaret Thatcher (1979–1990) and John Major (1990–1997). In the last two decades the Conservative Party has pursued policies of fiscal discipline, private ownership, free enterprise, deregulation, law and order, and has been skeptical of the European monetary union. While the Labour Party has traditionally been concerned with nationalization of industries, full employment, workers' rights, and social welfare, these demands have been moderated gradually during the past decade. In response, Labour has attempted to "modernize" the party and to broaden its electoral base of support. The latest election platforms reflect a narrowing of the ideological distance between the two major parties. While the single-member, "winner-take-all" electoral system tends to produce majorities in the House of Commons, and thus, favors the two major parties, the Liberal-Democrats (formed through the merger between the Liberal Party and the Social Democratic Party in 1988), have been gradually gaining electoral strength. Their current leader is Paddy Ashdown.

## PERSONAL BACKGROUND

Anthony Charles Lynton Blair, the second of three children, was born on 6 May 1953 in Edinburgh, Scotland, to Leo Blair and Hazel Corscadden. Blair grew up in Durham City in Northern England, where his father was a lawyer and university lecturer.

Chairman of the local Conservative association, Leo Blair is widely believed to have instilled in his son the values of ambition, initiative, hard work, responsibility, and competitiveness. It is from this middle-class background that Tony Blair developed his political views.

Blair was educated at Durham Choristers and then attended the prestigious Fetters College in Edinburgh in the early 1970s. While proving to be a dedicated and serious student, Blair also exhibited a gregarious personal side. During his formative years, Blair performed as an actor and was a singer in a rock band. After college he spent a year in London, where he drove a van, moved musical equipment, and worked in the basement of a department store. Blair continued his education at St. John's College, Oxford, where he studied law.

Upon completing his education, Blair became a barrister in London and practiced law until 1983, specializing in employment and industrial law. In 1980 Blair married Cherie Booth, a fellow barrister. Booth has since gone on to become one of London's most successful and best known lawyers. They have four children—Euan, Nicholas, Kathryn, and Leo. The youngest was born in May 2000 and was the first baby to be born at the residence of the prime minister in 150 years.

## RISE TO POWER

Tony Blair's first attempt to gain a seat in parliament was unsuccessful. He was defeated in the traditionally conservative district of Beaconsfield, west of London in 1982. Though this seat was considered unwinnable for a Labour candidate, Blair impressed several leaders by his ambition, dedication, and intelligence during the campaign. He was chosen to stand for elections in Sedgefield, near Durham, and gained the seat in 1983. After becoming a member of Parliament (MP), Blair's rise to power occurred rapidly. Some observers have stated that his "intelligence, energy, charm and discipline" helped to propel him through the ranks of the Labour Party.

During Labour's years as an opposition party, Blair was promoted to the treasury front bench in 1985 and in 1987 became spokesman on trade and industry, with special responsibility for consumer affairs and the city of London. He was promoted to the shadow cabinet in 1988 as shadow secretary of state for energy. In the following year, he was made shadow secretary of state for employment, and in 1992, he was appointed to the important post of shadow home secretary.

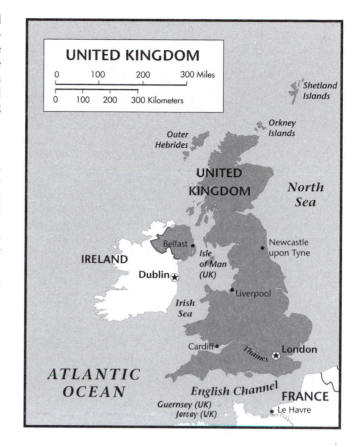

After Labour's fourth straight electoral defeat in 1992, Neil Kinnock resigned as Labour Party leader, replaced by his deputy, John Smith. Some people assumed that Smith would become the next prime minister, but with his unexpected death in 1994, the Labour Party sought a new leader who would lead them to victory. On 21 July 1994, at the age of 41, Blair became the youngest leader of the Labour Party. Three years later, Blair led the Labour Party to its first electoral victory since Harold Wilson, winning 419 seats in the House of Commons. On 1 May 1997, Blair became Britain's youngest prime minister in the 20th century.

## LEADERSHIP

Observers have noted in recent years that many parties of the left in Western Europe are becoming more centrist, concerned more with broadening their base of support and winning elections than with maintaining traditional socialist demands and ideological rigor. The Labour Party in Britain has gone through such a process, beginning in the mid-1980s under the leadership of Neil Kinnock (1983–1992). While the Labour Party has gradually become more ideologically pragmatic in the past 15 years, it has not come about without internal party struggles. Since becoming party leader in 1994, Tony Blair has adroitly held his party together while continuing the process of modernization, under the rubric of "New Labour."

Under Blair's leadership, the Labour Party voted in 1995 to drop the famous Clause Four of its party constitution, which defines one of Labour's aims as the "collective ownership of the means of production, distribution and exchange." This clause has been at the center of debate concerning the future of the Labour Party. Moreover, Blair has been able to reduce the traditionally powerful role of trade unions in the policy formulation and candidate selection processes within the Labour Party. Rather than making specific policy commitments, Blair has attempted to gain support from "middle England" and unify the party factions around the goal of winning the 1997 elections. His iron-hand style of rule has enhanced his reputation for strong leadership.

Blair led the Labour Party to a decisive victory in 1997, with a resounding majority in the House of Commons (419 seats for Labour, 165 seats for Conservatives, 46 seats for Liberal Democrats). This electoral success is more surprising given the economic growth, controlled inflation, increased investment, and decreasing unemployment Britain enjoyed under John Major's government. The electorate is thought to have embraced a "fresh new leader," as well as rejecting the divided and scandal-plagued Conservatives. In addition to losing 177 seats from the previous election, the Conservative Party also lost many of its leaders during the 1997 elections.

## DOMESTIC POLICY

Blair has stated that his government will not drastically diverge from the previous policies of limited government, fiscal discipline, private enterprise, and individual responsibility. He has promised no new nationalization of utilities, no new public spending, and no new taxes to buttress the welfare state. Blair has described New Labour as no longer a "tax and spend party, but rather a responsible party, a law and order party, a pro-business party." Soon after taking office, Blair signaled an historic change in economic policy by ceding control over interest rates to the central bank (Bank of England), drawing cheers from the Conservative opposition, European leaders and financial executives. Many have interpreted this decision as an indication of Blair's commitment to fiscal discipline. Mindful of the next general election in 2001, the government presented an expansionary fiscal policy in March 2000 with a sharp increase in spending on National Health Services (projected to be around 6% in real terms for three years).

Labour's victory brought several constitutional changes to the UK. After decades of debate, Labour organized a referendum on devolution or a Scottish and Welsh parliament. The referendum was held on 11 September 1997 and produced clear majorities for two propositions that created a separate regional parliament and gave these parliaments limited taxing powers. The Scottish and Welsh parliaments were formally opened in 1998.

Blair also proposed to reform the House of Lords to make it more "compatible with a democratic society." In October 1999, a new measure came into effect that abolished 650 hereditary peer seats in the House of Lords. Instead, the House of Lords elected 75 of their numbers to sit alongside 500 life peers, several senior judges, 26 bishops of the Church of England, and 15 deputy speakers elected by the whole house from among the hereditary peers. His government has already discontinued the practice of recommending knighthood for senior MPs leaving Parliament. Such awards are to be bestowed based strictly on merit.

Local council and city elections in 4 May 2000 sent a mixed message to the modernizing program of Tony Blair and the Labour party. Blair opposed the candidacy of Ken Living-stone, a former Labour politician for mayor of London. Because of Blair's heavy-handed attempt to prevent Livingstone from running for mayor, he was forced to run as an independent. The publicity served Livingstone well and London voters overwhelmingly supported him. The success of Livingstone seems to suggest that Blair is losing touch with the core voters of the old Labour party.

The Conservative party during the same election did well in some council or regional bodies and lost seats considered to be in secure districts. They ran on a populist line by politicizing asylum seekers and law and order issues. In response, Tony Blair's government has imposed further restrictions on who is eligible to receive asylum.

## FOREIGN POLICY

In contrast to the Conservative party, the Labour party under Tony Blair carries a more positive relationship with the European Union. Blair signed the social protocol, negotiated during the Maastricht summit in 1991 and aimed at protecting employees' rights and introducing a minimum wage (Britain is the only advanced industrial nation without one). The Thatcher and Major governments absolutely refused to consider the social protocol. Blair also signed the Amsterdam treaty in 1997, which gave more decision-making powers to the European parliament and moved some policy issues housed in the pillar on internal security and home affairs, to the Commission. Certainly, Blair wants greater British participation in the European integration process. But Blair has made no firm commitment to joining the euro and economic and monetary union. He has indicated that Britain would join as soon as the monetary and fiscal indicators are in alignment with that of the euro zone, but has not set any deadlines.

Blair has devoted himself to finding a lasting solution for Northern Ireland, which was also given new devolution powers. The problem was that the Unionists refused to share power with the IRA until the IRA had been disarmed and the IRA refused to comply with total decommissioning. Ireland and Britain signed an accord in 1998, which envisioned a Catholic-Protestant administration in Northern Ireland. The power-sharing government began operating in December 1999 but lasted only 11 weeks after the IRA refused to make any disarmament commitments. A breakthrough occurred in May 2000 when the IRA announced its readiness to permit outside observers to inspect arms dumps to ensure that no weapons had been removed. The Protestant party voted to revive a joint government with Catholics on 27 May 2000.

## ADDRESS

10 Downing Street
London SW1A 2AA
United Kingdom

## REFERENCES

Janet Matthews Information Services, 18 April 2000
Open.Gov.UK [Online] Available http//www.open.gov.uk (Accessed 5/00).

**Profile researched and written by S. Martin Hwang, Binghamton University (6/97; updated 5/2000).**

# UNITED STATES

## Bill Clinton
## President
*(pronounced "BILL CLIN-ton")*

*"We are going to build a bridge to the twenty-first century.
We just need to run our country the way we want to run our lives."*

The United States of America is located in the North American continent, bordering Canada to the north and Mexico to the south. Alaska sits to the northwest of Canada, and the Hawaiian Islands are situated in the Pacific Ocean, midway between the west coast of the US and eastern Asia. The US encompasses approximately 5.8 million sq km (3.6 million sq mi) and has a population of approximately 273 million. The largest religious groups are Protestants and Catholics. However, there are also great numbers of Jews, Muslims, Hindus, Buddhists, and other religious minorities. English is the primary language. With the exception of the Native American population, the US is a nation of immigrants, settled and developed by people from all over the world.

The unit of currency is the dollar, a strong currency that can often be used in many countries around the world. The per capita GDP has been estimated at $31,500. As the US has the world's largest economy, its trading partners are numerous, though most business is conducted with Canada, Japan, Europe, and Mexico. Major exports include machinery, chemicals, aircraft, motor vehicles, agricultural products, and entertainment. The US is also a leading producer of computer and communications technology.

## POLITICAL BACKGROUND

Consisting of 50 states and several territories, the US is a federal republic with its capital in Washington, DC. Any citizen over 18 years of age may vote, yet only about half of the people eligible to vote exercise this right. Those who do usually choose between candidates affiliated with the two major political parties, the Democrats and the Republicans. However, there are a number of smaller parties, such the Libertarian Party, the Green Party, and the recently founded Reform Party. Responsibility for governing is shared between the states and the federal government. The two levels maintain similar structures, as outlined in the US constitution, which set up a federal government consisting of three branches: legislative, judicial, and executive. The legislature, known as the Congress, is bicameral. The House of Representatives, whose 435 members face election every two years, are apportioned by the populations of the various states. The Senate is made up of 100 members, two from each state, elected for six-year terms. The judiciary is comprised of a Supreme Court and a series of lower courts. Executive power is vested in the president who serves a four-year term and can be re-elected only once. A variety of agencies operate under the president, making up a vast bureaucracy which carries out the day-to-day tasks of implementing and enforcing laws and regulations. Currently, the presidency is occupied by Bill Clinton, a Democrat who has held the office since January of 1993.

## PERSONAL BACKGROUND

Bill Clinton was born in Hope, Arkansas, on 19 August 1946. His father, William Blythe, was killed in a car accident before his son was born. When Bill was four years old, his mother married Roger Clinton, who legally adopted him and whose name Clinton would take when he was 15. Clinton attended public schools in Hot Springs, Arkansas, where he was an excellent student. Interested in politics at an early age, he was selected to participate in Boys Nation in Washington DC, where he was able to visit the White House and meet President John F. Kennedy. Attending college at Georgetown University, he earned an international relations degree and got marks high enough to win a Rhodes scholarship for study at Oxford University. While Clinton was in England, the Vietnam War was at its height. Clinton saw this war as immoral and participated in numerous protests. He eventually submitted to the draft upon his return to the US but was not called to serve in the armed forces. This circumstance allowed him to enter law school at Yale University. While attending Yale, Clinton met Hillary Rodham, who would become his wife and most important political advisor. A successful lawyer and feminist, Hillary kept her maiden name until it became an issue in her husband's political career. The Clintons have one child, a daughter named Chelsea.

## RISE TO POWER

Clinton's first venture into politics was unsuccessful. In the aftermath of the Watergate scandal, he challenged a Republican Congressman in a heavily Republican district of Arkansas but failed to unseat him. Clinton then turned toward state politics, making a successful bid for attorney general in 1976. Two years later, at 32, he became the youngest governor in the country. Attacking the job with his usual energy, he took on entrenched interests, raised taxes to fund state programs, and brought many people from outside Arkansas into his administration. In doing so much, so fast, Clinton alienated many in his state, seeming arrogant and unmindful of the people who elected him. He soon became the youngest ex-governor in the country.

Determined to run for governor again in 1982, he was careful not to repeat the same mistakes. Clinton issued a televised apology for raising taxes and promised to listen to voters more carefully. He was rewarded with another opportunity to serve as governor, a post he held until his election to the presidency. Clinton became active in various national political associations, serving as chairman of such groups as the National Conference of Democratic Governors and, more importantly, the Democratic Leadership Council, an organization designed to bring the party toward the center of the American political spectrum and end the Democrats' losing streak in presidential politics.

Clinton's road to the White House began with early losses in the primaries in New Hampshire and Maryland. However, he quickly bounced back, winning almost all the primary races on "Super Tuesday." As his campaign gathered momentum, it soon became apparent that he would be nominated by the Democratic National Convention in July 1992. On 3 November 1992, with 43% of the popular vote, Clinton emerged victorious over his opponents, incumbent Republican President George Bush, who received 38% of the vote, and independent H. Ross Perot, who received 19% of the vote. In the electoral college vote count, Clinton received 370 votes to Bush's 168. On 20 January 1993, Bill Clinton was inaugurated as the country's forty-second president.

## LEADERSHIP

The Clinton presidency got off to a rocky start with the defeat of the health care reform program that was his administration's first major initiative. However, Clinton proved able to work with both parties when necessary and won support from the opposition for a major legislative victory, the ratification of the North American Free Trade Agreement (NAFTA). In the 1994 mid-term Congressional elections, the Republicans gained control of both houses for the first time since 1954, and the vote was viewed by many as a referendum on the president's first two years.

However, Clinton soon rebounded as the nation's economy continued to improve. A budget dispute between his administration and the Republican-controlled Congress resulted in a shutdown of the federal government at the end of 1995, for which the Congress was widely blamed. Clinton's policies became more conservative, reflecting an awareness of political realities. In an effort to co-opt popular Republican issues, he approved a line-item veto, called for a balanced budget, and signed legislation to reform the welfare system. His success in moving to the center, combined with a general sense that he had matured in office, gave him a high approval rating across the country, and in 1996 he won a second term, with 49% of the vote against 42% for Republican Bob Dole.

Clinton's triumph in becoming the first Democrat since Franklin Delano Roosevelt to be elected to a second presidential term was sharply undercut during that term. The ongoing Whitewater investigation into alleged unethical past dealings by the president and his associates led to revelations of sexual misconduct in 1995 and 1996 involving a White House intern, Monica Lewinsky. After at first denying these revelations, which included charges of perjuring himself before a grand jury, Clinton admitted in August 1998 to having had an improper relationship with Lewinsky. The scandal led to impeachment proceedings in the House of Representatives, which in October impeached Clinton by a vote of 258 to 176, making him only the second president in US history to be impeached. However, in the Senate trial that took place the following February, Clinton was acquitted on both articles of impeachment.

Although Clinton continued to energetically fulfill his presidential duties in the conduct of both domestic and foreign policy, and public approval of his job performance remained high, his legacy as president was seen as inescapably tainted by the impeachment. By 2000, as his second term drew to a close, he was widely regarded as a "lame duck," and national attention focused increasingly on the presumptive presidential nominees of the major parties, Vice President Al Gore (Democrat) and Texas Governor George W. Bush (Republican), son of former President George Bush. (Elections were scheduled for 7 November 2000.)

Nevertheless, Clinton announced an ambitious agenda for 2000 that included reinvigorating the stalled Middle East peace process, expanding gun control, and shoring up Social Security. He also declared his intention to use the nation's budget surplus to pay down the national debt and strengthen its entitlement programs.

## DOMESTIC POLICY

Clinton's success in the 1992 campaign was attributed to a continual emphasis on the economy, pointing out its weaknesses and attributing them to President Bush. In fact, Clinton presided not only over an economic recovery but, during the eight years of his presidency, over an unprecedented period of extended economic growth, during which inflation was kept under control, unemployment reached a 30-year low, and the stock market soared to record heights.

Clinton's domestic policy accomplishments have included creating AmeriCorps, an government agency which provides money to pay off college loans in exchange for two years of national service; signing the Family and Medical Leave Act (allowing workers unpaid leave for family and medical emergencies); increasing the minimum wage; and signing a modest health care reform law (so workers can keep their health insurance when they change jobs). He has been an advocate of free trade, approving both NAFTA and the General Agreement on Tariffs and Trade (GATT).

In response to the chronic social problems of crime and poverty, Clinton signed laws outlawing assault rifles and overhauling the welfare system. The controversial welfare law, which fulfilled Clinton's campaign promise to "end welfare as we know it," turned over to the states responsibility for assisting the poor, with the federal government providing only a fixed sum of money, known as a "block grant." The law also required that no one be allowed to receive benefits for more than two years. After that, all able-bodied people would have to find work. Clinton claimed that this law would end a cycle of dependency by forcing people off welfare.

In his 2000 State of the Union address, Clinton outlined a large number of legislative proposals, including targeted tax cuts (most notably a reduction in the so-called marriage penalty) and measures to improve education, reform health care, fight crime, support workers and their families, and preserve the environment.

## FOREIGN POLICY

Clinton can be said to be the first post-Cold War president. While many old foreign-policy concerns could be laid to rest, there was a new set of problems to be confronted: nuclear proliferation, stability in Russia, the rise of China, and ethnic violence.

In Russia, Clinton supported the government of Boris Yeltsin, who presided over the transition away from Communism, and has expressed support for Yeltsin's successor, Vladimir Putin. Clinton met with Putin in Moscow in June 2000 at a summit meeting that included talks on arms control and missile defense. However, against Russia's wishes, Clinton has advocated expanding the NATO alliance to include countries from Eastern Europe.

Regarding China, Clinton has tried to keep relations cordial, focusing primarily on economic issues. He won a major victory toward the end of his presidency when the House voted to grant China permanent normal trade relations in June 2000, paving the way for China's admission to the WTO, probably early in 2001.

In addressing the problem of wars originating from ethnic nationalism, the US has been called upon to serve as broker between the warring sides, to lead a military intervention, or both, in countries including Bosnia, Somalia, and Haiti. In March 1999, the US spearheaded a series of NATO bombing raids on targets in Serbia to counter Serbian expulsion of ethnic Albanians from the Serbian province of Kosovo.

Clinton has also worked to broker peace in other regions. In the Middle East he helped mediate a historic agreement between Israel and her Arab neighbors, including Jordan and the Palestinians. In Northern Ireland too, the Clinton administration mediated talks between the various factions, helping to negotiate a ceasefire and peace agreement. However, as Clinton's final year in office began, stability in both regions was looking increasingly fragile.

## ADDRESS

The White House
1600 Pennsylvania Avenue
Washington, D.C. 20500
USA

## REFERENCES

"Bill Clinton's Final Days." *US News & World Report*, 20 December 1999, p. 16.

"Bill, Vlad, Dubya et al: Clinton's going to Moscow, but Bush or Gore will have to deal with Putin." *Time International*, 5 June 2000, p. 48.

"Clinton Comes Calling." *World Press Review*, May 2000, p. 27.

*Current Biography Yearbook*. New York: H.W. Wilson, 1988.

"The Long March Begins." *Newsweek*, 5 June 2000, p. 29.

*New Republic*, 9 November 1992, 11 November 1996.

*Newsweek*, 18 November 1996.

*Political Handbook of the World*. Ed. Arthur Banks and Thomas Muller. Binghamton, NY: CSA Publications, 1999.

"Star Wars II: Here We Go Again." *The Nation*, 19 June 2000, p. 11.

*Time*, 27 January 1992; 20 July 1992; 4, 11 November 1996.

*US News and World Report*, 30 March 1992; 4, 18 November 1996.

**Profile researched and written by David Bernell, Johns Hopkins University (12/96; updated 6/2000).**

# URUGUAY

### Jorge Luis Batlle Ibañez
### President
*(pronounced "YORJ LOO-ee BAT-il ih-BON-yez")*

*"Only those societies with open economies and with a high level of technology have acceptable levels of unemployment. Uruguay can and should transform itself into one of these nations."*

Slightly more than halfway down the South Atlantic coast of South America lies the Eastern Republic of Uruguay, second smallest country in South America, and a state where sheep outnumber people eight to one. Nestled between the southern tip of Brazil and a section of Argentina's eastern border, Uruguay covers 176,215 sq km (68,037 sq mi). Its seaside capital and largest city is Montevideo, with a population of 1.4 million.

Almost 90% of the country's 3.3 million people are of Spanish or Italian heritage. The population is 66% Catholic, 2% Protestant, and 2% Jewish. Spanish is the official language. The educational system is free from kindergarten through college, and the adult literacy rate is one of the continent's highest at 97.3%. Its 76-year average life expectancy sets it apart from many other Latin American countries. The currency unit is the new *peso*. Despite its 85% urban population, Uruguay's economy has traditionally been tied to the land, with livestock and agriculture constituting its mainstays. Principal exports are meat, wool, textiles and leather goods. Industrial production, the economy's most troubled sector, accounts for less than 19% of the country's GNP, down from 30% in 1986. Tourism, especially from Argentina, has been an important growth sector during the last several years. Uruguay's major trading partners are Argentina and Brazil, accounting for nearly 50% of the country's imports and 40% of its exports in recent years. Uruguay's rapidly growing trade deficit reached US$1 billion in 1997. The rate of inflation is 8.6%, down from 129% in 1990. Per capita GNP is US$8,600. The World Bank has classified Uruguay as a severely indebted country.

## POLITICAL BACKGROUND

Beginning in the mid-1600s this sparsely inhabited fertile plain, home to the semi-nomadic Charrua Indians, became a contested arena between the Spanish and the Portuguese. By the end of the 18th century most of the Portuguese had been driven out of the area. In the early part of the 19th century, the movement for independence that swept through Latin America took an interesting twist in Uruguay. In 1811, Jose Gervasio Artigas led a group of revolutionaries against the Spanish in Argentina. Although they successfully ousted the colonial rulers, they failed to establish an Argentine confederation among the provinces of the Rio de la Plata. Ten years later, Brazil tried unsuccessfully to annex the East Bank. Finally, in 1828 Uruguay became independent from both Argentina and Brazil, adopted its first constitution in 1830, and elected revolutionary leader Fructuoso Rivera, the country's first president.

After independence, the conflict became an internal one. When Rivera's term ended in 1836, he tried to overthrow his successor, Manuel Oribe. Civil war ensued and continued for the next 16 years. Oribe's faction became known as the Blancos, because they wore white hatbands, and Rivera's, who wore red hatbands, the Colorados. In 1865, the Colorados captured control of the government (in exchange for ceding control of the countryside to the Blancos) and held onto power for nearly a century. During the long reign of the Coloradoans, one person in particular put a distinctive mark upon the Uruguayan political system. Elected president twice, in 1903 and 1911, Jose Batile y Ordonez was a visionary who instituted a wide-ranging series of social and political reforms that transformed this tiny country into a modern socialist state. Batile established a social security system, unemployment insurance, and a penal system based on rehabilitation rather than punishment. Banking, insurance, and utilities were run by state corporations; divorce was legalized and freedom of the press protected. He made education universal and free.

The 1940s and 1950s were Uruguay's golden years. Bolstered by war-time Allied needs for wool and meat, Uruguay's economy boomed and the country enjoyed a period of prosperity and political stability. But the tensions in Uruguayan society re-emerged during the 1950s as foreign trade declined, the economy stagnated, inflationary pressures mounted, and government deficits rose dramatically. In 1958, the Blancos became the majority party for the first time since 1865. Social turmoil and political paralysis increasingly gripped the country during the next decade. Confronted with significant student and labor unrest and an incipient leftist, urban guerrilla movement, the *Tupamaros,* the military took over the government in June 1973. For the next 12 years, the country suffered brutal repression under authoritarian military rule. Thousands were tortured, unions were dissolved, and the universities were purged and restructured. Thirty-seven newspapers were shut down. Most writers, painters, and musicians were either arrested or fled the country. During this era Uruguay's external debt soared to more than US$5 billion dollars.

The return to civilian rule began in 1980 when Uruguayan voters rejected a referendum to institutionalize the military's ultimate authority over the country's political system. In November 1984, elections were held for a civilian president, and Julio Maria Sanguinetti, the Colorado candidate, won. Sanguinetti served a full term, and was followed by Luis Alberto Lacalle in 1989, a standard-bearer for the Blanco Party (now known as the National Party). Lacalle pursued an neo-conservative agenda of market-oriented economic changes, which included lowering tariffs, shrinking the government, reducing social security benefits, privatizing the national airline, and promoting Uruguay's participation in international trade and the regional trading bloc, Mercosur. However, Lacalle's 1992 referendum that proposed selling several state-run companies, including the phone company, was overwhelmingly rejected, and the legislature blocked many of his other attempts at reform.

In November 1994, after what most observers called the most bitterly contested and closest election ever, Sanguinetti was once again chosen president, becoming the second Uruguayan in the country's 160-year history to hold the office twice. In 1999, in his fifth attempt at the presidency, Jorge Batlle and his Colorado Party had to strike an alliance with the National Party to defeat a strong challenge from a rejuvenated left.

The Uruguayan constitution bars presidents from holding office for successive terms. Its unique, complex electoral system allows more than one presidential candidate from each party, with voters voting simultaneously for a party and for specific candidates within each party. Each party's first-place candidate then receives all his party's votes. Members of Congress are elected proportionally to the number of votes cast for their party. Suffrage is universal and mandatory for citizens 18 and older, with fines administered to those who fail to vote. All national and mayoral offices are elected simultaneously for five-year terms. The bicameral legislature has a 30-member senate and a 99-member house of deputies.

## PERSONAL BACKGROUND

Jorge Luis Batlle Ibañez was born on 25 October 1927. By 17, he already was working as a journalist for Radio Ariel, and later become its director. He joined the Colorado Party in 1945 when he was only 18. In 1956, he received a law degree from the Faculty of Law and Social Sciences at the University of Montevideo. By 1945, he was working as a journalist with *Diario Acción,* which was put out of circulation by the military dictatorship in the early 1970s. In 1998, he was recognized as distinguished citizen by the World Zionist Organization as part of Israel's 50th anniversary. He has represented his country at the United Nations. He is married to Mercedes Menafra. He has two children and three grandchildren.

## RISE TO POWER

Batlle comes from a distinguished political family. His great-uncle, José Batlle y Ordóñez, remains one of Uruguay's most respected former presidents. During his presidency (1903–07 and 1911–15), Uruguay experienced remarkable social progress. Welfare programs that he initiated remained part of the social structure at the beginning of the 21st century. Jorge Batlle came into politics in his teen years, joining the Colorado Party in 1945. Despite his name, Batlle slowly rose through the party ranks. He was elected to the Chamber of Deputies in 1958, and reelected four years later. In 1966 and 1971, he unsuccessfully ran for the presidency. Outside

politics, he spent the bulk of his time working as a journalist or editor of *Acción* newspaper, until it was closed during the dictatorship of 1973–84. During the military regime, Batlle worked in agribusiness, but remained politically active. He was arrested several times for his political opinions. At the return of democracy, Batlle, under the auspices of the Colorado Party, was elected senator in November 1984 and again in 1995. In 1989 and 1994, he unsuccessfully sought the presidency.

In 1999, Batlle was a presidential candidate for the Colorados. Traditionally, the Colorados and the National Party (formerly the Blanco Party) had dominated national politics. But in the 1990s, the leftists had made major gains at the polls. On 31 October 1999, Tabaré Vázquez, who was backed by a center-left coalition, gained 39% of the vote in the presidential election, not enough to prevent a second election between the top two vote getters. Batlle finished second with 31.7%. In the November runoff election, Batlle gained 51.59% of the vote to win the presidency. Vázquez had 44.07% of the vote.

## LEADERSHIP

The unexpected first place finish by Vázquez in the first round of the presidential election in October 1999 shocked the Colorados and the National Party. Vázquez had gained support by promising not to touch the country's generous welfare system. More importantly, he promised to slow down liberalization of the economy, which called for more privatization of state assets. Batlle was seen as an old-guard conservative whose views on the economy did not inspire much confidence in Uruguayans. Twice in plebiscites, Uruguayans had rejected proposed liberalization programs in the 1990s. Fearing a leftist victory, Batlle was forced to align the Colorados with their historic foes: the National Party. He positioned his party as a wiser and more moderate alternative to Broad Front, the leftist coalition. Yet, his economic positions remained quite similar to what Vázquez was offering: slow down the pace of liberalization and leave untouched the country's nearly 100-year old social safety net. It was his alliance with the National Party that brought victory. In exchange for their votes, Batlle named five Blancos to his cabinet.

At the beginning of 2000, the Colorados and the National Party Blancos held a slim majority in the Senate, with 17 of 31 seats, and a majority in the lower house, with 54 of 99 seats. The alliance was expected to allow Batlle more room to tinker with the economy. Faced with a shrinking economy, and 11% unemployment, Batlle faced tough fiscal decisions at the beginning of his presidency in 2000.

## DOMESTIC POLICY

While Batlle had promised a cautious approach to economic reforms, his inauguration speech gave hints that he was prepared to press for major reforms to change antiquated ways of doing business, bringing spending under control and making Uruguayan exports more competitive in the world market. Faced with a shrinking economy, he proposed cutting government expenses to reduce a fiscal deficit. He predicted that 2000 would be a difficult year, but expected the economy to rebound in 2001. The agribusiness was hit especially hard during the economic slowdown of 1998–99. Batlle wants state-owned companies to improve services, quality and prices, and compete at a regional level. He also called for more transparency, proposing a new government agency that would inform citizens about government expenditures. Shortly after his election, Batlle disclosed his salary and the salary of his closest associates on the presidential Internet web site. The Internet, and computer technology in general, was expected to be a main component of Batlle's development policies. He wants all Uruguayan students to become computer literate.

Shortly after his inauguration, Batlle met with families of Uruguayans who disappeared during the dictatorship years of the 1970s and early 1980s. The previous government had refused to meet with the families, simply saying that an amnesty law protected former and current military leaders and closed the issue. But Batlle said his government had a moral responsibility to bring closure to the approximately 159 unsolved disappearances. The issue remains an open wound in Uruguay. Batlle's government quickly dismissed a high-ranking member of the army in early 2000 for suggesting that the armed forces would someday have to stage another war against leftists.

## FOREIGN POLICY

Despite the close economic ties to Brazil and Argentina that created economic problems in Uruguay starting in 1998, Batlle remained deeply committed to Mercosur, the trade pact comprising Brazil, Argentina, Uruguay, and Paraguay. "We have grown with Mercosur, we aspire to keep growing with Mercosur. We believe in Mercosur and we are not bothered by crises because they help us correct errors," Batlle said in his inauguration speech. Soon after his speech, he met with the Brazilian and Argentinean presidents to discuss widening the scope of Mercosur, including a speedy process to accept Chile into the trade pact. Chile and Bolivia are associate members. Batlle firmly believes in a world economy, and was expected to press for greater ties with several nations. He envisions an economic pact that would cover all of the territories between Alaska and Patagonia. He also wants Mercosur to reach beyond the economy, acting as a cultural, intellectual and technological ambassador for the region.

## ADDRESS
Officina del Presidente
Montevideo, Uruguay

## REFERENCES
Agence France Presse.
CNN Online (English and Spanish) 1999 and 2000. [Online] Available http://www.cnn.com (Accessed 24 April 2000).
Latin American Weekly Report.
O'Donnell, Guillermo et al. *Transitions from Authoritarian Rule: Latin America.* Baltimore: Johns Hopkins, 1986.
Office of the President. [Online] Available http://www.presidencia.gub.uy (Accessed 24 April 2000).
"Uruguay: Batlle's Triumph." *The Economist,* 4 December 1999, p. 36.
"Uruguay: President Takes Office." *New York Times,* 2 March 2000, p. A12.
*Washington Post.*
Weinstein, Martin. *Uruguay: Democracy at the Crossroads.* Boulder: Westview, 1988.

**Profile researched and written by Ignacio A. Lobos (6/2000).**

# UZBEKISTAN

## Islam Karimov
## President
*(pronounced "iz-LAHM ka-REE-moff")*

*"A firm hand is needed in today's explosive situation, and the people of Uzbekistan will not accept Western-style democracy because of their history and national character."*

The Republic of Uzbekistan is by far the most populous of the predominantly Muslim Central Asian republics of the former Soviet Union. This landlocked nation shares borders with the other former Soviet republics of Turkmenistan, Kyrgyzstan, Tajikistan, and Kazakhstan, as well as with Afghanistan. It has a land area of 447,400 sq km (172,741 sq mi).

The rapidly growing population is estimated at 24.1 million. A Soviet-era census listed about 71% of the population as ethnic Uzbeks, 8% Russian (most of whom live in the capital of Tashkent), and the rest mainly other Central Asian peoples. By various estimates, between one-third and one-half of Uzbekistan's 1.65 million Russians have left. Despite decades of Soviet anti-religious propaganda, centers of Islamic study and religiosity continued to operate. Most Uzbeks belong to the Sunni branch of Islam. The population is predominantly rural (60%) and agrarian.

Nearly 75% of the arable land is dedicated to cotton, a legacy of Soviet central planning. Irrigating the arid land for cotton has led to the draining of the Aral Sea, formerly the fourth largest inland body of water in the world, of 65% of its volume. The sea's depletion and the resultant salinization of tens of thousands of square kilometers of land, together with extreme overuse of pesticides, have led to one of the world's worst ecological and public-health catastrophes. The economy is mostly based on agriculture and energy and mineral extraction. It has been the world's third or fourth largest producer of cotton, eighth largest producer of gold, and among the top ten in natural gas production. According to the U.S. Department of Energy, Uzbekistan has over one billion barrels of proven and possible oil reserves and 109–123 trillion cubic feet of gas reserves.

President Karimov aims to move gradually toward "market socialism" in order to ensure social stability. Uzbekistan put restrictive trade practices into effect after 1997, including high import tariffs that were imposed on CAEC members Kazakhstan and Kyrgyzstan in 1999. A restrictive currency conversion system also holds back exports. The economy began to recover in 1996. Consumer price inflation decreased to about 29% in 1998 (compared to 204% in 1995). Gross Domestic Product (GDP) is us$59.2 billion and per capita GDP is approximately us$2,500. A bad cotton harvest in 1998 and declines in world commodity prices contributed to a decline in exports, leading the government to increase foreign short-term debts and draw down international reserves. The Uzbek government has reported that industrial and agricultural production increases contributed to a 4.4% rise in GDP during the first nine months of 1999. Widespread poverty and unemployment provide grounds for religious extremism and dissent to grow, according to many observers. Most state-owned apartments and many small enterprises have been privatized.

## POLITICAL BACKGROUND

The Uzbek people stem from an amalgam of Central Asian Turkic tribes. Their language is Turkic. Central Asia was ruled for centuries by a succession of emirs, khans, and potentates. The most notable was Tamerlane, who conquered a vast empire in the 14th century and established his capital as Samarkand in present-day Uzbekistan. Russian penetration and annexation came in the second half of the 19th century. The Russians brought railroads, cities and cotton growing to what had been a largely nomadic society. In 1917 and 1918, following the collapse of the czarist regime and the Russian Revolution, pro-Bolshevik Russian workers in Tashkent and a rival Muslim Congress established competing governments. The intervention of the Red Army proved decisive, despite prolonged anti-Soviet resistance known as the Basmachi revolt. By 1924, a Soviet regime was established. To facilitate control, Central Asia was divided along ethnic and linguistic lines, leading to the creation of, among others, the Uzbek Soviet Socialist Republic.

Joseph Stalin, in power from 1924–53, transformed the USSR into a highly centralized totalitarian dictatorship with all control emanating from Moscow. Rigid centralization was relaxed somewhat under Khrushchev's administration, 1954–64, and markedly under Brezhnev and his immediate successors. In the Brezhnev era, republic Communist Party bosses came to exercise almost unlimited power locally, provided they remained loyal to Moscow on national issues. Sharaf Rashidov, head of the Uzbek Communist Party from 1959–84 ruled Uzbekistan virtually as a personal fiefdom in his later years. In Tashkent, as in Moscow, the government was subordinate to the Party leader and the legislature was a rubber-stamp nonentity.

Gorbachev's leadership in Moscow from 1985 until 1991 accelerated the decentralization of the USSR. Gorbachev also launched an anti-corruption campaign that hit hardest in Uzbekistan, where falsification of cotton production figures and massive skimming of state funds pervaded Uzbek politics. Many important Uzbek officials were accused of crimes and

some were imprisoned. Rashidov's immediate successor, Usmankhodzhayev, was forced out by Moscow in 1988. His successor, Nishanov, left Tashkent a year later for a leadership role in the USSR Supreme Soviet. Nishanov was succeeded as Uzbek Communist Party first secretary in March 1989 by Islam Karimov.

On 25 August 1991, days after the failed Soviet coup, Uzbekistan declared its independence and changed its name from the Uzbek Soviet Socialist Republic to the Republic of Uzbekistan. On 21 December 1991, it joined 10 other former Soviet republics in a loose association called the Commonwealth of Independent States (CIS).

## PERSONAL BACKGROUND

Islam Karimov was born on 30 January 1938 in Samarkand. His was a poor family. His father, an Uzbek, worked as a handyman. His mother was a Tajik. Young Karimov showed high intelligence and was able to attend the Russian high school in Samarkand. He then entered Tashkent's Central Asian Polytechnic Institute where he earned a degree in mechanical engineering. From 1960 to 1966 he advanced from assistant foreman to senior engineer, first in an agricultural machinery plant and then an aviation production association in Tashkent. In 1964, Karimov joined the Communist Party and in 1966, he shifted from engineering to work in the Uzbek government as an economic specialist. From 1966 to 1983, Karimov worked in the Uzbek State Planning Committee (GOSPLAN), eventually becoming first deputy chairman. During this period he also earned a Candidate of Economic Sciences degree, roughly equivalent to a PhD.

## RISE TO POWER

In 1983, Karimov was appointed Uzbek minister of finance, a post he held for three years. In 1983, he was also elected as a deputy to the Uzbek Supreme Soviet, or legislature. In 1986, he was appointed deputy chairman of the Uzbek Council of Ministers and chairman of the Uzbek GOSPLAN, holding both positions until 1989. At this time Karimov also took important posts in the Communist Party as an *oblast* (regional) first secretary and full member of the Uzbek Communist Party Central Committee.

Karimov reached a top leadership position in 1989. When Rafik Nishanov, head of the Uzbek Communist Party, became chairman of the upper chamber of the newly restructured USSR Supreme Soviet in the spring of 1989, Karimov, who had not been implicated in the corruption scandals of the Rashidov era, was selected to replace him as Uzbek Party first secretary, the de facto leader of Uzbekistan. This brought with it full membership in the Communist Party of the Soviet Union (CPSU) Central Committee and its Politburo in 1990. He orchestrated the election of the Uzbek Supreme Soviet in February 1990, forbidding the Birlik movement from fielding candidates, so that in many constituencies Uzbek Communist Party (UCP) candidates ran unopposed. Upon convening, this Supreme Soviet named Karimov to the new post of president. In November 1991, the UCP renamed itself the People's Democratic party of Uzbekistan (PDP), retaining Karimov as its head. (He remained its head until he resigned in June 1996, arguing that as president he should be above partisanship.) In November 1991, he restructured the Council of Ministers as a Cabinet of Ministers directly under the president. Karimov completed his consolidation of power in December 1991 by winning the presidency of Uzbekistan in a popular election. According to official results, 94% of eligible voters participated and 86% of those voted for Karimov, while opposition Erk Party candidate Mohammed Solikh received 12%. Birlik had been refused registration so was unable to field a candidate. International observers found widespread election fraud by government officials.

## LEADERSHIP

Karimov has shown himself to be a shrewd politician, one of the few old-line Communist Party leaders able to maintain himself in power through the post-Communist era. Under Karimov, Uzbekistan remains one of the most authoritarian of the former Soviet republics.

A new Constitution was adopted by the Oliy Majlis in 1992 by unanimous vote after two months of public discussion. It provides for a strong president and a weaker, 250-member unicameral legislature, termed the Oliy Majlis or Supreme Assembly. Although a multi-party system was proclaimed, the Oliy Majlis, just after enacting the constitution, banned Birlik as a subversive organization and removed the legislative mandate from a prominent human rights activist. As detailed in the constitution and by a law approved in September 1994, the Oliy Majlis adopts laws and amendments to the constitution, determines the direction of domestic and foreign policy, approves the budget, determines taxes, schedules legislative and presidential elections, elects the constitutional court, supreme court, and arbitration court, ratifies the president's choices for prime minister and other members of the cabinet, ratifies a presidential declaration of a state of emergency, and ratifies treaties, among other powers. In actuality, the Oliy-Majlis is closely controlled by Karimov.

On 26 March 1995, Karimov orchestrated a referendum to extend his presidential term until the year 2000, winning support by 99.6% of 11.25 million voters. Most international observers deemed these results questionable. Two candidates were registered to run in the 9 January 2000 presidential race, incumbent President Karimov and Abdulkhafiz Jalolov. Jalolov, a philosopher, was nominated by his People's Democratic Party (PDP), which Karimov formerly headed, to give the appearance of a contested race. All other registered parties and regional councils vied to support Karimov. His campaign pledges included extending privatization, promoting small business, and allowing currency convertibility for the Uzbek currency, the som, which would encourage foreign investment. He also appeared to extend an olive branch to some former opponents, such as exiled Sheikh Mohammed Sadeq, Uzbekistan's former Islamic leader, inviting him to return. Karimov won 91.9% of 12.1 million votes cast, with a reported 95.1% turnout. The US State Department announced on 12 January 2000, that "this election was neither free nor fair and offered Uzbekistan's voters no true choice," mentioning the Uzbek government's refusal to register opposition parties or candidates and that Jalalov had endorsed Karimov during the campaign. Some critics argued that the election illustrated groups competing for Karimov's favor and spoils.

Karimov's leadership was challenged in February 1999 by explosions in the capital city of Tashkent that Karimov denounced as a coup attempt. After the explosions, which by various reports killed 16–28 and wounded 100–351, Uzbek officials detained dozens of suspects, including political dissidents. The first trial of 22 suspects in June 1999 resulted in six receiving the death sentence. Karimov in April 1999 asserted that former Uzbek presidential candidate Mohammad Solikh had masterminded the plot, and had been supported by the Taliban group in Afghanistan and Uzbek Islamic extremist Tohir Yuldash. The 22 suspects were described in court proceedings as Islamic terrorists who received training in Afghanistan (by the Taliban), Tajikistan, Pakistan, and Russia (by the terrorist Khattab in Chechnya), and were led by Solikh and Yuldash and his ally Jama Namanganiy. Testimony alleged that Solikh had joined the Islamic Movement of Uzbekistan, led by Yuldash and Namanganiy, in mid-1997, and that Solikh, Yuldash, Namanganiy, and others had agreed that Solikh would be president and Yuldash defense minister after Karimov was overthrown and a caliphate established. According to an Uzbek media report in July 1999, the coup plot included a planned attack on Uzbekistan by Namanganiy and UTO allies transiting through Tajikistan and Kyrgyzstan. Another secret trial in August 1999 of six suspects in the bombings (brothers of Solikh or members of his Erk Party) resulted in sentences ranging from 8 to 15 years. Solikh rejected accusations of involvement in the bombings, alleging that court "confessions" were coerced and scripted. At the OSCE Summit in November 1999, Karimov called for the creation of OSCE special forces to combat terrorism. The OSCE more generally resolved that the international community should play a role in anti-terrorism and anti-crime efforts and in bolstering security cooperation in Central Asia.

Karimov faced another crisis in the latter part of 1999. Several hundred Islamic extremists and others fled repression in Uzbekistan and settled in Tajikistan but were being forced out at Uzbekistan's behest. Rogue groups from Tajikistan refused to disarm as part of the Tajik peace settlement and entered Kyrgyzstan in July–August 1999. Namanganiy headed the largest guerrilla group. The guerrillas seized hostages, including four Japanese geologists, and several Kyrgyz villages, stating that they would cease hostilities if Kyrgyzstan provided a safe haven for refugees and would release hostages if Uzbekistan released jailed extremists. The guerrillas were rumored to be seeking to create an Islamic state in south Kyrgyzstan as a springboard for a jihad in Uzbekistan. Kyrgyzstan's defense minister in October 1999 announced success in forcing guerrillas out of the southwestern mountains into Tajikistan. Karimov contributed air support that targeted several alleged guerrilla hideouts in Tajikistan, eliciting protests from Tajikistan of violations of its airspace. Karimov heavily criticized Kyrgyz President Askar Akayev for supposed laxity in suppressing the guerrillas. In November 1999, Karimov also denounced Tajik President Imomali Rakhmonov for allowing the guerrillas to enter Afghanistan rather than wiping them out.

## DOMESTIC POLICY

In November 1997, President Karimov admitted that "we do not fully meet many democratic standards today," blaming the "traditionalism" of the people and stating that he aimed to change this way of thinking "gradually and in stages." According to the U.S. State Department's *Country Reports on Human Rights Practices for 1998*, the Karimov regime severely limits human rights. Citizens cannot exercise their right to change their government peacefully because the government "severely represses opposition groups and individuals and applies strict limits on freedom of expression." No real opposition groups are allowed to legally function. Only approved public meetings and demonstrations may be held. Police and security forces use torture, harassment, illegal searches, property confiscations, and arbitrary arrest and detention to stifle dissent. Beating of detainees is routine. No opposition newspapers are allowed; the last was banned in 1993. Thirty to forty independent television companies have operated, though they practice self-censorship. The State Department's *Report on International Religious Freedom for 1999* states that the Uzbek government regards unofficial Islamic groups as threats and has increasingly restricted their activities. The government tolerates many Christian evangelical groups, but often harasses those that try to convert Muslims to Christianity. The head of the Uzbek Human Rights Society, Tolib Yoqubov (also a leading member of Birlik) in September 1999 reported that "tens of thousands of innocent religious people are being kept in prisons" in Uzbekistan.

In April 2000, Karimov issued a draft booklet of his speeches and writings on creating a national ideology to supplant the vestiges of Soviet-style "slavishness" and "hostility" among the people. This ideology would draw on the past and present to emphasize a "free and prosperous" Uzbekistan, and would be the lodestone of domestic and foreign policies, he stated. He stressed that it would be particularly useful in helping younger generations to be "conscious of their national identity, to stick to their national traditions, [and] to bring our sacred religion to a higher level." At the same time, he averred, other ideologies would also be allowed to exist in Uzbekistan. He described Uzbeks as "the most simple...but also the most magnanimous people in the world," able to be easily swayed by "evil forces," particularly Islamic extremism that is being exported to the country by outside powers. Pointing to the Autumn 1999 incursion into Kyrgyzstan by guerrillas aiming at invading Uzbekistan, he warned that hostile forces were again trying to invade, and called for "inculcating in our people's minds" the ability to repulse the "evil forces."

## FOREIGN POLICY

In January 1992, Uzbekistan was admitted to the UN and the Conference on Security and Cooperation in Europe and agreed to abide by their many conventions and declarations including those on human and political rights and peaceful settlement of disputes. In addition, Uzbekistan agreed to honor all relevant international commitments of the USSR. It is establishing diplomatic relations with countries around the world.

Uzbekistan seeks working relations with Russia that do not overly compromise its independence. Russia and Uzbekistan signed a Friendship Treaty in 1992 that includes collective security provisions. Uzbekistan, Russia, Armenia, and other Central Asian states signed a collective security pact in 1992, calling for mutual assistance in the case of aggression against the parties. Uzbekistan withdrew from this pact in early 1999, citing sovereignty issues, but in late 1999 stressed that it supported stepped-up bilateral security arrangements with Russia. Karimov refused to join an expanded customs union formed by Russia, Belarus, Kyrgyzstan, and Kazakhstan in 1996, calling its terms "categorically unacceptable" to Uzbekistan's independence. Many in Uzbekistan argue that it should be the "big brother" in relations with the rest of Central Asia. Uzbeks make up over 50% of Central Asians and, like Russians, are the targets of attacks by nationalist extremists in Tajikistan and

elsewhere. Karimov has eschewed such rhetoric but seeks to play a leading regional role. Karimov reportedly contributed arms and troops to help rout anti-government forces in Tajikistan in late 1992 and its troops were part of CIS "peacekeeping" forces sent to guard borders in Tajikistan. In late 1998, Tajik President Rakhmonov accused Karimov of supporting an uprising in northern Tajikistan. Karimov rejected the accusation and pulled Uzbekistan's 140–150 "peacekeeping" troops out of Tajikistan.

President Karimov's priority in foreign policy has been to establish good relations with regional powers such as Russia and Turkey, though he has also pursued ties with the United States and other nations. Karimov has raised concerns about the threat Islamic fundamentalism in Afghanistan poses to Uzbekistan and the region. As a member of the UN sponsored "6 plus 2" Afghan peace group, he hosted July 1999 peace talks. Karimov and other officials have voiced concerns about Iran's economic ties with Turkmenistan and other activities in the region. Recently, however, he has praised Iran's role in mediating the Tajik and Afghan civil wars and called for increased trade. Relations with Turkey have been friendly and it is the biggest investor in Uzbekistan. In March 1999, Turkish President Suleyman Demirel visited Uzbekistan and Karimov hailed Turkey as "our closest supporter, friend and brother," but by mid-1999 tensions had arisen over Turkey's hesitancy to hand over suspects in a bombing incident in Uzbekistan.

## REFERENCES

*AACAR Bulletin,* American Association for Central Asian Research, Spring 1992.

*CSCE Report: The Referendum on Independence and Presidential Election in Uzbekistan,* 31 January 1992.

*Far Eastern Economic Review,* 9 January 1992.

*FBIS Daily Report: Soviet Union* (before 1992), *Central Eurasia* (after 1992), various issues.

*RFE/RL Research Report,* 6 March 1992.

"Uzbekistan—Many Votes, Few Friends. (Islam Karimov Elected President of Uzbekistan)." *The Economist,* 15 January 2000, p. 39.

**Profile researched and written by Jim Nichol (May 2000).**

# VANUATU

## Donald Kalpokas
## Prime Minister
*(pronounced "kal-POE-kas")*

*"An economic policy is more than just trading, free enterprise, and people doing business.
It is the country's system of socio-economic everything."*

The Republic of Vanuatu is the name that these South Pacific islands adopted when they became an independent nation in 1980. Formerly, the archipelago was known as the New Hebrides, the name given to them by the English explorer James Cook in 1774. The country is located 2,172 km (1,347 mi) northeast of Sydney, Australia. It lies within the geographic region known as Melanesia. Its closest neighbors are Fiji to the east, New Caledonia to the south, and the Solomon Islands to the northwest. There are some 80 islands in the archipelago, with a land area totaling 14,763 sq km (5,700 sq mi). The major islands are Efate, Espiritu Santo, Malekula, and Tanna, where 70% of the population lives.

The population is estimated to be 189,000. Almost 18% of the populace live in the two largest towns, Port Vila on Efate and Luganville on Espiritu Santo. *Ni-Vanuatu* (People of Vanuatu) are ethnically Melanesian and constitute almost 98% of the population. The largest group of non-Melanesians are of European descent; smaller groups of Polynesians, Chinese, and Vietnamese make up the remainder. With a population density of about 13 people per sq km and an average growth rate of about 2%, Vanuatu does not face an overpopulation problem quite so severe as that of other Pacific Island nations. According to the constitution, Bislama, an English-based pidgin, is the national language, but both French and English are also used in government, business, and education. About 55% of children are educated in English-language schools and 35% in French-language schools. Although more than 100 indigenous languages are said to be spoken, Bislama now stands as the most widely understood tongue. Christianity in both Protestant and Catholic branches is the dominant faith. However, traditional religious practices that emphasize dependence on ancestral spirits have not entirely disappeared.

Vanuatu's economy is dominated by agriculture, with manufacturing being largely restricted to the processing of agricultural products. The major exports are copra (dried coconut), beef, veal, timber, and cocoa. Vegetable squash is emerging as a potentially significant export. A financial center opened in the capital city of Port Vila in 1971 and has become a significant provider of tax shelters and banking for offshore interests. Tourism is a growing sector with great potential. Vanuatu's unit of currency is the *vatu*, or stone. The per capita GNP is us$1,300. Vanuatu appears on the UN's list of least developed countries.

## POLITICAL BACKGROUND

The colonial history of Vanuatu is unique in the Pacific Islands. For 74 years prior to independence, the islands were ruled as a "condominium," controlled jointly by France and England. This meant that each colonial power maintained separate administrations. Though these were equal in theory, the actual amount of French and English influence varied greatly in different islands. This unusual history has important political consequences today. For example, the *Vanua'aku Pati* (Vanuatu Party—VP), led by Father Wlater Lini and which dominated politics from 1971 until 1991, is regarded as the representative of anglophone interests. It has been associated in the news media with Anglican and Presbyterian congregations.

At present the country is a republic, governed by a single-chamber parliament, or Representative Assembly, recently expanded to 52 members. This body is elected regionally at least every four years; the voting age is 18. Executive power is vested in the prime minister and a council of ministers. After a general election, parliament meets to elect a new prime minister who then proceeds to form a government. The number of ministers in the council must not be more than a quarter of the number of members of parliament. Vanuatu's head of state is the president, elected on a secret ballot by an electoral college of parliament and the presidents of the six provincial councils. His term of office is five years. The incumbent, Jean-Marie Leye, has recently taken a more active political role in dealing with political unrest. The constitution also allows for a national council of chiefs which meets at least once a year to discuss matters that will help promote and preserve *ni-Vanuatu* culture and languages.

## PERSONAL BACKGROUND

Donald Kalpokas was born in 1943 on Lelepa, a small islet near Efate. He was initially educated at schools in the Efate area, but completed his secondary education at King George VI School in the Solomon Islands. Kalpokas continued his education in New Zealand, where he studied at the Ardmore Teachers Training College. He taught for one year in Vanuatu before beginning advanced work in educational administration at the University of the South Pacific in Fiji.

Kalpokas comes from a family long associated with the Presbyterian Church, in which he serves as a lay preacher. He is married and has five children.

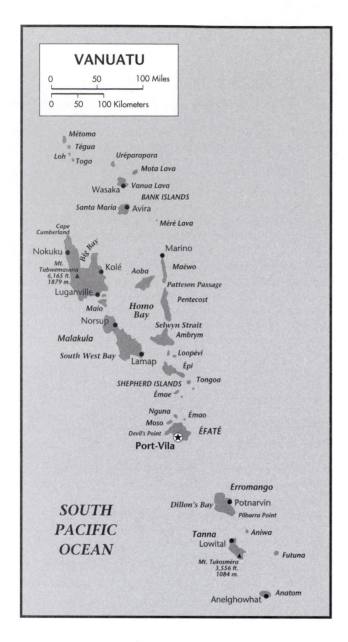

## RISE TO POWER

Kalpokas has taken an active role in politics ever since he met fellow student Walter Lini in New Zealand. While employed as a teacher in 1971, he helped to form the New Hebrides Cultural Association to represent *ni-Vanuatu* interests as the colonial period drew to a close. After a peaceful demonstration in support of regulations protecting village land tenure, this group reorganized itself as the New Hebrides National Party. In 1977, this party was renamed the *Vanua'aku Pati* (Vanuatu Party—VP). Two years later, a Representative Assembly was established in anticipation of eventual independence. In the first elections, VP candidates received 62% of the popular vote, winning 26 of the 39 seats. Kalpokas was elected to represent North Efate and has held that position ever since—making him one of only four parliamentarians who has served continuously since independence.

As a founding member of the VP, Kalpokas worked in close association with Lini for almost 20 years. However, their relationship began to show signs of strain in 1983. Kalpokas resigned his portfolio as minister for education in Lini's cabinet after a disagreement over the firing of a deputy prime minister. Lini survived a no-confidence motion put forth by Kalpokas. The rift was later healed, and Lini accepted him back into the VP's ranks. Under Lini's leadership, the VP continued to hold power, winning clear parliamentary majorities in both the 1983 and 1987 elections. There was growing dissatisfaction, however, with its economic policies.

The VP's success was overshadowed by concerns about Lini's health. He suffered a stroke in 1987 and a heart attack in April 1991. Kalpokas and other VP members felt that Lini was no longer the dependable leader he had once been. They complained that he had become high-handed and undemocratic when making important decisions. In August 1991, a party congress was convened, only to be boycotted by Lini. The congress elected Kalpokas party leader. Two months later he became prime minister after Lini was deposed by a no-confidence vote taken in an extraordinary session of parliament. Lini then broke away to form a new party, the National Unity Party (NUP), splitting what had long been the dominant political organization in Vanuatu.

The VP's internal struggles clearly affected the election of December 1991, when that party and the new NUP won 10 seats each. The francophone Union of Moderate Parties (UMP) won 19 seats, short of the majority necessary to form a government. The UMP and the NUP formed a coalition with Korman Maxime Carlot as prime minister. This coalition marked the beginning of new unrest in Vanuatu's political affairs.

Elections in 1995 continued this new pattern of shifting coalitions and personal rivalries as Serge Vohor and Carlot struggled over control of the UMP and the prime minister's office. Vohor replaced Carlot as prime minister in 1995 but lost the office to him after only two months. In 1996, Vohor formed a new coalition with VP support and returned to power, but by now the political scene had become increasingly confused.

The newly created position of ombudsman began to issue reports that added to this picture of instability. In that office, Marie-Noelle Ferrieux Patterson aggressively investigated charges of corruption and mismanagement. Her findings implicated Vohor, Carlot, and other political leaders. Vohor's government voted, over VP opposition, to repeal the act which had created ombudsman powers, but Vanuatu's president refused to promulgate this piece of legislation as law.

The president took further action to dissolve parliament in November 1997, in the face of ongoing political crises that included violent demonstrations in Port Vila. The ruling coalition refused to step down, claiming the president had no constitutional right to do this. In January 1998, however, the Court of Appeal ruled that the president's act had been legal—clearing the way for a new general election.

In the election of 6 March 1998, the VP improved its earlier performance to take 18 seats, but these were not enough to form a government in the enlarged 52-member Assembly. Kalpokas was able to rejoin forces with Lini, whose NUP had taken 11 seats. The addition of some minority party legislators enabled Kalpokas to form a new coalition with a clear majority of 31 members, which elected him prime minister. In November 1999, Kalpokas resigned to avoid a no-confidence vote, and he was succeeded by Barak Sope, leader of the Melanesian Progressive Party.

## LEADERSHIP

The image of Kalpokas as leader is well summarized in a recent article, which called him "Vanuatu's Mr. Clean." Ever since his days as student and schoolteacher, he has consistently pursued what he believes to be the best interests of *ni-Vanuatu*, without succumbing to the temptations of power or personal gain which have apparently lured others. Although willing to join in the coalition governments which Vanuatu's recent parliamentary elections have made necessary, he has always been loyal to the party which he helped found. His only real political defeat came because he did not anticipate that others would be more willing to sacrifice principle for power. When the VP's internal split in 1991 left the party with minority representation, he did not expect that Lini's group and the francophone UMP would join forces against him. It remains to be seen whether the disagreements between him and his old ally have been resolved so that he will be able to carry out the policies he has always supported.

## DOMESTIC POLICY

Kalpokas took over as prime minister after several years of political turmoil. Since the 1991 general election ended the VP's 20 years of political dominance, Vanuatu has presented to the world a picture of near-anarchy. In addition to the reshuffling of cabinets and coalitions, international news media have publicized charges of corruption in high places. Economic problems have been aggravated by the previous government's failure to approve a 1998 budget. Although the Vohor government had initiated a comprehensive reform program to strengthen the country's fragile economy, little progress had been made toward its implementation. The new prime minister has made it clear that addressing such domestic problems is his highest priority.

To achieve this, Kalpokas wants to restore the Ombudsman's Act, which the Vohor government had repealed. He has also set a high priority on enacting a leadership code, drafted but not passed in 1997. Kalpokas hopes to introduce legislation for a value added tax to reduce public debt.

Because of his training and early career as a teacher, Kalpokas has long argued for a master plan to improve Vanuatu's schools, with the goal of increasing the number of *ni-Vanuatu* with marketable skills. Even though some 90% of the country's children have primary education, only about 9% go on to secondary school. Better educated *ni-Vanuatu* could also form a more efficient and smaller civil service. Like many Pacific Island nations, Vanuatu is burdened by a bloated public payroll.

## FOREIGN POLICY

Because of the domestic problems that he has inherited, Kalpokas has so far made few foreign policy statements. Vanuatu's continuing dependence on foreign aid connects foreign policy to domestic economic concerns. Even before attaining his present office, Kalpokas had in 1995 admitted that the VP's foreign policy required rethinking, especially to attract foreign investment and expertise. If his government follows a common pattern among Pacific nations, this will include overtures to Asian countries like Japan, which provide the bulk of aid to the area. Within the Pacific Island region, Kalpokas is expected to be enthusiastic toward the Melanesian Spearhead Group, formed in March 1988 by representatives of the pidgin-speaking nations of Papua New Guinea, the Solomon Islands, and Vanuatu. Such a policy would be consistent with the VP's long identification with the anglophone party. However, in this as in other political decisions, Kalpokas must remain sensitive to the historically rooted and conflicting claims of anglophone and francophone Vanuatu.

At the South Pacific Forum in June 1999, Vanuatu supported a Pacific Free Trade Area (FTA) that would initially include 14 countries in the region, with the possibility of future expansion. The proposed FTA would offset ramifications of the expiration of the Lome Convention agreement between the European Union (EU) and 71 African, Caribbean, and Pacific (ACP) countries. The Lome Convention agreement is subject to a World Trade Organization (WTO) waiver that expired in February 2000, though the EU announced plans to petition for an extension to 2006. The South Pacific FTA would also buffer its members against the expiration in 2006 of the WTO waiver for the US Compact of Free Association, which selectively offers trade preferences to member countries. An official of the South Pacific Forum mentioned Vanuatu's production of kava and beef as an example of the regional diversity of goods that can be traded to the mutual benefit of FTA member nations.

## ADDRESS

Office of the Prime Minister
P.O. Box 110
Port Vila, Vanuatu

## REFERENCES

Ambrose, David. *A Coup That Failed? Recent Political Events in Vanuatu.* The Australian National University, 1996.

*Country Profile: Vanuatu, 1996–97.* Economist Intelligence Unit Ltd., 1997.

*Islands Business Pacific,* April 1998.

Van Trease, Howard, ed. *Melanesian Politics: Stael Blong Vanuatu.* New Zealand: University of the South Pacific and University of Canterbury, 1995.

*Vanuatu Weekly,* January 1996–March 1998.

**Profile researched and written by Eugene Ogan, Professor Emeritus, University of Minnesota. (9/98; updated 5/2000).**

# VATICAN CITY

### John Paul II
### Pope
*(pronounced "JON PALL")*

*"I was afraid to receive this nomination, but I did it in the spirit of obedience to Our Lord and in the total confidence in his mother, the most holy Madonna."*

The official name of the Vatican, or Vatican City as it is interchangeably called, is *Lo Stato de la Citta del Vaticano* (State of the Vatican City). It is not a country, but rather an independent city-state and is the smallest state in the world. It is somewhat triangularly shaped and covers an area of 0.44 sq km (0.11 sq mi) lying entirely within the city of Rome near the west bank of the Tiber River and west of the Castet Sant'Angelo. To the west and south it is bounded by the Leonine Wall. The Vatican is famous for its gardens which contain fine collections of orchids and exotic flora. The population of the Vatican is less than 900. The Vatican unit of currency is the Vatican *lira* (plural-lire) which is interchangeable with the Italian *lira*. Italian is the official language of the Vatican, however, Latin is the official language of the Holy See (the seat of jurisdiction of the pope as spiritual leader) and is used for most formal papal acts and addresses. Although the citizens within the Vatican represent countries from all over the world, most of the inhabitants of the Vatican are Italian. The entrances to the Vatican City are guarded by Swiss Papal Guards. The Vatican City is the center of the Roman Catholic Church and the seat of its holy leader, the pope. The Vatican economy is supported by contributions, known within the Catholic Church as Peter's pence, and tourism. The only industries of the Vatican produce a limited amount of mosaics, religious publications, and staff uniforms. The Vatican is active worldwide in banking and financial activities. Other than postage stamps, the Vatican produces no exports.

## POLITICAL BACKGROUND

The Vatican City is the physical seat of the Holy See which is the central government of the Roman Catholic Church. For many centuries, the popes of the Roman Catholic Church held sovereignty over a wide band of territory across central Italy. However, in 1861 these Papal States fell under the control of the Kingdom of Sardinia. The pope's sovereignty was limited to Rome and its surrounding areas. In 1870 even Rome itself was forcibly incorporated into the new Kingdom of Italy. In 1871 the Italian Parliament passed the Law of Guarantees which secured the pope's spiritual freedom, an income, and special status for the Vatican area. Unwilling to accept this arrangement, however, the popes remained as self-imposed prisoners in the Vatican until a more permanent political and financial agreement, the Lateran Treaty, was signed with the Italian government in 1929. A new concordat

was signed in 1984 that further specified church-state relations between the Holy See and Italy.

A constitution published at the time the Lateran Treaty went into effect provided for the pope to exercise supreme legislative, executive and judicial power within the Vatican City. However, the pope delegates internal administration to the Pontifical Commission for the State of the Vatican City, which is assisted by the Administration of the Patrimony of the Apostolic City. The Pontifical Commission consists of seven cardinals of the Roman Catholic Church and a lay special delegate, with the assistance of a board of 21 lay advisors. The principal government officials other than the pope are the secretary of state and the secretary of the Sacred Council for Public Affairs.

Following the death of a reigning pope, the College of Cardinals is called into conclave to choose a successor from their number. The cardinal who receives two-thirds of the vote is elected pope for life. There are no political parties and no local government. Much of the government's work is devoted to the needs or the Catholic Church and is conducted by offices called Sacred Councils. Each office is headed by a cardinal who holds his position for five years. Thus the Vatican can be characterized as a monarchical-sacerdotal state.

The Vatican issues its own currency, stamps and passports. Defense is the responsibility of Italy, but internal security is maintained by a contingent of the Swiss Guard and a civilian security corps. Judicial authority for criminal cases resides in the Vatican Courts. For ordinary legal matters, which typically involve religious cases, there are tribunals inside the Vatican to decide issues. Appeals can be made to the Roman Rota or, in exceptional cases, to the Supreme Tribunal of the Apostolic Signature.

## PERSONAL BACKGROUND

Pope John Paul II was born Karol Jozef Wojtyla (pronounced "voy-TEE-wah") in Wadowice, Poland on 18 May 1920. He was the second of two children born to a strict Catholic family. His mother Emilia (Kaczorowska) Wojtyla, who was or Lithuanian descent, died when he was only nine. His brother Edmund, who was much older than Karol, died four years later. His father, Karol Wojtyla, Sr. was a pensioned army sergeant and died in 1942.

In school, the young Karol Wojtyla excelled in sports, dramatics and academic subjects. He enrolled in the field of literature at Jagiellonian University in Krakow, Poland in

1938. There he acted with an amateur theatrical troupe and participated in poetry readings and literary discussions. He began his seminary studies in secret while earning a living as a manual laborer in a quarry and a chemical factory during Poland's occupation by the Nazis in World War II.

Wojtyla was ordained in Krakow in 1946, after which he worked in France as pastor to French working-class youth and Polish refugees. He then went on to further his studies at the Pontifical Angelicum University in Rome. After graduating, he returned to Poland to serve a parish for some years and then went on to become a professor of ethics at the Catholic University of Lublin.

"Pilgrim Pope" John Paul II, as he is affectionately called, is an enormously popular pope. Besides being an accomplished philosopher and well-versed in Marxist theory, he has also written books and treatises dealing with religion as well as literary poems and plays. He has recorded an album of religious hymns and he enjoys staying physically fit through both swimming and jogging. His outgoing nature has attracted millions. He is on record as having celebrated the largest Mass ever when 1.2 million people attended his Mass in Dublin, Ireland on 30 September 1979. His weekly audiences, or public appearances, at the Vatican City attract such huge crowds that the meetings have had to be moved from St. Peter's Church to the square outside. During one such appearance there in May of 1981, he was shot and seriously wounded by Mehmet Ali Agca, a Turkish terrorist. Pope John Paul II completely recovered from the attack. He has been plagued with illness in the 1990s mostly due to old-age.

In addition to his native Polish, the pope speaks fluent Italian and flawless Latin. He is also quite conversant in English, French, German and Spanish. He is the first non-Italian pope since the year 1522 and the first Slavic pope ever.

## RISE TO POWER

In 1958, Wojtyla was consecrated auxiliary bishop of Krakow, Poland under Archbishop Eugeniusz Baziak. Four years later the archbishop died and Bishop Wojtyla was named vicar capitular and placed in charge of the archdiocese of Krakow. In 1964, he was officially appointed archbishop of Krakow. From 1962 to 1965, Wojtyla addressed the Vatican Council II on several occasions concerning important doctrines of the Catholic Church. In 1967, the then Pope Paul VI elevated Wojtyla to a cardinal. During his cardinalate, Cardinal Wojtyla began to make the first of his many future international journeys, including trips to the US in 1969 and 1976.

With the deaths of Pope Paul VI in August 1978 and Pope John Paul I in September of 1978, a secret conclave in the Vatican was called by the College of Cardinals to elect the 263rd successor to St. Peter as bishop of Rome. Cardinal Wojtyla was elected in October 1978, at which time he chose the new name John Paul II. With tears in his eyes he accepted the position. The new pope made his first public appearance shortly afterwards from the balcony overlooking St Peter's Square in which he announced to the gathered crowd, "I was afraid to receive this nomination, but I did it in the spirit of obedience to Our Lord and in the total confidence in his mother, the most holy Madonna." Humility and professed

obedience to God have characterized his papacy. Like his predecessor, John Paul I, he declined coronation and one month later was installed as pope in a simple Mass in St. Peter's Square on 22 October 1978.

## LEADERSHIP

As the head of the Roman Catholic Church, the pope has an international constituency. However, given the ever greater complexity of society, religious authorities can no longer assume that believers will automatically accept all, or perhaps even most, of the tenets of their religion. This is especially true when church dogma conflicts with personal beliefs, an especially common phenomenon today in industrialized countries. John Paul II has addressed this issue directly by reinforcing church teachings through numerous public addresses and visits to foreign countries. The pope has traveled widely since assuming his title, visiting many of the least developed countries and speaking out for greater reliance on spiritual faith and condemning what he sees as an overemphasis on material goods. In this regard, he is considered a conservative on Catholic doctrine. He condemns the use of artificial forms of contraception, denies the right of priests to actively participate in the political and economic affairs of their host countries, and is against allowing women into the priesthood. At the same time though, the pope has spoken forcefully for the need to respect human rights and the need for the world community to act with greater unity. He has been especially vocal in calling upon the rich world to share its wealth with poor regions and has tried to build bridges with the Islamic world in the 1990s.

## DOMESTIC POLICY

Since the pope is the leader of the Roman Catholic Church, domestic policy of the Vatican City is primarily devoted to the health, maintenance and augmentation of the church worldwide. The Vatican City labor force consists mainly of priests and other ecclesiastics who naturally accept the leading role of the pope. Adult literacy is close to 100% and about 65 papal educational institutions are located throughout Rome. One of the major responsibilities of the Vatican is to be the voice of the Catholic Church for its members. To that end, the Vatican publishes a newspaper and magazine devoted to Catholic affairs and prints official church documents that are communicated throughout the world.

John Paul II has made himself and his papacy part of the global scene through worldwide traveling, a papal first. These journeys are used to show the universal character of the Roman Catholic Church and to personally deliver the pope's message to all interested peoples. This universality of the church, combined with a call for greater religious toleration, has long been a personal doctrine for the pope. At the Vatican Council II (1962–1965), the future Pope John Paul II pointed out that the church could not claim religious liberty for itself without conceding it to others.

The Jubilee Year 2000 turned out to be a bonanza for the Vatican and for small businesses licensed to sell Holy Year trinkets. It brought thousands of extra tourists to the area.

## FOREIGN POLICY

Many nations today recognize the State of the Vatican City as an independent sovereign state under the temporal jurisdiction of the pope. The Vatican also has permanent observer status in the UN. Until recently, the Vatican had uneven relations with the Communist nations of Eastern Europe and the USSR. With the dramatic political and social changes now taking place within these countries, relations between the Roman Catholic Church and these governments have markedly improved. However relations with other communist or socialist countries in Asia, Africa, and Latin America remain somewhat tense. The major principles behind the Vatican's foreign policy are neutrality and the demand for greater international cooperation.

From 1870 to 1984, the US had no formal diplomatic relations with the Holy See. Since 1984, the Pope has visited the US regularly, the last time being January 1999 when he went to St. Louis for a quick 30 hour tour. In March 2000, the Pope made a historic trip to Israel where he visited Holocaust memorials and spoke of the Church's culpability in fostering anti-Semitism. During this trip, he also went to Bethlehem and reaffirmed the Holy See's support for an independent Palestinian homeland.

## ADDRESS

Supreme Pontiff of the Roman Catholic Church
Vatican City

## REFERENCES

*Agence France Presse*, 15 December 1999.
*Current Biography*, 1979, pp 194–197.
*Financial Times*, 12 March 1999.
*International Herald Tribune*, 24 March 2000.
*New Catholic Encyclopedia*, 1967, pp. 555–558.
*Worldmark Encyclopedia of the Nations: Europe*, 1984. pp 311–320.

**Profile researched and written by Laurence Marcus, Washington University (4/91; updated 5/2000).**

# VENEZUELA

## Hugo Chavez
## President
*(pronounced "OO-go CHAH-ves")*

*"This will be a government of neither the left nor the right...It will be a civic humanist government because it will put in first place, at the center of its attention, human beings."*

The Republic of Venezuela sits on the northern tip of the continent of South America, directly east of Colombia. Its northern boundary is 2,800 km (1,739 mi) of Caribbean Sea coastline. Guyana and Brazil share borders on Venezuela's east and southeastern sides, respectively. Venezuela covers an area of 912,050 sq km (352,143 sq mi) and is shaped somewhat like a saddle. The capital and largest city is Caracas.

Venezuela's population is estimated at 23.2 million. Approximately 67% of the people are mestizo (half-Indian, half-Spanish), 21% white (Spanish), 10% black, and 2% Indian (largely Yanonami, living in the Amazon jungle along the border with Brazil). The official language is Spanish, spoken by all except the Indians. Christianity is the main religion, with Roman Catholicism predominant. Adult literacy was 90% in 1998.

The unit of currency is the *bolivar*. Although Venezuela is Latin America's fourth largest economy, about 75% of the population live in poverty. Petroleum accounts for nearly 80% of the export revenue. In addition to oil, the country is resource-rich with iron ore, bauxite, gold, diamonds, and other valuable minerals, plus vast expanses of untapped forests and excellent grazing and agricultural lands producing coffee, rice, and cotton.

## POLITICAL BACKGROUND

As Latin America's second oldest democracy, Venezuela is a federal republic, operating under its 1961 constitution. Since 1958, it has functioned as a free, populist democracy, and has been considered one of the most stable governments in Latin America. Suffrage is universal and compulsory for anyone over the age of 18. Members of the bicameral Congress are elected every five years. The judicial system is weak and generally politicized. Supreme Court members are appointed by the legislature. The president is ineligible for reelection for ten years after leaving office.

The first Europeans to set foot on Venezuelan soil came with Christopher Columbus in 1498. Prior to Columbus, the territory was home to the Carib and Arawak Indians. The Spaniards thought the Indian pile dwellings on Lake Maracaibo resembled buildings in Venice, Italy and named the area Venezuela or "little Venice." It remained a remote outpost of Spanish administration until the 18th century, when cacao, tobacco, and coffee companies were given charters by the Spanish crown. Venezuela gained its independence from Spain in 1821, after a 10 year struggle led by

Simón Bolívar, Francisco Miranda, and others. Between 1821 and 1830, it belonged to the Gran Colombia confederation with Ecuador and Colombia.

Venezuela became an independent republic in 1830. The 19th century witnessed dictatorships, civil war, and intermittent forays by foreign commercial interests. By 1930, Venezuela had become a major petroleum producer and exporter. Between 1935 and 1958, the country vacillated between dictatorship and democracy.

Until recently, Venezuela had a two-party political system that resulted from the Pact of Punto Fijo, a power-sharing arrangement reached during the transition to democracy in December 1958. *Acción Democrática* (AD) is a social democratic party founded in 1941 with a strong base of support in organized labor. *Comité de Organización Electoral Independiente* (COPEI) is a Christian Democratic party slightly right of center. Traditionally, these two parties commanded widespread support from across Venezuelan classes, occupational groups, and regions, effectively marginalizing parties on both the left and right. For 40 years they had largely alternated in office. Since 1988, however, both parties had been suffering internal leadership rifts. Moreover, the Venezuelan public had grown increasingly disaffected with what they frequently refer to as their *partidocracia* (or "partyarchy"), a government run by the party for the party. By the early 1990s, the perception of widespread corruption among public officials, confirmed by revelations of specific instances, brought public disenchantment to an all-time high.

In 1992, two coup attempts were sparked by junior military officers who were dissatisfied with President Carlos Andres Perez's stringent economic reforms and evidence of political corruption. The leader of the first failed coup was Hugo Chavez, a lieutenant colonel. In May 1993 Perez left office in disgrace after being impeached by the Senate for his participation in a misappropriation and embezzlement scheme. Elections held in December 1993 returned Rafael Caldera, a Venezuelan political institution, to the presidency after 20 years. Caldera was the first president since 1958 not elected as the candidate of either AD or COPEI. He won a mere 30% plurality of the vote. Over the next five years the country was plunged into recession three times and the gap between rich and poor grew wider. By the time Caldera left office, Venezuela was in a state of political and economic disarray.

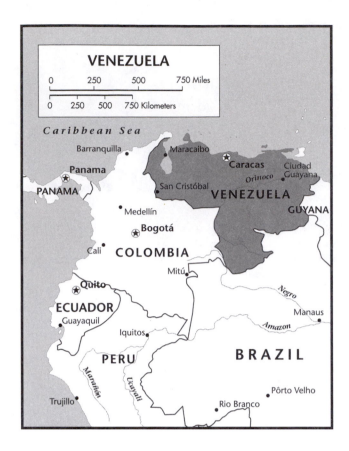

## PERSONAL BACKGROUND

Hugo Chavez Frias was born 28 July 1954, the son of school-teachers from Sabaneta, a poor farming town in the western state of Barinas. He studied at the Military Academy of Venezuela in Caracas and later earned a graduate degree in international relations. Chavez spent years building an underground organization inside the army to oppose military corruption. As head of an elite paratrooper unit, he led 12,000 troops in the first of two failed coup attempts against President Carlos Andres Perez in 1992.

Chavez is an avid baseball player. He enjoys traditional Venezuelan food, the popular *joropo* dance, and native art. Chavez is well read, and has dabbled in playwriting. He has been married twice and has four children with his second wife, Marisabel. His political inspiration is Simón Bolívar, who is often invoked in his speeches. Chavez is a devout Catholic who often quotes passages from the Bible.

## RISE TO POWER

Since 1989, Chavez and a group of fellow soldiers had worked clandestinely to build the Bolivarian Revolutionary Movement. The movement first surfaced in 1992 during a time of riots, strikes, and scandals that were threatening the long-touted stability of the country. Chavez led insurgent troops in a bloody but unsuccessful attempt to overthrow the Perez government. After the failed coup, he was jailed for two years before being pardoned by Rafael Caldera. Upon his release in 1994, Chavez visited Cuba and praised President Fidel Castro and "the Cuban way." A charismatic figure and

fiery orator, he formed the *Polo Patriotico* (Patriotic Pole), an alliance of 14 minor parties across a wide political spectrum.

In March 1998 Chavez reappeared on the political scene, mounting a populist campaign which harnessed discontent among ordinary citizens and disadvantaged groups who were angered by the corruption and cronyism of Venezuela's political system. He accused the country's traditional parties of being dishonest, of catering to the elite and to foreign investors, and of mismanagement of the oil revenues. Chavez enjoys the support of leftist intellectuals and the Fifth Republic Movement, a largely leftist party led by former coup leaders. However, he also has the backing of nationalists, large landowners, and conservative business leaders in agriculture and manufacturing who hope he will keep out foreign investors. Among his legions of mostly poor supporters he is known as *El Comandante*. At his closing campaign rally, he drew more than 700,000 people, many of whom wore the red parachutist's beret that had become his trademark on the campaign trail. On 6 December 1998 Chavez became the youngest elected president in Venezuelan history, defeating his closest challenger, Henrique Salas Romer, a Yale-educated economist, by 56.5% to 39.5%. About 65% of registered voters went to the polls.

## LEADERSHIP

Chavez came to office at a difficult time. Venezuelans, whose standard of living has been steadily declining for more than 15 years, saw consumer prices rise 33% in 1998. Chavez's opponent had received the endorsement of Venezuela's political establishment, including the two traditional parties and 15 of the 23 state governors. The Patriotic Pole coalition, which united around Chavez's criticisms of neo-liberalism and its standard package of free-market economic prescriptions, won a plurality (35%) of the 208 congressional seats in the November 1998 regional elections, breaking the 40-year political stranglehold of the two traditional parties.

Intransigence within the legislature was expected to make Chavez's task difficult. For the first time in 40 years, none of the top leadership positions in Congress went to members of the AD, despite its hold on 30% of the seats. Moreover, the election of Luis Manuel Davila, a member of Chavez's Fifth Republic Movement, as president of Congress signaled that Chavez might be able to find the political backing he needed to accomplish his reform agenda. Chavez's cabinet, announced on the eve of his inauguration, included the same broad spectrum as his Patriotic Pole: soldiers, leftist intellectuals, business and labor leaders, and a native Wayu Indian activist. Yet, none of those expected political battles took place. By mid-1999, Chavez's supporters had effectively shut down the Senate, and by December, with a new constitution in place, there was no Senate.

Throughout the political turmoil, Chavez sought to assure Venezuela's business class and foreign investors that his election would pursue prudent economic policies. Local investors had taken their money out of the country before the December 1998 election, but brought it back after they saw the results. Taking a conciliatory posture in his acceptance speech, Chavez said he would pursue a "third way" between socialism and unbridled capitalism. The retention of Maritza Izaguirre as finance minister was viewed by business leaders, investors, and international financial institutions as an indication of his seriousness in pursuing a market-oriented approach to his economic reform measures.

## DOMESTIC POLICY

To reform Venezuela's political system, Chavez pledged to ask for a popular referendum calling for a constituent assembly to rewrite the 1961 Constitution, reorganize the judiciary, and extend his presidential authority. In July 1999, voters gave Chavez's supporters 121 of 131 seats in the Constitutional Assembly, which was given the task of rewriting the constitution. In December 1999, 47% of the country's 11 million voters went to the polls to vote on the new document. Of those who voted, 71% approved the reforms. Chavez was clearly the major political winner. The new constitution, which came into effect on 30 December 1999, replaced the Senate with a unicameral National Assembly and consolidated power in the executive branch. It extended the presidential term from five to six years and eliminated a law that prevented the president from seeking two consecutive terms. Critics said the new constitution would allow Chavez to hold on to power for more than a decade. To meet Chavez's wishes, the constitution renamed the country to Republica Bolivariana de Venezuela (Bolivarian Republic of Venezuela) to honor Bolívar.

Chavez had asked for an extension of his presidential authority in order to fight poverty, reform the fiscal system, and restructure the foreign debt. Political opponents feared the changes had given Chavez too much power. Not of all these changes went into effect without resistance. By early 2000, Chavez had grown increasingly more critical with anyone who opposed his plans for the nation. In April 2000, journalists symbolically refused to ask any questions during a presidential press conference, in part to protest against a constitutional mandate that could be used to censor the press. While Chavez remained popular, more Venezuelans became critical. By May 2000, Chavez held a 15 to 20-point lead over his presidential opponent, Francisco Arias Cardenas, a former state governor.

General elections were to take place in May 2000, but were suspended by the nation's high court, which ruled technical problems with the balloting would have prevented free and fair elections. Venezuelans had been expected to elect more than 6,000 public officials, including the president, throughout the nation. Chavez praised the court's decision, saying it reaffirmed the nation's commitment to democracy.

The economy also continued to be a problem. The decline in oil revenues, combined with high interest rates, pushed the country into a deep recession. Venezuela's gross domestic product shrank 1% in 1998 and was expected to contract 1.5% in 1999. Unemployment remained in double digits in 2000. The budget deficit, which was more than US$3 billion in 1998, was expected to reach US$8 billion in 1999. Chavez promised to cut the budget by over 11%, raise the sales tax, and encourage foreign investment.

Chavez also said he intended to reduce the bloated, inefficient public sector by cutting more than half of Venezuela's state ministries and accelerating the privatization of state-owned firms. About 33% of the population is employed by the government. Although Chavez promised not to privatize the huge state oil company, Petroleos de Venezuela (PDVSA), he forced its president to resign in a bitter power struggle. He replaced him with his vice president, Hector Ciavaldini, who was supposed to cut waste and use the company's profits to help Venezuelans.

## FOREIGN POLICY

Venezuela is the world's second largest oil exporter and the largest source for US oil. About 75% of its export earnings, 25% of GDP, and nearly half of all government revenues come from petroleum. But with oil prices at under US$10 a barrel, Venezuelan foreign indebtedness has grown to US$36 billion, and nearly 40% of the budget is devoted to meeting debt service obligations. Chavez intended to support efforts by the Organization of Petroleum Exporting Countries (OPEC) to raise the price of crude oil. But in the long run, he hopes to diversify the economy in order to lessen the impact of fluctuations in oil prices. Reduction of foreign debt burdens is a top priority of the Chavez government. Although he had been denied a visa to the US prior to his election because of his participation in the 1992 coup attempt, Chavez wants to improve relations. He is hoping for technological and commercial exchanges as well as political support from the international financial institutions, where he will be seeking assistance for the reorientation of the economy.

Chavez made it clear that he welcomed foreign investors from every part of the world. Initially, investors were cautious because of his vague proposals and fiery populist rhetoric during the campaign. During 1999 he embarked on long international trips with visits to China, Malaysia, Singapore, Japan, the Philippines, Spain and France. He has sought foreign investment, but has clearly worked to improve his international image, which has been tainted in some nations by his close ties to Cuba's Fidel Castro and his attacks against free market economics.

Chavez's goodwill has not been extended to his neighbors. He has been critical of Colombia's president, but has been more hostile to neighboring Guyana. In October 1999, Venezuela reiterated its claim to a large piece of that country, raising tensions between the two nations.

## ADDRESS
Oficina del Presidente
Palacios de Miraflores
Caracas, Venezuela

## REFERENCES

*Agence France Presse,* 6 December 1998–2 February 1999.
*Boston Globe,* 6–7 December 1998.
*Business Week,* 1 February 1999.
Economist Intelligence Unit, *Country Reports,* 4th Qtr 1998, 1st Qtr 1999.
Inter Press Service, 3–7 December 1998.
*Latin American Weekly Report,* 5 January 1999.
*Latin Finance,* January 1999.
*Los Angeles Times,* 6 December 1998.
*Notisur* 11 December 1998–12 February 1999.
*Toronto Star,* 1 January 1999.
*Washington Post,* various issues, 1998, 1999, and 2000.
*Washington Times,* 10 February 1999.

**Profile researched and written by James L. McDonald, Senior International Policy Analyst, Bread for the World, Silver Spring, MD (6/99; revised 6/2000).**

# VIETNAM

### Le Kha Phieu
### Secretary General
(pronounced "LEE KAH FEW")

*"There have appeared potential dangers of social and political instability."*

The Socialist Republic of Vietnam extends nearly 1,000 miles along the eastern part of the Indochina peninsula. It is bordered by China to the north, Laos and Cambodia to the west, and the South China Sea and the Gulf of Tonkin to the east. Its area is 332,561 sq km (128,402 sq mi). The two largest cities are Ho Chi Minh City and Hanoi.

Vietnam's rapidly growing population is estimated at 77.3 million, with a density of 600 people per sq mi. Its ethnically diverse population consists of more than 60 groups, including many highland tribes, Chinese, Khmer, and other non-Vietnamese people. Although religion is discouraged by the state, many Vietnamese are nominally Buddhist, Taoist, or Roman Catholic. The official language is Vietnamese, but French and Chinese are also spoken. The literacy rate is 94% and the life expectancy for males and females is 65 and 70 years, respectively.

The Vietnamese economy is largely agricultural. Traditionally, northern Vietnam has been more industrialized. Since the recent opening of the economy, commerce in Ho Chi Minh City is flourishing. Vietnam is becoming self-sufficient in food production. Its per capita GDP is us$1,770. Major trading partners are Japan and former Eastern bloc countries. Exports include processed foods, rice, rubber, cement, and textiles. Currently, Vietnam suffers from large trade deficits. The national currency is the *dong*.

## POLITICAL BACKGROUND

The defining feature of Vietnamese history is nationalism. Throughout its history, Vietnam experienced foreign domination. Despite 1,000 years of Chinese rule (111 BC to 939 AD), Vietnam emerged with many of its cultural and historical traditions intact. From 1862 until 1893, the French established control over the entire Indochina region, including Vietnam, Laos, and Cambodia. They administered the area as French Indochina until World War II. Following the Japanese occupation of 1945, the French allowed the formation of the Democratic Republic of Vietnam under Ho Chi Minh's nationalist resistance movement, the Vietminh. Ho's group subscribed to a nationalistic brand of communism while another organization, consisting of royalist and anticommunist groups, supported Emperor Bao Dai.

After World War II, the French attempted to reestablish control over the region. While they provisionally recognized Ho's government in the north, the French sought to negotiate the future of South Vietnam. However, negotiations broke down and the Vietminh attacked French forces. In 1949, the French recognized the authority of the Bao Dai government over southern Vietnam. Fighting between the French and the Vietminh continued until a humiliating French defeat at Dien Bien Phu in May 1954. At the Geneva Conference of July 1954, an armistice ended the fighting and Vietnam was divided at the 17th parallel into two nations: the Democratic Republic of Vietnam, headed by the communists and the southern Republic of Vietnam, led by the anticommunist forces, organized around Bao Dai. While this north-south divide was intended to be a temporary measure, Ngo Dinh Diem proclaimed himself the first president of the Republic of Vietnam and repudiated the provisions of the Geneva Accords. Thereafter, Vietnam remained a politically divided and conflict-ridden place until 1975.

After the French withdrew from Vietnam, the US became steadily involved in propping up the southern regime. However, a groundswell of opposition emerged against the repressive Diem regime in the late 1950s, led by the National Liberation Front (NLF) and its military arm, the Viet Cong. As US involvement in the country increased, so did North Vietnam's control over the Viet Cong. By the mid-1960s, protecting South Vietnam became a cornerstone of US foreign policy in Asia. At the peak of its military involvement, 500,000 US troops were stationed in Vietnam to fight the Viet Cong. Massive US aid, however, failed to shore up the South Vietnamese government and communist victory became increasingly inevitable, as domestic opposition undermined the American will to fight. After a 1973 peace agreement, the US withdrew its troops and the South Vietnamese government continued its downward spiral. Without US assistance, Saigon (then capital of South Vietnam) fell to the Viet Cong and, in April 1975, the South Vietnamese government surrendered.

The reunification of the country gave birth to the Socialist Republic of Vietnam, with its capital at Hanoi. The North Vietnamese quickly consolidated their control over the south and dominated its politics. The new leaders imposed re-education camps to instill socialist values and moved to collectivize farms and nationalize business operations. Saigon was renamed Ho Chi Minh City, honoring the founder of the Democratic Republic of Vietnam. The National Assembly approved a new constitution which declared the state to be a "proletarian dictatorship" and proclaimed the Communist Party as the "only force leading the state and society." Later constitutional revisions introduced major political and economic reforms, including the right to private property. Over the years, many refugees fled Vietnam and settled in the West, fearing political persecution and diminished economic opportunities.

At present, the Constitution designates the 395-member National Assembly as the supreme organ of the state. In practice, however, power is in the hands of party elites who hold important administrative positions in government. The Vietnamese Communist Party (VCP) is the country's only political party. Based on constitutional revisions in 1992, the president is elected by and from the National Assembly. The president in turn, nominates the vice-president, the prime minister, the chief justice of the Supreme Court, and the head of the Supreme People's Inspectorate—all of whom must be approved by the Assembly. The day-to-day affairs of governing are entrusted to the prime minister, the five deputy ministers, and cabinet ministers. The VCP's Central Committee (161 members) and Politburo (17 members) exercise considerable influence. In the 1996 VCP Congress, a new five-member standing committee was set up within the Politburo. Those holding senior positions in the party need a correspondingly important government position to wield influential power. The VCP began a youth movement, with many senior leaders moving out of government positions, despite maintaining key posts within the party. The appointment of Le Kha Phieu as secretary general of the VCP, Phan Van Khai as prime minister, and Tran Duc Luong as president, solidified the transition of power from Do Muoi and his generation of leaders.

## PERSONAL BACKGROUND

Le Kha Phieu was born to peasant farmers on 27 December 1931 in the Dong Khe community, Thanh Hoa province, in north central Vietnam. This region, known as the cradle of the revolutionary movement, produced such national leaders as Ho Chi Minh. During French colonization, it resisted colonial rule more actively than other regions. The local revolutionary movement produced a strong sense of community and a social network through which Phieu still operates.

Phieu joined the Communist Party on 14 June 1949, after having been one of the original revolutionaries against Japanese and French domination. During the French Resistance, Phieu became an army officer and received training from the Vietnamese Military Academy, where he studied Marxist-Leninist ideology and military strategy. He was also a leader of a communist cell, the basic unit of political organization, in Thanh Hoa province. During the Vietnam War, Phieu operated in the northern, central, and southern parts of Vietnam. As the war spread to Cambodia and Laos, he became a regimental commander in those nations. In the late 1960s, he became deputy chief commissar of the Thien Military Zone, consisting of the Quang Tri and Thuo Thien provinces in central Vietnam. He was viewed as a front-line officer who had the skill to command military forces in battle. During the war, he was promoted to the rank of general and then became chief commissar of the Second Army Corps. Toward the end of the war, he was sent south to

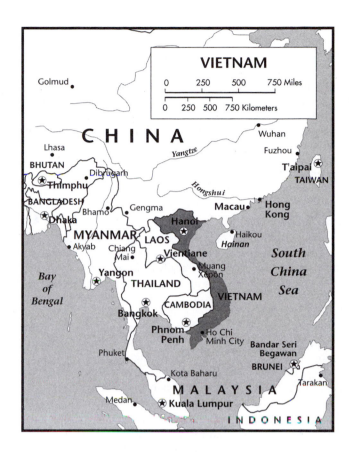

command a North Vietnamese infiltration unit, and was promoted to lieutenant general.

After the war, Phieu remained active in the military leadership, and eventually became the chief of political council of the Vietnamese Peoples Army. In that capacity, he served as the primary architect of the military's education and indoctrination policies.

## RISE TO POWER

Throughout the 1990s, Phieu and his cohort represented the second line of leadership behind the troika consisting of Vo Van Kiet, Le Duc Ahn, and Do Muoi. Phieu built his base of support by allying with party conservatives and the military. While Kiet and Ahn were considered to be reform oriented, conservative Muoi became the architect of Vietnam's economic restructuring, known as *Doi Moi*. He supported Phieu, whom many came to regard as even more conservative than Muoi. Phieu, along with Muoi, became the ideological torchbearers for conservatives and the military as those two groups held onto power through the 1990s.

After serving as a member of the Central Committee of the Vietnamese Communist Party in the 1980s, Phieu became a member of the Central Committee's Secretariat in 1992. Later, he became the permanent secretary of the Central Committee. In January 1994, he was elevated to membership in the ruling Politburo, the primary executive organ of the party. As a Politburo member, he supported a conservative and gradual opening of the Vietnamese economy to the international market. He often pointed to the inherent problems of rapid social and political change caused by uncontrolled economic growth. Supported strongly by the military and handpicked by Muoi to succeed him, Phieu became the secretary general of the Vietnamese Communist Party on 29 December 1997. He maintains close ties with Muoi, who retired from the Politburo along with Anh and Kiet, to make way for a new generation of leaders. Muoi now plays an advisory role to the party. He remains so influential that Phieu sometimes appears weak due to his reliance on the "retired" leader's guidance. Any leanings Phieu might have toward the progressive side have been seemingly stifled by Muoi's overbearing Marxist conservatism.

## LEADERSHIP

The departure of the old leadership led by Muoi, Anh, and Kiet ushered Vietnam into uncharted territory. As in the past, the rivalry between the secretary general, the prime minister, and the president appears to continue on personal lines—as each position has weakly institutionalized functions. Phieu's leadership has continued to seek a consensus based on personal abilities rather than any inherent institutional strengths. During the later 1990s, as economic growth followed by economic stagnation brought about social dislocations, the party and the military reasserted their desire to control Vietnamese political and economic development.

Phieu is conservative in ideology, supporting gradual economic liberalization through a socialist market system with continued party control over the political system. Most observers state that his orientation toward governance is law-and-order and pro-military. His fiery editorials criticizing the market system and extolling socialism appear frequently in government-sponsored newspapers.

## DOMESTIC POLICY

Vietnam's domestic policy focuses on balancing the benefits of economic growth with controlling social dislocations produced by modernization. Following the era of economic liberalization initiated in the late 1980s, Vietnam's economy grew steadily at about 9% per year. However, such rapid growth was uneven. While Ho Chi Minh City benefited from the influx of foreign investment, much of the countryside remains gripped by poverty and the lack of modern amenities. Rural dissatisfaction has on occasion led to violent protests. In particular, the collectivist agricultural practices undermine the farmer's independence. They also object to the effects of massive corruption. In response, the government has jailed local officials, and strengthened the grievance procedures for peasants.

While Phieu opposes rapid deregulation and privatization of state-owned industry, Prime Minister Phan Van Khai favors the synchronization of Vietnam's economy with market forces. Phieu distrusts global capitalism and its possible by-product—political liberalization. In particular, traditionalists within the party look to him to speak on issues of corruption and social decay: increased petty crime, fraud, prostitution, and political apathy. Phieu's conservative ideology makes the prospect of dramatic and swift economic deregulation unlikely, further dampening prospects for sustained future growth. Given his Marxist ideology and close ties to party traditionalists and the military, Phieu is not likely to become an advocate for economic reform.

## FOREIGN POLICY

The demise of the Eastern bloc fundamentally altered Vietnam's foreign policy and forced it to reach out to noncommunist states. This process began in conjunction with domestic economic liberalization in 1988. The withdrawal of Vietnamese forces from Cambodia led to a dramatic improvement in relations with China. The foreign policy emphasis shifted from emphasizing ideological solidarity with the Communist bloc, toward a pragmatic attempt to attract overseas investors.

In November 1991, China and Vietnam normalized relations, effectively ending Vietnam's international isolation. Meanwhile, Vietnam made a rapprochement to the West, in particular with Germany and the US. Vietnam also launched an initiative to improve relations with Japan, Russia, and its Southeast Asian neighbors. As a result, the US lifted its trade embargo against Vietnam in 1994 and normalized diplomatic relations the following year. In return, Vietnam pledged continued cooperation in locating and returning the remains of US soldiers. German, Japanese, and other Asian firms have invested heavily in Vietnam since 1994. These achievements culminated with Vietnam's entry into the Association of Southeast Asian Nations (ASEAN) on 28 July 1995.

When the economic meltdown hit Asia in the late 1990s, Vietnam was affected by the drying up of investments. The government's unwillingness to bow to the demands of foreign investors and their governments also hampered growth. Following the investor euphoria of Vietnam's opening up, a sense of disappointment with red tape, Party control, and corruption set in. The Party was perceived as being in denial about the state of its economy, even as it became more dependent on foreign aid. Reforms promoted by lenders such as the International Monetary Fund (IMF) were rejected when they did not fit into the leadership's socialist vision for the nation. International lenders and investors want a reformed legal code and greater convertibility for the *dong* in international currency markets. If the economy continues to slide significantly, Vietnam may need to seek assistance from the IMF, which will demand significant changes in how the economy is being managed. Such a situation could undermine support for Phieu within the military and party.

While the 25th Anniversary of Vietnam's reunification following the war with the US was cause for celebration in high government circles as well as in the streets, rivalry within the hierarchy darkened the picture in April 2000. Phieu is perceived as trying to push the other troika members out of the way where any meaningful policy issues are concerned. Anti-corruption drives appear to be directed only at the more reform-minded members of the elite. The Party itself seems unable to act decisively to recharge the nation's economy. Phieu is holding on very hard and despite his own plea for more open criticism, does not appear to entertain any views other than those of his elderly Communist mentors.

## ADDRESS

Governmental Offices
1 Hoang Hoa Tham St., Hanoi, Vietnam

## REFERENCES

*Asiaweek,* 29 January 1999; 14 April 2000.

Banks, Arthur, Alan Day, and Thomas Muller. *Political Handbook of the World, 1996–97.* Binghamton, NY: CSA Publications, 1996.

*The Economist,* 3 January 1998.

*Facts on File,* 31 December 1997.

*Far Eastern Economic Review,* 18 December 1997; 1 May 2000.

Human Rights Watch. *Vietnam: Silencing of Dissent.* New York: May 2000.

*Keesing's Record of World Events,* December 1997.

*New York Times,* 31 December 1997.

*Nguoi Lao Dong* (Vietnam), 31 December 1997.

Templer, Robert. *Shadows and Wind: A View of Modern Vietnam.* Boston, MA: Little, Brown, 1999.

*Quan Doi Nhan Dan* (Vietnam), 6 January 1998.

**Profile researched and written by Robert W. Compton, Jr., Binghamton University (SUNY) (6/98; updated 5/2000).**

# YEMEN

### Ali Abdullah Saleh
### President
*(pronounced "ah-LEE ab-DAH-la sah-LEE")*

*"The Republic of Yemen will be a factor for stability and security in the Arabian Peninsula and the Gulf region and a strong bastion for the Arab Nations, the Arab League and joint Arab action."*

The Republic of Yemen was established on 22 May 1990 from the union of the two formerly independent states of the Yemen Arab Republic (YAR) and People's Democratic Republic of Yemen (PDRY). Yemen borders on the Kingdom of Saudi Arabia, the Sultanate of Oman, the Arabian Sea, the Gulf of Aden, and the Red Sea. It should be noted however, that like most other borders in the Arabian peninsula, Yemen's borders with its neighbors are not well defined and are open to dispute.

Yemen covers an area of 528,106 sq km (203,645 sq mi) and controls the strategic strait of Bah al-Mandeb, connecting the Arabian Sea and the Indian Ocean to the Red Sea. Yemen's population is estimated at 17 million, most of whom belong to various tribes. It is believed that about two million Yemeni nationals live outside the country, working as laborers in Saudi Arabia and other Gulf countries. Large numbers of Yemenis also live in the United States, mainly in southern California.

Yemen's political capital is San'a (the former capital of YAR) with a population of 280,000. The economic capital of the state is Aden (the former capital of PDRY). Islam is the official religion of the state, and its official language is Arabic. Yemen's exports include cotton, coffee, hides, vegetables, and salted and dried fish. The per capita GDP is US$740; the currency is the Yemini rial.

## POLITICAL BACKGROUND
Once the home to the ancient kingdom of Sheba (950 to 115 BC), Yemen was part of the Ottoman Empire from 1517 until the end of World War I. However, Ottoman power in Yemen was always limited, and in reality, the province was ruled by the Zaidi (a branch of Shi'a Islam) Imams who had established the Rassid dynasty in the ninth century. The last of the Imams was overthrown in the early 1960s.

In 1839, British forces, who had established their presence in the area as early as 1799, occupied the strategic port of Aden and its surrounding countryside. While the Aden Colony was administered by the British, the rest of Yemen remained under Ottoman/Zaidi control until 1918 when it became an independent kingdom ruled by the Zaidi Imams. The Imams' position, however, was challenged in 1962 and the dynasty was overthrown, resulting in a civil war between the pro-monarchy forces supported by Saudi Arabia and the republican forces supported by Egypt. The republican forces established the Yemen Arab Republic (North Yemen) in

San'a, which was recognized by the superpowers and admitted to the UN in 1963. The Yemeni civil war, however, continued until 1969.

Upon the withdrawal of British forces from the Aden Colony in 1967, Marxist elements took over and established an independent state known as the People's Republic of Southern Yemen. The name was later changed to the People's Democratic Republic of Yemen (South Yemen). For the most part, relations between the conservative and pro-West government in the north and the Marxist pro-Soviet government in the south were troublesome, culminating in numerous military clashes, including a full-scale war in September 1970 and attempts to overthrow each other's regimes. In June 1978, for example, the North Yemeni president was assassinated when a bomb carried in the briefcase of a South Yemeni envoy exploded. North Yemen accused Aden of involvement in the assassination, and fighting broke out between the two countries.

Despite their differences, however, the two Yemens had engaged in unity talks as early as 1972. Plans for a unified Yemen were originally drawn up in the mid-1980s, but the 1986 coup in South Yemen and the subsequent civil war postponed reunification. In 1989, the two countries announced that they would merge on 30 November 1990. On 22 May 1990, however, six months ahead of schedule, the parliaments of the two countries approved the plan for unification, and the two Yemens formally merged to form the Republic of Yemen.

On the same day, the parliaments of the two countries elected Ali Abdullah Saleh, President of North Yemen, as the President of the newly established Republic. The former Secretary-General of the Yemen Socialist Party, the ruling party of South Yemen, Ali Salim al-Baid was elected as his vice president.

## PERSONAL BACKGROUND
His excellency Ali Abdullah Saleh was born circa 1942 in the village of Bayt al-Ahmar. Saleh's family belongs to the Sanhan tribe, which is part of the Hashid tribal confederacy. He received his early education in the village's religious school and is a follower of the Zaidi branch of Shi'a Islam. Saleh is married and has five children.

## RISE TO POWER
Saleh's military and political career began in 1958 when he joined the irregular tribal forces of Imam Ahmad, the last

Rassad ruler of Yemen. In 1958, Saleh joined the regular armed forces, and by 1970 he was enrolled in a non-commissioned officer's school. At the time of the 1962 revolution, which overthrew the Imam's regime and precipitated the Yemeni civil war, Saleh was an army sergeant who chose to side with the revolutionary republican forces; he was wounded in the line of duty. He was commissioned as a second lieutenant in 1963 and enrolled in the armored school for officers in 1964. In 1974 Saleh was one of the chief participants in the military coup that brought Lt. Colonel al-Hamdi to power. After the coup, he held a number of military commands, including armament chief of armory corps, armor battalion commander, staff officer of the armor division, and the commander of the Taiz Brigade, a position that he held through to the time of his election to the presidency in 1988. In 1982, Ali Abdullah Saleh was promoted to the rank of colonel.

After the assassination of President al-Ghashami on 24 June 1978, Saleh became a member of the temporary council of the presidency and used his position to defeat other contenders for the presidency. On July 17, the People's Constituent Assembly (the North Yemeni Parliament) elected him president and commander in chief of the armed forces. He was re-elected for a third term on 17 July 1988, and became the first president of unified Yemen in May 1990. In September 1999, the Republic of Yemen carried out the first direct presidential elections ever held on the Arabian peninsula, and voters returned Saleh to office for another five-year term.

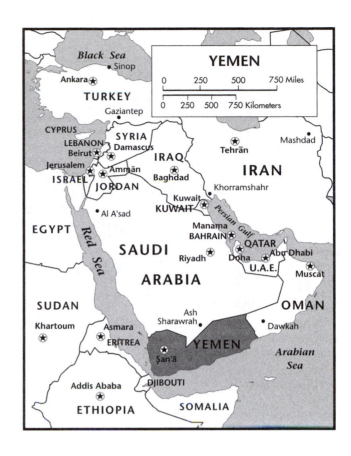

## LEADERSHIP

As President of North Yemen, Saleh's policies were guided by three principles: stabilization of the domestic scene, improving the economic situation, and union with the South.

In general, both South and North Yemen suffered from political instability beginning in the early 1960s. Both countries were the victims of numerous military coup d'etats, revolutions, assassinations, and civil wars. Yemen's tribal structure and the fact that two governments with opposing political ideologies ruled in San'a and Aden made it fertile for violent uprisings often backed by foreign powers. Until unification, the two regimes were often actively involved in plots to overthrow each other. In addition, foreign powers like Saudi Arabia, Egypt, and the superpowers, often tried to exploit the differences between the two regimes and the various social groups. Hence, when President Saleh took office, his first task was to build a national consensus. He did this by improving relations between San'a and its neighbors, in particular South Yemen, and by devising a mechanism through which different social groups could voice their grievances.

Saleh's tribal background has given him an appreciation of the importance of tribes in the Yemeni society. Whereas Yemeni leaders before Saleh had tried to eliminate the tribes and exclude them from participation in the political life of the country, Saleh has actively courted the tribes and tried to integrate them into Yemeni society and politics. At the same time he has also been responsive to the needs of other groups. Under Saleh's leadership, Yemen has developed democratic institutions, and in 1988 it became the first country on the Arabian peninsula to have an elected parliament.

## DOMESTIC POLICY

As one of the poorest countries in the region, Yemen is highly dependent on foreign economic aid and remittances from Yemenis working abroad. The economic situation, however, was helped enormously by the discovery of oil in the summer of 1984 in the border area between the two Yemens. In January of 1989, the two countries established the Yemeni Company for Investment in Oil and Mineral Resources for the development of the oil fields along their common border.

In 1999, like other oil-producing states, Yemen—where oil accounts for more than 80% of exports—was hard hit by falling world oil prices. The government's income was cut in half, necessitating major budget cuts, and unemployment was in the double digits. Low oil prices also endangered another major source of Yemeni income—remittances by Yemenis working abroad, since the neighboring Gulf states that usually host these workers were in trouble themselves. Adding to the nation's problems, Yemen's tourist industry, which normally plays an important role in its economy, was endangered by a rash of kidnappings and killings of Westerners that had been brought to the forefront of public attention by a major kidnapping incident at the end of 1998.

## FOREIGN POLICY

Saleh's foreign policy as the leader of North Yemen was characterized by the principles of "positive neutrality" and Arab unity. Under Saleh, Yemen cultivated close ties with Saudi Arabia and other pro-West states in the region. He also purchased military equipment from the US and expanded economic relations with the West. At the same time, Saleh also tried to maintain friendly relations with the Soviet Union. In October 1984, he renewed the treaty of Friendship and Cooperation that was originally signed in 1964 by San'a and Moscow.

Saleh has emerged as one of the staunchest supporters of Arab unity. After the 1982 Israeli invasion of Lebanon, he sent Yemeni volunteers to assist Palestinian fighters in Lebanon and provided the Palestine Liberation Organization with training facilities in Yemen. During the Iran-Iraq War, Yemeni volunteers were dispatched to fight alongside the Iraqis. In 1989, Yemen along with Egypt, Iraq, and Jordan formed the Arab Cooperation Council to facilitate the movement of capital and labor among member states. Yemen's refusal to publicly condemn the Iraqi invasion of Kuwait of August 1990 indicated that the new Republic's foreign policy would continue to be guided by the principle of Arab unity. In 1999, Yemen was one of nine Arab parliaments that appealed to UN Secretary-General Kofi Annan to lift the sanctions on Iraq, which they claimed amounted to genocide.

Also in 1999, Yemen called on Saudi Arabia for a specific time table to resolve a border dispute between the two countries dating back to the 1930s. Saudi Arabia had resumed issuing visas to Yemenis in 1998 after a seven-year break caused by differences over the Gulf crisis. However, in December 1999 the Saudis deported some 3,000 Yemenis, claiming they had violated Saudi immigration laws. The Saudi move followed Yemen's request for resolution to the frontier demarcation talks.

## ADDRESS
Office of the President
San'a, Yemen

## REFERENCES
*The Economist,* 9 December 1989.
*The Middle East and North Africa,* 1990.
*New York Times,* various issues.
*Political Leaders of the Contemporary Middle East and North Africa.*

**Profile researched and written by Hootan Shambayati (8/90; updated 5/2000).**

# YUGOSLAVIA

## Slobodan Milosevic
## President

*(pronounced "SLOW-boh-dahm mee-LOH-shev-eech")*

*"Yugoslavia must remain peaceful, free, and independent."*

The Federal Republic of Yugoslavia is made up of the republics of Serbia and Montenegro, and is one of the five successor states to Tito's Socialist Federal Republic of Yugoslavia. It borders on Bosnia-Herzegovina and Croatia to the west; Hungary to the north; Romania and Bulgaria to the east; and Albania and Macedonia to the south, with a 100 km (62 mi) shoreline on the Adriatic Sea. This new Yugoslav state covers an area of 102,500 sq km (39,575 sq mi).

Yugoslavia has a population of 11.2 million, of which 94% live in Serbia. The major ethnic groups include 63% Serbs, 17% Albanians, 5% Montenegrins, 3% Hungarians, 3% Slavic Muslims, and 9% various other nationalities. The official language is Serbian, written with the Cyrillic alphabet. The population is heavily Eastern Orthodox Christian, with a minority of about 17% Sunni Muslim.

The official currency is the Yugoslav *dinar*. The per capita GNP of Yugoslavia is us$2,300.

## POLITICAL BACKGROUND

After World War I the Serbian kingdom joined with the kingdom of Montenegro and the Austro-Hungarian lands inhabited by Slovenes, Croats, Slavic Muslims and Serbs. A new state of South Slavs (Yugoslavia) was formed, ruled by an authoritarian Serbian king and dominated by Serbia. When World War II broke out, the Axis powers dismembered Yugoslavia. Much of the territory of Serbia and Montenegro was divided among neighboring German allies.

Following World War II, with the victory of Josip Broz Tito's Communist partisans over the Germans and the local forces loyal to the Serbian king, a new country was formed, with six constituent republics. Tito became the nation's president in 1953 and had himself declared president for life under a revised constitution ten years later. After Tito's death in 1980, Yugoslavia adopted a rotating presidency to defuse tensions between its multiple ethnic groups, but these tensions ultimately resulted in the breakup of the country and declarations of independence by the constituent republics of Croatia, Slovenia, Macedonia, and Bosnia and Herzegovina, leaving a "rump Yugoslavia" composed solely of Serbia and Montenegro. In 1992 these two republics proclaimed a new Federal Republic of Yugoslavia.

Hostilities in the region continued into the 1990s. In 1995 the Dayton peace accord was signed by representatives of Serbia, Croatia, and Bosnia, but sporadic fighting continued. The major flare-up in the succeeding years was the Kosovo crisis of 1998–99, resulting from the persecution and evacu-ation of the majority Albanian population in the Serbian province of Kosovo and ending in the intensive bombing of Serbia by NATO forces in the spring of 1999.

## PERSONAL BACKGROUND

Slobodan Milosevic was born on 20 August 1941 in Pozarevac, in eastern Serbia, the son of an Orthodox priest and a Communist school teacher. In 1964 he received his law degree from the University of Belgrade, where he was an active Communist. He subsequently held a number of positions in the Communist Party's economic apparatus until 1968, when he obtained an executive position at the large state-owned gas company, Tehnogas. He went on to become the president of Tehnogas, and then president of a large state-owned bank. He is married to Mirjana Markovic, a professor and the ideologist of the "Yugoslav United Left," a coalition of left and hard-line Communist forces allied with Milosevic's own Socialist Party of Serbia. They have a son and a daughter.

## RISE TO POWER

Milosevic became a member of the Serbian Communist Party's central committee and of its top decision-making body (presidium) in 1982. In 1984, he led the local Communist Party organization in Belgrade, and two years later was elected president of the ruling Serbian Communist Party, League of Communists of Serbia (LCS).

In the early 1980s the economic crisis continued to deepen. By 1985 moderate reformers had agreed with reformers in other Yugoslav republics on the need for changes in the economic and political system, including the status of Kosovo within the Yugoslav federation. Threatened by these impending changes, conservatives in the Serbian party, allied with nationalist intellectuals, provoked confrontations and violence in Kosovo, accused the dominant moderate wing of the LCS of not defending Serbs in Kosovo, and complained that Yugoslavia had subordinated Serbia to the interests of other republics. In the forefront of this strategy was Milosevic, who used the issue of Kosovo to remove his moderate opponents from the Serbian party and replace them with ideological conservatives loyal to him. Outside the party he cracked down on non-Communist opposition forces, took control of the once-autonomous Serbian media, and imposed military rule in Kosovo. Using mob rallies that focused on alleged corruption as well as betrayal of Serbs in Kosovo, Milosevic and his allies in 1988 and 1989 managed to replace

the leaders of the Montenegro and Vojvodina Communist parties with his own allies. But these events alarmed the party leaders in the other Yugoslav republics, who responded by seeking the support of their own populations, calling for greater political freedom. By the spring of 1990 the republics of Slovenia and Croatia had held multi-party elections, won by anticommunist parties promising greater independence for their republics.

Within Serbia itself Milosevic soon came under increasing pressure to hold elections. In the summer of 1990, he renamed the LCS the Socialist Party of Serbia (SPS). The SPS controlled the media, appealed to the themes of peace and prosperity, and painted the opposition as dangerous, irrational nationalists. Consequently, Milosevic's party won 194 of 250 parliamentary seats in the November elections. Milosevic himself was elected president of Serbia with 65% of the vote.

## LEADERSHIP
Milosevic's main challenge has been to maintain power in the face of strong pressures for political and economic change. In 1991, drawing on the history of violence against Serbs in Croatia during World War II, Milosevic and his allies provoked violent conflicts in that republic, accusing the newly elected nationalists of seeking to exterminate Serbs. Milosevic thereby sought to silence domestic political opposition and to destroy the Yugoslav state by getting Croatia and Slovenia out of the federation so that Serbia could dominate it.

From May to December 1991, Serbia and the Yugoslav army waged war throughout Croatia, which in late June announced its decision to pull out of the Yugoslav federation. Next, warfare broke out in Bosnia in March 1992 and lasted until the end of 1995. Most of the violence, however, took place in the first months, when non-Serbs were "cleansed" from Serbian-held territory through massacres, rapes, and expulsions. Throughout the Bosnian war, the international community identified Serbia as being responsible. In May 1992 Serbia and Montenegro proclaimed a new Federal Republic of Yugoslavia. The first president was Dobrica Cosic, a nationalist writer who had been instrumental in the provocation of conflict in Kosovo, Croatia, and Bosnia. Yet the true power in the new state was the Serbian president Milosevic, who continued at least covertly to aid the Bosnian Serb forces.

By the summer of 1995, the international community called for a halt to the fighting, and the Bosnian, Croat, Serb, and Muslim leaders, along with Croatian President Tudjman and Serbian President Milosevic, met in November 1995 outside of Dayton, Ohio. They agreed to a compromise peace plan that maintained Bosnia as one state, divided into two ethnically-defined "entities." Milosevic's role in coming to an agreement and overcoming the opposition of the Bosnian Serbs was crucial.

Since the Dayton agreement ended the war in Bosnia, Milosevic has faced a number of challenges to his power from within Serbia. Local elections in the fall of 1996 resulted in victories for opposition parties. When Milosevic annulled the results, opposition forces and students took to the streets. For four months the streets of Belgrade and other major cities in Serbia saw massive protests against the regime's control of the media, corruption, lack of democracy, and the poor state of the economy. Eventually, Milosevic compromised and allowed opposition forces to take power in a number of cities.

In July 1997, Milosevic successfully arranged to have himself elected president of the Yugoslav federation, since he was not eligible to run for another term as president of Serbia. But elections in November 1997, in both Serbia and Montenegro, demonstrated growing disenchantment with Milosevic's rule. In Serbia, his handpicked candidate for president failed to get sufficient votes, and in parliamentary elections his political allies failed to gain the majority of seats. In Montenegro, Milosevic's longtime ally lost in the presidential race to an opponent who openly denounced Milosevic and his ruling party.

In 1998 and 1999, Milosevic once again gained international attention because of the crisis in the primarily Albanian-populated province of Kosovo, where a crackdown by Serbian security forces ultimately escalated to Bosnian-style "ethnic cleansing." Numerous reports of human rights violations led to the involvement of the international community and a 10-week intensive bombing campaign by NATO forces in the spring of 1999. In May 1999, a UN international tribunal indicted Milosevic, together with four top Serbian officials, for war crimes in Kosovo based on their responsibility for mass deportations and the murder of over 300 Kosovars. Milosevic thus became the first sitting head of state to receive such an indictment.

## DOMESTIC POLICY
Politically, Milosevic faces challenges from the democratic opposition as well as from extreme nationalist forces. Thus

far, however, no single opposition party or candidate has been able to gather enough support to topple the tenacious leader. Although surveys in early 2000 gave Milosevic a low approval rating of 17% with the Yugoslavian people, this figure was still higher than that for all opposition leaders combined. Meanwhile, Milosevic's government continued to quash dissent through media control, political intimidation, and other means.

The Yugoslav economy suffers from international economic sanctions and the loss of export markets in the rest of the world as well as in other former Yugoslav republics. Although the regime initially claimed to favor a move to privatization, the dominant coalition parties prefer a reinvigorated state socialism. In spite of predictions that infrastructure damage from the NATO bombing would create sufficient hardship to oust Milosevic from power, Yugoslavia maintained its power supply (and political stability) throughout the following winter. By the first half of 2000, the government claimed to have repaired a significant portion of the damage incurred in the bombing. In addition, government-subsidized prices for essential commodities had kept living standards from sinking to a point that would spur acute discontent and civil unrest.

## FOREIGN POLICY

Yugoslavia has become increasingly isolated due to international disapproval of Milosevic's activities, and the country became even more discredited in the international community with Milosevic's 1999 indictment for war crimes by a UN tribunal. Yugoslavia has yet to be admitted to the UN, the Organization for Security and Cooperation in Europe (OSCE), or most other international organizations and has also been excluded from participation in international financial institutions. Close cooperation with the US and EU also seem unlikely as long as Milosevic remains in power.

Yugoslavia has maintained good relations with Greece, but has pinned its international economic and political hopes on Russia. Milosevic also has sought to improve relations with China, visiting Beijing in November 1997. A major theme on this visit was the future of socialism and economic cooperation between the two socialist countries. Both Russia and China provided aid to help Yugoslavia through the first winter following the NATO bombing campaign in the spring of 1999; aid included a US$300 million loan from the Chinese.

## ADDRESS

President of the Federal Republic
Andricev Venac 1
11000 Belgrade, Yugoslavia

## REFERENCES

B92 Open Serbia. [Online] Available http://b92eng.opennet.org (Accessed 3/98).

Banks, Arthur and Thomas Muller, eds. *Political Handbook of the World*. Binghamton, NY: CSA Publications, 1999.

Bennett, Christopher. *Yugoslavia's Bloody Collapse*. New York: NYU Press, 1995.

Federal Republic of Yugoslavia. [Online] Available http://www.gov.yu (Accessed 3/98).

*International Security*, Winter 1994–95.

"Milosevic in His Bunker." *Newsweek*, 7 June 1999, p.49.

"Milosevic, the Comeback Kid." *National Affairs*, 15 May 2000, p.26.

*New York Times*, 23 November 1995.

"No Impunity for Milosevic." *The Nation*, 21 June 1999, p.3.

Official Yugoslavia information. [Online] Available http://www.yugoslavia.com (Accessed 3/98).

Radio Free Europe/Radio Liberty Daily Reports. [Online] Available http://www.rferl.org/newsline (Accessed 3/98).

"Serbia—A Glimmer of Opposition." *The Economist*, 15 April 2000, p.46.

Silber, Laura and Allan Little. *Yugoslavia: Death of a Nation*. New York: Penguin Books, 1997.

*Vreme* (Belgrade), 20 January 1992–8 November 1997.

**Profile researched and written by V.P. Gagnon, Jr., Ithaca College (3/98; updated 5/00).**

# ZAMBIA

### Frederick Chiluba
### President
*(pronounced "chi-LOO-bah")*

*"Behind this velvet glove lies an iron fist."*

The Republic of Zambia is a landlocked country located in the heart of southern Africa. The national territory occupies 752,614 sq km (290,584 sq mi) and consists primarily of grasslands and forests. Zambia is bordered to the north by Zaire and Tanzania; to the east by Malawi and Mozambique; to the south by Zimbabwe and Namibia; and to the west by Angola. The population is estimated to be just over 9.5 million with an annual growth rate of 2.1%. More than 1.5 million people live in the capital city of Lusaka and almost half of the nation's population is clustered in the densely populated Copperbelt. The largest segment of the population is composed of various Bantu-speaking groups, notably the Bemba in the north and the Lozi in the southwest. A handful of whites, Asians, and people of mixed descent are concentrated in the Copperbelt in the north. The official language is English, but Afrikaans and more than 70 other languages are also spoken. Almost 75% of Zambians are Christian; the remainder practice either traditional religions or Islam. The Zambian economy is almost entirely based on mineral extraction and commercial agriculture. Copper accounts for about 90% of Zambia's total exports. Cobalt, lead, manganese, and zinc are also mined. Commercial crops include maize, peanuts, tobacco, and cotton. Agriculture employs about 85% of the labor force, while producing 12% of the GDP. Zambian per capita GDP is estimated to be us$880. The national currency is the *kwacha*.

## POLITICAL BACKGROUND

Zambia, formerly the British protectorate of Northern Rhodesia, was under British dominion from 1888 until 24 October 1964, when it became an independent republic within the Commonwealth under the leadership of Kenneth David Kaunda and his United National Independence Party (UNIP). Kaunda consolidated control over the nation in the ensuing years, culminating in the 1972 abolition of political parties other than the UNIP. Elections continued to be held, but only UNIP members could stand for office. No one dared to oppose Kaunda as president.

In December 1990, bowing to persistent demands for democratization and rioting over rises in food prices, Kaunda legalized opposition political parties. The Movement for Multi-Party Democracy (MMD) quickly organized itself as the primary opposition to the UNIP. A broad-based, diverse coalition of interest groups, MMD's sole unifying principle was its opposition to UNIP and continued political domination by Kaunda.

According to Zambia's constitution, the president is elected to a five-year term by universal suffrage. The constitution also provides for a prime minister and cabinet, both appointed by the president, and a 150-member National Assembly, elected simultaneously with the president.

## PERSONAL BACKGROUND

The son of a copper miner, Frederick Jacob Titus Chiluba was born on 30 April 1943, in Kitwe, one of the major cities in the northern copperbelt. Forced to drop out of school for financial reasons, he completed his secondary education through London correspondence courses in 1971.

As a young man, Chiluba worked as a personnel clerk on a Tanzanian sisal plantation, where he developed an interest in the labor movement. In 1966, he joined a Swedish mining equipment company. He remained with that company, rising from accounts assistant to credit manager, until 1990, when he took a leave of absence.

Chiluba started in the labor movement as a shop steward for the National Union of Building, Electrical and General Workers (NUBEGW), and was elected its president in 1971. He subsequently became president of the Zambian Congress of Trade Unions (ZCTU)—a labor group whose membership had grown to 300,000. In 1987 he left NUBEGW, the loser in an intramural political fight, and quickly formed his own labor union, thus retaining leadership of the ZCTU. Under Chiluba's leadership, ZCTU became increasingly vocal in its opposition to Kaunda and UNIP. In 1981, Chiluba was jailed without trial for allegedly destabilizing the country in an attempt to overthrow the government. He was released three months later without charge.

Frederick Chiluba, who stands just under five feet tall, is a born-again Christian and is married with nine children. Asked how he planned to celebrate his electoral victory, he said, "I am a teetotaler. I have been trying non-alcoholic champagne in Zambia, but there is none."

## RISE TO POWER

As head of the ZCTU, Chiluba held a position of national importance and prominence for 16 years. In July 1990, he was present at the founding of a pressure group for multi-party elections. Eight months later, after opposition parties had been legalized, he became the president of the new Movement for Multi-party Democracy, by then a full-fledged political party.

Despite several restrictions on access to the state-run media during the six-week campaign for the presidency, Chiluba received enormous support in his far-flung campaign throughout Zambia. Encumbered by state-of-emergency regulations, which forced him to apply to the government for permission to hold campaign rallies, and despite fear among many Zambians that opposition to Kaunda and UNIP would result in some form of retribution, Chiluba often found himself addressing crowds whose numbers exceeded 100,000. Kaunda, in contrast, faced no more than 10,000 supporters—many of whom were state workers whose offices had been closed to encourage their attendance at his rallies.

When he legalized political parties, Kaunda maintained tight control over the pace of change. He refused to set a date for elections until the last possible moment. He chose to select a committee to draft a new constitution, rather than eliminate by presidential fiat constitutional provisions inimical to multi-party democracy. However, the opposition was so strongly united, the populace so weary of Kaunda's policies and heavy-handed paternalistic leadership, and the economy in such a shambles, that it was almost a foregone conclusion that Kaunda would lose the first democratic elections held in the state he helped to found 27 years earlier.

On 31 October 1991, Chiluba and the MMD swept to victory over Kaunda and the UNIP. Chiluba was elected by a margin of 76% to 24% and MMD took 125 of 150 seats in the National Assembly.

## LEADERSHIP

Once in office Chiluba set out to liberalize Zambia's faltering economy and to clean up a government notorious for its corruption. His first year in office went well, since as Chiluba put it, "we had the support of the people." But, by the middle of his second year, the situation was not so rosy. In March of 1993, Chiluba declared a state of emergency on the grounds that, "Zambia is threatened. Our young democracy is at stake. The danger is real and the consequences if not attended to are grave. The political climate is being poisoned by a few of our citizens who are bent on plunging this nation into chaos."

The "citizens" in question turned out to be members of the UNIP, 14 of whom were arrested without charges, shortly after the imposition of the state of emergency. The state of emergency immediately cast a pall over the future of democracy in Zambia in the eyes of the Zambians and the members of the international community who had viewed this transition to multi-party democracy as a model for other African nations.

Since then there have been allegations of corruption in the cabinet, including drug smuggling by ministers. While Chiluba himself has not been implicated, his unwillingness to investigate the charges has not inspired confidence. One of Zambia's independent newspapers, *The Post,* has charged Chiluba with having an illegitimate child whom he refused to recognize and even of being an impostor named Titus Mpundu who adopted the name Chiluba after he was expelled from secondary school. The editor of *The Post* has since been jailed for contempt of parliament, but was released.

The worst blot on Chiluba's record has been his handling of the 1996 elections, the first since he ousted Kaunda. His main opponent was Kaunda. Although most observers agreed that Kaunda's candidacy was a long shot, Chiluba chose to amend the constitution in such a way that Kaunda was barred from running. The new rules required that the candidates' parents be from Zambia. Kaunda, whose parents came from what is now Malawi, was not allowed to run. The voting went ahead on November 18, despite a boycott by Kaunda's supporters and protest from the international community. Chiluba was re-elected with 70% of the vote and the MMD took 131 of 150 parliamentary seats. Voter turnout was low—only 40% of registered voters participated. International observers declared the election to be neither free nor fair, complaining of irregularities in voter registration, vote buying and Kaunda's exclusion.

## DOMESTIC POLICY

Though Chiluba's handling of the 1996 elections has brought little but opprobrium, his handling of the economy has gotten high marks from the international community. The economy he inherited from Kaunda was a shambles. Roughly 80% of the economy had been state-owned and poorly managed. The copper industry, Zambia's main money maker, was milked to support other state-run enterprises, leaving the industry without the means to buy new equipment or even spare parts for old equipment. Maize prices were heavily subsidized and every attempt to reduce the subsidy ended in riots.

Faced with these challenges, Chiluba has embarked on an aggressive campaign of privatization and deregulation of the economy. The currency is no longer controlled, the price of maize meal has been allowed to rise to five times its former price, and 140 state run enterprises have been sold off to foreign investors. As Zambia entered the 21st century, the giant mining Anglo-American Corporation was poised to buy the state owned Zambia Consolidated Mines. The Anglo-American Corporation has formed a minor subsidiary company in Zambia to take care of its interests in the Konkola Copper Mine, the only remaining government asset other than the Nkana smelter and refinery, which the government soon will privatize as well. South African conglomerates have also shown keen interest in buying some of the state owned mining assets.

These efforts have begun to show results, but for many Zambians the results have come at too high a price. Although inflation has fallen from 200% to below 50%, unemployment is high at approximately 22%. Privatization of the copper mines may mean the loss of additional jobs. Furthermore the mines have long provided their employees with some of the best schools and medical care in Zambia. Labor leaders fear that new mine owners might sell off the schools and hospitals, leaving those who retain their jobs with reduced social services. Chiluba is thought to have put off the sale of the mines until after the election for this very reason. Maintaining the pace of the privatization campaign in the face of growing political discontent will be Chiluba's main domestic policy challenge.

## FOREIGN POLICY
Chiluba began his term as the darling of the international community. Despite approval for his economic reforms, his handling of the election has cost him much support. Early in his first term he severed diplomatic relations with Iran and Iraq over an alleged attempt to destabilize his government. When allegations of rampant corruption began to surface, the

Consultative Group on Zambia, a coalition of Western aid donors, threatened to cut off aid if this issue was not addressed. In 1996, when it became clear that Chiluba was going to bar Kaunda from participation in the elections, the major donors cut their aid packages by 10% in protest. The IMF and the World Bank have not curtailed their lending.

If Chiluba can hold the course on his economic reforms and permit greater freedom for political opponents, he can probably regain the backing of major donor nations. It is unlikely, however, that he will ever regain the unreserved support he enjoyed in 1992.

## ADDRESS
State House
PO Box 135
Lusaka, Zambia

## REFERENCES
*Africa Report*, January–February 1993, p. 36; May–June 1993, p. 13; March–April 1994, p. 58.
*Brookings Review*, Spring 1992, p. 40.
Bwalya, Mwimba. "There Is a Hole in Zambia's Economy." *The Times of Zambia (Lusaka)*, 6 July 1999.
Chipungu, Joel. "Tuberculosis Kills 600 in Kitwe." *PanAfrican News Agency*, 29 September 1999.
*The Economist*, various issues 1996–2000.
*New York Times*, various issues, 1995–2000.
*Washington Post*, 12 September 1995; 25 July 1996; 11 August 1996.

**Profile researched and written by Erik O. Gilbert, Ph.D., Boston University (12/96; updated by Ezekiel Kalipeni, University of Illinois at Urbana-Champaign 4/2000).**

# ZIMBABWE

**Robert Mugabe**
**Executive President**
*(pronounced "moo-GAH-bay")*

*"Radical leftism is being cast aside all over the world, so there is no reason to stick it out."*

The Republic of Zimbabwe is a landlocked nation in south-central Africa bordered by South Africa to its south, Botswana to the west, Zambia to the south, and Mozambique to its north and east. Most of its 390,580 sq km (150,803 sq mi) occupies fertile plateaus and mountainous regions between the Zambezi and Limpopo Rivers. Zimbabwe's population is 11,271,000, with 30 people per sq km (75 per sq mi).

Zimbabwe's population is composed of two broad multi-tribal groupings, the Shona (about 77%) primarily located in the north, and the Ndebele (about 18%) who are concentrated in the southern area of Matabeleland. Less than 1% of the population is of European descent, with even fewer Asians and people of mixed race. The major religions in Zimbabwe are traditional animism (often in combination with Christianity), 50%; Christianity (Anglican), 24%; and Islam, 24%. Zimbabwe's official language is English but Shona and Sindebele are widely spoken.

The Zimbabwean economy is endowed with rich resources including minerals and fertile soil. In the 1990s, however, a series of severe droughts crippled the economy by reducing agricultural exports and increasing the need for food importation. Over 60% of the people are engaged in subsistence agriculture and 16% in industry and services. An estimated 45% of the population is unemployed. The per capita GDP is estimated to be US$2,400. Zimbabwe has one of the most industrialized economies in Africa; its primary industrial products are processed metals, clothing, and chemicals. Primary agricultural products include tobacco, sugar, cotton, and maize. Mining, especially that of gold, nickel, chrome, and copper also contributes to foreign exchange earnings. South Africa is Zimbabwe's major trading partner. The national currency is the Zimbabwean dollar.

## POLITICAL BACKGROUND

Originally administered by the British South Africa Company, Southern Rhodesia (as it was then known) became an internally self-governing British colony in 1923. In 1953, it joined Northern Rhodesia (now Zambia) and Nyasaland (now Malawi) to form the Federation of Rhodesia and Nyasaland, but in 1963 it reverted to a separate status. On 11 November 1965, Prime Minister Ian Smith unilaterally declared Rhodesia's independence cementing white control over the government. Great Britain refused to accept Rhodesia's Unilateral Declaration of Independence (UDI) because the Smith government systematically prevented black majority rule and practiced economic exclusion. After a 1965 meeting between British Prime Minister Harold Wilson and Ian Smith failed to produce any progress toward majority rule, the United Nations imposed international sanctions on Rhodesia. Subsequently on 20 June 1969, Rhodesia declared itself a republic and Britain suspended diplomatic and economic ties with Rhodesia.

A decade of armed struggle in the 1970s, led by Joshua Nkomo's Zimbabwe African People's Union (ZAPU) and Ndabaningi Sithole and Robert Mugabe's Zimbabwe African National Union (ZANU), followed the UDI. On 18 April 1980, Zimbabwe/Rhodesia became the Republic of Zimbabwe with Robert Mugabe as prime minister. Under the constitution that went into effect that day, 20 of the 100 seats in the national assembly were reserved for a white constituency, while the remaining 80 seats were elected by registered voters (excluding those who were white). In 1987, the constitution was amended to end the separate roll for white voters, effectively diminishing white participation in the national assembly. Furthermore, the position of prime minister was replaced in favor of an executive president who is elected for a six-year term. Members of the national assembly elected Robert Mugabe as president on 30 December 1987 and he was popularly elected on 28–30 March 1990 following a constitutional revision. Also in 1987, ZANU and ZAPU merged and Joshua Nkomo became one of two vice-presidents.

As of 1990, the upper house (Senate) was abolished and the present legislature consists of 150 members, of which 120 are popularly elected to six year terms. The House of Assembly contains 10 members appointed by traditional chiefs and 20 presidential appointees. While the House of Assembly theoretically possesses primary legislative power, dominant policy-making power drifted to the cabinet and Mugabe's party. A new party constitution (1989) enlarged the ZANU's Politburo from 15 to 26 and the Central Committee was expanded to 150 members. Mugabe's attempt to create a de facto one-party state in 1990 was defeated by the politburo but Mugabe remained firmly in control as party president.

## PERSONAL BACKGROUND

Robert Gabriel Mugabe was born on 21 February 1924 in Kutama, Zimbabwe (then Southern Rhodesia) to Gabriel, a mission carpenter, and Bona Mugabe. Initially educated at missionary schools, Robert completed his secondary and

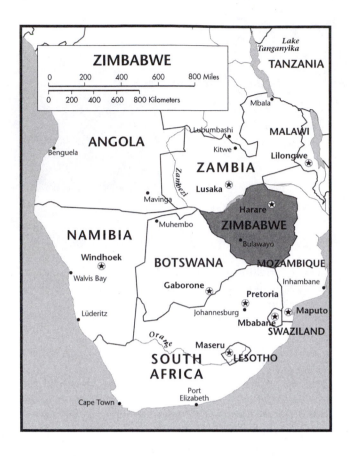

century," was attended by 40,000 people. Mugabe's contribution to Zimbabwean and African development are widely recognized; he holds many honorary degrees and two awards for public service: Africa Prize for Leadership for the Sustainable End of Hunger (1988) and the Jawaharlal Nehru Award (1989). He and his wife have a residence at Zvimba, a rural village 50 miles (80 km) west of Harare.

## RISE TO POWER

Throughout the 1970s, Mugabe played a major role in providing ZANU with leadership stability and a united sense of purpose as he led the armed struggle against the white minority regime. After the assassination of ZANU National Chairman Herbert Chitepo in 1975 and a popular rebellion against former ZANU head, Reverend Sithole, for his relationship with the Smith government, Mugabe became the undisputed leader of ZANU. From 1974 to 1979 Mugabe led the armed struggle from Mozambique by building a highly effective liberation army that eventually helped bring the Smith government to the negotiating table. He succeeded in establishing himself as the primary independence leader.

In 1976, Mugabe formed an uneasy alliance with Joshua Nkomo's ZAPU party to create a united front against the Smith government. While the alliance was uneasy, it directly contributed to the Mugabe victory in the February 1980 elections. Mugabe's major constituency was the Shona tribe, which represented the majority population, and ZANLA troops. Mugabe was considered a nationalist and liberator of Zimbabwe, and therefore, he had wide-ranging popular support.

Despite ZANU's landslide victory, Mugabe sought to form a government of national unity by naming a cabinet that included ZAPU and white members. Furthermore, Mugabe initiated policies designed to stabilize a war-torn nation by promoting a gradual change toward socialism that also upheld the property rights of white landowners. His rival, Joshua Nkomo was given the position of minister of home affairs in the first government.

## LEADERSHIP

Mugabe has maintained virtually unchallenged political control of Zimbabwe since independence. His popularity has waned in the 1990s as continuous economic stagnation afflicted the nation. Mugabe is considered a man of high integrity and moderation, but corruption among the rank-and-file ZANU officials has become a serious political liability.

During the 1980s, Mugabe's political power expanded dramatically. In June 1985, in the first elections since independence, ZANU increased its House of Assembly seats by six. However, ZANU was unable to secure any seats in Matabeleland, the traditional stronghold of Joshua Nkomo's ZAPU. Mugabe dealt effectively with a serious ethnic rift between the Shona and Ndebele by pulling off a stunning political maneuver that caused a reconciliation between ZAPU and ZANU. In an agreement signed between Robert Mugabe and Joshua Nkomo in December 1987, the two leaders merged their political parties and Mugabe named Nkomo as vice-president. Furthermore, in September of that year, the 20 seats set aside for the white minority were abolished.

early college studies through correspondence, qualifying as a secondary school teacher in 1941. He taught at a variety of mission schools before going to South Africa, graduating with a BA in English and history from Fort Hare University in 1951. Upon returning home in 1952, Mugabe taught at Highfield (Harare) and Mambo (Gwelo) government schools. In 1955, Mugabe moved to Northern Rhodesia to teach at Chalimbana Teacher Training College after obtaining a bachelor's in education by correspondence.

In 1957, Robert Mugabe went to Ghana to teach at St. Mary's College. It was there that he developed an interest in politics after being inspired by Ghanaian independence and charismatic leaders including Ghana's Kwame Nkrumah and Malawi's Hastings Kamuzu Banda. It was there that he met his first wife, Sally Hayfron (later deceased).

Upon Mugabe's return from Ghana in 1960, he entered the political arena by becoming the publicity secretary and youth organizer for the National Democratic Party (NDP). The NDP was banned on 9 December 1961, but Mugabe became deputy secretary-general for the Zimbabwe African People's Union (ZAPU). In 1962, authorities banned ZAPU and arrested Mugabe. He was placed under detention from 1964–74, when international pressures secured his release along with other nationalist leaders. From 1974–79, Mugabe commanded guerilla forces from Mozambique. He was elected ZANU president and the commander-in-chief of the Zimbabwe National Liberation Army (ZANLA) in 1977 and ultimately led ZANU to the Lancaster House agreements in 1979.

On 16 August 1996, Mugabe married Grace Marufu, his former secretary. The wedding, dubbed "wedding of the

Mugabe's inauguration as executive president, a position that combined the roles of prime minister and ceremonial president, represented the apex of his power. However, by 1988 citizens' discontent increased and Mugabe found that his nationalistic appeal no longer appealed to the masses. In the 1990s, Mugabe increasingly abandoned his Marxist-Leninist rhetoric and attempted to stimulate the sagging economy by appealing for international investment. However, he continued to direct the expropriation of white-held land for distribution to black peasant farmers. Amid charges against ZANU officials for hoarding land originally intended for distribution to peasants, the integrity of the Mugabe regime suffered and public trust in ZANU declined. While Mugabe's party continued to control nearly all seats in the House of Assembly, the departure of trusted aides weakened his leadership. Mugabe was reelected as executive president on 17 March 1996, but he subsequently acknowledged that most leaders of the independence era faced serious health problems. His successor is presently undetermined.

## DOMESTIC POLICY

On 9 May 1996, the Mugabe government reshuffled its cabinet and named Herbert Murerwa as the official finance minister. It is hoped that the move will curtail public criticism of the government and rebuild public trust in ZANU as it prepares to launch new domestic initiatives. Improving the condition of the economy is likely to remain a major concern of the Mugabe regime. In previous years a structural adjustment program, corruption in land reform procedures, and serious drought imposed severe economic hardship on Zimbabwe. Unemployment, inflation, a trade imbalance, and government deficits are serious economic policy issues that need resolution. To stimulate the economy, the government has begun a series of privatization maneuvers, but the economy remains largely monopolized by government and quasi government-run enterprises.

Traditionally, Zimbabwe has been an exporter of food, but recent droughts resulted in the need for imported grain. Another factor contributing to lower food yields is the privatization of land into smaller parcels. The absence of technological advancements of small peasant-operated land continues to hamper attempts at agricultural recovery.

The current political situation in Zimbabwe is becoming less predictable as a new generation of leaders emerges. Political dissatisfaction is on the rise, and the Mugabe government desperately needs to begin a process of political liberalization if it wants to remain in power over the long term.

Economic recovery is vital if political transition is to proceed smoothly. Mugabe has come to realize that corruption in the top echelons of government needs to be dealt with seriously. In early 2000 he earnestly embarked upon a strong campaign to rid of the government of corruption by arresting and charging several top officials in his government, such as the Minister of Agriculture and the Minister of Energy who were accused of graft. Confidence in Mugabe's government has waned substantially, so much so that a national referendum in February 2000 resulted in the defeat of a government sponsored draft constitution.

## FOREIGN POLICY

Zimbabwe's foreign policy in the 1980s was characterized by nonalignment, opposition to South Africa, support for the Mozambican government in a civil war, and stormy relations with the United States. Since independence, Mugabe had officially followed a course of active nonalignment that sought to avoid entanglement with the United States or Soviet Union. Often, Mugabe's pronouncements at the United Nations angered American diplomats and led to cut-offs of American aid. Although Zimbabwe always had extensive trade relations with South Africa, it was a member of the Frontline States—a group of southern and central African states critical of the white South African regime. The Frontline States worked together to find alternatives to South African trade.

Since the 1980s, the Zimbabwean government provided military and technical assistance to Mozambique in its fight against the Mozambique National Resistance (RENAMO), that was supported by South Africa. After Mugabe reiterated his support for Mozambique's government in October 1986 following the death of then President Samora Machel in a suspicious plane crash, RENAMO declared war on the Zimbabwean government. RENAMO forces frequently crossed into Zimbabwe and inflicted civilian casualties. Meanwhile, Zimbabwe stationed troops in Mozambique and was host to over 100 thousand refugees. After the late 1992–early 1993 cease fire in Mozambique, Zimbabwean troops were withdrawn and a repatriation of refugees began. As of 2000, Zimbabwe-Mozambique relations are strong and friendly.

Since the establishment of a democratic South Africa in 1994, relations with that country have improved. Zimbabwe also played an important role on the UN Security Council during the Gulf War. That, coupled with adherence to International Monetary Fund structural adjustment plans, have led to improved relations with the United States. Zimbabwe continues to play an active role in African affairs; from 1992 through 1995 Zimbabwe contributed peacekeeping troops to UN missions in Mozambique, Rwanda, Angola, and Somalia. In May 1995, President Mugabe visited the US in a bid to obtain foreign aid and investment.

In the late 1990s, Mugabe entangled himself in the civil war in the Democratic Republic of the Congo (formerly Zaire). He deployed thousands of troops in support of President Laurent Kabila. The involvement in the war proved very costly for the Zimbabwean economy prompting the International Monetary Fund to suspend its loan program to Zimbabwe pending Mugabe's explanation of the source of funds used to support his involvement in the Congo.

## ADDRESS

Office of the President
Private Bag 7708, Causeway
Harare
Zimbabwe

## REFERENCES

*Africa Confidential*, 2 February 1996, no. 3, p. 6–7; 15 March 1996, no. 6, p. 6–7; 24 May 1996, no. 11, p. 4–5.
*Africa News*. [Online] courtesy of Panafrican News Agency.
*Africa South of the Sahara*. 25th ed. London: Europa Publications Ltd., 1996.

Banks, Arthur, Alan Day, and Thomas Muller, eds. *Political Handbook of the World, 1995–6.*

Brockman, Norbert C. *An African Biographical Dictionary.* Santa Barbara, CA: ABC-CLIO, 1994.

Hayes, S.V. *Who's Who of Southern Africa.* Johannesburg: Who's Who of Southern Africa, 1996.

"Mugabe Says Zimbabwean Troops in DRCongo to Defend Kabila Against Invasion." ZBC Radio, Harare, BBC Monitoring International Reports, 12 August 1999.

*The New York Times,* 27 April 1996.

Rake, Alan. *New African Yearbook, 1995–96.* Edison, NJ: Hunter Publishing Inc., 1995.

———. *Who's Who in Africa: Leaders for the 1990s.* Metuchen, NJ: The Scarecrow Press, 1992.

Profile researched and written by Robert W. Compton, Jr., Department of Political Science, Binghamton University (SUNY) and Keuka College (10/96; updated by Ezekiel Kalipeni, University of Illinois at Urbana-Champaign 4/2000).

# INDEX OF NAMES

601